A Cultural Studies Reader

History, Theory, Practice

Edited by

Jessica Munns and Gita Rajan

With the British section edited and
introduced by

Roger Bromley

Longman
London and New York

Longman Group Limited,
Longman House, Burnt Mill,
Harlow, Essex CM20 2JE, England
and Associated Companies throughout the world.

Published in the United States of America
by Longman Publishing, New York

First published 1995

ISBN 0 582 214106 CSD
ISBN 0 582 214114 PPR

British Library Cataloguing-in-Publication Data

A catalogue record for this book is
available from the British Library

Library of Congress Cataloging-in-Publication Data

A Cultural Studies Reader: History, Theory, Practice / edited by Jessica
   Munns and Gita Rajan; with the British section edited and
   introduced by Roger Bromley.
      p.   cm.
   Includes bibliographical references and index.
   ISBN 0-582-21410-6. -- ISBN 0-582-21411-4 (pbk.)
   1. Popular culture -- Study and teaching -- United States.
   2. Culture -- Study and teaching -- United States. 3. Popular culture –
   Study and teaching -- Great Britain. 4. Culture -- Study and teaching –
   Great Britain. 5. Criticism -- United States. 6. Criticism -- Great
   Britain. 7. Mass media – United States. 8. Mass media – Great
   Britain.   I. Munns, Jessica, 1949-   .   II. Rajan, Gita, 1952-   .
   III. Bromley, Roger.
   E169.04.C85   1995
   306 -- dc20   95-16009
                                                                           CIP

Set by 8 in Ehrhardt 10/11.5pt
Produced by Longman Singapore Publishers (Pte) Ltd.
Printed in Singagpore

Contents

Acknowledgements

The editors would like to thank the University of New Orleans for providing them with a Summer Research Grant in 1991 which enabled them to start this project. The editors would also like to thank the following scholars who have variously advised them, drawn their attention to essays, read over their introductions, and encouraged them: Charles Bassett, Daniel Bivona, Roger Bromley, Robert Bourdette, Jr., Robert Con Davis, Melissa Hearn, Cynthia Hogue, Betty Katrovas, Sally Mooney, Bonnie Noonan, Penny and Neil Richards, and David Suchoff, and members of the University of Pennsylvania Cultural Studies group, especially Eric Cheyfitz, Peter Stallybrass, and Liliane Weissberg. We would also like to thank Dean Jean Wu of Bryn Mawr College. We are also very grateful to Stuart Hall and J. Hillis Miller for responding so helpfully and fully to our requests for interviews.

We would also like to thank Karen M. Sheriff who was largely responsible for the writing and editing of the headnotes in this collection. She would like to thank Ronald Schleiffer and her graduate student colleagues at the University of Oklahoma, Melody Brown, Susan Halloran, Scott Kelley, R. Scott LaMascus, Trevor Montroy, Samantha Ward and Craig Womack for their assistance in writing the headnotes. Initials after each headnote indicate the author. We would also like to thank the editors at Longman; and finally, we are, as always, grateful to our families for their patience and support.

Toward A Definition of a Specular Border Intellectual' in *Edward Said: A Critical Reader* ed. Michael Sprinker; Basil Blackwell Inc for the article 'Minority Discourse & the Pitfalls of Canon Formation' by Cornell West in *Yale Journal of Criticism* Vol. 1:1, fall 1987; Brown University for the article 'Dyes and Dolls: Multicultural Barbie and the Merchandising of Difference' by Ann duCille in *Differences: A Journal of Feminist Cultural Studies* 6.1 (1994); Charter 88 Trust Publications Ltd for the paper 'The Media and the Constitution' by Jean Seaton. © Jean Seaton, ('The Media and the Constitution' is one of a series of Manchester Papers published by Charter 88 Trust Publications, following the Charter 88 Constitutional Convention); *Daedalus* Journal of the American Academy of Arts & Sciences for the essay 'Interpretive Communities and Variable Literacies: The Functions of Romance Reading' by Janice Radway from the issue entitled 'Anticipations', Summer 1984, Vol. 113, No. 3; Dalhousie University Press/the authors for the article 'The Need for Cultural Studies: Resisting Intellectuals and Oppositional Public Spheres' by Henry Giroux, David Shumway, Paul Smith & James Sosnoski from *The Dalhousie Review*, Vol 64, 1985; Duke University Press for the articles 'On Cultural Studies' by Fredric Jameson in *Social Text*, 34. © 1993 by Duke University Press, 'What is Cultural Studies Anyway?' by Richard Johnson in *Social Text* 16, 1986/87, 'Across Gender, Across Sexuality: Willa Cather and Others' by Eve Ksofosky Sedgwick from *South Atlantic Quarterly*, 88:1, pp 53–72. © 1989 by Duke University Press; the author, Professor Stuart Hall for his article 'Cultural Studies: Two Paradigms' from *Culture, Ideology and Social Practice: A Reader* ed. Tony Bennett et al (Batsford Academic & Educational Ltd with Open University Press, 1981). © Stuart Hall, & extracts from an interview by Roger Bromley; Harcourt Brace Inc for an extract from 'Feminine Stereotypes' by Mary Ellmann in *Thinking About Women*, © 1968 by Mary Ellmann; Harvard University Press, Cambridge, Mass. for ch. XXII 'Myth of the Garden & Turner's Frontier Hypothesis' from *Virgin Land: The American West as a Symbol and Myth* by Henry Nash Smith. © 1950 by the President and Fellows of Harvard College, © 1978 by Henry Nash Smith; the author, J. Hillis Miller for an extract from an interview with Gita Rajan and Jessica Munns; Johns Hopkins University Press for the chapter 'The Violence of the Letter: From Levi-Strauss to Rousseau' from *Of Grammatology* by Jacques Derrida (1974) & the article 'The Good, the Bad and the Indifferent: Defending Popular Culture from the Populists' by Simon Frith in *Diacritics*, Vol 21: 4, Winter 1991; Lawrence & Wishart Ltd for the extract 'I Intellectuals' from *A Gramsci Reader* edited by David Forgacs; the author's agent for the poem 'Discretion' by Roger McGough from Watchwords, pubd. Jonathan Cape Ltd; McGraw-Hill Inc. for the chapter 'The Stereotype' from The Female Eunuch by Germaine Greer (1st edition, McGraw-Hill, 1970) & the chapter 'The Medium is the Message' from *Understanding Media: the Extensions of Man* by Marshall McLuhan (McGraw-Hill, 1970); New Left Review for the article 'The Long Revolution' by E.P. Thompson from *New Left Review* (1961); W.W. Norton & Co Inc for extracts from *The Marx-Engels Reader*, Second Edition by Robert C. Tucker, editor. © 1978, 1972 by W.W. Norton & Co. Inc; the Editor, The Oxford Literary Review for the articles 'Homophobia and Sexual Difference' by Jonathan Dollimore in *The Oxford Literary Review* 8 (1986) & 'The Banality of Gender' by Simon Watney in *The Oxford Literary Review* 8 (1986). © 1986 The Oxford Literary Review; Penguin Books Ltd for an extract from GRUNDRISSE: *Foundations of the Critique of Political Economy* by Karl Marx, translated by Martin

Nicolaus (Penguin Books, 1973) translation © Martin Nicolaus, 1973; Penguin Books Ltd/Georges Borcnardt Inc for Part One from *The History of Sexuality* Vol. 1 by Michel Foucault, translated by Robert Hurley (Allen Lane, 1979) © Editions Gallimard, 1976, Translation © Random House Inc, 1978; Random Century Group for the article 'Illustrations for Popular Art – Peg's Paper' by Richard Hoggestt from *The Uses of Literature*, pubd. Chatto & Windus Ltd & the chapter 'Conclusion' by Raymond Williams to *Culture and Society*, (1st edition, Chatto & Windus Ltd, 1958); Random Century Group/Harcourt Brace Inc. & Surhkamp Verlag for extracts from the article 'The Work of Art in the age of Mechanical Reproduction' from *Illuminations* by Walter Benjamin, ed. by Hannah Arendt, translated by Harry Zohn (Jonathan Cape, 1970), © 1955 by Suhrkamp Verlag, English translation © 1968 by Harcourt Brace Inc; Random Century Group/Georges Borchardt, Inc for the article 'A Writing Lesson' from *Tristes Topiques* by Claude Levi-Strauss. © 1955 by Librarie Plon. English translation © 1973 by Jonathan Cape Ltd; Routledge/W.W. Norton Inc/Editions du Seuil for chapter 1 'The mirror stage as formative of the function of the I as revealed in psychoanalytic experience' from *ECRITS: A Selection* by Jacques Lacan, translated from the French by Alan Sherida. © 1966 by editions du Seuil. English translation © 1977 by Tavistock Publications Ltd; Routledge Inc/the author, Lawrence Grossberg for his article 'MTV: Swinging on the (Postmodern) Star' from *Cultural Politics in Contemporary America*, edited by Ian Angus & Sut Jhally, (Routledge, 1989); Routledge Inc/the author, Gayatri Chakravorty Spivak for her article 'The Politics of Translation' from *Outside the Teaching Machine*, (Routledge, 1993); the Editors, *Screen*/the author, Laura Mulvey for her essay 'Visual Pleasure and Narrative Cinema' in *Screen*, Vol 16, no 3, pp 6–18; Serpent's Tail Publishers for the chapter 'Cruciality and the Frog's Perspective' by Paul Gilroy from *Small Acts*, (London: Serpent's Tail, 1993); Simon & Schuster Education, Hemel Hempstead, UK. for the article 'Oppressive dichotomies: the nature/culture debate' by Penelope Brown and Ludmilla Jordanova from *The Changing Experience of Women*, edited by E. Whitelegg et al (Basil Blackwell in association with the Open Univerity, 1982); Stanford University Press for the article 'Is Female to Male as Nature is to Culture?' by Sherry B. Ortner from *Women, Culture and Society*, edited by Michelle Zimbalist Rosaldo & Louise Lamphere. © 1974 by the Board of Trustees of the Leland Stanford Junior University; University of California Press Journals/the author, James Clifford for his article 'On Ethnographic Authoriy' from *Representations*, Vol. 1:2, Spring 1983; University of Minnesota Press for the 'Introduction' by Seamus Deane from *Nationalism, Colonialism and Literature*, Terry Eagleton, Fredric Jameson and Edward Said; Verso/Suhrkamp Verlag for a letter dated 18.3.36 from Theodor Adorno to Walter Benjamin from *Aesthetics and Politics* by Ernst Block et al (1980) & *Uber Walter Benjamin*, © Suhrkamp Verlag 1979.

We have unfortunately been unable to trace the copyright holder of 'Doublespeak and Ideology in Ads: A Kit for Teachers' by Richard Ohmann from *Teaching About Doublespeak* ed. Daniel Dietrich, and would appreciate any information which would enable us to do so.

General introduction

Cultural studies, as a discipline, occupies a relatively new space in American and British universities. Most scholars in both countries see it emerging as an area of academic research, and consequently, a pedagogical practice from different socio-political and economic changes that followed the second world war. A series of world events validate such a view, and a major factor is the rise in the political status of America above that of Europe (and Britain) during the middle of the twentieth century, which in turn created new power trajectories in the global arena. This power differential created 'first' and 'second' worlds, situating countries in a hierarchy based upon economic and political cartographies rather than categories of geographic location or cultural community. This in turn created a new space called the 'third' world that was soon occupied by the growing number of previously colonized nations breaking free from 'empires'.

Another factor is the rise of a modern society with a large consumer capacity which re-configured trade and labour along lines of technocratic capital. And finally, the rise in democratic values in America and Britain gave the middle class, with its distinct needs and desires, a valid space for creating and enjoying popular culture. All these massive factors (and several smaller, individual ones) contributed in various ways to the intellectual endeavour of cultural critique. Contrary to what some scholars have argued however, cultural critique itself, i.e., critique as mode of challenging and refining the foundational assumptions of any field of enquiry, has always been a clear voice in the liberal humanist tradition. It is, as Con Davis and Schliefer point out in *Criticism and Culture* (1991) not completely an invention of the late twentieth century scholar. One force that shapes this book is this historiography of cultural critique that is vital to cultural studies as a discipline. Another major force is the impact of such a critique on the various cultural forms in contemporary society.

In a lecture, 'The Future of Cultural Studies' given in 1986, Raymond Williams stated, 'you cannot understand an intellectual or artistic project without also understanding its formation; that the relation between a project and a formation is always

1

decisive; and . . . the emphasis of Cultural Studies is precisely that it engages with both.' With this double agenda, with regard to cultural studies as both an academic project and a particular social formation, we hope to bring together an energetic mode of enquiry and one of the most dynamic and vital disciplines to be taught in the academy in recent years.

Historicizing contexts

If the post-war scene created neat divisions of first/second worlds, then the crumbling of the Berlin wall in the 1980s, the fracture of the Soviet Union in the 1990s, and the gradual and unwelcome increase in economic and political strength in the Far and Near East demanded another scale for cultural critique. For example, the North Atlantic Free Trade Agreement recently adopted by the United States, Canada, and Mexico, the negotiations of the European Economic Community, and the much-debated General Agreement on Tariffs and Trade proposition, on the one hand signal a move towards homogenizing global markets, and on the other wipe out the distinct signatures of each country's culture that were so eminently marketable. In this frame, questions regarding an inalienable essence of America or an intrinsic nature of (Europe) Britain as they become global phenomena have become urgent and intensified. Commonly challenged and critiqued issues in such a globalization centre around some basic structures. For example, one area of debate is the relationship of cultural productions such as art, literature, music, and theatre, and the social value of these forms in a democratized and computerized *multi-media* society. In today's hyper-technological world, concepts such as 'interactive video' or 'information super-highways' are not jargons in the audio-visual industry, but emerging forms of cultural production and daily consumption. Also, questions of cultural identity *vis-à-vis* the roles played by citizens in these societies are raised where *gender*, *class*, and *race* factor into their value as citizens. Similar questions as to the meaning of migrant, diasporic, and transnational identities have been raised by post-colonials, where the politics of *representation and nationhood* come into play. Yet, none of these issues can be singled out, or compartmentalized, or read as discreet units, especially since the intellectuals engaged in such enquiries have been drawn into old and new centres of world power and have fed into American and British universities and their systems of thought. Thus, cultural critique is more than an interdisciplinary solution, it provides a spectrum of approaches to questions that are raised in today's global, multi-classed, multi-racial, and multi-cultural societies. While most of the major factors initiating cultural critique are shared by America and Britain, the methods, milieux, and trajectories of these movements varied considerably in each country.

The discussions and analyses of culture, the alternations between jeremiad and optimistic belief in progress, however, are not new. Jürgen Habermas, in 'Modernity: An Incomplete Project', quotes Octavio Paz who remarked 'the avant-garde of 1967 repeats the deeds and gestures of 1917' (6). Frequently, arguments from the post-war period to the present have their roots in earlier discourses, or unknowingly echo earlier anxieties and critiques. Indeed, most of the arguments demarcating high/low culture inevitably rehearse Matthew Arnold's thesis from *Culture and Anarchy* (1867), making it important to recognize Arnold's double position as both creating and critiquing a concept of culture. In this vein, Gerald Graff in a recent interview pointed out the impossibility of escaping Arnold's over-arching presence in cultural studies, for both Right- and Left-wing intellectuals.

As the intellectual emerged in American and European societies in the eighteenth and nineteenth centuries, his (and eventually her) task was not, as was the case for the clerical class of previous ages, to pass on a set body of knowledge but to critique the state of the very bodies of knowledge. Karl Marx declared that the role of philosophy was not to understand society but to change it, and although the revolution he advocated was not endorsed by all social thinkers, the principle of change was. From Marx to Arnold, the great cultural critics of the nineteenth century sought not only to understand their age but to remedy its flaws, and for these purposes roamed freely across those disciplinary boundaries which subsequent educational systems created. Gerald Graff has documented in *Professing Literature* (1987) that American universities started creating departments to teach specific, national literatures only by the end of the nineteenth century. Similarly, in Britain, Chris Baldick in *The Social Mission of English Criticism* (1983) and Peter Widdowson in *Re-Reading English* (1982) have pointed that the academization of 'English' had a certain social and cultural inflection. And, tracing the idea of culture even further back to the late eighteenth century, Raymond Williams in *Culture and Society* (1958) also points to the ever-present battle between democracy and industrialization and culture and education. The nineteenth-century view that fruitful change was more likely to be located in a return to an earlier and stronger value system than through a radical reorganization of contemporary culture is a remedy that is suggested even today by Right-wing pundits. In so many of its concerns and approaches, cultural studies is not so much a new and terrifying subject, as it is a re-examination, a re-negotiation, and a re-interpretation of major Enlightenment and humanist ideals, especially with a contemporary temper of sustained critique. This is not to argue that cultural studies is an endless repetition of older ideas and themes, but to suggest that cultural studies has a comprehensible origin and a genealogy of analytical methodologies, which needs to be taken into account. In so far as cultural studies is forging new ground, even sometimes to dissociate itself from the assumptions of the past, it is as vital to scrutinize the materials of our study of culture as it is to study the materials of culture.

Most cultural-studies scholars use the second world war as a historical marker for tracing the growth of the field. The post-war scene created a demand for the provision of higher-level education to suit the needs of increasingly technological societies, and this, in turn, stimulated a recognition by first-wave cultural-studies scholars of the inter-related nature of culture and society. There began a move to 'build' universities in America and Britain in the 1960s and 1970s. This resulted in a massive increase in university populations, and areas such as sociology and cultural anthropology started establishing both empirical and theoretical models for tracing connections between culture and society. More recently, the role of the citizen, specifically, the gender, class, and race of the citizen have come into play in the methodological analysis of culture. This in turn has resulted in a re-examination of a largely male, Eurocentric world view. This move has been matched by the development of a growing body of texts concerned with previously marginalized areas, such as the works of women and ethnic minorities, 'unacademic' subjects such as TV, pop music, comic books, as well as the once taboo field of diverse sexuality. In such a climate cultural studies has moved from a minority discourse pursued mostly at the graduate level at a few specially focused institutions to an increasingly integral element of the modern university curriculum at both undergraduate and graduate levels.

In Britain certain works and dates can be established as formative in the development of a cultural studies consciousness. Richard Hoggart's influential *The Uses of Literacy* (1957), focused attention on alterations in the traditional class system in Britain as it nostalgically looked back to a community of 'working-class' people. And E. P. Thompson's interpretation of the 'worker' in British society in *The Making of the English Working Class* (1968) is another index in the formation of cultural studies. The National Union of Teachers conference in Britain in 1960 took as its subject matter the critical responses of teachers to television and film, which led directly to Paddy Whannel and Stuart Hall's ground-breaking book, *The Popular Arts* (1964). In America, an infinitely larger and less centralized country, the movement towards such a consciousness is more diffused, although the Taniment Institute Conference in 1959 parallels the concerns of the NUT conference and similarly brought together scholars from a range of disciplines. So too, the landmark case in Mississippi for integrating high-school education of black and white students generated a new paradigm for racial equality in America. Meanwhile, at the university level, American studies programmes pioneered interdisciplinary methods to define and often celebrate a unique national culture. While in Britain, new universities broke from traditional syllabi to create Common First Year programmes of study, in America, the move was more gradual. In both countries entirely new areas of study, such as women's studies, black studies, film studies, studies in Commonwealth literature, communications studies, and sociology of literature crossed hitherto separated disciplinary boundaries.

In Britain, the critique of contemporary culture was largely a dialogue of the New Left-wing intellectuals, even if many of its roots lay in the despair of Right-wing intellectuals like T. S. Eliot and F. R. Leavis at changes in traditional ways and values. British cultural studies formed itself out of many sources but predominantly by braiding together works in different areas with a debate with Marxism. In America, the impetus to study culture has always been as much the province of the Right as of the Left, but with, perhaps, a more nationalistic bias as European theories were often regarded with suspicion. Consequently, in America, cultural anthropology, American studies, and media studies tended to provide a viable methodology for cultural studies. Due to this documentary and explanatory principle, American cultural studies, on the surface at least, can be seen as less overtly engaged in political critique. While a Marxist heritage has made British cultural studies alert to issues of class, popular culture, and subcultures, initially at the expense of issues of race and gender, American forms of cultural studies focused upon ethnographic approaches, making them more open to questions of gender and race but obscuring issues of class. Black studies and women's studies, for instance, both emerged in America first.

Britain had to fight a double-edged battle against traditionalist disapproval and Marxist tendencies to subsume all struggles of power under the category of class struggle.

An interesting fact that is overlooked while creating such epistemological charts is the 'cultural' exchange that took place between the first and second worlds, especially in the light of the present breakdown of the Russian empire. The cold war was often also a culture war as each bloc sent its artists to perform in each other's capital cities, and the cold war, whether producing intellectuals supporting or contesting the superiority-claims of their bloc, made 'culture' by show-casing systems of habits, customs, practices, and beliefs. This need to define a cultural territory spilled, not fortuitously, into the expanding arena of higher education. While the flexing of political and nuclear muscle is well known, what often gets elided in these conflicts is the common ground that a European culture forged between the two blocs as a space for mediations.

Contemporary contexts

While the topics mentioned above provide a glimpse into the background of cultural studies, there are a number of anthologies in the market today that deal with theories and methodologies already at work. The publications of the Open University in support of its ground-breaking courses in cultural studies and women's studies, for instance, provide basic collections of contemporary materials largely based on the works of British practitioners. The publications of the University of Essex conferences on the sociology of literature similarly collect together innovative materials, mostly by British and European scholars, focused around interdisciplinary issues of culture, gender, class, and race. In America since the 1970s collections of essays devoted to black studies, women's studies, chicana/o and native-American cultures have highlighted the importance of the issues of race and gender to modern culture. While the general emphasis tends to be on literature and media, their significance to all branches of cultural enquiry is clear. An informative over-view of the development of cultural studies as a discipline is provided by Graeme Turner in *British Cultural Studies: An Introduction* (1990). American publications such as Cary Nelson and Lawrence Grossberg's *Marxism and the Interpretation of Culture* (1989) gather together a massive collection of essays covering a wide range of cultural issues offering students and scholars important resources. Grossberg and Nelson have re-negotiated the very terrain that cultural critique has occupied in its engagement with traditional Marxism. Their agenda is ambitious, poly-directional, and deliberately heterogenous, making the anthology, in turn, multi-textured, and uneven in presentation. This is partly due to the fact that their work is one of the first 'cultural studies' collections in America (a collection of the first cultural studies conference organized at the University of Illinois), and, unlike British scholars, they are not seeking to create a foundational text for the field. Since then, various other cultural studies anthologies have also been published. An interesting, if polemical, over-view of the rise of cultural studies is provided in Patrick Brantlinger's *In Crusoe's*

Footprints (1990). His most recent anthology, *Modernity and Mass Culture* (1992), reflects his major concern with the relations between mass and elite culture and between modernity and postmodernity.

Cultural studies anthologies indicate the political nature of cultural critique which is always embroiled in contradictory and conflicting discourses. One factor that is undebatable about the nature of cultural studies, however, is its immense political potential. Whether cultural critique rests on Marxist or continental theories of subjectivity (both as physical potential and/or psychological interpolations), or on oppositional dialogues with Right-wing reactionaries (Reaganites in America and Thatcherites in Britain), or is faced with constant interruptions by race and gender analysts, the field continues to challenge every shift in global culture. Cultural studies is therefore championed as an energetic, polysemic, multi-disciplinary field by its advocates, or is denounced by its opponents as a parasitic, cacophonous phenomenon capable of wrecking culture as it is known today. This is because all parties involved agree that cultural studies is an inherently powerful tool with a radical potential for intervening in the education and socialization, i.e., acculturation, of future generations of students.

Our *Reader* attempts to provide a brief context of ideas that are crucial to cultural critique and presents a survey of some of the major texts in the field thus far. The introductory essay and the nineteenth-century section are designed to draw attention to the central issues of cultural criticisms in America and Britain, and each of the sections on British and American cultural studies shows the distinct traditions and trends in the two countries. While we hope to draw a comprehensive map, this is not intended as a 'world' reader; work carried out by 'Third World', Australian, Canadian, and Eastern European cultural critics has not been included. We have not, however, enforced an essentialist paradigm, i.e., insisted that all our authors be either American or British by birth or nationality, but rather that their work is conducted in the contexts of American and British cultural and academic life and responsive to the particular strains, movements and tendencies of these cultures. However, even with the latitude that the American–British locus provides, we have not been able to include certain works by major figures in cultural theory or any work by Right-wing intellectuals such as Allan Bloom, due to the sheer economics of production.

Textual contexts

As an area of academic enquiry, cultural studies, inevitably, is textually based and with this *Reader* we hope to provide a series of texts, some very well known and some less known outside their particular country of origin or discipline, which will contribute to the study of culture/s. We are, however, very aware that cultural studies, more perhaps than many other academic areas, both in its formation and in its objects of study resists, as much as it consists of, textualization. Cultural studies can only partially be undertaken through the study of written texts. Films, videos, music disks, trips to shopping malls, museums and art galleries all have their place in any study of the materials of culture. Essays by Stuart Hall, James Clifford and Richard Johnson included in the *Reader* specifically address what are in many ways the paradoxes and problematics of an area of study which defies easy and singular definition and which is constantly enmeshed in mediating between experience as a lived process and as a textualized critique. In Williamsesque terms, cultural studies is, perhaps, a 'structure of feeling', as well as, or even more than, a 'discipline'—and hence the ability of cultural studies to colonize and combine varied disciplinary areas.

Our *Reader* offers an historical perspective on the field of enquiry and a selection focused around strong thematic markers which signal the significant fields of cultural enquiry. There are three basic organizational movements: chronological growth, national concerns, and thematic areas. These groupings in themselves indicate the development of cultural studies from nineteenth-century reactions to a mass society, to specific national concerns, and then to the interdisciplinary productions of an increasingly international/cross-national body of scholars. The *Reader* is not, however, a history of ideas but offers an interpretation of how certain ways of thinking about culture have come into being in relation to cultural phenomena, such as urbanization, technology, and the increasing presence of women and peoples of colour in the public sphere.

In the first section we provide basic texts from Arnold to Marx which plot the field for subsequent formations and reactions. Essays in cultural studies frequently refer to the importance of Marx to the study of culture as a social construct, and/or to the elitist critique of Arnold. Similarly, they refer to the central role of Frederick Jackson Turner's thesis of 'frontierism' in the American imagination, or to Frederick Douglass's questions on race politics. We have thus sought to present selections from nineteenth-century cultural thought which will serve as a useful background.

The following three sections, The impact of European theory, Cultural studies in Britain, and Cultural studies in America, indicate certain moments in cultural theory and critique which could be summarized as: European theories shaping cultural criticism, British formulations of critique and resistance, and American reflections and re-conceptions of culture. The selections here chart the specific national and cultural-historical boundaries which mark the emergence of cultural studies as an academic discipline in America and Britain. The selection of major European texts indicates the significance of a theoretical discourse which created a specific vocabulary for analytical methodologies. One criterion for including a theoretical section was to familiarize students with certain foundational concepts that are used in many of the essays in the *Reader*.

The four following sections are thematically organized and simply titled: Media Studies, Race Studies, Gender Studies, and Voice-Overs. The point in keeping the titles direct is to indicate the concrete nature of these constructs within culture, while the essays themselves bring out the theoretical complexity within these constructs. We hope to create a play in these sections ranging from media as the scene of representation, gender as the deployment of sexuality, and race as presenting the politics of multi-culturalisms and colour. All the sections represent major areas of cultural concern/critique carried out on both sides of the Atlantic by an increasingly international body of scholars. Our final section is deliberately heterogenous, moving from monographs to dialogues and from manifestoes to pedagogic paradigms in an effort to invite scholars, critics and students to talk to each other. An important contribution that we see our *Reader* making is in presenting a body of knowledge to students as one view of the origin of cultural studies, and the consequent development of cultural critique as an intellectual endeavour and a disciplinary practice. We hope that teachers and students will be able to use this knowledge (in its metalanguage of analysis) as a productive pedagogical practice. In other words, what impact does the field of cultural studies have on the academic growth of students in today's multi-cultural environment? How do students learn the meanings and values of cultures as both lived-in experiences and as intellectual tools of critique? This *Reader* presents students with concrete examples of the various constructions and practices of culture. Quite specifically, this step into the classroom at this precise socio–political and cultural moment, with Right-wing opponents of cultural studies in America blocking its entrance into the academy, is a direct way of empowering students. Given the marbled nature of the demographics of today's student populations on both sides of the Atlantic, Henry Giroux's comment in 'Post-Colonial Ruptures and Democratic Possibilities' is very valid. He writes that cultural studies has given 'a new twist to the political and the personal, [since] the conservative backlash has attempted to reverse many of the gains made by women, gays and lesbians, ethnic and racial minorities, and other subordinated groups who have organized [themselves] around a politics of identity' (6).

REFERENCES AND FURTHER READING

Aronowitz, Stanley, *Dead Artists, Live Theories, and Other Cultural Problems*, London and New York: Routledge, 1993.
Barrell, John, Jacqueline Rose, and Peter Stallybrass eds, with an Intro. by Stuart Hall, *Carnival, Hysteria, and Writing: Collected Essays and 'Autobiography' of Allon White*, Oxford: Oxford University Press, 1993.
Bennett, T., *Outside Literature*, London: Routledge, 1990.
Bhabha, Homi K., *Location of Culture*, London and New York: Routledge, 1993.
Bloom, Allan, *The Closing of the American Mind: How Higher Education has Failed Democracy and the Souls of Today's Students*, New York: Simon and Schuster, 1987.
Brantlinger, Patrick, *Crusoe's Footprints: Cultural Studies in Britain and America*, London and New York: Routledge, 1990.
Carey, James, *Communication as Culture: Essays on Media and Society*, Boston: Unwin Hyman, 1989.
Centre for Contemporary Cultural Studies, *Unpopular Education: Schooling and Social Democracy in England since 1944*, London: Hutchinson, 1981.
Centre for Contemporary Cultural Studies, *Making Histories: Studies in History-Writing and Politics*, London: Hutchinson, 1982.
Centre for Contemporary Cultural Studies, *The Empire Strikes Back: Race and Racism in 70s Britain*, London: Hutchinson, 1982.
Chambers, Iain, *Popular Culture: The Metropolitan Experience*, New York: Methuen, 1986.
Clarke, J., C. Critcher, and Richard Johnson, *Working Class Culture: Studies in History and Theory*, New York: St. Martin's Press, 1979.
Clifford, J., and V. Dhareshwar eds, 'Traveling Theory, Traveling Theorists', *Inscriptions* 5 (1989).
Con Davis, Robert, and Ronald Schliefer, *Criticism and Culture*, London and New York: Longman, 1991.
Crimp, D. ed., *AIDS: Cultural Analysis/Cultural Activism*, Cambridge, Mass.: MIT Press, 1988.
Czitrom, Daniel, *Media and the American Mind: From Morse to McLuhan*, Chapel Hill: University of North Carolina Press, 1982.
D'Souza, Dinesh, *Illiberal Education: The Politics of Race and Sex on Campus*, New York: Free Press, 1991.

During, Simon, *The Cultural Studies Reader*, London and New York: Routledge, 1993.

Easthope, Anthony, and Kate McGowan eds, *A Critical And Cultural Theory Reader*, Buckingham: Open University Press, 1993.

Fiske, John, *Understanding Popular Culture*, Boston: Unwin Hyman, 1989.

Fiske, John, *Reading the Popular*, Boston: Unwin Hyman, 1989.

Frith, Simon, and Andrew Goodwin eds, *On Record: Rock, Pop, and the Written Word*, New York: Pantheon, 1990.

Glazer, Nathan, and Daniel Patrick Moynihan, *Beyond the Melting Pot*, Cambridge, Mass.: Harvard University Press, 1963.

Giroux, A. Henry, and Peter McLaren, *Between Borders: Pedagogy and the Politics of Cultural Studies*, London and New York: Routledge, 1993.

Giroux, A. Henry, 'Post-Colonial Ruptures and Democratic Possibilities: Multiculturalism as Anti-Racist Pedagogy', *Cultural Critique* (1992): 5–39.

Graff, Gerald, *How Teaching the Conflicts Can Revitalize American Education*, New York: Norton, 1992.

Habermas, Jürgen, 'Modernity: an Incomplete Project' in *Anti-Aesthetic: Postmodern Culture*, ed. Hal Foster, London: Pluto Press, 1983.

Inglis, Fred, *Cultural Studies*, Oxford: Blackwell, 1993.

Katsiaficas, George, *The Imagination of the New Left: A Global Analysis of 1968*, Boston: South End Press, 1987.

Milner, Andrew, *Contemporary Cultural Theory: An Introduction*, London: UCL Press, 1993.

Omi, Michael, and Howard Winant, *Racial Formation in the United States: From the 1960s to the 1980s*, London and New York: Routledge, 1986.

Punter, David ed., *Introduction to Contemporary Cultural Studies*, London: Longman, 1986.

Ross, Andrew, *No Respect: Intellectuals and Popular Culture*, London: Routledge, 1989.

Sill, Geoffrey M. et al. eds, *Opening the American Mind: Race, Ethnicity, and Gender in Higher Education*, Newark, NJ: University of Delaware Press, 1993.

Trend, David, *Cultural Pedagogy: Art/Education/Politics*, New York: Bergin, 1992.

Wagner, Roy, *The Invention of Culture*, Chicago: Chicago University Press, 1981.

JOURNALS

Cultural Critique.
Cultural Dynamics.
Cultural Studies.
Diaspora.
Explorations.
New Formations.
Notebooks in Cultural Analysis.

Postmodern Culture.
Public Culture.
Representations.
Temple University Working Papers in Culture and Communication.
Transitions.

1 The nineteenth century

Introduction

American and British nineteenth-century thinkers represented in this section are heirs to the rational, humanist philosophy of the Enlightenment. Enlightenment philosophy is generally optimistic, believing that 'man' is able to perfect himself and society through the exercise of reason. It also asserts that human autonomy and human action contribute to the making of culture. Voltaire, a major Enlightenment figure, used reason to satirize and defamiliarize social customs and hierarchies, and Jean Jacques Rousseau, another prominent thinker of the era, questioned the 'naturalness' of social inequality. René Déscartes and Immanuel Kant took the concept of rationality even further to interrogate the ability of reason itself as a tool of critique. The Enlightenment ideal of reasoned human agency implicitly promoted culture as knowable and perfectible. This framework of rational criteria and analytical methodology was transmitted to the nineteenth-century thinkers, who challenged and modified these views based upon new cultural forces.

By the early nineteenth century in Britain, the optimistic rationalism of the Enlightenment was assailed by competing forces—the impact of scientific discoveries, breakdown of established religious beliefs, industrialization, the simultaneous growth of democratization on national territory and the expansion of Empire to Africa and Asia—all of which produced massive cultural and social destabilization. Victorians viewed scientific developments both positively and negatively, industrialization produced unprecedented levels of prosperity together with the first recorded instances of migrating slums. Industrialization also led to fears that materialism was replacing spirituality. The apogee of this mood of Victorian optimism and sense of progress was 'The Great Exhibition of the Works of All Nations' inaugurated by Queen Victoria in 1851, an event considered by some cultural critics to be the ironic wedding of art and commerce. Industrial growth, which harnessed reason for liberal and progressive ends, also resulted in unleashing an onslaught of scepticism. On a different level, new ideas ranging from Charles Darwin's evolutionary theory of the species to religious concepts of creationism radically undermined the traditional

13

authority of the Bible. Religious certitude and unity were eroded partially by the rise of nonconformists, the doctrinaire religiosity of Tractarians like Cardinal Newman, and by analytical works like David Friedrich Strauss's *The Life of Jesus* (1835, trans. George Eliot, 1846), which interpreted the New Testament as a historical and literary text. Major shifts in defining 'identity' occurred at the socio-political level as well. The political map of Britain changed gradually which in turn re-configured the distribution of power. Some notable acts were the passing of the first and second Reform Bills (1832 and 1867), which ensured 'manhood' suffrage, Home Rule, and the First Education Act (1868) all of which indicate the intervention of the state into the lives of working-class people.

The revolutionary societies of America (1776) and France (1789) stimulated radical movements in Britain as well. Mary Wollstonecraft had already noted discrepancies between enlightened thinking with regard to men and their rights, and traditional thinking with regard to women and their lack of rights. John Stuart Mill, the liberal humanist, wrote that 'what is now called the nature of women is an eminently artificial thing—the result of forced repression in some directions, unnatural stimulation in others.' This debate on construction of 'woman' as a gendered, cultural construct, is a central issue for feminists even today (see Gender Studies section). Similarly, Imperial expansion produced its own stereotypes of other races, their mythologies, which were often pejorative, and this is a central issue for postcolonial scholars today (see Race Studies section). In effect, contemporary debates on essentialism and constructionism (the former indicating a biological force or 'naturalness' in discourses on identity and the latter dealing with the cultural forces shaping one's identity) were also being conducted by nineteenth-century critics.

Wollstonecraft advocated educational reform because she believed that only through more equitable education would women and men be redeemed from a degrading relationship. Many nineteenth-century thinkers, from Karl Marx to Matthew Arnold, if very differently, believed that through education 'man' could harness knowledge and reason to create a better world. Marx is both the product of the Enlightenment and also the prophet of its destruction. In place of the autonomous rational subject—the development of Déscartes and Kant—Marx placed an economically determined subject and developed a model of economic determinism to read the entire fabric of relationships in Western culture, ranging from religious beliefs to aesthetics, philosophy, art, and kinship systems. (See the section on the Impact of European Theory for Levi-Strauss's and Gramsci's shifts in this perspective.) Marx envisioned a revolutionary philosophy, arguing in the 'Feuerbach Theses' that 'philosophers have only *interpreted* the world, in various ways; the point, however, is to change it' (*Thesis* 11).

Matthew Arnold, unlike Marx who attempted to synthesize or systematize cultural relationships, pointed out the negative influence on the arts, and on the tastes and values of the Victorian people, of the expanding machine age and the emergence of a mass-society. Arnold believed that art and literature reflect the aesthetics of the age, representing what is best in the human spirit. In *Culture and Anarchy*, Arnold defines culture as an internal factor, a humanistic temper capable of understanding experiential reality in relation to an abstract human ideal. Arnold attempted through his (élitist) position to use culture to counter the erosion caused by the disruptive social forces of Victorian England and, indeed, what Marx would term 'laissez-faire capitalism'. For Arnold, culture healed this breach and created a new paradigm of beliefs, morals, education, art, and tradition. Therefore, he argued that culture aspiring through 'sweetness and light' could achieve a kind of perfection through guiding one's intellect with the Will of God. Since literature for Arnold provided the 'touchstones' of greatness, the function of criticism was to select and canonize those works of literature which would uplift the human spirit. Thus, Arnold argued that education could erase class barriers and produce a nation whose citizens share a high and noble culture. In this sense, literature is a substitute religion, and literary criticism which sustains that literature from the inroads of the barbarians and philistines is also cultural criticism.

British nineteenth-century thinkers, however different their analysis of social problems, sought overarching models of explanation which attempted to relate social, artistic, and material changes to industrial/economic developments. For many like Arnold, Carlyle, even Pater and Newman, the material connection was negative, and they hoped to stem a new barbarism through disseminating the culture of the élite. However, for others such as William Morris and John Ruskin, the revitalization of folk arts and crafts offered a socialist alternative to the machine age. Still others followed Marx and Engels in envisioning a radical and revolutionary change. Meanwhile, the widening horizons of the British Empire allowed statesmen like Clive, Hastings, and Macaulay to mandate cultural policy in India and Africa, the intent and implications of which scholars are trying to unravel even today. On the whole, thinkers from all disciplines were aware of the need to re-configure relations of labour, class, gender, and race consciousness in their attempts to create a stable, national culture.

American thinkers, never too isolated from their British counterparts, also had to relate to and theorize the nature of meaning of their new society. Britain (and Europe) offered models both negative and positive—corrupt and civilized—against which America fashioned a belief in vigorous individualism, self-reliance, and initiative. The people of this new land wanted to create a virile and vital culture through their belief in democracy. Ralph Waldo Emerson captured this burgeoning spirit of freedom and enterprise in his poetics of the 'Man Thinking' in 'The American Scholar' (1897), a concept which is often referred to in American literature as the myth of the New Adam. Emerson envisions America as a 'whole man' whose legs represent an energetic mobility, the arms the agrarian potential, and the head, more importantly, the 'eyes' (an Emersonian metaphor for the scholar poet), the ability to gaze at this glorious new land. A series of monumental and interconnected issues were addressed during the nineteenth century in America—the Suffrage movement, the abolition of slavery, which coincided with the civil-war years, and the settlement of the new land, which meant westward expansion—shaped the cultural milieu of this new land.

In 1869 the National Suffrage Association was established in New York and the spirit of this movement spanned across the land, and was first enacted into law the same year in Wyoming Territory. Two major organizers of the women's suffrage movement in America were Elizabeth Cady Stanton and Susan B. Anthony. The ideology behind the American Suffrage movement reveals that the enfranchisement of women coincided with a fundamental change in social values concerning the role of the two other radical groups in America—the activists in the prohibition movement and the immigration restriction movement. This moment also reveals a moralistic and nativistic attitude in nascent American culture that is evidenced even today in the debates between the 'reactionary' right and the 'liberal' left. The nineteenth-century historian Alex de Tocqueville, in *Democracy in America* (1835), traced the connection between history and religion, remarking that Protestantism was a pivotal factor in accelerating the spread of 'egalitarianism' in America. He noted that the basic religious belief of the people supported the Suffrage movement because of its implied tenet of equality: 'no free community existed without morals; . . . morals are the work of women. Consequently, whatever affects the conditions of women, their habits, their opinions, has great political importance in my eyes' (391).

The feminist movement of nineteenth-century America, like the Civil Rights movement of the 1960s, not only sponsored immediate economic and educational reforms for women but was also concerned with a broad range of other issues. Abolition of slavery, building a manageable workforce in the country, and temperance (prohibition) were some of the projects that the leaders of the movement undertook. In this emergent revolution, categorized broadly as women's suffrage, a new ethic for a new country was being forged. But, as American-studies scholars point out now, this ethic had a Eurocentric bias. Angela Davis, making an accurate connection between feminisms and color biases across the span of two centuries, points out in *Woman, Race, and Class* (1983), that the new ethic did not guarantee equal rights for black women. She writes

> if and when a historian sets the record straight on the experiences of enslaved Black women, he or she would have performed an inestimable service. . . . Judged by the evolving nineteenth century ideology of femininity, which emphasized women's roles as nurturing mothers and gentle companions and housekeepers for their husbands, Black women were practically anomalies. (4–5)

Slavery and abolition of slavery became the centre of both ideological and intellectual conflict during the civil-war years. Frederick Douglass's autobiographical narrative of the life of a slave (1882), only one of the few stark narratives of oppression and degradation, is an eloquently written work in 'white' English for a white audience, and contrasted very dramatically with the vernacular tone of Sojourner Truth who campaigned vigorously for the enfranchisement of black women. These two voices, the cultivated voice of Douglass and the raw passion in Truth, represent significantly different strategies of political intervention and social inclusion which are with us even today. Houston A. Baker, Jr. reads the slave narrative through a slightly different lens, contrasting the 'lawful sovereigns' with the 'plantation chattels' to argue that even though both groups belong to the nineteenth century, the former category encompasses canonical writers such as Emerson, Thoreau, and Whitman who are considered to be the sustained voice of American culture and humanism, while the latter category signals such 'slave' writers as Douglass or Henry Bibb, who have been retrieved, almost archivally, only as recently as the middle of the twentieth century. In the realm of critique, the marginals represent the other American voice and the other side of American culture. Within this logic, today's cultural critics argue that the slave narrative is essential to understanding the geography of the American literary imagination as a whole.

Besides being actively engaged in the Suffrage issue and the abolition of slavery, American pioneers made the settlement of this fertile new land a priority. A great deal of thought went into the selection of its peoples and population, a thought almost Darwinian in its logic of natural selection. This mentality brought to the fore issues such as race, gender, and class, all of which were occluded in the universalist and political terminology of democracy. Social historians and cultural anthropologists are re-examining the 'settlement' issue, and interrogating the complex intersection of influences—race, gender, class, and ethnicity—in re-charting the carefully masked policies of confining native Americans to reservations, or denying blacks the right to own land in the new territories, or selective immigration quotas, to show that such state policing distorted the melting-pot theory of American culture. (This idea is now being scrutinized as post-identity politics, see Race Studies section.)

The expansion of the boundaries of 'civilization' and 'culture' westward is not merely a historical or a geographical reality in America but a fundamentally political, religious, and social issue. Frederick Jackson Turner's essay 'The Significance of the Frontier in American History' (1926), often referred to as the Turner thesis, is the first formulation of the importance of the concept of the frontier in the cultural imagination of America, and carefully summarizes the effects of the numerous co-existing cultural forces of the nineteenth century that are catalogued above. Turner argued that while older societies were defined by clear, social and cultural boundaries, the western or frontier society, due to its inherent youthful exuberance, buoyant optimism and energetic activity, neither had nor needed social stratification. Turner connects the burgeoning impulses of the 'new Adam' to the basic premise of democracy in a classless America and sees the spirit of frontierism as more than an exploration of the land. He writes 'The American frontier is sharply distinguished from the European frontier—a fortified boundary line running through dense populations.' Literary figures like James Fennimore Cooper and Mark Twain, among others, concur with this view.

Another major figure in the American cultural scene at the beginning of the twentieth century is Charles Sanders Peirce, the founder of pragmatic philosophy and semiotics. Peirce, who was 'discovered' only during the middle of the twentieth century, actually participated in the intellectual founding of America, and developed a theory of signs independent of the Swiss linguist Ferdinand de Saussure, who is referred to as the European father of semiotics. Basing his work on principles of scientific enquiry, Peirce examined the pragmatic nature of language as a sign system, a system that was clearly constructed on cultural norms and usage. Peirce's work has a different texture from that of literary scholars such as Whitman or Thoreau, or the pamphlets of the Suffrage writers, or the tone of slave narratives. In other words, Peirce's discourse reveals yet another side of American culture, one which is closer to the intellectual life of Europe, wherein the mating of scientific enquiry and humanistic beliefs resembled Kant's exposition of the world through *pragmatische*, which explained laws empirically. (A companion in this enquiry was William James, the pragmatist philosopher.) A pioneer of modern logic, Peirce followed a rational mode of enquiry and systematic deductions, as seen in his letters to Lady Welby. While

17

some critics tend to see Peirce more as a religious philosopher or a liberal humanist, instead of a pragmatic semiotician, most cultural critics recognize the value of his contribution in furthering cultural studies via semiotics.

On both sides of the Atlantic rapid and far-reaching social change stimulated the need to interpret emerging cultural forces. Whether welcomed or abhorred, a mass society of increasing material prosperity was being born that challenged traditional understanding of social and cultural relationships. The essays in this section address issues of class, gender, and race, and their connections to lived-in experiences of everyday culture. These essays also serve another important function—that of providing a blueprint for the development of cultural hierarchies, critiques, and studies in our own times.

G.R. and J.M.

FURTHER READING

Armstrong, Nancy, *Desire and Domestic Fiction: A Political History of the Novel*, New York: Oxford University Press, 1987.

Asad, Talal ed., *Anthropology and the Colonial Encounter*, New York: Humanities Press, 1973.

Baker, Houston, Jr., *Blues, Ideology, and Afro-American Literature*, Chicago: Chicago University Press, 1989.

Baldick, Chris, *The Social Mission of English Criticism*, Oxford: Clarendon Press, 1983.

Barker, Martin, *The New Racism*, London: Junction Press, 1982.

Blackburn, Robin, *The Overthrow of Colonial Slavery*, London: Verso, 1988.

Boime, Albert, *The Art of Exclusion: Representing Blacks in the Nineteenth Century*, London: Thames & Hudson, 1990.

Buckley, Jerome, *The Victorian Temper*, Cambridge, Mass.: Harvard University Press, 1951.

Colls, Robert, and Phillip Dodd eds, *Englishness: Politics and Culture 1880-1920*, London: Croom Helm, 1987.

Davidoff, L., and Catherine Hall, *Family Fortunes: Men and Women of the English Middle Class 1780-1850*, London: Hutchinson, 1987.

Fuentes, Carlos, *A Change of Skin*, trans. S. Hileman, New York: Farrar, Straus & Giroux, 1968.

Gallagher, Catherine, and T. Laqueur eds, *The Making of the Modern Body: Sexuality and Society in the Nineteenth Century*, Berkeley: University of California Press, 1987.

Gates, Henry L., Jr., *Figures in Black: Words, Signs, and the 'Racial' Self*, New York: Oxford University Press, 1987.

Green, Martin, *Dreams of Adventure, Deeds of Empire*, London: Routledge, 1980.

Hall, Stuart, 'The Emergence of Cultural Studies and the Crisis of the Humanities', *October* 53 (1990): 11–90.

LaCapra, Dominick, *History and Criticism*, Ithaca, New York: Cornell University Press, 1985.

Marable, Manning, *Race, Reform and Rebellion: The Reconstruction of Black America 1945-1982*, London: Macmillan, 1984.

Miller, J. Hillis, *The Disappearance of God: Five Nineteenth-Century Writers*, Cambridge, Mass.: Harvard University Press, 1963.

Morgan, Thais E. ed., *Victorian Sages and Cultural Discourse: Renegotiating Gender and Power*, New Brunswick: Rutgers University Press, 1990.

Pratt, Mary Louise, *Imperial Eyes: Studies in Travel Writing and Transculturation*, London and New York: Routledge, 1992.

Stansell, Christine, *City of Women: Sex and Class in New York, 1789-1860*, Urbana: University of Illinois Press, 1987.

Wolf, Eric, *Europe and the People Without History*, Berkeley: University of California Press, 1982.

Wolf, Janet, and John Seed eds, *The Culture of Capital: Art, Power, and the Nineteenth-Century Middle Class*, Manchester: Manchester University Press, 1988.

Matthew Arnold (1822–1888)

Matthew Arnold enjoyed the privileged life of an English intellectual, attended Oxford, and eventually got the prestigious position of Professor of Poetry at Oxford in 1857. He began his career as a poet; his famous poem 'Dover Beach' (written 1851, published 1867) is frequently anthologized and often quoted as the quintessential Victorian statement. As an Inspector of Schools from 1851 onward, he instituted several educational reform policies, got promoted to Chief Inspector of Schools in 1884, and retired from the post in 1886. Arnold was actively engaged in the controversies of Victorian England on issues of education, politics, religion, and literary criticism. His prose works include 'The Function of Criticism at the Present Time' (1864), *Essays in Criticism* (1865/1869), *Culture and Anarchy* (1869), and *Literature and Dogma* (1872).

Culture and Anarchy is Arnold's most incisive assessment of the problems facing Victorian society. In the first chapter 'Sweetness and Light', excerpted here, Arnold's thesis, that culture bears the responsibility for political progress and societal well-being, comes out of a mid-nineteenth-century Germanic notion of culture which is founded upon his study of Goethe and Schiller. He defines culture as 'the best knowledge and thought of the time' capable, like religion, of transcending sectarian bickering and reductive economic determinism. Arnold chides the middle class for its Philistine views, equating 'democracy' with 'anarchy', and believes that culture has the ability to transform and improve human character. He advocates a sound training in classical texts and believes that such an education would instil values, which would in turn ameliorate class conflict, leading the way to a more egalitarian social order. Although such an effect may seem to be doubtful, it is invoked even today in arguments for personal and societal improvement.
T.M.

Sweetness and light

The disparagers of culture make its motive curiosity; sometimes, indeed, they make its motive mere exclusiveness and vanity. The culture which is supposed to plume itself on a smattering of Greek and Latin is a culture which is begotten by nothing so intellectual as curiosity; it is valued either out of sheer vanity and ignorance or else as an engine of social and class distinction, separating its holder, like a badge or title, from other people who have not got it. No serious man would call this *culture*, or attach any value to it, as culture, at all. To find the real ground for the very different estimate which serious people will set upon culture, we must find some motive for culture in the terms of which may lie a real ambiguity; and such a motive the word *curiosity* gives us.

I have before now pointed out that we English do not, like the foreigners, use this word in a good sense as well as in a bad sense. With us the word is always used in a somewhat disapproving sense. A liberal and intelligent eagerness about the things of the mind may be meant by a foreigner when he speaks of curiosity, but with us the word always conveys a certain notion of frivolous and unedifying activity. In the *Quarterly Review*, some little time ago, was an estimate of the celebrated French critic, M. Sainte-Beuve, and a very inadequate estimate it in my judgment was. And its inadequacy consisted chiefly in this: that in our English way it left out of sight the double sense really involved in the word *curiosity*, thinking enough was said to stamp M. Sainte-Beuve with blame if it was said that he was impelled in his operations as a critic by curiosity, and omitting either to perceive that M. Sainte-Beuve himself, and many other people with him, would consider that this was praiseworthy and not blameworthy, or to point out why it ought really to be accounted worthy of blame and not of praise. For as there is a curiosity about intellectual matters which is futile, and merely a disease, so there is certainly a curiosity,—a desire after the things of the mind simply for their own sakes and for the pleasure of seeing them as they are,— which is, in an intelligent being, natural and laudable. Nay, and the very desire to see things as they are implies a balance and regulation of mind which is not often attained without fruitful effort, and which is the very opposite of the blind and dis- eased impulse of mind which is what we mean to blame when we blame curiosity. Montesquieu says: 'The first motive which ought to impel us to study is the desire to augment the excellence of our nature, and to render an intelligent being yet more intelligent.' This is the true ground to assign for the genuine scientific passion, how- ever manifested, and for culture, viewed simply as a fruit of this passion; and it is a worthy ground, even though we let the term *curiosity* stand to describe it.

But there is of culture another view, in which not solely the scientific passion, the sheer desire to see things as they are, natural and proper in an intelligent being, appears as the ground of it. There is a view in which all the love of our neighbour, the impulses towards action, help, and beneficence, the desire for removing human error, clearing human confusion, and diminishing human misery, the noble aspira- tion to leave the world better and happier than we found it,—motives eminently such as are called social,—come in as part of the grounds of culture, and the main and preeminent part. Culture is then properly described not as having its origin in curiosity, but as having its origin in the love of perfection; it is *a study of perfection*. It moves by the force, not merely or primarily of the scientific passion for pure knowledge, but also of the moral and social passion for doing good. As, in the first view of it, we took for its worthy motto Montesquieu's words: 'To render an intelligent being yet more intelligent!' so, in the second view of it, there is no better motto which it can have than these words of Bishop Wilson: 'To make reason and the will of God prevail!'

Only, whereas the passion for doing good is apt to be over-hasty in determining what reason and the will of God say, because its turn is for acting rather than think-ing and it wants to be beginning to act; and whereas it is apt to take its own conceptions, which proceed from its own state of development and share in all the imperfections and immaturities of this, for a basis of action; what distinguishes cul-ture is, that it is possessed by the scientific passion as well as by the passion of doing good; that it demands worthy notions of reason and the will of God, and does not readily suffer its own crude conceptions to substitute themselves for them. And knowing that no action or institution can be salutary and stable which is not based on reason and the will of God, it is not so bent on acting and instituting, even with the great aim of diminishing human error and misery ever before its thoughts, but that it can remember that acting and instituting are of little use, unless we know how and what we ought to act and to institute.

This culture is more interesting and more far-reaching than that other, which is founded solely on the scientific passion for knowing. But it needs times of faith and ardour, times when the intellectual horizon is opening and widening all round us, to flourish in. And is not the close and bounded intellectual horizon within which we have long lived and moved now lifting up, and are not new lights finding free passage to shine in upon us? For a long time there was no passage for them to make their way in upon us, and then it was of no use to think of adapting the world's action to them. Where was the hope of making reason and the will of God prevail among people who had a routine which they had christened reason and the will of God, in which they were inextricably bound, and beyond which they had no power of looking? But now the iron force of adhesion to the old routine,—social, political, religious,—has won-derfully yielded; the iron force of exclusion of all which is new has wonderfully yielded. The danger now is, not that people should obstinately refuse to allow any-thing but their old routine to pass for reason and the will of God, but either that they should allow some novelty or other to pass for these too easily, or else that they should underrate the importance of them altogether, and think it enough to follow action for its own sake, without troubling themselves to make reason and the will of God prevail therein. Now, then, is the moment for culture to be of service, culture which believes in making reason and the will of God prevail, believes in pefection, is the study and pursuit of perfection, and is no longer debarred, by a rigid invincible exclusion of whatever is new, from getting acceptance for its ideas, simply because they are new.

The moment this view of culture is seized, the moment it is regarded not solely as the endeavour to see things as they are, to draw towards a knowledge of the universal order which seems to be intended and aimed at in the world, and which it is a man's happiness to go along with or his misery to go counter to,—to learn, in short, the will of God,—the moment, I say, culture is considered not merely as the endeavour to *see* and *learn* this, but as the endeavour, also, to make it *prevail*, the moral, social, and beneficent character of culture becomes manifest. The mere endeavour to see and learn the truth for our own personal satisfaction is indeed a commencement for making it prevail, a preparing the way for this, which always serves this, and is wrongly, therefore, stamped with blame absolutely in itself and not only in its caricature and degeneration. But perhaps it has got stamped with blame, and disparaged with the dubious title of curiosity, because in comparison with this wider endeavour of such great and plain utility it looks selfish, petty, and unprofitable.

And religion, the greatest and most important of the efforts by which the human race has manifested its impulse to perfect itself,—religion, that voice of the deepest human experience,—does not only enjoin and sanction the aim which is the great aim of culture, the aim of setting ourselves to ascertain what perfection is and to make it prevail; but also, in determining generally in what human perfection consists, religion comes to a conclusion identical with that which culture,—culture seeking the determination of this question through *all* the voices of human experience which have been heard upon it, of art, science, poetry, philosophy, history, as well as of religion, in order to give a greater fulness and certainty to its solution,—likewise reaches. Religion says: *The kingdom of God is within you*; and culture, in like manner, places human perfection in an *internal* condition, in the growth and predominance of our humanity proper, as distinguished from our animality. It places it in the ever-increasing efficacy and in the general harmonious expansion of those gifts of thought and feeling, which make the peculiar dignity, wealth, and happiness of human nature. As I have said on a former occasion: 'It is in making endless additions to itself, in the endless expansion of its powers, in endless growth in wisdom and beauty, that the spirit of the human race finds its ideal. To reach this ideal, culture is an indispensable aid, and that is the true value of culture.' Not a having and a resting, but a growing and a becoming, is the character of perfection as culture conceives it; and here, too, it coincides with religion.

And because men are all members of one great whole, and the sympathy which is in human nature will not allow one member to be indifferent to the rest or to have a perfect welfare independent of the rest, the expansion of our humanity, to suit the idea of perfection which culture forms, must be a *general* expansion. Perfection, as culture conceives it, is not possible while the individual remains isolated. The individual is required, under pain of being stunted and enfeebled in his own development if he disobeys, to carry others along with him in his march towards perfection, to be continually doing all he can to enlarge and increase the volume of the human stream sweeping thitherward. And here, once more, culture lays on us the same obligation as religion, which says, as Bishop Wilson has admirably put it, that 'to promote the kingdom of God is to increase and hasten one's own happiness.'

But, finally, perfection,—as culture from a thorough disinterested study of human nature and human experience learns to conceive it,—is a harmonious expansion of *all* the powers which make the beauty and worth of human nature, and is not consistent with the over-development of any one power at the expense of the rest. Here culture goes beyond religion, as religion is generally conceived by us.

If culture, then, is a study of perfection, and of harmonious perfection, general perfection, and perfection which consists in becoming something rather than in having something, in an inward condition of the mind and spirit, not in an outward set of circumstances,—it is clear that culture, instead of being the frivolous and useless thing which Mr. Bright, and Mr. Frederic Harrison, and many other Liberals are apt to call it, has a very important function to fulfil for mankind. And this function is particularly important in our modern world, of which the whole civilisation is, to a much greater degree than the civilisation of Greece and Rome, mechanical and external, and tends constantly to become more so. But above all in our own country has culture a weighty part to perform, because here that mechanical character, which civilisation tends to take everywhere, is shown in the most eminent degree. Indeed nearly all the characters of perfection, as culture teaches us to fix them, meet in this country with some powerful tendency which thwarts them and sets them at defiance. The idea of perfection as an *inward* condition of the mind and spirit is at variance with the mechanical and material civilisation in esteem with us, and nowhere, as I have said, so much in esteem as with us. The idea of perfection as a *general* expansion of the human family is at variance with our strong individualism, our hatred of all limits to the unrestrained swing of the individual's personality, our maxim of 'every man for himself.' Above all, the idea of perfection as a *harmonious* expansion of human nature is at variance with our want of flexibility, with our inaptitude for seeing more than one side of a thing, with our intense energetic absorption in the particular pursuit we happen to be following. So culture has a rough task to achieve in this country. Its preachers have, and are likely long to have, a hard time of it, and they will much oftener be regarded, for a great while to come, as elegant or spurious Jeremiahs than as friends and benefactors. That, however, will not prevent their doing in the end good service if they persevere. And, meanwhile, the mode of action they have to pursue, and the sort of habits they must fight against, ought to be made quite clear for every one to see, who may be willing to look at the matter attentively and dispassionately.

Faith in machinery is, I said, our besetting danger; often in machinery most absurdly disproportioned to the end which this machinery, if it is to do any good at all, is to serve, but always in machinery, as if it had a value in and for itself. What is freedom but machinery? what is population but machinery? what is coal but machinery? what are railroads but machinery? what is wealth but machinery? what are, even, religious organisations but machinery? Now almost every voice in England is accustomed to speak of these things as if they were precious ends in themselves, and therefore had some of the characters of perfection indisputably joined to them.

[. . .]

And in the same way with respect to railroads and coal. Every one must have observed the strange language current during the late discussions as to the possible failure of our supplies of coal. Our coal, thousands of people were saying, is the real basis of our national greatness; if our coal runs short, there is an end of the greatness of England. But what *is* greatness?—culture makes us ask. Greatness is a spiritual condition worthy to excite love, interest, and admiration; and the outward proof of possessing greatness is that we excite love, interest, and admiration. If England were swallowed up by the sea tomorrow, which of the two, a hundred years hence, would most excite the love, interest, and admiration of mankind,—would most, therefore, show the evidences of having possessed greatness,—the England of the last twenty years, or the England of Elizabeth, of a time of splendid spiritual effort, but when our coal, and our industrial operations depending on coal, were very little developed? Well, then, what an unsound habit of mind it must be which makes us talk of things like coal or iron as constituting the greatness of England, and how salutary a friend is culture, bent on seeing things as they are, and thus dissipating delusions of this kind and fixing standards of perfection that are real!

Wealth, again, that end to which our prodigious works for material advantage are directed,—the commonest of commonplaces tells us how men are always apt to regard wealth as a precious end in itself; and certainly they have never been so apt thus to regard it as they are in England at the present time. Never did people believe anything more firmly than nine Englishmen out of ten at the present day believe that our greatness and welfare are proved by our being so very rich. Now, the use of culture is that it helps us, by means of its spiritual standard of perfection, to regard wealth as but machinery, and not only to say as a matter of words that we regard wealth as but machinery, but really to perceive and feel that it is so. If it were not for this purging effect wrought upon our minds by culture, the whole world, the future as well as the prsent, would inevitably belong to the Philistines. The people who believe most that our greatness and welfare are proved by our being very rich, and who most give their lives and thoughts to becoming rich, are just the very people whom we call Philistines. Culture says: 'Consider these people, then, their way of life, their habits, their manners, the very tones of their voice; look at them attentively; observe the literature they read, the things which give them pleasure, the words which come forth out of their mouths, the thoughts which make the furniture of their minds; would any amount of wealth be worth having with the condition that one was to become just like these people by having it?' And thus culture begets a dissatisfaction which is of the highest possible value in stemming the common tide of men's thoughts in a wealthy and industrial community, and which saves the future, as one may hope, from being vulgarised, even if it cannot save the present.

Population, again, and bodily health and vigour, are things which are nowhere treated in such an unintelligent, misleading, exaggerated way as in England. Both are really machinery; yet how many people all around us do we see rest in them and fail to look beyond them! Why, one has heard people, fresh from reading certain articles of the *Times* on the Registrar-General's returns of marriages and births in this country, who would talk of our large English families in quite a solemn strain, as if they had something in itself beautiful, elevating, and meritorious in them; as if the British Philistine would have only to present himself before the Great Judge with his twelve children, in order to be received among the sheep as a matter of right!

But bodily health and vigour, it may be said, are not to be classed with wealth and population as mere machinery; they have a more real and essential value. True; but only as they are more intimately connected with a perfect spiritual condition than wealth or population are. The moment we disjoin them from the idea of a perfect spiritual condition, and pursue them, as we do pursue them, for their own sake and as ends in themselves, our worship of them becomes as mere worship of machinery, as our worship of wealth or population, and as unintelligent and vulgarising a worship as that is. Every one with anything like an adequate idea of human perfection has distinctly marked this subordination to higher and spiritual ends of the cultivation of bodily vigour and activity. 'Bodily exercise profiteth little; but godliness is profitable unto all things,' says the author of the Epistle to Timothy. And the utilitarian Franklin says just as explicitly:—'Eat and drink such an exact quantity as suits the constitution of thy body, *in reference to the services of the mind.*' But the point of view of culture, keeping the mark of human perfection simply and broadly in view, and not assigning to this perfection, as religion or utilitarianism assigns to it, a special and limited character, this point of view, I say, of culture is best given by these words of Epictetus:—'It is a sign of αφυΐα,' says he,—that is, of a nature not finely tempered,—'to give yourselves up to things which relate to the body; to make, for instance, a great fuss about exercise, a great fuss about eating, a great fuss about drinking, a great fuss about walking, a great fuss about riding. All these things ought to be done merely by the way: the formation of the spirit and character must be our real concern.' This is admirable; and, indeed, the Greek word εὐφυΐα, a finely tempered nature, gives exactly the notion of perfection as culture brings us to conceive it: a harmonious perfection, a perfection in which the characters of beauty and intelligence are both present, which unites 'the two noblest of things,'—as Swift, who of one of the two, at any rate, had himself all too little, most happily calls them in his *Battle of the Books,*—'the two noblest of things, *sweetness and light.*' The εὐφυής is the man who tends towards sweetness and light; the ἀφυής, on the other hand, is our Philistine. The immense spiritual significance of the Greeks is due to their having been inspired with this central and happy idea of the essential character of human perfection; and Mr. Bright's miconception of culture, as a smattering of Greek and Latin, comes itself, after all, from this wonderful significance of the Greeks having affected the very machinery of our education, and is in itself a kind of homage to it.

In thus making sweetness and light to be characters of perfection, culture is of like spirit with poetry, follows one law with poetry. Far more than on our freedom, our population, and our industrialism, many amongst us rely upon our religious organisations to save us. I have called religion a yet more important manifestation of human nature than poetry, because it has worked on a broader scale for perfection, and with greater masses of men. But the idea of beauty and of a human nature perfect on all its sides, which is the dominant idea of poetry, is a true and invaluable idea, though it has not yet had the success that the idea of conquering the obvious faults of our animality, and of a human nature perfect on the moral side,—which is the dominant idea of religion,—has been enabled to have; and it is destined, adding to itself the religious idea of a devout energy, to transform and govern the other.

The best art and poetry of the Greeks, in which religion and poetry are one, in which the idea of beauty and of a human nature perfect on all sides adds to itself a religious and devout energy, and works in the strength of that, is on this account of such surpassing interest and instructiveness for us, though it was,—as, having regard to the human race in general, and, indeed, having regard to the Greeks themselves, we must own,—a premature attempt, an attempt which for success needed the moral and religious fibre in humanity to be more braced and developed than it had yet been. But Greece did not err in having the idea of beauty, harmony, and complete human perfection, so present and paramount. It is impossible to have this idea too present and paramount; only, the moral fibre must be braced too. And we, because we have braced the moral fibre, are not on that account in the right way, if at the same time the idea of beauty, harmony, and complete human perfection, is wanting or misapprehended amongst us; and evidently it *is* wanting or misapprehended at present. And when we rely as we do on our religious organisations, which in themselves do not and cannot give us this idea, and think we have done enough if we make them spread and prevail, then, I say, we fall into our common fault of overvaluing machinery.

Nothing is more common than for people to confound the inward peace and satisfaction which follows the subduing of the obvious faults of our animality with what I may call absolute inward peace and satisfaction,—the peace and satisfaction which are reached as we draw near to complete spiritual perfection, and not merely to moral perfection, or rather to relative moral perfection. No people in the world have done more and struggled more to attain this relative moral perfection than our English race has. For no people in the world has the command to *resist the devil*, to *overcome the wicked one*, in the nearest and most obvious sense of those words, had such a pressing force and reality. And we have had our reward, not only in the great worldly prosperity which our obedience to this command has brought us, but also, and far more, in great inward peace and satisfaction. But to me few things are more pathetic than to see people, on the strength of the inward peace and satisfaction which their rudimentary efforts towards perfection have brought them, employ, concerning their incomplete perfection and the religious organisations within which they have found it, language which properly applies only to complete perfection, and is a far-off echo of the human soul's prophecy of it. Religion itself, I need hardly say, supplies them in abundance with this grand language. And very freely do they use it; yet it is really the severest possible criticism of such an incomplete perfection as alone we have yet reached through our religious organisations.

The impulse of the English race towards moral development and self-conquest has nowhere so powerfully manifested itself as in Puritanism. Nowhere has Puritanism found so adequate an expression as in the religious organisation of the Independents. The modern Independents have a newspaper, the *Nonconformist*, written with great sincerity and ability. The motto, the standard, the profession of faith which this organ of theirs carries aloft, is: 'The Dissidence of Dissent and the Protestantism of the Protestant religion.' There is sweetness and light, and an ideal of complete harmonious human perfection! One need not go to culture and poetry to find language to judge it. Religion, with its instinct for perfection, supplies language to judge it, language, too, which is in our mouths every day. 'Finally, be of one mind, united in feeling,' says St. Peter. There is an ideal which judges the Puritan ideal: 'The Dissidence of Dissent and the Protestantism of the Protestant religion!' And religious organisations like this are what people believe in, rest in, would give their lives for! Such, I say, is the wonderful virtue of even the beginnings of perfection, of having conquered even the plain faults of our animality, that the religious organisation which has helped us to do it can seem to us something precious, salutary, and to be propagated, even when it wears such a brand of imperfection on its forehead as this. And men have got such a habit of giving to the language of religion a special application, of making it a mere jargon, that for the condemnation which religion itself passes on the shortcomings of their religious organisations they have no ear; they are sure to cheat themselves and to explain this condemnation away. They can only be reached by the criticism which culture, like poetry, speaking a language not to be sophisticated, and resolutely testing these organisations by the ideal of a human perfection complete on all sides, applies to them.

But men of culture and poetry, it will be said, are again and again failing, and failing conspicuously, in the necessary first stage to a harmonious perfection, in the subduing of the great obvious faults of our animality, which it is the glory of these religious organisations to have helped us to subdue. True, they do often so fail. They have often been without the virtues as well as the faults of the Puritan; it has been one of their dangers that they so felt the Puritan's faults that they too much neglected the practice of his virtues. I will not, however, exculpate them at the Puritan's expense. They have often failed in morality, and morality is indispensable. And they have been punished for their failure, as the Puritan has been rewarded for his performance. They have been punished wherein they erred; but their ideal of beauty, of sweetness and light, and a human nature complete on all its sides, remains the true ideal of perfection still; just as the Puritan's ideal of perfection remains narrow and inadequate, although for what he did well he has been richly rewarded. Notwithstanding the mighty results of the Pilgrim Fathers' voyage, they and their standard of perfection are rightly judged when we figure to ourselves Shakspeare or Virgil,—souls in whom sweetness and light, and all that in human nature is most humane, were eminent,—accompanying them on their voyage, and think what intolerable company Shakspeare and Virgil would have found them! In the same way let us judge the religious organisations which we see all around us. Do not let us deny the good and the happiness which they have accomplished; but do not let us fail to see clearly that their idea of human perfection is narrow and inadequate, and that the Dissidence of Dissent and the Protestantism of the Protestant religion will never bring humanity to its true goal. As I said with regard to wealth: Let us look at the life of those who live in and for it,—so I say with regard to the religious organisations. Look at the life imaged in such a newspaper as the *Nonconformist*,—a life of jealousy of the Establishment, disputes, tea-meetings, openings of chapels, sermons; and then think of it as an ideal of a human life completing itself on all sides, and aspiring with all its organs after sweetness, light, and perfection!

Another newspaper, representing, like the *Nonconformist*, one of the religious organisations of this country, was a short time ago giving an account of the crowd at Epsom on the Derby day, and of all the vice and hideousness which was to be seen in that crowd, and then the writer turned suddenly round upon Professor Huxley, and asked him how he proposed to cure all this vice and hideousness without religion. I confess I felt disposed to ask the asker this question: And how do you propose to cure it with such a religion as yours? How is the ideal of a life so unlovely, so unattractive, so incomplete, so narrow, so far removed from a true and satisfying ideal of human perfection, as is the life of your religious organisation as you yourself reflect it, to conquer and transform all this vice and hideousness? Indeed, the strongest plea for the study of perfection as pursued by culture, the clearest proof of the actual inadequacy of the idea of perfection held by the religious organisations,—expressing, as I have said, the most widespread effort which the human race has yet made after perfection,—is to be found in the state of our life and society with these in possession of

27

it, and having been in possession of it I know not how many hundred years. We are all of us included in some religious organisation or other; we all call ourselves, in the sublime and aspiring language of religion which I have before noticed, *children of God*. Children of God;—it is an immense pretension!—and how are we to justify it? By the works which we do, and the words which we speak. And the work which we collective children of God do, our grand centre of life, our *city* which we have builded for us to dwell in, is London! London, with its unutterable external hideousness, and with its internal canker of *publice egestas, privatim opulentia,*—to use the words which Sallust puts into Cato's mouth about Rome,—unequalled in the world! The word, again, which we children of God speak, the voice which most hits our collective thought, the newspaper with the largest circulation in England, nay, with the largest circulation in the whole world, is the *Daily Telegraph*! I say that when our religious organisations,—which I admit to express the most considerable effort after perfection that our race has yet made,—land us in no better result than this, it is high time to examine carefully their idea of perfection, to see whether it does not leave out of account sides and forces of human nature which we might turn to great use; whether it would not be more operative if it were more complete. And I say that the English reliance on our religious organisations and on their ideas of human perfection just as they stand, is like our reliance on freedom, on muscular Christianity, on population, on coal, on wealth,—mere belief in machinery, and unfruitful; and that it is wholesomely counteracted by culture, bent on seeing things as they are, and on drawing the human race onwards to a more complete, a harmonious perfection.

Culture, however, shows its single-minded love of perfection, its desire simply to make reason and the will of God prevail, its freedom from fanaticism, by its attitude towards all this machinery, even while it insists that it *is* machinery. Fanatics, seeing the mischief men do themselves by their blind belief in some machinery or other,— whether it is wealth and industrialism, or whether it is the cultivation of bodily strength and activity, or whether it is a political organisation, or whether it is a religious organisation,—oppose with might and main the tendency to this or that political and religious organisation, or to games and athletic exercises, or to wealth and industrialism, and try violently to stop it. But the flexibility which sweetness and light give, and which is one of the rewards of culture pursued in good faith, enables a man to see that a tendency may be necessary, and even, as a preparation for something in the future, salutary, and yet that the generations or individuals who obey this tendency are sacrificed to it, that they fall short of the hope of perfection by following it; and that its mischiefs are to be criticised, lest it should take too firm a hold and last after it has served its purpose.

Mr. Gladstone well pointed out, in a speech at Paris,—and others have pointed out the same thing,—how necessary is the present great movement towards wealth and industrialism, in order to lay broad foundations of material well-being for the society of the future. The worst of these justifications is, that they are generally addressed to the very people engaged, body and soul, in the movement in question; at all events, that they are always seized with the greatest avidity by these people, and taken by them as quite justifying their life; and that thus they tend to harden them in their sins. Now, culture admits the necessity of the movement towards fortune-making and exaggerated industrialism, readily allows that the future may derive benefit from it; but insists, at the same time, that the passing generations of industrialists,—forming, for the most part, the stout main body of Philistinism,—are sacrificed to it. In the same way, the result of all the games and sports which occupy the passing generation of boys and young men may be the establishment of a better and sounder physical type for the future to work with. Culture does not set itself against the games and sports; it congratulates the future, and hopes it will make a good use of its improved physical basis; but it points out that our passing generation of boys and young men is, meantime, sacrificed. Puritanism was perhaps necessary to develop the moral fibre of the English race, Noncomformity to break the yoke of ecclesiastical domination over men's minds and to prepare the way for freedom of thought in the distant future; still, culture points out that the harmonious perfection of generations of Puritans and Nonconformists has been, in consequence, sacrificed. Freedom of speech may be necessary for the society of the future, but the young lions of the *Daily Telegraph* in the meanwhile are sacrificed. A voice for every man in his country's government may be necessary for the society of the future, but meanwhile Mr. Beales and Mr. Bradlaugh are sacrificed.

Oxford, the Oxford of the past, has many faults; and she has heavily paid for them in defeat, in isolation, in want of hold upon the modern world. Yet we in Oxford, brought up amidst the beauty and sweetness of that beautiful place, have not failed to seize one truth,—the truth that beauty and sweetness are essential characters of a complete human perfection. When I insist on this, I am all in the faith and tradition of Oxford. I say boldly that this our sentiment for beauty and sweetness, our sentiment against hideousness and rawness, has been at the bottom of our attachment to so many beaten causes, of our opposition to so many triumphant movements. And the sentiment is true, and has never been wholly defeated, and has shown its power even in its defeat. We have not won our political battles, we have not carried our main points, we have not stopped our adversaries' advance, we have not marched victoriously with the modern world; but we have told silently upon the mind of the country, we have prepared currents of feeling which sap our adversaries' position when it seems gained, we have kept up our own communications with the future. Look at the course of the great movement which shook Oxford to its centre some thirty years ago! It was directed, as any one who reads Dr. Newman's *Apology* may see, against what in one word may be called 'Liberalism.' Liberalism prevailed; it was the appointed force to do the work of the hour; it was necessary, it was inevitable that it should prevail. The Oxford movement was broken, it failed; our wrecks are scattered on every shore:—

Quæ regio in terris nostri non plena laboris?

But what was it, this liberalism, as Dr. Newman saw it, and as it really broke the Oxford movement? It was the great middle-class liberalism, which had for the cardinal points of its belief the Reform Bill of 1832, and local self-government, in politics; in the social sphere, free-trade, unrestricted competition, and the making of large industrial fortunes; in the religious sphere, the Dissidence of Dissent and the Protestantism of the Protestant religion. I do not say that other and more intelligent forces than this were not opposed to the Oxford movement: but this was the force which really beat it; this was the force which Dr. Newman felt himself fighting with;

this was the force which till only the other day seemed to be the paramount force in this country, and to be in possession of the future; this was the force whose achievements fill Mr. Lowe with such inexpressible admiration, and whose rule he was so horror-struck to see threatened. And where is this great force of Philistinism now? It is thrust into the second rank, it is become a power of yesterday, it has lost the future. A new power has suddenly appeared, a power which it is impossible yet to judge fully, but which is certainly a wholly different force from middle-class liberalism; different in its cardinal points of belief, different in its tendencies in every sphere. It loves and admires neither the legislation of middle-class Parliaments, nor the local self-government of middle-class vestries, nor the unrestricted competition of middle-class industrialists, nor the dissidence of middle-class Dissent and the Protestantism of middle-class Protestant religion. I am not now praising this new force, or saying that its own ideals are better; all I say is, that they are wholly different. And who will estimate how much the currents of feeling created by Dr. Newman's movement, the keen desire for beauty and sweetness which it nourished, the deep aversion it manifested to the hardness and vulgarity of middle-class liberalism, the strong light it turned on the hideous and grotesque illusions of middle-class Protestantism,—who will estimate how much all these contributed to swell the tide of secret dissatisfaction which has mined the ground under the self-confident liberalism of the last thirty years, and has prepared the way for its sudden collapse and supersession? It is in this manner that the sentiment of Oxford for beauty and sweetness conquers, and in this manner long may it continue to conquer!

In this manner it works to the same end as culture, and there is plenty of work for it yet to do. I have said that the new and more democratic force which is now superseding our old middle-class liberalism cannot yet be rightly judged. It has its main tendencies still to form. We hear promises of its giving us administrative reform, law reform, reform of education, and I know not what; but those promises come rather from its advocates, wishing to make a good plea for it and to justify it for superseding middle-class liberalism, than from clear tendencies which it has itself yet developed. But meanwhile it has plenty of well-intentioned friends against whom culture may with advantage continue to uphold steadily its ideal of human perfection; that this is *an upward spiritual activity, having for its characters increased sweetness, increased light, increased life, increased sympathy*. Mr. Bright, who has a foot in both worlds, the world of middle-class liberalism and the world of democracy, but who brings most of his ideas from the world of middle-class liberalism in which he was bred, always inclines to inculcate that faith in machinery to which, as we have seen, Englishmen are so prone, and which has been the bane of middle-class liberalism. [. . .] It is the same fashion of teaching a man to value himself not on what he *is*, not on his progress in sweetness and light, but on the number of the railroads he has constructed, or the bigness of the tabernacle he has built. Only the middle classes are told they have done it all with their energy, self-reliance, and capital, and the democracy are told they have done it all with their hands and sinews. But teaching the democracy to put its trust in achievements of this kind is merely training them to be Philistines to take the place of the Philistines whom they are superseding; and they too, like the middle class, will be encouraged to sit down at the banquet of the future without having on a wedding garment, and nothing excellent can then come from them. Those who know their besetting faults, those who have watched them and listened to them, or those who will read the instructive account recently given of them by one of themselves, the *Journeyman Engineer*, will agree that the idea which culture sets before us of perfection,—an increased spiritual activity, having for its characters increased sweetness, increased light, increased life, increased sympathy,—is an idea which the new democracy needs far more than the idea of the blessedness of the franchise, or the wonderfulness of its own industrial performances.

Other well-meaning friends of this new power are for leading it, not in the old ruts of middle-class Philistinism, but in ways which are naturally alluring to the feet of democracy, though in this country they are novel and untried ways. I may call them the ways of Jacobinism. Violent indignation with the past, abstract systems of renovation applied wholesale, a new doctrine drawn up in black and white for elaborating down to the very smallest details a rational society for the future,—these are the ways of Jacobinism. [. . .] Culture is always assigning to system-makers and systems a smaller share in the bent of human destiny than their friends like. A current in people's minds sets towards new ideas; people are dissatisfied with their old narrow stock of Philistine ideas, Anglo-Saxon ideas, or any other; and some man, some Bentham or Comte, who has the real merit of having early and strongly felt and helped the new current, but who brings plenty of narrowness and mistakes of his own into his feeling and help of it, is credited with being the author of the whole current, the fit person to be entrusted with its regulation and to guide the human race.

[. . .]

The pursuit of perfection, then, is the pursuit of sweetness and light. He who works for sweetness and light, works to make reason and the will of God prevail. He who works for machinery, he who works for hatred, works only for confusion. Culture looks beyond machinery, culture hates hatred; culture has one great passion, the passion for sweetness and light. It has one even yet greater!—the passion for making them *prevail*. It is not satisfied till we *all* come to a perfect man; it knows that the sweetness and light of the few must be imperfect until the raw and unkindled masses of humanity are touched with sweetness and light. If I have not shrunk from saying that we must work for sweetness and light, so neither have I shrunk from saying that we must have a broad basis, must have sweetness and light for as many as possible. Again and again I have insisted how those are the happy moments of humanity, how those are the marking epochs of a people's life, how those are the flowering times for literature and art and all the creative power of genius, when there is a *national* glow of life and thought, when the whole of society is in the fullest measure permeated by thought, sensible to beauty, intelligent and alive. Only it must be *real* thought and *real* beauty; *real* sweetness and *real* light. Plenty of people will try to give the masses, as they call them, an intellectual food prepared and adapted in the way they think proper for the actual condition of the masses. The ordinary popular literature is an example of this way of working on the masses. Plenty of people will try to indoctrinate the masses with the set of ideas and judgments constituting the creed of their own profession or party. Our religious and political organisations give an example of this way of working on the masses. I condemn neither way; but culture works differently. It does not try to teach down to the level of inferior classes; it does not try to win them for this or that sect of its own, with ready-made judgments and

31

watchwords. It seeks to do away with classes; to make the best that has been thought and known in the world current everywhere; to make all men live in an atmosphere of sweetness and light, where they may use ideas, as it uses them itself, freely,—nourished, and not bound by them.

This is the *social idea*; and the men of culture are the true apostles of equality. The great men of culture are those who have had a passion for diffusing, for making prevail, for carrying from one end of society to the other, the best knowledge, the best ideas of their time; who have laboured to divest knowledge of all that was harsh, uncouth, difficult, abstract, professional, exclusive; to humanise it, to make it efficient outside the clique of the cultivated and learned, yet still remaining the *best* knowledge and thought of the time, and a true source, therefore, of sweetness and light. Such a man was Abelard in the Middle Ages, in spite of all his imperfections; and thence the boundless emotion and enthusiasm which Abelard excited. Such were Lessing and Herder in Germany, at the end of the last century; and their services to Germany were in this way inestimably precious. Generations will pass, and literary monuments will accumulate, and works far more perfect than the works of Lessing and Herder will be produced in Germany; and yet the names of these two men will fill a German with a reverence and enthusiasm such as the names of the most gifted masters will hardly awaken. And why? Because they *humanised* knowledge; because they broadened the basis of life and intelligence; because they worked powerfully to diffuse sweetness and light, to make reason and the will of God prevail. With Saint Augustine they said: 'Let us not leave thee alone to make in the secret of thy knowledge, as thou didst before the creation of the firmament, the division of light from darkness; let the children of thy spirit, placed in their firmament, make their light shine upon the earth, mark the division of night and day, and announce the revolution of the times; for the old order is passed, and the new arises; the night is spent, the day is come forth; and thou shalt crown the year with thy blessing, when thou shalt send forth labourers into thy harvest sown by other hands than theirs; when thou shalt send forth new labourers to new seed-times, whereof the harvest shall be not yet.'

Karl Marx (1818–1883) and Friedrich Engels (1820–1895)

The works of Karl Marx and Friedrich Engels are among the most influential political documents presented to the Western world in the last 200 years. Marx, born in Trier in 1818, of a German-Jewish family which had been converted to Christianity, was a philosopher, economist and historian. Assisted and supported by Engels, who was born into a wealthy manufacturing family in 1820, Marx wrote a number of treatises which reflected the tenets of scientific socialism, or Marxism, as his approach came to be called.

Many of those important tenets are included in the excerpts from their works which follow. In 'Ideology in General', which was first published in *The German Ideology* (largely written between 1845 and 1846) 'the connections between the social and political structure with production' are emphasized. Here Marx and Engels argue that citizens' 'real lives' determine a state's ideology; therefore, they demand recognition of the value of working-class people in society. The next excerpt, 'Concerning the Production of Consciousness', also from *The German Ideology*, extends this position to a 'revolutionary class', which according to Marx and Engels, must be created to counter those in society who have control over the means of production and thus have enough leisure-time to create consciousness. It is therefore critical that those working-class people who actually produce the goods in society be roused to revolution, and participate in the changing of the societal consciousness. The next excerpt, 'Production', from the *Grundrisse* (1858) reveals Marx's view of history. It addresses the issue of art and its relationship to societal structure and change, suggesting that human consciousness operates in cycles of progress, and that the human intellect matures over time. The final two selections are from Marx's *Capital* (1867). 'On the Realm of Necessity and the Realm of Freedom' is a projection of the writer's hopes for the future when technology will be advanced enough to allow working-class people time enough to think for themselves; even so, Marx allows that time must always be set aside for production. In 'Classes' Marx challenges common identifications of three social classes—always a crucial concern in his

33

writings. Throughout their works, perhaps the most famous of which was the *Communist Manifesto* (1848), Marx and Engels stress issues of power, production, intellectual activity, and social change. Various forms of Marxism have been deployed in political, academic, and social settings since its beginning. Contemporary scholars in cultural and literary studies continue to appropriate and respond to the ideas of these two writers and their successors.
M.B.

From *The German Ideology* (1846)

The fact is, therefore, that definite individuals who are productively active in a definite way enter into these definite social and political reactions. Empirical observations must in each separate instance bring out empirically, and without any mystification and speculation, the connection of the social and political structure with production. The social structure and the State are continually evolving out of the life process of definite individuals, but of individuals, not as they may appear in their own and other people's imagination, but as they *really* are; i.e., as they operate, produce materially, and hence as they work under definite material limits, presuppositions and conditions independent of their will.

The production of ideas, of conceptions, of consciousness, is at first directly interwoven with the material activity and the material intercourse of men, the language of real life. Conceiving, thinking, the mental intercourse of men, appear at this stage as the direct efflux of their material behaviour. The same applies to mental production as expressed in the language of politics, laws, morality, religion, metaphysics, etc., of a people. Men are the producers of their conceptions, ideas, etc.—real, active men, as they are conditioned by a definite development of their productive forces and of the intercourse corresponding to these, up to its furthest forms. Consciousness can never be anything else than conscious existence, and the existence of men is their actual life-process. If in all ideology men and their circumstances appear upside-down as in a *camera obscura*, this phenomenon arises just as much from their historical life-process as the inversion of objects on the retina does from their physical life-process.

In direct contrast to German philosophy which descends from heaven to earth, here we ascend from earth to heaven. That is to say, we do not set out from what men say, imagine, conceive, nor from men as narrated, thought of, imagined, conceived, in order to arrive at men in the flesh. We set out from real, active men, and on the basis of their real life-process we demonstrate the development of the ideological reflexes and echoes of this life-process. The phantoms formed in the human brain are also, necessarily, sublimates of their material life-process, which is empirically verifiable and bound to material premises. Morality, religion, metaphysics, all the rest of ideology and their corresponding forms of consciousness, thus no longer retain the semblance of independence. They have no history, no development; but men, developing their material production and their material intercourse, alter, along with this their real existence, their thinking and the products of their thinking. Life is not determined by consciousness, but consciousness by life. In the first method of approach the starting-point is consciousness taken as the living individual; in the second method, which conforms to real life, it is the real living individuals themselves, and consciousness is considered solely as *their* consciousness.

[. . .]

The ideas of the ruling class are in every epoch the ruling ideas: i.e., the class which is the ruling *material* force of society, is at the same time its ruling *intellectual* force. The class which has the means of material production at its disposal, has control at the same time over the means of mental production, so that thereby, generally speaking, the ideas of those who lack the means of mental production are subject to it. The ruling ideas are nothing more than the ideal expression of the dominant material relationships, the dominant material relationships grasped as ideas; hence of the relationships which make the one class the ruling one, therefore, the ideas of its dominance. The individuals composing the ruling class possess among other things consciousness, and therefore think. Insofar, therefore, as they rule as a class and determine the extent and compass of an epoch, it is self-evident that they do this in its whole range, hence among other things rule also as thinkers, as producers of ideas, and regulate the production and distribution of the ideas of their age: thus their ideas are the ruling ideas of the epoch. For instance, in an age and in a country where royal power, aristocracy and bourgeoisie are contending for mastery and where, therefore, mastery is shared, the doctrine of the separation of powers proves to be the dominant idea and is expressed as an 'eternal law.'

The division of labour, which we have already seen above as one of the chief forces of history up till now, manifests itself also in the ruling class as the division of mental and material labour, so that inside this class one part appears as the thinkers of the class (its active, conceptive ideologists, who make the perfecting of the illusion of the class about itself their chief source of livelihood), while the others' attitude to these ideas and illusions is more passive and receptive, because they are in reality the active members of this class and have less time to make up illusions and ideas about themselves. Within this class this cleavage can even develop into a certain opposition and hostility between the two parts, which, however, in the case of a practical collision, in which the class itself is endangered, automatically comes to nothing, in which case there also vanishes the semblance that the ruling ideas were not the ideas of the ruling class and had a power distinct from the power of this class. The existence of revolutionary ideas in a particular period pre-supposes the existence of a revolutionary class; about the premises for the latter sufficient has already been said above.

If now in considering the course of history we detach the ideas of the ruling class from the ruling class itself and attribute to them an independent existence, if we confine ourselves to saying that these or those ideas were dominant at a given time, without bothering ourselves about the conditions of production and the producers of these ideas, if we thus ignore the individuals and world conditions which are the source of the ideas, we can say, for instance, that during the time that the aristocracy was dominant, the concepts honour, loyalty, etc., were dominant, during the dominance of the bourgeoisie the concepts freedom, equality, etc. The ruling class itself on the whole imagines this to be so. This conception of history, which is common to all historians, particularly since the eighteenth century, will necessarily come up against the phenomenon that increasingly abstract ideas hold sway, i.e., ideas which increasingly take on the form of universality. For each new class which puts itself in the place of one ruling before it, is compelled, merely in order to carry through its aim, to represent its interest as the common interest of all the members of society, that is, expressed in ideal form: it has to give its ideas the form of universality, and represent them as the only rational, universally valid ones. The class making a revolution appears from the very start, if only because it is opposed to a *class*, not as a class but as the representative of the whole of society; it appears as the whole mass of society confronting the one ruling class.* It can do this because, to start with, its interest really is more connected with the common interest of all other non-ruling classes, because under the pressure of hitherto existing conditions its interest has not yet been able to develop as the particular interest of a particular class. Its victory, therefore, benefits also many individuals of the other classes which are not winning a dominant position, but only insofar as it now puts these individuals in a position to raise themselves into the ruling class. When the French bourgeoisie overthrew the power of the aristocracy, it thereby made it possible for many proletarians to raise themselves above the proletariat, but only insofar as they became bourgeois. Every new class, therefore, achieves its hegemony only on a broader basis than that of the class ruling previously, whereas the opposition of the non-ruling class against the new ruling class later develops all the more sharply and profoundly. Both these things determine the fact that the struggle to be waged against this new ruling class, in its turn, aims at a more decided and radical negation of the previous conditions of society than could all previous classes which sought to rule.

This whole semblance, that the rule of a certain class is only the rule of certain ideas, comes to a natural end, of course, as soon as class rule in general ceases to be the form in which society is organised, that is to say, as soon as it is no longer necessary to represent a particular interest as general or the 'general interest' as ruling.

Once the ruling ideas have been separated from the ruling individuals and, above all, from the relationships which result from a given stage of the mode of production, and in this way the conclusion has been reached that history is always under the sway of ideas, it is very easy to abstract from these various ideas '*the* idea,' the notion, etc., as the dominant force in history, and thus to understand all these separate ideas and concepts as 'forms of self-determination' on the part of *the* concept developing in history. It follows then naturally, too, that all the relationships of men can be derived from the concept of man, man as conceived, the essence of man, *Man*.

---

*Marginal note by Marx: 'Universality corresponds to (1) the class versus the estate, (2) the competition, world-wide intercourse, etc., (3) the great numerical strength of the ruling class, (4) the illusion of the *common* interests (in the beginning this illusion is true), (5) the delusion of the ideologists and the division of labour.'

From *Grundrisse* (1858)

(1) In the case of the arts, it is well known that certain periods of their flowering are out of all proportion to the general development of society, hence also to the material foundation, the skeletal structure as it were, of its organization. For example, the Greeks compared to the moderns or also Shakespeare. It is even recognized that certain forms of art, e.g. the epic, can no longer be produced in their world epoch-making, classical stature as soon as the production of art, as such, begins: that is, that certain significant forms within the realm of the arts are possible only at an undeveloped stage of artistic development. If this is the case with the relation between different kinds of art within the realm of the arts, it is already less puzzling that it is the case in the relation of the entire realm to the general development of society. The difficulty consists only in the general formulation of these contradictions. As soon as they have been specified, they are already clarified.

Let us take e.g. the relation of Greek art and then of Shakespeare to the present time. It is well known that Greek mythology is not only the arsenal of Greek art but also its foundation. Is the view of nature and of social relations on which the Greek imagination and hence Greek [mythology] is based possible with self-acting mule spindles and railways and locomotives and electrical telegraphs? What chance has Vulcan against Roberts & Co., Jupiter against the lightning-rod and Hermes against the Credit Mobilier? All mythology overcomes and dominates and shapes the forces of nature in the imagination and by the imagination: it therefore vanishes with the advent of real mastery over them. What becomes of Fama alongside Printing House Square? Greek art presupposes Greek mythology, i.e. nature and the social forms already reworked in an unconsciously artistic way by the popular imagination. This is its material. Not any mythology whatever, i.e. not an arbitrarily chosen unconsciously artistic reworking of nature (here meaning everything objective, hence including society). Egyptian mythology could never have been the foundation or the womb of Greek art. But, in any case, a *mythology*. Hence, in no way a social development which excludes all mythological, all mythologizing relations to nature; which therefore demands of the artist an imagination not dependent on mythology.

From another side, is Achilles possible with powder and lead? Or the *Iliad* with the printing press, not to mention the printing machine? Do not the song and the saga and the muse necessarily come to an end with the printer's bar, hence do not the necessary conditions of epic poetry vanish?

But the difficulty lies not in understanding that the Greek arts and epic are bound up with certain forms of social development. The difficulty is that they still afford us artistic pleasure and that in a certain respect they count as a norm and as an unattainable model.

A man cannot become a child again, or he becomes childish. But does he not find joy in the child's naiveté, and must he himself not strive to reproduce its truth at a higher stage? Does not the true character of each epoch come alive in the nature of its children? Why should not the historic childhood of humanity, its most beautiful unfolding, as a stage never to return, exercise an eternal charm? There are unruly

37

children and precocious children. Many of the old peoples belong in this category. The Greeks were normal children. The charm of their art for us is not in contradiction to the undeveloped stage of society on which it grew. [It] is its result, rather, and is inextricably bound up, rather, with the fact that the unripe social conditions under which it arose, and could alone arise, can never return.

From *Capital*, vol. 3 (1894)

On the realm of necessity and the realm of freedom

We have seen that the capitalist process of production is a historically determined form of the social process of production in general. The latter is as much a production process of material conditions of human life as a process taking place under specific historical and economic production relations, producing and reproducing these production relations themselves, and thereby also the bearers of this process, their material conditions of existence and their mutual relations, i.e., their particular socio-economic form. For the aggregate of these relations, in which the agents of this production stand with respect to Nature and to one another, and in which they produce, is precisely society, considered from the standpoint of its economic structure. Like all its predecessors, the capitalist process of production proceeds under definite material conditions, which are, however, simultaneously the bearers of definite social relations entered into by individuals in the process of reproducing their life. Those conditions, like these relations, are on the one hand prerequisites, on the other hand results and creations of the capitalist process of production; they are produced and reproduced by it. We saw also that capital—and the capitalist is merely capital personified and functions in the process of production solely as the agent of capital—in its corresponding social process of production, pumps a definite quantity of surplus labour out of the direct producers, or labourers; capital obtains this surplus labour without an equivalent, and in essence it always remains forced labour—no matter how much it may seem to result from free contractual agreement. This surplus labour appears as surplus value, and this surplus value exists as a surplus product. Surplus labour in general, as labour performed over and above the given requirements, must always remain. In the capitalist as well as in the slave system, etc., it merely assumes an antagonistic form and is supplemented by complete idleness of a stratum of society. A definite quantity of surplus labour is required as insurance against accidents, and by the necessary and progressive expansion of the process of reproduction in keeping with the development of the needs and the growth of population, which is called accumulation from the viewpoint of the capitalist. It is one of the civilizing aspects of capital that it enforces this surplus labour in a manner and under conditions which are more advantageous to the development of the productive forces, social relations, and the creation of the elements for a new and higher form than under the preceding forms of slavery, serfdom, etc. Thus it gives rise to a stage, on the one hand, in which coercion and monopolization of social development (including its material and intellectual advantages) by one portion of society at the expense of the other are eliminated; on the other hand, it creates the material means and embryonic conditions, making it possible in a higher form of society to combine this surplus labour with a greater reduction of time devoted to material labour in general. For, depending on the development of labour productivity, surplus labour may be large in a small total working day, and relatively small in a large total working day. If the necessary labour time = 3 and the surplus labour = 3, then the total working day = 6 and the rate of surplus labour = 100%. If the necessary labour = 9 and the surplus labour = 3, then the total working day = 12 and the rate of surplus labour only $3\frac{1}{3}$%. In that case, it depends upon the labour productivity how much use value shall be produced in a definite time, hence also in a definite surplus labour time. The actual wealth of society, and the possibility of constantly expanding its reproduction process, therefore, do not depend upon the duration of surplus labour, but upon its productivity and the more or less copious conditions of production under which it is performed. In fact, the realm of freedom actually begins only where labour which is determined by necessity and mundane considerations cease; thus in the very nature of things it lies beyond the sphere of actual material production. Just as the savage must wrestle with Nature to satisfy his wants, to maintain and reproduce life, so must civilized man, and he must do so in all social formations and under all possible modes of production. With his development this realm of physical necessity expands as a result of his wants; but, at the same time, the forces of production which satisfy these wants also increase. Freedom, in this field can only consist in socialized man, the associated producers, rationally regulating their interchange with Nature, bringing it under their common control, instead of being ruled by it as by the blind forces of Nature; and achieving this with the least expenditure of energy and under conditions most favourable to, and worthy of, their human nature. But it nonetheless still remains a realm of necessity. Beyond it begins that development of human energy which is an end in itself, the true realm of freedom, which, however, can blossom forth only with the realm of necessity as its basis. The shortening of the working day is its basic prerequisite.

Classes

The owners merely of labour-power, owners of capital, and land-owners, whose respective sources of income are wages, profit and ground-rent, in other words, wage-labourers, capitalists and land-owners, constitute then three big classes of modern society based upon the capitalist mode of production.

In England, modern society is indisputably most highly and classically developed in economic structure. Nevertheless, even here the stratification of classes does not appear in its pure form. Middle and intermediate strata even here obliterate lines of demarcation everywhere (although incomparably less in rural districts than in the cities). However, this is immaterial for our analysis. We have seen that the continual tendency and law of development of the capitalist mode of production is more and more to divorce the means of production from labour and more and more to concentrate the scattered means of production into large groups, thereby transforming labour into wage-labour and the means of production into capital. And to this tendency, on the other hand, corresponds the independent separation of landed property from capital and labour, or the transformation of all landed property into the form of landed property corresponding to the capitalist mode of production.

The first question to be answered is this: What constitutes a class?—and the reply to this follows naturally from the reply to another question, namely: What makes wage-labourers, capitalists and landlords constitute the three great social classes?

At first glance—the identity of revenues and sources of revenue. These are three great social groups whose members, the individuals forming them, live on wages, profit and ground-rent respectively, on the realisation of their labour-power, their capital, and their landed property.

However, from this standpoint, physicians and officials, e.g., would also constitute two classes, for they belong to two distinct social groups, the members of each of these groups receiving their revenue from one and the same source. The same would also be true of the infinite fragmentation of interest and rank into which the division of social labour splits labourers as well as capitalists and landlords–the latter, e.g., into owners of vineyards, farm owners, owners of forests, mine owners and owners of fisheries.*

*Here the manuscript breaks off.

Sojourner Truth (?–1883)
Elizabeth Cady Stanton (1815–1902)
Susan Brownell Anthony (1820–1906)

As a black woman, Sojourner Truth was born into slavery in the late eighteenth century in Ulster County, New York. At this time, New York and New Jersey were the only northern states that sanctioned slavery. After her release from slavery in 1827, Truth became involved in the abolitionist movement, and her book (which she dictated since she could not read or write), *Narrative of Sojourner Truth: A Northern Slave* (1850) led to numerous public-speaking engagements, especially as an advocate of abolition. At the same time she began to speak for the rights of women too. Truth can be legitimately seen as one of the pioneering activists in matters of racial and gender equality in the American scene. As her speech here indicates, she believed that ending slavery was only half the battle for human rights, the other was the recognition of black women as citizens.

Although both came from white middle-class backgrounds, Elizabeth Cady Stanton and Susan Brownell Anthony also began their political activism in the abolitionist movement, but by the 1840s were working more strenuously for women's rights. Stanton campaigned for women's enfranchisement, property rights, and control of their bodies. These issues were to occupy her for the duration of her career as a writer, speaker, and activist. In her speech here, Stanton argues that until equal rights of women are fully realized women should concede nothing to the men who oppress them. Anthony, who was raised in a Quaker family, worked in the temperance movement, and it was through this activity that she met Stanton in 1851. The two became lifelong friends and colleagues in their efforts for the battle for the rights of women. The document reprinted here is a partial transcript of Anthony's trial in 1873 where she was found guilty of having voted illegally in the presidential election of 1872. Her words on her own behalf eloquently and forcefully articulate the position that without the right to vote her trial has been in no way fair and that she is a subject, not a citizen, of the United States.

T.M.

41

Sojourner Truth, Address to the First Annual Meeting of the American Equal Rights Association, New York City, May 9, 1867

'My friends, I am rejoiced that you are glad, but I don't know how you will feel when I get through. I come from another field—the country of the slave. They have got their liberty—so much good luck to have slavery partly destroyed; not entirely. I want it root and branch destroyed. Then we will all be free indeed. I feel that if I have to answer for the deeds done in my body just as much as a man, I have a right to have just as much as a man. There is a great stir about colored men getting their rights, but not a word about the colored women; and if colored men get their rights, and not colored women theirs, you see the colored men will be masters over the women, and it will be just as bad as it was before. So I am for keeping the thing going while things are stirring; because if we wait till it is still, it will take a great while to get it going again. White women are a great deal smarter, and know more than colored women, while colored women do not know scarcely anything. They go out washing, which is about as high as a colored woman gets, and their men go about idle, strutting up and down; and when the women come home, they ask for their money and take it all, and then scold because there is no food. I want you to consider on that, chil'n. I call you chil'n; you are somebody's chil'n, and I am old enough to be mother of all that is here. I want women to have their rights. In the courts women have no right, no voice; nobody speaks for them. I wish woman to have her voice there among the pettifoggers. If it is not a fit place for women, it is unfit for men to be there.

'I am above eighty years old; it is about time for me to be going. I have been forty years a slave and forty years free, and would be here forty years more to have equal rights for all. I suppose I am kept here because something remains for me to do; I suppose I am yet to help to break the chain. I have done a great deal of work; as much as a man, but did not get so much pay. I used to work in the field and bind grain, keeping up with the cradler; but men doing no more, got twice as much pay; so with the German women. They work in the field and do as much work, but do not get the pay. We do as much, we eat as much, we want as much. I suppose I am about the only colored woman that goes about to speak for the rights of the colored women. I want to keep the thing stirring, now that the ice is cracked. What we want is a little money. You men know that you get as much again as women when you write, or for what you do. When we get our rights we shall not have to come to you for money, for then we shall have money enough in our own pockets; and may be you will ask us for money. But help us now until we get it. It is a good consolation to know that when we have got this battle once fought we shall not be coming to you any more. You have been having our rights so long, that you think, like a slave-holder, that you own us. I know that it is hard for one who has held the reins for so long to give up; it cuts like a knife. It will feel all the better when it closes up again. I have been in

Washington about three years, seeing about these colored people. Now colored men have the right to vote. There ought to be equal rights now more than ever, since colored people have got their freedom. I am going to talk several times while I am here; so now I will do a little singing. I have not heard any singing since I came here.'

Accordingly, suiting the action to the word, Sojourner sang, 'We are going home.' 'There, children,' she said, 'in heaven we shall rest from all our labors; first do all we have to do here. There I am determined to go, not to stop short of that beautiful place, and I do not mean to stop till I get there, and meet you there, too.'

Elizabeth Cady Stanton, Letter, NWSA Convention, Washington, D.C., January 21–23, 1889

I notice that in some of our conventions resolutions of thanks are passed to senators, congressmen and legislators for advocating some minor privileges which have been conceded to women, such as admission to colleges and professions, limited forms of suffrage, etc. Now I do not see any occasion for gratitude to these honorable gentlemen who, after robbing us of all our fundamental rights as citizens, propose to restore a few minor privileges. There is not one impulse of gratitude in my soul for any of the fragmentary privileges, which by slow degrees we have wrung out of our oppressors during the last half century, nor will there be so long as woman is robbed of all the essential rights of citizenship.

If strong appeals could induce the highway robber to return a modicum of what he had stolen, it might mitigate the miseries of his victim, but surely there would be no reason for gratitude, and an expression of thanks to him would be quite as much out of place as are complimentary resolutions passed in our conventions to legislators for their concessions to women. They deserve nothing at our hands until they make full restitution of all we possessed in the original compact under the colonial constitutions—rights over which in the nature of things men could have no lawful jurisdiction whatever. . . . Woman has the same right to a voice in this government that man has, and it is based on the same natural desire and capacity for self-government and self-protection. . . .

Until woman is recognized as an equal factor in civilization, and is possessed of her personal property, civil and political rights, all minor privileges and concessions are but so many added aggravations, and are insulting mockeries of that justice, liberty and equality which are the birthright of every citizen of a republic. 'Universal suffrage,' said Charles Sumner, 'is the first proof and only basis of a genuine republic.'

The United States of America vs. Susan B. Anthony, Circuit Court, Northern District of New York, June 17–18, 1873

UNITED STATES CIRCUIT COURT. (NORTHERN DISTRICT OF NEW YORK.) The United States of America *vs.* Susan B. Anthony; Hon. Ward Hunt, Presiding. Appearances: For the United States: Hon: Richard Crowley, U.S. District Attorney; For the Defendant: Hon. Henry R. Selden, John Van Voorhis, Esq.

Tried at Canandaigua, Tuesday and Wednesday, June 17th and 18th, 1878, before Hon. Ward Hunt, and a jury. Jury impaneled at 2:30 P.M.

Mr. Crowley opened the case as follows:

May it please the Court and Gentlemen of the Jury:

On the 5th of November, 1872, there was held in this State, as well as in other States of the Union, a general election for different officers, and among those, for candidates to represent several districts of this State in the Congress of the United States. The defendant, Miss Susan B. Anthony, at that time resided in the city of Rochester, in the county of Monroe, Northern District of New York, and upon the 5th day of November, 1872, she voted for a representative in the Congress of the United States, to represent the 29th Congressional District of this State, and also for a representative at large for the State of New York, to represent the State in the Congress of the United States. At that time she was a woman. I suppose there will be no question about that. The question in this case, if there be a question of fact about it at all, will, in my judgment, be rather a question of law than one of fact. I suppose that there will be no question of fact, substantially, in the case when all of the evidence is out, and it will be for you to decide under the charge for his honor, the Judge, whether or not the defendant committed the offense of voting for a representative in Congress upon that occasion. We think, on the part of the Government, that there is no question about it either one way or the other, neither a question of fact, nor a question of law, and that whatever Miss Anthony's intentions may have been— whether they were good or otherwise—she did not have a right to vote upon that question, and if she did vote without having a lawful right to vote, then there is no question but what she is guilty of violating a law of the United States in that behalf enacted by the Congress of the United States.

We don't claim in this case, gentlemen, that Miss Anthony is of that class of people who go about 'repeating.' We don't claim that she went from place to place for the purpose of offering her vote. But we do claim that upon the 5th of November, 1872, she voted, and whether she believed that she had a right to vote or not, it being a question of law, that she is within the statute. Congress in 1870 passed the following statute: (Reads 19th Section of the Act of 1870, page 144, 15th statutes at large). It is not necessary for me, gentlemen, at this stage of the case, to state all the facts which will be proven on the part of the Government. I shall leave that to be shown by the evidence and by the witnesses, and if any question of law shall arise his Honor will undoubtedly give you instructions as he shall deem proper. Conceded, that on the 5th day of November, 1872, Miss Susan B. Anthony was a woman.

* * *

The Court, after listening to an argument from the District Attorney, denied the motion for a new trial.

The COURT: The prisoner will stand up. Has the prisoner anything to say why sentence shall not be pronounced?

Miss ANTHONY: Yes, your honor, I have many things to say; for in your ordered verdict of guilty, you have trampled underfoot every vital principle of our government. My natural rights, my civil rights, my political rights, are all alike ignored. Robbed of the fundamental privilege of citizenship, I am degraded from the status of a citizen to that of a subject; and not only myself individually, but all of my sex, are, by your honor's verdict, doomed to political subjection under this so-called Republican government.

Judge HUNT: The Court can not listen to a rehearsal of arguments the prisoner's counsel has already consumed three hours in presenting.

Miss ANTHONY: May it pleasure your honor, I am not arguing the question, but simply stating the reasons why sentence can not, in justice, be pronounced against me. Your denial of my citizen's right to vote is the denial of my right of consent as one of the governed, the denial of my right of representation as one of the taxed, the denial of my right to a trial by a jury of my peers as an offender against law, therefore, the denial of my sacred rights to life, liberty, property, and—

Judge HUNT: The Court can not allow the prisoner to go on.

Miss ANTHONY: But your honor will not deny me this one and only poor privilege of protest against this high-handed outrage upon my citizen's rights. May it please the Court to remember that since the day of my arrest last November, this is the first time that either myself or any person of my disfranchised class has been allowed a word of defense before judge or jury—

Judge HUNT: The prisoner must sit down; the Court can not allow it.

Miss ANTHONY: All my prosecutors, from the 8th Ward corner grocery politician, who entered the complaint, to the United States Marshal, Commissioner, District Attorney, District Judge, your honor on the bench, not one is my peer, but each and all are my political sovereigns; and had your honor submitted my case to the jury, as was clearly your duty, even then I should have had just cause of protest, for not one of those men was my peer; but, native or foreign, white or black, rich or poor, educated or ignorant, awake or asleep, sober or drunk, each and every man of them was my political superior; hence, in no sense, my peer. Even, under such circumstances, a commoner of England, tried before a jury of lords, would have far less cause to complain than should I, a woman, tried before a jury of men. Even my counsel, the Hon. Henry R. Selden, who has argued my cause so ably, so earnestly, so unanswerably before your honor, is my political sovereign. Precisely as no disfranchised person is entitled to sit upon a jury, and no woman is entitled to the franchise, so, none but a regularly admitted lawyer is allowed to practice in the courts, and no woman can gain admission to the bar—hence, jury, judge, counsel, must all be of the superior class.

Judge HUNT: The Court must insist—the prisoner has been tried according to the established forms of law.

45

Miss ANTHONY: Yes, your honor, but by forms of law all made by men, interpreted by men, administered by men, in favor of men, and against women; and hence, your honor's ordered verdict of guilty, against a United States citizen for the exercise of 'that citizen's right to vote,' simply because that citizen was a woman and not a man. But, yesterday, the same man-made forms of law declared it a crime punishable with $1,000 fine and six months' imprisonment, for you, or me, or any of us, to give a cup of cold water, a crust of bread, or a night's shelter to a panting fugitive as he was tracking his way to Canada. And every man or woman in whose veins coursed a drop of human sympathy violated that wicked law, reckless of consequences, and was justified in so doing. As then the slaves who got their freedom must take it over, or under, or through the unjust forms of law, precisely so now must women, to get their right to a voice in this Government, take it; and I have taken mine, and mean to take it at every possible opportunity.

Judge HUNT: The Court orders the prisoner to sit down. It will not allow another word.

Miss ANTHONY: When I was brought before your honor for trial, I hoped for a broad and liberal interpretation of the Constitution and its recent amendments, that should declare all United States citizens under its protecting ægis—that should declare equality of rights the national guarantee to all persons born or naturalized in the United States. But failing to get this justice—failing, even, to get a trial by a jury *not* of my peers—I ask not leniency at your hands—but rather the full rigors of the law.

Judge HUNT: The Court must insist— (Here the prisoner sat down.)

Judge HUNT: The prisoner will stand up. (Here Miss Anthony arose again.) The sentence of the Court is that you pay a fine of one hundred dollars and the costs of the prosecution.

Miss ANTHONY: May it please your honor, I shall never pay a dollar of your unjust penalty. All the stock in trade I possess is a $10,000 debt, incurred by publishing my paper,—*The Revolution*—four years ago, the sole object of which was to educate all women to do precisely as I have done, rebel against your man-made, unjust, unconstitutional forms of law, that tax, fine, imprison, and hang women, while they deny them the right of representation in the Government; and I shall work on with might and main to pay every dollar of that honest debt, but not a penny shall go to this unjust claim. And I shall earnestly and persistently continue to urge all women to the practical recognition of the old revolutionary maxim, that 'Resistance to tyranny is obedience to God.'

Judge HUNT: Madam, the Court will not order you committed until the fine is paid.

Frederick Douglass (1817–1895)

Frederick Douglass was born a slave in Maryland in 1817. After escaping from bondage as a young man, he spent the rest of his life fighting the institution of slavery on a national level. Language was an important part of Douglass's anti-slavery platform, and he delivered stirring speeches around the country, challenging blacks to rise up against the oppression of 'negroes'. He worked for William Lloyd Garrison's anti-slavery publication, the *Liberator*, and later edited and published his own paper, the *North Star*, which was renamed *Frederick Douglass' Paper*.

The reading below is an excerpt from another of Douglass's important publications, his autobiography, *Life and Times of Frederick Douglass*. This chapter, 'Hope for the Nation', is a powerful personal narrative which includes Douglass's reflections on a crucial period in the abolition movement—the last stages of the civil war up to the assassination of President Abraham Lincoln. In it, Douglass recounts the anticipation and reception of the Emancipation Proclamation, and evaluates the document's impact on himself and 'those in like condition'. He discusses the ways in which this proclamation changed the meaning of the civil war, and reveals his own lasting belief in the abolition of slavery. Equally important in this piece is Douglass's personal view of Abraham Lincoln as a great leader. Ultimately, in 'Hope for the Nation' Douglass pays tribute to the slain President, refutes commonly held negative opinions of him, and makes an effort to solidify his own connection with him. The beautifully crafted prose, skilfully deployed rhetoric, and tremendous historical relevance of this piece and Douglass's other writings make them a pivotal area of exploration in contemporary culture studies.
M.H.

Hope for the nation

The first of January, 1863, was a memorable day in the progress of American liberty and civilization. It was the turning-point in the conflict between freedom and slavery. A death-blow was given to the slaveholding rebellion. Until then the federal arm had been more than tolerant to that relic of barbarism. It had defended it inside the slave States; it had countermanded the emancipation policy of John C. Fremont in Missouri; it had returned slaves to their so-called owners; it had threatened that any attempt on the part of the slaves to gain their freedom by insurrection, or otherwise, should be put down with an iron hand; it had even refused to allow the Hutchinson family to sing their anti-slavery songs in the camps of the Army of the Potomac; it had surrounded the houses of slaveholders with bayonets for their protection; and through its secretary of war, William H. Seward, had given notice to the world that, 'however the war for the Union might terminate, no change would be made in the relation of master and slave.' Upon this pro-slavery platform the war against the rebellion had been waged during more than two years. It had not been a war of conquest, but rather a war of conciliation. McClellan, in command of the army, had been trying, apparently, to put down the rebellion without hurting the rebels, certainly without hurting slavery, and the government had seemed to coöperate with him in both respects. Charles Sumner, William Lloyd Garrison, Wendell Phillips, Gerrit Smith and the whole anti-slavery phalanx at the North, had denounced this policy, and had besought Mr. Lincoln to adopt an opposite one, but in vain. Generals in the field, and councils in the Cabinet, had persisted in advancing this policy through defeats and disasters, even to the verge of ruin. We fought the rebellion, but not its cause. The key to the situation was the four millions of slaves; yet the slave who loved us, was hated, and the slaveholder who hated us, was loved. We kissed the hand that smote us, and spurned the hand that helped us. When the means of victory was before us,—without our grasp,—we went in search of the means of defeat. And now, on this day of January 1st, 1863, the formal and solemn announcement was made that thereafter the government would be found on the side of emancipation. This proclamation changed everything. It gave a new direction to the councils of the Cabinet, and to the conduct of the national arms. I shall leave to the statesman, the philosopher and the historian, the more comprehensive discussion of this document, and only tell how it touched me, and those in like condition with me at the time. I was in Boston, and its reception there may indicate the importance attached to it elsewhere. An immense assembly convened in Tremont Temple to await the first flash of the electric wires announcing the 'new departure.' Two years of war, prosecuted in the interests of slavery, had made free speech possible in Boston, and we were now met together to receive and celebrate the first utterance of the long-hoped-for proclamation, *if* it came, and, if it did *not* come, to speak our minds freely; for, in view of the past, it was by no means certain that it would come. The occasion, therefore, was one of both hope and fear. Our ship was on the open seas, tossed by a terrible storm; wave after wave was passing over us, and every hour was fraught with increasing peril. Whether we should survive or perish depended in large measure upon the coming of this proclamation. At least so we felt. Although the conditions on which Mr. Lincoln had promised to withhold it had not been complied with, yet, from many considerations, there was room to doubt and fear. Mr. Lincoln was known to be a man of tender heart, and boundless patience: no man could tell to what length he might go, or might refrain from going, in the direction of peace and reconciliation. Hitherto, he had not shown himself a man of heroic measures, and, properly enough, this step belonged to that class. It must be the end of all compromises with slavery—a declaration that thereafter the war was to be conducted on a new principle, with a new aim. It would be a full and fair assertion that the government would neither trifle, or be trifled with, any longer. But would it come? On the side of doubt, it was said that Mr. Lincoln's kindly nature might cause him to relent at the last moment; that Mrs. Lincoln, coming from an old slaveholding family, would influence him to delay, and to give the slaveholders one other chance.* Every moment of waiting chilled our hopes, and strengthened our fears. A line of messengers was established between the telegraph office and the platform of Tremont Temple, and the time was occupied with brief speeches from Hon. Thomas Russell of Plymouth, Miss Anna E. Dickinson (a lady of marvelous eloquence), Rev. Mr. Grimes, J. Sella Martin, William Wells Brown, and myself. But speaking or listening to speeches was not the thing for which the people had come together. The time for argument was passed. It was not logic, but the trump of jubilee, which everybody wanted to hear. We were waiting and listening as for a bolt from the sky, which should rend the fetters of four millions of slaves; we were watching, as it were, by the dim light of the stars, for the dawn of a new day; we were longing for the answer to the agonizing prayers of centuries. Remembering those in bonds as bound with them, we wanted to join in the shout for freedom, and in the anthem of the redeemed.

Eight, nine, ten o'clock came and went, and still no word. A visible shadow seemed falling on the expecting throng, which the confident utterances of the speakers sought in vain to dispel. At last, when patience was well-nigh exhausted, and suspense was becoming agony, a man (I think it was Judge Russell) with hasty step advanced through the crowd, and with a face fairly illumined with the news he bore, exclaimed in tones that thrilled all hearts, 'It is coming!' 'It is on the wires!!' The effect of this announcement was startling beyond description, and the scene was wild and grand. Joy and gladness exhausted all forms of expression, from shouts of praise to sobs and tears. My old friend Rue, a colored preacher, a man of wonderful vocal power, expressed the heartfelt emotion of the hour, when he led all voices in the anthem, 'Sound the loud timbrel o'er Egypt's dark sea, Jehovah hath triumphed, his people are free.'

About twelve o'clock, seeing there was no disposition to retire from the hall, which must be vacated, my friend Grimes (of blessed memory), rose and moved that the meeting adjourn to the Twelfth Baptist church, of which he was pastor, and soon that church was packed from doors to pulpit, and this meeting did not break up till near the dawn of day. It was one of the most affecting and thrilling occasions I ever witnessed, and a worthy celebration of the first step on the part of the nation in its departure from the thraldom of ages.

*I have reason to know that this supposition did Mrs. Lincoln great injustice.

There was evidently no disposition on the part of this meeting to criticise the proclamation; nor was there with any one at first. At the moment we saw only its anti-slavery side. But further and more critical examination showed it to be extremely defective. It was not a proclamation of 'liberty throughout all the land, unto all the inhabitants thereof,' such as we had hoped it would be, but was one marked by discriminations and reservations. Its operation was confined within certain geographical and military lines. It only abolished slavery where it did not exist, and left it intact where it did exist. It was a measure apparently inspired by the low motive of military necessity, and by so far as it was so, it would become inoperative and useless when military necessity should cease. There was much said in this line, and much that was narrow and erroneous. For my own part, I took the proclamation, first and last, for a little more than it purported, and saw in its spirit a life and power far beyond its letter. Its meaning to me was the entire abolition of slavery, wherever the evil could be reached by the Federal arm, and I saw that its moral power would extend much further. It was, in my estimation, an immense gain to have the war for the Union committed to the extinction of slavery, even from a military necessity. It is not a bad thing to have individuals or nations do right, though they do so from selfish motives. I approved the one-spur-wisdom of 'Paddy,' who thought if he could get one side of his horse to go, he could trust the speed of the other side.

The effect of the proclamation abroad was highly beneficial to the loyal cause. Disinterested parties could now see in it a benevolent character. It was no longer a mere strife for territory and dominion, but a contest of civilization against barbarism.

The proclamation itself was throughout like Mr. Lincoln. It was framed with a view to the least harm and the most good possible in the circumstances, and with especial consideration of the latter. It was thoughtful, cautious, and well guarded at all points. While he hated slavery, and really desired its destruction, he always proceeded against it in a manner the least likely to shock or drive from him any who were truly in sympathy with the preservation of the Union, but who were not friendly to emancipation. For this he kept up the distinction between loyal and disloyal slaveholders, and discriminated in favor of the one, as against the other. In a word, in all that he did, or attempted, he made it manifest that the one great and all-commanding object with him was the peace and preservation of the Union, and that this was the motive and main-spring of all his measures. His wisdom and moderation at this point were for a season useful to the loyal cause in the border States, but it may be fairly questioned whether it did not chill the union ardor of the loyal people of the North in some degree, and diminish rather than increase the sum of our power against the rebellion; for moderate, cautious, and guarded as was this proclamation, it created a howl of indignation and wrath amongst the rebels and their allies. The old cry was raised by the copperhead organs of 'an abolition war,' and a pretext was thus found for an excuse for refusing to enlist, and for marshaling all the negro prejudice of the North on the rebel side. Men could say they were willing to fight for the Union, but that they were not willing to fight for the freedom of the negroes; and thus it was made difficult to procure enlistments or to enforce the draft. This was especially true of New York, where there was a large Irish population. The attempt to enforce the draft in that city was met by mobs, riot, and bloodshed. There is perhaps no darker chapter in the whole history of the war than this cowardly and bloody uprising in July, 1863.

[. . .]

In connection with George L. Stearns, Thomas Webster, and Col. Wagner, I had been at Camp William Penn, Philadelphia, assisting in the work of filling up the colored regiments, and was on my way home from there just as these events were transpiring in New York.

[. . .]

This was not the first time I had been in imminent peril in New York city. My first arrival there, after my escape from slavery, was full of danger. My passage through its borders after the attack of John Brown on Harper's Ferry was scarcely less safe. I had encountered Isaiah Rynders and his gang of ruffians in the old Broadway Tabernacle at our anti-slavery anniversary meeting, and I knew something of the crazy temper of such crowds; but this anti-draft, anti-negro mob, was something more and something worse—it was a part of the rebel force, without the rebel uniform, but with all its deadly hate; it was the fire of the enemy opened in the rear of the loyal army. Such men as Franklin Pierce and Horatio Seymour had done much in their utterances to encourage resistance to the drafts. Seymour was then Governor of the State of New York, and while the mob was doing its deadly work he addressed them as 'My friends,' telling them to desist then, while he could arrange at Washington to have the draft arrested. Had Governor Seymour been loyal to his country, and to his country's cause, in this her moment of need, he could have burned his tongue with a red hot iron sooner than allow it to call these thugs, thieves, and murderers his 'friends.'

My interviews with President Lincoln and his able Secretary, before narrated, greatly increased my confidence in the anti-slavery integrity of the government, although I confess I was greatly disappointed at my failure to receive the commission promised me by Secretary Stanton. I, however, faithfully believed, and loudly proclaimed my belief, that the rebellion would be suppressed, the Union preserved, the slaves emancipated and that the colored soldiers would in the end have justice done them. This confidence was immeasurably strengthened when I saw Gen. George B. McClellan relieved from the command of the army of the Potomac and Gen. U. S. Grant placed at its head, and in command of all the armies of the United States. My confidence in Gen. Grant was not entirely due to his brilliant military successes, but there was a moral as well as military basis for my faith in him. He had shown his single-mindedness and superiority to popular prejudice by his prompt cooperation with President Lincoln in his policy of employing colored troops and by his order commanding his soldiers to treat such troops with due respect. In this way he proved himself to be not only a wise general, but a great man—one who could adjust himself to new conditions, and adopt the lessons taught by the events of the hour.

[. . .]

It was when General Grant was fighting his way through the Wilderness to Richmond, on the 'line' he meant to pursue 'if it took all summer,' and every reverse to his arms was made the occasion for a fresh demand for peace without emancipation, that [. . .]. The increasing opposition to the war, in the North, and the mad cry against it, because it was being made an abolition war, alarmed Mr. Lincoln, and made him apprehensive that a peace might be forced upon him which would leave still in slavery all who had not come within our lines. What he wanted was to make his proclamation as effective as possible in the event of such a peace. He said, in a regretful tone, 'The slaves are not coming so rapidly and so numerously to us as I had hoped.' I replied that the slaveholders knew how to keep such things from their slaves, and probably very few knew of his proclamation. 'Well,' he said, 'I want you to set about devising some means of making them acquainted with it, and for bringing them into our lines.'

[. . .]

I listened with the deepest interest and profoundest satisfaction, and, at his suggestion, agreed to undertake the organizing a band of scouts, composed of colored men, whose business should be somewhat after the original plan of John Brown, to go into the rebel States, beyond the lines of our armies, and carry the news of emancipation, and urge the slaves to come within our boundaries.

This plan, however, was very soon rendered unnecessary, by the success of the war in the Wilderness and elsewhere, and by its termination in the complete abolition of slavery.

I refer to this conversation because I think that, on Mr. Lincoln's part, it is evidence conclusive that the proclamation, so far at least as he was concerned, was not effected merely as a 'necessity.'

An incident occurred during this interview which illustrates the character of this great man, though the mention of it may savor a little of vanity on my part. While in conversation with him his Secretary twice announced 'Governor Buckingham of Connecticut,' one of the noblest and most patriotic of the loyal governors. Mr. Lincoln said, 'Tell Governor Buckingham to wait, for I want to have a long talk with my friend Frederick Douglass.' I interposed, and begged him to see the Governor at once, as I could wait; but no, he persisted that he wanted to talk with me and that Governor Buckingham could wait. This was probably the first time in the history of this Republic when its chief magistrate had found an occasion or shown a disposition to exercise such an act of impartiality between persons so widely different in their positions and supposed claims upon his attention. From the manner of the Governor, when he was finally admitted, I inferred that he was as well satisfied with what Mr. Lincoln had done, or had omitted to do, as I was.

I have often said elsewhere what I wish to repeat here, that Mr. Lincoln was not only a great President, but a GREAT MAN—too great to be small in anything. In his company I was never in any way reminded of my humble origin, or of my unpopular color. While I am, as it may seem, boasting of the kind consideration which I have reason to believe that Mr. Lincoln entertained towards me, I may mention one thing more. At the door of my friend John A. Gray, where I was stopping in Washington, I found one afternoon the carriage of Secretary Dole, and a messenger from President Lincoln with an invitation for me to take tea with him at the Soldiers' Home, where he then passed his nights, riding out after the business of the day was over at the Executive Mansion. Unfortunately, I had an engagement to speak that evening, and having made it one of the rules of my conduct in life never to break an engagement if possible to keep it, I felt obliged to decline the honor. I have often regretted that I did not make this an exception to my general rule. Could I have known that no such opportunity could come to me again, I should have justified myself in disappointing a large audience for the sake of such a visit with Abraham Lincoln.

[. . .]

The Emancipation proclamation by Abraham Lincoln, had given slavery many and deadly wounds, yet it was in fact only wounded and crippled, not disabled and killed. With this condition of national affairs came the summer of 1864, and with it the revived Democratic party with the story in its mouth that the war was a failure, and with it Gen. George B. McClellan, the greatest failure of the war, as its candidate for the presidency.

[. . .]

All that had been done toward suppressing the rebellion and abolishing slavery would have proved of no avail, and the final settlement between the two sections of the Republic touching slavery and the right of secession would have been left to tear and rend the country again at no distant future.

It was said that this Democratic party, which under Mr. Buchanan had betrayed the government into the hands of secession and treason, was the only party which could restore the country to peace and union. No doubt it would have 'patched up' a peace, but it would have been a peace more to be dreaded than war. So at least I felt and worked. When we were thus asked to exchange Abraham Lincoln for George B. McClellan—a successful Union President for an unsuccessful Union general—a party earnestly endeavoring to save the Union, torn and rent by a gigantic rebellion, I thought with Mr. Lincoln that it was not wise to 'swap horses while crossing a stream.' Regarding, as I did, the continuance of the war to the complete suppression of the rebellion and the retention in office of President Lincoln as essential to the total destruction of slavery, I certainly exerted myself to the uttermost in my small way to secure his reelection. This most important object was not attained, however, by speeches, letters, or other electioneering appliances. The staggering blows dealt upon the rebellion that year by the armies under Grant and Sherman, and his own great character, ground all opposition to dust and made his election sure even before the question reached the polls. Since William the Silent, who was the soul of the mighty war for religious liberty against Spain and the Spanish inquisition, no leader of men has been loved and trusted in such generous measures as was Abraham Lincoln. His election silenced in a good degree the discontent felt at the length of the war and the complaints of its being an abolition war. Every victory of our arms on flood and field was a rebuke to McClellan and the Democratic party, and an indorsement of Abraham Lincoln for President and of his new policy. It was my good fortune to be present at his inauguration in March, and to hear on that occasion his remarkable inaugural address. On the night previous I took tea with Chief Justice Chase and assisted his beloved daughter, Mrs. Sprague, in placing over her honored father's shoulders the new robe then being made, in which he was to administer the oath of office to the reëlected President. There was a dignity and grandeur about the Chief Justice which marked him as one born great. He had known me in early anti-slavery days and had welcomed me to his home and his table when to do so was a strange thing in Washington, and the fact was by no means an insignificant one.

The inauguration, like the election, was a most important event. Four years before, after Mr. Lincoln's first election, the pro-slavery spirit determined against his

53

inauguration, and it no doubt would have accomplished its purpose had he attempted to pass openly and recognized through Baltimore. There was murder in the air then, and there was murder in the air now. His first inauguration arrested the fall of the Republic, and the second was to restore it to enduring foundations. At the time of the second inauguration the rebellion was apparently vigorous, defiant, and formidable, but in reality, weak, dejected, and desperate. It had reached that verge of madness when it had called upon the negro for help to fight against the freedom which he so longed to find, for the bondage he would escape—against Lincoln the emancipator for Davis the enslaver. But desperation discards logic as well as law, and the South was desperate. Sherman was marching to the sea, and Virginia with its rebel capital was in the firm grasp of Ulysses S. Grant. To those who knew the situation it was evident that unless some startling change was made the Confederacy had but a short time to live, and that time full of misery. This condition of things made the air at Washington dark and lowering. The friends of the Confederate cause here were neither few nor insignificant. They were among the rich and influential. A wink or a nod from such men might unchain the hand of violence and set order and law at defiance. To those who saw beneath the surface it was clearly perceived that there was danger abroad, and as the procession passed down Pennsylvania avenue I for one felt an instinctive apprehension that at any moment a shot from some assassin in the crowd might end the glittering pageant and throw the country into the depths of anarchy. I did not then know, what has since become history, that the plot was already formed and its execution which, though several weeks delayed, at last accomplished its deadly work was contemplated for that very day. Reaching the Capitol, I took my place in the crowd where I could see the presidential procession as it came upon the east portico, and where I could hear and see all that took place. There was no such throng as that which celebrated the inauguration of President Garfield nor that of President Rutherford B. Hayes. The whole proceeding was wonderfully quiet, earnest, and solemn. From the oath as administered by Chief Justice Chase, to the brief but weighty address delivered by Mr. Lincoln, there was a leaden stillness about the crowd. The address sounded more like a sermon than like a state paper. In the fewest words possible he referred to the condition of the country four years before on his first accession to the presidency, to the causes of the war, and the reasons on both sides for which it had been waged. 'Neither party,' he said, 'expected for the war the magnitude or the duration which it had already attained. Neither anticipated that the cause of the conflict might cease with or even before the conflict itself should cease. Each looked for an easier triumph and a result less fundamental and astounding.' Then in a few short sentences admitting the conviction that slavery had been the 'offense which in the providence of God must needs come, and the war as the woe due to those by whom the offense came,' he asks if there can be 'discerned in this any departure from those Divine attributes which the believers in a loving God always ascribe to him? Fondly do we hope,' he continued, 'fervently do we pray, that this mighty scourge of war may speedily pass away. Yet if God wills that it continue until all the wealth piled by the bond-man's two hundred and fifty years of unrequited toil shall be sunk, and until every drop of blood drawn with the lash shall be paid for by another drawn with the sword, as was said three thousand years ago, so still it must be said, "The judgments of the Lord are true and righteous altogether."

'With malice toward none, with charity for all, with firmness in the right as God gives us to see the right, let us strive to finish the work we are in, to bind up the nation's wounds, to care for him who shall have borne the battle, and for his widow and his orphans, to do all which may achieve and cherish a just and lasting peace among ourselves and with all nations.'

I know not how many times and before how many people I have quoted these solemn words of our martyred President. They struck me at the time, and have seemed to me ever since to contain more vital substance than I have ever seen compressed in a space so narrow; yet on this memorable occasion, when I clapped my hands in gladness and thanksgiving at their utterance, I saw in the faces of many about me expressions of widely different emotion.

On this inauguration day, while waiting for the opening of the ceremonies, I made a discovery in regard to the Vice President, Andrew Johnson. There are moments in the lives of most men when the doors of their souls are open, and, unconsciously to themselves, their true characters may be read by the observant eye. It was at such an instant that I caught a glimpse of the real nature of this man, which all subsequent developments proved true. I was standing in the crowd by the side of Mrs. Thomas J. Dorsey, when Mr. Lincoln touched Mr. Johnson and pointed me out to him. The first expression which came to his face, and which I think was the true index of his heart, was one of bitter contempt and aversion. Seeing that I observed him, he tried to assume a more friendly appearance, but it was too late; it is useless to close the door when all within has been seen. His first glance was the frown of the man; the second was the bland and sickly smile of the demagogue. I turned to Mrs. Dorsey and said, 'Whatever Andrew Johnson may be, he certainly is no friend of our race.'

No stronger contrast between two men could well be presented than the one exhibited on this day between President Lincoln and Vice-President Johnson. Mr. Lincoln was like one who was treading the hard and thorny path of duty and self-denial; Mr. Johnson was like one just from a drunken debauch. The face of the one was full of manly humility, although at the topmost height of power and pride; that of the other was full of pomp and swaggering vanity. The fact was, though it was yet early in the day, Mr. Johnson was drunk.

In the evening of the day of the inauguration, another new experience awaited me. The usual reception was given at the executive mansion, and though no colored persons had ever ventured to present themselves on such occasions, it seemed, now that freedom had become the law of the republic, and colored men were on the battle-field mingling their blood with that of white men in one common effort to save the country, that it was not too great an assumption for a colored man to offer his congratulations to the President with those of other citizens. I decided to go, and sought in vain for some one of my own color to accompany me. It is never an agreeable experience to go where there can be any doubt of welcome, and my colored friends had too often realized discomfiture from this cause to be willing to subject themselves to such unhappiness; they wished me to go, as my New England colored friends in the long-ago liked very well to have me take passage on the first-class cars, and be hauled out and pounded by rough-handed brakemen, to make way for them. It was plain, then, that some one must lead the way, and that if the colored man would have his rights, he must take them; and now, though it was plainly quite the thing for me to attend President Lincoln's reception, 'they all with one accord began to make excuse.' It was finally arranged that Mrs. Dorsey should bear me company, so together we joined in the grand procession of citizens from all parts of the country, and moved slowly towards the executive mansion. I had for some time looked upon myself as a man, but now in this multitude of the élite of the land, I felt myself a man among men. I regret to be obliged to say, however, that this comfortable assurance was not of long duration, for on reaching the door, two policemen stationed there took me rudely by the arm and ordered me to stand back, for their directions were to admit no persons of my color. The reader need not be told that this was a disagreeable set-back. But once in the battle, I did not think it well to submit to repulse. I told the officers I was quite sure there must be some mistake, for no such order could have emanated from President Lincoln; and that if he knew I was at the door he would desire my admission. They then, to put an end to the parley, as I suppose, for we were obstructing the doorway, and were not easily pushed aside, assumed an air of politeness, and offered to conduct me in. We followed their lead, and soon found ourselves walking some planks out of a window, which had been arranged as a temporary passage for the exit of visitors. We halted so soon as we saw the trick, and I said to the officers: 'You have deceived me. I shall not go out of this building till I see President Lincoln.' At this moment a gentleman who was passing in recognized me, and I said to him: 'Be so kind as to say to Mr. Lincoln that Frederick Douglass is detained by officers at the door.' I was not long before Mrs. Dorsey and I walked into the spacious East Room, amid a scene of elegance such as in this country I had never before witnessed. Like a mountain pine high above all others, Mr. Lincoln stood, in his grand simplicity, and *home-like beauty*. Recognizing me, even before I reached him, he exclaimed, so that all around could hear him, 'Here comes my friend Douglass.' Taking me by the hand, he said, 'I am glad to see you. I saw you in the crowd to-day, listening to my inaugural address; how did you like it?' I said, 'Mr. Lincoln, I must not detain you with my poor opinion, when there are thousands waiting to shake hands with you.' 'No, no,' he said, 'you must stop a little, Douglass; there is no man in the country whose opinion I value more than yours. I want to know what you think of it?' I replied, 'Mr. Lincoln, that was a sacred effort.' 'I am glad you liked it!' he said; and I passed on, feeling that any man, however distinguished, might well regard himself honored by such expressions, from such a man.

It came out that the officers at the White House had received no orders from Mr. Lincoln, or from any one else. They were simply complying with an old custom, the outgrowth of slavery, as dogs will sometimes rub their necks, long after their collars are removed, thinking they are still there. My colored friends were well pleased with what had seemed to them a doubtful experiment, and I believe were encouraged by its success to follow my example. I have found in my experience that the way to break down an unreasonable custom, is to contradict it in practice. To be sure in pursuing this course I have had to contend not merely with the white race, but with the black. The one has condemned me for my presumption in daring to associate with it, and the other for pushing myself where it takes it for granted I am not wanted. I am pained to think that the latter objection springs largely from a consciousness of inferiority, for as colors alone can have nothing against each other, and the conditions of human association are founded upon character rather than color, and character depends upon mind and morals, there can be nothing blameworthy in people thus equal meeting each other on the plane of civil or social rights.

[. . .]

I was in Rochester, N.Y., where I then resided, when news of the death of Mr. Lincoln was received. Our citizens, not knowing what else to do in the agony of the hour, betook themselves to the city hall. Though all hearts ached for utterance, few felt like speaking. We were stunned and overwhelmed by a crime and calamity hitherto unknown to our country and our government. The hour was hardly one for speech, for no speech could rise to the level of feeling. Doctor Robinson, then of Rochester University, but now of Brown University, Providence, R.I., was prevailed upon to take the stand, and made one of the most touching and eloquent speeches I ever heard. At the close of his address, I was called upon, and spoke out of the fullness of my heart, and, happily, gave expression to so much of the soul of the people present that my voice was several times utterly silenced by the sympathetic tumult of the great audience. I had resided long in Rochester, and had made many speeches there which had more or less touched the hearts of my hearers, but never till this day was I brought into such close accord with them. We shared in common a terrible calamity, and this 'touch of nature made us' more than countrymen, it made us 'kin.'

Frederick Jackson Turner (1861–1932)

Frederick Jackson Turner, a man credited with re-shaping American historiography, studied history and literature at the University of Wisconsin, Johns Hopkins University, and Harvard. He was also a tutor of rhetoric and oratory at the University of Wisconsin. His Master's thesis and doctoral dissertation were on the influence of Indian Trade in Wisconsin. He was a history professor at the University of Wisconsin and Harvard. He is the author of *The Character and Influence of the Indian Trade in Wisconsin* (1891), *The Rise of the New West, 1819–1829* (1906), *List of References on History of the West* (1911), *The Frontier in American History* (1920), 'Sections and the Nation' (*Yale Review*, 1922) and *The United States, 1830–50: The Nation and Its Sections* (1935). He edited a *Guide to the Study and Reading of American History* (1912) with Edward Channing and Albert Bushnell Hart and was a member of the board of editors for *American Historical Review* from 1910 to 1915. Jackson Turner's book *The Significance of Sections in American History*, published the year he died, was awarded the Pulitzer Prize posthumously.

Jackson Turner's 'The Significance of the Frontier in American History' was originally a paper presented at the Chicago meeting of the American Historical Association in 1893. In this essay Jackson Turner argues that American social development is analogous to American westward settlement. He suggests that America's attempts to transform the 'primitive' wilderness into cities full of complex economic, political, and sociological systems comprise America's history. He points out that the westward expansion consolidates a series of quintessentially 'American' experiences. He claims that the 'wilderness masters the colonist' and in the westward expansion of the frontier, American people grew away from the initial European influence to establish a unique, 'American part of our history'.
K.M.S.

The significance of the frontier in American history[1]

In a recent bulletin of the Superintendent of the Census for 1890 appear these significant words: 'Up to and including 1880 the country had a frontier of settlement, but
at present the unsettled area has been so broken into by isolated bodies of settlement
that there can hardly be said to be a frontier line. In the discussion of its extent, its
westward movement, etc., it can not, therefore, any longer have a place in the census
reports.' This brief official statement marks the closing of a great historic movement.
Up to our own day American history has been in a large degree the history of the colonization of the Great West. The existence of an area of free land, its continuous
recession, and the advance of American settlement westward, explain American
development.

   Behind institutions, behind constitutional forms and modifications, lie the vital
forces that call these organs into life and shape them to meet changing conditions.
The peculiarity of American institutions is, the fact that they have been compelled to
adapt themselves to the changes of an expanding people—to the changes involved in
crossing a continent, in winning a wilderness, and in developing at each area of this
progress out of the primitive economic and political conditions of the frontier into
the complexity of city life. Said Calhoun in 1817, 'We are great, and rapidly—I was
about to say fearfully—growing!'[2] So saying, he touched the distinguishing feature of
American life. All peoples show development; the germ theory of politics has been
sufficiently emphasized. In the case of most nations, however, the development has
occurred in a limited area; and if the nation has expanded, it has met other growing
peoples whom it has conquered. But in the case of the United States we have a different phenomenon. Limiting our attention to the Atlantic coast, we have the
familiar phenomenon of the evolution of institutions in a limited area, such as the rise
of representative government; the differentiation of simple colonial governments into
complex organs; the progress from primitive industrial society, without division of
labor, up to manufacturing civilization. But we have in addition to this a recurrence
of the process of evolution in each western area reached in the process of expansion.
Thus American development has exhibited not merely advance along a single line,
but a return to primitive conditions on a continually advancing frontier line, and a
new development for that area. American social development has been continually
beginning over again on the frontier. This perennial rebirth, this fluidity of American
life, this expansion westward with its new opportunities, its continuous touch with
the simplicity of primitive society, furnish the forces dominating American character. The true point of view in the history of this nation is not the Atlantic coast, it is
the Great West. Even the slavery struggle, which is made so exclusive an object of
attention by writers like Professor von Holst, occupies its important place in
American history because of its relation to westward expansion.

   In this advance, the frontier is the outer edge of the wave—the meeting point
between savagery and civilization. Much has been written about the frontier from the

point of view of border warfare and the chase, but as a field for the serious study of the economist and the historian it has been neglected.

The American frontier is sharply distinguished from the European frontier—a fortified boundary line running through dense populations. The most significant thing about the American frontier is, that it lies at the hither edge of free land. In the census reports it is treated as the margin of that settlement which has a density of two or more to the square mile. The term is an elastic one, and for our purposes does not need sharp definition. We shall consider the whole frontier belt, including the Indian country and the outer margin of the 'settled area' of the census reports. This paper will make no attempt to treat the subject exhaustively; its aim is simply to call attention to the frontier as a fertile field for investigation, and to suggest some of the problems which arise in connection with it.

In the settlement of America we have to observe how European life entered the continent, and how America modified and developed that life and reacted on Europe. Our early history is the study of European germs developing in an American environment. Too exclusive attention has been paid by institutional students to the Germanic origins, too little to the American factors. The frontier is the line of most rapid and effective Americanization. The wilderness masters the colonist. It finds him a European in dress, industries, tools, modes of travel, and thought. It takes him from the railroad car and puts him in the birch canoe. It strips off the garments of civilization and arrays him in the hunting shirt and the moccasin. It puts him in the log cabin of the Cherokee and Iroquois and runs an Indian palisade around him. Before long he has gone to planting Indian corn and plowing with a sharp stick; he shouts the war cry and takes the scalp in orthodox Indian fashion. In short, at the frontier the environment is at first too strong for the man. He must accept the conditions which it furnishes, or perish, and so he fits himself into the Indian clearings and follows the Indian trails. Little by little he transforms the wilderness, but the outcome is not the old Europe, not simply the development of Germanic germs, any more than the first phenomenon was a case of reversion to the Germanic mark. The fact is, that here is a new product that is American. At first, the frontier was the Atlantic coast. It was the frontier of Europe in a very real sense. Moving westward, the frontier became more and more American. As successive terminal moraines result from successive glaciations, so each frontier leaves its traces behind it, and when it becomes a settled area the region still partakes of the frontier characteristics. Thus the advance of the frontier has meant a steady movement away from the influence of Europe, a steady growth of independence on American lines. And to study this advance, the men who grew up under these conditions, and the political, economic, and social results of it, is to study the really American part of our history.

In the course of the seventeenth century the frontier was advanced up the Atlantic river courses, just beyond the 'fall line,' and the tidewater region became the settled area. In the first half of the eighteenth century another advance occurred. Traders followed the Delaware and Shawnese Indians to the Ohio as early as the end of the first quarter of the century.[3] Gov. Spotswood, of Virginia, made an expedition in 1714 across the Blue Ridge. The end of the first quarter of the century saw the advance of the Scotch-Irish and the Palatine Germans up the Shenandoah Valley into the western part of Virginia, and along the Piedmont region of the Carolinas.[4]

The Germans in New York pushed the frontier of settlement up the Mohawk to German Flats.[5] In Pennsylvania the town of Bedford indicates the line of settlement. Settlements had begun on New River, a branch of the Kanawha, and on the sources of the Yadkin and French Broad.[6] The King attempted to arrest the advance by his proclamation of 1763,[7] forbidding settlements beyond the sources of the rivers flowing into the Atlantic; but in vain. In the period of the Revolution the frontier crossed the Alleghanies into Kentucky and Tennessee, and the upper waters of the Ohio were settled.[8] When the first census was taken in 1790, the continuous settled area was bounded by a line which ran near the coast of Maine, and included New England except a portion of Vermont and New Hampshire, New York along the Hudson and up the Mohawk about Schenectady, eastern and southern Pennsylvania, Virginia well across the Shenandoah Valley, and the Carolinas and eastern Georgia.[9] Beyond this region of continuous settlement were the small settled areas of Kentucky and Tennessee, and the Ohio, with the mountains intervening between them and the Atlantic area, thus giving a new and important character to the frontier. The isolation of the region increased its peculiarly American tendencies, and the need of transportation facilities to connect it with the East called out important schemes of internal improvement, which will be noted farther on. The 'West,' as a self-conscious section, began to evolve.

From decade to decade distinct advances of the frontier occurred. By the census of 1820[10] the settled area included Ohio, southern Indiana and Illinois, southeastern Missouri, and about one-half of Lousiana. This settled area had surrounded Indian areas, and the management of these tribes became an object of political concern. The frontier region of the time lay along the Great Lakes, where Astor's American Fur Company operated in the Indian trade,[11] and beyond the Mississippi, where Indian traders extended their activity even to the Rocky Mountains; Florida also furnished frontier conditions. The Mississippi River region was the scene of typical frontier settlements.[12]

The rising steam navigation[13] on western waters, the opening of the Erie Canal, and the westward extension of cotton[14] culture added five frontier states to the Union in this period. Grund, writing in 1836, declares: 'It appears then that the universal disposition of Americans to emigrate to the western wilderness, in order to enlarge their dominion over inanimate nature, is the actual result of an expansive power which is inherent in them, and which by continually agitating all classes of society is constantly throwing a large portion of the whole population on the extreme confines of the State, in order to gain space for its development. Hardly is a new State of Territory formed before the same principle manifests itself again and gives rise to a further emigration; and so is it destined to go on until a physical barrier must finally obstruct its progress.'[15]

In the middle of this century the line indicated by the present eastern boundary of Indian Territory, Nebraska, and Kansas marked the frontier of the Indian country.[16] Minnesota and Wisconsin still exhibited frontier conditions,[17] but the distinctive frontier of the period is found in California, where the gold discoveries had sent a sudden tide of adventurous miners, and in Oregon, and the settlements of Utah.[18] As the frontier had leaped over the Alleghanies, so now it skipped the Great Plains and the Rocky Mountains; and in the same way that the advance of the frontiersmen

61

beyond the Alleghanies had caused the rise of important questions of transportation and internal improvement, so now the settlers beyond the Rocky Mountains needed means of communication with the East, and in the furnishing of these arose the settlement of the Great Plains and the development of still another kind of frontier life. Railroads, fostered by land grants, sent an increasing tide of immigrants into the Far West. The United States Army fought a series of Indian wars in Minnesota, Dakota, and the Indian Territory.

By 1880 the settled area had been pushed into northern Michigan, Wisconsin, and Minnesota, along Dakota rivers, and into the Black Hills region, and was ascending the rivers of Kansas and Nebraska. The development of mines in Colorado had drawn isolated frontier settlements into that region, and Montana and Idaho were receiving settlers. The frontier was found in these mining camps and the ranches of the Great Plains. The superintendent of the census for 1890 reports, as previously stated, that the settlements of the West lie so scattered over the region that there can no longer be said to be a frontier line.

In these successive frontiers we find natural boundary lines which have served to mark and to affect the characteristics of the frontiers, namely: the 'fall line'; the Alleghany Mountains; the Mississippi; the Missouri where its direction approximates north and south; the line of the arid lands, approximately the ninety-ninth meridian; and the Rocky Mountains. The fall line marked the frontier of the seventeenth century; the Alleghanies that of the eighteenth; the Mississippi that of the first quarter of the nineteenth; the Missouri that of the middle of this century (omitting the California movement); and the belt of the Rocky Mountains and the arid tract, the present frontier. Each was won by a series of Indian wars.

At the Atlantic frontier one can study the germs of processes repeated at each successive frontier. We have the complex European life sharply precipitated by the wilderness into the simplicity of primitive conditions. The first frontier had to meet its Indian question, its question of the disposition of the public domain, of the means of intercourse with older settlements, of the extension of political organization, of religious and educational activity. And the settlement of these and similar questions for one frontier served as a guide for the next. The American student needs not to go to the 'prim little townships of Sleswick' for illustrations of the law of continuity and development. For example, he may study the origin of our land policies in the colonial land policy; he may see how the system grew by adapting the statutes to the customs of the successive frontiers.[19] He may see how the mining experience in the lead regions of Wisconsin, Illinois, and Iowa was applied to the mining laws of the Sierras,[20] and how our Indian policy has been a series of experimentations on successive frontiers. Each tier of new States has found in the older ones material for its constitutions.[21] Each frontier has made similar contributions to American character, as will be discussed farther on.

But with all these similarities there are essential differences, due to the place element and the time element. It is evident that the farming frontier of the Mississippi Valley presents different conditions from the mining frontier of the Rocky Mountains. The frontier reached by the Pacific Railroad, surveyed into rectangles, guarded by the United States Army, and recruited by the daily immigrant ship, moves forward at a swifter pace and in a different way than the frontier reached by the birch canoe or the pack horse. The geologist traces patiently the shores of ancient seas, maps their areas, and compares the older and the newer. It would be a work worth the historian's labors to mark these various frontiers and in detail compare one with another. Not only would there result a more adequate conception of American development and characteristics, but invaluable additions would be made to the history of society.

Loria,[22] the Italian economist, has urged the study of colonial life as an aid in understanding the stages of European development, affirming that colonial settlement is for economic science what the mountain is for geology, bringing to light primitive stratifications. 'America,' he says, 'has the key to the historical enigma which Europe has sought for centuries in vain, and the land which has no history reveals luminously the course of universal history.' There is much truth in this. The United States lies like a huge page in the history of society. Line by line as we read this continental page from West to East we find the record of social evolution. It begins with the Indian and the hunter; it goes on to tell of the disintegration of savagery by the entrance of the trader, the path-finder of civilization; we read the annals of the pastoral stage in ranch life; the exploitation of the soil by the raising of unrotated crops of corn and wheat in sparsely settled farming communities; the intensive culture of the denser farm settlement; and finally the manufacturing organization with city and factory system.[23] This page is familiar to the student of census statistics, but how little of it has been used by our historians. Particularly in eastern States this page is a palimpsest. What is now a manufacturing State was in an earlier decade an area of intensive farming. Earlier yet it had been a wheat area, and still earlier the 'range' had attracted the cattle-herder. Thus Wisconsin, now developing manufacture, is a State with varied agricultural interests. But earlier it was given over to almost exclusive grain-raising, like North Dakota at the present time.

Each of these areas has had an influence in our economic and political history; the evolution of each into a higher stage has worked political transformations. But what constitutional historian has made any adequate attempt to interpret political facts by the light of these social areas and changes?[24]

The Atlantic frontier was compounded of fisherman, fur-trader, miner, cattle-raiser, and farmer. Excepting the fisherman, each type of industry was on the march toward the West, impelled by an irresistible attraction. Each passed in successive waves across the continent. Stand at Cumberland Gap and watch the procession of civilization, marching single file—the buffalo following the trail to the salt springs, the Indian, the fur-trader and hunter, the cattle-raiser, the pioneer farmer—and the frontier has passed by. Stand at South Pass in the Rockies a century later and see the same procession with wider intervals between. The unequal rate of advance compels us to distinguish the frontier into the trader's frontier, the rancher's frontier, or the miner's frontier, and the farmer's frontier. When the mines and the cow pens were still near the fall line the traders' pack trains were tinkling across the Alleghanies, and the French on the Great Lakes were fortifying their posts, alarmed by the British trader's birch canoe. When the trappers scaled the Rockies, the farmer was still near the mouth of the Missouri.

Why was it that the Indian trader passed so rapidly across the continent? What effects followed from the trader's frontier? The trade was coeval with American discovery. The Norsemen, Vespuccius, Verrazani, Hudson, John Smith, all trafficked for furs. The Plymouth pilgrims settled in Indian cornfields, and their first return cargo was of beaver and lumber. The records of the various New England colonies show how steadily exploration was carried into the wilderness by this trade. What is true for New England is, as would be expected, even plainer for the rest of the colonies. All along the coast from Maine to Georgia the Indian trade opened up the river courses. Steadily the trader passed westward, utilizing the older lines of French trade. The Ohio, the Great Lakes, the Mississippi, the Missouri, and the Platte, the lines of western advance, were ascended by traders. They found the passes in the Rocky Mountains and guided Lewis and Clark,[25] Frémont, and Bidwell. The explanation of the rapidity of this advance is connected with the effects of the trader on the Indian. The trading post left the unarmed tribes at the mercy of those that had purchased fire-arms—a truth which the Iroquois Indians wrote in blood, and so the remote and unvisited tribes gave eager welcome to the trader. 'The savages', wrote La Salle, 'take better care of us French than of their own children; from us only can they get guns and goods.' This accounts for the trader's power and the rapidity of his advance. Thus the disintegrating forces of civilization entered the wilderness. Every river valley and Indian trail became a fissure in Indian society, and so that society became honeycombed. Long before the pioneer farmer appeared on the scene, primitive Indian life had passed away. The farmers met Indians armed with guns. The trading frontier, while steadily undermining Indian power by making the tribes ultimately dependent on the whites, yet, through its sale of guns, gave to the Indian increased power of resistance to the farming frontier. French colonization was dominated by its trading frontier; English colonization by its farming frontier. There was an antagonism between the two frontiers as between the two nations. Said Duquesne to the Iroquois, 'Are you ignorant of the difference between the king of England and the king of France? Go see the forts that our king has established and you will see that you can still hunt under their very walls. They have been placed for your advantage in places which you frequent. The English, on the contrary, are no sooner in possession of a place than the game is driven away. The forest falls before them as they advance, and the soil is laid bare so that you can scarce find the wherewithal to erect a shelter for the night.'

And yet, in spite of this opposition of the interests of the trader and the farmer, the Indian trade pioneered the way for civilization. The buffalo trail became the Indian trail, and this became the trader's 'trace;' the trails widened into roads, and the roads into turnpikes, and these in turn were transformed into railroads. The same origin can be shown for the railroads of the South, the Far West, and the Dominion of Canada.[26] The trading posts reached by these trails were on the sites of Indian villages which had been placed in positions suggested by nature; and these trading posts, situated so as to command the water systems of the country, have grown into such cities as Albany, Pittsburgh, Detroit, Chicago, St. Louis, Council Bluffs, and Kansas City. Thus civilization in America has followed the arteries made by geology, pouring an ever richer tide through them, until at last the slender paths of aboriginal intercourse have been broadened and interwoven into the complex mazes of modern commercial lines; the wilderness has been interpenetrated by lines of civilization growing ever more numerous. It is like the steady growth of a complex nervous system for the originally simple, inert continent. If one would understand why we are to-day one nation, rather than a collection of isolated states, he must study this economic and social consolidation of the country. In this progress from savage conditions lie topics for the evolutionist.[27]

The effect of the Indian frontier as a consolidating agent in our history is important. From the close of the seventeenth century various intercolonial congresses have been called to treat with Indians and establish common measures of defense. Particularism was strongest in colonies with no Indian frontier. This frontier stretched along the western border like a cord of union. The Indian was a common danger, demanding united action. Most celebrated of these conferences was the Albany congress of 1754, called to treat with the Six Nations, and to consider plans of union. Even a cursory reading of the plan proposed by the congress reveals the importance of the frontier. The powers of the general council and the officers were, chiefly, the determination of peace and war with the Indians, the regulation of Indian trade, the purchase of Indian lands, and the creation and government of new settlements as a security against the Indians. It is evident that the unifying tendencies of the Revolutionary period were facilitated by the previous coöperation in the regulation of the frontier. In this connection may be mentioned the importance of the frontier, from that day to this, as a military training school, keeping alive the power of resistance to aggression, and developing the stalwart and rugged qualities of the frontiersman.

It would not be possible in the limits of this paper to trade the other frontiers across the continent. Travelers of the eighteenth century found the 'cowpens' among the cane-brakes and peavine pastures of the South, and the 'cow drivers' took their droves to Charleston, Philadelphia, and New York.[28] Travelers at the close of the War of 1812 met droves of more than a thousand cattle and swine from the interior of Ohio going to Pennsylvania to fatten for the Philadelphia market.[29] The ranges of the Great Plains, with ranch and cowboy and nomadic life, are things of yesterday and of to-day. The experience of the Carolina cowpens guided the ranchers of Texas. One element favoring the rapid extension of the rancher's frontier is the fact that in a remote country lacking transportation facilities the product must be in small bulk, or must be able to transport itself, and the cattle raiser could easily drive his product to market. The effect of these great ranches on the subsequent agrarian history of the localities in which they existed should be studied.

The maps of the census reports show an uneven advance of the farmer's frontier, with tongues of settlement pushed forward and with indentations of wilderness. In part this is due to Indian resistance, in part to the locations of river valleys and passes, in part to the unequal force of the centers of frontier attraction. Among the important centers of attraction may be mentioned the following: fertile and favorably situated soils, salt springs, mines, and army posts.

The frontier army post, serving to protect the settlers from the Indians, has also acted as a wedge to open the Indian country, and has been a nucleus for settlement.[30] In this connection mention should also be made of the government military and exploring expeditions in determining the lines of settlement. But all the more important expeditions were greatly indebted to the earliest pathmakers, the Indian guides, the traders and trappers, and the French voyageurs, who were inevitable parts of governmental expeditions from the days of Lewis and Clark.[31] Each expedition was an epitome of the previous factors in western advance.

In an interesting monograph, Victor Hehn[32] has traced the effect of salt upon early European development, and has pointed out how it affected the lines of settlement and the form of administration. A similar study might be made for the salt springs of the United States. The early settlers were tied to the coast by the need of salt, without which they could not preserve their meats or live in comfort. Writing in 1752, Bishop Spangenburg says of a colony for which he was seeking lands in North Carolina, 'They will require salt & other necessaries which they can neither manufacture nor raise. Either they must go to Charleston, which is 300 miles distant . . . Or else they must go to Boling's Point in V^a on a branch of the James & is also 300 miles from here . . . Or else they must go down the Roanoke—I know not how many miles—where salt is brought up from the Cape Fear.'[33] This may serve as a typical illustration. An annual pilgrimage to the coast for salt thus became essential. Taking flocks or furs and ginseng root, the early settlers sent their pack trains after seeding time each year to the coast.[34] This proved to be an important educational influence, since it was almost the only way in which the pioneer learned what was going on in the East. But when discovery was made of the salt springs of the Kanawha, and the Holston, and Kentucky, and central New York, the West began to be freed from dependence on the coast. It was in part the effect of finding these salt springs that enabled settlement to cross the mountains.

From the time the mountains rose between the pioneer and the seaboard, a new order of Americanism arose. The West and the East began to get out of touch of each other. The settlements from the sea to the mountains kept connection with the rear and had a certain solidarity. But the over-mountain men grew more and more independent. The East took a narrow view of American advance, and nearly lost these men. Kentucky and Tennessee history bears abundant witness to the truth of this statement. The East began to try to hedge and limit westward expansion. Though Webster could declare that there were no Alleghanies in his politics, yet in politics in general they were a very solid factor.

The exploitation of the beasts took hunter and trader to the west, the exploitation of the grasses took the rancher west, and the exploitation of the virgin soil of the river valleys and prairies attracted the farmer. Good soils have been the most continuous attraction to the farmer's frontier. The land hunger of the Virginians drew them down the rivers into Carolina, in early colonial days; the search for soils took the Massachusetts men to Pennsylvania and to New York. As the eastern lands were taken up migration flowed across them to the west. Daniel Boone, the great backwoodsman, who combined the occupations of hunter, trader, cattle-raiser, farmer, and surveyor—learning, probably from the traders, of the fertility of the lands of the upper Yadkin, where the traders were wont to rest as they took their way to the Indians, left his Pennsylvania home with his father, and passed down the Great Valley road to that stream. Learning from a trader of the game and rich pastures of Kentucky, he pioneered the way for the farmers to that region. Thence he passed to the frontier of Missouri, where his settlement was long a landmark on the frontier. Here again he helped to open the way for civilization, finding salt licks, and trails, and land. His son was among the earliest trappers in the passes of the Rocky Mountains, and his party are said to have been the first to camp on the present site of Denver. His grandson, Col. A. J. Boone, of Colorado, was a power among the Indians of the Rocky Mountains, and was appointed as agent by the government. Kit Carson's mother was a Boone.[35] Thus this family epitomizes the backwoodsman's advance across the continent.

The farmer's advance came in a distinct series of waves. In Peck's New Guide to the West, published in Boston in 1837, occurs this suggestive passage:

> Generally, in all the western settlements, three classes, like the waves of the ocean, have rolled one after the other. First comes the pioneer, who depends for the subsistence of his family chiefly upon the natural growth of vegetation, called the 'range', and the proceeds of hunting. His implements of agriculture are rude, chiefly of his own make, and his efforts directed mainly to a crop of corn and a 'truck patch.' The last is a rude garden for growing cabbage, beans, corn for roasting ears, cucumbers, and potatoes. A log cabin, and, occasionally, a stable and corn-crib, and a field of a dozen acres, the timber girdled or 'deadened', and fenced, are enough for his occupancy. It is quite immaterial whether he ever becomes the owner of the soil. He is the occupant for the time being, pays no rent, and feels as independent as the 'lord of the manor.' With a horse, cow, and one or two breeders of swine, he strikes into the wood with his family, and becomes the founder of a new county, or perhaps state. He builds his cabin, gathers around him a few other families of similar tastes and habits, and occupies till the range is somewhat subdued, and hunting a little precarious, or, which is more frequently the case, till the neighbors crowd around, roads, bridges, and fields annoy him, and he lacks elbow room. The preëmption law enables him to dispose of his cabin and corn-field to the next class of emigrants; and, to employ his own figures, he 'breaks for the high timber,' 'clears out for the New Purchase,' or migrates to Arkansas or Texas, to work the same process over.
>
> The next class of emigrants purchase the lands, add field to field, clear out the roads, throw rough bridges over the streams, put up hewn log houses with glass windows and brick or stone chimneys, occasionally plant orchards, build mills, school-houses, court-houses, etc., and exhibit the picture and forms of plain, frugal, civilized life.
>
> Another wave rolls on. The men of capital and enterprise come. The settler is ready to sell out and take the advantage of the rise in property, push farther into the interior and become, himself, a man of capital and enterprise in turn. The small village rises to a spacious town or city; substantial edifices of brick, extensive fields, orchards, gardens, colleges, and churches are seen. Broad-cloths, silks, leghorns, crapes, and all the refinements, luxuries, elegancies, frivolities, and fashions are in vogue. Thus wave after wave is rolling westward; the real Eldorado is still farther on.
>
> A portion of the two first classes remain stationary amidst the general movement, improve their habits and condition, and rise in the scale of society.
>
> The writer has traveled much amongst the first class, the real pioneers. He has lived many years in connection with the second grade; and now the third wave is sweeping over large districts of Indiana, Illinois, and Missouri. Migration has become almost a habit in the West. Hundreds of men can be found, not over 50

years of age, who have settled for the fourth, fifth, or sixth time on a new spot. To sell out and remove only a few hundred miles makes up a portion of the variety of back-woods life and manners.[36]

Omitting those of the pioneer farmers who move from the love of adventure, the advance of the more steady farmer is easy to understand. Obviously the immigrant was attracted by the cheap lands of the frontier, and even the native farmer felt their influence strongly. Year by year the farmers who lived on soil whose returns were diminished by unrotated crops were offered the virgin soil of the frontier at nominal prices. Their growing families demanded more lands, and these were dear. The competition of the unexhausted, cheap, and easily tilled prairie lands compelled the farmer either to go west and continue the exhaustion of the soil on a new frontier, or to adopt intensive culture. Thus the census of 1890 shows, in the Northwest, many counties in which there is an absolute or a relative decrease of population. These States have been sending farmers to advance the frontier on the plains, and have themselves begun to turn to intensive farming and to manufacture. A decade before this, Ohio had shown the same transition stage. Thus the demand for land and the love of wilderness freedom drew the frontier ever onward.

Having now roughly outlined the various kinds of frontiers, and their modes of advance, chiefly from the point of view of the frontier itself, we may next inquire what were the influences on the East and on the Old World. A rapid enumeration of some of the more noteworthy effects is all that I have time for.

First, we note that the frontier promoted the formation of a composite nationality for the American people. The coast was preponderantly English, but the later tides of continental immigration flowed across to the free lands. This was the case from the early colonial days. The Scotch-Irish and the Palatine Germans, or 'Pennsylvania Dutch,' furnished the dominant element in the stock of the colonial frontier. With these peoples were also the freed indented servants, or redemptioners, who at the expiration of their time of service passed to the frontier. Governor Spotswood of Virginia writes in 1717, 'The inhabitants of our frontiers are composed generally of such as have been transported hither as servants, and, being out of their time, settle themselves where land is to be taken up and that will produce the necessarys of life with little labour.'[37] Very generally these redemptioners were of non-English stock. In the crucible of the frontier the immigrants were Americanized, liberated, and fused into a mixed race, English in neither nationality nor characteristics. The process has gone on from the early days to our own. Burke and other writers in the middle of the eighteenth century believed that Pennsylvania[38] was 'threatened with the danger of being wholly foreign in language, manners, and perhaps even inclinations.' The German and Scotch-Irish elements in the frontier of the South were only less great. In the middle of the present century the German element in Wisconsin was already so considerable that leading publicists looked to the creation of a German state out of the commonwealth by concentrating their colonization.[39] Such examples teach us to beware of misinterpreting the fact that there is a common English speech in America into a belief that the stock is also English.

In another way the advance of the frontier decreased our dependence on England. The coast, particularly of the South, lacked diversified industries, and was dependent on England for the bulk of its supplies. In the South there was even a dependence on the Northern colonies for articles of food. Governor Glenn, of South Carolina, writes in the middle of the eighteenth century: 'Our trade with New York and Philadelphia was of this sort, draining us of all the little money and bills we could gather from other places for their bread, flour, beer, hams, bacon, and other things of their produce, all which, except beer, our new townships begin to supply us with, which are settled with very industrious and thriving Germans. This no doubt diminishes the number of shipping and the appearance of our trade, but it is far from being a detriment to us.'[40] Before long the frontier created a demand for merchants. As it retreated from the coast it became less and less possible for England to bring her supplies directly to the consumer's wharfs, and carry away staple crops, and staple crops began to give way to diversified agriculture for a time. The effect of this phase of the frontier action upon the northern section is perceived when we realize how the advance of the frontier aroused seaboard cities like Boston, New York, and Baltimore, to engage in rivalry for what Washington called 'the extensive and valuable trade of a rising empire.'

The legislation which most developed the powers of the national government, and played the largest part in its activity, was conditioned on the frontier. Writers have discussed the subjects of tariff, land, and internal improvement, as subsidiary to the slavery question. But when American history comes to be rightly viewed it will be seen that the slavery question is an incident. In the period from the end of the first half of the present century to the close of the Civil War slavery rose to primary, but far from exclusive, importance. But this does not justify Dr. von Holst (to take an example) in treating our constitutional history in its formative period down to 1828 in a single volume, giving six volumes chiefly to the history of slavery from 1828 to 1861, under the title 'Constitutional History of the United States.' The growth of nationalism and the evolution of American political institutions were dependent on the advance of the frontier. Even so recent a writer as Rhodes, in his 'History of the United States since the Compromise of 1850,' has treated the legislation called out by the western advance as incidental to the slavery struggle.

This is a wrong perspective. The pioneer needed the goods of the coast, and so the grand series of internal improvement and railroad legislation began, with potent nationalizing effects. Over internal improvements occurred great debates, in which grave constitutional questions were discussed. Sectional groupings appear in the votes, profoundly significant for the historian. Loose construction increased as the nation marched westward.[41] But the West was not content with bringing the farm to the factory. Under the lead of Clay—'Harry of the West'—protective tariffs were passed, with the cry of bringing the factory to the farm. The disposition of the public lands was a third important subject of national legislation influenced by the frontier.

The public domain has been a force of profound importance in the nationalization and development of the government. The effects of the struggle of the landed and the landless States, and of the Ordinance of 1787, need no discussion.[42] Administratively the frontier called out some of the highest and most vitalizing activities of the general government. The purchase of Lousiana was perhaps the constitutional turning point in the history of the Republic, inasmuch as it afforded both a new area for national legislation and the occasion of the downfall of the policy of strict construction. But the purchase of Lousiana was called out by frontier needs and demands. As frontier States accrued to the Union the national power grew. In a speech on the dedication of the Calhoun monument Mr. Lamar explained: 'In 1789 the States were the creators of the Federal Government; in 1861 the Federal Government was the creator of a large majority of the States.'

When we consider the public domain from the point of view of the sale and disposal of the public lands we are again brought face to face with the frontier. The policy of the United States in dealing with its lands is in sharp contrast with the European system of scientific administration. Efforts to make this domain a source of revenue, and to withhold it from emigrants in order that settlement might be compact, were in vain. The jealousy and the fears of the East were powerless in the face of the demands of the frontiersmen. John Quincy Adams was obliged to confess: 'My own system of administration, which was to make the national domain the inexhaustible fund for progressive and unceasing internal improvement, has failed.' The reason is obvious; a system of administration was not what the West demanded; it wanted land. Adams states the situation as follows: 'The slaveholders of the South have bought the coöperation of the western country by the bribe of the western lands, abandoning to the new Western States their own proportion of the public property and aiding them in the design of grasping all the lands into their own hands. Thomas H. Benton was the author of this system, which he brought forward as a substitute for the American system of Mr. Clay, and to supplant him as the leading statesman of the West. Mr. Clay, by his tariff compromise with Mr. Calhoun, abandoned his own American system. At the same time he brought forward a plan for distributing among all the States of the Union the proceeds of the sales of the public lands. His bill for that purpose passed both Houses of Congress, but was vetoed by President Jackson, who, in his annual message of December, 1832, formally recommended that all public lands should be gratuitously given away to individual adventurers and to the States in which the lands are situated.'[43]

'No subject,' said Henry Clay, 'which has presented itself to the present, or perhaps any proceeding, Congress, is of greater magnitude than that of the public lands.' When we consider the far-reaching effects of the government's land policy upon political, economic, and social aspects of American life, we are disposed to agree with him. But this legislation was framed under frontier influences, and under the lead of Western statesmen like Benton and Jackson. Said Senator Scott of Indiana in 1841: 'I consider the preëmption law merely declaratory of the custom or common law of the settlers.'

It is safe to say that the legislation with regard to land, tariff, and internal improvements—the American system of the nationalizing Whig party—was conditioned on frontier ideas and needs. But it was not merely in legislative action that the frontier worked against the sectionalism of the coast. The economic and social characteristics of the frontier worked against sectionalism. The men of the frontier had closer resemblances to the Middle region than to either of the other sections. Pennsylvania had been the seed-plot of frontier emigration, and, although she passed on her settlers along the Great Valley into the west of Virginia and the Carolinas, yet the industrial society of these Southern frontiersmen was always more like that of the Middle region than like that of the tide-water portion of the South, which later came to spread its industrial type throughout the South.

The Middle region, entered by New York harbor, was an open door to all Europe. The tide-water part of the South represented typical Englishmen, modified by a warm climate and servile labor, and living in baronial fashion on great plantations; New England stood for a special English movement—Puritanism. The Middle region was less English than the other sections. It had a wide mixture of nationalities, a varied society, the mixed town and county system of local government, a varied economic life, many religious sects. In short, it was a region mediating between New England and the South, and the East and the West. It represented that composite nationality which the contemporary United States exhibits, that juxtaposition of non-English groups, occupying a valley or a little settlement, and presenting reflections of the map of Europe in their variety. It was democratic and nonsectional, if not national; 'easy, tolerant, and contented;' rooted strongly in material prosperity. It was typical of the modern United States. It was least sectional, not only because it lay between North and South, but also because with no barriers to shut out its frontiers from its settled region, and with a system of connecting waterways, the Middle region mediated between East and West as well as between North and South. Thus it became the typically American region. Even the New Englander, who was shut out from the frontier by the Middle region, tarrying in New York or Pennsylvania on his westward march, lost the acuteness of his sectionalism on the way.[44]

The spread of cotton culture into the interior of the South finally broke down the contrast between the 'tide-water' region and the rest of the State, and based Southern interests on slavery. Before this process revealed its results the western portion of the South, which was akin to Pennsylvania in stock, society, and industry, showed tendencies to fall away from the faith of the fathers into internal improvement legislation and nationalism. In the Virginia convention of 1829–30, called to revise the constitution, Mr. Leigh, of Chesterfield, one of the tide-water counties, declared:

> One of the main causes of discontent which led to this convention, that which had the strongest influence in overcoming our veneration for the work of our fathers, which taught us to contemn the sentiments of Henry and Mason and Pendleton, which weaned us from our reverence for the constituted authorities of the State, was an overweening passion for internal improvement. I say this with perfect knowledge, for it has been avowed to me by gentlemen from the West over and over again. And let me tell the gentleman from Albemarle (Mr. Gordon) that it has been another principal object of those who set this ball of revolution in motion, to overturn the doctrine of State rights, of which Virginia has been the very pillar, and to remove the barrier she has interposed to the interference of the Federal Government in that same work of internal improvement, by so reorganizing the legislature that Virginia, too, may be hitched to the Federal car.

It was this nationalizing tendency of the West that transformed the democracy of Jefferson into the national republicanism of Monroe and the democracy of Andrew Jackson. The West of the War of 1812, the West of Clay, and Benton and Harrison, and Andrew Jackson, shut off by the Middle States and the mountains from the coast sections, had a solidarity of its own with national tendencies.[45] On the tide of the Father of Waters, North and South met and mingled into a nation. Interstate migration went steadily on—a process of cross-fertilization of ideas and institutions. The fierce struggle of the sections over slavery on the western frontier does not diminish

71

the truth of this statement; it proves the truth of it. Slavery was a sectional trait that would not down, but in the West it could not remain sectional. It was the greatest of frontiersmen who declared: 'I believe this Government can not endure permanently half slave and half free. It will become all of one thing or all of the other.' Nothing works for nationalism like intercourse within the nation. Mobility of population is death to localism, and the western frontier worked irresistibly in unsettling population. The effect reached back from the frontier and affected profoundly the Atlantic coast and even the Old World.

But the most important effect of the frontier has been in the promotion of democracy here and in Europe. As has been indicated, the frontier is productive of individualism. Complex society is precipitated by the wilderness into a kind of primitive organization based on the family. The tendency is anti-social. It produces antipathy to control, and particularly to any direct control. The tax-gatherer is viewed as a representative of oppression. Prof. Osgood, in an able article,[46] has pointed out that the frontier conditions prevalent in the colonies are important factors in the explanation of the American Revolution, where individual liberty was sometimes confused with absence of all effective government. The same conditions aid in explaining the difficulty of instituting a strong government in the period of the confederacy. The frontier individualism has from the beginning promoted democracy.

The frontier States that came into the Union in the first quarter of a century of its existence came in with democratic suffrage provisions, and had reactive effects of the highest importance upon the older States whose peoples were being attracted there. An extension of the franchise became essential. It was *western* New York that forced an extension of suffrage in the constitutional convention of that State in 1821; and it was *western* Virginia that compelled the tide-water region to put a more liberal suffrage provision in the constitution framed in 1830, and to give to the frontier region a more nearly proportionate representation with the tide-water aristocracy. The rise of democracy as an effective force in the nation came in with western preponderance under Jackson and William Henry Harrison, and it meant the triumph of the frontier—with all of its good and with all of its evil elements.[47] An interesting illustration of the tone of frontier democracy in 1830 comes from the same debates in the Virginia convention already referred to. A representative from western Virginia declared:

> But, sir, it is not the increase of population in the West which this gentleman ought to fear. It is the energy which the mountain breeze and western habits impart to those emigrants. They are regenerated, politically I mean, sir. They soon become *working politicians*; and the difference, sir, between a *talking* and a *working* politician is immense. The Old Dominion has long been celebrated for producing great orators; the ablest metaphysicians in policy; men that can split hairs in all abstruse questions of political economy. But at home, or when they return from Congress, they have negroes to fan them asleep. But a Pennsylvania, a New York, an Ohio, or a western Virginia statesman, though far inferior in logic, metaphysics, and rhetoric to an old Virginia statesman, has this advantage, that when he returns home he takes off his coat and takes hold of the plow. This gives him bone and muscle, sir, and preserves his republican principles pure and uncontaminated.

So long as free land exists, the opportunity for a competency exists, and economic power secures political power. But the democracy born of free land, strong in selfishness and individualism, intolerant of administrative experience and education, and pressing individual liberty beyond its proper bounds, has its dangers as well as its benefits. Individualism in America has allowed a laxity in regard to governmental affairs which has rendered possible the spoils system and all the manifest evils that follow from the lack of a highly developed civic spirit. In this connection may be noted also the influence of frontier conditions in permitting lax business honor, inflated paper currency and wild-cat banking. The colonial and revolutionary frontier was the region whence emanated many of the worst forms of an evil currency.[48] The West in the War of 1812 repeated the phenomenon on the frontier of that day, while the speculation and wild-cat banking of the period of the crisis of 1837 occurred on the new frontier belt of the next tier of States. Thus each one of the periods of lax financial integrity coincides with periods when a new set of frontier communities had arisen, and coincides in area with these successive frontiers, for the most part. The recent Populist agitation is a case in point. Many a State that now declines any connection with the tenets of the Populists, itself adhered to such ideas in an earlier stage of the development of the State. A primitive society can hardly be expected to show the intelligent appreciation of the complexity of business interests in a developed society. The continual recurrence of these areas of paper-money agitation is another evidence that the frontier can be isolated and studied as a factor in American history of the highest importance.[49]

The East has always feared the result of an unregulated advance of the frontier, and has tried to check and guide it. The English authorities would have checked settlement at the headwaters of the Atlantic tributaries and allowed the 'savages to enjoy their deserts in quiet lest the peltry trade should decrease.' This called out Burke's splendid protest:

> If you stopped your grants, what would be the consequence? The people would occupy without grants. They have already so occupied in many places. You can not station garrisons in every part of these deserts. If you drive the people from one place, they will carry on their annual tillage and remove with their flocks and herds to another. Many of the people in the back settlements are already little attached to particular situations. Already they have topped the Appalachian Mountains. From thence they behold before them an immense plain, one vast, rich, level meadow; a square of five hundred miles. Over this they would wander without a possibility of restraint; they would change their manners with their habits of life; would soon forget a government by which they were disowned; would become hordes of English Tartars; and, pouring down upon your unfortified frontiers a fierce and irresistible cavalry, become masters of your governors and your counselers, your collectors and comptrollers, and of all the slaves that adhered to them. Such would, and in no long time must, be the effect of attempting to forbid as a crime and to suppress as an evil the command and blessing of Providence, 'Increase and multiply'. Such would be the happy result of an endeavor to keep as a lair of wild beasts that earth which God, by an express charter, has given to the children of men.

But the English Government was not alone in its desire to limit the advance of the frontier and guide its destinies. Tide-water Virginia[50] and South Carolina[51] gerry-

73

mandered those colonies to insure the dominance of the coast in their legislatures. Washington desired to settle a State at a time in the Northwest; Jefferson would reserve from settlement the territory of his Louisiana Purchase north of the thirty-second parallel, in order to offer it to the Indians in exchange for their settlements east of the Mississippi. 'When we shall be full on this side,' he writes, 'we may lay off a range of States on the western bank from the head to the mouth, and so range after range, advancing compactly as we multiply.' Madison went so far as to argue to the French minister that the United States had no interest in seeing population extend itself on the right bank of the Mississippi, but should rather fear it. When the Oregon question was under debate, in 1824, Smyth, of Virginia, would draw an unchangeable line for the limits of the United States at the outer limit of two tiers of States beyond the Mississippi, complaining that the seaboard States were being drained of the flower of their population by the bringing of too much land into market. Even Thomas Benton, the man of widest views of the destiny of the West, at this stage of his career declared that along the ridge of the Rocky mountains 'the western limits of the Republic should be drawn, and the statue of the fabled god Terminus should be raised upon its highest peak, never to be thrown down.'[52] But the attempts to limit the boundaries, to restrict land sales and settlement, and to deprive the West of its share of political power were all in vain. Steadily the frontier of settlement advanced and carried with it individualism, democracy, and nationalism, and powerfully affected the East and the Old World.

The most effective efforts of the East to regulate the frontier came through its educational and religious activity, exerted by interstate migration and by organized societies. Speaking in 1835, Dr. Lyman Beecher declared: 'It is equally plain that the religious and political destiny of our nation is to be decided in the West,' and he pointed out that the population of the West 'is assembled from all the States of the Union and from all the nations of Europe, and is rushing in like the waters of the flood, demanding for its moral preservation the immediate and universal action of those institutions which discipline the mind and arm the conscience and the heart. And so various are the opinions and habits, and so recent and imperfect is the acquaintance, and so sparse are the settlements of the West, that no homogeneous public sentiment can be formed to legislate immediately into being the requisite institutions. And yet they are all needed immediately in their utmost perfection and power. A nation is being "born in a day." . . . But what will become of the West if her prosperity rushes up to such a majesty of power, while those great institutions linger which are necessary to form the mind and the conscience and the heart of that vast world. It must not be permitted. . . . Let no man at the East quiet himself and dream of liberty, whatever may become of the West. . . . Her destiny is our destiny.'[53]

With the appeal to the conscience of New England, he adds appeals to her fears lest other religious sects anticipate her own. The New England preacher and school-teacher left their mark on the West. The dread of Western emancipation from New England's political and economic control was paralleled by her fears lest the West cut loose from her religion. Commenting in 1850 on reports that settlement was rapidly extending northward in Wisconsin, the editor of the *Home Missionary* writes: 'We scarcely know whether to rejoice or mourn over this extension of our settlements. While we sympathize in whatever tends to increase the physical resources and prosperity of our country, we can not forget that with all these dispersions into remote and still remoter corners of the land the supply of the means of grace is becoming relatively less and less.' Acting in accordance with such ideas, home missions were established and Western colleges were erected. As seaboard cities like Philadelphia, New York, and Baltimore strove for the mastery of Western trade, so the various denominations strove for the possession of the West. Thus an intellectual stream from New England sources fertilized the West. Other sections sent their missionaries; but the real struggle was between sects. The contest for power and the expansive tendency furnished to the various sects by the existence of a moving frontier must have had important results on the character of religious organization in the United States. The multiplication of rival churches in the little frontier towns had deep and lasting social effects. The religious aspects of the frontier make a chapter in our history which needs study.

From the conditions of frontier life came intellectual traits of profound importance. The works of travelers along each frontier from colonial days onward describe certain common traits, and these traits have, while softening down, still persisted as survivals in the place of their origin, even when a higher social organization succeeded. The result is that to the frontier the American intellect owes its striking characteristics. That coarseness and strength combined with acuteness and inquisitiveness; that practical, inventive turn of mind, quick to find expedients; that masterful grasp of material things, lacking in the artistic but powerful to effect great ends; that restless, nervous energy;[54] that dominant individualism, working for good and for evil; and withal that buoyancy and exuberance which comes with freedom—these are traits of the frontier, or traits called out elsewhere because of the existence of the frontier. Since the days when the fleet of Columbus sailed into the waters of the New World, America has been another name for opportunity, and the people of the United States have taken their tone from the incessant expansion which has not only been open but has even been forced upon them. He would be a rash prophet who should assert that the expansive character of American life has now entirely ceased. Movement has been its dominant fact, and, unless this training has no effect upon a people, the American energy will continually demand a wider field for its exercise. But never again will such gifts of free land offer themselves. For a moment, at the frontier, the bonds of custom are broken and unrestraint is triumphant. There is not *tabula rasa*. The stubborn American environment is there with its imperious summons to accept its conditions; the inherited ways of doing things are also there; and yet, in spite of environment, and in spite of custom, each frontier did indeed furnish a new field of opportunity, a gate of escape from the bondage of the past; and freshness, and confidence, and scorn of older society, impatience of its restraints and its ideas, and indifference to its lessons, have accompanied the frontier. What the Mediterranean Sea was to the Greeks, breaking the bond of custom, offering new experiences, calling out new institutions and activities, that, and more, the ever retreating frontier has been to the United States directly, and to the nations of Europe more remotely. And now, four centuries from the discovery of America, at the end of a hundred years of life under the Constitution, the frontier has gone, and with its going has closed the first period of American history.

NOTES

1. A paper read at the meeting of the American Historical Association in Chicago, July 12, 1893.
2. 'Abridgment of Debates of Congress,' v, p. 706.
3. Bancroft (1860 ed.), iii, pp. 344, 356, citing Logan MSS.; [Mitchell] 'Contest in America,' etc. (1752), p. 237.
4. Kercheval, 'History of the Valley'; Bernheim, 'German Settlements in the Carolinas'; Winsor, 'Narrative and Critical History of America,' v, p. 304; Colonial Records of North Carolina, iv, p. xx; Weston, 'Documents Connected with the History of South Carolina,' p. 82; Ellis and Evans, 'History of Lancaster County, Pa.,' chs. iii, xxvi.
5. Parkman, 'Pontiac,' ii; Griffis, 'Sir William Johnson,' p. 6; Simms's 'Frontiersmen of New York.'
6. Monette, 'Mississippi Valley,' i, p. 311.
7. Wis. Hist. Cols., xi, p. 50; Hinsdale, 'Old Northwest,' p. 121; Burke, 'Oration on Conciliation,' Works (1872 ed.), i, p. 473.
8. Roosevelt, 'Winning of the West,' and citations there given; Cutler's 'Life of Cutler.'
9. Scribner's Statistical Atlas, xxxviii, pl. 13; McMaster, 'Hist. of People of U.S.,' i, pp. 4, 60, 61; Imlay and Filson, 'Western Territory of America' (London, 1793); Rochefoucault-Liancourt, 'Travels Through the United States of North America' (London, 1799); Michaux's 'Journal,' in *Proceedings American Philosophical Society*, xxvi, No. 129; Forman, 'Narrative of a Journey Down the Ohio and Mississippi in 1780–'90' (Cincinnati, 1888); Bartram, 'Travels Through North Carolina,' etc. (London, 1792); Pope, 'Tour Through the Southern and Western Territories,' etc. (Richmond, 1792); Weld, 'Travels Through the States of North America' (London, 1799); Baily, 'Journal of a Tour in the Unsettled States of North America, 1796–'97' (London, 1856); Pennsylvania Magazine of History, July, 1886; Winsor, 'Narrative and Critical History of America,' vii, pp. 491, 492, citations.
10. Scribner's Statistical Atlas, xxxix.
11. Turner, 'Character and Influence of the Indian Trade in Wisconsin' (Johns Hopkins University Studies, Series ix), pp. 61 ff.
12. Monette, 'History of the Mississippi Valley,' ii; Flint, 'Travels and Residence in Mississippi;' Flint, 'Geography and History of the Western States;' 'Abridgment of Debates of Congress,' vii, pp. 397, 398, 404; Holmes, 'Account of the U.S.'; Kingdom, 'America and the British Colonies' (London, 1820); Grund, 'Americans,' ii, chs. i, iii, vi (although writing in 1836, he treats of conditions that grew out of western advance from the era of 1820 to that time); Peck, 'Guide for Emigrants' (Boston, 1831); Darby, 'Emigrants' Guide to Western and Southwestern States and Territories'; Dana, 'Geographical Sketches in the Western Country'; Kinzie, 'Waubun'; Keating, 'Narrative of Long's Expedition'; Schoolcraft, 'Discovery of the Sources of the Mississippi River,' 'Travels in the Central Portions of the Mississippi Valley,' and 'Lead Mines of the Missouri'; Andreas, 'History of Illinois,' i, 86–99; Hurlbut, 'Chicago Antiquities'; McKenney, 'Tour to the Lakes'; Thomas, 'Travels Through the Western Country,' etc. (Auburn, N.Y., 1819).
13. Darby, 'Emigrants' Guide,' pp. 272 ff; Benton, 'Abridgment of Debates,' vii, p. 397.
14. De Bow's *Review*, iv, p. 254; xvii, p. 428.
15. Grund, 'Americans,' ii, p. 8.
16. Peck, 'New Guide to the West' (Cincinnati, 1848), ch. iv; Parkman, 'Oregon Trail'; Hall, 'The West' (Cincinnati, 1848); Pierce, 'Incidents of Western Travel'; Murray, 'Travels in North America'; Lloyd, 'Steamboat Directory' (Cincinnati, 1856); 'Forty Days in a Western Hotel' (Chicago), in *Putnam's Magazine*, December, 1894; Mackay, 'The Western World,' ii, ch. ii, iii; Meeker, 'Life in the West'; Bogen, 'German in America' (Boston, 1851); Olmstead, 'Texas Journey'; Greeley, 'Recollections of a Busy Life'; Schouler, 'History of the United States,' v, 261–267; Peyton, 'Over the Alleghanies and Across the Prairies' (London, 1870); Loughborough, 'The Pacific Telegraph and Railway' (St. Louis, 1849); Whitney, 'Project for a Railroad to the Pacific' (New York, 1849); Peyton, 'Suggestions on Railroad Communication with the Pacific, and the Trade of China and the Indian Islands'; Benton, 'Highway to the Pacific' (a speech delivered in the U.S. Senate, December 16, 1850).
17. A writer in *The Home Missionary* (1850), p. 239, reporting Wisconsin conditions, exclaims: 'Think of this, people of the enlightened East. What an example, to come from the very frontier of civilization!' But one of the missionaries writes: 'In a few years Wisconsin will no longer be considered as the West, or as an outpost of civilization, any more than Western New York, or the Western Reserve.'

18. Bancroft (H.H.), 'History of California, History of Oregon, and Popular Tribunals'; Shinn, 'Mining Camps.'

19. See the suggestive paper by Prof. Jesse Macy, 'The Institutional Beginnings of a Western State.'

20. Shinn, 'Mining Camps.'

21. Compare Thorpe, in *Annals American Academy of Political and Social Science*, September, 1891; Bryce, 'American Commonwealth' (1888), ii, p. 689.

22. Loria, 'Analisi della Proprieta Capitalista', ii, p. 15.

23. Compare 'Observations on the North American Land Company,' London, 1796, pp. xv, 1244; Logan, 'History of Upper South Carolina,' i, pp. 149–151; Turner, 'Character and Influence of Indian Trade in Wisconsin,' p. 18; Peck, 'New Guide for Emigrants' (Boston, 1837), ch. iv; 'Compendium Eleventh Census,' i, p. xl.

24. See *post*, for illustrations of the political accompaniments of changed industrial conditions.

25. But Lewis and Clark were the first to explore the route from the Missouri to the Columbia.

26. 'Narrative and Critical History of America,' viii, p. 10; Sparks' 'Washington Works,' ix, pp. 303, 327; Logan, 'History of Upper South Carolina,' i; McDonald, 'Life of Kenton,' p. 72; Cong. Record, xxiii, p. 57.

27. On the effect of the fur trade in opening the routes of migration, see the author's 'Character and Influence of the Indian Trade in Wisconsin.'

28. Lodge, 'English Colonies,' p. 152 and citations; Logan, 'Hist. of Upper South Carolina,' i, p. 151.

29. Flint, 'Recollections,' p. 9.

30. See Monette, 'Mississippi Valley,' i, p. 344.

31. Coues', 'Lewis and Clark's Expedition,' i, pp. 2, 253–259; Benton, in Cong. Record, xxiii, p. 57.

32. Hehn, *Das Salz* (Berlin, 1873).

33. Col. Records of N. C., v, p. 3.

34. Findley, 'History of the Insurrection in the Four Western Counties of Pennsylvania in the Year 1794' (Philadelphia, 1796), p. 35.

35. Hale, 'Daniel Boone' (pamphlet).

36. Compare Baily, 'Tour in the Unsettled Parts of North America' (London, 1856), pp. 217–219, where a similar analysis is made for 1796. See also Collot, 'Journey in North America' (Paris, 1826), p. 109; 'Observations on the North American Land Company' (London, 1796), pp. xv, 144; Logan, 'History of Upper South Carolina.'

37. 'Spotswood Papers,' in Collections of Virginia Historical Society, i, ii.

38. [Burke], 'European Settlements' (1765 ed.), ii, p. 200.

39. Everest, in 'Wisconsin Historical Collections,' xii, pp. 7 ff.

40. Weston, 'Documents connected with History of South Carolina,' p. 61.

41. See, for example, the speech of Clay, in the House of Representatives, January 30, 1824.

42. See the admirable monograph by Prof. H. B. Adams, 'Maryland's Influence on the Land Cessions'; and also President Welling, in *Papers American Historical Association*, iii, p. 411.

43. Adams' Memoirs, ix, pp. 247, 248.

44. Author's article in *The Ægis* (Madison, Wis.), November 4, 1892.

45. Compare Roosevelt, 'Thomas Benton,' ch. i.

46. *Political Science Quarterly*, ii, p. 457. Compare Sumner, 'Alexander Hamilton,' chs. ii–vii.

47. Compare Wilson, 'Division and Reunion,' pp. 15, 24.

48. On the relation of frontier conditions to Revolutionary taxation, see Sumner, Alexander Hamilton, ch. iii.

49. I have refrained from dwelling on the lawless characteristics of the frontier, because they are sufficiently well known. The gambler and desperado, the regulators of the Carolinas and the vigilantes of California, are types of that line of scum that the waves of advancing civilization bore before them, and of the growth of spontaneous organs of authority where legal authority were absent. Compare Barrows, 'United States of Yesterday and To-morrow'; Shinn, 'Mining Camps'; and Bancroft, 'Popular Tribunals.' The humor, bravery, and rude strength, as well as the vices of the frontier in its worst aspect, have left traces on American character, language, and literature, not soon to be effaced.

50. Debates in the Constitutional Convention, 1829–1830.

51. [McCrady] 'Eminent and Representative Men of the Carolinas', i, p. 43; Calhoun's Works, i, pp. 401–406.

52. Speech in the Senate, March 1, 1825; Register of Debates, i, 721.

53. Plea for the West (Cincinnati, 1835), pp. 11 ff.

54. Colonial travelers agree in remarking on the phlegmatic characteristics of the colonists. It has frequently been asked how such a people could have developed that strained nervous energy now characteristic of them. Compare Sumner, 'Alexander Hamilton,' p. 98, and Adams, 'History of the United States,' i, p. 60; ix, pp. 240, 241. The transition appears to become marked at the close of the War of 1812, a period when interest centered upon the development of the West, and the West was noted for restless energy. Grund, 'Americans,' ii, ch. i.

2 The impact of European theory

Introduction

Enquiries into the nature of the subject in culture, or elaborations of subjectivity, or identity-politics in society have been areas of theoretical speculations from the Enlightenment era onwards. Such theoretical formulations, inherently interdisciplinary in their foundations and implications, range from philosophy, religion, art, history, philology, literature, psychology, biology, to economics and politics. Most of these theories provide models for understanding the formation/construction of *agency* for the human subject, the implicit and explicit drives that *motivate or hinder* such an agency in a socio-cultural arena, and explanations of *sign systems* (ranging from language to myths) which produce meanings. All these theories help to explain practices and regulate behaviour within a culture-specific context. As this theoretical section shows, the subject is constructed in and between layers of language and cultural experiences, encompassing socio-economic, psychological, historical, political, biological, ethnic and religious realities. The value of these theories, now more in the nature of a mediated study of concrete human sciences and abstract speculations, lies in their capacity to provide a methodology for producing, reading, and consuming cultures and cultural practices. Specific theoretical models have had huge impacts upon the analyses of culture, and they are listed here in a chronological order. Adaptations of Marxism have influenced early British cultural studies while structuralism and semiotics influenced American cultural studies, film and media studies, and feminisms on both sides of the Atlantic. Post-structuralism and deconstruction have had their impact upon historiography, subsequent forms of feminisms, and a major part of cultural critique in minority discourses. And lastly, psychoanalysis, post-structuralism, and post-modernism have influenced film, media, and gay/lesbian studies. Yet, it is also important to note that these theories are not used as discrete or exclusive methods for specific fields of inquiries, there is often an overlapping of theories and methods in cultural critique.

Antonio Gramsci represents a unique theory of human subjectivity and assesses culture in general and cultural practices in Fascist Italy in particular in *Prison*

Notebooks (1965) which were written as private thoughts to his sister-in-law, Tatiana Schuct. He argues that all cultural practices ranging from art, literature, education, architecture, theatre, philosophy, and religion exert 'hegemonic' influences in society. Because of this over-arching claim, echoes of Marx, Lenin, Trotsky, Hegel, Croce, and Nietzsche are inevitable in Gramsci's work, especially in his essays on the 'organic individual' as a person who can transform a hegemony to a 'regulated society'. While some critics have compared the centre/periphery trope in Gramsci's work to the base/superstructure model of Marx, it is accurate to state, as does Joseph Buttigeig in his article, 'The Legacy of Antonio Gramsci', in *Boundary* 2 (Spring 1986), that Gramsci's *Prison Notebooks* does not lay out a 'grand theory or a metaphysics of power but rather a material political significance and consequences of the distribution and exercise of power in specific societies at given moments' (7) (see Voice-Overs section for Hall's interview). Gramsci can be seen as a precursor to Michel Foucault whose syllogism of history/power/knowledge has wide-ranging implications for reading culture. While Foucault is looking at culture through institutional structures, Gramsci seeks to work through the individual. Gramsci says the concept of the

> organic intellectual leads to certain definitions of the . . . State which is normally understood as political society . . . and not as an equilibrium between political society and civil society . . . and it is precisely within civil society that the intellectuals carry out their special work.
>
> *(PN* 481)

Gramsci's political/philosophical speculations, especially in his 'Subaltern' essays, have proved invaluable to studies in race politics (see sections on Race Studies and Voice-Overs). Theodor Adorno, Max Horkheimer, and Herbert Marcuse belong to the 'Frankfurt School' of criticism that espouses a 'revised' version of Marxism coupled with modernism in envisioning the role of art in a modern, capitalist society as having a utopian, revolutionary potential. Adorno and Horkheimer in *The Dialectic of Enlightenment* (1972) elaborate on the notion of a 'culture industry' as being exploitative of avant-garde modernist art through mass production. Adorno is thus sceptical of Walter Benjamin's influential thesis in 'The Work of Art in the Age of Mechanical Reproduction', where Benjamin argues for the possibility of a liberatory politics in intervening mechanically in producing art so as to make it more accessible to the masses. In contrast, Adorno feels that it is precisely for this reason that art gets subordinated to forces of market capital and loses its radical quality and aesthetic integrity (see section on Media Studies). In *Aesthetic Theory* (1984) Adorno emphasizes this point by saying that only art can say what 'is barred to politics' (194).

Structuralism as a school of thought, inaugurated by Ferdinand de Saussure in *Course in General Linguistics* (1915), situates language in a scientific frame, analyses its components (signifier/signified) to reveal the properties of language as both (a) an arbitrary sign-system (where a culture imposes meaning through words, rather than language itself having an inherent/natural meaning), and (b) as a differential sign-system (meaning is generated by opposing words/concepts to each other instead of, again, language having an inherent/natural content). In Europe, structuralism shifted language from the domain of philology and history to that of science, and

82

consequently situated it on a more objective/analytical plane. In America, Charles Sanders Peirce in *Collected Papers* (8 vols., 1931–58) emphasized a more pragmatic aspect of structural semiotics, one concerned with the functions and logic of language in culture.[1] From the perspective of cultural studies, the legacy of both strands of structuralist thought is the positioning of language as a 'performative' within culture. One facet of this vital function is revealed through myth-making which is one of the main tenets of the anthropological enquiry in Claude Lévi-Strauss's *Triste Tropiques* (1955). He opposes two foundational terms like 'nature' and 'culture' to document the various cultural practices performed within 'primitive societies'. He situates the more 'primitive' cultures of South American Indians in the nature column and shows that the act of writing is a cultural practice adopted by more 'advanced' civilizations to access power, authority, and capital (see 'A Writing Lesson', below). While comparative and/or oppositional enquiry is an insightful moment in cultural anthropology, Lévi-Strauss is blind to the fact that his own bipolar structure is an imposition of the West. Consequently, the post-structural agenda (quite literally, a temporal and spatial afterthought) is to critique the presuppositions within structures as a whole.

Post-structuralism, largely a European phenomenon, was formally imported into America during the 'Languages of Criticism and the Sciences of Man' Colloquium in 1966 at Johns Hopkins University, mainly through the radical ideas presented by Jacques Derrida, Jacques Lacan, Lucien Goldmann, Tzvetan Todorov, Roland Barthes and others. A notable cultural moment is Derrida's essay 'Structure, Sign, and Play in the Human Sciences' which is a rigorous and carefully executed critique of Claude Lévi-Strauss's model of structural anthropology employed in *The Elementary Structures of Kinship* (1965), especially in the nature–culture opposition and the explanation of the incest-taboo. Structuralism, which was posited as a scientific, objective enquiry, i.e., a positive truth claim in philosophical parlance, is revealed as being grounded in subjective, experiential reality, unable to transcend its place in the structure of civilization/culture as it is presently situated. Derrida's deconstructive analysis resulted in his famous remark on the process of writing/reading always being hindered by its own 'structurality'. Gayatri Chakravorty Spivak in her brilliant introduction to and translation of Derrida's *Of Grammatology* (1976) explains his notion that deconstruction must be treated as a methodological 'event' and not a theoretical school. A useful contextualization of Derrida's nomenclature of 'deconstruction' is Martin Heidigger's theory of time as interrupting experiential reality which he called this 'destructive' analysis.

Deconstruction/post-structuralism achieved three important things as a theoretical model: (a) it yoked together numerous disciplines such as art, literature, philosophy, law, politics, economics, history, and aesthetics to show how clearly knowledge is produced and circulated, *and* ultimately textualized within Western culture; (b) argued that knowledge, as it is constructed, is implicated in language as a sign-system, thus meaning is arbitrary or locked into the power of the person who 'owns' the language (a point that is especially prevalent in post-colonial studies); and (c) demonstrated how such knowledge is deployed discursively in culture. Thus, language both creates knowledge and becomes the tool of its own critique. Derrida says in *Writing in Difference* (1967) that deconstruction allows one to view the world against the grain, 'read philosophers in a *certain way*' (288; emphasis added) to keep a vigil over truth-claims. Very much like Derrida's serious questioning of the arbitrariness of language in structuralism is Julia Kristeva's agenda in her essay, 'Stabat Mater' in *Tel Quel* (Winter 1977).

Kristeva, an original thinker from the Continental branch of feminism, shows the paucity of Lévi-Strauss' culture-nature opposition in 'Stabat Mater' by using the Virgin Mary as an example. The essay employs writing itself as a semiological tool in the sign-system. 'Stabat Mater', written in a double column, reveals distinct differences in the discourse levels: the left-hand column, written in academic (phallic and male centred) discourse, positions the Virgin Mary as an arch symbol of Western culture; and the right-hand column catalogues the 'experiences' of motherhood conveying an effect of uncontrolled, un-ordered, 'pulsing', fluid emotionality, which she suggests is pre-linguistic. Through this double-columned articulation Kristeva shows that structuralist models of grounding meaning in categories of nature/culture, and by extension, masculine/feminine, civilized/uncivilized, linguistic/pre-linguistic, are inadequate (yet, she too uses Lacanian notions of Symbolic/Imaginary). Finally, the double-column strategy also points to the paradoxical and simultaneous folding-over of woman as sign and signifier.[2] Recent criticism of the essay focuses upon Kristeva's premise of a biological essence in the position woman occupies. With regard to the impact of European theory on cultural critique, however, Kristeva's work signals an insight that is feminist and cultural in its intent, and her technique of exposing the constructed divide between nature and culture is analogous to the formulations of Clifford Geertz and James Clifford in ethnographic studies (see sections on Cultural Studies in America and Race Studies). Geertz and Clifford show the overlapping areas of kinship/societal practices, demonstrating that nature and culture cannot be compartmentalized into sealed structural units in everyday experiential reality.

Roland Barthes, one of the more flamboyant yet rigorous cultural critics, maintains that structural semiotics is an 'activity' (much like Derrida's 'event' in deconstruction) rather than a 'theory' of criticism. In works such as *Mythologies* (1957), *Elements of Semiology* (1964), *The Pleasure of the Text* (1975) and *Image-Music-Text* (1977) he engages in this activity to read both high and low cultural practices, and to trace their allegiances with and resistance to established 'traditions'. Addressing cultural issues more specifically by reading media images, but with a different 'take' on the sign-system of contemporary culture, Jean Baudrillard argues in *Simulations* (1976) that American culture of mass-consumerism combined with technological advances (using Disneyland as an example) has made American culture a 'simulacra' of the real, or more accurately, a media-generated reality. In contrast, Pierre Bourdieu, in *Distinctions: A Social Critique of the Judgement of Taste* (1984) is more concerned with analysing the premises of high culture and exposes the élitist nature of good 'taste'. As a post-structuralist historian, Michel Foucault's major contribution lies in his insights into the role of language within culture, mainly for its discursive potential and regulatory function. For example, in his work *The History of Sexuality* (1976) he shows how sex and sexuality move from being private, pleasurable, socio-cultural interactive practices into medical, juridical, and moral/ethical discourses of disease, control, and reproduction. In other words, Foucault shows how tracks of power undergird knowledge, how politics intersects with history, and how these seemingly disparate forces collude to regulate and convert actual lived-in sexual/cultural norms into sterile language and discourse. He documents such reversals between discourse modes and discursive practices (or lived-in practices) from the sixteenth century onwards as a trend in Western culture.

Just as structuralism served as the ground for deconstruction/post-structuralism, Sigmund Freud's work on human psychology and sexuality helped shape both Jacques Lacan's psychoanalytic theory and a large part of contemporary feminist thought. Freud's work in *The Interpretation of Dreams* (1917) challenges the notion of a rational subject by reading dreams like a rebus, i.e., quite literally. In displacing the Western subject from a cognitive, humanistic being to a sexually/ impulsively driven one, he establishes the idea of male superiority, which in turn systematically invalidates 'woman' as incapable of functioning except through lack and disease, and most importantly, over-determines heterosexuality. He takes his thesis that anatomy is destiny quite literally. Jacques Lacan, in his semiotic re-reading of Freud in 'The Insistence of the Letter in the Unconscious' (1957) claims that the 'unconscious is structured like a language', thus dreams must not be read literally but must be seen as figurative representations of repressed desires. In other words, dream images do not signal actual events, but suggest anxieties and preoccupations of the dreamer. Using Saussurian and Jakobsonian linguistics, Lacan shifts dream images into the register of language, such that metaphors signal unconscious desires which are substitutive in character and metonymies represent unconscious drives which are contiguous in function. Lacan argues that language creates the illusion of both authority and presence in conscious and unconscious realms through the 'Name of the Father' via an abstract 'transcendental signifier' and a concrete series of unending and linked signifiers (where new meaning *comes to be* because of a previous notation). Much like psychotherapy, psychoanalytic interpretations in literature and the arts are seen as a 'cure' for the text. The strength of psychoanalytic theory lies in its ability to create different positions for the subject, largely a Western male subject, and in its articulations of cultural critique. Consequently, a good deal of energy in feminist thought is spent on 'curing' psychoanalytic theory of its masculinist biases. 'Feminine Sexuality' (Juliet Mitchell, *Psychoanalysis and Feminism*, 1974) is a useful cliché to have come out of psychoanalytic theory; and feminist discourse which engages the experiences of female, gay, and lesbian sexualities is in some form an oppositional discourse, in others a supplemental dialogue with psychoanalysis.

If Luce Irigaray's *Speculum of the Other Woman* (1977) is seen as an attack on Freudian/Lacanian phallocentric models of male/female identities in culture and their proliferation in language, then Gilles Deleuze and Felix Gauttari's *Anti-Oedipus: Capitalism and Schizophrenia* (1972) and *A Thousand Plateaus* (1980) serve as an even sharper critique of post-structuralist/ psychoanalytic theories. Deleuze and Gauttari systematically unravel the truth claims of psychoanalysis as a whole, which in an attempt to make meaning of the text/culture braids together metaphors of Oedipus, castration, and repression, all of which are signs of absence and trauma. They argue that the values in these terms are vested in bourgeois interests of masculine presence, heterosexual, familial structures, and controlled/monitored libidinal expressions. While they agree with Freud on the crucial role of the unconscious, they

85

do not read it in idealistic or mythic terms. Instead, in *Anti-Oedipus* they posit the 'order of desire' as multiple, 'polymorphous', with a potential for cultural 'production' (as opposed to repression) not limited to 'two sexes, but *n* sexes' even a 'hundred thousand' (296).

In conclusion, it is important to stress that the impact of European theories becomes evident in American and British cultural critiques only after these works were translated into English and circulated during the 1970s and early 1980s. It is accurate to say that before such an intrusion of continental theory, British analyses relied heavily on Marxism as a tool while American analyses made use of methodologies provided by Lévi-Strauss's structural paradigms. (See Hall's discussion of the impact of theory on British and American cultural studies in the Voice-Overs section.)

GR and JM

NOTES

1. Similarly, Edward Sapir in *Language* (1921) overrides the notion of naturalness in language to focus on structural configurations which generate meaning when they 'hit points in a pattern' (Hawkes, *Structuralism and Semiotics*, Berkeley: University of California Press, 1977, 30). Roman Jakobson, an influential figure from the Moscow Linguistic Circle and Prague School, interjects a new perspective by yoking together utterance and the unconscious (philology and psychology) through rhetorical tropes of metaphor and metonymy. This technique will prove invaluable to Jacques Lacan, who later posits a whole branch of psychoanalytic theory on the troping of desire. One of the innovations of this branch of structural semiotics was to emphasize the systematic and constructed form of culture (and literature), and this is evidenced in Viktor Shklovsky's 'Art as Techné' (1917), and Vladimir Propp's *Morphology of the Folktale* (1928). In America, Northrop Frye's *Anatomy of Criticism* (1958) wedded together methodologies from New Criticism, Russian formalism, and Jungian notions of archetypes. Other influential structuralist critics whose work is more directly situated in rhetorical/literary analysis are A. J. Greimas, Jean Piaget, Emile Beneviste, Mukarovsky Jan, Thomas Sebeok, Benjamin Whorf, Tzvetan Todorov, Luciene Goldmann, Gerald Genet, and Jonathan Culler.
2. Equally important are feminist critiques by Hélène Cixous (*ecriture feminine and jouissance*), Monique Wittig, Sarah Kofman, Michele Montreley, Juliet Mitchell, Elaine Showalter, Diana Fuss, Gayatri Chakravorty Spivak, Sandra Gilbert, Susan Gubar, Annette Kolodny, Tania Modleski, and others.

FURTHER READING

Adorno, Theodor, *Prisms*, trans. S. and S. Weber, London: Neville Spearman, 1967.

Adorno, Theodor, and Max Horkheimer, *Dialectic of Enlightenment*, trans. John Cumming, London: Allen Tate, 1972.

Barthes, Roland, 'The Structuralist Activity', in *Critical Essays*, trans. Richard Howard, Evanston, Illinois: Northwestern University Press, 1972, 13–20.

Barthes, Roland, *Elements of Semiology*, trans. Annette Lavers and Colin Smith, New York: Hill and Wang, 1968.

Barthes, Roland, *Image-Music-Text*, trans. Stephen Heath, London: Fontana, 1977.

Baudrillard, Jean, *Simulations*, trans. Foss, Patton, and Beitchman, New York: Semiotext(e), 1983.

Benhabib, Seyla, *Critique, Norm and Utopia: A Study of the Foundations of Critical Theory*, New York: Columbia University Press, 1986.

Benjamin, Walter, *Illuminations*, ed. Hannah Arendt, London: Collins/Fontana, 1973.

Davis, R. C., and Ronald Schleifer, *Criticism and Culture: The Role of Critique in Modern Literary Theory*, London: Longman, 1991.

Deleuze, Gilles, and Felix Gauttari, *A Thousand Plateaus*, trans. Brian Massumi, Minneapolis: University of Minnesota Press, 1987.

Deleuze, Gilles, and Felix Gauttari, *Anti-Oedipus: Capitalism and Schizophrenia*, trans. Robert Hurley, Mark Seem, and Helen Lane, Minneapolis: University of Minnesota Press, 1983.

Derrida, Jacques, 'Structure, Sign, and Play in the Discourse of the Human Sciences', in *The Structuralist Controversy*, ed. Richard Macksey and Eugenio Donato, Baltimore: Johns Hopkins University Press, 1966, 247–72.

Derrida, Jacques, *Of Grammatology*, trans. Gayatri C. Spivak, Baltimore: Johns Hopkins University Press, 1976.

Foucault, Michel, *Madness and Civilization: A History of Insanity in the Age of Reason*, trans. Richard Howard, New York: Random House, 1973.

Foucault, Michel, *The Order of Things: An Archeology of the Human Sciences*, New York: Vintage/Random House, 1970.

Foucault, Michel, *The History of Sexuality*, trans. Robert Hurley, New York: Random House, 3 vols, 1984–6.

Freud, Sigmund, *Interpretation of Dreams*, Standard Edition, vols. 4–5, trans. and ed. J. Strachey, London: Hogarth Press, 1953–74.

Gramsci, Antonio, *Selected Writings: 1916–1935*, ed. David Forgacs, New York: Schocken Books, 1988.

Kristeva, Julia, *Desire in Language*, trans. Léon Roudiez et al., New York: Columbia University Press, 1980.

Lacan, Jacques, *Ecrits: A Selection*, trans. Alan Sheridan, New York: Norton, 1977.

Lévi-Strauss, Claude, *The Elementary Structures of Kinship*, trans. Belle and Strumer, London: Jonathan Cape, 1969.

Lévi-Strauss, Claude, *Structural Anthropology*, trans. Jacobson and Schoepf, New York: Basic Books, 1958.

Rorty, Richard, *Consequences of Pragmatism*, Minneapolis: University of Minnesota Press, 1982.

Said, Edward, *The World, the Text, and the Critic*, Cambridge, Mass.: Harvard University Press, 1983.

Walter Benjamin (1892–1940) and Theodor Wiesengrund Adorno (1903–1969)

Walter Benjamin studied philosophy and literature in Germany, and was greatly influenced by Baudelaire, Mallarmé, and Brecht. Early in his career he published two books: *The Concept of Art in German Romanticism* (1920) and *The Origin of German Tragedy* (1928). He worked at the Institute of Social Research in New York in the mid-1930s, and was constantly engaged in debates with Theodor Adorno, who was a leading member of the Institute, regarding the nuances of Marxist interpretations. Later Benjamin wrote *Understanding Brecht* (1973), *Charles Baudelaire: A Lyric Poet in the Era of High Capitalism* (1973), and a collection of essays titled *Illuminations* (1970). One of his best-known essays, 'The Work of Art in The Age of Mechanical Reproduction', is from *Illuminations*, and is printed in part here. Though trained in Marxism, Benjamin's brilliant analysis of the connections between art, technology, and value is entirely original. Benjamin problematizes the connections between the modern, i.e., progress which prioritizes technology in society, and modernity, which alienates the artist from society in an effort to gauge the value of art in society. In this essay, he argues that 'mechanical reproduction' or mass art takes away the elitist 'aura' surrounding a work of art, thereby making it more accessible, more democratic, and consequently, more political. Benjamin's work has influenced cultural critics, specifically those in film, art, and media studies.

Theodor Adorno was born in Frankfurt, studied philosophy and music at Vienna, and has taught in Britain, the United States, and Germany. As a leading member of the Institute of Social Research in New York, Adorno was constantly engaged in debates with American scholars. He wrote *Prisms* (1967), *The Philosophy of Modern Music* (1973), *Negative Dialectics* (1973), *Aesthetic Theory* (1984), and, with Max Horkheimer, *The Dialectic of Enlightenment* (1972). This co-authored work specifically analyses the 'culture industry', and has had a considerable impact in shaping the field of cultural studies. Adorno belongs to the Frankfurt school of critics, is therefore more of a traditional Hegelian Marxist, and disagrees with Benjamin on the role of art in society. In his reply to Benjamin's letter which is printed here, Adorno criticizes Benjamin's position, especially since he sees the loss of 'autonomy' of a work of art through reproduction as an encroachment of capitalism into the creativity of the artist. Adorno's analyses have influenced the first generation of British cultural theorists, American-studies scholars and literary critics.

G.R.

Walter Benjamin, from 'The work of art in the age of mechanical reproduction'

The uniqueness of a work of art is inseparable from its being imbedded in the fabric of tradition. This tradition itself is thoroughly alive and extremely changeable. An ancient statue of Venus, for example, stood in a different traditional context with the Greeks, who made it an object of veneration, than with the clerics of the Middle Ages, who viewed it as an ominous idol. Both of them, however were equally confronted with its uniqueness, that is, its aura. Originally the contextual integration of art in tradition found its expression in the cult. We know that the earliest art works originated in the services of a ritual—first the magical, then the religious kind. It is significant that the existence of the work of art with reference to its aura is never entirely separated from its ritual function. In other words, the unique value of the 'authentic' work of art has its basis in ritual, the location of its original use value. This ritualistic basis, however remote, is still recognizable as secularized ritual even in the most profane forms of the cult of beauty. The secular cult of beauty, developed during the Renaissance and prevailing for three centuries, clearly showed that ritualistic basis in its decline and the first deep crisis which befell it. With the advent of the first truly revolutionary means of reproduction, photography, simultaneously with the rise of socialism, art sensed the approaching crisis which has become evident a century later. At the time, art reacted with the doctrine of *l'art pour l'art*, that is, with a theology of art. This gave rise to what might be called a negative theology in the form of the idea of 'pure' art, which not only denied any social function of art but also any categorizing by subject matter. (In poetry, Mallarmé was the first to take this position.)

An analysis of art in the age of mechanical reproduction must do justice to these relationships, for they lead us to an all-important insight: for the first time in world history, mechanical reproduction emancipates the work of art from its parasitical dependence on ritual. To an ever greater degree the work of art reproduced becomes the work of art designed for reproducibility. From a photographic negative, for example, one can make any number of prints; to ask for the 'authentic' print makes no sense. But the instant the criterion of authenticity ceases to be applicable to artistic production, the total function of art is reversed. Instead of being based on ritual, it begins to be based on another practice—politics.

Mechanical reproduction of art changes the reaction of the masses toward art. The reactionary attitude toward a Picasso painting changes into the progressive reaction toward a Chaplin movie. The progressive reaction is characterized by the direct, intimate fusion of visual and emotional enjoyment with the orientation of the expert. Such fusion is of great social significance. The greater the decrease in the social significance of an art form, the sharper the distinction between criticism and enjoyment by the public. The conventional is uncritically enjoyed, and the truly new is criticized with aversion. With regard to the screen, the critical and the receptive attitudes of the public coincide. The decisive reason for this is that individual reactions are predetermined by the mass audience response they are about to produce, and this is nowhere more pronounced than in the film. The moment these responses become manifest they control each other. Again, the comparison with painting is fruitful. A painting has always had an excellent chance to be viewed by one person or by a few. The simultaneous contemplation of paintings by a large public, such as developed in the nineteenth century, is an early symptom of the crisis of painting, a crisis which was by no means occasioned exclusively by photography but rather in a relatively independent manner by the appeal of art works to the masses.

Painting simply is in no position to present an object for simultaneous collective experience, as it was possible for architecture at all times, for the epic poem in the past, and for the movie today. Although this circumstance in itself should not lead one to conclusions about the social role of painting, it does constitute a serious threat as soon as painting, under special conditions and, as it were, against its nature, is confronted directly by the masses. In the churches and monasteries of the Middle Ages and at the princely courts up to the end of the eighteenth century, a collective reception of paintings did not occur simultaneously, but by graduated and hierarchized mediation. The change that has come about is an expression of the particular conflict in which painting was implicated by the mechanical reproducibility of paintings. Although paintings began to be publicly exhibited in galleries and salons, there was no way for the masses to organize and control themselves in their reception. Thus the same public which responds in a progressive manner toward a grotesque film is bound to respond in a reactionary manner to Surrealism.

One of the foremost tasks of art has always been the creation of a demand which could be fully satisfied only later. The history of every art form shows critical epochs in which a certain art form aspires to effects which could be fully obtained only with a changed technical standard, that is to say, in a new art form. The extravagances and crudities of art which thus appear, particularly in the so-called decadent epochs, actually arise from the nucleus of its richest historical energies. In recent years, such barbarisms were abundant in Dadaism. It is only now that its impulse becomes discernible: Dadaism attempted to create by pictorial—and literary—means the effects which the public today seeks in the film.

Every fundamentally new, pioneering creation of demands will carry beyond its goal. Dadaism did so to the extent that it sacrificed the market values which are so characteristic of the film in favor of higher ambitions—though of course it was not conscious of such intentions as here described. The Dadaists attached much less importance to the sales value of their work than to its uselessness for contemplative immersion. The studied degradation of their material was not the least of their means to achieve this uselessness. Their poems are 'word salad' containing obscenities and every imaginable waste produce of language. The same is true of their paintings, on which they mounted buttons and tickets. What they intended and achieved was a relentless destruction of the aura of their creations, which they branded as reproductions with the very means of production. Before a painting of Arp's or a poem by August Stramm it is impossible to take time for contemplation and evaluation as one would before a canvas of Derain's or a poem by Rilke. In the decline of middle-class society, contemplation became a school for asocial behavior; it was countered by distraction as a variant of social conduct. Dadaistic activities actually assured a rather vehement distraction by making works of art the center of scandal. One requirement was foremost: to outrage the public.

From an alluring appearance or persuasive structure of sound the work of art of the Dadaists became an instrument of ballistics. It hit the spectator like a bullet, it happened to him, thus acquiring a tactile quality. It promoted a demand for the film, the distracting element of which is also primarily tactile, being based on changes of place and focus which periodically assail the spectator. Let us compare the screen on which a film unfolds with the canvas of a painting. The painting invites the spectator to contemplation; before it the spectator can abandon himself to his associations. Before the movie frame he cannot do so. No sooner has his eye grasped a scene than it is already changed. It cannot be arrested. Duhamel, who detests the film and knows nothing of its significance, though something of its structure, notes this circumstance as follows: 'I can no longer think what I want to think. My thoughts have been replaced by moving images'.[1] The spectator's process of association in view of these images is indeed interrupted by their constant, sudden change. This constitutes the shock effect of the film, which, like all shocks, should be cushioned by heightened presence of mind. By means of its technical structure, the film has taken the physical shock effect out of the wrappers in which Dadaism had, as it were, kept it inside the moral shock effect.

NOTE

1. Georges Duhamel, *Scènes de la vie future*, Paris, 1930, p. 52.

Theodor Adorno, 'Letter to Walter Benjamin'*

London, 18 March 1936

Dear Herr Benjamin,

If today I prepare to convey to you some notes on your extraordinary study ('The Work of Art in the Age of Mechanical Reproduction'), I certainly have no intention of offering you criticism or even an adequate response. The terrible pressure of work

* Trans. Harry Zohn, reprinted from Ernst Bloch et al., *Aesthetics and Politics*, London and New York: Verso, pp. 120–6.

on me—the big book of logic,[1] the completion of my contribution to the monograph on Berg,[2] which is ready except for two analyses, and the study on jazz[3]—makes any such endeavour hopeless. This is especially true of a work in the face of which I am very seriously aware of the inadequacy of written communication, for there is not a sentence which I would not wish to discuss with you in detail. I cling to the hope that this will be possible very soon, but on the other hand I do not want to wait so long before giving you some kind of response, however insufficient it may be.

Let me therefore confine myself to one main theme. My ardent interest and my complete approval attach to that aspect of your study which appears to me to carry out your original intention—the dialectical construction of the relationship between myth and history—within the intellectual field of the materialistic dialectic: namely, the dialectical self-dissolution of myth, which is here viewed as the disenchantment of art.

You know that the subject of the 'liquidation of art' has for many years underlain my aesthetic studies and that my emphatic espousal of the primacy of technology, especially in music, must be understood strictly in this sense and in that of your second technique. It does not surprise me if we find common ground here; it does not surprise me, because in your book on the Baroque you accomplished the differentiation of the allegory from the symbol (in the new terminology, the 'aural' symbol) and in your *Einbahnstrasse*[4] you differentiated the work of art from magical documentation. It is a splendid confirmation—I hope it does not sound immodest if I say: for both of us—that in an essay on Schönberg which appeared in a *Festschrift* two years ago[5] and with which you are not familiar, I proposed formulations about technology and dialectics as well as the alteration of relationships to technology, which are in perfect accord with your own.

It is this accord which for me constitutes the criterion for the differences that I must now state, with no other aim than to serve our 'general line', which is now so clearly discernible. In doing so, perhaps I can start out by following our old method of immanent criticism. In your earlier writings, of which your present essay is a continuation, you differentiated the idea of the work of art as a structure from the symbol of theology and from the taboo of magic. I now find it disquieting—and here I see a sublimated remnant of certain Brechtian motifs—that you now casually transfer the concept of magical aura to the 'autonomous work of art' and flatly assign to the latter a counter-revolutionary function. I need not assure you that I am fully aware of the magical element in the bourgeois work of art (particularly since I constantly attempt to expose the bourgeois philosophy of idealism, which is associated with the concept of aesthetic autonomy, as mythical in the fullest sense). However, it seems to me that the centre of the autonomous work of art does not itself belong on the side of myth—excuse my topic parlance—but is inherently dialectical; within itself it juxtaposes the magical and the mark of freedom. If I remember correctly, you once said something similar in connection with Mallarmé, and I cannot express to you my feeling about your entire essay more clearly than by telling you that I constantly found myself wishing for a study of Mallarmé as a counterpoint to your essay, a study which, in my estimation, you owe us as an important contribution to our knowledge. Dialectical though your essay may be, it is not so in the case of the autonomous work of art itself; it disregards an elementary experience which becomes more evident to me every day in my own musical experience—that precisely the uttermost consistency in the pursuit of the technical laws of autonomous art changes this art and instead of rendering it into a taboo or fetish, brings it close to the state of freedom, of something that can be consciously produced and made. I know of no better materialistic programme than that statement by Mallarmé in which he defines works of literature as something not inspired but made out of words; and the greatest figures of reaction, such as Valéry and Borchardt (the latter with his essay about villas[6] which, despite an unspeakable comment about workers, could be taken over in a materialistic sense in its entirety), have this explosive power in their innermost cells. If you defend the *kitsch* film against the 'quality' film, no one can be more in agreement with you than I am; but *l'art pour l'art* is just as much in need of a defence, and the united front which exists against it and which to my knowledge extends from Brecht to the Youth Movement, would be encouragement enough to undertake a rescue.

[In your essay on *The Elective Affinities*][7] you speak of play and appearance as the elements of art; but I do not see why play should be dialectical, and appearance—the appearance which you have managed to preserve in Ottilie who, together with Mignon and Helena,[8] now does not come off so well—should not. And at this point, to be sure, the debate turns political quickly enough. For if you render rightly technicization and alienation dialectical, but not in equal measure the world of objectified subjectivity, the political effect is to credit the proletariat (as the cinema's subject) directly with an achievement which, according to Lenin, it can realize only through a theory introduced by intellectuals as dialectical subjects, who themselves belong to the sphere of works of art which you have consigned to Hell.

Understand me correctly. I would not want to claim the autonomy of the work of art as a prerogative, and I agree with you that the aural element of the work of art is declining—not only because of its technical reproducibility, incidentally, but above all because of the fulfilment of its own 'autonomous' formal laws (this is the subject of the theory of musical reproduction which Kolisch and I have been planning for years). But the autonomy of the work of art, and therefore its material form, is not identical with the magical element in it. The reification of a great work of art is not just loss, any more than the reification of the cinema is all loss. It would be bourgeois reaction to negate the reification of the cinema in the name of the ego, and it would border on anarchism to revoke the reification of a great work of art in the spirit of immediate use-values. '*Les extrèmes me touchent*' [Gide], just as they touch you—but only if the dialectic of the lowest has the same value as the dialectic of the highest, rather than the latter simply decaying. Both bear the stigma of capitalism, both contain elements of change (but never, of course, the middle-term between Schönberg and the American film). Both are torn halves of an integral freedom, to which however they do not add up. It would be romantic to sacrifice one to the other, either as the bourgeois romanticism of the conservation of personality and all that stuff, or as the anarchistic romanticism of blind confidence in the spontaneous power of the proletariat in the historical process—a proletariat which is itself a product of bourgeois society.

To a certain extent I must accuse your essay of this second romanticism. You have swept art out of the corners of its taboos—but it is as though you feared a consequent inrush of barbarism (who could share your fear more than I?) and protected yourself by raising what you fear to a kind of inverse taboo. The laughter of the audience at a cinema—I discussed this with Max, and he has probably told you about it already—is anything but good and revolutionary; instead, it is full of the worst bourgeois sadism. I very much doubt the expertise of the newspaper boys who discuss sports; and despite its shock-like seduction, I do not find your theory of distraction convincing—if only for the simple reason that in a communist society work will be organized in such a way that people will no longer be so tired and so stultified that they need distraction. On the other hand, certain concepts of capitalist practice, like that of the test, seem to me almost ontologically congealed and taboo-like in function—whereas if anything does have an aural character, it is surely the film which possesses it to an extreme and highly suspect degree. To select only one more small item: the idea that a reactionary is turned into a member of the avant-garde by expert knowledge of Chaplin's films strikes me as out-and-out romanticization. For I cannot count Kracauer's[9] favourite director, even after *Modern Times*, as an avant-garde artist (the reason will be perfectly clear from my article on jazz), nor do I believe that any of the decent elements in this work will attract attention. One need only have heard the laughter of the audience at the film to know what is actually happening.

Your dig at Werfel gave me great pleasure. But if you take Mickey Mouse instead, things are far more complicated, and the serious question arises as to whether the reproduction of every person really constitutes that *a priori* of the film which you claim it to be, or whether instead this reproduction belongs precisely to that 'naïve realism' whose bourgeois nature we so thoroughly agreed upon in Paris. After all, it is hardly an accident if that modern art which you counterpose to technical art as aural, is of such inherently dubious quality as Vlaminck[10] and Rilke. The lower sphere, to be sure, can score an easy victory over this sort of art; but if instead there were the names of, let us say, Kafka and Schönberg, the problem would be posed very differently. Certainly Schönberg's music is *not* aural.

Accordingly, what I would postulate is *more* dialectics. On the one hand, dialectic penetration of the 'autonomous' work of art which is transcended by its own technology into a planned work; on the other, an even stronger dialecticization of utilitarian art in its negativity, which you certainly do not fail to note but which you designate by relatively abstract categories like 'film capital', without tracking it down to its ultimate lair as immanent irrationality. When I spent a day in the studios of Neubabelsberg two years ago, what impressed me most was how *little* montage and all the advanced techniques that you emphasize are actually used; rather, reality is everywhere *constructed* with an infantile mimetism and then 'photographed'. You underestimate the technicality of autonomous art and overestimate that of dependent art; this, in plain terms, would be my main objection. But this objection could only be given effect as a dialectic between extremes which you tear apart. In my estimation, this would involve nothing else than the complete liquidation of the Brechtian motifs which have already undergone an extensive transformation in your study—above all, the liquidation of any appeal to the immediacy of interconnected aesthetic effects, however fashioned, and to the actual consciousness of actual workers who have absolutely no advantage over the bourgeois except their interest in the revolution, but otherwise bear all the marks of mutilation of the typical bourgeois character. This prescribes our function for us clearly enough—which I certainly do not mean in the sense of an activist conception of 'intellectuals'. But it cannot mean either that we may only escape the old taboos by entering into new ones—'tests', so to speak. The goal of the revolution is the abolition of fear. Therefore we need have no fear of it, nor need we ontologize our fear. It is not bourgeois idealism if, in full knowledge and without mental prohibitions, we maintain our solidarity with the proletariat instead of making our own necessity a virtue of the proletariat, as we are always tempted to do—the proletariat which itself experiences the same necessity and needs us for knowledge as much as we need the proletariat to make the revolution. I am convinced that the further development of the aesthetic debate which you have so magnificently inaugurated, depends essentially on a true accounting of the relationship of the intellectuals to the working-class.

Excuse the haste of these notes. All this could be seriously settled only on the basis of the details in which the Good Lord—possibly not magical after all—dwells.[11] Only the shortage of time leads me to use the large categories which you have taught me strictly to avoid. In order at least to indicate to you the concrete passages to which I refer, I have left my spontaneous pencilled annotations on the manuscript, though some of them may be too spontaneous to be communicated. I beg your indulgence for this as well as for the sketchy nature of my letter.

I am going to Germany on Sunday. It is possible that I shall be able to complete my jazz study there, something that I unfortunately did not have time to do in London. In that case I would send it to you without a covering letter and ask you to send it on to Max immediately after reading it (it probably will amount to more than twenty-five printed pages). This is not certain, because I do not know whether I shall find the time or, especially, whether the nature of this study will permit me to send it from Germany without considerable danger. Max has probably told you that the idea of the clown is its focal point. I would be very pleased if it appeared together with your study. Its subject is a very modest one, but it probably converges with yours in its decisive points, and will attempt to express positively some of the things that I have formulated negatively today. It arrives at a complete verdict on jazz, in particular by revealing its 'progressive' elements (semblance of montage, collective work, primacy of reproduction over production) as façades of something that is in truth quite reactionary. I believe that I have succeeded in really decoding jazz and defining its social function. Max was quite taken with my study, and I could well imagine that you will be, too. Indeed I feel that our theoretical disagreement is not really a discord between us but rather, that it is my task to hold your arm steady until the sun of Brecht has once more sunk into exotic waters. Please understand my criticisms only in this spirit.

I cannot conclude, however, without telling you that your few sentences about the disintegration of the proletariat as 'masses' through revolution[12] are among the profoundest and most powerful statements of political theory that I have encountered since I read *State and Revolution*.

Your old friend,

Teddie Wiesengrund[13]

I should also like to express my special agreement with your theory of Dadaism. It fits into the essay as nicely as the 'bombast' and the 'horrors' fit into your Baroque book.

NOTES

1. This was the philosophical work, a critique of phenomenology, on which Adorno was engaged while at Oxford. It was eventually published in Stuttgart in 1956 as *Zur Metakritik der Erkenntnistheorie. Studien über Husserl and die phänomenologischen Antinomien.*
2. Included in Willi Reich (ed.), *Alban Berg*, Vienna, 1937.
3. Published as 'Über Jazz' in the *Zeitschrift für Sozialforschung*, 5 (1936), and later included in Adorno's volume *Moments Musicaux*, Frankfurt, 1964. For Adorno's views on Jazz, see also his essay 'Perennial Fashion—Jazz', *Prisms*, London, 1967.
4. Benjamin's volume of aphorisms *Einbahnstrasse* was published in Berlin in 1928 and then later included in Adorno's collection *Impromptus*, Frankfurt, 1968.
5. This essay, 'Der dialektische Komponist', was originally published in Vienna in 1934.
6. Rudolf Borchardt (1877–1945) was a prominent litterateur in Germany, whose essay on Tuscan villas is included in the edited volume of his writings, *Prosa III*, Stuttgart, 1960, pp. 38–70.
7. Benjamin's essay, *Goethes Wahlverwandtschaften* was published in Hofmannsthal's journal *Neue Deutsche Beiträge* in 1924–5.
8. Characters in Goethe's *Elective Affinities*, *Wilhelm Meister's Apprenticeship*, and *Faust II*, respectively.
9. Siegfried Kracauer, long a friend of Adorno, was the author of *From Caligari to Hitler*, Princeton, 1947, an attack on German expressionist cinema.
10. Changed to Derain in the published version of Benjamin's essay.
11. A reference to the programmatic dictum of the art historian Aby Warburg: *Der liebe Gott steckt im Detail* (The Good Lord dwells in detail).
12. This passage does not appear in any of the published versions of Benjamin's essay.
13. Wiesengrund was Adorno's paternal name.

Antonio Gramsci (1891–1937)

Antonio Gramsci was born in Sardinia, Italy, and is considered a visionary theorist. In 1911 he began to study linguistics at the University of Turin, made contact with members of the socialist movement in 1913, and then joined the Italian Socialist Party. His journalistic activity began in 1914 when he wrote a controversial article to the Turinese socialist paper challenging the passive socialist attitude towards World War I. At this time he also became an active theatre critic and gave political speeches to several workers' cultural clubs. By 1917 he was writing pieces exalting Lenin and the Russian Revolution. During this same year, at a time when several socialist leaders were arrested, he became the editor of the *Il Grido del Popolo*, the Turinese socialist paper. In 1919 he helped found the weekly paper, *Ordine Nuovo*, and later edited this as a daily paper where he analysed the crisis of Italian liberal democracy and the fascist movement. In 1922, Gramsci moved to Moscow and worked for the Communist Third International party, and by 1926 Gramsci, along with other Communist leaders, was arrested despite his parliamentary immunity. Under incredible odds in prison, Gramsci wrote approximately nineteen notebooks which contained his thoughts on political reform. Most of these notebooks were written to his sister-in-law Tatiana Schucht, and were posthumously published in 1947. It was not until 1975, however, that translations of a definitive version of Gramsci's notebooks appeared in print. Four volumes of his pre-prison writings have also been published.

Gramsci proposed the idea of 'hegemony' to describe the state's hidden and coercive power over the people, and showed how hegemony influences the members of the working class to believe in principles and act in ways that are not in their class interests. He also discussed the role of the intellectual, and in this piece 'Intellectuals', Gramsci considers two groups: the 'organic' and the 'traditional' intellectuals. He asks 'are intellectuals an autonomous and independent social group, or does every social group have its own particular specialized category of intellectuals?' He answers this question by moving away from static categories, and pointing out that every social group which articulates the development of an economic, social, or political structure finds 'categories of intellectuals already in existence', which represents a historical continuity uninterrupted even by the most complicated and radical changes in political and social forms. He concludes this essay by identifying the function of the modern political party which 'is precisely the mechanism that carries out in civil society the same function as the state. . . . In other words it is responsible for welding together the organic intellectuals of a given group—the dominant one—and the traditional intellectuals.'

K.M.S.

Intellectuals

Are intellectuals an autonomous and independent social group, or does every social group have its own particular specialized category of intellectuals? The problem is a complex one, because of the variety of forms assumed to date by the real historical process of formation of the different categories of intellectuals. The most important of these forms are two:

1. Every social group, coming into existence on the original terrain of an essential function in the world of economic production, creates together with itself, organically, one or more strata of intellectuals which give it homogeneity and an awareness of its own function not only in the economic but also in the social and political fields. The capitalist entrepreneur creates alongside himself the industrial technician, the specialist in political economy, the organizer of a new culture, of a new legal system, etc. It should be noted that the entrepreneur himself represents a higher level of social elaboration, already characterized by a certain directive [*dirigente*] and technical (i.e. intellectual) capacity: he must have a certain technical capacity, not only in the limited sphere of his activity and initiative but in other spheres as well, at least in those which are closest to economic production. He must be an organizer of masses of men; he must be an organizer of the 'confidence' of investors in his business, of the customers for his product, etc.

If not all entrepreneurs, at least an elite amongst them must have the capacity to be an organizer of society in general, including all its complex organism of services, right up to the state organism, because of the need to create the conditions most favourable to the expansion of their own class; or at the least they must possess the capacity to choose the deputies (specialized employees) to whom to entrust this activity of organizing the general system of relationships external to the business itself. It can be observed that the 'organic' intellectuals which every new class creates alongside itself and elaborates in the course of its development, are for the most part 'specializations' of partial aspects of the primitive activity of the new social type which the new class has brought into prominence. Even feudal lords were possessors of a particular technical capacity—military capacity—and it is precisely from the moment at which the aristocracy loses its monopoly of technico-military capacity that the crisis of feudalism begins. But the formation of intellectuals in the feudal world and in the preceding classical world is a question to be examined separately: this formation and elaboration follows ways and means which must be studied concretely. 'Thus it is to be noted that the mass of the peasantry, although it performs an essential function in the world of production, does not elaborate its own 'organic' intellectuals, nor does it 'assimilate' any stratum of 'traditional' intellectuals, although it is from the peasantry that other social groups draw many of their intellectuals and a high proportion of traditional intellectuals are of peasant origin.)

2. However, every 'essential' social group which emerges into history out of the preceding economic structure, and as an expression of a development of this structure, has found (at least in all of history up to the present) categories of intellectuals already in existence and which seemed indeed to represent a historical continuity uninterrupted even by the most complicated and radical changes in political and social forms.

The most typical of these categories of intellectuals is that of the ecclesiastics, who for a long time (for a whole phase of history, which is partly characterized by this very monopoly) held a monopoly of a number of important services: religious ideology, that is the philosophy and science of the age, together with schools, education, morality, justice, charity, good works, etc. The category of ecclesiastics can be considered the category of intellectuals organically bound to the landed aristocracy. It had equal status juridically with the aristocracy, with which it shared the exercise of feudal ownership of land, and the use of state privileges connected with property. But the monopoly held by the ecclesiastics in the superstructural field (from this monopoly derived the general meeting of 'intellectual' or 'specialist' of the word *cleric* in many Romance languages, or those influenced through Church Latin by the Romance languages, together with its correlative *layman* in the sense of 'profane', 'non-specialist') was not exercised without a struggle or without limitations, and hence there took place the birth, in various forms (to be gone into and studied concretely), of other categories, favoured and enabled to expand by the growing strength of the central power of the monarch, right up to absolutism. Thus we find the formation of the *noblesse de robe*, with its own privileges, a stratum of administrators, etc., scholars and scientists, theorists, non-ecclesiastical philosophers, etc.

Since these various categories of traditional intellectuals experience through an '*esprit de corps*' their uninterrupted historical continuity and their special qualification, they thus put themselves forward as autonomous and independent of the dominant social group. This self-assessment is not without consequences in the ideological and political field, consequences of wide-ranging import. The whole of idealist philosophy can easily be connected with this position assumed by the social complex of intellectuals and can be defined as the expression of that social utopia by which the intellectuals think of themselves as 'independent', autonomous, endowed with a character of their own, etc.

One should note however that if the Pope and the leading hierarchy of the Church consider themselves more linked to Christ and to the apostles than they are to senators Agnelli and Benni, the same does not hold for Gentile and Croce, for example: Croce in particular feels himself closely linked to Aristotle and Plato, but he does not conceal, on the other hand, his links with senators Agnelli and Benni, and it is precisely here that one can discern the most significant character of Croce's philosophy.

(This research into the history of the intelletuals will not be of a 'sociological' character but will lead to a series of essays of 'cultural history' (*Kulturgeschichte*) and history of political science. All the same, it will be difficult to avoid certain schematic and abstract forms that will be reminiscent of those of 'sociology': it will therefore be necessary to find the most suitable form of writing for making this exposition 'non-sociological'. The first part of the research could be a methodical critique of existing works on intellectuals, which are nearly all of a sociological type. It is therefore indispensable to collect a bibliography on the subject.)

What are the 'maximum' limits of acceptance of the term 'intellectual'? Can one find a unitary criterion to characterize equally all the diverse and disparate activities of intellectuals and to distinguish these at the same time and in an essential way from the activities of other social groupings? The most widespread error of method seems to me that of having looked for this criterion of distinction in the intrinsic nature of intellectual activities, rather than in the ensemble of the system of relations in which these activities (and therefore the intellectual groups who personify them) have their place within the general complex of social relations. Indeed the worker or proletarian, for example, is not specifically characterized by his manual or instrumental work, but by performing this work in specific conditions and in specific social relations (apart from the consideration that purely physical labour does not exist and that even Taylor's phrase of 'trained gorilla' is a metaphor to indicate a limit in a certain direction: in any physical work, even the most degraded and mechanical, there exists a minimum of technical qualification, that is, a minimum of creative intellectual activity). And we have already observed that the entrepreneur, by virtue of his very function, must have to some degree a certain number of qualifications of an intellectual nature although his part in society is determined not by these, but by the general social relations which specifically characterize the position of the entrepreneur within industry.

All men are intellectuals, one could therefore say; but not all men have in society the function of intellectuals (thus, because it can happen that everyone at some time fries a couple of eggs or sews up a tear in a jacket, we do not necessarily say that everyone is a cook or a tailor). Thus there are historically formed specialized categories for the exercise of the intellectual function. They are formed in connection with all social groups, but especially in connection with the most important social groups, and they undergo more extensive and complex elaboration in connection with the dominant social group. One of the most important characteristics of any group that is developing towards dominance is its struggle to assimilate and to conquer 'ideologically' the traditional intellectuals, but this assimilation and conquest is made quicker and more efficacious the more the group in question succeeds in simultaneously elaborating its own organic intellectuals.

The enormous development of activity and organization of education in the broad sense in the societies that emerged from the medieval world is an index of the importance assumed in the modern world by intellectual functions and categories. Parallel with the attempt to deepen and to broaden the 'intellectuality' of each individual, there has also been an attempt to multiply and narrow the various specializations. This can be seen from educational institutions at all levels, up to and including the organisms that exist to promote so-called 'high culture' in all fields of science and technology.

(The education system is the instrument through which intellectuals of various levels are elaborated. The complexity of the intellectual function in different states can be measured objectively by the number and gradation of specialized schools: the more extensive the 'area' covered by education and the more numerous the 'vertical' 'levels' of schooling, the more complex is the cultural world, the civilization, of a particular state. A point of comparison can be found in the sphere of industrial technology: the industrialization of a country can be measured by how well equipped it is in the production of machines with which to produce machines, and in the manufacture of ever more accurate instruments for making both machines and further instruments for making machines, etc. The country which is best equipped in the construction of instruments for experimental scientific laboratories and in the construction of instruments with which to test the first instruments, can be regarded as the most complex in the technical–industrial field, with the highest level of civilization, etc. The same applies to the preparation: schools and institutes of high culture can be assimilated to each other.) (In this field also, quantity cannot be separated from quality. To the most refined technical–cultural specialization there cannot but correspond the maximum possible diffusion of primary education and the maximum care taken to expand the middle grades numerically as much as possible. Naturally this need to provide the widest base possible for the selection and elaboration of the top intellectual qualifications—i.e. to give a democratic structure to high culture and top-level technology—is not without its disadvantages: it creates the possibility of vast crises of unemployment for the middle intellectual strata, and in all modern societies this actually takes place.)

It is worth noting that the elaboration of intellectual strata in concrete really does not take place on the terrain of abstract democracy but in accordance with very concrete traditional historical processes. Strata have grown up which traditionally 'produce' intellectuals and these strata coincide with those which have specialized in 'saving', i.e. the petty and middle landed bourgeoisie and certain strata of the petty and middle urban bourgeoisie. The varying distribution of different types of school (classical and professional) over the 'economic' territory and the varying aspirations of different categories within these strata determine, or give form to, the production of various branches of intellectual specialization. Thus in Italy the rural bourgeoisie produces in particular state functionaries and professional people, whereas the urban bourgeoisie produces technicians for industry. Consequently it is largely northern Italy which produces technicians and the South which produces functionaries and professional men.

The relationship between the intellectuals and the world of production is not as direct as it is with the fundamental social groups but is, in varying degrees, 'mediated' by the whole fabric of society and by the complex of superstructures, of which the intellectuals are, precisely, the 'functionaries'. It should be possible both to measure the degree of 'organicism' of the various intellectual strata and their degree of connection with a fundamental social group, and to establish a gradation of their functions and of the superstructures from the bottom to the top (from the structural base upwards). What we can do, for the moment, is to fix two major superstructural 'levels': the one that can be called 'civil society', that is the ensemble of organisms commonly called 'private', and that of 'political society' or 'the state'. These two

101

levels correspond on the one hand to the function of 'hegemony' which the dominant group exercises throughout society and on the other hand to that of 'direct domination' or command exercised through the state and 'juridical' government. The functions in question are precisely organizational and connective. The intellectuals are the dominant group's 'deputies' exercising the subaltern functions of social hegemony and political government. These comprise:

1. The 'spontaneous' consent given by the great masses of the population to the general direction imposed on social life by the dominant fundamental group; this consent is 'historically' caused by the prestige (and consequent confidence) which the dominant group enjoys because of its position and function in the world of production.

2. The apparatus of state coercive power which 'legally' enforces discipline on those groups who do not 'consent' either actively or passively. This apparatus is, however, constituted for the whole of society in anticipation of moments of crisis of command and direction when spontaneous consent has failed.

This way of posing the problem has as a result a considerable extension of the concept of intellectual, but it is the only way which enables one to reach a concrete approximation of reality. It also clashes with preconceptions of caste. The function of organizing social hegemony and state domination certainly gives rise to a particular division of labour and therefore to a whole hierarchy of qualifications in some of which there is no apparent attribution of directive or organizational functions. For example, in the apparatus of social and state direction there exists a whole series of jobs of a manual and instrumental character (non-executive work, agents rather than officials or functionaries). It is obvious that such a distinction has to be made just as it is obvious that other distinctions have to be made as well. Indeed, intellectual activity must also be distinguished in terms of its intrinsic characteristics, according to levels which in moments of extreme opposition represent a real qualitative difference—at the highest level would be the creators of the various sciences, philosophy, art, etc., at the lowest the most humble 'administrators' and divulgators of pre-existing, traditional, accumulated intellectual wealth. Here again military organization offers a model of complex gradations between subaltern officers, senior officers and general staff, not to mention the NCOs, whose importance is greater than is generally admitted. It is worth observing that all these parts feel a solidarity and indeed that it is the lower strata that display the most blatant *esprit de corps*, from which they derive a certain 'conceit' which is apt to lay them open to jokes and witticisms.

In the modern world the category of intellectuals, understood in this sense, has undergone an unprecedented expansion. The democratic-bureaucratic system has given rise to a great mass of functions which are not all justified by the social necessities of production, though they are justified by the political necessities of the dominant fundamental group. Hence Loria's conception of the unproductive 'worker' (but unproductive in relation to whom and to what mode of production?), a conception which could in part be justified if one takes account of the fact that these masses exploit their position to take for themselves a large cut out of the national income. Mass training has standardized individuals both psychologically and in terms of individual qualification and has produced the same phenomena as with other standardized masses: competition which creates the need for professional associations and leads to unemployment, over-production of qualified people by the education system, emigration, etc.

Different position of intellectuals of the urban type and the rural type. Intellectuals of the urban type have grown up along with industry and are linked to its fortunes. Their function can be compared to that of subaltern officers in the army. They have no autonomous initiative in elaborating plans for construction. Their job is to articulate the relationship between the entrepreneur and the instrumental mass and to carry out the immediate execution of the production plan decided by the industrial general staff, controlling the elementary stages of work. On the whole the average urban intellectuals are very standardized, while the top urban intellectuals are more and more identified with the industrial general staff itself.

Intellectuals of the rural type are for the most part 'traditional', that is they are linked to the social mass of country people and the town (particularly small-town) petty bourgeoisie, not as yet elaborated and set in motion by the capitalist system. This type of intellectual brings into contact the peasant masses with the local and state administration (lawyers, notaries, etc.). Because of this activity they have an important politico–social function, since professional mediation is difficult to separate from political. Furthermore: in the countryside the intellectual (priest, lawyer, notary, teacher, doctor, etc.), has on the whole a higher or at least a different living standard from that of the average peasant and consequently represents a social model for the peasant to look to in his aspiration to escape from or improve his condition. The peasant always thinks that at least one of his sons could become an intellectual (especially a priest), thus becoming a gentleman and raising the social level of the family by facilitating its economic life through the connections which he is bound to acquire with the rest of the gentry. The peasant's attitude towards the intellectual is double and appears contradictory. He respects the social position of the intellectuals and in general that of state employees, but sometimes affects contempt for it, which means that his admiration is mingled with instinctive elements of envy and impassioned anger. One can understand nothing of the collective life of the peasantry and of the germs and ferments of development which exist within it, if one does not take into consideration and examine concretely and in depth this effective subordination to the intellectuals. Every organic development of the peasant masses, up to a certain point, is linked to and depends on movements among the intellectuals.

With the urban intellectuals it is another matter. Factory technicians do not exercise any political function over the instrumental masses, or at least this is a phase that has been superseded. Sometimes, rather, the contrary takes place, and the instrumental masses, at least in the person of their own organic intellectuals, exercise a political influence on the technicians.

The central point of the question remains the distinction between intellectuals as an organic category of every fundamental social group and intellectuals as a traditional category. From this distinction there flows a whole series of problems and possible questions for historical research.

The most interesting problem is that which, when studied from this point of view, relates to the modern political party, its real origins, its developments and the forms which it takes. What is the character of the political party in relation to the problem of the intellectuals? Some distinctions must be made:

1. The political party for some social groups is nothing other than their specific way of elaborating their own category of organic intellectuals directly in the political and philosophical field rather than in the field of productive technique. These intellectuals are formed in this way and cannot indeed be formed in any other way, given the general character and the conditions of formation, life and development of the social group within whose productive technique those strata are formed which can be said to correspond to NCOs in the army, that is to say, for the town, skilled and specialized workers and, for the country (in a more complex fashion) share-croppers and tenant farmers—since in general terms these types of farmer correspond more or less to the type of the artisan, who is the skilled worker of a medieval economy.

2. The political party, for all groups, is precisely the mechanism which carries out in civil society the same function as the state carries out, more synthetically and over a larger scale, in political society. In other words it is responsible for welding together the organic intellectuals of a given group—the dominant one—and the traditional intellectuals. The party carries out this function in strict dependence on its basic function, which is that of elaborating its own component parts—those elements of a social group which has been born and developed as an 'economic' group—and of turning them into qualified political intellectuals, leaders and organizers of all the activities and functions inherent in the organic development of an integral society, both civil and political. Indeed it can be said that within its field the political party accomplishes its function more completely and organically than the state does within its admittedly far larger field. An intellectual who joins the political party of a particular social group is merged with the organic intellectuals of the group itself, and is linked tightly with the group. This takes place through participation in the life of the state only to a limited degree and often not at all. Indeed it happens that many intellectuals think that they *are* the state, a belief which, given the magnitude of the category, occasionally has important consequences and leads to unpleasant complications for the fundamental economic group which *really* is the state.

That all members of a political party should be regarded as intellectuals is an affirmation that can easily lend itself to mockery and caricature. But if one thinks about it nothing could be more exact. There are of course distinctions of level to be made. A party might have a greater or lesser proportion of members in the higher grades or in the lower, but this is not the point. What matters is the function, which is directive and organizational, i.e. educative, i.e. intellectual. A tradesman does not join a political party in order to do business, nor an industrialist in order to produce more at lower cost, nor a peasant to learn new methods of cultivation, even if some aspects of these demands of the tradesman, the industrialist or the peasant can find satisfaction in the party (common opinion tends to oppose this, maintaining that the tradesman, industrialist or peasant who engages in 'politicking' loses rather than gains, and is the worst type of all—which is debatable). For these purposes, within limits, there exists the professional association, in which the economic-corporate activity of the tradesman, industrialist or peasant is most suitably promoted. In the political party the elements of an economic social group get beyond that moment of their historical development and become agents of more general activities of a national and international character.

[. . .]

Claude Lévi-Strauss (1908–)

Claude Lévi-Strauss, a French social anthropologist, first studied Law and Philosophy, but became interested in anthropology while lecturing at São Paulo University in Brazil (1934–9). He worked in the New School for Social Research in New York before becoming the Director of Studies at the École Pratique des Hautes Études in Paris in 1950. Lévi-Strauss's innovative approaches to analysing kinship structures and ritual and mythic conventions of South Americans have influenced contemporary anthropology considerably. He investigates the systematic ordering of codes in cultural behavior by using linguistics models to analyse a wide range of the 'discourses' of culture. The purpose of 'myth', he argues, is the resolution of social contradictions, rather than the creation of positive cultural and discursive 'contents'. His book *Structural Anthropology* (1958) exemplifies the extent to which he was influenced by structural linguistics, especially the works of Ferdinand de Saussure and Roman Jakobson. His other major works include: *Tristes Tropiques* (1955), *Totemism* (1962), *The Savage Mind* (1962), *The Raw and the Cooked* (1964), *The Elementary Structures of Kinship* (1967), and *The Origin of Table Manners* (1968).

In 'A Writing Lesson' in *Tristes Tropiques*, Lévi-Strauss proposes the idea of written language as a pre-condition to man's evolution and civilization. He recalls an expedition he arranged with a group of Sabane people in order to investigate the relationship between writing and culture. He assesses the attempts of the tribal chief to act as an 'intermediary agent for the exchange of goods', and uses this episode to demonstrate that, for the Nambikwara, writing had been 'borrowed as a symbol . . . for a sociological rather than an intellectual purpose'. He reviews the development of agriculture, the domestication of animals, and various arts and crafts of this tribal group to argue that indeed their form of civilization did not need 'writing' as a precondition to culture. He identifies the facilitation of slavery as the only aspect of civilization which is concomitant with the development of written language. 'The integration of large numbers of individuals into a political system, and their grading into castes and classes' is, according to Lévi-Strauss, one of the major ends to which

written language has been put in Western civilizations. He admits, however, exceptions to this definition, yet maintains a parallel relationship between 'writing' and 'knowledge'. He concludes by noting that 'writing' must be common to all members of a specific group so that the authoritarians of the group can have control. Ironically, in analysing the Nambikwara system of exchange, he implicitly equates his ignorance of its processes to the Nambikwara's lack of knowledge of writing.
K.M.S.

A writing lesson

I was keen to find out, at least indirectly, the approximate size of the Nambikwara population. In 1915, Rondon had suggested a figure of twenty thousand, which was probably too high an estimate; but at that time, each group comprised several hundred members, and, according to information I had picked up along the line, there had since been a rapid decline. Thirty years ago, the known fraction of the Sabané group comprised more than a thousand individuals; when the group visited the telegraph station at Campos Novos in 1928, a hundred and twenty-seven men were counted in addition to women and children. However, in 1929 an influenza epidemic broke out when the group was camping in a locality known as Espirro. The illness developed into a form of pulmonary oedema and, within forty-eight hours, three hundred natives had died. The group broke up, leaving the sick and the dying behind. Of the thousand Sabané who were once known to exist, there remained in 1938 only nineteen men with their women and children. These figures are perhaps to be explained, not only by the epidemic, but also by the fact that, a few years before, the Sabané had started a war against some of their eastern neighbours. But a large group, which had settled not far from Tres Buritis, was wiped out by a flu epidemic in 1927, with the exception of six or seven individuals, of whom only three were still alive in 1938. The Tarundé group, which was once one of the largest, numbered only twelve men (plus the women and children) in 1936; of these twelve men four survived in 1939.

Now, there were perhaps no more than two thousand natives scattered across the area. A systematic census was out of the question, because of the permanent hostility shown by certain groups and the fact that all groups were on the move during the nomadic period. But I tried to persuade my Utiarity friends to take me to their village, after organizing some kind of meeting there with other groups to whom they were related either by kinship or marriage; in this way I would be able to gauge the size of a contemporary gathering and compare it in this respect with those previously observed. I promised to bring presents and to engage in barter. The chief of the group was rather reluctant to comply with my request: he was not sure of his guests, and if my companions and myself were to disappear in an area where no white men had set foot since the murder of the seven telegraph employees in 1925, the precarious peace which had prevailed since then might well be endangered for some time to come.

He finally agreed on condition that we reduced the size of our expedition, taking only four oxen to carry the presents. Even so, it would be impossible to follow the usual tracks along the valley bottoms where the vegetation was too dense for the animals to get through. We would have to go across the plateaux following a route specially worked out for the occasion.

In retrospect, this journey, which was an extremely hazardous one, seems to me now to have been like some grotesque interlude. We had hardly left Juruena when my Brazilian companion noticed that the women and children were not with us: we were accompanied only by the men, armed with bows and arrows. In travel books, such circumstances mean that an attack is imminent. So we moved ahead with mixed feelings, checking the position of our Smith-and-Wesson revolvers (our men pronounced the name as 'Cemite Vechetone') and our rifles from time to time. Our fears proved groundless: about midday we caught up with the rest of the group, whom the chief had taken the precaution of sending off the previous evening, knowing that our mules would advance more quickly than the basket-carrying women, whose pace was further slowed down by the children.

A little later, however, the Indians lost their way: the new route was not as straightforward as they had imagined. Towards evening we had to stop in the bush; we had been told that there would be game to shoot; the natives were relying on our rifles and had brought nothing with them; we only had emergency provisions, which could not possibly be shared out among everybody. A herd of deer grazing around a water-hole fled at our approach. The next morning, there was widespread discontent, openly directed against the chief who was held responsible for a plan he and I had devised together. Instead of setting out on a hunting or collecting expedition, all the natives decided to lie down under the shelters, leaving the chief to discover the solution to the problem. He disappeared along with one of his wives; towards evening we saw them both return, their heavy baskets full of the grasshoppers they had spent the entire day collecting. Although crushed grasshopper is considered rather poor fare, the natives all ate heartily and recovered their spirits. We set off again the following morning.

At last we reached the appointed meeting-place. It was a sandy terrace overlooking a stream lined with trees, between which lay half-hidden native gardens. Groups arrived intermittently. Towards evening, there were seventy-five persons representing seventeen families, all grouped together under thirteen shelters hardly more substantial than those to be found in native camps. It was explained to me that, during the rainy season, all these people would be housed in five round huts built to last for some months. Several of the natives appeared never to have seen a white man before and their surly attitude and the chief's edginess suggested that he had persuaded them to come rather against their will. We did not feel safe, nor did the Indians. The night promised to be cold, and as there were no trees on the terrace, we had to lie down like the Hambikwara on the bare earth. Nobody slept: the hours were spent keeping a close but polite watch on each other.

It would have been unwise to prolong such a dangerous situation, so I urged the chief to proceed without further delay to the exchange of gifts. It was at this point that there occurred an extraordinary incident that I can only explain by going back a little. It is unnecessary to point out that the Nambikwara have no written language, but they do not know how to draw either, apart from making a few dotted lines or zigzags on their gourds. Nevertheless, as I had done among the Caduveo, I handed out sheets of paper and pencils. At first they did nothing with them, then one day I saw that they were all busy drawing wavy, horizontal lines. I wondered what they were trying to do, then it was suddenly borne upon me that they were writing or, to be more accurate, were trying to use their pencils in the same way as I did mine, which was the only way they could conceive of, because I had not yet tried to amuse them with my drawings. The majority did this and no more, but the chief had further ambitions. No doubt he was the only one who had grasped the purpose of writing. So he asked me for a writing-pad, and when we both had one, and were working together, if I asked for information on a given point, he did not supply it verbally but drew wavy lines on his paper and presented them to me, as if I could read his reply. He was half taken in by his own make-believe; each time he completed a line, he examined it anxiously as if expecting the meaning to leap from the page, and the same look of disappointment came over his face. But he never admitted this, and there was a tacit understanding between us to the effect that his unintelligible scribbling had a meaning which I pretended to decipher; his verbal commentary fol- lowed almost at once, relieving me of the need to ask for explanations.

As soon as he had got the company together, he took from a basket a piece of paper covered with wavy lines and made a show of reading it, pretending to hesitate as he checked on it the list of objects I was to give in exchange for the presents offered me: so-and-so was to have a chopper in exchange for a bow and arrows, someone else beads in exchange for his necklaces . . . This farce went on for two hours. Was he perhaps hoping to delude himself? More probably he wanted to astonish his compan- ions, to convince them that he was acting as an intermediary agent for the exchange of the goods, that he was in alliance with the white man and shared his secrets. We were eager to be off, since the most dangerous point would obviously be reached when all the marvels I had brought had been transferred to native hands. So I did not try to explore the matter further, and we began the return journey with the Indians still acting as our guides.

. The abortive meeting and the piece of humbug of which I had unwittingly been the cause had created an atmosphere of irritation; to make matters worse, my mule had ulcers in its mouth which were causing it pain. It either rushed impatiently ahead or came to a sudden stop; the two of us fell out. Suddenly, before I realized what was happening, I found myself alone in the bush, with no idea which way to go.

Travel books tell us that the thing to do is attract the attention of the main party by firing a shot. I got down from my mount and fired. No response. At the second shot I seemed to hear a reply. I fired a third, the only effect of which was to frighten the mule; it trotted off and stopped some distance away.

I systematically divested myself of my weapons and photographic equipment and laid them all at the foot of a tree, carefully noting its position. Then I ran off to recapture my mule, which I had glimpsed in the distance, seemingly in docile mood. It waited till I got near, then fled just as I was about to seize the reins, repeating this little game several times and leading me further and further on. In despair I took a leap and hung on to its tail with both hands. Surprised at this unwonted procedure, it made no further attempt to escape from me. I climbed back into the saddle and tried to return to collect my equipment, but we had wandered round so much that I was unable to find it.

Disheartened by the loss, I then decided to try and rejoin the caravan. Neither the mule nor I knew which way it had gone. Either I would decide on one direction which the mule was reluctant to follow, or I would let it have its head, and it would start going round in circles. The sun was sinking towards the horizon, I had lost my weapons and at any moment I expected to be pierced by a shower of arrows. I might not be the first person to have entered that hostile area, but my predecessors had not returned, and, irrespective of myself, my mule would be a most desirable prey for people whose food supplies were scanty. While turning these sombre thoughts over and over in my mind, I waited for the sun to set, my plan being to start a bush fire, since at least I had some matches. Just when I was about to do this, I heard voices: two Nambikwara had turned back as soon as my absence was noticed and had been following my trail since midday; for them, finding my equipment was child's play. They led me back through the darkness to the encampment, where the others were waiting.

Being still perturbed by this stupid incident, I slept badly and whiled away the sleepless hours by thinking over the episode of the exchange of gifts. Writing had, on that occasion, made its appearance among the Nambikwara but not, as one might have imagined, as a result of long and laborious training. It had been borrowed as a symbol, and for a sociological rather than an intellectual purpose, while its reality remained unknown. It had not been a question of acquiring knowledge, of remembering or understanding, but rather of increasing the authority and prestige of one individual—or function—at the expense of others. A native still living in the Stone Age had guessed that this great means towards understanding, even if he was unable to understand it, could be made to serve other purposes. After all, for thousands of years, writing has existed as an institution—and such is still the case today in a large part of the world—in societies the majority of whose members have never learnt to handle it. The inhabitants of the villages I stayed in in the Chittagong hills in eastern Pakistan were illiterate, but each village had its scribe who acted on behalf of individuals or of the community as a whole. All the villagers know about writing, and make use of it if the need arises, but they do so from the outside, as if it were a foreign mediatory agent that they communicate with by oral methods. The scribe is rarely a functionary or employee of the group: his knowledge is accompanied by power, with the result that the same individual is often both scribe and money-lender; not just because he needs to be able to read and write to carry on his business, but because he thus happens to be, on two different counts, someone who *has a hold* over others.

Writing is a strange invention. One might suppose that its emergence could not fail to bring about profound changes in the conditions of human existence, and that these transformations must of necessity be of an intellectual manner. The possession of writing vastly increases man's ability to preserve knowledge. It can be thought of as an artificial memory, the development of which ought to lead to a clearer awareness of the past, and hence to a greater ability to organize both the present and the future. After eliminating all other criteria which have been put forward to distinguish between barbarism and civilization, it is tempting to retain this one at least: there are peoples with, or without, writing; the former are able to store up their past achievements and to move with ever-increasing rapidity towards the goal they have set themselves, whereas the latter, being incapable of remembering the past beyond the narrow margin of individual memory, seem bound to remain imprisoned in a fluctuating history which will always lack both a beginning and any lasting awareness of an aim.

Yet nothing we know about writing and the part it has played in man's evolution justifies this view. One of the most creative periods in the history of mankind occurred during the early stages of the neolithic age, which was responsible for agriculture, the domestication of animals and various arts and crafts. This stage could only have been reached if, for thousands of years, small communities had been observing, experimenting and handing on their findings. This great development was carried out with an accuracy and a continuity which are proved by its success, although writing was still unknown at the time. If writing was invented between 4000 and 3000 B.C., it must be looked upon as an already remote (and no doubt indirect) result of the neolithic revolution, but certainly not as the necessary precondition for it. If we ask ourselves what great innovation writing was linked to, there is little we can suggest on the technical level, apart from architecture. But Egyptian and Sumerian architecture was not superior to the achievements of certain American peoples who knew nothing of writing in the pre-Columbian period. Conversely, from the invention of writing right up to the birth of modern science, the world lived through some five thousand years when knowledge fluctuated more than it increased. It has often been pointed out that the way of life of a Greek or Roman citizen was not so very different from that of an eighteenth-century middle-class European. During the neolithic age, mankind made gigantic strides without the help of writing; with writing, the historic civilizations of the West stagnated for a long time. It would no doubt be difficult to imagine the expansion of science in the nineteenth and twentieth centuries without writing. But, although a necessary precondition, it is certainly not enough to explain the expansion.

To establish a correlation between the emergence of writing and certain characteristic features of civilization, we must look in a quite different direction. The only phenomenon with which writing has always been concomitant is the creation of cities and empires, that is the integration of large numbers of individuals into a political system, and their grading into castes or classes. Such, at any rate, is the typical pattern of development to be observed from Egypt to China, at the time when writing first emerged: it seems to have favoured the exploitation of human beings rather than their enlightenment. This exploitation, which made it possible to assemble thousands of workers and force them to carry out exhausting tasks, is a much more likely explanation of the birth of architecture than the direct link referred to above. My hypothesis, if correct, would oblige us to recognize the fact that the primary function of written communication is to facilitate slavery. The use of writing for disinterested purposes, and as a source of intellectual and aesthetic pleasure, is a secondary result, and more often than not it may even be turned into a means of strengthening, justifying or concealing the other.

There are, nevertheless, exceptions to the rule: there were native empires in Africa which grouped together several hundreds of thousands of subjects; millions lived under the Inca empire in pre-Columbian America. But in both continents such attempts at empire building did not produce lasting results. We know that the Inca empire was established around the twelfth century: Pizarro's soldiers would not have conquered it so easily, three centuries later, had they not found it in a state of advanced decay. Although we know little about ancient African history, we can sense that the situation must have been similar: great political groupings came into being and then vanished again within the space of a few decades. It is possible, then, that these examples confirm the hypothesis, instead of contradicting it. Although writing may not have been enough to consolidate knowledge, it was perhaps indispensable for the strengthening of dominion. It we look at the situation nearer home, we see that the systematic development of compulsory education in the European countries goes hand in hand with the extension of military service and proletarianization. The fight against illiteracy is therefore connected with an increase in governmental authority over the citizens. Everyone must be able to read, so that the government can say: Ignorance of the law is no excuse.

The process has moved from the national to the international level, thanks to a kind of complicity that has grown up between newly created states—which find themselves facing problems which we had to cope with a hundred or two hundred years ago—and an international society of privileged countries worried by the possibility of its stability being threatened by the reactions of peoples insufficiently trained in the use of the written word to think in slogans that can be modified at will or to be an easy prey to suggestion. Through gaining access to the knowledge stored in libraries, these peoples have also become vulnerable to the still greater proportion of lies propagated in printed documents. No doubt, there can be no turning back now. But in my Nambikwara village, the insubordinate characters were the most sensible. The villagers who withdrew their allegiance to their chief after he had tried to exploit a feature of civilization (after my visit he was abandoned by most of his people) felt in some obscure way that writing and deceit had penetrated simultaneously into their midst. They went off into a more remote area of the bush to allow themselves a period of respite. Yet at the same time I could not help admiring their chief's genius in instantly recognizing that writing could increase his authority, thus grasping the basis of the institution without knowing how to use it. At the same time, the episode drew my attention to another aspect of Nambikwara life: the political relationships between individuals and groups. I was soon to be able to observe them more directly.

While we were still at Utiarity, an epidemic of putrid ophthalmia had broken out among the natives. The infection, which was gonorrheal in origin, spread to the whole community, causing terrible pain and temporary blindness which could become permanent. For several days the group was completely paralysed. The natives treated the infection with water in which a certain kind of bark had been allowed to soak and which they injected into the eye by means of a leaf rolled into a cornet shape. The disease spread to our group: the first person to catch it was my wife who had taken part in all my expeditions so far, her speciality being the study of material culture and skills; the infection was so serious that she had to be evacuated. Then it affected most of the men, as well as my Brazilian companion. Soon the expedition was brought to a halt; I left the main body to rest, with our doctor to give them such treatment as they needed, and with two men and a few beasts I headed for

Campos Novos, near which post several bands of natives had been reported. I spent a fortnight there in semi–idleness, gathering barely ripe fruit in an orchard which had reverted to the wild state: there were guavas, the bitter taste and gritty texture of which always fall far short of their aroma, and caju, as brilliantly coloured as parrots, which contain an acid and strongly flavoured juice in the spongy cells of their coarse pulp. To get meat for our meals we had only to go a few hundred metres from the camp at dawn to a copse regularly visited by wood-pigeons, which were easy to shoot. It was at Campos Novos that I met with two groups, whom the expectation of my presents had lured down from the north.

These two groups were as ill-disposed towards each other as they both were towards me. From the start, they did not so much ask for my presents as demand to be given them. During the first few days, only one group was present, as well as a native from Utiarity who had gone on ahead of me. I think perhaps he was showing too great an interest in a young woman belonging to his hosts' group, since relations between the strangers and their visitor became strained almost at once and he started coming to my encampment in search of a more friendly atmosphere; he also shared my meals. This fact was noticed and one day while he was out hunting I received a visit from four natives forming a kind of delegation. In threatening tones, they urged me to put poison in my guest's food; they had, in fact, brought the necessary prepar- ation along with them, a grey powder packed in four little tubes tied together with thread. It was a very awkward situation: if I refused outright, I might well be attacked by the group, whose hostile intentions called for a prudent response. I therefore thought it better to exaggerate my ignorance of the language, and I pretended to understand nothing at all. After several attempts, during which I was told over and over again that my protégé was *kakoré*, that is, very wicked, and should be got rid of as soon as possible, the delegation withdrew with many expressions of displeasure. I warned the interested party, who at once disappeared; I did not see him again until I returned to the area several months later.

Fortunately, the second group arrived the next day, thus providing the first with a different object on which to vent their animosity. The meeting took place at my encampment which was both neutral territory and the goal of these various journey- ings. Consequently, I had a good view of the proceedings. The men had come alone, and almost immediately a lengthy conversation began between their respective chiefs. It might be more accurately termed a series of alternating monologues, uttered in plaintive, nasal tones which I had never heard before. 'We are extremely annoyed. You are our enemies!' moaned one group, whereupon the others replied more or less, 'We are not annoyed. We are your brothers. We are friends—friends! We can get along together! etc.'. Once this exchange of provocations and protestations was over, a communal camp was set up next to mine. After a few songs and dances, during which each group ran down its own performance by comparing it with that of its opponents ('The Taimaindé are good singers! We are poor singers!'), the quarrel was resumed, and before long the tension heightened. The night had only just begun when the mixture of songs and arguments produced a most extraordinary din, the meaning of which I failed to grasp. Threatening gestures were made, and sometimes scuffles broke out, and other natives intervened as peacemakers. All the threatening gestures centred round the sexual organs. A Nambikwara Indian expresses dislike by grasping his penis in both hands and pointing it towards his opponent. This gesture is followed by an assault on that person, the aim being to pull off the tuft of *buriti* straw attached to the front of the belt above the genitals. These 'are hidden by the straw', and 'the object of the fight is to pull off the straw.' The action is purely symbolical, because the genital covering of the male is made of such flimsy material and is so insubstantial that it neither affords protection nor conceals the organs. Attempts are also made to seize the opponent's bow and arrows and to put them beyond his reach. Throughout these actions, the natives remain extremely tense, as if they were in a state of violent and pent-up anger. The scuffles may sometimes degenerate into a free-for-all, but on this occasion the fighting subsided at dawn. Still in the same state of visible irritation and with gestures that were anything but gentle, the two sets of opponents then set about examining each other, fingering their ear-pendants, cotton bracelets and little feather ornaments, and muttering a series of rapid comments, such as 'Give it . . . give it . . . see, that's pretty,' while the owner would protest, 'It's ugly . . . old, . . . damaged!'

This 'reconciliatory inspection' marked the end of the quarrel, and initiated another kind of relationship between the groups: commercial exchanges. Rudimentary the material culture of the Nambikwara may be, but the crafts and produce of each group are highly prized by the others. The eastern Nambikwara need pottery and seeds; those from the north consider that their more southerly neighbours make particularly delicate necklaces. It follows that when a meeting between two groups is conducted peacefully, it leads to a reciprocal exchange of gifts; strife is replaced by barter.

Actually, it was difficult to believe that an exchange of gifts was in progress; the morning after the quarrel, each man went about his usual business and the objects or produce were passed from one to another without the giver calling attention to the fact that he was handing over a gift, and without the receiver paying any heed to his new acquisition. The items thus exchanged included raw cotton and balls of thread; lumps of wax or resin; urucu paste; shells, ear-drops, bracelets and necklaces; tobacco and seeds, feathers and bamboo laths to be made into arrow heads; bundles of palm fibres, porcupine quills; whole pots or fragments of pottery and gourds. This mysterious exchange of goods went on for half a day, after which the groups took leave of each other and went their separate ways.

The Nambikwara rely, then, on the generosity of the other side. It simply does not occur to them to evaluate, argue, bargain, demand or take back. I offered a native a machete as payment for taking a message to a neighbouring group. On his return, I omitted to hand over the agreed reward immediately, thinking that he would come to fetch it. He did not do so, and the next day I could not find him; he had departed in a rage, so his companions told me, and I never saw him again. I had to ask another native to accept the present on his behalf. This being so, it is hardly surprising that, when the exchanges are over, one group should go off dissatisfied with its share, and (taking stock of its acquisitions and remembering its own gifts) should build up feelings of resentment which become increasingly aggressive. Very often these feelings are enough to start a war; of course, there are other causes, such as the need to commit, or avenge, a murder or the kidnapping of a woman; however, it does not seem that a group feels collectively bound to exact reprisals for some injury done to one of

113

its members. Nevertheless, because of the hostility between the groups, such pretexts are often willingly accepted, especially if a particular group feels itself to be strong. The proposal is presented by a warrior who expounds his grievances in the same tone and style as is used for the inter-group speeches: 'Hallo! Come here! Come along! I am angry! very angry! arrows! big arrows!'

Clad in special finery, consisting of tufts of *buriti* straw daubed with red and helmets made from jaguar hides, the men assemble under the leadership of their chief and dance. A divinatory rite has to be performed: the chief, or the shaman in those groups which have one, hides an arrow somewhere in the bush. A search is made for it the following day. If it is stained with blood, war is decided upon; if not, the idea is dropped. Many expeditions begun in this way come to an end after a few kilometres' march. The excitement and enthusiasm abate, and the warriors return home. But some expeditions are carried through and may result in bloodshed. The Nambikwara attack at dawn and arrange their ambush by posting themselves at intervals in the bush. The signal for the attack is passed from man to man by means of the whistle which each carries slung around his neck. This consists of two bamboo tubes bound together with thread, and its sound approximates to the cricket's chirp; no doubt this is why its name is the same as that of the insect. The war arrows are identical to those normally used for hunting large animals, except that their spear-shaped tip is given a serrated edge. Arrows dipped in curare poison, which are commonly employed for hunting, are never used, because an opponent hit by one would be able to remove it before the poison had time to spread through his body.

Jacques Derrida (1930–)

Jacques Derrida is a professor at the École des Hautes Études en Sciences Sociales, Paris and at the University of California at Irvine. Derrida made his momentous début in America at a conference in Johns Hopkins University in 1966 with his paper 'Structure, Sign, and Play in the Discourse of the Human Sciences'. Considered to be the father of deconstruction, Derrida writes extensively on language, philosophy, religion, and psychoanalysis. He has published numerous books which have been translated into English, *Speech and Phenomena* (1973), *Of Grammatology* (1974), *Writing and Difference* (1978), *Dissemination* (1981), *The Post Card* (1980), *Margins of Philosophy* (1982), and *Spurs: Nietzsche's Styles* (1979).

Derrida's work represents a radical departure from traditional, European humanist scholarship and lays out his post-structural theory of language in which he critiques philosophical, phenomenological, and linguistic concepts regarding the relations of speech to writing. In the chapter re-printed here, from *Of Grammatology*, Derrida takes Claude Lévi-Strauss and Jean-Jacques Rousseau to task for privileging the primacy of speech over writing. Derrida grants that it is an empirical fact that writing historically followed speech in the development of the language, arts, and culture. He then goes on to argue that there is a writing-in-general, an arché-writing, that establishes a primal or metaphysical 'presence' which human beings seek to capture and express through language. This phenomenon governs the dualisms or binary oppositions that are foundational to Western metaphysics. Thus, when Lévi-Strauss and Rousseau reveal a nostalgia for the 'primitive' or 'organic' beginnings of oral communication because speech supposedly maintained the virtue of immediacy (i.e., presence), they construct a fundamental binary opposition of nature/culture (or physis/nomos) that governs their assumptions about the origins of both language and culture. Derrida argues that they both shun writing and exalt 'voice' which places them inside a Western metaphysical tradition extending from Plato's *Phaedrus* to Ferdinand de Saussure's *Course in General Linguistics*. Derrida counters this tradition by arguing that 'presence' itself is an effect of linguistic structures, and is constructed

115

as a binary opposition to 'absence' of the first speaker. This position invokes the logic of the supplement of 'The Violence of the Letter' to which the title of the chapter alludes.

T.M. and G.R.

The violence of the letter: from Lévi-Strauss to Rousseau

Shall I proceed to the teaching of writing? No, I am ashamed to toy with these trifles in a treatise on education.—Emile

It [writing] seems to favor rather the exploitation than the enlightenment of mankind. . . . Writing, on this its first appearance in their midst, had allied itself with falsehood.—'A Writing Lesson,' *Tristes Tropiques*.[1]

Metaphysics has constituted an exemplary system of defense against the threat of writing. What links writing to violence? What must violence be in order for something in it to be equivalent to the operation of the trace?

And why bring this question into play within the affinity or filiation that binds Lévi-Strauss to Rousseau? Another difficulty is added to the problem of the justification of this historical contraction; what is a lineage in the order of discourse and text? If in a rather conventional way I call by the name of *discourse* the present, living, conscious *representation* of a *text* within the experience of the person who writes or reads it, and if the text constantly goes beyond this representation by the entire system of its resources and its own laws, then the question of genealogy exceeds by far the possibilities that are at present given for its elaboration. We know that the metaphor that would describe the genealogy of a text correctly is still *forbidden*. In its syntax and its lexicon, in its spacing, by its punctuation, its lacunae, its margins, the historical appurtenance of a text is never a straight line. It is neither causality by contagion, nor the simple accumulation of layers. Nor even the pure juxtaposition of borrowed pieces. And if a text always gives itself a certain representation of its own roots, those roots live only by that representation, by never touching the soil, so to speak. Which undoubtedly destroys their *radical essence*, but not the necessity of their *racinating function*. To say that one always interweaves roots endlessly, bending them to send down roots among the roots, to pass through the same points again, to redouble old adherences, to circulate among their differences, to coil around themselves or to be enveloped one in the other, to say that a text is never anything but a *system of roots*, is undoubtedly to contradict at once the concept of system and the pattern of the root. But in order not to be pure appearance, this contradiction takes on the meaning of a contradiction, and receives its 'illogicality,' only through being thought within a finite configuration—the history of metaphysics—and caught within a root system which does not end there and which as yet has no name.

The text's self-consciousness, the circumscribed discourse where genealogical representation is articulated (what Lévi-Strauss, for example, makes of a certain 'eighteenth century,' by quoting it as the source of his thought), without being confused with genealogy itself, plays, precisely by virtue of this divergence, an organizing role in the structure of the text. Even if one did have the right to speak of retrospective illusion, it would not be an accident or a theoretical falling off; one would have to account for its necessity and its positive effects. A text always has several epochs and reading must resign itself to that fact. And this genealogical self-representation is itself already the representation of a self-representation; what, for example, 'the French eighteenth century,' if such a thing existed, already constructed as its own source and its own presence.

Is the play of these appurtenances, so manifest in texts of anthropology and the 'sciences of man,' produced totally within a 'history of metaphysics?' Does it somewhere force the closure? Such is perhaps the widest horizon of the questions which will be supported by a few examples here. To which proper names may be assigned: the sustainers of the discourse, Condillac, Rousseau, Lévi-Strauss; or common names: concepts of analysis, of genesis, of origin, of nature, of culture, of sign, of speech, of writing, etc.; in short, the common name of the proper name.

In linguistics as well as in metaphysics, *phonologism* is undoubtedly the exclusion or abasement of writing. But it is also the granting of authority to a science which is held to be the model for all the so-called sciences of man. In both these senses Lévi-Strauss's structuralism is a phonologism. As for the 'models' of linguistics and phonology, what I have already brought up will not let me skirt around a structural anthropology upon which phonological science exercises so *declared* a fascination, as for instance in 'Language and Kinship';[2] it must be questioned line by line.

The advent of structural linguistics [*phonologie*] completely changed this situation. Not only did it renew linguistic perspectives; a transformation of this magnitude is not limited to a single discipline. Structural linguistics will certainly play the same renovating role with respect to the social sciences that nuclear physics, for example, has played for the physical sciences [*l'ensemble des sciences exactes*] (p. 39) [p. 31].

If we wished to elaborate the question of the *model*, we would have to examine all the 'as'-s and 'likewise'-s that punctuate the argument, ordering and authorizing the analogy between phonology and sociology, between phonemes and the terms of kinship. 'A striking analogy,' we are told, but the functioning of its 'as' shows us quickly enough that this is a very infallible but very impoverished generality of structural laws, no doubt governing the systems considered, but also dominating many other systems without privilege; a phonology exemplary as the example in a series and not as the regulative model. But on this terrain questions have been asked, objections articulated; and as the *epistemological* phonologism establishing a science as a master-model presupposes a *linguistic* and *metaphysical* phonologism that raises speech above writing, it is this last that I shall first try to identify.

For Lévi-Strauss has written of writing. Only a few pages, to be sure[3] but in many respects remarkable; very fine pages, calculated to amaze, enunciating in the form of paradox and modernity the anathema that the Western world has obstinately mulled over, the exclusion by which it has constituted and recognized itself, from the *Phaedrus* to the *Course in General Linguistics*.

Another reason for rereading Lévi-Strauss: if, as I have shown, writing cannot be felt without an unquestioning faith in the entire system of differences between *physis* and its other (the series of its 'others:' art, technology, law, institution, society, immotivation, arbitrariness, etc.), and in all the conceptuality disposed within it, then one should follow with the closest attention the troubled path of a thinker who some-times, at a certain stage in his reflections, bases himself on this difference, and sometimes leads us to its point of effacement: 'The opposition between nature and culture to which I attached much importance at one time . . . now seems to be of primarily methodological importance.'[4] Undoubtedly Lévi-Strauss has only travelled from one point of effacement to another. *Les structures élémentaires de la parenté* (1949),[5] dominated by the problem of the prohibition of incest, already credited dif-ference only around a suture. As a result both the one and the other became all the more enigmatic. And it would be risky to decide if the seam—the prohibition of incest—is a strange exception that one happened to encounter within the transparent system of difference, a 'fact,' as Lévi-Strauss says, with which 'we are then con-fronted' (p. 9) [p. 8]; or is rather the origin of the difference between nature and culture, the condition—outside of the system—of the system of difference. The con-dition would be a 'scandal' only if one wished to comprehend it *within* the system whose condition it precisely is.

> Let us suppose then that everything universal in man relates to the natural order, and is characterized by spontaneity, and that everything subject to a norm is cul-tural and is both relative and particular. We are then confronted with a fact, or rather, a group of facts, which, in the light of previous definitions, are not far removed from a scandal: . . . [for] the prohibition of incest . . . presents, without the slightest ambiguity, and inseparably combines, the two characteristics in which we recognize the conflicting features of two mutually exclusive orders. It consti-tutes a rule, but a rule which, alone among all the social rules, possesses at the same time a universal character (p. 9) [pp. 8–9].

But the 'scandal' appeared only at a certain moment of the analysis; the moment when, giving up a 'real analysis' which will never reveal any difference between nature and culture, one passed to an 'ideal analysis' permitting the definition of 'the double criterion of norm and universality.' It is thus from the confidence placed in the difference between the two analyses that the scandal took its scandalous meaning. What did this confidence signify? It appeared to itself as the scholar's right to employ 'methodological tools' whose 'logical value' is anticipated, and in a state of precipita-tion, with regard to the 'object,' to 'truth,' etc., with regard, in other words, to what science works toward. These are the first words—or nearly so—of *Structures*:

> It is beginning to emerge that this distinction between the state of nature and the state of society (today I would rather say state of nature and state of culture) while of no acceptable historical significance, does contain a logic, fully justifying its use by modern sociology as a methodological tool (p. 1) [p. 3].

This is clear: in regard to the 'chiefly methodological value' of the concepts of nature and culture, there is no evolution and even less retraction from *Structures* to *The Savage Mind*. Nor is there either evolution or retraction with regard to this concept of methodological tool; *Structures* announces most precisely what, more than a decade later, will be said of '*bricolage*,' of tools such as 'means' 'collected or retained on the principle that "they may always come in handy."' 'Like "*bricolage*" on the technical plane, mythical reflection can reach brilliant unforeseen results on the intellectual plane. Conversely, attention has often been drawn to the mytho-poetical nature of "*bricolage*" ' (pp. 26 f.) [pp. 17–18]. To be sure, it would still remain to be asked if the anthropologist considers himself 'engineer' or '*bricoleur*.' *Le cru et le cuit* [Paris, 1964] is presented as 'the myth of mythology' ('Preface,' p. 20).[6]

Nevertheless, the effacement of the frontier between nature and culture is not produced by the same gesture from *Structures* to *The Savage Mind*. In the first case, it is rather a question of respecting the originality of a scandalous suture. In the second case, of a reduction, however careful it might be not to 'dissolve' the specificity of what it analyses:

> . . . it would not be enough to reabsorb particular humanities into a general one. This first enterprise opens the way for others which Rousseau [whose 'usual acumen' Lévi-Strauss has just praised] would not have been so ready to accept and which are incumbent on the exact natural sciences: the reintegration of culture in nature and finally of life within the whole of its physio-chemical conditions (p. 327) [p. 247].

At once conserving and annulling inherited conceptual oppositions, this thought, like Saussure's, stands on a borderline: sometimes within an uncriticized conceptuality, sometimes putting a strain on the boundaries, and working toward deconstruction.

Finally, why Lévi-Strauss *and* Rousseau? The quotation above necessarily leads us to this question. This conjunction must be justified gradually and intrinsically. But it is already known that Lévi-Strauss not only feels himself to be *in agreement* with Jean-Jacques, to be his heir at heart and in what might be called theoretical affect. He also often presents himself as Rousseau's modern disciple; he reads Rousseau as the *founder*, not only the prophet, of modern anthropology. A hundred texts glorifying Rousseau may be cited. Nevertheless, let us recall, at the end of *Totémisme aujourd'hui*,[7] the chapter on 'Totemism from Within:' 'a . . . militant fervor for ethnography,' the 'astonishing insight' of Rousseau who, 'more prudent . . . than Bergson' and 'before even the "discovery" of totemism' 'penetrate[d]' (p. 147) that which opens the possibility of totemism in general, namely:

1. *Pity*, that fundamental affection, as primitive as the love of self, which unites us to others naturally: to other human beings, certainly, but also to all living beings.

2. The *originarily metaphoric*—because it belongs to the passions, says Rousseau— essence of our *language*. What authorizes Lévi-Strauss's interpretation is the *Essay on the Origin of Languages*, which we shall try to read closely later: 'As man's first motives for speaking were of the passions [and not of needs], his first expressions were tropes. Figurative language was the first to be born' [p. 12]. It is again in 'Totemism from Within' that the second *Discourse* is defined as 'the first treatise of general anthropology in French literature. In almost modern terms, Rousseau poses

119

the central problem of anthropology, viz., the passage from nature to culture' (p. 142) [p. 99]. And here is the most systematic homage: 'Rousseau did not merely foresee anthropology; he founded it. First in a practical way, in writing that *Discours sur l'origine et les fondements de l'inégalité parmi les hommes* which poses the problem of the relationships between nature and culture, and which is the first treatise of general anthropology; and later on the theoretical plane, by distinguishing, with admirable clarity and concision, the proper object of the anthropologist from that of the moralist and the historian: "When one wants to study men, one must consider those around one. But to study man, one must extend the range of one's vision. One must first observe the differences in order to discover the properties" (*Essay on the Origin of Languages*, Chapter VIII) [pp. 30–31].'[8]

It is therefore a declared and militant Rousseauism. Already it imposes on us a very general question that will orient all our readings more or less directly: to what extent does Rousseau's appurtenance to logocentric metaphysics and within the philosophy of presence—an appurtenance that we have already been able to recognize and whose exemplary figure we must delineate—to what extent does it limit a scientific discourse? Does it necessarily retain within its boundaries the Rousseauist discipline and fidelity of an anthropologist and of a theorist of modern anthropology?

If this question is not sufficient to link the development which will follow with my initial proposition, I should perhaps recapitulate:

1. that digression about the violence that *does not supervene* from without upon an innocent language in order to surprise it, a language that suffers the aggression of writing as the accident of its disease, its defeat and its fall; but is the originary violence of a language which is always already a writing. Rousseau and Lévi-Strauss are not for a moment to be challenged when they relate the power of writing to the exercise of violence. But radicalizing this theme, no longer considering this violence as *derivative* with respect to a naturally innocent speech, one reverses the entire sense of a proposition—the unity of violence and writing—which one must therefore be careful not to abstract and isolate.

2. that other ellipsis of the metaphysics or onto-theology of the logos (par excellence in its Hegelian moment) as the powerless and oneiric effort to master absence by reducing the metaphor within the absolute parousia of sense. Ellipsis of the originary writing within language as the irreducibility of metaphor, which it is necessary here to think in its possibility and short of its rhetorical repetition. The irremediable absence of the proper name. Rousseau no doubt believed in the figurative initiation of language, but he believed no less, as we shall see, in a progress toward literal (proper) meaning. 'Figurative language was the first to be born,' he says, only to add, 'proper meaning was discovered last' (*Essay*).[9] It is to this eschatology of the *proper* (*prope*, *proprius*, self-proximity, self-presence, property, own-ness) that we ask the question of the *graphein*.

The Battle of
Proper Names

But how is one to distinguish, in writing, between a man one mentions and a man one addresses. There really is an equivocation which would be eliminated by a vocative mark.—*Essay on the Origin of Languages*

Back now from *Tristes Tropiques* to the *Essay on the Origin of Languages*, from 'A Writing Lesson' given to the writing lesson refused by the person who was 'ashamed to toy' with the 'trifl[ing]' matter of writing in a treatise on education. My question is perhaps better stated thus: do they say the same thing? Do they do the same thing?

In that *Tristes Tropiques* which is at the same time *The Confessions* and a sort of supplement to the *Supplément au voyage de Bougainville*,[10] the 'Writing Lesson' marks an episode of what may be called the anthropological war, the essential confrontation that opens communication between peoples and cultures, even when that communication is not practiced under the banner of colonial or missionary oppression. The entire 'Writing Lesson' is recounted in the tones of violence repressed or deferred, a violence sometimes veiled, but always oppressive and heavy. Its weight is felt in various places and various moments of the *narrative*: in Lévi-Strauss's account as in the relationship among individuals and among groups, among cultures or within the same community. What can a relationship to writing signify in these diverse instances of violence?

Penetration in the case of the Nambikwara. The anthropologist's affection for those to whom he devoted one of his dissertations, *La vie familiale et sociale des Indiens Nambikwara* (1948). Penetration, therefore, into 'the lost world' of the Nambikwara, 'the little bands of nomads, who are among the most genuinely "primitive" of the world's peoples' on 'a territory the size of France,' traversed by a *picada* (a crude trail whose 'track' is 'not easily distinguished from the bush' [p. 262]; one should meditate upon all of the following together: writing as the possibility of the road and of difference, the history of writing and the history of the road, of the rupture, of the *via rupta*, of the path that is broken, beaten, *fracta*, of the space of reversibility and of repetition traced by the opening, the divergence from, and the violent spacing, of nature, of the natural, savage, salvage, forest. The *silva* is savage, the *via rupta* is written, discerned, and inscribed violently as difference, as form imposed on the *hylè*, in the forest, in wood as matter; it is difficult to imagine that access to the possibility of a road-map is not at the same time access to writing). The territory of the Nambikwara is crossed by the line of an autochthonic picada. But also by another *line*, this time imported:

> [An abandoned telephone line] obsolete from the day of its completion [which] hung down from poles never replaced when they go to rot and tumble to the ground. (Sometimes the termites attack them, and sometimes the Indians, who mistake the humming of the telegraph wires for the noise of bees on their way to the hive.) [p. 262]

The Nambikwara, whose tormenting and cruelty—presumed or not—are much feared by the personnel of the line, 'brought the observer back to what he might readily, though mistakenly, suppose to be the childhood of our race' [p. 265]. Lévi-Strauss describes the biological and cultural type of this population whose technology, economy, institutions, and structures of kinship, however primitive, give them of course a rightful place within humankind, so-called human society and the 'state of culture.' They speak and prohibit incest. 'All were interrelated, for the Nambikwara prefer to marry a niece (their sister's daughter), or a kinswoman of the kind which anthropologists call "cross-cousin": the daughter of their father's sister,

121

or of their mother's brother' [p. 269]. Yet another reason for not allowing oneself to be taken in by appearances and for not believing that one sees here the 'childhood of our race:' the structure of the language. And above all its *usage*. The Nambikwara use several dialects and several systems according to situations. And here intervenes a phenomenon which may be crudely called 'linguistic' and which will be of central interest to us. It has to do with a *fact* that we have not the means of interpreting beyond its general conditions of possibility, its *a priori*; whose factual and empirical causes—as they open within this determined situation—will escape us, and, moreover, call forth no question on the part of Lévi-Strauss, who merely notes them. This fact bears on what we have proposed about the essence or the energy of the *graphein* as the originary effacement of the proper name. From the moment that the proper name is erased in a system, there is writing, there is a 'subject' from the moment that this obliteration of the proper is produced, that is to say from the first appearing of the proper and from the first dawn of language. This proposition is universal in essence and can be produced *a priori*. How one passes from this *a priori* to the determination of empirical facts is a question that one cannot answer in general here. First because, by definition, there is no general answer to a question of this form.

It is therefore such a *fact* that we encounter here. It does not involve the structural effacement of what we believe to be our proper names; it does not involve the obliteration that, paradoxically, constitutes the originary legibility of the very thing it erases, but of a prohibition heavily superimposed, in certain societies, upon the use of the proper name: 'They are not allowed . . . to use proper names' [p. 270], Lévi-Strauss observes.

Before we consider this, let us note that this prohibition is necessarily derivative with regard to the constitutive erasure of the proper name in what I have called arche-writing, within, that is, the play of difference. It is because the proper names are already no longer proper names, because their production is their obliteration, because the erasure and the imposition of the letter are originary, because they do not supervene upon a proper inscription; it is because the proper name has never been, as the unique appellation reserved for the presence of a unique being, anything but the original myth of a transparent legibility present under the obliteration; it is because the proper name was never possible except through its functioning within a classification and therefore within a system of differences, within a writing retaining the traces of difference, that the interdict was possible, could come into play, and, when the time came, as we shall see, could be transgressed; transgressed, that is to say restored to the obliteration and the non-self-sameness [*non-propriété*] at the origin.

This is strictly in accord with one of Lévi-Strauss's intentions. In 'Universalization and Particularization' (*The Savage Mind*, Chapter VI) it will be demonstrated that 'one . . . never names: one classes someone else . . . [or] one classes oneself.'[11] A demonstration anchored in some examples of prohibitions that affect the use of proper names here and there. Undoubtedly one should carefully distinguish between the essential necessity of the disappearance of the proper name and the determined prohibition which can, contingently and ulteriorly, be added to it or articulated within it. Nonprohibition, as much as prohibition, presupposes fundamental obliteration. Nonprohibition, the *consciousness* or exhibition of the proper name, only makes up for or uncovers an essential and irremediable impropriety.

When within *consciousness*, the name *is called* proper, it is already classified and is obliterated in *being named*. It is already no more than a *so-called* proper name.

If writing is no longer understood in the narrow sense of linear and phonetic notation, it should be possible to say that all societies capable of producing, that is to say of obliterating, their proper names, and of bringing classificatory difference into play, practice writing in general. No reality or concept would therefore correspond to the expression 'society without writing.' This expression is dependent on ethnocentric oneirism, upon the vulgar, that is to say ethnocentric, misconception of writing. The scorn for writing, let us note in passing, accords quite happily with this ethnocentrism. The paradox is only apparent, one of those contradictions where a perfectly coherent desire is uttered and accomplished. By one and the same gesture, (alphabetic) writing, servile instrument of a speech dreaming of its plenitude and its self-presence, is scorned and the dignity of writing is refused to nonalphabetic signs. We have peceived this gesture in Rousseau and in Saussure.

The Nambikwara–the *subject* of 'A Writing Lesson'—would therefore be one of these peoples without writing. They do not make use of what *we* commonly call writing. At least that is what Lévi-Strauss tells us: 'That the Nambikwara could not write goes without saying' [p. 288]. This incapacity will be presently thought, within the ethico-political order, as an innocence and a non-violence interrupted by the forced entry of the West and the 'Writing Lesson'. We shall be present at that scene in a little while.

How can access to writing in general be refused to the Nambikwara except by determining writing according to a model? Later on we shall ask, confronting many passages in Lévi-Strauss, up to what point it is legitimate not to call by the name of writing those 'few dots' and 'zigzags' on their calabashes, so briefly evoked in *Tristes Tropiques*. But above all, how can we deny the practice of writing in general to a society capable of obliterating the proper, that is to say a violent society? For writing, obliteration of the proper classed in the play of difference, is the originary violence itself: pure impossibility of the 'vocative mark,' impossible purity of the mark of vocation. This 'equivocation,' which Rousseau hoped would be 'eliminated' by a 'vocative mark,' cannot be effaced. For the existence of such a mark in any code of punctuation would not change the problem. The death of absolutely proper naming, recognizing in a language the other as pure other, invoking it as what it is, is the death of the pure idiom reserved for the unique. Anterior to the possibility of violence in the current and derivative sense, the sense used in 'A Writing Lesson,' there is, as the space of its possibility, the violence of the arche-writing, the violence of difference, of classification, and of the system of appellations. Before outlining the structure of this implication, let us read the scene of proper names; with another scene, that we shall shortly read, it is an indispensable preparation for the 'Writing Lesson.' This scene is separated from the 'Writing Lesson' by one chapter and another scene: 'Family Life.' And it is described in Chapter 26 [23] 'On the Line.'

> The Nambikwara make no difficulties and are quite indifferent to the presence of the anthropologist with his notebooks and camera. But certain problems of language complicated matters. They are not allowed, for instance, to use proper names. To tell one from another we had to do as the men of the line do and agree

with the Nambikwara on a set of nicknames which would serve for identification. Either Portuguese names, like Julio, Jose-Maria, Luisa; or sobriquets such as Lebre, *hare*, or Assucar, *sugar*. I even knew one whom Rondon or one of his companions had nicknamed Cavaignac on account of his little pointed beard–a rarity among Indians, most of whom have no hair on their faces. One day, when I was playing with a group of children, a little girl was struck by one of her comrades. She ran to me for protection and began to whisper something, a 'great secret,' in my ear. As I did not understand I had to ask her to repeat it over and over again. Eventually her adversary found out what was going on, came up to me in a rage, and tried in her turn to tell me what seemed to be another secret. After a little while I was able to get to the bottom of the incident. The first little girl was trying to tell me her enemy's name, and when the enemy found out what was going on she decided to tell me the other girl's name, by way of reprisal. Thenceforward it was easy enough, though not very scrupulous, to egg the children on, one against the other, till in time I knew all of their names. When this was completed and we were all, in a sense, one another's accomplices, I soon got them to give me the adults' names too. When this [cabal] was discovered the children were reprimanded and my sources of information dried up.[12]

We cannot enter here into the difficulties of an empirical deduction of this prohibition, but we know a priori that the 'proper names' whose interdiction and revelation Lévi-Strauss describes here are not proper names. The expression 'proper name' is improper, for the very reasons that *The Savage Mind* will recall. What the interdict is laid upon is the uttering of what *functions* as the proper name. And this function is *consciousness* itself. The proper name in the colloquial sense, in the sense of consciousness, is (I should say 'in truth' were it not necessary to be wary of that phrase)[13] only a designation of appurtenance and a linguistico-social classification. The lifting of the interdict, the great game of denunciation and the great exhibition of the 'proper' (let us note that we speak here of an act of war and there is much to say about the fact that it is little girls who open themselves to this game and these hostilities) does not consist in revealing proper names, but in tearing the veil hiding a classification and an appurtenance, the inscription within a system of linguistico-social differences.

What the Nambikwara hid and the young girls lay bare through transgression, is no longer the absolute idioms, but already varieties of invested common names, 'abstracts' if, as we read in *The Savage Mind* (p. 242) [p. 182], 'systems of appellations also have their "abstracts." '

The concept of the proper name, unproblematized as Lévi-Strauss uses it in *Tristes Tropiques*, is therefore far from being simple and manageable. Consequently, the same may be said of the concepts of violence, ruse, perfidy, or oppression, that punctuate 'A Writing Lesson' a little further on. We have already noted that violence here does not unexpectedly break in all at once, starting from an original innocence whose nakedness is *surprised* at the very moment that the secret of the *so-called* proper names is violated. The structure of violence is complex and its possibility— writing—no less so.

There was in fact a first violence to be named. To name, to give names, that it will on occasion be forbidden to pronounce, such is the originary violence of language which consists in inscribing within a difference, in classifying, in suspending the vocative absolute. To think the unique *within* the system, to inscribe it there, such is the gesture of the arche-writing: arche-violence, loss of the proper, of absolute proximity, of self-presence, in truth the loss of what has never taken place, of a self-presence which has never been given but only dreamed of and always already split, repeated, incapable of appearing to itself except in its own disappearance. Out of this arche-violence, forbidden and therefore confirmed by a second violence that is reparatory, protective, instituting the 'moral,' prescribing the concealment of writing and the effacement and obliteration of the so-called proper name which was already dividing the proper, a third violence can *possibly* emerge or not (an empirical possibility) within what is commonly called evil, war, indiscretion, rape; which consists of revealing by effraction the so-called proper name, the originary violence which has severed the proper from its property and its self-sameness [*propreté*]. We could name a third violence of reflection, which denudes the native non-identity, classification as denaturation of the proper, and identity as the abstract moment of the concept. It is on this tertiary level, that of the empirical consciousness, that the common concept of violence (the system of the moral law and of transgression) whose possibility remains yet unthought, should no doubt be situated. The scene of proper names is written on this level; as will be later the writing lesson.

This last violence is all the more complex in its structure because it refers at the same time to the two inferior levels of arche-violence and of law. In effect, it reveals the first nomination which was already an expropriation, but it denudes also that which since then functioned as the proper, the so-called proper, substitute of the deferred proper, *perceived* by the *social* and *moral consciousness* as the proper, the reassuring seal of self-identity, the secret.

Empirical violence, war in the colloquial sense (ruse and perfidy of little girls, *apparent* ruse and perfidy of little girls, for the anthropologist will prove them innocent by showing himself as the true and only culprit; ruse and perfidy of the Indian chief playing at the comedy of writing, *apparent* ruse and perfidy of the Indian chief borrowing all his resources from the Occidental intrusion), which Lévi-Strauss always thinks of as an *accident*. An accident occurring, in his view, upon a terrain of innocence, in a 'state of culture' whose *natural* goodness had not yet been degraded.[14]

Two pointers, seemingly anecdotal and belonging to the decor of the representation to come, support this hypothesis that the 'Writing Lesson' will confirm. They announce the great staging of the 'lesson' and show to advantage the art of the composition of this travelogue. In accordance with eighteenth-century tradition, the anecdote, the page of confessions, the fragment from a journal are knowledgeably put in place, calculated for the purposes of a philosophical demonstration of the relationships between nature and society, ideal society and real society, most often between the *other* society and our *society*.

What is the first pointer? The battle of proper names follows the arrival of the foreigner and that is not surprising. It is born in the presence and even from the presence of the anthropologist who comes to disturb order and natural peace, the complicity which peacefully binds the good society to itself in its play. Not only have the people of the Line imposed ridiculous sobriquets on the natives, obliging them to assume these intrinsically (hare, sugar, Cavaignac), but it is the anthropological eruption which breaks the secret of the proper names and the innocent complicity governing the play of young girls. It is the anthropologist who violates a virginal space so accurately connoted by the scene of a game and a game played by little girls. The mere presence of the foreigner, the mere fact of his having his eyes open, cannot not provoke a violation: the *aside*, the secret murmured in the ear, the successive movements of the 'stratagem,' the acceleration, the precipitation, a certain increasing jubilation in the movement before the falling back which follows the consummated fault, when the 'sources' have 'dried up,' makes us think of a dance and a fête as much as of war.

The mere presence of a spectator, then, is a violation. First a pure violation: a silent and immobile foreigner attends a game of young girls. That one of them should have 'struck' a 'comrade' is not yet true violence. No integrity has been breached. Violence appears only at the moment when the intimacy of proper names can be opened to forced entry. And that is possible only at the moment when the space is shaped and reoriented by the glance of the foreigner. The eye of the other calls out the proper names, spells them out, and removes the prohibition that covered them.

At first the anthropologist is satisfied merely to see. A fixed glance and a mute presence. Then things get complicated, become more tortuous and labyrinthine, when he becomes a party to the play of the rupture of play, as he lends an ear and broaches a first complicity with the victim who is also the trickster. Finally, for what counts is the names of the adults (one could say the eponyms and the secret is violated only in the place where the names are attributed), the ultimate denunciation can no longer do without the active intervention of the foreigner. Who, moreover, claims to have intervened and accuses himself of it. He has seen, then heard; but, passive in the face of what he already knew he was provoking, he still waited to hear the master-names. The violation was not consummated, the naked base of the proper was still reserved. As one cannot or rather must not incriminate the innocent young girls, the violation will be accomplished by the thenceforward active, perfidious, and rusing intrusion of the foreigner who, having seen and heard, is now going to 'excite' the young girls, loosen their tongues, and get them to divulge the precious names: those of the adults (the dissertation tells us that only 'the adults possessed names that were proper to them,' p. 39). With a bad conscience, to be sure, and with that pity which Rousseau said unites us with the most foreign of foreigners. Let us now reread the *mea culpa*, the confession of the anthropologist who assumes entire responsibility for a violation that has satisfied him. After *giving* one another *away*, the young girls *gave away* the adults.

> The first little girl was trying to tell me her enemy's name, and when the enemy found out what was going on she decided to tell me the other girl's name, by way of reprisal. Thenceforward it was easy enough, though not very scrupulous, to egg the children on, one against the other, till in time I knew all their names. When this was completed and we were all, in a sense, one another's accomplices, I soon got them to give me the adults' names too [p. 270].

The true culprit will not be punished, and this gives to his fault the stamp of the irremediable: 'When this [cabal] was discovered the children were reprimanded and my sources of information dried up.'

One already suspects—and all Lévi-Strauss's writings would confirm it—that the critique of ethnocentrism, a theme so dear to the author of *Tristes Tropiques*, has most often the sole function of constituting the other as a model of original and natural goodness, of accusing and humiliating oneself, of exhibiting its being-unacceptable in an anti-ethnocentric mirror. Rousseau would have taught the modern anthropologist this humility of one who knows he is 'unacceptable,' this remorse that produces anthropology.[15] That is at least what we are told in the Geneva lecture:

> In truth, I am not 'I,' but the feeblest and humblest of 'others.' Such is the discovery of the *Confessions*. Does the anthropologist write anything other than confessions? First in his own name, as I have shown, since it is the moving force of his vocation and his work; and in that very work, in the name of the society, which, through the activities of its emissary, the anthropologist, chooses for itself other societies, other civilizations, and precisely the weakest and most humble; but only to verify to what extent that first society is itself 'unacceptable' (p. 245).

Without speaking of the point of mastery thus gained by the person who conducts this operation at home, one rediscovers here a gesture inherited from the eighteenth century, from a certain eighteenth century at any rate, for even in that century a certain sporadic suspicion of such an exercise had already commenced. Non-European peoples were not only studied as the index to a hidden good Nature, as a native soil recovered, of a 'zero degree' with reference to which one could outline the structure, the growth, and above all the degradation of our society and our culture. As always, this archeology is also a teleology and an eschatology; the dream of a full and immediate presence closing history, the transparence and indivision of a parousia, the suppression of contradiction and difference. The anthropologist's mission, as Rousseau would have assigned it, is to work toward such an end. Possibly against the philosophy which 'alone' would have sought to 'excite' 'antagonisms' between the 'self and the other.'[16] Let us not be accused here of forcing words and things. Let us rather read. It is again the Geneva lecture, but a hundred similar passages may be found:

> The Rousseauist revolution, pre-forming and initiating the anthropological revolution, consists in refusing the expected identifications, whether that of a culture with that culture, or that of an individual, member of one culture, with a personage or a social function that the same culture wishes to impose upon him. In both cases the culture or the individual insists on the right to a free identification which can only be realized *beyond* man: an identification with all that lives and therefore suffers; and an identification which can also be realized *short of* the function or the person; with a yet unfashioned, but given, being. Then the self and the other, freed of an antagonism that only philosophy seeks to excite, recover their unity. An original alliance, at last renewed, permits them to found together the *we* against the *him*, against a society inimical to man, and which man finds himself all the more ready to challenge because Rousseau, by his example, teaches him how to elude the intolerable contradictions of civilized life. For if it is true that Nature has expelled man, and that society persists in oppressing him, man can at least reverse the horns of the dilemma to his own advantage, *and seek out the society of nature in order to meditate*

127

there upon the nature of society. This, it seems to me, is the indissoluble message of *The Social Contract*, the *Lettres sur la botanique*, and the *Reveries.*[17]

'A Little Glass of Rum,' which is a severe criticism of Diderot and a glorification of Rousseau ('[who] of all the *philosophes*, came nearest to being an anthropologist . . . our master . . . our brother, great as has been our ingratitude toward him; and every page of this book could have been dedicated to him, had the object thus proffered not been unworthy of his great memory') concludes thus: '. . . the question to be solved is whether or not these evils are themselves inherent in that state [of society]. We must go beyond the evidence of the injustices or abuses to which the social order gives rise and discover the unshakeable basis of human society.'[18]

The diversified thinking of Lévi-Strauss would be impoverished if it were not emphatically recalled here that this goal and this motivation do not exhaust, though they do more than connote, the task of science. They mark it profoundly in its very content. I had promised a second pointer. The Nambikwara, around whom the 'Writing Lesson' will unfold its scene, among whom evil will insinuate itself with the intrusion of writing come from *without* (*exothen*, as the *Phaedrus* says)—the Nambikwara, who do not know how to write, are *good*, we are told. The Jesuits, the Protestant missionaries, the American anthropologists, the technicians on the Line, who believed they perceived violence or hatred among the Nambikwara are not only mistaken, they have probably projected their own wickedness upon them. And even provoked the evil that they then believed they saw or wished to perceive. Let us reread the end of Chapter 17 [24], entitled, always with the same skill, 'Family Life.' This passage immediately precedes 'A Writing Lesson' and is, in a certain way, indespensable to it. Let us first confirm what goes without saying: if we subscribe to Lévi-Strauss's declarations about their innocence and goodness, their 'great sweetness of nature,' 'the most . . . authentic manifestations of human tenderness,' etc. only by assigning them a totally derived, relative, and empirical place of legitimacy, regarding them as descriptions of the empirical affections of the *subject* of this chapter—the Nambikwara as well as the author—if then we subscribe to these descriptions only as *empirical relation*, it does not follow that we give credence to the moralizing descriptions of the American anthropologist's converse deploring of the hatred, surliness, and lack of civility of the natives. In fact these two accounts are symmetrically opposed, they have the same dimensions, and arrange themselves around one and the same axis. After having cited a foreign colleague's publication, which is very severe toward the Nambikwara for their complacency in the face of disease, their filthiness, wretchedness, and rudeness, their rancorous and distrustful character, Lévi-Strauss argues:

> When I myself had known them, the diseases introduced by white men had
> already decimated them; but there had not been, since Rondon's always humane
> endeavors, any attempt to enforce their submission. I should prefer to forget Mr.
> Oberg's harrowing description and remember the Nambikwara as they appear in a
> page from my notebooks. I wrote it one night by the light of my pocket-lamp:
> 'The camp-fires shine out in the darkened savannah. Around the hearth which is
> their only protection from the cold, behind the flimsy screen of foliage and palm-
> leaves which had been stuck into the ground where it will best break the force of

wind and rain, beside the baskets filled with the pitiable objects which comprise all their earthly belongings, the Nambikwara lie on the bare earth. Always they are haunted by the thought of other groups, as fearful and hostile as they are themselves, and when they lie entwined together, couple by couple, each looks to his mate for support and comfort and finds in the other a bulwark, the only one he knows, against the difficulties of every day and the meditative melancholia which from time to time overwhelms the Nambikwara. The visitor who camps among the Indians for the first time cannot but feel anguish and pity at the sight of a people so totally dis-provided for; beaten down into the hostile earth, it would seem, by an implacable cataclysm; naked and shivering beside their guttering fires. He gropes his way among the bushes, avoiding where he can the hand, or the arm, or the torso that lies gleaming in the firelight. But this misery is enlivened by laughing whispers. Their embraces are those of couples possessed by a longing for a lost oneness; their caresses are in no wise disturbed by the footfall of a stranger. In one and all there may be glimpsed a great sweetness of nature, a profound nonchalance, an animal satisfaction as ingenuous as it is charming, and, beneath all this, something that can be recognized as one of the most moving and authentic manifestations of human tenderness' [p. 285].

The 'Writing Lesson' follows this description, which one may indeed read for what it claims, at the outset, to be: a page 'from my notebooks' scribbled one night in the light of a pocket lamp. It would be different if this moving painting were to belong to an anthropological discourse. However, it certainly sets up a premise—the goodness or innocence of the Nambikwara—indispensable to the subsequent demonstration of the conjoint intrusion of violence and writing. Here a strict separation of the anthropological confession and the theoretical discussion of the anthropologist must be observed. The difference between empirical and essential must continue to assert its rights.

We know that Lévi-Strauss has very harsh words for the philosophies that have made the mind aware of this distinction, and which are, for the most part, philosophies of consciousness, of the cogito in the Cartesian or Husserlian sense. Very harsh words also for *L'Essai sur les données immédiates de la conscience*,[19] which Lévi-Strauss reproaches his old teachers for having pondered too much instead of studying Saussure's *Course in General Linguistics*.[20] Now whatever one may finally think of philosophies thus incriminated or ridiculed (and of which I shall say nothing here except to note that only their ghosts, which sometimes haunt school manuals, selected extracts, or popular opinion, are evoked here), it should be recognized that the difference between empirical affect and the structure of essence was for them a major rule. Neither Descartes nor Husserl would ever have suggested that they considered an empirical modification of their relationship with the world or with others as scientific truth, nor the quality of an emotion as the premise of a syllogism. Never in the *Regulae* does one pass from the phenomenologically irrefutable truth of 'I see yellow' to the judgment 'the world is yellow.' Let us not pursue this direction. Never, at any rate, would a rigorous philosopher of consciousness have been so quickly persuaded of the fundamental goodness and virginal innocence of the Nambikwara merely on the strength of an empirical account. From the point of view of anthropological science, this conclusion is as surprising as the wicked American anthropologist's might be 'distressing' (Lévi-Strauss's word). Surprising, indeed, that this unconditional affirmation of the radical goodness of the Nambikwara comes from the pen of an anthropologist who sets against the bloodless phantoms of the philosophers of consciousness and intuition, those who have been, if the beginning of *Tristes Tropiques* is to be believed, his only true masters: Marx and Freud.

The thinkers assembled hastily at the beginning of that book under the banner of metaphysics, phenomenology, and existentialism, would not be recognized in the lineaments ascribed to them. But it would be wrong to conclude that, conversely, Marx and Freud would have been satisfied by the theses written in their name—and notably the chapters that interest us. They generally demanded to see proof when one spoke of 'great sweetness of nature,' 'profound nonchalance,' 'animal satisfaction as ingenuous as it is charming,' and 'something that can be recognized as one of the most moving and authentic manifestations of human tenderness.' They wanted to see proof and would undoubtedly not have understood what could possibly be referred to as 'the original alliance, later renewed,' permitting 'the found[ing] together of the *we* against the *him*' (already quoted), or as 'that regular and, as it were crystalline structure which the best-preserved of primitive societies teach us is not antagonistic to the human condition' (*Leçon inaugurale au Collège de France*, p. 49).

Within this entire system of philosophical kinship and claims of genealogical filiations, not the least surprised might well be Rousseau. Had he not asked that he be allowed to live in peace with the philosophers of consciousness and of interior sentiment, in peace with that sensible cogito,[21] with that interior voice which, he believed, never lied? To reconcile Rousseau, Marx, and Freud, is a difficult task. Is it possible to make them agree among themselves in the systematic rigor of conceptuality?

NOTES

1. Claude Lévi-Strauss, *Tristes Tropiques* (Paris, 1955), pp. 344, 345, translated as *Tristes Tropiques* by John Russell (New York, 1961), pp. 292, 293.
2. In *Structural Anthropology*. Cf. also 'Introduction à l'oeuvre de Marcel Mauss,' *Sociologie et Anthropologie* (Paris: Presses Universitaires de France), p. xlix.
3. It is especially *Tristes Tropiques*, all through that 'Writing Lesson' (chap. 18) whose theoretical substance is to be found also in the second of the 'Entretiens avec Claude Lévi-Strauss,' G. Charbonnier, 'Primitifs et civilisés,' [*Les lettres nouvelles* 10 (1961), pp. 24–33; translated as *Conversations with Claude Lévi-Strauss*, by John and Doreen Weightman (London, 1969), pp. 21–31]. It is also *Structural Anthropology* ('Problems of Method and Teaching,' particularly in the chapter speaking of the 'criterion of authenticity,' p. 400 [p. 363]). Finally, less directly, *The Savage Mind*, the part seductively entitled 'Time Recaptured.'
4. *The Savage Mind*, p. 327 [p. 247], cf. also p. 169 [p. 127].
5. *Les structures élémentaires de la parenté*, 2nd edn (Paris, 1967); translated as *The Elementary Structures of Kinship*, Rodney Needham et al. (Boston, 1969).
6. Tr. John and Doreen Weightman, *The Raw and the Cooked* (Harper Torchbooks edition New York, 1970), p. 12.
7. *Totémisme aujourd'hui*, 2nd edn (Paris, 1965); translated as *Totemism*, Rodney Needham (Boston, 1963).
8. 'Jean-Jacques Rousseau, fondateur des sciences de l'homme,' p. 240. It deals with a lecture included in the volume *Jean-Jacques Rousseau—La Baconnière—1962*. A theme dear to Merleau-Ponty is recognizable here: the work of anthropology *realizes* the imaginary variation in search of the essential invariant.

9. The idea of an originarily figurative language was pretty widespread at this time; it is to be found particularly in Warburton and in Condillac, whose influence on Rousseau is massive in this area. As for Vico: Bernard Gagnebin and Marcel Raymond have asked in connection with the *Essay on the Origin of Languages*, if Rousseau had not read the *Scienza Nuova* when he was Montaigu's secretary in Venice. But if Rousseau and Vico both affirm the metaphoric nature of primitive languages, Vico alone attributes to them this divine origin, also the theme of disagreement between Condillac and Rousseau. Moreover, Vico is one of the rare believers, if not the only believer, in the contemporaneity of origin between writing and speech: 'Philologists [Derrida's version would incorrectly read "philosophers"] have believed that among the nations languages first came into being and then letters; whereas . . . letters and languages were born twins and proceeded apace through all their three stages' (*Scienza Nuova* 3, 1) [*The New Science of Giambattista Vico*, tr. Thomas Goddard Bergin and Max Harold Fisch (Ithaca, 1968), p. 21]. Cassirer does not hesitate to affirm that Rousseau has 'summarized' in the *Essay* Vico's theories on Language (*Philosophie der symbolischen Formen* [(Berlin, 1923–9); translated as *The Philosophy of Symbolic Form*, by Ralph Manheim (New Haven, 1953)], I, I, 4).

10. Denis Diderot, *Oeuvres complètes*, Pléiade edition (Paris, 1935), pp. 993–1032; 'Supplement to Bougainville's "Voyage",' *Rameau's Nephew and Other Works*, ed. Jacques Barzun and Ralph H. Bowen (Garden City, 1956), pp. 187–239.

11. 'What we have here are thus two extreme types of proper name between which there are a whole series of intermediate cases. At one extreme, the name is an identifying mark which, by the application of a rule, establishes that the individual who is *named* is a member of a preordained class (a social group in a system of groups, a status by birth in a system of statuses). At the other extreme, the name is a free creation on the part of the individual who *gives the name* and expresses a transitory and subjective state of his own by means of the person he names. But can one be said to be really naming in either case? The choice seems only to be between identifying someone else by assigning him to a class or, under cover of giving him a name, identifying oneself through him. One therefore never names: one classifies someone else if the name is given to him in virtue of his characteristics and one classifies oneself if, in the belief that one need not follow a rule, one names someone else "freely," that is, in virtue of characteristics of one's own. And most commonly one does both at once' (p. 240) [p. 181]. Cf. also 'The Individual as A Species' and 'Time Recaptured' (chapters 7 and 8): 'In every system, therefore, proper names represent the quanta of *signification* below which one no longer does anything but point. This brings us to the root of the parallel mistakes committed by Peirce and by Russell, the former's in defining proper names as "indices" and the latter's in believing that he had discovered the logical model of proper names in demonstrative pronouns. This amounts in effect to allowing that the act of naming belongs to a continuum in which there is an imperceptible passage from the act of signifying to that of pointing. I hope that I have succeeded in showing that this passage is in fact discontinuous although each culture fixes its thresholds differently. The natural sciences put theirs on the level of species, varieties or subvarieties as the case may be. So terms of different degrees of generality will be regarded each time as proper names' (pp. 285–60) [p. 215].

Radicalizing this intention, it should perhaps be asked if it is any longer legitimate to refer to the prenominal 'property' of pure 'monstration'—pointing at—if pure indication, as the zero degree of language, as 'sensible certitude,' is not a myth always already effaced by the play of difference. It should perhaps be said of indication 'proper' what Lévi-Strauss says of proper names: 'At the lower end there is no external limit to the system either, since it succeeds in treating the qualitative diversity of natural species as the symbolic material of an order, and its progress towards the concrete, particular and individual is not even arrested by the obstacle of personal appellations: even proper names can serve as terms for a classification' (p. 288) [p. 218] (cf. also p. 242) [pp. 182–3].

12. [Pp. 269–70]. Since we read Rousseau in the transparence of the texts, why not slide under this scene that other taken out of a *Promenade* (9)? In spelling out all its elements one by one and minutely, I shall be less attentive to the opposition of term to term than to the rigorous symmetry of such an opposition. Everything happens as if Rousseau had developed the reassuring positive whose impression Lévi-Strauss gives us in the negative. Here is the scene: 'But, soon weary of emptying my purse to make people crush each other, I left the good company and went to walk alone in the fair. The variety of the objects there amused me for a long time. I perceived among others five or six boys from Savoy, around a small girl who had still on her tray a dozen meagre apples, which she was anxious to get rid of; the Savoyards, on their side, would have gladly freed her of them; but they had only two or three

131

pence among them all, and that was not much to make a great breach among the apples. This tray was for them the garden of the Hesperides; and the young girl was the dragon who guarded it. This comedy amused me for a long time; I finally created a climax by paying for the apples from the young girl and distributing them among the small boys. I had then one of the finest spectacles that can flatter a man's heart, that of seeing joy united with the innocence of youth, spreading everywhere about me. For the spectators themselves, in seeing it, partook of it, and I, who shared at such cheap expense this happiness, had in addition the joy of feeling that it was my work' (*Pléiade*, I, pp. 1092–3; [*The Reveries of a Solitary*, tr. John Gould Fletcher (New York, 1927), pp. 184–5]).

13. Of that word and that concept which, as I had suggested at the outset, has sense only within the logocentric closure and the metaphysics of presence. When it does not imply the possibility of an intuitive or judicative *adequation*, it nevertheless continues in *aletheia* to privilege the instance of a vision filled and satisfied by presence. It is the same reason that prevents the thought of writing to be simply contained within a science, indeed an epistemological circle. It can have neither that ambition nor that modesty.

14. A situation difficult to describe in Rousseauist terms, the professed absence of writing complicating things yet further: *The Essay on the Origin of Languages* would perhaps give the name 'savagery' to the state of society and writing described by Lévi-Strauss: 'These three ways of writing correspond almost exactly to three different stages according to which one can consider men gathered into a nation. The depicting of objects is appropriate to a savage people; signs of words and of propositions, to a barbaric people, and the alphabet to civilized peoples [*peuples policés*]' [p. 17].

15. 'If the West has produced anthropologists, it is because it was so tormented by remorse' ('A Little Glass of Rum,' *Tristes Tropiques*, chap. 38) [(p. 449) [p. 388]].

16. What one may read between the lines of the second *Discourse*: 'It is reason that engenders self-love, and reflection that confirms it: it is reason which turns man back upon himself, and divides him from everything that disturbs or afflicts him. It is philosophy that isolates him, and it is through philosophy that he says in secret, at the sight of the misfortunes of others: "Perish if you will, I am secure" ' (p. 60) [p. 184].

17. [*Jean-Jacques Rousseau*], p. 245. Italics author's.

18. *Tristes Tropiques*, chap. 18. With respect to Diderot, let us note in passing that the severity of his judgment on writing and the book does not in any way yield to Rousseau. The article 'book' [*livre*] which he wrote for the *Encyclopédie* is a most violent indictment.

19. Henri Bergon (Paris, 1889); translated as *Time and Free Will*, by F. L. Pogson (London and New York, 1910).

20. *Tristes Tropiques*, chap. 6. 'How I Became an Anthropologist.'

21. In the Geneva lecture [see n. 4] Lévi-Strauss believes he can simply oppose Rousseau to the philosophies that take their 'point of departure in the cogito' (p. 242).

Jacques Lacan (1901–1981)

Jacques Lacan, the most important psychoanalytical theorist since Freud, was born in Paris at the beginning of the twentieth century. He trained in medicine, psychiatry, and psychoanalysis, and worked with Henri Claude, one of the foremost French psychiatrists of the twentieth century, at the Clinique des Maladies Mentales et de L'Encephale. He also worked at the Infirmerie Spéciale Prés de la Préfecture de Police where he trained with Georges de Clerambault, whose theory of mental automatism (compulsion) greatly influenced Lacan, and at Carl Jung's clinic. In his academic and medical training, Lacan soon realized the limits of Freudian psychoanalysis. In 1953 Lacan began weekly seminars which provided the basis for much of his important work, and these seminars have been published as *Ecrits*.

Lacan re-interpreted Freud, holding the unconscious, rather than the ego, as the true subject of psychoanalysis and discourse. He did not see the unconscious as a material, concrete thing, and treated the idea of the unified subject as illusory. Lacan, like Lévi-Strauss, Foucault, Barthes, and Derrida, grounded his work in structural linguistics. Working from Saussure's sign theory, Lacan argued that the unconscious is structured like a language and maintained that meaning was available through connecting signifiers. Lacan claimed that in a fundamental way language mediated between the unconscious and the conscious in producing meaning.

In his lecture 'The mirror stage as formative of the function of the I as revealed in psychoanalytic experience', presented at the 16th International Congress of Psychoanalysis in Zurich on 17 July 1949, Lacan argued that, 'we have only to understand the mirror stage as an *identification*.' The most significant aspect of an infant's first identification with his/her reflection in a mirror is that it is the 'symbolic matrix in which the "I" is precipitated in a primordial form, before it is objectified in the dialectic of identification with the other, and before language restores to it, in the universal, its function as subject'. Since the image the infant sees is a contrasting image, one which mimics him/her, the identification 'prefigures its alienating destiny' because it is an other that he/she recognizes. Since the function of the mirror stage is to establish a relationship between the organism and its reality, the 'I' is inevitably fragmented. Lacan's concluding statements reveal a certain anxiety in positing such a splintered 'I' which is both determined by the subject in the mirror and by society's or culture's subsequent reading of the 'I'. Lacan's theories of the 'gaze' and subject formation are used widely by literary, film, and media critics.

K.M.S.

The mirror stage as formative of the function of the *I* as revealed in psychoanalytic experience

The conception of the mirror stage that I introduced at our last congress, thirteen years ago, has since become more or less established in the practice of the French group. However, I think it worthwhile to bring it again to your attention, especially today, for the light it sheds on the formation of the *I* as we experience it in psychoanalysis. It is an experience that leads us to oppose any philosophy directly issuing from the *Cogito*.

Some of you may recall that this conception originated in a feature of human behaviour illuminated by a fact of comparative psychology. The child, at an age when he is for a time, however short, outdone by the chimpanzee in instrumental intelligence, can nevertheless already recognize as such his own image in a mirror. This recognition is indicated in the illuminative mimicry of the *Aha-Erlebnis*, which Köhler sees as the expression of situational apperception, an essential stage of the act of intelligence.

This act, far from exhausting itself, as in the case of the monkey, once the image has been mastered and found empty, immediately rebounds in the case of the child in a series of gestures in which he experiences in play the relation between the movements assumed in the image and the reflected environment, and between this virtual complex and the reality it reduplicates—the child's own body, and the persons and things, around him.

This event can take place, as we have known since Baldwin, from the age of six months, and its repetition has often made me reflect upon the startling spectacle of the infant in front of the mirror. Unable as yet to walk, or even to stand up, and held tightly as he is by some support, human or artificial (what, in France, we call a '*trotte-bébé*'), he nevertheless overcomes, in a flutter of jubilant activity, the obstructions of his support and, fixing his attitude in a slightly leaning-forward position, in order to hold it in his gaze, brings back an instantaneous aspect of the image.

For me, this activity retains the meaning I have given it up to the age of eighteen months. This meaning discloses a libidinal dynamism, which has hitherto remained problematic, as well as an ontological structure of the human world that accords with my reflections on paranoiac knowledge.

We have only to understand the mirror stage *as an identification*, in the full sense that analysis gives to the term: namely, the transformation that takes place in the subject when he assumes an image—whose predestination to this phase-effect is sufficiently indicated by the use, in analytic theory, of the ancient term *imago*.

This jubilant assumption of his spectacular image by the child at the *infans* stage, still sunk in his motor incapacity and nursling dependence, would seem to exhibit in an exemplary situation the symbolic matrix in which the *I* is precipitated in a primordial form, before it is objectified in the dialectic of identification with the other, and before language restores to it, in the universal, its function as subject.

This form would have to be called the Ideal-I,[1] if we wished to incorporate it into our usual register, in the sense that it will also be the source of secondary identifications, under which term I would place the functions of libidinal normalization. But the important point is that this form situates the agency of the ego, before its social determination, in a fictional direction, which will always remain irreducible for the individual alone, or rather, which will only rejoin the coming-into-being (*le devenir*) of the subject asymptotically, whatever the success of the dialectical syntheses by which he must resolve as *I* his discordance with his own reality.

The fact is that the total form of the body by which the subject anticipates in a mirage the maturation of his power is given to him only as *Gestalt*, that is to say, in an exteriority in which this form is certainly more constituent than constituted, but in which it appears to him above all in a contrasting size (*un relief de stature*) that fixes it and in a symmetry that inverts it, in contrast with the turbulent movements that the subject feels are animating him. Thus, this *Gestalt*—whose pregnancy should be regarded as bound up with the species, though its motor style remains scarcely recognizable—by these two aspects of its appearance, symbolizes the mental permanence of the *I*, at the same time as it prefigures its alienating destination; it is still pregnant with the correspondences that unite the *I* with the statue in which man projects himself, with the phantoms that dominate him, or with the automaton in which, in an ambiguous relation, the world of his own making tends to find completion.

Indeed, for the *imagos*—whose veiled faces it is our privilege to see in outline in our daily experience and in the penumbra of symbolic efficacity[2]—the mirror-image would seem to be the threshold of the visible world if we go by the mirror disposition that the *imago of one's own body* presents in hallucinations or dreams, whether it concerns its individual features, or even its infirmities, or its object-projections; or if we observe the role of the mirror apparatus in the appearances of the *double*, in which psychical realities, however heterogeneous, are manifested.

That a *Gestalt* should be capable of formative effects in the organism is attested by a piece of biological experimentation that is itself so alien to the idea of psychical causality that it cannot bring itself to formulate its results in these terms. It nevertheless recognizes that it is a necessary condition for the maturation of the gonad of the female pigeon that it should see another member of its species, of either sex; so sufficient in itself is this condition that the desired effect may be obtained merely by placing the individual within reach of the field of reflection of a mirror. Similarly, in

135

the case of the migratory locust, the transition within a generation from the solitary to the gregarious form can be obtained by exposing the individual, at a certain stage, to the exclusively visual action of a similar image, provided it is animated by movements of a style sufficiently close to that characteristic of the species. Such facts are inscribed in an order of homeomorphic identification that would itself fall within the larger question of the meaning of beauty as both formative and erogenic.

But the facts of mimicry are no less instructive when conceived as cases of heteromorphic identification, in as much as they raise the problem of the signification of space for the living organism—psychological concepts hardly seem less appropriate for shedding light on these matters than ridiculous attempts to reduce them to the supposedly supreme law of adaptation. We have only to recall how Roger Caillois (who was then very young, and still fresh from his breach with the sociological school in which he was trained) illuminated the subject by using the term '*legendary psychasthenia*' to classify morphological mimicry as an obsession with space in its derealizing effect.

I have myself shown in the social dialectic that structures human knowledge as paranoiac[3] why human knowledge has greater autonomy than animal knowledge in relation to the field of force of desire, but also why human knowledge is determined in that 'little reality' (*ce peu de réalité*), which the Surrealists, in their restless way, saw as its limitation. These reflections lead me to recognize in the spatial captation manifested in the mirror-stage, even before the social dialectic, the effect in man of an organic insufficiency in his natural reality—in so far as any meaning can be given to the word 'nature'.

I am led, therefore, to regard the function of the mirror-stage as a particular case of the function of the *imago*, which is to establish a relation between the organism and its reality—or, as they say, between the *Innenwelt* and the *Umwelt*.

In man, however, this relation to nature is altered by a certain dehiscence at the heart of the organism, a primordial Discord betrayed by the signs of uneasiness and motor unco-ordination of the neo-natal months. The objection notion of the anatomical incompleteness of the pyramidal system and likewise the presence of certain humoral residues of the maternal organism confirm the view I have formulated as the fact of a real *specific prematurity of birth* in man.

It is worth noting, incidentally, that this is a fact recognized as such by embryologists, by the term *foetalization*, which determines the prevalence of the so-called superior apparatus of the neurax, and especially of the cortex, which psycho-surgical operations lead us to regard as the intra-organic mirror.

This development is experienced as a temporal dialectic that decisively projects the formation of the individual into history. The *mirror stage* is a drama whose internal thrust is precipitated from insufficiency to anticipation—and which manufactures for the subject, caught up in the lure of spatial identification, the succession of phantasies that extends from a fragmented body-image to a form of its totality that I shall call orthopaedic—and, lastly, to the assumption of the armour of an alienating identity, which will mark with its rigid structure the subject's entire mental development. Thus, to break out of the circle of the *Innenwelt* into the *Umwelt* generates the inexhaustible quadrature of the ego's verifications.

This fragmented body—which term I have also introduced into our system of theoretical references—usually manifests itself in dreams when the movement of the analysis encounters a certain level of aggressive disintegration in the individual. It then appears in the form of disjointed limbs, or of those organs represented in exoscopy, growing wings and taking up arms for intestinal persecutions—the very same that the visionary Hieronymus Bosch has fixed, for all time, in painting, in their ascent from the fifteenth century to the imaginary zenith of modern man. But this form is even tangibly revealed at the organic level, in the lines of 'fragilization' that define the anatomy of phantasy, as exhibited in the schizoid and spasmodic symptoms of hysteria.

Correlatively, the formation of the *I* is symbolized in dreams by a fortress, or a stadium—its inner arena and enclosure, surrounded by marshes and rubbish-tips, dividing it into two opposed fields of contest where the subject flounders in quest of the lofty, remote inner castle whose form (sometimes juxtaposed in the same scenario) symbolizes the id in a quite startling way. Similarly, on the mental plane, we find realized the structures of fortified works, the metaphor of which arises spontaneously, as if issuing from the symptoms themselves, to designate the mechanisms of obsessional neurosis—inversion, isolation, reduplication, cancellation and displacement.

But if we were to build on these subjective givens alone—however little we free them from the condition of experience that makes us see them as partaking of the nature of a linguistic technique—our theoretical attempts would remain exposed to the charge of projecting themselves into the unthinkable of an absolute subject. This is why I have sought in the present hypothesis, grounded in a conjunction of objective data, the guiding grid for a *method of symbolic reduction*.

It establishes in the *defences of the ego* a genetic order, in accordance with the wish formulated by Miss Anna Freud, in the first part of her great work, and situates (as against a frequently expressed prejudice) hysterical repression and its return at a more archaic stage than obsessional inversion and its isolating processes, and the latter in turn as preliminary to paranoic alienation, which dates from the deflection of the specular *I* into the social *I*.

This moment in which the mirror-stage comes to an end inaugurates, by the identification with the *imago* of the counterpart and the drama of primordial jealousy (so well brought out by the school of Charlotte Bühler in the phenomenon of infantile *transitivism*), the dialectic that will henceforth link the *I* to socially elaborated situations.

It is this moment that decisively tips the whole of human knowledge into mediatization through the desire of the other, constitutes its objects in an abstract equivalence by the co-operation of others, and turns the *I* into that apparatus for which every instinctual thrust constitutes a danger, even though it should correspond to a natural maturation—the very normalization of this maturation being henceforth dependent, in man, on a cultural mediation as exemplified, in the case of the sexual object, by the Oedipus complex.

In the light of this conception, the term primary narcissism, by which analytic doctrine designates the libidinal investment characteristic of that moment, reveals in those who invented it the most profound awareness of semantic latencies. But it also throws light on the dynamic opposition between this libido and the sexual libido, which the first analysts tried to define when they invoked destructive and, indeed,

137

death instincts, in order to explain the evident connection between the narcissistic libido and the alienating function of the *I*, the aggressivity it releases in any relation to the other, even in a relation involving the most Samaritan of aid.

In fact, they were encountering that existential negativity whose reality is so vigorously proclaimed by the contemporary philosophy of being and nothingness.

But unfortunately that philosophy grasps negativity only within the limits of a self-sufficiency of consciousness, which, as one of its premises, links to the *méconnaissances* that constitute the ego, the illusion of autonomy to which it entrusts itself. This flight of fancy, for all that it draws, to an unusual extent, on borrowings from psychoanalytic experience, culminates in the pretention of providing an existential psychoanalysis.

At the culmination of the historical effort of a society to refuse to recognize that it has any function other than the utilitarian one, and in the anxiety of the individual confronting the 'concentrational'[4] form of the social bond that seems to arise to crown this effort, existentialism must be judged by the explanations it gives of the subjective impasses that have indeed resulted from it; a freedom that is never more authentic than when it is within the walls of a prison; a demand for commitment, expressing the impotence of a pure consciousness to master any situation; a voyeuristic–sadistic idealization of the sexual relation; a personality that realizes itself only in suicide; a consciousness of the other that can be satisfied only by Hegelian murder.

These propositions are opposed by all our experience, in so far as it teaches us not to regard the ego as centred on the *perception–consciousness system*, or as organized by the 'reality principle'—a principle that is the expression of a scientific prejudice most hostile to the dialectic of knowledge. Our experience shows that we should start instead from the *function of méconnaissance* that characterizes the ego in all its structures, so markedly articulated by Miss Anna Freud. For, if the *Verneinung* represents the patent form of that function, its effects will, for the most part, remain latent, so long as they are not illuminated by some light reflected on to the level of fatality, which is where the id manifests itself.

We can thus understand the inertia characteristic of the formations of the *I*, and find there the most extensive definition of neurosis—just as the captation of the subject by the situation gives us the most general formula for madness, not only the madness that lies behind the walls of asylums, but also the madness that deafens the world with its sound and fury.

The sufferings of neurosis and psychosis are for us a schooling in the passions of the soul, just as the beam of the psychoanalytic scales, when we calculate the tilt of its threat to entire communities, provides us with an indication of the deadening of the passions in society.

At this junction of nature and culture, so persistently examined by modern anthropology, psychoanalysis alone recognizes this knot of imaginary servitude that love must always undo again, or sever.

For such a task, we place no trust in altruistic feeling, we who lay bare the aggressivity that underlies the activity of the philanthropist, the idealist, the pedagogue, and even the reformer.

In the recourse of subject to subject that we preserve, psychoanalysis may accompany the patient to the ecstatic limit of the '*Thou art that*', in which is revealed to him the cipher of his mortal destiny, but it is not in our mere power as practitioners to bring him to that point where the real journey begins.

NOTES

1. Throughout this article I leave in its peculiarity the translation I have adopted for Freud's *Ideal-Ich* [i.e., 'je-idéal'], without further comment, other than to say that I have not maintained it since.
2. Cf. Claude Lévi-Strauss, *Structural Anthropology*, Chapter X.
3. Cf. 'Aggressivity in Psychoanalysis', p. 8 and *Écrits*, p. 180.
4. '*Concentrationnaire*', an adjective coined after World War II (this article was written in 1949) to describe the life of the concentration-camp. In the hands of certain writers it became, by extension, applicable to many aspects of 'modern' life [Tr.].

Michel Foucault (1926–1984)

Michel Foucault was born in Poitiers, France, studied at Sorbonne and then received his philosophy degree at the École Normale Supérieure in 1948. He was briefly a member of the Communist party and studied the politics of the Paris Communist Front until 1950. In the same year he also earned a degree in psychology, did extensive research in psychopathology, and published *Mental Illness and Psychology*. In 1964, he became the Chair and Professor of Philosophy at the University of Clermont-Ferrand. He also taught at the University of Vincennes, before naming his own position, 'Professor of the History of Systems of Thought', at the Collège de France in 1970. The relationship of power to knowledge and the dynamics between language and social institutions (rather than language as a static sign system), were two areas of enquiry that Foucault researched extensively and helped to define within the academy. He called the practice of concretizing relationships between language and social institutions 'discourse'. Studying language at the level of discourse, he identified underlying rules that govern particular forms of signification, which in turn create and perpetuate certain forms of knowledge. Foucault's early works include *Madness and Civilization* (1961), *The Birth of the Clinic* (1963), *The Order of Things* (1966), and *The Archeology of Knowledge* (1969). The use of language as a manipulative 'discursive practice' led him to examine the disciplining of the human body as a sexual object *vis-à-vis* the cultural practices of European society. *Discipline and Punish* (1975) and *The History of Sexuality* (4 vols., 1976–84) are his later works which grew out of this interest in 'discursive practices' and have been tremendously influential.

The essay included here, 'We "Other Victorians"', is from Foucault's *The History of Sexuality*. In it he contrasts the beginning of the seventeenth century, a period in which bodies unabashedly 'displayed' themselves, with the prudery of the Victorian bourgeoisie, and maintains that this Victorian attitude towards sexuality continues to dictate our cultural behavior even today. He discusses the influence of 'modern puritanism' with its 'triple edict' and agrees with Freud's speculation on the potency of repressed sexuality. He too believes that it coincides with the development of capitalism, and claims that defining the relationship between power and sex in terms of repression is 'gratifying for us' because repression can be easily analysed and discussed. He outlines a mechanism called the 'repressive hypothesis' in order to 'define the regime of power–knowledge–pleasure that sustains the discourse on human sexuality in our part of the world'. Foucault's work has been used extensively by critics in media and gender studies, especially in the analyses of knowledge, power, control, and sexuality.

K.M.S.

We 'other Victorians'

For a long time, the story goes, we supported a Victorian regime, and we continue to be dominated by it even today. Thus the image of the imperial prude is emblazoned on our restrained, mute, and hypocritical sexuality.

At the beginning of the seventeenth century a certain frankness was still common it would seem. Sexual practices had little need of secrecy; words were said without undue reticence, and things were done without too much concealment; one had a tolerant familiarity with the illicit. Codes regulating the coarse, the obscene, and the indecent were quite lax compared to those of the nineteenth century. It was a time of direct gestures, shameless discourse, and open transgressions, when anatomies were shown and intermingled at will, and knowing children hung about amid the laughter of adults: it was a period when bodies 'made a display of themselves.'

But twilight soon fell upon this bright day, followed by the monotonous nights of the Victorian bourgeoisie. Sexuality was carefully confined; it moved into the home. The conjugal family took custody of it and absorbed it into the serious function of reproduction. On the subject of sex, silence became the rule. The legitimate and procreative couple laid down the law. The couple imposed itself as model, enforced the norm, safeguarded the truth, and reserved the right to speak while retaining the principle of secrecy. A single locus of sexuality was acknowledged in social space as well as at the heart of every household, but it was a utilitarian and fertile one: the parents' bedroom. The rest had only to remain vague; proper demeanor avoided contact with other bodies, and verbal decency sanitized one's speech. And sterile behavior carried the taint of abnormality; if it insisted on making itself too visible, it would be designated accordingly and would have to pay the penalty.

Nothing that was not ordered in terms of generation or transfigured by it could expect sanction or protection. Nor did it merit a hearing. It would be driven out, denied, and reduced to silence. Not only did it not exist, it had no right to exist and would be made to disappear upon its least manifestation—whether in acts or in words. Everyone knew, for example, that children had no sex, which was why they were forbidden to talk about it, why one closed one's eyes and stopped one's ears whenever they came to show evidence to the contrary, and why a general and studied

141

silence was imposed. These are the characteristic features attributed to repression, which serve to distinguish it from the prohibitions maintained by penal law: repression operated as a sentence to disappear, but also as an injunction to silence, an affirmation of nonexistence, and, by implication, an admission that there was nothing to say about such things, nothing to see, and nothing to know. Such was the hypocrisy of our bourgeois societies with its halting logic. It was forced to make a few concessions, however. If it was truly necessary to make room for illegitimate sexualities, it was reasoned, let them take their infernal mischief elsewhere: to a place where they could be reintegrated, if not in the circuits of production, at least in those of profit. The brothel and the mental hospital would be those places of tolerance: the prostitute, the client, and the pimp, together with the psychiatrist and his hysteric—those 'other Victorians,' as Steven Marcus would say—seem to have surreptitiously transferred the pleasures that are unspoken into the order of things that are counted. Words and gestures, quietly authorized, could be exchanged there at the going rate. Only in those places would untrammeled sex have a right to (safely insularized) forms of reality, and only to clandestine, circumscribed, and coded types of discourse. Everywhere else, modern puritanism imposed its triple edict of taboo, nonexistence, and silence.

But have we not liberated ourselves from those two long centuries in which the history of sexuality must be seen first of all as the chronicle of an increasing repression? Only to a slight extent, we are told. Perhaps some progress was made by Freud; but with such circumspection, such medical prudence, a scientific guarantee of innocuousness, and so many precautions in order to contain everything, with no fear of 'overflow,' in that safest and most discrete of spaces, between the couch and discourse: yet another round of whispering on a bed. And could things have been otherwise? We are informed that if repression has indeed been the fundamental link between power, knowledge, and sexuality since the classical age, it stands to reason that we will not be able to free ourselves from it except at a considerable cost: nothing less than a transgression of laws, a lifting of prohibitions, an irruption of speech, a reinstating of pleasure within reality, and a whole new economy in the mechanisms of power will be required. For the least glimmer of truth is conditioned by politics. Hence, one cannot hope to obtain the desired results simply from a medical practice, not from a theoretical discourse, however rigorously pursued. Thus, one denounces Freud's conformism, the normalizing functions of psychoanalysis, the obvious timidity underlying Reich's vehemence, and all the effects of integration ensured by the 'science' of sex and the barely equivocal practices of sexology.

This discourse on modern sexual repression holds up well, owing no doubt to how easy it is to uphold. A solemn historical and political guarantee protects it. By placing the advent of the age of repression in the seventeenth century, after hundreds of years of open spaces and free expansion, one adjusts it to coincide with the development of capitalism: it becomes an integral part of the bourgeois order. The minor chronicle of sex and its trials is transposed into the ceremonious history of the modes of production; its trifling aspect fades from view. A principle of explanation emerges after the fact: if sex is so rigorously repressed, this is because it is incompatible with a general and intensive work imperative. At a time when labor capacity was being systematically exploited, how could this capacity be allowed to dissipate itself in pleasurable pursuits, except in those—reduced to a minimum—that enabled it to reproduce itself? Sex and its effects are perhaps not so easily deciphered; on the other hand, their repression, thus reconstructed, is easily analysed. And the sexual cause—the demand for sexual freedom, but also for the knowledge to be gained from sex and the right to speak about it—becomes legitimately associated with the honor of a political cause: sex too is placed on the agenda for the future. A suspicious mind might wonder if taking so many precautions in order to give the history of sex such an impressive filiation does not bear traces of the same old prudishness: as if those valorizing correlations were necessary before such a discourse could be formulated or accepted.

But there may be another reason that makes it so gratifying for us to define the relationship beween sex and power in terms of repression: something that one might call the speaker's benefit. If sex is repressed, that is, condemned to prohibition, nonexistence, and silence, then the mere fact that one is speaking about it has the appearance of a deliberate transgression. A person who holds forth in such language places himself to a certain extent outside the reach of power; he upsets established law; he somehow anticipates the coming freedom. This explains the solemnity with which one speaks of sex nowadays. When they had to allude to it, the first demographers and psychiatrists of the nineteenth century thought it advisable to excuse themselves for asking their readers to dwell on matters so trivial and base. But for decades now, we have found it difficult to speak on the subject without striking a different pose: we are conscious of defying established power, our tone of voice shows that we know we are being subversive, and we ardently conjure away the present and appeal to the future, whose day will be hastened by the contribution we believe we are making. Something that smacks of revolt, of promised freedom, of the coming age of a different law, slips easily into this discourse on sexual oppression. Some of the ancient functions of prophecy are reactivated therein. Tomorrow sex will be good again. Because this repression is affirmed, one can discreetly bring into coexistence concepts which the fear of ridicule or the bitterness of history prevents most of us from putting side by side: revolution and happiness; or revolution and a different body, one that is newer and more beautiful; or indeed, revolution and pleasure. What sustains our eagerness to speak of sex in terms of repression is doubtless this opportunity to speak out against the powers that be, to utter truths and promise bliss, to link together enlightenment, liberation, and manifold pleasures; to pronounce a discourse that combines the fervor of knowledge, the determination to change the laws, and the longing for the garden of earthly delights. This is perhaps what also explains the market value attributed not only to what is said about sexual repression, but also to the mere fact of lending an ear to those who would eliminate the effects of repression. Ours is, after all, the only civilization in which officials are paid to listen to all and sundry impart the secrets of their sex: as if the urge to talk about it, and the interest one hopes to arouse by doing so, have far surpassed the possibilities of being heard, so that some individuals have even offered their ears for hire.

But it appears to me that the essential thing is not this economic factor, but rather the existence in our era of a discourse in which sex, the revelation of truth, the overturning of global laws, the proclamation of a new day to come, and the promise of a certain felicity are linked together. Today it is sex that serves as a support for the ancient form—so familiar and important in the West—of preaching. A great sexual sermon—which has had its subtle theologians and its popular voices—has swept through our societies over the last decades; it has chastised the old order, denounced hypocrisy, and praised the rights of the immediate and the real; it has made people dream of a New City. The Franciscans are called to mind. And we might wonder how it is possible that the lyricism and religiosity that long accompanied the revolutionary project have, in Western industrial societies, been largely carried over to sex.

The notion of repressed sex is not, therefore, only a theoretical matter. The affirmation of a sexuality that has never been more rigorously subjugated than during the age of the hypocritical, bustling, and responsible bourgeoisie is coupled with the grandiloquence of a discourse purporting to reveal the truth about sex, modify its economy within reality, subvert the law that governs it, and change its future. The statement of oppression and the form of the sermon refer back to one another; they are mutually reinforcing. To say that sex is not repressed, or rather that the relationship between sex and power is not characterized by repression, is to risk falling into a sterile paradox. It not only runs counter to a well-accepted argument, it goes against the whole economy and all the discursive 'interests' that underlie this argument.

This is the point at which I would like to situate the series of historical analyses that will follow, the present volume being at the same time an introduction and a first attempt at an overview: it surveys a few historically significant points and outlines certain theoretical problems. Briefly, my aim is to examine the case of a society which has been loudly castigating itself for its hypocrisy for more than a century, which speaks verbosely of its own silence, takes great pains to relate in detail the things it does not say, denounces the powers it exercises, and promises to liberate itself from the very laws that have made it function. I would like to explore not only these discourses but also the will that sustains them and the strategic intention that supports them. The question I would like to pose is not, Why are we repressed? but rather, Why do we say, with so much passion and so much resentment against our most recent past, against our present, and against ourselves, that we are repressed? By what spiral did we come to affirm that sex is negated? What led us to show, ostentatiously, that sex is something we hide, to say it is something we silence? And we do all this by formulating the matter in the most explicit terms, by trying to reveal it in its most naked reality, by affirming it in the positivity of its power and its effects. It is certainly legitimate to ask why sex was associated with sin for such a long time— although it would remain to be discovered how this association was formed, and one would have to be careful not to state in a summary and hasty fashion that sex was 'condemned'—but we must also ask why we burden ourselves today with so much guilt for having once made sex a sin. What paths have brought us to the point where we are 'at fault' with respect to our own sex? And how have we come to be a civilization so peculiar as to tell itself that, through an abuse of power which has not ended, it has long 'sinned' against sex? How does one account for the displacement which, while claiming to free us from the sinful nature of sex, takes us with a great historical wrong which consists precisely in imagining that nature to be blameworthy and in drawing diastrous consequences from that belief?

It will be said that if so many people today affirm this repression, the reason is that it is historically evident. And if they speak of it so abundantly, as they have for such a long time now, this is because repression is so firmly anchored, having solid roots and reasons, and weighs so heavily on sex that more than one denunciation will be required in order to free ourselves from it; the job will be a long one. All the longer, no doubt, as it is in the nature of power—particularly the kind of power that operates in our society—to be repressive, and to be especially careful in repressing useless energies, the intensity of pleasures, and irregular modes of behavior. We must not be surprised, then, if the effects of liberation vis-à-vis this repressive power are so slow to manifest themselves; the effort to speak freely about sex and accept it in its reality is so alien to a historical sequence that has gone unbroken for a thousand years now, and so inimical to the intrinsic mechanisms of power, that it is bound to make little headway for a long time before succeeding in its mission.

One can raise three serious doubts concerning what I shall term the 'repressive hypothesis.' First doubt: Is sexual repression truly an established historical fact? Is what first comes into view—and consequently permits one to advance an initial hypothesis—really the accentuation or even the establishment of a regime of sexual repression beginning in the seventeenth century? This is a properly historical question. Second doubt: Do the workings of power, and in particular those mechanisms that are brought into play in societies such as ours, really belong primarily to the category of repression? Are prohibitions, censorship, and denial truly the forms through which power is exercised in a general way, if not in every society, most certainly in our own? This is a historico-theoretical question. A third and final doubt: Did the critical discourse that addresses itself to repression come to act as a roadblock to a power mechanism that had operated unchallenged up to that point, or is it not in fact part of the same historical network as the thing it denounces (and doubtless misrepresents) by calling it 'repression'? Was there really a historical rupture between the age of repression and the critical analysis of repression? This is a historico-political question. My purpose in introducing these three doubts is not merely to construct counterarguments that are symmetrical and contrary to those outlined above; it is not a matter of saying that sexuality, far from being repressed in capitalist and bourgeois societies, has on the contrary benefitted from a regime of unchanging liberty; nor is it a matter of saying that power in societies such as ours is more tolerant than repressive, and that the critique of repression, while it may give itself airs of a rupture with the past, actually forms part of a much older process and, depending on how one chooses to understand this process, will appear either as a new episode in the lessening of prohibitions, or as a more devious and discreet form of power.

The doubts I would like to oppose to the repressive hypothesis are aimed less at showing it to be mistaken than at putting it back within a general economy of discourses on sex in modern societies since the seventeenth century. Why has sexuality been so widely discussed, and what has been said about it? What were the effects of power generated by what was said? What are the links between these discourses, these effects of power, and the pleasures that were invested by them? What knowledge (*savoir*) was formed as a result of this linkage? The object, in short, is to define the regime of power-knowledge-pleasure that sustains the discourse on human sexuality in our part of the world. The central issue, then (at least in the first instance), is not to determine whether one says yes or no to sex, whether one formulates prohibitions or permissions, whether one asserts its importance or denies its effects, or whether one refines the words one uses to designate it; but to account for the fact that it is spoken about, to discover who does the speaking, the positions and viewpoints from which they speak, the institutions which prompt people to speak about it and which store and distribute the things that are said. What is at issue, briefly, is the over-all 'discursive fact,' the way in which sex is 'put into discourse.' Hence, too, my main concern will be to locate the forms of power, the channels it takes, and the discourses it permeates in order to reach the most tenuous and individual modes of behavior, the paths that give it access to the rare or scarcely perceivable forms of desire, how it penetrates and controls everyday pleasure—all this entailing effects that may be those of refusal, blockage, and invalidation, but also incitement and intensification: in short, the 'polymorphous techniques of power.' And finally, the essential aim will not be to determine whether these discursive productions and these effects of power lead one to formulate the truth about sex, or on the contrary false-hoods designed to conceal that truth, but rather to bring out the 'will to knowledge' that serves as both their support and their instrument.

Let there be no misunderstanding: I do not claim that sex has not been prohibited or barred or masked or misapprehended since the classical age; nor do I even assert that it has suffered these things any less from that period on than before. I do not maintain that the prohibition of sex is a ruse; but it is a ruse to make prohibition into the basic and constitutive element from which one would be able to write the history of what has been said concerning sex starting from the modern epoch. All these nega-tive elements—defenses, censorships, denials—which the repressive hypothesis groups together in one great central mechanism destined to say no, are doubtless only component parts that have a local and tactical role to play in a transformation into discourse, a technology of power, and a will to knowledge that are far from being reducible to the former.

In short, I would like to disengage my analysis from the privileges generally accorded the economy of scarcity and the principles of rarefaction, to search instead for instances of discursive production (which also administer silences, to be sure), of the production of power (which sometimes have the function of prohibiting), of the propagation of knowledge (which often cause mistaken beliefs or systematic miscon-ceptions to circulate); I would like to write the history of these instances and their transformations. A first survey made from this viewpoint seems to indicate that since the end of the sixteenth century, the 'putting into discourse of sex,' far from under-going a process of restriction, on the contrary has been subjected to a mechanism of increasing incitement; that the techniques of power exercised over sex have not obeyed a principle of rigorous selection, but rather one of dissemination and implant-ation of polymorphous sexualities; and that the will to knowledge has not come to a halt in the face of a taboo that must not be lifted, but has persisted in constituting—despite many mistakes, of course—a science of sexuality. It is these movements that I will now attempt to bring into focus in a schematic way, bypassing as it were the repressive hypothesis and the facts of interdiction or exclusion it invokes, and start-ing from certain historical facts that serve as guidelines for research.

146

3 *Cultural studies in Britain*

Edited by Roger Bromley

Introduction

All the standard accounts of British cultural studies trace its origins to the 1950s and to the emergence of three key texts. However, as Stuart Hall, whose 1980 essay remains in many ways the most precise and critically informed version, reminds us, there are no 'absolute beginnings' to the project of cultural studies. Even if this is so, it would be foolish to under-estimate the impact of the works which marked its formal, textual starting point: Richard Hoggart's *The Uses of Literacy* (1957); Raymond Williams's *Culture and Society* (1958); and E. P. Thompson's *The Making of the English Working Class* (1963).

None of these texts was conceived in isolation, nor did they 'arrive unaccompanied'. Each was part of a wider context which tends to be ignored by accounts which stress the coherence and intentionality of its formative moments. In one of his last public lectures, Raymond Williams (1989) spent time reminding his audience of how much cultural-studies work was being carried out prior to the 1950s by people, influenced by but critical of I. A. Richards, F. R. Leavis, and *Scrutiny*, who were engaged in detailed analyses of popular fiction, cinema, advertising, and newspapers from a number of perspectives and under various headings. Some of this work was undertaken by acolytes of Leavis in the grammar schools, but much of it occurred in evening classes and weekend schools under the auspices of the Workers Educational Association (WEA) and the extra-mural departments of the universities. Far from being simply a matter of the founding texts, cultural studies is shown to have a longer history and deeper roots, extending back as far as army education in the second world war and before, and being conducted very much as a vocation and a political commitment. As Williams acknowledges, many of the pioneers of cultural studies were extremely active in adult education, inspired by a dedication to popular, democratic and participatory education. Understandably, there were conflicts between the analytical procedures of 'close reading' designed to educate a moral minority, and the desire for a democratized culture which generated pressures for alternative, class-responsive ways of understanding.

149

With the exception of Germaine Greer, all of the writers here represented chose to work in adult education for a number of years, and their writings were produced under the stimulus of this experience and as part of a search to valorize other histories and other narratives than those taught in the universities of the period. These writings are now rightly seen as foundation documents, but they are only a fractional representation of a complex cultural moment, a profound engagement with traditions, class, work, and leisure gradually brought in from the margins by hundreds of mostly unknown, but intrepid, trespassers on the 'intellectual property' of an educational élite.

There is a danger of 'romancing the margins', of sentimentalizing the origins of what is now an institutionalized academic practice but, as the field of study becomes so extensive, it is timely to recall its materialist beginnings, its radical and practical intervention at a time of deep conservatism profoundly shaped by a colonial mentality and imperial modes of self-understanding. Oddly enough, perhaps the initial stages of the cultural-studies project were, in some inchoate fashion, a local instance of liberation from a colonizing authority, although there can be no doubt that, in its emphasis on the analysis of the national culture, it was still deeply marked by this. Certainly, many of its early practitioners were either from, or actively identified with, the margins of that regime of authority.

If most accounts of the origins tend to ignore the local educational and political aspects of its shaping, they nearly all refer to the wider context of the cold war, McCarthyism, the Hungarian uprising in 1956 which depleted the British Communist Party of many of its intellectuals, the Bomb and CND, the Suez crisis, decolonization and the recurring 'problems' with the Empire, and the growing impact of American power. While, to my knowledge, there is no systematic analysis of this precise conjuncture, much has been written about the apparent influence of the 'New Left' and the Communist Party. With hindsight, both of these influences have perhaps been over-emphasized at the expense of active Labour-Party constituencies as a site for setting the agenda for much of the progressive thinking around education, welfare and the media. As McGuigan (1992) points out, the National Union of Teachers conference on 'Popular Culture and Personal Responsibility' in 1960 helped produce Williams's 1962 publication, *Communications* and Denys Thompson's *Discrimination and Popular Culture* (1964), both widely used in schools, further education, and adult education, especially in liberal-studies programmes. Many of the people involved in this conference and its related events were Labour-Party activists (Williams was a member from 1961 to 1966) and it is difficult to imagine from this point in time how seriously cultural debate around the arts, communications, and education was taken in this period. I am not speaking of the official organization of the Party, nor of its leadership, but of the sense in which, as Williams writing of the 'culture of politics' in 1959 expressed it, the new generation came to think of the Labour Party as its own movement.

It is not too fanciful to claim that those involved in cultural studies at that time (even if many did not use the term) saw themselves as engaged in transforming British society to such an extent that the cultural privilege, political power, and social authority of the class which had shaped the nation until the second world war would never again be regarded as legitimate currency. It was naive, evolutionary and, ultimately, a 'whig' view of the historical process but it was nevertheless the dominant strain in radical thinking. 'Agency', 'intervention', 'effect', were, at that time, not just items in a cultural discourse. 'Class' was the primary analytical resource; education, at all levels, seen as the principal medium of empowerment and change. For a number of years cultural studies has ceased to have this activist inflection, but, interestingly, the Institute for Cultural Policy Studies set up by Tony Bennett and colleagues at Griffith University in Australia, renews this original project by asserting the need 'to include policy considerations in the definition of culture in viewing it as a particular field of government' and 'for intellectual work to be conducted in a manner such that, in both its substance and its style, it can be calculated to influence or service the conduct of identifiable agents within the region of culture concerned' (Grossberg et al., 1992, 23).

Textually, Hoggart's *The Uses of Literacy* (1957) marks the first stages of this phase of development; arguably, *Policing the Crisis* (1978) the last. The former was written in the period 1952 to 1956, about changes in working-class culture during the preceding thirty or forty years, particularly as these were being shaped by mass publications. Although it is more concerned with methodology than is sometimes remembered (in fact, its major influence has been on what we would now call the ethnographic tradition) it is addressed to 'the serious common reader' or 'the intelligent layman [*sic*] from any class'. Already in a few lines of the Preface a number of loaded terms—'serious', 'common', 'intelligent', 'mass'—are introduced. In a sense, also, the outcome of the study is announced in advance by the description of 'the extraordinarily low level of the organs of mass communication'. This assumption remained a given of the study of popular culture for at least two decades.

Unsystematic, autobiographical, puritanical, impressionistic and nostalgic though it might be, *The Uses of Literacy* did attempt to discriminate between 'mass' and 'popular' (the 'Leavisite' use of 'discrimination' was ubiquitous but it tended to see the 'mass' and the 'popular' as co-terminous in many respects), and allowed scope for agency, choice, negotiation and the creative use of cultural resources. The traces of Leavisite élitism, the easy-target anti-Americanisms, and the occasionally patronizing tone can all now be seen as fundamental weaknesses, but in the immediate post-second-world-war period there was deep and understandable anxiety that the hard-won literacy of the working class might not be used as part of an education for democracy and citizenship (to adopt some of the left rhetoric of the 1930s and the war period) but simply as an instrument of 'the culture industry'. Hoggart had a high profile as a policy-maker concerned with the arts, broadcasting and youth and community services.

Policing the Crisis (1978) researched and written in the period from 1973 to 1977, was a work of 'intervention', designed to have an effect on social policy ('to do something about the present conditions') and to produce the basis of a political judgement on issues of crime, race, youth and black struggle. It was also a book about a society which was perceived as slipping into a certain mode of crisis. In many ways this was a landmark in the work of the Centre for Contemporary Cultural Studies (CCCS) at the University of Birmingham, one of its finest achievements. It may seem strange to link it with *The Uses of Literacy* as, with its collectively authored approach, explicit political intent, and complex theoretical ambition, it would seem an entirely different phenomenon. All that is being argued is that it continued, and for the moment marked the end of, the 'interventionist' academic work of British cultural studies— work that was conducted as if its outcome mattered, that could influence 'identifiable agents', and had some urgent connection with the material conditions of people's lived experience. (In a much attenuated form, Paul Willis's work continues this tradition; see *Common Culture*, 1990.)

Of course, this kind of approach did not cease in 1978 but, arguably, it was continued in the work of feminist history and in writings on race, ethnicity, and black struggle rather than in conjunctural cultural analysis of this kind. Saying this does not devalue the work done in the 1980s under the pressure of very different political circumstances, it suggests that 'interventionist' research was not the most prominent feature of British cultural studies, partly because its twin axes of class analysis and a democratic socialist agenda had yielded to a more theoreticist approach and these no longer had the same resonance or salience.

This is not to propose a crude homology between the growth of British cultural studies and some kind of social democratic consensus in the period 1957 to 1978, but an attempt to indicate that, for all its radicalism, oppositional discourse, institutional marginality, and theoretical de-familiarization, cultural studies developed in a relatively uncontested space as a sustained and substantial critique of a society which, however inarticulately and indirectly, acknowledged itself to be in crisis with no immediate likelihood of cultural, social, or political resolution. In other words, presumptuous though it may seem, the minor presence in British academic life of cultural studies exercised an influence out of all proportion to its size, in so far as the currency of much of the cultural, political and social debate around the notion of 'crisis' took its bearings from agendas established by cultural studies and, of course, sociology harnessed to, or by, mainstream political discourse (I am thinking particularly of debates around the inner cities, schooling, youth subcultures, gendered discourse and behaviour, and the significant cultural impact of the Greater London Council—until its demise was engineered by the Thatcher government in 1986—and other radical local authorities).

Initially blunted by, and limited in its response to, the Thatcherite project, cultural studies has been subject to prolific growth in academic institutions in the late 1980s and the early 1990s. Much of this growth has been shaped by the influence of postmodernist theory, is consequently lacking at times in historicized particularity, and, despite efforts to the contrary, is still rather bound by a preoccupation with a national culture focused upon a critique of 'Englishness' which, on occasion comes suspiciously close to celebrating it; or, at least, seeking to find/found a Left version of it. (See Gilroy's essay in the section on Race Studies.)
R.B.

REFERENCES AND FURTHER READING

Brantlinger, Patrick, *Crusoe's Footprints—Cultural Studies in Britain and America*, London: Routledge, 1990.
Gilroy, Paul, *The Black Atlantic: Modernity and Double Consciousness*, London: Verso, 1993.
Grossberg, Lawrence, C. Nelson, and P. Treichler, eds, *Cultural Studies*, New York: Routledge, 1992.

Hall, Stuart, and Paddy Whannel, *The Popular Arts*, London: Hutchinson, 1964.

Hall, Stuart, and Tony Jefferson, eds, *Resistance Through Rituals: Youth Subcultures in Post-War Britain*, London: Hutchinson, 1976.

Hall, Stuart, et al., *Culture, Media, Language*, London: Hutchinson, 1980.

Harris, D., *From Class Struggle to the Politics of Pleasure: the Effects of Gramscianism on Cultural Studies*, London: Routledge, 1992.

Hoggart, Richard, *Speaking to Each Other*, 2 vols., London: Chatto & Windus, 1970.

Leavis, F. R., *Mass Civilization and Minority Culture*, Cambridge: Gordon Fraser, 1930.

Leavis, F. R., and Denys Thompson, *Culture and Environment*, London: Chatto & Windus, 1933.

McGuigan, J., *Cultural Populism*, London: Routledge, 1992.

O'Connor, Alan, *Raymond Williams: Writing, Culture, Politics*, Oxford: Blackwell, 1989.

Oxford English Limited, 'Raymond Williams: Third Generation', *News from Nowhere*, No. 6, February 1989.

Turner, Graeme, *British Cultural Studies—An Introduction*, London: Unwin Hyman, 1990.

Widdowson, Peter, ed., *Re-Reading English*, London: Methuen, 1982.

Willis, Paul, *Common Culture*, London: Open University Press, 1990.

Women's Study Group, CCCS, eds, *Women Take Issue*, London: Hutchinson, 1978.

Richard Hoggart (1918–)

Institutionally, Hoggart was the most significant of the founding figures in cultural studies. *The Uses of Literacy* (1957) certainly had a far wider readership for a time than any of the other 'seminal' texts. In 1963, he moved to the University of Birmingham to take up a professorship of English and a year later, with modest financial support from the Rowntree Trust and Penguin Books, he established the Centre for Contemporary Cultural Studies (CCCS) at the university. Subsequently, and under the directorship of Stuart Hall and Richard Johnson, this centre was to become the major influence on the institutional development of cultural studies (in some accounts, seemingly the only influence). Hoggart's initial presence helped establish the first serious, non-élitist, study of popular culture in the United Kingdom. The first seven projects of the Centre (not all of which were completed) indicate the 'populist' nature of the original enterprise and residual traces of the Leavis and Thompson culture and environment approach of the 1930s: Orwell and the Climate of the Thirties; Growth and Change in the Local Press; Folk Song and Folk Idioms in Popular Music; Levels of Fiction and Changes in Contemporary Society; Domestic Art and Iconography in the Home; Pop Music and Adolescent Culture; The Meaning of Sport and its Presentation. The stress on the local, the domestic, and the 'folk' suggests an endeavour which attempts to secure a 'people-scale' culture, active and experiential, against a 'mass culture', impersonal, national and designed for passivity.

The passage from *The Uses of Literacy* reprinted below is class-specific in its reference and informed by the practices of 'close reading'. It is also filled with a range of terms and assumptions, used uncritically and unreflectively, like 'genuinely working class', 'homely', 'ordinary', 'sensible', 'sound and practical', 'extraordinary fidelity to the details of readers' lives', and 'a solid and relevant way of life', which, while they seek to describe (inscribe) a way of life positively that is conventionally regarded as a deficit culture, are prompted by a series of negatives and opposites seen as the currency of mass culture and treated in the second half of the book. The phrases also

154

form a litany of values which attempt to give shape, depth, and continuity to a class confronted by the meretricious and the ephemeral.

All of this is nostalgic, generalized and, in a sense, undiscriminating (i.e. the readings are actually not very 'close') but it is written against the sententiousness of works like Q. D. Leavis's *Fiction and the Reading Public* which sought to 'police' all popular reading matter. If it proposes (or constructs) an 'organic community' at least it is northern, urban, and working-class, rather than the 'classless' pastoral of the cottage in the Cotswolds. And if its values are unexamined and, to a large extent, 'imagined', rather than 'lived', the fears of 'mass production', 'standardization', 'levelling-down', 'the loss of the organic community', and of 'substitute-living' (these are all chapter headings taken from *Culture and Environment: The Training of Critical Awareness*, 1933) which, undoubtedly, shadow the writing of the book, do not lead to a call to 'train' the working class in the values of an embattled petit-bourgeoisie, but to a recognition of the need for the exercise of democratic vigilance and active participation.

Although the formative work of Hoggart, Williams and Thompson is written specifically for, and on behalf of, the working class its addressee, explicit or otherwise, is also a ruling class, and its 'companionable' bourgeoisie, which privileges its values in the name of objectivity and universality but obscures their partiality and class-particularity through the exercise of power and authority which subordinates, and silences by contempt, alternative voices, oppositional values. By the end of the 1960s, Hoggart's influence at CCCS had waned, and he subsequently became more involved in cultural policy-making (he had already served on the Pilkington Broadcasting Committee and the Albemarle Committee on Youth Services) as Deputy-Director of UNESCO, and Vice-Chairman of the Arts Council of Great Britain. He returned to academic life as the Warden of Goldsmith's College, University of London at the end of the 1970s and remained there until his retirement. Recently, his series of autobiographical writings have given his work renewed popularity.

R.B.

The 'real' world of people: illustrations from popular art—*Peg's Paper*

This overriding interest in the close detail of the human condition is the first pointer to an understanding of working-class art. To begin with, working-class art is essentially a 'showing' (rather than an 'exploration'), a presentation of what is known already. It starts from the assumption that human life is fascinating in itself. It has to deal with recognisable human life, and has to begin with the photographic, however fantastic it may become; it has to be underpinned by a few simple but firm moral rules.

Here is the source of the attraction, the closely, minutely domestic attraction, of *Thompson's Weekly News*. It is this, more than a vicarious snobbery, which makes radio serials with middle-class settings popular with working-class people, since these serials reflect daily the minutiæ of everyday life. It is this which helps to ensure that the news-presentation of most popular newspapers belongs to the realms of imaginative or fictional writing of a low order. Those special favourites of working-class people, the Sunday gossip-with-sensation papers, the papers for the free day, assiduously collect from throughout the British Isles all the suitable material they can find, for the benefit of almost the whole of the adult working-class population. It is true that their interest, whether in news-reporting or in fiction, is often increased by the 'ooh-aah' element—a very 'ordinary' girl is knocked down by a man who proves to be a film-star; an attractive young widow proves to have disposed of two husbands with arsenic and popped them under the cellar-flagstones—and it is easy to think that most popular literature is of the 'ooh-aah' kind. One should think first of the photographically detailed aspect; the staple fare is not something which suggests an escape from ordinary life, but rather it assumes that ordinary life is intrinsically interesting. The emphasis is initially on the human and detailed, with or without the 'pepping-up' which crime or sex or splendour gives. De Rougemont speaks of millions (though he has in mind particularly the middle-classes) who 'breathe in . . . a romantic atmosphere in the haze of which passion seems to be the supreme test'. As we shall see, there is much in working-class literature too which gives support to this view; but it is not the first thing to say about the more genuinely working-class publications which persist. For them passion is no more interesting than steady home-life.

Some B.B.C. programmes underline the point. Notice how popular the 'homely' programmes are, not simply such programmes as *Family Favourites* ('for Good Neighbours') nor simply the family serials and feature-programmes such as *Mrs. Dale's Diary*, *The Archers*, *The Huggetts*, *The Davisons*, *The Grove Family*, *The Hargreaves*; but the really ordinary homely programmes, often composed, rather like the more old-fashioned papers, of a number of items linked only by the fact that they all deal with the ordinary lives of ordinary people. I have in mind programmes like Wilfred Pickles's *Have a Go* and Richard Dimbleby's *Down Your Way*. They have no particular shape; they do not set out to be 'art' or entertainment in the music-hall sense; they simply 'present the people to the people' and are enjoyed for that. So are the programmes which still make use of the music-hall 'comic's' tradition of handling working-class life, programmes like Norman Evans's *Over the Garden Wall* and Al Read's superb sketches. It is not necessary, for success, that the programme should be a form of professional art; if it is really homely and ordinary it will be interesting and popular.

I have suggested that it is commonly thought that some magazines—for example, those predominantly read by working-class women and usually spoken of as '*Peg's Paper* and all that'—provide little other than undiluted fantasy and sensation. This is not true; in some ways the more genuinely working-class magazines are preferable to those in the newer style. They are in some ways crude, but often more than that; they still have a felt sense of the texture of life in the group they cater for. I shall refer to them as 'the older magazines' because they carry on the *Peg's Paper* tradition, and reflect the older forms of working-class life: in fact, most of them, under their present titles, are between ten and twenty years old.

Almost all are produced by three large commercial organizations: Amalgamated

Press, the Newnes Group, and Thomson and Leng. But the authors and illustrators seem to have a close knowledge of the lives and attitudes of their audience. One wonders whether the publishers take in much of their material piece-meal from outside, rather as the stocking-makers of Nottingham once did. Most of the material is conventional—that is, it mirrors the attitudes of the readers; but those attitudes are by no means as ridiculous as one might at first be tempted to think. In comparison with these papers, some of those more recently in the front are as a smart young son with a quick brain and a bundle of up-to-date opinions beside his sentimental, superstitious and old-fashioned mother.

These older magazines can often be recognised by their paper, a roughly-textured newsprint which tends to have a smell—strongly evocative to me now, because it is also that of the old boys' magazines and comics—of something slightly damp and fungoid. They can be recognised also by their inner lay-out, in which only a few kinds of type are likely to be used; by their covers, which are usually 'flat' and boldly coloured in a limited range—almost entirely of black with strong shades of blue, red and yellow, with few intermediates. They usually sell at threepence each, and have such titles as *Secrets*, *Red Star Weekly*, *Lucky Star* (which now incorporates *Peg's Paper*), *The Miracle*, *The Oracle*, *Glamour*, *Red Letter* and *Silver Star*. They are apparently designed for adolescent girls and young married women in particular; thus, two in three of the readers of *Red Letter* are under thirty-five. There is some provision for older readers. The number of their readers varies between one-third and three-quarters of a million each, with most of them above the half-million. There will be much overlapping, but the total number of readers remains considerable, and they are almost entirely from the working-classes.

In composition they are all much alike. There are many advertisements, scattered throughout in penny packets, on the back cover and over large parts of the last couple of text-pages; there are usually no advertisements on the front cover pages and first text-pages. After the coloured cover, the inner cover page is generally given to some regular editorial feature; or the main serial, or the week's 'dramatic long complete novel', begins there. The advertisements, regularly recurring throughout the whole group of magazines, cover a narrow range of goods. Some cosmetics still use an aristocratic appeal, with photographs of titled ladies dressed for a ball. The same ailments appear so often in the advertisements for proprietary remedies that a hasty generaliser might conclude from them that the British working-classes are congenitally both constipated and 'nervy'. There are many announcements of cures for disabilities which are likely to make a girl a 'wall-flower'. The 'scientists tell us' approach is there, but so still is its forerunner, the 'gypsy told me' approach. Thus, there are occasionally esoteric Indian remedies in this manner—'Mrs. Johnson learned this secret many years ago from her Indian nurse in Bombay. Since then, many thousands have had cause to be glad that they reposed confidence in her system.' For married women there are washing-powder advertisements, and those for headache powders or California Syrup of Figs for children. But, in general, the assumption is that the married women readers are young enough to want to keep up with the unmarried by the use of cosmetics and hair-shampoos. Mail-order firms advertise fancy wedge-shoes, nylon underwear for—I suppose—the younger women, and corsets for the older. For all groups, but especially, it appears, for the youngish

157

married women with little spare money, there are large advertisements (much the biggest in these magazines) inviting them to become agents for one of the great Clothing or General Credit Clubs which proliferate, chiefly from the Manchester area, and usually give their agents two shillings in the pound, a fat catalogue and free notepaper.

Stories make up the body of the text-pages, but interspersed are the regular and occasional features. There are no politics, no social questions, nothing about the arts. This is neither the world of the popular newspapers which still purport to be alive to events, nor that of those women's magazines which have an occasional flutter with 'culture'. There are beauty hints, often over the signature of a well-known film-star: and some very homely home hints; there is a half-page of advice from an 'aunt' or a nurse on personal problems—the kind of thing laughed at as 'Auntie Maggie's advice'; in fact, it is usually very sensible. I do not mean, though this is true, that there is never a breath which is not firmly moral. But the general run of the advice is practical and sound, and when a problem arises whose answer is beyond the competence of the journalist, the enquirer is told to go to a doctor or to one of the advisory associations. There is a fortune-teller's section, based on the stars or birthday dates.

The stories divide easily into the serials, the long complete story of the week and the short stories (probably only one page in length). The long stories and the serials often have startling surprises, as a young man proves to be really wealthy or a girl finds she wins a beauty competition, even though she has always thought of herself as a plain Jane. This is particularly the case with the serials, which must be 'dramatic' and mount their accumulated series of suspended shocks as week follows week. So they tend to deal in what are called wild passions and in murder. There are handsome men on the loose, usually called Rafe. But much more interesting, because much more obviously feared, are the 'fascinating bitches', the Jezebels, as most advance trailers dub them. These are the women who set up in provincial towns and fail to report that they have a 'dreadful past' or that a 'dreadful secret' lies in their previous home a hundred miles away; or they get rid of pretty young girls by whom the man they are after is really attracted, by tipping them overboard from a rowing-boat, trussed in a cabin-trunk; or they convert an electric-kettle into a lethal weapon: 'She did not look evil—yet her presence was like a curse'—'She was a woman fashioned by the Devil himself into the mould of the fairest of angels.'

The strong case against this kind of literature is well known, and I do not mean to take that case lightly. It applies, one should remember, to popular literature for all classes. When one has said that some of these stories supply the thrill of the wicked or evil, can one go farther? Can one distinguish them from the general run of this kind of popular writing? Denis de Rougemont points out that this type of story, especially when it is written for the middle-classes, usually manages to have things both ways, that though the villains never triumph in fact, they do triumph emotionally; that where, for instance, adulterous love is the subject, these stories imply an emotional betrayal. They 'hold the chains of love to be indefeasible and [imply] the superiority from a "spiritual" standpoint of mistress over wife'. 'Therefore', M. de Rougemont continues, 'the institution of marriage comes off rather badly, but that does not matter . . . since the middle-class (especially on the Continent) is well aware that this institution is no longer grounded in morality or religion, but rests securely upon financial foundations.' M. de Rougemont also emphasises the fascination of the love/death theme, of an adulterous love-relationship which can find some sort of resolution only in death.

There seems to me a difference between this and most of the 'thrilling' stories in these 'older' magazines. There seems to be little emotional betrayal of the explicit assumptions here; the thrill comes because the villain is striking—'making passes at'—some things still felt underneath to be important, at a sense of the goodness of home and married life, above individual relations of passion. Thus there is no use of the love/death theme, since that would be to kill altogether the positive and actual home/marriage theme. The villain, inviting an adulterous relationship, seems to be found interesting less because he offers a vicarious enjoyment of a relationship which, though forbidden, is desired, as because he makes a shocking attack on what is felt to count greatly. He is a kind of bogy-man rather than a disguised hero. He does not usually triumph emotionally in the way he does in that more sophisticated literature which I take M. de Rougemont to be describing; this is, in fact, an extremely uncomplicated kind of literature.

These stories differ yet more obviously from many later versions of the sex-and-violence tale, from the kind of tale which is serialised in some of the Sunday papers. In those the author tries—while the rape or violence is being committed—to give a mild thrill and then laps the whole in hollow moral triteness. They are even further from the two-shilling sex-and-violence novelettes. They have no sexual excitement at all, and no description aiming to arouse it; and this, I think, is not only because women are not usually as responsive as men to that kind of stimulus, but because the stories belong to different worlds. These stories from the working-class women's magazines belong neither to the middle-class world, nor to that of the more modern Sunday papers, nor to that of the later novelettes, nor, even less, to an environment in which illicit relations can be spoken of as 'good fun', as 'smart' or 'progressive'. If a girl does lose her virginity here, or a wife commit adultery, you hear, 'And so that night I fell,' or 'I committed the great sin': and though a startled thrill is evident there, you feel that the sense of a fall and a sin is real also.

The strongest impression, after one has read a lot of these stories, is of their extraordinary fidelity to the detail of the readers' lives. The short stories take up as much space as the serial or long story, and they seem to be mainly faithful transcripts of minor incidents, amusing or worrying, from ordinary life. The serials may erupt into the startlingly posh world of what are still called 'the stately homes of England', or present a Rajah or a Sheik: but often the world is that the readers live in, with a considerable accuracy in its particulars. A fair proportion of the crime is of that world too—the distress when Mrs. Thompson is suspected of shoplifting, and so on. I open *Silver Star*: on the inner front cover the complete long novel, *Letters of Shame*, begins:

> As Stella Kaye unlatched the gate of number 15, the front door opened and her mother beckoned agitatedly.
> 'Whatever's made you so late?' she whispered. 'Did you remember the sausages? Oh, good girl!'
> Stella looked at her mother's flushed face and best flowered apron.
> Visitors! Just when she was bursting to spring her news on them all! It would have to keep.

159

A typical copy of *Secrets* has as its week's verse, 'Mother's Night Out', about the weekly visit by Father and Mother to the pictures: 'It's Monday night and at No. 3, Mother and Dad are hurrying tea. In fact, poor Dad has scarcely done before Mother's urging, "Fred, come on!" '

A short story at the back of the *Oracle*, 'Hero's Homecoming', opens: 'Most of the women who dealt at the little general store on the corner of Roper's Road were rather tired of hearing about Mrs. Bolsom's boy, but they couldn't very well tell her so because she was so obliging and so handy to run to at times of emergency.' A typical *Lucky Star* one-page story starts: 'Lilian West glanced at the clock on the kitchen wall. "My goodness," she thought. "How quickly I get through the housework these days!" ' It goes on to tell how, after deciding to leave her married children alone so as not to be thought a nuisance, she found fresh happiness in realising how much she was still needed. 'Mary was an ordinary girl doing an ordinary job in a factory,' another story begins, and incidentally epitomises the points of departure for almost all of them.

The illustrations help to create the same atmosphere. Some of the newer magazines specialise in photographic illustrations of the candid camera kind. The 'older' ones still use black-and-white drawings in an unsophisticated style. There exist, particularly in more modern publications, black-and-white line drawings which are very sophisticated: compared with them the cartoons still to be found in some provincial newspapers, drawn by a local man, belong to thirty years ago. So it is with most of the drawings here (the main illustration to the serial or the long complete novel is sometimes an exception); they are not smart in their manner, and their detail is almost entirely unromanticised. The girls are usually pretty (unless the burden is that even a plain girl can find a good husband), but they are pretty in an unglamorous way, in the way working-class girls are often very pretty. They wear blouses and jumpers with skirts, or their one dance-dress. The factory chimney can be seen sticking up in one corner and the street of houses with intermittent lamp-posts stretches behind; there are the buses and the bikes and the local dance-halls and the cinemas.

Such a nearness to the detail of the lives of readers might be simply the prelude to an excursion into a wish-fulfilment story about the surprising things that can happen to someone from that world. Sometimes this is so, and there is occasionally a stepping-up of the social level inside the stories, so that people can feel how nice it would be to be a member of the villa or good-class housing groups. But often what happens is what might happen to anyone, and the environment is that of most readers.

If we look more closely at the stories, we are reminded at once of the case against 'stock responses': every reaction has its fixed counter for presentation. I run through the account of a trial: the mouths are 'set', the faces 'tense with excitement'; tremors run down spines; the hero exhibits 'iron control' and faces his captors with a 'stony look'; his watching girl-friend is the victim of an 'agonised heart' as 'suspense thickens in the air'. But what does this indicate? That the writers use cliché, and that the audience seems to want cliché, that they are not exploring experience, realising experience through language? That is true. But these are first, I repeat, statements; picture presentations of the known. A reader of them is hardly likely to tackle anything that could be called serious literature; but there are worse diets, especially today. If we regard them as faithful but dramatised presentations of a life whose form and values are known, we might find it more useful to ask what are the values they embody. There is no virtue in merely laughing at them: we need to appreciate first that they may in all their triteness speak for a solid and relevant way of life. So may the tritest of Christmas and Birthday card verses; that is why those cards are chosen with great care, usually for the 'luvliness' and 'rightness' of their verse. The world these stories present is a limited and simple one, based on a few accepted and long-held values. It is often a childish and garish world, and the springs of the emotions work in great gushings. But they do work; it is not a corrupt or a pretentious world. It uses boldly words which serious writers for more sophisticated audiences understandably find difficulty in using today, and which many other writers are too knowing to be caught using. It uses, as I noted in another connection, words like 'sin', 'shame', 'guilt', 'evil', with every appearance of meaningfulness. It accepts completely, has as its main point of reference, the notion that marriage and a home, founded on love, fidelity and cheerfulness, are the right purpose of a woman's life. If a girl 'sins' the suggestion is—and this reinforces what I said earlier about the ethical emphasis in working-class beliefs—not that the girl has 'sinned against herself', as another range of writers would put it, or that she has fallen short in some relationship other than the human and social, but that she has spoiled her chances of a decent home and family. One of the commoner endings to this kind of serial is for the girl either to find again the man responsible, and marry him, or to find another man who, though he knows all, is prepared to marry her and be a father to the child, loving them both. One can appreciate the force of the mistrust of 'the other woman', the Jezebel, the home-breaker, the woman who sets out to wreck an existing marriage or one just about to start. Even the man with a roving eye gets short shrift if he goes in for marriage-breaking; before that he comes under dispensations more indulgent than those accorded to women on the loose.

It is against this ground-pattern that the thrills throw their bold reliefs, and to which they are indissolubly bound. I do not think that the thrills tempt the readers to imitate them, or much to dream of them in a sickly way. They bear the same relation to their lives as the kite to the solid flat common from which it is flown. The ground-pattern of ordinary life weaves its strands in and out through the serials and the short stories, in all the magazines. It is the pattern of the main assumptions:

> Don't spoil today because some friend has left you; you cannot say of ALL God has bereft you. Life is too brief for anger or for sorrow . . .

or:

> Happiness is made up
> Of a million tiny things
> That often pass unnoticed . . .

In its outlook, this is still substantially the world of Mrs. Henry Wood (*East Lynne*; *Danesbury House*; *Mrs. Halliburton's Troubles*), of Florence L. Barclay (one million copies of *The Rosary* sold), of Marie Corelli (*The Sorrows of Satan*—a 'classic' to my aunts), of Silas K. Hocking (*Ivy*; *Her Benny*; *His Father*), of Annie S. Swan (*A Divided House*), or Ruth Lamb (*A Wilful Ward*; *Not Quite a Lady*; *Only a Girl Wife*; *Thoughtful Joe and How He Gained His Name*), and of a great number of others, often

161

published by the Religious Tract Society and given as prizes in the upper classes of Sunday schools. It is being ousted now by the world of the newer kind of magazine. I wonder, incidentally, whether it is resisting longer in Scotland: a very plain but attractive threepenny weekly, *People's Friend*, is still published there; a similar magazine, the *Weekly Telegraph* from Sheffield, died only a few years ago, I believe. Some of the 'older' magazines are trying to preserve themselves by producing the glamour of the newer magazines, often linked to an inflated form of the older thrills. Tense and gripping new serials are announced on the placards, with large illustrations compounded of the old-style ordinariness and the new-style close-up.

But a few of the newer kind of magazines continue to increase their already phenomenal circulations. In many ways they embody the same attitudes as the 'older' magazines, though they aim at too large an audience to be able to identify themselves with one social class. They are considerably smarter in presentation and presumably can provide more specialised articles on home problems than the 'older' magazines. There are crudities in the 'older' magazines whose removal ought not to be regretted. I have not stressed these qualities because I have been concerned to show the better links with working-class life. But the smartness of the newer magazines often extends, it seems to me, to their attitudes, and the change is not always for the good. The smartness easily becomes a slickness; there is an emphasis on money-prestige (—figures of salaries or winnings are given in brackets after the names of people in the news), much 'fascinated' attention is given to public personalities such as the gay wives of industrial magnates, or radio and film-stars; there is a kittenish domesticity and a manner predominantly arch or whimsical.

The 'glossies' are aiming, successfully, to attract the younger women who want to be smart and up to date, who do not like to seem old-fashioned. The 'older' magazines would perhaps like to catch up with the 'glossies', but that would be very costly; and there is still presumably a large enough audience for them to be profitably produced in much their old form. When that ceases to be the case they will, I suppose, either make really radical changes in the direction indicated by the 'glossies', or die.

Raymond Williams (1921–1988)

Industrialization and democratization, Williams argues in *Culture and Society* (1958) were the key processes which led to the focus on the idea of culture as a response to revolutionary social change. Written consciously in a tradition—*Culture and Anarchy, Culture and Environment*—which sees culture as the primary (privileged) site for the transformation of 'social being', the book begins with the response of the Romantic movement to industrialization and ends with a brief study of Orwell. *Culture and Society* is the first major text in Williams's monumental contribution to cultural studies which includes *The Long Revolution* (1961), *The Country and the City* (1973), *Television: Technology and Cultural Form* (1974), *Keywords* (1976; 1983), *Marxism and Literature* (1977), *Politics and Letters* (1979), *Problems in Materialism and Culture* (1980), *Culture* (1981), *Towards 2000* (1983), *Writing in Society* (1984). There have been at least three posthumously published volumes since his death in January, 1988.

The impetus for *Culture and Society* lay in the publication of T. S. Eliot's *Notes towards the Definition of Culture* (1948) which led Williams to trace, in an adult education class, the idea of culture through the study of a number of writers, all contemporary apart from Matthew Arnold. He was motivated to write the book as a way of countering a long line of thinking about culture from reactionary perspectives, especially to refute what he perceived as a growing contemporary use of the concept of culture against democracy, socialism, the working class and popular education.

Williams describes the context in which he wrote *Culture and Society*, 'a time when my separation from the possibilities of political action and collaboration were virtually complete. There was a breakdown of any collective project that I could perceive, political, cultural, or literary' (*Politics and Letters*, 102). Given the high premium placed on collaborative and collective work in cultural studies this is a telling comment. When the book was finished Williams became involved with a range of political activities, including CND, writing for *Tribune*, contributing to the 'Left-Labour' collection of essays, *Conviction* (1958), and, in 1961, joining the

Labour Party (although not a member, he had worked full-time for it at a by-election in 1939 and in the 1950 and 1955 elections). All of these social movements used his intellectual work together with the ideas of a number of others, to generate a level of cultural debate in political organizations which has rarely been matched since.

Williams's essay in *Conviction*, 'Culture is Ordinary', needs to be read alongside the Conclusion re-printed here, with its arguments for community and a common culture, as it combines his cultural criticism with a clear political commitment. In the essay he argues that the making of a society is 'the finding of common meanings and directions, and its growth is an active debate and amendment under the pressures of experience, contact, and discovery, writing themselves into the land'. There is also the important, and much quoted, formulation: 'There are in fact no masses, but only ways of seeing people as masses.' Both the *Conviction* essay and the Conclusion seek to sustain the idea of a democratic culture and a popular education against the new commercial culture, and to establish an idea of value which is not merely elitist or which automatically demeans anything of a working class or popular 'belonging'. In both pieces, Williams is writing explicitly as a 'socialist intellectual'.
R.B.

Conclusion to *Culture and Society 1780–1950*

The history of the idea of culture is a record of our reactions, in thought and feeling, to the changed conditions of our common life. Our meaning of culture is a response to the events which our meanings of industry and democracy most evidently define. But the conditions were created and have been modified by men. Record of the events lies elsewhere, in our general history. The history of the idea of culture is a record of our meanings and our definitions, but these, in turn, are only to be understood within the context of our actions.

The idea of culture is a general reaction to a general and major change in the conditions of our common life. Its basic element is its effort at total qualitative assessment. The change in the whole form of our common life produced, as a necessary reaction, an emphasis on attention to this whole form. Particular change will modify an habitual discipline, shift an habitual action. General change, when it has worked itself clear, drives us back on our general designs, which we have to learn to look at again, and as a whole. The working-out of the idea of culture is a slow reach again for control.

Yet the new conditions, which men have been striving to understand, were neither uniform nor static. On the contrary, they have, from the beginning, contained extreme diversity of situation, in a high and moving tension. The idea of culture describes our common inquiry, but our conclusions are diverse, as our starting points were diverse. The word, culture, cannot automatically be pressed into service as any kind of social or personal directive. Its emergence, in its modern meanings, marks the effort at total qualitative assessment, but what it indicates is a process, not a conclusion. The arguments which can be grouped under its heading do not point to any inevitable action or affiliation. They define, in a common field, approaches and conclusions. It is left to us to decide which, if any, we shall take up, that will not turn in our hands.

In each of the three major issues, those of Industry, of Democracy and of Art, there have been three main phases of opinion. In industry, there was the first rejection, alike of machine-production and of the social relations embodied in the factory system. This was succeeded by a phase of growing sentiment against the machine as such, in isolation. Thirdly, in our own period, machine production came to be accepted, and major emphasis transferred to the problem of social relations within an industrial system of production.

In the question of democracy, the first phase was one of concern at the threat to minority values with the coming of popular supremacy: a concern which was emphasized by general suspicion of the power of the new masses. This, in turn, was succeeded by a quite different tendency, in which emphasis fell on the idea of community, of organic society, as against the dominant individualistic ethic and practice. Thirdly, in our own century, the fears of the first phase were strongly renewed, in the particular context of what came to be called mass democracy in the new world of mass communications.

In the question of art, the first emphasis fell, not only on the independent value of art, but on the importance to the common life of the qualities which it embodied. The contingent element of defiant exile passed into the second phase, in which the stress fell on art as a value in itself, with at times an open separation of this value from common life. Thirdly, emphasis came to be placed on a deliberate effort towards the reintegration of art with the common life of society: an effort which centred around the word 'communication'.

In these three questions I have listed the phases of opinion in the order in which they appeared, but of course opinion is persistent, and whether in relation to industry, to democracy or to art, each of the three phases could easily be represented from the opinions of our own day. Yet it is possible in retrospect to see three main periods, within each of which a distinct emphasis is paramount. In the first period, from about 1790 to 1870, we find the long effort to compose a general attitude towards the new forces of industrialism and democracy; it is in this period that the major analysis is undertaken and the major opinions and descriptions emerge. Then, from about 1870 to 1914, there is a breaking-down into narrower fronts, marked by a particular specialism in attitudes to art, and, in the general field, by a preoccupation with direct politics. After 1914 these definitions continue, but there is a growing preoccupation, approaching a climax after 1945, with the issues raised not only by the inherited problems but by new problems arising from the development of mass media of communication and the general growth of large-scale organizations.

A great deal of what has been written in each of these three periods retains its relevance and importance. In particular, it is impossible to over-emphasize our debt to the first great critical period which gave us, in relation to these problems, the greater part of our language and manner of approach. From all the periods, indeed, certain decisive statements stand. Yet even as we learn, we realize that the world we see through such eyes is not, although it resembles, our world. What we receive from the tradition is a set of meanings, but not all of these will hold their significance if, as we must, we return them to immediate experience.

[. . .]

It is important to remember that, in judging a culture, it is not enough to concentrate on habits which coincide with those of the observer. To the highly literate observer there is always a temptation to assume that reading plays as large a part in the lives of most people as it does in his own. But if he compares his own kind of reading with the reading-matter that is most widely distributed, he is not really comparing levels of culture. He is, in fact, comparing what is produced for people to whom reading is a major activity with that produced for people to whom it is, at best, a minor. To the degree that he acquires a substantial proportion of his ideas and feelings from what he reads he will assume, again wrongly, that the ideas and feelings of the majority will be similarly conditioned. But, for good or ill, the majority of people do not yet give reading this importance in their lives; their ideas and feelings are, to a large extent, still moulded by a wider and more complex pattern of social and family life. There is an evident danger of delusion, to the highly literate person, if he supposes that he can judge the quality of general living by primary reference to the reading artifacts. He will, in particular, be driven to this delusion if he retains, even in its most benevolent form, the concept of the majority of other people as 'masses', whom he observes as a kind of block. The error resembles that of the narrow reformer who supposes that farm labourers and village craftsmen were once uneducated, merely because they could not read. Many highly educated people have, in fact, been so driven in on their reading, as a stabilizing habit, that they fail to notice that there are other forms of skilled, intelligent, creative activity: not only the cognate forms of theatre, concert and picture-gallery; but a whole range of general skills, from gardening, metalwork and carpentry to active politics. The contempt for many of these activities, which is always latent in the highly literate, is a mark of the observers' limits, not those of the activities themselves. Neglect of the extraordinary popularity of many of these activities, as evidence of the quality of living in contemporary society, is the result of partisan selection for the reasons given.

This point comes to be of particular importance when we remember that the general tendency of modern development has been to bring many more levels of culture within the general context of literacy than was ever previously the case. A number of tastes which would formerly have been gratified in pre-literate and therefore largely unrecorded ways are now catered for and even fostered in print. Or, to put it in another way, the historical counterpart of a modern popular newspaper, in its informing function, is not an earlier minority newspaper, but that complex of rumour and travellers' tales which then served the majority with news of a kind. This is not to surrender the finest literacy we have, which at all times offers a standard for the newly literate functions. But, equally, to look at the matter in this way helps us to keep a just sense of proportion.

Our problem is one of adapting our social training to a widely literate culture. It is clear that the highest standards of literacy in contemporary society depend on a level of instruction and training far above that which is commonly available. For this reason it is still much too early to conclude that a majority culture is necessarily low in taste. The danger of such a judgement is that it offers a substitute righteousness—

the duty of defending a standard against the mob. Right action is not of this kind, but is a matter of ensuring that the technical changes which have made our culture more dependent on literate forms are matched by a proportionate increase in training for literacy in its full sense. It is obvious that we have allowed the technical changes to keep far ahead of the educational changes, and the reasons for this neglect, which in its own terms is so plainly foolish, lie in a combination of interest and inertia, deeply rooted in the organization of society.

[. . .]

Such a view might settle the matter if we could be sure that our only problem was to ensure that educational provision matched the extension of literacy. A generation of work would lie ahead of us, but the path at least would be clear. Yet evidently such questions are not settled within a specialized field. The content of education, as a rule, is the content of our actual social relations, and will only change as part of a wider change. Further, the actual operation of the new techniques is extremely complicated, in social terms, because of their economic bearings. The technical changes made necessary a great increase in the amount and concentration of capital, and we are still on the upward curve of this increase, as is most evident in the management of newspapers and television. These facts have led, in our society, to an extreme concentration of production of work of this kind, and to extraordinary needs and opportunities for controlling its distribution. Our new services tend to require so much capital that only a very large audience can sustain them. This in itself is not a difficulty; the potential audience is there. But everything depends on the attitude of those who control these services to such an audience. Our broadcasting corporation, for example, holds, in general, a reasonable interpretation of its particular responsibilities in this situation, even if this is no more surely founded than in a vestigial paternalism. Yet we are constantly being made aware how precarious this interpretation must be, under the pressures which come from a different attitude. The scale of capital involved has given an entry to a kind of person who, a hundred years ago, would never have thought of running a newspaper or a theatre. The opportunity to exploit the difficulties of a transitional culture was open, and we have been foolish enough to allow it to be widely taken. The temptation to make a profit out of ignorance or inexperience is present in most societies. The existence, in our own, of powerful media of persuasion and suggestion made it virtually irresistible.

[. . .]

Culture and which way of life?

We live in a transitional society, and the idea of culture, too often, has been identified with one or other of the forces which the transition contains. Culture is the product of the old leisured classes who seek now to defend it against new and destructive forces. Culture is the inheritance of the new rising class, which contains the humanity of the future; this class seeks, now, to free it from its restrictions. We say things like this to each other, and glower. The one good thing, it seems, is that all the contending parties are keen enough on culture to want to be identified with it. But then, we are none of us referees in this; we are all in the game, and playing in one or other direction.

I want to say something about the idea of 'working-class culture', because this seems to me to be a key issue in our own time, and one in which there is a considerable element of misunderstanding. I have indicated already that we cannot fairly or usefully describe the bulk of the material produced by the new means of communication as 'working-class culture'. For neither is it by any means produced exclusively for this class, nor, in any important degree, is it produced by them. To this negative definition we must add another: that 'working-class culture', in our society, is not to be understood as the small amount of 'proletarian' writing and art which exists. The appearance of such work has been useful, not only in its more self-conscious forms, but also in such material as the post-Industrial ballads, which were worth collecting. We need to be aware of this work, but it is to be seen as a valuable dissident element rather than as a culture. The traditional popular culture of England was, if not annihilated, at least fragmented and weakened by the dislocations of the Industrial Revolution. What is left, with what in the new conditions has been newly made, is small in quantity and narrow in range. It exacts respect, but it is in no sense an alternative culture.

This very point of an alternative is extremely difficult, in terms of theory. If the major part of our culture, in the sense of intellectual and imaginative work, is to be called, as the Marxists call it, bourgeois, it is natural to look for an alternative culture, and to call it proletarian. Yet it is very doubtful whether 'bourgeois culture' is a useful term. The body of intellectual and imaginative work which each generation receives as its traditional culture is always, and necessarily, something more than the product of a single class. It is not only that a considerable part of it will have survived from much earlier periods than the immediately pre-existing form of society; so that, for instance, literature, philosophy and other work surviving from before, say, 1600, cannot be taken as 'bourgeois'. It is also that, even within a society in which a particular class is dominant, it is evidently possible both for members of other classes to contribute to the common stock, and for such contributions to be unaffected by or in opposition to the ideas and values of the dominant class. The area of a culture, it would seem, is usually proportionate to the area of a language rather than to the area of a class. It is true that a dominant class can to a large extent control the transmission and distribution of the whole common inheritance; such control, where it exists, needs to be noted as a fact about that class. It is true also that a tradition is always selective, and that there will always be a tendency for this process of selection to be related to and even governed by the interests of the class that is dominant. These factors make it likely that there will be qualitative changes in the traditional culture when there is a shift of class power, even before a newly ascendant class makes its own contributions. Points of this kind need to be stressed, but the particular stress given by describing our existent culture as bourgeois culture is in several ways misleading. It can, for example, seriously mislead those who would now consider themselves as belonging to the dominant class. If they are encouraged, even by their opponents, to think of the existing culture (in the narrow sense) as their particular product and legacy, they will deceive themselves and others. For they will be encouraged to argue that, if their class position goes, the culture goes too; that standards depend on the restriction of a culture to the class which, since it has produced it, alone understands it. On the other hand, those who believe themselves to be representatives of a new rising class will, if they accept the proposition of 'bourgeois culture', either be tempted to neglect a common human inheritance, or, more intelligently, be perplexed as to how, and how much of, this bourgeois culture is to be taken over. The categories are crude and mechanical in either position. Men who share a common language share the inheritance of an intellectual and literary tradition which is necessarily and constantly revalued with every shift in experience. The manufacture of an artificial 'working-class culture', in opposition to this common tradition, is merely foolish. A society in which the working class had become dominant would, of course, produce new valuations and new contributions. But the process would be extremely complex, because of the complexity of the inheritance, and nothing is now to be gained by diminishing this complexity to a crude diagram.

[. . .]

The most difficult task confronting us, in any period where there is a marked shift of social power, is the complicated process of revaluation of the inherited tradition. The common language, because in itself it is so crucial to this matter, provides an excellent instance. It is clearly of vital importance to a culture that its common language should not decline in strength, richness and flexibility; that it should, further, be adequate to express new experience, and to clarify change. But a language like English is still evolving, and great harm can be done to it by the imposition of crude categories of class. It is obvious that since the development, in the nineteenth century, of the new definition of 'standard English', particular uses of the common language have been taken and abused for the purposes of class distinction. Yet the dialect which is normally equated with standard English has no necessary superiority over other dialects. Certain of the grammatical clarifications have a common importance, but not all even of these. On the other hand, certain selected sounds have been given a cardinal authority which derives from no known law of language, but simply from the fact that they are habitually made by persons who, for other reasons, possess social and economic influence. The conversion of this kind of arbitrary selection into a criterion of 'good' or 'correct' or 'pure' English is merely a subterfuge. Modern communications make for the growth of uniformity, but the necessary selection and clarification have been conducted, on the whole, on grounds quite irrelevant to language. It is still thought, for instance, that a double negative ('I don't want none') is *incorrect* English, although millions of English-speaking persons use it regularly: not, indeed, as a misunderstanding of the rule, which they might be thought too ignorant to apprehend; but as the continuation of a habit which has been in the language continuously since Chaucer. The broad 'a', in such words as 'class', is now taken as the mark of an 'educated person', although till the eighteenth century it was mainly a rustic habit, and as such despised. Or 'ain't', which in the eighteenth century was often a mark of breeding, is now supposed to be a mark of vulgarity: in both cases, the valuation is the merest chance. The extraordinary smugness about aspirates, vowel-sounds, the choice of this or that synonym ('couch' 'sofa'), which has for so long been a normal element of middle-class humour, is, after all, not a concern for good English, but parochialism. (The current controversy about what are called 'U' and 'non-U' speech habits clearly illustrates this; it is an aspect, not of major social differences, but of the long difficulty of drawing the lines between the upper and lower sections of the *middle* class.) Yet, while this is true, the matter is complicated by the fact that in a society where a particular class and hence a particular use of the common language is dominant a large part of the literature, carrying as it does a body of vital common experience, will be attracted to the dominant language mode. At the same time, a national literature, as English has never ceased to be, will, while containing this relation, contain also elements of the whole culture and language. If we are to understand the process of a selective tradition, we shall not think of exclusive areas of culture but of degrees of shifting attachment and interaction, which a crude theory either of class or of standards is incompetent to interpret.

[. . .]

We may now see what is properly meant by 'working-class culture'. It is not proletarian art, or council houses, or a particular use of language; it is, rather, the basic collective idea, and the institutions, manners, habits of thought and intentions which proceed from this. Bourgeois culture, similarly, is the basic individualist idea and the institutions, manners, habits of thought and intentions which proceed from that. In our culture as a whole, there is both a constant interaction between these ways of life and an area which can properly be described as common to or underlying both. The working class, because of its position, has not, since the Industrial Revolution, produced a culture in the narrower sense. The culture which it has produced, and which it is important to recognize, is the collective democratic institution, whether in the trade unions, the cooperative movement or a political party. Working-class culture, in the stage through which it has been passing, is primarily social (in that it has created institutions) rather than individual (in particular intellectual or imaginative work). When it is considered in context, it can be seen as a very remarkable creative achievement.

[. . .]

The idea of community

The development of the idea of culture has, throughout, been a criticism of what has been called the bourgeois idea of society. The contributors to its meaning have started from widely different positions, and have reached widely various attachments and loyalties. But they have been alike in this, that they have been unable to think of society as a merely neutral area, or as an abstract regulating mechanism. The stress has fallen on the positive function of society, on the fact that the values of individual men are rooted in society, and on the need to think and feel in these common terms. This was, indeed, a profound and necessary response to the disintegrating pressures which were faced.

Yet, according to their different positions, the idea of community, on which all in general agree, has been differently felt and defined. In our own day we have two major interpretations, alike opposed to bourgeois liberalism, but equally, in practice, opposed to each other. These are the idea of service, and the idea of solidarity. These have in the main been developed by the middle class and the working class respectively. From Coleridge to Tawney the idea of function, and thence of service to the community, has been most valuably stressed, in opposition to the individualist claim. The stress has been confirmed by the generations of training which substantiate the ethical practice of our professions, and of our public and civil service. As against the practice of *laissez-faire*, and of self-service, this has been a major achievement which has done much for the peace and welfare of our society. Yet the working-class ethic, of solidarity, has also been a major achievement, and it is the difference of this from the idea of service which must now be stressed.

[...]

How we are Governed, as an explanation of democracy, is an expression of the idea of service at its psychological limit. The break through to 'How we govern ourselves' is impossible, on the basis of such a training: the command to conformity, and to respect for authority as such, is too strong. Of course, having worked for improvement in the conditions of working people, in the spirit of service, those who are ruled by the idea of service are genuinely dismayed when the workers do not fully respond: when, as it is put, they don't play the game, are lacking in team-spirit, neglect the national interest. This has been a crisis of conscience for many middle-class democrats and socialists. Yet the fact is that working-class people cannot feel that this *is* their community in anything like the sense in which it is felt above them. Nor will education in their responsibilities to a community thus conceived convince them. The idea of service breaks down because while the upper servants have been able to identify themselves with the establishment, the lower servants have not. What 'they' decide is still the practical experience of life and work.

The idea of service, ultimately, is no substitute for the idea of active mutual responsibility, which is the other version of community. Few men can give the best of themselves as servants; it is the reduction of man to a function. Further, the servant, if he is to be a good servant, can never really question the order of things; his sense of authority is too strong. Yet the existing order is in fact subject to almost overwhelming pressures. The break through, into what together we want to make of our lives, will need qualities which the idea of service not only fails to provide, but, in its limitation of our minds, actively harms.

[...]

The development of a common culture

In its definition of the common interest as true self-interest, in its finding of individual verification primarily in the community, the idea of solidarity is potentially the real basis of a society. Yet it is subject, in our time, to two important difficulties. For it has been, basically, a defensive attitude, the natural mentality of the long siege. It has in part depended, that is to say, on an enemy; the negative elements thus produced will have to be converted into positives in a fully democratic society. This will at best be profoundly difficult, for the feelings involved are fundamental.

The issue can be defined as one in which diversity has to be substantiated within an effective community which disposes of majority power. The feeling of solidarity is, although necessary, a primitive feeling. It has depended, hitherto, on substantial identity of conditions and experience. Yet any predictable civilization will depend on a wide variety of highly specialized skills, which will involve, over definite parts of the culture, a fragmentation of experience. The attachment of privilege to certain kinds of skill has been traditionally clear, and this will be very difficult to unlearn, to the degree that is necessary if substantial community of condition is to be assured. A culture in common, in our own day, will not be the simple all-in-all society of old dreams. It will be a very complex organization, requiring continual adjustment and redrawing. At root, the feeling of solidarity is the only conceivable element of stabilization in so difficult an organization. But in its issue it will have to be continually redefined, and there will be many attempts to enlist old feelings in the service of an emerging sectional interest. The emphasis that I wish to place here is that this first difficulty—the compatibility of increasing specialization with a genuinely common culture—is only soluble in a context of material community and by the full democratic process.

[. . .]

No community, no culture, can ever be fully conscious of itself, ever fully know itself. The growth of consciousness is usually uneven, individual and tentative in nature. An emphasis of solidarity which, by intention or by accident, stifles or weakens such growth may, evidently, bring a deep common harm. It is necessary to make room for, not only variation, but even dissidence, within the common loyalty. Yet it is difficult to feel that, even in the English working-class movement, with its long democratic tradition, this need has been clearly and practically recognized.

A culture, while it is being lived, is always in part unknown, in part unrealized. The making of a community is always an exploration, for consciousness cannot precede creation, and there is no formula for unknown experience. A good community, a living culture, will, because of this, not only make room for but actively encourage all and any who can contribute to the advance in consciousness which is the common need. Wherever we have started from, we need to listen to others who started from a different position. We need to consider every attachment, every value, with our whole attention; for we do not know the future, we can never be certain of what may enrich it; we can only, now, listen to and consider whatever may be offered and take up what we can.

[. . .]

We have to plan what can be planned, according to our common decision. But the emphasis of the idea of culture is right when it reminds us that a culture, essentially, is unplannable. We have to ensure the means of life, and the means of community. But what will then, by these means, be lived, we cannot know or say. The idea of culture rests on a metaphor: the tending of natural growth. And indeed it is on growth, as metaphor and as fact, that the ultimate emphasis must be placed. Here, finally, is the area where we have most need to reinterpret.

[. . .]

172

The forces which have changed and are still changing our world are indeed industry and democracy. Understanding of this change, this long revolution, lies at a level of meaning which it is not easy to reach. We can in retrospect see the dominative mood as one of the mainsprings of industry: the theory and practice of man's mastering and controlling his natural environment. We are still rephrasing this, from experience, as we learn the folly of exploiting any part of this environment in isolation. We are learning, slowly, to attend to our environment as a whole, and to draw our values from that whole, and not from its fragmented parts, where a quick success can bring long waste. In relation to this kind of learning, we come to realize, again slowly, that where the dominative mood extends to man himself, where human beings also are isolated and exploited, with whatever temporary success, the issue in the long run is a cancelling in spirit of the full opportunities offered by the material gains. A knot is tied, that has come near to strangling our whole common life, in this century. We live in almost overwhelming danger, at a peak of our apparent control. We react to the danger by attempting to take control, yet still we have to unlearn, as the price of survival, the inherent dominative mode. The struggle for democracy is the pattern of this revalution, yet much that passes as democratic is allied, in spirit, with the practice of its open enemies. It is as if, in fear or vision, we are now all determined to lay our hands on life and force it into our own image, and it is then no good to dispute on the merits of rival images. This is a real barrier in the mind, which at times it seems almost impossible to break down: a refusal to accept the creative capacities of life; a determination to limit and restrict the channels of growth; a habit of thinking, indeed, that the future has now to be determined by some ordinance in our own minds. We project our old images into the future, and take hold of ourselves and others to force energy towards that substantiation.

[. . .]

There are still major material barriers to democracy, but there is also this barrier in our minds, behind which, with an assumption of virtue, we seek to lay hands on others, and, from our own constructions, determine their course. Against this the idea of culture is necessary, as an idea of the tending of *natural* growth. To know, even in part, any group of living processes, is to see and wonder at their extraordinary variety and complexity. [. . .] Any culture, in its whole process, is a selection, an emphasis, a particular tending. The distinction of a culture in common is that the selection is freely and commonly made and remade.

[. . .]

The evident problems of our civilization are too close and too serious for anyone to suppose that an emphasis is a solution. In every problem we need hard, detailed inquiry and negotiation. Yet we are coming increasingly to realize that our vocabulary, the language we use to inquire into and negotiate our actions, is no secondary factor, but a practical and radical element in itself. To take a meaning from experience, and to try to make it active, is in fact our process of growth. Some of these meanings we receive and re-create. Others we must make for ourselves, and try to communicate. The human crisis is always a crisis of understanding: what we genuinely understand we can do. I have written this book because I believe the tradition it records is a major contribution to our common understanding, and a major incentive to its necessary extensions. There are ideas, and ways of thinking, with the seeds of life in them, and there are others, perhaps deep in our minds, with the seeds of a general death. Our measure of success in recognizing these kinds, and in naming them making possible their common recognition, may be literally the measure of our future.

E. P. Thompson (1924–1992)

Thompson's critique of Raymond Williams's theory of culture is still regarded as one of the formative texts in the development of cultural studies. In his review of *The Long Revolution* by Raymond Williams (*New Left Review*, Nos. 9 and 10 (1961)), Thompson points to particular limitations of the arguments in *The Long Revolution*, especially the lack of emphasis on struggle, the neglect of alternative reading publics and oppositional cultural forms, the suspect use of the 'whole way of life' concept, a failure to come to terms with the problem of ideology, and the primacy given to the process of communication at the expense of an analysis of power. Throughout the two-part review Thompson is seeking to establish a meaningful distinction between 'culture' and 'not culture', a distinction which, he argues, Williams consistently blurs. Interestingly, Thompson is already arguing for the abandonment of the mechanical metaphor of base/superstructure and suggests that if this were to happen and if Williams were to discard his vocabulary of 'systems' and 'elements', then common ground might be established by recognizing that 'the mode of production and productive relationships determine cultural processes in an epochal sense.' In the last section of the review ('History of Human Culture') Thompson argues for seeing history as a way of conflict, and of class relationships shaping 'the way of life', not patterns of culture. He reiterates Marx's claim that in class society 'social being determines social consciousness' and is critical of the primacy which Williams gives to cultural history.

Two years after the writing of this review, Thompson published *The Making of the English Working Class* (1963), a monumental study of enormous influence on a whole generation of social and cultural historians. In this he stresses that it is a study of an active process: 'The working class did not rise like the sun at an appointed time. It was present at its own making' (Preface, 8). Like so much else which has shaped the growth of cultural studies, this is a work of rescue and recovery, restoring the histories and practices of minorities, dissenters, and radical cultural forms. In line with the positions argued in the review, *The Making of the English Working Class* insists upon class as a cultural and economic formation, and stresses human agency, conflict, tension and active struggle. It is this materialist, historicizing dimension of cultural studies which has been neglected by some of its recent post-structuralist exponents. R.B.

From E. P. Thompson's review of Raymond Williams's *The Long Revolution*

I will take two examples of the way in which the pressures of the past decade can be seen as a limitation upon *The Long Revolution*. In his chapter on 'The Growth of the Popular Press' Williams is at pains to demolish the 1870 Education Act=*Titbits*=*Daily Mail* myth. This he does effectively—so much so that the business of demolition can be seen as the active principle according to which his evidence is selected. But as a consequence a number of questions highly relevant to the historian of the working-class movement are never asked at all—questions of quality, of the relation of the press to popular movements, and of the relation of ownership to political power. While the struggle to establish an alternative popular press is mentioned, it is done so in an annexe apart from the main narrative—it is not seen as a continuing part of the same story, where power, the pursuit of profit, and the response of democracy interlock. The *Northern Star*—the most impressive 19th-century working-class newspaper—is not mentioned here, nor in the analysis of culture in the 1840s, although it offers substantial evidence on the other side of the story. The collapse of this press—and the decline in quality when contrasted with *Reynold's* or *Lloyds* two decades later—remain unexplained. As the story proceeds into this century, the quantitative narrative passes by all those points at which power intervened or at which choices were involved which might have led to a different outcome. We are left with an impression of a great 'expansion' and of a concentration of ownership, and if this was the story then it had to be so. This must lead on—as it does in the final section of the book—to the conclusion that if there is to be a remedy it must come through far-reaching administrative measures which will ensure a newly independent press. But I hold this to be utopian. We shall never develop an opinion strong enough in this country to force such measures, which oppose at a critical point the interests of the capitalist class, unless we are strong enough to found an independent socialist press which can voice and organise this opinion. It is one of the paradoxes of the critical younger generation, that one may hear on every side voices deploring the effects of advertising and of the centralised media, but scarcely a voice which goes on to say: we must combine to produce, finance, and sell an independent paper. Sooner or later the attempt must be made once more; and if it should be made I have no doubt that Mr. Williams would give it immediate support. But my point is that his analysis does not lead people towards this kind of active confrontation, because he has given a record of impersonal forces at work and not a record of struggle.

In this case I think he has asked the wrong questions. In his analysis of culture in the 1840s, and of the growth of the reading public, I think he has excluded a whole area of relevant evidence. Both studies abound in new insights, and it would be ungrateful to quarrel with them if this is all that is being claimed. But Mr. Williams makes a greater claim:

> Cultural history must be more than the sum of the particular histories, for it is with the relations between them, the particular forms of the whole organisation, that it is especially concerned.

And the analysis of the 1840s is offered as a paradigm in application of 'the theory of culture as the study of relationships between elements in a whole way of life' (46). I have spent a good deal of time in the 1840s, and his 1840s are not mine. He deals splendidly with the popular novel and reveals unsuspected connections: with the Chartist press and the teeming political theory of the time he deals scarcely at all. The seven 'factors' which he offers as dominating 'the general political and social history' of the period are an arbitrary selection; and to abstract factors in this way is the first step towards muddling problems of relationship and causation. Points of conflict are blurred: defeats and failures are minimised: the dominant social character is tricked up in its Sunday best, and the charges against the middle-class (brought by Dickens or Oastler or Fielden or any Chartist branch) of hypocrisy, dual standards, and self-interest, go unexamined—there are no good or bad men in Mr. Williams' history, only dominant and subordinate 'structures of feeling'. In the result, we are left with a general euphoria of 'progress'; whatever has happened the emphasis lingers upon 'growth', 'expansion', 'new patterns'. All three social characters (he tells us)

> contribute to the growth of society: the aristocratic ideals tempering the harshness of middle-class ideals at their worst; working-class ideals entering into a fruitful and decisive combination with middle-class ideals at their best (63).

This is indeed a complacent judgment upon a decade which saw the Duke of Wellington (aristocratic ideals?) commanding a mob of middle-class specials against a Chartist demonstration; and which ended (to mention some of the negative evidence which is not considered) with scores of gifted working-men in jail, transported, or emigrating from tyranny—with tens of thousands of handloom weavers starved out of their 'whole way of life' at home and with millions starved out of theirs in Ireland—and with the first great working-class party in Europe in total defeat. For such a decade as this (and I do not mean to deny the positive evidence) 'growth' can be a misleading term. Suffering is not just a wastage in the margin of growth: for those who suffer it is absolute.

177

Reading publics

The 'reading public' is another misleading term. Given this simple undifferentiated notion we become committed to a simple quantitative narrative. But in fact there have always been a number of reading publics, differentiated not only according to educational and social levels, but, crucially, in their manner of production and distribution of the product and in the relation between the writer and his audience. It is not enough for Mr. Williams to note a rise in the number of pamphlets, etc., during the Civil War which can be correlated with 'a rise in social and especially political interests'. We miss the understanding of a new *kind* of reading public, hinted at by one Puritan divine:

> When I came to the Army, among Cromwell's soldiers, I found a new face of things which I never dreamed of. I heard the plotting heads very hot upon that which intimated their intention to subvert both Church and State . . . A few fiery, self-conceited men among them kindled the rest and made all the noise and bustle, and carried about the Army as they pleased . . . A great part of the mischief they did among the soldiers was by pamphlets which they abundantly dispersed . . .
> And soldiers being usually dispersed in their quarters, they had such books to read when they had none to contradict them.

And the same inadequacy is even more marked in Williams' treatment of the 1790s, where he notes the extraordinary sale of Paine's *Rights of Man*, and adds as his only comment:

> It seems clear that the extension of political interest considerably broadened the reading public by collecting a new class of readers, from groups hardly touched by the earlier expansion (163).

Notice once again the impersonal construction: it is the 'extension' of interest which 'broadens' the public and 'collects' a new class of readers. This enables us to side-step the fact that we are considering an *alternative* reading-public and an *alternative* press, created by the initiative of a 'few fiery, self-conceited men' in the face of Church, Commerce, and State. Everything is different. So far from being rewarded or held in esteem for their work, the writers—Lilburne or Paine—were jailed or driven into exile; their work was circulated by illegal, voluntary means in the face of many hazards; and the very *manner* of reading was different—in the London Corresponding Society and among Sheffield cutlers it was the common procedure that a chapter of Paine's work would be 'set' and then it would be read aloud and discussed at the next week's meeting. Perhaps these are over-dramatic examples: but the 'few fiery, self-conceited men' have been at their work of kindling an alternative public for several centuries now, and they constitute a tradition which is not sufficiently taken into Mr. Williams' survey of the evidence.

I would not make so much of these criticisms if I did not think them pertinent to Mr. Williams' main claim—to have offered a new general theory of culture. These criticisms might be merely local, and indicate some deficiency, at these points, in Mr. Williams' equipment.

A comparison between the inadequacy of his treatment of the popular press and the superb chapter on 'The Social History of Dramatic Forms' is instructive; in the latter there is a sense of conflict, paradox, of cultural 'lag' and contradiction, which his own expert knowledge and sense of the medium has brought into the very texture of his style, and which is so signally absent from the former. And yet I am convinced that these deficiencies are not only local, but are symptomatic of general limitations in Mr. Williams' method.

We may start by noting the limitations of the tradition out of which Mr. Williams' work arises. The Tradition (if there is one) is a very English phenomena: it is comprised in the main of publicists, writers, critics and philosophers (of an English variety): throughout *Culture and Society* there is no frontal encounter with an historian, an anthropologist, a sociologist of major stature. If Williams had allowed himself to look beyond this island, he might have found a very different eleven of Players fielding against him, from Vico through Marx to Weber and Mannheim, beside whom his own team might look, on occasion, like gentlemen amateurs. Even within this island there are other traditions which he might have consulted: I think of the life-long engagement with the problem of culture of Professor Gordon Childe. And the omission is significant: the archeologist, or the student of primitive society, in his consideration of the idea of culture, must be governed by peculiarly stubborn material which resists the tendency towards idealist speculation—or, frankly, talking 'out of the top of one's head'—which is the vice of the amateur gentleman tradition. Moreover, in common with the conceptual historian, he must be aware that definitions alone are sterile. False definitions will certainly lead on to bad history, bad sociology, bad archaeology; and Raymond Williams' patient work of clarification has cleared away a great deal of litter of the past two decades. But to adumbrate a theory of culture it is necessary to proceed from definitions to evidence and back from the evidence to definitions once again; if the anthropological and historical evidence is not fully consulted, then we may not know what it is that we should ask, nor what it is that we must define. And for an adequate theory of human culture, the evidence to be consulted is very wide: we must be able to think of a Mesolithic or an Aztec culture, and of feudal and capitalist culture in their epochal (not their pejorative) sense.

Is there a tradition?

When the problem is seen in this perspective it is self-evident that its solution is beyond the reach of any one man: this must be the work of many men, contributing to a tradition. But such traditions exist, and notably that tradition which originates in Marx. It is here that I find a curious ambiguity in all of Mr. Williams' work. In one sense, a great part of both books can be seen as an oblique running argument with Marxism: in another sense Marx is never confronted at all. In *Culture and Society* there is a chapter in which the confusions of certain English Marxist critics are exposed: as one of those pilloried I may take the opportunity of saying that I found the criticism wholly constructive and helpful. But by abstracting some Marxist criticism from the main tradition ('the validity of his (Marx's) economic and political theory cannot here be discussed') Williams evaded the point that what Marx offered was not a theory of art and a theory of politics and another theory of economics but *a theory of history*, of the processes of historical change as (in Williams' own notion of 'culture') 'the study of relationships between elements in a whole way of life'. Now the point here is not whether Marx's theory was essentially *right*: it is evident that Mr. Williams is critical of its tendency towards economic and technological reductionism (although it is not always clear whether he is arguing here with Marx or with his vulgarisers), and that he holds—as I do—that the imagery of basis and superstructure is far too mechanical to describe the logic of change. The point is, rather, is there a tradition there to which—despite all that has happened, all that must be revalued, and all the new evidence that must be taken in—we can return? Or must we start at the beginning again?

It is this tendency to 'write off' the socialist tradition which is so disturbing in *The Long Revolution*. It can be noted in a dozen ways, and it is evident throughout the four conceptual chapters with which the book opens. For a socialist thinker Mr. Williams is extraordinarily curt with the socialist tradition—and indeed in his reference to *any* minority radical tradition. One might never suppose that socialism, in the 19th and 20th centuries, is a major direction of European thought. The Labour movement is credited from time to time with the creation of new *institutions*: but it is never credited with a *mind*. On the one side the 'older human systems', on the other side 'expansion', 'growth', and new institutions, and in the middle The Tradition, savouring the complexities dispassionately and trying to think out the right thing to do in response to 'industry' and 'democracy'. At times Mr. Williams seems to lean over backwards in the attempt to evade making an obvious connection with Marx: for example, his enlightening discussion of exiles, vagrants and rebels (90–94) demands but does not receive some correlation with Marx's notion of alienation: and in his attempts to break down the subject/object antithesis (23, 99) one feels impelled to scribble *Theses of Feuerbach* in the margin. At other times Mr. Williams' self-isolation from any tradition leads to statements so portentous as to appear arrogant, as in his initial discussion of creativity where (as it seems to me) he is not upsetting our whole received outlook but is bringing important new evidence to support a way of looking at the problem which has already been reached independently by some anthropologists and historians:

> To take account of human creativity the whole received basis of social thinking, its conception of what man in society is, must be deeply revised (115).

Yes, but Marx wrote something of this sort, in relation to Promethean man, back in the 1840s; and the renewed interest—in Poland, France and this country—in the 1844 MSS indicates that Mr. Williams is not as isolated at this point as his claim implies.

New and old vocabularies

The evasion of this confrontation involves him at times in thinking which I would almost describe as shoddy: as, for example, his reference to 'socialists such as Marx' who related 'the system of decision (politics) to the system of maintenance (economics)' but who excluded from their thinking 'the system of learning and communication' and relationships based on 'the generation and nurture of life' (114). This is a strange accusation against the authors of *The German Ideology* and *The Origin of the Family*. The point, once again, is not whether Marx and Engels saw these 'systems' in the right relationship—nor whether, in the state of knowledge then available to them, it was possible for them to do so. There is room for argument here: but Williams refuses to retrace the argument. It seems evident to him that in the later Marxist tradition 'art is degraded as a mere reflection of the basic economic and political process, on which it is thought to be parasitic . . . But the creative element in man is the root both of his personality and his society; it can neither be confined to art nor excluded from the systems of decision and maintenance' (115). Amen to this: an amen which found dramatic expression in the squares of Warsaw and Budapest in 1956. But we do not owe this insight to the discoveries of Professor J. Z. Young, however valuable his supporting evidence may be. It is also explicit in Marx's view of *homo faber*:

> We presuppose labour in a form that stamps it as exclusively human. A spider conducts operations that resemble those of a weaver, and a bee puts to shame many an architect in the construction of her cells. But what distinguishes the worst architect from the best of bees is this, that the architect raises his structure in imagination before he erects it in reality. (*Capital*, I, iii, VII.)

Oh, *that* book! Do we really have to go over all that old nineteenth-century stuff again! We have all felt this response: Marx has become not only an embarrassment but a bore. But *The Long Revolution* has convinced me, finally, that go over it again we must. If Mr. Williams had done so—if he had had any frontal encounter with historical materialism—I cannot believe that he could have left his chapter on 'Images of Society' unrevised: nor that he could have discussed 'the crucial question of the nature and origin of change' in the space of four pages (118–121), without stumbling upon the crucial arguments of agency and determinism. His conclusion (if it is a conclusion)—'people change and are changed'—is of course the beginning of the problem: and it is exactly here, in 1844, that Marx began. I can understand only too well the temptation to avoid a discussion in a field so confused and so highly charged with irrelevant emotion. But the fact is that we need a book as good as *Culture and Society* discussing the Marxist and *marxisan* tradition in the same definitive way. The alternative for which Williams has opted demands no less than the creation of a new vocabulary; and the danger here is that Williams is making a dialogue between himself and (among others) historians and economists extraordinarily difficult. I think that his terms for 'politics' and 'economics'—the 'system of decision' and the 'system of maintenance'—are misleading in a number of ways, and contribute to a fragmented view of the social process which makes more difficult his own avowed

181

intention of synthesising 'an adequate sense of general human organisation': they make it more difficult, for example, to conceive of relationships of power, property and exploitation as co-existing simultaneously within all the 'systems'. Further, if we segregate these four activities as co-equal 'systems' (politics, economics, communications, and the family) then we must look to some other discipline to examine the manner according to which the systems are related to each other; and this synthesising discipline will very soon make imperialist claims. These claims are commonly made today by sociology, and Williams has now staked a counter-claim in the name of 'cultural history':

> I see this cultural history as more than a department, a special area of change. In this creative area the changes and conflicts of the whole way of life are necessarily involved (122).

I must dispute this claim. Now if Williams by 'the whole way of life' really means the *whole* way of life he is making a claim, not for cultural history, but for history. The fact that this claim can now be made, with some colour, against history by both critics and sociologists is a devastating comment upon the relegation of history to an inferior status in this country. I can only speculate here upon the reasons for this: one part may be found in the failure of Marxist historians to take into account whole areas of concern disclosed by sociologists and critics (although there is a sturdy minority tradition associated with Dona Torr, Mr. Christopher Hill, and contributors to *Past and Present* which may assume greater importance in the future). Another part is analysed in Mr. E. H. Carr's splendid Trevelyan Lectures, whose quality serves to emphasise the absence of conceptual historical thinking of this order in this country for some years. A further part lies in the eagerness with which academics in the empirical tradition have taken upon themselves the role of narrative drudges, making whole history schools into a kind of piece-meal baggage-train serving more ambitious departments. And yet another, I suspect, can be attributed to a mere shift in fashion and a recrudescence of the amateur gentleman tradition (you have to slog at economics or philosophy but anyone's opinion about 'culture' or 'society' is as good as anyone else's).

I do not dispute, then, that Mr. Williams may have been provoked into making his claim by the eagerness with which historians, under the chiding of Sir Lewis Namier and Professor Popper, have abandoned theirs. The place has been widely advertised as being 'To Let'. But before we accept the new occupant we must first look at the references of a 'whole way of life'. This is Mr. Williams' talisman. It is being suggested that society is constituted of elements (or activities or systems) which, when taken together in their mutual interaction, constitute 'a whole way of life'. At this point we become involved in abstractions which teeter again and again on the cliffs of tautology. If way of life equals culture then what is society apart from way of life: does society equal culture also? We are dragged from the edge by the word 'organisation':

> The 'pattern of culture' is a selection and configuration of interests and activities, and a particular valuation of them, producing a distinct organisation, a 'way of life' (47).

The point, then, is that culture is more than the elements or activities in inter-relation: it is the way in which, in a given society, these elements are related, giving rise to a distinct organisation or meaningful form to the whole society. 'The analysis of culture is the attempt to discover the nature of the organisation which is the complex of these relationships' (46). But we are now surrounded with cliffs: I find it difficult to conceive of a society apart from the complex of its relationships or apart from its organisation, and I had supposed that historians, sociologists, anthropologists, in their different ways, were—or ought to be—concerned with exactly these questions of relationship between elements and principles of organisation. If Mr. Williams wishes to colonise all this in the name of culture, we need not argue about the name. And yet it is obvious that something more than this is being claimed, both in Mr. Williams' own practice and in the manner in which the claim is phrased—'. . . is the attempt to discover the nature of . . .'—this surely suggests a process so delicate, a responsiveness to 'social character' and 'structures of feeling', for which the discipline of the critic will be more appropriate than the blundering discipline of the historian? What then is the 'cultural historian' who (we must remember) is specially concerned with the 'creative area' where 'changes and conflicts . . . are necessarily involved?' He cannot be a whole-way-of-life historian or we are back in a tautological teeter. He must have the equipment of a critic with that kind of literary-sociological flair which is so interesting (and so refreshing) a phenomenon of contemporary American and British writing. Good: I am ready to root for Richard Hoggart as King and David Riesman as President USA. But there is a simple assertion: in all those coils of abstraction nothing has been proved.

A principle of selection

Raymond Williams is offering creative definitions, and I am asking questions, and mine is the easier and less worthy task. But I think he has tried to take in too much, over-reached himself, and is in danger of losing some of the ground he has really gained. If he had argued that the social 'sciences' had neglected a crucial area of culture which cannot be evaluated or interpreted without the equipment of the critic, I would have fought by his side. But this 'whole way of life' is suspect for several reasons. It derives from Eliot: and in its first assertion is associated with religion:

> . . . there is an aspect in which we can see a religion as the *whole way of life* of a people, from birth to the grave, from morning to night and even in sleep, and that way of life is also its culture.

Mr. Williams noted of this, in *Culture and Society*, that in this sense of 'culture'— 'Eliot, like the rest of us, has been at least casually influenced' by anthropology and sociology. One might wish that the acquaintance had been less 'casual'. For Eliot went on, in a well-known passage, to argue that the term 'culture':

> includes all the characteristic activities and interests of a people: Derby Day, Henley Regatta, Cowes, the 12th of August, a cup final, the dog races, the pin

table, the dart board, Wensleydale cheese, boiled cabbage cut into sections, beet-root in vinegar, 19th-century Gothic churches and the music of Elgar. The reader can make his own list.

The point, of course, is that while 'the reader' may make his own list the serious stu-dent of society may *not*. To decide which activities are characteristic implies some principle of selection and some theory of social process. Mr. Williams, in his essay on Eliot, notes that he has here selected examples of 'sport, food and a little art'; and suggests that characteristic activities should 'also include steelmaking, touring in motor-cars, mixed farming, the Stock Exchange, coalmining, and London Transport.' And this is the only serious qualification which he offers to Eliot's piece of sloppy and amateurish thinking. The reader can still make his own list: but it ought to take in rather more.

There are a lot of points here. To begin with, despite the qualification, Eliot's ghost haunts Mr. Williams—and other *NLR* writers—whenever they mention the 'whole way of life'. Whatever is claimed, the predominant associations are with leis-ure activities, the arts and the media of communication. 'Whole' is forgotten (unless in the sense of the integrating *ethos*) and we slide from 'way of life' into 'style of life'. When we speak of an individual's way of life, we usually mean to indicate his style of living, personal habits, moral conduct, and the rest, rather than his position, work, power, ideas and beliefs—and the same range of associations has become attached to the term in the literary-sociological tradition. But if Mr. Williams is serious about including steelmaking, coalmining and the Stock Exchange in his list, then we are back at the beginning again (culture equals society) or still searching for a principle of selection. The way of life associated with coalmining cannot be considered apart from the 'elements': we must know a lot about technological conditions (are women chained to tubs or is there an automated coalface?), about who owns the pits, and whether the miners are tied in conditions of servitude or have the vote and a strong trade union. I am sorry to be so obvious: but we are concerned with definitions, and this phrase must be cross-examined in its turn.

But we must be more obvious still. Why must the list stop here? Why not also include, as 'characteristic activities', strikes, Gallipolli, the bombing of Hiroshima, corrupt trade union elections, crime, the massive distortion of news, and Aldermaston marches? Why not indeed? The 'whole way of life' of European culture in this century (as the Eichmann trial reminds us) has included many things which may make future generations surprised at our 'characteristics'. But not one example is included in Eliot's nor in Mr. Williams' list which forces to the front the problems of power and of conflict. If such examples had been there we might have been impelled to go on and question the word 'life'. I am not being flippant—'life' is a 'good' word, with associations of unconscious vitalism: life 'flows', it is 'ever-chang-ing', in 'flux', and so on—and so indeed it is. But I think it has flowed through chinks in Mr. Williams' reasoning into a pervasive euphoria of 'expansion' and 'new pat-terns'. It is perhaps the mindless force which has built the institutions of the Labour movement and which is there behind his impersonal constructions. I wish that he had remembered of 'life', as (Mr. Carr has just now reminded us) Marx insisted of 'history':

History does nothing, it possesses no immense wealth, fights no battles. It is rather *man*, real living *man* who does everything, who possesses and fights.

We might note a tentative definition from the archaeologist, Professor Grahame Clark:

Culture . . . may be defined as the measure of man's control over nature, a control exercised through experience among social groups and accumulated through the ages.

I do not offer this as a final definition: it is formulated in reply to different questions. But it seems to me to have two merits which are not to be found in the amateur tradition. First, it is a definition in terms of *function*: it raises the question of what culture *does* (or fails to do). Second, it introduces the notion of culture as experience which has been 'handled' in specifically human ways, and so avoids the life equals way-of-life tautology. Any theory of culture must include the concept of the dialectical interaction between culture and something that is *not* culture. We must suppose the raw material of life-experience to be at one pole, and all the infinitely complex human disciplines and systems, articulate and inarticulate, formalised in institutions or dispersed in the least formal ways, which 'handle', transmit, or distort this raw material to be at the other. It is the active *process*—which is at the same time *the process through which men make their history*—that I am insisting upon: I would not dare, in this time of linguistic hypertension, to offer a new definition. What matters, in the end, is that the definition will help us to understand the processes of social change. And if we were to alter one word in Mr. Williams' definition, from 'way of life' to 'way of *growth*', we move from a definition whose associations are passive and impersonal to one which raises questions of activity and agency. And if we change the word again, to delete the associations of 'progress' which are implied in 'growth', we might get: 'the study of relationships between elements in a whole way of *conflict*'. And a way of conflict is a way of *struggle*. And we are back with Marx.

Germaine Greer (1939–)

Until the ubiquitous Camille Paglia was beamed around the world, Germaine Greer was virtually the only woman the British media recognized as having something to say about feminism. *The Female Eunuch* (1970) became *the* feminist book, its author a media celebrity, alternately outrageous or 'intellectual', depending on the genre of the programme. Twenty or more years later, she is still a 'household' name and appears, periodically, in colour supplements, on chat shows or late shows. Part of the counter-culture of the latter part of the 1960s, contributor to *Oz* magazine and *Suck*, and also lecturer in English at Warwick University from 1968 to 1973, there was a self-marketing aspect of Greer which partly obscured the serious influence and effect of *The Female Eunuch* (1970) which became an international bestseller and was, for many women, their first engagement with 'second wave' feminism. Her description of the 'stereotype': 'To her belongs all that is beautiful, even the very word beauty itself. All that exists, exists to beautify her . . . she is the crown of creation . . . weeping, pouting or smiling, running or reclining, she is a doll,' resonated with large numbers of women who recognized the 'madonna/whore/Lolita' syndrome long before Madonna re-packaged it. Though used in academic contexts, Greer's book was not written primarily for an academic audience, but to stimulate debate and, above all, *action* around the politics of gender representation (compare the picketing of Miss America contests, the debate with Mailer at City Hall, New York) and a positive female sexuality. The book was written against the grain of constitutional, or reformist, feminism and in the context of the 'New Left' seen as 'the forcing house for most movement' in which 'liberation is dependent upon the coming of the classless society and the withering away of the state' (11).

The extract from *The Female Eunuch* included here is directed towards what Greer calls 'the compound of induced characteristics of soul and body [which] is the myth of the Eternal Feminine, nowadays called the Stereotype. This is the dominant image of femininity which rules our culture and to which all women aspire' (15). A generation later, in a so-called 'post-feminist' moment, thousands of young women, who may never have heard of Germaine Greer, will recognize the popular cultural artifact she describes which, despite Madonna, still has currency as a goddess of consumer culture. Cultural studies had been preoccupied with advertising and 'mass culture' since the early 1930s and would have shared Greer's anxiety about consumerism, but at the time when she published *The Female Eunuch*, there was little or no institutional space for issues of gender. The work of Juliet Mitchell (who wrote for *New Left Review* in the 1960s) and Sheila Rowbotham was acknowledged in *Women Take Issue* (CCCS, 1978) a publication that was deeply critical of the CCCS precisely because of its marginalizing of gender issues. As Catherine Hall still needed to say, as late as 1990, 'The complexities of the relation between class and culture have received much attention. It is time for gender and culture to be subjected to more critical scrutiny.' There is perhaps a certain irony that this was being said at the end of a decade when 'class' had ceased to have much currency as a resource for cultural analysis.

R.B.

The stereotype

In that mysterious dimension where the body meets the soul the stereotype is born and has her being. She is more body than soul, more soul than mind. To her belongs all that is beautiful, even the very word beauty itself. All that exists, exists to beautify her.

> Taught from infancy that beauty is woman's sceptre, the mind shapes itself to the body, and roaming round its gilt cage, only seeks to adorn its prison.
>
> Mary Wollstonecraft,
> *A Vindication of the Rights of Women*, 1792, p. 90

The sun shines only to burnish her skin and gild her hair; the wind blows only to whip up the color in her cheeks; the sea strives to bathe her; flowers die gladly so that her skin may luxuriate in their essence. She is the crown of creation, the masterpiece. The depths of the sea are ransacked for pearl and coral to deck her; the bowels of the earth are laid open that she might wear gold, sapphires, diamonds and rubies. Baby seals are battered with staves, unborn lambs ripped from their mothers' wombs, millions of moles, musk-rats, squirrels, minks, ermines, foxes, beavers, chinchillas, ocelots, lynxes, and other small and lovely creatures die untimely deaths that she might have furs. Egrets, ostriches and peacocks, butterflies and beetles yield her their plumage. Men risk their lives hunting leopards for her coats, and crocodiles for her handbags and shoes. Millions of silkworms offer her their yellow labours; even the seamstresses roll seams and whip lace by hand, so that she might be clad in the best that money can buy.

The men of our civilization have stripped themselves of the fineries of the earth so that they might work more freely to plunder the universe for treasures to deck my lady in. New raw materials, new processes, new machines are all brought into her service. My lady must therefore be the chief spender as well as the chief symbol of spending ability and monetary success. While her mate toils in his factory, she totters about the smartest streets and plushiest hotels with his fortune upon her back and bosom, fingers and wrists, continuing that essential expenditure in his house which is her frame and her setting, enjoying that silken idleness which is the necessary condition of maintaining her mate's prestige and her qualification to demonstrate it.[1] Once upon a time only the aristocratic lady could lay claim to the title of crown of creation: only her hands were white enough, her feet tiny enough, her waist narrow enough, her hair long and golden enough; but every well-to-do burgher's wife set herself up to ape my lady and to follow fashion, until my lady was forced to set herself out like a gilded doll overlaid with monstrous rubies and pearls like pigeons' eggs. Nowadays the Queen of England still considers it part of her royal female role to sport as much of the family jewelery as she can manage at any one time on all public occasions, although the male monarchs have escaped such showcase duty, which devolves exclusively upon their wives.

At the same time as woman was becoming the showcase for wealth and caste, while men were slipping into relative anonymity and 'handsome is as handsome does,' she was emerging as the central emblem of western art. For the Greeks the male and female body had beauty of a human, not necessarily a sexual, kind; indeed they may have marginally favored the young male form as the most powerful and perfectly proportioned. Likewise the Romans showed no bias towards the depiction of femininity in their predominantly monumental art. In the Renaissance the female form began to predominate, not only as the mother in the predominant emblem of *madonna col bambino*, but as an aesthetic study in herself. At first naked female forms took their chances in crowd scenes or diptychs of Adam and Eve, but gradually Venus claims ascendancy, Mary Magdalene ceases to be wizened and emaciated, and becomes nubile and ecstatic, portraits of anonymous young women, chosen only for their prettiness, begin to appear, are gradually disrobed, and renamed Flora or Primavera. Painters began to paint their own wives and mistresses and royal consorts as voluptuous beauties, divesting them of their clothes if desirable, but not of their jewelery. Susanna keeps her bracelets on in the bath, and Hélène Fourment keeps ahold of her fur as well!

What happened to women in painting happened to her in poetry as well. Her beauty was celebrated in terms of the riches which clustered around her: her hair was gold wires, her brow ivory, her lips ruby, her teeth gates of pearl, her breasts alabaster veined with lapis lazuli, her eyes as black as jet.[2] The fragility of her loveliness was emphasized by the inevitable comparisons with the rose, and she was urged to employ her beauty in love-making before it withered on the stem.[3] She was for consumption; other sorts of imagery spoke of her in terms of cherries and cream, lips as sweet as honey and skin white as milk, breasts like cream uncrudded, hard as apples.[4] Some celebrations yearned over her finery as well, her lawn more transparent than morning mist, her lace as delicate as gossamer, the baubles that she toyed with and the favors that she gave.[5] Even now we find the thriller hero describing his classy dame's elegant suits, cheeky hats, well-chosen accessories and footwear; the imagery no longer dwells on jewels and flowers but the consumer emphasis is the same. The mousy secretary blossoms into the feminine stereotype when she reddens her lips, lets down her hair, and puts on something frilly.

Nowadays women are not expected, unless they are Paola di Liegi or Jackie Onassis, and then only on gala occasions, to appear with a king's ransom deployed upon their bodies, but they are required to look expensive, fashionable, well-groomed, and not to be seen in the same dress twice. If the duty of the few may have become less onerous, it has also become the duty of the many. The stereotype marshals an army of servants. She is supplied with cosmetics, underwear, foundation garments, stockings, wigs, postiches and hairdressing as well as her outer garments, her jewels and furs. The effect is to be built up layer by layer, and it is expensive. Splendor has given way to fit, line and cut. The spirit of competition must be kept up, as more and more women struggle towards the top drawer, so that the fashion industry can rely upon an expanding market. Poorer women fake it, ape it, pick up on the fashions a season too late, use crude effects, mistaking the line, the sheen, the gloss of the high-class article for a garish simulacrum. The business is so complex that it must be handled by an expert. The paragons of the stereotype must be dressed, coifed and painted by the experts and the style-setters, although they may be encouraged to give heart to the housewives studying their lives in pulp magazines by claiming a lifelong fidelity to their own hair and soap and water. The boast is more usually discouraging than otherwise, unfortunately.

As long as she is young and personable, every woman may cherish the dream that she may leap up the social ladder and dim the sheen of luxury by sheer natural loveliness; the few examples of such a feat are kept before the eye of the public. Fired with hope, optimism and ambition, young women study the latest forms of the stereotype, set out in *Vogue*, *Nova*, *Queen* and other glossies, where the mannequins stare from among the advertisements for fabulous real estate, furs and jewels. Nowadays the uniformity of the year's fashions is severely affected by the emergence of the pert female designers who direct their appeal to the working girl, emphasizing variety, comfort, and simple, striking effects. There is no longer a single face of the year: even Twiggy has had to withdraw into marketing and rationed personal appearances, while the Shrimp works mostly in New York. Nevertheless the stereotype is still supreme. She has simply allowed herself a little more variation.

The stereotype is the Eternal Feminine. She is the Sexual Object sought by all men, and by all women. She is of neither sex, for she has herself no sex at all. Her value is solely attested by the demand she excites in others. All she must contribute is her existence. She need achieve nothing, for she is the reward of achievement. She need never give positive evidence of her moral character because virtue is assumed from her loveliness, and her passivity. If any man who has no right to her be found with her she will not be punished, for she is morally neuter. The matter is solely one of male rivalry. Innocently she may drive men to madness and war. The more trouble she can cause, the more her stocks go up, for possession of her means more the more demand she excites. Nobody wants a girl whose beauty is imperceptible to all but him; and so men welcome the stereotype because it directs their taste into the most commonly recognized areas of value, although they may protest because some aspects of it do not tally with their fetishes. There is scope in the stereotype's variety for most fetishes. The leg man may follow miniskirts, the tit man can encourage see-through blouses and plunging necklines, although the man who likes fat women may feel constrained to enjoy them in secret. There are stringent limits to the variations on the stereotype, for nothing must interefere with her function as sex object. She may wear leather, as long as she cannot actually handle a motorbike: she may wear rubber, but it ought not to indicate that she is an expert diver or waterskier. If she wears athletic clothes the purpose is to underline her unathleticism. She may sit astride a horse, looking soft and curvy, but she must not crouch over its neck with her rump in the air.

The myth of the strong black woman is the other side of the coin of the myth of the beautiful dumb blonde. The white man turned the white woman into a weak-minded, weak-bodied, delicate freak, a sex pot, and placed her on a pedestal; he turned the black woman into a strong self-reliant Amazon and deposited her in his kitchen. . . . The white man turned himself into the Omnipotent Administrator and established himself in the Front Office.

Eldridge Cleaver,
'The Allegory of the Black Eunuchs,'
Soul on Ice, 1968, p. 162

Because she is the emblem of spending ability and the chief spender, she is also the most effective seller of this world's goods. Every survey ever held has shown that the image of an attractive woman is the most effective advertising gimmick. She may sit astride the mudguard of a new car, or step into it ablaze with jewels; she may lie at a man's feet stroking his new socks; she may hold the petrol pump in a challenging pose, or dance through woodland glades in slow motion in all the glory of a new shampoo; whatever she does her image sells. The gynolatry of our civilization is written large upon its face, upon hoardings, cinema screens, television, newspapers, magazines, tins, packets, cartons, bottles, all consecrated to the reigning deity, the female fetish. Her dominion must not be thought to entail the rule of women, for she is not a woman. Her glossy lips and mat complexion, her unfocused eyes and flawless fingers, her extraordinary hair all floating and shining, curling and gleaming, reveal the inhuman triumph of cosmetics, lighting, focusing and printing, cropping and composition. She sleeps unruffled, her lips red and juicy and closed, her eyes as crisp and black as if new painted, and her false lashes immaculately curled. Even when she

---

She was created to be the toy of man, his rattle, and it must jingle in his ears whenever, dismissing reason, he chooses to be amused.

Mary Wollstonecraft,
A Vindication of the Rights of Women, 1792, p. 66

washes her face with a new and creamier toilet soap her expression is as tranquil and vacant and her paint as flawless as ever. If ever she should appear tousled and troubled, her features are miraculously smoothed to their proper veneer by a new washing powder or a bouillon cube. For she is a doll: weeping, pouting or smiling, running or reclining, she is a doll. She is an idol, formed of the concatenation of lines and masses, signifying the lineaments of satisfied impotence.

Her essential quality is castratedness. She absolutely must be young, her body hairless, her flesh buoyant, and *she must not have a sexual organ*. No musculature must distort the smoothness of the lines of her body, although she may be painfully slender or warmly cuddly. Her expression must betray no hint of humor, curiosity or intelligence, although it may signify hauteur to an extent that is actually absurd, or smoldering lust, very feebly signified by drooping eyes and a sullen mouth (for the stereotype's lust equals irrational submission), or, most commonly, vivacity and idiot happiness. Seeing that the world despoils itself for this creature's benefit, she must be happy; the entire structure would topple if she were not. So the image of woman appears plastered on every surface imaginable, smiling interminably. An apple pie evokes a glance of tender beatitude, a washing machine causes hilarity, a cheap box of chocolates brings forth meltingly joyous gratitude, a Coke is the cause of a rictus of unutterable brilliance, even a new stick-on bandage is saluted by a smirk of satisfaction. A real woman licks her lips and opens her mouth and flashes her teeth when photographers appear: *she* must arrive at the premiere of her husband's film in a paroxysm of delight, or his success might be murmured about. The occupational hazard of being a Playboy Bunny is the aching facial muscles brought on by the obligatory smiles.

Discretion is the better part of Valerie
though all of her is nice
lips as warm as strawberries
eyes as cold as ice
the very best of everything
only will suffice
not for her potatoes
and puddings made of rice

Roger McGough, *Discretion*

So what is the beef? Maybe I couldn't make it. Maybe I don't have a pretty smile, good teeth, nice tits, long legs, a cheeky arse, a sexy voice. Maybe I don't know how to handle men and increase my market value, so that the rewards due to the feminine will accrue to me. Then again, maybe I'm sick of the masquerade. I'm sick of pretending eternal youth. I'm sick of belying my own intelligence, my own will, my own sex. I'm sick of peering at the world through false eyelashes, so everything I see is mixed with a shadow of bought hairs; I'm sick of weighting my head with a dead mane, unable to move my neck freely, terrified of rain, of wind, of dancing too vigorously in case I sweat into my lacquered curls. I'm sick of the Powder Room. I'm sick of pretending that some fatuous male's self-important pronouncements are the objects of my undivided attention, I'm sick of going to films and plays when someone else wants to, and sick of having no opinions of my own about either. I'm sick of being a transvestite. I refuse to be a female impersonator. I am a woman, not a castrate.

To what end is the laying out of the embroidered Hair, embared Breasts; vermilion Cheeks, alluring looks, Fashion gates, and artfull Countenances, effeminate intangling and insnaring Gestures, their Curls and Purls of proclaiming Petulancies, boulstered and laid out with such example and authority in these our days, as with Allowance and beseeming Conveniency?

Doth the world wax barren through decrease of Generations, and become, like the Earth, less fruitful heretofore? Doth the Blood lose his Heat or do the Sunbeams become waterish and less fervent, than formerly they have been, that men should be thus inflamed and persuaded on to lust?

Alex. Niccholes, *A Discourse of Marriage and Wiving*,
1615, pp. 143–52

April Ashley was born male. All the information supplied by genes, chromosomes, internal and external sexual organs added up to the same thing. April was a man. But he longed to be a woman. He longed for the stereotype, not to embrace, but to be. He wanted soft fabrics, jewels, furs, makeup, the love and protection of men. So he was impotent. He couldn't fancy women at all, although he did not particularly welcome homosexual addresses. He did not think of himself as a pervert, or even as a transvestite, but as a woman cruelly transmogrified into manhood. He tried to die, became a female impersonator, but eventually found a doctor in Casablanca who came up with a more acceptable alternative. He was to be castrated, and his penis used as the lining of a surgically constructed cleft, which would be a vagina. He would be infertile, but that has never affected the attribution of femininity. April returned to England, resplendent. Massive hormone treatment had eradicated his beard, and formed tiny breasts: he had grown his hair and bought feminine clothes during the time he had worked as an impersonator. He became a model, and began to illustrate the feminine stereotype as he was perfectly qualified to do, for he was elegant, voluptuous, beautifully groomed, and in love with his own image. On an ill-fated day he married the heir to a peerage, the Hon. Arthur Corbett, acting out the highest achievement of the feminine dream, and went to live with him in a villa in Marbella. The marriage was never consummated. April's incompetence as a woman is what we must expect from a castrate, but it is not so very different after all from the impotence of feminine women, who submit to sex without desire, with only the infantile pleasure of cuddling and affection, which is their favorite reward. As long as the feminine stereotype remains the definition of the female sex, April Ashley is a woman, regardless of the legal decision ensuing from her divorce.[6] She is as much a casualty of the polarity of the sexes as we all are. Disgraced, unsexed April Ashley is our sister and our symbol.

NOTES

1. Thorstein Veblen, *The Theory of Leisure Class* (London and New York: Macmillan, 1989), *passim*.
2. E.g.,

   I thought my mistress' hairs were gold,
   And in her locks my heart I fold;
   Her amber tresses were the sight
   That wrapped me in vain delight;

   Her ivory front, her pretty chin,
   Were stales that drew me on to sin;
   Her starry looks, her crystal eyes
   Brighter than the sun's arise.

   > (Robert Greene, *Francesco's Fortunes*)

3. E.g.,

   When I admire the rose,
   That Nature makes repose
   In you the best of many,
   And see how curious art
   Hath decked every part,
   I think with doubtful view
   Whether you be the rose or the rose be you.

   > (Thomas Lodge, *William Longbeard*)

4. E.g.,

   Her cheeks like apples which the sun hath rudded,
   Her lips like cherries charming men to bite,
   Her breasts like to a bowl of cream uncrudded . . .

   > (Edmund Spenser, *Epithalamion*)

5. E.g.,

   The outside of her garments were of lawn,
   The lining purple silk, with gilt stars drawn,
   Her wide sleeves green and bordered with many a grove . . .
   Buskins of shells all silvered used she
   Branched with blushing coral to the knee,
   Where sparrows perched, of hollow pearl and gold,
   Such as the world would wonder to behold;
   Those with sweet water oft her handmaid fills,
   Which as she went would chirrup through the bills.

   It is only proper to point out that in this passage Marlowe is setting Hero up as a foil to the natural beauty of Leander, beloved of the gods, who is presented quite naked. Hero as a stereotype might be considered one of the themes of the poem.

6. *Corbett v. Corbett* (otherwise Ashley) before Mr. Justice Ormerod (Law Report, February 2, 1970, Probate, Divorce and Admiralty Division). *News of the World*, February 8, 1970, *Sunday Mirror*, February 3, 8, 15, 1970.

Stuart Hall (1932–)

Apart from Raymond Williams, Stuart Hall has been the most influential figure in British cultural studies. Outside of Britain, his work has probably been more responsible than any other for the spread of the field. Unlike Williams, his significance cannot be measured by a series of landmark books (not that Williams's role should be confined to these) but has manifested itself in an astonishing range of articles and co-authored books, many of which have a definitive place in the literature of the field. As director of the Birmingham Centre for Contemporary Cultural Studies throughout the 1970s, he helped to make its break with a Left-Leavisite, humanist, cultural populism and, with others, steered it towards an engagement with European structuralist and Marxist theories, especially the work of Gramsci and Althusser. Expressed simply, the key concepts to emerge from this engagement were encoding and decoding in the television discourse, hegemony, ideology, the epistemological break in Marx's theoretical development, and the abandoning of the base/superstructure metaphor. These conceptual shifts were not, of course, restricted to Birmingham but received their most pronounced institutional inflection at the Centre.

'Cultural Studies: Two paradigms' (1980) is a summative account of the theoretical growth of cultural studies up until the end of the 1970s, and focuses upon its dominant methodologies—culturalism and structuralism—supplemented by reference to the post-structuralisms shaped by the work of Lacan and Foucault. It marks the end of Hall's period at Birmingham, prior to his becoming professor of sociology at the Open University. As well as this, it is the most sustained expression of his own appropriation of Gramscian ideas in which concepts of ideology and culture are not seen as being opposed to each other but are re-articulated in different ways. Throughout the 1980s, although he produced a considerable amount of material for innovative OU courses, he has been identified primarily with the definition of the concept of 'Thatcherism', mainly through a series of analytical essays in *Marxism Today* which depended upon his thesis of 'authoritarian populism'. He was also one of the principal architects of *Marxism Today*'s 'new times' project with its somewhat

194

surprising articulation of postmodernism with what came to be called (after Gramsci) postFordism. Hall's political journalism has been subject to extensive criticism for what opponents have considered to be its excessive 'culturalism' and 'opportunism'.

Interestingly, however much criticized, out of this same concern with postmodernist ideas of identity, re-thinking the subject, and difference came the ICA lecture, 'Minimal Selves' (1987) which has been extremely influential. Throughout his career, Hall has always been involved with black cultural history and theory and with community politics, and the highly-praised six-part television series, *Redemption Song* (1991) which Hall presented, emerged from this conjuncture and, although not explicitly autobiographical as such, enabled him to explore questions of post-colonial identity and cultural difference in the Caribbean which he left more than forty years ago.
R.B.

Cultural studies: two paradigms*

In serious, critical intellectual work, there are no 'absolute beginnings' and few unbroken continuities. . . . What we find, instead, is an untidy but characteristic unevenness of development. What is important are the significant *breaks*—where old lines of thought are disrupted, older constellations displaced, and elements, old and new, are regrouped around a different set of premises and themes.
[. . .]
Cultural Studies, as a distinctive problematic, emerges from one such moment, in the mid-1950s. It was certainly not the first time that its characteristic questions had been put on the table. Quite the contrary. The two books which helped to stake out the new terrain—Hoggart's *Uses of Literacy* and Williams's *Culture and Society*— were both, in different ways, works (in part) of recovery. Hoggart's book took its reference from the 'cultural debate', long sustained in the arguments around 'mass society' and in the tradition of work identified with Leavis and *Scrutiny*. *Culture and Society* reconstructed a long tradition which Williams defined as consisting, in sum, of 'a record of a number of important and continuing reactions to . . . changes in our social, economic and political life' and offering 'a special kind of map by means of which the nature of the changes can be explored' (Williams, 1963, p. 16). The books looked, at first, simply like an updating of these earlier concerns, with reference to the post-war world. Retrospectively, their 'breaks' with the traditions of thinking in which they were situated seems as important, if not more so, than their continuity with them. The *Uses of Literacy* did set out—much in the spirit of 'practical criticism'—to 'read' working class culture for the values and meanings embodied in its patterns and arrangements: as if they were certain kinds of 'texts'. But the application of this method to a living culture, and the rejection of the terms of the 'cultural debate' (polarized around the high/low culture distinction) was a thorough-going

*Source: *Media, Culture and Society*, No. 2, 1980, pp. 57–72.

departure. *Culture and Society*—in one and the same movement—constituted a tradition (*the* 'culture-and-society' tradition), defined its 'unity' (not in terms of common positions but in its characteristic concerns and the idiom of its inquiry), itself made a distinctive modern contribution to it—*and* wrote its epitaph. The Williams book which succeeded it—*The Long Revolution*—clearly indicated that the 'culture-and-society' mode of reflection could only be completed and developed by moving somewhere else—to a significantly different kind of analysis. The very difficulty of some of the writing in *The Long Revolution*—with its attempt to 'theorize' on the back of a tradition resolutely empirical and particularist in its idiom of thought . . . stems, in part, from this determination to *move on*. The 'good' and the 'bad' parts of *The Long Revolution* both arise from its status as a work 'of the break'. The same could be said of E. P. Thompson's *Making of the English Working Class*, which belongs decisively to this 'moment', even though, chronologically it appeared somewhat later. It, too, had been 'thought' within certain distinctive historical traditions: English marxist historiography, Economic and 'Labour' History. But in its foregrounding of the questions of culture, consciousness and experience, and its accent on agency, it also made a decisive break: with a certain kind of technological evolutionism, with a reductive economism, and an organizational determinism.

[. . .]

Two rather different ways of conceptualizing 'culture' can be drawn out of the many suggestive formulations in Raymond Williams's *Long Revolution*. The first relates 'culture' to the sum of the available descriptions through which societies make sense of and reflect their common experiences. This definition takes up the earlier stress on 'ideas', but subjects it to a thorough reworking. The conception of 'culture' is itself democratized and socialized. It no longer consists of the sum of the 'best that has been thought and said', regarded as the summits of an achieved civilization—that ideal of perfection to which, in earlier usage, all aspired. Even 'art'—assigned in the earlier framework a privileged position, as touchstone of the highest values of civilization—is now redefined as only one, special, form of a general social process: the giving and taking of meanings, and the slow development of 'common' meanings—a common culture: 'culture', in this special sense, 'is ordinary' (to borrow the title of one of Williams's earliest attempts to make this general position more widely accessible—see Williams, 1958). If even the highest, most refined of descriptions offered in works of literature are also 'part of the general process which creates conventions and institutions, through which the meanings that are valued by the community are shared and made active' (Williams, 1965, p. 55), then there is no way in which this process can be hived off or distinguished or set apart from the other practices of the historical process. . . . Accordingly, there is no way in which the communication of descriptions, understood in this way, can be set aside and compared externally with other things.

[. . .]

If this first emphasis takes up and re-works the connotation of the term 'culture' with the domain of 'ideas', the second emphasis is more deliberately anthropological, and emphasizes that aspect of 'culture' which refers to social *practices*. It is from this second emphasis that the somewhat simplified definition—'culture is a whole way of life'—has been rather too neatly abstracted. Williams did relate this aspect of the concept to the more 'documentary'—that is, descriptive, even ethnographic—usage of the term. But the earlier definition seems to me the more central one, into which 'way of life' is integrated. The important point in the argument rests on the active and indissoluble relationships between elements or social practices normally separated out. It is in *this* context that the 'theory of culture' is defined as 'the study of relationships between elements in a whole way of life'. 'Culture' is not *a* practice; nor is it simply the descriptive sum of the 'mores and folkways' of societies—as it tended to become in certain kinds of anthropology. It is threaded through *all* social practices, and is the sum of their inter-relationship. The question of what, then, is studied, and how, resolves itself. The 'culture' is those patterns of organization, those characteristic forms of human energy which can be discovered as revealing themselves—in 'unexpected identities and correspondences' as well as in 'discontinuities of an unexpected kind' (*ibid* p. 63)—within or underlying *all* social practices. The analysis of culture is, then, 'the attempt to discover the nature of the organization which is the complex of these relationships'. It begins with 'the discovery of patterns of a characteristic kind'. One will discover them, not in the art, production, trading, politics, the raising of families, treated as separate activities, but through 'studying a general organisation in a particular example' (*ibid* p. 61). Analytically, one must study 'the relationships between these patterns'. The purpose of the analysis is to grasp how the interactions between all these practices and patterns are lived and experienced as a whole, in any particular period. This is its 'structure of feeling'.

It is easier to see what Williams was getting at, and why he was pushed along this path, if we understand what were the problems he addressed, and what pitfalls he was trying to avoid. This is particularly necessary because *The Long Revolution* (like many of Williams's works) carries on a submerged, almost 'silent' dialogue with alternative positions, which are not always as clearly identified as one would wish. There is a clear engagement with the 'idealist' and 'civilizing' definitions of culture—both the equation of 'culture' with *ideas*, in the idealist tradition; and the assimilation of culture to an *ideal*, prevalent in the elitist terms of the 'cultural debate'. But there is also a more extended engagement with certain kinds of Marxism, against which Williams's definitions are consciously pitched. He is arguing against the literal operations of the base/superstructure metaphor, which in classical Marxism ascribed the domain of ideas and of meanings to the 'superstructures', themselves conceived as merely reflective of and determined in some simple fashion by 'the base'; without a social effectivity of their own. That is to say, his argument is constructed against a vulgar materialism and an economic determinism. He offers, instead, a radical interactionism: in effect, the interaction of all practices in and with one another, skirting the problem of determinacy.

[. . .]

There have been several, radical revisions of this early position: and each has contributed much to the redefinition of what Cultural Studies is and should be. We have acknowledged already the exemplary nature of Williams's project, in constantly rethinking and revising older arguments—in going on thinking. Nevertheless, one is struck by a marked line of continuity through these seminal revisions.

[. . .]

Williams takes on board E. P. Thompson's critique of *The Long Revolution* (Thompson, 1961) that no 'whole way of life' is without its dimension of struggle and confrontation between opposed *ways* of life—and attempts to rethink the key issues of determination and domination via Gramsci's concept of 'hegemony'. This essay ('Base and Superstructure in Marxist Cultural Theory', Williams, 1973) is a seminal one, especially in its elaboration of dominant, residual and emergent cultural practices, and its return to the problematic of determinacy as 'limits and pressures'. None the less, the earlier emphases recur, with force: 'we cannot separate literature and art from other kinds of social practice, in such a way as to make them subject to quite special and distinct laws'. . . . And this note is carried forward—indeed, it is radically accented—in Williams's most sustained and succinct recent statement of his position: the masterly condensations of *Marxism and Literature*. Against the structuralist emphasis on the specificity and 'autonomy' of practices, and their analytic separation of societies into their discrete instances, Williams's stress is on 'constitutive activity' in general, on 'sensuous human activity, as practice'.

[. . .]

The organizing terrain of Thompson's work—classes as relations, popular struggle, and historical forms of consciousness, class cultures in their historical particularity—is foreign to the more reflective and 'generalizing' mode in which Williams typically works. . . . Thompson also operates with a more 'classical' distinction than Williams, between 'social being' and 'social consciousness' (the terms he infinitely prefers, from Marx, to the more fashionable 'base and superstructure'). Thus, where Williams insists on the absorption of all practices into the totality of 'real, indissoluble practice', Thompson does deploy an older distinction between what is 'culture' and what is 'not culture'. 'Any theory of culture must include the concept of the dialectical interaction between culture and something that is *not* culture.' Yet the definition of culture is not, after all, so far removed from Williams's: 'We must suppose the raw material of life experience to be at one pole, and all the infinitely complex human disciplines and systems, articulate and inarticulate, formalised in institutions or dispersed in the least formal ways, which "handle", transmit or distort this raw material to be at the other'. Similarly, with respect to the commonality of 'practice' which underlies all the distinct practices: 'It is the active process—which is at the same time the process through which men make their history—that I am insisting upon' (Thompson, 1961, p. 33). [. . .] And—a simple statement which may be taken as defining virtually the whole of Thompson's historical work, from *The Making* to *Whigs and Hunters*, *The Poverty of Theory* and beyond—'capitalist society was founded upon forms of exploitation which are simultaneously economic, moral and cultural. Take up the essential defining productive relationship . . . and turn it round, and it reveals itself now in one aspect (wage-labour), now in another (an acquisitive ethos), and now in another (the alienation of such intellectual facilities as are not required by the worker in his productive role)' (Thompson, 1965, p. 356).

Here, then, despite the many significant differences, is the outline of one significant line of thinking in Cultural Studies—some would say, *the* dominant paradigm. . . . In its different ways, it conceptualizes culture as interwoven with all social practices; and those practices, in turn, as a common form of human activity: sensuous human praxis, the activity through which men and women make history. It is opposed to the base-superstructure way of formulating the relationship between ideal and material forces, especially where the 'base' is defined as the determination by 'the economic' in any simple sense. It prefers the wider formulation—the dialectic between social being and social consciousness: neither separable into its distinct poles. . . . It defines 'culture' as *both* the meanings and values which arise amongst distinctive social groups and classes, on the basis of their given historical conditions and relationships, through which they 'handle' and respond to the conditions of existence; *and* as the lived traditions and practices through which those 'understandings' are expressed and in which they are embodied. Williams brings together these two aspects—definitions and ways of life—around the concept of 'culture' itself. Thompson brings together the two elements—consciousness and conditions—around the concept of 'experience'. Both positions entail certain difficult fluctuations around these key terms. Williams so totally absorbs 'definitions of experience' into our 'ways of living', and both into an indissoluble real material practice-in-general, as to obviate any distinction between 'culture' and 'not-culture'. Thompson sometimes uses 'experience' in the more usual sense of consciousness, as the collective ways in which men 'handle', transmit or 'distort' their given conditions, the raw materials of life; sometimes as the domain of the 'lived', the mid-term *between* 'conditions' and 'culture'; and sometimes as the objective conditions themselves—against which particular modes of consciousness are counterposed. But, whatever the terms, both positions tend to read structures of relations in terms of how they are 'lived' and 'experienced'. . . . This is a consequence of giving culture-consciousness and experience so pivotal a place in the analysis. The *experiential pull* in this paradigm, and the emphasis on the creative and on historical agency, constitute the two key elements in the *humanism* of the position outlined. Each, consequently accords 'experience' an authenticating position in any cultural analysis. [. . .] In 'experience', all the different practices intersect; within 'culture' the different practices interact—even if on an uneven and mutually determining basis. This sense of cultural totality—of *the whole* historical process—over-rides any effort to keep the instances and elements distinct. Their real interconnection, under given historical conditions, must be matched by a totalizing movement 'in thought', in the analysis.

[. . .]

The 'culturalist' strand in Cultural Studies was interrupted by the arrival on the intellectual scene of the 'structuralisms'. These, possibly more varied than the 'culturalisms', nevertheless shared certain positions and orientations in common which makes their designation under a single title not altogether misleading. It has been remarked that whereas the 'culturalist' paradigm can be defined without requiring a conceptual reference to the term 'ideology' (the *word*, of course, does appear: but it is not a key concept), the 'structuralist' interventions have been largely articulated around the concept of 'ideology': in keeping with its more impeccably Marxist lineage, 'culture' does not figure so prominently. Whilst this may be true of the Marxist structuralists, it is at best less than half the truth about the structuralist enterprise as such. But it is now a common error to condense the latter exclusively around the impact of Althusser and all that has followed in the wake of his interventions—where 'ideology' has played a seminal, but modulated rôle: and to omit the significance of Lévi-Strauss. Yet, in strict historical terms, it was Lévi-Strauss, and the early semiotics, which made the first break. And though the Marxist structuralisms have

199

superseded the latter, they owed, and continued to owe, an immense theoretical debt . . . to his work. It was Lévi-Strauss's structuralism which, in its appropriation of the linguistic paradigm, after Saussure, offered the promise to the 'human sciences of culture' of a paradigm capable of rendering them scientific and rigorous in a thoroughly new way. And when, in Althusser's work, the more classical Marxist themes were recovered, it remained the case that Marx was 'read'—and reconstituted— through the terms of the linguistic paradigm. In *Reading Capital*, for example, the case is made that the mode of production–to coin a phrase—could best be understood as if 'structured like a language' (through the selective combination of invariant elements). The a-historical and synchronic stress, against the historical emphasis of 'culturalism', derived from a similar source. So did a pre-occupation with 'the social, *sui generis*'—used not adjectivally but substantively: a usage Lévi-Strauss derived, not from Marx, but from Durkheim. . . .

This structuralism shared with culturalism a radical break with the terms of the base/superstructure metaphor, as derived from the simpler parts of the *German Ideology*. And though 'It is to this theory of the superstructures, scarcely touched on by Marx' to which Lévi-Strauss aspired to contribute, his contribution was such as to break in a radical way with its whole terms of reference, as finally and irrevocably as the 'culturalists' did. Here—and we must include Althusser in this characterization—culturalists and structuralists alike ascribed to the domains hitherto defined as 'superstructural' a specificity and effectivity, a constitutive primacy, which pushed them beyond the terms of reference of 'base' and 'superstructure'. Lévi-Strauss and Althusser, too, were anti-reductionist and anti-economist in their very cast of thought, and critically attacked that transitive causality which, for so long, had passed itself off as 'classical Marxism'.

Lévi-Strauss worked consistently with the term 'culture'. [. . .] First, he conceptualized 'culture' as the categories and frameworks in thought and language through which different societies classified out their conditions of existence—above all (since Lévi-Strauss was an anthropologist), the relations between the human and the natural worlds. Second, he thought of the manner and practice through which these categories and mental frameworks were produced and transformed, largely on an analogy with the ways in which language itself—the principal medium of 'culture'— operated. He identified what was specific to them and their operation as the 'production of meaning': they were, above all, *signifying* practices. Third, . . . he largely gave up the question of the relation *between* signifying and non-signifying practices—between 'culture' and 'not-culture', to use other terms—for the sake of concentrating on the *internal* relations within signifying practices by means of which the categories of meaning were produced. This left the question of determinacy, of totality, largely in abeyance. The causal logic of determinacy was abandoned in favour of a structuralist causality—a logic of *arrangement*, of internal relations, of articulation of parts within a structure. Each of these aspects is also positively present in Althusser's work and that of the Marxist structuralists, even when the terms of reference had been regrounded in Marx's 'immense theoretical revolution'. We can see this in Althusser's seminal formulations about ideology—defined as the themes, concepts and representations through which men and women 'live', in an imaginary relation, their relation to their real conditions of existence (see Althusser, 1971). . . .

'Ideologies' are here being conceptualized, not as the contents and surface forms of ideas, but as the unconscious categories through which conditions are represented and lived. We have already commented on the active presence in Althusser's thinking of the linguistic paradigm—the second element identified above. And though, in the concept of 'over-determination'—one of his most seminal and fruitful contributions—Althusser did return to the problems of the relations *between* practices and the question of determinacy, . . . he did tend to reinforce the 'relative autonomy' of different practices, and their internal specificities, conditions and effects at the expense of an 'expressive' conception of the totality, with its typical homologies and correspondences.

Aside from the wholly distinct intellectual and conceptual universes within which these alternative paradigms developed, there were certain points where, despite their apparent overlaps, culturalism and structuralism were starkly counterposed. We can identify this counterposition at one of its sharpest points precisely around the concept of 'experience', and the rôle the term played in each perspective. Whereas, in 'culturalism', experience was the ground—the terrain of 'the lived'—where consciousness and conditions intersected, structuralism insisted that 'experience' could not, by definition, be the ground of anything, since one could only 'live' and experience one's conditions *in and through* the categories, classifications and frameworks of the culture. These categories, however, did not arise from or in experience: rather, experience was their 'effect'. The culturalists had defined the forms of consciousness and culture as collective. But they had stopped far short of the radical proposition that, in culture and in language, the subject was 'spoken by' the categories of culture in which he/she thought, rather than 'speaking them'. These categories were, however, not merely collective rather than individual productions: they were for the structuralists, *unconscious* structures. That is why, though Lévi-Strauss spoke only of 'Culture', his concept provided the basis for an easy translation, by Althusser, into the conceptual framework of ideology: 'Ideology is indeed a system of "representations", but in the majority of cases these representations have nothing to do with "consciousness": . . . it is above all as structures that they impose on the vast majority of men, not via their "consciousness" . . . it is within this ideological unconsciousness that men succeed in altering the "lived" relation between them and the world and acquiring that new form of specific unconsciousness called "consciousness" ' (Althusser, 1969, p. 233). It was, in this sense, that 'experience' was conceived, not as an authenticating source but as an effect: not as a reflection of the real but as an 'imaginary relation'. It was only a short step . . . to the development of an account of how this 'imaginary relation' served, not simply the dominance of a ruling class over a dominated one, but (through the reproduction of the relations of production, and the constitution of labour-power in a form fit for capitalist exploitation) the expanded reproduction of the mode of production itself. Many of the other lines of divergence between the two paradigms flow from this point: the conception of 'men' as bearers of the structures that speak and place them, rather than as active agents in the making of their own history: the emphasis on a structural rather than a historical 'logic'; . . . the recasting of history as a march of the structures: . . . the structuralist 'machine' . . .

[. . .]

Without suggesting that there can be any easy synthesis between them, it might usefully be said at this point that neither 'culturalism' nor 'structuralism' is, in its present manifestation, adequate to the task of constructing the study of culture as a conceptually clarified and theoretically informed domain of study. Nevertheless, something fundamental to it emerges from a rough comparison of their respective strengths and limitations.

The great strength of the structuralisms is their stress on 'determinate conditions'. They remind us that, unless the dialectic really can be held, in any particular analysis, between both halves of the proposition—that 'men make history . . . on the basis of conditions which are not of their making'—the result will inevitably be a naïve humanism, with its necessary consequence: a voluntarist and populist political practice. The fact that 'men' can become conscious of their conditions, organize to struggle against them and in fact transform them—without which no active politics can even be conceived, let alone practised—must not be allowed to override the awareness of the fact that, in capitalist relations, men and women are placed and positioned in relations which constitute them as agents. 'Pessimism of the intellect, optimism of the will' is a better starting point than a simple heroic affirmation. Structuralism does enable us to begin to think—as Marx insisted—of the *relations* of a structure on the basis of something other than their reduction to relationships between 'people'. This was Marx's privileged level of abstraction: that which enabled him to break with the obvious but incorrect starting point of 'political economy'— bare individuals.

But this connects with a second strength: the recognition by structuralism not only of the necessity of abstraction as the instrument of thought through which 'real relations' are appropriated, but also of the presence, in Marx's work, of a continuous and complex movement *between different levels of abstraction*. It is, of course, the case—as 'culturalism' argues—that, in historical reality, practices do not appear neatly distinguished out into their respective instances. However, to think about or to analyse the complexity of the real, the act of practice of thinking is required; and this necessitates the use of the power of abstraction and analysis, the formation of concepts with which to cut into the complexity of the real, in order precisely to reveal and bring to light relationships and structures which cannot be visible to the naïve naked eye, and which can neither present nor authenticate themselves. . . . Of course, structuralism has frequently taken this proposition to its extreme. Because thought is impossible without 'the power of abstraction', it has confused this with giving an absolute primacy to the level of the formation of concepts—and at the highest, most abstract level of abstraction only: Theory with a capital 'T' then becomes judge and jury. But this is precisely to lose the insight just won from Marx's own practice. For it is clear in, for example, *Capital*, that the *method*— whilst, of course, taking place 'in thought' (as Marx asked in the 1857 Introduction, where else?)—rests, not on the simple exercise of abstraction but on the movement and relations which the argument is constantly establishing between *different levels* of abstraction: at each, the premises in play must be distinguished from those which—for the sake of the argument—have to be held constant. . . . This method is adequately represented in *neither* the absolutism of Theoretical Practice, in structuralism, nor in the anti-abstraction (of E. P. Thompson's) 'Poverty Of Theory' position into which, in reaction, culturalism appears to have been driven or driven itself. Nevertheless it is intrinsically *theoretical*, and must be. Here, structuralism's insistence that thought does not reflect reality, but is articulated on and appropriates it, is a necessary starting point. An adequate *working through* of the consequences of this argument might begin to produce a method which takes us outside the permanent oscillations between abstraction/anti-abstraction and the false dichotomies of Theoreticism *vs*. Empiricism which have both marked and disfigured the structuralism/culturalism encounter to date.

Structuralism has another strength, in its conception of 'the whole'. There is a sense in which, though culturalism constantly insists on the radical particularity of its practices, its mode of conceptualizing the 'totality' has something of the complex simplicity of an expressive totality behind it.[1] Its complexity is constituted by the fluidity with which practices move into and out of one another. [. . .] Structuralism goes too far in erecting the machine of a 'Structure', with its self-generating propensities, . . . equipped with its distinctive instances. Yet it represents an advance over culturalism in the conception it has of the necessary *complexity* of the unity of a structure. . . . Moreover, it has the conceptual ability to think of a unity which is constructed through the *differences* between, rather than the homology of, practices. [. . .] But the emphasis on unity-in-difference, on complex unity—can be worked in another, and ultimately more fruitful direction: towards the problematic of relative autonomy and 'over-determination', and the study of *articulation*. Again, articulation contains the danger of a high formalism. But it also has the considerable advantage of enabling us to think of how specific practices (articulated around contradictions which do not all arise in the same way, at the same point, in the same moment), can nevertheless be thought *together*. The structuralist paradigm thus does—if properly developed—enable us to begin really to *conceptualize* the specificity of different practices (analytically distinguished, abstracted out), without losing its grip on the ensemble which they constitute. Culturalism constantly affirms the specificity of different practices—'culture' must not be absorbed into 'the economic': but it lacks an adequate way of establishing this specificity theoretically.

The third strength which structuralism exhibits lies in its decentering of 'experience' and its seminal work in elaborating the neglected category of 'ideology'. It is difficult to conceive of a Cultural Studies thought within a Marxist paradigm which is innocent of the category of 'ideology'. Of course, culturalism constantly makes reference to this concept: but it does not in fact lie at the centre of its conceptual universe. The authenticating power and reference of 'experience' imposes a barrier between culturalism and a proper conception of 'ideology'. Yet, without it, the effectivity of 'culture' for the reproduction of a particular mode of production cannot be grasped. It is true that there is a marked tendency in the more recent structuralist conceptualisations of 'ideology' to give it a functionalist reading—as the necessary cement of the social formation. From this position, it is indeed impossible—as culturalism would correctly argue—to conceive either of ideologies which are not, by definition, 'dominant': or of the concept of struggle (the latter's appearance in Althusser's famous ISA's article being—to coin yet another phrase—largely 'gestural'). Nevertheless, work is already being done which suggests ways in which the field of ideology may be adequately conceptualized as a terrain of struggle (through the work of Gramsci, and more recently, of Laclau—see Laclau, 1977), and these have structuralist rather than culturalist bearings.

Culturalism's strengths can almost be derived from the weaknesses of the structuralist position already noted, and from the latter's strategic absences and silences. It has insisted, correctly, on the affirmative moment of the development of conscious struggle and organization as a necessary element in the analysis of history, ideology and consciousness: against its persistent down-grading in the structuralist paradigm. Here, again, it is largely Gramsci who has provided us with a set of more refined terms through which to link the largely 'unconscious' and given cultural categories of 'common sense' with the formation of more active and organic ideologies, which have the capacity to intervene in the ground of common sense and popular traditions and, through such interventions, to organize masses of men and women. In this sense, culturalism *properly* restores the dialectic between the unconsciousness of cultural categories and the moment of conscious organization: even if, in its characteristic movement, it has tended to match structuralism's over-emphasis on 'conditions' with an altogether too-inclusive emphasis on 'consciousness'. It therefore not only recovers—as the necessary moment of any analysis—the process by means of which classes-in-themselves, defined primarily by the way in which economic relations position 'men' as agents—become active historical and political forces-for-themselves: it also—against its own anti-theoretical good sense—*requires* that, when properly developed, each moment must be understood in terms of the level of abstraction at which the analysis is operating. Again, Gramsci has begun to point a way through this false polarization in his discussion of 'the passage between the structure and the sphere of the complex superstructures', and its distinct forms and moments.

[. . .]

I have said enough to indicate that, in my view, the line in Cultural Studies which has attempted to *think forwards* from the best elements in the structuralist and culturalist enterprises, by way of some of the concepts elaborated in Gramsci's work, comes closest to meeting the requirements of the field of study. And the reason for that should by now also be obvious. Though neither structuralism nor culturalism will do, as self-sufficient paradigms of study, they have a centrality to the field which all the other contenders lack because, between them (in their divergences as well as their convergences) they address what must be the *core problem* of Cultural Studies. They constantly return us to the terrain marked out by those strongly coupled but not mutually exclusive concepts culture/ideology. They pose, together, the problems consequent on trying to think *both* the specificity of different practices and the forms of the articulated unity they constitute. They make a constant, if flawed, return to the base/superstructure metaphor. They are correct in insisting that this question— which resumes all the problems of a non-reductive determinacy—is the heart of the matter: and that, on the solution of this problem will turn the capacity of Cultural Studies to supersede the endless oscillations between idealism and reductionism. They confront—even if in radically opposed ways—the dialectic between conditions and consciousness. At another level, they pose the question of the relation between the logic of thinking and the 'logic' of historical process. They continue to hold out the promise of a properly materialist theory of culture. In their sustained and mutually reinforcing antagonisms they hold out no promise of an easy synthesis. But, between them, they define where, if at all, is the space, and what are the limits within which such a synthesis might be constituted. In Cultural Studies, theirs are the 'names of the game'.

NOTE

1. The concept of 'expressive totality' was developed by Althusser in his critique of Hegelian forms of Marxism. According to these, the structure of the social whole is said to be determined by an essential or single contradiction—between the forces and the relations of production, for instance. Ideological and political contradictions are then viewed as the 'expressions'—that is, particular forms of the appearance—of this essential and determining contradiction.

REFERENCES

Althusser, L., *For Marx*, Allen Lane, 1969.
Althusser, L., 'Ideology and Ideological State Apparatuses', in *Lenin and Philosophy, and other Essays*, New Left Books, 1971.
Althusser, L. and Balibar, E., *Reading Capital*, New Left Books, 1970.
Hoggart, R., *The Uses of Literacy*, Penguin, 1969.
Laclau, E., *Politics and Ideology in Marxist Theory*, New Left Books, 1977.
Marx, K. and Engels, F., *The German Ideology*, Lawrence and Wishart, 1965.
Marx, K., *Grundrisse: Foundations of the Critique of Political Economy*, Penguin, 1973.
Marx, K., *Capital: A Critique of Political Economy*, 3 vols, Lawrence and Wishart, 1970.
Thompson, E. P., *The Making of the English Working Class*, Penguin, 1968.
Thompson, E. P., 'Peculiarities of the English', *Socialist Register*, 1965.
Thompson, E. P., Reviews of Raymond Williams's *The Long Revolution*, *New Left Review*, Nos. 9 and 10, 1961.
Thompson, E. P., *Whigs and Hunters*, Allen Lane, 1975.
Thompson, E. P., *The Poverty of Theory*, Merlin Press, 1978.
Williams, R., *Culture and Society 1780–1950*, Penguin, 1963.
Williams, R., *The Long Revolution*, Penguin, 1965.
Williams, R., 'Culture is Ordinary', *Conviction*, 1958.
Williams, R., 'Literature and Sociology: in memory of Lucien Goldmann', *New Left Review*, No. 67, 1971.
Williams, R., 'Base and Superstructure in Marxist Cultural Theory', *New Left Review*, No. 82, 1973.
Williams, R., *Marxism and Literature*, Oxford University Press, 1977.
Williams, R., *The Country and the City*, Chatto and Windus, 1973.

4 Cultural studies in America

Introduction

As with the growth of cultural studies in Britain, cultural studies in America has had varied and plural origins by no means limited to or determined by movements inside academia. However, its origins can be argued to be more heterogeneous and less politically leftist than in Britain. Less than in Britain can one point (even if erroneously) to specific founding texts and founding figures, but rather to a wide range of movements and issues, such as the GI Bill, which enabled an older generation of students to enter the universities in the post-war years, political realities, such as the cold war, and material developments, especially inside communications technology. The social issues of race and gender were first felt outside the academy in racial confrontations at Little Rock and via the influx of women into the labour-force. Media studies emerged from commercial needs as well as from academic concerns, and cultural critique was as much the province of the Beat poets and liberal journalists as university intellectuals. In both countries, however, both non-academic and academic studies of the national and other cultures were deeply influenced by America's post-war rise to global domination and by the influx of a new generation of university students drawn from broader social and ethnic categories than before the second world war.

The rise of American studies provided an important arena for the emergence of interdisciplinary studies engaged in understanding the genesis and development of the national culture through a study of 'great' works and movements. American studies itself has many possible origins: Frederick Jackson Turner's *The Significance of the Frontier in American History* (1893) (see section on the Nineteenth Century), the Progressive era revolt against formalism; early academic programmes—in 1936 George Washington University began a programme in American studies and in the same year Harvard University established a graduate programme in the History of American Civilization; and particular books such as V. L. Parrington's *Main Currents in American Thought* (1927–30) or F. O. Mathiessen's *American Renaissance* (1941). Gene Wise has characterized the aim of Americanist scholars from the 1930s to the

1950s as probing for the 'fundamental meaning of America' and as working with a series of assumptions—that 'there is an "American Mind" . . . more or less homogenous' moulded by living in a 'New World' to be 'hopeful, innocent, individualistic, pragmatic, idealist'. Further, these qualities although present in 'popular minds', are seen as best expressed by writers such as Emerson, Thoreau, Whitman, Twain ('"Paradigm Dramas" in American Studies: A Cultural and Institutional History of the Movement', *American Quarterly*, 31, 2, 1979). As Wise notes, basic to the search for the meaning of America was the view that '"thought" in America is an integrated whole', hence, the need for interdisciplinary studies became integral to the inquiries. What developed was an interdisciplinary field which was humanistic in its assumptions about the significance of individual experience and art-works.

In his 1957 essay, 'Can "American Studies" Develop a Method?' (*American Studies Quarterly*), Henry Nash Smith argued that American studies was challenged by sociology's concern with generalized mass experience and New Criticism's divorce of text from social/historical context. He looked forward to the emergence of some method to unite the general with the particular and concluded with a defence of studying the 'masterpiece of literature, or the extraordinarily productive career' as 'valid expressions of the culture'. The myth-symbol approach Nash Smith evolved provided the field with a range of powerful metaphors for the analysis of American literature and history and can be seen at work in *Virgin Land: The American West as Symbol and Myth* (1950). Leo Marx, one of Nash Smith's most brilliant followers, defined myth as 'a combination of symbols, held together by narrative, which embodies the virtually all-encompassing conception of reality—the world view—of a group' ('American Studies—A Defence of an Unscientific Method', *New Literary History*, 1, 1969). The myth-symbol approach, however, has been criticized for working within a model of historical consensus, reflecting cold war politics, for its unexplored humanistic assumptions, and for avoiding discussion of myth as an ideological formation or analytic tool. By the late 1960s, the concept of homogeneity that underwrote much work in the field was fractured with the emergence of new fields of cultural and interdisciplinary study—such as black, hispanic, native American and women's studies. Nevertheless, by moving history, to some extent, from background to context, by looking at popular as well as canonical works, by insisting on an interdisciplinary approach, and by raising questions of method, the Americanists made a vital contribution to the scholarly study of culture.

The second world war brought a series of eminent German intellectuals to America, such as Hannah Arendt and the members of the Frankfurt School of post-Marxist critical theory, Max Horkeimer, Theodor Adorno and Herbert Marcuse, who set up the Institute for Social Research at Columbia University. From their experience of Nazi Germany, they brought with them a fear of the transformation of liberal political institutions and social culture into totalitarian state formations. They also brought with them an awareness of the ability of the media—film, radio, newspapers—to control and manipulate the mass, substituting irrational desires for rational and 'real' wants and needs. In his study of a popular Los Angeles astrology column, *The Stars Down to Earth* (Heidelberg, 1957), for instance, Adorno argued that the column 'by strengthening the sense of fatality, dependence and obedience . . . paralyses the will to change objective conditions in any respect and relegates all worries to a private plane promising a cure-all by the very same compliance which prevents a change of conditions' (72).

Mass culture as mass commodification purveyed through the mass media is seen not merely as engrossing people with fictions but also as turning people into fictions. Indeed, in Horkheimer's and Adorno's famous essay, 'The Culture Industry: Enlightenment as Mass Deception', they conclude that 'personality scarcely signifies anything more than shining white teeth and freedom from body odor and emotions' (first edition in German, 1944). Herbert Marcuse attained guru status on American campuses with two books, *Eros and Civilization* (1955) and *One Dimensional Man* (1964). Marcuse's basic argument is that advanced technological-industrial societies sustain and reproduce themselves by creating and satisfying material needs. Marcuse argues that a society of material abundance is able to cancel out the voices and forces of dissent active in eras of scarcity:

> If the worker and his boss enjoy the same television programme and visit the same resort places, if the typist is as attractively made up as the daughter of her employer, if the Negro owns a Cadillac, if they all read the same newspaper, then this assimilation indicates not the disappearance of classes, but the extent to which the needs and satisfactions that serve the preservation of the Establishment are shared by the underlying population.

(*One Dimensional Man*, 8)

The Frankfurt School continues to exert considerable influence on cultural studies on both sides of the Atlantic, but its élitism has increasingly been attacked by those who argue that despite (or, indeed, because of) commercialization popular cultural forms, such as popular music, represent pertinent and valid forms of cultural experience.

Criticism of mass-consumerism and the media's role in purveying material desires and forming opinions was not limited to Marxists but was also the province of liberals who saw the mass media as threatening individualism. Walter Lippman's *Public Opinion* (1922) can be identified as having inaugurated modern media studies in America and established many of its concerns. His book is focused on the news media, and articulates fears of stereotyping and the manipulation of public opinion. The Commission on Freedom of the Press publication, *A Free and Responsible Press* (1947), is indicative of the growing awareness during the post-war period of the social and ethical issues raised by an era of mass communications. The power and potential for change signalled by the spread of television into most homes in America, as in England, increased concern over the ethics and politics of the mass media. In 1959 a three-day colloquium on Mass Culture organized by the Tamiment Institute and the journal *Daedalus* gathered together sociologists such as Edward Shils, philosophers such as Hannah Arendt, and historians such as Arthur Schlesinger, Jr., as well as representatives of the mass media, to debate on the nature and relationship of culture and communications. As with the National Union of Teachers conference 'Popular Culture and Personal Responsibility' in 1960 in England, this conference can be regarded as a seminal event during which arguments on the gap between high and popular culture and the relationship of media and mass were structured. For Shils, in effect, the 'brutal culture' offered to the masses more or less suited them, as it always had, and 'superior culture' continued, as it always had, to be a minority activity untouched by the mass (*Culture for the Millions? Mass Media in Modern Society*, 1964). Works such as C. Wright Mills' *The Power Elite* (1959) offered a leftist critique of media as manipulative and exploitative.

An alternative approach to the media, differing from either élitist indifference or disparagement toward the mass media or leftist and liberal concern with its commodification of life, was explored by the Canadian academic Mashall McLuhan. His publications, as well as his frequent television appearances, made his 'message' influential in the 1960s and 1970s. McLuhan's basic thesis, as in the extract in this section from *Understanding the Media: The Extensions of Man* (1965), is that each communications medium—the print word of the Gutenberg era or the electronic media of the present age—alters beyond our recognition our ways of thinking and perceiving. He argues that whereas print media created a linear and sequential concept of knowledge and modes of thought, the electronic media create a complex and stimulating social and mental culture of immediacy. For McLuhan, the 'electric media' have the effect of homogenizing culture and also dispersing it to create the 'global village'. There is no centre left but only isolated groups of media participants—the media 'extensions of man'. However, even as issues of the mass were in debate, the nature of the mass was altering.

The post-war cultural commentators, looking at the effects of industrial technology and the mass media on society, were only very marginally, if at all, concerned with issues of ethnic minorities and gender. The female metaphors of land passively awaiting male impregnation, analysed by Annette Kolodny in *The Lay of the Land* (1975), for instance, were barely examined in Nash Smith's work *Virgin Land* (1950), although its title might seem to call for such investigation. With regard to race, it is perhaps not unfair to cite Talcott Parson's introduction to *The Negro American* (1965) which looks forward to total assimilation:

> Only in a highly urbanized, hence individualized and pluralized, society does the opportunity emerge for a saliently different minority group to diffuse itself through the society. Only then does its position become so anomalous as to activate strong pressures to break up its monolithic separateness, even if, as in some historic cases (for example, certain Jewish communities), it is a privileged separateness.

By the late 1960s and early 1970s, the women's movement and the civil rights movement generated new analyses of culture by forcing recognition of the importance of gender and race in the construction of patterns of domination and subordination. With regard to both movements, the analysis of the ways in which cultural domination is achieved and operates was given a new concreteness by the political and legal demands of ethnic minorities and women, subjects largely subsumed and undifferentiated in the critiques and defences of American culture. At the same time, the full media coverage of the war in Vietnam, whose images of carnage appeared in news broadcasts every evening, altered America's self- and world-image and stimulated an era of political and cultural reassessment which marks the end of the post-war era of cultural consensus.

The speeches and essays of Martin Luther King Jr. and Malcolm X, and King's assassination in 1965, and the activities of political groups such as the Black Panthers, radically challenged the 'melting-pot' paradigm and made rethinking on race/ethnic issues essential. The effects of this radical re-thinking can be traced in the section below on Race, as well as in Ann duCille's essay, 'Dyes and Dolls: Multicultural Barbie and the Merchandising of Difference' in the section on Gender.

Similarly, feminist activism and works such as Betty Freidan's *The Feminine Mystique* (1963), Mary Ellmann's *Thinking About Women* (1968), and Kate Millet's *Sexual Politics* (1970), re-thought gender as political rather than biological issues. Ellmann's concern with the female 'stereotype' can be compared with Germaine Greer's approach (see section on British Cultural Studies). Feminism, socialism and black activism came together in the writings of Angela Davis, whose *Women, Sex, Race and Class* (1982) offers a route through American history and society, deploying analytic criteria increasingly recognized as interdependent. The ideology sustaining the construction of race and gender in the media and in social norms, habits and customs was investigated as new programmes opened up in the fields of black, hispanic, native American and women's studies. In the process, the paradigm of the homogenizing dominion of a mass commodity culture was joined by that of contestatory sub- and counter-cultures (see sections on Race and Media Studies).

Cultural studies in America has been characterized by Stefan Collini as 'being shaped above all by the marriage between literary theory and what has been called "the politics of identity"'. In comparison, he argues, the British field 'still tends to be more historical, more empirical, and perhaps more nostalgic' ('Escape from DWEMsville', *Times Literary Supplement*, May 27, 1994; see also Stuart Hall in Voice-Overs). Certainly, a literary and ethnographic/anthropological strain can be discerned in American cultural studies. The study of culture draws directly and indirectly on the ethnographic methods of anthropology—recording and describing languages, customs, beliefs and habits. As anthropologists increasingly sought to develop methods for interpreting cultural activity in terms of interconnection, they turned to literary texts as models and metaphors, and to the interpretive methods (and problems) of literary theory, such as are articulated in Paul Ricour's influential essay 'The Model of the Text: Meaningful Action Considered as Text' (*Social Research*, 38, 1971). Clifford Geertz's methodology, 'Thick Description', has had a very considerable effect on the wide field of cultural studies, especially in America, influencing the New Historicist literary studies of Stephen J. Greenblatt and the work of cultural historians such as Natalie Zemon Davies. Geertz's style is very different from McLuhan's, but his assertion that 'anthropological writings are always in themselves interpretations', can be compared with McLuhan's insistence that the medium is the message. The Anglo-American and European enthnographic traditions are examined in James Clifford's essay, 'On Ethnographic Authority', which can be compared with Stuart Hall's 'Cultural Studies: Two Paradigms' (see section on British Cultural Studies) as it reviews experiential and textual approaches to enthnography.

From their different standpoints in terms of area of investigation and political colouration, a distinct and distinctly varied field of cultural studies has emerged in America. Certain areas of investigation, however, can be seen to represent common ground as conservative traditionalists, liberal humanists or left radicals formulate their topics in relation or reaction to the impact of mass-communications in an era of mass society. Similarly, certain approaches can be seen to develop as cultural commentators become increasingly concerned with the language—metaphors, styles and implicit assumptions—used both to convey and critique culture. The text has ceased to be seen as a transparent vehicle conveying cultural information and has become itself a culturally encoded form. Cultural studies has frequently been defined as studies in ideology; however, this ideological analysis has also emerged as deeply concerned with ideological representation.

J.M. and G.R.

FURTHER READING

Bell, Daniel, *The End of Ideology: On the Exhaustion of Ideas in the Fifties*, New York: Free Press, 1960.

Bercovitch, Sacvan and Myra Jehlen, eds, *Ideology and Classic American Literature*, Cambridge: Cambridge University Press,1986.

Bernstein, Barton, ed., *Towards a New Past: Dissenting Essays in American History*, New York: Random House, 1968.

Cleaver, Eldridge, *Soul on Ice*, New York: McGraw-Hill, 1968.

Drucker, Peter, *The Age of Discontinuity: Guidelines to Our Changing Society*, New York: Harper & Row, 1969.

Horkheimer, Max, and Theodor Adorno, 'The Culture Industry: Enlightenment as Mass Deception', *The Dialectic of Enlightenment*, trans. John Cumming, New York: Continuum, 1987.

Kuhn, Thomas S., *The Structure of Scientific Revolutions*, 2nd edn, Chicago: University of Chicago Press, 1970.

Lewis, Richard W. B., *The American Adam; Innocence, Tragedy, and Tradition in the Nineteenth Century*, Chicago: University of Chicago Press, 1955.

Marx, Leo, *The Machine in the Garden: Technology and the Pastoral Ideal in America*, Oxford and New York: Oxford University Press, 1964.

Michaels, Walter Benn, and Donald E. Pease, eds, *The American Renaissance Reconsidered*, Baltimore and London: Johns Hopkins University Press, 1985.

Riesman, David, *The Lonely Crowd: A Study of the Changing American Character*, New Haven: Yale University Press, 1961.

Rosenberg, Bernard, and David M. White, eds, *Mass Culture: the Popular Arts in America*, Glencoe, Illinois: Free Press, 1957.

Schramm, Wilbur L., ed., *Mass communications: A Book of Readings selected and edited for the Institute of Communications Research in the University of Illinois*, Urbana: University of Illinois Press, 1949.

Slotkin, Richard, *Regeneration Through Violence: The Mythology of the American Frontier, 1600–1860*, Middletown, Conn.: Wesleyan University Press, 1973.

Trachtenberg, Alan, *Brooklyn Bridge: Fact and Symbol*, Chicago: University of Chicago Press, 1979.

Trilling, Lionel, *The Liberal Imagination: Essays on Literature and Society*, New York: Viking Press, 1950.

Henry Nash Smith (1906–1986)

Henry Nash Smith was born in Dallas and educated at Southern Methodist University and Harvard. He taught at both these institutions, and at the Universities of Texas at Austin, and Minnesota before being named professor of English at the University of California at Berkeley in 1953. His seminal work in American literature, *Virgin Land: The American West as Symbol and Myth*, was published in 1950. His other works include *Mark Twain's Fable of Progress* (1964), *Mark Twain: The Development of a Writer* (1971), and *Democracy and the Novel: Popular Resistance to Classic American Writers* (1978).

The essay which follows is the last chapter from *Virgin Land*, in which Smith takes Frederick Jackson Turner to task for the contradictory assumptions behind his 1893 frontier hypothesis. Turner states that the 'existence of an area of free land, its continuous recession, and the advance of American settlement westward explain American development', and Smith interjects two pivotal factors—culture and ideology—in reading the American context. After having developed in the earlier chapters the actualities of the frontier, in the final chapter of *Virgin Land* Smith feels that Turner relies very heavily on the myth of the 'pastoral' or the garden metaphor to signal the superiority of agrarian environments in analyses of democracy, 'regeneration', and progress. Smith complains: 'Turner's metaphors threaten to become themselves a means of cognition and to supplant discursive reasoning.' Especially problematic for Smith is Turner's habit of combining the agrarian ideal with the theory of progressive, social development: two systems which Smith argues are contradictory because they position the yeoman farmer as both the fortunate object of utopian nature and as a backward, inferior stage in the hierarchy of civilization. Smith also accuses Turner of incomplete analysis, especially in ignoring the 'European exploitation of native peoples all over the world'. Ultimately, Smith faults Turner for his distrust of the city and his failure to deal cogently with industrial revolution. As a result, Smith highlights crucial questions for American studies— questions which also focus on the significance of what are called 'identity politics' in

American studies. How can American development be measured without reliance on European standards? Smith does not attempt to fully answer this question, but sets a challenging agenda for a 'new intellectual system' to interrogate American literature, culture, and new-world ideology.

R.S.L.

The myth of the garden and Turner's frontier hypothesis

By far the most influential piece of writing about the West produced during the nineteenth century was the essay on 'The Significance of the Frontier in American History' read by Frederick Jackson Turner before the American Historical Association at Chicago in 1893. The 'frontier hypothesis' which he advanced on that occasion revolutionized American historiography and eventually made itself felt in economics and sociology, in literary criticism, and even in politics.[1]

Turner's central contention was that 'the existence of an area of free land, its continuous recession, and the advance of American settlement westward explain American development.'[2] This proposition does not sound novel now because it has been worked into the very fabric of our conception of our history, but in 1893 it was a polemic directed against the two dominant schools of historians: the group interpreting American history in terms of the slavery controversy, led by Hermann Edouard von Holst, and the group headed by Turner's former teacher, Herbert B. Adams of Johns Hopkins, who explained American institutions as the outgrowth of English, or rather ancient Teutonic germs planted in the New World. Turner maintained that the West, not the proslavery South or the antislavery North, was the most important among American sections, and that the novel attitudes and institutions produced by the frontier, especially through its encouragement of democracy, had been more significant than the imported European heritage in shaping American society.

To determine whether Turner's hypothesis is or is not a valid interpretation of American history forms no part of the intention of this book.[3] The problem here is to place his main ideas in the intellectual tradition that has been examined in earlier chapters. Whatever the merits or demerits of the frontier hypothesis in explaining actual events, the hypothesis itself developed out of the myth of the garden. Its insistence on the importance of the West, its affirmation of democracy, and its doctrine of geographical determinism derive from a still broader tradition of Western thought that would include Benton and Gilpin as well, but its emphasis on agricultural settlement places it clearly within the stream of agrarian theory that flows from eighteenth-century England and France through Jefferson to the men who elaborated the ideal of a society of yeoman farmers in the Northwest from which Turner sprang. Turner's immersion in this stream of intellectual influence had an unfortunate effect in committing him to certain archaic assumptions which hampered his approach to twentieth-century social problems. But one must not forget that the tradition was richer than these assumptions, and that it conferred on him the authority of one who speaks from the distilled experience of his people.[4] If the myth of the garden embodied certain erroneous judgments made by these people concerning the economic forces that had come to dominate American life, it was still true to their experience in the large, because it expressed beliefs and aspirations as well as statistics. This is not the only kind of historical truth, but it is a kind historians need never find contemptible.

Turner's most important debt to his intellectual tradition is the ideas of savagery and civilization that he uses to define his central factor, the frontier. His frontier is explicitly 'the meeting point between savagery and civilization.'[5] For him as for his predecessors, the outer limit of agricultural settlement is the boundary of civilization, and in his thought as in that of so many earlier interpreters we must therefore begin by distinguishing two Wests, one beyond and one within this all-important line.

From the standpoint of economic theory the wilderness beyond the frontier, the realm of savagery, is a constantly receding area of free land. Mr. Fulmer Mood has demonstrated that Turner derived this technical expression from a treatise on economics by Francis A. Walker used as a text by one of his teachers at Johns Hopkins, Richard T. Ely. In Walker's analysis Turner found warrant for his belief that free land had operated as a safety valve for the East and even for Europe by offering every man an opportunity to acquire a farm and become an independent member of society. Free land thus tended to relieve poverty outside the West, and on the frontier itself it fostered economic equality. Both these tendencies made for an increase of democracy.[6] Earlier writers from the time of Franklin had noted that the West offered freedom and subsistence to all,[7] but Turner restated the idea in a more positive form suggested by his conviction that democracy, the rise of the common man, was one of the great movements of modern history.

[. . .]

This is the background of the proposition in the 1893 essay that 'democracy [is] born of free land,'[8] as well as of the celebrated pronouncement made twenty years later: 'American democracy was born of no theorist's dream; it was not carried in the Susan Constant to Virginia, nor in the Mayflower to Plymouth. It came stark and strong and full of life out of the American forest, and it gained new strength each time it touched a new frontier.'[9]

But while economic theory still underlies this later statement, the change of terminology has introduced new and rich overtones. We have been transferred from the plane of the economist's abstractions to a plane of metaphor, and even of myth—for the American forest has become almost an enchanted wood, and the image of Antaeus has been invoked to suggest the power of the Western earth. Such intimations reach beyond logical theory. They remind us that the wilderness beyond the limits of civilization was not only an area of free land; it was also nature. The idea of nature suggested to Turner a poetic account of the influence of free land as a rebirth, a regeneration, a rejuvenation of man and society constantly recurring where civilization came into contact with the wilderness along the frontier.[10]

Rebirth and regeneration are categories of myth rather than of economic analysis, but ordinarily Turner kept his metaphors under control and used them to illustrate

217

and vivify his logical propositions rather than as a structuralist principle or a means of cognition: that is, he used them rhetorically not poetically. The nonpoetic use of a vivid metaphor is illustrated in a speech he delivered in 1896:

> Americans had a safety valve for social danger, a bank account on which they might continually draw to meet losses. This was the vast unoccupied domain that stretched from the borders of the settled area to the Pacific Ocean. . . . No grave social problem could exist while the wilderness at the edge of civilizations [sic] opened wide its portals to all who were oppressed, to all who with strong arms and stout heart desired to hew out a home and a career for themselves. Here was an opportunity for social development continually to begin over again, wherever society gave signs of breaking into classes. Here was a magic fountain of youth in which America continually bathed and was rejuvenated.[11]

The figure of the magic fountain is merely a rhetorical ornament at the end of a paragraph having a rational structure and subject to criticism according to recognized canons. But sometimes, especially when the conception of nature as the source of occult powers is most vividly present, Turner's metaphors threaten to become themselves a means of cognition and to supplant discursive reasoning. This seems to happen, for example, in an essay he wrote for the *Atlantic* in 1903. After quoting a clearly animistic passage from Lowell's Harvard Commemoration Ode on how Nature had shaped Lincoln of untainted clay from the unexhausted West, 'New birth of our new soil, the first American,' Turner builds an elaborate figurative structure:

> Into this vast shaggy continent of ours poured the first feeble tide of European settlement. European men, institutions, and ideas were lodged in the American wilderness, and this great American West took them to her bosom, taught them a new way of looking upon the destiny of the common man, trained them in adaptation to the conditions of the New World, to the creation of new institutions to meet new needs; and ever as society on her eastern border grew to resemble the Old World in its social forms and its industry, ever, as it began to lose faith in the ideal of democracy, she opened new provinces, and dowered new democracies in her most distant domains with her material treasures and with the ennobling influence that the fierce love of freedom, the strength that came from hewing out a home, making a school and a church, and creating a higher future for his family, furnished to the pioneer.[12]

It would be difficult to maintain that all these metaphors are merely ornamental. Is it wholly meaningless, for example, that the West, the region close to nature, is feminine, while the East, with its remoteness from nature and its propensity for aping Europe, is neuter?

In the passage just quoted, a beneficent power emanating from nature is shown creating an agrarian utopia in the West. The myth of the garden is constructed before our eyes. Turner is asserting as fact a state of affairs that on other occasions he recognized as merely an ideal to be striven for. Earlier in the same essay, for example, he had summarized Jefferson's 'platform of political principles' and his 'conception that democracy should have an agricultural basis.'[13] The 'should' easily becomes 'did': Jefferson's agrarian ideal proves to be virtually identical with the frontier democracy that Turner believed he had discovered in the West. To imagine an ideal

218

so vividly that it comes to seem actual is to follow the specific procedure of poetry.

The other member of the pair of ideas which defined the frontier for Turner was that of civilization. If the idea of nature in the West provided him with a rich and not always manageable store of metaphorical coloring, his use of the idea of civilization had the equally important consequence of committing him to the theory that all societies, including those of successive Wests, develop through the same series of progressively higher stages. Mr. Mood has traced this conception also to Ely and to Walker, and back of them to the German economic theorist Friedrich List.[14] But, as we have had occasion to notice earlier in this study, the idea had been imported into the United States from France soon after 1800 and by the 1820s had become one of the principal instruments for interpreting the agricultural West.

Turner's acceptance of this theory involved him in the difficulties that it had created for earlier observers of frontier society, such as Timothy Flint. For the theory of social stages was basically at odds with the conception of the Western farmer as a yeoman surrounded by utopian splendor. Instead, it implied that the Western farmer was a coarse and unrefined representative of a primitive stage of social evolution. Turner's adoption of these two contradictory theories makes it difficult for him to manage the question of whether frontier character and society, and frontier influence on the rest of the country, have been good or bad. As long as he is dealing with the origins of democracy in the West he evidently considers frontier influence good. A man who refers to 'the familiar struggle of West against East, of democracy against privileged classes'[15] leaves no doubt concerning his own allegiance. This attitude was in fact inevitable as long as one maintained the doctrine that frontier society was shaped by the influence of free land, for free land was nature, and nature in this system of ideas is unqualifiedly benign. Indeed, it is itself the norm of value. There is no way to conceive possible bad effects flowing from the impact of nature on man and society.

But when Turner invokes the concept of civilization, the situation becomes more complex. His basic conviction was that the highest social values were to be found in the relatively primitive society just within the agricultural frontier. But the theory of social stages placed the highest values at the other end of the process, in urban industrial society, amid the manufacturing development and city life which Jefferson and later agrarian theorists had considered dangerous to social purity. Turner wavered between the two views. In the 1893 essay, to take a minute but perhaps significant bit of evidence, he referred to the evolution of each successive region of the West 'into a higher stage'—in accord with the orthodox theory of civilization and progress. When he revised the essay for republication in 1899, he realized that such an assumption might lead him into inconsistency and substituted 'a different industrial stage.'[16]

But he could not always maintain the neutrality implied in this revision. For one thing, he strongly disapproved of the Western love of currency inflation, which he considered a consequence of the primitive state of frontier society. 'The colonial and Revolutionary frontier,' he asserted in the 1893 essay, 'was the region whence emanated many of the worst forms of an evil currency,' and he pointed out that each of the periods of lax financial integrity in American history had coincided with the rise of a new set of frontier communities. The Populist agitation for free coinage of silver was a case in point.

219

Many a state that now declines any connection with the tenets of the Populists [he wrote] itself adhered to such ideas in an earlier stage of the development of the state. A primitive society can hardly be expected to show the intelligent appreciation of the complexity of business interests in a developed society.[17]

In his revision of the essay in 1899 Turner noted with satisfaction that Wisconsin had borne out his principles:

Wisconsin, to take an illustration, in the days when it lacked varied agriculture and complex industrial life, was a stronghold of the granger and greenback movements; but it has undergone an industrial transformation, and in the last presidential contest Mr. Bryan carried but one county in the state.[18]

Here the evolution of society from agrarian simplicity toward greater complexity is assumed to bring about improvement.

Yet if Turner could affirm progress and civilization in this one respect, the general course of social evolution in the United States created a grave theoretical dilemma for him. He had based his highest value, democracy, on free land. But the westward advance of civilization across the continent had caused free land to disappear. What then was to become of democracy? The difficulty was the greater because in associating democracy with free land he had inevitably linked it also with the idea of nature as a source of spiritual values. All the overtones of his conception of democracy were therefore tinged with cultural primitivism, and tended to clash with the idea of civilization. In itself this was not necessarily a disadvantage; the conception of civilization had been invoked to justify a number of dubious undertakings in the course of the nineteenth century, including European exploitation of native peoples all over the world. Furthermore, as we have had occasion to observe in studying the literary interpretation of the agricultural West, the theory of social progress through a uniform series of stages was poor equipment for any observer who wished to understand Western farmers. But Turner had accepted the idea of civilization as a general description of the society that had been expanding across the continent, and with the final disappearance of free land this idea was the only remaining principle with which he could undertake the analysis of contemporary American society.

Since democracy for him was related to the idea of nature and seemed to have no logical relation to civilization, the conclusion implied by his system was that post-frontier American society contained no force tending toward democracy. Fourierists earlier in the century, reaching a conclusion comparable to this, had maintained that civilization was but a transitory social stage, and that humanity must transcend it by advancing into the higher stage of 'association.' Henry George in Turner's own day had announced that progress brought poverty, that civilization embodied a radical contradiction and could be redeemed only by a revolutionary measure, the confiscation of the unearned increment in the value of natural resources. But Turner did not share the more or less revolutionary attitude that lay back of these proposals.[19] On the contrary, he conceived of social progress as taking place within the existing framework of society, that is, within civilization. Whatever solution might be found for social problems would have to be developed according to the basic principles already accepted by society. This meant that his problem was to find a basis for democracy in some aspect of civilization as he observed it about him in the United

States. His determined effort in this direction showed that his mind and his standards of social ethics were subtler and broader than the conceptual system within which the frontier hypothesis had been developed, but he was the prisoner of the assumptions he had taken over from the agrarian tradition.[20] He turned to the rather unconvincing idea that the Midwestern state universities might be able to save democracy by producing trained leaders,[21] and later he placed science beside education as another force to which men might turn for aid in their modern perplexity. But these suggestions were not really satisfying to him, and he fell back at last on the faith he had confided to his Commonplace Book as an undergraduate—a faith neither in nature nor in civilization but simply in man, in the common people. In 1924, after reviewing the most urgent of the world's problems, Turner declared with eloquence and dignity:

> I prefer to believe that man is greater than the dangers that menace him; that education and science are powerful forces to change these tendencies and to produce a rational solution of the problems of life on the shrinking planet. I place my trust in the mind of man seeking solutions by intellectual toil rather than by drift and by habit, bold to find new ways of adjustment, and strong in the leadership that spreads new ideas among the common people of the world; committed to peace on earth, and ready to use the means of preserving it.[22]

This statement is an admission that the notion of democracy born of free land, colored as it is by primitivism, is not an adequate instrument for dealing with a world dominated by industry, urbanization, and international conflicts. The first World War had shaken Turner's agrarian code of values as it destroyed so many other intellectual constructions of the nineteenth century. He continued to struggle with the grievous problems of the modern world, but his original theoretical weapons were no longer useful.

Turner's predicament illustrates what has happened to the tradition within which he worked. From the time of Franklin down to the end of the frontier period almost a century and a half later, the West had been a constant reminder of the importance of agriculture in American society. It had nourished an agrarian philosophy and an agrarian myth that purported to set forth the character and destinies of the nation. The philosophy and the myth affirmed an admirable set of values, but they ceased very early to be useful in interpreting American society as a whole because they offered no intellectual apparatus for taking account of the industrial revolution. A system which revolved about a half-mystical conception of nature and held up as an ideal a rudimentary type of agriculture was powerless to confront issues arising from the advance of technology. Agrarian theory encouraged men to ignore the industrial revolution altogether, or to regard it as an unfortunate and anomalous violation of the natural order of things. In the restricted but important sphere of historical scholarship, for example, the agrarian emphasis on the frontier hypothesis has tended to divert attention from the problems created by industrialization for a half century during which the United States has become the most powerful industrial nation in the world.[23] An even more significant consequence of the agrarian tradition has been its effect on politics. The covert distrust of the city and of everything connected with industry that is implicit in the myth of the garden has impeded coöperation between

221

farmers and factory workers in more than one crisis of our history, from the time of Jefferson to the present.

The agrarian tradition has also made it difficult for Americans to think of themselves as members of a world community because it has affirmed that the destiny of this country leads her away from Europe toward the agricultural interior of the continent. This tendency is quite evident in Turner.[24] Although he devoted much attention to the diplomatic issues arising out of westward expansion, the frontier hypothesis implied that it would be a last misfortune for American society to maintain close connections with Europe. The frontier which produced Andrew Jackson, wrote Turner with approval in 1903, was 'free from the influence of European ideas and institutions. The men of the "Western World" turned their backs upon the Atlantic Ocean, and with a grim energy and self-reliance began to build up a society free from the dominance of ancient forms.'[25] It was only later, when he was trying to find a theoretical basis for democracy outside the frontier, that Turner criticized the American attitude of 'contemptuous indifference' to the social legislation of European countries.[26]

But if interpretation of the West in terms of the idea of nature tended to cut the region off from the urban East and from Europe, the opposed idea of civilization had even greater disadvantages. It not only imposed on Westerners the stigma of social, ethical, and cultural inferiority, but prevented any recognition that the American adventure of settling the continent had brought about an irruption of novelty into history. For the theory of civilization implied that America in general, and the West *a fortiori*, were meaningless except in so far as they managed to reproduce the achievements of Europe. The capital difficulty of the American agrarian tradition is that it accepted the paired but contradictory ideas of nature and civilization as a general principle of historical and social interpretation. A new intellectual system was requisite before the West could be adequately dealt with in literature or its social development fully understood.

NOTES

1. *References on the Significance of the Frontier in American History*, compiled by Everett E. Edwards (United States Department of Agriculture Library, Bibliographical Contributions, No. 25, 2nd ed. [April, 1939]. Mimeographed), lists 124 items bearing on the subject, ranging in date from Franklin's 'Observations on the Peopling of Countries' (1751) to 1939. A passage from a radio address by Franklin D. Roosevelt in 1935 which Dr. Edwards quotes in his excellent Introduction illustrates the political application of Turner's ideas: 'Today we can no longer escape into virgin territory. We must master our environment. . . . We have been compelled by stark necessity to unlearn the too comfortable superstition that the American soil was mystically blessed with every kind of immunity to grave economic maladjustments . . .' (p. 3).
2. 'The Significance of the Frontier in American History,' in *The Early Writings of Frederick Jackson Turner, with a List of All His Works Compiled by Everett E. Edwards and an Introduction by Fulmer Mood* (Madison, Wisconsin, 1938), p. 186.
3. A growing body of scholarship is being devoted to this challenging question. George W. Pierson has called attention to inconsistencies in Turner's doctrines and has inquired into the extent of their currency among historians at the present time: 'The Frontier and Frontiersman of Turner's Essays: A Scrutiny of the Foundations of the Middle Western Tradition,' *Pennsylvania Magazine of History and Biography*, LXIV, 449–478 (October, 1940); 'The Frontier and American Institutions: A Criticism of

the Turner Theory,' *New England Quarterly*, XV, 224–55 (June, 1942); 'American Historians and the Frontier Hypothesis in 1941,' *Wisconsin Magazine of History*, XXVI, 36–60, 170–85 (September, December, 1942). I am indebted to Professor Pierson for many ideas, especially the remark he quotes from a colleague to the effect that Turner's frontiersman closely resembles the stock eighteenth-century picture of the small farmer in Britain (*Wisconsin Magazine of History*, XXVI, 183–4) and the suggestion that Turner's 'poetic interpretations' revived 'the grandest ideas that had gone to make up the American legend' (*idem*).

4. James C. Malin points out that most of Turner's ideas were 'in the air.' He remarks that great thinkers are normally 'the beneficiaries of the folk process and are probably seldom so much true creators as channels through which the folk process finds its fullest expression in explicit language . . .' ('Space and History: Reflections on the Closed-Space Doctrines of Turner and Mackinder and the Challenge of Those Ideas by the Air Age,' *Agricultural History*, XVII, 67–8, April, 1944).

5. *Early Writings*, p. 187.

6. Fulmer Mood, 'The Development of Frederick Jackson Turner as a Historical Thinker,' *Publications of the Colonial Society of Massachusetts*, XXXIV: *Transactions 1937–1942* (Boston, 1943), pp. 322–5.

7. Turner copied into a Commonplace Book that he kept in 1886, during his first year of teaching, a quotation ascribed to Franklin: 'The boundless woods of America which are sure to afford freedom and subsistence to any man who can bait a hook or pull a trigger' (Commonplace Book [II], p. [1]. Turner Papers, Henry E. Huntington Library). The idea occurs often in Franklin but I have not been able to find these words.

8. *Early Writings*, p. 221.

9. 'The West and American Ideals,' an address delivered at the University of Washington, June 17, 1914, *Washington Historical Quarterly*, V, 245 (October, 1914). When Turner revised this address for inclusion in the volume of collected papers *The Frontier in American History* in 1920, he omitted the words 'stark and strong and full of life' (New York, 1920, reprint ed., 1931, p. 293). Although Turner repudiated the 'germ theory' of constitutional development in his 1893 essay (*Early Writings*, p. 188), he had accepted it for a time after he left Herbert B. Adams' seminar at Johns Hopkins. Reviewing the first two volumes of Theodore Roosevelt's *The Winning of the West* in the Chicago *Dial* in August of 1889 (X, 72), he remarked that 'the old Germanic "tun" ' reappeared in the 'forted village' of early Kentucky and Tennessee, the 'folkmoot' in popular meetings of the settlers, and the 'witenagemot' in representative assemblies like the Transylvania legislature. 'These facts,' he added, 'carry the mind back to the warrior-legislatures in the Germanic forests, and forward to those constitutional conventions now at work in our own newly-made states in the Far West; and they make us proud of our English heritage.' In an undergraduate address he had asserted that 'The spirit of individual liberty slumbered in the depths of the German forest' from the time of the barbarian invasions of Rome until it burst forth in the American and French Revolutions (Madison University Press [May 26, 1883], p. 4). Turner's discovery of the American frontier as a force encouraging democracy may exhibit some imaginative persistence of this association between desirable political institutions and a forest.

10. A characteristic phrase is the reference to 'this rebirth of American society' that has gone on, decade after decade, in the West (from an essay in the *Atlantic*, 1896, reprinted in *The Frontier in American History*, p. 205). In his undergraduate Commonplace Book Turner had jotted down, among notes for an oration, 'See Emerson's preface to "Nature" . . .' and had added part of a sentence: '. . . let us believe in the eternal genesis, the freshness & value of things present, act as though, just created, we stood looking a new world in the face and investigate for ourselves and act regardless of past ideas' (Commonplace Book [I], p. [3]). This is quite Emersonian; it might well be a paraphrase of the familiar first paragraph of Emerson's essay: 'Why should not we also enjoy an original relation to the universe? Embosomed for a season in nature, whose floods of life stream around and through us, and invite us, by the powers they supply, to action proportioned to nature, why should we grope among the dry bones of the past, or put the living generation into masquerade out of its faded wardrobe?' (*Complete Works*, Volume I: *Nature, Addresses, and Lectures* [Boston, 1903], p. [3]). Turner said in 1919 that he had been impressed with Woodrow Wilson's emphasis on Walter Bagehot's idea of growth through 'breaking the cake of custom' (Frederick Jackson Turner to William E. Dodd, Cambridge, Mass., October 7, 1919, copy in Turner Papers, Henry E. Huntington Library). The phrase appears in the *Atlantic* essay (*The Frontier in American History*, p. 205).

11. Address at the dedication of a new high school building at Turner's home town of Portage, Wisconsin, January 1, 1896, reported in the Portage *Weekly Democrat*, January 3, 1896 (clipping in Turner Papers,

Henry E. Huntington Library).

12. *The Frontier in American History*, pp. 255, 267.

13. *Ibid.*, p. 250.

14. *Publications of the Colonial Society of Massachusetts*, XXXIV, 304–7. Mr. Mood says that the idea of applying the theory of evolution to social phenomena was the 'fundamental, unifying concept' of Turner's early writings (p. 304), but adds that the *a priori* idea of a sequence of social stages 'can be asserted to be, as a universal rule . . . fallacious. . . . It is one component element in Turner's [1893] essay that will not now stand the test of inspection' (p. 307n).

15. *The Frontier in American History*, p. 121 (1908).

16. *Early Writings*, pp. 199, 285.

17. *Ibid.*, p. 222.

18. *Ibid.*, p. 285.

19. Frederick Jackson Turner to Merle E. Curti, San Marino, Cal., January 5, 1931. Copy in Turner Papers, Henry E. Huntington Library. Turner says he had not read George before writing the 1893 essay and that he had never accepted the single-tax idea.

20. Professor Malin has emphasized the fact that in his later career Turner was 'baffled by his contemporary world and had no satisfying answer to the closed-frontier formula in which he found himself involved' (*Essays on Historiography*, Lawrence, Kansas, 1946, p. 38).

21. *The Frontier in American History*, p. 285 (1910).

22. 'Since the Foundation,' an address delivered at Clark University, February 4, 1924, *Publications of the Clark University Library*, VII, No. 3, p. 29. After the words 'dangers that menace him' Turner has indicated in his personal copy in the Henry E. Huntington Library (No. 222544) the addition of the following words: 'that there are automatic adjustments in progress.'

23. Charles A. Beard makes this point in what seems to me a convincing manner in 'The Frontier in American History,' *New Republic*, XCVII, 359–62 (February 1, 1939). Professor Malin asserts vigorously that 'among other things, the frontier hypothesis is an agricultural interpretation of American history which is being applied during an industrial urban age . . .' ('Mobility and History,' *Agricultural History*, XVII, 177, October, 1943).

24. Benjamin F. Wright has a similar comment in his review of *The Significance of Sections in American History*, *New England Quarterly*, VI, 631 (September, 1933). Professor Malin calls the frontier hypothesis 'an isolationist interpretation in an international age' (*Agricultural History*, XVII, 177). 'It seemed to confirm the Americans,' he remarks elsewhere, 'in their continental isolationism. Was not their United States a unique civilization; was it not superior to that of Europe and Asia?' (*ibid.*, XVIII, 67, April, 1944).

25. *The Frontier in American History*, p. 253 (1903).

26. *Ibid.*, p. 294 (1914). In the 1903 article Turner had emphasized the contrast between American democracy, which was 'fundamentally the outcome of the experiences of the American people in dealing with the West,' and the 'modern efforts of Europe to create an artificial democratic order by legislation' (*ibid.*, p. 266). The implication is clearly that American democracy is the opposite of artificial, i.e., natural, and that this natural origin establishes its superiority.

Marshall McLuhan (1911–1980)

Born in Canada and educated both in Canada and in England, Marshall McLuhan began his career in 1944 as a professor of English literature. Early on, he demonstrated an ability to address a wide range of literary figures and genres, writing essays on Shakespeare, T. S. Eliot, Tennyson, Gerard Manley Hopkins, John Dos Passos. By the early 1950s, however, McLuhan's interests shifted from literature to media. Beginning with the publication of his first book, *The Mechanical Bride: Folklore of Industrial Man* (1951), McLuhan turned his attention to mass media, to show both its operations in a technological society and its influence on society. His two most important works on the relationships among humans, media and technology—works which alone secure his reputation as a philosopher of mass media—are *The Gutenberg Galaxy: The Making of Typographic Man* (1962) and *Understanding Media: The Extensions of Man* (1964).

Originally written for the US Office of Education, *Understanding Media* (from which the following essay is taken) explores what McLuhan calls the 'extended beings'. Building on the idea that humans master nature through the use of tools, and that these tools are no more than extensions of the individual, McLuhan expands his sense of 'tools' to include information technology. As mechanical tools determine the kind of physical work we can do, so do electronic tools (television for example) shape intellectual 'work' on the abstract level of thought. The problem in all this, however, is that with each successive extension of the self through media, the individual loses a sense of form altogether, resulting in the illusion that all media are totally objective, transparent packages for making meaning. In 'The Medium is the Message', both the title and thesis of the essay, McLuhan demonstrates that throughout the history of mechanical print (since the sixteenth century), the idea that the form communication assumes (its medium) is something independent of its content (the message), has been a widespread source of debate—up until the twentieth century. With the transformation from mechanical to electric and electronic communication technology (telephone, radio, TV), the temporal and spatial scale on which we exchange information shifted so radically—and so quickly—that we have become desensitized to how such media shape our instantaneously meaning-saturated lives. In other words, we forget that information can only fit the shape and contours of its container. Our failure to see the potential for such instruments to construct, limit, and control thought is the subject to which McLuhan turns.

S.R.

The medium is the message

In a culture like ours, long accustomed to splitting and dividing all things as a means of control, it is sometimes a bit of a shock to be reminded that, in operational and practical fact, the medium is the message. This is merely to say that the personal and social consequences of any medium—that is, of any extension of ourselves—result from the new scale that is introduced into our affairs by each extension of ourselves, or by any new technology. Thus, with automation, for example, the new patterns of human association tend to eliminate jobs, it is true. That is the negative result. Positively, automation creates roles for people, which is to say depth of involvement in their work and human association that our preceding mechanical technology had destroyed. Many people would be disposed to say that it was not the machine, but what one did with the machine, that was its meaning or message. In terms of the ways in which the machine altered our relations to one another and to ourselves, it mattered not in the least whether it turned out cornflakes or Cadillacs. The restructuring of human work and association was shaped by the technique of fragmentation that is the essence of machine technology. The essence of automation technology is the opposite. It is integral and decentralist in depth, just as the machine was fragmentary, centralist, and superficial in its patterning of human relationships.

The instance of the electric light may prove illuminating in this connection. The electric light is pure information. It is a medium without a message, as it were, unless it is used to spell out some verbal ad or name. This fact, characteristic of all media, means that the 'content' of any medium is always another medium. The content of writing is speech, just as the written word is the content of print, and print is the content of the telegraph. If it is asked, 'What is the content of speech?,' it is necessary to say, 'It is an actual process of thought, which is in itself nonverbal.' An abstract painting represents direct manifestation of creative thought processes as they might appear in computer designs. What we are considering here, however, are the psychic and social consequences of the designs or patterns as they amplify or accelerate existing processes. For the 'message' of any medium or technology is the change of scale or pace or pattern that it introduces into human affairs. The railway did not introduce movement or transportation or wheel or road into human society, but it accelerated and enlarged the scale of previous human functions, creating totally new kinds of cities and new kinds of work and leisure. This happened whether the railway functioned in a tropical or a northern environment, and is quite independent of the freight or content of the railway medium. The airplane, on the other hand, by accelerating the rate of transportation, tends to dissolve the railway form of city, politics, and association, quite independently of what the airplane is used for.

Let us return to the electric light. Whether the light is being used for brain surgery or night baseball is a matter of indifference. It could be argued that these activities are in some way the 'content' of the electric light, since they could not exist without the electric light. This fact merely underlines the point that 'the medium is the message' because it is the medium that shapes and controls the scale and form of human association and action. The content or uses of such media are as diverse as they are ineffectual in shaping the form of human association. Indeed, it is only too typical that the 'content' of any medium blinds us to the character of the medium. It is only today that industries have become aware of the various kinds of business in which they are engaged. When IBM discovered that it was not in the business of making office equipment or business machines, but that it was in the business of processing information, then it began to navigate with clear vision. The General Electric Company makes a considerable portion of its profits from electric light bulbs and lighting systems. It has not yet discovered that, quite as much as A.T.&T., it is in the business of moving information.

The electric light escapes attention as a communication medium just because it has no 'content.' And this makes it an invaluable instance of how people fail to study media at all. For it is not till the electric light is used to spell out some brand name that it is noticed as a medium. Then it is not the light but the 'content' (or what is really another medium) that is noticed. The message of the electric light is like the message of electric power in industry, totally radical, pervasive, and decentralized. For electric light and power are separate from their uses, yet they eliminate time and space factors in human association exactly as do radio, telegraph, telephone, and TV, creating involvement in depth.

A fairly complete handbook for studying the extensions of man could be made up from selections from Shakespeare. Some might quibble about whether or not he was referring to TV in these familiar lines from *Romeo and Juliet*:

But soft! what light through yonder window breaks?
It speaks, and yet says nothing.

In *Othello*, which, as much as *King Lear*, is concerned with the torment of people transformed by illusions, there are these lines that bespeak Shakespeare's intuition of the transforming powers of new media:

Is there not charms
By which the property of youth and maidhood
May be abus'd? Have you not read Roderigo,
Of some such thing?

In Shakespeare's *Troilus and Cressida*, which is almost completely devoted to both a psychic and social study of communication, Shakespeare states his awareness that true social and political navigation depend upon anticipating the consequences of innovation:

> The providence that's in a watchful state
> Knows almost every grain of Plutus' gold,
> Finds bottom in the uncomprehensive deeps,
> Keeps place with thought, and almost like the gods
> Does thoughts unveil in their dumb cradles.

The increasing awareness of the action of media, quite independently of their 'content' or programming, was indicated in the annoyed and anonymous stanza:

> In modern thought, (if not in fact)
> Nothing is that doesn't act,
> So that is reckoned wisdom which
> Describes the scratch but not the itch.

The same kind of total, configurational awareness that reveals why the medium is socially the message has occurred in the most recent and radical medical theories. In his *Stress of Life*, Hans Selye tells of the dismay of a research colleague on hearing of Selye's theory:

> When he saw me thus launched on yet another enraptured description of what I had observed in animals treated with this or that impure, toxic material, he looked at me with desperately sad eyes and said in obvious despair: 'But Selye, try to realize what you are doing before it is too late! You have now decided to spend your entire life studying the pharmacology of dirt!'

> (Hans Selye, *The Stress of Life*)

As Selye deals with the total environmental situation in his 'stress' theory of disease, so the latest approach to media study considers not only the 'content' but the medium and the cultural matrix within which the particular medium operates. The older unawareness of the psychic and social effects of media can be illustrated from almost any of the conventional pronouncements.

In accepting an honorary degree from the University of Notre Dame a few years ago, General David Sarnoff made this statement: 'We are too prone to make technological instruments the scapegoats for the sins of those who wield them. The products of modern science are not in themselves good or bad; it is the way they are used that determines their value.' That is the voice of the current somnambulism. Suppose we were to say, 'Apple pie is in itself neither good nor bad; it is the way it is used that determines its value.' Or, 'The smallpox virus is in itself neither good nor bad; it is the way it is used that determines its value.' Again, 'Firearms are in themselves neither good nor bad; it is the way they are used that determines their value.' That is, if the slugs reach the right people firearms are good. If the TV tube fires the right ammunition at the right people it is good. I am not being perverse. There is simply nothing in the Sarnoff statement that will bear scrutiny, for it ignores the nature of the medium, of any and all media, in the true Narcissus style of one hypnotized by the amputation and extension of his own being in a new technical form. General Sarnoff went on to explain his attitude to the technology of print, saying that it was true that print caused much trash to circulate, but it had also disseminated the Bible and the thoughts of seers and philosophers. It has never occurred to General Sarnoff that any technology could do anything but *add* itself on to what we already are.

Such economists as Robert Theobald, W. W. Rostow, and John Kenneth Galbraith have been explaining for years how it is that 'classical economics' cannot explain change or growth. And the paradox of mechanization is that although it is itself the cause of maximal growth and change, the principle of mechanization excludes the very possibility of growth or the understanding of change. For mechanization is achieved by fragmentation of any process and by putting the fragmented parts in a series. Yet, as David Hume showed in the eighteenth century, there is no principle of causality in a mere sequence. That one thing follows another accounts for nothing. Nothing follows from following, except change. So the greatest of all reversals occurred with electricity, that ended sequence by making things instant. With instant speed the causes of things began to emerge to awareness again, as they had not done with things in sequence and in concatenation accordingly. Instead of asking which came first, the chicken or the egg, it suddenly seemed that a chicken was an egg's idea for getting more eggs.

Just before an airplane breaks the sound barrier, sound waves become visible on the wings of the plane. The sudden visibility of sound just as sound ends is an apt instance of that great pattern of being that reveals new and opposite forms just as the earlier forms reach their peak performance. Mechanization was never so vividly fragmented or sequential as in the birth of the movies, the moment that translated us beyond mechanism into the world of growth and organic interrelation. The movie, by sheer speeding up the mechanical, carried us from the world of sequence and connections into the world of creative configuration and structure. The message of the movie medium is that of transition from lineal connections to configurations. It is the transition that produced the now quite correct observation: 'If it works, it's obsolete.' When electric speed further takes over from mechanical movie sequences, then the lines of force in structures and in media become loud and clear. We return to the inclusive form of the icon.

To a highly literate and mechanized culture the movie appeared as a world of triumphant illusions and dreams that money could buy. It was at this moment of the movie that cubism occurred, and it has been described by E. H. Gombrich (*Art and Illusion*) as 'the most radical attempt to stamp out ambiguity and to enforce one reading of the picture—that of a man-made construction, a colored canvas.' For cubism substitutes all facets of an object simultaneously for the 'point of view' or facet of perspective illusion. Instead of the specialized illusion of the third dimension on canvas, cubism sets up an interplay of planes and contradiction or dramatic conflict of patterns, lights, textures that 'drives home the message' by involvement. This is held by many to be an exercise in painting, not in illusion.

In other words, cubism, by giving the inside and outside, the top, bottom, back, and front and the rest, in two dimensions, drops the illusion of perspective in favor of instant sensory awareness of the whole. Cubism, by seizing on instant total awareness, suddenly announced that *the medium is the message*. Is it not evident that the moment that sequence yields to the simultaneous, one is in the world of the structure

229

and of configuration? Is that not what has happened in physics as in painting, poetry, and in communication? Specialized segments of attention have shifted to total field, and we can now say, 'The medium is the message' quite naturally. Before the electric speed and total field, it was not obvious that the medium is the message. The message, it seemed, was the 'content,' as people used to ask what a painting was *about*. Yet they never thought to ask what a melody was about, nor what a house or a dress was about. In such matters, people retained some sense of the whole pattern, of form and function as a unity. But in the electric age this integral idea of structure and configuration has become so prevalent that educational theory has taken up the matter. Instead of working with specialized 'problems' in arithmetic, the structural approach now follows the line of force in the field of number and has small children meditating about number theory and 'sets.'

Cardinal Newman said of Napoleon, 'He understood the grammar of gunpowder.' Napoleon had paid some attention to other media as well, especially the semaphore telegraph that gave him a great advantage over his enemies. He is on record for saying that 'Three hostile newspapers are more to be feared than a thousand bayonets.'

Alexis de Tocqueville was the first to master the grammar of print and typography. He was thus able to read off the message of coming change in France and America as if he were reading aloud from a text that had been handed to him. In fact, the nineteenth century in France and in America were just such an open book to de Tocqueville because he had learned the grammar of print. So he, also, knew when that grammar did not apply. He was asked why he did not write a book on England, since he knew and admired England. He replied:

> One would have to have an unusual degree of philosophical folly to believe oneself able to judge England in six months. A year always seemed to me too short a time in which to appreciate the United States properly, and it is much easier to acquire clear and precise notions about the American Union than about Great Britain. In America all laws derive in a sense from the same line of thought. The whole of society, so to speak, is founded upon a single fact; everything springs from a simple principle. One could compare America to a forest pierced by a multitude of straight roads all converging on the same point. One has only to find the center and everything is revealed at a glance. But in England the paths run criss-cross, and it is only by travelling down each one of them that one can build up a picture of the whole.

De Tocqueville, in earlier work on the French Revolution, had explained how it was the printed word that, achieving cultural saturation in the eighteenth century, had homogenized the French nation. Frenchmen were the same kind of people from north to south. The typographic principles of uniformity, continuity, and lineality had overlaid the complexities of ancient feudal and oral society. The Revolution was carried out by the new literati and lawyers.

In England, however, such was the power of the ancient oral traditions of common law, backed by the medieval institution of Parliament, that no uniformity or continuity of the new visual print culture could take complete hold. The result was that the most important event in English history has never taken place; namely, the English Revolution on the lines of the French Revolution. The American Revolution had no medieval legal institutions to discard or to root out, apart from monarchy. And many have held that the American Presidency has become very much more personal and monarchical than any European monarch ever could be.

De Tocqueville's contrast between England and America is clearly based on the fact of typography and of print culture creating uniformity and continuity. England, he says, has rejected this principle and clung to the dynamic or oral common-law tradition. Hence the discontinuity and unpredictable quality of English culture. The grammar of print cannot help to construe the message of oral and nonwritten culture and institutions. The English aristocracy was properly classified as barbarian by Matthew Arnold because its power and status had nothing to do with literacy or with the cultural forms of typography. Said the Duke of Gloucester to Edward Gibbon upon the publication of his *Decline and Fall*: 'Another damned fat book, eh, Mr. Gibbon? Scribble, scribble, scribble, eh, Mr. Gibbon?' De Tocqueville was a highly literate aristocrat who was quite able to be detached from the values and assumptions of typography. That is why he alone understood the grammar of typography. And it is only on those terms, standing aside from any structure or medium, that its principles and lines of force can be discerned. For any medium has the power of imposing its own assumption on the unwary. Prediction and control consist in avoiding this subliminal state of Narcissus trance. But the greatest aid to this end is simply in knowing that the spell can occur immediately upon contact, as in the first bars of a melody.

A Passage to India by E. M. Forster is a dramatic study of the inability of oral and intuitive oriental culture to meet with the rational, visual European patterns of experience. 'Rational,' of course, has for the West long meant 'uniform and continuous and sequential.' In other words, we have confused reason with literacy, and rationalism with a single technology. Thus in the electric age man seems to the conventional West to become irrational. In Forster's novel the moment of truth and dislocation from the typographic trance of the West comes in the Marabar Caves. Adela Quested's reasoning powers cannot cope with the total inclusive field of resonance that is India. After the Caves: 'Life went on as usual, but had no consequences, that is to say, sounds did not echo nor thought develop. Everything seemed cut off at its root and therefore infected with illusion.'

A Passage to India (the phrase is from Whitman, who saw America headed Eastward) is a parable of Western man in the electric age, and is only incidentally related to Europe or the Orient. The ultimate conflict between sight and sound, between written and oral kinds of perception and organization of existence is upon us. Since understanding stops action, as Nietzsche observed, we can moderate the fierceness of this conflict by understanding the media that extend us and raise these wars within and without us.

Detribalization by literacy and its traumatic effects on tribal man is the theme of a book by the psychiatrist J. C. Carothers, *The African Mind in Health and Disease* (World Health Organization, Geneva, 1953). Much of his material appeared in an article in *Psychiatry* magazine, November, 1959: 'The Culture, Psychiatry, and the Written Word.' Again, it is electric speed that has revealed the lines of force operating from Western technology in the remotest areas of bush, savannah, and desert. One example is the Bedouin with his battery radio on board the camel. Submerging

231

natives with floods of concepts for which nothing has prepared them is the normal action of all of our technology. But with electric media Western man himself experiences exactly the same inundation as the remote native. We are no more prepared to encounter radio and TV in our literate milieu than the native of Ghana is able to cope with the literacy that takes him out of his collective tribal world and beaches him in individual isolation. We are as numb in our new electric world as the native involved in our literate and mechanical culture.

Electric speed mingles the cultures of prehistory with the dregs of industrial marketeers, the nonliterate with the semiliterate and the postliterate. Mental breakdown of varying degrees is the very common result of uprooting and inundation with new information and endless new patterns of information. Wyndham Lewis made this a theme of his group of novels called *The Human Age*. The first of these, *The Childermass*, is concerned precisely with accelerated media change as a kind of massacre of the innocents. In our own world as we become more aware of the effects of technology on psychic formation and manifestation, we are losing all confidence in our right to assign guilt. Ancient prehistoric societies regard violent crime as pathetic. The killer is regarded as we do a cancer victim. 'How terrible it must be to feel like that,' they say. J. M. Synge took up this idea very effectively in his *Playboy of the Western World*.

If the criminal appears as a nonconformist who is unable to meet the demand of technology that we behave in uniform and continuous patterns, literate man is quite inclined to see others who cannot conform as somewhat pathetic. Especially the child, the cripple, the woman, and the colored person appear in a world of visual and typographic technology as victims of injustice. On the other hand, in a culture that assigns roles instead of jobs to people—the dwarf, the skew, the child create their own spaces. They are not expected to fit into some uniform and repeatable niche that is not their size anyway. Consider the phrase 'It's a man's world.' As a quantitative observation endlessly repeated from within a homogenized culture, this phrase refers to the men in such a culture who have to be homogenized Dagwoods in order to belong at all. It is in our I.Q. testing that we have produced the greatest flood of misbegotten standards. Unaware of our typographic cultural bias, our testers assume that uniform and continuous habits are a sign of intelligence, thus eliminating the ear man and the tactile man.

C. P. Snow, reviewing a book of A. L. Rowse (*The New York Times Book Review*, December 24, 1961) on *Appeasement* and the road to Munich, describes the top level of British brains and experience in the 1930s. 'Their I.Q.s were much higher than usual among political bosses. Why were they such a disaster?' The view of Rowse, Snow approves: 'They would not listen to warnings because they did not wish to hear.' Being anti-Red made it impossible for them to read the message of Hitler. But their failure was as nothing compared to our present one. The American stake in literacy as a technology or uniformity applied to every level of education, government, industry, and social life is totally threatened by the electric technology. The threat of Stalin or Hitler was external. The electric technology is within the gates, and we are numb, deaf, blind, and mute about its encounter with the Gutenberg technology, on and through which the American way of life was formed. It is, however, no time to suggest strategies when the threat has not even been acknowledged to exist. I am in the position of Louis Pasteur telling doctors that their greatest enemy was quite invisible, and quite unrecognized by them. Our conventional response to all media, namely that it is how they are used that counts, is the numb stance of the technological idiot. For the 'content' of a medium is like the juicy piece of meat carried by the burglar to distract the watch-dog of the mind. The effect of the medium is made strong and intense just because it is given another medium as 'content.' The content of a movie is a novel or a play or an opera. The effect of the movie form is not related to its program content. The 'content' of writing or print is speech, but the reader is almost entirely unaware either of print or of speech.

Arnold Toynbee is innocent of any understanding of media as they have shaped history, but he is full of examples that the student of media can use. At one moment he can seriously suggest that adult education, such as the Workers Educational Association in Britain, is a useful counterforce to the popular press. Toynbee considers that although all of the oriental societies have in our time accepted industrial technology and its political consequences: 'On the cultural plane, however, there is no uniform corresponding tendency' (Somervell, I. 267). This is like the voice of the literate man, floundering in a milieu of ads, who boasts, 'Personally, I pay no attention to ads.' The spiritual and cultural reservations that the oriental peoples may have toward our technology will avail them not at all. The effects of technology do not occur at the level of opinions or concepts, but alter sense ratios or patterns of perception steadily and without any resistance. The serious artist is the only person able to encounter technology with impunity, just because he is an expert aware of the changes in sense perception.

The operation of the money medium in seventeenth-century Japan had effects not unlike the operation of typography in the West. The penetration of the money economy, wrote G. B. Sansom (in *Japan*, Cresset Press, London, 1931) 'caused a slow but irresistible revolution, culminating in the breakdown of feudal government and the resumption of intercourse with foreign countries after more than two hundred years of seclusion.' Money has reorganized the sense life of peoples just because it is an *extension* of our sense lives. This change does not depend upon approval or disapproval of those living in the society.

Arnold Toynbee made one approach to the transforming power of media in his concept of 'etherialization,' which he holds to be the principle of progressive simplification and efficiency in any organization or technology. Typically, he is ignoring the *effect* of the challenge of these forms upon the response of our senses. He imagines that it is the response of our opinions that is relevant to the effect of media and technology in society, a 'point of view' that is plainly the result of the typographic spell. For the man in a literate and homogenized society ceases to be sensitive to the diverse and discontinuous life of forms. He acquires the illusion of the third dimension and the 'private point of view' as part of his Narcissus fixation, and is quite shut off from Blake's awareness or that of the Psalmist, that we become what we behold.

Today when we want to get our bearings in our own culture, and have need to stand aside from the bias and pressure exerted by any technical form of human expression, we have only to visit a society where that particular form has not been felt, or a historical period in which it was unknown. Professor Wilbur Schramm made such a tactical move in studying *Television in the Lives of Our Children*. He

233

found areas where TV had not penetrated at all and ran some tests. Since he had made no study of the peculiar nature of the TV image, his tests were of 'content' preferences, viewing time, and vocabulary counts. In a word, his approach to the problem was a literary one, albeit unconsciously so. Consequently, he had nothing to report. Had his methods been employed in 1500 A.D. to discover the effects of the printed book in the lives of children or adults, he could have found out nothing of the changes in human and social psychology resulting from typography. Print created individualism and nationalism in the sixteenth century. Program and 'content' analysis offer no clues to the magic of these media or to their subliminal charge.

Leonard Dooh, in his report *Communication in Africa*, tells of one African who took great pains to listen each evening to the BBC news, even though he could understand nothing of it. Just to be in the presence of those sounds at 7 P.M. each day was important for him. His attitude to speech was like ours to melody—the resonant intonation was meaning enough. In the seventeenth century our ancestors still shared this native's attitude to the forms of media, as is plain in the following sentiment of the Frenchman Bernard Lam expressed in *The Art of Speaking* (London, 1696):

> 'Tis an effect of the Wisdom of God, who created Man to be happy, that whatever is useful to his conversation (way of life) is agreeable to him . . . because all victual that conduces to nourishment is relishable, whereas other things that cannot be assimulated and be turned into our substance are insipid. A Discourse cannot be pleasant to the Hearer that is not easie to the Speaker; nor can it be easily pronounced unless it be heard with delight.

Here is an equilibrium theory of human diet and expression such as even now we are only striving to work out again for media after centuries of fragmentation and specialism.

Pope Pius XII was deeply concerned that there be serious study of the media today. On February 17, 1950, he said:

> It is not an exaggeration to say that the future of modern society and the stability of its inner life depend in large part on the maintenance of an equilibrium between the strength of the techniques of communication and the capacity of the individual's own reaction.

Failure in this respect has for centuries been typical and total for mankind. Subliminal and docile acceptance of media impact has made them prisons without walls for their human users. As A. J. Liebling remarked in his book *The Press*, a man is not free if he cannot see where he is going, even if he has a gun to help him get there. For each of the media is also a powerful weapon with which to clobber other media and other groups. The result is that the present age has been one of multiple civil wars that are not limited to the world of art and entertainment. In *War and Human Progress*, Professor J. U. Nef declared: 'The total wars of our time have been the result of a series of intellectual mistakes . . .'

If the formative power in the media are the media themselves, that raises a host of large matters that can only be mentioned here, although they deserve volumes. Namely, that technological media are staples or natural resources, exactly as are coal and cotton and oil. Anybody will concede that society whose economy is dependent upon one or two major staples like cotton, or grain, or lumber, or fish, or cattle is going to have some obvious social patterns of organization as a result. Stress on a few major staples creates extreme instability in the economy but great endurance in the population. The pathos and humor of the American South are embedded in such an economy of limited staples. For a society configured by reliance on a few commodities accepts them as a social bond quite as much as the metropolis does the press. Cotton and oil, like radio and TV, become 'fixed charges' on the entire psychic life of the community. And this pervasive fact creates the unique cultural flavor of any society. It pays through the nose and all its other senses for each staple that shapes its life.

That our human senses, of which all media are extensions, are also fixed charges on our personal energies, and that they also configure the awareness and experience of each one of us, may be perceived in another connection mentioned by the psychologist C. G. Jung:

> Every Roman was surrounded by slaves. The slave and his psychology flooded ancient Italy, and every Roman became inwardly, and of course unwittingly, a slave. Because living constantly in the atmosphere of slaves, he became infected through the unconscious with their psychology. No one can shield himself from such an influence (*Contributions to Analytical Psychology*, London, 1928).

Clifford Geertz (1926–)

As a cultural anthropologist and ethnographer, Clifford Geertz has conducted extensive research on the peoples and cultures of Indonesia and Morocco. Geertz believes that ethnography is an empirical and theoretical model for interpreting specific contexts. Its aim is to understand how human beings fashion their lives through their social interactions and cultural specificity. Thus, understanding the signs of outward human behavior provides a semiotic grid for deciphering culture. It is then the ethnographer's task to read the signs for their significance in specific contexts. His books include, *Agricultural Involution: The Processes of Ecological Change in Indonesia* (1963), *The Social History of an Indonesian Town* (1965), *Islam Observed: Religious Development in Morocco and Indonesia* (1968), *The Interpretation of Cultures* (1973), *Local Knowledge: Further Essays in Interpretive Anthropology* (1983), and *Works and Lives: The Anthropologist As Author* (1989). Geertz also contributes essays to journals such as the *New York Review of Books*.

In the essay re-printed here, which is the opening chapter of *The Interpretation of Cultures*, Geertz explains the methodologies and assumptions that have guided his research. He begins by recounting a narrative he collected in the field in Morocco and uses this story as a model for the various challenges that an ethnographer must confront. He calls ethnographic description a 'thick description [because] what we call our data are really our own construction of other people's constructions of what they and their compatriots are up to.' The ethnographer must sort out the meaning by examining the multi-layered narrativès, and Geertz compares this work to that of literary critics. Geertz deals at length with the hazard of using literary techniques to analyse culture, which is part of his scientific, ethnographic project, because, he argues, ethnographic description must render social discourse readable and not resort to mere literary finesse. 'The whole point of a semiotic approach to culture is', Geertz writes, 'to aid us in gaining access to the conceptual world in which we our subjects live so that we can, in some extended sense of the term, converse with them.'
T.M.

Thick description: toward an interpretive theory of culture

I

In her book, *Philosophy in a New Key*, Susanne Langer remarks that certain ideas burst upon the intellectual landscape with a tremendous force. They resolve so many fundamental problems at once that they seem also to promise that they will resolve all fundamental problems, clarify all obscure issues. Everyone snaps them up as the open sesame of some new positive science, the conceptual center-point around which a comprehensive system of analysis can be built. The sudden vogue of such a *grande idée*, crowding out almost everything else for a while, is due, she says, 'to the fact that all sensitive and active minds turn at once to exploiting it. We try it in every connection, for every purpose, experiment with possible stretches of its strict meaning, with generalizations and derivatives.'

After we have become familiar with the new idea, however, after it has become part of our general stock of theoretical concepts, our expectations are brought more into balance with its actual uses, and its excessive popularity is ended. A few zealots persist in the old key-to-the-universe view of it; but less driven thinkers settle down after a while to the problems the idea has really generated. They try to apply it and extend it where it applies and where it is capable of extension; and they desist where it does not apply or cannot be extended. It becomes, if it was, in truth, a seminal idea in the first place, a permanent and enduring part of our intellectual armory. But it no longer has the grandiose, all-promising scope, the infinite versatility of apparent application, it once had. The second law of thermodynamics, or the principle of natural selection, or the notion of unconscious motivation, or the organization of the means of production does not explain everything, not even everything human, but it still explains something; and our attention shifts to isolating just what that something is, to disentangling ourselves from a lot of pseudoscience to which, in the first flush of its celebrity, it has also given rise.

Whether or not this is, in fact, the way all centrally important scientific concepts develop, I don't know. But certainly this pattern fits the concept of culture, around which the whole discipline of anthropology arose, and whose domination that discipline has been increasingly concerned to limit, specify, focus, and contain. It is to this cutting of the culture concept down to size, therefore actually insuring its continued importance rather than undermining it, that the essays below are all, in their several ways and from their several directions, dedicated. They all argue, sometimes explicitly, more often merely through the particular analysis they develop, for a narrowed, specialized, and, so I imagine, theoretically more powerful concept of culture to replace E. B. Tylor's famous 'most complex whole,' which, its originative power not denied, seems to me to have reached the point where it obscures a good deal more than it reveals.

The conceptual morass into which the Tylorean kind of *pot-au-feu* theorizing about culture can lead, is evident in what is still one of the better general introductions to anthropology, Clyde Kluckhohn's *Mirror for Man*. In some twenty-seven pages of his chapter on the concept, Kluckhohn managed to define culture in turn as: (1) 'the total way of life of a people'; (2) 'the social legacy the individual acquires from his group'; (3) 'a way of thinking, feeling, and believing'; (4) 'an abstraction from behavior'; (5) a theory on the part of the anthropologist about the way in which a group of people in fact behave; (6) a 'storehouse of pooled learning'; (7) 'a set of standardized orientations to recurrent problems'; (8) 'learned behavior'; (9) a mechanism for the normative regulation of behavior; (10) 'a set of techniques for adjusting both to the external environment and to other men'; (11) 'a precipitate of history'; and turning, perhaps in desperation, to similes, as a map, as a sieve, and as a matrix. In the face of this sort of theoretical diffusion, even a somewhat constricted and not entirely standard concept of culture, which is at least internally coherent and, more important, which has a definable argument to make is (as, to be fair, Kluckhohn himself keenly realized) an improvement. Eclecticism is self-defeating not because there is only one direction in which it is useful to move, but because there are so many: it is necessary to choose.

The concept of culture I espouse is essentially a semiotic one. Believing, with Max Weber, that man is an animal suspended in webs of significance he himself has spun, I take culture to be those webs, and the analysis of it to be therefore not an experimental science in search of law but an interpretive one in search of meaning. It is explication I am after, construing social expressions on their surface enigmatical. But this pronouncement, a doctrine in a clause, demands itself some explication.

II

Operationalism as a methodological dogma never made much sense so far as the social sciences are concerned, and except for a few rather too well-swept corners— Skinnerian behaviorism, intelligence testing, and so on—it is largely dead now. But it had, for all that, an important point to make, which, however we may feel about trying to define charisma or alienation in terms of operations, retains a certain force: if you want to understand what a science is, you should look in the first instance not at its theories or its findings, and certainly not at what its apologists say about it; you should look at what the practitioners of it do.

In anthropology, or anyway social anthropology, what the practitioners do is ethnography. And it is in understanding what ethnography is, or more exactly *what doing ethnography is*, that a start can be made toward grasping what anthropological analysis amounts to as a form of knowledge. This, it must immediately be said, is not a matter of methods. From one point of view, that of the textbook, doing ethnography is establishing rapport, selecting informants, transcribing texts, taking genealogies, mapping fields, keeping a diary, and so on. But it is not these things, techniques and received procedures, that define the enterprise. What defines it is the kind of intellectual effort it is: an elaborate venture in, to borrow a notion from Gilbert Ryle, 'thick description.'

Ryle's discussion of 'thick description' appears in two recent essays of his (now reprinted in the second volume of his *Collected Papers*) addressed to the general question of what, as he puts it, '*Le Penseur*' is doing: 'Thinking and Reflecting' and 'The Thinking of Thoughts.' Consider, he says, two boys rapidly contracting the eyelids

238

of their right eyes. In one, this is an involuntary twitch; in the other, a conspiratorial signal to a friend. The two movements are, as movements, identical; from an I-am-a-camera, 'phenomenalistic' observation of them alone, one could not tell which was twitch and which was wink, or indeed whether both or either was twitch or wink. Yet the difference, however unphotographable, between a twitch and a wink is vast; as anyone unfortunate enough to have had the first taken for the second knows. The winker is communicating, and indeed communicating in a quite precise and special way: (1) deliberately, (2) to someone in particular, (3) to impart a particular message, (4) according to a socially established code, and (5) without cognizance of the rest of the company. As Ryle points out, the winker has now done two things, contracted his eyelids and winked, while the twitcher has done only one, contracted his eyelids. Contracting your eyelids on purpose when there exists a public code in which so doing counts as a conspiratorial signal *is* winking. That's all there is to it: a speck of behavior, a fleck of culture, and—*voilà!*—a gesture.

That, however, is just the beginning. Suppose, he continues, there is a third boy, who, 'to give malicious amusement to his cronies,' parodies the first boy's wink, as amateurish, clumsy, obvious, and so on. He, of course, does this in the same way the second boy winked and the first twitched: by contracting his right eyelids. Only this boy is neither winking nor twitching, he is parodying someone else's, as he takes it, laughable, attempt at winking. Here, too, a socially established code exists (he will 'wink' laboriously, overobviously, perhaps adding a grimace—the usual artifices of the clown); and so also does a message. Only now it is not conspiracy but ridicule that is in the air. If the others think he is actually winking, his whole project misfires as completely, though with somewhat different results, as if they think he is twitching. One can go further: uncertain of his mimicking abilities, the would-be satirist may practice at home before the mirror, in which case he is not twitching, winking, or parodying, but rehearsing; though so far as what a camera, a radical behaviorist, or a believer in protocol sentences would record he is just rapidly contracting his right eyelids like all the others. Complexities are possible, if not practically without end, at least logically so. The original winker might, for example, actually have been fake-winking, say, to mislead outsiders into imagining there was a conspiracy afoot when there in fact was not, in which case our descriptions of what the parodist is parodying and the rehearser rehearsing of course shift accordingly. But the point is that between what Ryle calls the 'thin description' of what the rehearser (parodist, winker, twitcher . . .) is doing ('rapidly contracting his right eyelids') and the 'thick description' of what he is doing ('practicing a burlesque of a friend faking a wink to deceive an innocent into thinking a conspiracy is in motion') lies the object of ethnography: a stratified hierarchy of meaningful structures in terms of which twitches, winks, fake-winks, parodies, rehearsals of parodies are produced, perceived, and interpreted, and without which they would not (not even the zero-form twitches, which, *as a cultural category*, are as much nonwinks as winks are nontwitches) in fact exist, no matter what anyone did or didn't do with his eyelids.

Like so many of the little stories Oxford philosophers like to make up for them-selves, all this winking, fake-winking, burlesque-fake-winking, rehearsed-burlesque-fake-winking, may seem a bit artificial. In way of adding a more empirical note, let me give, deliberately unpreceded by any prior explanatory comment at all, a not untypical excerpt from my own field journal to demonstrate that, however evened off for didactic purposes, Ryle's example presents an image only too exact of the sort of piled-up structures of inference and implication through which an ethnographer is continually trying to pick his way:

The French [the informant said] had only just arrived. They set up twenty or so small forts between here, the town, and the Marmusha area up in the middle of the mountains, placing them on promontories so they could survey the country-side. But for all this they couldn't guarantee safety, especially at night, so although the *mezrag*, trade-pact, system was supposed to be legally abolished it in fact continued as before.

One night, when Cohen (who speaks fluent Berber), was up there, at Marmusha, two other Jews who were traders to a neighboring tribe came by to purchase some goods from him. Some Berbers, from yet another neighboring tribe, tried to break into Cohen's place, but he fired his rifle in the air. (Traditionally, Jews were not allowed to carry weapons; but at this period things were so unsettled many did so anyway.) This attracted the attention of the French and the marauders fled.

The next night, however, they came back, one of them disguised as a woman who knocked on the door with some sort of a story. Cohen was suspicious and didn't want to let 'her' in, but the other Jews said, 'oh, it's all right, it's only a woman.' So they opened the door and the whole lot came pouring in. They killed the two visiting Jews, but Cohen managed to barricade himself in an adjoining room. He heard the robbers planning to burn him alive in the shop after they removed his goods, and so he opened the door and, laying about him wildly with a club, managed to escape through a window.

He went up to the fort, then, to have his wounds dressed, and complained to the local commandant, one Captain Dumari, saying he wanted his *'ar*—i.e., four or five times the value of the merchandise stolen from him. The robbers were from a tribe which had not yet submitted to French authority and were in open rebellion against it, and he wanted authorization to go with his *mezrag*-holder, the Marmusha tribal *sheikh*, to collect the indemnity that, under traditional rules, he had coming to him. Captain Dumari couldn't officially give him permission to do this, because of the French prohibition of the *mezrag* relationship, but he gave him verbal authorization, saying, 'If you get killed, it's your problem.'

So the *sheikh*, the Jew, and a small company of armed Marmushans went off ten or fifteen kilometers up into the rebellious area, where there were of course no French and, sneaking up, captured the thief-tribe's shepherd and stole its herds. The other tribe soon came riding out on horses after them, armed with rifles and ready to attack. But when they saw who the 'sheep thieves' were, they thought better of it and said, 'all right, we'll talk.' They couldn't really deny what had happened—that some of their men had robbed Cohen and killed the two visi-tors—and they weren't prepared to start the serious feud with the Marmusha a scuffle with the invading party would bring on. So the two groups talked, and talked, and talked, there on the plain amid the thousands of sheep, and decided finally on five-hundred-sheep damages. The two armed Berber groups then lined up on their horses at opposite ends of the plain, with the sheep herded beween them, and Cohen, in his black gown, pillbox hat, and flapping slippers, went out alone among the sheep, picking out, one by one and at his own good speed, the best ones for his payment.

So Cohen got his sheep and drove them back to Marmusha. The French, up in their fort, heard them coming from some distance ('Ba, ba, ba' said Cohen, happily, recalling the image) and said, 'What the hell is that?' And Cohen said, 'That is my *'ar*. The French couldn't believe he had actually done what he said he had done, and accused him of being a spy for the rebellious Berbers, put him in prison, and took his sheep. In the town, his family, not having heard from him in so long a time, thought he was dead. But after a while the French released him and he came back home, but without his sheep. He then went to the Colonel in the town, the Frenchman in charge of the whole region, to complain. But the Colonel said, 'I can't do anything about the matter. It's not my problem.'

Quoted raw, a note in a bottle, this passage conveys, as any similar one similarly presented would do, a fair sense of how much goes into ethnographic description of even the most elemental sort—how extraordinarily 'thick' it is. In finished anthropological writings, including those collected here, this fact—that what we call our data are really our own constructions of other people's constructions of what they and their compatriots are up to—is obscured because most of what we need to comprehend a particular event, ritual, custom, idea, or whatever is insinuated as background information before the thing itself is directly examined. (Even to reveal that this little drama took place in the highlands of central Morocco in 1912—and was recounted there in 1968—is to determine much of our understanding of it.) There is nothing particularly wrong with this, and it is in any case inevitable. But it does lead to a view of anthropological research as rather more of an observational and rather less of an interpretive activity than it really is. Right down at the factual base, the hard rock, insofar as there is any, of the whole enterprise, we are already explicating: and worse, explicating explications. Winks upon winks upon winks.

Analysis, then, is sorting out the structures of signification—what Ryle called established codes, a somewhat misleading expression, for it makes the enterprise sound too much like that of the cipher clerk when it is much more like that of the literary critic—and determining their social ground and import. Here, in our text, such sorting would begin with distinguishing the three unlike frames of interpretation ingredient in the situation, Jewish, Berber, and French, and would then move on to show how (and why) at that time, in that place, their copresence produced a situation in which systematic misunderstanding reduced traditional form to social farce. What tripped Cohen up, and with him the whole, ancient pattern of social and economic relationships within which he functioned, was a confusion of tongues.

I shall come back to this too-compacted aphorism later, as well as to the details of the text itself. The point for now is only that ethnography is thick description. What the ethnographer is in fact faced with—except when (as, of course, he must do) he is pursuing the more automatized routines of data collection—is a multiplicity of complex conceptual structures, many of them superimposed upon or knotted into one another, which are at once strange, irregular, and inexplicit, and which he must contrive somehow first to grasp and then to render. And this is true at the most down-to-earth, jungle field work levels of his activity: interviewing informants, observing rituals, eliciting kin terms, tracing property lines, censusing households

... writing his journal. Doing ethnography is like trying to read (in the sense of 'construct a reading of') a manuscript—foreign, faded, full of ellipses, incoherencies, suspicious emendations, and tendentious commentaries, but written not in conventionalized graphs of sound but in transient examples of shaped behavior.

III

Culture, this acted document, thus is public, like a burlesqued wink or a mock sheep raid. Though ideational, it does not exist in someone's head; though unphysical, it is not an occult entity. The interminable, because unterminable, debate within anthropology as to whether culture is 'subjective' or 'objective,' together with the mutual exchange of intellectual insults ('idealist!'—'materialist!'; 'mentalist!'—'behaviorist!'; 'impressionist!'—'positivist!') which accompanies it, is wholly misconceived. Once human behavior is seen as (most of the time; there *are* true twitches) symbolic action—action which, like phonation in speech, pigment in painting, line in writing, or sonance in music, signifies—the question as to whether culture is patterned conduct or a frame of mind, or even the two somehow mixed together, loses sense. The thing to ask about a burlesqued wink or a mock sheep raid is not what their ontological status is. It is the same as that of rocks on the one hand and dreams on the other—they are things of this world. The thing to ask is what their import is: what it is, ridicule or challenge, irony or anger, snobbery or pride, that, in their occurrence and through their agency, is getting said.

This may seem like an obvious truth, but there are a number of ways to obscure it. One is to imagine that culture is a self-contained 'super-organic' reality with forces and purposes of its own; that is, to reify it. Another is to claim that it consists in the brute pattern of behavioral events we observe in fact to occur in some identifiable community or other; that is, to reduce it. But though both these confusions still exist, and doubtless will be always with us, the main source of theoretical muddlement in contemporary anthropology is a view which developed in reaction to them and is right now very widely held—namely, that, to quote Ward Goodenough, perhaps its leading proponent, 'culture [is located] in the minds and hearts of men.'

Variously called ethnoscience, componential analysis, or cognitive anthropology (a terminological wavering which reflects a deeper uncertainty), this school of thought holds that culture is composed of psychological structures by means of which individuals or groups of individuals guide their behavior. 'A society's culture,' to quote Goodenough again, this time in a passage which has become the *locus classicus* of the whole movement, 'consists of whatever it is one has to know or believe in order to operate in a manner acceptable to its members.' And from this view of what culture is follows a view, equally assured, of what describing it is—the writing out of systematic rules, an ethnographic algorithm, which, if followed, would make it possible so to operate, to pass (physical appearance aside) for a native. In such a way, extreme subjectivism is married to extreme formalism, with the expected result: an explosion of debate as to whether particular analyses (which come in the form of taxonomies, paradigms, tables, trees, and other ingenuities) reflect what the natives 'really' think or are merely clever simulations, logically equivalent but substantively different, of what they think.

As, on first glance, this approach may look close enough to the one being developed here to be mistaken for it, it is useful to be explicit as to what divides them. If, leaving our winks and sheep behind for the moment, we take, say, a Beethoven quartet as an, admittedly rather special but, for these purposes, nicely illustrative, sample of culture, no one would, I think, identify it with its score, with the skills and knowledge needed to play it, with the understanding of it possessed by its performers or auditors, nor, to take care, *en passant*, of the reductionists and reifiers, with a particular performance of it or with some mysterious entity transcending material existence. The 'no one' is perhaps too strong here, for there are always incorrigibles. But that a Beethoven quartet is a temporally developed tonal structure, a coherent sequence of modeled sound—in a word, music—and not anybody's knowledge of or belief about anything, including how to play it, is a proposition to which most people are, upon reflection, likely to assent.

To play the violin it is necessary to possess certain habits, skills, knowledge, and talents, to be in the mood to play, and (as the old joke goes) to have a violin. But violin playing is neither the habits, skills, knowledge, and so on, nor the mood, nor (the notion believers in 'material culture' apparently embrace) the violin. To make a trade pact in Morocco, you have to do certain things in certain ways (among others, cut, while chanting Quranic Arabic, the throat of a lamb before the assembled, undeformed, adult male members of your tribe) and to be possessed of certain psychological characteristics (among others, a desire for distant things). But a trade pact is neither the throat cutting nor the desire, though it is real enough, as seven kinsmen of our Marmusha sheikh discovered when, on an earlier occasion, they were executed by him following the theft of one mangy, essentially valueless sheepskin from Cohen.

Culture is public because meaning is. You can't wink (or burlesque one) without knowing what counts as winking or how, physically, to contract your eyelids, and you can't conduct a sheep raid (or mimic one) without knowing what it is to steal a sheep and how practically to go about it. But to draw from such truths the conclusion that knowing how to wink is winking and knowing how to steal a sheep is sheep raiding is to betray as deep a confusion as, taking thin descriptions for thick, to identify winking with eyelid contractions or sheep raiding with chasing woolly animals out of pastures. The cognitivist fallacy—that culture consists (to quote another spokesman for the movement, Stephen Tyler) of 'mental phenomena which can [he means 'should'] be analyzed by formal methods similar to those of mathematics and logic'—is as destructive of an effective use of the concept as are the behaviorist and idealist fallacies to which it is a misdrawn correction. Perhaps, as its errors are more sophisticated and its distortions subtler, it is even more so.

The generalized attack on privacy theories of meaning is, since early Husserl and late Wittgenstein, so much a part of modern thought that it need not be developed once more here. What is necessary is to see to it that the news of it reaches anthropology; and in particular that it is made clear that to say that culture consists of socially established structures of meaning in terms of which people do such things as signal conspiracies and join them or perceive insults and answer them, is no more to say that it is a psychological phenomenon, a characteristic of someone's mind, personality, cognitive structure, or whatever, than to say that Tantrism, genetics, the progressive form of the verb, the classification of wines, the Common Law, or the

243

notion of 'a conditional curse' (as Westermarck defined the concept of '*ar* in terms of which Cohen pressed his claim to damages) is. What, in a place like Morocco, most prevents those of us who grew up winking other winks or attending other sheep from grasping what people are up to is not ignorance as to how cognition works (though, especially as, one assumes, it works the same among them as it does among us, it would greatly help to have less of that too) as a lack of familiarity with the imaginative universe within which their acts are signs. As Wittgenstein has been invoked, he may as well be quoted:

> We . . . say of some people that they are transparent to us. It is, however, important as regards this observation that one human being can be a complete enigma to another. We learn this when we come into a strange country with entirely strange traditions; and, what is more, even given a mastery of the country's language. We do not *understand* the people. (And not because of not knowing what they are saying to themselves.) We cannot find our feet with them.

IV

Finding our feet, an unnerving business which never more than distantly succeeds, is what ethnographic research consists of as a personal experience; trying to formulate the basis on which one imagines, always excessively, one has found them is what anthropological writing consists of as a scientific endeavor. We are not, or at least I am not, seeking either to become natives (a compromised word in any case) or to mimic them. Only romantics or spies would seem to find point in that. We are seeking, in the widened sense of the term in which it encompasses very much more than talk, to converse with them, a matter a great deal more difficult, and not only with strangers, than is commonly recognized. 'If speaking *for* someone else seems to be a mysterious process,' Stanley Cavell has remarked, 'that may be because speaking *to* someone does not seem mysterious enough.'

Looked at in this way, the aim of anthropology is the enlargement of the universe of human discourse. That is not, of course, its only aim—instruction, amusement, practical counsel, moral advance, and the discovery of natural order in human behavior are others; nor is anthropology the only discipline which pursues it. But it is an aim to which a semiotic concept of culture is peculiarly well adapted. As interworked systems of construable signs (what, ignoring provincial usages, I would call symbols), culture is not a power, something to which social events, behaviors, institutions, or processes can be causally attributed; it is a context, something within which they can be intelligibly—that is, thickly—described.

The famous anthropological absorption with the (to us) exotic—Berber horsemen, Jewish peddlers, French Legionnaires—is, thus, essentially a device for displacing the dulling sense of familiarity with which the mysteriousness of our own ability to relate perceptively to one another is concealed from us. Looking at the ordinary in places where it takes unaccustomed forms brings out not, as has so often been claimed, the arbitrariness of human behavior (there is nothing especially arbitrary about taking sheep theft for insolence in Morocco), but the degree to which its meaning varies according to the pattern of life by which it is informed. Understanding a people's culture exposes their normalness without reducing their particularity. (The more I manage to follow what the Moroccans are up to, the more logical, and the more singular, they seem.) It renders them accessible: setting them in the frame of their own banalities, it dissolves their opacity.

It is this maneuver, usually too casually referred to as "seeing things from the actor's point of view,' too bookishly as 'the *verstehen* approach,' or too technically as 'emic analysis,' that so often leads to the notion that anthropology is a variety of either long-distance mind reading or cannibal-isle fantasizing, and which, for some-one anxious to navigate past the wrecks of a dozen sunken philosophies, must therefore be executed with a great deal of care. Nothing is more necessary to compre-hending what anthropological interpretation is, and the degree to which it *is* interpretation, than an exact understanding of what it means—and what it does not mean—to say that our formulations of other peoples' symbol systems must be actor-oriented.[1]

What it means is that descriptions of Berber, Jewish, or French culture must be cast in terms of the constructions we imagine Berbers, Jews, or Frenchmen to place upon what they live through, the formulae they use to define what happens to them. What it does not mean is that such descriptions are themselves Berber, Jewish, or French—that is, part of the reality they are ostensibly describing; they are anthropo-logical—that is, part of a developing system of scientific analysis. They must be cast in terms of the interpretations to which persons of a particular denomination subject their experience, because that is what they profess to be descriptions of; they are anthropological because it is, in fact, anthropologists who profess them. Normally, it is not necessary to point out quite so laboriously that the object of study is one thing and the study of it another. It is clear enough that the physical world is not physics and *A Skeleton Key to Finnegan's Wake* not *Finnegan's Wake*. But, as, in the study of culture, analysis penetrates into the very body of the object—that is, *we begin with our own interpretations of what our informants are up to, or think they are up to, and then systematize those*—the line between (Moroccan) culture as a natural fact and (Moroccan) culture as a theoretical entity tends to get blurred. All the more so, as the latter is presented in the form of an actor's-eye description of (Moroccan) concep-tions of everything from violence, honor, divinity, and justice, to tribe, property, patronage, and chiefship.

In short, anthropological writings are themselves interpretations, and second and third order ones to boot. (By definition, only a 'native' makes first order ones: it's *his* culture.)[2] They are, thus, fictions; fictions, in the sense that they are 'something made,' 'something fashioned'—the original meaning of *fictiˉo*—not that they are false, unfactual, or merely 'as if' thought experiments. To construct actor-oriented descriptions of the involvements of a Berber chieftain, a Jewish merchant, and a French soldier with one another in 1912 Morocco is clearly an imaginative act, not all that different from constructing similar descriptions of, say, the involvements with one another of a provincial French doctor, his silly, adulterous wife, and her feckless lover in nineteenth century France. In the latter case, the actors are represented as not having existed and the events as not having happened, while in the former they are represented as actual, or as having been so. This is a difference of no mean importance; indeed, precisely the one Madame Bovary had difficulty grasping. But the importance does not lie in the fact that her story was created while Cohen's was

245

only noted. The conditions of their creation, and the point of it (to say nothing of the manner and the quality) differ. But the one is as much a *ficti‾o*—'a making'—as the other.

Anthropologists have not always been as aware as they might be of this fact: that although culture exists in the trading post, the hill fort, or the sheep run, anthropology exists in the book, the article, the lecture, the museum display, or, sometimes nowadays, the film. To become aware of it is to realize that the line between mode of representation and substantive content is as undrawable in cultural analysis as it is in painting; and that fact in turn seems to threaten the objective status of anthropological knowledge by suggesting that its source is not social reality but scholarly artifice.

It does threaten it, but the threat is hollow. The claim to attention of an ethnographic account does not rest on its author's ability to capture primitive facts in faraway places and carry them home like a mask or a carving, but on the degree to which he is able to clarify what goes on in such places, to reduce the puzzlement— what manner of men are these?—to which unfamiliar acts emerging out of unknown backgrounds naturally give rise. This raises some serious problems of verification, all right—or, if 'verification' is too strong a word for so soft a science (I, myself, would prefer 'appraisal'), of how you can tell a better account from a worse one. But that is precisely the virtue of it. If ethnography is thick description and ethnographers those who are doing the describing, then the determining question for any given example of it, whether a field journal squib or a Malinowski-sized monograph, is whether it sorts winks from twitches and real winks from mimicked ones. It is not against a body of uninterpreted data, radically thinned descriptions, that we must measure the cogency of our explications, but against the power of the scientific imagination to bring us into touch with the lives of strangers. It is not worth it, as Thoreau said, to go round the world to count the cats in Zanzibar.

V

Now, this proposition, that it is not in our interest to bleach human behaviour of the very properties that interest us before we begin to examine it, has sometimes been escalated into a larger claim: namely, that as it is only those properties that interest us, we need not attend, save cursorily, to behavior at all. Culture is most effectively treated, the argument goes, purely as a symbolic system (the catch phrase is, 'in its own terms'), by isolating its elements, specifying the internal relationships among those elements, and then characterizing the whole system in some general way— according to the core symbols around which it is organized, the underlying structures of which it is a surface expression, or the ideological principles upon which it is based. Though a distinct improvement over 'learned behavior' and 'mental phenomena' notions of what culture is, and the source of some of the most powerful theoretical ideas in contemporary anthropology, this hermetical approach to things seems to me to run the danger (and increasingly to have been overtaken by it) of locking cultural analysis away from its proper object, the informal logic of actual life. There is little profit in extricating a concept from the defects of psychologism only to plunge it immediately into those of schematicism.

Behavior must be attended to, and with some exactness, because it is through the flow of behavior—or, more precisely, social action—that cultural forms find articulation. They find it as well, of course, in various sorts of artifacts, and various states of consciousness; but these draw their meaning from the role they play (Wittgenstein would say their 'use') in an ongoing pattern of life, not from any intrinsic relationships they bear to one another. It is what Cohen, the sheikh, and 'Captain Dumari' were doing when they tripped over one another's purposes—pursuing trade, defending honor, establishing dominance—that created our pastoral drama, and that is what the drama is, therefore, 'about.' Whatever, or wherever, symbol systems 'in their own terms' may be, we gain empirical access to them by inspecting events, not by arranging abstracted entities into unified patterns.

A further implication of this is that coherence cannot be the major test of validity for a cultural description. Cultural systems must have a minimal degree of coherence, else we would not call them systems; and, by observation, they normally have a great deal more. But there is nothing so coherent as a paranoid's delusion or a swindler's story. The force of our interpretations cannot rest, as they are now so often made to do, on the tightness with which they hold together, or the assurance with which they are argued. Nothing has done more, I think, to discredit cultural analysis than the construction of impeccable depictions of formal order in whose actual existence nobody can quite believe.

If anthropological interpretation is constructing a reading of what happens, then to divorce it from what happens—from what, in this time or that place, specific people say, what they do, what is done to them, from the whole vast business of the world—is to divorce it from its applications and render it vacant. A good interpretation of anything—a poem, a person, a history, a ritual, an institution, a society—takes us into the heart of that of which it is the interpretation. When it does not do that, but leads us instead somewhere else—into an admiration of its own elegance, of its author's cleverness, or of the beauties of Euclidean order—it may have its intrinsic charms; but it is something else than what the task at hand—figuring out what all that rigamarole with the sheep is about—calls for.

The rigamarole with the sheep—the sham theft of them, the reparative transfer of them, the political confiscation of them—is (or was) essentially a social discourse, even if, as I suggested earlier, one conducted in multiple tongues and as much in action as in words.

Claiming his *'ar*, Cohen invoked the trade pact; recognizing the claim, the sheikh challenged the offenders' tribe; accepting responsibility, the offenders' tribe paid the indemnity; anxious to make clear to sheikhs and peddlers alike who was now in charge here, the French showed the imperial hand. As in any discourse, code does not determine conduct, and what was actually said need not have been. Cohen might not have, given its illegitimacy in Protectorate eyes, chosen to press his claim. The sheikh might, for similar reasons, have rejected it. The offenders' tribe, still resisting French authority, might have decided to regard the raid as 'real' and fight rather than negotiate. The French, were they more *habile* and less *dur* (as, under Mareschal Lyautey's seigniorial tutelage, they later in fact became), might have permitted Cohen to keep his sheep, winking—as we say—at the continuance of the trade pattern and its limitation to their authority. And there are other possibilities: the Marmushans might have regarded the French action as too great an insult to bear and gone into dissidence themselves; the French might have attempted not just to

247

clamp down on Cohen but to bring the sheikh himself more closely to heel; and Cohen might have concluded that between renegade Berbers and Beau Geste soldiers, driving trade in the Atlas highlands was no longer worth the candle and retired to the better-governed confines of the town. This, indeed, is more or less what happened, somewhat further along, as the Protectorate moved toward genuine sovereignty. But the point here is not to describe what did or did not take place in Morocco. (From this simple incident one can widen out into enormous complexities of social experience.) It is to demonstrate what a piece of anthropological interpretation consists in: tracing the curve of a social discourse; fixing it into an inspectable form.

The ethnographer 'inscribes' social discourse; *he writes it down*. In so doing, he turns it from a passing event, which exists only in its own moment of occurrence, into an account, which exists in its inscriptions and can be reconsulted. The sheikh is long dead, killed in the process of being, as the French called it, 'pacified'; 'Captain Dumari,' his pacifier, lives, retired to his souvenirs, in the south of France; and Cohen went last year, part refugee, part pilgrim, part dying patriarch, 'home' to Israel. But what they, in my extended sense, 'said' to one another on an Atlas plateau sixty years ago is—very far from perfectly—preserved for study. 'What,' Paul Ricoeur, from whom this whole idea of the inscription of action is borrowed and somewhat twisted, asks, 'what does writing fix?'

> Not the event of speaking, but the 'said' of speaking, where we understand by the 'said' of speaking that intentional exteriorization constitutive of the aim of discourse thanks to which the *sagen*—the saying—wants to become *Aus-sage*—the enunciation, the enunciated. In short, what we write is the *noema* ['thought,' 'content,' 'gist'] of the speaking. It is the meaning of the speech event, not the event as event.

This is not itself so very 'said'—if Oxford philosophers run to little stories, phenomenological ones run to large sentences; but it brings us anyway to a more precise answer to our generative question, 'What does the ethnographer do?'—he writes.[3] This, too, may seem a less than startling discovery, and to someone familiar with the current 'literature,' an implausible one. But as the standard answer to our question has been, 'He observes, he records, he analyzes'—a kind of *veni, vidi, vici* conception of the matter—it may have more deep-going consequences than are at first apparent, not the least of which is that distinguishing these three phases of knowledge-seeking may not, as a matter of fact, normally be possible; and, indeed, as autonomous 'operations' they may not in fact exist.

The situation is even more delicate, because, as already noted, what we inscribe (or try to) is not raw social discourse, to which, because, save very marginally or very specially, we are not actors, we do not have direct access, but only that small part of it which our informants can lead us into understanding.[4] This is not as fatal as it sounds, for, in fact, not all Cretans are liars, and it is not necessary to know everything in order to understand something. But it does make the view of anthropological analysis as the conceptual manipulation of discovered facts, a logical reconstruction of a mere reality, seem rather lame. To set forth symmetrical crystals of significance, purified of the material complexity in which they were located, and then attribute their existence to autogenous principles of order, universal properties of the human mind, or vast, a priori *weltanschauungen*, is to pretend a science that does not exist and imagine a reality that cannot be found. Cultural analysis is (or should be) guessing at meanings, assessing the guesses, and drawing explanatory conclusions from the better guesses, not discovering the Continent of Meaning and mapping out its bodiless landscape.

VI

So, there are three characteristics of ethnographic description: it is interpretive; what it is interpretive of is the flow of social discourse; and the interpreting involved consists in trying to rescue the 'said' of such discourse from its perishing occasions and fix it in perusable terms. The *kula* is gone or altered; but, for better or worse, *The Argonauts of the Western Pacific* remains. But there is, in addition, a fourth characteristic of such description, at least as I practice it: it is microscopic.

This is not to say that there are no large-scale anthropological interpretations of whole societies, civilizations, world events, and so on. Indeed, it is such extension of our analyses to wider contexts that, along with their theoretical implications, recommends them to general attention and justifies our constructing them. No one really cares anymore, not even Cohen (well . . . maybe, Cohen), about those sheep as such. History may have its unobtrusive turning points, 'great noises in a little room'; but this little go-round was surely not one of them.

It is merely to say that the anthropologist characteristically approaches such broader interpretations and more abstract analyses from the direction of exceedingly extended acquaintances with extremely small matters. He confronts the same grand realities that others—historians, economists, political scientists, sociologists—confront in more fateful settings: Power, Change, Faith, Oppression, Work, Passion, Authority, Beauty, Violence, Love, Prestige; but he confronts them in contexts obscure enough—places like Marmusha and lives like Cohen's—to take the capital letters off them. These all-too-human constancies, 'those big words that make us all afraid,' take a homely form in such homely contexts. But that is exactly the advantage. There are enough profundities in the world already.

Yet, the problem of how to get from a collection of ethnographic miniatures on the order of our sheep story—an assortment of remarks and anecdotes—to wall-sized culturescapes of the nation, the epoch, the continent, or the civilization is not so easily passed over with vague allusions to the virtues of concreteness and the down-to-earth mind. For a science born in Indian tribes, Pacific islands, and African lineages and subsequently seized with grander ambitions, this has come to be a major methodological problem, and for the most part a badly handled one. The models that anthropologists have themselves worked out to justify their moving from local truths to general visions have been, in fact, as responsible for undermining the effort as anything their critics—sociologists obsessed with sample sizes, psychologists with measures, or economists with aggregates—have been able to devise against them.

Of these, the two main ones have been: the Jonesville-is-the-USA 'microcosmic' model; and the Easter-Island-is-a-testing-case 'natural experiment' model. Either heaven in a grain of sand, or the farther shores of possibility.

The Jonesville-is-America writ small (or America-is-Jonesville writ large) fallacy is so obviously one that the only thing that needs explanation is how people have managed to believe it and expected others to believe it. The notion that one can find the essence of national societies, civilizations, great religions, or whatever summed up and simplified in so-called 'typical' small towns and villages is palpable nonsense. What one finds in small towns and villages is (alas) small-town or village life. If localized, microscopic studies were really dependent for their greater relevance upon such a premise—that they captured the great world in the little—they wouldn't have any relevance.

But, of course, they are not. The locus of study is not the object of study. Anthropologists don't study villages (tribes, towns, neighborhoods . . .) they study *in* villages. You can study different things in different places, and some things—for example, what colonial domination does to established frames of moral expectation— you can best study in confined localities. But that doesn't make the place what it is you are studying. In the remoter provinces of Morocco and Indonesia I have wrestled with the same questions other social scientists have wrestled with in more central locations—for example, how comes it that men's most importunate claims to humanity are cast in the accents of group pride?—and with about the same conclusiveness. One can add a dimension—one much needed in the present climate of size-up-and-solve social science; but that is all. There is a certain value, if you are going to run on about the exploitation of the masses in having seen a Javanese sharecropper turning earth in a tropical downpour or a Moroccan tailor embroidering kaftans by the light of a twenty-watt bulb. But the notion that this gives you the thing entire (and elevates you to some moral vantage ground from which you can look down upon the ethically less privileged) is an idea which only someone too long in the bush could possibly entertain.

The 'natural laboratory' notion has been equally pernicious, not only because the analogy is false—what kind of a laboratory is it where *none* of the parameters are manipulable?—but because it leads to a notion that the data derived from ethnographic studies are purer, or more fundamental, or more solid, or less conditioned (the most favored word is 'elementary') than those derived from other sorts of social inquiry. The great natural variation of cultural forms is, of course, not only anthropology's great (and wasting) resource, but the ground of its deepest theoretical dilemma: how is such variation to be squared with the biological unity of the human species? But it is not, even metaphorically, experimental variation, because the context in which it occurs varies along with it, and it is not possible (though there are those who try) to isolate the y's from x's to write a proper function.

The famous studies purporting to show that the Oedipus complex was backwards in the Trobriands, sex roles were upside down in Tchambuli, and the Pueblo Indians lacked aggression (it is characteristic that they were all negative—'but not in the South'), are, whatever their empirical validity may or may not be, not 'scientifically tested and approved' hypotheses. They are interpretations, or misinterpretations, like any others, arrived at in the same way as any others, and as inherently inconclusive as any others, and the attempt to invest them with the authority of physical experimentation is but methodological sleight of hand. Ethnographic findings are not privileged, just particular: another country heard from. To regard them as anything more (*or anything less*) than that distorts both them and their implications, which are

250

far profounder than mere primitivity, for social theory.

Another country heard from: the reason that protracted descriptions of distant sheep raids (and a really good ethnographer would have gone into what kind of sheep they were) have general relevance is that they present the sociological mind with bodied stuff on which to feed. The important thing about the anthropologist's findings is their complex specificness, their circumstantiality. It is with the kind of material produced by long-term, mainly (though not exclusively) qualitative, highly participative, and almost obsessively fine-comb field study in confined contexts that the meta-concepts with which contemporary social science is afflicted—legitimacy, modernization, integration, conflict, charisma, structure, . . . meaning—can be given the sort of sensible actuality that makes it possible to think not only realistically and concretely *about* them, but, what is more important, creatively and imaginatively *with* them.

The methodological problem which the microscopic nature of ethnography presents is both real and critical. But it is not to be resolved by regarding a remote locality as the world in a teacup or as the sociological equivalent of a cloud chamber. It is to be resolved—or, anyway, decently kept at bay—by realizing that social actions are comments on more than themselves; that where an interpretation comes from does not determine where it can be impelled to go. Small facts speak to large issues, winks to epistemology, or sheep raids to revolution, because they are made to.

VII

Which brings us, finally, to theory. The besetting sin of interpretive approaches to anything—literature, dreams, symptoms, culture—is that they tend to resist, or to be permitted to resist, conceptual articulation and thus to escape systematic modes of assessment. You either grasp an interpretation or you do not, see the point of it or you do not, accept it or you do not. Imprisoned in the immediacy of its own detail, it is presented as self-validating, or, worse, as validated by the supposedly developed sensitivities of the person who presents it; any attempt to cast what it says in terms other than its own is regarded as a travesty—as, the anthropologist's severest term of moral abuse, ethnocentric.

For a field of study which, however timidly (though I, myself, am not timid about the matter at all), asserts itself to be a science, this just will not do. There is no reason why the conceptual structure of a cultural interpretation should be any less formulable, and thus less susceptible to explicit canons of appraisal, than that of, say, a biological observation or a physical experiment—no reason except that the terms in which such formulations can be cast are, if not wholly nonexistent, very nearly so. We are reduced to insinuating theories because we lack the power to state them.

At the same time, it must be admitted that there are a number of characteristics of cultural interpretation which make the theoretical development of it more than usually difficult. The first is the need for theory to stay rather closer to the ground than tends to be the case in sciences more able to give themselves over to imaginative abstraction. Only short flights of ratiocination tend to be effective in anthropology; longer ones tend to drift off into logical dreams, academic bemusements with formal symmetry. The whole point of a semiotic approach to culture is, as I have said, to aid us in gaining access to the conceptual world in which our subjects live so that we can, in some extended sense of the term, converse with them. The tension between the pull of this need to penetrate an unfamiliar universe of symbolic action and the requirements of technical advance in the theory of culture, between the need to grasp and the need to analyze, is, as a result, both necessarily great and essentially irremovable. Indeed, the further theoretical development goes, the deeper the tension gets. This is the first condition for cultural theory: it is not its own master. As it is unseverable from the immediacies thick description presents, its freedom to shape itself in terms of its internal logic is rather limited. What generality it contrives to achieve grows out of the delicacy of its distinctions, not the sweep of its abstractions.

And from this follows a peculiarity in the way, as a simple matter of empirical fact, our knowledge of culture . . . cultures . . . a culture . . . grows: in spurts. Rather than following a rising curve of cumulative findings, cultural analysis breaks up into a disconnected yet coherent sequence of bolder and bolder sorties. Studies do build on other studies, not in the sense that they take up where the others leave off, but in the sense that, better informed and better conceptualized, they plunge more deeply into the same things. Every serious cultural analysis starts from a sheer beginning and ends where it manages to get before exhausting its intellectual impulse. Previously discovered facts are mobilized, previously developed concepts used, previously formulated hypotheses tried out; but the movement is not from already proven theorems to newly proven ones, it is from an awkward fumbling for the most elementary understanding to a supported claim that one has achieved that and surpassed it. A study is an advance if it is more incisive—whatever that may mean—than those that preceded it; but it less stands on their shoulders than, challenged and challenging, runs by their side.

It is for this reason, among others, that the essay, whether of thirty pages or three hundred, has seemed the natural genre in which to present cultural interpretations and the theories sustaining them, and why, if one looks for systematic treatises in the field, one is so soon disappointed, the more so if one finds any. Even inventory articles are rare here, and anyway of hardly more than bibliographical interest. The major theoretical contributions not only lie in specific studies—that is true in almost any field—but they are very difficult to abstract from such studies and integrate into anything one might call 'culture theory' as such. Theoretical formulations hover so low over the interpretations they govern that they don't make much sense or hold much interest apart from them. This is so, not because they are not general (if they are not general, they are not theoretical), but because, stated independently of their applications, they seem either commonplace or vacant. One can, and this in fact is how the field progresses conceptually, take a line of theoretical attack developed in connection with one exercise in ethnographic interpretation and employ it in another, pushing it forward to greater precision and broader relevance; but one cannot write a 'General Theory of Cultural Interpretation.' Or, rather, one can, but there appears to be little profit in it, because the essential task of theory building here is not to codify abstract regularities but to make thick description possible, not to generalize across cases but to generalize within them.

To generalize within cases is usually called, at least in medicine and depth psychology, clinical inference. Rather than beginning with a set of observations and attempting to subsume them under a governing law, such inference begins with a set of (presumptive) signifiers and attempts to place them within an intelligible frame. Measures are matched to theoretical predictions, but symptoms (even when they are measured) are scanned for theoretical peculiarities—that is, they are diagnosed. In the study of culture the signifiers are not symptoms or clusters of symptoms, but symbolic acts or clusters of symbolic acts, and the aim is not therapy but the analysis of social discourse. But the way in which theory is used—to ferret out the unapparent import of things—is the same.

Thus we are led to the second condition of cultural theory: it is not, at least in the strict meaning of the term, predictive. The diagnostician doesn't predict measles; he decides that someone has them, or at the very most *anticipates* that someone is rather likely shortly to get them. But this limitation, which is real enough, has commonly been both misunderstood and exaggerated, because it has been taken to mean that cultural interpretation is merely post facto: that, like the peasant in the old story, we first shoot the holes in the fence and then paint the bull's-eyes around them. It is hardly to be denied that there is a good deal of that sort of thing around, some of it in prominent places. It is to be denied, however, that it is the inevitable outcome of a clinical approach to the use of theory.

It is true that in the clinical style of theoretical formulation, conceptualization is directed toward the task of generating interpretations of matters already in hand, not toward projecting outcomes of experimental manipulations or deducing future states of a determined system. But that does not mean that theory has only to fit (or, more carefully, to generate cogent interpretations of) realities past; it has also to survive—intellectually survive—realities to come. Although we formulate our interpretation of an outburst of winking or an instance of sheep-raiding after its occurrence, sometimes long after, the theoretical framework in terms of which such an interpretation is made must be capable of continuing to yield defensible interpretations as new social phenomena swim into view. Although one starts any effort at thick description, beyond the obvious and superficial, from a state of general bewilderment as to what the devil is going on—trying to find one's feet—one does not start (or ought not) intellectually empty-handed. Theoretical ideas are not created wholly anew in each study; as I have said, they are adopted from other, related studies, and, refined in the process, applied to new interpretive problems. If they cease being useful with respect to such problems, they tend to stop being used and are more or less abandoned. If they continue being useful, throwing up new understandings, they are further elaborated and go on being used.[5]

Such a view of how theory functions in an interpretive science suggests that the distinction, relative in any case, that appears in the experimental or observational sciences between 'description' and 'explanation' appears here as one, even more relative, between 'inscription' ('thick description') and 'specification' ('diagnosis')—between setting down the meaning particular social actions have for the actors whose actions they are, and stating, as explicitly as we can manage, what the knowledge thus attained demonstrates about the society in which it is found and, beyond that, about social life as such. Our double task is to uncover the conceptual structures that inform our subjects' acts, the 'said' of social discourse, and to construct a system of analysis in whose terms what is generic to those structures, what belongs to them because they are what they are, will stand out against the other determinants of human behavior. In ethnography, the office of theory is to provide a vocabulary in which what symbolic action has to say about itself—that is, about the role of culture in human life—can be expressed.

Aside from a couple of orienting pieces concerned with more foundational matters, it is in such a manner that theory operates in the essays collected here. A repertoire of very general, made-in-the-academy concepts and systems of concepts—'integration,' 'rationalization,' 'symbol,' 'ideology,' 'ethos,' 'revolution,' 'identity,' 'metaphor,' 'structure,' 'ritual,' 'world view,' 'actor,' 'function,' 'sacred,' and, of course, 'culture' itself—is woven into the body of thick-description ethnography in the hope of rendering mere occurrences scientifically eloquent. The aim is to draw large conclusions from small, but very densely textured facts; to support broad assertions about the role of culture in the construction of collective life by engaging them exactly with complex specifics.

Thus it is not only interpretation that goes all the way down to the most immediate observational level: the theory upon which such interpretation conceptually depends does so also. My interest in Cohen's story, like Ryle's in winks, grew out of some very general notions indeed. The 'confusion of tongues' model—the view that social conflict is not something that happens when, out of weakness, indefiniteness, obsolescence, or neglect, cultural forms cease to operate, but rather something which happens when, like burlesqued winks, such forms are pressed by unusual situations or unusual intentions to operate in unusual ways—is not an idea I got from Cohen's story. It is one, instructed by colleagues, students, and predecessors, I brought to it.

Our innocent-looking 'note in a bottle' is more than a portrayal of the frames of meaning of Jewish peddlers, Berber warriors, and French proconsuls, or even of their mutual interference. It is an argument that to rework the pattern of social relationships is to rearrange the coordinates of the experienced world. Society's forms are culture's substance.

VIII

There is an Indian story—at least I heard it as an Indian story—about an Englishman who, having been told that the world rested on a platform which rested on the back of an elephant which rested in turn on the back of a turtle, asked (perhaps he was an ethnographer; it is the way they behave), what did the turtle rest on? Another turtle. And that turtle? 'Ah, Sahib, after that it is turtles all the way down.'

Such, indeed, is the condition of things. I do not know how long it would be profitable to meditate on the encounter of Cohen, the sheikh, and 'Dumari' (the period has perhaps already been exceeded); but I do know that however long I did so I would not get anywhere near to the bottom of it. Nor have I ever gotten anywhere near to the bottom of anything I have ever written about, either in the essays below or elsewhere. Cultural analysis is intrinsically incomplete. And, worse than that, the more deeply it goes the less complete it is. It is a strange science whose most telling assertions are its most tremulously based, in which to get somewhere with the matter at hand is to intensify the suspicion, both your own and that of others, that you are not quite getting it right. But that, along with plaguing subtle people with obtuse questions, is what being an ethnographer is like.

There are a number of ways to escape this—turning culture into folklore and collecting it, turning it into traits and counting it, turning it into institutions and classifying it, turning it into structures and toying with it. But they *are* escapes. The fact is that to commit oneself to a semiotic concept of culture and an interpretive approach to the study of it is to commit oneself to a view of ethnographic assertion as, to borrow W. B. Gallie's by now famous phrase, 'essentially contestable.' Anthropology, or at least interpretive anthropology, is a science whose progress is marked less by a perfection of consensus than by a refinement of debate. What gets better is the precision with which we vex each other.

This is very difficult to see when one's attention is being monopolized by a single party to the argument. Monologues are of little value here, because there are no conclusions to be reported; there is merely a discussion to be sustained. Insofar as the essays here collected have any importance, it is less in what they say than what they are witness to: an enormous increase in interest, not only in anthropology, but in social studies generally, in the role of symbolic forms in human life. Meaning, that elusive and ill-defined pseudoentity we were once more than content to leave philosophers and literary critics to fumble with, has now come back into the heart of our discipline. Even Marxists are quoting Cassirer; even positivists, Kenneth Burke.

My own position in the midst of all this has been to try to resist subjectivism on the one hand and cabbalism on the other, to try to keep the analysis of symbolic forms as closely tied as I could to concrete social events and occasions, the public world of common life, and to organize it in such a way that the connections between theoretical formulations and descriptive interpretations were unobscured by appeals to dark sciences. I have never been impressed by the argument that, as complete objectivity is impossible in these matters (as, of course, it is), one might as well let one's sentiments run loose. As Robert Solow has remarked, that is like saying that as a perfectly aseptic environment is impossible, one might as well conduct surgery in a sewer. Nor, on the other hand, have I been impressed with claims that structural linguistics, computer engineering, or some other advanced form of thought is going to enable us to understand men without knowing them. Nothing will discredit a semiotic approach to culture more quickly than allowing it to drift into a combination of intuitionism and alchemy, no matter how elegantly the intuitions are expressed or how modern the alchemy is made to look.

The danger that cultural analysis, in search of all-too-deep-lying turtles, will lose touch with the hard surfaces of life—with the political, economic, stratificatory realities within which men are everywhere contained—and with the biological and physical necessities on which those surfaces rest, is an ever-present one. The only defense against it, and against, thus, turning cultural analysis into a kind of sociological aestheticism, is to train such analysis on such realities and such necessities in the first place. It is thus that I have written about nationalism, about violence, about identity, about human nature, about legitimacy, about revolution, about ethnicity, about urbanization, about status, about death, about time, and most of all about particular attempts by particular peoples to place these things in some sort of comprehensible, meaningful frame.

To look at the symbolic dimensions of social action—art, religion, ideology, science, law, morality, common sense—is not to turn away from the existential dilemmas of life for some empyrean realm of deemotionalized forms; it is to plunge

255

into the midst of them. The essential vocation of interpretive anthropology is not to answer our deepest questions, but to make available to us answers that others, guarding other sheep in other valleys, have given, and thus to include them in the consultable record of what man has said.

NOTES

1. Not only other peoples': anthropology *can* be trained on the culture of which it is itself a part, and it increasingly is; a fact of profound importance, but which, as it raises a few tricky and rather special second order problems, I shall put to the side for the moment.

2. The order problem is, again, complex. Anthropological works based on other anthropological works (Lévi-Strauss', for example) may, of course, be fourth order or higher, and informants frequently, even habitually, make second order interpretations—what have come to be known as 'native models.' In literate cultures, where 'native' interpretation can proceed to higher levels—in connection with the Maghreb, one has only to think of Ibn Khaldun; with the United States, Margaret Mead—these matters become intricate indeed.

3. Or, again, more exactly, 'inscribes.' Most ethnography is in fact to be found in books and articles, rather than in films, records, museum displays, or whatever; but even in them there are, of course, photographs, drawings, diagrams, tables, and so on. Self-consciousness about modes of representation (not to speak of experiments with them) has been very lacking in anthropology.

4. So far as it has reinforced the anthropologist's impulse to engage himself with his informants as persons rather than as objects, the notion of 'participant observation' has been a valuable one. But, to the degree it has lead the anthropologist to block from his view the very special, culturally bracketed nature of his own role and to imagine himself something more than an interested (in both senses of that word) sojourner, it has been our most powerful source of bad faith.

5. Admittedly, this is something of an idealization. Because theories are seldom if ever decisively disproved in clinical use but merely grow increasingly awkward, unproductive, strained, or vacuous, they often persist long after all but a handful of people (though *they* are often most passionate) have lost much interest in them. Indeed, so far as anthropology is concerned, it is almost more of a problem to get exhausted ideas out of the literature than it is to get productive ones in, and so a great deal more of theoretical discussion than one would prefer is critical rather than constructive, and whole careers have been devoted to hastening the demise of moribund notions. As the field advances one would hope that this sort of intellectual weed control would become a less prominent part of our activities. But, for the moment, it remains true that old theories tend less to die than to go into second editions.

James Clifford (1945–)

James Clifford teaches in the history of consciousness programme at the University of California, Santa Cruz. He is the author of *The Predicament of Culture* (1988), *Writing Culture: The Poetics and Politics of Ethnography* (1986), and *Person and Myth: Maurice Leenhardt in the Melanesian World* (1982). His work speaks to the dilemmas of cultural dynamics as indigenous groups in various localities around the globe interact with the new technology and mass culture of the hegemonic order of the post-industrial societies. He warns against reductivist claims that this interaction will erase cultural differences and denies the foregone conclusion that the people of these cultures are either doomed or blessed when they are assimilated. Instead, he sees local cultural differentiation continuing in unpredictable patterns that ethnographers will be obliged to track in an enterprise of the ethnography of modernity.

Clifford discusses this kind of ethnography in the following essay and shows how recording or 'writing' such research may be carried out. He argues that ethnography begins and ends in writing and that this writing is largely interpretive (rather than explanative) of the cultures with which it interacts. This thesis is a radical shift in cultural anthropology which had hitherto seen the function of the recorder or writer as a 'truth' teller. He says that ethnographers write with a variety of strategies of 'textualization' which do not necessarily preclude one another. In addition, ethnographic research is intersubjective, and ethnographers' discursive moves establish and circumscribe the rhetorical situation in which they work. Clifford traces the constitution of this situation in the work of ethnographers from the past 100 years and examines their work both as science and literature. Recent literary theory informs Clifford's analyses and supports his thesis that ethnographic writing is a literary genre that is subject to the same discursive formations as other kinds of writing and to the same interpretive techniques. He believes that ethnographers can no longer rely upon a single mode of realism to either establish their authority as writers or grant verisimilitude to their findings.

T.M.

On ethnographic authority*

The 1724 frontispiece of Father Lafitau's *Moeurs des sauvages ameriquains* portrays the ethnographer as a young woman sitting at a writing table amidst artifacts from the New World and from classical Greece and Egypt. The author is accompanied by two cherubs who assist in the task of comparison and by the bearded figure of Time who points toward a tableau representing the ultimate source of the truths issuing from the writer's pen. The image toward which the young woman lifts her gaze is a bank of clouds where Adam, Eve and the serpent appear. Above them stand the redeemed man and woman of the Apocalypse on either side of a radiant triangle bearing the Hebrew script for Yahweh.

The frontispiece for Malinowski's *Argonauts of the Western Pacific* is a photograph with the caption 'A Ceremonial Act of the Kula.' A shell necklace is being offered to a Trobriand chief who stands at the door of his dwelling. Behind the man presenting the necklace is a row of six bowing youths, one of them sounding a conch. All the figures stand in profile, their attention apparently concentrated on the rite of exchange, a real event of Melanesian life. But on closer inspection one of the bowing Trobrianders may be seen to be looking at the camera.

Lafitau's allegory is the less familiar: his author transcribes rather than originates. Unlike Malinowski's photo, the engraving makes no reference to ethnographic experience—despite Lafitau's five years of research among the Mohawks, research that has earned him a respected place among the fieldworkers of any generation. His account is presented not as the product of first-hand observation but of writing, in a crowded workshop. The frontispiece from *Argonauts*, like all photographs, asserts presence, that of the scene before the lens. But it suggests also another presence—the ethnographer actively composing this fragment of Trobriand reality. Kula exchange, the subject of Malinowski's book, has been made perfectly visible, centered in the perceptual frame. And a participant's glance redirects our attention to the observational standpoint we share, as readers, with the ethnographer and his camera. The predominant mode of modern fieldwork authority is signaled: 'You are there, because I was there.'

The present essay traces the formation and breakup of this authority in twentieth century social anthropology. It is not a complete account, nor is it based on a fully realized theory of ethnographic interpretation and textuality.[1] Such a theory's contours are problematic, since the activity of cross cultural representation is now more than usually in question. The present predicament is linked to the breakup and redistribution of colonial power in the decades after 1950 and to the echoes of that process in the radical cultural theories of the 1960s and 1970s. After the Negritude movement's reversal of the European gaze, after anthropology's *crise de confiance* with respect to its liberal status within the imperial order, and now that the West can no

*An early version of this essay was presented at the American Anthropological Association in December of 1980. For helpful criticisms I would like to thank Talal Assad, Vincent Crapanzano, Joel Fineman, Thomas Laqueur, Joan Larcom, George Marcus, T. N. Pandey, Mary Pratt, Richard Randolph, Renato Rosaldo, George Stocking, Sharon Traweek, Steven Webster.

longer present itself as the unique purveyor of anthropological knowledge about others, it has become necessary to imagine a world of generalized ethnography. With expanded communication and intercultural influence, people interpret others, and themselves, in a bewildering diversity of idioms—a global condition of what Bakhtin called 'heteroglossia.'[2] This ambiguous, multi-vocal world makes it increasingly hard to conceive of human diversity as inscribed in bounded, independent cultures. Difference is an effect of inventive syncretism. In recent years works like Edward Said's *Orientalism* and Paulin Hountondji's *Sur la 'philosophie africaine'* have cast radical doubt on the procedures by which alien human groups can be represented, without proposing systematic, sharply new methods or epistemologies. These studies suggest that while ethnographic writing cannot entirely escape the reductionist use of dichotomies and essences, it can at least struggle self-consciously to avoid portraying abstract, a-historical 'others.'[3] It is more than ever crucial for different peoples to form complex concrete images of one another, as well as of the relationships of knowledge and power that connect them. But no sovereign scientific method or ethical stance can guarantee the truth of such images. They are constituted—the critique of colonial modes of representation has shown at least this much—in specific historical relations of dominance and dialogue.

The experiments in ethnographic writing surveyed below do not fall into a clear reformist direction or evolution. They are *ad hoc* inventions and cannot be seen in terms of a systematic analysis of post-colonial representation. They are perhaps best understood as components of that 'toolkit' of engaged theory recently recommended by Deleuze and Foucault.

> The notion of theory as a toolkit means (i) The theory to be constructed is not a system but an instrument, a *logic* of the specificity of power relations and the struggles around them; (ii) That this investigation can only be carried out step by step on the basis of reflection (which will necessarily be historical in some of its aspects) on given situations.[4]

We may contribute to a practical reflection on cross cultural representation by undertaking an inventory of the better, though imperfect, approaches currently at hand. Of these, ethnographic fieldwork remains an unusually sensitive method. Participant observation obliges its practitioners to experience, at a bodily as well as intellectual level, the vicissitudes of translation. It requires arduous language learning, some degree of direct involvement and conversation, and often a derangement of personal and cultural expectations. There is, of course, a myth of fieldwork, and the actual experience, hedged around with contingencies, rarely lives up to the ideal. But as a means for producing knowledge from an intense, intersubjective engagement, the practice of ethnography retains a certain exemplary status. Moreover, if fieldwork has for a time been identified with a uniquely Western discipline and a totalizing science of 'anthropology,' these associations are not necessarily permanent. Current styles of cultural description are historically limited and undergoing important metamorphoses.

The development of ethnographic science cannot ultimately be understood in isolation from more general political-epistemological debates about writing and the representation of otherness. However, in the present discussion I have maintained a

259

focus on professional anthropology and specifically on developments within interpretive ethnography since 1950.[5] The current crisis—or better, dispersion—of ethnographic authority makes it possible to mark off a rough period, bounded by the years 1900 and 1960, during which a new conception of field research established itself as the norm for European and American anthropology. Intensive fieldwork, pursued by university trained specialists, emerged as a privileged, sanctioned source of data about exotic peoples. It is not a question, here, of the dominance of a single research method. 'Intensive' ethnography was variously defined.[6] Moreover, the hegemony of fieldwork was established earlier and more thoroughly in America and England than it was in France. The early examples of Boas and the Torres Straits Expedition were matched only belatedly by the founding of the Institut d'Ethnologie in 1925 and the much-publicized Mission Dakar-Djibouti of 1932.[7] Nevertheless, by the mid-1930s one can fairly speak of a developing international consensus: valid anthropological abstractions were to be based, wherever possible, on intensive cultural descriptions by qualified scholars. By the mid-1930s the new style had been made popular, institutionalized, and embodied in specific textual practices.

It has recently become possible to identify and take a certain distance from these conventions.[8] If ethnography produces cultural interpretations through intense research experiences, how is unruly experience transformed into an authoritative written account? How, precisely, is a garrulous, overdetermined, cross cultural encounter shot through with power relations and personal cross purposes circumscribed as an adequate version of a more-or-less discrete 'other world,' composed by an individual author?

In analyzing the complex transformation one must bear in mind the fact that ethnography is from beginning to end enmeshed in writing. This writing includes, minimally, a translation of experience into textual form. The process is complicated by the action of multiple subjectivities and political constraints beyond the control of the writer. In response to these forces ethnographic writing enacts a specific strategy of authority. This has classically involved an unquestioned claim to appear as the purveyor of truth in the text. A complex cultural experience is enunciated by an individual: *We the Tikopia*, by Raymond Firth; *Nous avons mangé la forêt*, by Georges Condominas; *Coming of Age in Samoa*, by Margaret Mead; *The Nuer*, by Evans-Pritchard.

The discussion that follows first locates this authority historically—in the development of a twentieth-century science of participant-observation. It then proceeds to a critique of underlying assumptions and a review of emerging textual practices. Alternate strategies of ethnographic authority may be seen in recent experiments by ethnographers who self-consciously reject scenes of cultural representation in the style of Malinowski's frontispiece. Different secular versions of Lafitau's crowded scriptorial workshop are emerging. In the new paradigms of authority the writer is no longer fascinated by transcendent figures—by a Hebrew-Christian deity or its twentieth-century replacements, 'Man' and 'culture.' Nothing remains of the heavenly tableau except the anthropologist's scumbled image in a mirror. And the silence of the ethnographic workshop has been broken—by insistent, heteroglot voices, by the scratching of other pens.[9]

At the close of the nineteenth century nothing guaranteed, *a priori*, the ethnographer's status as the best interpreter of native life—as opposed to the traveller, and especially to the missionary and administrator, some of whom had been in the field far longer and had better research contacts and linguistic skills. The development of the fieldworker's image in America, from Cushing (an oddball) to Margaret Mead (a national figure) is significant. During this period a particular form of authority was created, an authority both scientifically validated and based on a unique personal experience. During the 1920s Malinowski played a central role in establishing credit for the fieldworker, and we should recall in this light his attacks on the competence of competitors in the field. For example, the colonial magistrate Rentoul, who had the temerity to contradict science's findings concerning Trobriand conceptions of paternity, was excommunicated in the pages of *Man* for his unprofessional 'police court perspective.' The attack on amateurism in the field was pressed even further by Radcliffe-Brown who, as Ian Langham has shown, came to epitomize the scientific professional, discovering rigorous social laws, etc.[10] What emerged during the first half of the twentieth century, with the success of professional fieldwork, was a new fusion of general theory and empirical research, of cultural analysis with ethnographic description.

The fieldworker-theorist replaced an older partition between the 'man on the spot' (in Frazer's words) and the sociologist or anthropologist in the metropole. This division of labor varied in different national traditions. In America, for example, Morgan had personal knowledge of at least some of the cultures that were raw material for his sociological syntheses; and Boas, rather earlier than elsewhere, made intensive fieldwork the *sine qua non* of serious anthropological discourse. But in general, before Malinowski, Radclife-Brown, and Mead had successfully established the norm of the university trained scholar testing and deriving theory from first-hand research, a rather different economy of ethnographic knowledge prevailed. For example, Codrington's *The Melanesians* (1891) is a detailed compilation of folklore and custom, drawn from a relatively long term of research as an evangelist and based on intensive collaboration with indigenous translators and informants. The book is not organized around a fieldwork 'experience,' and it does not advance a unified interpretative hypothesis, functional, historical or otherwise. It is content with low level generalizations and the amassing of an eclectic range of information. Codrington is acutely aware of the incompleteness of his knowledge, believing that real understanding of native life begins only after a decade or so of experience and study.[11] This understanding of the difficulty of grasping the world of alien peoples—the many years of learning and unlearning needed, the problems of acquiring a thorough linguistic competence—tends to dominate the most serious ethnographic work of Codrington's generation. But such assumptions would soon be challenged by the more confident cultural relativism of the Malinowskian model. The new fieldworkers sharply distinguished themselves from the earlier 'men on the spot,' the missionary, the administrator, the trader, and the traveller, whose knowledge of indigenous peoples, they argued, was not informed by the best scientific hypotheses or a sufficient neutrality.

Before the emergence of professional ethnography, writers like McLennan, Lubbock, and Tylor had attempted to control the quality of the reports on which their anthropological syntheses were based. They did this by means of the guidelines of *Notes and Queries* and, in Tylor's case, by cultivating long-term working relations with sophisticated researchers in the field like the missionary Lorimer Fison. After 1883, as newly appointed Reader in Anthropology at Oxford, Tylor worked to encourage the systematic gathering of ethnographic data by qualified professionals. The United States Bureau of Ethnology, already committed to the undertaking, provided a model. Tylor was active in founding a Committee on the North-Western Tribes of Canada. The Committee's first agent in the field was the nineteen-year veteran missionary among the Ojibwa, E. F. Wilson. He was replaced, before long, by Franz Boas, a physicist in the process of turning to professional ethnography. George Stocking has persuasively argued that the replacement of Wilson by Boas 'marks the beginning of an important phase in the development of British ethnographic method: the collection of data by academically trained natural scientists defining themselves as anthropologists, and involved also in the formulation and evaluation of anthropological theory.' With Boas' early survey work and the emergence in the 1890s of other natural-scientist fieldworkers like A. C. Haddon and Baldwin Spencer, the move toward professional ethnography was underway. The Torres Straits Expedition of 1899 may be seen as a culmination of the work of this 'intermediate generation,' as Stocking calls them. The new style of research was clearly different from that of missionaries and other amateurs in the field, and part of a general trend, since Tylor, 'to draw more closely together the empirical and theoretical components of anthropological inquiry.'[12]

However, the establishment of intensive participant-observation as a professional norm would have to await the Malinowskian cohort. The 'intermediate generation' of ethnographers did not, typically, live in a single locale for a year or more, mastering the vernacular and undergoing a personal learning experience comparable to an initiation. They did not speak as cultural insiders, but retained the natural scientist's documentary, observational stance. The principal exception, before the third decade of the century, Frank Hamilton Cushing, remained an isolated instance. As Curtis Hinsley has suggested, Cushing's long first-hand study of the Zunis, his quasi-absorption into their way of life, 'raised awkward problems of verification and accountability. . . . A community of scientific anthropology on the model of other sciences required a common language of discourse, channels of regular communication, and at least minimal consensus on judging method.'[13] Cushing's intuitive, excessively personal understanding of the Zuni could not confer scientific authority.

Schematically put, before the late nineteenth century the ethnographer and the anthropologist, the describer/translator of custom and the builder of general theories about humanity, were distinct. (A clear sense of the *tension* between ethnography and anthropology is important in correctly perceiving the recent, and perhaps temporary, conflation of the two projects.) Malinowski gives us the imago of the new 'anthropologist'—squatting by the campfire, looking, listening and questioning, recording, and interpreting Trobriand life. The literary charter of this new authority is the first chapter of *Argonauts*, with its prominently displayed photographs of the ethnographer's tent pitched among Kiriwinian dwellings. The sharpest methodological justification for the new mode is to be found in Radcliffe-Brown's *Andaman Islanders*. The two books were published within a year of each other. And although their authors developed quite different fieldwork styles and visions of cultural science, both early texts provide explicit arguments for the special authority of the ethnographer-anthropologist.

Malinowski, as his notes for the crucial Introduction to *Argonauts* show, was greatly concerned with the rhetorical problem of convincing his readers that the facts he was putting before them were objectively acquired, not subjective creations.[14] Moreover, he was fully aware that 'In Ethnography, the distance is often enormous between the brute material of information—as it is presented to the student in his own observations, in native statement, in the kaleidoscope of tribal life—and the final authoritative presentation of the results.'[15] Stocking has nicely analyzed the various literary artifices of *Argonauts* (its engaging narrative constructs, use of active voice in the 'ethnographic present,' illusive dramatizations of the author's participation in scenes of Trobriand life), techniques Malinowski used so that 'his own experience of the natives' experience (might) become the reader's experience as well.'[16] The problems of verification and accountability that had relegated Cushing to the professional margin were very much on Malinowski's mind. This anxiety is reflected in the mass of data contained in *Argonauts*, its sixty-six photographic plates, the now rather curious 'Chronological list of Kula Events Witnessed by the Writer,' the constant alternation between impersonal description of typical behavior and statements on the order of 'I witnessed . . .,' and 'Our party, sailing from the North. . . .'

Argonauts is a complex narrative, simultaneously of Trobriand life and of ethnographic fieldwork. It is archetypical of the generation of ethnographies that successfully established participant-observation's scientific validity. The story of research built into *Argonauts*, into Mead's popular work on Samoa, into *We the Tikopia*, became an implicit narrative underlying all professional reports on exotic worlds. If subsequent ethnographers did not need to include developed fieldwork accounts, it was because such accounts were assumed, once a statement was made on the order of, for example, Godfrey Lienhardt's single sentence at the beginning of *Divinity and Experience*: 'This book is based upon two years' work among the Dinka, spread over the period 1947–1950.'[17]

In the 1920s, the new fieldworker-theorist brought to completion a powerful new scientific and literary genre, the ethnography, a synthetic cultural description based on participant-observation.[18] The new style of representation depended on institutional and methodological innovations circumventing the obstacles to rapid knowledge of other cultures that had preoccupied the best representatives of Codrington's generation. These may be briefly summarized.

First, the persona of the fieldworker was validated, both publicly and professionally. In the popular domain, visible figures like Malinowski, Mead, and Griaule communicated a vision of ethnography as both scientifically demanding and heroic. The professional ethnographer was trained in the latest analytic techniques and modes of scientific explanation. This conferred an advantage over amateurs in the field: the professional could claim to get to the heart of a culture more quickly, grasping its essential institutions and structures. A prescribed attitude of cultural relativism distinguished the fieldworker from missionaries, administrators, and others whose view of natives was, presumably, less dispassionate, who were preoccupied with the problems of government, or conversion. In addition to scientific sophistication and relativist sympathy, a variety of normative standards for the new form of research emerged: the fieldworker was to live in the native village, use the vernacular, stay a sufficient (but seldom specified) length of time, investigate certain classic subjects, and so on.

Second: it was tacitly agreed that the new-style ethnographer, whose sojourn in the field seldom exceeded two years, and more frequently was much less, could efficiently 'use' native languages without 'mastering' them. In a significant article of 1939 Margaret Mead argued that the ethnographer following the Malinowskian prescription to avoid interpreters and to conduct research in the vernacular did not, in fact, need to attain 'virtuosity' in native tongues, but could 'use' the vernacular to ask questions, maintain rapport, and generally get along in the culture while obtaining good research results in particular areas of concentration.[19] This, in effect, justified her own practice, which featured relatively short stays and a focus on specific domains, like childhood, or 'personality.' These foci would function as 'types' for a cultural synthesis. But her attitude toward language 'use' was broadly characteristic of an ethnographic generation that could, for example, credit an authoritative study called *The Nuer*, that was based on only eleven months of difficult research. Mead's article provoked a sharp response from Robert Lowie, writing from the older Boasian tradition, more philological in its orientation.[20] But he was a rearguard action; the point had been generally established that valid research could, in practice, be accomplished on the basis of a one or two-year familiarity with a foreign vernacular (even though, as Lowie suggested, no one would credit a translation of Proust that was based on an equivalent knowledge of French).

Third: the new ethnography was marked by an increased emphasis on the power of observation. Culture was construed as an ensemble of characteristic behaviors, ceremonies and gestures, susceptible to recording and explanation by a trained onlooker. Mead pressed this point furthest (indeed, her own powers of visual analysis were extraordinary). As a general trend the participant-*observer* emerged as a research norm. Of course, successful fieldwork mobilized the fullest possible range of interactions, but a distinct primacy was accorded to the visual: interpretation was tied to description. After Malinowski, a general suspicion of 'privileged informants' reflected this systematic preference for the (methodical) observations of the ethnographer over the (interested) interpretations of indigenous authorities.

Fourth: certain powerful theoretical abstractions promised to help academic ethnographers 'get to the heart' of a culture more rapidly than someone undertaking, for example, a thorough inventory of customs and beliefs. Without spending years getting to know natives, their complex languages and habits, in intimate detail, the researcher could go after selected data that would yield a central armature of structure of the cultural whole. Rivers' 'genealogical method,' followed by Radcliffe-Brown's model of 'social structure,' provided this sort of shortcut. One could, it seemed, elicit kin terms without a deep understanding of lcoal vernacular, and the range of necessary contextual knowledge was conveniently limited.

Fifth: since culture, seen as a complex whole, was always too much to master in a short research span, the new ethnographer tended to focus thematically on particular institutions. The aim was not to contribute to a complete inventory or description of custom, but rather to get at the whole through one or more of its parts. We have noted the privilege given, for a time, to social structure. An individual life-cycle, a ritual complex like the Kula ring or the Naven ceremony could also serve, as could categories of behavior like 'economics,' 'politics,' and the like. In the predominantly synecdochic rhetorical stance of the new ethnography, parts were assumed to be microcosms or analogies of wholes. This setting of institutional foregrounds against cultural backgrounds in the portrayal of a coherent world lent itself to realist literary conventions.

Sixth: the wholes thus represented tended to be synchronic, products of short-term research activity. The intensive fieldworker could plausibly sketch the contours of an 'ethnographic present'—the cycle of a year, a ritual series, patterns of typical behavior. To introduce long-term historical inquiry would have impossibly complicated the task of the new-style fieldwork. Thus, when Malinowski and Radcliffe-Brown established their critique of the 'conjectural history' of the diffusionists it was all too easy to exclude diachronic processes as objects of fieldwork, with consequences that have by now been sufficiently denounced.

These innovations served to validate an efficient ethnography based on scientific participant-observation. Their combined effect may be seen in what may well be the *tour de force* of the new ethnography, Evans-Pritchard's *The Nuer*, published in 1940. Based on eleven months of research conducted—as the book's remarkable introduction tells us—in almost impossible conditions, Evans-Pritchard nonetheless was able to compose a classic. He arrived in Nuerland on the heels of a punitive military expedition and at the urgent request of the government of the Anglo-Egyptian Sudan. He was the object of constant and intense suspicion. Only in the final few months could he converse at all effectively with informants who, he tells us, were skilled at evading his questions. In the circumstances his monograph is a kind of miracle.

While advancing limited claims and making no secret of the restraints on his research, Evans-Pritchard manages to present his study as a demonstration of the effectiveness of theory. He focuses on Nuer political and social 'structure,' analyzed as an abstract set of relations between territorial segments, lineages, age-sets, and other more fluid groups. This analytically derived ensemble is portrayed against an 'ecological' backdrop composed of migatory patterns, relationships with cattle, notions of time and space. Evans-Pritchard sharply distinguishes his method from what he calls 'haphazard' (Malinowskian) documentation. *The Nuer* is not an extensive compendium of observations and vernacular texts in the style of Malinowski's *Argonauts* and *Coral Gardens*. Evans-Pritchard argues rigorously that 'facts can only be selected and arranged in the light of theory.' The frank abstraction of a political-social structure offers the necessary framework. If I am accused of describing facts as exemplifications of my theory, he then goes on to note, I have been understood.[21]

In *The Nuer*, Evans-Pritchard makes strong claims for the power of scientific abstraction to focus research and arrange complex data. The book often presents itself as an argument, rather than a description. But not consistently: its theoretical argument is surrounded by skilfully observed and narrated evocations and interpretations of Nuer life. These passages function rhetorically as more than simple 'exemplifications,' for they effectively implicate readers in the complex subjectivity of participant-observation. This may be seen in a characteristic paragraph which progresses through a series of discontinuous discursive positions:

265

It is difficult to find an English word that adequately describes the social position of *diel* in a tribe. We have called them aristocrats, but do not wish to imply that Nuer regard them as of superior rank, for, as we have emphatically declared, the idea of a man lording it over others is repugnant to them. On the whole—we will qualify the statement later—the *diel* have prestige rather than rank and influence rather than power. If you are a *dil* of the tribe in which you live you are more than a simple tribesman. You are one of the owners of the country, its village sites, its pastures, its fishing pools and wells. Other people live there by virtue of marriage into your clan, adoption into your lineage, or of some other social tie. You are a leader of the tribe and the spear-name of your clan is invoked when the tribe goes to war. Whenever there is a *dil* in the village, the village clusters around him as a herd of cattle clusters around its bull.[22]

The first three sentences are presented as an argument about translation, but in passing they attribute to 'Nuer' a stable set of attitudes. (I will have more to say later about this style of attribution.) Next, in the four sentences beginning 'If you are a *dil* . . .', the second-person construction brings together reader and native in a textual participation. The final sentence, offered as a direct description of a typical event (which the reader now assimilates from the standpoint of a participant-observer) evokes the scene by means of Nuer cattle metaphors. In the paragraph's eight sentences an argument about translation passes through a fiction of participation to a metaphorical fusion of external and indigenous cultural descriptions. The subjective joining of abstract analysis and concrete experience is accomplished.

Evans-Pritchard would later move away from the theoretical position of *The Nuer*, rejecting its advocacy of 'social structure' as a privileged framework. Indeed, each of the fieldwork 'shortcuts' enumerated above was, and remains, contested. Yet by their deployment in different combinations, the authority of the academic field-worker-theorist was established in the years between 1920 and 1950. This peculiar amalgam of intense personal experience and scientific analysis (understood in this period as *both* 'rite of passage' and 'laboratory') emerged as a method: participant-observation. Though variously understood, and now disputed in many quarters, this method remains the chief distinguishing feature of professional anthropology. Its complex subjectivity is routinely reproduced in the writing and reading of ethnographies.

'Participant-observation' serves as shorthand for a continuous tacking between the 'inside' and 'outside' of events: on the one hand grasping the sense of specific occurrences and gestures empathetically, on the other stepping back to situate these meanings in wider contexts. Particular events thus acquire deeper or more general significance, structural roles, and so forth. Understood literally, participant-observation is a paradoxical, misleading formula. But it may be taken seriously if reformulated in hermeneutic terms as a dialectic of experience and interpretation. This is how the method's most persuasive recent defenders have restated it, in the tradition that leads from Dilthey, via Weber, to 'symbols and meanings anthropologists' like Geertz. Experience and interpretation have, however, been accorded different emphases when presented as claims to authority. In recent years, there has been a marked shifted of emphasis from the former to the latter. This section and the one that follows will explore the rather different claims of experience and interpretation as well as their evolving interrelation.

The growing prestige of the fieldworker-theorist downplayed (without eliminating) a number of processes and mediators that had figured more prominently in previous methods. We have seen how language mastery was defined as a level of use adequate for amassing a discrete body of data in a limited period of time. The tasks of textual transcription and translation along with the crucial dialogical role of interpreters and 'privileged informants' were relegated to a secondary, sometimes even despised, status. Fieldwork was now centered on the *experience* of the participant-observing scholar. A sharp image, or narrative, made its appearance—that of an outsider entering a culture, undergoing a kind of initiation leading to 'rapport' (minimally, acceptance and empathy, but usually implying something akin to friendship). Out of this experience emerged, in unspecified ways, a representational text authored by the participant-observer. As we shall see, this version of textual production obscures as much as it reveals. But it is worth taking seriously its principal assumption, that the experience of the researcher can serve as a unifying source of authority in the field.

Experiential authority is based on a 'feel' for the foreign context, a kind of accumulated savvy and sense of the style of a people or place. Such an appeal is frequently explicit in the texts of the early professional participant-observers. Margaret Mead's claim to grasp the underlying principle or ethos of a culture through a heightened sensitivity to form, tone, gesture, and behavioral styles, or Malinowski's stress on his life *in* the village and the comprehension derived from the 'imponderabilia' of daily existence, are prominent cases in point. Many ethnographies, Colin Turnbull's *The Forest People* for example, are still cast in the experiential mode, asserting, prior to any specific research hypothesis or method, the 'I was there' of the ethnographer as insider and participant.

Of course, it is difficult to say very much about experience. Like 'intuition' one has it or not, and its invocation often smacks of mystification. Nevertheless one should resist the temptation to translate all meaningful experience into interpretation. If the two are reciprocally related, they are not identical. It makes sense here to hold them apart, if only because appeals to experience often act as validations for ethnographic authority. The most serious argument for the role of experience in the historical and cultural sciences is contained in the general notion of *Verstehen*.[23] In Dilthey's influential view, understanding others arises initially from the sheer fact of coexistence in a shared world. But this experiential world, an intersubjective ground for objective forms of knowledge, is precisely what is missing or problematic for an ethnographer entering an alien culture. Thus during the early months in the field (and indeed throughout the research) what is going on is language-learning in the broadest sense. Dilthey's 'common sphere' must be established and re-established, building up a shared experiential world in relation to which all 'facts,' 'texts,' 'events,' and their interpretations will be constructed. This process of living one's way into an alien expressive universe is, in his scheme, always subjective in nature. But it quickly becomes dependent on what he calls 'permanently fixed expressions,' stable forms to which understanding can return. The exegesis of these fixed forms provides the content of all systematic historical-cultural knowledge. Thus experi-

267

ence, for Dilthey, is closely linked to interpretation (and he is among the first modern theorists to compare the understanding of cultural forms to the reading of 'texts'). But this sort of reading or exegesis cannot occur without an intense, personal participation, an active at-homeness in a common universe.[24]

Following Dilthey, ethnographic 'experience' can be seen as the building-up of a common, meaningful world, drawing on intuitive styles of feeling, perception, and guesswork. This activity makes use of clues, traces, gestures, and scraps of sense prior to the development of developed, stable interpretations. Such piecemeal forms of experience may be classified as esthetic and/or divinatory. There is space here for only a few words about such styles of comprehension as they relate to ethnography. An evocation of an esthetic mode is conveniently provided by A. L. Kroeber's 1931 review of Mead's *Growing up in New Guinea*.

> First of all, it is clear that she possesses to an outstanding degree the faculties of swiftly apperceiving the principal currents of a culture as they impinge on individuals, and of delineating these with compact pen-pictures of astonishing sharpness. The result is a representation of quite extraordinary vividness and semblance to life. Obviously, a gift of intellectualized but strong sensationalism underlies this capacity; also, obviously, a high order of intuitiveness, in the sense of the ability to complete a convincing picture from clues, for clues is all that some of her data can be, with only six months to learn a language and enter the inwards of a whole culture, besides specializing on child behavior. At any rate, the picture, so far as it goes, is wholly convincing to the reviewer, who unreservedly admires the sureness of insight and efficiency of stroke of the depiction.[25]

A different formulation is provided by Maurice Leenhardt in *Do Kamo: Person and Myth in the Melanesian World*, a book which, in its sometimes cryptic mode of exposition, requires of its readers just the sort of esthetic, gestaltist perception at which both Mead and Leenhardt excelled. Leenhardt's endorsement of this approach is significant since, given his extremely long field experience and profound cultivation of a Melanesian language, his 'method' cannot be seen as a rationalization for short-term ethnography.

> In reality, our contact with another is not accomplished through analysis. Rather, we apprehend him in his entirety. From the outset, we can sketch our view of him using an outline or symbolic detail which contains a whole in itself and evokes the true form of his being. This latter is what escapes us if we approach our fellow creature using only the categories of our intellect.[26]

Another way of taking experience seriously as a source of ethnographic knowledge is provided by Carlo Ginzburg's recent investigations into the complex tradition of divination.[27] His research ranges from early hunters' interpretations of animal tracks, to Mesopotamian forms of prediction, the deciphering of symptoms in Hippocratic medicine, to the focus on details in detecting art forgeries, to Freud, Sherlock Holmes, and Proust. These styles of nonecstatic divination apprehend specific, circumstantial relations of meaning, and are based on guesses, on the reading of apparently disparate clues and 'chance' occurrences. Ginzburg proposes his model of 'conjectural knowledge' as a disciplined, nongeneralizing mode of comprehension that is of central, though unrecognized, importance for the cultural sciences. It may be added to a rather meager stock of resources for understanding rigorously how one feels one's way into an unfamiliar ethnographic situation.

Precisely because it is hard to pin down, 'experience' has served as an effective guarantee of ethnographic authority. There is, of course, a telling ambiguity in the term. Experience evokes a participatory presence, a sensitive contact with the world to be understood, a rapport with its people, a concreteness of perception. And experience suggests also a cumulative, deepening knowledge ('. . . her ten years' experience of New Guinea'). The senses work together to authorize an ethnographer's real, but ineffable, feel or flair for his or her people. But it is worth noticing that this 'world,' when conceived as an experiential creation, is subjective, not dialogical or intersubjective. The ethnographer *accumulates* personal knowledge of the field. (The possessive form, 'my people,' has until recently been familiarly used in anthropological circles; but the phrase in effect signifies 'my experience.')

It is understandable, given their vagueness, that experiential criteria of authority— unexamined beliefs in the 'method' of participant-observation, in the power of rapport, empathy, and so on—have come under criticism by hermeneutically sophisticated anthropologists. In recent years the second moment in the dialectic of experience and interpretation has received increasing attention and elaboration.[28] Interpretation, based on a philological model of textual 'reading,' has emerged as a sophisticated alternative to the now apparently naive claims for experiential authority. Interpretive anthropology demystifies much of what had previously passed unexamined in the construction of ethnographic narratives, types, observations, and descriptions. It contributes to an increasing visibility of the creative (and in a broad sense, poetic) processes by which 'cultural' objects are invented and treated as meaningful.

What is involved in looking at culture as an assemblage of texts to be interpreted? A classic account has been provided by Paul Ricoeur, notably in his 1971 essay, 'The Model of the Text: Meaningful Action Considered as a Text.'[29] Clifford Geertz, in a number of stimulating and subtle discussions, has adapted Ricoeur's theory to anthropological fieldwork.[30] 'Textualization' is understood as a prerequisite to interpretation, the constitution of Dilthey's 'fixed expressions.' It is the process through which unwritten behavior, speech, beliefs, oral tradition or ritual, come to be marked as a corpus, a potentially meaningful ensemble separated out from an immediate discursive or performative situation. In the moment of textualization this meaningful corpus assumes a more or less stable relation to a context, and we are familiar with the end result of this process in much of what counts as ethnographic thick description. For example, we say that a certain institution or segment of behavior is typical of, or a communicative element within, a surrounding culture. (Geertz's famous cockfight becomes an intensely significant locus of Balinese culture.) Fields of synecdoches are created in which parts are related to wholes—and by which the whole, what we often call culture, is constituted.

Ricoeur does not actually privilege part-whole relations and the specific sorts of analogies that constitute functionalist or realist representations. He merely posits a necessary relation between text and 'world.' A world cannot be apprehended directly; it is always inferred on the basis of its parts, and the parts must be conceptually and

269

perceptually cut out of the flux of experience. Thus, textualization generates sense through a circular movement which isolates and then contextualizes a fact or event in its englobing reality. A familiar mode of authority is generated which claims to represent discrete, meaningful words. Ethnography is the interpretation of cultures.

A second key step in Ricoeur's analysis is his account of the process by which 'discourse' becomes text. Discourse, in Benveniste's classic discussion, is a mode of communication where the presence of the speaking subject and of the immediate situation of communication are intrinsic.[31] Discourse is marked by pronouns (pronounced or implied) 'I' and 'You,' and by deictic indicators, 'this,' 'that,' 'now,' and so on, which signal the present instance of discourse rather than something beyond it. Discourse does not transcend the specific occasion in which a subject appropriates the resources of language in order to communicate dialogically. Ricoeur argues that discourse cannot be interpreted in the open-ended, potentially public way that a text is 'read.' To understand discourse you 'had to have been there,' in the presence of the discoursing subject. For discourse to become text it must become 'autonomous,' in Ricoeur's terms, separated from a specific utterance and authorial intention. Interpretation is not interlocution. It does not depend on being in the presence of a speaker.

The relevance of this distinction for ethnography is perhaps too obvious. The ethnographer always ultimately departs, taking away texts for later interpretation. (And among those 'texts' taken away we can include memories—events patterned, simplified, stripped of immediate context in order to be interpreted in later reconstruction and portrayal.) The text, unlike discourse, can travel. If much ethnographic writing is produced in the field, actual composition of an ethnography is done elsewhere. Data constituted in discursive, dialogical conditions are appropriated only in textualized form. Research events and encounters become field notes. Experiences become narratives, meaningful occurrences, or examples.

This translation of the research experience into a textual corpus separate from its discursive occasions of production has important consequences for ethnographic authority. The data thus reformulated need no longer be understood as the communication of specific persons. An informant's explanation or description of custom need not be cast in a form that includes the message 'so and so said this.' A textualized ritual or event is no longer closely linked to the production of that event by specific actors. Instead, these texts become evidences of an englobing context, a 'cultural' reality. Moreover, as specific authors and actors are severed from their productions, a generalized 'author' must be invented to account for the world or context within which the texts are fictionally relocated. This generalized author goes under a variety of names: the native point of view, 'the Trobrianders,' 'the Nuer,' 'the Dogon,' as these and similar phrases appear in ethnographies. 'The Balinese' function as author of Geertz's textualized cockfight.

The ethnographer thus enjoys a special relationship with a cultural origin, or 'absolute subject.'[32] It is tempting to compare the ethnographer with the literary interpreter (and this comparison is increasingly commonplace)—but more specifically with the traditional critic, who sees the task at hand as locating the unruly meanings of a text in a single, coherent intention. By representing the Nuer, the Trobrianders, or the Balinese as whole subjects, sources of a meaningful intention, the ethnographer transforms the research situation's ambiguities and diversities of meaning into an integrated portrait. But it is important to notice what has dropped out of sight. The research process is separated from the texts it generates and from the fictive world they are made to call up. The actuality of discursive situations and individual interlocutors is filtered out. But informants—along with field notes—are crucial intermediaries, typically excluded from authoritative ethnographies. The dialogical, situational aspects of ethnographic interpretation tend to be banished from the final representative text. Not entirely banished, of course; there exist approved *topoi* for the portrayal of the research process.

We are increasingly familiar with the separate fieldwork account (a sub-genre which still tends to be classified as subjective, 'soft,' or unscientific). But even within classic ethnographies, more or less stereotypic 'fables of rapport' narrate the attainment of full participant-observer status. These fables may be told elaborately or in passing, naively or ironically. They normally portray the ethnographer's early ignorance, misunderstandings, lack of contact, frequently a sort of childlike status within the culture. In the *Bildungsgeschichte* of the ethnography these states of innocence or confusion are replaced by adult, confident, disabused knowledge. We may cite again Geertz's cockfight, where an early alienation from the Balinese, a confused, 'non-person' status, is transformed by the appealing fable of the police raid with its show of complicity.[33] The anecdote establishes a presumption of connectedness which permits the writer to function in his subsequent analyses as an omnipresent, knowledgeable exegete and spokesman. This interpreter situates the ritual sport as a text in a contextual world and brilliantly 'reads' its cultural meanings. Geertz's abrupt disappearance into his rapport—the quasi-invisibility of participant-observation—is paradigmatic. Here he makes use of an established convention for staging the attainment of ethnographic authority. As a result, we are seldom made aware of the fact that an essential part of the cockfight's construction as a text is dialogical, talking face-to-face with particular Balinese rather than reading culture 'over the[ir] shoulders.'[34]

Interpretive anthropology, by viewing cultures as assemblages of texts, loosely and sometimes contradictorily united, and by highlighting the inventive poesis at work in all collective representations, has contributed significantly to the defamiliarization of ethnographic authority. But in its mainstream realist strands it does not escape the general strictures of those critics of 'colonial' representation who, since 1950, have rejected discourses that portray the cultural realities of other peoples without placing their own reality in jeopardy. In Leiris's early critiques, by way of Maquet, Asad and many others, the unreciprocal quality of ethnographic interpretation has been called to account.[35] Henceforth, neither the experience nor the interpretive activity of the scientific researcher can be considered innocent. It becomes necessary to conceive ethnography, not as the experience and interpretation of a circumscribed 'other' reality, but rather as a constructive negotiation involving at least two, and usually more, conscious, politically significant subjects. Paradigms of experience and interpretation are yielding to paradigms of discourse, of dialogue and polyphony. The remaining sections of my essay will survey these emergent modes of authority.

A discursive model of ethnographic practice brings into prominence the

271

intersubjectivity of all speech, along with its immediate performative context. Benveniste's work on the constitutive role of personal pronouns and deixis highlights just these dimensions. Every use of 'I' presupposes a 'you,' and every instance of discourse is immediately linked to a specific, shared situation. No discursive meaning, then, without interlocution and context. The relevance of this emphasis for ethnography is evident. Fieldwork is significantly composed of language events; but language, in Bakhtin's words, 'lies on the borderline between oneself and the other. The word in language is half someone else's.' The Russian critic urges a rethinking of language in terms of specific discursive situations: 'There are,' he writes, 'no "neutral" words and forms—words and forms that can belong to "no one"; language has been completely taken over, shot through with intentions and accents.' The words of ethnographic writing, then, cannot be construed as monological, as the authoritative statement about, or interpretation of, an abstracted, textualized reality. The language of ethnography is shot through with other subjectivities and specific contextual overtones; for all language, in Bakhtin's view, is 'a concrete heteroglot conception of the world.'[36]

Forms of ethnographic writing which present themselves in a 'discursive' mode tend to be concerned with the representation of research contexts and situations of interlocution. Thus a book like Paul Rabinow's *Reflections on Fieldwork in Morocco* is concerned with the representation of a specific research situation (a series of constraining times and places) and (in somewhat fictionalized form) a sequence of individual interlocutors.[37] Indeed, an entire new sub-genre of 'fieldwork accounts' (of which Rabinow's is one of the most trenchant) may be situated within the discursive paradigm of ethnographic writing. Jeanne Favret-Saada's *Les mots, la mort, les sorts* is an insistent, self-conscious experiment with ethnography in a discursive mode.[38] She argues that the event of interlocution always assigns to the ethnographer a specific position in a web of intersubjective relations. There is no neutral standpoint in the power-laden field of discursive positionings, in a shifting matrix of relationships, of 'I's' and 'you's.'

A number of recent works have chosen to present the discursive processes of ethnography in the form of a dialogue between two individuals. Lacoste-Dujardin's *Dialogue des femmes en ethnologie* and Shostak's *Nisa: The Life and Words of a !Kung Woman* are noteworthy examples.[39] The dialogical mode is advocated with considerable sophistication in two other texts. The first, Kevin Dwyer's theoretical reflections on 'The Dialogic of Ethnology' springs from a series of interviews with a key informant and justifies Dwyer's decision to structure his ethnography in the form of a rather literal record of these exchanges.[40] The second work is Vincent Crapanzano's more complex *Tuhami: Portrait of a Moroccan*, another account of a series of interviews which rejects any sharp separation of an interpreting self from a textualized other.[41] Both Dwyer and Crapanzano locate ethnography in a process of dialogue where interlocutors actively negotiate a shared vision of reality. Crapanzano argues that this mutual construction must be at work in any ethnographic encounter, but that participants tend to assume they have simply acquiesced to the reality of their counterpart. Thus, for example, the ethnographer of the Trobriand Islanders does not openly concoct a version of reality in collaboration with his informants but rather interprets the 'Trobriand point of view.' Crapanzano and Dwyer offer sophisticated attempts to break with this literary/hermeneutical convention. In the process, the ethnographer's authority as narrator and interpreter is altered. Dwyer proposes a hermeneutics of 'vulnerability,' stressing the ruptures of fieldwork, the divided position and imperfect control of the ethnographer. Both Crapanzano and Dwyer seek to represent the research experience in ways that tear open the textualized fabric of the other and thus, also, of the interpreting self.[42] (Here etymologies are evocative: the word text is related, as is well known, to weaving, vulnerability to rending or wounding, in this instance the opening up of a closed authority.)

The model of dialogue brings to prominence precisely those discursive—circumstantial and intersubjective—elements that Ricoeur had to exclude from his model of the text. But if interpretive authority is based on the exclusion of dialogue, the reverse is also true: a purely dialogical authority would repress the inescapable fact of textualization. While ethnographies cast as encounters between two individuals may successfully dramatize the intersubjective, give-and-take of fieldwork and introduce a counterpoint of authoritative voices, they remain *representations* of dialogue. As texts they may not be dialogical in structure. (Although Socrates appears as a decentered participant in his encounters, Plato retains full control of the dialogue.[43]) This displacement but not elimination of monological authority is characteristic of any approach that portrays the ethnographer as a discrete character in the fieldwork narrative. Moreover, there is a frequent tendency in fictions of dialogue for the ethnographer's counterpart to appear as a representative of his or her culture—a type, in the language of traditional realism—through which general social processes are revealed.[44] Such a portrayal reinstates the synecdochic interpretive authority by which the ethnographer reads text in relation to context, thereby constituting a meaningful 'other' world. But if it is difficult for dialogical portrayals to escape typifying procedures, they can, to a significant degree, resist the pull toward authoritative representation of the other. This depends on their ability fictionally to maintain the strangeness of the other voice and to hold in view the specific contingencies of the exchange.

To say that an ethnography is composed of discourses and that its different components are dialogically related, is not to say that its textual form should be that of a literal dialogue. Indeed, as Crapanzano recognizes in *Tuhami*, a third participant, real or imagined, must function as mediator in any encounter between two individuals.[45] The fictional dialogue is, in fact, a condensation, a simplified representation of complex, multi-vocal processes. An alternative way of representing this discursive complexity is to understand the overall course of the research as an on-going negotiation. The case of Marcel Griaule and the Dogon is well known and particularly clear-cut. Griaule's account of his instruction in Dogon cosmological wisdom, *Dieu d'Eau (Conversations with Ogotemmêli)*, was an early exercise in dialogical ethnographic narration. But beyond this specific interlocutory occasion, a more complex process was at work. For it is apparent that the content and timing of the Griaule team's long-term research, spanning decades, was closely monitored and significantly shaped by Dogon tribal authorities.[46] This is no longer news. Many ethnographers have commented on the ways, both subtle and blatant, in which their research was directed or circumscribed by their informants. In his provocative discussion of this issue, Ioan Lewis even calls anthropology a form of 'plagiarism.'[47]

The give and take of ethnography is clearly portrayed in a recently published study, noteworthy for its presentation within a single work of both an interpreted other reality *and* the research process itself: Renato Rosaldo's *Ilongot Headhunting*.[48] Rosaldo arrives in the Philippine highlands intent on writing a synchronic study of social structure. But again and again, over his objections, he is forced to listen to endless Ilongot narratives of their local history. Dutifully, dumbly, in a kind of bored trance, he transcribes these stories, filling notebook after notebook with what he considers disposable texts. Only after leaving the field, and after a long process of reinterpretation (a process made manifest in the ethnography) does it become clear that these obscure tales have in fact provided Rosaldo with his final topic, the culturally distinctive Ilongot sense of narrative and history. Rosaldo's experience of what might be called 'directed writing' sharply poses a fundamental question. Who is actually the author of field notes?

The issue is a subtle one, and deserves systematic study. But enough has been said to make the general point, that indigenous control over knowledge gained in the field can be considerable, and even determining. Current ethnographic writing is seeking new ways to adequately represent the authority of informants, and there are few models to look to. But it is worth reconsidering the older textual compilations of Boas, Malinowski, Leenhardt, and others. In these works, the ethnographic genre has not coalesced around the modern interpretational monograph closely identified with a personal fieldwork experience. We can contemplate an ethnographic mode that is not yet authoritative in those specific ways that are now politically and epistemologically in question. These older assemblages include much that is actually or all but written by informants. One thinks of the role of George Hunt in Boas's ethnography, or of the fifteen '*transcripteurs*' listed in Leenhardt's *Documents néo-calédoniens*.[49]

Malinowski is a complex transitional case. His ethnographies reflect the incomplete coalescence of the modern monograph. If he was centrally responsible for the welding of theory and description into the authority of the professional fieldworker, Malinowski nonetheless included material that did not directly support his own all-too-clear interpretive slant. In the many dictated myths and spells which fill his books he published much data that he frankly did not understand. The result was an open text subject to multiple reinterpretations. It is worth comparing such older compendia with the recent model ethnography, which cites evidence to support a focused interpretation, and little else. In the modern, authoritative monograph there are, in effect, no strong voices present except that of the writer. But, in *Argonauts* and *Coral Gardens* we read page after page of magical spells, none in any essential sense the ethnographer's words. These dictated texts, in all but their physical inscription, are written by specific, unnamed Trobrianders. Indeed, any continuous ethnographic exposition routinely folds into itself a diversity of descriptions, transcriptions, and interpretations by a variety of indigenous 'authors.' How should these authorial presences be made manifest?

A useful—if extreme—standpoint is provided by Bakhtin's analysis of the 'polyphonic' novel. A fundamental condition of the genre, he argues, is that it represents speaking subjects in a field of multiple discourses. The novel grapples with, and enacts, heteroglossia. For Bakhtin, preoccupied with the representation of non-homogeneous wholes, there are no integrated cultural worlds or languages. All attempts to posit such abstract unities are constructs of monological power. A 'culture' is, concretely, an open-ended, creative dialogue of subcultures, of insiders and outsiders, of diverse factions; a 'language' is the interplay and struggle of regional dialects, professional jargons, generic commonplaces, the speech of different age groups, individuals, and so forth. For Bakhtin, the polyphonic novel is not a tour de force of cultural or historical totalization (as realist critics like Lukàcs and Auerbach have argued), but rather a carnivalesque arena of diversity. Bakhtin discovers a utopian textual space where discursive complexity, the dialogical interplay of voices, can be accommodated. In the novels of Dostoyevski or Dickens, he values precisely their resistance to totality, and his ideal novelist is a ventriloquist—in nineteenth-century parlance, 'polyphonist.' 'He do the police in different voices,' a listener exclaims admiringly of the boy, Sloppy, who reads publicly from the newspaper in *Our Mutual Friend*. But Dickens, the actor, oral performer, and polyphonist, must be set against Flaubert, the master of authorial control moving godlike among the thoughts and feelings of his characters. Ethnography, like the novel, wrestles with these alternatives. Does the ethnographic writer portray what natives think by means of Flaubertian 'free indirect style,' a style that suppresses direct quotation in favor of a controlling discourse always more-or-less that of the author? (In a recent essay Dan Sperber, taking Evans-Pritchard as his example, has convincingly shown that *style indirect* is indeed the preferred mode of ethnographic interpretation.[50]) Or, does the portrayal of other subjectivities require a version that is stylistically less homogeneous, filled with Dickens' 'different voices?'

Some use of indirect style is inevitable, unless the novel or ethnography be composed entirely of quotations, which is theoretically possible but seldom attempted.[51] In practice, however, the ethnography and the novel have recourse to indirect style at different levels of abstraction. We need not ask how Flaubert knows what Emma Bovary is thinking, but the ability of the fieldworker to inhabit indigenous minds is always in doubt: indeed this is a permanent, unresolved problem of ethnographic method. Ethnographers have generally refrained from ascribing beliefs, feelings, and thoughts to individuals. They have not, however, hesitated to ascribe subjective states to a culture. Sperber's analysis reveals how phrases such as 'The Nuer think . . .' or 'The Nuer sense of time . . .' are fundamentally different from quotations or translations of indigenous discourse. Such statements are 'without any specified speaker,' and are literally equivocal, combining in an unspecified way the ethnographer's affirmations with that of an informant or informants.[52] Ethnographies abound in unattributed sentences like 'The spirits return to the village at night,' descriptions of beliefs in which the writer assumes, in effect, the voice of culture.

At this 'cultural' level, ethnographers aspire to a Flaubertian omniscience that moves freely throughout a world of indigenous subjects. But beneath the surface their texts are more unruly and discordant. Victor Turner's work provides a telling case in point, worth investigating more closely as an example of the interplay of monophonic and polyphonic exposition. Turner's ethnographies offer superbly complex portrayals of Ndembu ritual symbols and beliefs; and he has provided, too, an unusually explicit glimpse behind the scenes. In the midst of the essays collected in *The Forest of Symbols*, his third book on the Ndembu, Turner offers a portrait of his best informant, 'Muchona the Hornet, Interpreter of Religion.'[53] Muchona, a ritual healer, and Turner are drawn together by their shared interest in traditional symbols, etymologies, and esoteric meanings. They are both 'intellectuals,' passionate interpreters of the nuances and depths of custom; both are uprooted scholars sharing 'the quenchless thirst for objective knowledge.' Turner compares Muchona to a university don; his account of their collaboration includes more than passing hints of a strong psychological doubling, linking ethnographer and informant.

But there is a third present in their dialogue, Windson Kashinakaji, a Ndembu senior teacher at the local mission school. He brought Muchona and Turner together, and shares their passion for the interpretation of customary religion. Through his Biblical education he 'acquired a flair for elucidating knotty questions.' Newly skeptical of Christian dogma and missionary privileges, he is looking sympathetically at pagan religion. Kashinakaji, Turner tells us, 'spanned the cultural distance between Muchona and myself, transforming the little doctor's technical jargon and salty village argot into a prose I could better grasp.' The three intellectuals soon 'settled down into a sort of daily seminar on religion.' Turner's accounts of this seminar are stylized: 'eight months of exhilarating quickfire talk among the three of us, mainly about Ndembu ritual.' They reveal an extraordinary ethnographic 'colloquy.' But significantly, Turner does not make this three-way collaboration the crux of his essay. Rather he focusses on Muchona, thus transforming trialogue into dialogue and flattening a complex productive relation into the 'portrait' of an 'informant.' (This reduction was in some degree required by the format of the book in which the essay first appeared, Joseph Casagrande's important collection of 'Twenty Portraits of Anthropological Informants,' *In the Company of Man*.[54])

Turner's published works vary considerably in their discursive structure. Some are largely composed of direct quotations; in at least one essay Muchona is identified as the principal source of the overall interpretation; elsewhere he is invoked anonymously, for example as 'a male ritual specialist.'[55] Windson Kashinakaji is usually identified as an assistant and translator rather than as a source of interpretations. Overall, Turner's ethnographies are unusually polyphonic, openly built from quotations. ('According to an adept . . .', or, 'One informant guesses . . .'.) He does not, however, do the Ndembu in different voices, and we hear little 'salty village argot.' All the voices of the field have been smoothed into the expository prose of more-or-less interchangeable 'informants.' The staging of indigenous speech in an ethnography, the degree of translation and familiarization necessary, are complicated practical and rhetorical problems.[56] But Turner's works, by giving visible place to indigenous interpretations of custom, expose concretely these issues of textual dialogism and polyphony.

The inclusion of Turner's portrait of Muchona in *The Forest of Symbols* (1967) may be seen as a sign of the times. The Casagrande collection (1961) in which it originally appeared had the effect of segregating the crucial issue of relations between ethnographers and their indigenous collaborators. Discussion of these issues still had no place *within* scientific ethnographies. But Casagrande's collection shook the post-Malinowski professional taboo on 'privileged informants.' Raymond Firth on Pa

Fenuatara, Robert Lowie on Jim Carpenter—a long list of distinguished anthropologists described the indigenous 'ethnographers' with whom they shared, to some degree, a distanced, analytic, even ironic view of custom. These individuals became valued informants because they understood, often with real subtlety, what an *ethnographic* attitude toward culture entailed. In Lowie's quotation of his Crow interpreter (and fellow 'philologist') Jim Carpenter, one senses a shared outlook: 'When you listen to the old men telling about their visions, you've just *got* to believe them.'[57] And there is considerably more than a wink and a nod in a story recounted by Firth about his best Tikopia friend and informant.

> On another occasion talk turned to the nets set for salmon trout in the lake. The nets were becoming black, possibly with some organic growth, and tended to rot easily. Pa Fenuatara then told a story to the crowd assembled in the house about how, out on the lake with his nets one time, he felt a spirit going among the net and making it soft. When he held the net up he found it slimy. The spirit had been at work. I asked him then if this was a traditional piece of knowledge that spirits were responsible for the deterioration of the nets. He answered, 'No, my own thought.' Then he added with a laugh, 'My own piece of traditional knowledge.'[58]

The full methodological impact of Casagrande's collection remains latent, especially the significance of its accounts for the dialogical production of ethnographic texts and interpretations. This significance is obscured by a tendency to cast it as a universalizing, humanist document revealing 'a hall of mirrors . . . in full variety the endless reflected image of man.'[59] However, in the light of the present crisis in ethnographic authority, these revealing portraits spill into the oeuvres of their authors, altering the way they can be read. If ethnography is part of what Roy Wagner calls 'the invention of culture,' its activity is plural and beyond the control of any individual.[60]

One increasingly common way to manifest the collaborative production of ethnographic knowledge is to quote regularly and at length from informants. (A striking recent example is June Nash, *We Eat the Mines, the Mines Eat Us*.[61]) But such a tactic only begins to break up monophonic authority. Quotations are always staged by the quoter, and tend to serve merely as examples, or confirming testimonies. Looking beyond quotation, one might imagine a more radical polyphony that would 'do the natives and the ethnographer in different voices.' But this, too, would only displace ethnographic authority, still confirming the final, virtuoso orchestration by a single author of all the discourses in his or her text. And in this sense Bakhtin's polyphony, too narrowly identified with the novel, is a domesticated heteroglossia. Ethnographic discourses are not, in any event, the speeches of invented characters. Informants are specific individuals with real proper names—names to be cited, in altered form when tact requires. Informants' intentions are overdetermined, their words politically and metaphorically complex. Ethnography is invaded by heteroglossia. If accorded an autonomous textual space, transcribed at sufficient length, indigenous statements make sense on terms different from those of the arranging ethnographer.

This suggests an alternate textual strategy, a utopia of plural authorship that accords to collaborators, not merely the status of independent enunciators, but that of writers. As a form of authority it must still be considered utopian for two reasons.

First, the few recent experiments with multiply-authored works appear to require, as an instigating force, the research interest of an ethnographer, who in the end assumes an executive, editorial position. The authoritative stance of 'giving voice' to the other is not fully transcended. Second, the very idea of plural authorship challenges a deep Western identification of any text's order with the intention of a single author. If this identification was less strong when Latifau wrote his *Moeurs des sauvages ameriquains*, and if recent criticism has thrown it into question, it is still a potent constraint on ethnographic writing. Nonetheless, there are signs of movement in this domain, and we may anticipate a gradual increase in experiments with multiple authorship. Anthropologists will increasingly have to share their texts, and sometimes their title pages, with those indigenous collaborators for whom the term 'informants' is no longer adequate, if it ever was.

Ralph Bulmer and Ian Majnep's *Birds of My Kalam Country* is an important prototype.[62] (Separate typefaces distinguish the juxtaposed contributions of ethnographer and New Guinean, collaborators for more than a decade.) Even more significant is the collectively produced study, *Piman Shamanism and Staying Sickness (Ka:cim Mumkidag)* which lists on its title page, without distinction (though not, it may be noted, in alphabetical order): Donald M. Bahr, anthropologist; Juan Gregorio, shaman; David I. Lopez, interpreter; Albert Alvarez, editor. Three of the four are Papago Indians, and the book is consciously designed 'to transfer *to a shaman* as many as possible of the functions normally associated with authorship. These include the selection of an expository style, the duty to make interpretations and explanations, and the right to judge which things are important and which are not.'[63] Bahr, the initiator and organizer of the project, opts to share out authority as much as possible. Gregorio, the shaman, appears as the principal source of the 'theory of disease' which is transcribed and translated, at two separate levels, by Lopez and Alvarez. Gregorio's vernacular texts include compressed, often gnomic, explanations, which are themselves interpreted and contextualized by Bahr's separate commentary. The book is unusual in its textual enactment of the interpretation of interpretations.

In *Piman Shamanism* the transition from individual enunciations to cultural generalizations is always visible in the separation of Gregorio's and Bahr's voices. The authority of Lopez, less visible, is akin to that of Windson Kashinakaji in Turner's work. His bilingual fluency guides Bahr through the subtleties of Gregorio's language, thus permitting the shaman 'to speak at length on theoretical topics.' Neither Lopez nor Alvarez appear as specific voices in the text, and their contribution to the ethnography remains largely invisible to all but qualified Papagos, able to gauge the accuracy of the translated texts and the vernacular nuance of Bahr's interpretations. Alvarez's authority inheres in the fact that *Piman Shamanism* is a book directed at separate audiences. For most readers focussing on the translations and explanations the texts printed in Piman will be of little or no interest. However, the linguist Alvarez corrected the transcriptions and translations with an eye to their use in language teaching, using an orthography he had developed for that purpose. Thus the book contributes to Papagos' literary invention of their culture. This different reading, built into *Piman Shamanism*, is of more than local significance.

It is intrinsic to the breakup of monological authority that ethnographies no longer address a single general type of reader. The multiplication of possible readings reflects the fact that self-conscious 'ethnographic' consciousness can no longer be seen as the monopoly of certain Western cultures and social classes. Even in ethnographies lacking vernacular texts, indigenous readers will decode differently the textualized interpretations and lore. Polyphonic works are particularly open to readings not specifically intended. Trobriand readers may find Malinowski's interpretations tiresome but his examples and extensive transcriptions still evocative. And Ndembu will not gloss as quickly as European readers over the different voices embedded in Turner's works.

Recent literary theory suggests that the ability of a text to make sense in a coherent way depends less on the willed intentions of an originating author than on the creative activity of a reader. In Barthes' words, if a text is 'a tissue of quotations drawn from innumerable centers of culture,' then 'a text's unity lies not in its origin but in its destination.'[64] The writing of ethnography, an unruly, multisubjective activity, is given coherence in particular acts of reading. But there is always a variety of possible readings (beyond merely individual appropriations), readings beyond the control of any single authority. One may approach a classic ethnography seeking simply to grasp the meanings that the researcher derives from represented cultural facts. But, as we have suggested, one may also read against the grain of the text's dominant voice, seeking out other, half-hidden authorities, reinterpreting the descriptions, texts and quotations gathered together by the writer. With the recent questioning of colonial styles of representation, with the expansion of literacy and ethnographic consciousness, new possibilities for reading (and thus for writing) cultural descriptions are emerging.[65]

The textual embodiment of authority is a recurring problem for recent experiments in ethnography.[66] An older, realist mode—figures in the frontispiece to *Argonauts of the Western Pacific* are based on the construction of a cultural *tableau vivant* designed to be seen from a single vantage point, that of the writer and reader—can now be identified as only one possible paradigm for authority. Political and epistemological assumptions are built into this and other styles, assumptions the ethnographic writer can no longer afford to ignore. The modes of authority reviewed in this essay—experiential, interpretive, dialogical, polyphonic—are available to all writers of ethnographic texts, Western and non-Western. None is obsolete, none pure: there is room for invention within each paradigm. For example, interpretation—as conceived by Gadamer—can aspire to a radical dialogism. We have seen, too, how new approaches tend to rediscover discarded practices. Polyphonic authority looks with renewed sympathy to compendia of vernacular texts—expository forms distinct from the focused monograph tied to participant-observation. And now that naive claims to the authority of experience have been subjected to hermeneutic suspicion, we may anticipate a renewed attention to the subtle interplay of personal and disciplinary components in ethnographic research.

Experiential, interpretive, dialogical, and polyphonic processes are at work, discordantly, in any ethnography. But coherent presentation presupposes a controlling mode of authority. I have argued that this imposition of coherence on an unruly textual process is now, inescapably, a matter of strategic choice. I have tried to distinguish important styles of authority as they have become visible in recent

279

decades. If ethnographic writing is alive, as I believe it is, it is struggling within and against these possibilities.

NOTES

1. Only English, American, and French examples are discussed. If it is likely that the modes of authority analyzed here are able widely to be generalized, no attempt has been made to extend them to other national traditions. It is assumed, also, in the antipositivist tradition of Dilthey, that ethnography is a process of interpretation, not of explanation. Modes of authority based on natural-scientific epistemologies are not discussed. In its focus on participant-observation as an intersubjective process at the heart of twentieth-century ethnography, the essay scants a number of contributing sources of authority: for example, the weight of accumulated 'archival' knowledge about particular groups, of a cross cultural comparative perspective, and of statistical survey work.
2. See M. Bakhtin, 'Discourse in the Novel' (1935), in Michael Holquist, ed., *The Dialogic Imagination: Four Essays by M. M. Bakhtin* (Austin and London, 1981), pp. 259–442. 'Heteroglossia' assumes that 'languages do not *exclude* each other, but rather intersect with each other in many different ways (the Ukranian language, the language of the epic poem, of early Symbolism, of the student, of a particular generation of children, of the run-of-the-mill intellectual, of the Nietzschean and so on). It might even seem that the very word "language" loses all meaning in this process—for apparently there is no single plane on which all these "languages" might be juxtaposed to one another.' What is said of languages applies equally to 'cultures' and 'subcultures.' See also V. N. Vološinov (Bakhtin?), *Marxism and the Philosophy of Language* (New York and London, 1973), esp. Chaps. 1–3; and Tzvetan Todorov, *Mikhail Bakhtine: le principe dialogique* (Paris, 1981), pp. 88–93.
3. Edward Said, *Orientalism* (New York, 1978); Paulin Hountondji, *Sur la 'philosophie africaine'* (Yaounde Cameroon, 1980); for more on this ambiguous predicament, J. Clifford, review of Said, *History and Theory*, 19:2 (1980), 204–23.
4. Michel Foucault, *Power/Knowledge* (New York, 1980), p. 145; see also 'Intellectuals and Power: A Conversation between Michel Foucault and Gilles Deleuze,' in Foucault, *Language, Counter-Memory, Practice* (Ithaca, N.Y., 1977), pp. 208–9. A recent unpublished essay by Edward Said, 'The Text's Slow Politics and the Prompt Language of Criticism,' has sharpened my conception of a historically contingent, engaged theory.
5. I have not attempted to survey new styles of ethnographic writing that may be originating from outside the West. As Said, Hountondji, and others have shown, a considerable work of ideological 'clearing,' an oppositional, critical work remains, and it is to this that non-Western intellectuals have been devoting a great part of their energies. My essay remains inside, but at the experimental boundaries of, a realist cultural science elaborated in the Occident. It does not consider, as areas of innovation, the 'para-ethnographic' genres of oral history, the non-fiction novel, the 'new journalism,' travel literature, and the documentary film.
6. Compare, for example, Marcel Griaule's idea of team research (with repeated visits to the field) and Malinowski's extended solo sojourn: Griaule, *Méthode de l'ethnographie* (Paris, 1957); Malinowski, *Argonauts of the Western Pacific* (London, 1922), Chapter 1.
7. Victor Karady, 'Le problème de la légitimité dans l'organisation historique de l'ethnologie française,' *Revue française de sociologie*, 23:1 (1982), 17–36; George Stocking, 'The Ethnographer's Magic: the Development of Fieldwork in British Anthropology from Tylor to Malinowski,' *History of Anthropology* 1 (1983).
8. In the present crisis of authority, ethnography has emerged as a subject of historical scrutiny. For new critical approaches see: François Hartog, *Le miroir d'Hérodote: essai sur la représentation de l'autre* (Paris, 1980); K. O. L. Burridge, *Encountering Aborigines* (New York, 1973), Chapter 1; Michèle Duchet, *Anthropologie et Histoire au siècle des lumières* (Paris, 1971); James Boon, 'Comparative De-enlightenment: Paradox and Limits in the History of Ethnology,' *Daedalus*, Spring 1980, 73–90; Michel de Certeau, 'Writing vs. Time: History and Anthropology in the Works of Lafitau,' *Yale French Studies*, 59 (1980), 37–64; Edward Said, *Orientalism*; George Stocking, ed., 'Observers Observed: Essays on Ethnographic Fieldwork,' *History of Anthropology* 1 (1983), Madison, Wisconsin.
9. On the suppression of dialogue in Lafitau's frontispiece, and the constitution of a textualized, ahistori-

cal, and visually oriented 'anthropology,' see Michel de Certeau's detailed analysis in 'Writing vs. Time.'

10. B. Malinowski, 'Pigs, Papuans and Police Court Perspective,' *Man*, 32 (1932), 33–8; Alex Rentoul, 'Physiological paternity and the Trobrianders,' and 'Papuans, Professors and Platitudes,' *Man*, 31 (1931), 153–4, and 32 (1932), 274–6. Ian Langham, *The Building of British Social Anthropology* (Dordrecht, London, 1981), Chapter VII.

11. R. H. Codrington, *The Melanesians* (1891), Dover reprint (New York, 1972), pp. vi–vii.

12. George Stocking, 'The Ethnographer's Magic.'

13. Curtis Hinsley, 'Ethnographic Charisma and Scientific Routine: Cushing and Fewkes in the American Southwest,' *History of Anthropology*, 1 (1983).

14. Stocking, 'The Ethnographer's Magic.'

15. Malinowski, *Argonauts of the Western Pacific* (1922), pp. 3–4.

16. Stocking, 'The Ethnographer's Magic.' See also Harry Payne, 'Malinowski's Style,' *Proceedings of the American Philosophical Society*, forthcoming.

17. G. Lienhardt, *Divinity and Experience: the Religion of the Dinka* (Oxford, 1961), p. vii.

18. I am indebted to two impotant unpublished papers by Robert Thornton of the University of Capetown: 'The Rise of Ethnogaphy in South Africa: 1860–1920,' and 'The Rise of the Ethnographic Monograph in Eastern and Southern Africa.'

19. Margaret Mead, 'Native languages as Field-Work. Tools,' *American Anthropologist*, 41:2 (1939), 189–205.

20. Robert Lowie, 'Native Languages as Ethnographic Tools,' *American Anthropologist*, 42:1 (1940), 81–9.

21. E. Evans-Pritchard, *The Nuer* (New York, Oxford, 1969), p. 261.

22. *Ibid.*, p. 215.

23. The concept is sometimes too readily associated with intuition or empathy, but as a description of ethnographic knowledge, *Verstehen* properly involves a critique of empathetic experience. The exact meaning of the term is a matter of debate among Dilthey scholars. See Rudolf Makkreel, *Dilthey: Philosopher of the Human Sciences* (Princeton, 1975), pp. 6–7, and *passim*.

24. This bare summary is drawn from H. P. Rickman, ed., *W. Dilthey: Selected Writings* (Cambridge, 1976), pp. 168–245. 'The Construction of the Historical World in the Human Studies,' Vol. VII of the *Gesammelte Schriften* (Leipzig, 1914).

25. *American Anthropologist*, 33 (1931), p. 248.

26. Maurice Leenhardt, *Do Kamo* (Chicago, 1979), p. 2; see J. Clifford, *Person and Myth: Maurice Leenhardt in the Melanesian World* (Berkeley, 1982).

27. Carlo Ginzburg, 'Morelli, Freud and Sherlock Holmes: Clues and Scientific Method,' *History Workshop*, 9 (Spring 1980), 5, 36.

28. For example: Clifford Geertz, *The Interpretation of Cultures* (New York, 1973); 'From the Native's Point of View: on the Nature of Anthropological Understanding,' in K. Basso and H. Selby, eds., *Meaning in Anthropology* (Albuquerque, 1976), pp. 221–38; Paul Rabinow and William Sullivan, eds., *Interpretive Social Science* (Berkeley, 1979); Irene and Thomas Winner, 'The Semiotics of Cultural Texts,' *Semiotica*, 18:2 (1976), 101–56; Dan Sperber, 'L'Intérprétation en Anthropologie,' *L'Homme*, XXI:I (1981), 69–92.

29. *Social Research*, 38 (1971), 529–62.

30. See especially, 'Thick Description: Toward an Interpretive Theory of Culture,' Chapter 1 of *The Interpretation of Cultures*.

31. Emile Benveniste, 'The Nature of Pronouns,' and 'Subjectivity in Language,' *Problems in General Linguistics* (Coral Gables, Fla., 1971), pp. 217–30.

32. Françoise Michel-Jones, *Retour au Dogon: Figure du double et ambivalence* (Paris, 1978), p. 14.

33. Clifford Geertz, 'Deep Play: Notes on the Balinese Cockfight,' *Daedalus*, 101:1 (1972), reprinted in *The Interpretation of Cultures*, pp. 412–53.

34. *Ibid.*, p. 452.

35. Michel Leiris, 'L'ethnographe devant le colonialisme,' *Les Temps Modernes*, 58 (1950); reprinted in Leiris, *Brisées* (Paris, Mercure de France, 1966), pp. 125–45; Jacques Maquet, 'Objectivity in Anthropology,' *Current Anthropology*, 5 (1964), 47–55; Talal Asad, ed., *Anthropology and the Colonial Encounter* (London, 1973).

36. M. Bakhtin, 'Discourse in the Novel,' p. 293.

37. P. Rabinow, *Reflections on Fieldwork in Morocco* (Berkeley, 1977).
38. Paris, 1977; translated as *Deadly Words* (Cambridge, England, 1980). See especially Chapter 2. Her experience has been rewritten at another fictional level in J. Favret-Saada and Josée Contreras, *Corps pour corps: Enquête sur la sorcellerie dans le Bocage* (Paris, 1981).
39. Camille Lacoste-Dujardin, *Dialogue des femmes en ethnologie* (Paris, 1977); Marjorie Shostak, *Nisa: The Life and Words of a !Kung Woman* (Cambridge, Mass., 1981).
40. Kevin Dwyer, 'On the Dialogic of Field Work,' and 'The Dialogic of Ethnology,' *Dialectical Anthropology*, 2:2 (1977), 143–51, and 4:3 (1979), 205–24.
41. Vincent Crapanzano, *Tuhami: Portrait of a Moroccan* (Chicago, 1980); and 'On the Writing of Ethnography,' *Dialectical Anthropology*, 2:1 (1977), 69–73.
42. It would be wrong to gloss over the differences between Dwyer's and Crapanzano's theoretical positions. Dwyer, following Lukàcs, translates dialogic into Marxian/Hegelian dialectic, thus holding out the possibility of a restoration of the human subject, a kind of completion in and through the other. Crapanzano refuses any anchor in an englobing theory, his only authority being that of the dialogue's writer, an authority undermined by an inconclusive narrative of encounter, rupture, and confusion. (It is worth noting that dialogic, as used by Bakhtin, is not reducible to dialectic.)
43. On this see Stephen Tylor's 'Words for Deeds and the Doctrine of the Secret World: Testimony to a Chance Encounter Somewhere in the Indian Jungle,' forthcoming in *Proceedings of the Chicago Linguistic Society*.
44. On realist 'types,' see G. Lukàcs, *Studies in European Realism*, *passim*. The tendency to transform an individual into a cultural enunciator may be observed in M. Griaule's *Dieu d'Eau* (Paris, 1948). It occurs ambivalently in Shostak's *Nisa*. (For a discussion of this ambivalence and of the book's resulting discursive complexity see my review, *London Times Literary Supplement*, Sept. 17, 1982, 994–5.)
45. Crapanzano, *Tuhami*, pp. 147–51.
46. James Clifford, 'Power and Dialogue in Ethnography: Marcel Griaule's Initiation,' *History of Anthropology 1*, forthcoming.
47. I. Lewis, *The Anthropologist's Muse* (London, 1973).
48. R. Rosaldo, *Ilongot Headhunting 1883–1974: A Study in Society and History* (Stanford, 1980).
49. Paris, 1932; for a study of this mode of textual production see J. Clifford, 'Fieldwork, Reciprocity, and the Making of Ethnographic Texts,' *Man* 15 (1980), 518–32. See also, in this context, B. Fontana, Introduction to Frank Russell, *The Pima Indians* (Tucson, 1975), on the book's hidden co-author, the Papago Indian José Lewis; M. Leiris, 'Avant-propos,' *La langue secrète des Dogons de Sanga* (Paris, 1948), pp. ix–xxv, discusses collaboration as co-authorship, as does I. M. Lewis, in *The Anthropologist's Muse*. For a forward-looking defense of Boas' emphasis on vernacular texts and his collaboration with Hunt, see Irving Goldman, 'Boas on the Kwakiutl: the Ethnographic Tradition,' in S. Diamond, ed., *Theory and Practice: Essays presented to Gene Weltfish* (The Hague, 1980), pp. 334–6.
50. D. Sperber, 'L'Interprétation en Anthropologie,' *L'Homme*, XXI:I (1981), esp. pp. 76–9.
51. Such a project is announced by Evans-Pritchard in his introduction to *Man and Woman among the Azande* (London, 1974), a late work which may be seen as a reaction against the closed, analytic nature of his own earlier ethnographies. His acknowledged inspiration is Malinowski.
52. Sperber, 'L'Interprétation en Anthropologie,' p. 78.
53. V. Turner, *The Forest of Symbols: Aspects of Ndembu Ritual* (Ithaca, N.Y., and London, 1967), pp. 131–50.
54. New York, 1960, pp. 333–56. For a 'group dynamics' approach to ethnography, see T. Yannopoulos and Denis Martin, 'De la question au dialogue: à propos des enquêtes en Afrique noire,' *Cahiers d'études africaines*, 71 (1978), 421–42. For an ethnography explicitly based on native 'seminars' see N. Blurton Jones and M. Konner, '!Kung Knowledge of Animal Behavior,' in R. Lee and I. De Vore, eds., *Kalahari Hunter-Gatherers* (Cambridge, 1976), pp. 325–48.
55. V. Turner, *Revelation and Divination in Ndembu Ritual* (Ithaca, NY: 1975), pp. 40–2, 87, 154–6, 244; *Forest of Symbols*, p. 21.
56. Favret-Saada's use of dialect and italic type in *Les Mots, la mort, les sorts* is one solution among many to a problem that has long preoccupied realist novelists.
57. J. Casagrande, ed., *In the Company of Man*, p. 428.
58. *Ibid.*, pp. 17–18.
59. *Ibid.*, p. xiii.

60. Roy Wagner, *The Invention of Culture* (Chicago, 1980).

61. New York, 1980.

62. Auckland, London, 1977.

63. Bahr et al., *Piman Shamanism* (Tucson, 1974), p. 7.

64. R. Barthes, *Image, Music, Text* (New York, 1977), pp. 146. 148.

65. An extremely suggestive model of polyphonic exposition is offered by the projected four-volume edition of the ethnographic texts written, provoked, and transcribed between 1896 and 1914 by James Walker, on the Pine Ridge Sioux Reservation. Two titles have appeared so far: James Walker, *Lakota Belief and Ritual*, Raymond DeMallie and Elaine Jahner, eds., and *Lakota Society*, Raymond DeMallie, ed. (Lincoln, Nebraska, and London, 1980, 1982). These engrossing volumes in effect re-open the textual homogeneity of Walker's classic monograph of 1917, *The Sun Dance*, a summary of the individual statements here published in translation. These statements, by more than thirty named 'authorities,' complement and transcend Walker's synthesis. A long section of *Lakota Belief and Ritual* was written by Thomas Tyon, Walker's interpreter. And the collection's fourth volume will be a translation of the writings of George Sword, an Oglala warrior and judge encouraged by Walker to record and interpret the traditional way of life. The first two volumes present the unpublished texts of knowledgeable Lakota and Walker's own descriptions in identical formats. Ethnography appears as a process of collective production. It is essential to note that the Colorado Historical Society's decision to publish these texts was provoked by increasing requests from the Oglala Community at Pine Ridge for copies of Walker's materials to use in Oglala history classes.

66. For a very useful and complete survey of recent experimental ethnographies see George Marcus and Dick Cushman, 'Ethnographies as Texts,' *Annual Review of Anthropology*, 11 (1982), pp. 25–69; Steven Webster, 'Dialogue and Fiction in Ethnography,' *Dialectical Anthropology* 7:2 (1982); and Hussein Fahim, ed., *Indigenous Anthropology in Non-Western Countries* (Durham, North Carolina, 1982).

Mary Ellmann

Just as Mary Ellmann's book *Thinking About Women* (1968) is often read by feminist critics as brilliant but elusive, biographical details about the author too are not easily available. Patricia Meyer Spacks remarking on Ellmann's elegantly witty book made the famous pun that Ellmann left the reader with the 'triumph and limitation of *Thinking About Women*'. Ellmann was educated at the University of Massachusetts and Yale University and has taught at Oxford and Emory Universities. In her review work *Sexual/Textual Politics: Feminist Literary Theory*, Toril Moi notes Ellmann's sardonic and satirical style, but comments on the lack of an explicitly political thrust or historical perspective in *Thinking About Women*. But Ellmann, working with her own agenda in critiquing patriarchy, stated in her preface to the book: 'I am most interested in women as *words*.' And true to her credo she writes in 'Phallic Criticism', the chapter frequently anthologized from her book, 'the working rule is simple, basic: there must always be two literatures like two public toilets, one for Men and one for Women.' Her book is filled with such sharp and graphic moments that show the systematic positioning of women in culture as 'secondary'. Ellmann has also published critical essays on twentieth-century writers such as John Barth, Edith Wharton, Nabokov, Sylvia Plath, etc. Her work, together with Kate Millet's *Sexual Politics* (1969) is seen as part of the canonical, Anglo-American feminist tradition.

The essay printed here focuses upon the fact that patriarchy in general has created a convenient category of 'stereotypes' for both placing women within a culture and circumscribing the boundaries beyond which she cannot go. This double focus of Ellmann's work—literary and cultural—mirrors Germaine Greer's work in Britain, but also increases the scope of analysing the real and mythic place that women occupy in Western culture.

G.R.

Feminine stereotypes

Even individual character is finally impenetrable, and the character, say, of an entire nation so obscure that to offer its definition is considered obscurantism, or worse. At the end of the Second World War, with the full exposure of the Germans' 'Final Solution' of the Jews, it was still felt to be an intellectual impropriety to characterize the moral nature of Germany. Particularly then, since revulsion seems the least proper motive of characterization. But even those who despise the mode of thought cannot help but practice it. And a hope to repress sexual characterization, the most entrenched form of the general mode, would be as futile as a hope to end prostitution or even all sexual intercouse. There is perhaps nothing to which we are more accustomed, nothing which we digest more easily, than such an excursion as the following, from Mary McCarthy's short story, 'The Genial Host':

> Most Jewish men were more feminine than Gentile men of similar social background. You had noticed this and had supposed, vaguely, that it was the mark matriarchy had left on them, but looking at Pflaumen you saw the whole process dramatically. The matriarch had begun by being married off to a husband who was prosperous and settled and older than herself, and her sons she had created in her own image, forlorn little bridegrooms to a middle-aged bride.
>
> In most of the men, the masculine influence had, in the end, overridden or absorbed the feminine, and you saw only vestigial traces of the mother. There might be a tendency to hypochondria, a readiness to take offense, personal vanity, love of comfort, love of being waited on and made much of; and, on the other hand, there would be unusual intuitive powers, sympathy, loyalty, tenderness, domestic graces and kindnesses unknown to the Gentile.

The stereotypes of feminine character are embedded within those of Jewish character, and subscription to the one lot seems entirely at home with subscription to the other.[1] Of course, Mary McCarthy certainly would not have wanted to write the passage, to play the poor woman's Otto Weininger, after the Second World War, when even kind generalizations about the Jews fell into extreme disrepute. Still, their characterization here takes on an illusory strength through its connection with the characterization of women, which in turn is fortified by all physical interest—of which curiosity, speculation and assertion are, for human beings, natural extensions.

These intellectual exercises are the conventional means of distinguishing us from other land animals, who show no discernible inclination to *understand* their sexes. There are stereotyped conceptions of animals, as of Jews and of women, but these conceptions are not supposed to exist in the minds of the animals themselves. A rabbit, unlike a woman, does not know its own reputation either for timidity or fecundity. Instead, the preference of most animals, if they are allowed to pursue it, seems to be for thoughtless sexual agreement[2] or complete separation, depending only upon the season. The attempt of the sexes, in the intervals between copulation, to study each other is human, and accounts in turn for the singular capacity of human beings to experience attraction and animosity simultaneously. This cannot be considered their fault. They are the only mammals, with the exception of white mice, whose mating season is not defined,[3] and therefore they are obliged to study each other (as mice are not) even as they are attracted to each other. If they were perfect beings, this study would intensify the bliss, or perhaps the boredom, of their encounters. As they are, study makes it possible, as it is not possible for animals, for the one sex to disapprove of the other sex with which it must join.[4] In fact, this obligation works almost invariably against enjoyment of the study. The profound trial of having always not only to deal with, but to think about, those who are different from themselves, combining with the elusive nature of this difference, produces a large body of opinions which, if it is no more precise, is certainly more irritable than other bodies of opinion.

These opinions swarm particularly about the topic of femininity. Quantity here, as elsewhere, suggests the strength of the proleptic impulse: the desire to prove is abundant even when proof is not. But this form of wealth, like most other forms, is on the whole a comfort. Capacity for belief, at least in mundane matters, is limited, and it is impossible for women to believe so much about themselves. If they were to believe that all opinions about them are true, they would also have to believe that there is too much truth, a conclusion to which experience in all other situations does not lead either men or women. In fact, the increasing presence of women in the audience which receives these opinions, and the palpable incredulity which their presence projects,[5] seems already to have impeded somewhat the flow of the same opinions in the past—imposing at least some caution or some covering of tracks. It is perhaps for this reason that the opinions have now, for the most part, retreated into fiction, the conventional sanctuary of impeachable utterance.

A second impediment to belief is the element of contradiction which is inescapably felt in any set of these characterizations. It is not easy for a person to suppose, for example, that she is at once conservative and extravagant, or at once pious and materialistic. No doubt some eager ingenuity could provide the needed links—perhaps the pious woman counts up her sacraments and sins and indulgences and penances like so much loose change of different denominations. But the final efficacy of this labor is doubtful, and it is at any rate the job of those who have promulgated the incongruity. As John Stuart Mill argued in a similar context (under that fine, stout Victorian title, *On the Subjection of Women*), the burden of proof lies with the affirmative. For myself, I am less concerned at the moment with the self-evident disarray of these pronouncements than with certain consistent patterns underlying them.

In the stereotypes which follow, a repeated association of women is with nature and of men with art. In fact, this familiar sexual conception accounts for several of the most amiable stereotypes. As long as the two basic equations can be kept quite clear of each other, good will can prevail. Even if art is considered superior to nature, nature in its place is an agreeable phenomenon. Men may be wheat but, as the Wife of Bath noticed, even the Apostles fed well on barley. And then, nature sometimes not only supplements but charms art. Self-consciousness, the advantage of which people are ordinarily vain, seems occasionally burdensome; and they then admire and envy what seems instead the natural, physical and oblivious being of others—of animals, of children, of women and, often in American society, of Negroes. From this point of view, no revelations have been less welcome in the twentieth century than those of the complexity of Negroes (to white supremacists) and of the complexity of children (to parents, supremacists by age). The mind, Valéry felt, constantly tries to prevent or combat the person's sheer being. Others, then, who seem to the person less·mindful than himself, seem also to live more easily, happily, effortlessly. *Being*, Valéry's Monsieur Teste calls Madame Teste, instead of Emilie. And as childbirth (to those incapable of it) seems the most natural and least self-conscious of human experiences,[6] it is particularly the capacity to which the praise of feminine being is attached.

The celebration of thoughtless achievement is, nonetheless, subject to at least two qualifications. The first is made when the observer reconsiders his own condition and, experiencing a revived gratification on its account, finds the same supposed thoughtlessness of others contemptibly naive. Or artless, and in that sense not comparable to designed and directed achievements. At this juncture, very often, careful differences, instead of similarities, will be described between the production of the child and the production, say, of rhymed verse. A useful example of the workings of this much argued issue occurs incidentally in an article by Milton Himmelfarb:

> A few years back I read a neo-feminist's approving review of another neo-feminist's book. The reviewer said she agreed with the author that for a woman, a career is more creative than being a mother. That puzzled me: without having given much thought to it, I had assumed that about the closest the human race can get to creation is when a woman bears a child, nurtures him, and cares for him. A little later I was looking through the racks in a drugstore and came across a specimen of a common subliterary genre—books for adolescent girls about a young heroine with an interesting/creative job/career. The title of the book was *Phyllis White, TV Secretary*. Then I understood, How can being a mother compare in creativity with being a TV secretary?[7]

The predictable slur of the neo-feminist reference can be ignored. The phrase *without having given much thought to it* is more interesting. It is precisely with this air of vague benevolence that maternity is always patted on the head—with one hand, while TV secretaries are cuffed with the other. The confusion of sexual function and personal worth seems inevitably to coarsen judgment and restrict choice: the same intellectual vulgarity that brushes off the little Phyllis Whites expands easily to snigger at the unmarried or the impotent and, particularly in the United States, to persecute the homosexual. At the same time, this idealization of childbirth obscures the distinction between involuntary and voluntary achievement which we depend upon in descrbing any achievement as *creative*. When, as for Indian women, the sequence of conception, birth and starvation is invariable, this distinction remains clear; and the creative act (at once voluntary and socially beneficial) is to procure the means of birth control. But even in middle-class American society, does anyone seriously believe that women, in giving birth, get 'the closest the human race can get to creation'? Closer than Bach, whose wives between them produced twenty children? When we think of our primary metaphor of creation, God's creation of the world, we think of the world as an idea in His head (not as a foetus in His belly) and of His deliberately choosing to bring this idea into existence. That is, our concept of creation is profoundly intellectual and self-directed. Adam is formed out of dust, Eve out of Adam's rib: God plays the first sculptor and the first surgeon, He begins Art and Science. In the same way, Vladimir Nabokov speaks of the creation of the novel as a blasphemy, a small but insolent ambition for divinity.

There are, of course, reasons for women to value pregnancy and childbirth, but they are, I think, slowly persuaded to befuddle the issue (in every sense) with creativity. Women may want to be involved in a particular physiological process for nine months: some enjoy the process itself and most rejoice in its conclusion. But not on the grounds of creativity. The astonishment of childbirth is the unimaginable result of having done no more than indulge the body in a prolonged vagary of its own design. And even this detached impression of *uterine* accomplishment is brief: almost at once, the child appears always to have been a separate and complete being, whose body cannot be seen as the product of cellular multiplication. In this sense, prenatal development is *known* but not *believed*. A hubris of childbirth is the opposite, a moral conviction beyond natural verification. It marks an extraordinary schism between the self and the body in which the self acquires conscious pride in the unconscious workings of its container.

Another common deterrent to full enthusiasm in the contemplation of feminine 'being' itself denies any such primitive purity in this form of being. It is generally suspected that women infect their nature, not with art but with artifice. They appear, after all, to partake of at least a bastard self-consciousness, which leads them into contrived postures, deceptions and pretences. These are thought of as almost ineradicable blemishes upon a fundamental artlessness, and it is sometimes indicated that one of the beauties of the primary natural function, childbirth, is its temporary restoration of utter artlessness. At the moment that the child's head emerges from the vagina, it is possible for everyone to *trust* a woman. So Freud, on the day of his first child's birth, wrote his wife's mother:

> I have never seen her so magnificent in her simplicity and goodness as on this critical occasion, which after all doesn't permit any pretences.[8]

A second consistent quality of feminine stereotypes is the repeated effort to move women in two directions away from a premised, though indefinable, human center. These movements, like those of an autistic child, perhaps signify no more than obsessive attention to a single subject. But they result in an odd effect of hoisting up or lowering down, as elevators move from the basement to the roof and back again, all day long, or as pieces of clothing, once they are bought, must steadily alternate being being dirtied and cleaned. In this sense, opinions of women reflect two volatile impulses, to set things apart by distinction but also to return them—and then to less than even the common stock. An ideal seems formulated only to be regretted or begrudged, as every feminine virtue implies a feminine vice (chastity and frigidity, intuition and irrationality, motherhood and domination). It was Emerson's impression that this form of volatility was especially prominent in American life—to the extent, as he suggested, that election to office in the United States might be looked upon as a man's most reliable guarantee of impeachment.

Perhaps the most extreme range, between elevation and descent, in feminine stereotypes lies between a statement like Addison's:

Women in their nature are much more gay and joyous than men; whether it be that their blood is more refined, their fibres more delicate, and their animal spirits more light; vivacity is the gift of women, gravity that of men.

And the Marquis de Sade's observation:

... I believe that the flesh of women, as the flesh of all female animals, is necessarily very inferior to that of the male species.[9]

All that links the two is the unlikelihood of ever proving either one. Sade, of course, seems extraordinarily rude: one does not want to be eaten, but being eaten, one does not want to be thought an inferior dish. At the same time, a sentimental exaggeration of virtues, like Addison's, is paid for in an equal exaggeration of defects—usually discovered upon a close examination of the body in which the light and delicate spirit resides. It was, after all, Addison's contemporary, Swift, who focussed for horror upon the Brobdingnagian nurse's breast (rather than, say, the Brobdingnagian butler's buttocks) and who asked that portentous question, Does Celia shit? (Yes, competently. Hence her gayety, her vivacity, her refined blood.) Just as on the same seesaw principle, all sexual diseases are named for Venus. It is really this effect of alternation, the sheer coexistence of irreconcilable opinions, which breeds dissent. The impression is not one of definition so much as of the subject's being tossed up and down in a sport called Definition.

The directions of movement are not, however, entirely erratic. They involve at least two fixed moral judgments. The first is that women unfortunately *are* women, and that their ideal condition is attained by rising above themselves. When his sister-in-law, Mary Hogarth, died at seventeen, Dickens praised her character:

She had not a single fault, and was in life almost as far above the foibles and vanity of her sex and age as she is now in Heaven.[10]

On the other hand, men are not men without effort, and their ideal condition is attained by their *becoming*, and (with luck) remaining, simply men. It is by this route that a perverse appetite for unpleasant experiences, at least in the lives of *others*, develops: various regimens (sleeping in a wet sleeping bag, going to a military academy, etc.) are commonly said to 'make a man' out of a man. But copulation too, of course, presumably has this goal, among others. In *My Secret Life*, for example, at the conclusion of an abysmal first performance (which involves the kindest and most patient cook in London at the time), the protagonist crows, 'Now I am a man!' It is an index of grimness still at work, however, that copulation is the only shared, innocuous and more entertaining than competitive experience which is felt to have the desired effect of virilism.

These two variant conditions of ideal can perhaps be clarified by diagram:

Super-sexual IDEAL

⬆

WOMEN = DEFECT   MEN = IDEAL

⬆

Sub-sexual DEFECT

A third consistent pattern is that of complementary qualities. This is perhaps the pattern toward which everyone can feel some cordiality, since it shows an understandable desire for sexual order as well as a pretty confidence that balance and economy actually prevail. The feeling is that there must not, cannot, be waste by duplication, that the complementary nature of the male and female reproductive systems must have intellectual and emotional parallels. Ideally, from this point of view, men should have ears (to hear lectures with) and women eyes (to see trinkets with), in which case eyes would be sufficiently defined as 'those organs which, unlike ears, cannot take in sound.' One might in that way avoid the disturbing sense of overlapping and disorder which, as things are, must constantly be warded off by assertions to the contrary. For example, Otto Weininger established, at least to his own satisfaction (in 1904), that blood transfusions should be carried out only within each sex: since all cells of the female body were female, their being set free in the individual male system, as in all social systems, would cause an immediate internecion. The complementary impulse seems particularly strong in those, like Weininger, whose chief sources of anxiety are mobility, diversity, fluctuation—Keats's 'negative capability' of the poet. Such anxiety must urge a uniform commitment to fixed characteristics, an insistence upon the tidy and immutable properties of a reality which, as Bertrand Russell has said, suggests to others only the 'higgledy-piggledy':

> I think the universe is all spots and jumps, without unity, without continuity, without coherence or orderliness or any of the other properties that governesses love. The external world may be an illusion, but if it exists, it consists of events, short, small, and haphazard. Order, unity, and continuity are human inventions, just as are catalogues and encyclopaedias.[11]

The fourth consistent pattern is related to the third, though its effect is to disturb and confuse what, left to itself, might be the limpidity of the third. In the fourth, women tend to be not merely what men are not, but what the individual speaker is not, and even what he is not *at any given moment*. In the third pattern, let us say, the man is quite steadily direct and forceful, the woman oblique and fugitive. But in the fourth pattern, the woman's nature may be determined largely by the temperament of the person who describes her. The dispassionate sense, for example, of Defoe's judgment of women seems consistent with the temper of all his observations—upon the plague as upon Moll Flanders. Similarly now, in a novel like Philip Roth's *When She Was Good*, which attempts to describe a vindictive and merciless young woman—stones are brought in to hint that she is *stony*—the basic impression is one of the generally vindictive temper of the novel itself.

And beyond temperament, single and passing moods can govern contrasts. If the first seems at any moment lusty, the second seems prudish: but at another moment, if the first seems moral, the second is sluttish. Even a quality which is invariably ascribed to women, like compliancy, will be a defect in some circumstances, a virtue in others, rather as curly hair is sometimes chic, sometimes not, but always curly.

The sense of this erratic direction by mood, in an area formerly governed (with some startling exceptions) by a fairly benevolent certitude, seems now particularly strong. At least since the Second World War, the work of assigning stereotypes, not only to racial groups but to men and women, has of course continued, but in a

markedly distressed and even demoralized manner. The more stable sexual stereotypes of, say, the mid-nineteenth century provided some tranquillity for those who
framed them and perhaps also for some of those who bore them.[12] A perceptible dis-
turbance has now replaced that calm, in relation to all contrasts but especially in
relation to the former contrast of strength and weakness and to its former reconciliation: the tolerable exchange of male protection for female helplessness. Among the
varieties of suffering which have always been abundantly available, the suffering of
men as protectors of women and children was traditionally considered the most
severe, and therefore the most valid proof of sexual superiority. Whatever revision of
this point the peaceful society might suggest, the always present threat of war denied.
This balance of roles, for which everyone must feel nostalgia, was thrown off by the
Second World War, which replaced it with an appalling equality in suffering. In the
atomic bombing of Hiroshima and Nagasaki, and in the murder of six million Jewish
men, women and children in Europe, in the same manner and for the same cause,
without distinctions in age, sex or responsibility (all were equally responsible for
being alive and human), the modern concept of mutual vulnerability was established,
before which the traditional sexual contrasts of strength and weakness, courage and
timidity, authority and subservience became meaningless.

The Japanese of Hiroshima should seem to us to have died like women since many
of them died in the light, restless sleep of early morning, and all sleep (like night
itself) might be stereotyped as feminine—passive, thoughtless, pacific, unresisting.
But within the same daylight, masculine ethic of aggressive action, what is to be said
of the European Jews who died awake? It is possible for some critics, like Bruno
Bettelheim, to deplore their not countering the aggression of the Nazis with aggression of their own. Some yielded (we must always say *yielded*) to despair, others clung
to life on *passive* and *subservient* terms. But it is equally possible to suppose that the
ethic itself died at that time, extended into monstrosity by those whose minds and
bodies were equipped to kill indiscriminately, and exposed as anachronism by their
victims. This ethic collapsed before the modern exigencies which the Jews faced and
has not applied convincingly to those which have since prevailed. Starvation, racial
injustice and atomic fear are also mutual exigencies to which monosexual responses
are irrelevant. It is true that American engagement in warfare has, so far, retained a
conventional masculinity (and so President Johnson retains the 'our boys' rhetoric of
World War I). But this rule would disintegrate before the bombing of American
cities, as it has disintegrated in those places which we bomb. American women are
still divorced, then, from the personal experience of war which American men are
obliged to confer upon the women of other countries. Most soldiers must intend to
kill only other soldiers, but their weapons erase distinctions in both sex and age. It is
not that Vietnamese women are 'neo-feminists.' It is not that they refuse protection
or prefer napalm to a double standard, but that no one can provide protection for
them.

In consequence of such changes, inherited Western stereotypes are weakened, and
their continued endorsement is forced to be frantic. When Norman Mailer talks
about feisty men and languid women, one touches the past—hardly in the form in
which it persists in bourgeois enclaves, but as it drags at a mind attempting to reconcile an acute appreciation of the present with a passionate attachment to a masculine

291

ideal. The difficulty, and perhaps the futility, of such a reconciliation account for Mailer's always thrashing quality. At his best, he has a desperate bravado, a last-standness which becomes a way of extracting some vitality, like clotting blood, from defunct opinions.

Ordinarily, the chief mark of sexual stereotypes is their tedium. As the body comes to sexual adulthood, the mind seems to exchange spontaneity, like a secondary inno-cence, for conviction. But a surfeit is felt increasingly with set formulations, and a hunger renewed for idiosyncratic and isolated phenomena. Both help to account for the present unsuccess of the realistic novel whose main source of energy has been, and still is, psychosexual comparison and contrast. In turn, the reader recognizes the patterns of distinction, and closes the book. Even various degrees of plausibility within the stereotypes no longer hold an audience for them. Most seem ready to give up the chance (now, at any rate, diminished) of 'This is how it is' to avoid the cer-tainty of 'This is how they always say it is.' The original exhilaration of the chance slides irresistibly, through repetition, into banality.

NOTES

1. The one preoccupation seems quite generally to accompany the other. In Mailer's *An American Dream*, for example, references to Polish brutality, Irish treachery, German physiognomy, etc., occur almost as regularly as generic references to women. And all Leslie Fiedler's characters, men and women, take fixed positions on his compass of Jews, WASPs, Negroes and Indians.
2. I do not mean to suggest that periods of agreement among animals are necessarily shorter than those among human beings, or more brutal. Animal forms of courtship are studiously observed: male pen-guins, for example, bring gifts of pebbles (preferably red ones) and execute an awkward but (one must assume) suggestive dance. Penguins also show a rudimentary fidelity. Often the same couples will find each other year after year, in the midst of the large, unruly and raucous crowd which regularly gathers. (See Susan Michelmore, *Sex*, London, Pan Books, 1964.)
3. It is, evidently, for this reason that white mice also commit rape. Cf. the mouse riddle in Dryden's *Riddles and Rounds*:
   Before you mock my timorous shape
   Remark my wee penchant for rape.
4. Homosexuals are, of course, relieved of this necessity, but to judge from their printed opinions, some are not relieved of a similar, and seemingly still more intense, animosity.
   The exception is Oscar Wilde, who was incapable of animosity, even toward women. He could bring himself only to be witty at their light expense. Mrs. Radcliffe, 'who introduced the romantic novel, and has consequently much to answer for.' And 'the admirable Mrs. Chapone, whose *Ode to Solitude* always fills me with the wildest passion for society.' And Mrs. E. B. Browning: 'In philosophy she was a Platonist, in politics an Opportunist.'
5. A general levelling of education is in their favor: women know a bit more, and men a bit less. For example, Chaucer had this trick available for his cock Chaunticleer to play on Pertelote:
   In principio,
   Mulier est hominis confusio,
   Madame, the sentence of this Latin is,
   'Womman is mannes joye and al his blis. . . .
   The erudite thing doesn't work any more: women still don't know Latin but now men don't either.
6. It would be valuable to have a psychological study of women's states of *mind* in childbirth. The lapsing of ordinary interests, observations and criticisms is, one suspects, commonly exaggerated. A woman has been known, for example, to suffer acute embarrassment throughout her delivery because her hair is up in curlers. Moreover, while the recollection of pain fades quickly, what is *said* during the delivery is remembered. I myself recall a shoppy discussion of various antiseptics, and I have known women

who could mimic the manners and the remarks of obstetricians years after their children were born.

7. Milton Himmelfarb, 'Varieties of Jewish Experience,' *Commentary*, July 1967, p. 59.

8. *The Letters of Sigmund Freud* (Standard Edition, 1900), p. 224.

9. From 'Juliette' in *The Marquis de Sade* (An Essay by Simone de Beauvoir and Selections from His Writing, Chosen by Paul Dinnage), (London, John Calder, 1962), p. 171.

10. *Letters of Charles Dickens*, edited by Madeline House and Graham Storey (Oxford, Clarendon Press, 1965), p. 263.

11. Bertrand Russell, *The Scientific Outlook* (New York, W. W. Norton, 1931), pp. 94–5. Russell assigns the appetite for order to clergymen and journalists as well—i.e., to the sanctimonious on the one hand and the sensational on the other. Clearly, both states of mind are also prominent in the propagation of feminine stereotypes.

12. In *Middlemarch*, for example, George Eliot remarks on Mrs. Garth's hearty endorsement of the 'principle of subordination': 'On ninety-nine points Mrs. Garth decided, but on the hundredth she was often aware that she would have to perform the singularly difficult task of carrying out her own principle, and to make herself subordinate.'

5 Media studies

Introduction

Media studies lies at the heart of cultural studies and draws on many disciplines, such as literature, history, education, linguistics, sociology, semiotics, film studies and political science. Studies of the media can range from technical accounts of electronic processes to politically orientated investigations into representations of gender and race and concerns with the freedom of the press. Specific institutions have been set up to study media communications, such as the Leicester Centre for Mass Communications Research, the Glasgow Media Group (UK), and the Institute of Communications Research at the University of Illinois (USA). There have also long been departments in American universities offering degrees at all levels in communication studies which are also degrees in professional areas, such as press and television journalism. American media studies tended initially to be more empirically based than its British counterpart, using and developing methods of market research to see how audiences are targeted and looking at how media organizations work as an industrial practice.

Raymond Williams, in his ground-breaking work *Communications* (1962) which was deeply influenced by American empirical studies, uses the term communications—agreed meanings and the transmission of ideas and information—as almost synonymous with culture. As James Carey points out in *Communication as Culture* (1989) inside cultural studies, communications is not a neutral word. It can be taken as referring to the wide range of ritual enactments which define and consolidate a culture as well as to mass communications, the media industry and its audience. Cultural studies looks at communication in both of these ways. Studies of the media use empirical data and develop theoretical models to investigate the generation and transmission of cultural materials via specific media channels and modes of communication.

The liberal tradition inherited from the nineteenth century regards the press and other mass media as representative institutions—the fourth estate—which function to expose government institutions and commercial organizations to public opinion.

297

However, the liberal endorsement of a free press was joined early on by a concern over its coercive and manipulative potential. Empirical work, such as that carried out by the Glasgow Media Group in *Bad News* (1976), *More Bad News* (1980) and *Really Bad News* (1982) offers a detailed description of the various institutional and commercial influences which 'make' news into television programmes. James Curran's and Jean Seaton's seminal *Power without Responsibility: The Press and Broadcasting in Britain* (1981, 2nd edn 1985), offers a critical historical, institutional, and sociological account of the media in Britain. Seaton's discussion below addresses a specifically British movement to institute constitutional media controls. The question of the degree to which government can control or guarantee the freedom of the media is, however, of general application and concern to all societies whose information and 'culture' is widely disseminated through media organs.

Alongside the issue of press/media freedom from governmental or commercial control, there are also the debates structured around questions of whether the media reflect or distort *reality*, and enrich or impoverish the consumers' sense of life. A distinction which emerged early in media/communication studies and which gets replayed with variations was articulated by Dwight Macdonald. He argued that 'Folk Art grew from below. It was a spontaneous, autochthonous expression of the people, shaped by themselves . . . to suit their own needs. Mass culture is imposed from above. It is fabricated by technicians hired by businessmen; its audiences are passive consumers' (*Against the American Grain*, 1962). From what may be characterized as either the high left or the high right, there is considerable suspicion of the seductive power of the popular media seen as manipulative and self-serving. In his 1954 essay, 'How to Look at Television', Theodor Adorno, for instance, argued that 'the technology of television production makes stereotypy almost inevitable' and warned that through this process, 'people may not only lose true insight into reality, but ultimately their very capacity for life experiences may be dulled' (*The Quarterly of Film, Radio, and Television*, 3). From a very different political perspective, Allan Bloom in *The Closing of the American Mind* (1987) indicts the popular media for distracting attention from the 'great tradition'.

As well as articulating concerns with value and quality, freedom and control, media studies has increasingly developed in theoretical and methodological sophistication and created its own vocabulary drawn from specific media practices. For example, using technical vocabulary such as close-ups, visual clichés, sound-bites, or down-loading information, as well as tools of analysis from semiotic and literary theory has made media studies quite rigorous in its interpretive strategies. Semiotics, the study of the sign, word, image, note of music, gesture, item of adornment, by which communication is effected is also a study of how signs are culturally inflected and in turn inflect the culture. Signs, in communicating the meanings of a culture, also often carry an over-load or excess of meaning. A picture of a pair of jeans can be seen as an apt example of a sign with excess meaning; for instance, it does not just signify an article of working attire, but is also an inducement to purchase, carrying meanings about wealth, age, leisure, sexual allure and availability, general hipness, power. It can even act as a symbol of America.

Marxist/post-Marxist theories of ideology have had a great influence, particularly in British cultural studies, on the way semiotics has entered media studies. Their focus is on the way that signifying systems are deployed in an economy of production and consumption. Roland Barthes's essay 'Myth Today', for instance, looks at the way cultural meanings attach themselves to signs which are then attached to further signs in a signifying chain to produce what he calls the myths of bourgeois capitalist society. (See introduction to the Impact of Theory section for a comparison with Jacques Lacan.) The idea of media as part of the ideological state apparatus was developed by Louis Althusser who argued that a series of independent yet related social systems—law, education, media—cooperate not only to legitimate social norms but also to produce our consciousness of ourselves. In media studies, the study of signs includes a linguistic concern with how meaning is transmitted and also how particular and preferred meanings are transmitted through signifying systems. A great deal of work has been done, as in Judith Williamson's *Decoding Advertisements: Ideology and Meaning in Advertising* (1978), on the ways in which advertisements not only convey inducements to purchase particular goods but also carry messages concerning race, gender, and status. Richard Ohman's handy 'kit' of ideological terms used in advertising also addresses this issue and articulates a common concern in both British and American cultural studies to equip teachers and students with the critical tools for responding to the blandishments of the media and, in particular, advertisements. Denys Thompson's *Discrimination and Popular Culture* (1964), widely used in schools and further education colleges in Britain in the 1970s, was a pioneering work in this field.

Structuralist uses of semiotics for cultural analysis, such as in the work of the anthropologist Claude-Lévi Strauss (see section on Impact of Theory), look for the universal narrative paradigms organized along the 'deep structure' of binary opposition: high/low, male/female, hero/villain, nature/culture, etc. Semiotic and structuralist approaches have been very successfully applied to film (Peter Wollen's *Signs and Meaning in the Cinema*, 1969) and television serials (John Fiske, *Television Culture*, 1987), as well as prose (Tzvatan Todorov, *The Poetics of Prose*, 1977). Structuralist morphologies indicate the extent to which the narrative is impelled by its own structural determinants—narrative codes—rather than by verisimilitude, and have been fruitfully applied to such apparently truth-telling forms as documentaries and newscasts. Recent interest in this direction is catalogued as the 'politics of realism'.

However, assumptions about the universal nature of narrative codes hurrying towards closure are also the problematics of the structuralist approach. Working with narratives of tribal/folk societies, it may be possible to erase the gap between the teller, the tale and the told, but the media messages of advanced industrial-technological societies are not necessarily focused around agreed codes of story-telling and are not necessarily transmitted to audiences sharing common systems of thought. The same narrative may be received differently by different segments of the audience who, in turn, relate to different segments of the narrative. Here theorists have often turned to the work of Antonio Gramsci (see section on Impact of Theory) on hegemony, which grants an important role to resistance to the 'organic intellectual' and argues that social domination is achieved through reasoned consent. This process, however, involves an area of negotiation, and, some theorists would argue, there is always a residue of resistance left as an active area of cultural critique. Initially, media studies tended to concentrate on representation, the construction of images and narratives. Increasingly, however, studies have also focused on audiences and the processes of reception.

Psychoanalytic theories, especially those concerned with identity and gender construction, have been fruitfully applied to the analysis of media messages and reception (see section on Gender Studies). Laura Mulvey's famous essay, 'Visual Pleasure and Narrative Cinema', combines semiotic and narrative theories to subvert Lacanian theories of the 'gaze' to argue that 'the look of the camera' controls and limits the audience's range of reaction and reduces female figures to fetishized and passive bearers of the male gaze. Mulvey's approach, which concludes by looking to the works of 'radical film-makers' to deconstruct the camera's narrative control, can be contrasted with Janice Radway's essay on romance novels. Radway draws on the reader-response theories of Stanley Fish to discuss 'the social context surrounding a reader's activity'. She argues that different 'interpretive communities' react variously to reading romance novels and, far from condemning the Harlequin-style romance, suggests that socially, spatially, and sexually, romances can provide women 'with a kind of tacit, minimal protest against the patriarchal construction of women'. Radway's approach is typical of more recent approaches in media studies that grant consumers an active rather than a passive role in their encounters with media products.

Generally, there has been a move towards analyses of the media as complex transactions involving not only messages and meanings, but multi-valenced media formats and a wide range of audience variables which inflect the ways in which the media text is received and interpreted. With regard to format, Raymond Williams's comment that viewers 'watch television' rather than specific programmes—the experience being one of 'flow' without the logic of cause and effect—has, arguably, even more relevance nowadays with the advent of remote control which has produced the habits of 'zapping' and 'grazing' (*Television: Technology and Cultural Form*, 1974).

Stuart Hall's influential essay 'Encoding/Decoding' (*Culture, Media, Language*, 1980) furthered the move to develop complex and plural readings both of media messages and of audience composition and reception. In this essay Hall critiques American empiricist and behavioural communications theories which created the 'encoder-signal-decoder' paradigm of direct transmission. He argues that 'the codes of encoding and decoding may not be perfectly symmetrical' and that differences in audience relations to the 'dominant-hegemonic position' will inflect the ways in which decoding operates. The processes involved in the production of the signal are never simple but are variously constructed and open to diverse influences. On the reception end, David Morely applied Hall's hypothetical construction of three possible decoding positions, as preferred, negotiated and/or oppositional, in his ethnographic and semiotic study of a British news programme, *The 'Nationwide' Audience* (1980). Morely's findings indicated that there was no clear correlation between the reactions of his informer groups and their socio-economic status but that 'the crucial factor in the encounter of audience/subject and text will be the range of discourses at the disposal of the audience.' The ability of the audience to produce meanings from a text, he suggests, depends on their 'cultural competences', a concept adapted from the Saussurean model of linguistic competence.

As media studies has shifted away from assumptions of audience passivity, an alternative view, particularly associated with the work of John Fiske, has emerged. Fiske stresses audience creativity and emphasizes the pleasure involved in making meanings. In this context, the work of Marshall McLuhan has re-emerged as significant (see section on Cultural Studies in America). As in Radway's essay, such an approach sees audiences/readers actively appropriating elements in the text which they can apply to their lives. For instance, viewers can make up their own videos from clips which restructure the 'original' work, or produce 'fanzines' which elaborate on meanings embedded in or imposed on the 'original' work. At issue in the debate over the processes of audience reception is a political agenda to grant agency to consumers and theorize them as reacting against and transgressing the political and/or commercial content of the text.

Every new mass-media development re-arouses fears of cultural degradation and audience entrapment, and MTV, with its close association with advertising—each clip an advertisement for a group and a record label—has been greeted with what Lawrence Grossberg describes as a 'moral panic'. In response to this 'panic', he places MTV within existing media traditions and trends and also characterizes its nature in terms of the 'postmodern condition' in which 'we are condemned to try and make sense of our lives in structures that clearly contradict our experience'. Similarly, Simon Frith also investigates responses to the 'popular' media. He takes on the tradition of 'élite' disapproval of 'popular' media products, as well as its counter-formation of uncritical approval of the 'popular', as he queries the distinction in media and cultural studies between 'popular/low' and 'high' culture (see Bourdieu's analysis of the process of acquiring a cultured taste in the Impact of Theory section). The issue of the active/passive consumption of media products is addressed by Simon Frith, who while critical of 'romantic' readings of audience activity wishes to instantiate through the concept of taste an area of active consumption.

All media-studies critics agree that we are witnessing an information revolution with a proliferation of the means of communication which bypass the traditional information-communication circuits. There is, however, little agreement about how computer information and communication technology has and will affect society (see interview with J. Hillis Miller, in Voice-Overs section). The decentralization of knowledge can be seen as liberating and democratizing or, alternatively, the age of computer-information technology can be seen as franchising the indiscrete dissemination of global information to multinational corporations. There can be no doubt but that media studies, particularly as studies of mass media, are at the centre of the 'culture wars', and that studies of how different media work, how their products reflect or constitute or are used by their audiences, and what interests are served by their producers, are always and rightly political issues.

J.M. and G.R.

FURTHER READING

Allen, Robert, *Channels of Discourse: Television and Contemporary Criticism*, London: Methuen, 1987.
Curran, James, Michael Gurevitch, and Janet Wollacott, eds, *Mass Communication and Society*, London: Edward Arnold, 1977.

301

Jean Baudrillard, *The Mirror of Production*, trans. Mark Poster, St. Louis: Telos Press, 1975.

Bennet, Tony, Colin Mercer, and Janet Wollacott, eds, *Popular Culture and Social Relations*, Milton Keynes and Philadelphia: Open University Press, 1986.

De Lauretis, Teresa, *Alice Doesn't: Feminism, Semiotics and Cinema*, Bloomington: Indiana University Press, 1984.

Dyer, Richard, *Now You See It: Studies on Lesbian and Gay Film*, London and New York: Routledge, 1990.

Frith, Simon, Andrew Goodwin, and Lawrence Grossberg, eds, *Sound and Vision: The Music Television Reader*, Boston: Unwin & Hyman, 1991.

Gurevitch, Michael, Tony Bennet, James Curran, and Janet Wollacott, eds, *Culture, Society and the Media*, London: Methuen, 1982.

Hall, Stuart, 'Signification, representation, ideology: Althusser and the post-structuralist debates', *Critical Studies in Mass Communication*, 2 (1985), 91–114.

Hebdige, Dick, *Subculture: The Meaning of Style*, London and New York: Routledge, 1979.

Marcus, Greil, *Mystery Train: Images of America in Rock 'n' Roll*, New York: Dutton, 1975.

McCabe, Colin, *Theoretical Essays*, Manchester: Manchester University Press, 1985.

Morely, David, *Family Television: Cultural Power and Domestic Leisure*, London: Comedia, 1986.

Morris, Meghan, 'Banality in Cultural Studies', in *The Logics of Television*, ed. Patricia Mellencamp, Bloomington, Indiana: Indiana University Press, 1990, 14–43.

Penley, Constance, *Feminism and Film Theory*, New York and London: Routledge, 1988.

Waites, Bernard, Tony Bennet, and Graham Martin, eds, *Popular Culture, Past and Present*, London: Croom Helm, 1982.

Williams, Raymond, *Television: Technology and Cultural Form*, New York: Schocken Books, 1975.

Williamson, Judith, *Consuming Passions*, London: Marion Boyars, 1987.

Richard Ohmann (1931–)

Richard Ohmann is a professor of English at Wesleyan University. He received his BA from Oberlin in 1952 and his PhD from Harvard in 1960. He has been the recipient of a Guggenheim Fellowship and a Rockefeller Foundation Fellowship and written several books including *English in America: A Radical View of the Profession* (1976) and *Shaw: The Style and the Man* (1962). His essay, 'Doublespeak and Ideology in Ads: A Kit for Teachers', is from an edited anthology, *Teaching About Doublespeak* (1976).

In this essay, Ohmann attempts to alert students to manipulative advertisements that 'sell ideas, with or without products' by bringing 'doublespeak' to their attention, and explains how ideology works in general and in specific advertisements. The naturalization of doublespeak, he argues, makes us forget that it is ideologically contrived. He provides a list of ideological themes to look for in American industry, semantics, and rhetoric, admitting they have merit, but also pointing out that it is the abuse of these themes which we must attend to in order to keep them from determining our perspective.
K.M.S.

Doublespeak and ideology in ads: a kit for teachers

Compiled by Richard Ohmann and the Amherst Conference on Public Doublespeak, Summer 1974*

*Those who helped put together these materials at the Amherst conference were: Susan Allen, Meramec Community College, Missouri; John Bacich, Diablo Valley College, California; John Black, Darien High School, Connecticut; Jack Boozer, Warren Wilson College, North Carolina; Stella Bruton,

How can business defend itself? The answer is not distant. . . . Pick up the weapon lying idle at your side, your advertising budgets.

Patrick Buchanan

Mr. Buchanan, a speechwriter for former President Nixon, was talking about difficulties the oil companies had in 1974 in telling the public their views on energy and the environment. He went on to say, 'Oil companies spend billions each year in advertising, Mobil's creation of "idea advertising," in lieu of the happy-motoring nonsense, is a first step.' Whenever Mobil follows Buchanan's advice—as it has often done and will doubtless continue to do—it uses money spent by consumers for gas in order to educate those same customers in Mobil's *ideas*. Not having either the billions or the organization of oil companies, there's little that consumers can do to control such education except be alert to and critical of such ideas.

The following material, and abbreviated version of a teaching kit prepared at a workshop in Amherst in the summer of 1974, is about the kind of advertising that Patrick Buchanan had in mind, and about any ads that sell ideas, with or without products. It offers ways to help alert students to business ideas, and to ways of expressing them that are misleading, confusing, deceptive, manipulative. In other words, to what members of this NCTE committee have come to call 'doublespeak.'

You could think of the kit as an aid to self-defense, since without critical instruments a student has a handicap in sorting out the hundreds of messages she or he gets daily from advertisers. But we hope that the kit will be more than that, too. We'd like it to help you help students understand how ideology works, *whoever* the seller or giver. We'd like it to help you and your students define and understand the widespread thing we call doublespeak. And we think it will be useful in teaching some general points of rhetoric and semantics.

One obvious deficiency of the kit needs mentioning. We haven't been able to reproduce the photographs or layout of print ads, or the music or voice of radio ads, or the visual sequences of TV ads. These modes of presentation may contain nonverbal doublespeak, if you will, and we hope you will supplement the kit with whatever criticism you can bring to bear on the sounds and sights of advertising.

The explanations, checklists, and analyses here are addressed to you. They are no more than a sketch of the one- to three-week unit we imagine you may teach on doublespeak. And most of this material will need expansion or simplification, depending on the level of your college or high school students. Further—and perhaps this goes without saying—an effective unit on this subject cannot be 'canned' for students. Everything depends on their becoming actively critical, finding their own instances, doing their own analyses.

Continued from p. 303
West Chester State College, Pennsylvania; Walker Gibson, University of Massachusetts, Amherst; Francine Hardaway, Scottsdale Community College, Arizona; Andrea Johnson, Trinity College, Vermont; Howard Livingston, Pace University, New York; Dwight Marsh, Hastings College, Nebraska; David Milan, Tacoma Community College, Washington; Lee Morgan, Centenary College, Louisiana; Karl Oelke, Union College, New Jersey; Richard Ohmann, Wesleyan University, Connecticut; Jeffrey Roberts, Worcester State College, Massachusetts; Arthur Young, Michigan Technical University, Michigan.

Basic principles

Ideology is the ideas of a group of people with common interests—a nation, a party, a government, a social or economic class, an occupational group, an industry, etc. The most common tactic of ideology is to show how the interests of the group are 'really' the same as the interests of the whole society or of humanity in general. The famous remark of Charles Wilson some years back, 'What's good for General Motors is good for the country,' encapsulates the root principle of ideology. General Motors, the American Medical Association, the AFL-CIO, the National Rifle Association, garment workers, English teachers, college professors, businessmen—whatever group is organized and conscious of a common interest turns out ideology.

Ideological talk does not always amount to doublespeak, but it easily can. And for a simple reason: the interests of various groups in a society are *not* all compatible—not all the time in all respects. Poll taxes were good for white politicians but not for black tenant farmers. Higher faculty salaries at a private university with finite resources may mean *lower* salaries for secretaries or less scholarship money for students. And so on. Usually the conflict of interest is not so dramatic. Then ideology has its best opportunity—and runs its greatest risk of doublespeak. For then it can be rather abstract, hitching on to generally accepted ideas like (in this society) freedom, technological problem-solving, individualism, the family, 'ecology.' And if conflicts are obscure or buried, the grand concepts smooth a surface over them. Oil companies and consumers are both for a clean environment, and also for free choices in the market-place; so (say the oil companies) let us work together to solve our problem. To paraphrase an anecdote of Lincoln's, the wolf and the sheep are both for liberty. So long as the discussion remains on this level, bystanders might be content to let the wolf and the sheep resolve their own differences, not noticing that the wolf's desired liberty is to eat the sheep, the sheep's not to be eaten. One person's solution may be the other person's problem. Not *always*, but often. And in such a situation ideology is often doublespeak.

It's an important kind of doublespeak for people to study, for these reasons: (1) If they can't decode it, they are likely to make major social choices for bad reasons, and against their interest. (2) Powerful groups in a society have ideological advantage over the poor, weak, or unorganized. Welfare mothers doubtless have an ideology, too, but lacking the resources to buy prime TV time they are less able to confuse us with doublespeak than groups that *can* buy prime time. (Remember Buchanan's advice to business.) Ideological doublespeak always tends to keep power where it is in a society. So in the Soviet Union it would be well if young people could detect Communist Party doublespeak. Here, the doublespeak of the U.S. Communist Party is less a force to contend with than that of the Pentagon. Ideology-detection is a weapon mainly of those without much wealth or power—e.g., most of us and most of our students. (3) For all that, much ideology does not *intend* to deceive. People often deeply believe their own doublespeak. And sincerity and good will make ideological doublespeak especially hard to detect.

This 'kit' concentrates on advertisements. But early in a unit on this subject it is useful to have students look at some examples of more direct ideological argument, to see how it works, and how deception (conscious or unconscious) is likely to creep in. Choose one example of ideology that is unfamiliar to your students and one that is familiar. Needless to say, the choice will differ from one group of students to another, depending on their experience and stations in American society. It may be well to start with an argument quite foreign (literally) to them—say some Soviet or Chinese ideology.

How to look for ideology and doublespeak in ads: questions to ask

1 Who is the advertiser?
2 What is the explicit purpose of the ad?
3 Does the advertiser have any purpose other than the explicit one?
4 What kind of person or company does the advertiser claim to represent?
5 What audience does the advertiser assume?
6 To what qualities of that audience does the advertiser appeal?
7 What self-interests does the advertiser assume the audience to have? To *think* it has?
8 How does the advertiser relate the product, company, industry, or ideas to the audience's self-interest?
9 What common interests does the advertiser claim or imply between the company or person and the audience?
10 Are there possible *conflicts* of interest between advertisers and audience?
11 Does the ad refer, directly or obliquely, to such conflicts?
12 Does the advertiser call any widely accepted values or beliefs into play in pointing to the audience's and the company or person's common interest?
13 What words does the advertiser use for such values and beliefs? How abstract are these words? How easy are they to tie down to concrete situations and events?
14 What language does the advertiser use to suggest harmony between the company or person and the audience. Is it warranted?

Thirteen ideas of ideological stock in trade

Here's a highly selective list of ideological themes to look for in what American industry says:
1 Anything wrong in our society is a problem, amenable to a solution in the interest of all.

2 Corollary: all conflicts of interest are only apparent.

3 We'll all be best off if business manages the development of resources in the future.

4 It can do this only if (a) profits are high, and (b) there is a minimum of government interference.

5 Solutions to problems are generally technical; we need new technology, but not any change in the system.

6 Hence, what the experts decide is best for all. The people are often deficient in understanding.

7 On the other hand, neither business nor technocrats have much power: in the present system, *the people* are the ones who decide.

8 They decide best through individual purchases in a free market; voting is secondary, other kinds of politics a potential threat to free choice.

9 The United States can solve its problems apart from those of the rest of the world, and do so without creating problems elsewhere.

10 Freedom is good for both individuals and corporations, and pretty much the same thing for both.

11 Growth and productivity are good for all.

12 Our needs—for pleasure, love, approval, security, etc.—can best be met by consuming products.

13 Consumption should generally be done by units no larger than the nuclear family. And the nuclear family is the social ideal.

(Remember: Taken as ideas, these are of varying merit. They can be openly debated. Certainly they are not in themselves doublespeak. What earns them their places on this list is their very wide acceptance, coupled with their loose formulation: they can easily be appropriated for almost any purpose, including honest and dishonest ones. It is their abuse we should attend to.)

Short guide to ideological doublespeak

Look for doublespeak in these areas of semantics and rhetoric:

1 *What you mean 'we,' paleface?* The homogenizing 'we,' and 'us,' and 'our.' Particularly, watch for shifts in the reference of 'we,' and for instances where 'we' purports to refer to everyone in the society, but where what is said is in fact only true of some. (Recall the Lone Ranger's saying 'There are Indians closing in from all sides, Tonto: we're in trouble.' Tonto: 'What you mean "we," paleface?')

2 *'America.'* And 'the people,' 'our society,' etc. When you read 'America needs . . .' stop and ask if all Americans need it, or only some, or some more than others. The use of 'America' is often coercive, not referential.

3 *Abstraction away from people.* When someone proposes to fight 'poverty,' does that mean getting more money to poor people, and perhaps less to the wealthy? If

not, what? Again, can we be for 'ecology' without being against those who upset the ecological balance?

4   *Liberty. Or, the sheep and the wolf.* Both are for liberty, but one's liberty is the other's death. Watch for plus-words like 'liberty,' used as if they had the same meaning for all. In many situations they conceal conflict of interest.

5   *It's a problem.* An American habit of mind conceives any difficulty, crisis, disaster, social conflict—ANYthing BAD—as a problem. This move always implies that we're in it together, faced with the same problem, and all with the same interest in a solution. Remember that your solution *may* be my problem, or that your problem may even be *me.* Be watchful, especially, for disinterested formulation of 'problems' by those who have helped create them, and whose livelihoods are at stake. Another thing: labeling something a problem obviously implies that there *is* a solution—but in some situations there may be no approved solution, or even no solution at all.

6   *The technological fix.* Fusion will solve our problem, or a new emission control device, or a new ingredient, or a new kind of glass, or just 'research.' The technological fix is usually aimed at symptoms, not causes. Now sometimes technical solutions are what we (all of us) need. But often they're *more* needed by those who supply the technology. And very often the technological fix is offered as remedy for social or political problems. When some technological term is the subject of an active verb, try to put people back in the picture: Technology does nothing by itself. *Who* will set the machine going? With what interest?

7   *Experts know best.* A corollary of the above, this idea always merits some skepticism. But it leads to doublespeak especially when the ideologue says (a) the people must decide, (b) the people don't/can't understand what the experts understand, (c) let the experts decide.

8   *Hard facts or iron laws.* 'The hard fact is that America progresses only if business prospers.' Query: What makes a fact hard? Query: What issues are excluded from debate by this hard fact? Well, the equation of progress with economic growth, for one. And the question of alternatives to free enterprise for another. The hard fact move leads to doublespeak when it treats a present social arrangement as iron law, and so rules out choices that might not be good for the advertiser. Watch for law-like statements in present tense (like the invented one above), which foreclose discussion of the system itself and its assumptions. And watch for coercive uses of words and phrases like 'necessary,' 'only possible,' 'required,' 'essential to economic health,' and 'inevitable unless.'

9   *There's nobody here but us chickens.* Watch for formulations like 'the people will decide,' or 'we will all be ruled by free choices in a free market.' They imply that no one has more power than anyone else in determining the future—or even that big corporations have *less* power than ordinary people. Check these formulas against the facts of how decisions will be made on a particular issue. And remember to ask who paid for the ad, and whether ordinary people have any matching power.

308

10   *What can one man do?* To stop pollution, buy brand X gasoline. To handle the trash menace, dispose of your bottle properly. To deal with the energy shortage, turn your lights off when not using them. Some of this may be good advice (but not *all* of it), but none of the individual actions proposed will make a dent in the 'problem.' Watch for ads that urge independent acts of consumers, and stay silent about broader 'solutions,' like new laws, regulations of industry, etc.

11   *Corporations equal people.* A blend of 9 and 10. 'We're all in this together—*you* conserve heat in your house, and *we'll* build more nuclear plants.' Beware of hearty invitations to collaborate in making America better; ask whether the proposed 'part-nership' is one of equals, or one of chickens and foxes.

12   *Blurred ownership.* 'The people's coal.' 'Your power company.' 'American's resources.' 'Our industrial system.' And so on. Ask who, in cold financial and legal facts, owns the thing in question, who has power to determine its future, and why the possessive noun or pronoun is so generalized.

Kinds of ads, and how they sell ideas (not just products)

Probably all advertisements contain or imply some ideology. They are trying to get the audience to do something or believe something that's in the advertiser's interest. One natural meeting ground of audience and advertiser is broad ideas or images of the good life, the good society. As lots of people have said, advertising as a whole conveys some important ideological messages:[1] commodities can solve just about all human problems; business is meeting 'our' deepest needs; the American way of life is OK basically as it is; there are always problems, but they will be solved by business and consumers in league with each other—and solving problems is progress.

But these and other points of ideology appear very differently in different kinds of ads, and only some involve doublespeak. It helps, then, to have a classification of ads for this particular purpose. Here's a handy one, moving from specific to general rhet-orical aims.

1   Ads that make a factual claim about a product to persuade you to buy it. (Our razor blade lasts longer; our car gets the best mileage.) Subject to empirical test; no ideology in the foreground; doublespeak at a minimum.

2   Ads that sell a product by vague and untestable claims about it ('gets teeth whiter'), or by associating it with some reliable image—the happy family, youth, sex-ual success, etc. There's a good deal of deception in such ads through implied associations (cigarettes don't make you young, fresh, and healthy, in spite of what the picture suggests). Doublespeak here resides mainly in vagueness, evasion, empty lang-uage, rather than in ideology.

3   Ads that invoke current social concerns and the anxieties they stir, in order to

increase the motivation for buying the product. (Your house will be cold this winter; buy sweaters.) Ideology in the background, except for the usual implication that social problems can be solved by individuals, for themselves.

4   Ads that refer to the same current problems, but say that the consumer can help solve them—not just for the individual, but for all of us—by making the right purchase. (You can help the energy crisis by buying our gas.) Much ideology here, and often much doublespeak.

5   Ads that sell a company or an industry, not a product, by showing how its activities benefit all. These ads are a goldmine of ideological doublespeak.

6   'Responsible' ads that state the manufacturer's concern over the social consequences of the use of a product. The product, say the ads, is beneficial to all, *if* used properly. Where does responsibility lie for abuse, bad side effects, and the like? In the area of this question there is much room for doublespeak.

7   Explicitly ideological ads that defend high profits, argue against government regulation, etc.

8   And most general, what we might call 'philosophy of life ads.' They seem not to be about a product, a company, an industry, *or* the American way of life, but to offer disinterested wisdom. Great ideas (of Plato, Shakespeare, etc.) presented as a public service by the X Company. Ideology is deeply buried here.

A unit on ideological doublespeak in ads should concentrate on types 4–6. But we'll at least glance at the doublespeak potential in each category.

1   Watch for the general motto that sometimes accompanies class 1 ads. An insurance company ad describes the economic difficulties a small business can get in when its owner is disabled; then it offers a policy to prevent such difficulties. All factual. The motto at the end is 'We add assurance to life in an unsure world.' Here is ideological doublespeak of the 'hard fact' type. *Is* the world simply 'unsure'? Well, yes, continued life and good health are always unsure. But no, the world is not inherently unsure in the other sense required—economic consequences of accidents could be absorbed by the entire society, not left to individuals. The ad makes a social choice seem an inevitability. Why? Insurance companies, of course, have an interest in keeping the world economically unsure, and in convincing us that it *is* intrinsically unsure. Therefore, the role of insurance companies is in the interest of all of us.

2   A Colgate ad explains that Billie Jean King wins friends as easily as tennis tournaments. 'Liking people comes naturally to Billie Jean. Which is one reason she's a long-time user of Colgate.' The ideology is in the casual connective, which not only sells Colgate as a friend-maker (garden-variety doublespeak), but also reinforces the idea that social anxieties, personal failures, loneliness, can all be resolved by buying something. Ideology in class 2 ads is mainly on this level of abstraction. Get students to ask what assumptions these ads make about the kind of society we have, and how to face problems within it.

310

3   Closer to ideology here. Libbey-Owens-Ford titles an ad 'INSULATION YOU CAN SEE THROUGH, FROM LOF,' and goes on to cite rising energy costs as a reason for buying two special kinds of glass, to keep your view and still 'save . . . energy dollars.' Here the garden-variety doublespeak is in the implication that glass insulates better than other materials. 'Save energy dollars' compared to what? Not to insulated walls, but only to ordinary, cheaper glass. Glass is not 'insulation.' But the ideological doublespeak lies in the casual implication: energy crisis—buy glass. No real sacrifice is necessary, no change in our pattern of life or the economic system, not even the loss of your picture window. The crisis is presented as a problem of individuals, not a social problem. LOF asks us to rely on patchwork technological remedies, and on the market. This approach rules out, of course, the possibility of legally limiting the amount of glass in the new buildings, and so forecloses the possibility of a conflict between LOF's interests and ours. In class 3 ads, get students to look at the casual connections between the social crisis and the individual act recommended: what possibilities for action are omitted? Why?

4   What class 3 ads imply, class 4 ads more directly state.
What can one man do, my friend,
What can one man do,
To fight pollution in the air,
That's closin' in from everywhere?

There's a lead-free gasoline, my friend,
And its name is Amoco,®
Two lead free brands, one for every car,
The one sure way to go.

Lots of doublespeak here.

a   Abstracting. Not 'fight polluters,' but 'fight pollution.' Not 'that's coming from combustion of gas,' but 'that's closin' in from everywhere.'

b   Presenting individual purchases as a general problem-solver. The pertinent chemistry is such that if *you* switch to an unleaded or low lead gas, then either you increase hydrocarbon pollution by your own car or you leave *me* to purchase gasoline with *more* lead in it. Always ask of class 4 ads: What would be the result if everyone did what the ad recommends? And: *Could* everyone do what it recommends? Generally, class 4 ads imply the impossible.

c   The 'one person' ploy is common in free enterprise ideology. The point is to defer collective action in favor of individual action. Needless to say, one person can't do anything to fight pollution so long as he or she is restricted to choosing among brands, disposing of containers 'properly,' and the like. But encouraging this approach leads a consumer to (1) feel personally responsible, (2) overlook the advertiser's responsibility, and (3) accept the present means of making social decisions. 'One person' is led to believe he or she has power that in fact could only be possessed in league with many men and women.

5   Here's an example of a sort common today:

311

What's my electric company doing about the energy problem?

America's fuel shortage problem is so big that it seems difficult for one individual or even one industry to influence it very much. And there are no quick and easy solutions to the fuel shortage facing the nation.

But almost every individual and every company uses energy so we all should try to help by using fuels wisely.

The electric light and power industry is helping because we have some degree of flexibility in the way we can design our plants to use various fuels now and in the future.

Using fuels wisely

At the present time, about half of America's electric power is generated with coal. Natural gas and oil account for a little more than a third.

As we all know, supplies of oil are limited.

So, where changes are feasible, electric companies are burning coal in some of their power plants that once depended on oil. And the expanded utilization of coal, America's most plentiful fuel, is an important goal in our immediate and long term generating plans. Along with the increased use of nuclear energy.

Searching for new ways

The electric companies, in partnership with the federal government and others, are involved in research and development in a wide variety of new methods of power generation: developing nuclear 'Breeder' reactors that would create more useable nuclear fuel than they consume; experimenting with fusion which would create energy by combining the atoms available in ordinary water; producing electricity directly from the sun's energy; using the earth's heat, deep underground, as a generating source.

Research has been going on in these areas for a number of years, and it will continue long into the future, for there are no instant answers.

But the important thing is, we in the electric companies are doing everything we can today to find ways to ease the energy problem. We are also doing everything we can for tomorrow.

Outlook for the future

The time is past when any of us can use energy carelessly. But if everyone uses energy wisely in his home, or at his place of business, or when he travels, he will be helping with the nation's fuel shortage problem.

And if we in the electric industry can use those fuels to generate power that best conserve the nation's reserves, America will have gone a long way toward assuring an ample supply of energy for generations to come.

312

The people at your Investor-Owned Electric Light and Power Companies.

Places to look for doublespeak:

a   The generalization of a problem: 'America's fuel shortage problem.' The power companies' problem is, in part, to stay in command of this economic area, to keep Nader-like consumers from interfering with free choice and profits. The consumer's problem is, in part, to get the power companies to be more far-sighted and public spirited in the future than in the past. (The wolf and the sheep again.)

b   Equating corporations and individuals through the familiar doublespeak 'we': 'we all should try to help by using fuels wisely.' But 'we' consumers can only choose among fuels and technologies made available to us by the power companies and others. The we're-all-in-this-together approach is particularly misleading here.

c   Excluding the layman: See the paragraph about new ways to generate power. Only big industry in 'partnership' (suppression of conflict, again) with government could do research on this scale. No effort made here to explain to consumers what the experts are doing, or what consequences to expect from one or another of these technologies. In what sense is it, then, 'my' electric company?

d   The technological fix. This is so universal in American society that it passes almost unnoticed. We read that the power companies are 'doing everything we can today to find ways to ease the energy problem.' What is that 'everything'? Trying out technical solutions. Other possibilities occur: helping to reduce our dependence on power (who encourages us to buy all those appliances in the first place?); submitting energy decisions to voters; changing the companies from 'investor-owned' to public. Ads like this treat technology as the only way out, and do not explain why the technological fixes of the future will be better than those of the past, which created the 'problem' in the first place. And they assume that technology is, simply, good. Look in such ads for the presentation of social and political problems as purely technological. This tactic makes it seem that our interest is in leaving the problem to the companies, since they are the ones with the technical expertise.

e   America as abstraction. 'America's electric power,' 'America's most plentiful fuel,' 'America will have gone a long way toward assuring an ample supply of energy for years to come.' Who, specifically, uses the power? produces it? owns the fuel? will make the crucial decisions about energy in the future? Confront these aggregates with questions that make the concrete situation visible and like as not you'll uncover doublespeak.

6   An ad of the Distilled Spirits Council of the United States:

What's the best way to enjoy a drink? Slowly.

A social drink with good food and good friends. That's a traditional custom observed by most people in this country.

Like any other custom, of course, it can be abused.

Hastily downing glass after glass, for example. Or drinking with no food and no company. That's hardly the way to enjoy the products we make so carefully.

Most Americans, fortunately, make responsible decisions in this respect—drinking
and dining leisurely in a relaxed setting.
And with ordinary common sense, that's what liquor is—a pleasure, not a problem.
If you choose to drink, drink responsibly.

This ad trades mainly on 'There's nobody here but us chickens' and 'What can one
man do?' Liquor is traditional, a 'custom,' etc. But 'it can be abused.' So you individual drinkers should moderate your drinking, and that will make liquor 'a pleasure,
not a problem,' i.e., no social control is needed; the problem is some people who
abuse alcohol, and it can be solved by continuing the free economic relationship
between drinkers and distillers—if the drinkers will just be reasonable. (As usual in
this type of ideology, the people are held responsible for all problems.)

'If you choose to drink, drink responsibly.' Is the word 'choose' appropriate, for
many drinkers? Is this really an area where the concept of free individual choice
applies? The *New York Times* on July 11, 1974 carried a front page story headlined
'Alcoholism Cost to Nation Put at $25-Billion a Year.' Among other things, the
study suggested that 'alcohol control laws and regulations are grossly ineffective in
dealing with alcohol problems.' But it's in the interest of the distillers to conceive of
these as basically individual problems, hence matters of free choice, hence not amenable to social control.

7   In these ads, the argument is openly ideological. A United States Steel ad (written by the Chairman of the General Electric Company) explains that 'we' need to
have higher profits between now and 1985 so that 'we' can meet the 'capital needs of
this country,' so that 'we' won't have to live with worsening shortages. Note shifts in
reference. The homogenized 'we' are also asked 'to improve our personal productivity on the job. . . . This will not only help industry earn more and invest more in
America's future, it will also help each of us earn more as we produce more.' The
'personal productivity' of assembly line workers may be in the interest of the Board,
but is the Board's productivity so certainly in the interest of workers? It's a debatable
question, side-stepped by 'we' and 'our.' The same ad also relies heavily on the hard
facts approach: In the next twelve years our capital *needs* will come to $3 trillion.
Most of it 'will *have to* be raised and invested by the business community.' And the
iron law approach: 'The capital available to business comes *only* from profits. . . . The
higher the profits, the higher the levels of investment that are *possible.*' (Italics added.)
Ask students to imagine alternatives to these hard facts and iron laws, and consider
why the language might be excluding them. And in such ads, watch also for leave-it-
to-the-experts, for the portrayal of conflicts as 'problems,' and for blurred
ownership. (On this last: an ad of the American Electric Power system asks for the
Government to 'release' the resources of coal it 'owns' in the West. 'This coal is the
people's coal and the people need it.' Query: Is the government the people? Are the
power companies the people? Just who is to release whose coal and to whom?)

8   The Atlantic Richfield Company has a series of philosophy of life ads under way
at this writing. One begins with 'the real': 'People become obsolete before their time
in our assembly line culture,' talks about how 'we' have made the aged into a problem, offers examples of achievements by old people (Churchill, Sandburg, Grandma

314

Moses, Frank Lloyd Wright, Schweitzer), and ends with 'the ideal': 'The maturity and social flexibility to recognize that for some, life reserves its greatest rewards until later.' In such ads doublespeak is muted or absent. But they bear examination for the usual marks of ideology. How did 'our assembly line culture' get that way? Whose interest is served by automatic retirement? By making it hard for older people to find work? What do 'maturity and social flexibility' boil down to? What attitude do such ads encourage toward social 'problems'? Toward the status quo? And, of course, why is Atlantic Richfield spending money in this way?

NOTE

1. See, for instance, Marcuse's *One Dimensional Man*, or Ronald Gross's short essay, 'The Language of Advertising,' in *Language in America*, ed. Neil Postman, Charles Weingartner, and Terence P. Moran.

Jean Seaton (1947–)

Jean Seaton was educated at the universities of Leicester and Essex and is currently Director of Media Studies at the University of the South Bank in London. With James Curren she is the author of *Power Without Responsibility: The Press and Broadcasting in Britain* (first published in 1985 and now in its sixth edition), a highly influential study which applies industrial, institutional, political, historical, and ideological analyses to its subject. Seaton's interests are consistently with the history, politics and policies of broadcasting, and her ideas are theoretically informed and empirically grounded. Her work, which is directly concerned with British policies in broadcasting, unwittingly points to a subtle difference between Britain and America, where academic work can intervene in the socio-political arena—or, at least, can still imagine such intervention even if the Oxford-to-London train is no longer crammed with academics on their way to 'think-tanks'.

In 'The Media and the Constitution', Seaton considers whether or not a written constitution concerning the media would protect or threaten the rights of the media, its viewers, and readers. The consequences are debatable says Seaton and she addresses the positive as well as negative effects of the constitutionalists' case. Seaton also acknowledges the various and changing functions of the media. However, after reviewing the effects of the 'enshrined freedom of speech in the American constitution', she asserts that, for Britain, constitutional reform will not guarantee a 'better, more responsible, more inquiring, more honest political media'.

Seaton points to the long period of Thatcher and her one-party domination with its many 'attempts to circumvent press freedom' as two factors which 'contributed to a climate of cynicism in which politicians have ceased to expect freedom of speech to be respected'. Seaton argues that 'the real difficulty with the freedom of speech clause is not that it is wrong, or even that it is inadequate', but that 'it concentrates on a small corner while ignoring the whole crumbling edifice.' She points out the extent to which economic factors influence

316

the media, which ultimately prioritize the quality of production over the content of the message.
K.M.S.

The media and the constitution

Would a written constitution together with a Bill of Rights improve the British mass media, make them worse, or leave them little affected? Like many aspects of our political system, the principles underlying political communication have scant recognition in law. The biggest obstacle to enshrining them in a constitutional clause is deciding what they are.

It might be said that the basic functions of political discussion in newspapers and broadcasting are to inform and to express: to tell the public what it needs to know, to reflect public demand, and to organize, anticipate, and even at times to lead public opinion. It might also be said that the objective of journalism should not merely be to relay the facts, but to act as a channel between expert and lay person, to translate specialist knowledge into accessible common sense.

It is obvious to everybody, however, that the framing of such principles has little to do with the actual experience of most editors, producers, journalists, readers and viewers. The real function of all but a tiny segment of mass communication is entertainment. A raised legal or constitutional status for the press and broadcasting might successfully erect ramparts around the service provided to a small minority, while doing nothing to protect or improve the quality of the media diet of the overwhelming majority.

Clearly there is a persuasive case for the constitutional entrenchment of media rights, and it has been greatly strengthened over recent years. The long period of one-party domination in Britain encouraged a level of government interference which would not previously have been tolerated. The Thatcher era was scarred with politically-inspired attempts to circumvent press freedom: the Northern Ireland broadcasting ban; the injunctions against the publication of Spycatcher by the retired intelligence officer Peter Wright; the prosecution of Clive Ponting and Sarah Tisdale for passing information which in other, more liberal systems would have been freely available; and a series of interventions against the makers and producers of television documentaries (of which *Real Lives* and *Death on the Rock* were the most notable examples). These have all contributed to a climate of cynicism in which politicians have ceased to expect freedom of expression to be respected. If an informal system has broken down, it is certainly arguable that a formal system, with precise and enforceable rules, is required to take its place. A freedom of speech clause might render illegal many of the infringements of press and broadcasting freedoms against which there is at present no redress. It would have the additional advantage of reducing the gagging effect of Britain's quixotic libel laws, in so far as they affect matters of legitimate public interest.

317

Such a clause might be invoked to prevent the recent, disgraceful practice of packing the Board of Governors of the BBC with political stooges and using them not to defend the Corporation's independence but to secure its compliance. It might prevent the effective waiving of monopoly legislation to permit the takeover of newspapers by pro-government proprietors. But above all—and this is the crux of the constitutionalists' case—the existence of a carefully defined right to freedom of speech and expression would provide a benchmark against which all controversies involving alleged infringements could be judged. Thus the duties and obligations of the media could reasonably be raised in a discussion of the future of the level of BBC licence fees. At the same time, an agreed clause might be expected to become the starting point of all debate about the media and (so some would contend) the continuing guarantor of a fundamental liberty.

Many of these arguments stem from a disturbing sense of traditional freedoms slipping away. Such a feeling underlines the need for reform. It does not, however, ensure that reform will work. The real difficulty with a freedom of speech clause is not that it is wrong, or even that it is inadequate. It is rather that it concentrates on a small corner, while ignoring the whole crumbling edifice; and in so doing, fails even to recognise the possible side-effects.

There are a number of points. First, challenging governmental actions in the courts on constitutional grounds is almost always easier for the rich than for the poor. This has certainly been the experience of both the United States and Germany, where the 'right to be heard' is much more frequently invoked by individuals and interests with the resources to fight costly court actions than by those that lack them. In the USA, corporations have successfully begun to claim the speech rights of individuals through appeals to the constitution in the courts. Second, the existence of a constitutional provision does not in itself ensure that it will be respected. Where it runs against political or corporate interest, these interests will do all in their power to evade it.

Third, enshrined constitutional clauses are necessarily short, while the range of possible threats to the media freedom is infinite. Even the best drafted clause cannot cover every situation and—as the history of constitutions everywhere shows—is liable to a wide range of possible interpretations, varying over time, including many which the constitution makers may never have envisaged. When the founding fathers enshrined freedom of speech in the American constitution, it is unlikely that they imagined that it would be taken to mean that any upper limit on election spending by candidates or their backers is unconstitutional—which is how the US courts have recently interpreted the clause. The borderline between 'unlimited freedom of speech' and 'unlimited freedom to pay for advertising and propaganda' is not one that is easy for even the best constitutional lawyers to define.

Beneath the pressure for a free speech clause lies a presumption that the problem in political communication is one of censorship and muzzling, as in the fashionable 'right to reply' which was taken up by media unions in the 1970s and 1980s. According to this view, any group or organised interest suffering a criticism which it deemed unfair should be able to reply in kind and insist that its riposte is given equal prominence to the original attack. This could be invoked to give less powerful or less affluent groups a voice. Such a right, however, does nothing to ensure that anyone will listen. For in a highly competitive market place of media entertainment, sensation and debate, only the most powerful and innovatory messages of protest will stand any chance. If the issue is how to produce a better, more responsible, more inquiring, more honest political media, the answer is not to be found in constitutional reform but in the nature of the industries and how they are managed.

The pressures against responsible and challenging political journalism have little to do with formal rules and are unlikely to be affected by any change in them. A constitutional clause might, perhaps, inhibit the grosser forms of political bias and might even increase the opportunities for contrary opinions to be expressed. But it would not make bad good, or render the acceptable shocking, or make the complacent challenging or turn the banal into something imaginative. It would not remove the intense commercial pressure on newspapers and broadcasting companies to go for the cheapest, the least problematic, and choose material that is likely to reach the biggest audiences of the right social profiles. To take one obvious, though little discussed example: children are big consumers of television, they are the most impressionable section of the audience, and deserve the best, in terms of the social, political, creative and broadly educational quality of what they are served up. Yet without the restrictions posed by public service regulation the resources devoted to children's broadcasting are proportionately tiny because, though numerous, children are not big enough spenders to generate the advertising revenue which makes it possible to raise standards and make better programmes.

It is not the state of the law, but the commercial environment, which provides the American public with a wide range of low budget, low quality television channels whose political content, such as it is, is blander, less controversial and less directed at contemporary problems that do not have an instant entertainment value, than in Britain. It is not the law in Italy—where there is both a written constitution and a radically de-regulated television service—that provides the hapless Italian public with a remorseless diet of packaged American news reports, old American movies, American and Japanese cartoons, and low-cost chat shows; that has rendered careful documentary making, or serious television drama, not so much an endangered as an extinct species. In Britain the Conservative government's most powerful weapon against broadcasters has not been political censorship but the determined assault on the financial basis of public service broadcasting.

In some circumstances the state is undoubtedly the enemy of media freedom but it can also be a friend, one whose role it would be foolish to exclude. State interference is one thing, state regulation and state patronage another. Who would not agree that the involvement of the state in broadcasting over a long period in Britain has been beneficial, in terms of the variety, quality and political 'balance' of what the public has been provided and that the nation has been better served than would have been the case if the media had simply been left to the ravages of the ungoverned market? So successful has been the history of state involvement in broadcasting that, at a time when all the pressures favour disengagement, a powerful argument can be made for applying lessons learnt from radio and television to newspapers and introducing similar forms of regulation to curb the wilder abuses of the popular press.

Thus the emphasis of the constitutional reformers may be in the wrong place. It should be less concerned with guaranteeing opportunities to publish, and more with

319

stimulating creativity and innovation; less concerned with formal rights and more about the structures which encourage good quality. The preoccupation with real or supposed state censorship may be misplaced. The recent history of countries where censorship has been absolute for generations does not suggest that people can easily be brainwashed. The citizens of democratic countries are far less handicapped by the comparatively minor restrictions to freedom of speech that exist than by the suffocating pressure of triviality and blandness which rampant economic forces are permitted to produce, often in the name of political freedom.

In short, as far as the media are concerned, two cheers for a written constitution with a freedom of speech clause. To enshrine such a right that is widely seen as important would at least encourage people to cherish what they have taken for granted. But it will only begin to solve the problems of inadequate and deteriorating political communication. 'Where there is much desire to learn,' wrote Milton, 'there will be of necessity much desire to argue, much writing and many opinions.' Constitutional reform may provide formal protection for the freedom of the media but there is no substitute for a difficult, complex and bold policy initiative to improve quality.

Laura Mulvey (1941–)

Laura Mulvey was one of the first feminists to bring psychoanalysis as a critical tool to film studies. Her ground-breaking essay, 'Visual Pleasure and Narrative Cinema' (written in 1975), continues to be one of the most widely cited works and has been tremendously influential in feminist theory as well. Aside from articles in film and art journals, Mulvey has published a selection of her essays in *Visual and Other Pleasures* (1989) and contributed to *Goddard: Images, Sounds, Politics* (1980). She has also worked with Peter Wollen as an experimental film-maker.

In this essay Mulvey shows how Hollywood uses women to generate 'visual plea-sure' for the consumption of male viewers. Male protagonists, whose lives and actions the story follows, essentially 'drive' traditional Hollywood film narrative. Her thesis, that mainstream film uses women erotically to undermine the autonomy of male characters, reveals the adversarial relationship between women and narrative. However, Mulvey shows that tension between erotic and narrative registers on the screen is reinforced by the cinematic experience itself: the male viewer's pleasure in looking at women 'scopophilically' re-enacts a primary psychosexual drama (between mother and son) that triggers feelings of both desire for and fear of women. This conflict has deep roots in Freudian and Lacanian formulations of childhood fantasies and desires in the unconscious. For Mulvey, cinema resolves the conflict between scopophilia and the desire for differentiation through a 'beautifully complementary fantasy world'. Through readings of Hitchcock and Sternberg films, she convinc-ingly shows how this drama is replayed on the screen: as objects of the male characters' and male viewers' gaze, women disrupt narrative action (through sexual tension) and must eventually be overcome.
S.R.

Visual pleasure and narrative cinema*

I Introduction

(a) A political use of psychoanalysis

This paper intends to use psychoanalysis to discover where and how the fascination of film is reinforced by pre-existing patterns of fascination already at work within the individual subject and the social formations that have moulded him. It takes as its starting-point the way film reflects, reveals and even plays on the straight, socially established interpretation of sexual difference which controls images, erotic ways of looking and spectacle. It is helpful to understand what the cinema has been, how its magic has worked in the past, while attempting a theory and a practice which will challenge this cinema of the past. Psychoanalytic theory is thus appropriated here as a political weapon, demonstrating the way the unconscious of patriarchal society has structured film form.

The paradox of phallocentrism in all its manifestations is that it depends on the image of the castrated woman to give order and meaning to its world. An idea of woman stands as linchpin to the system: it is her lack that produces the phallus as a symbolic presence, it is her desire to make good the lack that the phallus signifies. Recent writing in *Screen* about psychoanalysis and the cinema has not sufficiently brought out the importance of the representation of the female form in a symbolic order in which, in the last resort, it speaks castration and nothing else. To summarise briefly: the function of woman in forming the patriarchal unconscious is twofold: she firstly symbolises the castration threat by her real lack of a penis and secondly thereby raises her child into the symbolic. Once this has been achieved, her meaning in the process is at an end. It does not last into the world of law and language except as a memory, which oscillates between memory of maternal plenitude and memory of lack. Both are posited on nature (or on anatomy in Freud's famous phrase). Woman's desire is subjugated to her image as bearer of the bleeding wound; she can exist only in relation to castration and cannot transcend it. She turns her child into the signifier of her own desire to possess a penis (the condition, she imagines, of entry into the symbolic). Either she must gracefully give way to the word, the name of the father and the law, or else struggle to keep her child down with her in the half-light of the imaginary. Woman then stands in patriarchal culture as a signifier for the male other, bound by a symbolic order in which man can live out his fantasies and obsessions through linguistic command by imposing them on the silent image of woman still tied to her place as bearer, not maker, of meaning.

There is an obvious interest in this analysis for feminists, a beauty in its exact rendering of the frustration experienced under the phallocentric order. It gets us nearer to the roots of our oppression, it brings closer an articulation of the problem, it faces

*Written in 1973 and published in 1975 in *Screen*.

us with the ultimate challenge: how to fight the unconscious structured like a language (formed critically at the moment of arrival of language) while still caught within the language of the patriarchy? There is no way in which we can produce an alternative out of the blue, but we can begin to make a break by examining patriarchy with the tools it provides, of which psychoanalysis is not the only but an important one. We are still separated by a great gap from important issues for the female unconscious which are scarcely relevant to phallocentric theory: the sexing of the female infant and her relationship to the symbolic, the sexually mature woman as non-mother, maternity outside the signification of the phallus, the vagina. But, at this point, psychoanalytic theory as it now stands can at least advance our understanding of the *status quo*, of the patriarchal order in which we are caught.

(b)   Destruction of pleasure as a radical weapon
As an advanced representation system, the cinema poses questions about the ways the unconscious (formed by the dominant order) structures ways of seeing and pleasure in looking. Cinema has changed over the last few decades. It is no longer the monolithic system based on large capital investments exemplified at its best by Hollywood in the 1930s, 1940s and 1950s. Technological advances (16mm and so on) have changed the economic conditions of cinematic production, which can now be artisanal as well as capitalist. Thus it has been possible for an alternative cinema to develop. However self-conscious and ironic Hollywood managed to be, it always restricted itself to a formal *mise en scène* reflecting the dominant ideological concept of the cinema. The alternative cinema provides a space for the birth of a cinema which is radical in both a political and an aesthetic sense and challenges the basic assumptions of the mainstream film. This is not to reject the latter moralistically, but to highlight the ways in which its formal preoccupations reflect the psychical obsessions of the society which produced it and, further, to stress that the alternative cinema must start specifically by reacting against these obsessions and assumptions. A politically and aesthetically avant-garde cinema is now possible, but it can still only exist as a counterpoint.

The magic of the Hollywood style at its best (and of all the cinema which fell within its sphere of influence) arose, not exclusively, but in one important aspect, from its skilled and satisfying manipulation of visual pleasure. Unchallenged, mainstream film coded the erotic into the language of the dominant patriarchal order. In the highly developed Hollywood cinema it was only through these codes that the alienated subject, torn in his imaginary memory by a sense of loss, by the terror of potential lack in fantasy, came near to finding a glimpse of satisfaction: through its formal beauty and its play on his own formative obsessions. This article will discuss the interweaving of that erotic pleasure in film, its meaning and, in particular, the central place of the image of woman. It is said that analysing pleasure, or beauty, destroys it. That is the intention of this article. The satisfaction and reinforcement of the ego that represent the high point of film history hitherto must be attacked. Not in favour of a reconstructed new pleasure, which cannot exist in the abstract, nor of intellectualised unpleasure, but to make way for a total negation of the ease and plenitude of the narrative fiction film. The alternative is the thrill that comes from leaving the past behind without simply rejecting it, transcending outworn or oppressive

323

forms, and daring to break with normal pleasurable expectations in order to conceive a new language of desire.

II Pleasure in looking/fascination with the human form

A The cinema offers a number of possible pleasures. One is scopophilia (pleasure in looking). There are circumstances in which looking itself is a source of pleasure, just as, in the reverse formation, there is pleasure in being looked at. Originally, in his *Three Essays on Sexuality*, Freud isolated scopophilia as one of the component instincts of sexuality which exist as drives quite independently of the erotogenic zones. At this point he associated scopophilia with taking other people as objects, subjecting them to a controlling and curious gaze. His particular examples centre on the voyeuristic activities of children, their desire to see and make sure of the private and forbidden (curiosity about other people's genital and bodily functions, about the presence or absence of the penis and, retrospectively, about the primal scene). In this analysis scopophilia is essentially active. (Later, in 'Instincts and Their Vicissitudes', Freud developed his theory of scopophilia further, attaching it initially to pre-genital auto-eroticism, after which, by analogy, the pleasure of the look is transferred to others. There is a close working here of the relationship between the active instinct and its further development in a narcissistic form.) Although the instinct is modified by other factors, in particular the constitution of the ego, it continues to exist as the erotic basis for pleasure in looking at another person as object. At the extreme, it can become fixated into a perversion, producing obsessive voyeurs and Peeping Toms whose only sexual satisfaction can come from watching, in an active controlling sense, an objectified other.

At first glance, the cinema would seem to be remote from the undercover world of the surreptitious observation of an unknowing and unwilling victim. What is seen on the screen is so manifestly shown. But the mass of mainstream film, and the conventions within which it has consciously evolved, portray a hermetically sealed world which unwinds magically, indifferent to the presence of the audience, producing for them a sense of separation and playing on their voyeuristic fantasy. Moreover the extreme contrast between the darkness in the auditorium (which also isolates the spectators from one another) and the brilliance of the shifting patterns of light and shade on the screen helps to promote the illusion of voyeuristic separation. Although the film is really being shown, is there to be seen, conditions of screening and narrative conventions give the spectator an illusion of looking in on a private world. Among other things, the position of the spectators in the cinema is blatantly one of repression of their exhibitionism and projection of the repressed desire onto the performer.

B The cinema satisfies a primordial wish for pleasurable looking, but it also goes further, developing scopophilia in its narcissistic aspect. The conventions of mainstream film focus attention on the human form. Scale, space, stories are all anthropomorphic. Here, curiosity and the wish to look intermingle with a fascination with likeness and recognition: the human face, the human body, the relationship between the human form and its surroundings, the visible presence of the person in the world. Jacques Lacan has described how the moment when a child recognises its own image in the mirror is crucial for the constitution of the ego. Several aspects of this analysis are relevant here. The mirror phase occurs at a time when children's physical ambitions outstrip their motor capacity, with the result that their recognition of themselves is joyous in that they imagine their mirror image to be more complete, more perfect than they experience in their own body. Recognition is thus overlaid with misrecognition: the image recognised is conceived as the reflected body of the self, but its misrecognition as superior projects this body outside itself as an ideal ego, the alienated subject which, re-introjected as an ego ideal, prepares the way for identification with others in the future. This mirror moment predates language for the child.

Important for this article is the fact that it is an image that constitutes the matrix of the imaginary, of recognition/misrecognition and identification, and hence of the first articulation of the I, of subjectivity. This is a moment when an older fascination with looking (at the mother's face, for an obvious example) collides with the initial inklings of self-awareness. Hence it is the birth of the long love affair/despair between image and self-image which has found such intensity of expression in film and such joyous recognition in the cinema audience. Quite apart from the extraneous similarities between screen and mirror (the framing of the human form in its surroundings, for instance), the cinema has structures of fascination strong enough to allow temporary loss of ego while simultaneously reinforcing it. The sense of forgetting the world as the ego has come to perceive it (I forgot who I am and where I was) is nostalgically reminiscent of that pre-subjective moment of image recognition. While at the same time, the cinema has distinguished itself in the production of ego ideals, through the star system for instance. Stars provide a focus or centre both to screen space and screen story where they act out a complex process of likeness and difference (the glamorous impersonates the ordinary).

C Sections A and B have set out two contradictory aspects of the pleasurable structures of looking in the conventional cinematic situation. The first, scopophilic, arises from pleasure in using another person as an object of sexual stimulation through sight. The second, developed through narcissism and the constitution of the ego, comes from identification with the image seen. Thus, in film terms, one implies a separation of the erotic identity of the subject from the object on the screen (active scopophilia), the other demands identification of the ego with the object on the screen through the spectator's fascination with and recognition of his like. The first is a function of the sexual instincts, the second of ego libido. This dichotomy was crucial for Freud. Although he saw the two as interacting and overlaying each other, the tension between instinctual drives and self-preservation polarises in terms of pleasure. But both are formative structures, mechanisms without intrinsic meaning. In themselves they have no signification, unless attached to an idealisation. Both pursue aims in indifference to

325

perceptual reality, and motivate eroticised phantasmagoria that affect the subject's perception of the world to make a mockery of empirical objectivity.

During its history, the cinema seems to have evolved a particular illusion of reality in which this contradiction between libido and ego has found a beautifully complementary fantasy world. In *reality* the fantasy world of the screen is subject to the law which produces it. Sexual instincts and identification processes have a meaning within the symbolic order which articulates desire. Desire, born with language, allows the possibility of transcending the instinctual and the imaginary, but its point of reference continually returns to the traumatic moment of its birth: the castration complex. Hence the look, pleasurable in form, can be threatening in content, and it is woman as representation/image that crystallises this paradox.

III   Woman as image, man as bearer of the look

A   In a world ordered by sexual imbalance, pleasure in looking has been split between active/male and passive/female. The determining male gaze projects its fantasy onto the female figure, which is styled accordingly. In their traditional exhibitionist role women are simultaneously looked at and displayed, with their appearance coded for strong visual and erotic impact so that they can be said to connote *to-be-looked-at-ness*. Woman displayed as sexual object is the *leitmotif* of erotic spectacle: from pin-ups to strip-tease, from Ziegfeld to Busby Berkeley, she holds the look, and plays to and signifies male desire. Mainstream film neatly combines spectacle and narrative. (Note, however, how in the musical song-and-dance numbers interrupt the flow of the diegesis.) The presence of woman is an indispensable element of spectacle in normal narrative film, yet her visual presence tends to work against the development of a story-line, to freeze the flow of action in moments of erotic contemplation. This alien presence then has to be integrated into cohesion with the narrative. As Budd Boetticher has put it:

> What counts is what the heroine provokes, or rather what she represents. She is the one, or rather the love or fear she inspires in the hero, or else the concern he feels for her, who makes him act the way he does. In herself the woman has not the slightest importance.

(A recent tendency in narrative film has been to dispense with this problem altogether; hence the development of what Molly Haskell has called the 'buddy movie', in which the active homosexual eroticism of the central male figures can carry the story without distraction.) Traditionally, the woman displayed has functioned on two levels: as erotic object for the characters within the screen story, and as erotic object for the spectator within the auditorium, with a shifting tension between the looks on either side of the screen. For instance, the device of the show-girl allows the two looks to be unified technically without any apparent break in the diegesis. A woman

performs within the narrative; the gaze of the spectator and that of the male characters in the film are neatly combined without breaking narrative verisimilitude. For a
moment the sexual impact of the performing woman takes the film into a no man's
land outside its own time and space. Thus Marilyn Monroe's first appearance in *The
River of No Return* and Lauren Bacall's songs in *To Have and Have Not*. Similarly,
conventional close-ups of legs (Dietrich, for instance) or a face (Garbo) integrate into
the narrative a different mode of eroticism. One part of a fragmented body destroys
the Renaissance space, the illusion of depth demanded by the narrative; it gives flat-
ness, the quality of a cut-out or icon, rather than verisimilitude, to the screen.

B An active/passive heterosexual division of labour has similarly controlled narrative structure. According to the principles of the ruling ideology and the psychical
structures that back it up, the male figure cannot bear the burden of sexual objectification. Man is reluctant to gaze at his exhibitionist like. Hence the split between
spectacle and narrative supports the man's role as the active one of advancing the
story, making things happen. The man controls the film fantasy and also emerges as
the representative of power in a further sense: as the bearer of the look of the spectator, transferring it behind the screen to neutralise the extra-diegetic tendencies
represented by woman as spectacle. This is made possible through the processes set
in motion by structuring the film around a main controlling figure with whom the
spectator can identify. As the spectator identifies with the main male protagonist, he
projects his look onto that of his like, his screen surrogate, so that the power of the
male protagonist as he controls events coincides with the active power of the erotic
look, both giving a satisfying sense of omnipotence. A male movie star's glamorous
characteristics are thus not those of the erotic object of the gaze, but those of the
more perfect, more complete, more powerful ideal ego conceived in the original
moment of recognition in front of the mirror. The character in the story can make
things happen and control events better than the subject/spectator, just as the image
in the mirror was more in control of motor co-ordination.

In contrast to woman as icon, the active male figure (the ego ideal of the identification process) demands a three-dimensional space corresponding to that of the mirror
recognition, in which the alienated subject internalised his own representation of his
imaginary existence. He is a figure in a landscape. Here the function of film is to
reproduce as accurately as possible the so-called natural conditions of human perception. Camera technology (as exemplified by deep focus in particular) and camera
movements (determined by the action of the protagonist), combined with invisible
editing (demanded by realism), all tend to blur the limits of screen space. The male
protagonist is free to command the stage, a stage of spatial illusion in which he articulates the look and creates the action. (There are films with a woman as main
protagonist, of course. To analyse this phenomenon seriously here would take me too
far afield. Pam Cook and Claire Johnston's study of *The Revolt of Mamie Stover* in
Phil Hardy (ed.), *Raoul Walsh* (Edinburgh, 1974), shows in a striking case how the
strength of this female protagonist is more apparent than real.)

C1 Sections III A and B have set out a tension between a mode of representation of
woman in film and conventions surrounding the diegesis. Each is associated with a

look: that of the spectator in direct scopophilic contact with the female form displayed for his enjoyment (connoting male fantasy) and that of the spectator fascinated with the image of his like set in an illusion of natural space, and through him gaining control and possession of the woman within the diegesis. (This tension and the shift from one pole to the other can structure a single text. Thus both in *Only Angels Have Wings* and in *To Have and Have Not*, the film opens with the woman as object of the combined gaze of spectator and all the male protagonists in the film. She is isolated, glamorous, on display, sexualised. But as the narrative progresses she falls in love with the main male protagonist and becomes his property, losing her outward glamorous characteristics, her generalised sexuality, her showgirl connotations; her eroticism is subjected to the male star alone. By means of identification with him, through participation in his power, the spectator can indirectly possess her too.)

But in psychoanalytic terms, the female figure poses a deeper problem. She also connotes something that the look continually circles around but disavows: her lack of a penis, implying a threat of castration and hence unpleasure. Ultimately, the meaning of woman is sexual difference, the visually ascertainable absence of the penis, the material evidence on which is based the castration complex essential for the organisation of entrance to the symbolic order and the law of the father. Thus the woman as icon, displayed for the gaze and enjoyment of men, the active controllers of the look, always threatens to evoke the anxiety it originally signified. The male unconscious has two avenues of escape from this castration anxiety: preoccupation with the re-enactment of the original trauma (investigating the woman, demystifying her mystery), counterbalanced by the devaluation, punishment or saving of the guilty object (an avenue typified by the concerns of the *film noir*); or else complete disavowal of castration by the substitution of a fetish object or turning the represented figure itself into a fetish so that it becomes reassuring rather than dangerous (hence overvaluation, the cult of the female star).

This second avenue, fetishistic scopophilia, builds up the physical beauty of the object, transforming it into something satisfying in itself. The first avenue, voyeurism, on the contrary, has associations with sadism: pleasure lies in ascertaining guilt (immediately associated with castration), asserting control and subjugating the guilty person through punishment or forgiveness. This sadistic side fits in well with narrative. Sadism demands a story, depends on making something happen, forcing a change in another person, a battle of will and strength, victory/defeat, all occurring in a linear time with a beginning and an end. Fetishistic scopophilia, on the other hand, can exist outside linear time as the erotic instinct is focused on the look alone. These contradictions and ambiguities can be illustrated more simply by using works by Hitchcock and Sternberg, both of whom take the look almost as the content or subject matter of many of their films. Hitchcock is the more complex, as he uses both mechanisms. Sternberg's work, on the other hand, provides many pure examples of fetishistic scopophilia.

C2 Sternberg once said he would welcome his films being projected upside-down so that story and character involvement would not interfere with the spectator's undiluted appreciation of the screen image. This statement is revealing but ingenuous:

ingenuous in that his films do demand that the figure of the woman (Dietrich, in the cycle of films with her, as the ultimate example) should be identifiable; but revealing in that it emphasises the fact that for him the pictorial space enclosed by the frame is paramount, rather than narrative or identification processes. While Hitchcock goes into the investigative side of voyeurism, Sternberg produces the ultimate fetish, taking it to the point where the powerful look of the male protagonist (characteristic of traditional narrative film) is broken in favour of the image in direct erotic rapport with the spectator. The beauty of the woman as object and the screen space coalesce; she is no longer the bearer of guilt but a perfect product, whose body, stylised and fragmented by close-ups, is the content of the film and the direct recipient of the spectator's look.

Sternberg plays down the illusion of screen depth; his screen tends to be one-dimensional, as light and shade, lace, steam, foliage, net, streamers and so on reduce the visual field. There is little or no mediation of the look through the eyes of the main male protagonist. On the contrary, shadowy presences like La Bessière in *Morocco* act as surrogates for the director, detached as they are from audience identification. Despite Sternberg's insistence that his stories are irrelevant, it is significant that they are concerned with situation, not suspense, and cyclical rather than linear time, while plot complications revolve around misunderstanding rather than conflict. The most important absence is that of the controlling male gaze within the screen scene. The high point of emotional drama in the most typical Dietrich films, her supreme moments of erotic meaning, take place in the absence of the man she loves in the fiction. There are other witnesses, other spectators watching her on the screen, their gaze is one with, not standing in for, that of the audience. At the end of *Morocco*, Tom Brown has already disappeared into the desert when Amy Jolly kicks off her gold sandals and walks after him. At the end of *Dishonoured*, Kranau is indifferent to the fate of Magda. In both cases, the erotic impact, sanctified by death, is displayed as a spectacle for the audience. The male hero misunderstands and, above all, does not see.

In Hitchcock, by contrast, the male hero does see precisely what the audience sees. However, although fascination with an image through scopophilic eroticism can be the subject of the film, it is the role of the hero to portray the contradictions and tensions experienced by the spectator. In *Vertigo* in particular, but also in *Marnie* and *Rear Window*, the look is central to the plot, oscillating between voyeurism and fetishistic fascination. Hitchcock has never concealed his interest in voyeurism, cinematic and non-cinematic. His heroes are exemplary of the symbolic order and the law—a policeman (*Vertigo*), a dominant male possessing money and power (*Marnie*)—but their erotic drives lead them into compromised situations. The power to subject another person to the will sadistically or to the gaze voyeuristically is turned onto the woman as the object of both. Power is backed by a certainty of legal right and the established guilt of the woman (evoking castration, psychoanalytically speaking). True perversion is barely concealed under a shallow mask of ideological correctness—the man is on the right side of the law, the woman on the wrong. Hitchcock's skilful use of identification processes and liberal use of subjective camera from the point of view of the male protagonist draw the spectators deeply into his position, making them share his uneasy gaze. The spectator is absorbed into a voyeuristic situation within the screen scene and diegesis, which parodies his own in the cinema.

In an analysis of *Rear Window*, Douchet takes the film as a metaphor for the cinema. Jeffries is the audience, the events in the apartment block opposite correspond to the screen. As he watches, an erotic dimension is added to his look, a central image to the drama. His girlfriend Lisa had been of little sexual interest to him, more or less a drag, so long as she remained on the spectator side. When she crosses the barrier between his room and the block opposite, their relationship is reborn erotically. He does not merely watch her through his lens, as a distant meaningful image, he also sees her as a guilty intruder exposed by a dangerous man threatening her with punishment, and thus finally giving him the opportunity to save her. Lisa's exhibitionism has already been established by her obsessive interest in dress and style, in being a passive image of visual perfection; Jeffries's voyeurism and activity have also been established through his work as a photo-journalist, a maker of stories and captor of images. However, his enforced inactivity, binding him to his seat as a spectator, puts him squarely in the fantasy position of the cinema audience.

In *Vertigo*, subjective camera predominates. Apart from one flashback from Judy's point of view, the narrative is woven around what Scottie sees or fails to see. The audience follows the growth of his erotic obsession and subsequent despair precisely from his point of view. Scottie's voyeurism is blatant: he falls in love with a woman he follows and spies on without speaking to. Its sadistic side is equally blatant: he has chosen (and freely chosen, for he had been a successful lawyer) to be a policeman, with all the attendant possibilities of pursuit and investigation. As a result, he follows, watches and falls in love with a perfect image of female beauty and mystery. Once he actually confronts her, his erotic drive is to break her down and force her *to tell* by persistent cross-questioning.

In the second part of the film, he re-enacts his obsessive involvement with the image he loved to watch secretly. He reconstructs Judy as Madeleine, forces her to conform in every detail to the actual physical appearance of his fetish. Her exhibitionism, her masochism, make her an ideal passive counterpart to Scottie's active sadistic voyeurism. She knows her part is to perform, and only by playing it through and then replaying it can she keep Scottie's erotic interest. But in the repetition he does break her down and succeeds in exposing her guilt. His curiosity wins through; she is punished.

Thus, in *Vertigo*, erotic involvement with the look boomerangs: the spectator's own fascination is revealed as illicit voyeurism as the narrative content enacts the processes and pleasures that he is himself exercising and enjoying. The Hitchcock hero here is firmly placed within the symbolic order, in narrative terms. He has all the attributes of the patriarchal superego. Hence the spectator, lulled into a false sense of security by the apparent legality of his surrogate, sees through his look and finds himself exposed as complicit, caught in the moral ambiguity of looking. Far from being simply an aside on the perversion of the police, *Vertigo* focuses on the implications of the active/looking, passive/looked-at split in terms of sexual difference and the power of the male symbolic encapsulated in the hero. Marnie, too, performs for Mark Rutland's gaze and masquerades as the perfect to-be-looked-at image. He, too, is on the side of the law until, drawn in by obsession with her guilt, her secret, he longs to see her in the act of committing a crime, make her confess and thus save her. So he, too, becomes complicit as he acts out the implications of his power. He controls money and words; he can have his cake and eat it.

IV Summary

The psychoanalytic background that has been discussed in this article is relevant to the pleasure and unpleasure offered by traditional narrative film. The scopophilic instinct (pleasure in looking at another person as an erotic object) and, in contradistinction, ego libido (forming identification processes) act as formations, mechanisms, which mould this cinema's formal attributes. The actual image of woman as (passive) raw material for the (active) gaze of man takes the argument a step further into the content and structure of representation, adding a further layer of ideological significance demanded by the patriarchal order in its favourite cinematic form— illusionistic narrative film. The argument must return again to the psychoanalytic background: women in representation can signify castration, and active voyeuristic or fetishistic mechanisms to circumvent this threat. Although none of these interacting layers is intrinsic to film, it is only in the film form that they can reach a perfect and beautiful contradiction, thanks to the possibility in the cinema of shifting the emphasis of the look. The place of the look defines cinema, the possibility of varying it and exposing it. This is what makes cinema quite different in its voyeuristic potential from, say, strip-tease, theatre, shows and so on. Going far beyond highlighting a woman's to-be-looked-at-ness, cinema builds the way she is to be looked at into the spectacle itself. Playing on the tension between film as controlling the dimension of time (editing, narrative) and film as controlling the dimension of space (changes in distance, editing), cinematic codes create a gaze, a world and an object, thereby producing an illusion cut to the measure of desire. It is these cinematic codes and their relationship to formative external structures that must be broken down before mainstream film and the pleasure it provides can be challenged.

To begin with (as an ending), the voyeuristic-scopophilic look that is a crucial part of traditional filmic pleasure can itself be broken down. There are three different looks associated with cinema: that of the camera as it records the pro-filmic event, that of the audience as it watches the final product, and that of the characters at each other within the screen illusion. The conventions of narrative film deny the first two and subordinate them to the third, the conscious aim being always to eliminate intrusive camera presence and prevent a distancing awareness in the audience. Without these two absences (the material existence of the recording process, the critical reading of the spectator), fictional drama cannot achieve reality, obviousness and truth. Nevertheless, as this article has argued, the structure of looking in narrative fiction film contains a contradiction in its own premises: the female image as a castration threat constantly endangers the unity of the diegesis and bursts through the world of illusion as an intrusive, static, one-dimensional fetish. Thus the two looks materially present in time and space are obsessively subordinated to the neurotic needs of the male ego. The camera becomes the mechanism for producing an illusion of Renaissance space, flowing movements compatible with the human eye, an ideology of representation that revolves around the perception of the subject; the camera's look is disavowed in order to create a convincing world in which the spectator's surrogate can perform with verisimilitude. Simultaneously, the look of the audience is denied an intrinsic force: as soon as fetishistic representation of the female image threatens to break the spell of illusion, and the erotic image on the screen appears directly (without mediation) to the spectator, the fact of fetishisation, concealing as it does castration fear, freezes the look, fixates the spectator and prevents him from achieving any distance from the image in front of him.

This complex interaction of looks is specific to film. The first blow against the monolithic accumulation of traditional film conventions (already undertaken by radical film-makers) is to free the look of the camera into its materiality in time and space and the look of the audience into dialectics and passionate detachment. There is no doubt that this destroys the satisfaction, pleasure and privilege of the 'invisible guest', and highlights the way film has depended on voyeuristic active/passive mechanisms. Women, whose image has continually been stolen and used for this end, cannot view the decline of the traditional film form with anything much more than sentimental regret.

Janice Radway (1949–)

Janice Radway, a professor in the programme in literature at Duke University, has done extensive research on communications, the history of women, literacy, and popular fiction in the United States. Her most recent work focuses on the Book-of-the Month Club and its impact on American reading and culture. Radway is the author of *Reading the Romance: Women, Patriarchy, and Popular Literature* (1984), and numerous journal articles and book chapters. She is the co-editor, together with Lawrence Grossberg, of the journal *Cultural Studies*.

The essay below, 'Interpretive Communities and Variable Literacies: The Function of Romance Reading', was first published in *Daedalus: Journal of the American Academy of Arts and Sciences* (1974). In it Radway offers a brief explanation of some important contemporary theoretical camps, including 'the *rezeptionästhetik* of the Constance school, the structuralism of Roland Barthes, the semiotics of Umberto Eco and Jonathan Culler, the "interactionist" work of Louise Rosenblatt and Stanley Fish, and the subjectivist arguments of David Bleich and Norman Holland'. Accepting some basic tenets of reader-response or reception theory, Radway presents the results of a research project which analysed a group of women who purchase romance novels from a bookstore in a small American town. Her major goal is to determine whether or not these readers constitute what Stanley Fish calls an 'interpretive community'. In the essay she reports some basic demographic information about the women, and offers an analysis of their views on reading by addressing issues such as (a) the reasons they give for reading, (b) the ways in which they use their reading, (c) the ways in which they describe the characters in the books, and (d) the connections they perceive between the books and their own lives. Notably, she considers the connection between the literacy levels of these women and the patriarchal culture in which they live to be a major factor. Citing the example of this group of readers, she argues that 'there may be, in fact, as many different forms of literate behavior as there are interpretive communities who buy and use books.'
M.B.

Interpretive communities and variable literacies: the functions of romance reading

One of the most engaging volumes yet published on the subject of reading is the marvelous collection of photographs by André Kertész titled simply, *On Reading*.[1] Presented without commentary, this series of images of readers absorbed in apparently diverse materials, in both expected and unexpected contexts, is eloquent in its insistence that books and reading serve myriad purposes and functions for a wide variety of individuals. For that reason alone, this simple photographic essay provides an implicit but nonetheless profound commentary on some entrenched and familiar assumptions about literacy.

By grouping together readers as different as the well-dressed man perched on a library ladder in a book-lined study and the ragged young boy sprawled across a pile of discarded newspapers in the street, Kertész is able to suggest that whatever the differences and merits of the materials they peruse, all are engaged in some form of the engrossing behavior through which print is transformed into a world.[2] The very inclusiveness of the series equalizes readers and reading processes that would, in other contexts, be ranked hierarchically on an imaginary literary scale. On that scale, the grade of 'truly literate' would be reserved for those educated individuals who were not only capable of reading texts that the culture deems 'literature,' but who also regularly choose to read such texts for utilitarian purposes, however broadly conceived. As Raymond Williams has observed, literature and literacy within this sort of system would be inextricably linked with the bourgeois ideology of taste and its concomitant construction of the 'literary tradition.'[3]

Kertész's book is useful, therefore, precisely because its resolutely democratic presentation of reading refuses to make the usual distinctions through which the truly literate are distinguished from the merely functionally literate or illiterate, and 'literature' is segregated from all that is subliterature, paraliterature, or simple entertainment. Although his photographs are all in some sense 'about' reading, what they demonstrate is the astonishing variety of circumstances within which reading occurs. Because they function at least partially as signifiers of 'context' and difference, the photographs direct our attention to the question of whether such contexts are mere 'settings' within which a single unitary process is carried on, or whether they are more significant situations that actively affect the character of that process and thus differentially transform the valence of the act. Kertész's photographs seem to suggest that we must give up our search for the essence and effects of literacy as a single process and look instead at the varied kinds of literate behaviors that people really engage in. The photographs, I would argue, pose the question of *how* each of these unique readers is literate in a particular time and place.

In effect, I am suggesting that Kertész's book echoes John Szwed's call for ethno-

Reprinted by permission of *Daedalus*, Journal of the American Academy of Arts and Sciences, 'Anticipations,' 113, no. 3 (Summer 1974).

graphic studies of different kinds of literate behavior.[4] Like Kertész, Szwed fore-grounds context and argues that in place of the usual theoretical accounts of the unavoidable psychological consequences of acquiring print literacy, we must have more specific studies of what people do with printed texts. I would repeat Szwed's call and suggest, additionally, that such ethnographies can be made more effective investigative tools for the study of literacy if they are grounded upon some recent theoretical arguments in reader-response criticism. Although reader criticism has been developed to explain the interpretation of literary texts, it has implications for the way we think about how people operate upon and use all sorts of printed matter.[5]

The reader and the reading process have come to occupy a central place in literary criticism in recent years, but investigators of these phenomena share no unified theor-etical position. Indeed, reception theory or reader-response criticism includes approaches as diverse as the *rezeptionsästhetik* of the Constance school, the structural-ism of Roland Barthes, the semiotics of Umberto Eco and Jonathan Culler, the 'interactionist' work of Louise Rosenblatt and Stanley Fish, and the subjectivist arguments of David Bleich and Norman Holland. Most of these reader theories were developed in response to the textual formalism associated with New Criticism and its caveat against the 'affective fallacy.' As participants in a widespread conceptual shift in the intellectual community from positivist positions to contextual or interpretive schemas, the various reader theorists sought to challenge the New Critical insistence on the absolute autonomy of the text. Troubled by the complete exclusion of the reader from accounts of the interpretive process, these theorists sought ways to reas-sert the essential dependency of meaning upon the interaction between the reader and the text.[6]

Yet, despite their preoccupation with the activities of readers, the theorists show a lingering tendency to grant primacy and ultimate power to the text itself. Although willing to acknowledge the reader's contribution to the process of producing a read-ing of a text, theorists like Roman Ingarden and Wolfgang Iser eventually claim priority for the text because they believe it inevitably directs, governs, controls, indeed, determines the reader's response to it.[7] To name their theories 'reception theories' and their method 'reader-response criticism' is entirely accurate, since they continue to posit a confrontation between two distinct and quite different entities, the reader and the text. The reader receives the text and responds to it in such a manner that the meaning—what its author desired to communicate and embodied within its textual structures—is, in Iser's words, 'concretized' by the reader. Theories like Iser's are variations of the simple transmission-reception model of communication, whereby a sender's message is transmitted to a receiver via the medium of the printed text.

In continuing to accord primacy to texts, the theories remain compatible with the determinism inherent in many traditional conceptions of literacy and, accordingly, in the understanding of reading they imply. Previous theories of literacy have assumed that the character of print itself determines what can be done with it, and thus what it means to be literate. These more recent reading theories also argue implicitly that reading is a singular, skilled process, which many readers only partially master and some texts do not fully require. Thus their adherents can continue to accept the divi-sion of texts into the complex, or 'great,' and the simple, or subliterary, as well as the

335

distinction between readers who are fully literate and those who are not. Despite their apparent interest in readers and reading activities, such theories continue to support the notion that all readers are alike and all reading really one, simply because they assume that the technology of print and the character of individual texts together determine the activities they initiate.

There are other reading theories, however, that call for a rethinking of the concept of literacy, precisely because they maintain it is the reader who controls the reading process, not the text. Although these theories are often lumped together with other reader-oriented criticisms as 'reception theory' or 'response criticism,' they should not be so labeled. In fact, such versions of reader theory conceive of reading as 'pro-duction' or 'construction,' as opposed to reception or even simple consumption. The individuals who have elaborated these theories do not belong to a single school, nor do they adhere to the same theoretical approach. Yet all hold that reading is a pro-ductive activity in which a reader actively *makes* sense of the verbal inscriptions on the page. The most important theorists in this branch of reader theory are Umberto Eco, Stanley Fish, Louise Rosenblatt, and Jonathan Culler.[8] The four vary in the degree to which they employ the jargon now associated with semiotic theory, but each has nonetheless elaborated a model of the text-reader interaction that can be called semiotic.

All, that is, conceive of textual meaning as the product of a complex transaction between an inert textual structure, composed of verbal signifiers, and an actively pro-ductive reader, who constructs those signifiers as meaningful signs on the basis of previously learned interpretive procedures and cultural codes. Although the reader often attempts to construe the text by referring to the codes and strategies she believes the author intended her to use, nothing in the text constrains her to do so, nor, if she does, is she necessarily successful. As Eco has observed, 'The multiplicity of codes, contexts, and circumstances shows us that the same message can be decoded from different points of view and by reference to diverse systems of conven-tions.'[9] Interpretation and textual meaning, then, are as dependent on who the reader is, on how she understands the process of reading, and on the cultural context within which she operates, as they are on the text's verbal structure itself.

Print is not determinant in such a view, nor is reading a simple mechanical matter of processing what is on the page. Rather, print functions as a kind of material with which and upon which readers operate in order to produce meaning. Reading, then, is a complicated semiotic and fundamentally social process that varies both in place and in time. That is to say, different readers read differently because they belong to what are known as various interpretive communities, each of which acts upon print differently and for different purposes.

The concept of the interpretive community, of course, has been discussed most recently by Stanley Fish.[10] Fish defines the notion rather narrowly, however, because he is interested only in different forms of academic literary criticism. For him, an interpretive community is a loosely connected group of literary scholars who share basic assumptions about the nature of literature, about the goals of literary criticism, and about the nature of the interpretive process. Different interpretive communities, therefore, at least as Fish discusses them, are composed of readers who may disagree about how to construct a literary interpretation, but who are nonetheless equally and similarly literate because all can produce coherent readings of difficult texts.

In spite of Fish's own lack of interest in other than professional readers, his concept of the interpretive community can be fruitfully rethought to apply more generally to readers outside the literary academy to help us understand why some readers prefer Westerns to the classics, detective stories to poetry, or the *Enquirer* to Shakespeare. Interpretive communities may not simply differ over what to do with metaphors and tropes; they may disagree even more fundamentally over the nature and purpose of reading itself. Different interpretive communities may actually be differently literate. We need to know, therefore, what exactly divides the vast community of individuals who buy and read books—in short, how book or print-related behaviors vary according to place and over time.

To call for such a project, however, is to confront obvious methodological problems almost at once. Because we do not know what an interpretive community actually is, we cannot identify one in order to study the ways in which its members are literate. Are such communities formally constituted groups to which individual members *know* they belong? Or are they much larger collections of people who, by virtue of a common social position and demographic character, unconsciously share certain assumptions about reading as well as preferences for reading material? Assuming that the latter is true, it is not at all obvious how we could ferret out the existence of such a group without first sharpening our understanding of how more formalized interpretive communities operate. If we can detect exactly what it is the readers in a formally recognized group share, and how this common fund of knowledge affects what they 'do' with printed texts, we may be able to ask certain questions of apparently unconnected individuals that will also reveal the particular ways in which they behave with printed texts and, therefore, how they are literate.

A logical way to start such a project would be to make use of the publishing industry's own understanding of the book-buying public. The industry recognizes that certain readers are particularly interested in a specific 'category' of books, and it therefore identifies mass-produced texts as belonging to one or another, usually by cover iconography. This has proved to be a reliable technique because there is indeed a portion of the book-buying community that reads only one kind of text. Time after time, such 'category' readers, as they are known in the trade, will choose books from only this category. Many students of mass-produced literature, furthermore, assume that such readers choose their category because essential features of their social life create needs and demands that are somehow addressed and fulfilled by these books.[11] If this is true, an investigation of their preferences for, and interaction with, books of a particular category may in fact amount to an investigation of the place and function of literacy in their lives.

In this paper, I shall detail my attempt at just such a study, but must point out first that the group I investigated was even more formalized than the loose conglomerate who read a particular category—in this case, the romance.[12] It was necessary to begin with a small group of romance readers, one clustered about a bookstore clerk in 'Smithton,' because not enough information about this audience is available from publishers to construct a representative sample of romance readers as a whole. Thus my findings about the nature of romance reading are based on a self-selected group of women united by their reliance on a single individual who

337

advises them about 'good' and 'bad' romances. Since all of the women in the group have been consulting Dorothy Evans, the bookstore clerk, for several years, I was not surprised to learn that as readers they are united by common purposes, preferences, and interpretive procedures. I also found that these aspects of their reading behavior seem to be a function of certain common social factors of their lives, a point I shall return to.

I must add, however, that my interpretive community of romance readers may not extend beyond the area served by this particular bookstore. These women, in fact, may not be part of a larger, genre-based interpretive community. We will know that only when we can test my findings against those of a much larger study, one that attempts to survey the behavior of *all* women who think of themselves as romance readers. While all may read romances, they may do so differently or for different purposes. They may indeed be category readers, but they may not constitute an interpretive community in the sense that they all select, use, and operate on printed texts in certain socially specific ways.

In turning now to the Smithton women and to their characteristic reading behavior, it seems important to describe first exactly how information was elicited about what they 'did' with texts. Because I was interested in the women's own self-perceptions and understanding of romances and romance reading, I relied on ethnographic interviewing techniques to map the 'world' of the romance reader. I interviewed sixteen women in two groups about all aspects of their leisure activity, and then talked more extensively with five, including Evans. Because I was well aware of the romance reader's wariness about the general public's scorn for her activity, I hoped the group situation would reassure each enough to answer my questions honestly. I was also aware, however, that the group situation might lead to a greater uniformity in response than actually existed, because of the influence of a single reader. I therefore also administered an anonymous questionnaire to the sixteen women as well as to twenty-six others. Since I found little discrepancy between my informants' oral and written responses and between the responses of the sixteen and others of Evans's customers, I concluded that the material elicited in the oral interviews was a reasonably accurate account of what the women thought they were up to.

My first task was to determine exactly how the members of the group made the necessary discriminations in order to select the texts they wanted. Because they are category readers, what was at issue was their definition of the category or genre and how they identified individual texts as examples of it. I sought such a definition through a variety of related questions to see whether their conscious understanding of the genre coincided with the definition they actually relied on in selecting reading matter.

What I found was that a definition of the genre was implicit in the way they used cover blurbs and illustrations, in their reliance on previous readings of certain authors, and in their use of Evans's recommendations to select their texts. Indeed, all of these activities seemed to be governed by their sense that 'romance' had something to do with the manner and tone of presentation of a love relationship. Once I had determined the rudimentary content of the genre, I asked them to provide a 'definition' of it to see whether their genre theory actually coincided with how they used individual instances of the category. What they told me was interesting, both because it tended to confirm their implicitly reported requirements and proved to be at once formalist and functional.

Their definition—a man and a woman meeting, the problems they encounter, whether the relationship will gel or not—not only identified the fundamental characters and events in the story, but also specified the evolution of the action and, implicitly, the nature of the response (tension or anxiety) it ought to evoke in the reader. By beginning with the definition, I was led to mark off two areas for further study. First, I pursued the issue of the plot structure itself by attempting to determine exactly how the women processed textual inscriptions to arrive at that particular abstract structure. I was trying, especially, to describe their manner of textual production, to discover what they did with the text to produce their characteristic interpretation. At the same time, I attempted to explore the nature of their reaction to the plot structure, and thus got involved with questions of how the text made them feel and how it functioned in their daily lives. Here, I was investigating the readers' use of the activity of reading, asking what they accomplished *by* or *in* the process of reading these books. Before I pursue this aspect of their reading behavior, I would like to return briefly to the interpretive process itself and explore some of the problems encountered in trying to determine how people in real life arrive at a given reading of a particular book, and some of the possibilities as well.

It is somewhat difficult to shed light on the interpretive process simply because so much of it occurs automatically and unconsciously. While most readers can easily summarize a book or recount its plot, we have no sure way of knowing exactly what interpretive operations come into play in the redaction of a 200- or 300-page text. After hearing a plot summary, the investigator might read the text, noting both what the reader has designated as significant in her account and what she has ignored. These observations can then be used to infer the selection criteria that prompted the reader to identify the relevant textual features from which she constructed her final reading.[13] Those selection criteria themselves then point to what the romantic story is 'about,' at least for the individual summarizing the plot.

In the case of the romance readers, every plot summary ignored the fact that the hero and heroine were contrasted with foil figures with whom they were sometimes entangled. Their refusal to acknowledge these contrasts as essential to the plot suggested that the women's interest in the romance came not from any interest in sexual competition, same sex friendships, or contrasts, but from a deep-seated need to see an ideal relationship worked out between a man and a woman. Their responses to questions about the qualities of good and bad romances seemed to validate this inference. An ideal romance focused on 'one woman-one man,' while a poor example of the genre often involved the hero and heroine with too many other secondary characters. Their sense that the romance should be 'about' a single relationship governed their selective perception of the significant features and events in each tale. This fundamental desire was ultimately responsible for the particular story they constructed.

With the women's essential evaluative criteria thus established, I then questioned them about their understanding or interpretation of the story they had constructed from each text's myriad details and events. Although this led to further observations about how the women treated language, particularly declarative statements, it went

339

beyond simple textual operations and their conscious understanding of the story to the covert consequences of those operations and the tacit significance of that understanding. It was surprising to discover that the women saw these tales of 'a man and a woman meeting' as stories about a woman's triumph, surprising, because so many feminist literary critics of the genre have argued that romances are about helpless, passive, weak women who relinquish their sense of self in the arms of the more important man.[14] I was tempted to attribute the interpretive difference to varying standards of judgment about female behavior, but certain of the women's statements about the authors' attitudes toward their heroines caused me to think twice about formulating such a conclusion.

Several of the women had observed repeatedly that their favorite writers always wrote about intelligent and independent heroines, so I decided to check this against the texts. If one focused only on verbal assertion, this was indeed the case. The authors always declared at the outset that their heroines were unusual, special, bright, and self-reliant, but later portrayed them as victims of circumstance. Apparently, the Smithton readers do not see this as contradictory because they do not use subsequent narrative action to revise a character portrait established by description at the beginning. Feminist literary critics, of course, applying what Jonathan Culler has described as a rule of unity, *do* try to produce a unified characterization that takes all of these details into account.[15] In their literary universe, character behavior is meant to comment on and alter preliminary portraiture[16]— hence, their final and quite different account of the romantic heroine as only a superficially independent woman, who is, in reality, deeply dependent and incapable of action herself. The argument for the accuracy of their interpretation is that as feminist critics, they are formally trained and thus fully literate. Romance readers, on the other hand, are neither well-educated nor fully conscious of what they do, and therefore simply don't know what the story *really* means. And because these women are somehow incompletely literate, they don't know how to interpret characters correctly. Nonetheless, the romantic text manages to exert its conservative power over them and thus functions to reinforce the patriarchal status quo.

I would like to suggest, however, that there is another equally plausible explanation of this difference in interpretations. The romance reader's failure to unify action and description may, in fact, be a function of a particular 'philosophy' of language that effectively precludes such an operation. Their portrait of the heroine, in such a view, is not a result of their ignorance or lack of self-awareness, but a product of a particular attitude toward language. The women believe that words have meanings that are fixed and definite. Because those meanings are essentially contained *in* words, the women also believe that people choose words to say what they mean. Words are always already meaningful and can be selected for what they accurately say about a character or event. The Smithton readers assume that romance authors choose their words very carefully because they intend those words to describe correctly the characters in question. As a result, they do not judge verbal assertion by comparing it with the character's actions. If the writer says that her heroine is intelligent and independent, nothing she does or does not do later can alter her basic character. Consequently, the women believe that they are reading a story about an extraordinary woman who is overcome by unforeseen circumstances, but who nevertheless manages to teach the hero how to care for her and to appreciate her as she wishes to be appreciated. Because he always learns the lesson she has to teach and proposes a permanent commitment, the women can interpret this as the triumph of her values. Their interpretation follows logically from their textual operations, which are themselves dictated by a prior understanding of words and languages. It seems to me that what we have here is not a form of partial literacy, but a different form of literacy altogether, founded on its own conception of the word and what can be done with it.

Another consequence of this attitude toward language surfaced again in a discussion about the women's reasons for reading romantic fiction. Although they agreed overwhelmingly that they read principally for enjoyment and to escape their daily problems, the Smithton women also maintained that they read romances to learn—not, as one might expect, about how to conduct a relationship but, rather, because they acquired factual information about geography, culture, and history from these books. This is so because they operate under two assumptions.

To begin with, they firmly believe that all romance authors research the historical and physical backgrounds of their stories. In fact, this is true. One has only to read the prefaces to romantic fiction to detect how important it is to the author to portray accurately both the physical setting of the story and the period in which it takes place. Indeed, romance writers constantly thank librarians and archivists for their assistance, and for those authors who travel to the foreign locales that form the backgrounds to their stories, there is gratitude to their guides as well.[17] Second, romance readers assume that when an author makes a factual statement about the background, she does so because it is 'true.' They therefore mark that statement as 'information' and commit it to memory as 'knowledge.' Their *attitude* toward language, then, rather than the text alone, is responsible for one of their most important claims about the worth and function of romance reading. Although the books are works of fiction, the women use them as primers about the world. The romance for them is a kind of encyclopedia, and reading, a process of education.[18]

Romance readers are perhaps not alone in treating novels as compendia about the world. A good deal of popular fiction places important emphasis on setting and background. The readers of Irving Wallace and Arthur Hailey, for instance, believe they authentically experience the worlds of Hollywood, big city hotels, Hawaiian history, and Israeli culture because of the extensive research these authors conduct for their books. Louis L'Amour, perhaps the most popular writer of Westerns, is also well known as a careful student of the history of the American West. If his readers, as well as those of Wallace and Hailey, treat their texts as seriously as do the Smithton romance readers, it may well be that a large portion of the American public has learned its history and geography from the popular book. They must be considered literate despite the fact that they are uninterested in that large body of material sanctioned by the culture as 'literature.'

But for romance readers, we need to go beyond this level of analysis. Although romances clearly both provide an education and reassure their readers about the triumphant superiority of women and their values, it is likely that when the texts provide the opportunity for the women to realize these benefits through particular kinds of interpretive operations, those operations carry other tacit consequences and

341

effects that the women are not aware of. This is the most difficult interpretive move in any reader study, since it is not at all clear either what constitutes evidence for an effect or how one validates an intuition that a reader benefits in ways other than those she can attest to explicitly. However, because reading and comprehension are surely not entirely conscious activities, it seems advisable to attempt to infer possible meanings to the reader and the effects of interpretive operations that she carries out but which she may not fully apprehend.

As an example, let me cite something I inferred from my observations about how the Smithton women treated the language of romantic texts. In exploring their methods for formulating character portraits and for processing 'factual' material, I noticed that one of the reasons they operate on the texts as they do is a function of the fact that the authors had selected a vocabulary and syntax readily familiar to a middle-class housewife and mother with a year or two of college education. I inferred that this simple and resolutely familiar language use actually permits the women to rely heavily on their memory of previously learned cultural codes. When they encounter such a linguistic structure, they simply supply the most common referents for the words and phrases in question and thus actually construct a fictional duplicate of the world they are familiar with. Although the process of construction appears to the women as automatic and natural comprehension—as learning, in fact—it is actually a form of production that has the ultimate effect of naturalizing and therefore ratifying the world in which the women ordinarily live. Reading is a highly reassuring process, because it prompts them to use their most familiar methods for apprehending the world, and rewards them by enabling them to 'find' only what they would have expected. Romance reading, it appears, allows a woman to believe she is learning and changing herself at the very same time it is reassuring her that she already knows how to make sense of an existence which always is as she expects, even in fiction.

Assessing the ultimate impact of these contradictory effects of the romance reader's interpretive activity is as difficult a task as trying to validate the fact that the covert consequences one detects or infers are actually experienced by the reader. One might argue that in learning more and more about her world, the romance reader comes to value herself and her abilities more, and thus feels powerful enough to seek change. Yet it is equally possible that the conservative nature of the interpretive process actually reassures her that nothing need be changed at all, precisely because the world *is* readable and hence fully meaningful. Corroboration of either effect can be sought in the reader's daily activities, but even then it would be virtually impossible to state positively that the interpretive activities performed in reading romantic novels resulted in changed behavior.

This is the point at which the analyst of reading becomes aware of the limits of the ethnographic method, an awareness that is quite like the anthropologist's recognition of how difficult it is to pierce the veil of cultural behavior to fathom its meaning and its fundamental roots in ideology. Even though reading can be investigated empirically, and the readers' own interpretations of texts taken into account, analytic interpretation cannot be done away with entirely. As Clifford Geertz reminded ethnographic anthropologists, 'What we call our data are really our own constructions of other people's constructions of what they and their compatriots are up to. Cultural

analysis,' he concludes, 'is . . . guessing at meanings, assessing the guesses, and drawing explanatory conclusions from the better guesses.'[19] My account of what romance
readers do to a text in the process of constructing an interpretation is just such a
guess; but I think it is a better guess than it would have been if I had merely inferred
the existence of such behavior on the basis of my own reading of the texts, a reading
that none of the Smithton readers would have recognized as an interpretation of the
books she knows so well.

Not only, however, do the Smithton women have an elaborate theory about the
meaning and significance of the romance as a literary form, but they can articulate to
themselves a coherent explanation of the meaning of the act of reading itself as well.
It is true, of course, that all acts of reading involve particular texts, and thus the overall significance of each complex act is intimately bound up with the meaning of the
text and its implication in the reader's social and ideological life. Still, because the act
of picking up a book is a form of social behavior that permits the reader to suspend
momentarily all connections with the outside world, I think it is essential to make a
distinction between book reading itself and the text constructed as a consequence of
it.[20] Beyond knowing what the romantic story means to the Smithton reader, one
wants to know also how she uses the activity of burying herself in the pages of a book.
To ask this question is, in effect, to ask what she understands herself to be doing in
reading, as well as to ask what she believes she conveys to others by reading.

The importance of these questions was made clear to me by the women themselves. Early in my initial interview with Evans, for example, I asked her what
romantic novels 'do' better than other novels available today. In posing the question,
I expected her to concern herself with plots and ideas, that is, with the meaning and
value of the romantic story. But she misconstrued my use of 'do' and thought I had
asked about the effects the reading of such novels has upon the reader. She talked at
great length about the benefits these books provide the traditional wife and mother.
The typical woman, she said, has many, many caretaking duties that are part of those
intertwined roles, but her labors are inadequately appreciated by her family. Because
individual family members do not sufficiently recognize her efforts nor compensate
her for them by 'taking care' of her, Evans believes such a woman must find a legitimate way of releasing her from her duties temporarily and of replenishing the energy
that is constantly being drained in performing them. Romance reading, she
explained, is the perfect solution. I think it would be worthwhile to quote Evans herself here, precisely because her remarks indicate so tellingly how conscious she is of
reading as an activity that is an integral part of the readers' daily existence.

> As a mother, I have run 'em to the orthodontist. I have run 'em to the swimming
> pool. I have run 'em to baton twirling lessons. I have run up to school because
> they forgot their lunch. You know, I mean, really! And you do it. And it isn't that
> you begrudge it. That isn't it. Then my husband would walk in the door and he'd
> say, 'Well, what did you do today?' You know, it was like, 'Well, tell me how you
> spent the last eight hours, because I've been out working.' And I finally got to the
> point where I would say, 'Well, I read four books, and I did all the wash and got
> the meal on the table and the beds are all made, and the house is tidy.' And I
> would get defensive like, 'So what do you call all this? Why should I have to tell

343

you because I certainly don't ask you what you did for eight hours, step by step.'—But their husbands *do* do that. We've compared notes. They hit the house and it's like 'Well all right, I've been out earning a living. Now what have you been doin' with your time?' And you begin to be feeling, 'Now really, why is he questioning me?'

Evans maintains, in effect, that romance reading is a 'declaration of independence' for her and her customers. She believes that in picking up a book, each is effectively erecting a barrier between herself and the arena of her regular family ministrations. Because husband and children are told, 'This is my time, my space, now leave me alone,' they are expected to respect the signal of the book and to avoid interrupting her. Book reading allows the woman to free herself from her duties and responsibilities and provides a 'space' or 'time' within which she can attend to her own interests and needs.

It is here that the demographic character of this particular group of readers is relevant. For the most part, the Smithton women are married, middle-class mothers of children other than infants. More than 60 percent were between twenty-five and forty-four at the time of the study, and 70 percent had children younger than eighteen. Although 42 percent work outside the home, they nevertheless felt that family care was primarily their responsibility. In discussion after discussion, they referred to the unrelenting family demands made upon them and to the 'tensions' these produced. Then, with a combination of defensiveness and belligerence, the women asserted repeatedly that the very difficulty of their double work burden earned them the right to do something pleasurable for themselves alone.

In assessing the correlation between the social character of the lives of these women and their understanding of the value of romance reading, it seems clear that what the women are doing is allowing themselves to abandon temporarily the self-abnegation that had been engrained in them all their lives as the proper attitude for a wife and mother. Within the context of their lives, romance reading appeared to be both an assertion of a deeply felt psychological need and a means for satisfying that need. Although the women themselves accept their need for respite and replenishment and for self-involvement as part of a role they willingly adopt, that they feel their romance reading is not simply pleasurable but necessary testifies to the enduring force of that need. Several of the women equated their reading to a form of addiction, and most were quite comfortable with a view of themselves as dependent on romances. Something specific and integral to their situation as wives and mothers apparently is the ultimate source of the romance's significance to them and, consequently, of their preference for the category.

It was at this point that I moved beyond the women's own construction of their behavior to look for a structural explanation of the social facts of their existence that led not only to the behavior itself but to their construction of it as well. Here, I was helped by recent work on the nature of patriarchy and middle-class marriage.[21] Within the context of such work, it seemed clear that the Smithton readers' need for respite and replenishment was a function of the fact that within traditional patriarchal marriage, no one is charged with the affective and emotional reconstitution of women.[22] Indeed, as one of Evans's customers put it, 'You always have to be a Mary

Poppins. You can't be sad, you can't be mad, you have to keep everything bottled up inside.' Even if a woman is depleted by her efforts to care for others, she is nonetheless expected to restore and sustain herself within such a family structure, precisely because other family members do not conceive of their role as being one of nurturance. The women turn to romance reading because the activity itself temporarily permits them to identify with a heroine who receives all the attention and care of an extraordinary man. In effect, when they buy a romance, they are purchasing personal space and vicarious attention.

Before exploring exactly how the stories supply the longed-for reassurance and nurturance, we might take note of the fact that the Smithton readers feel a bit guilty about the time and money spent on indulging themselves in this way. Given their willing acceptance of the traditional female role with its implicit self-denial and self-abnegation, this is quite understandable. Although the women defiantly assert that they, too, have a right to some time for themselves (they often point to the amount of time their husbands spend watching televised sports), they worry about their families' disapproval of their book expenses and their self-preoccupation. Indeed, many of the women asked somewhat rhetorically whether I agreed that they had a right to do something for themselves alone, even though as a wife and mother they were supposed to be concerned with the interests of others. Their defensiveness and uncertainty suggests that their chronic reading causes them to experience a certain amount of role conflict. They feel a need to replenish the self and to attend to emotional needs created by the role they have willingly accepted, yet are not sure that this should be done at the expense of family responsibilities or through an activity that is so obviously pleasurable.

It is here that the other 'use' of romance reading becomes important, because it acts to justify the time and money spent on books and reading. The Smithton women read primarily 'to escape'—literally, to deny their presence in the family context. But they also read to learn. They enjoy the travelog and documentary aspects of the romance immensely, and even categorize books on the basis of their historical and geographic settings. More important, however, they actively use the factual materials they learn through reading to demonstrate to their skeptical families that they have indeed acquired something valuable in exchange for their expenditure of time and money. This strategy cannily defines the *act* of romance reading as goal-directed work, and therefore assigns to it a higher value in the male world, which is preoccupied with labor, self-improvement, and achievement.

Although the women are well aware of the fact that they use this aspect of romance reading to convince their husbands of the activity's validity, they are unaware of the benefits they derive by construing the activity in this way. Again, I am making an interpretive leap here, but it seems to be justified, given all the women have said about the confining aspects of domestic work and our culture's propensity to disparage women. By storing factual material as 'information,' and by displaying it to others as their own 'knowledge,' the women convince themselves that they have not languished as 'mere housewives' but have continued to better themselves and to demonstrate their fundamental abilities. Thus, at the same time that romance reading gives them much needed personal time and space, it also enables them to believe that they are capable individuals and that they are changing for the better. Both 'uses' of romance reading, therefore, act to deny the immediate present and to propel the women elsewhere. The act of romance reading first walls off pressing demands and then demonstrates to the participants that they are making themselves better or 'other' than they were.

I think it can be seen from this example why it is so helpful to distinguish between the book read by an individual and the act of reading itself carried on within a specific social context. Although it is true that the two are not actually distinct components of the individual's behavior—simply because the act of reading must involve a text, which cannot help but contribute to the meaning of the larger activity—by separating them analytically, one can then isolate the social and material situation surrounding the actual event of reading. Books are always read within a set of specific circumstances, and their final meaning and impact may well be a function of the way those circumstances constitute the reader as a social being. In thus developing an account of how the act of book reading fits within the complex set of relations and behaviors that characterize the reader's social world, we can understand better why she might select such specific reading material in the first place. An important correlation may exist, in fact, between the needs that prompt the decision to read and the character of the books that are chosen for that activity. By taking account of that possibility, one is better prepared, finally, to return to the issue of textual interpretation in an effort to understand how the reader's particular construction of a text provides certain forms of intellectual and emotional gratification. Having sketched out how a reader actually uses her literacy, one is then prepared to investigate why she does so on these particular texts.

I can best demonstrate how intricate the connections can be between the social context surrounding a reader's activity and the texts that an individual chooses to read by referring one last time to Dorothy Evans and the Smithton women. Although I cannot detail all the ways in which the texts they selected addressed the specific needs and concerns that originated with their social role and their situation in the family context, I can at least show that by reading romances, their reading activity was made even more meaningful and beneficial to them. I discovered the special significance of the romance to them when I asked whether all romances were the same. Of course they weren't, the women replied, and then showed me that they could clearly distinguish the good romances from the bad. I then began to probe more deeply into their evaluative procedures and to examine more carefully the differences between the books they actually read and those they rejected.

Their favorite books were indeed characterized by the 'one woman/one man' plot they claimed to prefer, stories in which the romantic hero focused all of his attention on a heroine with whom they identified. Although the initial interaction between the pair was characterized by the usual misunderstandings and emotional distance, the hero's treatment of the heroine was decidedly less cruel and violent than it was in what they considered to be poorer versions of the genre. In fact, his mistreatment of the heroine was always mitigated by temporary softenings of his demeanor, and his ultimate attitude toward her was transformed much earlier in the tale. Ideal heroes, it seemed, were also a good deal more androgynous than their less satisfying counterparts in that they combined masculine strength and power with a more feminine sensitivity and tenderness.

346

In indulging themselves in a few hundred pages of the hero's response to the heroine, the Smithton women allowed themselves to exist vicariously as the center of a spectacular man's attention. Not only did their reading activity permit them to give up their actively nurturant or servicing role in the family, but it also, because of the nature of the text, enabled them to become the passive recipient of another's total and tender care. What they achieved through romance reading was twofold: a temporary release from the demands of the social role that defined them, and psychological gratification for the needs they experienced because they had adopted that role. It might be said that romance reading functioned for the women as a kind of tacit, minimal protest against the patriarchal constitution of women: it enabled them to mark off a space where they could temporarily deny the selflessness usually demanded of them, to acknowledge the validity of the desires and needs created by the demeanor they otherwise accepted as part of that constitution, and to meet those needs by acquiring vicariously the nurturance and care that was lacking in their daily lives.

Before characterizing romance reading as incipiently subversive or oppositional behavior, however, we would do well to look carefully at the second way in which the reading of romances specifically addressed the Smithton readers' social situation as women. This aspect of romance reading was revealed to me through my exploration of their assertion that the stories were those of a woman's triumph. In looking at their favorite books very carefully, in fact, I could see a way in which their assertion was true. The typical ideal romance establishes at the outset that there is a clear opposition between the male and female worlds, the former dominated by competition, the desire for wealth, and the quest for social position, the latter characterized by the value placed on love and intimate human interactions. The romantic heroine, of course, as an inhabitant of the female world, understands the value of love, while the hero does not. Preoccupied with the goals of the typical male quest, he has no time in the beginning for sensitivity and tender gestures. In the course of the story, however, he learns the value of such things because he almost loses the heroine. In a sense, he is converted by the heroine into an occupant and proponent of the female world of love and emotional commitment—hence, the Smithton readers' understanding of these stories as tales of a woman's victory.

Romance reading, then, also demonstrates to these women that the domestic world they occupy is eminently valuable. They are told, in fact, that it is the way to true happiness, just as they are shown that it has the evangelical power to convert doubters to its purpose. The romance thus assures its readers that the world they have chosen already, or will likely choose in the future, is the world they ought to occupy. We might logically conclude, therefore, that one consequence of romance reading might be a reinforcement of the patriarchal constitution of women. Despite the fact that it enables women to resist some of that constitution's most difficult demands, romance reading might ultimately conserve patriarchy, because it reassures women that the sphere they occupy is right and fulfilling, and that all of their needs can be met within it. If so, this aspect of romance reading would contradict its existence as incipient opposition, and might override any positive force it could exert upon women to develop more effective ways of coping with their needs for nurturance and attentive care.

Unfortunately, assessment of the relative power of these two aspects of this highly complex form of behavior is nearly impossible without long-range, extensive observation of the women's actual behavior in the family. And should such a study be undertaken, it would still be extremely difficult to isolate and identify the causes of specific behavioral changes. Greater assertiveness on the part of the women might have nothing to do with the positive effects of romance reading, but might be the result of changes in the culture at large. In addition, continued acceptance of the traditional female role might in fact be the result of persistent economic dependence rather than the conservative impact of romance reading. Here again, we run up against the limitations of the ethnographic method. Although we can ask our informants what they believe they are accomplishing in reading—just as we can ask them to explain how they affect others *by* reading—we must get beyond their conscious comprehension and self-understanding if we are to make some sort of judgment about the cumulative impact of that activity both on them and on others. To ask about such an effect is, in fact, to pose a question about the relationship between the imaginary realm and the realm of material behavior in the world of actual social relations. The answer to this question can only be found through careful observation of just those behavioral changes over time. However, even when ethnographic observation leads to conclusions about significant alterations in women's behavior, attribution of those changes to specific causes will remain an inherently interpretive procedure, because the link between imagination and action will always be an inferred one.

Because I could not observe the behavior of the Smithton women over a long period of time, my account of their reading activity ends with an explanation of the multiple meanings that the activity has within the context of their daily lives. That explanation locates the ultimate source of the group's existence as an interpretive community in their roles as wives and mothers. Their preference for the romance genre, in my view, is a function of their particular social situation. The nature of their literacy, therefore—which is to say, the way they choose, understand, and use their books— is deeply affected by the circumstances of their lives. These, in fact, are both the very source of their desire to read and the set of conditions that determine and give meaning to the particular way in which they do.

The ultimate test of such an argument, of course, would be a series of related studies of romance readers that would begin by defining differently the interpretive communities to be investigated. One such study would have to begin with a group of unrelated romance readers who were demographically similar to the Smithton women. If these readers also read romances to escape and to learn, and chose only those books that supplied vicarious nurturance, then I think we might reasonably conclude that at least one form of romance reading is a function of the social and psychological consequences of patriarchal marriage. If a more extensive study of a demographically varied group of romance readers demonstrated that young, unmarried women, say, read different romances for different reasons, this would not necessarily upset that initial correlation. It is entirely possible, I think, that the interpretive community of romance readers, defined only by its members' preference for the romance category, may be subdivided into more specialized groups, whose reading behaviors vary with the particular circumstances of their daily lives. Although the interest of romance readers in the genre may be a function of the fact that all are women in a patriarchal society, and thus all fantasize about achieving self-definition through attachment to a spectacular man, the character of the man, the nature of the attachment, and the process of self-realization that are longed for may be determined by the particular situation of these women in patriarchal culture. All components of literate behavior, in short, including the desire to read, the decision to read a certain kind of material, the interpretation of that material, and the uses to which both the interpretation and the act of constructing it are put, may well be a consequence of the diverse material and social features that characterize the lives of real individuals. There may be, in fact, as many different forms of literate behavior as there are interpretive communities who buy and use books.

NOTES

Writing of this paper was supported by a commission from the Annenberg Scholars Program, Annenberg School of Communications, University of Southern California, and delivered at the Scholars Conference, 'Creating Meaning: Literacies of Our Time,' February 1984. Copyright, Annenberg School of Communications. I would like to thank Horace Newcomb for his very helpful comments and suggestions on an earlier version of this paper.

1. André Kertész, *On Reading* (New York: Penguin Books, 1982).
2. Ibid., pp. 37, 10.
3. Raymond Williams, *Marxism and Literature* (Oxford: Oxford University Press, 1977), pp. 45–54.
4. John Szwed, 'The Ethnography of Literacy,' in *Writing: The Nature, Development, and Teaching of Written Communication*, vol. 1. *Variation in Writing: Funtional and Linguistic Cultural Differences*, edited by Marcia Farr Whiteman (Hillsdale, N.J.: Lawrence Erlbaum Associates, 1981). I am grateful to Judy Levin for bringing this article to my attention in one of our many helpful conversations about literacy and romance reading.
5. For a good introduction to reader-response criticism, see Jane P. Tompkins, *Reader-Response Criticism: From Formalism to Post-Structuralism* (Baltimore: Johns Hopkins University Press, 1980), and Susan B. Suleiman and Inge Crosman, *The Reader in the Text: Essays on Audience and Interpretation* (Princeton: Princeton University Press, 1980).
6. For historical and critical discussion of reader theory, see Jonathan Culler, *The Pursuit of Signs: Semiotics, Literature, Deconstruction* (Ithaca, N.Y.: Cornell University Press, 1981), pp. 47–131, and *On Deconstruction: Theory and Criticism after Structuralism* (Ithaca, N.Y.: Cornell University Press, 1982), pp. 31–83. See also Terry Eagleton, *Literary Theory: An Introduction* (Minneapolis: University of Minnesota Press, 1983), pp. 54–90.
7. See Roman Ingarden, *The Literary Work of Art: An Investigation on the Borderlines of Ontology, Logic, and Theory of Literature*, translated by George Grabowicz (Evanston, Ill.: Northwestern University Press, 1973), and Wolfgang Iser, *The Act of Reading: A Theory of Aesthetic Response* (Baltimore: Johns Hopkins University Press, 1978).
8. See especially, Umberto Eco, *The Role of the Reader: Explorations in the Semiotics of Texts* (Bloomington: Indiana University Press, 1979) and *A Theory of Semiotics* (Bloomington: Indiana University Press, 1976); Jonathan Culler, *Structuralist Poetics: Structuralism, Linguistics, and the Study of Literature* (Ithaca, N.Y.: Cornell University Press, 1975); Stanley Fish, *Is There a Text in This Class?: The Authority of Interpretive Communities* (Cambridge: Harvard University Press, 1980); Louise Rosenblatt, *The Reader, the Text, the Poem: The Transactional Theory of the Literary Work* (Carbondale: Southern Illinois University Press, 1978).
9. Eco, *A Theory of Semiotics*, p. 139.
10. See especially part 2 of *Is There a Text in This Class?*, pp. 303–71.
11. See, for example, John Cawelti, *Adventure, Mystery, and Romance: Formula Stories as Art and Popular Culture* (Chicago: University of Chicago Press, 1976).
12. The present discussion of romance reading is based on my full-length study, *Reading the Romance: Women, Patriarchy, and Popular Literature* (Chapel Hill: University of North Carolina Press, 1984).

For another summary of my findings, see 'Women Read the Romance: The Interaction of Text and Context,' *Feminist Studies* 9 (Spring 1983): 53–78. The names Dorothy Evans and the Smithton women are pseudonyms designed to protect the privacy of my informants.

13. As Stanley Fish has argued, 'Linguistic and textual facts, rather than being the objects of interpretation, are its products' (*Is There a Text in This Class?*, p. 9). Accordingly, the literary features used by the Smithton readers as the internal skeleton of their readings are actually isolated and deemed significant by them precisely because they come to the texts with a prior conception of what the stories should and usually do mean.

14. See Ann Douglas, 'Soft Porn Culture,' *The New Republic*, August 30, 1980, pp. 25–9; Tania Modleski, 'The Disappearing Act: A Study of Harlequin Romances,' *Signs* 5 (Spring 1980): 435–48; Ann Barr Snitow, 'Mass Market Romance: Pornography for Women is Different,' *Radical History Review* 20 (Spring/Summer 1979): 141–61.

15. Culler, *Structuralist Poetics*, pp. 230–8. See also his *Ferdinand de Saussure* (New York: Penguin Books, 1976), pp. 117–18.

16. For a demonstration of how such a reading strategy works, see William Veeder's discussion of *Portrait of a Lady*, in *Henry James—The Lessons of the Master: Popular Fiction and Personal Style in the Nineteenth Century* (Chicago: University of Chicago Press, 1975), pp. 106–83.

17. In her acknowledgments to *The Proud Breed* (New York: Fawcett Crest Books, 1978), p. 7, for instance, Celeste De Blasis thanks the San Bernardino County library system as well as the Bancroft Library at Berkeley. She continues, 'The Roman Catholic pastors of St. Joan of Arc, Victorville, St. David's, Apple Valley, Christ the Good Shepherd, Adelanto, and San Juan Capistrano Mission, and a noted historian of the Archdiocese of Los Angeles were generous with their knowledge of early California's church ritual.'

18. In an essay on Ian Fleming's thrillers ('Narrative Structures in Fleming,' in *The Role of the Reader*, pp. 144–72), Umberto Eco has argued that Fleming also indulges in minute description of familiar objects that appear in the background to the melodramatic action. Eco calls this strategy 'the technique of the aimless glance' and maintains that it functions to seduce the reader into identifying with a character who thus appears to be 'real' even though his activities are otherwise preposterous. Because Fleming rarely describes the unusual, Eco concludes, those descriptions do not occur as 'encyclopedic information.' Although the description in romances appears somewhat similar to that found in Fleming, it differs precisely because it focuses on the historically and spatially distant and thus can function encyclopedically.

19. Clifford Geertz, 'Thick Description: Toward an Interpretive Theory of Culture,' in *The Interpretation of Cultures* (New York: Basic Books, 1973), pp. 9, 20.

20. See Robert Escarpit's discussion of reading in *The Sociology of Literature*, translated by Ernest Pick (Painesville, Ohio: Lake Erie College Press, 1965), p. 88.

21. See, for example, Kate Millett, *Sexual Politics* (Garden City, N.Y.: Doubleday, 1970), pp. 23–58; Heidi Hartmann, 'The Unhappy Marriage of Marxism and Feminism: Towards a More Progressive Union,' *Capital and Class* 8 (Summer 1979), pp. 1–33 and 'The Family as Locus of Gender, Class, and Political Struggle: The Example of Housework,' *Signs* 6 (Spring, 1981), pp. 366–94; Annette Kuhn, 'Structures of Patriarchy and Capitalism in the Family,' in *Feminism and Materialism: Women and Modes of Production*, edited by Annette Kuhn and AnnMarie Wolpe (London: Routledge & Kegan Paul, 1978), pp. 42–67; and Roisin McDonough and Rachel Harrison, 'Patriarchy and Relations of Production,' in *Feminism and Materialism*, pp. 11–41.

22. See Nancy Chodorow, *The Reproduction of Mothering: Psychoanalysis and the Sociology of Gender* (Berkeley: University of California Press, 1978).

Simon Frith (1951–)

Simon Frith is currently a professor and research director of the John Logie Baird Centre and the Head of the English Department at Strathclyde University. He chairs the International Association for the Study of Popular Music. His past accomplishments include writing music criticism for various British newspapers, *The Sunday Times*, the *Observer, Scotland on Sunday*, as well as the American newspaper, *Village Voice*. He has edited collections including *Facing the Music, World Music*, and *Politics and Social Change*. His books include *Art into Pop* (1987), *Music for Pleasure* (1988), and *Sound Effects: Youth, Leisure, and the Politics of Rock and Roll* (1981). He consistently provides his readers with innovative ideas concerning the cultural effects of music on society.

In this essay, from *Diacritics* (1991) he provides a witty and incisive exploration of assumptions inside media studies about 'popular' culture. Frith notes the move away from the Frankfurt school's castigation of the 'culture industry' to more positive evaluations and characterizes this move as one from 'if it's popular it must be bad' to 'if it's popular it must be bad, unless it's popular with the right people.' He describes most academic approaches to popular media products as condescending, arguing that standards of taste and judgment applied to 'high' cultural products are ignored when academics turn to 'popular' culture which are undifferentiated and assessed only in terms of their presumed 'transgressive' potential. In particular, Frith disagrees with a specific assessment that Pierre Bourdieu makes regarding taste as a cultural marker for 'class differentiation, a mark of distinction—[as being] specific to the bourgeoisie'. In a double-pronged argument, Frith questions the validity of clear demarcations between 'high' and 'low' or 'popular' media products, insisting instead on the instability of such boundaries and the existence of a 'common culture', as well as indicating the deployment of aesthetic hierarchies and moral criteria in consumers' evaluations of 'popular' media products. Frith's essay can be compared with Raymond Williams' essay 'Culture is Ordinary' in *Conviction* (1958).
J.M. and S.W.

The good, the bad, and the indifferent: defending popular culture from the populists

In his book *Origins of the Popular Style*, musicologist Peter Van Der Merwe suggests that 'reviewing the popular music of the twentieth century as a whole, most people would probably agree that some of it is excellent, some unbearable and most of it very indifferent. What the good, bad and indifferent share is a musical language' (3). Most people would probably agree with this statement; disagreement would be about which songs or genres or performers were good, which bad, which indifferent. And, as Van Der Merwe points out, such aesthetic arguments and distinctions (including that between the 'high' and the 'low') are possible (and impassioned) only because they take place within a shared musical and critical discourse, because they rest on an assumption that we know what the music we like and dislike 'means.'

Take, for example, the following three authoritative statements. The first comes from the most famous middlebrow intellectual of the 1980s—Allan Bloom. 'Rock music,' he wrote in *The Closing of the American Mind*, 'has one appeal only, a barbaric appeal, to sexual desire—not love, not *eros*, but sexual desire undeveloped and untutored . . . these are [its] three great lyrical themes: sex, hate and a smarmy, hypocritical version of brotherly love' (73–4).

The second comes from a leftist cultural critic—Mark Crispin Miller. 'The rock critic,' he wrote in the *New York Review of Books* in 1977, 'struggles to interpret something that requires no interpretation . . . tries to appraise and explicate a music whose artists and listeners are anti-intellectual and usually stoned, and whose producers want more than anything to own several cars' (175).

The third comes from *The Shoe*, a novel by a young Scottish writer, Gordon Legge, the best book I've read about what it means to be a pop fan. 'How could people get so worked up about relatives and cars when there were records?' asks *The Shoe*'s central character.

> Records cut so much deeper. For him Astral Weeks, Closer and For Your Pleasure (the three best LPs of all time, [he] said. No contest) articulated the mundanity, despair and joy of existence. . . . [He] said his records were the most important things in his life—more important than Celtic [football club] easily. . . . It's just that football was easier to talk about for five hours down the pub on a Saturday night. (36)

Several things could be said about these passages—not least about the remarkable assurance with which academics describe other people's pleasure—but I want to pick up immediately on Gordon Legge's point: the exercise of taste and aesthetic discrimination is as important in popular as in high culture but is more difficult to talk about. This means that the glib, professional talkers, the Blooms and Millers—and I could multiply examples of such confident accounts of the real worth or worthlessness of pop culture from both left and right—have the voices that are heard most often.

This is the case even after the rise of cultural studies as an academic concern. The aesthetics of popular culture is a neglected topic, and it is time we took it as seriously as Allan Bloom et al. One reason for this neglect is that cultural studies emerged from disciplines in which issues of taste and judgment are kept well away from issues of academic analysis and assessment: 'evaluation,' as Barbara Herrnstein Smith notes, was long ago 'exiled' from literary criticism, and has yet to be admitted to studies of popular culture.[1]

In universities, then, just as in high schools, there is still a split between what Frank Kogan describes as the discourse of the classroom (with its focus on a subject matter) and the discourse of the hallway (with its focus on one's feelings about a subject matter) (3–4). In this respect (and despite first impressions) academic approaches to popular culture still derive from the mass cultural critiques of the 1930s and 1940s, particularly from the Marxist critique of contemporary popular culture in terms of the production and circulation of commodities. For the Frankfurt School, analyzing the organization of mass production on the one hand, and the psychology of mass consumption on the other, the value issue was, in a sense, straightforward—if it's popular it must be bad!—and Adorno and his colleagues developed a number of concepts (such as standardization) to show why this must be so.

On the whole, the analytic move since then has been to accept the Frankfurt reading of cultural production and to look for the redeeming features of commodity culture in the act of consumption. The task, beginning with American liberal sociologists in the 1950s, has been to find forms of mass consumption that are not 'passive' and types of mass consumers who are not stupified, to provide a sociology of watching and reading and listening. If it is in the act of consumption that contemporary culture is lived, then it is in the process of consumption that contemporary cultural values must be located.

In the cultural studies tradition with which I'm most familiar, British subcultural theory, this reworking took on the particular form of identifying certain social groups with what we might call 'positive mass consumption' (which became—and remains—the pithiest academic definition of 'popular' culture). The value of cultural goods could therefore be equated with the value of the groups consuming them—youth, the working class, women, and so forth.

There are two points to note about this move from the position 'if it's popular it must be bad' to the position 'if it's popular it must be bad, unless it's popular with the right people.' First, this remains a highly politicized notion of popular cultural value, whether explicitly, as in the British use of terms like *resistance* and *empowerment*, or implicitly, as in the American celebration of opinion leaders and taste publics in the name of a pluralist democracy. Other value terms—beauty, say—are notable by their absence. To put it another way, cultural value is assessed according to measures of true and false consciousness: aesthetic issues, the politics of excitement, say, or grace, are subordinated to the necessities of ideological interpretation, to the call for 'demystification.'

Second, because such reclamation of popular culture from the machinations of capital is politically selective, those consumers who aren't approved are still dismissed as 'dupes' in conventional Marxist terms. This is the fate, to which I will return, of the middlebrow: the easy listener and light reader and Andrew Lloyd Webber fan. Indeed, it would be quite easy to produce a canon of popular texts

353

excluded from cultural studies, such exclusion reflecting a contempt for their consumers which derives, in turn, from assumptions about their class position and/or social passivity.

More recently, though, partly in response to the implicit elitism of this position, partly as an effect of the depoliticization of cultural studies as they enter the humanities curriculum, a new argument has emerged: if it's popular it must be good! I could point to specific examples of this approach—the Popular Culture Association, the work of John Fiske—but the questions that interest me here are whether a populist approach is the logical conclusion of subculturalism, and whether it is likely to be the norm of academic cultural studies in the 1990s. I fear that the answer to both questions is yes, that cultural studies will remain rooted in accounts of the consumer, every act of 'popular' consumption an excuse for celebration. This is the populist argument against which I want to defend popular culture, and I should begin my defense by sketching the problems I have with it. To begin with, it is based on inadequate empirical studies of consumption (and, indeed, production) as such. I suspect that less such empirical work is being done in cultural studies now than was done by positivist social scientists in the 1950s, and I'm not yet convinced that the so-called 'turn to ethnography,' with its focus on select groups of valorized fans, is going to solve this problem.

This has two consequences. First, for all the talk about process and modes of circulation, the definition of 'popularity' by default refers to consumption as measured by sales figures and market indicators—Neilsen ratings, the music charts, box office returns, bestseller lists, circulation statistics, and so on (figures that in turn become the regulators of popular cultural history). Even if such figures were accurate (which is doubtful), they provide no evidence as to why such goods are chosen by their consumers nor whether they are actually enjoyed or valued by them (it is a common enough experience to go to a blockbuster film, watch a high-rated TV program, read a bestselling book, or buy a chart record that turns out to be quite uninteresting). The elision between what sells and what is popular (the assumption that what sells is therefore 'valuable') is obvious in John Fiske's account of 'popular discrimination,' for example. He stresses rightly the inability of mass culture industries to predict or manipulate popular taste (as indicated by the vast number of 'failed' records, films, TV shows, magazines, and so forth) but does not question the assumption that a market failure is by definition unpopular or that a market success has by definition a popular audience [see Fiske]. In accounts of popular music, at least, this is to ignore the significant unpopularity of certain stars (Vanilla Ice, say) and the popular cult influence of such market failures as Velvet Underground or the Stone Roses. If nothing else, consumer research among pop fans immediately reveals the intensity with which music and musicians are loathed as well as loved.

Second, because of its lack of sociological sophistication, academic cultural analysis remains for the most part textual analysis. The popular text (the TV show or shopping mall, the Madonna video or Springsteen CD) is read for the positive or 'transgressive' values the 'popular' audience must have found there, which is to end up (as in E. Ann Kaplan's book on MTV) with the familiar argument that cultural consumers and their values are somehow determined by the text, that what Kaplan calls the 'historical viewer' is irrelevant to a theory of popular values. 'Evidence of specific spectator behavior,' she declares brazenly, 'in no way invalidates the theory of MTV as a postmodernist form' (159). This is an essentially condescending view of the people—Madonna fans, say—who are supposedly being celebrated (a condescension not tempered by the use of anachronistic terms like carnival to describe their fandom) and, in particular, has the effect of leveling the cultural experiences involved: the populist assumption is that all popular cultural goods and services are somehow the same in their empowering value (as they are in terms of exchange value); the populist suggestion is that we equate romance reading and *Star Trek* viewing, Madonna and metal fans, shoppers and surfers, each having their own form of 'resistance.' The aesthetic discrimination essential to cultural consumption and the considered judgments it involves are ignored.

It is hard to avoid the conclusion that the more celebratory the populist study, the more patronizing its tone, an effect, I think, of the explicit populist determination to deny (or reverse) the usual high/low cultural hierarchy. If one strand of the mass cultural critique was an indictment of low culture from the perspective of high art (as was obviously the case for Adorno, for example), then to assert the value of the popular is also, certainly, to query the superiority of high culture. Most populist writers, though, draw the wrong conclusion; what needs challenging is not the notion of the superior, but the claim that it is the exclusive property of the 'high.'

To deny the significance of value judgments in popular culture (to ignore popular taste hierarchies) is, if nothing else, hypocritical. How often, I wonder, do cultural studies theorists celebrate popular cultural forms which they themselves soon find boring? How are their own feelings for the good and the bad coded into their analyses? I'm sure in my own cultural practice that *Jane Eyre* is a better romance than a Mills and Boon or Harlequin title, just as I know that the Pet Shop Boys are a better group than U2 and that Aerosmith has no value at all. The problem is how best to argue this. To gloss over the ceaseless value judgments, the continuous exercise of taste, being made within popular audiences themselves is, in effect, to do their discriminating for them, to refuse to engage in those arguments which produce cultural values.

My defense of popular culture rests, then, on two assumptions: first, that the essence of cultural practice is making judgments and assessing differences.[2] Such judgments, distinctions, and choices are justified—to examine the question of value in popular culture is to examine the terms of such justifications. Second, there is no reason to believe *a priori* that such judgment processes work differently in different cultural spheres. There are obvious differences between operas and soap operas, between classical and country music, but the fact that the objects of judgment are different does not mean that the processes of judgment are. The conventional distinction between form (high culture) and function (low culture) is not sustainable for long, even in its populist reading as a contrast between measures of quality and aesthetics, on the one hand, and measures of relevance and productivity, on the other [for a discussion of these terms see Fiske].

In *Contingencies of Value*, her book about high cultural evaluation, Barbara Herrnstein Smith suggests that

what we are doing in making an explicit judgment of a literary work is

355

a) articulating an estimate of how well that work will serve certain implicitly defined functions

b) for a specific implicitly defined audience

c) who are conceived of as experiencing the work under certain implicitly defined conditions. (13)

This could equally well describe what's going on in the judgment of pop songs or TV shows, shopping centers or newsreaders. The implication is that to understand popular cultural values we need to look at the social contexts in which value judgments are deployed, to look at the social reasons why some aspects of a sound or spectacle are valued over others. Musical value judgments, for example, are most significantly made in three contexts:

First, among *musicians*. The value complex here is fairly straightforward: values emerging from the constraints of collaboration (trust, professionalism, reliability); values emerging from the constraints of craft (skill, technique, technical and technological expertise); values emerging from the experience of performance (revolving around a sense of difference).[3]

Second, among *producers*, by whom I mean the broad range of people concerned to turn a music or musician into a profitable commodity. The obvious values of productive efficiency in this group are overlaid, perhaps unexpectedly, by a Romantic belief in genius and originality, in the 'mystery' of both musical creation and audience taste. The cliched opposition of art and commerce is, in this context, misleading. What is actually judged to be at stake is the production of value: commerce *as* art [see Stratton].

Third, among *consumers*. There are various sociological approaches to consumer values: via 'homologies'—musical genres are valued for their representation or expression of a group's nonmusical concerns; via fantasy—a song or star is an object available for identification and individual use; via social settings—music works as a soundtrack, a background noise for dancing, praying, shopping, and so on.

What interests me, though, is not the precise concepts involved, but the general point that from a functional perspective there is inevitably a tension between musicians' and consumers' value terms and procedures (which, from the musicians' point of view, leads almost invariably to both a contempt for their 'popular' audience and a sense that popular music making is a matter of compromise).[4] That gap between the evaluative principles of music makers and music listeners is equally apparent in classical music. In both pop and classical worlds this gap is bridged by producers, who seek to bring creators and consumers into profitable alignment (a productive tension), and by critics, who function both as experts, teaching audiences how to listen and look, and as representatives, interpreting audiences for artists.[5] The commodification of culture, in short, in constituting a tripartite structure of communication— creator/producer/consumer—also constructed a series of evaluative oppositions (art vs. commerce, art vs. craft, the amateur vs. the professional) and a series of evaluative processes that are common to all contemporary cultural forms, that play across high and low cultural practices alike. One effect of this has been the rise of the cultural go-between, the publishers and critics who now play a central role in the making of meaning. Indeed, from this perspective, we could define high culture simply as that form of mass culture which is mediated by academics.

The importance of the critic's role leads me to a second sociological issue: not the context of cultural judgments, but the terms in which they are made. As I have argued elsewhere (drawing on the work of Howard Becker and Pierre Bourdieu), three discourses seem to dominate cultural judgments [see Frith, 'What Is Good Music?']:

an *art* discourse—the ideal of cultural experience is *transcendence*; art provides a means of rising above the everyday, leaving the body, denying the significance of historical time and geographical place;

a *folk* discourse—the ideal of cultural experience is *integration*; folk forms provide a means of placement—in a space, a season, a community;

a *pop* discourse—the ideal of cultural experience is *fun*; pop provides routinized pleasures, more intense than the everyday but bound into its rhythm, and legitimized emotional gratification, a play of desire and discipline.

The point to stress about these discourses (and this is where I part company with both Becker and Bourdieu) is that they describe neither separate art worlds nor different class attitudes but are, rather, all at play across all cultural practices and indeed produce each other (the ideologies of art and folk are thus equally the legacy of Romanticism, and were both, in turn, redefined by the emergence of mass entertainment) [see Shiach]. Value terms (most notoriously the concept of 'authenticity') are therefore shared. Aesthetically, there is no immediate reason to treat popular culture any differently from high culture (which is one reason, to return to Bourdieu, why class cultural rituals are so important: they mark out boundaries of taste that are, in fact, unstable).

In general, though, my argument is a deliberate departure from the claim that taste—the use of culture as a means of class differentiation, a mark of distinction—is specific to the bourgeoisie. Such a claim rests on dated evidence and an oversimple account of the class structure [for this argument see Bourdieu]. It is certainly easy enough to trace the historical origins of what Bourdieu calls bourgeois culture. In *Highbrow/Lowbrow*, for instance, Lawrence Levine shows how the cultural flexibility of eighteenth-century America had to be denied by the aesthetic ideology that emerged in the mid-nineteenth century: 'A concert given in Baltimore on September 12, 1796, attests to the prevalence of a musical ethos quite divergent from the one we have come to know, an ethos that thought it quite proper to follow a Haydn overture with the song "And All For My Pretty Brunette," and a Bach overture with the song "Oh, None Can Love Like an Irish Man" ' (107).

The development of a new musical ethos meant first promoting the concept of 'a sacralized art,' an art 'that makes no compromises with the "temporal" world, an art that remains spiritually pure and never becomes secondary to the performer or to the audience, an art that is uncompromising in its devotion to cultural perfection'—the words are taken from *Dwight's Journal of Music*—and then marking off this sort of cultural experience from all others:

> Thus by the early decades of this century the changes that had either begun or
> gained velocity in the last third of the nineteenth century were in place: the mas-

357

terworks of the classical composers were to be performed in their entirety by highly trained musicians on programmes free from the contamination of lesser works or lesser genres, free from the interference of audience or performer, free from the distractions of the mundane; audiences were to approach the masters and their works with proper respect and proper seriousness, for aesthetic and spiritual elevation rather than mere entertainment was the goal. This transition was not confined to the worlds of symphonic and operatic music or of Shakespearian drama; it was manifest in other important areas of expressive culture as well.

(Levine 120, 146)

And Paul Di Maggio has shown how this aesthetic argument was tied into the development of a class-conscious American bourgeoisie: the distinction between high and popular culture, he writes, emerged in the second half of the nineteenth century 'out of the efforts of urban elites to build organisational forms that, first, isolated high culture and, second, differentiated it from popular culture'; his examples are the Boston Symphony Orchestra (which sloughed off the Boston Pops) and the Boston Museum of Fine Arts. What became high art rituals, connoisseurship, and so on were, then, as Bourdieu argued, an aspect of bourgeois 'distinction': if art had become the experience of the transcendent and the ineffable, then it was also the exclusive property of 'those with the status to claim that their experience is the purest, the most authentic' (Di Maggio 317).

But whatever the role of this artistic ideology in shaping the bourgeois aesthetic, or the role of the *haute bourgeoisie* in defining art, it is misleading to fix the discourse of transcendence in a single social position or to assume that the late nineteenth-century urban bourgeoisie is exactly the same thing as the late twentieth-century middle class. Even in the nineteenth century the increasing concern to define taste boundaries reflected the extent to which tastes were actually shared across classes—the problem was the control of public space; the threat was social intermingling. 'The art must not be degraded,' complained a columnist in London's *Music World* in 1845 in response to an announcement of cheap concerts. 'To play the finest music to an audience which has been admitted at a shilling apiece is what I can never give consent to' (qtd. in Weber 26).

Despite such attempts to control taste by price, in England, at least, by the end of the nineteenth century 'something very close to a mass musical culture had emerged—a sharing of common taste across a broad social range.' On the one hand this meant 'popular musicians and audiences [drawing] upon what we tenuously call "art music" ': 'through the people's concert, the concert-hall, the music-hall, the choral contest, the brass band performance and other routes, Handel, Wagner and Donizetti to name but three, were known to many "ordinary people": vaguely by some, intimately and expertly by a significant minority' (Russell 6–7).

On the other hand, it meant the broad popularity of what Van Der Merwe calls 'parlour music' among all sectors of the population. This is not to say there was not, by the end of the nineteenth century, a 'Great Musical Schism' between classical and parlour music, but, rather, that the differences could not easily be mapped onto the class structure. Just as professional musicians of the time moved easily between opera and music hall pit bands, between winter seasons in symphony orchestras and summer seasons in pier shows, so listeners from all social spheres could well be fans of Wagner and Vesta Tilley, choral music and comedy turns. 'Highbrow and lowbrow lived in the same world,' as Van Der Merwe puts it, and 'quite often they were the same person' (3–4; and see Russell 7–8)—a fact that turn-of-the-century entrepreneurs were quick to exploit. In its 1934 obituary of the 'high' composer, Edward Elgar, the *Times* remembered what a 'rage' his first (1904) symphony had been: 'For some time the regular orchestras of London could not play it often enough, special concerts were arranged for it, [and] enterprising commercialists even engaged orchestras to play it in their lounges and palm courts as an attraction to their winter sales of underwear' (Crump 167).

To trace the social meaning of high and low culture, then, it is not enough to point to the aesthetic ideology of the nineteenth-century urban bourgeoisie; we also need to look at the effects of mass cultural production, which in key ways *followed* the emergence of bourgeois culture and worked on it (just as it worked on urban proletarian culture). The 'transcendent' meaning of classical music, for example, was both exploited and denied by its immediate use in the new movie houses, just as it has been since by radio and record and television companies, as the background sound of advertisements and airplanes and shopping malls.

I want to note three aspects of this approach to mass cultural history. First, if high culture is defined as bourgeois culture, it becomes a reflex to equate mass culture with the working class. In fact, though, mass culture (if we define it as the culture made possible by technological change, by the use of the means of mass cultural production) has always been a form of middle-class culture, characterized by middlebrow concerns. As Janice Radway has shown in her studies of the Book of the Month Club, the rise of mass culture at the beginning of this century actually meant a blurring of the distinctions between high and low, art and commerce, the sacred and the profane.

Second, if one aspect of the emergence of mass culture was the 'disciplining' of nineteenth-century 'unrespectable' culture, another, equally important, was the 'loosening up' of nineteenth-century respectable culture. There is, by now, much illuminating historical work on the former process. In *Rudeness and Civility* for example, John F. Kassan shows clearly how the rise of consumer culture, the 'orderly spectacle,' meant the decline of a participatory, communal leisure culture in American working-class neighborhoods, a move from 'enthusiasm' to 'disciplined spectatorship' (252–6). But the other side of this story is the development of 'safe' ways in which middle-class city dwellers (and the respectable working class) could enjoy proletarian patterns of sociability and noisy public behavior. Kathy Peiss, for example, suggests that the rise of mass culture (the cinema is a good example) meant developing those aspects of working-class leisure that the middle class found attractive and shedding those things of which they disapproved. Mass culture meant 'Polite Vaudeville,' 'regulated pleasure' for all classes, organized especially around heterosociability and a new valorization of youth and youth consumption. Her example is Coney Island:

> Steeplechase incorporated into its notion of mass entertainment cultural patterns derived from working class amusements, street life and popular entertainment.

> Like them, the park encouraged familiarity between strangers, permitted a free-and-easy sexuality, and structured heterosocial interaction. This culture was not adopted wholesale, but was transformed and controlled, reducing the threatening nature of sexual contact by removing it from the street, workplace and saloon. Within the amusement park, familiarity between women and men could be accept-able if tightly structured and made harmless through laughter. At Steeplechase, sexuality was constructed in terms of titillation, voyeurism, exhibitionism and a stress on a couple and romance. (Peiss 136)

From this historical perspective twentieth-century popular culture describes a process in which class and other group values and conflicts are mediated rather than directly expressed, which is one reason why popular commodities (*Hustler*, say, or heavy metal) can be and often are simultaneously 'transgressive' (of 'respectable' values) and reactionary (see Kipnis).

Third, if mass culture is not defined against middle-class culture, against art, but is a way of processing it, then the crucial high/low conflict is not that between social classes but that produced by the commercial process itself at *all* 'levels' of cultural expression, in pop as well as classical music, in sports as well as the cinema. High/low thus describes the emergence of consumer elites or cults, on the one hand (the bohemian *versus* the conformist), and the tension between artists and their audiences I've already described, on the other (the modernist and avant-gardist against the orthodox and the mainstream).[6]

Sometime in the opening decades of the twentieth century, notes Levin Schücking, the critical observation that 'the play succeeded with the public' became a standard line in the scathing review, as German theater critics sought to ally themselves with experimental playwrights (and the future) against audiences (and the past) (57). 'The crowd liked them,' remains a standard line in a scathing rock review—the more their fans liked, say, Genesis, the more I, as *Sunday Times* rock critic, felt moved to dismiss them.

Thus the themes that haunted modernist writers and critics at the turn of the century (their 'high' cultural concern to be true to their art, to disdain mere entertainment, to resist market forces, their longing for a 'sensitive minority' readership, for what Ezra Pound called 'a party of intelligence,' which meant, in practice, each other) have continued to haunt such low artists as jazz and rock musicians, such low audiences as pop fans.[7]

In Arnold Bennett's 1907 story 'The Death of Simon Fuge,' the narrator describes 'one of the two London evening papers that a man of taste may peruse without humiliating himself. How appealing a morsel, this sheet new and smooth from the press, this sheet written by an ironic, understanding small band of men just for a few thousand persons like me, ruthlessly scornful of the big circulations and the idols of the people!' (196). This could equally well be a description of *Melody Maker* and its readers in the 1960s or *New Musical Express* and its readers in the 1970s, or *The Face* and its readers in the 1980s.

And in his 1893 story 'Greville Fane,' Henry James remarks that his eponymous heroine, a decidedly middlebrow, commercial churn-'em-out novelist is, neverthe-less, 'haunted by solemn spinsters who came to tea from Continental pensions, and by unsophisticated Americans who told her she was just loved in *their* country. "I had rather just be paid there," she usually replied; for this tribe of transatlantic opinion was the only thing that galled her. The Americans went away thinking her coarse' (160). Which reminds me irresistibly of my friend Louise, who came from Baltimore to London in 1967 to read her poetry to Donovan. He was coarse, too.

But perhaps the most striking (and recurrent) feature of the continuing standoff of the aesthete and the philistine (a necessary discursive counterpoint) is that for both sides the other is feminine. The woman as materialist corruptor of the artist is a consistent theme of James's stories and of subsequent bohemian mythology—of Bob Dylan's early songs, for instance—just as the high cultural description of mass culture as 'feminine' by theorists from Adorno and Horkheimer to Baudrillard is echoed in rock fans' contemptuous dismissal of 'teenybop' music (see Huyssen).

Meanwhile, from the philistine side, the American bandmaster John Philip Sousa once stressed to a Houston reporter that 'the people who frequent my concerts are the strong and healthy. I mean healthy both of mind and body. These people like virile music. Longhaired men and shorthaired women you never see in my audience. And I don't want them' (qtd. in Levine 238). This equation of high art and sissiness and perversion is familiar today for us in Britain thanks to the efforts of Gary Bushall, punk-rock-writer-turned-TV-critic of the *Sun*.

But the point I want to stress here is that the sustenance of 'art' in Henry James's or Ezra Pound's terms became dependent, in the end, on the academy, and it is this institutional setting, rather than the value issues as such, that has come to differentiate high from popular culture. It is the academy, that is—the university, the conservatoire, the art school—that, as Pierre Bourdieu argues, nowadays sustains high culture and guarantees its reproduction: in the master/pupil relationship, in the continuity of knowledge and sense of tradition embodied in the library and gallery and concert hall, in the setting of the standards of creative skill and interpretative expertise. It is the academy that now provides the terms—the meaning—of high cultural experience; it is academic discourse that now shapes the newspaper review, the record sleeve note, the exhibition catalogue; it is the academic who makes possible the mass consumption of high culture (Henry James as a classic text). Matthew Arnold, who continues to hover over all discussions of cultural value, approvingly quoted Renan as saying that 'all ages have had their inferior literature, but the great danger of our time is that this inferior literature tends more and more to get the upper place. No one has the same advantage as the Academy for fighting against this mischief' (376–7). Academy here means the Académie Française, which, in Arnold's words, had special facilities 'for creating a form of intellectual culture *which shall impose itself on all around.*'

By 1913, when Sir Arthur Quiller-Couch came to give his inaugural lecture as the first Professor of English at Cambridge, this notion of the academy had a more general currency. The purpose of studying English literature, suggested Quiller-Couch, was 'the refining of critical judgment,' the Cambridge degree aimed to create 'a man of unmistakeable intellectual breeding, whose trained judgment we can trust to choose the better and reject the worse' (qtd. in Keating 456–7). The development of English literature as an academic discipline has become a familiar story, but it is still worth stressing that it involved not just a civilizing mission—sending discriminating readers out into the classroom and marketplace—but also a defensive move: the academy became a stockade within which the better and the superior could be defended from the philistines (and, in particular, from the philistines' literary representative, the journalist, the object of recurrent academic hostility).[8] Thus, to provide a random example of the embattled academic, defending the artist from commercial forces, here is a quote from Harvey Allen's 1938 introduction to the Modern Library edition of Edgar Allan Poe's complete tales and poems. Poe's 'misfortune,' writes Allen, was that

> The results of a labour of a lifetime, two decades of continuous and persistent writing both in verse and prose, lay scattered in the pages of obscure, provincial, female and piffling—not to say downright eccentric—magazines, newspapers, weeklies, journals, remaindered and suppressed books and prospectuses—the very names of which are frequently productive of ribaldry or conducive to nausea. *Only the cast-iron constitution of professional scholars can solemnly digest their contents with the bowels of compassion.* (v; my emphasis)

The imagery is of the scholar as knight, riding forth to rescue the innocent artist from the clammy, corrupting hands of the popular paper, the popular magazine, the popular reader.

It is not only our cast-iron constitution that enables academics to consider mass culture dispassionately, but also our institutional position: we're free of the material implications of the art-vs.-market dilemma of writers like Henry James or musicians like the Gang of Four. It is not surprising, then, that high cultural values are by now inextricably entangled with academic practices, rather than with bourgeois consumption as such. This has had a number of consequences both for the teaching of cultural and literary studies (hence, for example, the peculiar suggestion in every monthly magazine I read at present that changes in university reading lists mean the end of civilization as we know it) and, indeed, for pop culture itself (in the influence of art schools on British pop music, for example). But I want to make two rather different points about culture, the academy, and popular taste.

First, the equation of high and academic culture helps explain why the high/low culture distinction is still so consistently read as a mind/body split. This can be traced back to the mental/manual division of labor built into the Industrial Revolution and the consequent organization of education, and overlies the original Romantic dichotomy between feeling and reason—feelings, that is, are now taken to be best expressed in mental terms, in silent contemplation of great art or great music. Bodily responses are, it seems, by definition, mindless. 'The brain,' wrote Frank Howes in the *British Journal of Aesthetics* in 1962, is associated with art music; 'brainlessness' with pop. Popular music, agreed Peter Stadler in the same journal a couple of issues later, is music requiring 'a minimum of brain activity.'

By 1971 the same argument was still being made in the journal but now, by Raymond Durgnat, to the opposite effect. He was *celebrating* rock and roll for its sensual effects. This has become a familiar strand in the populist academic account of pop culture, as intellectuals fantasize about the pleasures of mindlessness, and echoes similar intellectual arguments about the thrills of sensational literature, the emotional impact of film and TV melodrama [see Durgnat; and Frith, 'Cultural Studies']. 'In show business,' wrote the Hungarian musicologist Janos Marothy in his exhaustive Marxist history of high and low music, 'audience demands . . . are determined by the taste of the bourgeoisie. With . . . a kind of romantic longing, the bourgeoisie lays claim to the popular in an attempt to compensate for the emptiness of its life by means of "exotic" stimulants' (530–1). In cultural studies, we might add, audience demands are determined by the taste of academics. With a kind of romantic longing, the academy lays claim to the popular in an attempt to compensate for the egghead-edness of its life by means of sensual stimulants. Academics have bodies, that is, even if the theoretical effects of this are carefully hidden.

Even more important, 'the people' have minds. 'Here, in reading together,' writes Levin Schücking about nineteenth-century German culture (and these days we would add, in going to the movies together, watching TV together, playing music together), 'the opportunity was gained [especially for the young] of securing from the other's judgement of men and things an insight into [their] thoughts and feelings; an insight likely to become the first bond between kindred souls' (Schücking 32). Exactly the same point is made in Gordon Legge's pop novel, *The Shoe*, in which a pub newcomer's character (his slobbishness, his conservatism, his potential violence) is immediately revealed to drinkers and readers alike by his jukebox choice: Jeff Beck's 'Hi Ho Silver Lining.'

As academics, it seems, we don't actually know much about such aesthetic alliances and distinctions or about their implications (though we live them ourselves all the time). Even when we claim to know what people like, we rarely have much interesting to say about how such liking is organized from the inside (an inside untrammeled by sociological questionnaires and unpatrolled by subcultural cheerleaders). Among the few studies I know that give a sense of the popular aesthetic in action are the Mass-Observation surveys of British film tastes in 1938 and 1943 (Richards and Sheridan).

In these essays in popular criticism there are several obvious evaluative themes:

—films are assessed in terms of technique, skill and craft; with reference to things (acting, lighting, staging—*details*) done well.

—films are assessed in terms of expense and spectacle; cheapness and tackiness are words of abuse.

These are judgments (echoed in popular music discourse) of what is perceived to have *gone into the production*; they measure the extent to which the audience (the viewer, the listener) is being taken seriously.

—films are assessed for their believability, their truth-to-life; the realist impulse (the pop concern for sincerity) means judging a film's (or song's) narrative against one's own 'reality' (and vice versa), a judgment commonly made via identification with a character or performer.

—films are assessed for their ability to take one out of oneself, a quality of experience measured by its intensity (thrills), its presence (laughter), its difference from the everyday, its quality, that is, as entertainment.

These apparently contradictory demands are brought together in an assessment of films according to the *range* of experiences they offer—a good laugh and a good cry, the believable and the unbelievable—and the most common complaint is that a film (or record or TV show or holiday resort or haircut) is disappointing, doesn't live up

363

to expectations or else meets them all too well. Such judgments rest on various sorts of prior knowledge (about genre distinctions, for example) but also on implicit aesthetic hierarchies: the popular consumer too distinguishes between the easy and the difficult, between trash and quality, between indulgence and education; the popular consumer too makes different sorts of demand (more or less aesthetic, more or less functional) of different sorts of cultural commodity.

I will end—appropriately—with another Mass-Observation theme, the suggestion that to be valuable a film should have a 'moral' (a word that substitutes, I suppose, for meaning). 'I don't know what that was about,' said someone behind us at *The Grifters*. 'What was the moral?' 'Never throw something at someone who's drinking,' her friend suggested. The pursuit of a moral (a point, a closure) is, in academic cultural studies, seen as naive if not reactionary; it ensures that commercial popular culture, whatever its supposed content, remains orderly. On the other hand, in pursuit of such order, a popular reading often has to ask what Jonathan Culler once called (with reference to the popular story of the Three Little Pigs) 'improper questions,' just as in their concern for the real the popular reader or viewer or listener is often in pursuit of improper detail, of gossip, anecdotal truth (Ray 284). How many children had Lady Macbeth? Elvis Presley? Paul de Man?

The compulsion to explain the inexplicable, a recurring theme of popular narrative, has the effect of making the remarkable banal and thus, literally, even more remarkable. This is not a political impulse (politics starts from the material conditions in which people live, not with the cultural strategies that make those conditions livable), but it does generate a certain critical momentum, and, as I began with two quotes from high cultural positions which dismissed low culture as having no intellectual interest at all, I want to end with two quotes from equally high positions which suggest that what's at stake in exploring popular cultural values is not just something out there (in the body), but involves a common culture, something in which we share, in the mind as well.

'When we love a book,' Catherine Stimpson wrote recently,

> we read energetically. We believe that if a beloved book were human it would embrace us. Our feeling is more intense than easy pleasure, more dashing and ferocious than delight, more generous than distraction. We are grateful to the beloved text for being there. . . . [Such books] provide some of love's relational and terrifying thrills . . . [provide] the sensation of inhabiting a world apart from the world that normally inhibits one; an oscillation between control and self-abandonment; a dance with the partners of amusement and consolation; the gratification of needs that [have been] concealed. (958)

To which I'd just add that the romance of reading defines popular culture too: records and films, cars and TV shows, sports teams and designer clothes are loved.

'When we study the great classics of literature,' notes Northrop Frye in his essays on popular romance,

> we are following the dictates of common sense, as embodied in the author of Ecclesiastes: 'Better is the sight of the eye than the wandering of desire.' Great literature is what the eye can see, it is the genuine infinite as opposed to the phony

infinite, the endless adventures and endless sexual stimulation of the wandering of desire. But I have a notion that if the wandering of desire did not exist, great literature would not exist either. (30)

And I have a notion—here's my moral—that if desire has, for a moment, wandered into the classroom we should now be ready to follow it out again.

NOTES

1. This has led, among other things, to the relentless drive of film, TV, and pop music studies to develop canons of texts-for-study even less open to challenge than the literary canon. For a general discussion of these issues see Smith.
2. One sign of this is the ubiquitous use of competitions in the popular arts.
3. For a useful survey of musicians' day-to-day assessment of their work see Wills and Cooper.
4. The classic discussion of popular musicians' attitudes toward popularity remains Becker.
5. For a brilliant account of the evaluative consequences of this 'gap' in classical music see Cook.
6. For the significance of bohemianism for pop culture see Frith and Horne.
7. For an entertaining and helpful account of these arguments among turn-of-the-century writers see Keating.
8. Most recently expressed in the arguments around Paul de Man and deconstruction.

REFERENCES

Allen, Harvey. 'Introduction.' *Edgar Allan Poe: Complete Tales and Poetry*. New York: Modern Library, 1938.

Arnold, Matthew. 'The Literary Influence of Academics.' *Matthew Arnold: Poetry and Prose*. Ed. John Bryson. London: Hart-Davis, 1954.

Becker, Howard. *Outsiders: Studies in the Sociology of Deviance*. New York: Free Press, 1963.

Bennett, Arnold. *The Grim Smile of the Five Towns*. Leipzig: Tauchnitz, 1907.

Bloom, Allan. *The Closing of the American Mind*. New York: Simon and Schuster, 1987.

Bourdieu, Pierre. *Distinction: A Social Critique of the Judgement of Taste*. 1979. London: Routledge, 1984.

Cook, Nicholas. *Music Imagination and Culture*. Oxford: Clarendon, 1990.

Crump, Jeremy. 'The Identity of English Music: The Reception of Elgar 1898–1935.' *Englishness: Politics and Culture, 1880–1920*. Ed. Robert Colls and Philip Dodd. London: Croom Helm, 1986.

Di Maggio, Paul. 'Cultural Entrepreneurship in Nineteenth Century Boston, Part II: The Classification and Framing of American Art.' *Media Culture and Society* 4.4 (1982): 303–22.

Durgnat, Raymond. 'Rock, Rhythm and Dance.' *British Journal of Aesthetics* 11 (1971): 28–47.

Fiske, John. 'Popular Discrimination.' *Modernity and Mass Culture*. Ed. James Naremore and Patrick Brantlinger. Bloomington: Indiana UP, 1991.

Frith, Simon. 'What Is Good Music?' *Canadian Universities Music Review* 10.2 (1990): 92–102.

——. 'Cultural Studies and Popular Music.' Grossberg et al. 174–86.

——. Simon, and Howard Horne. *Art into Pop*. London: Methuen, 1988.

Frye, Northrop. *The Secular Scripture: A Study of the Structure of Romance*. Cambridge: Harvard UP, 1976.

Grossberg, Lawrence et al. *Cultural Studies Now and in the Future*. London: Routledge, 1991.

Howes, Frank. 'A Critique of Folk, Popular and "Art" Music.' *British Journal of Aesthetics* 2.3 (1962): 239–48.

Huyssen, Andreas. 'Mass Culture as Woman: Modernism's Other.' *After the Great Divide*. Bloomington: Indiana UP, 1986.

James, Henry. *Stories of Writers and Artists*. 1903. New York: New Directions, 1944.

Kaplan, E. Ann. *Rocking Round the Clock: Music, Television, Postmodernism and Consumer Culture*. New York: Methuen, 1987.

Kassan, John F.. *Rudeness and Civility: Manners in Nineteenth Century Urban America*. New York: Hill and Wang, 1990.

Keating, Peter. 'Readers and Novelists.' *The Haunted Study: A Social History of the English Novel, 1875–1914*. London: Secker and Warburg, 1989.

Kipnis, Laura. '(Male) Desire and (Female) Disgust: Reading *Hustler*.' Grossberg et al. 373–91.

Kogan, Frank. *Why Music Sucks* 7 (1991).

Legge, Gordon. *The Shoe*. Edinburgh: Polygon, 1989.

Levine, Lawrence M.. *Highbrow/Lowbrow*. Cambridge: Harvard UP, 1988.

Marothy, Janos. *Music and the Bourgeois: Music and the Proletarian*. Budapest: Akademiai Kindo, 1974.

Miller, Mark Crispin. 'Where All the Flowers Went.' *Boxed In: The Culture of TV*. Evanston: Northwestern UP, 1989.

Peiss, Kathy. *Cheap Amusements: Working Women and Leisure in Turn-of-the-Century New York*. Philadelphia: Temple UP, 1986.

Radway, Janice. 'The Scandal of the Middlebrow: The Book of the Month Club, Class Fracture and Cultural Authority.' *South Atlantic Quarterly* 89.4 (1990): 603–36.

Ray, Robert B.. 'The Twelve Days of Christmas: A Response to Dudley Andrew.' *Strategies* 3 (1990): 268–85.

Richards, Jeffrey, and Dorothy Sheridan, eds. *Mass-Observation at the Movies*. London: Routledge, 1987.

Russell, Dave. *Popular Music in England, 1840–1914*. Manchester: Manchester UP, 1987.

Schücking, Levin L.. *The Sociology of Literary Taste*. 1931. London: Kegan Paul, 1944.

Shiach, Morag. *Discourse on Popular Culture*. Cambridge: Polity, 1989.

Smith, Barbara Herrnstein. *Contingencies of Value*. Cambridge: Harvard UP, 1988.

Stadler, Peter. 'The Aesthetics of Popular Music.' *British Journal of Aesthetics* 2.4 (1962): 351–61.

Stimpson, Catherine R.. 'Reading for Love: Canons, Paracanons, and Whistling Jo March.' *New Literary History* 21 (1990): 957–76.

Stratton, Jon. 'Capitalism and Romantic Ideology in the Record Business.' *Popular Music* 3 (1983): 143–56.

Van Der Merwe, Peter. *Origins of the Popular Style*. Oxford: Clarendon, 1989.

Weber, William. *Music and the Middle Class*. London: Croom Helm, 1975.

Wills, Geoff, and Cary L. Cooper. *Pressure Sensitive: Popular Musicians under Stress*. London: Sage, 1988.

Lawrence Grossberg (1947–)

Lawrence Grossberg earned his BA from the University of Rochester and went on to study under Stuart Hall at the Centre for Contemporary Cultural Studies at Birmingham. He got his doctorate from the University of Illinois at Urbana, Champaign, and has travelled extensively in Europe as part of an anarchist theatre commune. Currently, he is teaching philosophy, literary/critical theory, and media and communication studies at the University of Illinois, where he is also the assistant director of the Unit of Critical and Interpretive Theory.

As Grossberg notes, academic interest in the connections between MTV and post-modernism is growing, and his essay, 'MTV: Swinging on the (Postmodern) Star', can be compared to E. Anne Kaplan's discussion of MTV, 'Feminism/Oedipus/Postmodernism: The Case of MTV', in *Postmodernism and its Discontents* (1988). Grossberg identifies MTV as a 'new "snake" in the cultural garden', which has aroused the sort of 'moral panic' with which particular cultural forms are customarily greeted from both the 'moral' Right and the 'moral' Left.

Grossberg goes on to define three sets of relationships that need to be taken into account when investigating MTV—media, economic conditions, and communicative potential. In each of these categories, Grossberg indicates the nuanced and empirical distinctions that need to be made in investigating rock as a video experience, which in turn move MTV from being a total, unique and monolithic phenomenon to being part of 'the changes taking place in television itself'.
G.R. and J.M.

MTV: swinging on the (postmodern) star

There is a new 'snake' in the cultural garden. Music television is the latest in a series of moral panics organized around particular cultural forms. While different moral constituencies interpret its dangers differently, the attacks have been predictable and boring. Whether coming from the 'moral' Right, the 'moral' Left, or from rock and roll fans (usually baby boomers), the criticisms echo the fears that have greeted many other popular cultural forms: music television is *another* example (surprise!) of sexist, violent, hedonistic, commodified, and alienating discourse. Reading the various public discussions, one is always aware that the same statements, inflected just a bit differently, could be and have been made in other cultural arenas. The vehemence of the responses to music television seems to be less the result of its actual uniqueness than of its intersections with two powerfully contested domains within our cultural life: the struggle over the meanings and experience of youth, and the resurgence of a moral panic in response to rock and roll more generally (e.g., the Parents' Music Resource Center).

But unlike earlier moral panics, debates about music television have quickly entered the academy; it has already generated its own field of competing interpretations and evaluations. Discussions within the institutions of knowledge production display their own kind of panic-reaction to music television, and while the panic is less emotional, it is no less real. What is perhaps most remarkable is the speed with which this has been accomplished: unlike previous forms of post-World War Two popular culture (especially youth culture), music television has been rapidly incorporated into the canon of legitimated topics.[1] In these debates, music television is rarely offered as just *another* example; it is the *ultimate* example: of the commodification of culture, of the capitalist recuperation of 'authentic' forms of resistance, of textual and subjective schizophrenia, of the postmodern disappearance of reality, of orgasmic democracy, etc. If the more public disputes are often carried on unself-consciously, with little empirical research or theoretical reflection, the academic disputes demonstrate how easy it is to find empirical support for many interpretations of the world; isolating one aspect of reality, abstracting it out of its concrete existence and ignoring its specificity, one can readily find 'proof' of its absolute power to define and determine the world.

Speaking metaphorically, if you go marching into a jungle looking for snakes, you are bound to find a lot of them; they are, in fact, there. But to assume that the essence of the jungle is revealed in the snake, that the existence of snakes defines the jungle, misses the complexity and richness of the jungle. And it misses what is interesting about the sorts of snakes one finds in the jungle(s). Similarly, understanding music television requires us to identify and locate its specific complexity. We need to look at it contextually and relationally, to ask what is unique in the diverse practices of music television, and what they have in common with other cultural formations. Its current forms were introduced partly in response to significant technological, economic, and musical changes; but it has emerged as well within a particular set of historical conditions, generational struggles, and changes in people's everyday lives.

368

The complexity of music television is defined by the particular links it builds and builds upon, between economic, textual, and communicative practices, historical relations, and subjective identities and experiences. Since these articulations are never necessary, we need to ask how they have been and are being constructed; and, if there are reasons to oppose such ways of defining and producing the forms of music television, we need to ask where alternatives are available?

Further, music television, like our jungle, is full of contradictions and struggles. Recognizing these depends upon our assuming that people are not cultural dopes, nor passively determined by the conditions of their existence. While there are obviously real historical tendencies, lines of force, pushing people in particular directions and into specific relations, nevertheless people are always actively responding to their conditions, taking what they are given, bending it to their own needs, and trying to gain some improvement in their lives, trying to survive and win (as Rambo says). The fact that people are subordinated and often oppressed—and that they sometimes occupy the role of oppressor—does not mean that they have been manipulated, duped, or colonized. It means that people operate in a field of contradictory relations and forces, and within that field, they do what they deem best or, perhaps, what they see as the best they can do.

Rock and roll on television

In this paper, I want to briefly talk about three sets of relationships that define the forms and effects of music television in the 1980s: media, economic, and communicative. Let me begin with an obvious but not trivial observation: music television involves *rock and roll* (in its broadest sense) on television, and rock and roll on *television*.[2] It cannot be separated from the forms, histories, audiences, and economies of each of these two cultural formations. Music television refers to the complex set of different but interrelated places and ways in which rock and roll is currently inserted into the discourses of television. It involves us in examining a number of different relationships: the relation between rock and roll and visual images; between different forms of rock and roll and different media (e.g., films, concerts, etc.); between particular songs (genres and groups) and their visual presentations and styles (e.g., the construction of particular video clips); between individual video clips and the particular formats which have come to dominate the presentations of music television (e.g., MTV but also VHF 1, Night Flight, Friday Night Videos, etc.); between the different forms of music television and their overlapping rock and roll audiences; and finally, between the forms of music television and the broader developments within both rock and roll and televisual discourse. Specific phenomena—whether individual video clips or video channels like MTV—cannot be understood apart from this broad range of relationships.

In fact, one does not have to be a video addict to notice that rock and roll is omnipresent on our videoscreens. If it is true to say that television has incorporated rock and roll, it is equally true that rock and roll has conquered television. It not only pro-

369

vides the soundtrack of our lives but increasingly, the visual (video) track as well: in advertisements, sports events, movies, series, themes, it is both visually and sonorially changing the face (the ears and the mouth as much as the eyes) of television. This is neither surprising not necessarily bad; as the rock and roll generations have grown up and come to define the largest part of the population, it is their music which is taken for granted. And, speaking personally, if one has to hear music in commercials, is it not better to hear the music one likes? Rock and roll has moved into the center of contemporary culture, defining the mainstream of the dominant forms of cultural enjoyment and perhaps even legitimacy. But if rock and roll is increasingly the mainstream of popular culture, it is important to note that it is not only the mainstream of rock and roll that has entered television, nor is music television merely a reflection of the *Billboard* charts. Not only can television make (and in some cases, remake) hits, it has also appropriated rock and roll's wide range of styles and successes. If MTV is television's 'AM radio' (with some 1970s FM influences), there are alternative programs and other places to turn for music television. (Consider the diverse playlist of a typical episode of *Miami Vice*: Dire Straits, Bryan Adams, Shriekback, Mark Isham, Fernando Villolona, Grace Jones, and Belkis Concepcion y sus Chicas.)

There are three common but mistaken assumptions about music television. The first is that the televisual image is necessarily less ambiguous than the musical image. On this basis, music videos are often condemned as limiting fans' imaginative freedom by predefining the meaning of the song and thus reducing the fan to a passive recipient. But television is never passively received and its texts are as open to different interpretations as any rock and roll song. If anything, the explicit conjunction of visual images and songs seems to multiply the possibilities of interpretation rather than constrain them.

The second assumption is that music television, by placing rock and roll in the hands of commercial corporations, increases the distance between the fan and the musician, and decreases the ability of both to control the production of the music. But rock and roll has always existed in a variety of marketable and mediated forms: records, tapes, films, radios, etc. There is little reason to privilege the live performance as if it were unmediated or as the only viable source of an 'authentic' experience: how small does such a performance have to be, how much electronic equipment is permissible, for an 'authentic' rock and roll experience? Rock and roll has always been a part of a capitalist system of production, distribution, and consumption within which both musicians and fans have constantly struggled against the formal, economic, and technological demands of a profit-motivated industry. The so-called 'independents' still sell a commodity, although they may operate on a smaller scale and with a smaller profit margin, and with 'better' motives.

The third assumption is that there is something radically new about the association of rock and roll with both visual images and television. But, as any fan of rock and roll knows, rock and roll has always been as much about images—images of stars and performers, of fashion and aesthetics, of the body and romance, of dancing and sex, and most importantly, of attitudes—as it has been about sounds. The importance of images, the particular forms they take and the ways they are allowably produced varies, not only across genres but also over time. For example, as Andrew Goodwin has argued,[3] the emergence of MTV cannot be separated

370

from the ways in which punk foregrounded the deconstruction of images and 'new pop' legitimated their reconstruction, even through such self-consciously artificial practices as lip-synching. Further, as any historian of rock and roll knows, rock and roll has always been on television and it has used that connection, in different ways and forms, at different times, for different audiences: e.g., live performances (from *Ed Sullivan* to *Saturday Night Live*; from *Kasey Kasem* to *Midnight Special*, from *American Bandstand* to *Putting on the Hits*, from Ricky Nelson to *The Monkees* to *The Partridge Family*); in ads and sports events; as a topic in a series or a particular episode; as a news or feature story; as an image of a character (Kookie), a generation or lifestyle (*Happy Days*) or an attitude (*Miami Vice*, David Letterman).

This list is obviously neither complete nor definitive; among other things, it ignores the important stylistic differences within and between programs. Moreover, an adequate history of rock and roll television would have to take both the audience and history into account, because both program production and viewing are historical activities. Different audiences may watch the same program but interpret it differently, not only because of their own history and relations to rock and roll, but also because of the use to which they put particular images in the larger contexts of their cultural lives and rock and roll fandom. One can, for example, use a particular program for narrative pleasure; for background; for lessons in dance, style, and attitude; for the televisual equivalent of pinups; for dancing or socializing (whether in the home, at parties, or clubs). At certain moments, for particular audiences, television may provide the easiest if not the only access to rock and roll images and performances. Women may not be comfortable attending heavy metal concerts; adolescents may not have the opportunity to enter bars; people living in small towns may not have venues which regularly feature rock and roll; aging baby boomers may not feel comfortable placing themselves in the midst of young rock and roll audiences.

The emergence, the forms, and the effects of music television cannot be entirely separated from changes taking place in television itself. Television is, after all, not a simple, unchanging medium; it has multiple forms, both technologically and textually. Its audiences do not all respond in the same ways, and in fact, no audience has a simple, single response to it. Significant changes in the technology and the economy of hardware have had important effects on the ways in which individuals and groups appropriate the medium. The one family television located in the semi-public, domestically governed space, has given way to the proliferation of televisions, not only in the different spaces of the household but also in public spaces. The small television set, with its poor visual and sonorial quality, has been replaced by technologies with highly sophisticated reproduction capacities (including stereo television). Remote control has changed our ability to control reception (e.g., Zipping, Zapping, muting) at the same time that cable has increased the range of programs available. This has also produced new economic demands: not only to identify particular audiences which can be delivered to advertisers (e.g., narrowcasting), but also to develop more precise guarantees of what is on the screen at the moment. Video tape technology, finally, has opened up new contexts and practices for television viewing, including home editing, video–movies (and their associated rental clubs), videobars (which may play tapes without the sound, or with a different soundtrack), and videotape collecting.

371

Music television and the commodification of culture

Music television is not only a response to changing economic, technological, cultural, and sociological conditions, it also enters into and changes these relations.[4] It has changed the ways rock and roll (and perhaps television) works in our culture. I want to describe these effects in two domains: first, as a changing set of economic relations and second, as a changing structure of communication.

The fact that rock and roll and music television operate within a capitalist economy of commodification is hardly remarkable; no doubt, rock videos are not only self-promotions but advertisements for consumption itself. This tells us very little about their concrete relations to the cultural industries and their audiences. The commodification of cultural practices—the formation of the culture industries, including their incorporation into capitalist relations of marketing and production (and most recently distribution)—is neither new nor specific to music television.[5] Music television's economic existence is defined by its complex functions within the contemporary structures of capitalism. In many ways, music television merely continues forms of commodification, packaging, and promotion that have defined postwar popular culture. It also shares many features that are characteristic of the postwar record industry. And, it exhibits certain features which, while not totally unique to it, suggest that it can be seen as the 'flagship' or a significant reorganization of the entertainment industry.

Let me begin with some obvious statements: music television produces a number of different commodities: it sells not only advertisers' products but lifestyles and a commitment to consumption; it sells not only records but videos; it sells images and packaged tastes; and it sells audiences. These commercial relations do not all exist harmoniously together. As Will Straw points out, there is an increasing split between the audiences which purchase musical commodities, and those which purchase various consumer goods (especially those designed for the upper and upbeat side of the baby-boom generations). It is also true that the increasing use of videos to promote rock and roll has given the major record companies (with their financial and technological resources) yet another advantage in the struggle to control, if not popular taste, then the availability of particular instances of popular culture. As budgets for video production mount, the commitment to other forms of support (such as tours) decreases, and companies almost inevitably cut their lists as they face ever spiraling costs and risks: musical talent may be weighed against the additional requirement of one's talent as a video performer.

The particular programing formats—such as MTV—that have dominated music television are an appropriation of radio formats defined in the 1950s and refined in the 1970s: the emphasis on the single (as the object of listening if not as the ultimate product to be purchased, since singles are not the dominant market form of popular music in the 1980s), the use of chattering VJ's, the incorporation of 'news' and special features, the absence of the audience from the screen (compared with early programs like *American Bandstand*), etc. Yet while the fragmentation of radio formats in the

372

1970s was an early precursor of MTV's 'narrowcasting,' MTV offered record companies, musicians, and audiences something which had never been available in the United States: a national rock and roll network. This opens the possibility of new ways of organizing tastes, and of new speeds at which songs and musicians can be disseminated across the country and incorporated into the national consciousness. Music television also brought youth audiences to television which had previously remained largely inaccessible to television's advertising messages, audiences which no doubt increased the pressure on families to be hooked up to cable or satellite systems.

Yet the really interesting—and difficult—questions involve how music videos (whether singularly or in larger formats) work as promotions and as the occasion for advertisements. The two are not identical (although contemporary advertising styles may be erasing the difference); promotions do not make a direct appeal for purchasing a product. Rather, they create a context within which such a purchase is both sensible and desirable. A video clip promotes its own song, the single record, and the album (or tape), much as radio has always done. It may even promote a film or a television show. In this instance, the song is its own image. On the other hand, video clips, like advertisements, do seem to offer more than the musical product; the product is packaged in discourses that are apparently unnecessary to the function of the music itself. Of course, this 'packaging' is not extraneous if it is the video itself that is being commodified and promoted (and to some extent, this is certainly true in the marketplace). But more generally, the intricate and important links between rock and roll and images/attitudes make it difficult to separate the commodity from the packaging. One is always buying more than music when buying rock and roll. This leaves open the question of whether, as Simon Frith argues, videos offer the meaning of the song as a commodity.

The economics of music television, and of the video clip as a promotional device, point to a broad transformation of the forms of the commodification of entertainment. Frith has described some of the economic realignments operating here. The music business is increasingly incorporated into multinational corporations with diverse, trans-media interests in entertainment. The production of a hit song is less important than the production of the star as a marketable commodity. While stars have always been produced and promoted, and in some cases (like Elvis Presley) have moved across media and genres, there have always been limits to this mobility. These limits have not only disappeared in the contemporary forms of the production of stardom, but it is their absence which defines the star. The star does not need a history. The old model of a star building an ever wider audience while 'paying their dues' seems to have given way to the immediate insertion of a figure into a position of stardom already waiting for him or her. It is less a matter of talent than promotion and visibility; talent is less a necessary prerequisite than a 'resource-pool' available for corporate raiding. Stars need no origin or identity outside of their various appearances as stars. Their stardom does not rest on a particular activity which will forever provide the basis for their reputation. In fact, a star's ability to occupy this new dispersed position of stardom may depend on an ironic reference to his or her artistic skills, and it is perfectly reasonable (and common) for an audience to discover such talents only after identifying the star somewhere else. Not only is it increasingly difficult to distinguish between advertisements, videoclips, and episodic sequences from films or television programs, it is increasingly difficult to define where a video-star's popularity is located (e.g., Bruce Willis as a singer, the star of *Moonlighting*, and a spokesperson for Seagram's wine coolers; Phil Collins has probably won as many fans through his commercials as through his actual records).

The star has to remain distant from any particular activity in order to be free to occupy the space of a particular image or attitude. It is the star—as the emblem of a particular mood or attitude—who is the major product promoted by music television; the star is a mobile sign which can be linked to any practice, product, or language, freed from any particular message or set of values. It is the star who is produced and promoted by the discourses of music television, sold to its advertisers and producers, and delivered over to its audiences. Stars are no longer individuals measured by their creativity, their authentic relation to their performance, or even the possibilities of an audience's projecting their fantasies onto them. Within this new corporately constituted space of cultural images, the star becomes a commodified (and therefore mobile) sign, moving across the broad terrain of cultural tastes and entertainment.

Music television, communication, and post-modernity

Still the question remains, where do we locate music television's popularity, its cultural power, and its communicative effects?[6] Music television certainly communicates images and lifestyles, interpretations and ideologies. But it does something more; Robert Pittman, one of the 'designers' of MTV, described it as a 'mood enhancer.' We need to take this notion of the communication of mood, affect, and emotion seriously if we are to understand the particular force of music television's message. The meanings and images communicated by the different forms of music television are relevant only insofar as they get us somewhere else: to a particular attitude or mood. Moods are, after all, contentless, although they have both quality and quantity; they construct the 'tone,' 'texture,' or 'coloration' of the world within which particular experiences and meanings are located. Moods are also infectious; they do not follow linear paths from senders to receivers; nor are they easily controlled by the normal strategies of interaction.

Of course, music itself frequently works precisely by foregrounding affective and emotional responses. But the uniqueness of music television's communication is defined by the fact that the construction and dissemination of moods is increasingly separated from the communication of any particular meanings or values. This affective overindulgence is partly the result of a set of historical changes which cumulatively define a rather unique—postmodern—condition, especially for those generations which grew up after the Second World War: the relationship between affect and ideology has become increasingly tenuous. The postmodern condition can be described as the perception of a growing gap between these two aspects of our experience, between the meanings and values which are available to us to make sense of our lives and actions, and the places where it appears possible to care about something enough, to have enough faith that it matters, so that one can actually make a commitment, that one can invest oneself in it. Whatever the reality of such perceptions, the future has become increasingly uncertain (and its images bear a striking resemblance to contemporary Beirut!); it has become increasingly difficult to differentiate between reality and its images, and most of the traditional values and pleasures (love, family, sex) which may have given our lives some meaning in the past have become treacherous traps which never seem to deliver on their promises. The result is that it is ever more difficult to make sense of our affective experiences ('life's a bitch and then you die') and to put any faith in the taken for granted interpretations of the meanings of our lives and actions. We no longer trust our common sense even as we are compelled to live it. (Even the promise of 'sex and drugs and rock 'n' roll.') We are condemned to try to make sense of our lives in structures that clearly contradict our experiences.

The emergence of rock and roll in the 1950s, and its history since then, can be partly understood as a response to this postmodern condition. Rock and roll was never concerned with communicating meanings, but rather, with providing the energies and the attitudes with which you could reshape your own moods against the increasing pessimism, boredom, and terror of contemporary life. This 'empowerment' depended upon rock and roll's elitism, and its construction of 'affective alliances.' The definition of rock and roll, the boundaries which define, not what is good or bad, but what deserves to be included within the category itself, is never simply available. Different fans construct the boundaries in different places and different ways: to be a fan of rock and roll is precisely to claim that one has a privileged access to those affective stakes which allow one to understand what truly constitutes the power of rock and roll. By circumscribing the limits of rock and roll, the fans also draw a field, a mobile bubble, around themselves; although their relation to rock and roll need not define a particular identity for them, it marks them as different. It encapsulates them within the affective possibilities of their particular version of the rock and roll culture. There are always others (including many who think they are rock and roll fans) who are not within this space, who do not understand rock and roll, and who do not share in the 'secret' knowledge. The knowledge is not hidden but it is only available by entering into the particular conjunction of music, style, attitude, images, etc. that defines such a rock and roll culture. The knowledge is there, in the affective experiences that are constructed by the particular sets of relations. Rock and roll empowers its fans by placing them into a particular 'affective alliance' which marks their difference, not in terms of their beliefs and values as much as their ability to struggle against the dominant moods of contemporary life without being able to rely on its languages. Obviously, there is nothing about this strategy which necessarily implies any sort of political resistance, personal authenticity, or cultural marginality. On the contrary, rock and roll is always located within the mainstream of everyday life; knowing that anything you believe in or desire is likely to end up being another trap, rock and roll offers strategies to continue believing in something, if only the need to believe and the sense of difference (elitism) that being a fan defines.

375

What happens when rock and roll's elitism, and its fascination with mood and attitude as a viable response to one's historical situation, is transferred onto the television screen, into televisual modes of communication? Affective alliances are democratized in a new cultural logic of 'authentic inauthenticity.' Television negates rock and roll's elitism by locating it within its own democratizing impulses. Of course, television's democratic tendencies are always limited by the real economic and political interests involved in the selection, framing, and distribution of its images. But once any image, in whatever form, makes it onto the screen, it becomes equal to any other image. On the video screen, every image is equally available, equally real, equally artificial, and equally worthy of emulation. There is no secret knowledge on television, or rather, the secret knowledge is instantly available and constantly repeated for any viewer. While this doesn't guarantee that everone will 'get it,' television's power does not depend upon its encapsulating an audience in order to define it as different from those who do not 'get it.' Television's 'attitude' does not depend upon its limited availability but rather upon its knowing self-consciousness. Its 'hip-ness' can never be taken too seriously. Its secret knowledge is precisely that there are no secrets because there is nothing behind the screen. This 'hip' attitude is a kind of ironic nihilism in which ironic distance is offered as the only reasonable relation to a reality which is no longer reasonable. Television, however unreasonable (and it certainly is strange these days), is as reasonable as reality. In fact, reality is already stranger than any fantasy we could construct. Consequently, the strange is already disturbingly familiar. This estrangement from the familiar and the familiarization of the estranged means that the lines separating the comic and the terrifying, the mundane and the exotic, the boring and the exciting, the ordinary and the extraordinary, disappear. If reality is already cliched, cliches can be taken as reality. If we are in fact totally alienated, then alienation is the taken for granted ground upon which we build our lives.

Within the logic of authentic inauthenticity (quite different from inauthentic authenticity), one celebrates a difference knowing that its status depends on nothing but its being celebrated. In the end, only one's affective commitment, however temporary or superficial, matters. Authentic inauthenticity refuses to locate identity and difference outside the fact of temporary affective commitments. If every identity is equally fake, a pose that one takes on, then authentic inauthenticity celebrates the possibilities of poses without denying that that is all they are. It is a logic which allows one to seek satisfactions knowing that one can never be satisfied, and that any particular pleasure is likely, in the end, to be disappointing. For even if all images are equally artificial, and all satisfactions equally unsatisfying, one still needs some image, one still seeks satisfactions. Although no particular pose can make a claim to some intrinsic status, any pose can gain a status by virtue of one's commitment to it; it can become an important landmark on one's affective map of what matters.

This logic or attitude dominates MTV. I am always surprised that critics take MTV, and particular videos, so seriously. MTV is neither a contemplative text which is constantly demanding interpretation and attention, nor is it some wonderfully orgasmic pleasure. MTV's format and playlist is AM/AOR, but what makes it so powerful is not the particular videos but its hip attitude, its refusal to take anything—itself, its fans, and the world—seriously, even as it appears to do just that.

This attitude is captured most explicitly in its self-promos (e.g., in an apparent commercial for MTV beer, the beer is dismissed as tasting terrible, but, the actor concludes, at least the videos are *pretty good*). MTV, and music television more broadly, debunks every image, presenting it as precisely what it is—an image, but acknowledging that there is nothing else to choose from. Thus, paradoxically, music television has freed music from the image. For example, whether one likes Madonna—whose music always sounds the same but whose images are constantly changing—often depends upon whether one think she takes her images too seriously. Music television makes the specific content, the specific style, the specific tastes irrelevant; in their place, it foregrounds one's willingness to take on a pose and one's ability to invest in it precisely knowing that it is a pose, that the only reason it has any value or that it can make any claim on you is that one takes it on, one makes it matter.

This logic, and the aesthetic-textual forms which are often used to code it, are not only characteristic of music television. The use of fragmentation, of images without referents, of subjects without substance, of history without reality, and of narratives without coherence, is increasingly visible across the forms of popular culture. Texts no longer appear to seek their own originality or significance; they gleefully celebrate the sense of repetition and of the lack of difference, not only between messages, but between different genres. This is not merely an aesthetics of advertising (although it is often most effective in advertising). These techniques have a long history in both 'high art' and popular culture. What is unique is how widespread and common they have become, and the particular shapes these techniques take on in forms such as music television.

The fact that the basic attitude of music television is defined by this logic of authentic inauthenticity does not deny that there are real differences within its various practices. By embracing this broad communicative strategy, music television creates a series of images of stars who embody, not authentic instances of subjectivity and political resistance, but temporary attitudes and moods which can be appropriated by fans as impossible identities, strategies by which they can continue to struggle to make a 'difference'—if not in the world, at least in their lives—even though 'difference' has become for them impossible and irrelevant. Pee Wee Herman, Madonna, and Max Headroom are examples of an 'ironic authenticity' which foregrounds and self-consciously celebrates the artificial and fragmented nature of any identity. Many of the ads associated with music television and youth audiences define a second strategy of 'hyperreal inauthenticity' in which 'reality' itself—represented as bleak, dismal, gritty, and meaningless—becomes its own image (e.g., the Jordache commercial in which a young man is emotionally distraught over his parents' divorce; or the Converse commercial in which a couple is breaking up and the sentimental plea that they remain friends is greeted with an icecream cone in the face and the command, 'take a walk').

But perhaps the most compelling, and certainly the most successful strategy is the position occupied and offered by Bruce Springsteen. Springsteen's phenomenal success not only crosses age, gender, class, and national boundaries, it does not seem to depend upon how one interprets his songs or even whether one is able to identify with the particular narratives he constructs. His fans' passionate commitment to him enabled him to perform before 100,000 people and to incorporate video screens into the concert without apparently losing the sense of immediacy. Moreover, the stylistic diversity of his videos defies any generic identification of musical and visual style. Four observations may help to locate the source of his popularity. First, especially since *The River*, Springsteen has explicitly created pop images of the postmodern condition (e.g., 'Is a dream a lie if it don't come true, or is it something worse?'). Second, Springsteen's own image is that he is just like us, an ordinary person with the same emotional experiences. Third, his image of authenticity is artificial, and his fans know it (although they may constantly avoid admitting it). His performances are extraordinarily well-rehearsed and planned, his gestures and stories repeated over and over again. But this does not interfere with his image of authenticity (although it obviously should); in fact, his fans go to see him repeatedly, in order to see him repeat his 'spontaneous' performances. Finally, what makes Springsteen different is that anyone can see that he cares more about rock and roll, and his fans, than any other contemporary performer. In the perfectionism with which he produces records, in his concerts, and in his lifestyle (he refuses the pleasures of the rock and roll life so that he can make better rock and roll). Springsteen's 'sentimental inauthenticity' (which he shares with other stars like Sylvester Stallone) celebrates the magical possibility of making a 'difference' against 'impossible' odds simply on the basis of the intensity of his commitment to ordinary activities. One need not agree with his particular commitment; one need only recognize that something matters so much to someone that one is transformed from an ordinary individual into someone 'heroic'—if not superhuman.

Conclusion

Music television can only be understood if we understand its relations to economic, technological, historical, and cultural changes. Moreover, its real effects are not guaranteed in advance, by either its existence within capitalist circuits of commodification and ideologies, nor by the particular formal techniques used to construct its texts. In fact, one can argue that the construction of commodified stars as emblems of moods which can be attached to anything (e.g., Bill Cosby, David Bowie, or the current use of the cast of *Mash* in character to endorse IBM computers) has to be partly understood as the cultural industry's response to changing cultural as well as economic conditions. Whatever the economic and ideological intentions of such corporate relations, these mobile stars open up affective possibilities for responding to, surviving within, and perhaps even occasionally 'winning' against a world that seems increasingly hostile and disabling. In fact, the relations between these two domains— capitalism and affective communication—remain an open question. It is precisely here that fans, critics, and scholars continue to struggle over the politics of music television, each attempting to produce the reality they read onto its surfaces.

NOTES

This paper has benefited from conversations with my graduate students. I would particularly like to thank Charles Acland, Jon Crane and Phil Gordon for their comments and suggestions.

1. For example, see E. Ann Kaplan, *Rocking Around the Clock: Music Television, Post Modernism and Consumer Culture* (New York: Methuen, 1984); and the issue devoted to MTV of *Journal of Communication Inquiry*, 10 (Winter 1986).
2. This is not to deny that there are other musical forms involved in music television, including country and western and various forms of black music, but rock and roll is clearly the dominant and most influential form, not only in terms of its presence on the screen and its economics, but also in terms of its leading position in defining the forms and formats of music television.
3. Andrew Goodwin, 'From Anarchy to Chromakey: Music, Media, Video,' *One Two Three Four (A Rock 'n' Roll Quarterly)*, No. 5 (Spring 1987), pp. 16–32.
4. The following discussion draws heavily upon Goodwin, 'From Anarchy'; Simon Frith, 'Making Sense of Videos,' and Will Straw, 'Music Videos in its Contexts: Popular Music and Postmodernism in the 1980s.' The latter two articles appear in Simon Frith, Andrew Goodwin, and Lawrence Grossberg, eds., *Sound and Vision: The Music Video Reader* (forthcoming).
5. Academics would do well to remember that we are also implicated in capitalist relations, and produce knowledge as commodities: whether in the form of books, journals, discourses with limited intelligibility to broader audiences, or educational apparatuses increasingly defined by limited access.
6. The following argument is an abbreviated version of my 'Music Television and the Production of Postmodern Difference,' in Frith, Goodwin, and Grossberg, *Sound and Vision*. A fuller reading of Springsteen is offered in my 'Pedagogy in the Age of Reagan: Politics, Postmodernity and the Popular,' in Henry A. Giroux and Roger Simon, eds., *Critical Pedagogy and Popular Culture* (New York: Bergin and Garvey, forthcoming).

6 Race studies

Introduction

Racial difference as a critical category with an encoded politics of oppression has a traceable origin in liberal, humanist thought. A notable instance of such a moment is Shakespeare's construction of Caliban in *The Tempest*, one of the most widely used examples in English literature, and one which is critiqued for robbing the 'other' of language and identity. Similarly, T. B. Macaulay's minutes and speeches in the British Parliament on English education in the colonies, especially India, are now being re-read in light of colonial and post-colonial discourse, as is Thomas Carlyle's 'The Nigger Question', which is re-examined as a document of categoric discrimination. In America, the critiques of Frederick Douglass and Sojourner Truth on racial inequality in the contexts of the Civil War and the suffragette movement provide their own insight into the intersections of race, politics, and culture (see section on the nineteenth century). And Hegelian and Kantian treatises on aesthetics which posit a dichotomous and derogatory relationship between the sublime (Western and high culture) and barbaric (non-Western and mass culture) are now being scrutinized by media, race, and film critics. Critics argue that this concept of aesthetics is founded on a European tradition of classical beauty which systematically relegates all other forms of beauty and pleasure in the world to the margins. Even Marxist theories of economic and political inequalities, which are regularly used by post-colonial critics to challenge power relationships between the colonized and the colonizer, are problematic because, in the final analysis, class conflict cannot be directly equated with the politics of race (see section on Gender Studies for similar problems when substituting sex for class). Moreover, some sections of Marx's theories are now being read as paradoxical and Eurocentric by a younger generation of post-colonial theorists because, while Marx advocated revolutions against oppressive governments in Europe, he maintained, for example, that India was better governed by an Imperial force such as the English. A concrete example of a post-colonial voice interrupting the discourse of contemporary Marxist analysis is that of Aijaz Ahmad, even though it is an anachronistic interjection at this point in the introduction. Ahmad's *In Theory: Classes, Nations, Literatures* (1993), critiques both the Western, humanist tradition (most notably, its disciple Edward Said) and Western appropriations of Marxist thought (again, Jameson is its representative voice) as examples of colonizing the mind of the intellectual. *In Theory* has produced a furore of critical debate in the academy on the very state and nature of post-colonial and exilic theories.

Fundamental and philosophic oppositions between Europe and its others (or America and its inhabitants) are proving fertile ground for scholars in colonial, neo-colonial, and post-colonial studies who are attempting to document oppression and to re-imagine cultures and peoples before colonial domination. In short, the Enlightenment project, forged during a historical moment of colonial expansion, which helped to construct a rational and regulated notion of European identity, unwittingly also created a non-European identity as its unwelcome, specular image. It is this image with its spectre of racial difference that is now being categorically challenged. Yet, not all post-colonial scholarship is uniformly virulent. Eric Cheyfitz in *The Poetics of Imperialism* (1991) invokes Montaigne's 'Of the *Caniballes*', which is one of Europe's earliest inscriptions of another's culture, in a deliberate gesture of mediation, and says 'like Montaigne, I know no Indian languages. . . . For like Montaigne, I am not writing to understand Native American cultures but to critique the violence of my own culture, specifically the violence of my own language' (xv).

Over the span of the last four decades or so numerous scholars from various disciplines have discussed the connections between race and culture. Albert Memmi's *The Colonizer and the Colonized* (1965) sets the stage for exploring the epistemic violence done to the body of the colonized peoples, while Frantz Fanon's *The Wretched of the Earth* (1963), and *Black Skin, White Masks* (1967) focus more specifically on the damage done to the psyche of the dominated. He politicizes and reverses the quintessential Enlightenment dichotomy between the body and the mind in his epigraph 'O my body, make me always a man who questions!' Aimé Cesaire's *Discourse on Colonialism* (1972) is yet another critical examination of colonialism and racial difference. A tremendously influential work in re-examining the discursive proliferation of race was Edward W. Said's *Orientalism* (1978) which showed how clearly fact and fantasy were amalgamated by nineteenth-century European historians, literary scholars, cartographers, pseudo-scientists, and philologists to construct an Orient. He demonstrated that the 'Orient' is a fictive and inaccurate space concertized by opposing the civilized West to a primitive East, and how the 'East', as a cultural and political category, is deployed by the West to glamorize and eroticize its own art, literature, and culture. In a persuasive thesis of 'imaginative geography', Said argues that Europe emerges as powerful and articulate and Asia as defeated and distant, 'full of insinuating danger' in such an 'Oriental' endeavour, especially notable because 'Orientalism' is not matched in symmetry by a field called 'Occidentalism'.

While Said as a humanist scholar carefully outlines racist assumptions and discriminatory structures, Gayatri Chakravorty Spivak is more Marxist and deconstructionist in her exposé of these very problems. In *The Post Colonial Critic* (1991) she demands the 'unlearning of one's own privilege. So that, not only does one become able to listen to that other constituency, but one learns to speak in such a way that one will be taken seriously by that other constituency' (41). This demand to hear the 'other's' voice on co-equal terms is one of the most powerful strategies employed by post-colonial critics. Francis Barker *et al.* had attempted a move in this direction in their double volume of *Europe and its Others* (1986). As a way of 'unlearning' their privilege they provide a multi-disciplinary perspective on the debates surrounding racial difference and politics. What is even more telling than Barker's collection itself is the origin of this work in a unequivocally interdisciplinary conference in England which focused on the sociology of literature, signalling that race pervades every aspect of culture. Similarly, Henry Louis Gates' collection *'"Race", Writing, and Difference'* (1987) examines the unmistakable and unavoidable presence of race in cultural studies. Tackling the complexity and complicity of difference, Tzvetan Todorov in *The Conquest of America: The Question of the Other* (1984) reveals how Europeans systematically used their own privilege to turn Indian/Native American mores and superstitions against themselves to conquer North America. Wilcomb Washburn's *Red Man's Land/White Man's Law* (1971) and Calvin Martin's edited volume, *The American Indian and the Problem of History* (1987) depict in scrupulous detail the politics of representing the Native American as other in her/is own land. Roland Barthes, not usually seen as a critic in this field, makes an astute remark in *The Semiotic Challenge* (1987):

> what Semiology must attack is, not only as in the days of *Mythologies*, the petit-bourgeois good conscience, but the symbolic and semantic systems of our entire civilization; it is not enough to seek to change contents, we must above all aim at fissuring the meaning-system itself: we must emerge from the Occidental enclosure. (24)

Imperial policy formulated in the nineteenth century tended to draw boundaries around land, peoples, and cultures. For example, Macaulay (and later Arnold) debated the usefulness of an Anglican education over an Orientalist one in the colonies, where Macaulay clinched his argument by stating that all the knowledge contained in Indian and Persian books could fit into one shelf of a library stacked with Classical and English texts. Since knowledge and education were measured, at least in the realm of culture, as a mark of civilization in clearly European and Christian terms, the value and pleasure derived from these 'other' texts was seen as trivial and undecipherable. Therefore these texts, and consequently these cultures and societies, were relegated to the margins of the geo-political arena where much of today's battles for cultural authority are fought. Gauri Viswanathan's *The Masks of Conquest* (1992) provides an incisive analysis of this aspect of colonialism. While this gesture of imperialism is more occluded in the case of Britain (although Ireland stands as a very anomalous question mark at this point), America's past reveals the direct tracks of oppression in the treatment of slaves and 'Indians'. This is because, to a large extent, even when America maintained its unique national identity, it still held European notions of civilization and acculturation. Today's right-wing reactionary figures such as Allan Bloom, Diane Ravitch, Camille Paglia (literature), Dinesh D'Souza (education), Pat Buchanan, Senator Jesse Helms (politics) and Rush Limbaugh (TV personality) bear testimony to this strand of Eurocentrism. Both the Eurocentric bias and the ire that the Right feels at the indelible presence of racial

385

difference in American culture can be read in Arthur Schlessinger's comment in *The Disuniting of America* (1992):

> whatever the particular crimes of Europe, that continent is also the source—the *unique* source—of liberating ideas of individual liberty, political democracy, the rule of law, human rights and cultural freedom that constitute our most precious legacy and to which most of the world today aspires. These are *European* ideas, not Asian, nor African, nor Middle Eastern ideas, except by adoption. (127)

Simultaneous with the present explosion of post-colonial theories is the drive to produce concrete pedagogical tools. Helen Tiffin et al. in *The Empire Writes Back* (1989) give a methodology for analysing colonial literatures (mainly Anglophone) by explaining the meaning of the densely packed and packaged terms in the emerging field. So too, Chinua Achebe's critique of Conrad's *Heart of Darkness*, which is now printed as a foreword to most editions and anthologies, points out that a European, uncritical, anthropological impulse robs Africa of its land (nation), its speech (language), and cultural identity (humanity). Freire Paulo in *Pedagogy of the Oppressed* (1973) takes the problematics of race into the classroom in his argument for a deeper understanding of difference.

The essays in this section deal with the complexity, both theoretical and pedagogical, of representing the non-European 'other'. Major issues of critical and theoretical debate now focus on the role of 'language' in culture, the place of the 'nation' in identity formation (be it nativist, or exilic, or diasporic, or transnational), the significance of the 'border' as an enclosure (as freedom and limitation) of identity, the temporal factor of 'modernity' in measuring technological progress of Western, industrialized nations, and the nature of 'pleasure' sanctioned by European cultures. The discourse on race and racial politics has ranged over the asymmetrical relations of power between the West and the non-West, the hierarchies and values of knowledge in the understanding of cultures, the formations of literary canons, the writing of histories, and the locus of the woman of colour in society. Within the frame of imperial hegemony and race politics in Britain, Gilroy's 'Cruciality and the Frog's Perspective' is a sophisticated argument in reading the Black Arts movement, and represents a more theoretical analysis of Blacks than his earlier, empirical work, *There Ain't No Black in the Union Jack*. The Field Day enterprise simultaneously participates in the insurgent mood of British post-colonial scholarship and in the more experiential register of minority discourse in America. It concentrates its intellectual labour on re-claiming, re-producing, and re-situating Irish writers such as Joyce within a political space created by the extended colonial crisis. This space allows the Irish nation to function as an allegorical category. In this effort, it is able to disassociate itself from the homogenizing, and uni-dimensional nature of 'English' literature. Seamus Deane's essay explains the purpose of the Field Day project and lays out some its aims.

While Britain and its imperialist policies are analysed through tropes of temporality and history, native American, African American, and chicana/o American theories of cultural imposition rely more on questions of spatiality and geography— the inability to speak their own language in their own 'nation', the lack of 'space' to practice their own traditions, and the notations of cultural boundaries are the topics

386

of enquiry. And the total dehumanization and delegitimization of the native American, forced into living in reservations, is also read as the terrifying spectre of the Foucauldian metaphor of power of the panoptic gaze. The essays printed here accordingly discuss *race* as it intersects with American culture. Paula Gunn Allen's 'How the West was Really Won' brings an ironic twist to America's archetypical romance with the frontier (see Turner's thesis from the nineteenth-century section). Gloria Anzaldua's essay, 'How to Tame a Wild Tongue', explores the issue of language and boundaries that are crucial to chicana/o politics in America. Cornell West, in his work on African American culture, is engaged in retrieving a black artistic ethos and tradition by exploding mythologies of racial stereotypes.

Abdul R. JanMohamed introduces an international register in the usual dichotomy between colonizer and colonized in his essay, 'Worldliness-Without-World, Homelessness-as-Home: Toward a Definition of the Specular Border Intellectual'. Using Said as an exilic subject and as a specular border intellectual, he theorizes Said's intention behind inter-cultural/cross-cultural production. Distinguishing the syncretic border intellectual from the specular one such as Said, he says 'like Conrad, these intellectuals are located at the juncture of the world that formed them, and like [Eric] Auerbach, they transform their border-crossing into positive missions that lead to significant cultural acts' (98). In *Outside in the Teaching Machine* (1993) and specifically in the essay 'The Politics of Translation' Spivak analyses the role of the translator in an inter-cultural space. She argues that translating an Indian work into English for example, means that one must go beyond merely 'transferring bodies of knowledge' in another register, one must necessarily 'consider the role played by language for the *agent*, the person who acts' such that the 'task of the feminist translator is to consider language as a clue to the workings of gendered agency' (179).

While the numerous agendas of the various groups in postcolonial camps from America and Britain (and between borders) that are presented in this section may seem diffuse and chaotic, and their arguments often repetitive and contradictory, the logic behind the whole endeavour is based on challenging Euro-American domination. Since colonization itself traversed so many cultures, peoples, ethnicities, languages, and nations, the responses too are preoccupied with socio-specific anxieties. Some scholars feel that including race as a category in cultural studies dilutes the issues and theorizes post-colonial problems along different trajectories, mainly because it could become duplicitous in colluding with the colonizer (specifically in its use of the colonizer's language). Yet, in the academy, faced with a multi-racial and multi-ethnic student body, cultural studies clearly provides one with a viable space to address the issues outlined above.

G.R. and J.M.

REFERENCES AND FURTHER READING

Adam, Ian, and Helen Tiffin, eds, *Past the Last Post: Theorizing Post-Colonialism and Post-Modernism*, Calgary: University of Calgary Press, 1990.

Anderson, Benedict, *Imagined Communities: Reflections on the Origin and Spread of Nationalism*, London: Verso, 1983.

Ashcroft, Bill, et al., *The Empire Writes Back: Theory and Practice in Post-Colonial Literatures*, London and New York: Routledge, 1989.

Baker, Houston A., *Modernism and the Harlem Renaissance*, Chicago: University of Chicago Press, 1987.

Bernal, Martin, *Black Athena* (2 vols), New Brunswick: Rutgers University Press, 1989.

Bhabha, Homi, ed., *Nation and Narration*, London: Routledge, 1990.

Fanon, Frantz, *Wretched of the Earth*, New York: Grove, 1963.

Fanon, Frantz, *Black Skin, White Masks*. New York: Grove, 1967.

Ferguson, Russell, et al., eds, *Out There: Marginalization and Contemporary Culture*, Cambridge: MIT Press, 1991.

Gates, Henry Louis, *The Signifying Monkey*, London and New York: Oxford University Press, 1984.

hooks, bell, *Yearning: Race, Gender, and Politics*, Boston: South End Press, 1990.

JanMohamed, Abdul, and David Lloyd, eds, *Nature and Context of Minority Discourse*, London: Oxford University Press, 1990.

Memmi, Albert, *The Colonizer and the Colonized*, Boston: Beacon, 1965.

Ngugi Wa Thiong'O, *Decolonizing the Mind*, Portsmouth, England: Heinemann, 1966.

Parker, Andrew, et al., *Nationalisms and Sexualities*, London and New York: Routledge, 1992.

Rosaldo, Renato, *Culture and Truth*, Boston: Beacon, 1989.

Said, Edward W., *Culture and Imperialism*, New York: Knopf, 1993.

Sivanandan, A., *Communities of Resistance*, London: Verso, 1988.

Spivak, Gayatri Chakravorty, *In Other Worlds: Essays in Cultural Politics*, London and New York: Routledge, 1987.

Spivak, Gayatri Chakravorty, *Outside In the Teaching Machine*, London and New York: Routledge, 1993.

Viznor, Gerald, 'Serioacupunctures: Mythic Reversals and the Striptease in Four Scenes', *The American Indian and the Problem of History*, ed. C. Martin, New York: Oxford University Press, 1987.

Paula Gunn Allen

Paula Gunn Allen is currently a professor of English at the University of California, at Los Angeles. Her works include *Spider Woman's Granddaughters: Traditional Tales and Contemporary Writing by Native American Women*, which won an American Book Award in 1990, *Grandmothers of the Light: A Medicine Woman's Sourcebook* (1991) and *The Sacred Hoop: Recovering the Feminine in American Indian Traditions* (1986), from which the article 'How the West was Really Won' is taken. She has also written a novel called *The Woman Who Owned the Shadows*. Allen is a member of the Laguna, Pueblo, and Sioux nations, and writes consistently challenging works which examine the changing roles of native American women in contemporary American society. 'How the West was Really Won' is a scholarly look at the changing status of heterosexual women, lesbians, and homosexuals within Native American culture as a result of the encroachment of Anglo–European control.

Allen traces the roles of heterosexual women, lesbians, and homosexuals within native-American culture through 'a progressive shift from gynocentric, egalitarian, ritual-based social systems to secularized structures closely imitative of the European patriarchal system.' She locates the reasons for the non–coincidental shift in the fact that native-American societies, who celebrated woman-based, woman-centred traditions, were ritual-based rather than economically or politically constructed. She examines the difference in European gender-based roles and native-American function-based roles as a main difference. In native-American cultures, 'individuals fit into these roles on the basis of proclivity, inclination, and temperament.' Thus, people who, in contemporary American and European culture, would be considered gays or lesbians were gender-designated in pre-colonization native-American societies as belonging to the opposite gender.

Along with the devaluation of women comes the devaluation of traditional spiritual leaders, female and male, and largely because of their ritual power and status, the devaluation of lesbian and gay tribal members as leaders, shamans, healers, or ritual participants.

Despite popular opinion that American Indian men have suffered more than women, Allen believes women have suffered a greater loss due to the encroachment of Anglo-Europeans. 'While women still play the traditional role of housekeeper, childbearer, and nurturer, they no longer enjoy the unquestioned positions of power, respect, and decision making on local and international levels that were not so long ago their accustomed functions.' Allen also celebrates women's role in native-American cultures as healers, dreamers, and shamans, not only in the past but also as it is re-emerging in contemporary native-American cultures.

S. W.

How the West was really won

In the beginning were the people, the spirits, the gods; the four-leggeds, the two-leggeds, the wingeds, the crawlers, the burrowers, the plants, the trees, the rocks. There were the moon, the sun, the earth, the waters of earth and sky. There were the stars, the thunders, the mountains, the plains, the mesas and the hills. There was the Mystery. There were the Grandmothers, the Mothers, the clans, the people. At the end of the fifteenth century, Anglo-European time, the old world that the tribes, Nations, and Confederacies lived in began to be torn apart. At first the tear seemed small enough, and for various reasons we did not grasp the enormity of the threat; indeed, many tribes did not know there was a threat for another two to three hundred years.

The wars of conquest that began with the landing of Christopher Columbus on an isolated little island on the edge of the southeastern sea gained momentum until every tribe and every aspect of traditional life was swept up in it; during the centuries of those wars everything in our lives was affected and much was changed, even the earth, the waters, and the sky. We went down under wave after wave of settlement, each preceded, accompanied by, and followed by military engagements that were more often massacres of our people than declared wars. These wars, taken together, constitute the longest undeclared war neo-Americans have fought, and no end is in sight.

It is still being fought on reservations, in urban communities, along Indian-white frontiers (which occur wherever Indian and non-Indian interface); in Mexico and in Central America—Guatemala, El Salvador, Nicaragua, Honduras, and Costa Rica; in South America—Brazil, Argentina, Chile, Venezuela, Peru. In some areas we have been all but extinguished, as in the islands of the Caribbean, Canada, and the United States; in others we continue to survive in large numbers, though usually characterized as peasants and disguised as Hispanics by the Anglo-European/Hispanic media, scholars, officials, and political activists. Still we endure, and many of our old values, lifeways, and philosophies endure with us, for they, like us, are inextricably linked to the land, the sky, the waters, and the spirits of this Turtle Island, this Earth-Surface place, that the whites call 'the New World.'

From gynecentric to patriarchal

During the five hundred years of Anglo-European colonization, the tribes have seen a progressive shift from gynecentric, egalitarian, ritual-based social systems to secularized structures closely imitative of the European patriarchal system. During this time women (including lesbians) and gay men—along with traditional medicine people, holy people, shamans, and ritual leaders—have suffered severe loss of status, power, and leadership. That these groups have suffered concurrent degradation is not coincidental; the woman-based, woman-centered traditions of many precontact tribes were tightly bound to ritual, and ritual was based on spiritual understandings rather than on economic or political ones.

The genocide practiced against the tribes is aimed systematically at the dissolution of ritual tradition. In the past this has included prohibition of ceremonial practices throughout North and Meso-America, Christianization, enforced loss of languages, reeducation of tribal peoples through government-supported and Christian mission schools that Indian children have been forced to attend, renaming of the traditional ritual days as Christian feast days, missionization (incarceration) of tribal people, deprivation of language, severe disruption of cultures and the economic and resource bases of those cultures, and the degradation of the status of women as central to the spiritual and ritual life of the tribes.

Along with the devaluation of women comes the devaluation of traditional spiritual leaders, female and male, and, largely because of their ritual power and status, the devaluation of lesbian and gay tribal members as leaders, shamans, healers, or ritual participants. Virtually all customary sexual customs among the tribes were changed—including marital, premarital, homosexual, and ritual sexual practices, along with childhood and adult indulgence in open sexuality, common in many tribes.

Colonization means the loss not only of language and the power of self-government but also of ritual status of all women and those males labeled 'deviant' by the white Christian colonizers. The usual divisions of labor—generally gender-based (if you count homosexual men as women and dikes as men)—were altered, prohibited, or forced underground, from whence they have only recently begun to reemerge as the tribes find themselves engaged in a return to more traditional ways of life.

In considering gender-based roles, we must remember that while the roles themselves were fixed in most archaic American cultures, with divisions of 'women's work' and 'men's work,' the individuals fit into these roles on the basis of proclivity, inclination, and temperament. Thus men who in contemporary European and American societies are designated gay or homosexual were gender-designated among many tribes as 'women' in terms of their roles; women who in contemporary societies are designated as lesbians (actually, 'dikes' is more accurate) were designated as men in tribal cultures. As an example, the Kaska of Canada would designate a daughter in a family that had only daughters as a boy. When she was small, around five, her

391

parents would tie a pouch of dried bear ovaries to her belt. She would dress in male clothing and would function in the Kaska male role for the rest of her life. Interestingly, if a male attempted to make sexual advances to this male-designated person, he was liable to punishment, because the Kaska felt this violation would ruin the 'dike's' luck in hunting.[1]

The Yuma had a tradition of gender designation based on dreams; a female who dreamed of weapons became male for all practical purposes. In this the Yumas were similar to the neighboring Mohaves and Cocopah, except the gender-role designation was based on the choice of companions and play objects of a young person. In such systems a girl who chose to play with boys or with boys' objects such as a bow and arrow became a male functionary. Among the Mohave, another dream-culture people related to the Yuma, the hwame, a term roughly corresponding to 'dike' in English, took a male name and was in all respects subject to ritual male taboos vis à vis females, such as avoidance of contact with a menstruating wife. The hwame's wife was not considered hwame but simply a woman.[2]

In addition to these tribes, others that display a positive acceptance of lesbianism include the Navajo (who considered lesbians an asset), the Mohave (who thought that from the inception of the world homosexuals were a natural and necessary part of society), the Quinault, the Apache, the Ojibwa, and the Eskimo.[3]

In her brilliant, comprehensive gay cultural history *Another Mother Tongue: Gay Words, Gay Worlds*, poet and writer Judy Grahn devotes a large chapter to the existence of lesbians and homosexuals as ritually and socially valued tribal members. Citing numerous sources including Jonathan Katz, Sue Ellen Jacobs, myself, Carolyn Neithammer, Arthur Evans, Edward Carpenter, Michael Wilken, John (Fire) Lame Deer, Hamilton Tyler, John Gunn, and various contemporary gay and lesbian American Indian poets and writers, Grahn writes a lengthy chronicle about the place gays held among many American Indian peoples. Grahn cites anthropologist Sue Ellen Jacobs as listing eighty-eight tribes whose recorded cultural attributes include references to gayness, with twenty of these including specific references to lesbianism. According to Jacobs, eleven tribes denied any homosexuality to anthropologists or other writers (which doesn't necessarily mean it wasn't openly sanctioned and practiced, acknowledged, or valued), and those denials came from tribes located in areas of heaviest, lengthiest, and most severely puritanical white encroachment. Among the eighty-eight tribes who admitted homosexuality among them and referred to it in positive ways are the Apache, Navajo, Winnebago, Cheyenne, Pima, Crow, Shoshoni, Paiute, Osage, Acoma, Zuñi, Sioux, Pawnee, Choctaw, Creek, Seminole, Illinois, Mohave, Shasta, Aleut, Sac and Fox, Iowa, Kansas, Yuma, Aztec, Tlingit, Maya, Naskapi, Ponca, Menomini, Maricopa, Klamath, Quinault, Yuki, Chilula, and Kamia—indicating the presence of lesbianism and homosexuality in every area of North America.[4]

Some of the native names for gays that Grahn lists include Alyha and Hwame (Mohave), Nadle (Navajo), Siange (Winnebago), Winkte and Adi-wa-lona (male) and Koshkalaka (female) (Lakota), Mingu-ga (Omaha and Ponca), Ko'thlama (Zuñi), Wergern (Yurok), Bo-te (Crow), Kwerhame (lesbian) and Elxa (homosexual) (Yuma), and Joya (Chumash). About this last name, Grahn writes:

392

Gay queens among the Indians of the Santa Barbara region were called 'Jewel,' and so the Spanish recorded it as 'Joya' . . .

The European soldiers, trappers, explorers, and settlers were contemptuous of Gay traditions in their own cultures, and several centuries of persecution under the Inquisition had taught them to deny all Gayness. The heaviest persecutions in Europe ran concurrent to the heaviest periods of colonization of the Indians in North America . . . Small wonder, perhaps, that Gay people were often the first Indians killed and that even when tribes were tolerated by the white people, their Gay people were mocked and persecuted to the point of changing their behavior for the sake of the safety of their people. Balboa, for instance, set wild dogs on the Gay medicine men of California tribes, killing them, the 'Jewels' of their own people.[5]

Recent scholarly work reveals the universal or nearly universal presence of homosexuality and lesbianism among tribal peoples, the special respect and honor often accorded gay men and women, and the alteration in that status as a result of colonization of the continent by Anglo-Europeans. These studies demonstrate the process by which external conquest and colonization become internalized among the colonized with vivid clarity. Homophobia, which was rare (perhaps even absent entirely) among tribal peoples in the Americas, has steadily grown among them as they have traded traditional tribal values for Christian industrial ones.

Gay historian Walter Williams records particularly poignant stories about contemporary homosexuals in which colonization is clearly linked to homophobia and racist colonial attempts to eradicate tribal cultures. Citing numerous scholarly sources, Williams refers to homosexuality among the Maya, Ojibwa, various branches of the Sioux, the Sac and Fox, the Osage, unspecified California and Alaskan Indians, the Papago, Crow, Hopi, Navajo, Klamath, Winnebago, Yokuts, Zuñi, Iroquois, Cheyenne, Omaha, and Aleut.[6]

Among the many accounts Williams cites, the stark homophobia of the white recorders contrasts sharply with the easy acceptance the Indians accord the presence of gays among themselves. This is particularly notable in the earliest white reports; as colonization deepens its hold on tribal lifeways, the reported attitude of Indians splits: some, usually the most traditional, continue to accord high respect to homosexuals, even to the present day. Of these, many, perhaps most, will not discuss the subject with non-Indians because they are unwilling to have institutions or practices that they value subjected to ridicule or contempt. They also may feel a strong need to protect the homosexuals and lesbians among them and the tribe as a whole from further life-threatening assaults which for too long have been directed against them.

Other Indians, more acculturated and highly Christianized, treat the presence of lesbianism or homosexuality among them with fear and loathing. They do not confine that loathing to homosexuality but direct it to other aspects of tribal ceremonial life, particularly when it has to do with sexuality. Thus a Hopi man despairs of his people, saying that there is nothing good in the old Hopi ways. This man, Kuanwikvaya, testified to U.S. officials: 'There is nothing good in the Hopi religion. It is all full of adultery and immorality. I cannot tell all the dirt and filth that is in these ceremonies.' Another Hopi man, Tuwaletstiwa, testified that before he

393

accepted Christianity his life 'was unspeakably evil . . . When a Hopi becomes a Christian he quits attending these dances. He knows the evil in them is so great.'[7] These testimonies were taken in 1920, when U.S. officials suppressed the Hopi dances. The men's statements were used as 'local witness' proof that the traditional ceremonies were properly banned.

These men eerily echo earlier white commentaries on the subject of homosexuality. Hubert Bancroft, a scholar of considerable stature on Native American subjects, characterizes the ritual institutions of homosexuality as 'the most repugnant of all their practices' and 'a shameful custom.'[8]

Then there is George Catlin, the renowned painter and chronicler of what he took to be the 'vanishing' Indian way of life. Catlin was invited to attend a feast given to honor Sac and Fox 'berdaches' (berdache was the word of choice for gay males at the time Catlin wrote in the late nineteenth century—an unhappy choice as the term signifies Arab love boy or sex-slave boy and as such is entirely inapplicable to the homosexuality practiced among the Sac and Fox or other tribal peoples). Catlin remarked in summarizing his visit among the 'berdache': 'This is one of the most unaccountable and disgusting customs that I have ever met in Indian country.' He continues, in the words used over and over by whites as a justification for the removal, assimilation, or destruction of native tribes: 'For further account of [the berdache feast] I am constrained to refer the reader to the country where it is practiced, and where I should wish that it might be extinguished before it be more fully recorded.'[9]

But the pattern of colonized psychology and social valuation among Indian people may be being reversed. Recently, Russell Means of the American Indian Movement—a man not always noted for his liberal attitudes toward women and other devalued individuals—said, in defense of homosexuals and their anciently valued place among the people: 'The Indian looked upon these unique individuals as something special the Great Mystery created to teach us. These people had something special to tell us.'[10] And the Oglala Sioux holy man John (Fire) Lame Deer said, 'To us a man is what nature, or his dreams, make him. We accept him for what he wants to be. That's up to him . . . There are good men among the winktes and they have been given certain powers.'[11]

It is significant, I think, that those who are homophobic are also very likely to be misogynist. Indeed, the latter often masquerade as the former. The colonizers' treatment of gays is analogous to their treatment of healers, holy people, dreamers, and other traditional leaders, foremost among whom have traditionally been the women—the matrons, clan mothers, dreamers, and makers of ritual and tribal life in the western hemisphere.

Before the coming of the white man, or long ago, so far, as the people say, the Grandmother(s) created the firmament, the earth, and all the spirit beings in it. She (or they) created, by thinking into being, the Women, or the Woman, from whom the people sprang. The Women thus thought into being also gave thought, and the people and all the orders of being in this world came into being, including the laws, the sciences, agriculture, householding, social institutions—everything. Long ago the peoples of this hemisphere knew that their power to live came to them from the

Grandmother or Grandmothers (depending on the tribe) not only originally but continuously, even to the present. Many old mythologies and most ceremonial cycles (if taken within their entire cultural framework) reiterate and celebrate this central fact of tribal Native American existence. Many of the tribes retain this old knowledge—a knowledge that they have kept hidden from the whites and often from their own tribespeople but that they have preserved. Only recently have the women begun to raise our voices again, at the behest of the Grandmother(s), to tell the story as it is told and to lay claim to the ancient power that is vested in Woman since before time.

In a recent interview published in the West German feminist monthly *Emma*, three Native American representatives of a movement called Concerned Aboriginal Women discussed the present crisis among American Indians in Canada and the part the women are taking in their struggle to retain title to their lands. One of the women, identified as Vera, said: 'You know, for such a long long time our men struggled and struggled, and things got worse. Then the grandmothers and mothers decided that now we must intervene! Among our people we have a tradition that the women make the decisions. Later we can go back to taking care of our children.' Another woman, Judalon, continued: 'The government corrupted our leaders and it took the women to realize it.' The third woman, Dinah, added, 'They've turned our men around the way they want them, so that they have lost their direction and no longer know where they should be going.'

The interviewer asked the women why they sound like they want to 'step back' to taking care of the children when German women are struggling to do more than housework and childrearing. German women 'want to be able to participate in public decisions,' the interviewer said. Judalon explained that Native American women have always participated in public decisions.

For example, in my mother's tribe, the Mohawks, the women made all the decisions. In the Longhouse the clan mothers would gather and sit on one side. The chiefs would sit on the other side. On the other two sides, the rest of the people would sit and the current problem would be discussed. The clan mothers would decide what should happen, but the men would speak for them. The men never made decisions. It was that way in the tribe and also in a clan's household. The women were responsible and made the decisions.

Everything has changed since we've had contact with the Europeans. First, our leaders were brainwashed. They became vain and thought that they alone could decide things . . . Today many Indian men behave like European men.

The other two women agree, noting that traditionally respect for women by Indian men was high and that all work was valued because it was all important. At this the interviewer asked about division of labor into gender roles, and the Iroquois women responded that work was generally divided along gender lines,

but I think with us there were never such sharp divisions between these areas as with you. The men had to be able to cook since, for example, they were often away hunting or fighting. And there were also girl warriors. In some tribes there were also women leaders. Of course, there are great differences between the Indian nations, but most of them did not have this sharp division of roles. There were also girls who were raised as boys, if, for example, a family only had daughters.

395

And these women would then marry other women. We even have special initiation rites for transvestites . . . In those families which lead a traditional lifestyle, it is still the case that the men have great respect for the women. And with the help of the spiritual movement, things have been changing over the last ten years. More and more Indians are returning to the traditional ways. The old people are teaching us.[12]

The way it is now is generally very different from the way it was; the devaluation of women that has accompanied Christianization and westernization is not a simple matter of loss of status. It also involves increases in violence against women by men, a phenomenon not experienced until recently and largely attributable to colonization and westernization.

Many people believe that Indian men have suffered more damage to their traditional status than have Indian women, but I think that belief is more a reflection of colonial attitudes toward the primacy of male experience than of historical fact. While women still play the traditional role of housekeeper, childbearer, and nurturer, they no longer enjoy the unquestioned positions of power, respect, and decision making on local and international levels that were not so long ago their accustomed functions. Only in some tribes do they still enjoy the medicine or shamanistic power they earlier possessed. No longer, except in backwoods pockets of resistance, do they speak with the power and authority of inviolable law.

It is true that colonization destroyed roles that had given men their sense of self-esteem and identity, but the significant roles lost were not those of hunter and warrior. Rather, colonization took away the security of office men once derived from their ritual and political relationship to women. Men's status in all tribes that use clan systems, and perhaps in others, came to them through the agency of women, who got their own status from the spirit people, particularly the Grandmother powers that uphold and energize the universe. But with the coming of the white man and his patriarchal system, the powers of the women were systematically undermined in countless ways, and this undermining was and is reinforced willingly by many of the men.

The history of the subjugation of women under the dominant patriarchal control of males is a long and largely ugly one, and it affects every tribe and Nation now as much as ever. It is synchronistic rather than coincidental that most of the Indian women known to the general non-Indian public have been convicted of playing into the white man's game and betraying the Indian; all have been accused of doing so because of sexual or romantic connections with white men, and all have been blamed by many Indians for white conquest. Patriarchy requires that powerful women be discredited so that its own system will seem to be the only one that reasonable or intelligent people can subscribe to.

The nature of the change in the images of women and gays among American Indians caused by patriarchal propaganda is historical, cultural, and political. In that change can be seen the history of patriarchy on this continent and, by extension, all over the world. As American Indian women emerge from the patriarchally imposed ignominy of the past centuries, the falsity of all the colonizers' stories about Native Americans, about spirituality, gayness, and femaleness, becomes increasingly apparent. And as we articulate a feminine analysis of the effects of colonization, we are more and more able to demonstrate that the colonizers' image of Indian women has, more than any other factor, led to the high incidence of rape and abuse of Indian women by

396

Indian men. This violent behavior is tacitly approved of by the tribes through the refusal of tribal governments across the country and in urban Indian enclaves to address the issue and provide care, shelter, and relief for the women victims and competent, useful treatment for the offenders. The white and recently Indian image of powerful Indian women as traitors is another chapter in the patriarchal folktale that begins with Eve causing Adam's fall from grace into divine disgrace.

Women as healers, dreamers, and shamans

I met Essie Parrish on a field trip with my students to the Kashia Pomo reservation at Stewart's Point, California, in 1974. The next year I met and heard a lecture by the Pomo dreamer and basketmaker Mabel McCabe. The teachings of thse two women provide clear information about the ancient ritual power of Indian women.

Mrs. McCabe spoke about the meaning of having a tradition, about how a woman becomes a basketmaker among her people—a process that is guided entirely by a spirit-teacher when the woman is of the proper age. It is not transmitted to her through human agency. For Mrs. McCabe, having a tradition means having a spirit-teacher or guide. That is the only way she used the term 'tradition' and the only context in which she understood it. Pomo baskets hold psychic power, spirit power; so a basketmaker weaves a basket for a person at the direction of her spirit guide. Owning a basket should not be by purchase, but by gift.

Imagine how much spirit power of the tribes is locked away in museums or kept secured in white homes where their true significance goes unrecognized. Soul theft is a terrible crime, and while there are many museums and field workers who are concerned with this issue and are trying to restore the sacred objects to their owners, there are many more who are blissfully ignorant of the significance of their collecting instincts or the meaning of their possessions.

Essie Parrish, who died within the last few years, was the Dreamer of the Kashia Pomo. The Dreamer is the person responsible for the continued existence of the people as a psychic (that is, tribal) entity. It is through her dreams that the people have being; it is through her dreams that they find ways to function in whatever reality they find themselves. It is through her dreams that the women keep children safe in war, that healings are made possible, and that children are assured a safe passage through life.

Under the auspices of the University of California at Berkeley, Mrs. Parrish made several movies recording her dances and songs. In one of them, *Dream Dances of the Kashia Pomo*, she and others dance and display the dance costumes that are made under her direction, appliquéd with certain dream-charged designs that hold the power she brings from the spirit world. She tells about the role of the Dreamer, who is the mother of the people not because she gives physical birth (though Mrs. Parrish has done that) but because she gives them life through her power of dreaming—that is, she en-livens them. Actually, the power of giving physical birth is a consequence of the power of giving nonmaterial or, you might say, 'astral' birth.

The Dreamer, then, is the center of psychic/spiritual unity of the people. She is

397

the center, the hub of the wheel. It is by virtue of her gift, her ability, that the people live and are a people, connected to one another in ways more than mere language, culture, or proximity can assure.

The life force that is passed to the Dreamer from the nonmaterial planes is embodied in songs, dances, ritual objects, and garments that the women make. The songs are sung by the Dreamer or sometimes by the dancers. The drums or other accompaniment are played by men. In many tribes the singing is done only by men, corresponding, I think, to the Mohawk male function of speaker or agent of the women's decisions. In such dream systems, among them the Iroquois, the Pomo, the Maya, the Mohave, and many other Nations, decisions are made in ritual ways. That is, their rituals, customs, social institutions, food-stuffs, healing materials and methods, their 'magic' or paranormal competencies, architecture, agriculture (or horticulture), land use, water use, food production methods, relationships to animals, plants, mountains, clouds, rain, lightning, thunder, earthquakes—anything and everything—come to them through dreams or vision-based concourse with the world of the spirit people, the divinities and deities, the Grandmothers, and the other exotic powers.

Even among Plains people, long considered the most male-oriented Indians, at least by the media and its precursors in popular culture, power was and is gained, accrued, mediated, and dispensed only through the grace and beneficence of female influence. Thus the Kiowa take their tribal realization, their psychic commonality, from their sacred Grandmother bundles; the Sioux and other Sun Dance people perform their rites (which are inextricably interwoven with feminine power) within the secure psychic power-generating and protective 'battery' of the circle of Grandmothers, and the Sacred Pipe way of the Lakota comes to them from the spirit White Buffalo Woman.

In these and many other tribal systems, the oral tradition in its ceremonial and ritual aspects rests on female power; shamanism, which is accorded to certain persons, including gays and lesbians, derives from the power of dream/vision and the living presence of the Dreamer among the people.

In another film, *Pomo Shaman*, Mrs. Parrish demonstrates a healing ritual, in which she uses water and water power, captured and focused through her motions, words, and use of material water, to heal a patient. She demonstrates the means of healing, and in the short narrative segments, she repeats in English some of the ritual. It is about creation and creating and signifies the basic understanding the tribal peoples generally have about how sickness comes about and how its effects can be assuaged, relieved, and perhaps even removed.

The mental health practitioner Phyllis Old Dog Cross alludes to this belief when she quotes anthropologist Peggy Sanday: ' "Where men are in harmony with their environment rape is usually absent." '[13] That is, rape or other acts of political or power-based violence result from a disorder in the relationship between person and cosmos.

Traditional American Indian systems depended on basic concepts that are at present being reformulated and to some extent practiced by western feminists, including cooperation (but by that traditional Indians generally meant something other than noncompetitiveness or passivity), harmony (again, this did not necessarily mean

398

absence of conflict), balance, kinship, and respect. Their material, social, and ritual systems were predicated on these essential values, which might be seen as objectives, parameters, norms, or principles depending on how they were being applied in a given situation. They did not rely on external social institutions such as schools, court, and prisons, kings, or other political rulers, but rather on internal institutions such as spirit-messengers, guides, teachers, or mentors; on tradition, ritual, dream and vision; on personal inclination (understood more in a geological sense than in a hedonistic one) and the leadership of those who had demonstrated competence with the foregoing characteristics.

Thus to traditional American Indians, social and personal life is governed by internal rather than external factors, and systems based on spiritual orders rather than on material ones are necessarily heavily oriented toward internal governing mechanisms.

Among traditionals the psychospiritual characteristics of the individual are channeled to blend harmoniously with those of the rest of the group. This channeling is done by applying custom, by sharing appropriate items from the oral tradition, and by helping and encouraging children in tribally approved endeavors that are matched to individual inclinations but that will provide useful skills, understandings, and abilities for the good of the entire group. The young person is trained in a number of ways, formal and informal, and by a number of individuals in the tribe. Traditionally, female children (or female surrogates) are trained by women, while male children (or male surrogates) are trained by men in learning their ritual roles within their social system. In some groups such as the Cherokee, however, shamans are typically trained along cross-gender rather than same gender lines. Thus male shamans train female apprentices, and female shamans train male apprentices. Traditionally, proper behavior falls along gender lines, as did expectations, but gender is understood in a psychological or psychospiritual sense much more than in a physiological one.

Thus the high position held by women as a group and by certain women as individuals results from certain inclinations that the women are born with and that they demonstrate through temperament, interest, competence, spirit-direction, and guidance. Women are by the nature of feminine, 'vibration' graced with certain inclinations that make them powerful and capable in certain ways (all who have this temperament, ambience, or 'vibration' are designated women and all who do not are not so designated). Their power includes bearing and rearing children (but in tribal life everyone is in some sense 'raising' the children); cooking and similar forms of 'woman's work'; decision making; dreaming and visioning; prophesying; divining, healing, locating people or things; harvesting, preserving, preparing, storing, or transporting food and healing stuffs; producing finished articles of clothing; making houses and laying them out in the proper village arrangement; making and using all sorts of technological equipment such as needles, scrapers, grinders, blenders, harvesters, diggers, fire makers, lathes, spindles, looms, knives, spoons, and ladles; locating and/or allocating virtually every resource used by the people. Guiding young women through the complex duties of womanhood must have taxed the creative, physical, psychic, and spiritual powers of all the women. In addition, they bore responsibility for preserving and using the oral tradition; making important tribal decisions about the life or death of captives and other outsiders; and overseeing ritual occasions, including making spiritual and physical provisions for ceremonies in cultures that devoted as much as two-thirds of their time to ritual/ceremonial pursuits. In short, the women did—and wherever possible still do—everything that maintains the life and stability of their tribal people. It is no wonder that Indian people in general insist that among them women are considered sacred. Nor, as perhaps you can see, is this an empty compliment in a society that depends for its life upon the sacred.

As shamans, the women in many tribes function in all ways that male shamans are known to. They perform healings, hunting ceremonies, vision quests and the guidance for them, acts of psychokinesis, teleportation, weather direction, and more. In the various tribes according to each one's customs, the shaman also creates certain artifacts—clothing, baskets, ornaments, objects to be worn in pouches or under skirts or sewed into belts. She officiates at burials, births, child naming and welcoming into this world, menstrual and pregnancy rituals and rites, psychic manipulation of animals, metamorphoses or transformations. She does much of this through dancing and chanting, and a large part of the method, symbols, significances, and effects of her shamanic efforts are recorded in the stories she tells, the songs she sings, and the knowledge she possesses. Much of this knowledge she transmits to others in ways that will be of use to them, and much of it she keeps to herself, teaches in formal settings to her apprentices, or shares with other shamans.

One of the primary functions of the shaman is her effect on tribal understandings of 'women's roles,' which in large part are traditional in Mrs. McCabe's sense of the word. It is the shaman's connection to the spirit world that Indian women writers reflect most strongly in our poetry and fiction. If there is any Indian woman's tradition that informs our work, it is the spiritual understanding of womanhood as an expression of spirit. That understanding is formed on the recognition that everything is alive, that the spirit people are part of our daily world, that all life lives in harmony and kinship with and to all other life, and that sickness of all kinds and of all orders comes about because of our resistance to surrendering to the complexity and multidimensionality of existence.

So we acknowledge that the violation of the Mothers' and Grandmothers' laws of kinship, respect, balance, and harmony brings about social, planetary, and personal illness and that healing is a matter of restoring the balance within ourselves and our communities. To this restoration of balance, of health, and wellness (wealth) we contribute our energies. For we are engaged in the work of reclaiming our minds, our gods, and our traditions. The sacred hoop cannot be restored unless and until its sacred center is recognized.

NOTES

1. Carolyn Neithammer, *Daughters of the Earth* (New York: Collier, 1977), p. 231. It must be said that Neithammer is as homophobic in her reporting on lesbianism as she is racist in her accounts of tribal views of womanhood. In her three-page treatment, she begins with accounts of positive valuing of lesbians, then moves to tolerance of lesbianism, and ends the section with a rousing tale of how the good villagers of a heterosexist Eskimo village routed the evil lesbian and her lover and forced them to give

up their unconventional lifestyle and return to the ways of their village. Sadly, her book is often the main title featured on the Native American Women shelf at women's bookstores across the country.

2. Neithammer, *Daughters*, pp. 231–4.

3. In an unpublished paper, Evelyn Blackwood cites Kaj Birket-Smith's *The Chugach Eskimo* (Copenhagen: National Museum, 1953) on the interesting point that evidently only the Chugach Eskimo and the Navajo literally perceive the berdache as 'half-man/half-woman,' which, Blackwood says, is not a common perception. 'Sexuality, Gender and Mode of Production: The Case of Native American Female Homosexuality (Berdache),' unpublished manuscript, 1983.

4. Judy Grahn, *Another Mother Tongue: Gay Words, Gay Worlds* (Boston: Beacon Press, 1984), pp. 55–56.

5. Grahn, *Another Mother Tongue*, pp. 55–6.

6. Walter Williams, 'American Indian Responses to the Suppression of the Homosexual Berdache Tradition,' presented at the Organization of American Historians convention, Spring 1983.

7. Martin Duberman, ed., 'Documents in Hopi Indian Sexuality,' *Radical History Review* 20 (Spring 1979), pp. 109, 112, 113.

8. Hubert Howe Bancroft, *The Native Races of the Pacific States of North America*, vol. 1 (New York: Appleton, 1875), p. 82.

9. George Catlin, *Illustrations of the Manners, Customs, and Conditions of the North American Indians, with Letters and Notes*, 10th ed. (London: Henry Bohn, 1866), 2:214–15. Cited in Jonathon Katz, *Gay American History, Lesbians and Gay Men in the U.S.A.* (New York: Crowell, 1976), p. 302.

10. Russell Means, Interview, *Penthouse Magazine* (April 1981), p. 138.

11. John (Fire) Lame Deer and Richard Erdoes, *Lame Deer: Seeker of Visions* (New York: Simon and Schuster, 1972), p. 149.

12. Interview in *Emma* (June 1982). Reprinted in *Connexions: An International Women's Quarterly*, no. 8 (Spring 1983), pp. 6–8.

13. Phyllis Old Dog Cross, 'Sexual Abuse, a New Threat to the Native American Woman: An Overview,' *Listening Post: A Periodical of the Mental Health Programs, Indian Health Service*, vol. 4, no. 2 (April 1982), p. 22.

Gloria Anzaldua

Gloria Anzaldua is a Chicana poet studying literature at the University of California at Santa Cruz. She is the co-editor, along with Cherrie Moraga, of *This Bridge Called My Back: Writings by Radical Women of Color* (1981). Her article included here, 'How to Tame a Wild Tongue', is chapter five of her more recent book *Border Lands: La Frontera: The New Mestiza* (1987). In 'How to Tame a Wild Tongue', Anzaldua gives an autobiographical account of being denied the legitimacy of one's language. She focuses on chicano Spanish, while also enumerating other living languages of the complex and heterogeneous group of Spanish speaking people. She questions the recourse left to 'a people who cannot entirely identify with either standard (formal, Castillian) Spanish nor standard English.' Her answer is that these people create their own languages, sometimes deliberately and sometimes because of the distortion of words brought on by the combining of two or more languages. She recalls having to try to lose her Spanish accent, not being able to teach chicano literature, and the negative stereotyping of Mexican pop culture which made it difficult, if not impossible, to gain a sense of her self and her culture. She also explains how hierarchies of Spanish languages are inextricably tied to the class-status of the people who speak them.

She lists standard English, working-class and slang English, standard Spanish, standard Mexican Spanish, North Mexican Spanish dialect, chicano Spanish (Texas, New Mexico, Arizona and California have regional variations), Tex-Mex, and *Pachuco* (Spanish words distorted by English and vice versa) as some of the languages spoken by chicano Spanish people and expounds at least briefly on the nature of each of these languages. For instance, she lists *Pachuco* as specifically a language of Spanish speaking youths, a 'language of rebellion, both against Standard Spanish and Standard English . . . a secret language', as their way of creating an identity. Chicano Spanish, she writes, is not an incorrect but a 'living' language which 'sprang out of the Chicanos' need to identify ourselves as a distinct people'. She explains that being a 'synergy' of two cultures, full of 'borderland conflict[s]', can make chicanos 'feel

402

like one cancels out the other and [they] are zero, nothing, no one'. To call someone's language illegitimate is tantamount to robbing them of a legitimate identity. G.R. and K.M.S.

How to tame a wild tongue

'We're going to have to control your tongue,' the dentist says, pulling out all the metal from my mouth. Silver bits plop and tinkle into the basin. My mouth is a motherlode.

The dentist is cleaning out my roots. I get a whiff of the stench when I gasp. 'I can't cap that tooth yet, you're still draining,' he says.

'We're going to have to do something about your tongue,' I hear the anger rising in his voice. My tongue keeps pushing out the wads of cotton, pushing back the drills, the long thin needles. 'I've never seen anything as strong or as stubborn,' he says. And I think, how do you tame a wild tongue, train it to be quiet, how do you bridle and saddle it? How do you make it lie down?

('Who is to say that robbing a people of its language is less violent than war?',
Ray Gwyn Smith[1])

I remember being caught speaking Spanish at recess—that was good for three licks on the knuckles with a sharp ruler. I remember being sent to the corner of the classroom for 'talking back' to the Anglo teacher when all I was trying to do was tell her how to pronounce my name. If you want to be American, speak 'American.' If you don't like it, go back to Mexico where you belong.

'I want you to speak English. *Pa' hallar buen trabajo tienes que saber hablar el inglés bien. Qué vale toda tu educación si todavía hablas inglés con un* 'accent',' my mother would say, mortified that I spoke English like a Mexican. At Pan American University, I, and all Chicano students were required to take two speech classes. Their purpose: to get rid of our accents.

Attacks on one's form of expression with the intent to censor are a violation of the First Amendment. *El Anglo con cara de inocente nos arrancó la lengua.* Wild tongues can't be tamed, they can only be cut out.

Overcoming the tradition of silence

Ahogadas, escupimos el oscuro.
Peleando con nuestra propia sombra
el silencio nos sepulta.

En boca cerrada no entran moscas. 'Flies don't enter a closed mouth' is a saying I kept

403

hearing when I was a child. *Ser habladora* was to be a gossip and a liar, to talk too much. *Mucha-chitas bien criadas*, well-bred girls don't answer back. *Es una falta de respeto* to talk back to one's mother or father. I remember one of the sins I'd recite to the priest in the confession box the few times I went to confession: talking back to my mother, *hablar pa' 'tras, repelar. Hocicona, repelona, chismosa*, having a big mouth, questioning, carrying tales are all signs of being *mal criada*. In my culture they are all words that are derogatory if applied to women—I've never heard them applied to men.

The first time I heard two women, a Puerto Rican and a Cuban, say the word '*nosotras*,' I was shocked. I had not known the word existed. Chicanas use *nosotros* whether we're male or female. We are robbed of our female being by the masculine plural. Language is a male discourse.

> And our tongues have become
> dry the wilderness has
> dried out our tongues and
> we have forgotten speech.
> (Irena Klepfisz)[2]

Even our own people, other Spanish speakers *nos quieren poner candados en la boca.* They would hold us back with their bag of *reglas de academia.*

Oyé como ladra: el lenguaje de la frontera

Quien tiene boca se equivoca.
(Mexican saying)

'*Pocho*, cultural traitor, you're speaking the oppressor's language by speaking English, you're ruining the Spanish language,' I have been accused by various Latinos and Latinas. Chicano Spanish is considered by the purist and by most Latinos deficient, a mutilation of Spanish.

But Chicano Spanish is a border tongue which developed naturally. Change, *evolución, enriquecimiento de palabras nuevas por invención o adopción* have created variants of Chicano Spanish, *un nuevo lenguaje. Un lenguaje que corresponde a un modo de vivir.* Chicano Spanish is not incorrect, it is a living language.

For a people who are neither Spanish nor live in a country in which Spanish is the first language; for a people who live in a country in which English is the reigning tongue but who are not Anglo; for a people who cannot entirely identify with either standard (formal, Castillian) Spanish nor standard English, what recourse is left to them but to create their own language? A language which they can connect their identity to, one capable of communicating the realities and values true to themselves—a language with terms that are neither *español ni inglés*, but both. We speak a patois, a forked tongue, a variation of two languages.

Chicano Spanish sprang out of the Chicanos' need to identify ourselves as a distinct people. We needed a language with which we could communicate with ourselves, a secret language. For some of us, language is a homeland closer than the Southwest—for many Chicanos today live in the Midwest and the East. And because we are a complex, heterogeneous people, we speak many languages. Some of the languages we speak are:

1. Standard English
2. Working class and slang English
3. Standard Spanish
4. Standard Mexican Spanish
5. North Mexican Spanish dialect
6. Chicano Spanish (Texas, New Mexico, Arizona and California have regional variations)
7. Tex-Mex
8. *Pachuco* (called *caló*)

My 'home' tongues are the languages I speak with my sister and brothers, with my friends. They are the last five listed, with 6 and 7 being closest to my heart. From school, the media and job situations, I've picked up standard and working class English. From Mamagrande Locha and from reading Spanish and Mexican literature, I've picked up Standard Spanish and Standard Mexican Spanish. From *los recién llegados*, Mexican immigrants, and *braceros*, I learned the North Mexican dialect. With Mexicans I'll try to speak either Standard Mexican Spanish or the North Mexican dialect. From my parents and Chicanos living in the Valley, I picked up Chicano Texas Spanish, and I speak it with my mom, younger brother (who married a Mexican and who rarely mixes Spanish with English), aunts and older relatives.

With Chicanas from *Nuevo México* or *Arizona* I will speak Chicano Spanish a little, but often they don't understand what I'm saying. With most California Chicanas I speak entirely in English (unless I forget). When I first moved to San Francisco, I'd rattle off something in Spanish, unintentionally embarrassing them. Often it is only with another Chicana *tejana* that I can talk freely.

Words distorted by English are known as anglicisms or *pochismos*. The *pocho* is an anglicized Mexican or American of Mexican origin who speaks Spanish with an accent characteristic of North Americans and who distorts and reconstructs the language according to the influence of English.[3] Tex-Mex, or Spanglish, comes most naturally to me. I may switch back and forth from English to Spanish in the same sentence or in the same word. With my sister and my brother Nune and with Chicano *tejano* contemporaries I speak in Tex-Mex.

From kids and people my own age I picked up *Pachuco*. *Pachuco* (the language of the zoot suiters) is a language of rebellion, both against Standard Spanish and Standard English. It is a secret language. Adults of the culture and outsiders cannot understand it. It is made up of slang words from both English and Spanish. *Ruca* means girl or woman, *vato* means guy or dude, *chale* means no, *simón* means yes, *churro* is sure, talk is *periquiar*, *pigionear* means petting, *que gacho* means how nerdy, *ponte águila* means watch out, death is called *la pelona*. Through lack of practice and not having others who can speak it, I've lost most of the *Pachuco* tongue.

Chicano Spanish

Chicanos, after 250 years of Spanish/Anglo colonization have developed significant differences in the Spanish we speak. We collapse two adjacent vowels into a single syllable and sometimes shift the stress in certain words such as *maíz/maiz*, *cohete/cuete*. We leave out certain consonants when they appear between vowels: *lado/lao, mojado/mojao*. Chicanos from South Texas pronounce *f* as *j* as in *jue* (*fue*). Chicanos use 'archaisms,' words that are no longer in the Spanish language, words that have been evolved out. We say *semos, truje, haiga, ansina*, and *naiden*. We retain the 'archaic' *j*, as in *jalar*; that derives from an earlier *h* (the French *halar* or the Germanic *halon* which was lost to standard Spanish in the 16th century), but which is still found in several regional dialects such as the one spoken in South Texas. (Due to geography, Chicanos from the Valley of South Texas were cut off linguistically from other Spanish speakers. We tend to use words that the Spaniards brought over from Medieval Spain. The majority of the Spanish colonizers in Mexico and the Southwest came from Extremadura—Hernán Cortés was one of them—and Andalucía. Andalucians pronounce *ll* like a *y*, and their *d*'s tend to be absorbed by adjacent vowels: *tirado* becomes *tirao*. They brought *el lenguaje popular, dialectos y regionalismos*.[4])

Chicanos and other Spanish speakers also shift *ll* to *y* and *z* to *s*.[5] We leave out initial syllables, saying *tar* for *estar*, *toy* for *estoy*, *hora* for *ahora* (*cubanos* and *puertorriqueños* also leave out initial letters of some words.) We also leave out the final syllable such as *pa* for *para*. The intervocalic *y*, the *ll* as in *tortilla, ella, botella*, gets replaced by *tortia* or *tortiya, ea, botea*. We add an additional syllable at the beginning of certain words: *atocar* for *tocar*, *agastar* for *gastar*. Sometimes we'll say *lavaste las vacijas*, other times *lavates* (substituting the *ates* verb endings for the *aste*).

We use anglicisms, words borrowed from English: *bola* from ball, *carpeta* from carpet, *máchina de lavar* (instead of *lavadora*) from washing machine. Tex-Mex argot, created by adding a Spanish sound at the beginning or end of an English word such as *cookiar* for cook, *watchar* for watch, *parkiar* for park, and *rapiar* for rape, is the result of the pressures on Spanish speakers to adapt to English.

We don't use the word *vosotros/as* or its accompanying verb form. We don't say *claro* (to mean yes), *imagínate*, or *me emociona*, unless we picked up Spanish from Latinas, out of a book, or in a classroom. Other Spanish-speaking groups are going through the same, or similar, development in their Spanish.

Linguistic terrorism

Deslenguadas. Somos los del español deficiente. We are your linguistic nightmare, your linguistic aberration, your linguistic *mestisaje*, the subject of your *burla*. Because we speak with tongues of fire we are culturally crucified. Racially, culturally and linguistically *somos huérfanos*—we speak an orphan tongue.

Chicanas who grew up speaking Chicano Spanish have internalized the belief that we speak poor Spanish. It is illegitimate, a bastard language. And because we internalize how our language has been used against us by the dominant culture, we use our language differences against each other.

Chicana feminists often skirt around each other with suspicion and hesitation. For the longest time I couldn't figure it out. Then it dawned on me. To be close to another Chicana is like looking into the mirror. We are afraid of what we'll see there. *Pena.* Shame. Low estimation of self. In childhood we are told that our language is wrong. Repeated attacks on our native tongue diminish our sense of self. The attacks continue throughout our lives.

Chicanas feel uncomfortable talking in Spanish to Latinas, afraid of their censure. Their language was not outlawed in their countries. They had a whole lifetime of being immersed in their native tongue; generations, centuries in which Spanish was a first language, taught in school, heard on radio and TV, and read in the newspaper.

If a person, Chicana or Latina, has a low estimation of my native tongue, she also has a low estimation of me. Often with *mexicanas y latinas* we'll speak English as a neutral language. Even among Chicanas we tend to speak English at parties or conferences. Yet, at the same time, we're afraid the other will think we're *agringadas* because we don't speak Chicano Spanish. We oppress each other trying to out-Chicano each other, vying to be the 'real' Chicanas, to speak like Chicanos. There is no one Chicano language just as there is no one Chicano experience. A monolingual Chicana whose first language is English or Spanish is just as much a Chicana as one who speaks several variants of Spanish. A Chicana from Michigan or Chicago or Detroit is just as much a Chicana as one from the Southwest. Chicano Spanish is as diverse linguistically as it is regionally.

By the end of this century, Spanish speakers will comprise the biggest minority group in the U.S., a country where students in high schools and colleges are encouraged to take French classes because French is considered more 'cultured.' But for a language to remain alive it must be used.[6] By the end of this century English, and not Spanish, will be the mother tongue of most Chicanos and Latinos.

So, if you want to really hurt me, talk badly about my language. Ethnic identity is twin skin to linguistic identity—I am my language. Until I can take pride in my language, I cannot take pride in myself. Until I can accept as legitimate Chicano Texas Spanish, Tex-Mex and all the other languages I speak, I cannot accept the legitimacy of myself. Until I am free to write bilingually and to switch codes without having always to translate, while I still have to speak English or Spanish when I would rather speak Spanglish, and as long as I have to accommodate the English speakers rather than having them accommodate me, my tongue will be illegitimate.

I will no longer be made to feel ashamed of existing. I will have my voice: Indian, Spanish, white. I will have my serpent's tongue—my woman's voice, my sexual voice, my poet's voice. I will overcome the tradition of silence.

My fingers
move sly against your palm
Like women everywhere, we speak in code. . . .
       (Melanie Kaye/Kantrowitz)[7]

'Vistas,' corridos, y comida: my native tongue

In the 1960s, I read my first Chicano novel. It was *City of Night* by John Rechy, a gay Texan, son of a Scottish father and a Mexican mother. For days I walked around in stunned amazement that a Chicano could write and could get published. When I read *I Am Joaquín*[8] I was surprised to see a bilingual book by a Chicano in print. When I saw poetry written in Tex-Mex for the first time, a feeling of pure joy flashed through me. I felt like we really existed as a people. In 1971, when I started teaching High School English to Chicano students, I tried to supplement the required texts with works by Chicanos, only to be reprimanded and forbidden to do so by the principal. He claimed that I was supposed to teach 'American' and English literature. At the risk of being fired, I swore my students to secrecy and slipped in Chicano short stories, poems, a play. In graduate school, while working toward a Ph.D., I had to 'argue' with one advisor after the other, semester after semester, before I was allowed to make Chicano literature an area of focus.

Even before I read books by Chicanos or Mexicans, it was the Mexican movies I saw at the drive-in—the Thursday night special of $1.00 a carload—that gave me a sense of belonging. '*Vámonos a las vistas*,' my mother would call out and we'd all—grandmother, brothers, sister and cousins—squeeze into the car. We'd wolf down cheese and bologna white bread sandwiches while watching Pedro Infante in melodramatic tear-jerkers like *Nosotros los pobres*, the first 'real' Mexican movie (that was not an imitation of European movies). I remember seeing *Cuando los hijos se van* and surmising that all Mexican movies played up the love a mother has for her children and what ungrateful sons and daughters suffer when they are not devoted to their mothers. I remember the singing-type 'westerns' of Jorge Negrete and Miquel Aceves Mejía. When watching Mexican movies, I felt a sense of homecoming as well as alienation. People who were to amount to something didn't go to Mexican movies, or *bailes* or tune their radios to *bolero*, *rancherita*, and *corrido* music.

The whole time I was growing up, there was *norteño* music sometimes called North Mexican border music, or Tex-Mex music, or Chicano music, or *cantina* (bar) music. I grew up listening to *conjuntos*, three- or four-piece bands made up of folk musicians playing guitar, *bajo sexto*, drums and button accordion, which Chicanos had borrowed from the German immigrants who had come to Central Texas and Mexico to farm and build breweries. In the Rio Grande Valley, Steve Jordan and Little Joe Hernández were popular, and Flaco Jiménez was the accordian king. The rhythms of Tex-Mex music are those of the polka, also adapted from the Germans, who in turn had borrowed the polka from the Czechs and Bohemians.

I remember the hot, sultry evenings when *corridos*—songs of love and death on the Texas-Mexican borderlands—reverberated out of cheap amplifiers from the local *cantinas* and wafted in through my bedroom window.

Corridos first became widely used along the South Texas/Mexican border during the early conflict between Chicanos and Anglos. The *corridos* are usually about Mexican heroes who do valiant deeds against the Anglo oppressors. Pancho Villa's

408

song, 'La cucaracha,' is the most famous one. Corridos of John F. Kennedy and his death are still very popular in the Valley. Older Chicanos remember Lydia Mendoza, one of the great border corrido singers who was called la Gloria de Tejas. Her 'El tango negro,' sung during the Great Depression, made her a singer of the people. The everpresent corridos narrated one hundred years of border history, bringing news of events as well as entertaining. These folk musicians and folk songs are our chief cultural myth-makers, and they made our hard lives seem bearable.

I grew up feeling ambivalent about our music. Country-western and rock-and-roll had more status. In the 50s and 60s, for the slightly educated and agringado Chicanos, there existed a sense of shame at being caught listening to our music. Yet I couldn't stop my feet from thumping to the music, could not stop humming the words, nor hide from myself the exhilaration I felt when I heard it.

There are more subtle ways that we internalize identification, especially in the forms of images and emotions. For me food and certain smells are tied to my identity, to my homeland. Woodsmoke curling up to an immense blue sky; woodsmoke perfuming my grandmother's clothes, her skin. The stench of cow manure and the yellow patches on the ground; the crack of a .22 rifle and the reek of cordite. Homemade white cheese sizzling in a pan, melting inside a folded tortilla. My sister Hilda's hot, spicy menudo, chile colorado making it deep red, pieces of panza and hominy floating on top. My brother Carito barbequing fajitas in the backyard. Even now and 3,000 miles away, I can see my mother spicing the ground beef, pork and venison with chile. My mouth salivates at the thought of the hot steaming tamales I would be eating if I were home.

Si le preguntas a mi mamá, '¿Qué eres?'

'Identity is the essential core of who we are as individuals, the conscious experience of the self inside.'

(Kaufman)[9]

Nosotros los Chicanos straddle the borderlands. On one side of us, we are constantly exposed to the Spanish of the Mexicans, on the other side we hear the Anglos' incessant clamoring so that we forget our language. Among ourselves we don't say nosotros los americanos, o nosotros los españoles, o nosotros los hispanos. We say nosotros los mexicanos (by mexicanos we do not mean citizens of Mexico; we do not mean a national identity, but a racial one). We distinguish between mexicanos del otro lado and mexicanos de este lado. Deep in our hearts we believe that being Mexican has nothing to do with which country one lives in. Being Mexican is a state of soul—not one of mind, not one of citizenship. Neither eagle nor serpent, but both. And like the ocean, neither animal respects borders.

Dime con quien andas y te diré quien eres.
(Tell me who your friends are and I'll tell you who you are.)

(Mexican saying)

Si le preguntas a mi mamá, '¿Qué eres?' te dirá, 'Soy mexicana.' My brothers and sister say the same. I sometimes will answer *'soy mexicana'* and at others will say *'soy Chicana' o 'soy tejana.'* But I identified as *'Raza'* before I ever identified as *'mexicana'* or 'Chicana.'

As a culture, we call ourselves Spanish when referring to ourselves as a linguistic group and when copping out. It is then that we forget our predominant Indian genes. We are 70–80% Indian.[10] We call ourselves Hispanic[11] or Spanish-American or Latin American or Latin when linking ourselves to other Spanish-speaking peoples of the Western hemisphere and when copping out. We call ourselves Mexican-American[12] to signify we are neither Mexican nor American, but more the noun 'American' than the adjective 'Mexican' (and when copping out).

Chicanos and other people of color suffer economically for not acculturating. This voluntary (yet forced) alienation makes for psychological conflict, a kind of dual identity—we don't identify with the Anglo-American cultural values and we don't totally identify with the Mexican cultural values. We are a synergy of two cultures with various degrees of Mexicanness or Angloness. I have so internalized the borderland conflict that sometimes I feel like one cancels out the other and we are zero, nothing, no one. *A veces no soy nada ni nadie. Pero hasta cuando no lo soy, lo soy.*

When not copping out, when we know we are more than nothing, we call ourselves Mexican, referring to race and ancestry; *mestizo* when affirming both our Indian and Spanish (but we hardly ever own our Black ancestry); Chicano when referring to a politically aware people born and/or raised in the U.S.; *Raza* when referring to Chicanos; *tejanos* when we are Chicanos from Texas.

Chicanos did not know we were a people until 1965 when Ceasar Chavez and the farmworkers united and *I Am Joaquín* was published and *la Raza Unida* party was formed in Texas. With that recognition, we became a distinct people. Something momentous happened to the Chicano soul—we became aware of our reality and acquired a name and a language (Chicano Spanish) that reflected that reality. Now that we had a name, some of the fragmented pieces began to fall together—who we were, what we were, how we had evolved. We began to get glimpses of what we might eventually become.

Yet the struggle of identities continues, the struggle of borders is our reality still. One day the inner struggle will cease and a true integration take place. In the meantime, *tenémos que hacer la lucha. ¿Quién está protegiendo los ranchos de migente? ¿Quién está tratando de cerrar la fisura entre la india y el blanco en nuestra sangre? El Chicano, si, el Chicano que anda como un ladrón en su propria casa.*

Los Chicanos, how patient we seem, how very patient. There is the quiet of the Indian about us.[13] We know how to survive. When other races have given up their tongue, we've kept ours. We know what it is to live under the hammer blow of the dominant *norteamericano* culture. But more than we count the blows, we count the days the weeks the years the centuries the eons until the white laws and commerce and customs will rot in the deserts they've created, lie bleached. *Humildes* yet proud, *quietos* yet wild, *nosotros los mexicanos-Chicanos* will walk by the crumbling ashes as we go about our business. Stubborn, persevering, impenetrable as stone, yet possessing a malleability that renders us unbreakable, we, the *mestizas* and *mestizos*, will remain.

NOTES

1. Ray Gwyn Smith, Moorland is Cold Country, unpublished book.
2. Irena Klepfisz, 'Dirayze abaym/The Journey Home,' in *The Tribe of Dina: A Jewish Women's Anthology*, Melanie Kaye/Kantrowitz and Irena Keipfisz, eds, (Moorpeliar, VT: Sinister Wisdom Books, 1986), 49.
3. R.C. Orrega, *Dialectologia Del Barrio*, trans. Horrencia S. Alwaii (Los Angeles, CA: R.C. Orega Publishers/Bookseller, 1977), 132.
4. Eduardo Hernandex-Chavez, Andrew D. Coiteh, and Anthony F. Belssamo, *El Lingnajn da los Chicanos: Regional and Social Characteristics of Language Used By Mexican Americans* (Arlington, VA: Center for Applied Linguistics, 1975), 39.
5. Hernandez-Chavez, xvii.
6. Irena Klepfiaz, 'Secular Jewish Identity: Yidishkayt in America,' in *The Tribe of Dina*, Kaye/Kantrowitz and Kelpfidz, eds., 43.
7. Melanie Kaye/Kantrowitz, 'Sign,' in *'We Speak In Code' Poems and Other Writings* (Pittsburgh, PA: Motheroor Publications, Inc., 1980), 85.
8. Rodolfo Gonzales, *I Am Joaquin/Yo Soy Joaquin* (New York, NY: Bantam Books, 1972). It was first published in 1967.
9. Kaufman, 68.
10. Chavez, 88–90.
11. 'Hispanic' is derived from Hispanis (Espana, a name given to the Iberian Peninsula in ancient times when it was a part of the Roman Empire) and is a term designated by the U.S. government to make it easier to handle us on paper.
12. The Treaty of Guadalupe Hidalgo created the Mexican-American in 1848.
13. Anglos, in order to alleviate their guilt for dispossessing the Chicano, stressed the Spanish part of us and perpetrated the myth of the Spanish Southwest. We have accepted the fiction that we are Hispanic, that is Spanish, in order to accommodate ourselves to the dominant culture and its abhorrance of Indians, Chavez, 88–91.

Cornel West (1953–)

Cornel West received his BA from Harvard, and his MA and PhD in philosophy from Princeton. He currently teaches philosophy of religion at Yale University. As a teacher, scholar, and public speaker, he epitomizes the character of the dynamic and politically engaged intellectual. In his work, West invokes the Western intellectual tradition while at the same time critiquing it. He sees the recent demise of European cultural hegemony as an opportunity for non-Europeans and those who have been marked as 'other' to construct anew self-empowering subjectivities. Some of his major works are: *Prophesy Deliverance!: An Afro-American Revolutionary Christianity* (1982), *Post Analytic Philosophy* (1985), *Race Matters* (1992), *The Ethical Dimensions of Marxist Thought* (1991), *The American Evasion of Philosophy: A Genealogy of Pragmatism* (1989), and *Prophetic Fragments* (1988).

In the essay reprinted here, West addresses the controversy of canon formation from the perspective of an oppositional African-American cultural critic. He agrees that the traditional canon of the academy must be opened up, but he wishes to enlarge the procedures for doing so. He sets forth the design of this polemical stance by arguing that literary formalism as it has been practised in this century does not help the cause of African-American literature. The reification of literary works by such prominent authors as Jean Toomer, Ralph Ellison, James Baldwin, Toni Morrison, and Ishmael Reed has dehistoricized and depoliticized them and robbed these works of the political potency which could inform a genuine oppositional, cultural stance. West asserts that cultural critics should not limit their work to the tenets of literary criticism but rather relate literary texts to larger institutional and historical issues. Cultural critics then may promote the establishment of a revised canon that includes African-American literary texts not merely as a marginalized addendum but as a structurally integral part that enables them to posit an effective cultural criticism.

T. M. and G.R.

412

Minority discourse and the pitfalls of canon formation

What does it mean to engage in canon formation at this historical moment? In what ways does the prevailing crisis in the humanities impede or enable new canon formations? And what role do the class and professional interests of the canonizers play in either the enlarging of a canon or the making of multiple, conflicting canons? I shall address these questions in the form of a critical self-inventory of my own intellectual activity as an Afro-American cultural critic. This self-inventory shall consist of three moments. First, I shall locate my own cultural criticism against a particular historical reading of the contemporary crisis in the humanities. Second, I shall examine my own deeply ambiguous intellectual sentiments regarding the process of canon formation now afoot in Afro-American literary criticism. And third, I shall put forward what I understand to be the appropriate role and function of oppositional cultural critics in regard to prevailing forms of canon formation in our time.

Any attempt to expand old canons or constitute new ones presupposes particular interpretations of the historical moment at which canonization is to take place. The major Western male literary canonizers of our century—T. S. Eliot, F. R. Leavis, F. O. Matthiessen, Cleanth Brooks, Northrop Frye, M. H. Abrams, and Paul de Man—all assumed specific interpretations of why their canonizing efforts were required and how these efforts could play a positive role. Contemporary literary critics remain too preoccupied with the fascinating and ingenious ways in which these canonizers reevaluated and readjusted the old canon. As a cultural critic, I would like to see more attention paid to the prevailing historical interpretations of the cultural crisis which prompts, guides, and regulates the canonizing efforts. In this sense, attempts to revise or reconstitute literary canons rest upon prior—though often tacit—interpretative acts of rendering a canonical historical reading of the crisis that in part authorizes literary canons. So the first battle over literary canon formation has to do with one's historical interpretation of the crisis achieving canonical status.

For instance, the power of T. S. Eliot's canonizing efforts had as much to do with his canonical reading of the crisis of European civilization after the unprecedented carnage and dislocations of World War I as with his literary evaluations of the Metaphysicals and Dryden over Spenser and Milton or his nearly wholesale disapproval of Romantic and Victorian poetry. As the first moment of my own self-inventory as an Afro-American cultural critic, I focus not on the kinds of texts to choose for an enlargement of the old canon or the making of a new one but rather on a historical reading of the present-day crisis of American civilization, an aspiring canonical historical reading that shapes the way in which literary canon-formation itself ought to proceed and the kind of cultural archives that should constitute this formation. This reading is informed by a particular sense of history in which conflict, struggle, and contestation are prominent. It accents the complex interplay of rhetorical practices (and their effects, for example, rational persuasion and intellectual pleasure) and the operations of power and authority (and their effects, for example, subordination and resistance).

413

My historical reading of the present cultural crisis begins with a distinctive feature of the twentieth century: the decolonization of the Third World associated with the historical agency of those oppressed and exploited, devalued and degraded by European civilization. This interpretive point of entry is in no way exhaustive—it does not treat other significant aspects of our time—yet neither is it merely arbitrary. Rather it is a world-historical process that has fundamentally changed not only our conceptions of ourselves and those constituted as 'others' (non-Europeans, women, gays, lesbians) but, more important, our understanding of how we have constructed and do construct conceptions of ourselves and others as selves, subjects, and peoples. In short, the decolonization of the Third World has unleashed attitudes, values, sensibilities, and perspectives with which we have yet fully to come to terms.

More specifically, the decolonization process signaled the end of the European age—an age that extends from 1492 to 1945. The eclipse of European domination and the dwarfing of European populations enabled the intellectual activities of demystifying European cultural hegemony and of deconstructing European philosophical edifices. In other words, as the prolonged period of European self-confidence came to an end with the emergence of the United States as the major world power after World War II, the reverberations and ramifications of the decline of European civilization could be felt in the upper reaches of the WASP elite institutions of higher learning—including its humanistic disciplines. The emergence of the first major subcultures of American non-WASP intellectuals as exemplified by the so-called New York intellectuals, the abstract expressionists, and the bebop jazz artists constituted a major challenge to an American male WASP cultural elite loyal to an older and eroding European culture.

The first significant blow—a salutary one, I might add—was dealt when assimilated Jewish Americans entered the high echelons of the academy—especially Ivy league institutions. Lionel Trilling at Columbia, Oscar Handlin at Harvard, and John Blum at Yale initiated the slow but sure undoing of male WASP cultural homogeneity—that is, the snobbish gentility, tribal civility, and institutional loyalty that circumscribed the relative consensus which rests upon the Arnoldian conception of culture and its concomitant canon. The genius of Lionel Trilling was to appropriate this conception for his own political and cultural purposes—thereby unraveling the old male WASP consensus yet erecting a new liberal academic consensus around the cold war anticommunist rendition of the values of complexity, difficulty, and modulation. In addition, the professionalization and specialization of teaching in the humanities that resulted from the postwar American economic boom promoted the close reading techniques of the New Critics—severed from their conservative and organicist anticapitalist (or anti-industrialist) ideology. Like Trilling's revisionist Arnoldian criticism, the New Critics' academic preoccupation with paradox, irony, and ambiguity both helped to canonize modernist literature and provided new readers of literary studies with a formal rigor and intellectual vigor which buttressed beleaguered humanist self-images in an expanding, technocentric culture. The new programs of American studies provided one of the few discursive spaces—especially for second-generation immigrants with progressive sentiments—wherein critiques of the emerging liberal consensus could be put forward, and even this space was limited by the ebullient postwar American nationalism which partly fueled the new interdisciplinary endeavor and by the subsequent repressive atmosphere of McCarthyism, which discouraged explicit social criticism.

The sixties constitute the watershed period in my schematic sketch of our present cultural crisis. During that decade we witnessed the shattering of male WASP cultural homogeneity and the collapse of the short-lived liberal consensus. More pointedly, the inclusion of Afro-Americans, Hispanic Americans, Asian Americans, native Americans, and American women in the academy repoliticized literary studies in a way that went against the grain of the old male WASP cultural hegemony and the new revisionist liberal consensus. This repoliticizing of the humanities yielded disorienting intellectual polemics and inescapable ideological polarization. These polemics and this polarization focused primarily on the limits, blindnesses, and exclusions of the prevailing forms of gentility, civility, and loyalty as well as the accompanying notions of culture and canonicity.

The radical and thorough questioning of male Euro-American cultural elites by Americans of color, American women, and New Left white males highlighted three crucial processes in the life of the country. First, the reception of the traveling theories from continental Europe—especially the work of the Frankfurt school and French Marxisms, structuralisms, and poststructuralisms. A distinctive feature of these theories was the degree to which they grappled with the devastation, decline, and decay of European civilization since the defeat of Fascism and the fall of the British and French empires in Asia and Africa. The American reception of these theories undoubtedly domesticated them for academic consumption. But the theories also internationalized American humanistic discourses so that they extended beyond the North Atlantic connection. For the first time, significant Latin American, African, and Asian writers figured visibly in academic literary studies.

The second noteworthy process accelerated by the struggles of the sixties was the recovery and revisioning of American history in light of those on its underside. Marxist histories, new social histories, women's histories, histories of peoples of color, gay and lesbian histories all made new demands of scholars in literary studies. Issues concerning texts in history and history in texts loomed large. The third process I shall note is the onslaught of forms of popular culture such as film and television on highbrow literate culture. American technology—under the aegis of capital—transformed the cultural sphere and everyday life of people and thereby questioned the very place, presence, and power of the printed word.

The establishmentarian response in the humanities was to accommodate the new social forces. In order to avoid divisive infighting within departments and to overcome the incommensurability of discourses among colleagues, ideologies of pluralism emerged to mediate clashing methods and perspectives in structurally fragmented departments. These ideologies served both to contain and often conceal irresoluble conflict and to ensure slots for ambitious and upwardly mobile young professors who were anxiety-ridden about their professional-managerial class status and fascinated with their bold, transgressive rhetoric, given their relative political impotence and inactivity. Needless to say, conservative spokespersons both inside and especially outside the academy lamented what they perceived as an 'assault on the life of the mind' and made nostalgic calls for a return to older forms of consensus. Contemporary reflections on ideologies of canon formation take their place within

415

this context of cultural heterogeneity, political struggle, and academic dissensus—a context which itself is a particular historical reading of our prevailing critical struggle for canonical status in the midst of the battle over literary canon formation.

Not surprisingly, attempts to justify and legitimate canon formation in Afro-American literary criticism are made in the name of pluralism. In our present historical context (with its highly limited options), these efforts are worthy of critical support. Yet I remain suspicious of them for two basic reasons. First, they tend to direct the energies of Afro-American critics toward scrutinizing and defending primarily Afro-American literary texts for a new or emerging canon and away from demystifying the already existing canon. The mere addition of Afro-American texts to the present canon without any explicit and persuasive account of how this addition leads us to see the canon anew reveals the worst of academic pluralist ideology. Serious Afro-American literary canon formation cannot take place without a wholesome reconsideration of the canon already in place. This is so not because 'existing monuments form an ideal order among themselves which is modified by the introduction of the new (the really new) work of art among them'—as T. S. Eliot posited in his influential essay 'Tradition and the Individual Talent.' Rather the interdependence of the canonical and noncanonical as well as the interplay of the old canonical texts and the new canonical ones again require us to examine the crucial role of our historical readings of the current crisis that acknowledges this interdependence and promotes this interplay. Mere preoccupation with Afro-American literary texts— already marginalized and ghettoized in literary studies—which leads toward a marginal and ghetto status in an enlarged canon or independent canon, forecloses this broader examination of the present crisis and thereby precludes action to transform it.

This foreclosure is neither fortuitous nor accidental. Rather it is symptomatic of the class interests of Afro-American literary critics: they become the academic superintendents of a segment of an expanded canon or a separate canon. Such supervisory power over Afro-American literary culture—including its significant consulting activities and sometimes patronage relations to powerful white academic critics and publishers—not only ensures slots for black literary scholars in highly competitive English departments. More important, these slots are themselves held up as evidence for the success of prevailing ideologies of pluralism. Such talk of success masks the ever-growing power of universities over American literary culture and, more specifically, the increasing authority of black literary professional managers over Afro-American literary practices and products. This authority cannot but have a major impact on the kinds of literary texts produced—especially as Afro-American literary programs increasingly produce the people who write the texts. It is fortunate that Richard Wright, Ann Petry, and Ralph Ellison did not labor under such authority. In fact, I would go as far as to postulate that the glacier shift from an Afro-American literature of racial confrontation during the four decades of the forties to the seventies to one of cultural introspection in our time is linked in some complex and mediated way to the existential needs and accommodating values of the black and white literary professional-managerial classes who assess and promote most of this literature.

Lest I be misunderstood, I am not suggesting that literary studies would be better off without Afro-American literary critics or with fewer of them. Nor am I arguing that canon formation among Afro-American critics ought not to take place. Rather I am making three fundamental claims. First, that Afro-American canon formation regulated by an ideology of pluralism is more an emblem of the prevailing crisis in contemporary humanistic studies than a creative response to it. Second, that this activity—despite its limited positive effects, such as rendering visible Afro-American literary texts of high quality—principally reproduces and reinforces prevailing forms of cultural authority in our professionalized supervision of literary products. Third, that black inclusion into these forms of cultural authority—with black literary critics overseeing a black canon—primarily serves the class interests of Afro-American literary academic critics.

A brief glance at the history of Afro-American literary criticism—including its present state—bears out these claims. Like most black literate intellectual activity in the Western world and especially in the United States, Afro-American literary criticism has tended to take a defensive posture. That is, it has viewed itself as evidence of the humanity and intellectual capacity of black people that are often questioned by the dominant culture. This posture is understandably shot through with self-doubts and inferiority anxieties. And it often has resulted in bloated and exorbitant claims about black literary achievement. In stark contrast to black artistic practices in homiletics and music, in which blacks' self-confidence abounds owing to the vitality of rich and varied indigenous traditions, black literary artists and critics have proclaimed a Harlem Renaissance that never took place, novelistic breakthroughs that amounted to poignant yet narrow mediums of social protest (for example, *Native Son*), and literary movements that consist of talented though disparate women writers with little more than their gender and color in common. Such defensive posturing overlooks and downplays the grand contributions of the major twentieth-century Afro-American literary artists—Jean Toomer, Ralph Ellison, James Baldwin (more his essays than his fiction), Toni Morrison, and Ishmael Reed. Such diminishment takes place because these authors arbitrarily get lumped with a group of black writers or associated with a particular theme in Afro-American intellectual history, which obscures their literary profundity and accents their less important aspects.

For instance, Toomer's ingenious modernist formal innovations and his chilling encounter with black southern culture in *Cane* are masked by associating him with the assertion of pride by the 'new Negro' in the twenties. Ellison's existentialist blues novelistic practices, with their deep sources in Afro-American music, folklore, Western literary humanism, and American pluralist ideology, are concealed by subsuming him under a 'post-Wright school of black writing.' Baldwin's masterful and memorable essays that mix Jamesian prose with black sermonic rhythms are similarly treated. Toni Morrison's magic realist portrayal of forms of Afro-American cultural disruption and transformation links her more closely to contemporary Latin American literary treatments of the arrested agency of colonized peoples than with American feminist preoccupations with self-fulfillment and sisterhood. Last, Ishmael Reed's bizarre and brilliant postmodernist stories fall well outside black literary lineages and genealogies. In short, it is difficult to imagine an Afro-American canon formation that does not domesticate and dilute the literary power and historical significance of these major figures.

417

Recent developments in Afro-American literary criticism that focus on the figurative language of the texts are indeed improvements over the flat content analyses, vague black aesthetic efforts, and political didacticism of earlier critics of Afro-American literature. Yet this new black formalism—under whose auspices Afro-American literary canon formation will more than likely take place—overreacts to the limits of the older approaches and thereby captures only select rhetorical features of texts while dehistoricizing their form and content. It ignores the way in which issues of power, political struggle, and cultural identity are inscribed within the formal structures of texts and thereby misses the implicit historical readings of the crisis that circumscribes the texts and to which the texts inescapably and subtly respond.

This new formalism goes even farther astray when it attempts, in the words of critic Henry Louis Gates, Jr., to 'turn to the Black tradition itself to develop theories of criticism indigenous to our literature.' It goes farther astray because it proceeds on the dubious notion that theories of criticism must be developed from literature itself—be it vernacular, oral, or highbrow literature. To put it crudely, this notion rests upon a fetishism of literature—a religious belief in the magical powers of a glorified set of particular cultural archives somehow autonomous and disconnected from other social practices. Must film criticism develop only from film itself? Must jazz criticism emerge only from jazz itself? One set of distinctive cultural archives must never be reducible or intelligible in terms of another set of cultural archives—including criticism itself. Yet it is impossible to grasp the complexity and multidimensionality of a specific set of artistic practices without relating it to other broader cultural and political practices at a given historical moment. In this sense, the move Afro-American literary critics have made from a preoccupation with Northrop Frye's myth structuralism (with its assumption of the autonomy of the literary universe) and Paul de Man's rigorous deconstructive criticism (with its guiding notion of the self-reflexive and self-contradictory rhetorics of literary texts) to the signifying activity of dynamic black vernacular literature is but a displacement of one kind of formalism for another; it is but a shift from Euro-American elitist formalism to Afro-American populist formalism, and it continues to resist viewing political conflict and cultural contestation within the forms themselves.

The appropriate role and function of opposition cultural critics regarding current forms of canon formation is threefold. First, we must no longer be literary critics who presume that our cultivated gaze on literary objects—the reified objects of our compartmentalized and professionalized disciplines—yields solely or principally judgments about the literary properties of these objects. There is indeed an inescapable evaluative dimension to any valid cultural criticism. Yet the literary objects upon which we focus are themselves cultural responses to specific crises in particular historical moments. Because these crises and moments must themselves be mediated through textual constructs, the literary objects we examine are never merely literary, and attempts to see them as such constitute a dehistoricizing and depoliticizing of literary texts that should be scrutinized for their ideological content, role, and function. In this sense, canon formations that invoke the sole criterion of form—be it of the elitist or populist variety—are suspect.

Second, as cultural critics attuned to political conflict and struggle inscribed within the rhetorical enactments of texts, we should relate such conflict and struggle to larger institutional and structural battles occurring in and across societies, cultures, and economies. This means that knowledge of sophisticated versions of historiography and refined perspectives of social theory are indispensable for a serious cultural critic. In other words—like the cultural critics of old—we must simply know much more than a professional literary critical training provides. The key here is not mere interdisciplinary work that traverses existing boundaries of disciplines but rather the more demanding efforts of pursuing dedisciplinizing modes of knowing that call into question the very boundaries of the disciplines themselves.

Finally, cultural critics should promote types of canon formation that serve as strategic weapons in the contemporary battle over how best to respond to the current crisis in one's society and culture. This view does not entail a crude, unidimensional, instrumental approach to literature; it simply acknowledges that so-called noninstrumental approaches are themselves always already implicated in the raging battle in one's society and culture. The fundamental question is not how one's canon can transcend this battle but rather how old or new canons, enlarged or conflicting canons, guide particular historical interpretations of this battle and enable individual and collective action within it. I simply hope that as canon formation proceeds among Afro-American cultural critics and others we can try to avoid as much as possible the pitfalls I have sketched.

Paul Gilroy

Paul Gilroy, a black, British cultural theorist, has worked as a disc jockey, musician, and journalist, and currently lectures in sociology at Goldsmith's College, University of London. His book *There Ain't No Black in the Union Jack; The Cultural Politics of Race and Nation* (1987) explores the relationship between race, class, and nation in contemporary Britain. Here Gilroy provides an account of race that functions as a critique of, rather than an alternative to, sociology's present definition of 'race relations'. His co-authored book, *The Empire Strikes Back* (1989) is more systematically political. His *The Black Atlantic* (1992) and *Small Acts* (1993) represent a sophisticated analysis of the discursive status of race, i.e., the lived-in cultural reality of British Blacks *vis-à-vis* the hegemony of British cultural policies and tolerance.

The essay printed here, 'Cruciality and the Frog's Perspective', is a chapter from *Small Acts*, and discusses the Black Arts movement in Britain. Challenging a simplistic, Marxist view of the role of art, he says 'we must begin with the black artist as a public figure—a figure in public politics. The public sphere in which artist and people encounter each other does not coincide neatly with the contours of the British nation-state.' In an effort to theorize the nature and complexity of the Black Arts movement as a mode of cultural activism, which he sees as emanating from 'underground' spaces, Gilroy rejects the common myth that black cultural forms, such as rap music in the US for instance, cater to a faddish, white audience. Elaborating on this point, he also rejects a homogenizing move to subsume British black art as representative of all African art in the United States, Africa, Asia, the Caribbean, and Europe, in a sense, fighting the impulse to create 'overarching colonial discourse' categories. Situating race, aesthetics, modernism, postmodernism, and culture in a deliberately non-hierarchical agenda, he remarks that current debate on the lower value of non-Western art is 'perhaps only European hubris'. He concludes the essay by suggesting a coalesced Black-British identity which would use the syncretic potential of culture because 'there is inevitably more to black art and life than any answers they give to racism.'
G.R.

420

Cruciality and the frog's perspective: an agenda of difficulties for the black arts movement in Britain

Perspectives must be fashioned that displace and estrange the world, reveal it to be, with its rifts and crevices, as indigent and distorted as it will appear one day in the messianic light.

(T. W. Adorno)

It is of the reactions, tortured and turbulent, of those Asians and Africans, in the New and Old World, that I wish to speak to you. Naturally I cannot speak for those Asians and Africans who are still locked in their mystical or ancestor-worshipping traditions. They are the voiceless ones, the silent ones. Indeed, I think that they are the doomed ones, men in a tragic trap. Any attempt on their part to wage battle to protect their traditions and their religions is a battle that is lost before it starts. And I say frankly that I suspect any white man who loves to dote upon these 'naked nobles', who wants to leave them as they are, who finds them 'primitive and pure', for such mystical hankering is, in my opinion, the last refuge of reactionary racists and psychological cripples tired of their own civilisation.

(Richard Wright)

It has become commonplace to remark that it is in art alone that the consciousness of adversity can find its own voice or consolation without being immediately betrayed by it. In the ironic milieu of racial politics, where the most brutally dispossessed people have often also proved to be the most intensely creative, the idea that artists are representative public figures has become an extra burden for them to carry. Its weight can be felt in the tension between the two quite different senses of a word which refers not just to depiction but to the idea of delegation or substitution.

For black Britain, the supposedly representative practice of avowedly political artists obliges them to speak on behalf of a heterogeneous collectivity.[1] In this case, it is a grouping produced by poverty, racism, exploitation and subordination rather than spontaneous fellow feeling or collective purpose. This community is largely insouciant as far as the problems of the black artist or the black intellectual are concerned. But the ambiguous identity that community provides affords the black artist certain significant protections and compensations. We must begin therefore with the black artist as a public figure—a figure in public politics. The public sphere in which artist and people encounter each other does not coincide neatly with the contours of the British nation-state. The discontinuous histories of black populations in the United States, Africa, Asia, the Caribbean and Europe have contributed to the distinctive experiences of blacks in this country for several hundred years. The communicative networks produced across the Atlantic triangle are *pre*-colonial, and understanding their complex effects is only obscured by simplistic appeals to the unifying potency of an overarching 'colonial discourse'. This point can be extended by saying that, although this paper is primarily concerned with black Britain as a distinct location within the African diaspora, there are other diasporas which contribute directly to the experiences of black Britain. The traumas of migration, dispersal and exile may themselves have become potent forces in the formation of sororial political relations between groups whose memories of colonial society might otherwise serve only to accentuate the divisions between them. The histories of these different 'racial' groups, though connected, are markedly different even if the effects of racism contain a future promise of their reconciliation.

The value of the term 'diaspora' increases as its essentially symbolic character is understood. It points emphatically to the fact that there can be no pure, uncontaminated or essential blackness anchored in an unsullied originary moment. It suggests that a myth of shared origins is neither a talisman which can suspend political antagonisms nor a deity invoked to cement a pastoral view of black life that can answer the multiple pathologies of contemporary racism.

Artists who would climb out of the underground spaces that serve as the foundations for the British black arts movement, have developed a special skill. They must learn to address different constituencies simultaneously. The most politically astute of them anticipate not a single, uniform audience but a plurality of publics. These audiences often coexist within the same physical environment but they live non-synchronously. Cultural activists encounter them as a hierarchy in which profoundly antagonistic relations may exist between dominant and subordinate groups. Making sense of this configuration of publics and the aura of novelty currently being constructed around black art, requires both artist and critic to consider the difficulties that surround the heretical suggestion that white audiences may be becoming more significant in the development of British black art than any black ones. We must be prepared to assess the differential impact of white audiences on the mood and style of black cultural activism as well as its forms and its ideological coherence.

These questions necessarily assume different proportions in discussion of vernacular culture than they do in the increasingly rarefied atmosphere that shrouds more self-consciously 'high cultural' black film practice or black visual arts. The question of audience is thus answered differently in each sector of cultural expression. However, the problem of negotiating the relationship between vernacular and non-vernacular forms,· like the related problem of admitting to or ignoring white audiences, has become a constant source of uncertainty and friction. It is useful to consider the example of music at this point, not only because it nurtures the 'sui-generis black genius'[2] but because, as the dominant and primary mode of black cultural activism, it supplies a hermeneutic key to a medley of interrelated forms. Articulated in an aesthetic of performance which asserts the priority of expression over artefact, its special traditions of improvisation and antiphony are revealed to be more than merely technical attributes. The deeply encoded language that supports the social relations in which black music is actively consumed has proved to be an additional resource for artists working in a variety of media.

The specifics of black visual arts and film as determinedly non-vernacular forms made by and for the literate and displayed through some of the most marginal distributive networks that England's moribund cultural order can offer, must also be understood. It is a small step on from raising these questions to ask whether these contrasting yet equally black forms demand different political alliances.

Vernacular forms derive their conspicuous power and dynamism in part from the simple fact that they seek to avoid the prying eyes and ears of the white world, whereas black film production in particular is tightly shackled into a relationship of dependency on overground cultural institutions which are both capital- and labour-intensive. When, then, is it becoming illegitimate to ask how different are the black audiences for these forms from the white? This can be a polite way of formulating a deeper and more shocking question: namely, is there *any* black audience for some of the most highly prized products of the black arts movement? Is there a non-literate, black, working- or non-working-class audience eagerly anticipating these particular cultural products? Have 'our' film-makers given up the pursuit of an audience outside the immediate, symbiotic formation in which black 'filmic texts' originate?[3]

Getting a clear picture of these important issues and the questions of class and power that they inescapably entail is actively suppressed by the racial ideology of our times. Contemporary British political orthodoxy around 'race' endorses the idea that racial identities are somehow primary, yet their supposed importance is matched by fear of their increasing fragility. It is sometimes argued that these identities are so frail that they are threatened by the fact that black and white people may want to discuss questions of aesthetics and politics together. Meanwhile, the complex pluralism of Britain's inner-urban streets demonstrates that, among the poor, elaborate syncretic processes are under way. This is not simple integration, but a complex, non-linear phenomenon. Each contributory element is itself transformed in their coming together. The kaleidoscopic formations of 'trans-racial' cultural syncretism are growing daily more detailed and more beautiful. Yet where black art and aesthetics are debated in conference after conference it is becoming harder to dislodge the belief that ethnic differences constitute an absolute break in history and humanity. A commitment to the mystique of cultural insiderism and the myths of cultural homogeneity is alive not just among the Brit-nationalists and racists but among the anti-racists who strive to answer them. The rampant popularity of these opinions dissolves old ideas of left and right and is directly connected to a dangerous variety of political timidity that culminates in a reluctance to debate some racial subjects because they are too sensitive to be aired and too volatile to be discussed openly. A corresponding tide of anti-intellectualism has meant that some spokespeople inside the black communities have accepted the trap which racism lays and begun to celebrate an idea of themselves as people who are happy to feel rather than think. It is also significant that this strong attachment to ethnicity has appeared as class relations inside the black communities are in turmoil. We must face the fact that our communities are increasingly riven by class antagonism. Certain cultural forms, for example the travel writing of Salman Rushdie and Caryl Phillips, clearly aspire to be part of the making of the black middle class.

This peculiar situation demands that we return to some old issues: the autonomy of art and the issue of racial propaganda; whether the protest and affirmation couplet is an adequate framework for understanding black cultural politics. In what sense are artists to be loyal only to themselves? Can the obligations of black consciousness and

423

artistic freedom be complementary rather than mutually exclusive? Can there be a revolutionary core to what Richard Wright once called the aesthetics of 'personalism' and the matching politics of radical individualism which have characterized Western modernisms—their academicism, formal preoccupations and imaginative proximity to social revolution? Nowadays, these historic questions tend to appear in somewhat different form and in a wholly different conceptual vocabulary. They are present in the suggestion that something called 'post-modernism' may provide a ready-made 'decentering of imperial and patriarchal discourses'. They haunt Michael Thelwell's repeated suggestion that modernism for black artists is an indulgence or evasion of their unique responsibilities, and Houston Baker's provocative but rather sketchy remarks on the ways in which the idea of modernism might be rethought as part of the intellectual and political history of Afro-America.[4]

A preliminary resolution of these problems may lie in embracing an aesthetic and political strategy that many black artists have evolved in an apparently spontaneous manner. I will call this option 'populist modernism',[5] a deliberately contradictory term which suggests that black artists are not only both 'defenders and critics of modernism' but mindful of their historic obligation to interrogate the dubious legacies of occidental modernity premised on the exclusion of blacks. This distinctive aesthetic and ethico-political approach requires a special gloss on terms like reason, justice, freedom and 'communicative ethics'. It starts from recognition of the African diaspora's peculiar position as 'step-children' of the West and of the extent to which our imaginations are conditioned by an enduring proximity to regimes of racial terror. It seeks deliberately to exploit the distinctive quality of perception that Du Bois identified long ago as 'double consciousness'.[6] Whether this is viewed as an effect of oppression or a unique moral burden, it is premised on some sense of black cultures, not simply as significant repositories of anti-capitalist sensibility but as counter-cultures of modernity forged in the quintessentially modern condition of racial slavery.

The most basic formal expression of this approach is recognizable in the recurrent desire of black artists to re-articulate the positive core of aesthetic modernism into resolutely populist formats. The fiction of Richard Wright, Toni Morrison, Alice Walker and Cyrus Coulter, James Brown's music, Amiri Baraka's drama and criticism, and even Lenny Henry's recent performances in the role of Delbert Wilkins, provide myriad examples. However, 'populist modernism' does not simply mark out adventuresome black borrowings and adaptations from a pre-formed Western canon. It can also apply where autonomous and self-validating non-European expressive traditions have entered the institutionalized Western world of art and, most importantly, where the historical and cultural substance of black life in the West has spontaneously arrived at insights which appear in European traditions as the exclusive results of lengthy and lofty philosophical speculation. For example, some of the prized linguistic insights of post-structuralism are less than novel in the context of a cultural tradition in which writing, literation and auto-poesis are inextricably entangled. In an interesting polemic against the idea of 'black studies' C. L. R. James illuminates this point by describing an encounter with Richard Wright.[7]

Having gone to the country to spend the weekend with Wright and his family, James describes being ushered into their house and shown numerous volumes of Kierkegaard, Heidegger, Nietzsche and Husserl on the bookshelves. Wright, fresh from cooking chicken in the kitchen, points to the bound volumes, saying 'Look here Nello, you see those books there? . . . Everything that [they] write in those books I knew before I had them.' James suggests that Wright's apparently intuitive fore-knowledge of the issues raised by Kierkegaard and the rest was an elementary product of his historical experiences as a black growing up in the United States between the wars: 'What [Dick] was telling me was that he was a black man in the United States and that gave him an insight into what today is the universal opinion and attitude of the *modern* personality' (my emphasis).

This historic meeting of two great black minds constitutes an important cautionary tale for Britain's black arts movement. For one thing, it supplies a timely reminder that art history and criticism do not supply adequate answers to their own parochial questions. If we also remember that non-European expressive traditions have refused the caesura which Western high culture would introduce between art and life, the insights of Wright and James can also be read as an implicit questioning of the idea that occidental aesthetics and philosophy are best understood as cohesive yet auto-nomous projects. It is also a great relief to discover that these issues have been dealt with before by the artists and thinkers of the African diaspora. Yet their tradition of inquiry into what can loosely be called the politics of representation is itself obscure. It needs to be recovered and brought into debates which are just beginning in black Britain. Certain aspects of the aesthetic and philosophical traditions of the diaspora are particularly pertinent to black Britain's conditions of exile, voluntary and invol-untary. First, an understanding of 'racial' memory in affective and normative terms rather than as a problem of cognition is particularly pressing. Second, much work needs to be done on the distinctive intertextual patterns in which discrete texts and performances have echoed each other, corresponded, interacted and replied. Third, forms of black meta-communication, which require that surface and deep expres-sions diverge, pose special analytical problems. Fourth, the centrality of performance rather than text and the consequent priority accorded to the act of expression over the artefact require a distinct methodological orientation. These modes of significa-tion render the arbitrary relation between signs and referents in its most radical form. It cannot be said too often that they originate in a historical experience where the error of mistaking a sign for its referent becomes quite literally a matter of life and death. Fifth, these traditions have had plenty to say about the polysemic richness of black languages that pose a question mark over the adequacy of language in general as a vehicle for articulating the intensity of meaning that diaspora history necessitates. Finally, there is the problem of genre and the constant subversive desire originally clearly evident in the auto-poesis of the slave autobiography to blend and transcend key Western categories: narrative and documentary; history and literature; ethics and politics; word and sound. Why, for example, was it necessary for Du Bois's *The Souls of Black Folk* to bring together sociology, history, music and fiction into a unified, polyphonic cultural performance?

This new agenda means that it is no longer enough simply to recognize the dia-logic features of these forms before comparing their supposed openness to the closed monologues of the master discourses of the master race. The specific forms which that dialogism takes must themselves be probed. A gospel choir and soloist, an improvising jazz band, a reggae toaster, a scratch mixer and Keith Piper have all

425

developed the dialogic character of black expressive culture in different directions. Their expressive forms are dialogic, but that dialogism is of a special type and its irreducible complexity has moved beyond the grasp of the self/other dichotomy.

Identifying what these different performances might share and making explicit the deep and carefully concealed aesthetic and political structures that make sense of them requires additional, supplementary concepts. All, for example, play with the principle of antiphony (call and response), a term which is particularly appropriate because it underlies the special role of black music in articulating non-verbal—unspoken and unspeakable—formulations of ethics and aesthetics. Approaching contemporary black cultural politics by this route involves a sharp move away from the rigid nexus of modernism and post-modernism and the casual references to the 'technical successes of modernist culture' which emanate from it. It is a tenacious challenge to the nascent orthodoxies of post-modernism which can only see the distinctive formal features of black expressive culture in terms of pastiche, quotation, parody and paraphrase rather than a more substantive, political and aesthetic concern with polyphony and the value of different registers of address.

This leads directly to the significance of current debates around post-modernism for the British black arts movement. There are special reasons why black activists here should resist the idea that any struggle over images is necessarily a struggle over power. The problems in trying to hold the term together are now well known: how does it refer to modernization, what are its claims as a cognitive theory, is it doing more than merely register a change in the cultural climate? Can the logic of late capitalism be marked conceptually in a non-reductive way? I see no strong objection to the term as a purely heuristic device. But there is a tendency to make it something more than this, to use it as the conceptual cornerstone of another grand narrative—several perhaps, as well as fuel for the resolutely uncritical academic industry currently being built in Britain around the excuses it offers—what Zygmunt Bauman has called its philosophy of surrender.[8] Post-modernism fever is an ailment identified through symptoms that have been around within modernism for a long while. François Lyotard's ties to C. L. R. James through the Socialisme ou Barbarie group, and Frederic Jameson's appetite for a rather anachronistic 'base and superstructure' variety of Marxism, betoken some of the more significant continuities. These ties may be an indication that the grand narrative of reason is not currently being brought to an end but rather *transformed*. Forms of rationality are being created endlessly. Perhaps only European hubris claims that this particular moment of crisis is the fundamental moment of rupture, the new dawn. Another significant way in which post-modernist orthodoxy is reconstitutive of earlier, more obviously modernist, work is its persistence in dealing with the problem of the subject exclusively in terms of its formation rather than through the fundamental issues of agency, action, reason and rationality inherent in considering the relationship between master and slave. Robert Farris Thompson's provocative discussion of Ashe, the ancient Yoruba concept of the power to make things happen, shows that these do not have to be Eurocentric issues.[9] The strategic silences in post-modernist pronouncements constitute a glimpse of the sad predicament of a coterie of ailing Western intellectuals comforting themselves on the historic funeral pyre of their class with a hot water-bottle of realism. This gesture abdicates their responsibility, not to some abstract 'other' but to themselves. To point this out is not to say that I think older, grander formulations have any residual appeal. The only happy moment in this whole unsavoury explosion of enthusiasm for the 'post-modern' is its challenge to the theological authority of positivistic Marxism. We should not have to choose between the knackered phallocracy of the vanguard party and an 'anything goes' or 'anything does' position which, at its best, simply places a pluralist or 'realist' mask in front of genuine conservatism. At its worst, post-modernism fever offers an exclusively aesthetic radicalism as the substitute for a moral one.

> . . . the new political art if it is to be possible at all—will have to hold to the truth of post-modernism, that is to say, to its fundamental object—the world space of multi-national capital—at the same time at which it achieves a breakthrough to some as yet unimaginable new mode of representing this last, in which we may again begin to grasp our positioning as individual and collective subjects and regain a capacity to act and struggle which is at present neutralised by our spatial as well as our social confusion.[10]

It is time that Professor Jameson specified precisely who is included when he says 'we' and 'our'. Those of us who have been denied access to the diachronic payoff that people like him take for granted are just beginning to formulate our own grand narratives. They are narratives of redemption and emancipation. Our cultural politics is not therefore about depthlessness but about depth, not about the waning of affect but about its reproduction, not about the suppression of temporal patterns but about history itself. This realization is our cue to shift the centre of debate away from Europe, to look at other more peripheral encounters with modernity. It is worth underlining that for some of us the 'enthusiasm of 1789' relates more to Port au Prince than it does to Paris. Why is it so difficult to think through the relationship between these locations and their respective counter-powers? To put it another way, it is not just the 'annihilation named Auschwitz' which now requires a formal transformation of what counts as history and as reality, of our understanding of reference and the function of the proper name. These ethico-political problems have been the substance of black expressive culture since slavery; from the time we walked through the door of Christianity and became people of the West (in it but not organically of it) and acquired the 'double vision' that entails what Richard Wright, drawing on Nietzsche, called the Frog's Perspective.[11]

Wright is one of the handful of black writers who have seen black nationalism as a beginning rather than an end. His populist modernism, most cogently expressed in his 1953 novel *The Outsider*, is crucial not least because it allows for the possibility that non-black artists may be part of the inheritance of black artists. This is only one way of rethinking the question of racial identity, secure in the knowledge that people inhabit highly differentiated and complex, even de-centred, identities. Race carries with it no fixed corona of absolute meanings. Thus gender, class, culture and even locality may become more significant determinants of identity than either biological phenotype or the supposed cultural essences of what are now known as ethnic groups. Culture is not a final property of social life. It is a dynamic volatile force. It is made and remade and the culture of the English fragments of the black diaspora is a syncretic, synthetic one. This ought to be obvious but it is not. The most unwholesome ideas of ethnic absolutism hold sway and they have been incorporated into the structures of the political economy of funding black arts. The tokenism, patronage and nepotism that have become intrinsic to the commodification of black culture rely absolutely on an absolute sense of ethnic difference. This variety of absolutism is strongest and most theoretically coherent in non-vernacular cultural forms. It is most eloquent where white audiences are not simply assumed but actively sought out and where the glamour of ambivalent ethnicity borrows most heavily from the devious, rhetorical excesses of literary post-structuralism.

Happily, there are elements within Britain's emergent post-nationalist black arts movement that are prepared to move as earlier generations of black intellectuals and artists have done, not into the blind alley of ethnic particularity, but outwards into a global, populist-modernist perspective.

At this point, the word 'sponditious', Delbert Wilkins's favourite term of praise, provides an appropriate conceptual marker for a new relationship, between the black artist and the racial community. Misrecognized by the overground as nonsense rather than good sense, it asserts the primacy of the vernacular over the esoteric and specifies the redemptive uniqueness of emergent black-English cultural forms. Sponditiousness is a vital presence in the antiphonic work of a host of little-known photographers, film-makers and writers.

However difficult their work becomes, it is always aligned to vernacular forms and modes of expression. The underground is the source of their joyously productive break with the immediate political past and their striking ability to perceive 'race' not as a biological or even cultural essence but as an inherently unstable social and political construction. There is also a hesitant, tentative suggestion that the most urgent tasks of black artists might begin in the critical documentation and dismantling of those constructed differences, not just between black and white but within the black communities too. These cultural activists do not articulate blackness as a homogenous condition. Their work testifies to the fact that it is riven by gender, sexuality, generation and class. Their primary difficulty is that if they know where black art is to begin, they do not necessarily understand where it is to end: in what has been called the black artist's search for space and status? Space where? Status with whom? In the transcendence of 'racial' particularity? In defensive political action? At present, there is every danger that these questions will be buried by an enthusiasm for the dubious comforts provided by the belief in an eternal ethnic identity and a theory of post-modernism that is little more than a premature foreclosure of vital debate. Pre-emptive statements that invoke the authority of the very grand narratives they are supposedly committed to deconstructing suggest, for example, that an integration of Afro-Asian cultures in contemporary Britain is simply nostalgic.[12] But why should this be the case? If we accept the necessarily pluralistic and polyphonic character of black culture, if we understand syncretism as the organizing and disorganizing principle at work in the cultural lives of black city-dwellers who may never have lived anywhere else, then the forms of this supposedly naive desire to integrate may already be spontaneously under way.

The critical tools which will unlock and discipline this new movement of black arts are at present in an undeveloped foetal state. The movement's inspiration lies in an exploration of the idea of blackness in relation to the idea of Britishness, but this project does not even attempt to explain how blackness is itself to be understood. If it is not a primary identity, is it a metaphysical condition? Can it be a bit of both? Was Ellison right when he suggested that it is a state of the soul accessible to all? Or was Baldwin correct when he articulated it as a mark of pain and hardship which carries with it a special obligation to humanize the dry bones of modernity's arid landscapes? How are we to think of difference within the framework it provides? Can we, like the D-Max group of photographers[13] did with the clever name for their collective, find symbols to express a multiplicity of black tones? Perhaps the realization that blackness is a necessarily multi-accentual sign provides a means to escape either/or-ism. Blackness evolves in fractal patterns. What we can usefully say about it depends on the scale of the analysis which is being undertaken. It is only when viewed from above that Britain's black communities have the homogeneity of a neat Euclidean outline. Moving lower and closer reveals the infinite course of their expressive traditions even within a highly restricted space—the fractal geometry of black life's rifts and crevices. Expressive culture can, of course, provide a means for different groups to negotiate each other's definitions of what it means to be black in overdeveloped, besieged Britain now. There are several other things we need to be clear on before we proceed. It may be easier to talk about racism than about black emancipation but there is inevitably more to black art and life than any answers they give to racism.

If our artists are to be primarily judged on the basis of their answers to racism, and that is a real danger at present, it must also be borne in mind that racism changes. There is, for example, no point in answering culturalist racism with artistic and political tactics appropriate to biological definitions of race. We must also recognize how racism pushes those it subordinates outside history into the unacceptable twin forms of the problem and the victim. These repellent roles exist only in an unchanging present. A reply to this effect of racist discourse and practice can only be produced by representing black life in terms of active agency, however limited its scope. Problems over the relation of aesthetics, ethics and politics are further compounded by the question of how a sense of historical process, generational continuity and change can be restored. Here, we can begin to engage with the specific history of blacks in Britain and this is a far more complex matter than it appears from the preliminary pioneering work which has already been done. None of us enjoys a monopoly on black authenticity.

The inescapable tension between those who define themselves as artists or intellectuals and the mass of the black settler communities cannot be conjured away. I am suggesting that only by sharpening that antagonism can we make our notion of community a way of having disagreements productively among ourselves rather than a largely rhetorical means of rationalizing the domination and subordination which already exist.

NOTES

Thanks to Vron Ware, Karen Alexander, Isaac Julien, David A. Bailey, Kobena Mercer and Sonia Boyce who helped me put this together. We're droppin' science y'all.

1. A useful starting point for enquiries into the inner character of the black arts movement in Britain is provided by *Storm of the Heart*, edited by Kwesi Owusu, Camden Press, London 1988. Catalogues

produced for black art exhibitions: *The Thin Black Line*, Institute of Contemporary Art, London, 1985; *The Essential Black Art*, Chisenhale Gallery, London, 1988; *The Image Employed: The Use of Narrative in Black Art*, Cornerhouse, Manchester, 1987; *From Modernism to Postmodernism: Rasheed Araeen/A Retrospective 1959–1987*, Ikon Gallery, Birmingham, 1987–88; *From Two Worlds*, Whitechapel Gallery, London, 1986; *Sonia Boyce*, Air Gallery, London, 1986; *Black British Film Culture*, ICA Document No. 7, ICA, London.

2. Greg Tate, 'The Return of the Black Aesthetic Cult: Nats meet Freaky-Deke', *Village Voice* Literary Supplement, December 1986; 'Public Enemy, The Devil Made 'Em Do It', *Village Voice*, 19 July 1988; 'Uplift the Race', *Village Voice*, 22 March 1988.

3. This point came home to me forcefully when I received a press release from the Black Audio Film Collective, prize-winning authors of the celebrated *Handsworth Songs*. This press release chronicled the success of *Handsworth Songs* and its successor, their latest film, *Testament*:

> *Testament*, Black Audio Film Collective's new film, has won the 1988 Grand Prize at the Riminincinema International Film Festival in Italy. The award follows *Testament*'s premiere at the Cannes International Film Festival (May) and its subsequent screenings at the Munich Film Festival (June), Montreal World Film Festival (August), Toronto Festival of Festivals (September) and its British premiere at the Birmingham International Film Festival (September).
>
> It is possible that the group had simply overlooked or forgotten the possibility that black British film culture might have a different agenda of priorities from that set by international film festival circuits. On the other hand, they may be simply making explicit what we had all suspected, namely that there is no base or context for the type of films they want to make within the black communities in this country.

4. Michael Thelwell, *Duties, Pleasures and Conflicts*, University of Massachusetts Press, 1987; Houston Baker, *Modernism and the Harlem Renaissance*, Chicago University Press, 1987.

5. I borrowed this term from Werner Sollor's study *Amiri Baraka/Leroi Jones: The Quest for a Populist Modernism*, Columbia University Press, 1978.

6. See W. E. B. Du Bois, *The Souls of Black Folk*, Bantam, New York, 1989 and Robert C. Williams's 'W. E. B. Du Bois: Afro-American philosopher of social reality' in L. Harris (ed.), *Philosophy Born of Struggle*, Kendall Hunt, Iowa, 1983.

7. C. L. R. James, 'Black Studies and the Contemporary Student' in *At the Rendez-vous with Victory*, Allison & Busby, London, 1984.

8. Zygmunt Bauman, 'The Left as the Counterculture of Modernity', *Telos 70*, 1986–7.

9. Robert Farris Thompson, *Flash of the Spirit: African and Afro-American Art and Philosophy*, Vintage Books, New York, 1983.

10. Fredric Jameson, 'Postmodernism or the Cultural Logic of Late Capitalism', *NLR* 146, July/August 1984.

11. Richard Wright, 'Preface' to George Padmore's *Pan Africanism or Communism*, Dennis Dobson, London, 1956.

12. John Roberts, 'Postmodernism and the Critique of Ethnicity: The recent work of Rasheed Araeen' in the catalogue *From Modernism to Postmodernism*, Ikon Gallery, Birmingham, 1987.

13. *D-Max* catalogue, Photographers Gallery, London, 1988.

Seamus Deane (1940–)

Seamus Deane was educated at Queen's University, Belfast, and Cambridge University and has taught at several universities in the United States including the University of California at Berkeley and Notre Dame. He is professor of modern English and American literature at University College, Dublin, and has been Director of the Field Day Theatre Company since 1980. His works include *A Short History of Irish Literature* (1986), *The French Revolution and Enlightenment in England 1789–1832* (1988), and the three volume *The Field Day Anthology of Irish Writing* (1991).

The following essay is Deane's introduction to *Nationalism, Colonialism, and Literature* (1990), which also contains essays by Terry Eagleton, Fredric Jameson, and Edward Said. Although his essay provides an American audience with the substantial, summarizing ideas from the Field Day project, Deane also provides a map for the development of central issues in contemporary thought on colonialism. The essay contextualizes the Irish/English conflict within the global crises of community and subjectivity as they deal with discussions of feminism, modernism, and decolonization. Deane lays out the mechanisms of imperialism and the dynamics of the colonizing experience such as conflicts in writing nationalist narratives, attempts to engage and change narrative structures, the problematic mutuality of national and racial stereotypes, the dangerous tendency to universalize nationalisms, and the habit of modern nationalisms to make use of the pattern of the fall from Eden.

Deane also uses the essay to review the work of Field Day, including: (1) pamph-. lets which analyze the dynamics of colonization; (2) theatre productions which are primarily 'adaptations, readjustments, and reorientations' of methods of naming, speaking, or voicing colonial/colonized positions; and (3) *The Field Day Anthology of Irish Writing*, which Deane argues is an act of 'repossession' of Irish discourse without losing the 'ironic self-consciousness' that canons are themselves fictions. But Deane does not present these processes as a solution to the complexity of colonization, but moves to show how in the case of the Irish/English conflict, neither

431

'priority [as] a claim to power' nor the 'postmodern simulacrum of pluralism' lead to new positions outside the imperial setting. Instead, pluralism leads to additional problems. Deane's work is very much part of a new Irish scholarship, to be distinguished, for instance, from the Yeats industry. Among other works of interest in this new area is David Cairns' and Shaun Richards' *Writing Ireland: colonialism, nationalism and culture* (1988).

R.S.M. and G.R.

The Field Day enterprise

The Field Day enterprise holds the conviction that we need a new discourse for a new relationship between our idea of the human subject and our idea of human communities. What is now happening in Ireland, most especially in Northern Ireland (constitutionally an integral part of the United Kingdom), is only one of the many crises that have made the need for such a discourse peremptory. In Africa, South America, the Middle East, the Soviet Union, and Eastern Europe, the nature of the crisis is more glaringly exposed and its consequences seem both more ominous and far-reaching in their effects. Nevertheless, the Irish-English collision has its own importance. Ireland is the only Western European country that has had both an early and a late colonial experience. Out of that, Ireland produced, in the first three decades of this century, a remarkable literature in which the attempt to overcome and replace the colonial experience by something other, something that would be 'native' and yet not provincial, was a dynamic and central energy. The ultimate failure of that attempt to imagine a truly liberating cultural alternative is as well known as the brilliance of the initial effort. Now that the established system has again been called into question, even to the point where it must seriously alter or collapse, Irish writing, operating in the shadow or in the wake of the earlier attempt, has once more raised the question of how the individual subject can be envisaged in relation to its community, its past history, and a possible future.

[. . .]

Field Day Theatre Company was founded in 1980 when the present political crisis in Northern Ireland was already twelve years old. That crisis continues and shows every sign of prolonging itself for a considerable length of time. Field Day is a response to that situation. It is based in Derry (or Londonderry), the second city in Northern Ireland; six of its seven directors are from the North and all of its enterprises, in theater, in pamphlets, and in the *Field Day Anthology of Irish Writing* (1990) have a bearing upon the nature and genesis of the present impasse. Although Northern Ireland is the site of the conflict, the whole island, including the Republic of Ireland, is involved as is the United Kingdom.

Field Day's analysis of the situation derives from the conviction that it is, above all, a colonial crisis. This is not a popular view in the political and academic establishment in Ireland. Historians in particular have been engaged for more than twenty years in what is referred to as a revision of Irish history, the chief aim of which was to demolish the nationalist mythology that had been in place for over fifty years, roughly from 1916 to 1966. This polemical ambition has been in large part realized. The nationalist narrative, which told the story of seven hundred years of English misrule (finally brought to a conclusion by the heroic rebellion of 1916 and the violence of the following six years, and now culminating in the unfinished business of the North), has lost much of its appeal and legitimacy save for those who are committed to the IRA and the armed struggle. Revisionism defends itself against those who describe it as simply another orthodoxy, created in accord with the political circumstances of the moment, by claiming to have revealed such a degree of complexity in Irish and Anglo-Irish affairs that no systematic explanation is possible. It has effectively localized interpretation, confining it within groups, interests, classes, and periods; any attempt to see these issues as variations on a ghostly paradigm, like colonialism, is characterized as 'ideological' and, on that account, is doomed. Ultimately, there may have been no such thing as colonialism. It is, according to many historians, one of the phantoms created by nationalism, which is itself phantasmal enough.

Field Day regards this new orthodoxy with disfavor because it shows little or no capacity for self-analysis. Its own demolition of nationalism rebounds on itself. Moreover, it has paid no serious attention to the realm of culture, regarding it as in some sense separate from politics. In this it has been supported by many who still believe in the autonomy of cultural artifacts, and who, as a consequence, subscribe to the Arnoldian notion that the work of art that most successfully disengages itself from the particularities of its origin and production is, by virtue of that 'disengagement,' most fully and purely itself. It is 'universal,' the proper thing for art to be. Contrastingly, Field Day sees art as a specific activity indeed, but one in which the whole history of a culture is deeply inscribed. The interpretation of culture is not predicated on the notion that there is some universal quality or essence that culture alone can successfully pursue and capture. That is itself a political idea that has played a crucial role in Irish experience. One of Field Day's particular aims has been to expose the history and function of that idea and to characterize its disfiguring effects.

To do so, it has been necessary to engage again with the concept of nationalism. It is not, in the Irish context, an exclusively Irish phenomenon, for the island has now, particularly in the North, and has had for at least two hundred years, British nationalism as a predominant political and cultural influence. In fact, Irish nationalism is, in its foundational moments, a derivative of its British counterpart. Almost all nationalist movements have been derided as provincial, actually or potentially racist, given to exclusivist and doctrinaire positions and rhetoric. These descriptions fit British nationalism perfectly, as the contemporaries of any of its exponents on Ireland— Edmund Spenser, Sir John Davies, Sir William Temple, Coleridge, Carlyle, Arnold, Enoch Powell, Ian Paisley—will prove. The point about Irish nationalism, the features within it that have prevented it from being a movement toward liberation, is that it is, *mutatis mutandis*, a copy of that by which it felt itself to be oppressed. The collusion of Irish with British nationalism has produced contrasting stereotypes whose most destructive effect has been the laying of the cultural basis for religious sectarianism. It is perhaps stating the obvious to say that the competing nationalisms have always defined themselves in relation to either Protestantism or Catholicism. Every attempt to refuse that definition—by the United Irishmen in the late eighteenth century, by the trades union movement in the early twentieth century—has been defeated by ruthless and concerted efforts. We are not witnessing in Northern Ireland some outmoded battle between religious sects that properly belong to the seventeenth century. We are witnessing rather the effects of a contemporary colonialism that has retained and developed an ideology of dominance and subservience within the readily available idiom of religious division. Constitutionally, as Northern Ireland reminds us, Britain is a specifically Protestant country. That constitutional 'anachronism'—with its roots in London and its rank flowering in Belfast—is a political reality when the constitution is challenged.

All nationalisms have a metaphysical dimension, for they are all driven by an ambition to realize their intrinsic essence in some specific and tangible form. The form may be a political structure or a literary tradition. Although the problems created by such an ambition are sufficiently intractable in themselves, they are intensified to the point of absurdity when a nationalist self-conception imagines itself to be the ideal model to which all others should conform. That is a characteristic of colonial and imperial nations. Because they universalize themselves, they regard any insurgency against them as necessarily provincial. In response, insurgent nationalisms attempt to create a version of history for themselves in which their intrinsic essence has always manifested itself, thereby producing readings of the past that are as monolithic as that which they are trying to supplant. They are usually, as in Ireland, under the additional disadvantage that much of their past has been destroyed, silenced, erased. Therefore the amalgam that is produced is susceptible to attack and derision.

Nevertheless, nationalism of both kinds has been particularly effective in the modern period precisely because it contains within itself this metaphysical essentialism. It has been able, on that account, to tell a characteristically modern (or modernist) story, with a power and persuasiveness that even yet have appeal. The story is, in effect, the story of the fall of modern humankind from a state of bliss into the peculiarly modern condition of alienation. The imperial nationalism of Britain told this tale over and over in a series of brilliant and ingenious parables that sought to identify that originary moment of decline. In literary history, from Coleridge to Arnold to Eliot and Leavis, the new narrative rediscovered a seventeenth-century Eden with a subsequent decline that had come to a culmination in the present. In the novel, Conrad, Kipling, Ford, Forster, and Lawrence brooded upon the failure of Englishness in imperial and other foreign territories. Imperial nativism sought solace in time past for the problems of the present and often came up with the notion that present failure was the consequence of the decline of 'national character,' perhaps the most enduring and insubstantial creation of all nationalist mythologies. In Ireland, just at this time undergoing its literary revival, the Edenic moment was displaced back into the pre-Christian (and therefore presectarian) past, and the model figures that emerged as types of Irish identity were, of necessity, legendary—like Cuchalain—and, by nature, susceptible to almost any reformulation. The central point here is, that it was in the late years of the nineteenth and early years of the twentieth century that the political situations in Britain and in Ireland demanded a

434

reconstituted version of both the national characters and the literary traditions of each. This is one—but a crucial—example of the interaction between the political and cultural zones and of the interaction between the British and the Irish that has done so much to produce the present complex and stymied situation in which we find ourselves.

In previous pamphlets, Field Day has attempted to come to terms with this inherited situation by demonstrating that the interweave of political and cultural (largely literary) forces is now subject to a fresh analysis, stimulated by the pressure of the existing political crisis. It is a truism to say that no language is innocent. It is more difficult to trace, within the rhetorics of political and literary discourses, the forms and varieties of incrimination, subjection, insurgency, evasion, and stereotyping that determine or are determined by our past and present interpretations. It seemed to us that, by doing so, we could begin to reverse the effects of the colonialism that has wrought such devastating as well as subtle effects in Ireland and in the consciousness of its people.

At its most powerful, colonialism is a process of radical dispossession. A colonized people is without a specific history and even, as in Ireland and other cases, without a specific language. The recovery from the lost Irish language has taken the form of an almost vengeful virtuosity in the English language, an attempt to make Irish English a language in its own right rather than an adjunct to English itself. The virtuosity of early modern Irish writing and its hesitant relationship to the language revival movement exemplify this queasy condition. Yeats, Joyce, and Synge present its characteristic features most fully, but others do so in only slightly less complete array—Wilde, George Moore, Shaw, and Beckett. But the linguistic question, although important, seemed secondary to the question of repossession—that is to say, the repossession of these (and other) authors for an interpretation that was governed by a reading of the conditions in which their work was produced and in the Irish conditions in which it was read. It was inevitable that Yeats and Joyce would initially take most of our attention, since it was they, more than anyone else, who had been (mis)read in the light of what was understood to be English or British literature, international modernism, the plight of humankind in the twentieth century. Our reading of them was designed to restore them to the culture in which they were still alive as presences, to interpret the interpretations that mediated them for us, to repossess their revolutionary and authoritative force for the here and now of the present in Ireland.

There is an inevitable monotony involved here, inescapable in colonial conditions. What seems like an endless search for a lost communal or even personal identity is doubly futile. Just naming it indicates that it is lost; once named, it can never be unnamed. In the second place, such an identity is wholly unreal. It can be made manifest only by pretending that it is the conclusion to a search of which it was the origin. When Yeats invented an Irish literary tradition in the English language, he did not discover in Swift, Burke, and others the Protestant Irish essence for which he sought; he sought in them the essence that he then discovered. The same is true of versions of English literature that find in Shakespeare and in Keats a native English genius that is somehow deflected in Milton or Pope. The pursuit of such questions leads to notions of national character, questions of the language appropriate to its

435

proper expression and, by extension, to the stereotyping of groups, classes, races in relation to the kinds of writing (or music, architecture, whatever it may be) that they produce. Still, monotonous as it may be, it is inescapable. Otherwise we may never see the colonial forest for the nativist trees.

In the attempted discovery of its 'true' identity, a community often begins with the demolition of the false stereotypes within which it has been entrapped. This is an intricate process, since the stereotypes are successful precisely because they have been interiorized. They are not merely impositions from the colonizer on the colonized. It is a matter of common knowledge that stereotypes are mutually generative of each other, as in the case of the English and the Irish. Although the stereotyping initiative, so to speak, is taken by the community that exercises power, it has to create a stereotype of itself as much as it does of others. Indeed, this is one of the ways by which otherness is defined. The definition of otherness, the degree to which others can be persuasively shown to be discordant with the putative norm, provides a rationale for conquest. The Irish reluctance to yield to the caricature of themselves as barbarous or uncivilized exposed the nullity of the English rationale although it also aggravated the ferocity of the process of subjugation. But within the last one hundred years the terms of the exchange altered. In all kinds of places—in Renan, in Arnold, in Havelock Ellis, in the career of George Bernard Shaw—it was quite suddenly revealed that the English national character was defective and in need of the Irish, or Celtic, character in order to supplement it and enable it to survive. All the theorists of racial degeneration—Galton, Nordau, Lombroso, Spengler—shared with literary critics and poets and novelists the conviction that the decline of the West must be halted by some infusion or transfusion of energy from an 'unspoiled' source. The Irish seemed to qualify for English purposes. They were white, rural, and neither decadent nor intellectual. In fact, they were not Irish; they were Celts. Their homeland was what Europe had been before the Romans conquered it—a place innocent of complex political, economic, and military structures, inhabited by a fierce, imaginative, poetic tribe. At this point, faced with this precipitous revision of white European history, the Irish, who had shown a marked inclination toward this view of themselves, finally took possession of the stereotype, modified the Celt into the Gael, and began that new interpretation of themselves known as the Irish literary revival. The revival, like the rebellion and the War of Independence, the treaty of 1922 (which partitioned Ireland into its present form), and the subsequent civil war, were simultaneously causes and consequences of the concerted effort to renovate the idea of the national character and of the national destiny. It was only when the Celt was seen by the English as a necessary supplement to their national character that the Irish were able to extend the idea of supplementarity to that of radical difference. This is a classic case of how nationalism can be produced by the forces that suppress it and can, at that juncture, mobilize itself into a form of liberation.

Such liberation as was achieved—and it was considerable—necessarily had its limits. It was a liberation into a specifically Irish, not a specifically human, identity. Since 1922, the developments in the South (now the Republic of Ireland) have emphasized this aspect of things. The Catholic church has successfully emphasized the uniqueness of the Irish Catholic tradition, seeing its role as the defender of a pious and chaste race in a degenerate and promiscuous world. Yeats too, especially in his later poetry, also wished to bestow upon his culture a unique role in helping humankind to survive the onslaught of the 'filthy modern tide.' In other words, Irish freedom declined into the freedom to become Irish in predestined ways. In that deep sense, the revolutionary impulse of the early part of the century was aborted. Now we have begun to come full circle again, repudiating that nationalist revolution, wishing—in some quarters—that 1916 had never happened and rewriting our history to cast doubt on the reality and the scandal of colonialism. Weary of the misconstrued Irish identity and understandably skeptical or derisive of the notion of Ireland's unique destiny, the Republic has surrendered the notion of identity altogether as a monotonous and barren anachronism and rushed to embrace all of those corporate, 'international' opportunities offered by the European Economic Community and the tax-free visitations of international cartels.

It was then, in the midst of this process, that the North began its internecine conflict. This restored to center stage all those issues of communal identity, colonial interference, sectarianism, and racial stereotyping that had apparently been sidelined. It is at this juncture that Field Day positions itself.

The enterprise is threefold. It comprises theater, the Field Day pamphlets, and *The Field Day Anthology*. By 1990, Field Day will have completed the first phase of its operations. In the pamphlets, the general trend has been to analyze the various rhetorics of coercion and liberation that are so evident in modern Irish literature (particularly in Yeats and Joyce), in modern Irish political and legal discourse and practice, as well as in the systems of interpretation that have mediated these. As pamphlets, their nature and purpose require that they address these topics with some force and brevity in relation to the present northern or Anglo-Irish situation. In the theater, the central preoccupation has been with a particular experience of what we may call translation. By this I mean the adaptations, readjustments, and reorientations that are required of individuals and groups who have undergone a traumatic cultural and political crisis so fundamental that they must forge for themselves a new speech, a new history or life story that would give it some rational or coherent form. Brian Friels's plays, *Translations* (1980) and *Making History* (1988), Thomas Kilroy's *Double Cross* (1987), and Tom Paulin's adaptation of *Antigone* under the title *The Riot Act* (1985) are some of the most effective examples of the explorations characteristic of Field Day's theater. In all of them, a political crisis produces a clash of loyalties that is analyzable but irresolvable. In all three cases, the dramatic analysis centers on anxieties of naming, speaking, and voice and the relation of these to place, identity, and self-realization. The plays and the pamphlets are intimately related as parts of a single project although they of course employ entirely different cadences in their development of the central discourse. *The Field Day Anthology of Irish Writing*, covering a span of 1,500 years, derives from these other activities. It is an act of repossession, resuming into the space of three massive volumes a selection of Irish literary, political, economic, philosophical, and other writings and presenting it, with a degree of ironic self-consciousness, as an integral and unitary 'tradition' or amalgam of traditions. The point is not to establish a canon as such; it is to engage in the action of establishing a system that has an enabling, a mobilizing energy, the energy of assertion and difference, while remaining aware that all such systems—like anthologies of other national literature—are fictions that have inscribed within them principles of hierarchy and of exclusion, as well as inclusion, that become evident only when the mass of material is organized into a particular form. It is not merely an exercise in regaining Swift, Berkeley, Goldsmith, Burke, Shaw, Yeats, Joyce, Beckett, and so forth from the neighboring fiction of English or British literature or literary tradition. It is a recuperation of these writers into the so-called other context, the inside reading of them in relation to other Irish writing, in order to modify and perhaps even distress other 'outside' readings that have been unaware of that context and its force.

These three enterprises clearly involve a number of general questions, but they are addressed to a particular and tragic situation. The major communities in the North, Protestant and Catholic, unionist and nationalist, are compelled by the force of circumstances, some of which I have already mentioned, to rehearse positions from which there is no exit. Both communities have felt in the past and now do feel that the principles to which they are loyal are in grievous danger of being betrayed (or have already been betrayed) by those governments, in London and in Dublin, who were ostensibly their custodians. Each community feels that it is obliged, in the isolation subsequent to that betrayal, to retain the true faith, whether the faith of Irish republican nationalism, or of Protestant and British liberty. Each community sees the other as a threat to its existence. Each regards itself as, at one and the same time, the preserver of basic principle, caricatured by its erstwhile allies and friends into a blind and benighted tribe. Both communities are trapped within a tight geographic space, within a stifling set of stereotypes, half-persuaded that they are an embarrassment to the nation-states that cooperate to govern them. Even the usual vocabulary of democratic discourse fails to operate successfully. The Catholics are a minority in Northern Ireland but a majority in the island as a whole; they claim that their minority status was designed by the drawing of the border to perpetuate a Protestant majority. The Protestants are a majority in Northern Ireland and a minority in the whole island; they are also on occasion reminded that they are a minority within the United Kingdom. The structural similarities of their positions, their vacillation between feeling themselves a threatened minority or a powerful majority, their powerlessness in changing the situation and their power to sustain it, their demonizing of one another as a people natively given to violence, bigotry, and prejudice all combine with economic frailty to produce the sectarian dynamic. The much-vaunted British legal system has shown itself, both in Britain (when Irish people are involved) and in Ireland, to be nothing more than a system of political repression, because it too cannot afford to distinguish between the idea of the person as such and the idea of the person who can be understood to be such within the terms of the prevailing British ideology. In a crisis like this, the process of legitimation has a hard time of it; the scandalous corruption of law in Northern Ireland has made it clear that law is a matter of control, not of justice. This is in itself no stunning revelation; no colony or ex-colony needs to be reminded of it. But, like the bitter heritage of sectarianism, it shows that there is no basis for believing that the human being as such exists above and beyond the discriminations and categorizations that politics produce. A sectarian society kills people because they are Catholic or Protestant, republican, nationalist, unionist, terrorist, member of the security forces, or whatever. These distinctions are themselves the product of the very idea of society itself; they simply become more

438

emphatic and crucial when the society's legitimation procedures are questioned.

Field Day, therefore, addresses this issue. A society needs a system of legitimation and, in seeking for it, always looks to a point of origin from which it can derive itself and its practices. That origin may be a document like the 1916 Proclamation of the Irish Republic, it may be Magna Carta, the Scottish Covenant, the revolution of 1688, 1789, or 1917. The Irish Revival and its predecessors had the right idea in looking to some legendary past for the legitimating origin of Irish society as one distinct from the British, which had a different conception of origin. But the search for origin, like that for identity, is self-contradictory. Once the origin is understood to be an invention, however necessary, it can never again be thought of as something 'natural.' A culture brings itself into being by an act of cultural invention that itself depends on an anterior legitimating nature. This is not merely a paradoxical game whereby the answer to 'what came first?' is uselessly answered by 'whatever came second.' Nature may be a cultural invention, but it is nonetheless powerful for that. It is culture's most precious invention. In Northern Ireland that invention is not lost; it is in dispute. The terms of the dispute can be crude. The 'native' Irish can say they came first; the Protestant planters can say that they were the first to create a civil society. These are not nugatory distinctions, for it is from them that so much of the later history of strife and disagreement evolves. Priority is a claim to power.

That is the reason for Field Day's preoccupation with naming, evident in the first three pamphlets by Tom Paulin, Seamus Heaney, and myself and evident too in the plays by Brian Friel, Thomas Kilroy, and Tom Paulin to which I referred earlier. The naming or renaming of a place, the naming or renaming of a race, a region, a person, is, like all acts of primordial nomination, an act of possession. *The Field Day Anthology* is also an exercise in renaming, the resituation of many tests, well known and scarcely known, in a renovated landscape or context. All the various names for Ireland and for the Irish connection with Great Britain are themselves indications of the uncertainty, the failure of self-possession, which has characterized the various relationships and conditions to which the names refer. A selection of them would include Ireland, Eire, the Free State, the Republic of Ireland, the Twenty-Six Counties, the Six Counties, Ulster, Northern Ireland, the United Kingdom of Great Britain and Ireland, the United Kingdom of Great Britain and Northern Ireland. In a similar manner, one can point to the attempts to nominate literature in Ireland in its various forms; it is Irish Literature, Gaelic literature, Anglo-Irish literature, Irish literature in English, and so on. There are also Irish English, Hiberno-English, and Anglo-Irish as variations on the English spoken in Ireland. The multiplicity of these names is, of course, no bad thing in itself. They all refer to distinct and important differences of emphasis, meaning, interpretation. But their vigor conceals a corresponding weakness. That for which there is no all-embracing name cannot be comprehensively possessed. Instead of possession, we have various modes of sectarian appropriation.

In that respect, Northern Ireland enacts for us the more general crisis in which that which is an integral part of our history has become alien to us and known only to a sub-group or groups within the polity. The bulk of the Irish people are ignorant of and alien to the Irish language and its ancient literature; northern Protestants are alien to both that and to their own complex earlier history in Ireland. To remove ourselves from that condition into one in which all these lesions and occlusions are forgotten, in which the postmodernist simulacrum of pluralism supplants the search for a legitimating mode of nomination and origin, is surely to pass from one kind of colonizing experience into another. For such pluralism refuses the idea of naming; it plays with diversity and makes a mystique of it; it is the concealed imperialism of the multinational, the infinite compatibility of all cultures with one another envisaged in terms of the ultimate capacity of all computers to read one another.

Abdul R. JanMohamed (1945–)

Born in Kenya, and educated both there and in the United States, Abdul JanMohamed currently teaches at the University of California at Berkeley. He is the author of *Manichaean Aesthetics* (1989), one of the first political analyses of the literary works of Conrad, Forster, and others in relation to racial politics and Western aesthetics. He is also the co-editor of *The Nature and Context of Minority Discourse* (1991) which not only portrayed a spectrum of race- and ethnicity-related enquiries, but also signalled the hidden politics of major granting agencies such as the National Endowment for the Humanities (US) wherein the bias of the Right wing could directly stifle the cultural production of Left-wing intellectuals. Author of numerous articles in post-colonial discourse, JanMohamed is also the founding editor of *Cultural Critique*. One of his major research projects is to examine the literary and cultural contribution of Richard Wright.

In the essay, 'Worldliness-without-World, Homelessness-as-Home: Toward a Definition of the Specular Border Intellectual', JanMohamed examines two categories of exilic intellectuals: the syncretic border intellectual and the specular border intellectual, and notes the motivating agency in the works of such specular border intellectuals as Edward Said, W. E. B. DuBois, Richard Wright, Zora Neale Hurston, and others. Using tropes such as borders, home, cultural mediations, and agency, JanMohamed argues that Said's positionality in occupying the contradictory spaces of 'worldliness-without-world and homelessness-as-home' allows him to speculate on the aesthetics of 'socio-cultural-classed-gendered locations' without falling back on simplistic, ideological readings, while at the same time giving him the liberatory potential to engage in the 'jouissance of homeless-as-home'. Such a theoretical examination of borders allows JanMohamed to conduct a dialogue with both transnational subjects such as Said, and the more American, ethnic, chicana subject such as Gloria Anzaldua.

G.R.

Worldliness-without-world, homelessness-as-home: toward a definition of the specular border intellectual

[Because Conrad] had an extraordinarily persistent residual sense of his own exilic marginality, he instinctively protected his vision with the aesthetic restraint of someone who stood forever at the very juncture of *this* [i.e., the colonial] world with another, always unspecified but different, one.[1]

How did exile become converted from a challenge or a risk, or even from an active impingement on his [Auerbach's] European selfhood, into a positive mission, whose success would be a cultural act of great importance?

(SC, pp. 6–7)

I

What 'cannot be said' in *Beginnings*, without making the production of the book impossible, is just those latent aporias about the self and its intentions, about history, and about beginnings, out of which the book constantly goes on producing itself, like a mushroom out of its mycelium. *Beginnings* constantly recognizes these contradictions, without quite recognizing them, in passages which are like slips of the tongue or the pen . . .[2]

This remark by J. Hillis Miller, while specifically commenting on *Beginnings*, is, I believe, applicable to Edward W. Said's entire corpus, or indeed to that of any author who has produced a significant and innovative body of criticism. Among all the productive aporias that could be located in Said's work, this essay will be confined to that which surrounds the 'self and its intentions,' the self to be understood not as the individual, Edward W. Said, but as the authorial subject-position implicit in Said's work, a position I shall categorize as that of 'the *specular border intellectual*.'

While this essay will not fully elaborate a typology of border intellectuals, it may be useful to distinguish at the outset between the *specular border intellectual*, the focus here, and the *syncretic border intellectual*, to be explored in detail elsewhere. Said describes the awareness of intellectuals situated on cultural borders as 'contrapuntal.' This musical metaphor, while aptly defining a structural symmetry and tension that characterize the border intellectual's subject position, tends to obscure the border intellectual's agency as well as the orientation of his or her intentionality toward the two cultures. While both syncretic and specular border intellectuals find themselves located between two (or more) groups or cultures, with which they are more or less familiar, one can draw a distinction between them based on the *intentionality of their intellectual orientation* (as opposed to a categorical epistemic differentiation).

The syncretic intellectual, more 'at home' in both cultures than his or her specular

442

counterpart, is able to combine elements of the two cultures in order to articulate new syncretic forms and experiences. An apposite example of such syncretic intellectuals can be found in Third World artists such as Wole Soyinka, whose plays often combine Greek tragedy with Yoruba mythology, or Salman Rushdie, whose 'English' novels are often articulated in Urdu syntax, or Chinua Achebe, whose 'English' fiction is structured by Igbo oral narrative patterns, and so forth. Anton Shammas's novel *Arabesques*, written in Hebrew by a Christian Arab, brilliantly problematizes the positionality of specular and syncretic intellectuals.[3]

By contrast, the specular border intellectual, while perhaps equally familiar with two cultures, finds himself or herself unable or unwilling to be 'at home' in these societies. Caught between several cultures or groups, none of which are deemed sufficiently enabling or productive, the specular intellectual subjects the cultures to analytic scrutiny rather than combining them; he or she utilizes his or her interstitial cultural space as a vantage point from which to define, implicitly or explicitly, other, utopian possibilities of group formation. Intellectuals like Edward W. Said, W. E. B. DuBois, Richard Wright, and Zora Neale Hurston occupy the specular site, each in a distinctive way.

II

Perhaps the best place to begin an exploration of Said as a specular border intellectual is with his statements on exile. With his usual insight and eloquence, Said reminds us in his essay, 'The Mind of Winter: Reflections on Life in Exile' (MW, pp. 49–55), that we should not romanticize the exile's predicament; that we must avoid a redemptive, i.e., a primarily religious, view of exile; that the 'interplay between nationalism and exile is like Hegel's dialectic of servant and master,' wherein opposites inform and constitute each other; and, finally, that we must not allow the aura of isolation and spirituality surrounding exile to displace our awareness of 'refugees' who are often politically disenfranchised groups of innocent and bewildered people. Those who are exiles, he argues, know 'that in a secular and contingent world, homes are always provisional. Borders and barriers, which enclose us within the safety of familiar territory, can also become prisons, and are often defended beyond reason or necessity. Exiles cross borders, break barriers of thought and experience' (MW, p. 54). While this is surely true, the exile's manner of border-crossing can be usefully distinguished from those of the immigrant, the colonialist, the scholar, etc. The salient question is how, precisely, do exiles cross borders; what are their intentions and goals in crossing borders, and how do these in turn affect the kinds of barriers they are inclined to break?

Said's concern with exile manifests itself, among other instances, in his preoccupation with intellectuals who cross borders in various ways: most notably T. E. Lawrence, Joseph Conrad, Eric Auerbach, and Louis Massignon. The last two clearly occupy privileged, albeit distinct, positions in Said's canon of border intellectuals, and I shall be scrutinizing Said's treatment of both. But it must be noted in passing, as both the epigraphs to this essay indicate, that Said's fascination with all these individuals is in some sense specular. Like Conrad, these intellectuals are located at the juncture of the world that formed them, and, like Auerbach, they transform their border-crossing into positive missions that lead to significant cultural acts. Said's relation to them is specular because, from his very different location on the same border between European and non-European cultures, he faces these Western intellectuals across that border, so to speak, and crosses over into the West only to re-cross the border with them in order to map the politics of their forays into other cultures. Thus Said's commentaries on these individuals constitute a series of specular crossing and re-crossing of cultural borders.

Yet Said's appropriations and rearticulations of these intellectuals are often ambiguous about positionality and borders, a characteristic best exemplified by his treatment of Auerbach. In discussing the instrumentality of Auerbach's exile in the production of *Mimesis*, Said ascribes the 'existence [of the book] to the very fact of Oriental, non-Occidental exile and homelessness,' and the 'conditions and circumstances' of the book's existence not to European culture but to 'an agonizing distance from it' (SC, p. 8). While Auerbach's exile is clearly 'non-Occidental' in terms of specific location, it seems confusing to characterize it as 'Oriental' exile, since there is no evidence that Auerbach's views were modified by any aspect of 'Oriental' cultures: the book could have been written in any other part of the non-Occidental world without significant difference. I am teasing semantics here in order to ascertain the nature of Auerbach's allegiance to the culture that formed him and to ask whether that allegiance is modified significantly by the influence of an alien culture. If such were the case, then one could characterize the transformation as 'agonizing,' since it would call the very formation of the intellectual into question. If not, then the distance is sufficiently enabling rather than agonizingly debilitating. Auerbach seems inclined to see it as enabling: 'The most priceless and indispensable part of a philologist's heritage is still his own nation's culture and heritage. Only when he is first separated from this heritage, however, and then transcends it does it become truly effective' (cited in SC, p. 7). The ambiguity and slippage in Auerbach's use of 'heritage'—a slippage from a professional, methodological inheritance to a national patrimony, which after being 'transcended' returns in a more effective guise because it is now simultaneously professional and cultural, the latter having been subsumed by the former—emphasize that an enabling distance leads ultimately to a more profound suture between the subject and the culture that formed her or him. And this, it seems to me, is the central issue in defining exile: how that particular mode of crossing a border elucidates the politics of cultural construction of subjects and how the latter can begin to break free from their indigenous formation by crossing borders.

Said's specular appropriation of Auerbach for defining the value of exile seems to overlook some fundamental differences between the two men. While Auerbach writes about and for Western cultures, Said does not write principally for or about Middle Eastern cultures; he writes in the main for and about the West. Even *The Question of Palestine* is addressed, at least in part, as Said explicitly acknowledges, to a Euro-American audience. Thus, while Auerbach is an exile in the weak sense, that is, a subject who always belongs to his home culture in spite of, indeed because of, a circumstantial and temporary alienation, Said, who is neither quite an exile nor quite an immigrant, is able to develop, out of his more complicated border status, an enabling theory of 'exile' as an 'ascetic ode of *willed* homelessness' (SC, p. 7, emphasis added). However, the discomfort caused by this complicated status inhibits a systematic and clear articulation of the code, which remains embedded in the ambiguities and apor-ias of Said's entire *oeuvre*.

Said's ambivalence toward defining the nature of border-crossings is most dramat-ically revealed in his article on 'Traveling Theory,' the influence of which is amply illustrated by the special issue of *Inscriptions* devoted to this topic.[4] Said's essay, designed to demonstrate how ideas and theories are transformed when they cross borders, provocatively diagnoses the nature and the dangers of transformations that have taken place either in mutations of a given theoretical position or between con-crete historical analysis and general theory related to that analysis; however, his argument about the causes of these transformations remains vague. Hence, the essay offers an apposite instance of the combined insight and blindness that characterizes Said's thinking about border-crossings.

After a rather general reference to ideas moving from West to East (and vice versa) in the nineteenth century, Said focuses on the transformation of Georg Lukács' theory of reification as it is later taken up by Lucien Goldmann and turned into the theory of 'homologies.' This transmutation of a complex theory into a vague, formu-laic metaphor is rightly characterized by Said as a 'degradation.' Yet he seems unwilling to consider the possibility that this change may be produced by the failure of individual understanding or imagination; instead, he argues, it is 'just that the sit-uation has changed sufficiently for the degradation to have occurred.' One waits to see what specific modifications in the situation are responsible for this, what kind of border has in fact been crossed, what are the socio-political differences between the two locations that can bring about such changes. Perhaps because he senses the reader's expectations, Said insists several times that relocation *in itself* precipitates the transformation. The tension caused by the contradiction between the insistence that change in location produces transformations and the refusal to specify the nature of that cause reaches its climax in the following statement:

> In measuring Lukács and Goldmann against each other, then, we are also recog-nizing the extent to which theory is a response to a specific social and historical situation of which an intellectual occasion is a part. Thus what is insurrectionary consciousness in one instance becomes tragic vision in another, for reasons that are elucidated when the situations in Budapest and Paris are *seriously compared*. I do not wish to suggest that Budapest and Paris determined the kinds of theories produced by Lukács and Goldmann. I do mean that 'Budapest' and 'Paris' are irreducibly first conditions, and they provide limits and apply pressures to which each writer, given his own gifts, predilections, and interests, responds.
> (TT, p. 237)

One is no closer to understanding what kind of border has been crossed and how that might have contributed to the change. Said's equivocation about the relations between a subject and the determining socio-political situation has reached an infi-nitely periphrastic refusal to come to terms with the issue.

By the time he moves to Raymond Williams's meditation on Lukács' and Goldmann's ideas, the problem of crossing cultural borders has been displaced by epistemological questions. When Said turns to Michel Foucault, the last theoretician considered in the essay, his concern has shifted to the discrepancy between the value

of Foucault's detailed historical work and the weaknesses in his theoretical pronouncements about power/knowledge. By the end, 'travel' has become a general
metaphor covering a series of diverse theoretical transformations, but the effects of
crossing borders have not been illuminated. Said has a strong awareness of situations
and borders, yet he declines to specify the precise causes and effects of such crossings. Instead, he produces criticism that emanates from and reflects the difficult
predicament of border intellectuals in two ways: first, his criticism is a 'reflection,' an
indirect meditation, on the predicament; and, second, it occupies a specular position
in relation to Western culture.

III

Before proceeding to examine further Said's meditations on the nature of borders
and the relation of these meditations to his own location, a few clarifications about
different modes of border-crossing may be useful. A systematic scrutiny must avoid a
metaphoric use of the term 'exile,' which tends to be shrouded in the emotionally-
charged connotations of the exile's plight. One can schematically identify four
different modes of border-crossings: those used by the exile, the immigrant, the colonialist, and the scholar, the last typified by the anthropologist studying other cultures
(one might add the tourist and the traveler as subcategories of the scholar/anthropol-
ogist). While both the exile and the immigrant cross the border between one social or
national group and another, the exile's stance toward the new host culture is negative, the immigrant's positive. That is, the notion of exile always emphasizes the
absence of 'home,' of the cultural matrix that formed the individual subject; hence, it
implies an involuntary or enforced rupture between the collective subject of the original culture and the individual subject. The nostalgia associated with exile (a
nostalgia that is structural rather than idiosyncratic) often makes the individual indifferent to the values and characteristics of the host culture; the exile chooses, if indeed
s/he has any choice, to live in a context that is least inhospitable, most like 'home.'
The immigrant, on the other hand, is not troubled by structural nostalgia because his
or her status implies a purposive directedness toward the host culture, which has
been deliberately chosen as the new home. Most importantly, his or her status
implies a voluntary desire to become a full-fledged subject of the new society. Thus
the immigrant is often eager to discard with deliberate speed the formative influences
of his or her own culture and to take on the values of the new culture; indeed, his or
her success as an immigrant depends on what Said calls 'uncritical gregariousness,'
that is, on an ability to identify rapidly and to merge with the structure of the new
culture's collective subjectivity.[5]

Unlike the exile and the immigrant, for both of whom the problematic consists in a
rupture between and a re-suturing of individual and collective subjectivities, the
colonialist and the anthropologist, who also cross cultural borders, are not troubled
by this problem.[6] Colonial and anthropological projects are both characterized by a
deliberate denial and often an explicit, militant repression of the individual's desire
to become a subject of the host culture. Both must apprehend the new culture, not as
a field of subjectivity, but rather as an object of and for their gaze. For the colonialist
the new culture becomes an object of his military, administrative, and economic
skills, which, according to colonial theory and practice, remain objective and uncon-

taminated so long as the administrator is prevented from 'going native,' i.e., from becoming a subject of the new culture.[7] For the anthropologist the situation is, of course, more complicated. While he or she is professionally obliged to 'master' the language and culture of the host society, all aspects of his or her individual subjectivity—the fundamental epistemological structures of professional work or career, fundamental values and beliefs, even bodily well-being—remain under the discursive control of the home culture. The anthropologist, too, cannot afford to 'go native,' for to do so would mean the loss of an 'objectivity' essential to professional status.[8] For both the colonialist and the traditional anthropologist, the host culture ultimately remains an object of attention: the gaze of the former is military, administrative, and economic; that of the latter is epistemological and organizational. Both gazes, quite unlike the perspectives of the exile and the immigrant, are panoptic and thus dominating.

IV

If we begin to scrutinize Third World intellectuals like Edward Said and American minority intellectuals like Richard Wright, it quickly becomes evident that while they fit none of my four categories, their subject-positions do share some characteristics of all but one. Obviously, neither is a colonialist, but in some sense both are simultaneously exiles *and* immigrants. Said and Wright are both descendants of people forced to leave their original cultures, and, like immigrants, both operate more or less effectively in their new culture. However, neither becomes a full-fledged subject of the latter: Said because he chooses not to, because he does not wish to rush into what he calls an 'uncritical gregariousness'; Wright because racism would not permit blacks to become full members of white American culture. Somewhat like anthropologists, both are quasi-subjects who participate in the new culture yet stand on its border; however, unlike the anthropologist, neither is a full participant in any other culture. Both are subjects in a dominant culture, yet marginal to it. Hence, both are confined to the predicament of border intellectuals, neither motivated by nostalgia for some lost or abandoned culture nor at home in this or any other culture.

This predicament of the border intellectual must be carefully defined. How can one situate oneself on the border? What kind of space characterizes it? In theory, and effectively in practice, borders are neither inside nor outside the territory they define but simply designate the difference between the two. They are not really spaces at all; as the sites of differences between interiority and exteriority, they are points of infinite regression. Thus, intellectuals located on this site are not, so to speak, 'sitting' on the border; rather, they are forced *to constitute themselves as the border*, to coalesce around it as a point of infinite regression. In consciously or unconsciously constituting themselves in this manner, they have to guard themselves against the traps of specularity, for the border only functions as a mirror, as a site defining the 'identity' and 'homogeneity' of the group that has constructed it. Said is clearly aware of this paradox, and its resultant demand, but seems unwilling to unravel it explicitly:

> I am speaking of exile, [he says] not as a privileged site for self-reflection but as an *alternative* to the mass institutions looming over much of modern life. If the exile is neither going to rush into an uncritical gregariousness [like the immigrant] nor

sit on the sidelines nursing a wound [like the exile], he or she must cultivate a scrupulous (not indulgent or sulky) subjectivity. (MW, p. 54)

This formulation leads to two related questions. First, is it possible to cultivate a subjectivity, especially a 'scrupulous' one, without the aid of self-reflection? And second, what does 'scrupulous' mean in this context? Though Said never provides direct answers to these questions, the scrupulousness that is entailed in the subject-position of the border intellectual, it seems to me, is everywhere exemplified in his work.

V

Without going into the details of Said's forced migration from Palestine to Lebanon to Egypt and then eventually to permanent settlement in the US, or into other aspects of his biography, his work shows how he occupies a subject-position that is neither quite that of an exile nor quite that of an immigrant. As a Palestinian and an advocate of his people's rights and aspirations, Said, in spite of his Western education, functions as an exile on the borders of the dominant culture. Thus, even when articulating Palestinian aspiration, as for instance in *The Question of Palestine*, Said feels obliged to address the West, whose power greatly determines Palestinian destiny.

The Question of Palestine aims, Said says in the preface, to put 'before the American reader a broadly representative Palestinian position . . .' (QP, p. xi). The power of the US is more explicitly acknowledged when Said comments that 'there is an important place in the question of Palestine for what Jews and Americans now think and do. It is this place to which my book addresses itself' (QP, p. xvi). The politics underlying such an address account for Said's position as a subject: 'Every Palestinian,' he says, 'has no state as a Palestinian even though he is "of," without belonging to, a state in which at present he resides' (QP, p. 120). Though this is true of all Palestinians, and, I would add, of all border intellectuals, the statement defines the political position in cold, neutral terms; its affective results are exposed when Said permits himself to speak in a more subjective vein:

My hope is to have made clear the Palestinian interpretation of Palestinian experience, and to have shown the relevance of both to the contemporary political scene. To explain one's sense of oneself as a Palestinian in this way is to feel embattled. To the West, which is where I live, to be a Palestinian is in political terms to be an outlaw of sorts, or at any rate very much an outsider. But that is reality, and I mention it only as a way of indicating the peculiar loneliness of my undertaking in this book. (QP, p. xviii)

This sense of being an outsider is rearticulated in a different register as the collective obligation of Palestinians to negotiate constantly a variety of borders in order to define themselves individually and collectively. Hence Said's striking description of Palestinian reality as 'cubistic, all suddenly obtruding planes jutting out into one or another realm' (QP, p. 123).

However, Said's subject-position is only partly that of articulator and defender of Palestinian aspirations within the West; he is also an active and important producer of the evolving Palestinian identity. In the absence of an authoritative history of Palestinians, *The Question of Palestine* marks an early stage in the production of such a history, and, in the absence of an informed, sympathetic, and serious discussion of the Palestinian 'problem' in the West, the book plays an important role by inserting the question into Western discourse. As Said makes clear, his book is motivated not only by the current plight of Palestinians, but also by a utopian vision of Palestine, a 'nonplace,' an idea that galvanizes Palestinians everywhere. In relation to this utopian potential, as in relation to the American audience for whom Said articulates Palestine, he is a border intellectual, and this just because 'Palestine' is a most unusual 'place':

> If we think of Palestine as having a function of both a place to *return to* and of an *entirely new* place, a vision partially of a restored past and of a novel future, per-haps even of a historical disaster transformed into a hope for a different future, we will understand the word's meaning better. (*QP*, p. 125)

In the context of such a 'Palestine' and the US, where he is professionally located, Said can be seen as at once an 'exile' and an 'immigrant.' He is an exile from the land of his birth who has become an eminent member of the American academy but who refuses, unlike most immigrants, what he calls an 'uncritical gregariousness,' that is, an anxious desire to become an uncritical subject of the new culture. Yet in relation to 'Palestine' he is an exile waiting across the historical, temporal border for the establishment of a utopian state.[9]

Thus Said is enmeshed in a complicated border space, which is by no means the single source of his work but which does leave a singular trace throughout his writing. Quite often his position, which allows a kind of distance from Western literature and discursive practices, permits Said a specular role—that is, he is able to provide in his writing a set of mirrors allowing Western cultures to see their own structures and functions.

Said's most famous book, *Orientalism*, is just such a specular performance. It mir-rors analytically a Western mode of discursive control that Said labels 'orientalist': he reveals to Orientalists (those few who are willing to listen) their own hidden ideologi-cal procedures and programs. *Orientalism* is clearly not the product of a 'traditional' intellectual in Gramsci's sense, that is, of one who produces the ideology of the dominant class while believing that her or his work is neutral and unbiased. In fact, the book is a stringent critique of the traditional orientalist intellectuals who are blind to their ideological formation. On the other hand, *Orientalism* is not the product of an 'organic' intellectual either, since in producing his deconstruction of 'orientalism,' Said does not speak for any *particular* organic group outside the West; the book is not in the service of a *specific* counter-hegemonic formation,[10] though many Third World and American minority intellectuals have found it sympathetic. *Orientalism* is, instead, the work of a border intellectual: one who is the subject neither of the host culture or the dominant class, as are the immigrant and the traditional intellectual, respectively, nor of the 'home' culture or the subaltern class, as are the exile and the organic intellectual, respectively. Said's critique is articulated from the neutrality of the border: *Orientalism* is deeply 'interested' in unmasking the underlying, organiza-tional structure of the discourse that masquerades as truth, but Said is not motivated to offer an alternate positivity, whether in the guise of a truth or a set of alternative group 'interests.'

While the border status of *Orientalism* is virtually self-evident, that of Said's earlier book, *Beginnings*, is more complicated and intriguing. This work is clearly an important part of the structuralist and poststructuralist debate, a debate that it scrutinizes in the fifth chapter. However, *Beginnings* itself implicitly challenges one to look for the enabling and creative 'beginning' contradictions that make this very book possible.

Said's definition of 'beginnings' and 'intentionality,' the work's key concepts, is circular. '*The Beginning*,' he tells us, '*is the first step in the intentional production of meaning*' (*B*, p. 5). By intention, he 'mean[s] an appetite at the beginning intellectually to do something in a characteristic language—either consciously or unconsciously, but at any rate in a language that always (or nearly always) shows signs of the beginning intention in some form and is always engaged purposefully in the production of meaning' (*B*, p. 12). The term 'intention' also has two other important implications for Said. First, 'intention is the link between idiosyncratic view and the communal concern' (*B*, p. 13); second, it 'is a notion that includes everything that later develops out of it, no matter how eccentric the development or inconsistent the result' (*B*, p. 12). What is implicit in these tautological definitions is made more explicit when Said argues that for 'the great modern rethinkers,' like Marx and Freud, 'beginning is a way of grasping the whole project' (*B*, p. 41). That is to say, a study of beginnings implies a scrutiny of the entire project of a given culture or a given historical period. Since the choice of any given intention, implied in the concept of beginning, involves the rejection or bracketing of other intentions, one is obliged to examine the axiology according to which intentions are prioritized; hence, one has to study the entire cultural *gestalt*. Similarly, if intentions must be studied teleologically, and if they link the individual and collective cultural subjects (i.e., the idiosyncratic view and the communal concern), then a thorough scrutiny of beginnings necessarily involves an analysis of economic, political, social, ideological, and psychological relations.

However, Said explicitly refuses an analysis of the socio-political circumstances of beginnings, and he avoids any sustained comparisons of beginnings in Western and non-Western cultures. (It would be fascinating, for instance, to compare, as Said does not, the phenomenology of beginnings in oral-mythic cultures, on the one hand, with that in chirographic-historical cultures, on the other). Said *does* make a brief reference to the long shadow cast by the Koran on the development of modern Arabic fiction, which, from the viewpoint of the authorial subject-position, serves to define the nature of Said's attention. Having ruled out other cultures, as well as a socio-political examination of beginnings, Said can confine himself to a scrutiny of the literary, critical, and philosophical texts of Western high culture. The problem here is not that the field is artificially demarcated, but that, having limited himself to a field where writers are consciously concerned with the problem of beginnings, Said is then able to undertake an analysis that, to use his own terms, is neither quite intransitive nor quite transitive: it is an uneasy, though illuminating and stimulating, mixture.

Transitive and intransitive analyses of beginnings are, Said tells us, 'two styles of thought, and imagination, one projective and descriptive, the other tautological and endlessly self-mimetic.' The former leads to a 'beginning with (or for) an anticipated

450

end, or at least expected continuity'; the latter 'retains for the beginning its identity as *radical* starting point: the intransitive and conceptual aspect, that which has no object but its own constant clarification.' Said's work is clearly not a systemic and rigorous intransitive analysis similar to those of Husserl and Heidegger. Nor is it quite a transitive one, for its *telos* is never entirely clear. The intentionality of Said's book, it seems to me, is ambivalently caught between an attempt at a rigorous phenomenological reduction of the concept and experience of 'beginnings,' on the one hand, and a non-phenomenological, historical survey of the same topic, on the other. In effect, Said ends up with what one might call a 'transitive phenomenology' of 'beginnings.'

This particular form of analysis is privileged for various reasons. The one of greatest interest here stems from the structural position of the exile or immigrant in the new culture. In defining exteriority, Said links it with the feeling of what Lukács, echoing Novalis, calls 'transcendental homelessness,' which Said says 'is the result of discovering an absolute incompatibility between the realm of totality and the realm of personal interiority, of subjectivity' (*B*, p. 312). This is precisely the incongruity experienced by the exile and, in a less problematic manner, by the immigrant. The subjectivity or interiority of the immigrant or exile is formed and informed by the 'totality' of her or his 'home' culture. When individuals go to a new society, they experience a major gap between the alien culture and the self (in)formed elsewhere: collective and individual subjects no longer coincide. The immigrant who wishes to integrate himself into this new social structure will be forced to contemplate, first and foremost, how and where he must begin. How to enter the host culture and where to begin will become a transitive phenomenological problem for him. For the indigenous subject, who is a part of the prevailing cultural discourse, intentions and beginnings will at best be mundane problems. It is no accident, then, that a border intellectual like Said 'happens' to produce a massive, scholarly study of beginnings and that this study takes the form of a transitive phenomenology that Said repeatedly classifies as a 'meditation' about beginnings, nor, indeed, that Said 'begins' his own scholarly career with a study of Joseph Conrad, whose life and work exemplify the challenges and problems of exile and immigration.

One might reasonably expect a scholarly meditation on beginnings to scrutinize its own beginnings and intentionality, and one might assume that, for it to be rigorous and hence productive, such an endeavour would ultimately have to be either intransitive, thereby pushing the beginning of *Beginnings* to its fundamental epistemological and ontological ground, or specifically transitive, thereby providing a concrete sociopolitical and biographical account of the origin and *telos* of the task. Said not only avoids each alternative, he also evades biographical reflexivity about his project. Instead, he provides us with the most passive and impersonal account of the book's genesis. In discussing the circumstances that led to this meditation, Said promises to tell us 'why such a study proposed itself to its author, why it is pursued in this way in particular, and how a rationale for such a study is arrived at' (*B*, p. 5). Further, the argument of the book is based on 'what the subject of "beginning" *authorizes*' (*B*, pp. 16–17). Thus the agency of the writer is almost totally repressed, and the writing subject is implicitly split between the active scribe and the passive meditator. Indeed, the meditating mind turns itself into a reflecting mirror: 'constructing the tautology

451

that says one begins at the beginning depends on the ability of both mind and language to reverse themselves, and thus to move from present to past and back again, from a complex situation to an anterior simplicity and back again, or from one point to another as if in a circle' (*B*, pp. 29–30).

The mind not only becomes a reflecting surface, but also adopts a paradoxically passive form of volition—it elects to be passive: 'The form of writing I chose,' Said says, 'was the meditative essay—first, because I believed myself to be trying for a form of unity as I write; and second, *because I want to let beginnings generate in my mind the type of relationships and figures most suitable to them*' (*B*, p. 16, emphasis added). The meditating mind becomes a (relatively genial) host to the problematic of beginnings revealed in the canonical literature of the (relatively genial) host culture.

That specular meditation produces a transitive phenomenology of beginnings that is not particularly goal-oriented. Unlike the immigrant, whose life and well-being depend on a concrete transitive comprehension of the host culture's intentionalities, on his or her mastery of where and how to begin in this new milieu, Said, precisely because he is not motivated by the desire to become a full, uncritical subject, can embark on a teleologically 'neutral' transitive phenomenology of beginnings in Western societies. In so doing he once again constructs an analytic mirror that reflects and refracts the structures of the host culture.

These considerations of the authorial subject-position manifested in *Beginnings* lead to several conclusions. The first is an aporia that I will take up again in discussing Said's method. As Hayden White has noted, one of the cures that *Beginnings* seems to propose for the contemporary crisis in Western cultures is 'the revitalization of the will.'[11] Yet in Said's account of the origins of *Beginnings*, the authorial will seems to be subordinated drastically to the 'authority' (of others') beginnings, to the object of contemplation. (Said thereby raises, but does not pursue, the question of the extent to which and in what manner the meditating mind is active, as he later insists it is.) The aporia, however, revolves around the relation between the quieting of the authorial will and the advocacy, direct or indirect, of a revitalized will. It is the very same aporia Said subsequently explores in Louis Massignon's study of Islamic religious mysticism.

Of more immediate interest is the fact that, via his transitive phenomenology, Said has produced a new methodological emphasis. The procedure of *Beginnings* implies that phenomenological investigation need not be torn between the polar opposites of pure, idealist meditations or starkly materialist studies of worldly determinations. His transitive phenomenology points towards the possibility of a 'political phenomenology,' analogous to Alfred Schutz's social phenomenology, a procedure devoted to mapping the dynamic structures of the intentionality and teleology of power and of relations of domination, a typology of these structures from their macroscopic—the politics of group and cultural formations—to their microscopic manifestations—the politics of discursive constructions of 'individual' subjects.

Finally, the procedure of *Beginnings* sheds interesting light on the relations among the apparently discrete works within Said's critical corpus. As J. Hillis Miller observes,

[t]here is, in both Said and his work, that discontinuity which is one of the central

themes of *Beginnings*: the difficult concept of production or assemblage which is not disorder or heterogeneity, and yet not assimilable to the familiar models of order—organic unity, dialectical progression, or genealogical series—in which origin fathers forth a sequence leading without break to some foreordained end.[12]

This 'discontinuity' is informed, if not produced, by the position of the border intellectual and the very concern with beginnings. Each of Said's major works begins anew, striking out in a different direction from the previous studies; each opens up novel fields and provides different angles of vision. His work as a whole can be described, to borrow his own metaphor about Palestinian experience, as 'cubistic.' The cement holding the different planes and fields together is the fundamental procedures and attitudes of his never explicitly articulated method.

VI

Hayden White has perspicuously described the core of Said's method. *Beginnings*, he argues, does not 'authorize' either the logic of identity and contradiction ('the hypotactical principles of subordination and reductive inclusion') or the principle of analogy ('the paratactical principle of similitude or resemblance'). Said's method, rather, is based on 'notions of adjacency, complementarity, discontinuity—in other words, *contiguity*, which serves as both an ontological principle and a method of exposition. In Said's world-view, things exist side-by-side with one another, not in hierarchies of relative reality or ordered series of dynastically related groups. But the principle of contiguity here embraced is not a mechanistic one.'[13]

Examples of this method can be found throughout Said's work. 'Intellectuals in the Post-Colonial World' provides a striking instance:

> The comparative or, better, the contrapuntal perspective then proposes itself and with it, Ernst Bloch's notion of non-synchronous experience. That is we must be able to think through and interpret together discrepant experiences, each with its particular agendas and pace of development, its own formations, its own natural coherence and its system of external relationships. (IPW, p. 56)

This is followed by a fascinating comparison between Fournier's *Description de l'Egypte* and Abd al Rahman al Jabarti's *Journal*, both of which date from the 1820s, and by a sketch for an analysis of other texts that follow each of these writers on either side of the divide. The language of Said's articulation—'contrapuntal,' 'non-synchronous,' 'discrepant,' etc.—stresses separation rather than continuity, implicitly emphasizing the interpreting will of the critic who compares the two sides. Such a method, while obviously productive in Said's hands, raises questions about the nature of the critical will and Said's subsequent deep valorization of the term 'criticism.' To use this method productively, a critic must attain a certain 'neutrality'; he or she must transcend those deep ideological allegiances to 'group,' 'nation,' 'race,' 'gender,' or 'class' that lead to the manichean valorization of one side and reciprocal devaluation of the other that *Orientalism* and a variety of feminist texts have criticized in their respective fields. The critic, in short, must be able to transcend the ideological boundaries that are imposed upon him or her by 'home.'

'Secular Criticism' takes up the discussion of 'home' in terms of its binary opposite, 'homelessness.' These definitions ultimately remain metaphoric and generate an ambiguous proliferation of meanings. Thus, 'home' comes to be associated with 'culture' as an environment, process, and hegemony that determine individuals through complicated mechanisms. Culture is productive of the necessary sense of belonging, of 'home'; it attempts to suture, in as complete a manner as possible, collective and individual subjectivity. But culture is also divisive, producing boundaries that distinguish the collectivity and what lies outside it and define hierarchic organizations within the collectivity. 'Homelessness,' on the other hand, is first defined negatively via Matthew Arnold as the opposite of 'home': 'anarchy, the culturally disfranchised, those elements opposed to culture and State.' More positively, 'homelessness' as an enabling concept is associated, via Raymond Williams's rearticulation of Gramsci, with the civil and political space that hegemony cannot suture, a space in which 'alternative acts and alternative intentions which are not yet articulated as a social institution or even project' can survive. 'Homelessness,' then, is a situation wherein utopian potentiality can endure.

'Criticism,' which denotes an oppositional socio-political attitude as well as a method and procedure in this essay, can be seen to emanate from this space of 'homelessness.' Said, it seems, is deliberately employing and redefining 'criticism', an over-determined, emotionally charged term already over-used in literary and cultural studies, in order to shock critics into re-examining their practices and assumptions and into abandoning their 'home,' that is, the ideological attitudes constraining a freer, more 'neutral' pursuit of knowledge. Yet precisely in this forceful attempt to redirect our use of that term, 'Secular Criticism' produces a certain ambiguity: 'In its suspicion of totalizing concepts, in its discontent with reified objects, in its impatience with guilds, special interests, imperialized fiefdoms, and orthodox habits of mind, criticism is most itself and, if the paradox can be tolerated, most unlike itself at the moment it starts turning into organized dogma' (SC, p. 29). In this paradoxical formulation, criticism functions to define that which is simultaneously to be affirmed and denied. The same effect is produced by statements like the following: '. . . contemporary criticism is an institution for publicly affirming the values of ours, that is, European, dominant elite culture . . .' (SC, p. 25); 'Criticism in short is always situated, skeptical, secular, reflectively open to its own failings' (SC, p. 26). Such contradictions not only lead to the kind of debate on Said's work, essentially over terminology, that took place in *Diacritics*;[14] they also draw our attention away from a clarification of 'homelessness' that is crucial to Said's privileging of 'criticism.'

'Secular Criticism' hints at two crucial aspects of this border space that Said calls 'homelessness.' The first concerns the critic's location. After noting that intellectuals can collaborate with as well as oppose a dominant order, Said remarks: 'All this, then, shows us the individual consciousness placed at a sensitive nodal point, and it is this consciousness at that critical point which this book attempts to explore in the form of what I call *criticism*' (SC, p. 15). 'Criticism' here designates the distance, made possible by self-reflexivity, between a given hegemonic order and the individual critic. The 'sensitive nodal point,' then, in effect defines the location of the border intellectual, as Said's fascination with various individuals who cross borders indicates. The second concerns the nature of criticism itself: 'For in the main—and here I shall be explicit—criticism must think of itself as life-enhancing and constitutively opposed to every form of tyranny, domination and abuse; its social goals are non-coercive knowledge produced in the interest of human freedom' (SC, p. 29). The nature of this criticism will of course depend on how one defines 'human freedom,' about which there will surely be much disagreement. What seems beyond dispute, however, is the valorization of 'non-coercive knowledge.' 'Secular Criticism,' in keeping with its introductory function in the anthology, does not further articulate either the location of the border intellectual or the nature of non-coercive knowledge. That task is left to Said's commentary on Massignon.

Although Said's essay, 'Islam, Philology, and French Culture: Renan and Massignon,' sets out to demonstrate that humanistic fields, based not on criticism or discipline but on cultural prestige, are incapable of self-criticism, one is struck less by this purpose than by Said's warmth, generosity, and respect for Massignon; and one soon discovers beneath these sentiments an even finer appreciation of Massignon's method and style. Massignon's 'epistemological attitude' toward the Arab cultures he studied, characterized by Said as one of 'sympathetic assumption and rapprochement,' is ultimately responsible for his method. In Massignon's work, Said explains,

> the problem of language and of the philological vocation are considered within a *spatial* perspective, as aspects of a topography of distances, of geographical differentiation, of spirits of place separated from each other by a territory whose function for the scholar is that it must be charted as exactly as possible, and then in one way or another overcome. (IPFC, p. 284)

The imperative to chart cultural differences with exactitude in order to overcome them begins to define non-coercive knowledge. Clearly, Said values both Massignon's refusal to subordinate Islam and Arab cultures to Christianity and European cultures and the resultant analysis that is non-manichean, non-agonistic, and non-polemical. In Said's view, Massignon goes well beyond freeing himself from the negative, confining ideology of European superiority that is typical of orientalist thinking. He even seems to have based his method on a certain dialectical notion of relation between self and other in Arabic grammar and rhetoric:

> For language is both a 'pilgrimage' and a 'spiritual displacement,' since we only elaborate language in order to be able to go out from ourselves toward another, and also to evoke with this other an absent One, the third person, *al-Gha'ib*, as He is called by Arab grammarians. And we do this so as to discover and identify all these entities with each other. (cited in IPFC, p. 286)

Every aspect of Massignon's endeavour—his epistemology, his view of language, his approach to Arab cultures, even his view of the orientalist's vocation—is informed by a 'spiritual displacement' that permits him to understand the Arab in the latter's own terms. This open and generous approach, unfettered by the powerful ideological forces of his 'home' culture, is what I believe Said has in mind by 'non-coercive knowledge.' Massignon thus stands as Said's prime example of an intellectual who manages to overcome the powerful ideological confinements of 'home'; his capacity for 'spiritual displacement' symbolizes Said's valorization of 'homelessness.'

455

But 'homelessness' cannot be achieved without multiple border crossings, indeed, without a constant, keen awareness of the politics of borders. Such an awareness permeates Massignon's work and style, which Said characterizes as discontinuous and abrupt, 'as if it wishes constantly to embody distance and the alternation of presence and absence, the paradox of sympathy and alienation, the motif of inclusion and exclusion, grace and disgrace, apotropaic prayer and compassionate love' (IPFC, p. 287). Said aptly characterizes this constant oscillation in spatial terms, that is, not only as co-equivalence but also as repeated border crossings. Massignon, Said implies, was perfectly comfortable as a subject in his host culture and elsewhere; he was quite 'at home' without having to subordinate himself to the ideological constraints of any particular national or cultural group. The paradox of 'homelessness-as-home' is best captured by the ambiguity of the following statement: for Massignon, says Said, the Arabic language 'is a closed world with a certain number of stars in it; entering it, the scholar is both at home and repatriated from his own world' (IPFC, p. 286). Massignon is 'at home' in this tension, in the play between Arabic and European cultures. Said here transforms the border into 'homelessness-as-home' by turning a negative determination, i.e., the status of an outsider or marginalized border intellectual, into a positive vocation, mining that site for its political and epistemological wealth.

Bruce Robbins succinctly captures an aspect of this paradox:

> If criticism is not to be subsumed by the interest of the homeland, Said suggests, it can only be located in dislocation itself, in the always shifting, always empty space 'between culture and system.' But he also argues that if criticism is not to withdraw into harmless seclusion, it must accept the taint and constraint of placement in the world—and even, perhaps, make a home for itself there. Homelessness or worldliness? Between them there is nothing so satisfying as a choice or a contradiction, but there is a lively project of critical self-discovery.[15]

Robbins's characterization is generally accurate, except for the negative connotation that he attaches to worldliness and the potential opposition he perceives between it and homelessness. It seems to me that the opposition between 'secular' and 'religious' criticism implies that Said sees a certain kind of worldliness as being free precisely of the 'taint and constraint' produced by the attachment of 'religious' criticism to the 'parochial' interests of *particular* worlds. Worldliness represents in Said's criticism, for example in his analysis of Massignon, the critic's achieved freedom from loyalty and subordination to specific ideologies, cultures, systems, worlds. Seen in this way, worldliness is not opposed to homelessness, but is its complement. 'Worldliness-without-world' and 'homelessness-as-home' are different formulations privileging the same subject position: that of the specular border intellectual.

Borders, as implied earlier, are articulations of epistemic and socio-political differences; indeed, borders are digital punctuations of analog differences, that is, highly valorized, stylized, and formulaic punctuations of infinite, continuous, and heterotopic differences that fill a given continuum. In contrast to the analog differences, borders, digitalized articulations of differences, introduce categorial gaps in a continuum. In a socio-political register, borders that articulate or impose categorial 'differences' between groups—demarcated in terms of 'nations,' 'cultures,' 'classes,' 'genders,' 'races,' etc.—tend to reify analog relations into imaginary identities and oppositions. In the context of such charged gaps, *syncretic* border intellectuals are those whose work fills the gaps—for instance, between two cultures. (I have in mind here particularly the artistic production of authors such as Soyinka, Rushdie, etc., who bridge the gaps between different cultures.) By contrast, *specular* border intellectuals produce work that reflects (on) the gaps and that articulates their nature and structures. Indeed, 'worldliness-without-world/homelessness-as-home,' the paradoxical formulation that is embedded in Said's corpus, elucidates the relation between the task and the location of the specular border intellectual. 'Worldliness-without-world' represents a sophisticated awareness of the politics produced by socio-cultural-classed-gendered locations, an awareness, however, that does not subjugate itself to that politics. It represents a freedom, or at least an attempt to achieve freedom, from the politics of imaginary identification and opposition, from conflation of identity and location, and so on—in short, from the varied and powerful forms of suturing that are represented by and instrumental in the construction of 'home.' While 'worldliness-without-world' emphasizes the specular border intellectual's awareness of his or her location outside the group in question, 'homelessness-as-home' accentuates a *jouissance* derived from transitoriness, from privileging process and relationship over allegiance to groups or to objects representing reified relationships; it privileges the pleasure of border-crossing and transgression.

VII

The power of this formulation informs a large part of Said's work, but he never explicitly privileges either the 'identity' of the border intellectual or the productive site occupied by that intellectual, in part, perhaps, because to do so risks essentialism. On the other hand, not to generalize at all, to argue, for instance, that there are as many types of border intellectuals as there are individuals situated on borders, risks the chaos of infinite monadic specificity. This is not the place to attempt an encompassing or complete definition of the border intellectual that would systematically negotiate the twin dangers of essentialism and infinite heterogeneity, or to provide a typology of border intellectuals; yet it may be useful to essay *some* general statements about the circumstances of border intellectuals. Said is obviously not the only intellectual who speaks from the border. While his work provokes serious thought about the border as a site of intellectual work, other individuals, for example, W. E. B. DuBois, Zora Neale Hurston, or Richard Wright, have also written from that subject-position and yet articulated it differently because of their various historical, political, class, and gender determinations. Thus, while the specific *foci* and strategies of border intellectuals can vary considerably, the position that they find themselves in has certain common features.

To the extent that groups—whether organized around culture, nation, class, gender, or race—tend to define their identities, their 'homogeneity,' by differentiating themselves from others, and to the extent that the inscription of difference tends to be valorized in a more or less manichean fashion, border intellectuals, who are caught between various group formations, are often forced to internalize the manichean dichotomies. If a group defines itself, as all groups finally do, as 'human' in contrast to others who are classified as 'sub-human,' then the intellectual situated on the border of that group, that is, an intellectual who does not have (or chooses not to utilize) access to another group that will adequately and confidently empower him or her according to its alternate definition of itself as 'human,' will be torn between his or her aspiration for 'humanity' and the actual socio-historical experience of being treated as sub-human.

In the case of border intellectuals, the rupture between aspiration or ego-ideal valorized by the dominant culture and the experience of actual social devaluation cuts through the very center of subjectivity. This rupture, we must remember, is not inflicted on an already formed 'individual' or subject but is involved in the very process of formation.[16] Thus, not only are images of self-as-human and other-as-sub-human related in a binary opposition, but the very process of *suturing* a 'homogeneity,' which seems crucial to the cultural necessity of the group's 'identity,' is simultaneously the process of rupturing the subject on the border: the border subject becomes the site on which a group defines its identity. Among the many implications of this predicament, I can only touch on some of the more salient:

• If the border is the site of infinite regression and if the border subject is the site on which the group defines its identity, then the ruptured body of that subject becomes the text on which the structure of group identity is written in inverted form—the *in*-formation of the group is inscribed on the body of the border subject. The border intellectual willing to read his or her own body, his or her own formation, has ready access to the structures and values of the group in question as well as to alternate possibilities of individual and collective subject formation.

• If the border subject is a deeply ruptured one, then a contemplation of how that subject was formed can, given a certain utopian impulse, lead to a desire to purge all the manichean valences, all the negative inscriptions that the group projected in its formation. In its most radical instance, such as that of Richard Wright, such a desire to deconstruct that received, manichean subjectivity becomes a prolonged project, which in turn paradoxically constitutes the core around which a new subjectivity begins to coalesce. Caught between a white racist society that would not accept him and a black culture that he repudiated for complex (and ultimately mistaken) reasons, Wright dedicated his life to investigating the border space between the two. In his bifurcated *oeuvre*, his utopian, communitarian urge is almost totally relegated to his journalistic writing. By contrast, his fiction—which explores different facets of the question 'What quality of will must a Negro possess to live and die with dignity in a country that denied his humanity?'—is dedicated to excavating the individual subjectivity that has been formed by the struggle between black and white cultures. Each of Wright's novels successively probes and reveals a deeper stratum of the political, ideological, and cultural processes of subject formation on the racial border. In so doing, Wright in effect becomes an archaeologist of the site of his own formation, devoting most of his energies to deconstructing the black subject's formation, thereby re-forming his (Wright's) own subjectivity as a writer around the project of excavating the border. In short, Wright's work constitutes a systematic reading of the border subject's body.

• The site of the border subject is clearly one mode of what Foucault identifies as 'heterotopia,' even though he does not have this kind of subjectivity in mind.[17] Utopias and heterotopias are, according to Foucault, the two sites that 'have the curious property of being in relation with all other sites, but in such a way as *to suspect, neutralize, or invert the set of relations that they happen to designate, mirror, or reflect'* (emphasis added). These two sites are linked with all others, but primarily by a relation of contradiction. Heterotopias, like boundaries, established 'in the very founding of society,' are 'counter-sites' in which all the other real sites that can be found within a culture 'are simultaneously represented, contested, and inverted.' Foucault's subsequent elaboration of the specular nature of heterotopias and the principles according to which they function, while very suggestive for a more extended exploration of the border intellectual as a heterotopic site, cannot be taken up here. It is crucial, however, to make one distinction. While Foucault's heterotopic sites are all *social* and *institutional* spaces—cemeteries, fairs, libraries, prisons, etc.—the border intellectual, as I have defined that concept, is simultaneously a 'space' and a subject, is, indeed, a subject-as-space. Unlike Foucault's sites, which are inherently heterotopic, the transformation of the border subject, who is always constituted as a *potential* heterotopic site, into an *actual* heterotopic, specular border intellectual depends upon his or her own agency: only by directly or indirectly reading himself or herself as a heterotopic border constructed as such by society can the intellectual articulate his or her specular potentiality. In their own very different ways, both Said and Wright investigate this shifting site.

• If a constructive appropriation of the heterotopic site by the border intellectual depends on articulations of specularity, then one must guard against the varied traps of auto-affection, the most important of which is a disguised, if not open, desire for an 'authentic identity,' a self-presence that is somehow thought to lie beyond the politics of specularity. The self-reflection of the border intellectual privileges less a transitive search for what Said calls 'origins' than an intransitive hermeneutics of socio-cultural structuration, a political phenomenology attentive to the rhetorical construction of all discursive formations and subject-positions.

• In many ways the specular border intellectual is homologous with what Donna Haraway has defined as the 'Cyborg.' 'There is no drive in cyborgs to produce total theory,' she argues, 'but there is an intimate experience of boundaries, their constructions and deconstructions'; 'Cyborg imagery can suggest a way out of the maze of dualisms in which we have explained our bodies and our tools to ourselves. This is a dream not of a common language, but of a powerful infidel heteroglossia.'[18] Said's valorization of 'affiliation' over 'filiation' can be read as a form of 'infidel heteroglossia.' While the life of Joseph Conrad (with whose border crossing Said 'begins' his professional career) also exemplifies a certain type of heteroglossia, Conrad's discomfort with and desire to overcome the dilemma of the border intellectual is marked by a dual desire: to belong to a select group, to become an insider—'one of us'—as Marlow puts it in *Lord Jim* and to value 'fidelity' above all else. Unlike Conrad and like the Cyborg, the border intellectual must affirm the value of infidelity to cultures, nations, groups, institutions, etc., to the extent that these are defined in monologic, essentialist terms.

• For border intellectuals in the academy the political phenomenology founded on their positionality necessarily leads to two major consequences, both easily visible today. First, to what Aronowitz and Giroux call 'border pedagogy,' which urges students to scrutinize knowledge from the position of 'border-crossers, as people moving in and out of borders constructed around coordinates of difference and power.' This pedagogy encourages students 'to develop a relationship of non-identity with their own subject positions and the multiple cultural, political, and social codes that constitute established boundaries of power, dependency, and possibility.'[19]

Second, to the enormous amount of theoretical and archival work, begun during the 1960s and 70s and currently gathering greater momentum, by feminist and minority intellectuals, who have had to function on and against the borders of a Eurocentric and patriarchal cultural canon. Within this area, a great deal of criticism on the positionality of feminist and minority intellectuals—for instance, by Gayatri Spivak and bell hooks on minority/'Third World' feminist intellectuals, and by Harold Cruse and Cornel West on African-American intellectuals—has explored in diverse ways the power and limitations inherent in the border status of such intellectuals. A recent anthology of essays on Chicano literature and culture, *Criticism in the Borderlands*, foregrounds more deliberately the politics of border-crossing.[20]

Yet for minority and feminist intellectuals, the valorization of heterogeneity and a heterotopic site, of 'homelessness,' poses severe problems, for it tends to complicate the demands of and desire for identification and solidarity with the group from which the intellectual draws some of her or his power.

• The position of the border subject, complicated and precarious, can generate, when appropriately cultivated, as it is by intellectuals like Said and Wright, a tense productivity that resists stability and the coercive tendencies of fixed, indigenous identities. Such an appropriation can transform the predicament of the border intellectual into a fruitful and powerful asset.

NOTES

I would like to thank the following for commenting on earlier drafts of this essay: Nancy Armstrong, David Lloyd, Alicia Ostriker, Donna Przybylowicz, Mark Rose, Jochen Schulte-Sasse, Muhammad Siddiq, Michael Sprinker, and Leonard Tennenhouse; The Humanities Research Institute at UC, Irvine provided a fellowship that allowed me to begin the essay; the Literary Criticism conference at Georgetown University afforded an opportunity to present a part of it as a talk.

1. Edward W. Said, 'Intellectuals in the Post-Colonial World,' *Salmagundi*, no. 70–1 (Summer 1986), p. 49. Henceforth, citations from Edward Said's works will be included in the text and abbreviated as follows: *B—Beginnings: Intention and Method* (New York: Basic Books, 1979); IPFC—'Islam, Philology, and French Culture,' *The World, the Text, and the Critic* (Cambridge, Mass.: Harvard University Press, 1983); IPW—'Intellectuals in the Post-Colonial World'; MW—'The Mind in Winter: Reflections on Life in Exile,' *Harper's*, no. 269 (September 1984); *QP—The Question of Palestine* (New York: Times Books, 1979); SC—'Secular Criticism,' *The World, the Text, and the Critic*; TT— 'Travelling Theory,' *The World, the Text, and the Critic*.

2. J. Hillis Miller, 'Beginning with a Text,' *Diacritics*, 4, no. 3 (1976), p. 4.

3. Anton Shammas, *Arabesques*, trans. Vivian Eden (New York: Harper and Row, 1983).

4. See *Inscriptions*, no. 5 (1989), which is devoted to a consideration of 'Traveling Theories, *Traveling Theorists.*'

5. Robert A. Burt's book, *Two Jewish Justices: Outcasts in the Promised Land* (Berkeley: University of California Press, 1988), provides a fascinating study of the manner in which the stances of the exile and the immigrant taken up, respectively, by Justices Louis Brandeis and Felix Frankfurter, affected their legal opinions and attitudes and, in the long run, the Supreme Court itself. According to Burt,

Brandeis 'found a place to stand both in and apart from his society. He was neither insider nor outsider. He found a unique place for himself, poised always at the boundary.' By contrast, 'to become a full-fledged American . . . Frankfurter had to separate himself from his immigrant past—as it were, by *force majeure*, by corporal . . . punishment' (citations come from pp. 13 and 39 respectively).

6. I have in mind here the nineteenth- and twentiety-century European colonialist's relation to Third World colonies, which defined the European as the controller and administrator. Settler colonialism, of the kind that was practiced in the US, Canada, Australia, and for a time in Kenya and southern Africa, is significantly different. This difference is marked precisely by the fact that at a given historical point (i.e., after the natives are sufficiently subjugated, if not destroyed) the designation used for Europeans coming to these countries changes from 'colonialist' to 'immigrant' or 'settler.'

7. For an excellent analysis of the appropriating colonialist gaze, see Mary Louise Pratt, 'Scratches on the Face of the Country; or, What Mr Barrows Saw in the Land of the Bushmen,' in *'Race,' Writing, and Difference* (Chicago: University of Chicago Press, 1985), pp. 138–62.

8. I have in mind here, of course, a traditional, non-reflexive anthropological practice. James Clifford's analyses of the narrative structures of ethnographic accounts as well as what one might characterize, for the sake of brevity, as self-reflexive ethnography have successfully challenged the 'objectivist' model. See, for example, Paul Rabinow, *Reflections on Fieldwork in Morocco* (Berkeley: University of California Press, 1977) and, more recently, Michael Jackson, *Path Toward a Clearing: Radical Empiricism and Ethnographic Inquiry* (Bloomington: Indiana Univ. Press, 1989); Kirin Narayan, *Storytellers, Saints, and Scoundrels: Folk Narratives in Hindu Religious Teaching* (Philadelphia: University of Pennsylvania Press, 1989); Ted Swedenburg, 'Occupational Hazards: Palestine Ethnography,' *Cultural Anthropology*, vol. 4, no. 3 (1989), pp. 265–72; Dorinne Kondo, *Crafting Selves: Power, Gender, and Discourse of Identity in a Japanese Workplace* (Chicago: University of Chicago Press, 1990); Smadar Lavie, *The Poetics of Military Occupation: Mzeina Allegories of Bedouin Identity Under Israeli and Egyptian Rule* (Los Angeles: University of California Press, 1990); Brackette Williams, *Stains on My Name, War in My Veins: Guyana and the Politics of Cultural Struggle* (Durham: Duke University Press, 1991).

   Of particular relevance here are the meditations on border crossings and 'relational knowledge' by Renato Rosaldo in *Culture and Truth: The Remaking of Social Analysis* (Boston: Beacon Press, 1989), and, in a different register, by Gloria Anzaldua, *Borderlands/La Frontera: The New Mestiza* (San Francisco: Spinsters/Aunt Lute, 1987).

9. Said's refusal to become an uncritically gregarious member of the US community and his utopian use of 'Palestine' find fascinating parallels in (and invite a fuller comparison to) the stance of Justice Louis Brandeis, which is characterized by Robert Burt as follows: 'The only homeland that Brandeis wholeheartedly embraced was thus an imaginary place—not America as it was, but only a romanticized Jeffersonian vision of a past America, and not Palestine as it was, but this same romantic vision of a Zion' (*Two Jewish Justices*, p. 17). However, Said's vision, it seems to me, is not really romantic, as Brandeis' might have been.

10. I am thinking here of various non-Western cultures as potentially counter-hegemonic ones, for none of which Said speaks directly. Said is, of course, a specific intellectual in the Foucauldian sense, but then by definition he does not represent others.

11. Hayden White, 'Criticism as Cultural Politics,' *Diacritics*, 4, no. 3 (1976), p. 13.

12. Miller, 'Beginning with a Text,' p. 2.

13. White, 'Criticism as Cultural Politics,' p. 12.

14. See the exchange between Bruce Robbins and Catherine Gallagher, *Diacritics*, 13, no. 3 (Fall 1983), pp. 69–77; 15, no. 2 (Summer 1985), pp. 37–43; 16, no. 3 (Fall 1986), pp. 67–72.

15. Bruce Robbins, 'Homelessness and Worldliness,' *Diacritics*, 13, no. 3 (Fall 1983), p. 69.

16. The most dramatic and penetrating representation of this rupture I know of appears in Zora Neale Hurston's *Their Eyes Were Watching God*, where the young Janie, the protagonist, is initially unable to recognize her black self in a photograph with other white children.

17. Michael Foucault, 'Of Other Spaces,' *Diacritics*, 16, no. 1 (Spring 1986), pp. 22–7.

18. Donna Haraway, 'A Manifesto for Cyborgs: Science, Technology, and Socialist Feminism in the 1980s,' in *Coming to Terms: Feminism, Theory, Politics*, ed. Elizabeth Weed (New York: Routledge, 1989), p. 204.

19. Stanley Aronowitz and Henry A. Giroux, *Postmodern Education: Politics, Culture, and Social Criticism*

461

(Minneapolis: University of Minnesota Press, 1991), pp. 199 and 200.

20. Hector Calderón and José David Saldívar, eds., *Criticism in the Borderlands: Studies in Chicano Literature, Culture, and Ideology* (Durham: Duke University Press, 1991). According to the editors, this book is in part 'an invitation . . . for readers . . . to remap the borderlands of theory and theorists. Our work in the eighties and nineties, along with that of other postcolonial intellectuals, moves, travels, as they say, between first and third worlds, between cores and peripheries, centers and margins. The theorists in this book see their texts always "written for" in our local and global borderlands.'

Gayatri Chakravorty Spivak (1942—)

Born in Calcutta, Gayatri Chakravorty Spivak is one of the most eminent literary and cultural critics of our time. She was educated in India and America, and received her PhD from Cornell University. She has taught in universities in America, Australia, Saudi Arabia, Europe, and India. Currently a professor of Comparative Literature at Columbia University, she was the Andrew Mellon Professor of English at the University of Pittsburgh. Spivak made a tremendous impact upon the American academy with her introduction to and translation of Jacques Derrida's *Of Grammatology* (1976). Her recent works include, *In Other Worlds: Essays in Cultural Politics* (1987), *The Post-Colonial Critic: Interviews, Strategies, Dialogues* (1990), and *Outside In The Teaching Machine* (1993). She has collaborated with the 'Subaltern Group,' where she assumes a systematic Marxist/deconstructive feminist stance, critiquing the phenomenon of colonialism/nationalism, and theorizing its connection to consciousness and class issues. She has written numerous articles, including the famous one, 'Can the Subaltern Speak?' As a cultural critic, she scrupulously examines the power and locus of authority (in texts and society), emphasizing issues of class, gender, and race. She self-consciously positions herself in differing locations such as 'first world theorist,' 'diasporic intellectual,' 'teacher,' and 'Indian woman' deploying the tremendous power and privilege that go with these terms.

In the essay 'The Politics of Translation' reprinted here from *Outside in the Teaching Machine*, Spivak addresses the role of the translator, both in the familiar literal capacity and in a trans-cultural capacity, and says 'the experience of contained alterity in an unknown language spoken in a different cultural milieu is uncanny.' Actively seeking agency in language by commanding an ethical yet intimate translation *and transculturalation*, Spivak aims to question the very status of multicultural inquiries which focus on polarized notions of naive (indigenous criticisms) and sophisticated (postcolonial critiques), and says 'poststructuralism has shown some of us a staging of the agent within a three-tiered notion of language (as rhetoric, logic, silence).' By specifically invoking race and gender through the figures of Michele Barrett, Alice Walker, Monique Wittig, Luce Irigary, Mahasweta Devi, and Toni

Morrison, and deliberately mediating between French, English and Bengali, Spivak constructs and deconstructs the boundaries between inside/outside, self/other, logic/ rhetoric, male/female, and text/context.
G.R.

The politics of translation

The idea for this title comes from the British sociologist Michèle Barrett's feeling that the politics of translation takes on a massive life of its own if you see language as the process of meaning-construction.[1]

In my view, language may be one of many elements that allow us to make sense of things, of ourselves. I am thinking, of course, of gestures, pauses, but also of chance, of the subindividual force-fields of being which click into place in different situations, swerve from the straight or true line of language-in-thought. Making sense of ourselves is what produces identity. If one feels that the production of identity as self-meaning, not just meaning, is as pluralized as a drop of water under a microscope, one is not always satisfied, outside of the ethicopolitical arena as such, with 'generating' thoughts on one's own. (Assuming identity as origin may be unsatisfactory in the ethicopolitical arena as well, but consideration of that now would take us too far afield.) I have argued elsewhere that one of the ways of resisting capitalist multiculturalism's invitation to self-identity and compete is to give the name of 'woman' to the unimaginable other. The same sort of impulse is at work here in a rather more tractable form. For one of the ways to get around the confines of one's 'identity' as one produces expository prose is to work at someone else's title, as one works with a language that belongs to many others. This, after all, is one of the seductions of translating. It is a simple miming of the responsibility to the trace of the other in the self.

Responding, therefore, to Barrett with that freeing sense of responsibility, I can agree that it is not bodies of meaning that are transferred in translation. And from the ground of that agreement I want to consider the role played by language for the *agent*, the person who acts, even though intention is not fully present to itself. The task of the feminist translator is to consider language as a clue to the workings of gendered agency. The writer is written by her language, of course. But the writing of the writer writes agency in a way that might be different from that of the British woman/citizen within the history of British feminism, focused on the task of freeing herself from Britain's imperial past, its often racist present, as well as its 'made in Britain' history of male domination.

Translation as reading

How does the translator attend to the specificity of the language she translates? There is a way in which the rhetorical nature of every language disrupts its logical systematicity. If we emphasize the logical at the expense of these rhetorical interferences, we remain safe. 'Safety' is the appropriate term here, because we are talking of risks, of violence to the translating medium.

I felt that I was taking those risks when I recently translated some eighteenth-century Bengali poetry. I quote a bit from my 'Translator's Preface':

> I must overcome what I was taught in school: the highest mark for the most accurate collection of synonyms, strung together in the most proximate syntax. I must resist both the solemnity of chaste Victorian poetic prose and the forced simplicity of 'plain English,' that have imposed themselves as the norm . . . Translation is the most intimate act of reading. I surrender to the text when I translate. These songs, sung day after day in family chorus before clear memory began, have a peculiar intimacy for me. Reading and surrendering take on new meanings in such a case. The translator earns permission to transgress from the trace of the other—before memory—in the closest places of the self.[2]

Yet language is not everything. It is only a vital clue to where the self loses its boundaries. The ways in which rhetoric or figuration disrupt logic themselves point at the possibility of random contingency, beside language, around language. Such a *dis*semination cannot be under our control. Yet in translation, where meaning hops into the spacy emptiness between two named historical languages, we get perilously close to it. By juggling the disruptive rhetoricity that breaks the surface in not necessarily connected ways, we feel the selvedges of the language-textile give way, fray into *frayages* or facilitations.[3] Although every act of reading or communication is a bit of this risky fraying which scrambles together somehow, our stake in agency keeps the fraying down to a minimum except in the communication and reading of and in love. (What is the place of 'love' in the ethical? As we saw, Irigaray has struggled with this question.) The task of the translator is to facilitate this love between the original and its shadow, a love that permits fraying, holds the agency of the translator and the demands of her imagined or actual audience at bay. The politics of translation from a non-European woman's text too often suppresses this possibility because the translator cannot engage with, or cares insufficiently for, the rhetoricity of the original.

The simple possibility that something might not be meaningful is contained by the rhetorical system as the always possible menace of a space outside language. This is most eerily staged (and challenged) in the effort to communicate with other possible intelligent beings in space. (Absolute alterity or otherness is thus differed-deferred into an other self who resembles us, however minimally, and with whom we can communicate.) But a more homely staging of it occurs across two earthly languages. The experience of contained alterity in an unknown language spoken in a different cultural milieu is uncanny.

Let us now think that, in that other language, rhetoric may be disrupting logic in the matter of the production of an agent, and indicating the founding violence of the silence at work within rhetoric. Logic allows us to jump from word to word by means of clearly indicated connections. Rhetoric must work in the silence between and around words in order to see what works and how much. The jagged relationship between rhetoric and logic, condition and effect of knowing, is a relationship by which a world is made for the agent, so that the agent can act in an ethical way, a political way, a day-to-day way; so that the agent can be alive, in a human way, in the world. Unless one can at least construct a model of this for the other language, there is no real translation.

Unfortunately it is only too easy to produce translations if this task is completely ignored. I myself see no choice between the quick and easy and slapdash way, and translating well and with difficulty. There is no reason why a responsible translation should take more time in the doing. The translator's preparation might take more time, and her love for the text might be a matter of a reading skill that takes patience. But the sheer material production of the text need not be slow.

Without a sense of the rhetoricity of language, a species of neocolonialist construction of the non-Western scene is afoot. No argument for convenience can be persuasive here. That is always the argument, it seems. This is where I travel from Barrett's enabling notion of the question of language in poststructuralism. Poststructuralism has shown some of us a staging of the agent within a three-tiered notion of language (as rhetoric, logic, silence). We must attempt to enter or direct that staging, as one directs a play, as an actor interprets a script. That takes a different kind of effort from taking translation to be a matter of synonym, syntax, and local color.

To be only critical, to defer action until the production of the utopian translator, is impractical. Yet, when I hear Derrida, quite justifiably, point out the difficulties between French and English, even when he agrees to speak in English—'I must speak in a language that is not my own because that will be more just'—I want to claim the right to the same dignified complaint for a woman's text in Arabic or Vietnamese.[4]

It is more just to give access to the largest number of feminists. Therefore these texts must be made to speak English. It is more just to speak the language of the majority when through hospitality a large number of feminists give the foreign feminist the risk to speak, in English. In the case of the third world foreigner, is the law of the majority that of decorum, the equitable law of democracy, or the 'law' of the strongest? We might focus on this confusion. There is nothing necessarily meretricious about the Western feminist gaze. (The 'naturalizing' of Jacques Lacan's sketching out of the psychic structure of the gaze in terms of group political behavior has always seemed to me a bit shaky.) On the other hand, there is nothing essentially noble about the law of the majority either. It is merely the easiest way of being 'democratic' with minorities. In the act of wholesale translation into English there can be a betrayal of the democratic ideal into the law of the strongest. This happens when all the literature of the Third World gets translated into a sort of with-it translatese, so that the literature by a woman in Palestine begins to resemble, in the feel of its prose, something by a man in Taiwan. The rhetoricity of Chinese and Arabic! The cultural politics of high-growth, capitalist Asia-Pacific, and devastated West Asia! Gender difference inscribed and inscribing in these differences!

For the student, this tedious translatese cannot compete with the spectacular stylistic experiments of a Monique Wittig or an Alice Walker.

466

Let us consider an example where attending to the author's stylistic experiments can produce a different text. Mahasweta Devi's 'Stanadāyini' is available in two versions.[5] Devi has expressed approval for the attention to her signature style in the version entitled 'Breast-Giver.' The alternative translation gives the title as 'The Wet-Nurse,' and thus neutralizes the author's irony in constructing an uncanny word; enough like 'wet-nurse' to make that sense, and enough unlike to shock. It is as if the translator should decide to translate Dylan Thomas's famous title and opening line as 'Do not go gently into that good night.' The theme of treating the breast as organ of labor-power-as-commodity and the breast as metonymic part-object standing in for other-as-object—the way in which the story plays with Marx and Freud on the occasion of the woman's body—is lost even before you enter the story. In the text Mahasweta uses proverbs that are startling even in the Bengali. The translator of 'The Wet-Nurse' leaves them out. She decides not to try to translate these hard bits of earthy wisdom, contrasting with class-specific access to modernity, also represented in the story. In fact, if the two translations are read side by side, the loss of the rhetorical silences of the original can be felt from one to the other.

First, then, the translator must surrender to the text. She must solicit the text to show the limits of its language, because that rhetorical aspect will point at the silence of the absolute fraying of language that the text wards off, in its special manner. Some think this is just an ethereal way of talking about literature or philosophy. But no amount of tough talk can get around the fact that translation is the most intimate act of reading. Unless the translator has earned the right to become the intimate reader, she cannot surrender to the text, cannot respond to the special call of the text.

The presupposition that women have a natural or narrative-historical solidarity, that there is something in a woman or an undifferentiated women's story that speaks to another woman without benefit of language-learning, might stand against the translator's task of surrender. Paradoxically, it is not possible for us as ethical agents to imagine otherness or alterity maximally. We have to turn the other into something like the self in order to be ethical. To surrender in translation is more erotic than ethical. In that situation the good-willing attitude 'she is just like me' is not very helpful. In so far as Michèle Barrett is not like Gayatri Spivak, their friendship is more effective as a translation. In order to earn that right of friendship or surrender of identity, of knowing that the rhetoric of the text indicates the limits of language for you as long as you are with the text, you have to be in a different relationship with the language, not even only with the specific text.

Learning about translation on the job, I came to think that it would be a practical help if one's relationship with the language being translated was such that sometimes one preferred to speak in it about intimate things. This is no more than a practical suggestion, not a theoretical requirement, useful especially because a woman writer who is wittingly or unwittingly a 'feminist'—and of course all woman writers are not 'feminist' even in this broad sense—will relate to the three-part staging of (agency in) language in ways defined out as 'private,' since they might question the more public linguistic maneuvers.

Let us consider an example of lack of intimacy with the medium. In Sudhir Kakar's *The Inner World*, a song about Kāli written by the late nineteenth-century monk Vivekananda is cited as part of the proof of the 'archaic narcissism' of the Indian [sic] male.[6] (Devi makes the same point with a light touch, with reference to Krisna and Siva, tying it to sexism rather than narcissism and without psychoanalytic patter.)

From Kakar's description, it would not be possible to glimpse that 'the disciple' who gives the account of the singular circumstances of Vivekananda's composition of the song was an Irishwoman who became a Ramakrishna nun, a white woman among male Indian monks and devotees.[7] In the account Kakar reads, the song is translated by this woman, whose training in intimacy with the original language is as painstaking as one can hope for. There is a strong identification between Indian and Irish nationalists at this period; and Nivedita, as she was called, also embraced what she understood to be the Indian philosophical way of life as explained by Vivekananda, itself a peculiar, resistant consequence of the culture of imperialism, as has been pointed out by many. For a psychoanalyst like Kakar, this historical, philosophical, and indeed sexual text of translation should be the textile to weave with. Instead, the English version, 'given' by the anonymous 'disciple,' serves as no more than the opaque exhibit providing evidence of the alien fact of narcissism. It is not the site of the exchange of language.

At the beginning of the passage quoted by Kakar, there is a reference to Ram Prasad (or Ram Proshad; 1718–85). Kakar provides a footnote: 'Eighteenth century singer and poet whose songs of longing for the Mother are very popular in Bengal.' I believe this footnote is also an indication of what I am calling the absence of intimacy.

Vivekananda is, among other things, an example of the peculiar reactive construction of a glorious 'India' under the provocation of imperialism. The rejection of 'patriotism' in favor of 'Kāli' reported in Kakar's passage is played out in this historical theater, as a choice of the cultural female sphere rather than the colonial male sphere.[8] It is undoubtedly 'true' that for such a figure, Ram Proshad Sen provides a kind of ideal self. Sen had retired with a pension from a clerk's job with a rural landowner, when the English were already in Bengal but had not claimed territory officially. He was himself given some land by one of the great rural landowners the year after the battle that inaugurated the territorial enterprise of the East India Company. He died eight years before the Permanent Settlement would introduce a violent epistemic rupture.[9] In other words, Vivekananda and Ram Proshad are two related moments of colonial discursivity translating the figure of Kāli. The dynamic intricacy of that discursive textile is mocked by the useless footnote.

It would be idle here to enter the debate about the 'identity' of Kāli or indeed other goddesses in Hindu 'polytheism.' But simply to contextualize, let me add that it is Ram Proshad about whose poetry I wrote the 'Translator's Preface' quoted earlier. He is by no means simply an archaic stage-prop in the disciple's account of Vivekananda's 'crisis.' Some more lines from my 'Preface': 'Ram Proshad played with his mother tongue, transvaluing the words that are heaviest with Sanskrit meaning. I have been unable to catch the utterly new but utterly gendered tone of affectionate banter'—not only, not even largely, 'longing'—'between the poet and Kāli.' Unless Nivedita mistranslated, it is the difference in tone between Ram Proshad's innovating playfulness and Vivekananda's high nationalist solemnity that, in spite of the turn from nationalism to the Mother, is historically significant. The politics of translation has shifted into the register of reactive nativism. And that change is expressed in the gendering of the poet's voice.

How do women in contemporary polytheism relate to this peculiar mother, certainly not the psychoanalytic bad mother whom Kakar derives from Max Weber's misreading, not even an organized punishing mother, but a child-mother who punishes with astringent violence and is also a moral and affective mother?[10] Ordinary women, not saintly women. Why take it for granted that the invocation of goddesses in a historically masculinist polytheist sphere is more feminist than Nietzsche or Derrida claiming woman as model? I think it is a Western and male-gendered suggestion that powerful women in the Sākta (Sakti or Kāli-worshipping) tradition *necessarily* take Kāli as a role model.

Mahasweta's Jashoda tells me more about the relationship between goddesses and strong ordinary women than the psychoanalyst. And here too the example of an intimate translation that goes respectfully 'wrong' can be offered. The French wife of a Bengali artist translated some of Ram Proshad Sen's songs in the twenties to accompany her husband's paintings based on the songs. Her translations are marred by the pervasive orientalism ready at hand. Compare two passages, both translating the 'same' Bengali. I have at least tried, if failed, to catch the unrelenting mockery of self and Kāli in the original:

Mind, why footloose from Mother?
Mind mine, think power, for freedom's dower, bind bower with love-rope
In time, mind, you minded not your blasted lot.
And Mother, daughter-like, bound up house-fence to dupe her dense and devoted
     fellow.
Oh you'll see at death how much Mum loves you
A couple minutes' tears, and lashings of water, cowdung-pure.

Here is the French, translated by me into an English comparable in tone and vocabulary:

Pourquoi as-tu, mon âme, délaissé les pieds de Ma?
O esprit, médite Shokti, tu obtiendras la délivrance.
Attache-les ces pieds saints avec la corde de la dévotion.
Au bon moment tu n'as rien vu, c'est bien là ton malheur.
Pour se jouer de son fidèle, Elle m'est apparue
Sous la forme de ma fille et m'a aidé à réparer ma clôture.
C'est à la mort que tu comprendras l'amour de Mâ.
Ici, on versera quelques larmes, puis on purifiera le lieu.

Why have you, my soul [*mon âme* is, admittedly, less heavy in
     French], left Ma's feet?
O mind, meditate upon Shokti, you will obtain deliverance.
Bind those holy feet with the rope of devotion.
In good time you saw nothing, that is indeed your sorrow.
To play with her faithful one, She appeared to me
In the form of my daughter and helped me to repair my enclosure.
It is at death that you will understand Ma's love.
Here, they will shed a few tears, then purify the place.

And here the Bengali:

মন কেন মার চরণ-ছাড়া ।

ও মন, ভাব শক্তি, পাবে মুক্তি, বাঁধ দিয়ে ভক্তি-দড়া ।।

সময় থাকতে, না দেখলে মন, কেমন তোমার কপালপোড়া ।

মা ভক্তে ছলিতে, তনয়া রূপেতে বাঁধেন আসি ঘরের বেড়া ।।

মায়ে যত ভালবাসে, বুঝা যাবে মৃত্যুশেষে,

মোলে দন্ড-দুচার কান্নাকাটি, শেষে দিবে গোবরছড়া ।

I hope these examples demonstrate that depth of commitment to correct cultural politics, felt in the details of personal life, is sometimes not enough. The history of the language, the history of the author's moment, the history of the language-in-and-as-translation, must figure in the weaving as well.

Mere reasonableness will allow rhetoricity to be appropriated, put in its place, situated, seen as only nice. Rhetoricity is put in its place that way because it disrupts. Women within male-dominated society, when they internalize sexism as normality, act out a scenario against feminism that is formally analogical to this. The relationship between logic and rhetoric, between grammar and rhetoric, is also a relationship between social logic, social reasonableness, and the disruptiveness of figuration in social practice. These are the first two parts of our three-part model. But then, rhetoric points at the possibility of randomness, of contingency as such, dissemination, the falling apart of language, the possibility that things might not always be semiotically organized. (My problem with Kristeva and the 'presemiotic' is that she seems to want to expand the empire of the meaningful by grasping at what language can only point at.) Cultures that might not have this specific three-part model will still have a dominant sphere in its traffic with language and contingency. Writers like Ifi Amadiume show us that, without thinking of this sphere as biologically determined, one still has to think in terms of spheres determined by definitions of secondary and primary sexual characteristics in such a way that the inhabitants of the other sphere are para-subjective, not fully subject.[11] The dominant groups' way of handling the three-part ontology of language has to be learned as well—if the subordinate ways of rusing with rhetoric are to be disclosed.

To decide whether you are prepared enough to start translating, then, it might help if you have graduated into speaking, by choice or preference, of intimate matters in the language of the original. I have worked my way back to my earlier point: I cannot see why the publishers' convenience or classroom convenience or time convenience for people who do not have the time to learn should organize the construction of the rest of the world for Western feminism. Five years ago, berated as unsisterly, I would think, 'Well, you know one ought to be a bit more giving etc.,' but then I asked myself again, 'What am I giving, or giving up? To whom am I giving by assuring that you don't have to work that hard, just come and get it? What am I trying to promote?' People would say, you who have succeeded should not pretend to be a marginal. But surely by demanding higher standards of translation, I am not marginalizing myself or the language of the original?

I have learned through translating Devi how this three-part structure works differently from English in my native language. And here another historical irony has become personally apparent to me. In the old days, it was most important for a colonial

470

or postcolonial student of English to be as 'indistinguishable' as possible from the native speaker of English. I think it is necessary for people in the third world translation trade now to accept that the wheel has come around, that the genuinely bilingual postcolonial now has a bit of an advantage. But she does not have a real advantage as a translator if she is not strictly bilingual, if she merely speaks her native language. Her own native space is, after all, also class-organized. And that organization still often carries the traces of access to imperialism, often relates inversely to access to the vernacular as a public language. So here the requirement for intimacy brings a recognition of the public sphere as well. If we were thinking of translating Marianne Moore or Emily Dickinson, the standard for the translator could not be 'anyone who can conduct a conversation in the language of the original (in this case English).' When applied to a third world language, the position is inherently ethnocentric. And then to present these translations to our unprepared students so that they can learn about women writing!

In my view, the translator from a third world language should be sufficiently in touch with what is going on in literary production in that language to be capable of distinguishing between good and bad writing by women, resistant and conformist writing by women.

She must be able to confront the idea that what seems resistant in the space of English may be reactionary in the space of the original language. Farida Akhter has argued that, in Bangladesh, the real work of the women's movement and of feminism is being undermined by talk of 'gendering,' mostly deployed by the women's development wings of transnational nongovernment organizations, in conjunction with some local academic feminist theorists.[12] One of her intuitions was that 'gendering' could not be translated into Bengali. 'Gendering' is an awkward new word in English as well. Akhter is profoundly involved in international feminism. And her base is third world. I could not translate 'gender' into the U.S. feminist context for her. This misfiring of translation, between a superlative reader of the social text such as Akhter, and a careful translator like myself, speaking as friends, has added to my sense of the task of the translator.

Good and bad is a flexible standard, like all standards. Here another lesson of post-structuralism helps: these decisions of standards are made anyway. It is the attempt to justify them adequately that polices. That is why disciplinary preparation in school requires that you write examinations to prove these standards. Publishing houses routinely engage in materalist confusion of those standards. The translator must be able to fight that metropolitan materalism with a special kind of specialist's knowledge, not mere philosophical convictions.

In other words, the person who is translating must have a tough sense of the specific terrain of the original, so that she can fight the racist assumption that all third world women's writing is good. I am often approached by women who would like to put Devi in with just Indian women writers. I am troubled by this, because 'Indian women' is not a feminist category. (Elsewhere I have argued that 'epistemes'—ways of constructing objects of knowledge—should not have national names either.) Sometimes Indian women writing means American women writing or British women writing, except for national *origin*. There is an ethno–cultural agenda, an obliteration of third world specificity as well as a denial of cultural citizenship, in calling them merely 'Indian.'

My initial point was that the task of the translator is to surrender herself to the linguistic rhetoricity of the original text. Although this point has larger political implications, we can say that the not unimportant minimal consequence of ignoring this task is the loss of 'the literarity and textuality and sensuality of the writing' (Barrett's words). I have worked my way to a second point, that the translator must be able to discriminate on the terrain of the original. Let us dwell on it a bit longer.

I choose Devi because she is unlike her scene. I have heard an English Shakespearean suggest that every bit of Shakespeare criticism coming from the subcontinent was by that virtue resistant. By such a judgment, we are also denied the right to be critical. It was of course bad to have put the place under subjugation, to have tried to make the place over with calculated restrictions. But that does not mean that everything that is coming out of that place after a negotiated independence nearly fifty years ago is necessarily right. The old anthropological supposition (and that is bad anthropology) that every person from a culture is nothing but a whole example of that culture is acted out in my colleague's suggestion. I remain interested in writers who are against the current, against the mainstream. I remain convinced that the interesting literary text might be precisely the text where you do not learn what the majority view of majority cultural representation or self-representation of a nation state might be. The translator has to make herself, in the case of third world women in writing, almost better equipped than the translator who is dealing with the Western European languages, because of the fact that there is so much of the old colonial attitude, slightly displaced, at work in the translation racket. Poststructuralism *can* radicalize the field of preparation so that simply boning up on the language is not enough; there is also that special relationship to the staging of language as the production of agency that one must attend to. But the agenda of poststructuralism is mostly elsewhere, and the resistance to theory among metropolitan feminists would lead us into yet another narrative.

The understanding of the task of the translator and the practice of the craft are related but different. Let me summarize how I work. At first I translate at speed. If I stop to think about what is happening to the English, if I assume an audience, if I take the intending subject as more than a springboard, I cannot jump in, I cannot surrender. My relationship with Devi is easygoing. I am able to say to her: I surrender to you in your writing, not to you as intending subject. There, in friendship, is another kind of surrender. Surrendering to the text in this way means, most of the time, being literal. When I have produced a version this way, I revise. I review not in terms of a possible audience, but by the protocols of the thing in front of me, in a sort of English. And I keep hoping that the student in the classroom will not be able to think that the text is just a purveyor of social realism if it is translated with an eye toward the dynamic staging of language mimed in the revision by the rules of the inbetween discourse produced by a literalist surrender.

Vain hope, perhaps, for the accountability is different. When I translated Jacques Derrida's *De la grammatologie*, I was reviewed in a major journal for the first and last time. In the case of my translations of Devi, I have almost no fear of being accurately judged by my readership here. It makes the task more dangerous and more risky. And that for me is the real difference between translating Derrida and translating Mahasweta Devi, not merely the rather more artificial difference between deconstructive philosophy and political fiction.

The opposite argument is not neatly true. There is a large number of people in the

472

third world who read the old imperial languages. People reading current feminist fiction in the European languages would probably read it in the appropriate imperial language. And the same goes for European philosophy. The act of translating into the third world language is often a political exercise of a different sort. I am looking forward, as of this writing, to lecturing in Bengali on deconstruction in front of a highly sophisticated audience, knowledgeable both in Bengali and in deconstruction (which they read in English and French and sometimes write about in Bengali), at Jadavpur University in Calcutta. It will be a kind of testing of the postcolonial translator, I think.[13]

Democracy changes into the law of force in the case of translation from the third world and women even more because of their peculiar relationship to whatever you call the public/private divide. A neatly reversible argument would be possible if the particular Third World country had cornered the Industrial Revolution first and embarked on monopoly imperialist territorial capitalism as one of its consequences, and thus been able to impose a language as international norm. Something like that idiotic joke: if the Second World War had gone differently, the United States would be speaking Japanese. Such egalitarian reversible judgments are appropriate to counterfactual fantasy. Translation remains dependent upon the language skill of the majority. A prominent Belgian translation theorist solves the problem by suggesting that, rather than talk about the third world, where a lot of passion is involved, one should speak about the European Renaissance, since a great deal of wholesale cross-cultural translation from Greco-Roman antiquity was undertaken then. What one overlooks is the sheer authority ascribed to the originals in that historical phenomenon. The status of a language in the world is what one must consider when teasing out the politics of translation. Translatese in Bengali can be derided and criticized by large groups of anglophone and anglograph Bengalis. It is only in the hegemonic languages that the benevolent do not take the limits of their own often uninstructed good will into account. That phenomenon becomes hardest to fight because the individuals involved in it are genuinely benevolent and you are identified as a trouble-maker. This becomes particularly difficult when the metropolitan feminist, who is sometimes the assimilated postcolonial, invokes, indeed translates, a too quickly shared feminist notion of accessibility.

If you want to make the translated text accessible, try doing it for the person who wrote it. The problem comes clear then, for she is not within the same history of style. What is it that you are making accessible? The accessible level is the level of abstraction where the individual is already formed, where one can speak individual rights. When you hang out and with a language away from your own (*Mitwegsein*) so that you want to use that language by preference, sometimes, when you discuss something complicated, then you are on the way to making a dimension of the text accessible to the reader, with a light and easy touch, to which she does not accede in her everday. If you are making anything else accessible, through a language quickly learned with an idea that you transfer content, then you are betraying the text and showing rather dubious politics.

How will women's solidarity be measured here? How will their common experience be reckoned if one cannot imagine the traffic in accessibility going both ways? I think that idea should be given a decent burial as ground of knowledge, together with the idea of humanist universality. It is good to think that women have something in common, when one is approaching women with whom a relationship would not

473

otherwise be possible. It is a great first step. But, if your interest is in learning if there *is* women's solidarity, how about stepping forth from this assumption, appropriate as a means to an end like local or global social work, and trying a second step? Rather than imagining that women automatically have something identifiable in common, why not say, humbly and practically, my first obligation in understanding solidarity is to learn her mother tongue. You will see immediately what the differences are. You will also feel the solidarity every day as you make the attempt to learn the language in which the other woman learned to recognize reality at her mother's knee. This is preparation for the intimacy of cultural translation. If you are going to bludgeon someone else by insisting on your version of solidarity, you have the obligation to try out this experiment and see how far your solidarity goes.

In other words, if you are interested in talking about the other, and/or in making a claim to be the other, it is crucial to learn other languages. This should be distinguished from the learned tradition of language acquisition for academic work. I am talking about the importance of language acquisition for the woman from a hegemonic monolinguist culture who makes everybody's life miserable by insisting on women's solidarity at her price. I am uncomfortable with notions of feminist solidarity which are celebrated when everybody involved is similarly produced. There are countless languages in which women all over the world have grown up and been female or feminist, and yet the languages we keep on learning by rote are the powerful European ones, sometimes the powerful Asian ones, least often the chief African ones. We are quite at home, and helpful, when large migant populations are doing badly in the dominant countries, our own. The 'other' languages are learned only by anthropologists who *must* produce knowledge across an epistemic divide. They are generally (though not invariably) not interested in the three-part structure we are discussing.

If we are discussing solidarity as a theoretical position, we must also remember that not all the world's women are literate. There are traditions and situations that remain obscure because we cannot share their linguistic constitution. It is from this angle that I have felt that learning languages might sharpen out own presuppositions about what it means to use the sign 'woman.' If we say that things should be accessible to us, who is this 'us'? What does that sign mean?

Although I have used the examples of women all along, the arguments apply across the board. It is just that women's rhetoricity may be doubly obscured. I do not see the advantage of being completely focused on a single issue, although one must establish practical priorities. In the book where this chapter was first anthologized, the editors were concerned with poststructuralism and its effect on feminist theory. Where some poststructuralist thinking can be applied to the constitution of the agent in terms of the literary operations of language, women's texts might be operating differently because of the social differentiation between the sexes. Of course the point applies generally to the colonial context as well. When Ngugi decided to write in Kikuyu, some thought he was bringing a private language into the public sphere. But what makes a language shared by many people in a community private? I was thinking about those so-called private languages when I was talking about language learning. But even within those private languages it is my conviction that there is a difference in the way in which the staging of language produces not only the sexed subject but the gendered agent, by a version of centering, persistently disrupted by rhetoricity, indicating contingency. Unless demonstrated otherwise, this for me remains the condition and effect of dominant and subordinate gendering. If that is so, then we have some reason to focus on women's texts. Let us use the word 'woman' to name that space of parasubjects defined as such by the social inscription of primary and secondary sexual characteristics. Then we can cautiously begin to track a sort of commonality in being set apart, within the different rhetorical strategies of different languages. But even here, historical superiorities of class must be kept in mind. Bharati Mukherjee, Anita Desai, and Gayatri Spivak do not have the same rhetorical figuration of agency as an illiterate domestic servant.

Tracking commonality through responsible translation can lead us into areas of difference and different differentiations. This may also be important because, in the heritage of imperialism, the female legal subject bears the mark of a failure of Europeanization, by contrast with the female anthropological or literary subject from the area. For example, the division between French and Islamic codes in modern Algeria is in terms of family, marriage, inheritance, legitimacy, and female social agency. These are differences that we must keep in mind. And we must honor the difference between ethnic minorities in the first world and majority populations of the third.

In conversation, Barrett had asked me if I now inclined more toward Foucault. This is indeed the case. In 'Can the Subaltern Speak?,' I took a rather strong critical line on Foucault's work, as part of a general critique of imperialism.[14] As I have indicated elsewhere, I do, however, find, his concept of *pouvoir-savoir* immensely useful. Foucault has contributed to French this ordinary-language doublet (the ability to know [as]) to take its place quietly beside *vouloir-dire* (the wish to say—meaning to mean).

On the most mundane level, *pouvoir-savoir* is the shared skill which allows us to make (common) sense of things. It is certainly not only power/knowledge in the sense of *puissance/connaissance*. Those are aggregative institutions. The common way in which one makes sense of things, on the other hand, loses itself in the sub-individual.

Looking at *pouvoir-savoir* in terms of women, one of my focuses has been new immigrants and the change of mother-tongue and *pouvoir-savoir* between mother and daughter. When the daughter talks reproductive rights and the mother talks protecting honor, is this the birth or death of translation?

Foucault is also interesting in his new notion of the ethics of the care for the self. In order to be able to get to the subject of ethics it may be necessary to look at the ways in which an individual in that culture is instructed to care for the self rather than the imperialism-specific secularist notion that the ethical subject is given as human. In a secularism which is structurally identical with Christianity laundered in the bleach of moral philosophy, the subject of ethics is faceless. Breaking out, Foucault was investigating other ways of making sense of how the subject becomes ethical. This is of interest because, given the connection between imperialism and secularism, there is almost no way of getting to alternative general voices except through religion. And if one does not look at religion as mechanisms of producing the ethical subject, one gets various kinds of 'fundamentalism.' Workers in cultural politics and its connections to a new ethical philosophy have to be interested in religion in the production of ethical subjects. There is much room for feminist work here because Western feminists have not so far been aware of religion as a cultural instrument rather than a mark of cultural difference. I am currently working on Hindu performative ethics with Professor B. K. Matilal. He is an enlightened male feminist. I am an active feminist. Helped by his learning and his openness I am learning to distinguish between ethical catalysts and ethical motors even as I learn to translate bits of the Sanskrit epic in a way different from all the accepted translations, because I rely not only on learning, not only on 'good English,' but on that three-part scheme of which I have so lengthily spoken. I hope the results will please readers. If we are going to look at an ethics that emerges from something other than the historically secularist ideal—at an ethics of sexual differences, at an ethics that can confront the emergence of fundamentalisms without apology or dismissal in the name of the Enlightenment—then *pouvoir-savoir* and the care for the self in Foucault can be illuminating. And these 'other ways' bring us back to translation, in the general sense.

Translation in general

I want now to add two sections to what was generated from the initial conversation with Barrett. I will dwell on the politics of translation in a general sense, by way of three examples of 'cultural translation' in English. I want to make the point that the lessons of translation in the narrow sense can reach much further.

First, J. M. Coetzee's *Foe*. This book represents the impropriety of the dominant's desire to give voice to the native. When Susan Barton, the eighteenth-century Englishwoman from *Roxana*, attempts to teach a muted Friday (from *Robinson Crusoe*) to read and write English, he draws an incomprehensible rebus on his slate and wipes it out, withholds it. You cannot translate from a position of monolinguist superiority. Coetzee as white creole translates *Robinson Crusoe* by representing Friday as the agent of a withholding.

Second, Toni Morrison's *Beloved*.[15] Let us look at the scene of the change of the mother-tongue from mother to daughter. Strictly speaking, it is not a change, but a loss, for the narrative is not of immigration but of slavery. Sethe, the central character of the novel, remembers: 'What Nan'—her mother's fellow-slave and friend—'told her she had forgotten, along with the language she told it in. The same language her ma'am spoke, and which would never come back. But the message—that was—and had been there all along' (*B*, 62). The representation of this message, as it passes through the forgetfulness of death to Sethe's ghostly daughter Beloved, is of a withholding: 'This is not a story to pass on' (*B*, 275).

Between mother and daughter, a certain historical withholding intervenes. If the situation between the new immigrant mother and daughter provokes the question as to whether it is the birth or death of translation, here the author represents with violence a certain birth-in-death, a death-in-birth of a story that is not to translate or pass on. Strictly speaking, therefore, an aporia. And yet it is passed on, with the mark of *un*translatability on it, in the bound book, *Beloved*, that we hold in our hands. Contrast this to the confidence in accessibility in the house of power, where history is waiting to be restored.

The scene of violence between mother and daughter (reported and passed on by the daughter Sethe to her daughter Denver, who carries the name of a white trash

476

girl, in partial acknowledgment of women's solidarity in birthing) is, then, the condition of (im)possibility of *Beloved*.

> She picked me up and carried me behind the smokehouse. Back there she opened up her dress front and lifted her breast and pointed under it. Right on her rib was a circle and a cross burnt right in the skin. She said, 'This is your ma'am. This,' and she pointed . . . 'Yes, Ma'am,' I said. . . . 'But how will you know me? . . . Mark me, too,' I said . . . 'Did she?' asked Denver. 'She slapped my face.' 'What for?' 'I didn't understand it then. Not till I had a mark of my own' (*B*, 61).

This scene, of claiming the brand of the owner as 'my own,' to create, in this broken chain of marks owned by separate white male agents of property, an unbroken chain of rememory in (enslaved) daughters as agents of a history not to be passed on, is of necessity different from Friday's scene of withheld writing from the white woman wanting to create history by giving her 'own' language. And the lesson is the (im)possibility of translation in the general sense. Rhetoric points at absolute contingency, not the sequentiality of time, not even the cycle of seasons, but only 'weather.' 'By and by all trace is gone, and what is forgotten is not only the footprints but the water and what it is down there. The rest is weather. Not the breath of the disremembered and unaccounted for'—after the effacement of the trace, no project for restoring (women's?) history—'but wind in the eaves, or spring ice thawing too quickly. Just weather' (275).

With this invocation of contingency, where nature may be 'the great body without organs of woman,' we can align ourselves with Wilson Harris, the author of *The Guyana Quartet*, for whom trees are 'the lungs of the globe.'[16] Harris hails the (re)birth of the native imagination as not merely the trans-lation but the trans-substantiation of the species. What in more workaday language I have called the obligation of the translator to be able to juggle the rhetorical silences in the two languages, Harris puts this way, pointing at the need for translating the Carib's English:

> The Caribbean bone flute, made of human bone, is a seed in the soul of the Caribbean. It is a primitive technology that we can turn around [trans-version?]. Consuming our biases and prejudices in ourselves we can let the bone flute help us open ourselves rather than read it the other way—as a metonymic devouring of a bit of flesh.[17] The link of music with cannibalism is a sublime paradox. When the music of the bone flute opens the doors, absences flow in, and the native imagination puts together the ingredients for quantum immediacy out of unpredictable resources.

The bone flute has been neglected by Caribbean writers, says Wilson Harris, because progressive realism is a charismatic way of writing prize-winning fiction. Progressive realism measures the bone. Progressive realism is the too-easy accessibility of translation as transfer of substance.

The progressive realism of the West dismissed the native imagination as the place of the fetish. Hegel was perhaps the greatest systematizer of this dismissal. And psychoanalytic cultural criticism in its present charismatic incarnation sometimes measures the bone with uncanny precision. It is perhaps not fortuitous that the passage below gives us an account of Hegel that is the exact opposite of Harris's vision. The paradox of the sublime and the bone here lead to non-language seen as inertia,

477

where the structure of the passage is mere logic. The authority of the supreme language makes translation impossible:

> The Sublime is therefore the paradox of an object which, in the very field of representation, provides a view, in a negative way, of the dimension of what is unrepresentable . . . The bone, the skull, is thus an object which, by means of its *presence*, fills out the void, the impossibility of the signifying *representation* of the subject . . . The proposition 'Wealth is the Self' repeats at this level the proposition 'The Spirit is a bone' [both propositions are Hegel's]: in both cases we are dealing with a proposition which is at first sight absurd, nonsensical, with an equation the terms of which are incompatible; in both cases we encounter the same logical structure of passage: the subject, totally lost in the medium of language (language of gesture and grimaces; language of flattery), finds its objective counterpart in the inertia of a non-language object (skull, money).[18]

Wilson Harris's vision is abstract, translating Morrison's 'weather' into an oceanic version of quantum physics. But all three cultural translators cited in this section ask us to attend to the rhetoric which points to the limits of translation, in the creole's, the slave-daughter's, the Carib's use of 'English.' Let us learn the lesson of translation from these brilliant inside/outsiders and translate it into the situation of other languages.

Reading as translation

In conclusion, I want to show how the postcolonial as the outside/insider translates white theory as she reads, so that she can discriminate on the terrain of the original. She wants to use what is useful. Again, I hope this can pass on a lesson to the translator in the narrow sense.

'The link of music with cannibalism is a sublime paradox.' I believe Wilson Harris is using 'sublime' here with some degree of precision, indicating the undoing of the progressive Western subject as realist interpreter of history. Can a theoretical account of the aesthetic sublime in English discourse, ostensibly far from the bone flute, be of use? By way of answer, I will use my reading of Peter de Bolla's superb scholarly account of *The Discourse of the Sublime* as an example of sympathetic reading as translation, precisely not a surrender but a friendly learning by taking a distance.[19]

P. 4: 'What was it to be a subject in the eighteenth century?' The reader-as-translator (RAT) is excited. The long eighteenth century in Britain is the account of the constitution and transformation of nation into empire. Shall we read that story? The book will at least touch on that issue, if only to swerve. And women will not be seen as touched in their agency formation by that change. The book's strong feminist sympathies relate to the Englishwoman only as gender victim. But the erudition of the text allows us to think that this sort of rhetorical reading might be the method to open up the question 'What is it to be a postcolonial reader of English in the twentieth century?' The representative reader of *The Discourse of the Sublime* will be postcolonial. Has that law of the majority been observed, or the law of the strong? On p. 72 RAT comes to a discussion of Burke on the sublime:

> The internal resistance of Burke's text . . . restricts the full play of this trope [power . . . as a trope articulating the technologies of the sublime], thereby defeating a description of the sublime experience uniquely in terms of the enpowered [sic] subject. Put briefly, Burke, for a number of reasons, among which we must include political aims and ends, stops short of a discourse on the sublime, and in so doing he reinstates the ultimate power of an adjacent discourse, theology, which locates its own self-authenticating power grimly within the boundaries of god-head.

Was it also because Burke was deeply implicated in searching out the recesses of the mental theater of the English master in the colonies that he had some notion of different kinds of subject and therefore, like some Kurtz before Conrad, recoiled in horror before the sublimely empowered subject? Was it because, like some Kristeva before *Chinese Women*, Burke had tried to imagine the Begums of Oudh as legal subjects that he had put self-authentication elsewhere?[20] *The Discourse of the Sublime*, in noticing Burke's difference from the other discourses on the sublime, opens doors for other RATs to engage in such scholarly speculations and thus exceed and expand the book.

Pp. 106, 111–12, 131: RAT comes to the English National Debt. British colonialism was a violent deconstruction of the hyphen between nation and state. In imperialism the nation was subl(im)ated into empire. Of this, no clue in *The Discourse*. The Bank of England is discussed. Its founding in 1696, and the transformation of letters of credit to the ancestor of the modern cheque, had something like a relationship with the fortunes of the East India Company and the founding of Calcutta in 1690. The *national* debt is in fact the site of a crisis-management, where the nation, sublime object as miraculating subject of ideology, changes the sign 'debtor' into a catachresis or false metaphor by way of 'an acceptance of a permanent discrepancy between the total circulating specie and the debt.' The French War, certainly the immediate efficient cause, is soon woven into the vaster textile of crisis. *The Discourse* cannot see the nation covering for the colonial economy. As on the occasion of the race-specificity of gendering, so on the discourse of multinational capital, the argument is kept domestic, within England, European.[21] RAT snuffles off, disgruntled. She finds a kind of comfort in Mahasweta's livid figuration of the woman's body as body rather than attend to this history of the English body 'as a disfigurative device in order to return to [it] its lost literality.' Reading as translation has misfired here.

On p. 140 RAT comes to the elder Pitt. 'Although his functionality is initially seen as demanded . . . by the incorporation of nation,' it is not possible not at least to mention empire when speaking of Pitt's voice:

> the voice of Pitt . . . works its doubled intervention into the spirit and character of the times; at once the supreme example of the private individual in the service of the state, and the private individual eradicated by the needs of a public, nationalist, commercial empire. In this sense the voice of Pitt becomes the most extreme example of the textualization of the body for the rest of the century.[22]

479

We have seen a literal case of the textualization of the surface of the body between slave mother and slave daughter in *Beloved*, where mother hits daughter to stop her thinking that the signs of that text can be passed on, a lesson learned *après-coup*, literally after the blow of the daughter's own branding. Should RAT expect an account of the passing on of the textualization of the interior of the body through the voice, a metonym for consciousness, from master father to master son? The younger Pitt took the first step to change the nationalist empire to the imperial nation with the India Act of 1784. *Can The Discourse of the Sublime* plot that sublime relay? Not yet. But here, too, an exceeding and expanding translation is possible.

Predictably, RAT finds a foothold in the rhetoricity of *The Discourse*. Chapter Ten begins: 'The second part of this study has steadily examined how "theory" sets out to legislate and control a practice, how it produces the excess which it cannot legislate, and removes from the center to the boundary its limit, limiting case' (230). This passage reads to a deconstructive RAT as an enabling self-description of the text, although within the limits of the book, it describes, not itself, but the object of its investigation. By the time the end of the book is reached, RAT feels that she has been written into the text:

> As a history of that refusal and resistance [this book] presents a record of its own coming into being as history, the history of the thought it wants to think differently, over there. It is, therefore, only appropriate that its conclusion should gesture towards the limit, risk the reinversion of the boundary by speaking from the other, refusing silence to what is unsaid.[23]

Beyond this 'clamor for a kiss' of the other space, it is 'just weather.'

Under the figure of RAT (reader-as-translator), I have tried to limn the politics of a certain kind of clandestine postcolonial reading, using the master marks to put together a history. Thus we find out what books we can forage, and what we must set aside. I can use Peter de Bolla's *The Discourse on the Sublime* to open up dull histories of the colonial eighteenth century. Was Toni Morrison, a writer well-versed in contemporary literary theory, obliged to set aside Paul de Man's 'The Purloined Ribbon'?[24]

> Eighteen seventy-four and white folks were still on the loose . . . Human blood cooked in a lynch fire was a whole other thing . . . But none of that had worn out his marrow . . . It was the ribbon . . . He thought it was a cardinal feather stuck to his boat. He tugged and what came loose in his hand was a red ribbon knotted around a curl of wet woolly hair, clinging still to its bit of scalp . . . He kept the ribbon; the skin smell nagged him (*B*, 180–1).

Morrison next invokes a language whose selvedge is so frayed that no *frayage* can facilitate full passage: 'This time, although he couldn't cipher but one word, he believed he knew who spoke them. The people of the broken necks, of fire-cooked blood and black girls who had lost their ribbons' (*B*, 181). Did the explanation of promises and excuses in eighteenth-century Geneva not make it across into this 'roar'? I will not check it out and measure the bone flute. I will simply dedicate these pages to the author of *Beloved*, in the name of translation.

NOTES

1. The first part of this essay is based on a conversation with Michèle Barrett in the summer of 1990.
2. Forthcoming from Seagull Press, Calcutta.
3. 'Facilitation' is the English translation of the Freudian term *Bahnung* (pathing) which is translated *frayage* in French. The dictionary meaning is:

   Term used by Freud at a time when he was putting forward a neurological model of the functioning of the psychical apparatus (1895): the excitation, in passing from one neurone to another, runs into a certain resistance; where its passage results in a permanent reduction in this resistance, there is said to be facilitation; excitation will opt for a facilitated pathway in preference to one where no facilitation has occurred (J. B. Pontalis, *The Language of Psychoanalysis* [London: Hogarth Press, 1973], p. 157).

4. Jacques Derrida, 'The Force of Law,' p. 923.
5. 'The Wet-Nurse,' in Kali for Women, eds., *Truth Tales: Stories by Indian Women* (London: The Women's Press, 1987), pp. 1–50 (first published by Kali for Women, Delhi, 1986), and 'Breast-Giver,' in Spivak, *In Other Worlds*, pp. 222–40.
6. Sudhir Kakar, *The Inner World: A Psycho-Analytic Study of Childhood and Society in India*, 2nd ed. (Delhi: Oxford University Press, 1981), p. 171ff. Part of this discussion in a slightly different form is included in my 'Psychoanalysis in Left Field; and Fieldworking' (London: Routledge, forthcoming).
7. For a feminist attempt at understanding such figures, see Kumari Jayawardena, *The White Woman's Other Burden* (forthcoming).
8. See Partha Chatterjee, 'Nationalism and the Woman Question,' in *ReCasting Women*, ed. Kumkum Sangari and Sudesh Vaid (New Brunswick: Rutgers University Press, 1990), pp. 233–53, for a detailed discussion of this gendering in Indian nationalism.
9. I mention these details because Ram Proshad's dates and his rural situation make his pattern of recognition of the outsider on the landscape significantly different from that of the colonially educated, urban, ex-Communist, deeply nationalist/internationalist Vivekananda. Indeed, the latter's mediation into a text such as Ram Proshad's through the rural-origin urban-bound visionary Rama Krishna, his *guru*, makes his use precisely a 'citation,' in the most robust sense—'translation' into a displaced discursive formation. The first version of this essay was written at speed in Cambridge and reproduces a 'life-history' of Ram Proshad firmly entrenched in the Bengali imaginary. I have corrected the details in this version.
10. Max Weber, *The Religion of India: The Sociology of Hinduism and Buddhism*, trans. Hans. H. Gerth and Don Martindale (Glencoe, Ill.: Free Press, 1958).
11. Ifi Amadiume, *Male Daughters Female Husbands* (London: Zed Books, 1987).
12. For background on Akhter, already somewhat dated for this interventionist in the history of the present, see Yayori Matsui, ed., *Women's Asia* (London: Zed Books, 1989), chap. 1. See also her *Depopulating Bangladesh: Essays on the Politics of Fertility* (Dhaka: Narigrantha, 1992).
13. I have given an account of this in Spivak, 'Acting Bits/Identity Talk,' *Critical Inquiry* 18:4 (Summer 1992).
14. Spivak, 'Can the Subaltern Speak?,' in *Marxism and the Interpretation of Culture*, ed. Larry Grossberg and Cary Nelson (Urbana: University of Illinois Press, 1988), pp. 271–313.
15. Toni Morrison, *Beloved* (New York: Plume Books, 1987). Hereafter cited in text as *B* with page numbers included.
16. Wilson Harris, *The Guyana Quartet* (London: Faber, 1975). These quotations are from Wilson Harris, 'Cross-Cultural Crisis: Imagery, Language, and the Intuitive Imagination,' Commonwealth Lectures: University of Cambridge, Lecture no. 2 (October 31, 1990).
17. Derrida traces the trajectory of the Hegelian and pre-Hegelian discourse of the fetish in *Glas*. The worshipper of the fetish eats human flesh. The worshipper of God feasts on the Eucharist. Harris transverses the fetish here through the native imagination.
18. Slavoj Žižek, *The Sublime Object of Ideology*, trans. Jon Barnes (London: Verso, 1989), pp. 203, 208, 212.
19. Peter de Bolla, *The Discourse of the Sublime: Readings in History, Aesthetics, and the Subject* (Oxford: Blackwell, 1989). Page numbers are given in my text.
20. References and discussion of 'The Begums of Oudh,' and 'The Impeachment of Warren Hastings' are to be found in *The Writings and Speeches of Edmund Burke*, ed. P. J. Marshall (Oxford: Clarendon Press, 1981), vol. 5, *India, Madras and Bengal*, pp. 410–12, 465–6, 470; and in vol. 6, *India: Launching*

of the Hastings Impeachment, respectively.

21. See my 'Reading the Archives: The Rani of Sirmur,' in Francis Barker, ed., *Europe and Its Others* (Colchester: University of Essex, 1985), vol. 1, pp. 128–51.

22. De Bolla, *Discourse*, p. 182.

23. De Bolla, *Discourse*, p. 324.

24. Paul de Man, 'The Purloined Ribbon,' reprinted as 'Excuses (*Confessions*),' in de Man, *Allegories of Reading* (New Haven: Yale University Press, 1979), pp. 278–301.

7 Gender studies

Introduction

A major activity of all cultures is the distribution and definition of gender roles, that is, the processes of categorization by which biological bodies are inserted into a culture's signifying systems and assigned values and social roles. Gender studies looks at these processes of categorization and at the ways in which societies construct, articulate and police sexuality. Late nineteenth-century and early twentieth-century psychologists, anthropologists and sociologists pioneered studies of how gender identity and sexual object choice are acquired and given normative status.

The examination of gender emerged as a major feature of cultural studies via the women's liberation movements and the development of women's studies. These activist and academic movements in their turn were inspired by the Civil Rights movement and overlapped with the development of black studies (see sections on Cultural Studies in America and Race Studies). The institutionalization of women's studies has developed more rapidly in America than in Britain, where funding for new programmes is always more problematic. In both countries, however, there are common approaches: women's studies has always been interdisciplinary and implicitly or explicitly culturalist in its assumption that women's gender roles are culturally rather than biologically formed. And in both countries, the field draws on a variety of disciplines, such as history, psychology, anthropology, linguistics, biology to explore the social status of women and their works. There are also common goals: women's studies aims at 'consciousness raising' to query and dispel cultural paradigms which ensure that, whatever her legal and political rights, the construct 'woman' remains locked inside gender definitions and role models instituted by a patriarchal social and political system.

Patriarchy, as defined by Heidi Hartman, is 'a set of social relations between men, which have a material base, and which, though hierarchical, establish or create interdependence and solidarity among men that enable them to dominate women' ('The Unhappy Marriage of Marxism and Feminism: towards a more progressive Union',

Capital and Class, 8, 1979). While most feminist scholars would agree with that definition, there is considerable variation in the extent to which their work is engaged in a project to alter all social relations in hierarchy or rather is concerned with demanding a place for women inside the ranks of a hierarchy hitherto closed to them. There is also an increasing awareness of the differences that ethnicity and race bring to the formation and experience of gender identity and roles, topics explored, for instance, in the recent book, *Nationalisms and Sexualities* (1992). White academic feminists have often been criticized for an implicit assumption that their (white, middle-class) experience is universal. Barbara Christian, for instance, like many feminists of colour, has argued that white feminist theories frequently fail 'to take into account the complexity of life—that women are of many races and ethnic backgrounds with different histories and cultures' ('Race for Theory', *Cultural Critique*, 6, 1987). As Gloria Anzaldua and Paula Gunn Allen maintain (see section on Race Studies) race is seen as fundamentally re-configuring sexualities and social identities. In 'Dyes and Dolls: Multicultural Barbie and the Merchandizing of Difference', Ann duCille directly confronts issues of race and sexuality in relation to the culture of consumerism.

Gender studies is often implicitly coded as feminist. It is, however, concerned with the cultural significance of all formations in gender and sexuality. Few scholars would deny, for instance, that it is important to explore, as Kaja Silverman, Richard Dyer, and Michael Moon, among others have done, the characteristics, images and stereotypes of masculinity. Also gay and lesbian studies are beginning to make headway into academic institutions in England and America, for instance in pioneering programmes at the University of Sussex and the City University of New York. Like women's studies, these studies have entered academe via social/political movements, such as gay liberation, and have followed similar epistemological trajectories to those of women's studies. As explored in Simon Watney's essay, however, there are also marked divergences of concern and theoretical approach.

An important initial activity in both women's studies and gay and lesbian studies has been to reinstate the works and figures ignored in the traditional, heterosexual and male-dominated literary and artistic canons and historical accounts. Anthologies of women's and gays' and lesbians' writing, as well as single editions of the 'lost' works, such as Kate Chopin's *The Awakening*, or Radclyffe Hall's *The Well of Loneliness*, have been republished and re-examined, fundamentally altering the literary 'canon'. Generally, the work of scholars in a wide range of fields, including history, science, politics and philosophy, has helped to reveal the gender assumptions and sexual prejudices at work in orthodox delineations of Western culture.

In both feminist and gay and lesbian studies, however, the interpretation of the newly revealed past and enlarged present is in debate. For some the past may reveal a history of acceptance in certain periods and cultures—such as pederasty in Classical Athens—a grim history of discrimination, or, as in the feminist historical studies of Joan Kelly and Natalie Zemon Davis, arenas of (specific and limited) possibility. Some feminist literary scholars, such as Sandra Gilbert and Susan Gubar and Elaine Showalter find a rich legacy in the past of self-conscious, 'feminist' traditions of activity and creativity. But problems arise in setting up alternative traditions and canons which merely replicate the dominant habits of categorization. There are also problems in reading back into the past gender formations and the labels currently attached to sexual orientation.

Terms such as heterosexual, homosexual and lesbian, for instance, were coined by nineteenth-century studies of sexual pathologies. It can be argued that these terms represent a sex-gender, normal-deviant taxonomy which is itself the product of recent cultural imperatives replacing categories of sexual acts with definitions of sexual personalities. Jonathan Dollimore, for instance, argues that the 'crucial move was to see deviancy itself as a social construction and a process of ascription'. The gay liberation movement shifted the discourse of sexuality from demands/pleas for tolerance towards the project of interrogating the *political* nature of sexual-object-choice discrimination and ascription and, in the process, reopened the issue of gender definition. The premise, 'the personal is the political' animated much early feminist lesbian theorizing and in her influential essay, 'One is Not Born a Woman', (*Feminist Issues*, Winter 1981), Monique Wittig argued that lesbians are not women since 'the refusal to become heterosexual always meant to refuse to become a man or a woman, consciously or not. For a lesbian this goes further than the refusal of the *role* "woman". It is the refusal of the economic, ideological, and political power of a man.' This privileging of lesbian subjectivity as inherently more politically subversive than any other form of feminism, has tended to be replaced or, at least, modified by arguments such as Teresa de Lauretis' point that lesbianism is not 'a truer or essential or unifying identity, but precisely the critical vantage point' ('Eccentric Subjects: Feminist Theory and Historical Consciousness', *Feminist Studies*, 16 (1), 1990), by Ann Ferguson's critique of reifications of lesbianism as transcultural and transhistorical ('Is There a Lesbian Culture?' in *Lesbian Philosophies and Cultures*, 1990), by Diana Fuss' careful deconstruction of the essentialist/constructionist representation of female identity (*Essentially Speaking*, 1989), and by constructions such as Gloria Anzaldua's 'mestiza consciousness', which is profoundly alert to the multiplicity of cultural, racial and sexual existences (see section on Race Studies).

Increasingly the term 'Queer', itself open to controversy and debate, has been reappropriated, initially by the American movement Queer Nation, and as a term for a new field of academic work, 'queer theory'. In a recent article, Simon Watney describes the 'up-side' of 'queer' as its 'ability to articulate the complex, shifting contemporary alignments of class, race, gender, age and sexuality in the lives of individuals who frequently face multiple oppressions' ('Queer Epistemology: activism, "outing," and the politics of sexual identities', *Critical Quarterly*, 36, 1994). Eve Kosofsky Sedgwick in a recent interview also stresses the multiplicity of sexualities embraced by the term 'queer'—'it refers to people who have oblique or boundary-crossing or dissident relations to sex and gender' (*Times Higher Education Supplement*, 29 April 1994). In her essay Kosofsky Sedgwick argues for the greater significance for our culture of a homo/heterosexual dichotomy over a male/female split. In the process, she also reviews the debate between '"social constructionist" and "essentialist" understandings of homo/heterosexual identity' (also the subject of a special edition of *Differences*, Summer 1989).

Discussions over 'nature' and 'nurture'—the biologically essential or culturally constructed formation of gender and sexual orientation—are central to most studies

487

of gender. There is often a desire to assert the intrinsic difference between the experiences of a woman and man, or between heterosexual and homosexual desire and pleasure. These experiential differences have social, political and legal connotations and consequences, and debate centres on how far these experiences, desires and pleasures are intrinsic to specific biologies and/or psychologies or are themselves social products. There is much common ground between the 'essentialist' and 'constructionist' positions. At its most obvious, all grant that only women can give birth, but how childbirth is experienced and valued, how far that experience is shared with men or regarded as a uniquely female domain associated with nature and domesticity may vary considerably from culture to culture and from class and ethnic group to group. This differentiation fuels debate.

Two disciplines, anthropology and psychology, have been especially significant in generating materials relevant to the 'nature/culture' debate. From Bronislaw Malinowski's study of matriliny among the Trobriand Islanders to Margaret Mead's investigation of sexual customs in Samoa to Lévi-Strauss's work on taboos, a wide variety of behaviours associated with gender and range of socially acceptable sexual practices has been revealed. Two essays in this section take up the debate on the interpretation of anthropological and historical data on the character and distribution of gender roles. Sherry B. Ortner, drawing on ethnographic descriptions of cultural practices, argues for transcultural similarities, identified as a split between nature and culture, the former allied to the female and the latter allied to the male. Her thesis, which has been both influential and controversial, is contested in Penelope Brown's and Ludmilla Jordanova's argument that both 'nature' and 'culture' are themselves historically and culturally specific terms. That *our* culture, however, tends to mark a gender distinction in terms of an equation of nature = female and culture = male has been recently discussed by Marina Warner in her BBC Reith Lecture, 'Monstrous Mothers' (1994). In *Jurassic Park*, she argues, the park's collection of all-female dinosaurs defy masculine scientific control by spontaneously reproducing themselves, replaying a conflict between nature as female, culture as male in terms of a fear of uncontrollable female fertility. Nature and culture, as socially and politically loaded concepts placed in a bi-polar opposition and constantly capable of appropriating to themselves whatever are the current 'moral panics' over gender, remain important topics of theoretical and empirical investigation. Anthropology continues to offer both methods and materials for examinations of the diversity and structural significance of gender ascriptions. A distinct school of feminist anthropologists, such as Gayle Rubin, Rayna Rapp Reiter, and Henrietta Moore has emerged to challenge a previously largely male-dominated field and re-examine its taxonomies.

Psychoanalytic studies of the stages by which the human child acquires a sense of gender and sexual orientation have also provided materials for theorizing the relationship between biology, mind and culture. Sigmund Freud's studies in sexuality, such as *Three Essays on the Theory of Sexuality* (1905) and 'Some Psychical Consequences of the Anatomical Distinction Between the Sexes' (1925), assume a connection between genital identity and the acquisition of gender identity, and privilege the psychosexual experience of the male-child, seen as endowing men with stronger ego boundaries than women. These theories may now be seen themselves as rationalizations of culturally specific gender identities and roles rather than as concrete universals. Feminist psychologists have offered alternatives to Freud's theories of gender formation which are also alternatives to the value systems built up around traditional concepts of gender. As Carol Gilligan puts it, 'I reframe women's psychological development as centering on a struggle for connection rather than speaking about women in the way that psychologists have spoken about women—as having a problem in achieving separation' (*In a Different Voice*, xv).

Freudian theories on gender and sexuality have also been critiqued by Jacques Lacan and the continental school of feminists (see section on the Impact of European Theory). Jane Gallop's *The Daughter's Seduction* (1982), Alice Jardine's *Gynesis* (1985), and Toril Moi's *Sexual/Textual Politics* (1985) continue to disseminate the work of Lacan and the continental feminists in England and America. Lacan's modifications replaced Freud's fixed and unified sexual identity with more fluid and unstable formations and also, by relating subject and sexual identity to language acquisition, shifted 'sex' as a category from biology to culture. There is continued interest in moves to deconstruct the strict boundaries of binary thinking which, it is argued, reproduce subordination, marginalization and discrimination. The 'order of desire' according to Gilles Deleuze and Felix Gauttari in *Anti-Oedipus: Capitalism and Schizophrenia* (1972), need not be restricted (repressed) to 'two sexes, but *n* sexes' (see the introduction to The Impact of European Theory). Jessica Benjamin has argued for the need to find 'alternatives to phallic structures, to the symbolic mode' ('A Desire of One's Own: Psychoanalytic Feminism and Intersubjective Space', *Feminist Studies: Critical Studies*, 1986), and the recent work of Marjorie Garber, *Vested Interests: Cross-Dressing and Cultural Anxiety* (1992), offers a transcultural study of transvestitism as a 'third' position which disrupts the patterns of conventional binary thinking. Freudian and post-Freudian concepts of gender and sexuality permeate studies of how gender and sexuality function in the construction of national, cultural and subjective identities.

Marxism has provided another route for the investigation of social inequalities in gender roles and offers a theoretic for investigating the ways in which gender identity and roles and valuations of sexual object choice relate to political and social power. Classical Marxism is, however, primarily concerned with economic relations between classes. Since, neither women nor men, gays nor lesbians, form class entities, socialist scholars working in the area of gender have felt the need to modify or contest those aspects of Marxism which tend to subsume all struggles into the larger class struggle (see Heidi Hartman's essay cited above).

Cultural studies—perhaps in Britain, at least, because of its theoretical bias towards Marxist constructions—was not initially deeply concerned with issues of gender. Stuart Hall has recently drawn attention to the disruptive, but educative significance of the publication *Women Take Issue* (1976) which articulated feminist dissatisfaction with the implicitly masculinist bias of the Birmingham Centre—'As a thief in the night, it broke in; interrupted, made an unseemly noise, seized the time, crapped on the table of cultural studies' ('Cultural Studies and its Theoretical Legacies', in *Cultural Studies*, 1992). At least since then, however, the study of culture has hardly seemed possible without including the study of how cultures produce and reproduce concepts of gender and difference, how they ascribe, tolerate, and police sexualities and how issues of gender and difference interact with other systems

of identity and discrimination, such as class, religion, ethnicity, race, nationality. Overall studies of gender are highly eclectic and demonstrate the convergence of disciplines, methods and theories to investigate social representation and the construction of subjective identity which is the hallmark of cultural studies. Many of the essays in the other sections of this *Reader* address the issues of gender formation and sexual discrimination as they affect political life (see the section on the nineteenth century), the media and race (see sections on media and race studies).
J.M. and G.R.

REFERENCES AND FURTHER READING

Abelove, Henry, Michele Aina Barale, and David Halperin, eds, *The Lesbian and Gay Studies Reader*, London and New York: Routledge, 1993.

Boone, Joseph A., *Engendering Men: The Question of Male Feminist Criticism*, London and New York: Routledge, 1990.

Butler, Judith, *Gender Trouble: Feminism and the Subversion of Identity*, London and New York: Routledge, 1990.

Caughie, John, and Annette Kuhn, eds, *The Sexual Subject: A Screen Reader in Sexuality*, London and New York: Routledge, 1992.

Chodorow, Nancy, *The Reproduction of Mothering: Psychoanalysis and the Sociology of Gender*, Berkeley and Los Angeles: University of California Press, 1978.

de Beauvoir, Simone, *The Second Sex*, trans. H. M. Parshley, New York: Knopf, 1953.

Duberman, Martin, Martha Vicinus, and George Chauncey Jr., eds., *Hidden From History: Reclaiming the Gay and Lesbian Past*, New York and London: Meridian, 1989.

Fuss, Diana, ed., *Inside/Out: Lesbian Theories, Gay Theories*, London and New York: Routledge, 1991.

Gilligan, Carol, *In a Different Voice: Psychological Theory and Women's Development*, Cambridge, Mass.: Harvard University Press, first edn 1982, reprt 1993.

Kelly, Joan, *Women, History and Theory: The Essays of Joan Kelly*, Chicago and London: University of Chicago Press, 1984.

Lovell, Terry, ed., *British Feminist Thought: A Reader*, Oxford: Basil Blackwell, 1990.

Pateman, Carole, *The Sexual Contract*, Oxford: Polity Press in association with Basil Blackwell, 1988.

Rayna Rapp Reiter, *Toward an Anthropology of Women*, New York: Monthly Review Press, 1975.

Rich, Adrienne, *Of Woman Born: Motherhood as Experience and Institution*, New York: W. W. Norton, 1976.

Rowbotham, Shelia, *Hidden From History*, Middlesex: Penguin Books, 1968.

Scott, Joan W., 'Gender: A Useful Category of Historical Analysis', *American Historical Review*, 91, 5, 1986.

Showalter, Elaine, *A Literature of Their Own: British Women Novelists from Bronte to Lessing*, Princeton, New Jersey: Princeton University Press, 1977.

Showalter, Elaine, ed., *Speaking of Gender*, New York and London: Routledge, 1989.

Signs, Journal of Women in Culture and Society, Summer, 1993, for a series of essays on lesbianism.

Silverman, Kaja, *Male Subjectivity at the Margins*, London and New York: Routledge, 1992.

Snitow, Ann, Christine Stansell, and Sharon Thompson, eds, *Powers of Desire: The Politics of Sexuality*, New York: Monthly Review Press, 1983.

Walker, Alice, *In Search of Our Mothers' Gardens: Womanist Prose*, New York: Harcourt Brace Jovanovich, 1983.

Weeks, Jeffrey, *Against Nature: Essays on history, sexuality and identity*, London: Rivers Oram Press, 1991.

Woolf, Virginia, *A Room of One's Own*, New York: Harcourt Brace Jovanovich, 1981.

Sherry B. Ortner (1941–)

Sherry B. Ortner is a feminist historian who has written extensively on the subjects of culture and power. In her most recent book, *High Religion: A Cultural and Political History of Sherpa Buddhism* (1989), Ortner discusses the cultural conditions which led to the formation of a group of Buddhist monasteries in Nepal. The following essay, 'Is Female to Male as Nature Is to Culture?' was written in 1972, originally as a conference paper. The 1970s was a period when notions of gender, power, nature and culture were being fiercely debated, and the question in Ortner's title was on the minds of many who were grappling with those issues. The essay was published in 1974, and along with others written at around the same time, it helped to focus the debate over the oppositional relationship between women and nature and men and culture. Ortner's view is that the dichotomies (or two-part divisions) between women and men and nature and culture are negative and dangerous. In order to ask her important question, she begins by acknowledging that oppression and subordination of women takes place in every culture—is, indeed 'universal'—but that the variations and extent of that condition suggest that this fact is not based on some inherent issue linked to the nature of men and women. In other words, she argued that there was nothing 'essential' about being a woman, and like Simone de Beauvoir before her, shows that the category of 'woman' is indeed a cultural construct. Ortner explores ways in which women are linked to nature and men to culture and considers some reasons for those connections, but she problematizes them, arguing that women play a double role—both inside and outside of culture, which makes them inclined to serve as their own oppressors. As she draws on the ideas of such theorists as Lévi-Strauss, Rosaldo, and Chodorow, Ortner demands that women and men begin to question cultural constructions of gender and to take apart problematic dichotomies.

M.B.

Is female to male as nature is to culture?*

Much of the creativity of anthropology derives from the tension between two sets of demands: that we explain human universals, and that we explain cultural particulars. By this canon, woman provides us with one of the more challenging problems to be dealt with. The secondary status of woman in society is one of the true universals, a pan-cultural fact. Yet within that universal fact, the specific cultural conceptions and symbolizations of woman are extraordinarily diverse and even mutually contradictory. Further, the actual treatment of women and their relative power and contribution vary enormously from culture to culture, and over different periods in the history of particular cultural traditions. Both of these points—the universal fact and the cultural variation—constitute problems to be explained.

My interest in the problem is of course more than academic: I wish to see genuine change come about, the emergence of a social and cultural order in which as much of the range of human potential is open to women as is open to men. The universality of female subordination, the fact that it exists within every type of social and economic arrangement and in societies of every degree of complexity, indicates to me that we are up against something very profound, very stubborn, something we cannot rout out simply by rearranging a few tasks and roles in the social system, or even by reordering the whole economic structure. In this paper I try to expose the underlying logic of cultural thinking that assumes the inferiority of women; I try to show the highly persuasive nature of the logic, for if it were not so persuasive, people would not keep subscribing to it. But I also try to show the social and cultural sources of that logic, to indicate wherein lies the potential for change.

It is important to sort out the levels of the problem. The confusion can be staggering. For example, depending on which aspect of Chinese culture we look at, we might extrapolate any of several entirely different guesses concerning the status of women in China. In the ideology of Taoism, *yin*, the female principle, and *yang*, the male principle, are given equal weight; 'the opposition, alternation, and interaction of these two forces give rise to all phenomena in the universe' (Siu, 1968: 2). Hence we might guess that maleness and femaleness are equally valued in the general ideology of Chinese culture.[1] Looking at the social structure, however, we see the strongly emphasized patrilineal descent principle, the importance of sons, and the absolute authority of the father in the family. Thus we might conclude that China is the

---

*The first version of this paper was presented in October 1972 as a lecture in the course 'Women: Myth and Reality' at Sarah Lawrence College. I received helpful comments from the students and from my co-teachers in the course: Joan Kelly Gadol, Eva Kollisch, and Gerda Lerner. A short account was delivered at the American Anthropological Association meetings in Toronto, November 1972. Meanwhile, I received excellent critical comments from Karen Blu, Robert Paul, Michelle Rosaldo, David Schneider, and Terence Turner, and the present version of the paper, in which the thrust of the argument has been rather significantly changed, was written in response to those comments. I, of course, retain responsibility for its final form. The paper is dedicated to Simone de Beauvoir, whose book *The Second Sex* (1953), first published in French in 1949, remains in my opinion the best single comprehensive understanding of 'the woman problem.'

492

archetypal patriarchal society. Next, looking at the actual roles played, power and influence wielded, and material contributions made by women in Chinese society—all of which are, upon observation, quite substantial—we would have to say that women are allotted a great deal of (unspoken) status in the system. Or again, we might focus on the fact that a goddess, Kuan Yin, is the central (most worshiped, most depicted) deity in Chinese Buddhism, and we might be tempted to say, as many have tried to say about goddess-worshiping cultures in prehistoric and early histori-cal societies, that China is actually a sort of matriarchy. In short, we must be absolutely clear about *what* we are trying to explain before explaining it.

We may differentiate three levels of the problem:

1. The universal fact of culturally attributed second-class status of woman in every society. Two questions are important here. First, what do we mean by this; what is our evidence that this is a universal fact? And second, how are we to explain this fact, once having established it?

2. Specific ideologies, symbolizations, and socio-structural arrangements pertain-ing to women that vary widely from culture to culture. The problem at this level is to account for any particular cultural complex in terms of factors specific to that group—the standard level of anthropological analysis.

3. Observable on-the-ground details of women's activities, contributions, powers, influence, etc., often at variance with cultural ideology (although always constrained within the assumption that women may never be officially preeminent in the total system). This is the level of direct observation, often adopted now by feminist-ori-ented anthropologists.

This paper is primarily concerned with the first of these levels, the problem of the universal devaluation of women. The analysis thus depends not upon specific cultur-al data but rather upon an analysis of 'culture' taken generically as a special sort of process in the world. A discussion of the second level, the problem of cross-cultural variation in conceptions and relative valuations of women, will entail a great deal of cross-cultural research and must be postponed to another time. As for the third level, it will be obvious from my approach that I would consider it a misguided endeavor to focus only upon women's actual though culturally unrecognized and unvalued powers in any given society, without first understanding the overarching ideology and deeper assumptions of the culture that render such powers trivial.

The universality of female subordination

What do I mean when I say that everywhere, in every known culture, women are considered in some degree inferior to men? First of all, I must stress that I am talking about *cultural* evaluations; I am saying that each culture, in its own way and on its own terms, makes this evaluation. But what would constitute evidence that a parti-cular culture considers women inferior?

Three types of data would suffice: (1) elements of cultural ideology and infor-mants' statements that *explicitly* devalue women, according them, their roles, their tasks, their products, and their social milieux less prestige than are accorded men and the male correlates; (2) symbolic devices, such as the attribution of defilement, which may be interpreted as *implicitly* making a statement of inferior valuation; and (3) social-structural arrangements that exclude women from participation in or contact with some realm in which the highest powers of the society are felt to reside.[2] These three types of data may all of course be interrelated in any particular system, though they need not necessarily be. Further, any one of them will usually be sufficient to make the point of female inferiority in a given culture. Certainly, female exclusion from the most sacred rite or the highest political council is sufficient evidence. Certainly, explicit cultural ideology devaluing women (and their tasks, roles, products, etc.) is sufficient evidence. Symbolic indicators such as defilement are usually sufficient, although in a few cases in which, say, men and women are equally polluting to one another, a further indicator is required—and is, as far as my investigations have ascertained, always available.

On any or all of these counts, then, I would flatly assert that we find women subordinated to men in every known society. The search for a genuinely egalitarian, let alone matriarchal, culture has proved fruitless. An example from one society that has traditionally been on the credit side of this ledger will suffice. Among the matrilineal Crow, as Lowie (1956) points out, 'Women . . . had highly honorific offices in the Sun Dance; they could become directors of the Tobacco Ceremony and played, if anything, a more conspicuous part in it than the men; they sometimes played the hostess in the Cooked Meat Festival; they were not debarred from sweating or doctoring or from seeking a vision' (p. 61). Nonetheless, 'Women [during menstruation] formerly rode inferior horses and evidently this loomed as a source of contamination, for they were not allowed to approach either a wounded man or men starting on a war party. A taboo still lingers against their coming near sacred objects at these times' (p. 44). Further, just before enumerating women's rights of participation in the various rituals noted above, Lowie mentions one particular Sun Dance Doll bundle that was not supposed to be unwrapped by a woman (p. 60). Pursuing this trail we find: 'According to all Lodge Grass informants and most others, the doll owned by Wrinkled-face took precedence not only of other dolls but of all other Crow medicines whatsoever. . . . This particular doll was not supposed to be handled by a woman' (p. 229).[3]

In sum, the Crow are probably a fairly typical case. Yes, women have certain powers and rights, in this case some that place them in fairly high positions. Yet ultimately the line is drawn: menstruation is a threat to warfare, one of the most valued institutions of the tribe, one that is central to their self-definition; and the most sacred object of the tribe is taboo to the direct sight and touch of women.

Similar examples could be multiplied ad infinitum, but I think the onus is no longer upon us to demonstrate that female subordination is a cultural universal; it is up to those who would argue against the point to bring forth counterexamples. I shall take the universal secondary status of women as a given, and proceed from there.

Nature and culture[4]

How are we to explain the universal devaluation of women? We could of course rest the case on biological determinism. There is something genetically inherent in the male of the species, so the biological determinists would argue, that makes them the naturally dominant sex; that 'something' is lacking in females, and as a result women are not only naturally subordinate but in general quite satisfied with their position, since it affords them protection and the opportunity to maximize maternal pleasures, which to them are the most satisfying experiences of life. Without going into a detailed refutation of this position, I think it fair to say that it has failed to be established to the satisfaction of almost anyone in academic anthropology. This is to say, not that biological facts are irrelevant, or that men and women are not different, but that these facts and differences only take on significance of superior/inferior within the framework of culturally defined value systems.

If we are unwilling to rest the case of genetic determinism, it seems to me that we have only one way to proceed. We must attempt to interpret female subordination in light of other universals, factors built into the structure of the most generalized situation in which all human beings, in whatever culture, find themselves. For example, every human being has a physical body and a sense of nonphysical mind, is part of a society of other individuals and an inheritor of a cultural tradition, and must engage in some relationship, however mediated, with 'nature,' or the nonhuman realm, in order to survive. Every human being is born (to a mother) and ultimately dies, all are assumed to have an interest in personal survival, and society/culture has its own interest in (or at least momentum toward) continuity and survival, which transcends the lives and deaths of particular individuals. And so forth. It is in the realm of such universals of the human condition that we must seek an explanation for the universal fact of female devaluation.

I translate the problem, in other words, into the following simple question. What could there be in the generalized structure and conditions of existence, common to every culture, that would lead every culture to place a lower value upon women? Specifically, my thesis is that woman is being identified with—or, if you will, seems to be a symbol of—something that every culture devalues, something that every culture defines as being of a lower order of existence than itself. Now it seems that there is only one thing that would fit that description, and that is 'nature' in the most generalized sense. Every culture, or, generically, 'culture,' is engaged in the process of generating and sustaining systems of meaningful forms (symbols, artifacts, etc.) by means of which humanity transcends the givens of natural existence, bends them to its purposes, controls them in its interest. We may thus broadly equate culture with the notion of human consciousness, or with the products of human consciousness (i.e., systems of thought and technology), by means of which humanity attempts to assert control over nature.

Now the categories of 'nature' and 'culture' are of course conceptual categories—one can find no boundary out in the actual world between the two states or realms of being. And there is no question that some cultures articulate a much stronger opposition between the two categories than others—it has even been argued that primitive peoples (some or all) do not see or intuit any distinction between the human cultural state and the state of nature at all. Yet I would maintain that the universality of ritual betokens an assertion in all human cultures of the specifically human ability to act upon and regulate, rather than passively move with and be moved by, the givens of natural existence. In ritual, the purposive manipulation of given forms toward regulating and sustaining order, every culture asserts that proper relations between human existence and natural forces depend upon culture's employing its special powers to regulate the overall processes of the world and life.

One realm of cultural thought in which these points are often articulated is that of concepts of purity and pollution. Virtually every culture has some such beliefs, which seem in large part (though not, of course, entirely) to be concerned with the relationship between culture and nature (see Ortner, 1973, n.d.). A well-known aspect of purity/pollution beliefs cross-culturally is that of the natural 'contagion' of pollution; left to its own devices, pollution (for these purposes grossly equated with the unregulated operation of natural energies) spreads and overpowers all that it comes in contact with. Thus a puzzle—if pollution is so strong, how can anything be purified? Why is the purifying agent not itself polluted? The answer, in keeping with the present line of argument, is that purification is effected in a ritual context; purification ritual, as a purposive activity that pits self-conscious (symbolic) action against natural energies, is more powerful than those energies.

In any case, my point is simply that every culture implicitly recognizes and asserts a distinction between the operation of nature and the operation of culture (human consciousness and its products); and further, that the distinctiveness of culture rests precisely on the fact that it can under most circumstances transcend natural conditions and turn them to its purposes. Thus culture (i.e. every culture) at some level of awareness asserts itself to be not only distinct from but superior to nature, and that sense of distinctiveness and superiority rests precisely on the ability to transform—to 'socialize' and 'culturalize'—nature.

Returning now to the issue of women, their pan-cultural second-class status could be accounted for, quite simply, by postulating that women are being identified or symbolically associated with nature, as opposed to men, who are identified with culture. Since it is always culture's project to subsume and transcend nature, if women were considered part of nature, then culture would find it 'natural' to subordinate, not to say oppress, them. Yet although this argument can be shown to have considerable force, it seems to oversimplify the case. The formulation I would like to defend and elaborate on in the following section, then, is that women are seen 'merely' as being *closer* to nature than men. That is, culture (still equated relatively unambiguously with men) recognizes that women are active participants in its special processes, but at the same time sees them as being more rooted in, or having more direct affinity with, nature.

The revision may seem minor or even trivial, but I think it is a more accurate rendering of cultural assumptions. Further, the argument cast in these terms has several analytic advantages over the simpler formulation; I shall discuss these later. It simply might be stressed here that the revised argument would still account for the pan-cultural devaluation of women, for even if women are not equated with nature, they are nonetheless seen as representing a lower order of being, as being less transcendental of nature than men are. The next task of the paper, then, is to consider why they might be viewed in that way.

Why is woman seen as closer to nature?

It all begins of course with the body and the natural procreative functions specific to women alone. We can sort out for discussion three levels at which this absolute physiological fact has significance: (1) woman's *body and its functions*, more involved more of the time with 'species life,' seem to place her closer to nature, in contrast to man's physiology, which frees him more completely to take up the projects of culture; (2) woman's body and its functions place her in *social roles* that in turn are considered to be at a lower order of the cultural process than man's; and (3) woman's traditional social roles, imposed because of her body and its functions, in turn give her a different *psychic structure*, which, like her physiological nature and her social roles, is seen as being closer to nature. I shall discuss each of these points in turn, showing first how in each instance certain factors strongly tend to align woman with nature, then indicating other factors that demonstrate her full alignment with culture, the combined factors thus placing her in a problematic intermediate position. It will become clear in the course of the discussion why men seem by contrast less intermediate, more purely 'cultural' than women. And I reiterate that I am dealing only at the level of cultural and human universals. These arguments are intended to apply to generalized humanity; they grow out of the human condition, as humanity has experienced and confronted it up to the present day.

1. Woman's physiology seen as closer to nature. This part of my argument has been anticipated, with subtlety, cogency, and a great deal of hard data, by de Beauvoir (1953). De Beauvoir reviews the physiological structure, development, and functions of the human female and concludes that 'the female, to a greater extent than the male, is the prey of the species' (p. 60). She points out that many major areas and processes of the woman's body serve no apparent function for the health and stability of the individual; on the contrary, as they perform their specific organic functions, they are often sources of discomfort, pain, and danger. The breasts are irrelevant to personal health; they may be excised at any time of a woman's life. 'Many of the ovarian secretions function for the benefit of the egg, promoting its maturation and adapting the uterus to its requirements; in respect to the organism as a whole, they make for disequilibrium rather than for regulation—the woman is adapted to the needs of the egg rather than to her own requirements' (p. 24). Menstruation is often uncomfortable, sometimes painful; it frequently has negative emotional correlates and in any case involves bothersome tasks of cleansing and waste disposal; and—a point that de Beauvoir does not mention—in many cultures it interrupts a woman's routine, putting her in a stigmatized state involving various restrictions on her activities and social contacts. In pregnancy many of the woman's vitamin and mineral resources are channeled into nourishing the fetus, depleting her own strength and

497

energies. And finally, childbirth itself is painful and dangerous (pp. 24–7 *passim*). In sum, de Beauvoir concludes that the female 'is more enslaved to the species than the male, her animality is more manifest' (p. 239).

While de Beauvoir's book is ideological, her survey of woman's physiological situation seems fair and accurate. It is simply a fact that proportionately more of a woman's body space, for a greater percentage of her lifetime, and at some—sometimes great—cost to her personal health, strength, and general stability, is taken up with the natural process surrounding the reproduction of the species.

De Beauvoir goes on to discuss the negative implications of woman's 'enslavement to the species' in relation to the projects in which humans engage, projects through which culture is generated and defined. She arrives thus at the crux of her argument (pp. 58–9):

> Here we have the key to the whole mystery. On the biological level a species is maintained only by creating itself anew; but this creation results only in repeating the same Life in more individuals. But man assures the repetition of Life while transcending Life through Existence [i.e. goal-oriented, meaningful action]; by this transcendence he creates values that deprive pure repetition of all value. In the animal, the freedom and variety of male activities are vain because no project is involved. Except for his services to the species, what he does is immaterial. Whereas in serving the species, the human male also remodels the face of the earth, he creates new instruments, he invents, he shapes the future.

In other words, woman's body seems to doom her to mere reproduction of life; the male, in contrast, lacking natural creative functions, must (or has the opportunity to) assert his creativity externally, 'artificially,' through the medium of technology and symbols. In so doing, he creates relatively lasting, eternal, transcendent objects, while the woman creates only perishables—human beings.

This formulation opens up a number of important insights. It speaks, for example, to the great puzzle of why male activities involving the destruction of life (hunting and warfare) are often given more prestige than the female's ability to give birth, to create life. Within de Beauvoir's framework, we realize it is not the killing that is the relevant and valued aspect of hunting and warfare; rather, it is the transcendental (social, cultural) nature of these activities, as opposed to the naturalness of the process of birth: 'For it is not in giving life but in risking life that man is raised above the animal; that is why superiority has been accorded in humanity not to the sex that brings forth but to that which kills' (*ibid.*).

Thus if male is, as I am suggesting, everywhere (unconsciously) associated with culture and female seems closer to nature, the rationale for these associations is not very difficult to grasp, merely from considering the implications of the physiological contrast between male and female. At the same time, however, woman cannot be consigned fully to the category of nature, for it is perfectly obvious that she is a full-fledged human being endowed with human consciousness just as a man is; she is half of the human race, without whose cooperation the whole enterprise would collapse. She may seem more in the possession of nature than man, but having consciousness, she thinks and speaks; she generates, communicates, and manipulates symbols, categories, and values. She participates in human dialogues not only with other women but also with men. As Lévi-Strauss says, 'Woman could never become just a sign and nothing more, since even in a man's world she is still a person, and since insofar as she is defined as a sign she must [still] be recognized as a generator of signs' (1969a: 496).

Indeed, the fact of woman's full human consciousness, her full involvement in and commitment to culture's project of transcendence over nature, may ironically explain another of the great puzzles of 'the woman problem'—woman's nearly universal unquestioning acceptance of her own devaluation. For it would seem that, as a conscious human and member of culture, she has followed out the logic of culture's arguments and has reached culture's conclusions along with the men. As de Beauvoir puts it (p. 59):

> For she, too, is an existent, she feels the urge to surpass, and her project is not mere repetition but transcendence towards a different future—in her heart of hearts she finds confirmation of the masculine pretensions. She joins the men in the festivals that celebrate the successes and victories of the males. Her misfortune is to have been biologically destined for the repetition of Life, when even in her own view Life does not carry within itself its reasons for being, reasons that are more important than life itself.

In other words, woman's consciousness—her membership, as it were, in culture—is evidenced in part by the very fact that she accepts her own devaluation and takes culture's point of view.

I have tried here to show one part of the logic of that view, the part that grows directly from the physiological differences between men and women. Because of woman's greater bodily involvement with the natural functions surrounding reproduction, she is seen as more a part of nature than man is. Yet in part because of her consciousness and participation in human social dialogue, she is recognized as a participant in culture. Thus she appears as something intermediate between culture and nature, lower on the scale of transcendence than man.

2. Woman's social role seen as closer to nature. Woman's physiological functions, I have just argued, may tend in themselves to motivate[5] a view of woman as closer to nature, a view she herself, as an observer of herself and the world, would tend to agree with. Woman creates naturally from within her own being, whereas man is free to, or forced to, create artificially, that is, through cultural means, and in such a way as to sustain culture. In addition, I now wish to show how woman's physiological functions have tended universally to limit her social movement, and to confine her universally to certain social contexts which *in turn* are seen as closer to nature. That is, not only her bodily processes but the social situation in which her bodily processes locate her may carry this significance. And insofar as she is permanently associated (in the eyes of culture) with these social milieux, they add weight (perhaps the decisive part of the burden) to the view of woman as closer to nature. I refer here of course to woman's confinement to the domestic family context, a confinement motivated, no doubt, by her lactation processes.

Woman's body, like that of all female mammals, generates milk during and after pregnancy for the feeding of the newborn baby. The baby cannot survive without breast milk or some similar formula at this stage of life. Since the mother's body goes through its lactation processes in direct relation to a pregnancy with a particular child, the relationship of nursing between mother and child is seen as a natural bond, other feeding arrangements being seen in most cases as unnatural and makeshift. Mothers and their children, according to cultural reasoning, belong together. Further, children beyond infancy are not strong enough to engage in major work, yet are mobile and unruly and not capable of understanding various dangers; they thus require supervision and constant care. Mother is the obvious person for this task, as an extension of her natural nursing bond with the children, or because she has a new infant and is already involved with child-oriented activities. Her own activities are thus circumscrbed by the limitations and low levels of her children's strengths and skills:[6] she is confined to the domestic family group; 'woman's place is in the home.'

Woman's association with the domestic circle would contribute to the view of her as closer to nature in several ways. In the first place, the sheer fact of constant association with children plays a role in the issue; one can easily see how infants and children might themselves be considered part of nature. Infants are barely human and utterly unsocialized; like animals they are unable to walk upright, they excrete without control, they do not speak. Even slightly older children are clearly not yet fully under the sway of culture. They do not yet understand social duties, responsibilities, and morals; their vocabulary and their range of learned skills are small. One finds implicit recognition of an association between children and nature in many cultural practices. For example, most cultures have initiation rites for adolescents (primarily for boys; I shall return to this point below), the point of which is to move the child ritually from a less than fully human state into full participation in society and culture; many cultures do not hold funeral rites for children who die at early ages, explicitly because they are not yet fully social beings. Thus children are likely to be categorized with nature, and woman's close association with children may compound her potential for being seen as closer to nature herself. It is ironic that the rationale for boys' initiation rites in many cultures is that the boys must be purged of the defilement accrued from being around mother and other women so much of the time, when in fact much of the woman's defilement may derive from her being around children so much of the time.

The second major problematic implication of women's close association with the domestic context derives from certain structural conflicts between the family and society at large in any social system. The implications of the 'domestic/public opposition' in relation to the position of women have been cogently developed by Rosaldo, and I simply wish to show its relevance to the present argument. The notion that the domestic unit—the biological family charged with reproducing and socializing new members of the society—is opposed to the public entity—the superimposed network of alliances and relationships that *is* the society—is also the basis of Lévi-Strauss's argument in the *Elementary Structures of Kinship* (1969a). Lévi-Strauss argues not only that this opposition is present in every social system, but further that it has the significance of the opposition between nature and culture. The universal incest prohibition[7] and its ally, the rule of exogamy (marriage outside the group), ensure that 'the risk of seeing a biological family become established as a closed system is definitely eliminated; the biological group can no longer stand apart, and the bond of alliance with another family ensures the dominance of the social over the biological, and of the cultural over the natural' (p. 479). And although not every culture articulates a radical opposition between the domestic and the public as such, it is hardly contestable that the domestic is always subsumed by the public; domestic units are allied with one another through the enactment of rules that are logically at a higher level than the units themselves; this creates an emergent unit—society—that is logically at a higher level than the domestic units of which it is composed.

Now, since women are associated with, and indeed are more or less confined to, the domestic context, they are identified with this lower order of social/cultural organization. What are the implications of this for the way they are viewed? First, if the specifically biological (reproductive) function of the family is stressed, as in Lévi-Strauss's formulation, then the family (and hence woman) is identified with nature pure and simple, as opposed to culture. But this is obviously too simple; the point seems more adequately formulated as follows: the family (and hence woman) represents lower-level, socially fragmenting, particularistic sorts of concerns, as opposed to interfamilial relations representing higher-level, integrative, universalistic sorts of concerns. Since men lack a 'natural' basis (nursing, generalized to child care) for a familial orientation, their sphere of activity is defined at the level of interfamilial relations. And hence, so the cultural reasoning seems to go, men are the 'natural' proprietors of religion, ritual, politics, and other realms of cultural thought and action in which universalistic statements of spiritual and social synthesis are made. Thus men are identified not only with culture, in the sense of all human creativity, as opposed to nature; they are identified in particular with culture in the old-fashioned sense of the finer and higher aspects of human thought—art, religion, law, etc.

Here again, the logic of cultural reasoning aligning woman with a lower order of culture than man is clear and, on the surface, quite compelling. At the same time, woman cannot be fully consigned to nature, for there are aspects of her situation, even within the domestic context, that undeniably demonstrate her participation in the cultural process. It goes without saying, of course, that except for nursing newborn infants (and artificial nursing devices can cut even this biological tie), there is no reason why it has to be mother—as opposed to father, or anyone else—who remains identified with child care. But even assuming that other practical and emotional reasons conspire to keep woman in this sphere, it is possible to show that her activities in the domestic context could as logically put her squarely in the category of culture.

In the first place, one must point out that woman not only feeds and cleans up after children in a simple caretaker operation; she in fact is the primary agent of their early socialization. It is she who transforms newborn infants from mere organisms into cultured humans, teaching them manners and the proper ways to behave in order to become full-fledged members of the culture. On the basis of her socializing functions alone, she could not be more a representative of culture. Yet in virtually every society there is a point at which the socialization of boys is transferred to the hands of men. The boys are considered, in one set of terms or another, not yet 'really' socialized; their entrée into the realm of fully human (social, cultural) status can be accomplished only by men. We still see this in our own schools, where there is a gradual inversion in the proportion of female to male teachers up through the grades: most kindergarten teachers are female; most university professors are male.[8]

501

Or again, take cooking. In the overwhelming majority of societies cooking is the woman's work. No doubt this stems from practical considerations—since the woman has to stay home with the baby, it is convenient for her to perform the chores centered in the home. But if it is true, as Lévi-Strauss has argued (1969b), that transforming the raw into the cooked may represent, in many systems of thought, the transition from nature to culture, then here we have woman aligned with this important culturalizing process, which could easily place her in the category of culture, triumphing over nature. Yet it is also interesting to note that when a culture (e.g. France or China) develops a tradition of *haute cuisine*—'real' cooking, as opposed to trivial ordinary domestic cooking—the high chefs are almost always men. Thus the pattern replicates that in the area of socialization—women perform lower-level conversions from nature to culture, but when the culture distinguishes a higher level of the same function, the higher level is restricted to men.

In short, we see once again some sources of woman's appearing more intermediate than man with respect to the nature/culture dichotomy. Her 'natural' association with the domestic context (motivated by her natural lactation functions) tends to compound her potential for being viewed as closer to nature, because of the animal-like nature of children, and because of the infrasocial connotation of the domestic group as against the rest of society. Yet at the same time her socializing and cooking functions within the domestic context show her to be a powerful agent of the cultural process, constantly transforming raw natural resources into cultural products. Belonging to culture, yet appearing to have stronger and more direct connections with nature, she is once again seen as situated between the two realms.

3. Woman's psyche seen as closer to nature. The suggestion that woman has not only a different body and a different social locus from man but also a different psychic structure is most controversial. I will argue that she probably *does* have a different psychic structure, but I will draw heavily on Chodorow's paper (this volume) to establish first that her psychic structure need not be assumed to be innate; it can be accounted for, as Chodorow convincingly shows, by the facts of the probably universal female socialization experience. Nonetheless, if we grant the empirical near universality of a 'feminine psyche' with certain specific characteristics, these characteristics would add weight to the cultural view of woman as closer to nature.

It is important to specify what we see as the dominant and universal aspects of the feminine psyche. If we postulate emotionality or irrationality, we are confronted with those traditions in various parts of the world in which women functionally are, and are seen as, more practical, pragmatic, and this-worldly than men. One relevant dimension that does seem pan-culturally applicable is that of relative concreteness vs. relative abstractness: the feminine personality tends to be involved with concrete feelings, things, and people, rather than with abstract entities; it tends towards personalism and particularism. A second, closely related, dimension seems to be that of relative subjectivity vs. relative objectivity: Chodorow cites Carlson's study (1971), which concludes that 'males represent experiences of self, others, space, and time in individualistic, objective, and distant ways, while females represent experiences in relatively interpersonal, subjective, immediate ways' (this volume, p. 56, quoting Carlson, p. 270). Although this and other studies were done in Western societies, Chodorow sees their findings on the differences between male and female personality—roughly, that men are more objective and inclined to relate in terms of relatively abstract categories, women more subjective and inclined to relate in terms of relatively concrete phenomena—as 'general and nearly universal differences' (p. 43).

But the thrust of Chodorow's elegantly argued paper is that these differences are not innate or genetically programmed; they arise from nearly universal features of family structure, namely that 'women, universally, are largely responsible for early child care and for (at least) later female socialization' (p. 43) and that 'the structural situation of child rearing, reinforced by female and male role training, produces these differences, which are replicated and reproduced in the sexual sociology of adult life' (p. 44). Chodorow argues that, because mother is the early socializer of both boys and girls, both develop 'personal identification' with her, i.e. diffuse identification with her general personality, behavior traits, values, and attitudes (p. 51). A son, however, must ultimately shift to a masculine role identity, which involves building an identification with the father. Since father is almost always more remote than mother (he is rarely involved in child care, and perhaps works away from home much of the day), building an identification with father involves a 'positional identification,' i.e. identification with father's male role as a collection of abstract elements, rather than a personal identification with father as a real individual (p. 49). Further, as the boy enters the larger social world, he finds it in fact organized around more abstract and universalistic criteria; thus his earlier socialization prepares him for, and is reinforced by, the type of adult social experience he will have.

For a young girl, in contrast, the personal identification with mother, which was created in early infancy, can persist into the process of learning female role identity. Because mother is immediate and present when the daughter is learning role identity, learning to be a woman involves the continuity and development of a girl's relationship to her mother, and sustains the identification with her as an individual; it does not involve the learning of externally defined role characteristics (Chodorow, p. 51). This pattern prepares the girl for, and is fully reinforced by, her social situation in later life; she will become involved in the world of women, which is characterized by few formal role differences, and which involves again, in motherhood, 'personal identification' with *her* children. And so the cycle begins anew.

Chodorow demonstrates to my satisfaction at least that the feminine personality, characterized by personalism and particularism, can be explained as having been generated by social-structural arrangements rather than by innate biological factors. The point need not be belabored further. But insofar as the 'feminine personality' has been a nearly universal fact, it can be argued that its characteristics may have contributed further to the view of women as being somehow less cultural than men. That is, women tend to enter into relationships with the world that culture might see as being more 'like nature'—immanent and embedded in things as given—than 'like culture'—transcending and transforming things through the superimposition of abstract categories and transpersonal values. Woman's relationships tend to be, like nature, relatively unmediated, more direct, whereas man not only tends to relate in a more mediated way, but in fact ultimately often relates more consistently and strongly to the mediating categories and forms than to the persons or objects themselves.

It is thus not difficult to see how the feminine personality would lend weight to a view of women as being 'closer to nature.' Yet at the same time, the modes of relating characteristic of women undeniably play a powerful and important role in the cultural process. For just as relatively unmediated relating is in some sense at the lower end of the spectrum of human spiritual functions, embedded and particularizing rather than transcending and synthesizing, yet that mode of relating also stands at the upper end of that spectrum. Consider the mother-child relationship. Mothers tend to be committed to their children as individuals, regardless of sex, age, beauty, clan affiliation, or other categories in which the child might participate. Now any relationship with this quality—not just mother and child but any sort of highly personal, relatively unmediated commitment—may be seen as a challenge to culture and society 'from below,' insofar as it represents the fragmentary potential of individual loyalties vis-à-vis the solidarity of the group. But it may also be seen as embodying the synthesizing agent for culture and society 'from above,' in that it represents generalized human values above and beyond loyalties to particular social categories. Every society must have social categories that transcend personal loyalties, but every society must also generate a sense of ultimate moral unity for all its members above and beyond those social categories. Thus that psychic mode seemingly typical of women, which tends to disregard categories and to seek 'communion' (Chodorow, p. 55, following Bakan, 1966) directly and personally with others, although it may appear infracultural from one point of view, is at the same time associated with the highest levels of the cultural process.

The implications of intermediacy

My primary purpose in this paper has been to attempt to explain the universal secondary status of women. Intellectually and personally, I felt strongly challenged by this problem; I felt compelled to deal with it before undertaking an analysis of woman's position in any particular society. Local variables of economy, ecology, history, political and social structure, values, and world view—these could explain variations within this universal, but they could not explain the universal itself. And if we were not to accept the ideology of biological determinism, then explanation, it seemed to me, could only proceed by reference to other universals of the human cultural situation. Thus the general outlines of the approach—although not of course the particular solution offered—were determined by the problem itself, and not by any predilection on my part for global abstract structural analysis.

I argued that the universal devaluation of women could be explained by postulating that women are seen as closer to nature than men, men being seen as more unequivocally occupying the high ground of culture. The culture/nature distinction is itself a product of culture, culture being minimally defined as the transcendence, by means of systems of thought and technology, of the natural givens of existence. This of course is an analytic definition, but I argued that at some level every culture incorporates this notion in one form or another, if only through the performance of ritual as an assertion of the human ability to manipulate those givens. In any case, the core of the paper was concerned with showing why women might tend to be assumed, over and over, in the most diverse sorts of world views and in cultures of every degree of complexity, to be closer to nature than men. Woman's physiology, more involved more of the time with 'species of life'; woman's association with the structurally subordinate domestic context, charged with the crucial function of transforming animal-like infants into cultured beings; 'woman's psyche,' appropriately molded to mothering functions by her own socialization and tending toward greater personalism and less mediated modes of relating—all these factors make woman appear to be rooted more directly and deeply in nature. At the same time, however, her 'membership' and fully necessary participation in culture are recognized by culture and cannot be denied. Thus she is seen to occupy an intermediate position between culture and nature.

This intermediacy has several implications for analysis, depending upon how it is interpreted. First, of course, it answers my primary question of why woman is everywhere seen as lower than man, for even if she is not seen as nature pure and simple, she is still seen as achieving less transcendence of nature than man. Here intermediate simply means 'middle status' on a hierarchy of being from culture to nature.

Second, intermediate may have the significance of 'mediating,' i.e. performing some sort of synthesizing or converting function between nature and culture, here seen (by culture) not as two ends of a continuum but as two radically different sorts of processes in the world. The domestic unit—and hence woman, who in virtually every case appears as its primary representative—is one of culture's crucial agencies for the conversion of nature into culture, especially with reference to the socialization of children. Any culture's continued viability depends upon properly socialized individuals who will see the world in that culture's terms and adhere more or less unquestioningly to its moral precepts. The functions of the domestic unit must be closely controlled in order to ensure this outcome; the stability of the domestic unit as an institution must be placed as far as possible beyond question. (We see some aspects of the protection of the integrity and stability of the domestic group in the powerful taboos against incest, matricide, patricide, and fratricide.[9]) Insofar as woman is universally the primary agent of early socialization and is seen as virtually the embodiment of the functions of the domestic group, she will tend to come under the heavier restrictions and circumscriptions surrounding that unit. Her (culturally defined) intermediate position between nature and culture, here having the significance of her *mediation* (i.e. performing conversion functions) between nature and culture, would thus account not only for her lower status but for the greater restrictions placed upon her activities. In virtually every culture her permissible sexual activities are more closely circumscribed than man's, she is offered a much smaller range of role choices, and she is afforded direct access to a far more limited range of its social institutions. Further, she is almost universally socialized to have a narrower and generally more conservative set of attitudes and views than man, and the limited social contexts of her adult life reinforce this situation. This socially engendered conservatism and traditionalism of woman's thinking is another—perhaps the worst, certainly the most insidious—mode of social restriction, and would clearly be related to her traditional function of producing well-socialized members of the group.

Finally, woman's intermediate position may have the implications of greater symbolic ambiguity. Shifting our image of the culture/nature relationship once again, we may envision culture in this case as a small clearing within the forest of the larger natural system. From this point of view, that which is intermediate between culture and nature is located on the continuous periphery of culture's clearing; and though it may thus appear to stand both above and below (and beside) culture, it is simply outside and around it. We can begin to understand then how a single system of cultural thought can often assign to woman completely polarized and apparently contradictory meanings, since extremes, as we say, meet. That she often represents both life and death is only the simplest example one could mention.

For another perspective on the same point, it will be recalled that the psychic mode associated with women seems to stand at both the bottom and the top of the scale of human modes of relating. The tendency in that mode is to get involved more directly with people as individuals and not as representatives of one social category or another; this mode can be seen as either 'ignoring' (and thus subverting) or 'transcending' (and thus achieving a higher synthesis of) those social categories, depending upon the cultural view for any given purpose. Thus we can account easily for both the subversive feminine symbols (witches, evil eye, menstrual pollution, castrating mothers) and the feminine symbols of transcendence (mother goddesses, merciful dispensers of salvation, female symbols of justice, and the strong presence of feminine symbolism in the realms of art, religion, ritual, and law). Feminine symbolism, far more often than masculine symbolism, manifests this propensity toward polarized ambiguity—sometimes utterly exalted, sometimes utterly debased, rarely within the normal range of human possibilities.

If woman's (culturally viewed) intermediacy between culture and nature has this implication of generalized ambiguity of meaning characteristic of marginal phenomena, then we are also in a better position to account for those cultural and historical 'inversions' in which women are in some way or other symbolically aligned with culture and men with nature. A number of cases come to mind: the Sirionó of Brazil, among whom, according to Ingham (1971: 1098), 'nature, the raw, and maleness' are opposed to 'culture, the cooked, and femaleness';[10] Nazi Germany, in which women were said to be the guardians of culture and morals; European courtly love, in which man considered himself the beast and woman the pristine exalted object—a pattern of thinking that persists, for example, among modern Spanish peasants (see Pitt-Rivers, 1961). And there are no doubt other cases of this sort, including some aspects of our own culture's view of women. Each such instance of an alignment of women with culture rather than nature requires detailed analysis of specific historical and ethnographic data. But in indicating how nature in general, and the feminine mode of interpersonal relations in particular, can appear from certain points of view to stand both under and over (but really simply outside of) the sphere of culture's hegemony, we have at least laid the groundwork for such analyses.

In short, the postulate that woman is viewed as closer to nature than man has several implications for further analysis, and can be interpreted in several different ways. If it is viewed simply as a *middle* position on a scale from culture down to nature, then it is still seen as lower than culture and thus accounts for the pan-cultural assumption that woman is lower than man in the order of things. It is read as a *mediating* element in the culture-nature relationship, then it may account in part for the cultural tendency not merely to devalue woman but to circumscribe and restrict her functions, since culture must maintain control over its (pragmatic and symbolic) mechanisms for the conversion of nature into culture. And if it is read as an *ambiguous* status between culture and nature, it may help account for the fact that, in specific cultural ideologies and symbolizations, woman can occasionally be aligned with culture, and in any event is often assigned polarized and contradictory meanings within a single symbolic system. Middle status, mediating functions, ambiguous meaning—all are different readings, for different contextual purposes, of woman's being seen as intermediate between nature and culture.

Conclusions

Ultimately, it must be stressed again that the whole scheme is a construct of culture rather than a fact of nature. Woman is not 'in reality' any closer to (or further from) nature than man—both have consciousness, both are mortal. But there are certainly reasons why she appears that way, which is what I have tried to show in this paper. The result is a (sadly) efficient feedback system: various aspects of woman's situation (physical, social, psychological) contribute to her being seen as closer to nature, while the view of her as closer to nature is in turn embodied in institutional forms that reproduce her situation. The implications for social change are similarly circular: a different cultural view can only grow out of a different social actuality; a different social actuality can only grow out of a different cultural view.

It is clear, then, that the situation must be attacked from both sides. Efforts directed solely at changing the social institutions—through setting quotas on hiring, for example, or through passing equal-pay-for-equal-work laws—cannot have far-reaching effects if cultural language and imagery continue to purvey a relatively devalued view of women. But at the same time efforts directed solely at changing cultural assumptions—through male and female consciousness-raising groups, for example, or through revision of educational materials and mass-media imagery—cannot be successful unless the institutional base of the society is changed to support and reinforce the changed cultural view. Ultimately, both men and women can and must be equally involved in projects of creativity and transcendence. Only then will women be seen as aligned with culture, in culture's ongoing dialectic with nature.

NOTES

1. It is true of course that *yin*, the female principle, has a negative valence. Nonetheless, there is an absolute complementarity of *yin* and *yang* in Taoism, a recognition that the world requires the equal operation and interaction of both principles for its survival.

2. Some anthropologists might consider this type of evidence (social-structural arrangements that exclude women, explicitly or de facto, from certain groups, roles, or statuses) to be a subtype of the second type of evidence (symbolic formulations of inferiority). I would not disagree with this view, although most social anthropologists would probably separate the two types.

3. While we are on the subject of injustices of various kinds, we might note that Lowie secretly bought

this doll, the most sacred object in the tribal repertoire, from its custodian, the widow of Wrinkled-face. She asked $400 for it, but this price was 'far beyond [Lowie's] means,' and he finally got it for $80 (p. 300).

4. With all due respect to Lévi-Strauss (1969a, b, and *passim*).

5. Semantic theory uses the concept of motivation of meaning, which encompasses various ways in which a meaning may be assigned to a symbol because of certain objective properties of that symbol, rather than by arbitrary association. In a sense, this entire paper is an inquiry into the motivation of the meaning of woman as a symbol, asking why woman may be unconsciously assigned the significance of being closer to nature. For a concise statement on the various types of motivation of meaning, see Ullman (1963).

6. A situation that often serves to make her more childlike herself.

7. David M. Schneider (personal communication) is prepared to argue that the incest taboo is not universal, on the basis of material from Oceania. Let us say at this point, then, that it is virtually universal.

8. I remember having my first male teacher in the fifth grade, and I remember being excited about that—it was somehow more grown-up.

9. Nobody seems to care much about sororicide—a point that ought to be investigated.

10. Ingham's discussion is rather ambiguous itself, since women are also associated with animals: 'The contrasts man/animal and man/woman are evidently similar . . . hunting is the means of acquiring women as well as animals' (p. 1095). A careful reading of the data suggests that both women and animals are mediators beween nature and culture in this tradition.

Penelope Brown and
Ludmilla Jordanova

The voices of Penelope Brown and Ludmilla Jordanova are important in conversations about gender and power which have been ongoing for the last three decades. Brown has been most renowned for her work in the area of communication analysis; much of her research has centred on the issue of the relationships between gender and politeness in cultures around the world. One of her most cited articles is called 'How and Why Women Are More Polite: Some Evidence From a Mayan Community.' Jordanova has qualifications in both the humanities and the sciences, and is currently a professor of history at the University of York. Her book *Sexual Vision: Images of Gender in Science and Medicine Between the Eighteenth and Twentieth Centuries* (1989), is a gender-oriented cultural analysis of science and medicine.

In the essay which follows, Brown and Jordanova historicize the nature/culture dichotomy, following the trail of this debate from the writings of early twentieth century structuralists to the numerous writings on the subject which were produced in the early 1970s, and, in particular, Sherry B. Ortner's essay, 'Is Female to Male as Nature Is to Culture?' They argue that this historical task is critical for two reasons—first 'it sheds light on the difficulties of generalizing about alleged universals in the position of women', and second, 'it illustrates the prevalence and the persuasiveness of . . . essentialist thinking about the sexes.' Crucial to their argument is the issue of binary opposition in general, and they examine the ideas of Claude Lévi-Strauss, criticizing his emphasis on biology. They challenge the commonly held notion that biological differences between men and women create the social divisions in which they function, and argue that the rise of science since the mid-nineteenth century has strengthened the division between the sexes, as medicine claimed to demonstrate scientific reasons for the limited participation of women in 'culture'. The authors conclude that the nature/culture split and the specific associations with gender which it has in culture is a nineteenth-century Western creation, and the article ends in a call to feminists to examine this dichotomy and the surrounding issues in non-Western cultures in order to further illuminate its flaws.

M.B.

Oppressive dichotomies: the nature/culture debate*

Introduction

The distinction between nature and culture is basic to recent Western thought. It has so many varied manifestations that it takes considerable effort to make them explicit. Since the mid-nineteenth century, the opposition between nature and culture has become central to evolutionary theory and allied sciences, to debates on heredity and environment, nature *versus* nurture, the measurement of intelligence and educational methods. All these areas are informed by a distinction between unmediated, intractable nature, and a realm of human mastery where conscious social and individual action is accorded an important measure of power. The belief in human capacity to control nature is, in our culture, linked to the development of science, medicine and technology, and to the rational, refined analysis on which they are based. Our science based culture depends on abstract studies, mostly in the physical sciences, and on techniques relating to engineering skills. Both science and engineering are identified with male accomplishments, with the capacity for mathematical and logical reasoning, with mechanical skills; they are literally and metaphorically masculine activities. Women by contrast, are stereotypically identified with so-called caring jobs, nursing, teaching and social work. They are deemed to be uniquely gifted in the realm of human relationships by virtue of their greater emotional sensitivity. The model for female accomplishments is motherhood. The corresponding popular imagery is of soft, tender sympathy overriding reason and intellect. In the common emphasis on the unity of mother and child, the identification of women with nature is suggested. The biological functions of bearing and suckling children imply the privileged status of women with respect to nature. This is further reinforced by their care of defenceless, unformed children who are not yet fully social beings.

It would be possible to devote an entire chapter to detailing the various ways in which the nature/culture polarity functions both explicitly and implicitly in contemporary society. Our purpose here is different. We simply wish to note the pervasiveness of the dichotomy in our culture, and the power it has, and go on to suggest that we can learn a valuable object lesson from examining the history and use of these ideas, particularly as they are found in anthropological theories. Current debates in anthropology, like those in the natural sciences, rely on a certain approach to the interpretation of sex differences which we feel demands critical scrutiny. And it helps to realize that the presuppositions scientists and anthropologists use have a long and complex history. In what follows we shall outline the principal anthropolog-

*Source: Brown, P. and Jordanova, L. J. (1981) 'Oppressive dichotomies: the nature/culture debate', in *Women and Society: Interdisciplinary Essays*, Virago, London, Chapter 13.

510

ical arguments, indicate some of their main problems and then briefly place these debates in their historical context in Western thought.

An anthropological debate as object lesson

As we shall make clear later in the chapter, the association of women with nature and men with culture is by no means new. The recent debates within academic anthropology draw on assumptions and stereotypes which have been deeply embedded in our culture for several centuries. Currently, debate centres on the dichotomy between women being seen as closer to nature and men as closer to culture, and its use to 'explain' the apparently universal secondary status of women in all societies. The controversy is of interest to feminists for two reasons. First, it sheds light on the difficulties of generalizing about alleged universals in the position of women. Second, it illustrates the prevalence and the persuasiveness of what we shall call *essentialist* thinking about the sexes. By this we mean the common conviction that sex differences in the sense of gender ultimately refer to concrete, biological distinctions between men and women. We contrast this with a *relativist* position where, while granting biological sexual differences, emphasis is placed on the social construction of sexuality. From this latter perspective there is no such thing as woman or man in asocial terms; women and men, or rather femininity and masculinity, are constituted in specific cultural settings according to class, age, marital status and so on. We further contend that essentialist thinking about the sexes is part of a dominant ideology which is an impediment to our understanding of the ways societies construct the sexes.

The nature/culture debate has taken many different forms within twentieth-century social theory. Among the most important contributions is the work of Claude Lévi-Strauss. For him the human mind works through series of binary oppositions such as nature/culture, wild/tame, raw/cooked. He alleges that the nature/culture distinction is a universal folk concept, based on the equally universal human propensity to bound society off from non-society.[. . .] He also assumes that the human mind is specifically constructed to perceive binary oppositions. For him these dichotomies are in the unconscious; they need to be decided by the anthropologist, so that his model of what it is that social scientists do is of rational, logical deciphering.

A number of critiques have been made of Lévi-Strauss on the grounds that he bases culture in biology. They point out that nature and culture are not value-free terms which can safely be used to explain any phenomenon, for they carry the cultural biases of the meaning attached to them. Western ideas of nature and culture have, since the eighteenth century, focused on the origins and evolution of the human species. Thus, we take the 'natural' to be innate in our primitive heritage, while the 'cultural' is arbitrary and artificial. Furthermore, as will be made clear later, Western traditions lay particular emphasis on controlling nature by means of culture, especially through science, medicine and technology. But ideas of nature and culture can be entirely different in non-Western societies. So, in using our ideas of nature and culture to explain the beliefs and behaviour of other societies we run into the danger of confusing our theories with the cognitive structures of other societies.

The nature, culture and gender debates are best known to English speaking people through two articles published apparently independently in the early 1970s by Ardener and Ortner. They sparked off a heated argument which has resulted in a challenge, on both empirical and theoretical grounds, to the contention that women are universally seen as nearer to nature, men to culture. Critiques have come from two angles: theoretical ones which attack the logic of the arguments and the premises from which they start, and empirical ones using detailed ethnographic descriptions to show that in particular societies these concepts either do not exist in the forms claimed, or are not consistently associated with gender.[. . .]

Neither Ardener nor Ortner argue that women *are* closer to nature. Rather they try to explain how and why women are *seen* to be nearer to nature by members of very different societies. They agree in attributing the source of such a view of women to female biology as perceived by men, and to women's restriction to the domestic sphere. Both rely on the presumed readiness of human beings to attribute symbolic significance to female anatomy.

The underlying logic of both Ardener's and Ortner's arguments moves from the premise that the only unalterable sexual difference is reproductive structures and roles, to the conclusion that this must therefore be at the root of social differences based on the social identification of the sexes, i.e. gender. As we have already stressed, this is not a crude biological determinism where biology causes sex differences as sociobiologists might argue. Both Ardener and Ortner dissociate themselves from this position. But in fact what they do is simply add an extra link to the chain of causation. *Biological differences* provide a universal basis for *social definitions* which place women closer to nature than men, and this provides the basis for the *universal subordination* of women. Indeed both writers simply assume that women are universally subordinate to men, and see their task as explaining this 'fact'.[. . .]

As we mentioned earlier, ethnographic material has also been used to attack the identification of women with nature (MacCormack and Strathern, eds, 1980). Recent accounts show that nature and culture are *not* universal native categories, at least not in the form in which they are conceptualized in our society. The notion of culture as superior to and dominant over nature is not universal. Nor in societies which do have such concepts, is there necessarily a simple or consistent relationship with male and female. In both empirical and theoretical critiques of the debate, there is an implicit denial of the value of a rationalist discourse. Nature and culture are relativized concepts, their meaning derives from their place within a particular metaphysics; neither has a unique meaning either within Western thought or cross-culturally.

Many people dislike the ways in which the pair nature/culture has been associated with woman/man in anthropological theory. But it is not the belief that social groups tend to define themselves as 'us' and others as 'not us' which they object to. It is the assertion that 'not us' is equivalent to nature, and is therefore inferior, that they take issue with. The split between 'us' and 'not us' can be into two symmetrical halves rather hierarchically ordered.

Of course we now have to study the formation of 'not us' groups. It is plausible to suppose that at least some of the criteria differentiating 'us' and 'not us' will be sex based, but in gender, not in strictly biological terms. The placing of marginal persons such as childless women, widows, 'hermaphrodites', men who opt out of male activities, is highly culturally variable, and biological sex is not necessarily the determining factor.

Many of the comments we have made relate to the extraordinarily difficult questions of the use of dichotomous pairs in social theory as both explanations and descriptions of social behaviour. In part this brings us to the heart of philosophical disagreements about the form social theories should take, and of psychological disagreements about the way the human mind works and how psychoanalysis and theories of language are used. We are concerned here, however, with some rather simple errors which we believe are commonly made in analysing women. Even if we granted that there was a universal association of the form women are to nature as men are to culture, that would not sanction slipping into assertions about universal judgments of *value* (good/bad, superior/inferior), nor from there into issues of *control* (superordinate/subordinate). And this danger is not confined to anthropology.

The slippage referred to above is possible because of the way we conceptualize women and men as each possessing common features which constrain their lives. The feminist argument against this view is that what cultures make of sex differences is almost infinitely variable, so that biology cannot be playing a determining role. Women and men are products of social relations, if we change the social relations we change the categories 'woman' and 'man'. On both political and intellectual grounds we would argue that to put it at its bluntest, social relations determine sex differences rather than biological sex producing social divisions between the sexes.

The idea that biological differences between men and women cause social ones is, of course, extremely pervasive, and it has gained prominence through the recent spate of writings on sociobiology. Earlier we called it a dominant ideology. Now we want to argue that it is grounded in Western thought, and especially in science, medicine and technology; hence its dominance.

Science and sexuality

For many centuries there have been attempts to separate out what seemed intractable in the environment (nature), from what could easily be altered by human agency (culture). This division was bound up with notions about the form of God's power over both the natural world and over human beings. Only relatively recently it has been argued, did the idea that human beings had mastery over their surroundings assume more importance than the belief that they were impotent by comparison with the deity and were merely guarding the natural world on his behalf (Glacken 1967). The examples we use are drawn from the mid-eighteenth century on, the period when a secular and self-consciously scientific language began to be employed and when interest in the study of the physical and social aspects of 'man', nature and the environment began on a large scale (Jordanova 1979). During the nineteenth century, the nature/culture distinction seems to have applied more consistently to sexual divisions, with the result that stereotypes of women became more rigid. The ways in which this hardening of the divide between the sexes came about are of great interest, and all the more so as the rigid stereotypes were closely linked with a biological definition of sexuality.

As the anthropological material alluded to in the previous section suggested, the relationship between the metaphors people use and the aspects of lived experience they allegedly express are extremely complex. The metaphors contain contradictions, tensions or even what strike us as logical inconsistencies, but these in no way undermine the historical power of the images. For example, the eighteenth century use of women to symbolize truth in the sense of natural reason, virtue and clarity, coexisted with their simultaneous use to symbolize feelings and sentiment, also analogized to nature, but associated with irrationality and superstition. The nature/culture distinction has operated in Western traditions at many different levels. In addition to myths, pictures and symbols of all kinds, a coherent scientific self-consciousness played a crucial role in reinforcing and redefining the identification of female with nature and male with culture.

The scientific endeavour was linked with masculinity, while passive nature, unveiled and revealed by male science, was identified with femininity. The personification of nature as woman and as mother is prominent in much writing in English during the eighteenth and nineteenth centuries. Furthermore, the very process of constructing a scientific culture was conceived of as a struggle between the elements of male reason and female superstition. For civilization to progress, in other words, the forces of intellectual and social order had to triumph over the ignorant mysticism which kept back the human race. Men, in the name of science, would assert their culture over women and their religious creeds. For many people the battle for power between traditional and modern forces could be seen in the attempts by the intellectual élite of philosophers, savants and enlightened medical men on the side of science and reason to undermine the authority of superstitious and irrational practices exemplified by the Catholic church, and its main clientèle—women.[. . .]

The struggle between the sexes was, for Enlightenment thinkers, part of the history of the human race. The ideology of progress so deeply entrenched in Enlightenment thought suggested the importance of the growth of a rational, humane and civilized society with the development of knowledge and science as motors of change. Allowing the male value system to prevail was therefore an integral part of the process of developing culture with which nature, raw and unmediated, would be controlled. Human *mastery* over nature should ever increase, this was history, this was science. Women, as nature were to be controlled, or rather channelled into the correct role for nature in the history of the human race.

Although we are concerned with the manner in which men and women were conceptualized as opposite and complementary using the nature/culture dichotomy, it is important to stress that nature and culture were *not* seen as necessarily incommensurable categories in the eighteenth and nineteenth centuries. Obviously, for human beings to have culture, nature has to yield to their manipulations. Nature, including human beings, is modified as a result of culture. We must be careful therefore not to construe the concept of nature as implying simply a view of the world as composed of intractable, innate qualities. Although nature was distinguished from environment, culture, civilization and society, a continual interaction between them was envisaged. It is certainly true that what we have called essentialist thinking about the sexes is linked with a scientific view of nature, but it would be a drastic over-simplification to equate this with a crude deterministic position. In the natural philosophical and medical literatures of the eighteenth century there were extensive discussions on the ways in which behaviour, what we might call lifestyle, became incorporated into the body through diet, exercise, habits, occupation and so on. As a result, culture is continually affecting natural objects, particularly the human body; culture was identified as a major determinant of health and disease at both physical and moral levels. Both men and women were seen in terms of this continual dialectic between nature and culture.

Far from being defined exclusively in terms of their sex organs, women were, physiologically speaking, distinguished by the occupations and tasks of womanhood. Although these tended to be closely linked with their reproductive role, the emphasis on lifestyle as a determinant of the characteristics of the human body, provides important clues to the nature/culture relationship in the eighteenth and early nineteenth centuries. The emphasis on occupation as a determinant of health led to a radical boundary being drawn between the sexes. The theoretical basis for this was a physiology which recognized few boundaries; it conflated moral and physical, mind and body, and created a language capable of containing biological, psychological and social considerations. Physicians in late eighteenth-century France used these physiological presuppositions to argue that women were physiologically and automatically quite distinct from men (Knibiehler 1976). The total physiology of woman could, they argued, only be understood in terms of their lifestyle and the roles they ought to fulfil if they weren't doing so already. The occupational model of health tightly linked jobs performed in the social arena (for women, the production, suckling and care of children, the creation of a natural morality within the family) with health and disease. Of course the occupational model was applied to both men and women, but for the latter permissible occupation was tightly defined according to 'natural' criteria. Women's health therefore depended on their fulfilling a restricted social role which appeared to be an inevitable consequence of their ability to bear children. Men were members of the broadest social and cultural groups, while women's sphere of action was limited to the family—the ultimate guarantor of human stability since it was the essential *biological* unit of *social* life. These arguments led to women being conceptualized as physically feeble, unable to survive without male protection, frivolous and irrational. Women's minds worked differently from men's in making emotive associations rather than logical connections, a belief that became elaborated into a complex psychological theory in the nineteenth century which asserted women's incapacity for rational scientific thought and their superior talent for affective sentiments (Ploss et al 1935).[. . .]

There is no doubt that the question of power is the crucial one and it holds the key to the apparently contradictory ways in which women were associated with nature. As we stressed above, femininity was commonly equated with superstitions, that is, with irrational, illegitimate, mystical power. But it was also associated with moral regeneration; women as natural creatures held within them the possibility for growth and improvement, for the transcendence over evil by the forces of virtue. To be sure

515

this feminine harnessing of positive power also, by implication, involved mystical elements, notably the special bond between mother and child, but here it was safe, even desirable.[. . .]

Nineteenth-century interpretations of the nature/culture oppositions which extend the argument into an evolutionary framework were sometimes quite explicit about the struggle for power between men and women. These concerns came to the surface in a number of mid-nineteenth century works which dealt with the development of human society and attempted to grapple with the problems of whether all societies go through matriarchal stages (Fee 1974). Such works considered the economic foundations of sex roles and were closely related to prevalent beliefs about women's limited capacities for participation in the labour market.

Late nineteenth-century debates about the entry of women into the medical profession employ the same sexual polarities of nature and culture in an economic sense, for it was considered unseemly for women to compete publicly with men. The argument that women could not become doctors because of their inherent lack of scientific ability is now well known. It was also claimed that only married women had the necessary 'experience' for the job, but they were the very ones who were excluded by virtue of their childbearing and other family-based duties. Unmarried women, on the other hand, might have the life style compatible with a profession, but lacked, by definition, the 'experience' required (Donnison 1977, Delamont and Duffin, 1978, pp. 46–7).

The division between married and unmarried women is of great importance. At the end of the eighteenth century the medical literature emphasized the superior health of married women, and contained pleas to married women not to leave the home but to consider motherhood their occupation. At the same period, working women came increasingly from the ranks of young, unmarried girls. In terms of work the division was not just between women and men, but between men and single women on the one hand, and married women who were reproductively active, on the other. Women who worked presented a problem, for by selling their labour power, they entered a male world of abstract commodities with objective values. They violated the neat category distinction. The common nineteenth-century concern for the modesty of women workers should be seen in this context. A working woman carried with her, through her sexuality, the associations of a private, mystified arena connected with feelings in the family, not the public routines of work. She brought the potential for uncontrolled emotion into an arena of life which was held to epitomise control and objectivity, or put more concretely, men and money.

The economic inactivity of women was justified by the idealization of the home and family life as women's preserves. The dominance of women in the family was itself explained in terms of their reproductive and nurturing role which had arisen during the course of human evolution. There was thus a pleasing harmony between the biological, psychological and social division of labour. Female biological rhythms, especially the menstrual cycle, were taken as examples of natural laws at their most beautiful. Women had to submit to the fluctuations and changes of their bodies which were watched over by the benevolent eye of the husband and the physician.

In its application to sexual divisions, the nature/culture distinction mediated forms of power. But perceived distribution of power was not simply a question of male strength and female submission. In fact, two forms of power were envisaged and both had their positive and negative aspects. The first, identified with women, was potency in the realm of feeling which made women good wives and mothers and general upholders of morality. These praiseworthy features were matched by destructive ones; the tendency to be over-emotional, superstitious and credulous made women vulnerable to dogmatic religious and political practices. These two sides of female power express an ambivalence towards nature itself: it was the source of all knowledge, the ultimate ethical arbiter, and at the same time, capable of unpredictable destruction. Male domination, on the other hand, came into its own in the public rather than the private sphere. It was based on an understanding of natural laws and abstract relationships; it was ideally suited to surviving in the complex economy of nineteenth-century Europe. Male power expressed contemporary notions of culture, that it had penetrated nature's laws, understood them and was now in a position to manipulate them. Its negative aspect was a lack of sympathetic identification with others.

One of the most noteworthy features of this ideological construction was the association of each sex with universal biological categories, as if all women and all men were really the same regardless of class or other social differences. In fact class differences are explicitly denied in this view, which we characterized earlier as an *essentialist* approach to the sexes. Furthermore, the ways in which the behaviour of men and women were spoken about implied the life style of a bourgeoisie as the fundamental human standard not that of the working people. A basic question remains: what interests were, and are, served by elaborating a set of biologically based, opposed categories which deliberately ignored (or conveniently obscured) social divisions? We argued earlier that during the eighteenth century, male dominance was expressed through an area of human activity, science, which stands, then as now, for the capacity to control and manipulate the natural world. In this sense men possessed power through their identification with scientific knowledge. Simultaneously, women were conceptualized as the passive recipients of scientific manipulation. The dichotomy had implications for many areas of social life: the organization of work, the division of labour, the ways in which political and social stability were envisaged, and the respective roles of husband and wife in marriage and childbearing.

We are not suggesting that scientific thought was conveniently co-opted in the service of male domination, but that scientific theories and practices have provided our culture with one of the most fundamental ways in which sexual divisions were perceived and understood. We would also say that notions of sexuality were basic to the ways in which science as an activity was thought about. These divisions between male and female, science and nature, did not remain at the level of theorizing but set the terms for a whole range of concrete struggles which are still being enacted today in the Western world. It remains a task for feminist study to discover the situation in other cultures, and to be alert to the misuse of such ideas as the nature/culture dichotomy in the area of sexuality.

REFERENCES

Delamont, S. and Duffin, L., (eds) (1978) *The Nineteenth-century Woman: Her Cultural and Physical World*, London: Croom Helm.

Donnison, J. (1977) *Midwives and Medical Men: A History of Interprofessional Rivalries and Women's Rights*, London: Heinemann.

Fee, E (1974) 'The sexual politics of Victorian social anthropology.' In M. Hartmann and L. W. Banner (eds), *Clio's Consciousness Raised*, New York: Harper & Row.

Glacken, C. (1967) *Traces on the Rhodian Shore: Nature and Culture in Western Thought from Ancient Times to the End of the Eighteenth Century*, Berkeley, Cal: University of California Press.

Jordanova, L. J. (1979) 'Earth science and environmental medicine: the synthesis of the late Enlightenment.' In L. J. Jordanova and R. Porter (eds), *Images of the Earth: Essays in the History of the Environmental Sciences*, pp. 119–46, Chalfont St Giles: British Society for the History of Science.

Knibiehler, Y. (1976) 'Les médecins et la "nature feminine" au temps du Code Civile.' *Annales: Economies, Sociétés, Civilisations* 31 (4): 824–45.

MacCormack, Carol, and Strathern, M. (eds) (1980) *Nature Culture and Gender*, New York: Cambridge University Press.

Ploss, H. H. and Bartels, M. and P. (1935) *Woman: An Historical Gynaecological and Anthropological Compendium*, 3 vols London: Heinemann. (First published in German in 1885.)

Jonathan Dollimore (1942–)

Jonathan Dollimore, a professor of literature at the University of Sussex, is, together with Alan Sinfield, particularly associated with the British historical and ideological critique called 'cultural materialism'. This approach, often compared to American 'New Historicism', claims to be more politically orientated and materially based than the American intellectual movement. His publications include *Political Shakespeare: New Essays in Cultural Politics* (1985), *Radical Tragedy: Religion, Ideology, Power in the Drama of Shakespeare and his Contemporaries* (1984) and *Sexual Dissidence: Augustine to Wilde, Freud to Foucault* (1991).

Dollimore is also associated with the development of 'queer' theory in England and at the University of Sussex has pioneered programmes in sexuality and literature. His essay below, 'Homophobia and Sexual Difference', first delivered at the 'Sexual Difference' conference at the University of Southampton in July 1985, was published in the *Oxford Literary Review* (vol. 8, 1986). In terms of British studies of gender this was a ground-breaking conference which highlighted the emergence of 'queer' theory in a sometimes contestatory relationship with feminist theory. Dollimore's and Simon Watney's essays, therefore, emerge from a significant 'moment' in the academic discourse of sexuality in Britain. Both essays focus on homophobia and work with Michel Foucault's theories of the social and subjective construction of homosexuality, with Watney looking critically at various sociological and psychological theories of sexuality. Dollimore approaches the issue from a more cultural concern with the ways in which once identified 'homosexuality begins to speak on its own behalf; to forge its own identity and culture, *often in the self same terms* by which it had been produced and marginalised' coming eventually to 'challenge the very power structures which had produced and marginalized it'. He goes on to discuss concepts of repression and the return of the repressed and argues that while homophobia may be 'rooted in repressed desire' this is not its only condition. He concludes with a brief discussion of masculinity as a social and political formation and notes the intersection of social and class forces that combine racism, xenophobia, misogyny, and homophobia.

J.M.

Homophobia and sexual difference

The binary opposition, contends Derrida, is a violent hierarchy. He is surely right, and the opposition masculine/homosexual, a conflation of two classic binaries (masculine/feminine; hetero/homosexual) has been one of the most violent of all. I'm concerned here with something which serves directly to express that violence and which violently secures the opposition itself, namely homophobia. This is, I confess, an ambiguous and not entirely satisfactory term, though I don't propose to unpack that ambiguity except to say that the sense in which I'm using it is roughly descriptive of a manifest phenomenon: the hatred, fear and persecution of, the raging at, homosexuality.[1]

The wider project of which this paper is a part seeks to explain why the negation of homosexuality has been in direct proportion to its actual centrality, its cultural marginality in direct proportion to its cultural significance; why homosexuality is so strangely integral to the self same heterosexual cultures which obsessively denounce it, and why it is history—history rather than human nature—which has produced this paradoxical position.

There are two analytic perspectives which address first, this paradoxical centrality of homosexuality in our culture, second the phenomenon of homophobia, and third the construction of masculinity (the three things being closely related). The one is a radical psychoanalysis, the other a materialist account of deviance.

I'm aware of the theoretical tension—indeed incompatibility—between these two perspectives, and in a sense I welcome this, finding in that tension an impetus to recover the historical and political dimensions which theoretically self consistent (hermetically sealed?) critiques often gesture towards but rather more rarely engage with. Just now I'm interested in a cultural analysis generated both by the provocative convergences between otherwise incompatible theoretical perspectives—that is, incapable of synthesis—and also *across* their manifest divergences.

A psychoanalytic perspective can be sketched in terms of our related propositions:

1. In 1920 Freud declared: 'in addition to their manifest heterosexuality, a very considerable measure of latent or unconscious homosexuality can be detected in all normal people' (Pelican Freud, vol. 9, 1979: p. 399). Five years earlier, in an addition to the *Three Essays on the Theory of Sexuality* he had made the, in some ways, even more astonishing claim that 'all human beings are capable of making a homosexual object-choice and have in fact made one in their unconscious'; it follows then that 'from the point of view of psychoanalysis the exclusive sexual interest felt by men for women is also a problem that needs elucidating and is not a self-evident fact based upon an attraction that is ultimately of a chemical nature' (7: pp. 56–7). In a footnote

added in 1919 to his study of Leonardo, Freud reiterates this argument but with this significant addition; everyone has made a homosexual object choice 'and either still adheres to it in his unconscious or else protects himself against it by vigorous counter-attitudes' (14: p. 191). Such counter-attitudes help constitute homophobia and relate suggestively to Freud's account of negation (1915): 'the content of a repressed image or idea can make its way into consciousness, on condition that it is *negated*. Negation is a way of taking cognizance of what is repressed; indeed it is already a lifting of the repression, though not, of course, an acceptance of what is repressed' (11: pp. 437–38).

2. In the formation of the socialised, gendered subject—the production of sexual difference—this homosexuality, itself an aspect of an originally undifferentiated sexuality, i.e. polymorphous perversity, an innate bisexuality is repressed and sublimated. It is not of course thereby dispensed with: according to Freud repressed homosexuality helps constitute and maintain the very social order which requires its repression, helping, for example, 'to constitute the social instincts' (9: p. 198).

3. Certain kinds of paranoia are the expression of desublimated but still repressed homosexual desire. Paranoia in Freud's analysis is both less delusory and more revealing than its popular use currently allows: less delusory in the sense that it isn't just a delusion of being persecuted but an active homophobic attempt *to* persecute; more revealing in that, if Freud is correct, the popular remark 'just because we're paranoid it doesn't mean to say they're not after us' is complicated by the fact that 'us' may well in fact *be* 'them'.

4. The fourth proposition is implicit in the other three and relates to the more general process of identity formation. Achieving social identity is less a process of free growth than of restricted growth (7: p. 57); even of a stunted growth. But of course the growth metaphor must be dropped: identity is a construction and, as such, involves a process of exclusion, negation and repression. And this is a process which, even if successful, results in an identity intrinsically unstable. This is bad news for masculinity, one of whose self-conceptions is stability, and whose functions is to maintain it socially and psychically.

I haven't space to elaborate upon these propositions except to say that they have been appropriated, provocatively and selectively, for a radical homosexual politics: in France by Guy Hacquenghem, in Italy by Mario Mieli, in Germany by Martin Dannecker, in America and Australia by Dennis Altman.[2] At the same time as deploying Freudian categories, these writers explore the repression of homosexuality in the very practice of psychoanalysis itself, seeing this as an aspect of psychoanalysis as a vehicle of social control.

Among other things the materialist account of deviance addresses just this phenomenon of the social control of sexuality through the creation of categories like that of homosexual and the socio-political production of homophobia. This view is currently associated with Foucault but it has a much longer history, of which Foucault is only a recent part. It grows from anthropology, phenomenology, the sociology of deviance, radical criminology and Marxist sub-cultural theory. All these perspectives, though in very different ways, contest the ideas first that deviants are merely the waste product of civilisation, second that deviancy is somehow intrinsic to the deviant subject. The crucial move was to see deviancy itself as a social construction and a process of ascription. To retrace that process is to learn less and less about the deviant individual per se and more and more about him or her as the bearer of a social process, about the dominant social formations which identify him or her. For a variety of complex reasons society needs its deviants; in some cases for example a dominant culture needs its inferiors, its others, in order to consolidate itself. Often overlapping with such consolidation is a process of displacement: the demonised abnormal other, whose alienness reinforces through contrast the rightness of normality, serves at the same time as a scapegoat for normality's own sexual and not so sexual anxieties: homosexuals as corrupters of public morals, children, the family and even the armed forces; as conveying to other aliens (their external counterpart) the state's innermost secrets.

Consider as an instance Foucault's arguable claim that the homosexual was literally invented quite recently: 'the sodomite had been a temporary aberration; the homosexual was now a species'.[3] This was part of a wider process not of the repression of sexuality so much as its production, a production enabling new and quite complex forms of social control. But it was a control that could never be complete; once identified thus homosexuality begins to speak on its own behalf, to forge its own identity and culture, *often in the self same terms* by which it had been produced and marginalised, and eventually to challenge the very power structures which had produced and marginalised it. As Jeffrey Weeks has shown in his own work, this 'reverse discourse' as Foucault terms it, constitutes 'a complex and socially significant history of resistance and self-definition which historians have hitherto too easily ignored' (*Sex, Politics and Society*, Longman: 1988, p. 177). Its implications for a more general theory of political resistance are considerable, as can be seen from its points of convergence with the psychoanalytic perspective (and this despite the fact that in many ways it aims to repudiate psychoanalysis).

To begin with both perspectives suggest an eventual return to homosexuality—in the one it is a return from within, in the other a return from without; either an inner resurgence of desire through the breakdown of psychic repression, or the oppositional approach of the demonized other from beyond, from the social margins. Either way it returns to disturb the heterosexual and especially the masculine norm. In the first case, the psychoanalytic, homosexuality may become, in Hocquenghem's phrase, the 'killer of civilised egos' because such egos are rooted in and conditional upon the repression of that same homosexual desire which returns. In the second case the dominant is seen to create a discursive category which initially assists its domination but which subsequently comes to disrupt it.

We can see here a cultural complexity, and certain complex possibilities for cultural resistance, growing from the phenomenon of internal contradiction and negation. Both perspectives exemplify this and both can be related to other classic instances: for example to the more general Freudian proposition that the repressed may return disruptively via the very mechanisms and images of repression itself; to the Marxist analysis of the contradiction between the forces and relations of production and, beyond that, to the Hegelian contradiction intrinsic to the master/slave dialectic. And then most recently there is a certain emphasis in deconstruction which seeks to show that what the dominant excludes, negates or subordinates, remains intrinsic to it, actually or potentially, even though the process of (e.g.) exclusion represents the object of exclusion as quite alien—its alienness being the ostensible reason for its exclusion.

Not surprisingly this is an aspect of deconstruction which has found an illuminating and significant precedent in Freud. It's apparent for example that Freud problematises the category of normal sexuality by showing how its other, homosexuality, isn't at all over there, alien and removed (foreign), but at the very heart of heterosexuality itself. At the same time of course the authority of Freud has been a powerful force in our own century in reconstituting homosexuality as inferior, inadequate and marginal to heterosexuality. If his own categories of the Oedipus complex and of normal (i.e. normative) psychosexual development provide the basis for this renewed repression of homosexuality this is related to the fact that homosexuality remained a problem *for* Freud. On his own admission he never adequately accounted for it, though he tried to, and this despite the fact that his *Three Essays* suggested that it didn't need the kind of explaining which he subsequently wanted to give it. Homosexuality returns for Freud as well as for the subject of his case histories; his attention to it is symptomatic of, as well as an attempted explanation of, its troubling centrality to and disruption of the normal.

The cultural return of homosexuality in recent history has been well documented by Weeks; here it returns as a reverse discourse, moving from the margins to the centre, from construction to presence but a presence still in terms of the initial construction. From that history there is much to be learnt, even for a deconstructionist analysis. We see for example how the binary opposition normal/abnormal has worked by positing an absolute metaphysical difference (where the secondary or negative term has denoted *the alien*) which overlaps with the hierarchical assertion of another absolute—but now also relational—difference (where the secondary term denotes *the inferior*). Thus hierarchy, whereby metaphysical binarism is enforced, can also become a partial disclosure of the truth which metaphysics needs to efface: absolute difference is only ever a differential relation, a difference which is also a dependence. The master is dependent upon his slave in ways he never dreamed of, even the slave who doesn't work as such.

The second point at which the psychoanalytic and the materialist perspectives converge is around the question of identity, especially the emphasis on identity as negation. Both suggest that identity—individual and cultural—involves a process of exclusion and negation. In the first it is the negation of desire, in the second of the culturally defined other, of cultural difference. A yet further aspect of this convergence involves the intriguing phenomenon of the culturally negated other becoming the focus of the very desire which is being policed—within the dominant culture—in the process of the other's negation. Indeed the other, in the very process of being identified and negated may actually incite such desire. Romantics know about this.

These two areas of convergence also direct us to the main area of divergence: on the Freudian model it is the repression and sublimation of homosexual desire that helps secure identity and social organisation. Conversely, on the materialist model it is much more homophobia, as an aspect of the construction of homosexuality and independent of the question of the actual subjective repression of desire, which helps secure a coerced identity and social organisation, most especially the enforcing of a heterosexual norm and the policing of its boundaries: 'Homophobia is only incidentally directed against homosexuals—its more common use is against the 49% of the population which is male . . . The taunt "What are you, a fag?" is used in many ways to encourage certain types of male behaviour and to define the limits of "acceptable" masculinity'.[4] In the psychoanalytic account homophobia might well signal the precariousness and instability of identity, even of sexual difference itself; in the materialist it typically signals the reverse, that sexual difference is being secured.

If the trouble with the materialist view is its tendency to functionalist reduction, the Freudian position has even more intractable problems. Consider three: first it construes sexuality in terms of an original pre-social plenitude, an initially unstructured energy; second, and consequently, sexuality is construed in certain central texts of Freud as a drive with extreme hydraulic characteristics; third, a phenomenon like homophobia is explained too exclusively in terms of the subjective psychic repression of its agents. Even with these problems, and considerable as they are, the Freudian model must stand as an indispensable starting point for identifying a certain kind of homophobia, namely that conjunction of hatred, paranoia and desire which characterises some heterosexually identified men in their violent relationship with overtly homosexual men (especially those who take the sex before dispensing the violence).

Homophobia may then be rooted in repressed desire. But this can't be its necessary condition since it obviously circulates without it. Indeed, homophobia in this second, socio-political form, for example as 'a mechanism for regulating the behaviour of the many by the specific oppression of a few' (Sedgwick, p. 88) is much more effective than psychic repression as a mode of social control. Even so, since in cultural terms desiring the normal is inseparable from, conditional upon, not desiring the abnormal, repression remains central to identity, individual and cultural, even—or indeed especially—on the view of homophobia as a strategy of social control. Or should what is being identified here go by another name? Maybe we still need to pluralise the notion of repression, as we certainly need to pluralise that of homophobia: there are different kinds and the differences are crucial.

Historically what have made these crucial differences have been specific cultural and political determinations—those of religion, class and race for example.[5] And this tells us again that homophobia is something which may originate in, and constantly (as it circulates socially) reconnect with, psychic repression, but which also circulates without it.

Considering someone like D. H. Lawrence, it's clear that his antagonism to the Bloomsbury group focused homophobically on the homosexuality of some of its members. From his study of Lawrence at that time Paul Delany concludes that the writer has 'strong homosexual impulses which he felt morally bound to repress'.[6] It seems evident too that this repressed desire is displaced in this antagonism and becomes inextricably tangled with an equally powerful and important class hostility. Often however it is difficult in retrospect, or even contemporaneously for that matter, to discern the part that psychic repression plays in any instance of homophobia, or indeed if it is present what kind of repression it is; note that Delany writes of Lawrence's *moral* repression. But it's hardly imperative that we should, since the most pernicious forms of homophobia are also those whose social infiltration and political deployment don't presuppose psychic repression. A good instance of this would be the homophobic attack on Peter Tatchell during the Bermondsey by-election in 1983. Here there may indeed have been a displacement or projection of repressed desire. Indeed Tatchell, in his book on the events of those months, surveys the hate mail sent to him and concludes as much.[7]

More important though was a displacement onto the homosexual of a whole range of political fears and anxieties made possible by a prior social construction of the category homosexual:

Dear Mr Tatchell

When I lived in Bermondsey, until my family were bombed out while I was fighting to protect my country from outside evils, we had a saying. Bermondsey was a place where men were men, and women counted as 'manholes' and members of the 'Middlesex Regiment' would not be tolerated. So why don't you piss off back to where you came from and leave the decent people of that once great borough alone. This country is in enough trouble without the likes of you, and Tariq Ali etc, stirring it up . . .

(quoted from Tatchell, *Battle*, p. 72)

In this letter masculinity—'when men were men'—is vigilant against 'outside evils', racial infiltration, homosexuality conceived as sexual ambiguity ('Middlesex Regiment') and social decline—evoking perhaps imperial decline: 'that once great borough'. It's a letter which indicates at least two fundamental things about homophobia: first it's often bound into a certain kind of masculine identity, second both it and masculinity often intersect with other kinds of phobia and hatred: in this case racism, xenophobia and misogyny. Like many right wing hatreds this one is laced with nostalgia: that once great borough where men were men, women were manholes and queers were given short shrift. Manholes: many interrelated fears and phobias are suggested by that image. Perhaps the fear of sexual engulfment, perhaps the castration complex itself. But isn't it also an image which, like the letter as a whole, fearfully anticipates engulfment and contamination by the return of those others ('outside evils') whose marginality has hitherto seemed to guarantee a sexual, racial and national purity? I'm reminded that with the literal manhole—the thing in the street—well sure we can walk all over it. But don't we also know, if only in our dreams, that even as we do so we will one day just as surely fall down it?

NOTES

1. On homophobia see especially George Weinberg, *Society and the Healthy Homosexual* (New York, 1972); Mark Freedman, 'Homophobia: the Psychology of a Social Disease,' in *Body Politic*, 24 (June 1975); Ken Plummer, ed., *The Making of the Modern Homosexual* (London, 1981), esp. chs 3 and 6; Dennis Altman, *The Homosexualisation of America* (Boston, 1982); Eve Kosofsky Sedgwick, *Between Men: English Literature and Male Homosocial Desire* (New York, 1985).
2. Guy Hocquenghem, *Homosexual Desire* (London, 1978); Mario Mieli, *Homosexuality and Liberation: Elements of a Gay Critique* (London, 1980); Martin Dannecker, *Theories of Homosexuality* (London, 1981); Dennis Altman, *The Homosexualisation of America*.
3. *The History of Sexuality* (New York, 1980); see also Jeffrey Weeks, *Coming Out: Homosexual Politics in Britain from the Nineteenth Century to the Present* (London, 1977); and *Sex, Politics and Society: the Regulation of Sexuality Since 1800* (London, 1981).
4. G. K. Lehne, quoted from John Marshall, 'Pansies, Perverts and Macho Men' in Plummer, pp. 153–4.

5. A note on the issue of homophobia and class: in the last session of the Sexual Difference conference, in response to a question by Elaine Hobby about the lack of panels explicitly addressing gay and lesbian issues, Lisa Jardine invoked, somewhat gratuitously as it seemed, what she called the problem of 'the huge body of fascist gay men who I'm surrounded by in Cambridge'. Even in the absence of much direct experience of that institution, it seems imperative to make certain distinctions. The people impelled by her description, wherever they are, are best described not as fascist gays but fascists who are also homosexual. Not to make that distinction is to efface crucial political and cultural differences. Further, the fascism of such people almost invariably has less to do with their sexuality per se than with a whole range of other factors—e.g. the political culture of their institution, their own cultural trajectory, including class origins and current identifications. In the case of Cambridge (the University) such factors would seem to take an especially high priority.
6. *D. H. Lawrence's Nighmare* (Brighton, 1979), p. 50.
7. Peter Tatchell, *The Battle for Bermondsey* (London, 1983), p. 72.

Simon Watney

Simon Watney is a member of the communications faculty at the Central London Polytechnic and has written extensively on the cultural impact of Aids, see for instance his essay 'Emergent Sexual Identities and HIV/Aids', in P. Aggleton *et al.*, *AIDS: Facing the Second Decade* (1993). His publications include *Policing Desire: Pornography, Aids and the Media* (1987), *Taking Liberties: Aids and Cultural Politics* (1989), and *The Art of Duncan Grant* (1990). Like Jonathan Dollimore, he was a participant at the conference on sexual difference held at the University of Southampton in July 1985 and this essay, given as a paper at the conference, was published in the *Oxford Literary Review* (vol. 8, 1986).

Watney's essay begins with a critique of what he feels is an essentially heterosexual and collusive bias inside feminist gender studies leading to 'the significantly weak response of the Women's Movement to issues such as lesbian motherhood, or the AIDS epidemic as it affects gay men'. His essay goes on to discuss recent works on 'Coming Out' which, he argues are based on misinterpretations of the work of Michel Foucault. Where some have argued that 'Coming Out' is tantamount to asking for 'incorporation', 're-inscription', and a denial of rights of privacy, Watney asks whether '"Coming Out" does indeed constitute an exclusively personalized politics'. He suggests, instead, that Coming Out always involves a '*collective* identity', and a 'political-legal' programme. Watney criticizes psychoanalysis and sexual sociology for continuing to work inside parameters set by heterosexual concepts of sexual difference and suggests that what needs to be addressed is not homosexual desire (constantly confused with personal identity), but the 'problem of homophobia'.
J.M.

The banality of gender

'My dear Gladys!' cried Lord Henry. 'How can you say that? Romance lives by repetition, and repetition converts an appetite into an art. Besides, each time that one loves is the only time one has ever loved. Difference of object does not alter singleness of passion. It merely intensifies it. We can have in life but one great experience at best, and the secret of life is to reproduce that experience as often as possible.'

'Even when one has been wounded by it, Harry?' asked the Duchess, after a pause.

'Especially when one has been wounded by it,' answered Lord Henry.

(Oscar Wilde, *The Picture of Dorian Gray*)

In recent years it has proved convenient for the purposes of pedagogy to consider the demarcation of sexual difference in the likeness of those institutions which claim to speak on behalf of the human body, enouncing its many and various truths. At a certain risk of arbitrariness, we may initially distinguish between:

The Law—which considers sexual difference from the perspective of legitimacy, child-raising practices, inheritance, immigration rights, property, privacy, violence, work opportunities, standards of decency, notions of consent, and so on.

The State (national and local)—which thinks of sexual difference in relation to differentials of taxation, welfare benefits, sport, education, entertainment, transport, notions of decorum, and so on.

Sociology—which emphasises parallels and variables through the above structures in order to disclose the phenomenon. Society, and its articulation in the descriptive voices of social agents.

Anthropology—which maps these same variables across local and national boundaries, in order to disclose the phenomenon, Mankind.

History—which chronicles the causes and conditions of emergence of sexually derived practices, categories, mentalities, and institutions.

Cultural Studies—which examine the sex of cultural producers and consumers, and the mobilisation of sexual ideologies in cultural practices.

Psychoanalysis—which excavates the etiology and intentions of the desiring subjects who move across and motivate the above categories.

It should at once be noted that the sense of sexual difference which informs these overlapping institutions involves a taken-for-granted distinction between male and female, a sense of opposition which constitutes the bed-rock of their understanding of 'difference'. At the same time however, each reveals its own sexual unconscious in the degree to which it acknowledges, handles, disavows, or entirely represses the other major axis of sexual difference—that which Freud explores in the name of the object-choice, and to which Foucault gives the word 'sexuality'. From the choppy seas of epistemological confusion which surround the entire subject of sexual differences I should like to arrest two areas, first contemporary theories of gender in their political and ideological implications, and second the idea and practice of a specific gay politics. These are not unrelated topics, particularly if one accepts that the processes of identification which direct sexual differentiations are also fundamentally implicated in the fixity (or otherwise) of adult object-choice.

Gender versus identification

The resurgence of feminism as a political force since the 1950s has been largely dependent on its ability to offer a more persuasive account of the position of women than was claimed within any of the available Marxist traditions of social theory. Gender has been used as a central explanatory term across the entire spectrum of the Women's Movement, frequently being offered as an adequate and self-sufficient explanation of sexual difference, and a distinct arena for political contestation. According to this picture we are to distinguish two irreducible domains of human activity and awareness, stretched out above the fixed signs of biological sex difference. This account is almost invariably informed by a larger body of contingent political theory which, in the name of patriarchy, identifies a trans-historical and trans-cultural formation in human power relations, whereby men assume and sustain power at women's expense. Conflict and debate proceed from rival theories which regard gender characteristics as either biologically determined, and hence presumably immutable, or positioned by other forces, and hence open to modification. From this latter position derives a familiar set of political strategies aimed at the 'de-masculinising' of men, via the control of available representations, children's toys, and so on, the values of which supposedly are 'internalised' by male children, but not, somehow by female. Conversely women are to divest themselves of the traditional associations of 'submissive' femininity. That the categories of masculinity and femininity brought into play here brook no variants, or at least no explanation of variance, is an immediate and major problem, together with the excruciating voluntarism of the entire project, which involves at least three significant assumptions. First, that women and men can meaningfully be described as distinct socio-economic groups, who are dissatisfied with the *status quo*. Secondly, that 'feminised' men and 'masculinised' women would in any appreciable way change in their economic relations. And thirdly, that the organisation of all those phenomena which identify gender—dress-codes, speech, sexual fantasies and behaviour, hobbies, taste in films, career choices, and so on, are all equally determined by a single ur-code, and that this ur-code is immediately available to transformative strategies.

What has been entirely evacuated from this picture is the entire question of motivation, which in turn may be addressed more properly as the issue of *desire*. In the face of a theory which makes 'male' a unified and unitary sign of violence, and 'female' a sign of domesticity, psychoanalysis offers at the very least a range of terms which immediately opens out a terrain which the sociology of gender can scarcely perceive, let alone explain. The trivial, and trivialising notion of 'internalisation' is obliged either to admit that behind it lies a crude 'effects' theory of identity and behaviour, according to which we are all *tabulae rasae*, and infinitely open to the productive inscriptions of the social, or it collapses under the pressure of a coherent theory of sexed subjectivity, which would refuse to collapse the psychic into the social in the manner of the sociology of gender.

For Freud, the crucial mechanism involved in the organisation of sexual difference is that of identification, 'a psychological process whereby the subject assimilates an aspect, property or attribute of the other and is transformed, wholly or partially, after the model it provides. It is by a series of identifications that the personality is constituted and specified'.[1] We need however to be able to distinguish between the processes of identification which lead individual subjects to identify with others, requiring a recognition (or projection) of their otherness, and identifications based on the recognition (or projection) of significant similarities. Psychoanalysis thus invites us to explore sexual difference in terms of the various ways in which we identify ourselves with others, or others with ourselves, both of which processes require a sense of similarity *and* difference. It also emphasises that the overall organisation of a given individual's identifications is not necessarily cohesive or even coherent, in any unified and systematic way.

It is in this context that we need to consider the conflict in Freud's work between his emphasis on the mobility of fantasy, for example, or the principles of voyeurism and exhibitionism, and his tendency to employ highly reductive notions of activity and passivity as descriptive and evaluative terms in relation to sexuality, in much the same manner as more recent gender theorists. At the same time however he could note that 'we are accustomed to say that every human being displays both male and female instinctual impulses, needs and attributes; but though anatomy it is true, can point out the characteristic of maleness and femaleness, psychology cannot. For psychology the contrast between the sexes fades away into one between activity and passivity, in which we far too readily identify activity with maleness and passivity with femaleness, a view which is by no means universally confirmed . . .'.[2] This last point is of particular importance if we are concerned with the range and variety of sexual identifications, the implications of which are immediately stifled by gender theory, with its behaviourist dependence on observation, interpreting sexual activity in all its forms as variants of a one-directional process, proceeding from the supposedly 'active' penetrating male, to the receptive 'passive' female. In this manner gender theory colludes with the wider tendency to regard individual sexual preferences, of act or object, as aspective of other areas of identity. The slippage from 'male' to 'active' not only has profound ideological consequences in relation to the parallel slippage 'female' to 'passive', but also in relation to the evaluation of *all* non-heterosexual desires and practices. Unlike psychoanalysis, which proceeds from a radical distrust of any attempt to privilege one form of object-choice over another, gender theory tends inexorably to foreground an exclusively heterosexual model of sexual relations which is then found, as excess or as absence, in other sexualities.

At the same time gender theory tends to pay attention to the cultural signs and economic sites of gendered inequalities, to the neglect of actual sexual oppression. Hence the significantly weak response of the Women's Movement to issues such as lesbian motherhood, or the AIDS epidemic as it affects gay men, let alone the ordinary sexual misery of so many relationships. In this respect gender theory offers what

530

amounts to a 'false-consciousness' account of what sexual difference means to women and men. The intransigent structures of desire, based on the 'internalisation' of 'mis-representations' may be willed away, if only the system of sexual imagery can be itself transformed. Hence the central contemporary feminist emphasis on the category of pornography, which, we should note, does not exist in law. Gender theory thus also colludes with the formulation of laws articulating concepts of obscenity and inde-cency which are enacted in the name of community 'standards' which are exclusively heterosexual, and which in turn identify the 'average person' as the simultaneous locus of moral judgement and potential corruptibility, thus inscribing a normative heterosexual audience at the heart of the law *and* of the social which it seeks to 'pro-tect'. The immense convenience of this approach for gender theorists lies in its immediate reinforcement of the rhetorical and monolithic figures of man and woman, figures who recur throughout feminist cultural theory and linguistics, locked forever in post-Edenic opposition. What is clear is that this type of gender theory operates in the absence of any theory of sexual pleasure, and what that might have to do with power.

It remains a curious paradox that so many gay theorists coming from backgrounds in Marxism oriented themselves with this Radical Feminist approach to gender as the central term by which human history is to be analysed. For gender theory offers by far the least historically sophisticated position in contemporary sexual politics, whilst sharing with certain traditions of 'revolutionary' politics the same sense of a single all-determining factor: for class read gender.[3] It is of course impossible to rec-oncile any sense of this unitary stabilising factor which gender theory finds behind individual identity, with the uneven, unstable nature of subjectivity disclosed by Freud. It is therefore particularly important that we exercise great caution in respect of any metaphoric usage of the dualism 'active'/'passive' which might serve further to reinforce the banality of gender as constructed in such characteristically reductive humanist/universal terms. For it is this same couplet which, since Antiquity, has secured and validated the institutions and identities of patriarchy in all its forms. We should not confuse the possibility of a destabilising psychoanalytically informed poli-tics with the inanity of 'gender-bending', so dear to the humanist sociology of sex, which is hopelessly committed to the impossible project of 'restoring' a Mankind equal in (heterosexual) difference.

Confession versus assertion

One particular reading of Foucault's work on sexuality has become significantly influential in the 1980s. According to this position, psychoanalysis merely forces an ever closer union between sexuality and the concept of 'character', oblivious to the fact that Freud argues precisely that the structures of desire are *not* directly reducible to the historical and conscious organisation of sexual practice *or* identity. Thus we find the American critic Richard Sennet taking up a fashionable cry, understood to emanate from Foucault, against the assertion of homosexuality in the name of

'Coming Out' which, Sennett argues, merely authorises the State to propose 'Tell us who you are, how many you are, and we will incorporate you'.[4] Such a position however entirely overlooks the constant legal/medical/psychiatric policing of homosexuality as an inseparable by-product of the category itself. It also forbids *tout court* any sexual politics around non-heterosexual object-choice, either of collective affirmation or of specific institutional/discursive resistance. Sensitive to the slippage from sexual practice to 'character', it nonetheless perversely identifies it with psychoanalysis.

Sennett's position is closely aligned to various libertarian appeals against state intervention in matters of sexuality in the name of privacy. Privacy is thus mobilised as an individual right, aligned architecturally to the bedroom, understood as the site of sexuality. This merely affirms the private/public opposition which traditionally frames legislations surveying and surrounding homosexual acts, legislations which proceed from the visual perspective of an assumed 'general (heterosexual) public' which must not be scopically disturbed. As always, homosexuals are categorically excluded from the social formation, and are effectively privatised. Rights to Privacy campaigners may point to the impossibility of any totalising distinction between the realms of public and private, yet endlessly fall back into calls for the cessation of state/police invasions of gay privacy, understood to extend from bedrooms to bars, thus mapping out a distinct sexual geography of desire in law. At the same time it is demanded that *all* forms of sexuality be regarded and treated as private matters of individual moral choice, frequently calling upon 'commonsensical' notions of privacy in 'everyday life'. A more carefully argued version of this position is to be found in Jeff Minson's influential paper from 1981, *The Assertion of Homosexuality*.[5]

Minson outlines two sets of reservations concerning Coming Out. First, he argues, it 'fails to tap the material roots of homosexual oppression which lie in capitalist and/or patriarchal economico-political structures'. Coming out may 'achieve legal concessions' but cannot challenge 'heterosexual ideology' and power structures, which, apparently, 'will only tolerate homosexuality on condition that it retain its deviant status'. His second objection concerns 'the whole conceptualisation of homosexuality as an issue of personality and personal identity, which can simply be asserted'. We need however to immediately ask whether Coming Out does indeed constitute an exclusively personalised politics. On the contrary, I would suggest, Coming Out has since the late 1960s always involved a *collective* identity, and addresses not other individuals as such, but rather social/discursive institutions, especially those understood to possess the power to define sexual difference to the exclusion and/or obliteration of homosexual desire and practice.

Minson makes an important admission when he states his assumption that coming out involves the assertion of 'a difficult truth about one's personality'. There is, I think, an interesting inversion at work here, since Coming Out would not be compatible with the experience of homosexuality as a 'difficult truth', which would necessarily have to remain unspoken. Minson assumes that Coming Out *requires* that homosexuality be seen as an issue of personal identity, but by a now familiar slippage connects this to the argument that this merely reinforces the modern sexualisation of concepts of personal identity. He concludes that Coming Out assumes that speaking this identity is the most appropriate way of knowing it. However, this totally overlooks the strategic nature of Coming Out as a political/legal programme, and this in turn suggests a fundamental failure to perceive that the category 'gay' is not, and has never been, merely a personal label-like category, implying some kind of essence analogous or even synonymous with the term 'homosexual'. On the contrary, the term 'gay' specifically refutes the constitutive opposition hetero/homo sexuality as the central figure of our sexual 'truth'. What the term 'gay' does insist upon is a political and legal *unity of interests* between subjects variously categorised as perverse/sick/mad/queer/contagious and so on, in relation to those institutions and their attendent discursive formations which are able to define sexual difference as an exclusively biological dualism, 'male'—(hetero/sexual)—'female'. Minson's inability to recognise the enormous significance of the affirmative politico/legal discourse of gayness as a decisive break with the essentialist discourse of 'homosexuality' (and, by the same token, 'heterosexuality') is also apparent from his peculiar reading of Coming Out in the light of Foucault's Introduction to *The History of Sexuality*, as 'only the latest in a long line of organised and obligatory rituals of confession'.

Here the concept of confession is elided with his central idea of assertion. This slippage is all the more significant when one considers that the 'confession' of homosexuality would presumably involve either a total silence on the subject, or a self-denigratory identification as 'queer', 'perverse', 'sinful', or whatever. Besides, the very notion of a 'long line' of assertively confessional homosexuals insidiously suggests some kind of 'natural' lineage speaking identity from desire. The only 'long line' of which we can speak confidently is that of the prison-yard, or that of the gallows.[6] If there is a 'difficult truth' involved here, it can only concern those who casually inhabit the 'positive' category of heterosexuality. The discourse of homosexual 'confession', like that of other crimes without victims, is spoken only from the position of a psychotic disavowal of reality, as is abundantly apparent from the 'populist' coverage of the AIDS epidemic in the tabloid press and on television.[7] In relation to Coming Out, it is clear that Jeff Minson reads a technique for the destabilisation of the deployment of sexuality, as one of its primary instruments. Like Richard Sennett, Jeff Minson seems to hear the modern state 'positively soliciting' the very voice which undermines its medico/juridical authority. I am not familiar with these voices. Like Sennett, he also invokes a notion of the private in the name of sexual politics, distinct (apparently) from notions of the personal. Again, Minson fails to note that homosexuality is already specifically and carefully privatised by the prevailing legislation contained in the 1967 Sexual Offences Act.

In conclusion I note a conflict between on the one hand a picture of confession which requires, accepts, and validates, the authority of the confessor to define the guilt of the confessee, and then absolve or refuse absolution, and on the other a discourse of affirmation/assertion which involves coherent opposition to the institutional power and authority of the confessor. It is therefore *crucial* to be able to distinguish between confessional and affirmative discourses, the former admitting and legitimating notions of sin/transgression, the latter transvaluing the self-same actions/desires/identities. We should also note that Foucault himself expressed con-

533

cern about the promiscuous way in which this particular aspect of his work has been taken up, a concern which is not honoured by those who simply settle for lazy talk of 'secular confession' including, for example, psychoanalysis. If Freud's concepts of resistance, transference, and counter-transference have any psychic purchase, then it is exactly to deny the spurious descriptive analogy between the operations of the psychoanalyst and the Confessor.

What seems to be at work here is a curious and specific inability to distinguish between the organisation of desire in terms of sexual object-choice, and the mutability of identities opening from desire via shifting identifications, that is, via the operations of fantasy. I also note a significant parallel between the failure of the sociology of sex to interrogate sexual difference beyond the symbolic field which it identifies as 'gender', and an inability/refusal on the part of some *soi disant* Foucauldians to acknowledge the importance of a sexual politics organised strategically around notions of sexual choice. Leo Bersani reminds us that 'the deconstruction of the Self involves much more than a happy return to the polymorphous pleasures of sensual intensities not yet petrified (as a result of being denied) into fixed and partial character structures. Our thought about this process of deconstruction should engage us in a problematic reflection about different forms of psychic mobility'.[8] In this context I can see no point in criticising Foucault for failing to advance a theory of desire in the terms set by a discourse on sexual difference which only admits two terms—male and female. Rather, we should recognise that Coming Out for Foucault did not merely involve the re-inscription of a confessional 'homosexual' identity (how could it?), but had on the contrary a visionary and Utopic dimension. To be gay for Foucault was a state always waiting to be achieved. He believed passionately in the innovative potential of gay culture to *contest* disciplinary regimes of power organised in the body, and to construct totally new social, cultural and psychological forms. It was the image of diversity which he shared with Freud. For Foucault ecology, the sexual politics movements, prison reform and so on, constituted examples of such new political demands, as well as the conditions of emergence for new subjectivities outside and in advance of the ever narrowing domain of 'the political' which he understood to have been hijacked by specific political parties and institutions in the last century. What Foucault adds to Freud is this radical affirmation that exclusively heterosexual object-choice does not exhaust the territory of sexual difference, where its effective fetishisation—in 'theory' as elsewhere—only signals the failure of psychoanalysis to address itself to the problem of homophobia rather than to homosexual desire as such.

NOTES

1. Jean Laplanche and J-B. Pontalis, *The Language of Psycho-Analysis* (London: Hogarth Press, 1983), p. 205.
2. Freud, *Civilisation And Its Discontents*, Pelican Freud Library 12, p. 295, quoted by D. N. Rodowick, 'The Difficulty Of Difference', *Wide Angle*, 5:1 (1982), 15.
3. For example, see David Fernbach, *The Spiral Circle* (Gay Men's Press, 1981).
4. Richard Sennett, *Sexuality and Identity* (London: Brook Productions, 1982).
5. Jeff Minson, *The Assertion of Homosexuality*, m/f, 5/6 (1981).
6. See Louis Crompton, *Byron & Greek Love* (London: Faber, 1985), or Alan Bray, *Homosexuality in*

Renaissance England (London: Gay Men's Press, 1982).
7. See Simon Watney, 'The Rhetoric Of AIDS', *Screen*, 27:1 (1986).
8. Leo Bersani, *A Future For Astyanax: Character and Desire in Literature* (London: Marion Boyars, 1978), p. 5.
9. Michel Foucault, 'The Social Triumph of the Sexual Will: A Conversation', *Christopher Street*, 64 (1982).

Eve Kosofsky Sedgwick

Eve Kosofsky Sedgwick is currently the Newman Ivey White Professor of English at Duke University. She is a gay/lesbian and antihomophobic theorist whose braiding together of theoretical analysis, personal reflection and political commitment have gained her an international reputation, or as *Rolling Stone* magazine put it, she is the 'soft-spoken queen of gay studies'. In her critical enquiry, she identifies the binary distinction between homosexuality and heterosexuality as an ideal deconstructive site to analyse issues of race, class, and gender. This project was initiated in her first book, *Between Men: English Literature and Male Homosocial Desire* (1985), which is a study of the intricate masculine relations (homosocial bonds) that maintain power in a patriarchal society. In her subsequent books, *Epistemology of the Closet* (1990), and *Tendencies* (1993), she explores the contradictory homosexual models of gender inversion and gender separatism and offers alternative ways to conceptualize non-heterosexual relationships.

In 'Across Gender, Across Sexuality: Willa Cather and Others', Kosofsky Sedgwick focuses her discussion of the 'two conceptual impasses or incoherences, one concerning *gender* definition and the other concerning *sexual* definition' around an explication of Willa Cather's 1905 favourite and most frequently republished short story, 'Paul's Case: A Study in Temperament'. Kosofsky Sedgwick's essay was published in the *South Atlantic Quarterly*, 1988, and a slightly different version, 'Willa Cather and Others', can be found in *Tendencies*.

Kosofsky Sedgwick analyses the intersection of male and female homosexuality, seeing Cather (and others, such as Proust) as refracting 'queer' desires across the boundaries of gender, as she explores the possibilities for a cross-identification among various groups which would produce a pluralistic alliance between individuals of different genders and sexual orientations. As in all her works, Kosofsky Sedgwick can be seen as engaged in a project both personal, current, social and political to interrogate the axes of categorization. In Axiom 1 in *Epistemology*, Kosofsky Sedgwick explores the 'self-evident fact' that 'People are different from each other',

536

and in 'Queer and Now', she suggests that one of the things 'queer' can stand for is 'the open mesh of possibilities, gaps, overlaps, dissonances and resonances, lapses and excesses of meaning when the constituent elements of anyone's gender, anyone's sexuality aren't made (or *can't be* made) to signify monolithically' (*Tendencies*, 8). E.K and J.M.

Across gender, across sexuality: Willa Cather and others

I want to challenge the assumption that feminism is or should be the privileged site of a theory of sexuality. Feminism is the theory of gender oppression. . . . Gender affects the operation of the sexual system, and the sexual system has had gender-specific manifestations. But although sex and gender are related, they are not the same thing.

—*Gayle Rubin, 'Thinking Sex'*

Let's hypothesize, with Gayle Rubin, that the question of gender and the question of sexuality, inextricable from each other though they are in that each can be expressed only in the terms of the other, are nonetheless not the same question, that gender and sexuality represent two analytic axes that may productively be imagined as being as distinct from each other as, say, gender and class, or class and race.[1] Under this hypothesis, just as we've learned to assume that no issue of racial meaning fails to be embodied through the specificity of a particular class position—and no issue of class, for instance, through the specificity of a particular gender position—so we can assume that no issue of gender would fail to be embodied through the specificity of a particular sexuality, and vice versa; nonetheless, there could be use in keeping the analytic axes distinct.

Next, let's hypothesize that gay/lesbian and antihomophobic inquiry still has a lot to learn from asking the questions that feminist inquiry has learned to ask—but only so long as we don't demand to receive the same answers. Comparing feminist and gay theory as they currently stand, the newness and consequent relative underdevelopment of gay theory are most visible in two manifestations. First, we are by now very used to asking as feminists what we aren't yet used to asking as antihomophobic readers: how a variety of forms of oppression intertwine systemically with each other, and especially how the person who is disabled through one set of oppressions may *by the same positioning* be enabled through others. For instance, the understated demeanor of educated women in our society tends to mark both their deference to educated men and their expectation of deference from women and men of lower class. Again, a woman's use of a married name makes graphic her subordination as a woman and at the same time her privilege as a presumptive heterosexual. Or again, the distinctive vulnerability to rape of women of all races has become in this country a powerful tool

537

for the racist enforcement by which white people, including women, are privileged at the expense of black people of both genders. That one is *either* oppressed *or* an oppressor, on the other hand, or, if one happens to be both, that the two are not likely to have much to do with each other, still seems to be a common assumption in at least male gay writing and activism, as it hasn't for a long time been in careful feminist work.

Indeed, it was the long, painful realization, *not* that all oppressions are congruent, but that they are *differently* structured and so must intersect in complex embodiments, that has been the first great heuristic breakthrough of feminist thought. This realization has as its corollary that the comparison of different axes of oppression is a crucial task, not for any purpose of ranking oppressions, but to the contrary because each oppression is likely to be in a uniquely indicative relation to certain distinctive nodes of cultural organization. The *special* centrality of homophobic oppression in the twentieth century has been in its inextricability from the question of knowledge and the processes of knowing in modern Western culture at large.

The second and perhaps even greater heuristic leap of feminism has been the recognition that categories of gender—and hence oppressions of gender—can have a structuring force for axes of cultural discrimination whose thematic subject isn't explicitly gendered at all. We have now learned as feminist readers that dichotomies in a given text—of culture as opposed to nature, for instance, public as opposed to private, mind as opposed to body, activity as opposed to passivity—are, under particular pressures of culture and history, likely places to look for implicit allegories of the relations of men to women; more, that to fail to analyze such nominally ungendered constructs in gender terms can itself be a gravely tendentious move in the gender politics of reading. This has given us ways to ask the question of gender about texts even where the culturally 'marked' gender (female) is not present as either author or thematic. Coming of age at the same time as and in a synergistic relation to deconstruction, much feminist reading is moreover richly involved with the deconstructive understanding that categories presented in a culture as symmetrical binary oppositions—male/female, as well as culture/nature, etc.—actually subsist in a more unsettling and dynamic tacit relation according to which, first, term B is not symmetrical with but subordinated to term A; but, second, the ontologically valorized term A actually depends for its meaning on the simultaneous subsumption and exclusion of term B; hence, third, the question of priority between the supposed central and the supposed marginal category of each dyad is irresolvably unstable.

The dichotomy heterosexual/homosexual, as it has emerged through the last century of Western discourse, would seem to lend itself peculiarly neatly to a set of analytic moves learned from this deconstructive moment in feminist theory. One has perhaps only to remind oneself that the 'deviant' category 'homosexual' antedates the supposedly normative 'heterosexual': conceptually by something over a decade, and lexically, in American English, by at least two years.[2] In fact, heterosexual/homosexual fits the deconstructive template much more neatly than the dichotomy male/female does, and hence, importantly differently. The most dramatic difference between gender and sexual orientation—that virtually all people are publicly and unalterably assigned to one or the other gender, and from birth—seems if anything to mean that it is rather sexual orientation, with its far greater potential for rearrangement, ambiguity, and representational doubleness, that would offer the more apt deconstructive object. An essentialism of sexual object choice is far less easy to maintain, far more visibly incoherent, more visibly stressed and challenged at every point in the culture, than any essentialism of gender. Indeed the unbudging conceptual deadlock over the last hundred years between minoritizing views of homosexuality as the fixed trait of a distinct small percentage of the population, and universalizing views of it as a widely diffused potential in whole populations whom only its pointed repression renders heterosexual, answers the deconstructive analysis of the instability of binary oppositions with a congruence that may prove telling on both sides. And our developing understanding of the centrality of homosocial bonds to patriarchal heterosexist culture suggests ways of extending such an analysis from the individual to the systemic level.

A definitional and methodological caution concerning the relation of my current subject, gay/lesbian and antihomophobic theory, to the project alluded to by Gayle Rubin in the sentences I've used as an epigraph, a theory of sexuality [sic]. The two can after all scarcely be coextensive. And this is true not because 'gay/lesbian and antihomophobic theory' would fail to cover heterosexual as well as same-sex object choice (any more than 'feminist theory' would fail to cover men as well as women), but rather because sexuality extends along so many dimensions that aren't well described in terms of the gender of object choice at all. Some of these dimensions are habitually condensed under the rubrics of object choice, so that certain discriminations of (for instance) *act*, or of (for another instance) *erotic localization*, come into play however implicitly and however incoherently when categories of object choice are mobilized. For example, one used to hear a lot about a high developmental stage called 'heterosexual genitality'; or again, a certain anal-erotic salience of male homosexuality is if anything increasingly strong under the glare of heterosexist AIDS-phobia; while several different historical influences have led to the degenitalization and bodily diffusion of many popular, and indeed many lesbian, understandings of lesbian sexuality. Other dimensions of sexuality, however, distinguish object choice quite differently (for example, human/animal, adult/child, singular/plural, autoerotic/alloerotic) or are not even about object choice (e.g., orgasmic/nonorgasmic, noncommercial/commercial, using bodies only/using manufactured objects, in private/in public, spontaneous/scripted). Some of these other dimensions of sexuality have had high diacritical importance in different historical contexts (e.g., human/animal, autoerotic/alloerotic). Others, like adult/child object choice, visibly do have such importance today, but without being very fully subsumed under the homo/heterosexual binary. Still others, including a host of them I haven't mentioned or couldn't think of, subsist in this culture as nondiacritical differences, differences that seem to make little difference beyond themselves—except that the hyperintensive structuring of sexuality in our culture sets several of them at the exact border between legal and illegal. What I mean, at any rate, to emphasize is that the implicit condensation of 'sexual theory' into 'gay/lesbian and antihomophobic theory,' which corresponds roughly to our by now unquestioned reading of the ubiquitous 'sexual orientation' to mean 'gender of object choice,' is at the very least damagingly skewed by its present historical placement.

539

Even insofar as the question of sexuality can be condensed as the question of homo/heterosexuality, however, its conceptualization is anything but simple. In recent work, I have been arguing that our culture's crystallization of gay identities over the past hundred years has persistently been structured by two conceptual impasses or incoherences, one concerning *gender* definition, and the other concerning *sexual* definition.

	Separatist	Integrative
Homo/hetero *sexual* definition	*Minoritizing,* e.g., gay identity, 'essentialist,' third-sex models, civil rights models	*Universalizing,* e.g., bisexual potential, 'social constructionist,' 'sodomy' models, 'lesbian continuum'
Gender definition	*Gender separatist,* e.g., homosocial continuum, lesbian separatist, manhood-initiation, models	*Inversion/liminality/transitivity,* e.g., cross-sex, androgyny, gay/ lesbian solidarity models

With regard to gender, two quite opposite possibilities for defining the person who desires someone of their own gender have prevailed, often at the same time. One of these, the gender-integrative possibility manifest in the turn-of-the-century topos of inversion ('a woman's soul trapped in a man's body' or vice versa), but longer-lived in homophobia folklore and 'common sense,' in certain influential formulations of psychoanalysis and psychiatry, and also in many vibrant aspects of current gay and lesbian culture, points to an essential femininity in gay men and/or an essential masculinity in lesbians. While this topos of inversion or liminality places gay people exactly at the threshold between genders, its persistence has been yoked, at the same time, to that of its contradictory counterpart, the topos of gender separatism. Under this latter view, far from its being of the essence of desire (including same-sex desire) to cross boundaries of gender, it is instead the most natural thing in the world that people of the same gender, people grouped together under the single most determinative diacritical mark of social organization, people whose social needs and knowledges may have so much in common, should band together also on the axis of sexual desire. As the gender-separatist substitution of the concept 'woman-identified woman' for the gender-liminal stereotype of the mannish lesbian suggests, as indeed does the concept of the continuum of male or female homosocial desire, this topos tends to reassimilate identification with desire. Inversion models, by contrast, depend conceptually on the distinctness of identification from desire. Gender separatist models would thus place the woman-loving woman and the man-loving man each at the 'natural' defining center of their own gender, rather than, as gender-integrative models would, at the threshold between genders. The immanence of each of these models in the history of gay theory is clear from the early split in the German homosexual rights movement between Magnus Hirschfeld, who posited, in Donald

Mager's paraphrase, 'an exact equation . . . between cross-gender behaviors and homosexual desire,' and Benedict Friedländer, who concluded to the contrary 'that homosexuality was the highest, most perfect evolutionary stage of gender differentiation. Men who needed women were seen as less manly than those who could transcend the procreational imperative in favor of this higher "masculinity." '[3]

Along with the incoherence about *gender* definition, a deadlock or incoherence of definition prevails, as well, between separatist and integrative conceptualizations of homo/hetero*sexual* definition. Over the span of a century, definitions of homosexuality as a universal human potential have conflicted with definitions of it as the trait of a distinct and fixed minority. The most current form in which this conflict is visible is in the debate between 'social constructionist' and 'essentialist' understandings of homo/heterosexual identity. The conflict has a long history, however. Historical narratives since Foucault have seemed to show universalizing paradigms, such as the proscription of particular *acts* called 'sodomy' (acts that might be performed by anybody), as being displaced after the late nineteenth century by the definition of particular kinds of *persons*, specifically 'homosexuals.' But the truth seems to be that since the late nineteenth century the two understandings, contradictory though they are, have coexisted, creating in the space of their contradiction enormous potentials of discursive power. We have just at the moment of this writing (March 1988) a perfect example of this potent incoherence in the anomalous legal situation of gay people and acts in this country; while the Supreme Court in *Bowers v. Hardwick* has notoriously left the individual states free to prohibit any *acts* that they wish to define as 'sodomy,' by whomsoever performed, with no fear at all of impinging on any rights, and particularly privacy rights, safeguarded by the Constitution—at the same time a panel of the Ninth Circuit, Court of Appeals ruled last month (in *Sergeant Perry J. Watkins v. United States Army*) that homosexual *persons*, as a particular kind of person, *are* entitled to Constitutional protections under the Equal Protection clause. To be gay in this system is to come under the radically overlapping aegises of a universalizing discourse of acts and at the same time of a minoritizing discourse of persons. Just at the moment, at least in the institutions of law, the former aegis prohibits what the latter protects. But in the concurrent public health constructions around AIDS, for instance, it is far from clear that a minoritizing discourse of persons ('risk groups') is not even more oppressive than the competing, universalizing discourse of acts ('safer sex'). In the double binds implicit in the space overlapped by both, the stakes in matters of definitional control are extremely high.[4]

One thing that does emerge with clarity from this complex and contradictory map of sexual and gender definition is that the possible grounds to be found there for alliance and cross-identification among various groups will also be plural. To take the issue of gender definition alone: under a gender separatist topos, lesbians might look for identifications and alliances among women in general including straight women (as in Adrienne Rich's 'lesbian continuum' model); and gay men, as in Friedländer's model—or more recent 'male liberation' models—of masculinity, might look for them among men in general including straight men. Under a topos of gender inversion or liminality, on the other hand, gay men might look to identify with straight women (on grounds that they are also 'feminine' or also desire men), or with lesbians (on grounds that they similarly occupy a liminal position); while lesbians might analogously look to identify with gay men or, though this latter identification has not been strong since second-wave feminism, with straight men. Note, however, that this schematization over 'the issue of gender definition alone' also impinges on the issue of homo/heterosexual definition, and in an unexpectedly chiasmic way. Gender-*separatist* models like Rich's or Friedländer's seem to tend toward *universalizing* understandings of homo/heterosexual potential. To the degree that gender-*integrative* inversion or liminality models suggest an alliance or identity between lesbians and gay men, on the other hand, they tend toward gay-*separatist*, minoritizing models of specifically gay identity and politics. These crossings are quite contingent, however, as suggested by Freud's universalizing understanding of sexual definition which seems to go with an integrative, inversion model of gender definition. And more broadly, the routes to be taken across this misleadingly symmetrical map are fractured in a particular historical situation by the profound asymmetries of gender oppression and heterosexist oppression.

For a particular gay or lesbian subject, then, to choose a figure in a different position with whom to identify even partially always has the potential of being revelatory in *some* way about *some* aspect of the positioning of the subject her- or himself: not through a vague invocation of the commonality of all people of all genders and sexualities, though that may also be at work, but through the complex and conflictual specificities of what different positionings may have in common under the contradictory definitional aegises of our century.

Willa Cather's 1905 short story, 'Paul's Case: A Study in Temperament,' was her own lifelong favorite among her stories, the one she republished most and the only one she allowed to be anthologized by others. The *omphalos* of her continuing attachment to this story is oddly difficult to locate; but (if it's permissible to complicate the navel metaphor in this way) the knotted-up surgical scar of her *de*tachment from the story's main character is almost its first legible sign. 'It was Paul's afternoon to appear before the faculty of the Pittsburgh High School to account for his various misdemeanors,' the story begins; with a 'rancour and aggrievedness' for which they themselves feel shamed by their inability to account, the teachers of this tense, unlovely, effeminate, histrionic boy 'fell upon him without mercy, his English teacher leading the pack.'[5]

> Once, when he had been making a synopsis of a paragraph at the blackboard, his English teacher had stepped to his side and attempted to guide his hand. Paul had started back with a shudder and thrust his hands violently behind him. The astonished woman could scarcely have been more hurt and embarrassed had he struck at her. The insult was so involuntary and definitely personal as to be unforgettable. In one way and another, he had made all his teachers, men and woman alike, conscious of the same feeling of physical aversion.

The equivocalness of 'the same feeling of physical aversion'—does the aversion live in his body, or in theirs; or is the aversiveness tied up with a certain threat of de-differentiation between them?—seems fulfilled when it is the teachers, and not the object of their discipline, who 'left the building dissatisfied and unhappy; humiliated to have felt so vindictive toward a mere boy, to have uttered this feeling in cutting terms, and to have set each other on, as it were, in the grewsome game of intemperate reproach.' And that evening, when the English teacher arrives at a concert for which the boy is officiously acting as usher, it is she who betrays 'some embarrassment when she handed Paul the tickets, and a *hauteur* which subsequently made her feel very foolish.'

The Pittsburgh High School English teacher evaporates as a character from 'Paul's Case' shortly thereafter—'Paul forgot even the nastiness of his teacher's being there.' There is nothing in the story to suggest where her unushered homeward steps will take her, though they would have taken one Pittsburgh high school English teacher any evening in 1905 back to a bedroom shared with a sumptuously beautiful young woman, Isabelle McClung, who has defied her parents to the extent of bringing her imposing lover, Willa Cather, into the family home to live. While this English teacher doesn't require to be identified with that English teacher, it is also less easy than it might be to differentiate firmly their attitudes toward what Katherine Anne Porter confidently labels as 'a real "case" in the clinical sense of the word,' that is to say, 'boys like Paul.'[6]

Paul's teachers feel humiliated because they have found themselves momentarily unified in a ritual of scapegoating, without being at all clear what it is in the scapegoat that deserves torment or even what provokes this sudden communal construction. Cather herself had some history of being an effeminophobic bully; perhaps also of feeling shamed by being one. Ten years before 'Paul's Case,' for instance, in 1895, the year when a new homophobic politics of indignity had its watershed international premiere in the trials of Oscar Wilde, Cather published two columns on Wilde. In each of these, she harnesses her own prose eagerly to the accelerating rhetoric of the public auto-da-fé. Wilde is not just some random sinner—certainly not the object of any injustice—but something more, a signal criminal of Luciferian stature, the 'ghastly eruption that makes [society] hide its face in shame.'[7] Wilde 'is in prison now, most deservedly so. Upon his head is heaped the deepest infamy and the darkest shame of his generation. Civilization shudders at his name, and there is absolutely no spot on earth where this man can live. Cain's curse was light compared with his.' Joining so perfervidly in the public scapegoating of Wilde, Cather also seems, however, to assert a right, earned by the very excess of her revilement, to define for herself, and differently from the way the society or for that matter the courts have defined it, the 'true' nature of Wilde's sin and hence the true justification for his punishment of two years' imprisonment with hard labor. Wilde's disgrace is, in Cather's account, no isolated incident but 'the beginning of a national expiation' for 'the sin which insults the dignity of man, and of God in whose image he was made,' 'the potentiality of all sin, the begetter of all evil.' And that sin? '—Insincerity.' 'Art that is artificial and insincere' is the true 'sin against the holy spirit,' 'for which there is no forgiveness in Heaven, no forgetting in Hell.' The odd oversight of the framers of the Criminal Law Amendment Act and the 1885 Labouchère amendment to it, in omitting to include by name the unspeakable crimes of artificiality and insincerity, doesn't slow Cather a bit in this determined act of redefinition. Reactivating the ancient, barely latent cognitive antithesis between homosexual acts and *the natural*, Cather strongly reinforces the assaultive received association between Wilde's sexuality and a reprobated, putatively feminine love of artifice. At the same time, though, distinguishing however slightly and invidiously the one crime from the other ('The sins of the body are very small compared with that'), she also holds open a small shy gap of nonidentification between the two in which some nascent germ of gay-affirmative detachment, of critique, or even of outlaw love might shelter to await her own less terroristic or terrorized season.

Had that season arrived with the writing a decade later of 'Paul's Case'? In the early, Pittsburgh part of the story, it seems, quite to the contrary, that the identification between Paul's pathology on the one hand and his insincerity and artificiality on the other is so seamless that the former is to be fully evoked by the latter, through a mercilessly specular, fixated point of view that takes his theatrical self-presentation spitefully at its word. 'His eyes were remarkable for a certain hysterical brilliancy, and he continually used them in a conscious, theatrical sort of way, peculiarly offensive in a boy.' Paul's glance is a jerkily unsteady one—'Paul was always smiling, always glancing about him, seeming to feel that people might be watching him and trying to detect something'—but the gaze of the narrative at him is so unresting as to give point to his desperate way of regarding the world; one English teacher, at least, is eternally there to describe him 'looking wildly behind him now and then to see whether some of his teachers were not there to witness his light-heartedness.' Like Cather's Wilde a decade earlier, it seems as if Paul is to be hounded to exhaustion or death for a crime that hovers indeterminately between sex/gender irregularity and spoilt sensibility or bad art. The invidious need of a passionate young lesbian to place, and at a distance, the lurid, contagious scandal of male homosexuality: it is as if that were not quite to be disentangled from the invidious need of a hungry young talent to distinguish itself once and for all from the 'hysterical' artifice of the hapless youth who needs talent but hasn't it.

If the early parts of 'Paul's Case' seem written from the unloving compulsions of the English teacher, however, the latter part of the story, after Paul has stolen a thousand dollars from his father's employer and run away to New York, opens out to what seems to me an amazing tenderness of affirmation. How common is it, in a fictional tradition ruled by *le mensonge romantique*, for a powerfully desiring character to get the thing that he desires, and to learn immediately that he was right—that what he wanted really is the thing that would make him happy? And especially in the specific tradition of, shall we say, *Madame Bovary*, the fictional lineage whose geography consists solely of *the provinces* and the *capital*, and whose motive for desire is an acculturated stimulus that is explicitly said to be at once entire artifice and yet less than art? But this is what happens to the furtive, narrow-chested, nerve-twanging Paul in snowy New York. Furnished in one single expert shopping spree with suits, shoes, hat, scarfpin, brushes, handsome luggage, installed in a suite in the Waldorf, catered to with violets and jonquils, bathed, warmed, rested, and dressed, the opera in prospect and the popping of champagne corks to waltz music, Paul looks in the mirror the next day: 'Everything was quite perfect; he was exactly the kind of boy he had always wanted to be.' And it seems to be true. Even when, days later, running out of money and time he throws himself in front of a train and is crushed to atoms, nothing has undermined the preciousness for Paul of, not art, but the chrism of a feminized or homosexualized culture and artifice. 'He felt now that his surroundings explained him'; the lights forgivingly, expensively lowered, himself at last the seeing consciousness of the story, even the past of his life and his body are, as in a coming out, reknit with the new, authoritative fingers of his own eyes. 'He realized well enough that he had always been tormented by . . . a sort of apprehensive dread that, of late years, as the meshes of the lies he had told closed about him, had been pulling the muscles of his body tighter and tighter. . . .' This offering of Paul's proprioception is a new gift to the reader. 'There had always been the shadowed corner, the dark place into which he dared not look, but from which something seemed always to be watching him.' But now—'these were his people, he told himself.' 'It would be impossible for anyone to humiliate him.' If Cather, in this story, does something to cleanse her own sexual body of the carrion stench of Wilde's victimization, it is thus (unexpectedly) by identifying with what seems to be Paul's sexuality not in spite of but *through* its saving reabsorption in a gender-liminal (and very specifically classed) artifice that represents at once a particular subculture and culture itself.

Cather's implicit reading here of the gendering of sex picks out one possible path through the mazed junction at which long-residual issues of gender and class definition intersected new turn-of-the-century mappings of sexual choice and identification. In what I am reading as Cather's move in 'Paul's Case,' the mannish lesbian author's coming together with the effeminate boy on the ground of a certain distinctive position of gender liminality is also a move toward a minority gay identity whose more effectual cleavage, whose more determining separatism, would be that of homo/hetero*sexual* choice rather than that of male/female *gender*. The playing out of this story through the intertwinings of such gender-polarized terms as culture, artifice, and the punitive gaze, however, means that the thick semantics of gender asymmetry will cling to the syntax however airy of gender crossing and recrossing—clogging or rendering liable to slippage the gears of reader or authorial relation with a special insistence of viscosity.

Such formulations as these might push us toward some new hypotheses and new clusterings in the rich tradition of cross-gender inventions of homosexuality of the past century whose distinguished constituency might include—along with Cather—James, Proust, Yourcenar, Compton-Burnett, Renault, and more recent writers in sometimes less 'literary' forms such as Gayle Rubin, Esther Newton, Susan Sontag, Judy Grahn, Joanna Russ—or, I might add, Prince in his astonishingly Proustian recent hit single 'If I Was Your Girlfriend.' We could ask, for instance, about a text like James's *The Bostonians*, whether certain vindictive wrenchings of it out of 'shape,' warpings in its illusionistic surface of authorial control and address, might not represent less a static parti pris *against* women's desire for women than a dangerously unresolved question *about* it. How far, the novel asks, or more powerfully resists asking for fear of either the answer or no answer or too many answers—how far are these two things parallel or comparable: the ventriloquistic, half-contemptuous, hot desire of Olive Chancellor for a girl like Verena Tarrant; the ventriloquistic, half-contemptuous, hot desire of Henry James for a boy like Basil Ransome? To the degree that they aren't parallel, the intimate access of the authorial consciousness to the characters' must be dangerously compromised; to the degree that they are, so must its panoptic framing authority of distance and diagnostic privilege. Whether (in those waning decades of an intensive American homosociality) men's desire for men represents most the central and naturalizing maleness of its communicants, and women's for women an ultrafemininity unnatural only for its overtypifying concentration; or whether (in those inaugural years of medical, psychiatric, and legal discourses, both pro- and anti-gay, that variously distinguished 'homosexuals' male and female as a singular minority) a same-sex desire necessarily invoked, as well, a *cross*-gender liminality; the crisscrossed reading of such desires so ruptures the authorial surface of James's writing that what shoves through it here is the fist not of a male-erotic *écriture* but less daringly of a woman-hating and feminist-baiting violence of panic.

A more truly sexy moment, in Proust, gives the thrill of authorial availability through these eruptive diagonals of definition. After the flight and death of his probably lesbian mistress Albertine, the narrator of *A la recherche*, his jealousy only the more inflamed by its posthumousness, dispatches on an errand of detection and reconstruction along the trail of her elopement a functionary named Aimé, a head-waiter who has himself already been both a procurer and an object of desire both within and across gender through several volumes of this novel. Aimé sends back an account of Albertine which the narrator reproduces thus, its peculiarity being that Aimé, half-educated, 'when he meant to put inverted commas . . . put brackets, and when he meant to put something in brackets . . . put it in inverted commas':[8]

> 'The young laundry-girl confessed to me that she enjoyed playing around with her girlfriends and that seeing Mlle Albertine was always rubbing up against her in her bathing-wrap she made her take it off and used to caress her with her tongue along the throat and arms. . . . After that she told me nothing more, but being always at your service and ready to do anything to oblige you, I took the young laundry-girl to bed with me. She asked me if I would like her to do to me what she used to do to Mlle Albertine when she took off her bathing-dress. And she said to me: (If you could have seen how she used to wriggle, that young lady, she said to me (oh, it's too heavenly) and she got so excited that she could not keep from biting me.) I could still see the marks on the laundry-girl's arms.'[9]

The deroutinization of the subordinating work of punctuation here strips away the insulation of the text against every juxtaposition of sexualities. Albertine to the laundry-girl, the laundry-girl to Aimé, Aimé to the male narrator, the narrator to the reader: the insubordinated address of pain and ecstasy is anchored only at the last moment by its cryptic laundry-mark, residue of a rinsing and ravenous illegible rapture.

This highly chiasmic organization of homo/heterosexual definition in Proust, which prompts Leo Bersani to formulate 'the ontological necessity of homosexuality [in the other sex] in a kind of universal *hetero*sexual relation of all human subjects to their own desires,'[10] confirms that insofar as a growing minority gay identity does or did depend on a model of gender liminality, it tends to invest with meaning transpositions between *male* and *female* homosexuality, but also between the bonds of *homo*- and *hetero*sexuality. The Proustian example suggests that this choreography of crossings, identification, and momentary symmetries, this hummingbird ballet of within and without the parenthesis, represents a utopian possibility somewhere to one side of the stresses of gender or of other exploitations; I think there is evidence, however, that the truth of this choreography of cross-translation is at once less blithe and more interesting.

Back, for one final example, to Willa Cather: to her beautiful and difficult novel *The Professor's House*, whose eponymous domesticity (the house itself, that is to say, not the Professor) is biographically thought to allude to the enabling provision for Cather's own writing of a room of her own, first by Isabelle McClung and then perhaps by her more domesticated and serviceable companion/lover of decades, Edith Lewis. Though the love that sustains these necessary facilitations has been a lesbian one, its two crystallizations in the novel are both cross-translations: one across gender, into the gorgeous homosocial romance of two men on a mesa in New Mexico; the other across sexuality as well as gender, into the conventional but enabling heterosexual marriage of a historian of the Spanish in the New World. As with the subordinating parentheses in Proust, the male-homosocial romance represents at the same time the *inside* lining of the heterosexual bond (since the two segments of the domestic story flank their own history in the flashback interpolation of the mesa story) and equally its *exterior* landscape (since the Blue Mesa romance of Tom *Out*land, true to his name, is also figured in the 'single square window, swinging outward on hinges' that vents from the Professor's attic study the asphyxiating gas of his stove, and admits to it the 'long, blue, hazy smear'—the view of Lake Michigan 'like an open door that nobody could shut'—that makes the empowering distance for his intellectual achievements and desires).[11] The room of one's own, in short, as a room with a view: in this text the crossing of the upstairs/downstairs vertical axis of heterosexual domesticity *by* the space-clearing dash of a male-male romance may somehow refract and decompress the conditions of a lesbian love and creativity.

What become visible in this double refraction are the shadows of the brutal suppressions by which a lesbian love did not in Willa Cather's time and culture freely become visible as itself. Still, we can look for affordances offered by that love to these particular refractions. On the one hand, there is the distinctive sensuality attributed to the male-homosocial romance, its extravagant loyalties aerated by extroversion, eye-hunger, and inexpressiveness. On the other hand, there is the canny and manipulative relation to permeable privacies, of a tradition of heterosexual marriage in which marriage is inveterately reconstituted in relation to its others, in the age-old economy of the muse represented in this book by the memory of the dead boy Tom Outland. Each of these refractions seems moreover to be a way of telling the same story: the story of how expensive and wasteful a thing creative energy is, and how intimately rooted in a plot of betrayal or exploitation: Tom Outland's conscious and empowering betrayal of his beloved friend on the mesa, the Professor's self-deceived expropriation of the labor, vitality, and money of his wife and daughters. Certainly there is no reason why the right artist at the right moment cannot embody these truths that seem to be, among other things, lesbian truths, directly in the plots of lesbian desire, nurturance, betrayal, exploitation, creativity from which they here seem to have sprung. Then why *not* here? Among the reasons Cather may have had for not doing so must have been, besides the danger to herself and her own enabling privacy, the danger also from this particular steely and un–utopic plot to the early and still-fragile developing of *any* lesbian plot as a public possibility for carrying value and sustaining narrative.

She may also, however, have liked the advantage there was to be taken of these other, refracted plots as the most apt carriers, brewed in the acid nuance of centuries, for the exposition precisely of exploitation and betrayal. Anyone who knows how to read anything is experienced in reading, for instance, the story of a husband; we have all read that one all our lives, however resentfully or maybe all the better because resentfully. Our skills are honed to hear its finest vibrations and hollownesses: the constitutive one-sidedness of the story, the self-pity masquerading as toughness, self-ignorance as clearsightedness, abject exactions as rugged independence. We hear this and yet, in our immemorial heterosexist intimacy with this plot, we are also practiced in how not to stop listening there. We are experienced at looking in this place, even, for unrecognized pockets of value and vitality that can hit out in unpredictable directions.

The Professor's House ends with the exaction of such a reading, I think. Alone in his study while his family has summered in Europe, the Professor now feels he has taken the manful measure of the hard truths of life itself, the ones most alien, he insists, to the venal and feminized values of the familial (read female) life that had supported and must return to envelop him.

> He had never learned to live without delight. And he would have to learn to. . . .
> . . . He doubted whether his family would ever realize that he was not the same man they had said good-bye to; they would be too happily preoccupied with their own affairs. If his apathy hurt them, they could not possibly be so much hurt as he had been already. At least, he felt the ground under his feet. He thought he knew where he was, and that he could face with fortitude the *Berengaria* and the future.[12]

'Face with fortitude the *Berengaria* and the future,' the novel's last words. Conceivably it is the very coarseness and obviousness of the gender asymmetry of heterosexual marriage that licenses, here, a certain sadism of suspicious reading, that forces us not to take this straight as the zero-degree of revelation in Willa Cather's novel. It might impel us to want to lay our ear against the tight-stretched drum of that stirring nonsense word, the she-vessel's name *Berengaria*. (A nonsense word insofar as it is a proper noun, it has for the same reason its own attachments: Berengaria was the wife of Richard the Lion-Hearted, who was known for preferring to her intimacy that of men including, legendarily, his young minstrel.) *Berengaria*— a very mother-lode of anagrammatic *energia*; within language, a force of nature, a force of cleavage. Underneath the regimented grammatic f-f-fortitudes of the hetero-sexist orderings of marriage, there are audible in this alphabet the more purely semantic germs of any vital possibility: *Berengaria*, ship of women: the {green} {aria}, the {eager} {brain}, the {bearing} and the {bairn}, the {raring} {engine}, the {bargain} {binge}, the {ban} and {bar}, the {garbage}, the {barrage} of {anger}, the {bare} {grin}, the {rage} to {err}, the {rare} {grab} for {being}, the {begin} and {rebegin} {again}.

NOTES

The people who sparked my interest in 'Paul's Case' were an English teacher, Rita Kosofsky, and a graduate student, Eric Peterson (whose English teacher I was), on whose work on 'Paul's Case' this reading tries to build.

1. Gayle Rubin, 'Thinking Sex: Notes for a Radical Theory of the Politics of Sexuality,' in *Pleasure and Danger: Exploring Female Sexuality*, ed. Carole S. Vance (Boston, 1984), 307–8.

2. Jonathan Ned Katz, *Gay/Lesbian Almanac: A New Documentary* (New York, 1983), 145–50.

3. Donald Mager, 'Gay Theories of Gender Role Deviance,' *SubStance* 46 (1985): 35–36. His sources here are John Lauritsen and David Thorstad, *The Early Homosexual Rights Movement* (New York, 1974), and James D. Steakley, *The Homosexual Emancipation Movement in Germany* (New York, 1975).

4. This argument is given more fully in 'Epistemology of the Closet I,' *Raritan* 4 (Spring 1988): 39–69.

5. All quotations from 'Paul's Case' are from Willa Cather, *Five Stories* (New York, 1956), 149–74.

6. Katherine Anne Porter, 'A Note,' in Willa Cather, *The Troll Garden* (New York, 1971), 150–51.

7. *The Kingdom of Art: Willa Cather's First Principles and Critical Statements 1893–1896*, ed. Bernice Slote (Lincoln, Neb., 1966), 390. See also 389–93.

8. Marcel Proust, *Remembrance of Things Past*, trans. C. K. Scott-Moncrieff, Terence Kilmartin, and Andreas Mayor (New York, 1982), 3: 525.

9. Ibid., 535.

10. Leo Bersani, 'The Culture of Redemption: Marcel Proust and Melanie Klein,' *Critical Inquiry* 12 (Winter 1986): 416.

11. Willa Cather, *The Professor's House* (New York, 1973), 16, 28, 30.

12. Ibid., 282–83.

Ann duCille (1949–)

Ann duCille was born in Brooklyn, New York in 1949. She received her Bachelor's degree in English from Bridgewater State College in Massachusetts in 1971, a Master of Fine Arts in creative writing from Brown University in 1973, and a second Master's degree and a PhD, both in American civilization, from Brown University in 1988 and 1991, respectively. Currently associate professor of English and African American studies at Wesleyan University, duCille is the author of *The Coupling Convention: Sex, Text, and Tradition in Black Women's Fiction* (Oxford University Press, 1993), and is working on two other books: *The Black Feminist Reader*, an edited volume of black feminist criticism, and *Inconspicuous Consumption: Labor, Leisure, and the Lady in Black Middle-Class Culture*, in which Barbie figures in the last chapter. She holds a Guggenheim Fellowship for 1994–5.

In the witty and incisive essay, 'Multicultural Barbie and the Merchandizing of Difference', Ann duCille investigates the Barbie Doll as a 'gendered, racialized icon of contemporary culture', and argues that Barbie and similar dolls 'do the dirty work of patriarchy and capitalism in the most insidious way—in the guise of child's play'. duCille reviews the marketing history of the blond American Barbie as well as that of the more recent dyed, mildly physically altered and ethnically garbed Asian, African and Jamaican Barbies who come complete with language lessons in ethnic patois. duCille describes these multi-cultural play packages as 'quick-and-dirty ethnographies [which] only enhance the extent to which these would-be multicultural dolls treat race and ethnic difference like collectibles, contributing more to commodity culture than to the intercultural awareness they claim to inspire'. Meditating on her own childhood experiences happily playing with white dolls, but desiring a black doll, duCille investigates the appeal of Barbie as an image of female 'perfection' who purveys 'the dominant white Western ideal of beauty' and she concludes by suggesting that the current ethnic Barbies do not represent the triumph of 'difference' but rather that of similarity, 'a mediated text that no matter what its dye job ultimately must be readable as white'.

A.dC and J.M.

Dyes and dolls: multicultural Barbie and the merchandizing of difference

The white missionaries who came to Saint Aug's from New England were darling to us. They gave Bessie and me these beautiful china dolls that probably were very expensive. Those dolls were white, of course. You couldn't get a colored doll like that in those days. Well, I loved mine, just the way it was, but do you know what Bessie did? She took an artist's palette they had also given us and sat down and mixed the paints until she came up with a shade of brown that matched her skin. Then she painted that white doll's face! None of the white missionaries ever said a word about it. Mama and Papa just smiled.

(Sarah Delany, *Having Our Say*)

This is my doll story (because every black journalist who writes about race gets around to it sometime). Back when I started playing with Barbie, there were no Christies (Barbie's black friend, born in 1968) or black Barbies (born in 1980, brown plastic poured into blond Barbie's mold). I had two blonds, which I bought with Christmas money from girls at school.

I cut off their hair and dressed them in African-print fabric. They lived together (polygamy, I guess) with a black G.I. Joe bartered from the Shepp boys, my down-stairs neighbors. After an 'incident' at school (where all of the girls looked like Barbie and none of them looked like me), I galloped down our stairs with one Barbie, her blond head hitting each spoke of the banister, thud, thud, thud. And galloped up the stairs, thud, thud, thud, until her head popped off, lost to the graveyard behind the stairwell. Then I tore off each limb, and sat on the stairs for a long time twirling the torso like a baton.

(Lisa Jones, *Village Voice*)

Growing up in the 1950s—in the shadow of the second world war—it was natural for children—including little black children like my two brothers and me—to want to play war, to mimic what we heard on the radio, what we watched in black and white on our brand new floor model Motorola. In these war games, everyone wanted to be the Allied troops—the fearless, conquering white male heroes who had made the world safe for democracy, yet again, and saved us all from yellow peril. No one, of course, wanted to play the enemy—who most often was not the Germans or the Italians but the Japanese. So the enemy became or, more rightly, remained invisible, lurking in bushes we shot at with sticks we pretended were rifles and stabbed at with make-believe bayonets. 'Take that,' we shouted, liberally peppering our verbal

551

assaults with racial epithets. 'And that! And that!' It was all in fun —our venom and vigor. All's fair in wars of words. We understood little of what we said and nothing of how much our child's play reflected the sentiments of a nation that even in its finer, pre-war moments had not embraced as citizens its Asian immigrants or claimed as countrymen and women their American-born offspring.

However naively imitative, our diatribe was interrupted forever one summer afternoon by the angry voice of our mother, chastising us through the open window. 'Stop that,' she said. 'Stop that this minute. It's not nice. You're talking about the Japanese. *Japanese*, do you understand? And don't let me ever hear you call them anything else.' In the lecture that accompanied dinner that evening, we were made to understand not the history of Japanese-Americans, the injustice of internment, or the horror of Hiroshima, but simply that there were real people behind the names we called; that name-calling always hurts somebody, always undermines someone's humanity. Our young minds were led on the short journey from 'Jap' to 'nigger'; and if we were too young then to understand the origins and fine points of all such pejoratives, we were old enough to know firsthand the pain of one of them.

I cannot claim that this early experience left me free of prejudice, but it did assist me in growing up at once aware of my own status as 'different' and conscious of the exclusion of others so labeled. It is important to note, however, that my sense of my own difference was affirmed and confirmed not simply by parental intervention but also by the unrelenting sameness of the tiny, almost exclusively white town in which I was raised. There in the country confines of East Bridgewater, Massachusetts, the adults who surrounded me (except for my parents) were all white, as were the teachers who taught me, the authors who thrilled me (and instilled in me a love of literature), and the neighborhood children who called me nigger one moment and friend the next. And when my brothers and I went our separate ways into properly gendered spheres, the dolls I played with—like almost everything else about my environment—were also white: Betsy Wetsy, Tiny Tears, and Patty Play Pal.

It seems remarkable to me now, as I remember these childish things long since put away, that, for all the daily reminders of my blackness, I did not take note of its absence among the rubber-skin pinkness of Betsy Wetsy, the bald-headed whiteness of Tiny Tears, and the blue-eyed blondness of Patty Play Pal. I was never tempted like Elizabeth Delany to paint the dolls I played with brown like me or to dress them in African-print fabric like Lisa Jones. (Indeed, I had no notion of such fabrics and little knowledge of the 'dark continent' from which they came.) Caught up in fantasy, completely given over to the realm of make-believe, for most of my childhood I neither noticed nor cared that the dolls I played with did not look like me. The make-believe world to which I willingly surrendered more than just my disbelief was thoroughly and profoundly white. That is to say, the 'me' I invented, the 'I' I imagined, the Self I day-dreamed in technicolor fantasies was no more black like me than the dolls I played with. In the fifties and well into the sixties of my childhood, the black Other who was my Self, much like the enemy Other who was the foreign body of our war games, could only be imagined as faceless, far away, and utterly unfamiliar.

As suggested by my title, I am going to use the figure of multicultural Barbie to talk about the commodification of race and gender difference. I wanted to back into the present topic, however, into what I have to say about Barbie as a gendered, racialized icon of contemporary commodity culture, by reaching into the past—into the admittedly contested terrain of the personal—to evoke the ideological work of child's play. More than simple instruments of pleasure and amusement, toys and games play crucial roles in helping children determine what is valuable in and around them. Dolls in particular invite children to replicate them, to imagine themselves in their dolls' images. What does it mean, then, when little girls are given dolls to play with that in no way resemble them? What did it mean for me that I was nowhere in the toys I played with?

If the Japan and the Africa of my youth were beyond the grasp (if not the reach) of my imagination, children today are granted instant global gratification in their play—immediate, hands-on access to both Self and Other. Or so we are told by many of the leading fantasy manufacturers—Disney, Hasbro, and Mattel, in particular—whose contributions to multicultural education include such play things as Aladdin (movie, video, and dolls), G.I. Joe (male 'action figures' in black and white), and Barbie (now available in a variety of colors and ethnicities). Disneyland's river ride through different nations, like Mattel's Dolls of the World Collection, instructs us that 'It's a Small World After All.' Those once distant lands of Africa, Asia, Australia, and even the Arctic regions of the North Pole (yes, Virginia, there is an Eskimo Barbie) are now as close to home as the local Toys R Us and F.A.O. Schwarz. And lo and behold, the inhabitants of these foreign lands—from Disney's Princess Jasmine to Mattel's Jamaican Barbie—are just like us, dye-dipped versions of archetypal white American beauty. It is not only a small world after all, but, as the Grammy award-winning theme from *Aladdin* informs us, 'it's a whole new world.'

Many of the major toy manufacturers have taken on a global perspective, a kind of nearsightedness that constructs this whole new world as small and cultural difference as consumable. Perhaps nowhere is this universalizing myopia more conspicuous than in the production, marketing, and consumption of Barbie dolls. By Mattel's reckoning, Barbie enjoys 100 percent brand name recognition among girls ages three to ten, ninety-six percent of whom own at least one doll, with most owning an average of eight. Five years ago, as Barbie turned thirty, *Newsweek* noted that nearly 500 million Barbies had been sold, along with 200 million G.I. Joes—'enough for every man, woman, and child in the United States and Europe' (Kantrowitz 59-60). Those figures have increased dramatically in the past five years, bringing the current worldwide Barbie population to 800 million. In 1992 alone, $1 billion worth of Barbies and accessories were sold. Last year, Barbie dolls sold at an average of one million per week, with overall sales exceeding the $1 billion all-time high set the year before. As the Boston *Globe* reported on the occasion of Barbie's thirty-fifth birthday on March 9, 1994, nearly two Barbie dolls are sold every second somewhere in the world; about fifty percent of the dolls sold are purchased here in the United States (Dembner 16).

The current Barbie boom may be in part the result of new, multiculturally oriented developments both in the dolls and in their marketing. In the fall of 1990, Mattel, Inc. announced a new marketing strategy to boost its sales: the corporation would 'go ethnic' in its advertising by launching an ad campaign for the black and Hispanic versions of the already popular doll. Despite the existence of black, Asian, and Latina Barbies, prior to the fall of 1990 Mattel's print and TV ads featured only white dolls. In what *Newsweek* described as an attempt to capitalize on ethnic spending power, Mattel began placing ads for multicultural Barbies in such Afrocentric publications as *Essence* magazine and on such Latin-oriented shows as 'Pepe Plata' after market research revealed that most black and Hispanic consumers were unaware of the company's ethnic dolls. This targeted advertising was a smart move, according to the industry analysts cited by *Newsweek*, because 'Hispanics buy about $170 billion worth of goods each year, [and] blacks spend even more.' Indeed, sales of black Barbie dolls reportedly doubled in the year following this new ethnically-oriented ad campaign.[1] But determined to present itself as politically correct as well as financially savvy, Mattel was quick to point out that ethnic audiences, who are now able to purchase dolls who look like them, also have profited from the corporation's new marketing priorities. Barbie is a role model for all of her owners, according to product manager Deborah Mitchell, herself an African American. 'Barbie allows little girls to dream,' she asserted—to which the *Newsweek* reporter added (seemingly without irony): 'now, ethnic Barbie lovers will be able to dream in their own image' (Berkwitz 48).

Dream in their own image? The *Newsweek* columnist inadvertently put his finger on precisely what is so troubling to many parents, feminist scholars, and cultural critics about Barbie and dolls like her. Such toys invite, inspire, and even demand a potentially damaging process not simply of imagining but of interpellation. When little girls fantasize themselves into the conspicuous consumption, glamour, perfection, and, some have argued, anorexia of Barbie's world, it is rarely, if ever, 'in their own image that they dream.'[2] Regardless of what color dyes the dolls are dipped in or what costumes they are adorned with, the image they present is of the same mythically thin, long-legged, luxuriously-haired, buxom beauty. And while Mattel and other toy manufacturers may claim to have the best interests of ethnic audiences in mind in peddling their integrated wares, one does not have to be a cynic to suggest that profit remains the motivating factor behind this merchandising of difference.[3]

Far from simply playing with the sixty or so dolls I have acquired in the past year, then, I take them very seriously. In fact, I regard Barbie and similar dolls as Louis Althusser might have regarded them: as objects that do the dirty work of patriarchy and capitalism in the most insidious way—in the guise of child's play. But, as feminists have protested almost from the moment she hit the market, Barbie is not simply a child's toy or just a teenage fashion doll; she is an icon—perhaps *the* icon—of true white womanhood and femininity, a symbol of the far from innocent ideological stuff of which the (Miss) American dream and other mystiques of race and gender are made.

Invented by Ruth Handler, one of the founders of Mattel, and named after her daughter, Barbie dolls have been a very real force in the toy market since Mattel first introduced them at the American Toy Fair in 1959. In fact, despite the skepticism of toy store buyers—who at the time were primarily men—the first shipment of a half million dolls and a million costumes sold out immediately (Larcen A7). The first Barbies, which were modeled after a sexy German doll and comic strip character named Lilli, were all white, but in 1967 Mattel premiered a black version of the doll called 'Colored Francie.' 'Colored Francie,' like white 'Francie Fairchild' introduced the year before, was supposed to be Barbie's 'MOD'ern' younger cousin. As a white doll modeled and marketed in the image of Hollywood's Gidget, white Francie had been an international sensation, but Colored Francie was not destined to duplicate her prototype's success. Although the 'black is beautiful' theme of both the civil rights and black power movements may have suggested a ready market for a beautiful black doll, Colored Francie in fact did not sell well.

Evelyn Burkhalter, owner, operator, and curator of the Barbie Hall of Fame in Palo Alto, California—home to 16,000 Barbie dolls—attributes Colored Francie's commercial failure to the racial climate of the times. Doll purchasing patterns, it seems, reflected the same resistance to integration that was felt elsewhere in the nation. In her implied family ties to white Barbie, Colored Francie suggested more than simple integration. She implied miscegenation: a make-believe mixing of races that may have jeopardized the doll's real market value. Cynthia Roberts, author of *Barbie: Thirty Years of America's Doll* (1989), maintains that Colored Francie flopped because of her straight hair and Caucasian features (44), which seemingly were less acceptable then than now. No doubt Mattel's decision to call its first black Barbie 'Colored Francie' also contributed to the doll's demise. The use of the out-moded, even racist term 'colored' in the midst of civil rights and black power activism suggested that while Francie might be 'MOD'ern,' Mattel was still in the dark(y) ages. In any case, neither black nor white audiences bought the idea of Barbie's colored relations, and Mattel promptly took the doll off the market, replacing her with a black doll called Christie in 1968.

While a number of other black dolls appeared throughout the late sixties and seventies—including the Julia doll, modeled after the TV character played by black singer and actress Diahann Carroll—it was not until 1980 that Mattel introduced black dolls that were called Barbie like their white counterparts. Today, Barbie dolls come in a virtual rainbow coalition of colors, races, ethnicities, and nationalities—most of which look remarkably like the prototypical white Barbie, modified only by a dash of color and a change of costume. It is these would-be multicultural 'dolls of the world'—Jamaican Barbie, Nigerian and Kenyan Barbie, Malaysian Barbie, Chinese Barbie, Mexican, Spanish, and Brazilian Barbie, et cetera, et cetera, et cetera—that interest me. For me these dolls are at once a symbol and a symptom of what multiculturalism has become at the hands of contemporary commodity culture: an easy and immensely profitable way off the hook of Eurocentrism that gives us the face of cultural diversity without the particulars of racial difference.

If I could line up across the page the ninety 'different' colors, cultures, and other incarnations in which Barbie currently exists, the fact of her unrelenting sameness (or at least similarity) would become immediately apparent. Even two dolls might do the trick: 'My First Barbie' in white and 'My First Barbie' in black, for example, or white 'Western Fun Barbie' and black 'Western Fun Barbie.' Except for their dye jobs, the dolls are identical: the same body, size, shape, and apparel. Or perhaps I should say *nearly* identical because in some instances—with black and Asian dolls in particular—coloring and other subtle changes (stereotypically slanted eyes in the Asian dolls, thicker lips in the black dolls) suggest differently coded facial features.

In other instances, when Barbie moves across cultural as opposed to racial lines, it is costume rather than color that distinguishes one ethnic group or nation from another. Nigeria and Jamaica, for instance, are represented by the same basic brown body, dolled-up in different native garbs—or Mattel's interpretation thereof.[4] With other costume changes, this generic black body becomes Western Fun Barbie or Marine Barbie or Desert Storm Barbie, and even Presidential Candidate Barbie, who, by the way, comes with a Nancy Reagan-red taking-care-of-business suit as well as a red, white, and blue inaugural ball gown. Much the same is true of the generic Asian doll—sometimes called Kira—who reappears in a variety of different dress-defined ethnicities. In other words, where Barbie is concerned, clothes not only make the woman, they mark the racial and/or cultural difference.

Such difference is marked as well by the cultural history and language lessons that accompany each doll in Mattel's international collection. The back of Jamaican Barbie's box tells us, for example, 'How-you-du (Hello) from the land of Jamaica, a tropical paradise known for its exotic fruit, sugar cane, breathtaking beaches, and reggae beat!' The box goes on to explain that most Jamaicans have ancestors from Africa. Therefore, 'even though our official language is English, we speak patois, a kind of "*Jamaica Talk*," filled with English and African words.' The lesson ends with a brief glossary (eight words) and a few more examples of this 'Jamaica Talk,' complete with translations: 'A hope yu wi come-a Jamaica! (I hope you will come to Jamaica!); and 'Teck care a yusself, mi fren! (Take care of yourself, my friend!)' A nice idea, I suppose, but for me these quick-and-dirty ethnographies only enhance the extent to which these would-be multicultural dolls treat race and ethnic difference like collectibles, contributing more to commodity culture than to the intercultural awareness they claim to inspire.

Is the current fascination with the black or colored body—especially the female body—a contemporary version of the primitivism of the 1920s? Is multiculturalism to postmodernism what primitivism was to modernism? It was while on my way to a round table discussion on precisely this question that I bought my first black Barbie dolls in March of 1993. As carbon copies of an already problematic original, these colorized Mattel toys seemed to me the perfect tools with which to illustrate the point I wanted to make about the collapse of multiculturalism into an easy pluralism that simply adds what it constructs as the Other without upsetting the fundamental precepts and paradigms of Western culture or, in the case of Mattel, without changing the mold.

Not entirely immune to such critiques, Mattel sought expert advice from black parents and early childhood specialists in the development and marketing of its newest line of black Barbie dolls. Chief among the expert witnesses was clinical psychologist Darlene Powell Hopson, who co-authored with her husband Derek S. Hopson a study of racism and child development entitled *Different and Wonderful: Raising Black Children in a Race-Conscious Society* (1990). As part of their research for the book, the Hopsons repeated a ground-breaking study conducted by black psychologists Kenneth and Mamie Clark in the 1940s.

The Clarks used black and white dolls to demonstrate the negative effects of racism and segregation on black children. When given a choice between a white doll and a black doll, nearly 70 percent of the black children in the study chose the white doll. The Clarks' findings became an important factor in *Brown v. the Board of*

Education in 1954. More recently, some scholars have called into question not necessarily the Clarks' findings but their interpretation: the assumption that, in the realm
of make-believe, a black child's choosing a white doll necessarily reflects a negative
self concept.[5] For the Hopsons, however, the Clarks' research remains compelling.
In 1985 they repeated the Clarks' doll test and found that an alarming 65 percent of
the black children in their sample chose a white doll over a black one. Moreover, 76
percent of the children interviewed said that the black dolls 'looked bad' to them
(Hopsons xix).

In addition to the clinical uses they make of dolls in their experiments, the
Hopsons also give considerable attention to what they call 'doll play' in their book,
specifically mentioning Barbie. 'If your daughter likes "Barbie" dolls, by all means
get her Barbie,' they advise black parents. 'But also choose Black characters from the
Barbie world. *You do not want your child to grow up thinking that only White dolls, and
by extension White people, are attractive and nice*' (Hopsons 127, emphasis in the original). (Note that 'Barbie,' unmodified in the preceding passage, seems to mean *white*
Barbie dolls.) The Hopsons suggest that parents should not only provide their children with black and other ethnic dolls but that they should get involved in their
children's doll play. 'Help them dress and groom the dolls while you compliment
them both,' they advise, offering the following suggested routine: '"This is a beautiful doll. It looks just like you. Look at her hair. It's just like yours. Did you know
your nose is as pretty as your doll's?"' (119) They also suggest that parents use 'complimentary words such as *lovely, pretty, or nice* so that [the] child will learn to
associate them with his or her own image' (124).

Certainly it is important to help children feel good about themselves. One might
argue, however, that the 'just like you' simile and the beautiful doll imagery so central to these suggestions for what the Hopsons call positive play run the risk of
transmitting to the child a colorized version of the same old beauty myth. Like
Barbie dolls themselves, they make beauty—and by implication worth—a matter of
physical characteristics.

In spite of their own good intentions, the Hopsons, in linking play with 'beautiful'
dolls to positive self-imagining, echoed Mattel's own marketing campaign. It is not
surprising, then, that the Hopsons' findings and the interventional strategies they
designed for using dolls to instill ethnic pride caught the attention of Mattel. In 1990
Darlene Hopson was asked to consult with the corporation's product manager
Deborah Mitchell and designer Kitty Black-Perkins—both African Americans—in
the development of a new line of 'realistically sculpted' black fashion dolls. Hopson
agreed and about a year later Shani and her friends Asha and Nichelle became the
newest members of Barbie's ever-expanding family.

Shani means 'marvelous' in Swahili, according to the dolls' press kit. But as
Village Voice columnist Lisa Jones has noted, the name has other meanings as well:
'startling, a wonder, a novelty' (Jones 36). My own research indicates that while
Shani is a Swahili female name meaning marvelous, the Kiswahili word 'shani' translates as 'an adventure, something unusual' (Stewart 120). So it seems that Mattel's
new play thing is not just marvelous, too marvelous for words, but, as her name also
suggests, she is difference incarnate—a novelty, a new enterprise or, perhaps, as the
black female Other so often is, an exotic. Mattel, it seems to me, both plays up and

557

plays on what it presents as the doll's exotic black-is-beautiful difference. As the back of her package reads:

> Shani means marvelous in the Swahili language . . . and marvelous she is! With her friends Asha and Nichelle, Shani brings to life the special style and beauty of the African American woman.
>
> Each one is beautiful in her own way, with her own lovely skin shade and unique facial features. Each has a different hair color and texture, perfect for braiding, twisting and creating fabulous hair styles! Their clothes, too, reflect the vivid colors and ethnic accents that showcase their *exotic looks* and fashion flair! (my emphasis)
>
> Shani, Asha and Nichelle invite you into their glamorous world to share the fun and excitement of being a top model. Imagine appearing on magazine covers, starring in fashion shows, and going to Hollywood parties as you, Shani, Asha and Nichelle live your dreams of beauty and success, loving every marvelous minute!

While these words attempt to convey a message of black pride—after the fashion of the Hopsons' recommendations for positive play—that message is clearly tied to bountiful hair, lavish and exotic clothes, and other outward and visible signs not of brains but of beauty, wealth, and success. Shani may be a top fashion model, but don't look for her (or, if Mattel's own oft-articulated theory of Barbie as role model holds, yourself or your child) at M.I.T.

Like any other proud, well-to-do parents of a debutante, Mattel gave Shani her own coming out party at the International Toy Fair in February of 1991. This gala event included a tribute to black designers and an appearance by En Vogue singing the Negro National Anthem, 'Lift Every Voice and Sing'—evidently the song of choice of the doll Mattel describes as 'tomorrow's African American woman.' Also making their debuts were Shani's friends Asha and Nichelle, notable for the different hues in which their black plastic skin comes—an innovation due in part to Darlene Hopson's influence. Shani, the signature doll of the line, is what we call in the culture 'brown-skinned'; Asha is honey-colored (some would say 'high-yella'); and Nichelle is deep mahogany. Their male friend Jamal, added in 1992, completes the collection.

For the un(make-)believing, the three-to-one ratio of the Shani quartet—three black females to one black male—may be the most realistic thing about these dolls. In the eyes and the advertising of Mattel, however, Shani and her friends are the most authentic black female thing the mainstream toy market has yet produced. 'Tomorrow's African American woman' (an appellation which, as Lisa Jones has noted, both riffs and one-ups *Essence*'s 'Today's Black Woman') has broader hips, fuller lips, and a broader nose, according to product manager Deborah Mitchell. Principal designer Kitty Black-Perkins, who has dressed black Barbies since their birth in 1980, adds that the Shani dolls are also distinguished by their unique, culturally-specific clothes in 'spice tones, [and] ethnic fabrics,' rather than 'fantasy colors like pink or lavender' (as quoted by Jones 36)—evidently the colors of the faint of skin.

The notion that fuller lips, broader noses, wider hips, and higher derrieres somehow make the Shani dolls more realistically African American raises many difficult questions about authenticity, truth, and the ever-problematic categories of the real and the symbolic, the typical and the stereotypical. Just what are we saying when we claim that a doll does or does not 'look black'? How does black look? What would it take to make a doll look authentically African American? What preconceived, prescriptive ideals of legitimate blackness are inscribed in such claims of authenticity? How can doll manufacturers or any other image makers—the film industry, for example—attend to cultural, racial, and phenotypical differences without merely engaging the same simplistic big-lips/broad-hips stereotypes that make so many of us—blacks in particular—grit our (pearly white) teeth? What would it take to produce a line of dolls that more fully reflects the wide variety of sizes, shapes, colors, hair styles, occupations, abilities, and disabilities that African Americans—like all people—come in? In other words: what price difference?

If such specificity—such ethnic 'authenticity'—were possible to achieve in a doll, its purchase price, I suspect, would be much higher than a profit-driven corporation like Mattel would be willing to pay. Let me again invoke Shani to prove my point. On the one hand, Mattel was concerned enough about producing an ethnically correct black doll to seek the advice of black image specialists such as Darlene Hopson in the development and marketing of the Shani line. Ultimately, however, the company was not willing to follow the advice of such experts where doing so would cost the corporation more than the price of additional dyes and ethnic fabrics.

For example, Hopson reportedly argued not just for gradations in skin tones in the Shani dolls but also for variations in body type and lengths and styles of hair—for an Afro here or an asymmetrical cut there. But, while Mattel acknowledged both the legitimacy and the ubiquity of such arguments, profit motive mediated against the very realism the corporation set out to achieve in these dolls. 'To be truly realistic, one [Shani doll] should have shorter hair,' Deborah Mitchell confessed to Lisa Jones. 'But little girls of all races love hair play. We added more texture. But we can't change the fact that long, combable hair is still a key seller' (Jones 36).

Mitchell, of course, has a point. It is after all the taste of consumers that is inscribed in Barbie's long, combable hair. In the process of my own archival research—poking around in the dusty aisles of Toys R Us—I encountered a black teenage girl in search, like me, of the latest black Barbie. During the impromptu interview that ensued, my subject confessed to me in gory, graphic details the many Barbie murders and mutilations she had committed over the years. 'It's the hair,' she said emphatically several times. 'The hair, that hair; I want it. I want it.' Her words recalled my own torturous childhood struggles with the straightening combs, curling irons, and relaxers that bi-weekly transformed my wooly, 'just like a sponge' kinks into what the white kids at school marveled at as my 'Cleopatra [read straight] hair.' During one of those bi-weekly sessions with my mother and the straightening comb, I was foolish enough to say out loud what I had wished for a long time: that I had straight hair like the white girls at school. I still remember my mother's hurt, her sense of her daughter's racial heresy. Mitchell and Mattel indeed have a point. The difficult truth just may be that part of Shani's and black Barbie's attraction for little black girls in particular is the escape from their own often shorter, harder-to-comb hair that these dolls' lengthy straight locks represent.

Barbie's svelte figure, like her long combable hair, became Shani's body type as well. And, here, too marketability seems to have overruled professed attempts to capture the 'unique facial features' and the 'special style and beauty of the African American people.' Even the reported subtle changes that are supposed to signify Shani's black difference—her much-remarked broader hips and elevated buttocks, for example—are little more than optical illusions, according to anthropologists Jacqueline Urla and Alan Swedlund of the University of Massachusetts at Amherst. Urla and Swedlund, who have been studying the anthropometry—the body measurements—of Barbie for some time, argue that, while Shani's hips may appear to be wider, they are actually smaller in both circumference and breadth than those of other Barbie dolls. It is essential, after all, that all the dolls be able to share the same clothes, thus making any dramatic alterations in body type unlikely. The effect of a higher buttocks is achieved, Urla and Swedlund maintain, by changing the angle of the doll's back. In other words, the Shani doll's buttocks may appear stereotypically higher, but she is not really dimensionally different from all the other eleven-and-a-half inch fashion dolls.[6]

Lisa Jones concludes her *Village Voice* article on Barbie by noting that the women behind Shani—black women like Hopson and Mitchell—want the doll to be more than just a Barbie in blackface. While Hopson, in particular, certainly hoped for—shall I say—*different* difference she nevertheless maintains that the Shani dolls demonstrate 'social consciousness on Mattel's part' (Jones 36). British fashion designer and Barbie aficionado extraordinaire BillyBoy made a similar point in praising Mattel for integrating Barbie's family with first Colored Francie and then Christie in the late 1960s (BillyBoy 82). After nearly thirty years, I think we can forgive Mattel its Colored Francie faux pas and perhaps even applaud the attempt. But if Shani (who came out in a new scantily clad Soul Train edition in 1993) stands as Mattel's best effort to 'go ethnic,' as it were—to corner the contemporary mainstream market in 'realistically sculpted' black dolls that 'bring to life' the 'special style and beauty of the African-American people'—she stands on shaky ground.

And yet it may not be fair to single out Mattel as an example of what seems to be a national if not international phenomenon. Racial difference, like ethnic Barbie, is a hot commodity, and it isn't only Mattel who is making money. In the words of David Rieff, a contributing editor of *Harper's Magazine*:

> Everything is commodifiable, even Afrocentrism (there is money being made on all the Kinte [sic] cloth and Kwanza [sic] paraphernalia that are the rage among certain segments of the black community, and not only the black community), bilingualism (currently the hottest growth market in publishing is Spanish-language children's books), and the other 'multicultural' tendencies in American society that conservatives fear so desperately.
>
> (*Harper's*, August 1993)

Rieff goes so far as to call this newly globalized consumer economy multi-culturalism's silent partner. I want to be careful in expressing my own concerns about the relationship between multiculturalism and the conspicuous consumption of difference, however, lest my critique appear complicit with that of the conservatives to whom Rieff refers, who fear the possibilities of a truly transformative social, cultural, and economic order, which I in fact would welcome.

All cultural commodities are not created equal. It seems to me that however profitable their production may be for the publishing industry, Spanish-language children's books serve a useful, educational function for their target audiences. On the other hand, even taking into account the argument that black girls need black dolls to play with, I have a difficult time locating the redeeming social value in Mattel's little plastic women, even—or perhaps especially—when they are tinted brown and decorated in Kente cloth and Kufi hats, as the new Soul Train Shani dolls are. And while I am certain that hordes of black consumers are grateful for the black haircare products and cosmetics marketed by mainstream corporations such as Clairol, Revlon, and Mary Kay, I am less convinced that J.C. Penney's target audience will really find much cultural enlightenment in the Kente cloth potholders, napkin rings, and dish towels that the store is currently marketing as 'expressions of cultural pride.'

In *Fashion Influences*, a catalog clearly intended to cater to what it takes to be the tastes of black audiences, J.C. Penney advertises an assortment of housewares, ethnic artifacts, and exclusive designer fashions with 'Afrocentric flair.' Such specialty items as triple-woven cotton throws, which sell for $50 each, are available in four culturally edifying patterns: 01 Kwanzaa; 02 Kente; 03 Martin Luther King; and 04 Malcolm X. For another $40, customers can complement their Kwanzaa-patterned throw with a Kwanzaa needlepoint pillow. (For the not quite multiculturally literate shopper, Penney's provides a cultural history lesson: 'Kwanzaa means "first fruits of the harvest" in Swahili,' the catalog informs. 'Created in 1966, Kwanzaa is a seven-day celebration synthesizing elements from many African harvest festivals.') And just so consumers know precisely how politically correct their Penney's purchases are, many of the catalog descriptions inform shoppers that these Afrocentric items are made in the U.S.A. The Ivory Coast Table Linens, for example, are billed as an 'exuberantly colored interpretation of authentic African woven cloth. . . Made in the U.S.A.' The Kente-cloth pillows are made in the U.S.A. of fabric imported from Africa, but the MLK and Malcolm X throws are just plain made in the U.S.A. In other words, for not-so-modest prices, culturally and socially-conscious American consumers can look for the union label as they shop for these and other interpretations-of-authentic-African-inspired-made-in-America goods.

Thus it is that from custom-designed bedroom coordinates inspired by mud cloth from Mali in West Africa to an embroidered metallic caftan or 'Uwe (pronounced yoo-way, meaning dress)' inspired by 'garments worn by the royal court on special occasions,' what J.C. Penney is trading in and trading on in this blaxploitation catalog is cultural difference and, if you will, mis-spent racial pride. Although I doubt that Penney's cares who buys its Kufi hats, black-on-black dishware, and 'In Search of Identity' games, it is also clear that the company does not waste such catalogs on just any body. I, for example, have been a loyal Penney's catalog shopper for years; I receive the annual seasonal catalogs, as well as special fliers advertising queen-size fashions. I only happened upon Penney's blaxploitation catalog recently, however, when it was mailed not to me—faithful shopper—or to my home but to the Center for African American Studies at Wesleyan University. While my shopping history identified me as larger-sized, there was evidently nothing about my purchasing pattern that identified me as black. Penney's marketing division seems to have assumed—quite cleverly, I think—that a Center for African American Studies would be a likely place to find middle-class, culturally-conscious black consumers who might actually be able to afford the high-prized items in its Afrocentric catalog. (What a miscalculation in that last regard.)

I suspect that such catalogs are mailed not only to black studies departments but also to black beauty parlors (indeed I found a similar catalog from Spiegel at the shop where I get my hair cut) and black churches, where there is sure to be a ready-made market for the Sunday-go-to-meetin' hats, high-heel shoes, and church-lady suits 'with an Afrocentric flair' that fill their pages. Just to bring this discussion full circle, let me note that six Black Barbie dolls are available through this special catalog— Black Desert Storm Barbie and Ken and Soul Train Shani and her three friends Asha, Nichelle, and Jamal. Army Barbie and Ken are dressed in 'authentic desert fatigues with authentic insignias for enlisted personnel,' and the Shani dolls are decked out in 'cool hip-hop fashions inspired by the hot T.V. dance show.' But don't let these patriotic, all-American girls and boys fool you; they are all imported from Malaysia.

The body politic(s) of Barbie

> Barbie's body is a consumer object itself, a vehicle for the display of clothing and the spectacular trappings of a wealthy teenage fantasy life. Her extraordinary body exists not simply as an example of the fetishized female form typical of those offered up to the male gaze, but as a commodity vehicle itself whose form seduces the beholder and sells accessories, the real source of corporate profit. Like Lay's chips, no one can buy just one outfit for the doll. Barbie is the late capitalist girl incarnate.
>
> (Mel McCombie, 'Barbie: Toys Are Us?')

In focusing thus far on the merchandising of racial, perhaps more so than gender dif-ference, I do not mean to imply that racial and gender identities are divisible, even in dolls. Nor, in observing that most if not all of Mattel's 'dolls of the world' look remarkably like what the company calls the 'traditional, blond, blue-eyed Barbie,' do I mean to suggest that the seemingly endless recapitulation of the white prototype is the only way in which these dolls are problematic. In fact, the most alarming thing about Barbie may well be the extent to which she functions as what M.G. Lord calls a teaching tool for femininity, whatever her race or ethnicity. Lord, the author of *Forever Barbie: The Unauthorized Biography of a Real Doll*, due out later this year, describes Barbie as a 'space-age fertility icon. She looks like a modern woman, but she's a very primitive totem of female power' (Dembner 1).

Barbie has long had the eye and ire of feminists, who, for the most part, have reviled her as another manifestation of the damaging myths of female beauty and the feminine body that patriarchy perpetuates through such vehicles as popular and commodity culture. A counter narrative also exists, however, one in which Barbie is not an empty-headed, material girl bimbo, for whom math class is tough, but a feminist heroine, who has been first in war (a soldier who served in the Gulf, she has worn the colors of her country as well as the United Colors of Benetton), first in peace (she held her own summit in 1990 and she's a long-time friend of UNICEF, who 'loves all the children of the world'), and always in the hearts of her country (Americans buy her at the rate of one doll every second). While time does not allow me to reiterate or to assess here all the known critiques and defenses of Barbie, I do want to discuss briefly some of the gender ideals that I think are encoded in and transmitted by this larger-than-life little woman and what Barbie's escalating popularity says about contemporary American culture.

In *Touching Liberty: Abolition, Feminism, and the Politics of the Body* (1993), Karen Sanchez-Eppler argues that all dolls are intended to teach little girls about domesticity (133). If such tutelage is Barbie's not so secret mission, her methodology is far more complex and contradictory than that of the Betsy Wetsy and Tiny Tears baby dolls I played with thirty-five years ago. Those dolls invoked and evoked the maternal, as they and the baby bottles and diapers with which they were packaged invited us to nestle, nurse, and nurture. Barbie's curvaceous, big-busted, almost fully female body, on the other hand, summons not the maternal but the sexual, not the nurturant mother but the sensuous woman. As Mel McCombie has argued, rather than rehearsing parenting, as a baby doll does, Barbie's adult body encourages children to dress and redress a fashion doll that yields lessons about sexuality, consumption, and teenage life (3). Put another way, we might say that Barbie is literally and figuratively a titillating toy.

Bodacious as they may be, however, Barbie's firm plastic breasts have no nipples—nothing that might offend, nothing that might suggest her own pleasure. And if her protruding plastic mounds signify a simmering sensuality, what are we to make of her missing genitalia? McCombie suggests that Barbie's genital ambiguity can be read as an 'homage to "good taste"' and as a 'reflection of the regnant mores for teenage girls—to be both sexy and adult yet remain virginal' (4). I agree that her body invites such readings, but it also seems to me that there is nothing ambiguous about Barbie's crotch. It's missing in inaction. While male dolls like Ken and Jamal have bumps 'down there' and in some instances simulated underwear etched into the plastic, most Barbies come neither with drawers nor with even a hint of anything that needs covering, even as 'it' is already covered or erased. As an icon of idealized femininity, then, Barbie is locked into a never-never land in which she must be always already sexual without the possibility of sex. Conspicuously sensual on top but definitively nonsexual below, her plastic body indeed has inscribed within it the very contradictory, whore/madonna messages with which patriarchy taunts and even traumatizes young women in particular.

This kind of speculation about Barbie's breasts has led the doll's creator, Ruth Handler, to chide adults for their nasty minds. 'In my opinion people make too much of breasts,' Handler has complained. 'They are just part of the body' (BillyBoy 26). Mrs. Handler has a point (or maybe two). I feel more than just a little ridiculous myself as I sit here contemplating the body parts and sex life of a piece of plastic. What is fascinating, however, what I think is worth studying, what both invites and resists theorizing, is not the lump of molded plastic that is Barbie, but the imaginary life that is not—that is *our* invention. Barbie as a cultural artifact may be able to tell us more about ourselves and our society—more about society's attitudes toward *its* women—than anything we might say about the doll her- or, rather, *itself.*

In the nineteenth century, Alexis de Tocqueville and others argued that you could judge the character, quality, and degree of advancement of a civilization by the status and treatment of its women. What is the status of women in soon to be twenty-first-century America, and can Barbie serve as a barometer for measuring that status? Barbie, it seems to me, is a key player in the process of socialization—of engendering and racialization—that begins in infancy and is furthered by almost everything about our society, including the books children read, the toys they play with, and the cartoons they watch on television.

While changing channels one Saturday morning, I happened upon a cartoon, just a glimpse of which impelled me to watch on. At the point that I tuned in, a big, gray, menacingly male bulldog was barking furiously at a pretty, petite, light-colored cat, who simply batted her long lashes, meowed coquettishly, and rubbed her tiny feline body against his huge canine leg in response. The more the dog barked and growled, the softer the cat meowed, using her slinky feline body and her feminine wiles to win the dog over. Her strategy worked; before my eyes—and, I imagine, the eyes of millions of children, the ferocious beast was transformed into a lovesick puppy dog, who followed the cat everywhere, repeatedly saving her from all manner of evil and danger. Time and time again, the bulldog rescued the helpless, accident-prone pussy from falling girders, on-coming traffic, and other hazards to which she, in her innocent frailty, was entirely oblivious. By the end, the once ferocious bulldog was completely domesticated, as his no longer menacing body became a kind of bed for the cat to nestle in.

There are, of course, a number of ways to read the gender and racial politics of this cartoon. I suppose that the same thought process that theorizes Barbie as a feminist heroine for whom men are mere accessories might claim the kitty cat, too, as a kind of feminist feline, who uses her feminine wiles to get her way. What resonates for me in the cartoon, however, are its beauty and the beast, light/dark, good/evil, female/male race and gender codes: light, bright, cat-like femininity tames menacing black male bestiality. Make no mistake, however; it is not wit that wins out over barbarism but a mindless, can't-take-care-of-herself femininity.

Interestingly enough, these are the kinds of messages of which fairy tales and children's stories are often made. White knights rescue fair damsels in distress from dark, forbidding evils of one kind or another. As Darlene and Derek Hopson argue: 'Some of the most blatant and simplistic representations of white as good and black as evil are found in children's literature,' where evil black witches and good white fairies—heroes in white and villains in black—abound (121).

What Barbie dolls, cartoons like the one outlined above, and even the seemingly innocent fairy tales we read to our children seem to me to have in common are the mythologies of race and gender that are encoded in them. Jacqueline Urla and Alan Swedlund maintain that Barbie's body type constructs the bodies of other women as deviant and perpetuates an impossible standard of beauty. Attempting to live up to the Barbie ideal, others argue, fosters eating and shopping disorders in teenage girls—nightmares instead of dreams. BillyBoy, one of Barbie's most ardent supporters, defends his heroine against such charges by insisting that there is nothing abnormal about the proportions of Barbie's body. Rather, he asserts, 'she has the ideal that Western culture has insisted upon since the 1920s: long legs, long arms, small waist, high round bosom, and long neck' (22). The irony is that BillyBoy may be right. 'Unrealistic' or not, Barbie's weight and measurements (which if proportionate to those of a woman 5'6" tall would be something like 110 pounds and a top-heavy 39–18–33) are not much different from those of the beauty queens to whom Bert Parks used to sing 'Here she is, Miss America. Here she is, our ideal.'[7] If Barbie is a monster, she is our monster, our ideal.

But is Barbie bad?' Someone asked me the other day if a black doll that looks like a white doll isn't better than no black doll at all. I must admit that I have no ready answer for this and a number of other questions posed by my own critique. Although, as I acknowledged in the beginning, the dolls I played with as a child were white, I still remember the first time I saw a black doll. To me, she was the most beautiful thing I had ever seen; I wanted her desperately, and I was never again satisfied with white Betsy Wetsy and blonde, blue-eyed Patty Play Pal. She was something else, something *Other*, like me, and that, I imagine, was the source of her charm and my desire.

If I did not consciously note my own absence in the toys I played with, that absence, I suspect, had a profound effect on me nevertheless. We have only to read Toni Morrison's chilling tale *The Bluest Eye* to see the effect of the white beauty myth on the black child. And while they were by no means as dire for me as for Morrison's character Pecola Breedlove, I was not exempt from the consequences of growing up black in a white world that barely acknowledged my existence. I grew up believing I was ugly: my kinky hair, my big hips, the gap between my teeth. I have spent half my life smiling with my hand over my mouth to hide that gap, a habit I only began to get over in graduate school when a couple of Nigerian men told me that in their culture, where my body type is prized much more than Barbie's, such gaps are a sign of great beauty. I wonder what it would have meant for me as a child to see a black doll—or any doll—with big hips and a gap between her two front teeth.

Today, for $24.99, Mattel reaches halfway around the world and gives little girls— black like me—Nigerian Barbies to play with. Through the wonders of plastic, dyes, and mass production, the company brings into the homes of African American children a Nigeria that I as a young child did not even know existed. The problem is that Mattel's Nigeria does not exist either. The would-be ethnic dolls of the world Mattel sells, like their 'traditional, blond, blue-eyed' all-American girl prototype, have no gaps, no big ears, no chubby thighs or other 'imperfections.' For a modest price, I can dream myself into Barbie's perfect world, so long as I dream myself in her image. It may be a small world, a whole new world, but there is still no place for me as *me* in it.

This, then, is my final doll story. Groucho Marx said that he wouldn't want to belong to a club that would have him as a member. In that same vein, I am not so sure that most of us would want to buy a doll that 'looked like us.' Indeed, efforts to

565

produce and market such truer-to-life dolls have not met with much commercial success. Cultural critics like me can throw theoretical stones at her all we want, but part of Barbie's infinite appeal is her very perfection, the extent to which she is both product and purveyor of the dominant white Western ideal of beauty.

And what of black beauty? If Colored Francie failed thirty years ago in part because of her Caucasian features, what are we to make of the current popularity and commercial success of Black Barbie and Shani, straight hair and all? Have we progressed to a point where 'difference' makes no difference? Or have we regressed to such a degree that 'difference' is only conceivable as similarity—as a mediated text that no matter what its dye job ultimately must be readable as white. Listen to our language: we '*tolerate* difference'; we practice 'racial tolerance.' Through the compound fractures of interpellation and universalization, the Other is reproduced not in her own image but in ours. If we have gotten away from 'Us' and 'Them,' it may be only because Them R Us.

Is Barbie bad? Barbie is just a piece of plastic, but what she says about the economic base of our society—what she suggests about gender and race in our world—ain't good.

NOTES

I wish to thank the many friends and colleagues who have encouraged this project, especially Indira Karamcheti and her four-year-old daughter Gita, who introduced me to the miniature Barbies that come with McDonald's 'Happy Meals', and Erness Brody, who, with her daughter Jennifer Brody, is a veteran collector of vintage dolls. I owe a special debt to fellow 'Barbiologists' M.G. Lord, Mel McCombie, Jacqueline Urla, and Eric Swedlund, who have so generously shared their research, and to Darlene Powell Hopson for talking with me about her work with Mattel. I wish to acknowledge as well the work of Erica Rand, an art historian at Bates College, who is also working on Barbie.

1. Mattel introduced the Shani doll—a black, Barbie-like doll—in 1991, which also may have contributed to the rise in sales, particularly since the company engaged the services of a PR firm that specializes in targeting ethnic audiences.
2. Of course, the notion of 'dreaming in one's own image' is always problematic since dreams, by definition, engage something other than the 'real.'
3. Olmec Toys, a black-owned company headed by an African American woman named Yla Eason, markets a line of black and Latina Barbie-like dolls called the Imani Collection. Billed on their boxes as 'African American Princess' and 'Latin American Fantasy,' these dolls are also presented as having been designed with the self images of black children in mind. 'We've got one thing in mind with all our products,' the blurbs on the Imani boxes read; 'let's build self-esteem. Our children gain a sense of self importance through toys. So we make them look like them.' Given their obvious resemblance to Barbie dolls—their long, straight hair and pencil-thin plastic bodies—Imani dolls look no more 'like them,' like 'real' black children, than their prototype. Eason, who we are told was devastated by her son's announcement that he couldn't be a super-hero because he wasn't white, may indeed want to give black children toys to play with that 'look like them.' Yet, in order to compete in a market long dominated by Mattel and Hasbro, her company, it seems, has little choice but to conform to the Barbie mold.
4. After many calls to the Jamaican Embassy in Washington, D.C. and to various cultural organizations in Jamaica, I have determined that Jamaican Barbie's costume—a floor-length granny-style dress with apron and headrag—bears some resemblance to what is considered the island's traditional folk costume. I am still left wondering about the decision-making process, however: why the doll representing Jamaica is figured as a maid, while the doll representing Great Britain, for example, is presented as a lady—a blonde, blue-eyed Barbie doll dressed in a fancy riding habit with boots and hat.

5. See among others Morris Rosenburg's books *Conceiving the Self* (1979) and *Society and the Adolescent Self-Image* (1989) and William E. Cross's *Shades of Black: Diversity in African American Identity* (1991), all of which challenge the Clarks' findings. Cross argues, for example, that the Clarks confounded or conflated two different issues: attitude toward race in general and attitude toward the self in particular. How one feels about race is not necessarily an index of one's self-esteem.

6. Urla and Swedlund's findings are reported in an essay entitled 'The Anthropometry of Barbie: Unsettling Ideals of the Femine Body in Popular Culture,' in *Deviant Bodies*, eds. Jennifer Terry and Jacqueline Urla (Bloomington: Indiana Press), forthcoming.

7. In response to criticism from feminists in particular, the Miss America Pageant has attempted to transform itself from a beauty contest to a talent competition, whose real aim is to give college scholarships to smart, talented women (who just happen to look good in bathing suits and evening gowns). As part of its effort to appear more concerned with a woman's IQ than with her bra size, the Pageant did away with its longstanding practice of broadcasting the chest, waist, and hip measurements, as well as the height and weight, of each contestant.

REFERENCES

Berkwitz, David N. 'Finally, Barbie Doll Ads Go Ethnic.' *Newsweek* 13 August 1990: 48.

BillyBoy. *Barbie: Her Life and Times.* New York: Crown, 1987.

Cross, William E., Jr. *Shades of Black: Diversity in African American Identity.* Philadelphia: Temple University Press, 1991.

Dembner, Alice. 'Thirty-five and Still a Doll.' *Boston Globe* 9 March 1994: 1, 16.

Hopson, Darlene Powell and Derek S. *Different and Wonderful: Raising Black Children in a Race-Conscious Society.* New York: Simon & Schuster, 1990.

Jones, Lisa. 'A Doll Is Born.' *Village Voice.* 26 March 1991: 36.

Kantrowitz, Barbara. 'Hot Date: Barbie and G.I. Joe.' *Newsweek* 20 February 1989: 59–60.

Larcen, Donna. 'Barbie Bond Doesn't Diminish with Age.' *Hartford Current* 17 August 1993: A6–7.

Lorde, M.G. *Forever Barbie: The Unauthorized Biography of a Real Doll.* New York: William Morrow, 1994.

McCombie, Mel. 'Barbie: Toys Are Us.' Unpublished paper.

Roberts, Cynthia. *Barbie: Thirty Years of America's Doll.* Chicago: Contemporary Books, 1989.

Rosenberg, Morris. *Conceiving the Self.* New York: Basic Books, 1979.

——*Society and the Adolescent Self-Image.* Middletown, CT: Wesleyan University Press, 1989.

Sanchez-Eppler, Karen. *Touching Liberty: Abolition, Feminism, and the Politics of the Body.* Berkeley: University of California Press, 1993.

Stewart, Julia. *African Names.* New York: Carol, 1993.

Urla, Jacqueline and Alan Swedlund. 'The Anthropometry of Barbie: Unsettling Ideals of the Feminine in Popular Culture.' In *Deviant Bodies*, edited by Jennifer Terry and Jacqueline Urla. Bloomington: Indiana University Press. (Forthcoming).

8 Voice-overs: Definitions and Debates

Introduction

The essays presented in this section both provide a conclusion to the *Reader* and open up issues for further discussion. Issues that have been raised by scholars from earlier centuries which focus on traditional, humanist disciplines such as literature, art, philosophy, and history have been reframed continuously in the essays in this *Reader* in the language of cultural critique, racial difference and gender identity. Yet, while the inquiry has had a similar thrust, i.e., investigations by intellectuals into the impact of cultural norms and external practices on actual life experiences, it has also been markedly different in its answers and the scope of the analysis. Quite specifically, in tracing the epistemology of cultural critique, at least as far back as the nineteenth century, the *Reader* reveals the fact that culture is carefully constructed and elides the particular into the universal and the political into the personal. What this means is that formulations regarding the nature of culture are more than an élitist past-time, they are an investment made by a select few to regulate the conduct and values of whole societies. While this revelation is fundamental to philosophical thinking in Western culture since Plato, what is radical in the present move is the call to erase boundaries between high/low culture, speakable/unspeakable truth claims, civilized/barbaric pleasures, and master/disciple relationships.

More importantly, this breakdown of oppositions to expose the grids of culture is not post-structural play, or post-modern engagement with nothingness. It is meant instead to create a genuine climate of cultural critique that will systematically examine every rule and aspect of contemporary society. This is the spirit of Richard Johnson's essay which is playfully called 'What is Cultural Studies anyway?' Johnson begins by suggesting various working definitions for 'Cultural Studies', and stresses the positive contributions made by interdisciplinary approaches to the study of culture. The companion piece to this essay is the one by Fredric Jameson called 'On "Cultural Studies"', which states 'no group "has" a culture all by itself: culture is the nimbus perceived by one group when it comes into contact with and observes

571

another one. It is the objectification of everything alien and strange about the contact group'. They are similar in that they both work with Marxist parameters, yet they are completely different in their conclusions. Unlike Johnson's piece, Jameson's essay argues that cultural critique as a project and the inherent interdisciplinarity of cultural studies as a field are 'flawed' because they are incapable of engaging with the world at large—a world generated by late capitalism. Johnson's essay pre-dates Jameson's and contains the enthusiasm of new discoveries and potential alliances. Ironically, Jameson's work carries the ethos of the *fin de siècle*, it is full of criticisms of these very factors. If Johnson's is the voice, then Jameson's is the voice-over echoing and distorting the premises surrounding cultural studies. On a different level, Henry Giroux, *et al.* in 'The Need For Cultural Studies' have a pedagogic focus which advocates a continuous inquiry into the models and practice of cultural studies. Though their debate does not conduct a direct dialogue with any other essay in this section, it is certainly dialogic in its engagement with the academy. Theirs is the voice that is audible above the Jameson/Johnson debate, especially in the mediating remark 'in order to retain its theoretical and political integrity, Cultural Studies must develop forms of critical knowledge as well as a critique of knowledge itself'.

J. Hillis Miller's and Stuart Hall's interviews address cultural studies from different loci—the former as a humanist scholar and the latter as an agent of revolution. Their interviews are neither dialogues with one another nor are they dialogic in any immediate sense—theirs are the voices crucial to debates on cultural studies. The impact of post-colonial and feminist critique on an area of study initially inclined to subsume various othernesses into debates on class or the mass can be heard throughout this *Reader*, as the once-excluded voices of the 'other'. Their pieces resituate those makers of culture that need to be critiqued, mediated, and resisted. An aspect that all the essays and interviews in the *Reader* share is their sustained mode of inquiry. The invitation to the reader/student to enter the arena of discourse and participate in the debates makes this whole section and the *Reader* a collaborative project.

FURTHER READING

Arac, Jonathan, ed., *Postmodernism and Politics*, Manchester: Manchester University Press, 1986.
Aronowitz, Stanley, *Dead Artists, Live Theories, and Other Cultural Problems*, New York and London: Routledge, 1993.
Aronowitz, Stanley, and Henry A. Giroux, *Postmodern Education: Politics, Culture, and Social Criticism*, Minneapolis: University of Minnesota Press, 1991.
Bakhtin, Mikhail, *The Dialogic Imagination*, ed. M. Holquist, trans. C. Emerson and M. Holquist. Austin: Texas University Press, 1987.
Bell, David, *The Cultural Contradictions of Capitalism*, New York: Basic Books, 1976.
Bhabha, Homi, *Location of Culture*, London and New York: Routledge, 1993.
Durin, Simon, ed., *The Cultural Studies Reader*, London and New York: Routledge, 1993.
Foster, Hal, ed., *The Anti-Aesthetic: Essays on Postmodern Culture*, Seattle: Bay Press, 1983.
Giroux, A. Henry, and Peter McLaren, eds, *Between Borders: Pedagogy and the Politics of Cultural Studies*, London and New York: Routledge, 1993.
Graff, Gerald, *Beyond the Culture Wars*, New York: Norton, 1992.
Grossberg, Lawrence, *We Gotta Get Out Of This Place: Popular Conservatism and Postmodern Culture*, London and New York: Routledge, forthcoming.

Hirsch, E. D. Jr., *Cultural Literacy: What Every American Needs to Know*, Boston: Houghton, 1987.

Smithson, Isaiah, ed., *English Studies/Culture Studies*, Chicago and Evanston: University of Illinois Press, 1994.

Spivak, Gayatri Chakravorty, *Outside in the Teaching Machine*, London and New York: Routledge, 1993.

Richard Johnson (1939–)

Richard Johnson, who has recently formally retired from the University of Birmingham, now researches on a part-time basis at the Nottingham Trent University. He joined the Birmingham Centre for Contemporary Cultural Studies in the mid-1970s and took over from Stuart Hall as Director in 1980, a position he held into the late 1980s. Johnson's initial field was nineteenth-century social history. A very generous and modest scholar, Johnson's influence on cultural studies can, in part, be gauged by the frequency with which scholars in the field acknowledge his assistance. His career has also been marked by the principled positions he has taken up on issues of cultural and educational politics. Johnson has published a number of essays and his co-edited works include *Working-Class Culture: Studies in History and Theory* (1979), *Making Histories: Studies in History-Writing and Politics* (1982).

Undoubtedly, however, his most published and influential work is the essay reprinted in this section, 'What is Cultural Studies Anyway?' which was first circulated as a CCCS stencilled occasional paper (no. 74) in 1983. In this essay Johnson offers a defence of cultural studies as a mode of critique. He also undertakes a very full survey of the strategies of thought and the theoretical constructions—from Marxism to semiotics, from readers' response to post-structuralism—which have been applied in the field which he is seeking, through this survey, to define as cultural studies.

Johnson isolates three main models of cultural-studies research: production-based studies, text-based studies, and studies of lived cultures. Although Johnson acknowledges that these approaches cannot be easily added up together to produce a composite approach, he also argues that it may be 'transformative to rethink each moment in the light of the others, importing objects and methods of study usually developed in relation to one moment into the next'. Johnson's definitional divisions and critiques can be fruitfully compared to Stuart Hall's essay, 'Cultural Studies: Two Paradigms' (Section 3), James Clifford's essay, 'On Ethnographic Authority' (Section 4), and to Fredric Jameson's essay which follows.
J.M. and R.B.

What is cultural studies anyway?

Cultural studies is now a movement or a network. It has its own degree in several colleges and universities and its own journals and meetings. It exercises a large influence on academic disciplines, especially on English studies, sociology, media and communication studies, linguistics and history. In the first part of the article,[1] I want to consider some of the arguments for and against the academic codification of cultural studies. To put the question most sharply: should cultural studies aspire to be an academic discipline? In the second part, I'll look at some strategies of definition short of codification, because a lot hangs, I think, on the *kind* of unity or coherence we seek. Finally, I want to try out some of my own preferred definitions and arguments.

The importance of critique

A codification of methods or knowledges (instituting them, for example, in formal curricula or in courses on 'methodology') runs against some main features of cultural studies as a tradition: its openness and theoretical versatility, its reflexive even self-conscious mood, and, especially, the importance of critique. I mean critique in the fullest sense: not criticism merely, nor even polemic, but procedures by which other traditions are approached both for what they may yield and for what they inhibit. Critique involves stealing away the more useful elements and rejecting the rest. From this point of view cultural studies is a process, a kind of alchemy for producing useful knowledge; codify it and you might halt its reactions.

In the history of cultural studies, the earliest encounters were with literary criticism. Raymond Williams and Richard Hoggart, in their different ways, developed the Leavisite stress on literary-social evaluation, but turned the assessments from literature to everyday life.[2] Similar appropriations have been made from history. The first important moment here was the development of the post-war traditions of social history with their focus on popular culture, or the culture of 'the people' especially in its political forms. The Communist Party Historians' Group was central here, with its 1940s and early 1950s project of anglicizing and historicising old Marxism. In a way this influence was paradoxical; for the historians were less concerned with contemporary culture or even with the 20th century, putting energies instead into understanding the long British transition from feudalism to capitalism and the popular struggles and traditions of dissent associated with it. It was this work which became a second matrix for cultural studies.

Central in both literary and historical strands was the critique of old Marxism. The recovery of 'values' against Stalinism was a leading impulse of the first new left, but the critique of economism has been the continuous thread through the whole 'crisis of marxism' which has followed. Certainly cultural studies has been formed on this side of what we can call, paradoxically, a modern marxist revival, and in the

575

cross-national borrowings that were so marked a feature of the 1970s. It is important to note what different places the same figures have occupied in different national routes. The take-up of Althusserianism is incomprehensible outside the background of the dominant empiricism of British intellectual traditions. This feature helps to explain the appeal of philosophy, not as a technical pursuit, but as a generalised rationalism and excitement with abstract ideas.[3] Similarly, it is important to note how Gramsci, a version of whose work occupies a place of orthodoxy in Italy, was appropriated by us as a critical, heterodox figure. He provided mighty reinforcements to an already partly-formed cultural studies project, as late as the 1970s.[4]

Some students of culture remain 'marxist' in name (despite the 'crisis' and all that). It is more interesting, however, to note where cultural studies has been Marx-influenced. Everyone will have their own checklist. My own, which is not intended to sketch an orthodoxy, includes three main premises. The first is that cultural processes are intimately connected with social relations, especially with class relations and class formations, with sexual divisions, with the racial structuring of social relations and with age oppressions as a form of dependency. The second is that culture involves power and helps to produce assymetries in the abilities of individuals and social groups to define and realise their needs. And the third, which follows the other two, is that culture is neither an autonomous nor an externally determined field, but a site of social differences and struggles. This by no means exhausts the elements of Marxism that remain active and alive and resourceful in the existing circumstances, provided only they, too, are critiqued, and developed in detailed studies.

Other critiques have been distinctly philosophical. Cultural studies has been marked out, in the British context, for its concern with 'theory,' but the intimacy of the connection with philosophy has not been obvious until recently. Yet there is a very close cousinhood between epistemological problems and positions (e.g. empiricism, realism and idealism) and the key questions of 'cultural theory' (e.g. economism, materialism, or the problem of culture's specific effects). Again, for me, a lot of roads lead back to Marx, but the appropriations need to be wider ones. Lately there have been attempts to go beyond the rather sterile opposition of rationalism and empiricism in search of a more productive formulation of the relation between theory (or 'abstraction' as I now prefer) and 'concrete studies.'[5]

More important in our recent history have been the critiques deriving from the women's movement and from the struggles against racism.[6] These have deepened and extended the democratic and socialist commitments that were the leading principles of the first new left. If the personal was already political in the first phase of the Campaign for Nuclear Disarmament (CND), it was oddly ungendered. The democratic foundations of the early movements were therefore insecurely based as a new form of politics. Similarly there were (and are) deep problems about the ethno- and anglo-centricity of key texts and themes in our tradition.[7] The contemporary salience in Britain of a conservative-nationalist and racist politics means these flaws are all the more serious. It is incorrect therefore to see feminism or anti-racism as some kind of interruption or diversion from an original class politics and its associated research programme. On the contrary, it is these movements that have kept the new left new.

The specific results for cultural studies have been no less important.[8] Much more has been involved than the original question: 'what about women?' Feminism has influenced everyday ways of working and brought a greater recognition of the way that productive results depend upon supportive relationships. It has uncovered some unacknowledged premises of 'left' intellectual work and the masculine interests that held them in place. It has produced new objects of study and forced a rethinking of old ones. In media studies, for example, it has shifted attention from the 'masculine' genre of news and current affairs to the importance of 'light entertainment.' It has aided a more general turn from older kinds of ideology critique (which centred on maps of meaning or versions of reality) to approaches that centre on social identities, subjectivities, popularity and pleasure. Feminists also seem to have made a particular contribution to bridging the humanities/social science divide by bringing literary categories and 'aesthetic' concerns to bear on social issues.

I hope these cases show how central critique has been and how connected it is with political causes in the broader sense. A number of questions follow. If we have progressed by critique, are there not dangers that codifications will involve systematic closure? If the momentum is to strive for really useful knowledge, will academic codification help this? Is not the priority to become more 'popular' rather than more academic? These questions gain further force from immediate contexts. Cultural studies is now a widely taught subject, thus, unless we are very careful, students will encounter it as an orthodoxy. In any case, students now have lectures, courses and examinations in the study of culture. In these circumstances, how can they occupy a critical tradition critically?

This is reinforced by what we know—or are learning—about academic and other disciplinary dispositions of knowledge. Recognition of the forms of power associated with knowledge may turn out to be one of the leading insights of the 1970s. It is a very general theme: in the work of Pierre Bourdieu and Michel Foucault, in the radical philosophers' and radical scientists' critiques of science or scientism, in radical educational philosophy and sociology and in feminist critiques of the dominant academic forms. There has been a marked change from the singular affirmation of science in the early 1970s (with Althusser as one main figure) to the dissolution of such certainties (with Foucault as one point of reference) in our own times. Academic knowledge-forms (or some aspects of them) now look like part of the problem, rather than part of the solution. In fact, the problem remains much as it has always been—what can be won from the academic concerns and skills to provide elements of useful knowledge.

Pressures to define

Yet there are important pressures to define. There is the little daily politics of the college or the school—not so little since jobs, resouces and opportunities for useful work are involved. Cultural studies has won real spaces here and they have to be maintained and extended. The context of ('big') politics makes this still more important. We also have a Conservative Counter-Reformation in Britain and the U.S. One

577

manifestation is a vigorous assault on public educational institutions, both by cutting finance and by defining usefulness in strictly capitalist terms. We need definitions of cultural studies to struggle effectively in these contexts, to make claims for resources, to clarify our minds in the rush and muddle of everyday work, and to decide priorities for teaching and research.

Most decisively, perhaps, we need ways of viewing a vigorous but fragmented field of study, if not as a *unity* at least as a *whole*. If we do not discuss central directions of our own, we will be pulled hither and thither by the demands of academic self-reproduction and by the academic disciplines from which our subject, in part, grows. Academic tendencies, then, tend to be reproduced on the new ground: there are distinctively literary and distinctively sociological or historical versions of cultural studies, just as there are approaches distinguished by theoretical partisanship. This would not matter if any one discipline or problematic could grasp the objects of culture as a whole, but this is not, in my opinion, the case. Each approach tells us about a tiny aspect. If this is right, we need a particular kind of defining activity: one which reviews existing approaches, identifies their characteristic objects and their good sense, but also the limits of their competence. Actually it is not definition or codification that we need, but *pointers* to further transformations. This is not a question of aggregating existing approaches (a bit of sociology here, a spot of linguistics there) but of reforming the elements of different approaches in their relations to each other.

Strategies of definition

There are several different starting-points. Cultural studies can be defined as an intellectual and political tradition, in its relations to the academic disciplines, in terms of theoretical paradigms, or by its characteristic objects of study. The last starting-point now interests me most; but first a word about the others.

We need histories of cultural studies to trace the recurrent dilemmas and to give perspective to our current projects. But the informed sense of a 'tradition' also works in a more 'mythical' mode to produce a collective identity and a shared sense of purpose. To me, a lot of powerful continuities are wrapped up in the single term 'culture,' which remains useful not as a rigorous category, but as a kind of summation of a history. It references in particular the effort to heave the study of culture from its old inegalitarian anchorages in high-artistic connoisseurship and in discourses, of enormous condescension, on the not-culture of the masses. Behind this intellectual redefinition there is a somewhat less consistent *political* pattern, a continuity that runs from the first new left and the first Campaign for Nuclear Disarmament to the post-1968 currents. Of course there have been marked political antagonisms within the new left and between new left politics and the intellectual tendencies it has produced. The intellectual detours have often seemed politically self-indulgent. Yet what unites this sequence is the struggle to reform 'old left' politics. This includes the critique of old marxism but also of old social-democracy too. It involves a constructive quarrel with dominant styles within the Labour Movement, especially the neglect of cultural conditions of politics, and a mechanical narrowing of politics itself.

This sense of an intellectual-political connection has been important for cultural studies. It has meant that the research and the writing has been political, but not in any immediate pragmatic sense. Cultural studies is not a research programme for a particular party or tendency. Still less does it subordinate intellectual energies to any established doctrines. This political-intellectual stance is possible because the politics which we aim to create is not yet fully formed. Just as the politics involves a long haul, so the research must be as wide-ranging and as profound, but also as politically-directed, as we can make it. Above all, perhaps, we have to fight against the disconnection that occurs when cultural studies is inhabited for merely academic purposes or when enthusiasm for (say) popular cultural forms is divorced from the analysis of power and of social possibilities.

I have said a lot already about the second definitional strategy—charting our negative/positive relation to the academic disciplines. Cultural processes do not correspond to the contours of academic knowledges, as they are. No one academic discipline grasps the full complexity (or seriousness) of the study. Cultural studies must be inter-disciplinary (and sometimes anti-disciplinary) in its tendency. I find it hard, for example, to think of myself as an historian now, though perhaps historian-of-the-contemporary is a rough approximation in some contexts. Yet some historian's virtues seem useful for cultural studies—concerns for movement, particularity, complexity and context, for instance. I still love that combination of dense description, complex explanation and subjective even romantic evocation, which I find in the best historical writing. I still find most sociological description thin and obvious and much literary discourse clever but superficial! On the other hand, the rooted empiricism of historical practice is a real liability often blocking a properly cultural reading. I am sure it is the same for other disciplines too. Of course, there are lots of half-way houses, many of them serviceable workshops for cultural study, but the *direction* of movement, to my mind, has to be out, and away, and into more dangerous places!

Our third definitional strategy—the analysis and comparison of theoretical problematics—was, until recently, the favourite one.[9] I still see this as an essential component in all cultural study, but its main difficulty is that abstract forms of discourse disconnect ideas from the social complexities that first produced them, or to which they originally referred. Unless these are continuously reconstructed and held in the mind as a reference point, theoretical clarification acquires an independent momentum. In teaching situations or similar interchanges, theoretical discourse may seem, to the hearer, a form of intellectual gymnastics. The point appears to be to learn a new language, which takes time and much effort, in order, merely, to feel at ease with it. In the meantime there is something very silencing and perhaps oppressive about new forms of discourse. I think that this has been a fairly common experience, for students, even where, eventually, 'theory' has conferred new powers of understanding and articulation. This is one set of reasons why many of us now find it useful to start from concrete cases, either to teach theory historically, as a continuing, contextualised debate about cultural issues, or to hook up theoretical points and contemporary experiences.

This leads me to my preferred definitional strategy. The key questions are: what is the characteristic *object* of cultural studies? What is cultural studies *about*?

Simple abstractions: consciousness, subjectivity

I have suggested already that 'culture' has value as a reminder but not as a precise category; Raymond Williams has excavated its immense historical repertoire.[10] There is no solution to this polysemy: it is a rationalist illusion to think we can say 'henceforth this term will mean . . .' and expect a whole history of connotations (not to say a whole future) to fall smartly into line. So although I fly culture's flag anyway, and continue to use the word where imprecision matters, definitionally I seek other terms.

My key terms instead are 'consciousness' and 'subjectivity' with the key problems now lying somewhere in the relation between the two. For me cultural studies is about the historical forms of consciousness or subjectivity, or the subjective forms we live by, or, in a rather perilous compression, perhaps a reduction, the subjective side of social relations. These definitions adopt and gloss some of Marx's simple abstractions, but value them also for their contemporary resonance. I think of consciousness, first, in the sense in which it appears in *The German Ideology*. As a (fifth) premise for understanding human history, Marx and Engels add that human beings 'also possess consciousness.' This usage is echoed in later works too. Marx implies it when in *Capital*, volume I, he distinguishes the worst architect from the best bee by the fact that the architect's product has 'already existed ideally' before it is produced. It has existed in the consciousness, the imagination. In other words, human beings are characterised by an ideal or imaginary life, where will is cultivated, dreams dreamt, and categories developed. In his *1844 Manuscripts* Marx called this a feature of 'species being,' later he would have called it a 'general-historical' category, true of all history, a simple or universal abstraction.[11] Although the usage is less clear Marx also habitually refers to the 'subjective side' or 'subjective aspect' of social processes.

In marxist discourse (I am less sure of Marx) consciousness has overwhelmingly cognitive connotations: it has to do with knowledge (especially correct knowledge?) of the social and the natural worlds. I think Marx's consciousness was wider than this! It embraced the notion of a consciousness of self and an *active mental and moral self-production*. There is no doubt, however, that he was especially interested in conceptually-organised knowledge, especially in his discussions of particular ideological forms (e.g., political economy, Hegelian idealism, etc.). In his most interesting text on the character of thinking (the 1857 Introduction to the *Grundrisse*) other modes of consciousness, the aesthetic, the religious, etc., were bracketed out.

'Subjectivity' is especially important here, challenging the absences in consciousness. Subjectivity includes the possibility, for example, that some elements or impulses are subjectively active—they *move* us—without being consciously known. It highlights elements ascribed (in the misleading conventional distinction) to aesthetic or emotional life and to conventionally 'feminine' codes. It focuses on the 'who I am' or, as important, the 'who we are' of culture, on individual and collective identities. It connects with the most important structuralist insight: that subjectivities are produced, not given, and are therefore the objects of inquiry, not the premises or starting-points.

In all my thinking about cultural studies I find the notion of 'forms' also repeatedly recurs. Lying behind this usage are two major influences. Marx continuously uses the terms 'forms' or 'social forms' or 'historical forms' when he is examining in *Capital* (but especially in the *Grundrisse*) the various moments of economic circulation: he analyses the money form, the commodity form, the form of abstract labour, etc. Less often he used the same language in writing of consciousness or subjectivity. The most famous instance is from the 1859 *Preface*:

> a distinction should always be made between the material transformation of the economic conditions of production, which can be determined with the precision of natural science, and the legal, political, religious, aesthetic or philosophic—in short, ideological forms in which men become conscious of this conflict and fight it out (emphasis added).

What interests *me* about this passage is the implication of a different parallel project to Marx's own. His preoccupation was with those social forms through which human beings produce and reproduce their material life. He abstracted, analysed and sometimes reconstituted in more concrete accounts the economic forms and tendencies of social life. It seems to me that cultural studies too is concerned with whole societies (or broader social formations) and how they move. But it looks at social processes from another complimentary point of view. *Our* project is to abstract, describe and reconstitute in concrete studies the social forms through which human beings 'live,' become conscious, sustain themselves subjectively.

The stress on forms is reinforced by some broad structuralist insights. These have drawn out the structured character of the forms we inhabit subjectively: language, signs, ideologies, discourses, myths. They have pointed to regularities and principles of organisation—of form-ful-ness if you like. Though often pitched at too high a level of abstraction (e.g. language in general rather than languages in particular) they have strengthened our sense of the hardness, determinancy and, indeed, actual existence of social forms which exercise their pressures through the subjective side of social life. This is not to say that the description of form, in this sense, is enough. It is important to see the historical nature of subjective forms too. Historical in this context means two rather different things. First, we need to look at forms of subjectivity from the point of view of their pressures or tendencies, especially their contradictory sides. Even in abstract analysis, in order words, we should look for principles of movement as well as combination. Second, we need histories of the forms of subjectivity where we can see how these tendencies are modified by the other social determinations, including those that work through material needs.

As soon as we pose this as a project, we can see how the simple abstractions which we have thus far used, do not take us very far. Where are all the intermediate categories that would allow us to start to specify the subjective social forms and the different moments of their existence? Given our definition of culture, we cannot limit the field to specialised practices, particular genres, or popular leisure pursuits. *All social practices* can be looked at from a cultural point of view, for the work they do, subjectively. This goes, for instance, for factory work, for trade union organisation, for life in and around the supermarket, as well as for obvious targets like 'the media' (misleading unity!) and its (mainly domestic) modes of consumption.

Circuits of capital—circuits of culture?

So we need, first, a much more complex model, with rich intermediate categories, more layered than the existing general theories. It is here that I find it helpful to pose a kind of realist hypothesis about the existing state of theories. What if existing theories—and the modes of research associated with them—actually express different sides of the same complex process? What if they are all true, but only as far as they go, true for those parts of the process which they have most clearly in view? What if they are all false or incomplete, liable to mislead, in that they are only partial, and therefore cannot grasp the process as a whole? What if attempts to 'stretch' this competence (without modifying the theory) lead to really gross and dangerous (ideological?) conclusions?

I certainly do not expect immediate assent to the epistemological premises of this argument. I hope it will be judged in the light of its results. But its immediate merit is that it helps to explain one key feature: the theoretical and disciplinary fragmentations we have already noted. Of course these could be explained by the political, social and discursive differences we have also considered: especially the intellectual and academic divisions of labour and the social reproduction of specialist forms of cultural capital. Yet I find it more satisfactory to relate these manifest differences to the very processes they seek to describe. Maybe academic divisions also correspond to rather different social positions and viewpoints from which different aspects of cultural circuits acquire the greatest salience. This would explain not merely the fact of different theories, but the *recurrence* and *persistence* of differences, especially between large *clusters* of approaches with certain affinities.

The best way to take such an argument further would be to hazard some provisional description of the different aspects or moments of cultural processes to which we could then relate the different theoretical problematics. Such a model could not be a finished abstraction or theory, if such can exist. Its value would have to be heuristic or illustrative. It might help to explain why theories differ, but would not, in itself, sketch the ideal approach. At most it might serve as a guide to the desirable directions of future approaches, or to the way in which they might be modified or combined. It is important to bear these caveats in mind in what follows. I find it easiest (in a long CCCS tradition) to present a model diagrammatically (see below). The diagram is intended to represent a circuit of the production, circulation and consumption of cultural products. Each box represents a moment in this circuit. Each moment or aspect depends upon the others and is indispensable to the whole. Each, however, is distinct and involves characteristic changes of form. It follows that if we are placed at one point of the circuit, we do not necessarily see what is happening at others. The forms that have most significance for us at one point may be very differ-

582

ent from those at another. Processes disappear in results.[12] All cultural products, for example, require to be produced, but the conditions of their production cannot be inferred by scrutinising them as 'texts.' Similarly all cultural products are 'read' by persons other than professional analysts (if they weren't there would be little profit in their production), but we cannot predict these uses from our own analysis, or, indeed, from the conditions of production. As anyone knows, all our communications are liable to return to us in unrecognisable or at least transformed terms. We often call this *mis*understanding or, if we are being very academic, *mis*-readings. But these 'misses' are so common (across the range of a whole society) that we might well call them normal. To understand the transformations, then, we have to understand specific conditions of consumption or reading. These include asymmetries of resources and power, material and cultural. They also include the existing ensembles of cultural elements already active within particular social *milieux* ('lived cultures' in the diagram) and the social relations on which these combinations depend. These reservoirs of discourses and meanings are in turn raw material for fresh cultural production. They are indeed among the specifically cultural *conditions* of production.

In our societies, many forms of cultural production also take the form of capitalist commodities. In this case we have to supply specifically capitalist conditions of production (see the arrow pointing to moment 1) and specifically capitalist conditions of consumption (see the arrow pointing to moment 3). Of course this does not tell us all there is to know about these moments, which may be structured on other principles as well, but in these cases the circuit is, at one and the same time, a circuit of capital and its expanded reproduction *and* a circuit of the production and circulation of subjective forms.

Some implications of the circuit may be clearer if we take a particular case. We can, for example, whiz a Mini-Metro car around it. I choose the Mini-Metro because it is a pretty standard late 20th-century capitalist commodity that happened to carry a particularly rich accumulation of meanings. The Metro was the car that was going to save the British car industry, by beating rivals from the market and by solving British Leyland's acute problems of industrial discipline. It came to signify solutions to internal and external national threats. The advertising campaigns around its launching were remarkable. In one television ad, a band of Mini-Metros pursued a gang of foreign imports up to (and apparently over) the White Cliffs of Dover, whence they fled in what looked remarkably like landing-craft. This was a Dunkirk in reverse with the Metro as nationalist hero. Certainly these are some of the forms—nationalist epic, popular memory of World War II, internal/external threat—that I would want to abstract for further formal scrutiny. But this raises interesting questions too about what constitutes the 'text' (or raw material for such abstractions) in these cases. Would it be enough to analyse the design of the Metro itself as Barthes once analysed the lines of a Citroen? How could we exclude ads and garage showroom displays? Shouldn't we include, indeed, the Metro's place in discourses upon national economic recovery and moral renaissance?

Supposing that we answered these questions affirmatively (and gave ourselves more work) there would still be some unposed questions. What was *made* of the Metro phenomenon, more privately, by particular groups of consumers and readers? We would expect great diversity of response. Leyland workers, for example, were

583

likely to view the car differently from those who only bought it. Beyond this, the Metro (and its transformed meanings) became a way of getting to work or picking the kids up from school. It may also have helped to produce, for example, orientations towards working life, connecting industrial 'peace' with national prosperity. Then, of course, the products of this whole circuit returned once more to the moment of production—as profits for fresh investment, but also as market researcher's findings on 'popularity' (capital's own 'cultural studies'). The subsequent use, by British Leyland management, of similar strategies for selling cars and weakening workers suggests considerable accumulations (of both kinds) from this episode. Indeed the Metro became a little paradigm, though not the first, for a much more diffused ideological form, which we might term, with some compression, 'the nationalist sell.'

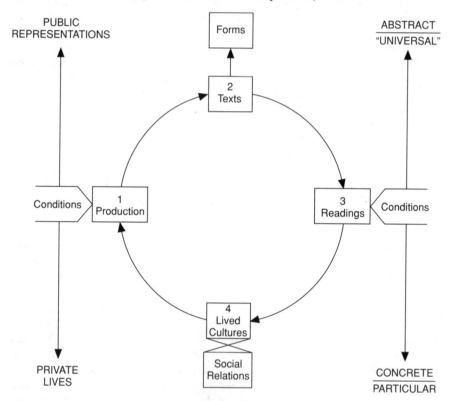

Publication and abstraction

So far I have talked rather generally about the transformations that occur around the circuit without specifying any. In so brief a discussion, I will specify two related changes of form indicated on the left and right hand sides of the circuit. The circuit involves movements between the public and the private but also movements between more abstract and more concrete forms. These two poles are quite closely related: private forms are more concrete, and more particular in their scope of reference; public forms are more abstract but also apply over a more general range. This may be clearer if we return to the Metro and, thence, to different traditions of cultural study.

As a designer's idea, as a manager's 'concept,' the Metro remained private.[13] It may even have been conceived in secret. It was known to a chosen few. At this stage, indeed, it would have been hard to separate it out from the social occasions at which it was discussed: board-room meetings, chats at the bar, Saturday's game of golf? But as ideas were 'put on paper' it started to take a more objective and more public form. The crunch came when decisions were made to go ahead with 'the concept' and, then again, to 'go public.' Finally, the Metro-idea, shortly followed by the Metro-car, moved into 'the full glare of publicity.' It acquired a more general significance, gathering around it, in fact, some pretty portentous notions. It became, in fact, a great public issue, or a symbol for such. It also took shape as an actual product and set of texts. In one obvious sense it was made 'concrete': not only could you kick it, you could drive it. But in another sense, this Metro was rather abstract. There it stood, in the showroom, surrounded by its texts of Britishness, a shiny, zippy thing. Yet who would know, from this display, who conceived it, how it was made, who suffered for it, or indeed what possible use it was going to have for the harassed-looking woman with two children in tow, who has just walked into the showroom. To draw out more general points, three things occurred in the process of public-ation. First, the car (and its texts) became *public* in the obvious sense: it acquired if not a *universal* at least a more *general* significance. Its messages too were generalised, ranging rather freely across the social surface. Second, at the level of *meaning*, publication involved *abstraction*. The car and its messages could now be viewed in relative isolation from the social conditions that formed it. Thirdly, it was subjected to a process of public *evaluation* (great public issue) on many different scales: as a technical-social instrument, as a national symbol, as a stake in class war, in relation to competing models, etc. It became a site of formidable struggles over meaning. In this process it was made to 'speak,' evaluatively, for 'us (British) all.' Note, however, in the moment of consumption or reading, represented here by the woman and her children (who have decided views about cars), we are forced back again to the private, the particular and concrete, however publicly displayed the raw materials for their readings may be.

I want to suggest that these processes are intrinsic to cultural circuits under modern social conditions, and that they are produced by, and are productive of, *relations of power*. But the most germane evidence for this lies in some repeated differences in the forms of cultural study.

Forms of culture—forms of study

One major division, theoretical and methodological, runs right through cultural studies. On the one side there are those who insist that 'cultures' must be studied as a whole, and *in situ*, located, in their material context. Suspicious of abstractions and of 'theory,' their practical theory is in fact 'culturalist.' They are often attracted to those formulations in Williams or E. P. Thompson that speak of cultures as whole ways of life or whole ways of struggle. Methodologically, they stress the importance of complex, concrete description, which grasps, particularly, the unity or homology of cultural forms and material life. Their preferences are therefore for social-historical recreations of cultures or cultural movements, or for ethnographic cultural description, or for those kinds of writing (e.g. autobiography, oral history, or realist forms of fiction) which recreate socially-located 'experience.'

On the other side, there are those who stress the relative independence or effect autonomy of subjective forms and means of signification. The practical theory here is usually structuralist, but in a form which privileges the discursive construction of situations and subjects. The preferred method is to treat the forms abstractly, sometimes quite formalistically, uncovering the mechanisms by which meaning is produced in language, narrative or other kinds of sign-system. If the first set of methods are usually derived from sociological, anthropological or social-historical roots, the second set owe most to literary criticism, and especially the traditions of literary modernism and linguistic formalism.[14]

In the long run, this division is, in my opinion, a sure impediment to the development of cultural studies. But it is important first to note the logic of such a division in relation to our sketch of cultural processes as a whole. If we compare, in more detail, what we have called the public and private forms of culture, the relation may be clearer.[15]

Private forms are not necessarily private in the usual sense of personal or individual, though they may be both. They may also be shared, communal and social in ways that public forms are not. It is their particularity or concreteness that marks them as private. They relate to the characteristic life experiences and historically-constructed needs of particular social categories. They do not pretend to define the world for those in other social groups. They are limited, local, modest. They do not aspire to universality. They are also deeply embedded in everyday social intercourse. In the course of their daily lives, women go shopping and meet and discuss the various doings of themselves, their families and their neighbours. Gossip is a private form deeply connected with the occasions and relations of being a woman in our society. Of course, it is *possible* to describe the discursive forms of gossip abstractly, stressing for instance the forms of reciprocity in speech, but this does seem to do a particular violence to the material, ripping it from the immediate and visible context in which these texts of talk arose.

An even more striking case is the working-class culture of the shop floor. As Paul Willis has shown there is a particularly close relationship here between the physical action of labour and the practical jokes and common sense of the workplace.[16] The whole discursive mode of the culture is to refuse the separations of manual practice and mental theory characteristic of public and especially academic knowledge forms. In neither case—gossip and shop-floor culture—is there a marked division of labour in cultural production. Nor are there technical instruments of production of any great complexity, though forms of speech and the symbolic uses of the human body are complex enough. Nor are the consumers of cultural forms formally or regularly distinguished from their producers, or far removed from them, in time or space.

I would argue that particular forms of inquiry and of representation have been developed to handle these features of private forms. Researchers, writers and all kinds of rapporteurs have adjusted their methods to what have seemed the most evident features of culture in this moment. They have sought to hold together the subjective and more objective moments, often not distinguishing them theoretically, or, in practice, refusing the distinction altogether. It is this stress of 'experience' (the term that perfectly captures this conflation or identity) that has united the practical procedures of social historians, ethnographers and those interested, say, in 'working-class writing.'

Compared with the thick, conjoined tissue of face-to-face encounters, the television programme 'going out on the air' seems a very abstracted, even ethereal product. For one thing it is so much more plainly a *re*presentation of 'real life' (at best) than the (equally constructed) narratives of everyday life. It takes a separated, abstracted or objective form, in the shape of the programme/text. It comes at us from a special, fixed place, a box of standardised shape and size in the corner of our sitting room. Of course, we apprehend it socially, culturally, communally, but it still has this separated moment, much more obviously than the private text of speech. This separated existence is certainly associated with an intricate division of labour in production and distribution and with the physical and temporal distance between the moment of production and that of consumption, characteristic of public knowledge forms in general. Public media of this kind, indeed, permit quite extraordinary manipulations of space and time as, for example, in the television revival of old movies.

I would argue that this apparent abstraction in the actual forms of public communication underlies the whole range of methods that focus on the construction of reality through symbolic forms themselves—with language as the first model, but the key moment as the objectification of language in text. It would be fascinating to pursue an historical inquiry linked to this hypothesis which would attempt to unravel the relationship between the real abstractions of communicative forms and the mental abstractions of cultural theorists. I do not suppose that the two processes go easily hand in hand or that changes occur synchronously. But I am sure that the notion of text—as something we can isolate, fix, pin down and scrutinise—depends upon the extensive circulation of cultural products which have been divorced from the immediate conditions of their production and have a moment of suspension, so to speak, before they are consumed.

Public–ation and power

The public and private forms of culture are not sealed against each other. There is a real circulation of forms. Cultural production often involves public-ation, the making public of private forms. On the other side, public texts are consumed or read in private. A girls' magazine, like *Jackie* for instance, picks up and represents some elements of the private cultures of femininity by which young girls live their lives. It instantaneously renders these elements open to public evaluation—as for example, 'girls' stuff,' 'silly' or 'trivial.' It also generalises these elements within the scope of the particular readership, creating a little public of its own. The magazine is then raw material for thousands of girl-readers who make their own *re*-appropriations of the elements first borrowed from their lived culture and forms of subjectivity.

It is important not to assume that public-ation only and always works in dominating or in demeaning ways. We need careful analyses of where and how public representa- tions work to seal social groups into the existing relations of dependence and where and how they have some emancipatory tendency. Short of this detail, we can nonetheless insist on the importance of *power* as an element in an analysis, by sug- gesting the main ways it is active in the public-private relationship.

Of couse there are profound differences in terms of access to the public sphere. Many social concerns may not acquire publicity at all. It is not merely that they remain private, but that they are actively privatised, *held* at the level of the private. Here, so far as formal politics and state actions are concerned, they are invisible, without public remedy. This means not only that they have to be borne, but that a consciousness of them, as evils, is held at a level of implicit or communal meanings. Within the group a knowledge of such sufferings may be profound, but not of such a kind that expects relief, or finds the sufferings strange.

As often, perhaps, such private concerns do appear publicly, but only on certain terms, and therefore transformed and framed in particular ways. The concerns of gossip, for example, do appear publicly in a wide variety of forms, but usually in the guise of 'entertainment.' They appear, for instance, in soap opera, or are 'dignified' only by their connection with the private lives of royalty, stars or politicians. Similarly, elements of shop-floor culture may be staged as comedy or variety acts. Such framings in terms of code or genre may not, as some theorists believe, alto- gether vitiate these elements as the basis of a social alternative, but they certainly work to contain them within the dominant public definitions of significance.

Public representations may also act in more openly punitive or stigmatising ways. In these forms the elements of private culture are robbed of authenticity or rational- ity, are constructed as dangerous, deviant, or dotty.[17] Similarly the experiences of subordinated social groups are presented as pathological, problems for intervention not in the organisation of society as a whole, but in the attitudes or behaviour of the suffering group itself. This is representation with a vengence: representation not as subjects demanding redress, but as objects at external intervention.

If space allowed it would be important to compare the different ways in which these processes may occur across the major social relationships of class, gender, race and age-dependence. One further general mechanism is the construction, in the pub- lic sphere, of definitions of the public/private division itself. Of course, these sound quite neutral definitions: 'everyone' agrees that the most important public issues are the economy, defence, law and order and, perhaps, welfare questions, and that other issues—family life, sexuality for example—are essentially private. The snag is that the dominant definitions of significance are quite socially specific and, in particular, tend to correspond to masculine and middle-class structures of 'interest' (in both the meanings of this term). It is partly because they start fundamentally to challenge

588

these dispositions that some feminisms, the peace movements and the Green parties are amongst the most subversive of modern developments.

I have stressed these elements of power, at the risk of some diversion from the main argument, because cultural studies practices must be viewed within this context. Whether it takes as its main object the more abstracted public knowledges and their underlying logics and definitions, or it searches out the private domains of culture, cultural studies is necessarily and deeply implicated in relations of power. It forms a part of the very circuits which it seeks to describe. It may, like the academic and the professional knowledges, police the public-private relation, or it may critique it. It may be involved in the surveillance of the subjectivities of subordinated groups, or in struggles to represent them more adequately than before. It may become part of the problem, or a part of the solution. That is why as we turn to the particular forms of cultural study, we need to ask not only about objects, theories and methods, but also about the political limits and potentials of different standpoints around the circuit.

From the perspective of production

This is a particularly wide and heterogeneous set of approaches. For I include under this head, approaches with very different political tendencies, from the theoretical knowledges of advertisers, persons involved in public relations for large organisations, many liberal-pluralist theorists of public communication and the larger part of writings on culture within the marxist and other critical traditions. As between disciplines, it is sociologists or social historians or political economists, or those concerned with the political organisation of culture, who have most commonly taken this viewpoint.

A more systematic approach to cultural production has been a relatively recent feature of the sociology of literature, art or popular cultural forms. These concerns parallel debates about the mass media and were originally deeply influenced by the early experiences of state propaganda under the conditions of the modern media, especially in Nazi Germany. Crossing the more aesthetic and political debates has been the pervasive concern with the influence of capitalist conditions of production and the mass market in cultural commodities on the 'authenticity' of culture, including the popular arts. Studies of production within these traditions have been equally varied: from grandiose critiques of the political economy and cultural pathology of mass communications (e.g. the early Frankfurt School) to close empirical inspections of the production of news or particular documentary series or soap operas on television.[18] In a very different way still, much modern social history has been concerned with 'cultural production,' though this time the cultural production of social movements or even whole social classes. It is important to accept E. P. Thompson's invitation to read *The Making of the English Working Class* from this cultural standpoint; Paul Willis' work, especially *Learning to Labour*, represents in many ways the sociological equivalent of this historiographical tradition.

What unites these diverse works, however, is that they all take, if not the view-

589

point of cultural producers, at least the *theoretical* standpoint of production. They are interested, first and foremost, in the production and the social organisation of cultural forms. Of course, it is here that marxist paradigms have occupied a very central place, even where continuously argued against. Early marxist accounts asserted the primacy of production conditions and often reduced these to some narrowly-conceived version of 'the forces and the relations of production.' Even such reductive analysis had a certain value: culture was understood as a social product, not a matter of individual creativity only. It was therefore subject to political organisation, whether by the capitalist state or by parties of social opposition.[19] In later marxist accounts, the historical forms of the production and organization of culture—'the superstructures'—have begun to be elaborated.

In Gramsci's writing the study of culture from the viewpoint of production becomes a more general interest with the cultural dimensions of struggles and strategies as a whole. The longstanding and baneful influence of 'high-cultural' or specialist definitions of 'Culture' *within* Marxism was also definitively challenged.[20] Gramsci was, perhaps, the first major marxist theorist and communist leader to take the cultures of the popular classes as a serious object of study and of political practice. All the more modern features of culture organisation also start to appear in his work: he writes of cultural organisers/producers not just as little knots of 'intellectuals' on the old revolutionary or Bolshevik model but as whole social strata concentrated around particular institutions—schools, colleges, the law, the press, the state bureaucracies and the political parties. Gramsci's work is the most sophisticated and fertile development of a traditional marxist approach via cultural production. Yet I think that Gramsci remains much more the 'Leninist' than is sometimes appreciated in new left or academic debates in Britain.[21] From the work available in English, it seems to me he was less interested in how cultural forms work, subjectively, than in how to 'organise' them, externally.

Limits of the viewpoint of production

I find two recurrent limits to looking at culture from this viewpoint. The first difficulty is the familiar one of 'economism,' though it is useful, I hope, to restate the problem in a different way. There is a tendency to neglect what is specific to *cultural* production in this model. Cultural production is assimilated to the model of capitalist (usually) production in general, without sufficient attention to the *dual* nature of the circuit of cultural commodities. The conditions of production include not merely the material means of production and the capitalist organisation of labour, but a stock of already existing *cultural* elements drawn from the reservoirs of lived culture or from the already public fields of discourse. This raw material is structured not only by capitalist production imperatives (i.e., commodified) but also by the indirect results of capitalist and other social relations on the existing rules of language and discourse, especially, class and gender-based struggles in their effects on different social symbols and signs. As against this, marxist political economy still goes for the more

590

brutally-obvious 'determinations'—especially mechanisms like competition, mono-polistic control, and imperial expansion.[22] This is why the claim of some semiologies to provide an alternative materalist analysis does have some force.[23] Many approaches to production, in other words, can be faulted on their chosen ground: as accounts of *cultural* production, of the production of *subjective* forms, they tell us at most about some 'objective' conditions and the work of some social sites—typically the ideological work of capitalist business (e.g. advertising, the work of commercial media) rather than that of political parties, schools, or the apparatuses of 'high cul-ture.'

The second difficulty is not economism but what we might call 'productivism.' The two are often combined but are analytically distinct. Gramsci's Marxism, for instance, is certainly not economistic, but it is, arguably, productivist. The problem here is the tendency to infer the character of a cultural product and its social use from the conditions of its production, as though, in cultural matters, production determines all. The common sense forms of this inference are familiar: we need only trace an idea to its source to declare it 'bourgeois' or 'ideological'—hence 'the bour-geois novel,' 'bourgeois science,' 'bourgeoise ideology' and, of course, all the 'proletarian' equivalents. Most critics of this reduction attack it by denying the con-nection between conditions of origin and political tendency.[24] I do not myself wish to deny that conditions of origin (including the class or gender position of producers) exercise a profound influence on the nature of the product. I find it more useful to question such identifications not as 'wrong' but as *premature*. They may be true as far as they go, according to the logics of that moment, but they neglect the range of pos-sibilities in cultural forms especially as these are realised in consumption or 'readership.' I do not see how any cultural form can be dubbed 'ideological' (in the usual marxist critical sense) until we have examined not only its origin in the primary production process, but also carefully analysed its textual forms *and* the modes of its reception. 'Ideological,' unless deployed as a neutral term, is the *last* term to use in such analysis, certainly not the first.[25]

I still find the debate between Walter Benjamin and Theodore Adorno about the tendency of mass culture a very instructive example.[26] Adorno swept on in his majes-tic polemic identifying capitalist production conditions, tracing effects in the 'fetishized' form of the cultural commodity and finding its perfect compliment in the 'regressive listening' of fans for popular music. There is a highly deductive or infer-ential element in his reasoning, often resting on some giant theoretical strides, plotted first by Lukacs. The conflations and reductions that result are well illustrated on one of his (few) concrete examples: his analysis of the British brewer's slogan— 'What We Want is Watneys.'

> The brand of beer was presented like a political slogan. Nor only does this bill-board give an insight into the nature of the up to date propaganda, which sells its slogans as well as its wares . . . the type of relationship which is suggested by the billboard, by which the masses make a commodity recommended to them the object of their own action, is in fact found again in the pattern of reception of light music. They need and demand what has been palmed off on them.[27]

The first four lines of this are fine. I like the insight about the parallel courses of political propaganda and commercial advertising, forced on as it was by the German situation. The reading of the slogan is also quite interesting, showing how advertising works to produce an *active* identification. But the analysis goes awry as soon as we get to 'the masses.' The actual differentiated drinkers of Watneys and readers of the slogan are assumed to act also as the brewer's ventriloquist's dummy, without any other determinations intervening. Everything specific to the enjoyment of slogans or the drinking of beer is abstracted away. Adorno is uninterested, for example, in the meaning of Watneys (or any other tipple) in the context of pub sociability, indexed by the 'we.' The possibility that drinkers may have their own reasons for consuming a given product and that drinking has a social use value is overlooked.[28]

This is quite an extreme case of productivism but the pressure to infer effects or readings from an analysis of production is a constant one. It is a feature, for example, of a rich vein of work in cultural studies which has mainly been concerned to analyse particular fields of public discourse. Among CCCS publications, *Policing the Crisis* and *Unpopular Education*[29] both were analyses of our first two moments—of texts, in this case the fields of discourse about law and order and about public education—and of their conditions and histories of production—law and order campaigns, media *cause célèbre*, the work of 'primary definers' like judges and the police, the role of a new political tendency, 'Thatcherism,' etc. Both studies proved to have considerable predictive value, showing the strengths and the popularity of new right politics before, in the case of *Policing*, Mrs Thatcher's first electoral victory in 1979.[30] Similarly, I believe that *Unpopular Education* contained what has turned out to be a percipient analysis of the fundamental contradictions of social-democratic politics in Britain and therefore of some of the agonies of the Labour Party. Yet, as political guides, both studies are incomplete: they lack an account of the crisis of '1945-ism' in the lived culture of, especially, working-class groups, or a really concrete rendering of the popular purchase of new right ideologies. They are limited, in other words, by reliance upon, for the most part, the 'public' knowledges of the media and of formal politics. Something more is required than this, especially if we are to go beyond critique to help in producing new political programmes and movements.

This argument may be capped if we turn to Walter Benjamin. Benjamin certainly took a more open view of the potentialities of mass cultural forms than Adorno. He was excited by their technical and educational possibilities. We urged cultural producers to transform not only their works, but also their ways of working. He described the techniques of a new form of cultural production: Brecht's 'epic theatre.' Yet we can see that all of these insights are primarily the comments of a critic upon the theories of producers, or take the standpoint of production. It is here, still with the creator, that the really revolutionary moves are to be made. It is true that Benjamin also had interesting ideas about the potentiality of modern forms to produce a new and more detached relationship between reader and text, but this insight remained abstract, as optimistic, in the same rather *a priori* way, as Adorno's pessimism. It was not rooted in any extended analysis of the larger experience of particular groups of readers.

Our first case (production) turns out to be an interesting instance of an argument the general form of which will recur. Of course, we must look at cultural forms from the viewpoint of their production. This must include the conditions and the means of

592

production, especially in their cultural or subjective aspects. In my opinion it must include accounts and understandings too of the actual moment of production itself— the labour, in its subjective and objective aspects. We canot be perpetually discussing 'conditions' and never discussing acts! At the same time, we must avoid the tempta- tion, signalled in marxist discussions of determination, to subsume all other aspects of culture under the categories of production-studies. This suggests two stages in a more sensible approach. The first is to grant independence and particularity to a dis- tinct production moment—and to do the same for other moments. This is a necessary, negative, holding of the line against reductionisms of all kinds. But once the line is held in our analysis, another stage becomes quite evident. The different moments or aspects are not in fact distinct. There is, for instance, a sense in which (rather carefully) we can speak of texts as 'productive' and a much stronger case for viewing reading or cultural consumption as a production process in which the first product becomes a material for fresh labour. The text-as-produced is a different object from the text-as-read. The problem with Adorno's analysis and perhaps with productivist approaches in general is not only that they infer the text-as-read from the text-as-produced, but that also, in doing this, they ignore the elements of pro- duction in other moments, concentrating 'creativity' in producer or critic. Perhaps this is the deepest prejudice of all among the writers, the artists, the teachers, the educators, the communicators and the agitators within the intellectual divisions of labour!

Text-based studies

A second whole cluster of approaches are primarily concerned with cultural prod- ucts. Most commonly these products are treated as 'texts'; the point is to provide more or less definitive 'readings' of them. Two developments seem especially impor- tant: the separation between specialist critics and ordinary readers, and the division between cultural practitioners and those who practice, primarily, by commenting on the works of others. Both developments have much to do with the growth and elabo- ration of educational and especially academic institutions, but it is interesting that the 'modernisms' which have so deeply influenced cultural studies, had their origins as producer's theories, but are now discussed most intensively in academic and educa- tional contexts. I am thinking particularly of the theories associated with Cubism and Constructivism, Russian formalism and film-making, and, of course, Brecht on theatre.[31]

Much of what is known about the textual organisation of cultural forms is now carried in the academic disciplines conventionally grouped together as the humani- ties or the arts. The major humanities disciplines, but especially linguistic and literary studies, have developed means of formal description which are indispensable for cultural analysis. I am thinking, for example, of the literary analysis of forms of narrative, the identification of different *genres*, but also of whole families of genre cat- egories, the analysis of syntactical forms, possibilities and transformations in linguistics, the formal analysis of acts and exchanges in speech, the analysis of some elementary forms of cultural theory by philosophers, and the common borrowings, by criticism and cultural studies, from semiology and other structuralisms.

Looking it at from outside, the situation in the humanities and especially in literature seems to me very paradoxical: on the one hand, the development of immensely powerful tools of analysis and description, on the other hand, rather meagre ambitions in terms of applications and objects of analysis. There is a tendency for the tools to remain obstinately technical or formal. The example I find most striking at the moment is linguistics, which seems a positive treasure-chest for cultural analysis but is buried in a heightened technical mystique and academic professionalism, from which, fortunately, it is beginning to emerge.[32] Other possibilities seem perpetually cooped up in the 'need' to say something new about some well-thumbed text or much disputed author. This sometimes encompasses a free-ranging amateurism whose general cultural credentials apparently sanction the liberal application of some pretty common sense judgments to almost everything. Yet the paradox is that humanities disciplines, which are pre-eminently concerned with identifying the subjective forms of life, are already cultural studies in embryo!

Forms, regularities and conventions first identified in literature (or certain kinds of music or visual art) often turn out to have a much wider social currency. Feminists working on romance, for example, have traced the correspondences between the narrative forms of popular romantic fiction, the public rituals of marriage (e.g. the Royal Wedding) and, if only through their own experience, the subjective tug of the symbolic resolutions of romantic love.[33] Provoked by this still-developing model, a similar set of arguments and researches are developing around conventional masculinity, the fighting fantasies of boy-culture, and the narrative forms of epic.[34] As if on a prompter's cue, the Falklands/Malvinas conflict crystallised both of these forms (and conjoined them) in a particularly dramatic and real public spectacle. There is no better instance, perhaps, of the limits of treating forms like romance or epic as merely *literary* constructions. On the contrary, they are among the most powerful and ubiquitous of *social* categories or *subjective* forms, especially in their constructions of conventional femininity and masculinity. Human beings live, love, suffer bereavement and go off and fight and die by them.

As usual, then, the problem is to appropriate methods that are often locked into narrow disciplinary channels and use their real insights more widely, freely. What kinds of text-based methods, then, are most useful? And what problems should we look for and try to overcome?

The importance of being formal

Especially important are all the modernist and post-modernist influences, particularly those associated with structuralism and post-Saussurean linguistics. I include the developments in semiology here, but would also want to include, as a kind of cousinhood, once-removed, some strands in 'Anglo-American' linguistics.[35] Cultural studies has often approached these strands quite gingerly, with heated battles, in particular, with those kinds of text-analysis informed by psycho-analysis,[36] but the fresh modernist infusions continue to be a source of developments. As someone coming from the other historical/sociological side, I am often surprised and uncritically entranced by the possibilities here.

Modern formal analysis promises a really careful and systematic description of subjective forms, and of their tendencies and pressures. It has enabled us to identify, for example, narrativity as a basic form of organisation of subjectivities.[37] It also gives us leads—or more—on the repertoire of narrative forms existing contemporaneously, the actual story-forms characteristic of different ways of life. If we treat these not as archetypes but as historically-produced constructions, the possibilities for fruitful concrete study on a wide range of materials are immense. For stories obviously come not merely in the form of bookish or filmic fictions but also in everyday conversation, in everyone's imagined futures and daily projections, and in the construction of identities, individual and collective, through memories and histories. What are the recurrent patterns here? What forms can we abstract from these texts most commonly? It seems to me that in the study of subjective forms, we are at the stage in political economy which Marx, in the *Grundrisse*, saw as necessary but primitive: 'when the forms had still to be laboriously peeled out from the material.'

There are a number of inhibitions here. One powerful one is an opposition to abstract categories and a terror of formalism. I think that this is often quite misplaced. We need to abstract forms in order to describe them carefully, clearly, noting the variations and combinations. I am sure that Roland Barthes was right when he argued against the quixotic rejection of 'the artifice of analysis':

> Less terrorised by the spectre of 'formalism,' historical criticism might have been less sterile; it would have understood that the specific study of forms does not in any way contradict the necessary principles of totality and History. On the contrary: the more a system is specifically defined in its forms, the more amenable it is to historical criticism. To parody a well-known saying, I shall say that a little formalism turns one away from History, but that a lot brings one back to it.[38]

Admittedly Barthes' 'History' is suspiciously capitalized and emptied of content: unlike Marxism, semiology does not present us with a practice (unless it be Barthes' little essays) for reconstituting a complex whole from the different forms. But I am sure we do end up with better, more explanatory, histories, if we have comprehended, more abstractly, some of the forms and relations which constitute them. In some ways, indeed, I find Barthes' work not formal enough. The level of elaboration in his later work sometimes seems gratuitous: too complex for clarity, insufficiently concrete as a substantive account. In these and other semiological endeavours do we mainly hear the busy whir of self-generating intellectual systems rapidly slipping out of control? If so, this is a different noise from the satisfying buzz of a really 'historical' abstraction?

Radical structuralisms excite me for another reason.[39] They are the furthest reach of the criticism of empiricism which, as I suggested earlier, founds cultural studies philosophically. This radical constructivism—nothing in culture taken as given, everything produced—is a leading insight we cannot fall behind. Of course, these two excitements are closely related, the second as a premise of the first. It is because we know we are not in control of our own subjectivities, that we need so badly to identify their forms and trace their histories and future possibilities.

What is a text anyway?

But if text analysis is indispensable, what is a text? Remember the Mini-Metro as an example of the tendency of 'texts' to a polymorphous growth; Tony Bennett's example of the James Bond genres is an even better case.[40] The proliferation of allied representations in the field of public discourses poses large problems for any practitioner of contemporary cultural studies. There are, however, better and worse ways of coping with them. Often, I think, it is a traditional literary solution that is reached for: we plump for an 'author' (so far as this is possible), a single work or series, perhaps a distinctive genre. Our choices may now be popular texts and perhaps a filmic or electronic medium, yet there are still limits in such quasi-literary criteria.

If, for example, we are really interested in how conventions and the technical means available within a particular medium structure representations, we need to work *across* genre and media, comparatively. We need to trace the differences as well as the similarities, for example, between literary romance, romantic love as public spectacle and love as a private form or narrative. It is only in this way that we can resolve some of the most important evaluative questions here: how far, for instance, romance acts merely to seal women into oppressive social conditions, and how far ideologies of love may nonetheless express utopian conceptions of personal relations. We certainly do not *have* to bound our research by literary criteria; other choices are available. It is possible for instance to take 'issues' or periods as the main criterion. Though restricted by their choice of rather 'masculine' genre and media, *Policing the Crisis* and *Unpopular Education* are studies of this kind. They hinge around a basically historical definition, examining aspects of the rise of the new right mainly from the early 1970s. The logic of this approach has been extended in recent CCCS media-based studies: a study of a wide range of media representations of the Campaign for Nuclear Disarmament in October 1981[41] and a study of the media in a 'post-Falklands' holiday period, from Christmas 1982 to New Year 1983.[42] This last approach is especially fruitful since it allows us to examine the construction of a holiday (and especially the play around the public/private division) according to the possibilities of different media and genres, for example, television soap opera and the popular daily press. By capturing something of the contemporary and combined 'effects' of different systems of representations, we also hope to get nearer to the commoner experience of listening, reading and viewing. This form of study, based upon a conjuncture which in this case is both historical (the post-Falklands moment of December 1982) and seasonal (the Christmas holiday), is premised on the belief that context is crucial in the production of meaning.

More generally, the aim is to decentre 'the text' as an object of study. 'The text' is no longer studied for its own sake, nor even for the social effects it may be thought to produce, but rather for the subjective or cultural forms which it realises and makes available. The text is only a *means* in cultural study; strictly, perhaps, it is a raw material from which certain forms (e.g. of narrative, ideological problematic, mode of address, subject position, etc.) may be abstracted. It may also form *part* of a larger discursive field or *combination* of forms occurring in other social spaces with some regularity. But the ultimate object of cultural studies is not, in my view, the text, but *the social life of subjective forms* at each moment of their circulation, including their textual embodiments. This is a long way from a literary valuing of texts for themselves, though, of course, the modes in which some textual embodiments of subjective forms come to be valued over others, especially by critics or educators—the problem especially of 'high' and 'low' in culture—is a central question, especially in theories of culture and class. But this is a problem which subsumes 'literary' concerns, rather than reproducing them. A key issue is how criteria of 'literariness' themselves come to be formulated and installed in academic, educational and other regulative practices.

Structuralist foreshortenings

How to constitute the text is one problem; another is the tendency of other moments, especially of cultural production and reading, but more generally of the more concrete, private aspects of culture, to disappear into a reading of the text. Around this tendency, we might write a whole complicated history of formalisms, using the term now in its more familiar critical sense. I understand formalism negatively, not as abstraction of forms from texts, but as the abstraction of texts from the other moments. For me this distinction is critical, marking the legitimate and excessive concerns with form. I would explain formalism in the negative sense in terms of two main sets of determinations: those that derive from the social location of 'critic' and the limits of a particular practice, and those that derive from particular theoretical problematics, the tools of different critical schools. Although there is a clear historical association, especially in the 20th century, between 'criticism' and 'formalism', there is no necessary connection.

The particular formalisms that interest me most—because there is the most to rescue—are those associated with the various structuralist and post-structuralist discussions of text, narrative, subject positions, discourses and so on. I include here, in a necessarily compressed way, the whole sequence that runs from Saussure's linguistics and Levi-Strauss' anthropology to early Barthes and what is sometimes called 'semiology mark 1'[43] to the developments set in train by May 1968 in film criticism, semiology and narrative theory, including the complicated intersection of Althusserian Marxism, later semiologies and psycho-analysis. Despite their variations, these approaches to 'signifying practices' share certain paradigmatic limits which I term the 'structuralist foreshortening.'

They are limited, in a very fundamental way, by staying within the terms of textual analysis. In so far as they go beyond it, they subordinate other moments *to*

597

textual analysis. In particular they tend to neglect questions of the production of cultural forms or their larger social organisation, or reduce questions of production to the 'productivity' (I would say 'capacity to produce') of the already existing systems of signification, that is the formal languages or codes. They also tend to neglect questions of readership, or subordinate them to the competencies of a textual form of analysis. They tend to derive an 'account' of readership, in fact, from the critic's own textual readings. I want to suggest that the common element in both these limits is a major theoretical lack—the absence of an adequate post-structuralist (or should I say post-post-structuralist) *theory of subjectivity*. This absence is one that is stressed within these approaches themselves; in fact, it is a major charge against old marxisms that they lacked 'a theory of the subject.' But the absence is supplied most unsatisfactorily by twinning textual analysis and psycho-analysis in an account of subjectivity which remains very abstract, 'thin' and un-historical and also, in my opinion, overly 'objective.' To sum up the limitations, there is not really an account or accounts here, of the *genesis* of subjective forms and the different ways in which human beings *inhabit* them.

The neglect of production

This is the easier point to illustrate. It is the difference, for example, between cultural studies in the CCCS tradition, and especially the CCCS appropriation of Gramsci's accounts of hegemony and, say, the main theoretical tendency in the magazine of film criticism associated with the British Film Institute, *Screen*. In the Italian context the comparison might be between the 'pure' semiological and cultural studies traditions. While cultural studies at Birmingham has tended to become *more* historical, more concerned with particular conjunctures and institutional locations, the tendency of film criticism in Britain has been, rather, the other way. Initially, an older marxist concern with cultural production, and, in particular with cinema as industry and with conjunctures in cinematic production was common both in Britain and in France. But like the French film magazines, *Screen* became in the 1970s, increasingly pre-occupied less with production as a social and historical process, and more with the 'productivity' of signifying systems themselves, in particular, with the means of representation of the cinematographic medium. This move was very explicitly argued for, not only in the critiques of realist theories of the cinema and of the realist structures of conventional film itself, but also in the critique of the 'super-realism' of (honoured) marxist practitioners like Einsenstein and Brecht.[44] It formed part of a larger movement which placed increasing emphasis on the means of representation in general and argued that we had to choose between the virtual autonomy and absolute determinacy of 'signification' or return to the consistency of orthodox Marxism. As the elegant one-sided exaggerations put it, it is the myths that speak the myth-maker, the language which speaks the speaker, the texts which read the reader, the theoretical problematic which produces 'science,' and ideology or discourse that produces 'the subject.'

There *was an* account of production in this work, but a very attenuated one. If we think of production as involving raw materials, tools or means of production, and socially-organised forms of human labour, *Screen*'s accounts of film, for instance, focussed narrowly on some of the tools or means of production/representation. I say 'some' because semiologically-influenced theories have tended to invert the priorities of older marxist approaches to production, focussing only on some of the *cultural* means, those, in fact, which political economy neglects. Film theory in the 1970s acknowledged the 'dual' nature of the cinematic circuit, but was mainly concerned to elaborate cinema as 'mental machinery.'[45] This was an understandable choice of *priorities*, but often pursued in a hyper-critical and non-accumulative way. More serious was the neglect of labour, of the actual human activity of producing. Again this may itself have been an exaggerated reaction against older fashions, especially, in this case *auteur* theory, itself an attenuated conception of labour! The neglect of (structured) human activity and especially of conflicts over all kinds of production seems in retrospect the most glaring absence. Thus, although the conception of 'practice' was much invoked (e.g. 'signifying practice') it was practice quite without 'praxis' in the older marxist sense. The effects of this were especially important in the debates, which we shall come to, about texts and subjects.

This criticism can be pushed, however, one stage further: a very limited conception of 'means.' In *Screen*'s theory there was a tendency to look only at the specifically cinematographic 'means'—the codes of cinema. The relations between these means and other cultural resources or conditions were not examined: for example, the relation between codes of realism and the professionalism of film-makers or the relation between media more generally and the state and formal political system. If these elements might be counted as means (they might also be thought of as social relations of production), the raw materials of production were also largely absent, especially in their cultural forms. For cinema, like other public media, takes its raw materials from the pre-existing field of public discourses—the whole field that is, not just from the bit called 'cinema'—and, under the kind of conditions we have examined, from private knowledges too. A critique of the very notion of representation (seen as indispensable to the critique of realism) made it hard for these theorists to pull into their accounts of film any very elaborate recognition of what an older, fuller theory might have called 'content.' Cinema (and then television) were treated as though they were, so to speak, only 'about' cinema or television, only reproducing or transforming the cinematographic or televisual forms, not pulling in and transforming discourses first produced elsewhere. In this way the cinematic text was abstracted from the whole ensemble of discourses and social relations which surrounded and formed it.

One further major limitation in much of this work was a tendency to refuse any explanatory move that went behind the existing means of representation, whether this was the language system, a particular 'signifying practice' or, indeed, the political system. The account was foreshortened to textual means and (just) textual 'effects.' The means were not conceived historically, as having their own moment of production. This was not a local difficulty in particular analyses, but a general theoretical absence, to be found in the earliest influential models of the theory. The same difficulty haunts Saussurean linguistics. Although the rules of language systems determine speech acts, the everyday deployment of linguistic forms appears not to touch the language system itself. This is partly because its principles are conceived so abstractly that historical change or social variation escapes detection, but it is also because there is no true production moment of the language system itself. Crucial insights into language and other systems of signification are therefore foreclosed: namely, that languages are produced (or differentiated), reproduced and modified by socially-organised human practice, that there can be no language (except a dead one) without speakers, and that language is continually fought over in its words, syntax and discursive deployments. In order to recover these insights, students of culture who are interested in language have had to go outside the predominantly French semiological traditions, back to the marxist philosopher of language Voloshinov or across to particular researches influenced by the work of Bernstein or Halliday.

Readers in texts; readers in society

The most characteristic feature of late semiologies has been the claim to advance a theory of the production of subjects. Initially, the claim was based on a general philo-sophical opposition to humanist conceptions of a simple, unified 'I' or subject, standing unproblematically at the centre of thought or moral or aesthetic evaluation. This feature of structuralism had affinities with similar arguments in Marx about the subjects of bourgeois ideologies, especially about the premises of political economy, and with Freud's anatomisation of the contradictions of human personality.

'Advanced semiology' presents several layers of theorisation of subjectivity which are difficult to unravel.[46] This complicated set of fusions and tangles combined fine lead-ing insights with theoretical disasters. The key insight, for me, is that narratives or images always imply or construct a position or positions from which they are to be read or viewed. Although 'position' remains problematic (is it a set of cultural com-petences, or, as the term implies, some necessary 'subjection' to the text?), the insight is dazzling, especially when applied to visual images and to film. We cannot perceive the work which cameras do from a new aspect, not merely presenting an object, but putting us in place before it. If we add to this, the argument that certain kinds of texts ('realism') naturalise the means by which positioning is achieved, we have a dual insight of great force. The particular promise is to render processes hitherto unconsciously suffered (and enjoyed) open to explicit analysis.

Within the context of my own argument, the importance of these insights is that they provide a way of *connecting* the account of textual forms with an exploration of intersections with readers' subjectivities. A careful, elaborated and hierarchised account of the reading positions offered in a text (in narrative structure or modes of address for instance) seems to me the most developed method we have so far within the limits of text analysis. Of course, such readings should not be taken to negate other methods: the reconstruction of the manifest and latent themes of a text, its denotative and connotative moments, its ideological problematic or limiting assump-tions, its metaphorical or linguistic strategies. The legitimate object of an identification of 'positions' is the *pressures* or *tendencies* of subjective forms, the *directions* in which they move us, their *force*—once inhabited. *The difficulties arise*—and they are very numerous—*if such tendencies are held to be realised in the subjectivities of readers, without additional and different forms of inquiry.*

The intoxications of the theory make such a move very tempting. But to slip from 'reader in the text' to 'reader in society' is to slide from the most abstract moment (the analysis of forms) to the most concrete object (actual readers, as they are constituted, socially, historically, culturally). This is conveniently to miss—but not explicitly as a rational abstraction—the huge number of fresh determinations or pressures of which we must now take account. In disciplinary terms we move from a ground usually covered by literary approaches to one more familiar to historical or sociological competences, but the common new element here is the ability to handle a mass of co-existing determinations, operating at many different levels.

It would take us into a long and complicated exploration of 'reading' to try and gauge the full enormity of the leap.[47] There is only room to stress a few difficulties in treating reading, not as reception or assimilation, but as itself an act of production. If the text is the raw material of this practice, we encounter, once again, all the problems of textual boundaries. The isolation of a text for academic scrutiny is a very specific form of reading. More commonly texts are encountered promiscuously; they pour in on us from all directions in diverse, coexisting media, and differently-paced flows. In everyday life, textual materials are complex, multiple, overlapping, co-existent, juxta-posed, in a word, 'inter-textual.' If we use a more agile category like discourse, indicating *elements* that cut across different texts, we can say that all readings are also 'inter-discursive.' No subjective form ever acts on its own. Nor can the *combinations* be predicted by formal or logical means, nor even from empirical analysis of the field of public discourse, though of course this may suggest hypotheses. The combinations stem, rather, from more particular logics—the structured life-activity in its objective and subjective sides, of readers or groups of readers: their social locations, their histories, their subjective interests, their private worlds.

The same problem arises if we consider the tools of this practice, or the codes, competences and orientations already present within a particular social *milieu*. Again these are not predictable from public texts. They belong to private *cultures*, in the way that term has usually been used in cultural studies. They are grouped according to 'ways of life.' They exist in the chaotic and historically-sedimented *ensembles* which Gramsci referred to as common sense. Yet these must determine the longer and shorter-range results of particular interpellative moments, or, as I prefer, the forms of cultural transformation which always occur in readings.

All this points to the centrality of what is usually called 'context.' Context determines the meaning, transformations or salience of a particular subjective form as much as the form itself. Context includes the cultural features described above, but also the contexts of immediate situations (e.g. the domestic context of the household) and the larger historical context or conjuncture.

Yet any account would remain incomplete without some attention to the act of reading itself and an attempt to theorise its products. The absence of action by the reader is characteristic of formalist accounts. Even those theorists (e.g. Brecht, *Tel Quel*, Barthes in *S/Z*) who are concerned with productive, deconstructive or critical

601

reading ascribe this capacity to types of text (e.g. 'writable' rather than 'readable' in Barthes' terminology) and not at all to a history of real readers. This absence of production in reading parallels the ascription of productivity to signifying systems which we have already noted. At best particular acts of reading are understood as a replaying of primary human experiences. Just as an older literary criticism sought universal values and human emotions in the text, so the new formalisms understand reading as the reliving of psycho-analytically-defined mechanisms. Analysis of the spectator's gaze, based on Lacanian accounts of the mirror phase, identify *some* of the motions of the way men use images of women and relate to heroes.[48] Such analyses *do* bridge text and reader. There is a huge potentiality, for cultural studies, in the critical use of Freudian categories, as critical that is, as the use of marxist categories has become or is becoming. Yet present uses often bridge text and reader at a cost: the radical simplification of the social subject, reducing him or her to the original, naked, infant needs. It is difficult on this basis to specify all the realms of difference which one wishes to grasp, even, surprisingly, gender. At worst the imputations about real subjects come down to a few universals, just as it is now only a few basic features of the text which interest us. There are distinct limits to a procedure which discovers, in otherwise varied phenomena, the same old mechanisms producing the same old effects.

One lack in these accounts is an attempt to describe more elaborately the surface forms—the flows of inner speech and narrative—which are the most empirically obvious aspect of subjectivity. Perhaps it is thought humanist to pay attention to consciousness in this way? But we all are (aren't we?) continuous, resourceful and absolutely frenetic users of narrative and image? And these uses occur, in part, inside the head, in the imaginative or ideal world which accompanies us in every action. We are not merely positioned by stories about ourselves, stories about others. We use realist stories about the future to prepare or plan, acting out scenarios of dangerous or pleasurable events. We use fictional or fantastical forms to escape or divert. We tell stories about the past in the form of memory which construct versions of who we presently are. Perhaps all this is simply pre-supposed in formalist analysis, yet to draw it into the foreground seems to have important implications.[49] It makes it possible to recover the elements of self-production in theories of subjectivity. It suggests that before we can gauge the productivity of new interpellations, or anticipate their like popularity, we need to know what stories are already in place.

All this involves a move beyond what seems to be an underlying formalist assumption: that real readers are 'wiped clean' at each textual encounter to be positioned (or liberated) anew by the next interpellation. Post-structuralist revisions, stressing the continuous productivity of language or discourse as *process*, do not necessarily help here, because it is not at all clear what all this productivity actually produces. There is no real theory of subjectivity here, partly because the *explanandum*, the 'object' of such a theory, remains to be specified. In particular there is no account of the carry-over or continuity of self-identities from one discursive moment to the next, such as a re-theorisation of memory in discursive terms might permit. Since there is no account of continuities or of what remains constant or accumulative, there is no account of structural shifts or major re-arrangements of a sense of self, especially in adult life. Such transformations are always, implicitly, referred to 'external' text-forms, for example revolutionary or poetic texts, usually forms of literature. There is no account of what predisposes the reader to use such texts productively or what conditions, other than the text-forms themselves, contribute to revolutionary conjunctures in their subjective dimensions. Similarly, with such a weight on the text, there is no account of how some readers (including, presumably, the analysts) can use conventional or realist texts critically. Above all, there is no account of what I would call *the subjective aspects of struggle*, no account of how there is a moment in subjective flux when social subjects (individual or collective) produce accounts of who they are, as conscious political agents, that is, constitute themselves, politically. To ask for such a theory is not to deny the major structuralist or post-structuralist insights: subjects *are* contradictory, 'in process,' fragmented, produced. But human beings and social movements also strive to produce some coherence and continuity, and through this, exercise some control over feelings, conditions and destinies.

This is what I mean by a 'post-post-structuralist' account of subjectivity. It involves returning to some older but reformulated questions—about struggle, 'unity,' and the production of a political will. It involves accepting structuralist insights as a statement of the problem, whether we are speaking of our own frag-mented selves or the objective and subjective fragmentation of possible political constituencies. But it also involves taking seriously what seems to me the most inter-esting theoretical lead: the notion of a discursive self-production of subjects, especially in the form of histories and memories.[50]

Social inquiries—logic and history

I hope that the logic of our third cluster of approaches, which focus on 'lived cul-ture,' is already clear. To recapitulate, the problem is how to grasp the more *concrete* and more *private* moments of cultural circulation. This sets up two kinds of pres-sures. The first is towards methods which can detail, recompose and represent complex ensembles of discursive and non-discursive features as they appear in the life of particular social groups. The second is towards 'social inquiry' or an active seeking out of cultural elements which do not appear in the public sphere, or only appear abstracted and transformed. Of course, students of culture have access to private forms through their own experiences and social worlds. This is a continuous resource, the more so if it is consciously specified and if its relativity is recognised. Indeed, a cultural self-criticism of this kind is *the* indispensable condition for avoid-ing the more grossly ideological forms of cultural study.[51] But the first lesson here is the recognition of *major cultural differences*, especially across those social relationships where power, dependence and inequality are most at stake. There are perils, then, in the use of a (limited) individual or collective self-knowledge where the limits of its representativeness are uncharted and its other sides—usually the sides of powerless-ness—are simply unknown. This remains a justification for forms of cultural study which take the cultural words of others (often reverse sides of one's own) as the main object.

603

We have to keep a discomforted eye on the historical pedigrees and current orthodoxies of what is sometimes called 'ethnography,' a practice of representing the cultures of others. The practice, like the word, already extends social distance and constructs relations of knowledge-as-power. To 'study' culture forms is already to differ from a more implicit inhabitation of culture which is the main 'common-sense' mode in *all* social groups. (And I mean *all* social groups—'intellectuals' may be great at describing *other* people's implicit assumptions, but are as 'implicit' as anyone when it comes to their own.)

The early years of new left research in particular—the 1940s, 50s and early 60s—involved a new set of relations between the subjects and objects of research, especially across class relations.[52] Intellectual movements associated with feminism and the work of some black intellectuals have transformed (but not abolished) these social divisions too. Experiments in community-based authorship have also, within limits, achieved new social relations of cultural production and publication.[53] Even so it seems wise to be suspicious, not necessarily of these practices themselves, but of all accounts of them that try to minimise the political risks and responsibilities involved, or to resolve magically the remaining social divisions. Since fundamental social relations have not been transformed, social inquiry tends constantly to return to its old anchorages, pathologising subordinated cultures, normalising the dominant modes, helping at best to build academic reputations without proportionate returns to those who are represented. Apart from the basic political standpoint—whose side the researchers are on—much depends on the specific theoretical forms of the work, the *kind* of ethnography.

Limits of 'experience'

There seems to be a close association beween ethnographies (or histories) based on sympathetic identification and empiricist or 'expressive' models of culture. The pressure is to represent lived cultures as authentic ways of life and to uphold them against ridicule or condescension. Research of this kind has often been used to criticise the dominant representations, especially those influencing state policies. Researchers have often mediated a private working-class world (often the world of their own childhood) and the definitions of the public sphere with its middle-class weighting. A very common way of upholding subordinated cultures has been to stress the bonds between the subjective and objective sides of popular practices. Working-class culture has been seen as the authentic expression of proletarian conditions, perhaps the only expression possible. This relation or identity has sometimes been cemented by 'old marxist' assumptions about the proper state of consciousness of the working-class. A similar set of assumptions can be traced in some feminist writings about culture which portray and celebrate a distinct feminine cultural world reflective of woman's condition. The term which most commonly indexes this theoretical framework is 'experience,' with its characteristic fusing of objective and subjective aspects.

Such frameworks produce major difficulties, not least for researchers themselves. Secondary analysis and re-presentation must always be problematic or intrusive if 'spontaneous' cultural forms are seen as a completed or necessary form of social knowledge. The only legitimate practice, in this framework, is to represent an unmediated chunk of authentic life experience itself, in something like its own terms. This form of cultural empiricism is a dead hand on the most important of cultural studies practices, and is one of the reasons why it is also the most difficult to deliver at all.

There is also a systematic pressure towards presenting lived cultures primarily in terms of their homogeneity and distinctiveness. This theoretical pressure, in conceptions like 'whole way of life,' becomes startlingly clear when issues of nationalism and racism are taken into account. There is a discomforting convergence between 'radical' but romantic versions of 'working-class culture' and notions of a shared Englishness or white ethnicity. Here too one finds the term 'way of life' used as though 'cultures' were great slabs of significance always humped around by the same set of people. In left ethnography the term has often been associated with an underrepresentation of non-class relations and of fragmentations within social classes.[54]

The main lack within expressive theories is attention to the means of signification as a specific cultural determination. There is no better instance of the divorce between formal analysis and 'concrete studies' than the rarity of linguistic analysis in historical or ethnographic work. Like much structuralist analysis, then, ethnographies often work with a foreshortened version of our circuit, only here it is the whole arc of 'public' forms which is often missing. Thus the creativity of private forms is stressed, the continuous cultural productivity of everyday life, but not its dependence on the materials and modes of public production. Methodologically, the virtues of abstraction are eschewed so that the separate (or separable) elements of lived cultures are not unravelled, and their real complexity (rather than their essential unity) is not recognised.

Best ethnography

I do not wish to imply that this form of cultural study is intrinsically compromised. On the contrary, I tend to see it as the privileged form of analysis, both intellectually and politically. Perhaps this will be clear if I briefly review some aspects of the best ethnographic studies at Birmingham.[55]

These studies have used abstraction and formal description to identify key elements in a lived cultural ensemble. Cultures are read 'textually.' But they have also been viewed alongside a reconstruction of the social position of the users. There is a large difference here between a 'structural ethnography' and a more ethno-methodological approach concerned exclusively with the level of meaning and usually within an individualistic framework. This is one reason, for instance, why feminist work in the Centre has been as much preoccupied with theorising the position of women as with 'talking to girls.' We have tried to ally cultural analysis with a (sometimes too generalised) structural sociology, centring upon gender, class and race.

Perhaps the most distinctive feature has been the connections made between lived cultural ensembles and public forms. Typically, studies have concerned the appropriation of elements of mass culture and their transformation according to the needs and cultural logics of social groups. Studies of the contribution of mass cultural forms (popular music, fashion, drugs or motor bikes) to sub-cultural styles, of girls' use of popular cultural forms, and of the lads' resistance to the knowledge and authority of school are cases in point. In other words the best studies of lived culture are also, necessarily, studies of 'reading.' It is from this point of view—the intersection of public and private forms—that we have the best chance of answering the two key sets of questions to which cultural studies—rightly—continually returns.

The first set concerns 'popularity,' pleasure and the *use value* of cultural forms. Why do some subjective forms acquire a popular force, become principles of living? What are the *different* ways in which subjective forms are inhabited—playfully or in deep seriousness, in fantasy or by rational agreement, because it is the thing to do or the thing *not* to do?

The second set of questions concerns the *outcomes* of cultural forms. Do these forms tend to reproduce existing forms of subordination or oppression? Do they hold down or contain social ambitions, defining wants too modestly? Or are they forms which permit a questioning of existing relations or a running beyond them in terms of desire? Do they point to alternative social arrangements? Judgments like these cannot be made on the basis of the analysis of production conditions or texts alone; they can best be answered once we have traced a social form right through the circuit of its transformations and made some attempt to place it within the whole context of relations of hegemony within the society.

Future shapes of cultural studies: directions

My argument has been that there are three main models of cultural studies research: production-based studies, text-based studies, and studies of lived cultures. This division conforms to the main appearances of cultural circuits, but inhibits the development of our understandings in important ways. Each approach has a rationality in relation to that moment it has most closely in view, but is quite evidently inadequate, even 'ideological,' as an account of the whole. Yet each approach also implies a different view of the politics of culture. Production-related studies imply a struggle to control or transform the most powerful means of cultural production, or to throw up alternative means by which a counter-hegemonic strategy may be pursued. Such discourses are usually addressed to institutional reformers or to radical political parties. Text-based studies, focussing on the forms of cultural products, have usually concerned the possibilities of a transformative cultural practice. They have been addressed most often to *avant-garde* practitioners, critics and teachers. These approaches have appealed especially to professional educators, in colleges or schools, because knowledges appropriate to radical practice have been adapted (not without problems) to a knowledge appropriate to critical readers. Finally, research into lived cultures has been closely associated with a politics of 'representation' upholding the ways of life of subordinated social groups and criticising the dominant public forms in the light of hidden wisdoms. Such work may even aspire to help to give a hegemonic or non-corporate turn to cultures that are usually privatised, stigmatised or silenced.

It is important to stress that the circuit has not been presented as an adequate account of cultural processes or even of elementary forms. It is not a completed set of abstractions against which every partial approach can be judged. It is not therefore an adequate strategy for the future just to add together the three sets of approaches, using each for its appropriate moment. This would not work without transformations of each approach and, perhaps, our thinking about 'moments.' For one thing there are some real theoretical incompatibilities between approaches; for another, the ambitions of many projects are already large enough! It is important to recognise that each aspect has a life of its own in order to avoid reductions, but, after that, it may be more transformative to rethink each moment in the light of the others, importing objects and methods of study usually developed in relation to one moment into the next. The moments, though separable, are not in fact discrete, therefore we need to trace what Marx would have called 'the inner connections' and 'real identities' between them.

Those concerned with production studies need to look more closely, for example, at the specifically cultural conditions of production. This would include the more formal semiological questions about the codes and conventions on which a television programme, say, draws, and the ways in which it reworks them. It would also have to include a wider range of discursive materials—ideological themes and problematics—that belong to a wider social and political conjuncture. But already, in the production moment, we would expect to find more or less intimate relations with the lived culture of particular social groups, if only that of the producers. Discursive and ideological elements would be used and transformed from there too. 'Already' then, in the study of the production moment, we can anticipate the other aspects of the larger process and prepare the ground for a more adequate account. Similarly we need to develop, further, forms of text-based study which hook up with the production and readership perspectives. It may well be, in the Italian context, where semiological and literary traditions are so strong, that those are the most important transformations. It *is* possible to look for the signs of the production process in a text: this is one useful way of transforming the very unproductive concern with 'bias' that still dominates discussion of 'factual' media. It *is* also possible to read texts as forms of representation, provided it is realised that we are always analysing a representation of a representation. The first object, that which is represented in the text, is not an objective event or fact, but has already been given meanings in some other social practice. In this way it is possible to consider the relationship, if any, between the characteristic codes and conventions of a social group and the forms in which they are represented in a soap opera or comedy. This is not merely an academic exercise, since it is essential to have such an account to help establish the text's salience for this group or others. There is no question of abandoning existing forms of text analysis, but these have to be adapted to, rather than superseding, the study of actual readerships. There seem to be two main requirements here. First, the formal reading

607

of a text has to be as open or as multi-layered as possible, identifying preferred positions or frameworks certainly, but also alternative readings and subordinated frameworks, even if these can only be discerned as fragments, or as contradictions in the dominant forms. Second, analysts need to abandon once and for all, both of the two main models of the critical reader: the primarily evaluative reading (is this a good/bad text?) and the aspiration to text-analysis as an 'objective science.' The problem with both models is that by de-relativising our acts of reading they remove from self-conscious consideration (but not as an active presence) our common sense knowledge of the larger cultural contexts and possible readings. I have already noted the difficulties here, but want also to stress the indispensability of this resource. The difficulties are met best, but not wholly overcome, when 'the analyst' is a group. Many of my most educative moments in cultural studies have come from these internal group dialogues about the readings of texts across, for example, gendered experiences. This is not to deny the real disciplines of 'close' reading, in the sense of *careful*, but not in the sense of *confined*.

Finally, those concerned with 'concrete' cultural description cannot afford to ignore the presence of text-like structures and particular forms of discursive organisation. In particular we need to know what distinguishes private cultural forms, in their basic modes of organisation, from the public forms. In this way we might be able to specify, linguistically for example, the differential relation of social groups to different media forms, and the real processes of reading that are involved.

Of course, the transformation of particular approaches will have effects on others. If linguistic analysis takes account of historical determinations, for example, or provides us with ways of analysing the operations of power, the division between language studies and concrete accounts will break down. This goes for the associated politics too. At the moment there are few areas so blocked by disagreement and incomprehension as the relationship between *avant-garde* theorists and practitioners of the arts and those interested in a more grass-roots entry through community arts, working-class writing, women's writing and so on. Similarly, it is hard to convey, just how mechanical, how unaware of cultural dimensions, the politics of most left factions remain. If I am right that theories are related to viewpoints, we are talking not just of theoretical developments, but about some of the conditions for effective political alliances as well.

NOTES

1. This paper is a revised and expanded version of talks given at the Department of English at Istituto Universitario Orientale in Naples and at the University of Palermo in April 1983. I am grateful to colleagues at Naples, Palermo, Pescara and from Bari for fruitful discussions around the themes raised here. In revising this paper, I have tried to respond to some comments, especially those concerning questions about consciousness and unconsciousness. I am grateful to Lidia Curti, Laura di Michele and Marina Vitale for encouraging the production of this paper and advising on its form, to the British Council for funding my visit, and to friends and students (not mutually exclusive categories) at Birmingham for bearing with very many different versions of 'the circuit.'
2. The key texts are Richard Hoggart, *The Uses of Literacy* (Penguin, 1958); Raymond Williams, *Culture and Society* (Penguin, 1958); Raymond Williams, *The Long Revolution* (Penguin, 1961).
3. For a still useful summary of CCCS responses to Althusser see McLennan, Molina and Peters,

'Althusser's Theory of Ideology,' in CCCS, *On Ideology* (Hutchinson, 1978).

4. See, for example, Hall, Lumley and McLennan, 'Politics and Ideology: Gramsci' in *On Ideology*. But Gramsci's theorisations are a main presence in much of the empirical work from the Centre from the mid-1970s.

5. See McLennan, *Marxism and Methodologies of History* (Verso, 1981) and Richard Johnson, 'Reading for the Best Marx: History-Writing and Historical Abstraction' in CCCS, *Making Histories: Studies in History-Writing and Politics* (Hutchinson, 1982).

6. These are difficult to represent bibliographically, but key points are marked by CCCS Womens Study Group: *Women Take Issue* (Hutchinson, 1978); CCCS, *The Empire Strikes Back* (Hutchinson, 1982). See also the series on Women and on Race in CCCS Stencilled Papers.

7. This is not a new criticism but given fresh force by the 1970s salience of race. See Paul Gilroy, 'Police and Thieves' in *Empire Strikes Back*, esp. pp. 147–51.

8. Some of these, at an early stage, are discussed in *Women Take Issue*, but there is need for a really full and consolidated account of the transformations in cultural studies stemming from feminist work and criticism. See also Angela McRobbie, 'Settling Accounts with Sub-Cultures,' *Screen Education* No. 34 (Spring, 1980) and the articles by Hazel Carby and Pratibha Parmar in *Empire Strikes Back*.

9. See, for example, Stuart Hall, 'Some Paradigms in Cultural Studies,' *Anglistica* (1978); Stuart Hall, 'Cultural Studies: Two Paradigms,' *Media, Culture and Society* No. 2 (1980) (reprinted in part in Tony Bennett *et al.* (eds.), *Culture, Ideology and Social Process* [Open University and Batsford, 1981]) and the introductory essays in Hall, Hobson, Lowe and Willis (eds.), *Culture, Media and Language* (Hutchinson, 1980). These essays are highly compressed versions of the MA Theory Course at CCCS which Stuart Hall taught and which comprised a comprehensive theoretical mapping of the field. See also my own attempts at theoretical clarification, much influenced by Stuart's, especially in, Clark, Critcher and Johnson (eds.), *Working Class Culture* (Hutchinson, 1979).

10. Raymond Williams, *Culture and Society* and the entry in *Keywords* (Fontana, 1976).

11. For a discussion of 'general-historical' abstraction in Marx see, Johnson, 'Best Marx,' p. 172.

12. The diagram is based, in its *general* forms, on a reading of Marx's account of the circuit of capital and its metamorphoses. For an important and original account of this, and of related questions (e.g. fetishism) see Victor Molina, 'Marx's Arguments About Ideology,' M. Litt. Thesis (University of Birmingham, 1982). This thesis is currently being revised for submission as a P.D. Also important is Stuart Hall, 'Encoding/Decoding' in *Culture, Media, Language*.

13. I am afraid this illustrative case is largely hypothetical since I have no contacts inside British Leyland management. Any resemblence to persons living or dead is entirely fortuitous and a pure instance of the power of theory!

14. This is the division between 'structuralist' and 'culturalist' approaches Stuart Hall and I, among others, have already discussed, but now in the form of 'objects' and methods, rather than 'paradigms.' See sources listed in note 9 above and add Richard Johnson, 'Histories of Culture/Theories of Ideology: Notes on an Impasse,' in Barrett *et al.* (eds.), *Ideology and Cultural Production*.

15. My thinking on 'the public and the private' is much influenced by certain German traditions, especially discussions around Jürgen Habermas' work on 'the public sphere.' This is now being interestingly picked up and used in some American work. See Jürgen Habermas, *Strukturwandel der Öffentlichkeit* (Neuweid, Berlin, 1962); Oskar Negt and Alexander Kluge, *Öffentlichkeit und Erfahrung: Zur Organisationsanalyse von Burgerlicher und proletarischer Öffentlichkeit* (Frankfurt am Main, 1972). For an extract of Negt and Kluge's work see A. Matterlart and S. Siegelaub (eds.), *Communication and Class Struggle*, vol. 2.

16. Paul Willis, 'Shop-floor Culture, Masculinity and the Wage Form' in Clarke, Critcher and Johnson (eds.), *Working Class Culture*.

17. There is a very large sociological literature on these forms of stigmatisation, especially of the deviant young. For a cultural studies development of this work see Stuart Hall *et al.*, *Policing the Crisis: 'Mugging,' the State and Law and Order* (Macmillan, 1978). For more subtle forms of marginalisation, see CCCS Media Group, 'Fighting Over Peace: Representations of the Campaign for Nuclear Disarmament in the Media,' CCCS Stencilled Paper, No. 72. For current treatment of the left and the trade unions in the British media see the sequence of studies by the Glasgow Media Group, starting with Glasgow University Media Group, *Bad News* (Routledge and Kegan Paul, 1976). Stanley Cohen and Jock Young (eds.), *The Manufacture of News* (Constable, 1973) was a pioneer collection.

18. Among the best close studies of this kind are Philip Elliott, *The Making of a Television Series: A Case Study in the Sociology of Culture* (Constable/Sage, 1972); Philip Schlesinger, *Putting 'Reality' Together: BBC News* (Constable/Sage, 1978); Jeremy Tunstall, *Journalists at Work* (Constable, 1971); Dorothy Hobson, *Crossroads*.

19. The forms of 'political organization' were often not specified in Marx or in the theorists who followed him, up to and including, in my view, Lenin. For Lenin, it seems to me, cultural politics remains a matter of organisation and 'propaganda' in quite narrow senses.

20. Althusser's exceptions of 'art' from ideology are an instance of the persistance of this view within marxism. It is interesting to compare Althusser's and Gramsci's views of 'philosophy' here too, Althusser tending to the specialist academic or 'high cultural' definition, Gramsci to the popular.

21. I think the predominant reception of Gramsci in Britain is 'anti-Leninist,' especially among those interested in discourse theory. But it may be that CCCS appropriations underestimate Gramsci's leninism too. I am grateful to Victor Molina for discussions on this issue.

22. See, for instance, the work of Graham Murdock and Peter Golding on the political economy of the mass media: e.g. 'Capitalism, Communication and Class Relations' in Curran *et al.* (eds.), *Mass Communication and Society*; Graham Murdock, 'Large Corporations and the Control of the Communications Industries' in Gurevitch *et al.* (eds.), *Culture, Society and the Media*; for a more explicitly polemical engagement with CCCS work see Golding and Murdock, 'Ideology and the Mass Media: the Question of Determination' in Barratt *et al.* (eds.), *Ideology and Cultural Production*. For a reply see I. Connell, 'Monopoly Capitalism and the Media: Definitions and Struggles' in S. Hibbin (ed.), *Politics, Ideology and the State* (Lawrence and Wishart, 1978).

23. These claims have their proximate origin in Althusser's statement that ideologies have a material existence. For a classic English statement of this kind of 'materialism' see Rosalind Coward and John Ellis, *Language and Materialism: Developments in Semiology and the Theory of the Subject* (Routledge and Kegan Paul, 1977). This is rather different from Marx's argument that under particular conditions ideologies acquire a 'material force' or Gramsci's elaboration of this in terms of the conditions of popularity.

24. This applies to a wide range of structuralist and post-structuralist theories from Poulantzas's arguments against class reductionist notions of ideology to the more radical positions of Barry Hindes and Paul Hirst and other theorists of 'discourse.'

25. In this respect I find myself at odds with many strands in cultural studies, including some influential ones, which opt for an expanded use of ideology rather in the bolshevik sense or in the more Leninist of Althusser's (several) uses. Ideology is applied, in Oxford's important popular culture course, for instance, to the formation of subjectivities as such. If stretched thus, I would argue that the term loses its usefulness—'discourse,' 'cultural form,' etc. would do quite as well. On the whole, I wish to retain the 'negative' or 'critical' connotations of the term 'ideology' in classic marxist discourse, though not, as it happens, the usual accompaniment, a 'hard' notion of Marxism-as-science. It may well be that all our knowledge of the world and all our conceptions of the self are 'ideological,' or more or less ideological, in that they are rendered partial by the operation of interests and of power. But this seems to me a proposition that has to be plausibly argued in particular cases rather than assumed at the beginning of every analysis. The expanded, 'neutral' sense of the term cannot altogether lay to rest the older negative connotations. The issues are interestingly stated in the work of Jorge Larrain. See *Marxism and Ideology* (Macmillan, 1983) and *The Concept of Ideology* (Hutchinson, 1979).

26. See especially Theodore Adorno, 'On the Fetish Character of Music and the Regression of Listening' in Arato and Gebhardt, (eds.), *The Essential Frankfurt School Reader* (New York: Continuum, 1982); Adorno & Horkheimer, *Dialectics of Enlightenment* (Allen Lane, 1973); Walter Benjamin, 'The Work of Art in an Age of Mechanical Reproduction' in *Illuminations* (Fontana, 1973).

27. 'Fetish Character in Music,' pp. 287–8. Later he gives slightly more rounded pictures of types of consumption of popular music, but even his fans' dancing resembles 'the reflexes of mutilated animals' (p. 292).

28. For more developed critiques see Dick Bradley, 'Introduction to the Cultural Study of Music,' CCCS Stencilled Paper, No. 61; Richard Middleton, 'Reading Popular Music,' *Oxford Popular Culture Course Unit*, Unit 16, Block 4 (Open University Press, 1981).

29. CCCS Education Group, *Unpopular Education: Schooling and Social Democracy in England since 1944* (Hutchinson, 1981).

30. The analysis of Thatcherism has continued to be one of Stuart Hall's major concerns. See the very important essays republished in Stuart Hall and Martin Jacques (eds.), *The Politics of Thatcherism* (Lawrence and Wishart/*Marxism Today*, 1983). 'The Great Moving Right Show,' written before the 1979 election, proved to be especially perceptive.

31. Particularly useful introductions in English to these combined impacts are Silvia Harvey, *May 1968 and Film Culture* (BFI, 1980); Tony Bennett, *Formalism and Marxism* (New Accents, Methuen, 1979).

32. See, for instance, the work of a group of 'critical linguists' initially based on the University of East Anglia, especially: R. Fowler *et al.*, *Language and Control* (Routledge and Kegan Paul, 1979). I am especially grateful to Gunther Kress, who spent some months at the Centre, and to Utz Maas of Osnabruck University for very fruitful discussions on the relationship of language studies and cultural studies. See also Utz Maas, 'Language Studies and Cultural Analysis,' Paper for a Conference on Language and Cultural Studies at CCCS, December 1982.

33. Much of this work remains unpublished. I very much hope that one of the next CCCS books will be a collection on romance. In the meantime see English Studies Group, 'Recent Developments' in *Culture, Media, Language*. Rachel Harrison, 'Shirley: Romance & Relations of Dependence' in CCCS Women's Studies Group, *Women Take Issue*; Angela McRobbie, 'Working-Class Girls and Femininity,' *ibid.*; Myra Connell, 'Reading and Romance,' Unpublished MA Dissertation (University of Birmingham, 1981); Christine Griffin, 'Cultures of Femininity: Romance Revisited,' CCCS Stencilled Paper, No. 69; Janice Winship, 'Woman Becomes an Individual: Femininity and Consumption in Women's Magazines,' CCCS Stencilled Paper, No. 65; Laura di Michele, 'The Royal Wedding,' CCCS Stencilled Paper, forthcoming.

34. Much of this work is in connection with the work of the Popular Memory Group in CCCS towards a book on the popularity of Conservative nationalism. I am especially grateful to Laura di Michele for her contribution in opening up these questions in relation to 'epic,' and to Graham Dawson for discussions on masculinity, war, and boy culture.

35. Especially those developing out of the work of M. A. K. Halliday which includes the 'critical linguistics' group. For Halliday see Gunther Kress (ed.), *Halliday: System and Function in Language* (Oxford University Press, 1976).

36. See especially the long, largely unpublished critique of *Screen* by the CCCS Media Group, 1977–78. Parts of this appear in Stuart Hall *et al.* (eds.), *Culture, Media, Language* (Hutchinson, 1980), pp. 157–173.

37. I take this to be the common message of a great range of work, some of it quite critical of structuralist formalism, on the subject of narrative in literature, film, television, folk tale, myth, history and political theory. I am in the middle of my own reading list, delving into this material from a quite unliterary background. My starting points are theories of narrative in general—compare Roland Barthes, 'Introduction to the Structural Analysis of Narratives' in Stephen Heath (ed.), *Barthes on Image, Music, Text* (Fontana, 1977) and Fredric Jameson, *The Political Unconscious: Narrative as A Socially-Symbolic Act* (Methuen, 1981), but I am most interested in work, at a lesser level of generality, that specifies the types or *genres* of narrative. Here I have found much stimulus in work on filmic or televisual narratives, see especially the texts collected in Tony Bennett *et al.* (eds.), *Popular Television and Film* (BFI/Open University, 1981), but also on 'archetypal' genre forms—epic, romance, tragedy, etc.—as in Northrop Frye, *Anatomy of Criticism* (Princeton University Press, 1957). My particular concern is with the stories we tell ourselves individually and collectively. In this respect the existing literature is, so far, disappointing.

38. Roland Barthes, *Mythologies* (Paladin, 1973), p. 112.

39. By which I mean 'post-structuralism' in the usual designation. This seems to me a rather misleading tag since it is hard to conceive of late semiology without early, or even of Foucault without Althusser.

40. Tony Bennett, 'James Bond as Popular Hero,' *Oxford Popular Culture Course Unit*, Unit 21, Block 5; 'Text and Social Process: The Case of James Bond,' *Screen Education* No. 41 (Winter/Spring, 1982).

41. 'Fighting Over Peace: Representations of CND in the Media,' CCCS Stencilled Paper, No. 72.

42. This project is not yet completed; provisional title: 'Jingo Bells: The Public and the Private in Christmas Media 1982.'

43. This term has been used to distinguish 'structuralist' and 'post-structuralist' semiologies, with the incorporation of emphases from Lacanian psycho-analysis as an important watershed.

44. The relation of *Screen*'s theory to Brecht and Eisenstein is rather odd. Characteristically, quotations

from Brecht were taken as starting-points for adventures which led to quite other destinations than Brecht's own thinking. See, for example, Colin MacCabe, 'Realism and the Cinema: Notes of Some Brechtian Theses' in Bennett *et al.* (eds.), *Popular Television and Film.*

45. 'The cinematic institution is not just the cinema industry (which works to fill cinemas, not to empty them), it is also the mental machinery—another industry—which spectators "accustomed to the cinema" have internalised historically and which has adapted them to the consumption of films.' C. Metz, 'The Imaginary Signifier,' *Screen*, vol. 16, no. 2 (Summer, 1975), p. 18.

46. What follows owes much to the CCCS *Screen* critique cited above (note 36).

47. There seem to be two rather distinct approaches to reading or 'audiences,' the one an extension of literary concerns, the other more sociological in approach and often growing out of media studies. I find David Morley's work in this area consistently interesting as an attempt to combine some elements from both sets of preoccupations, though I agree with his own assessment that the Centre's early starting-points, especially the notions of 'hegemonic,' 'negotiated' and 'alternative' readings were exceedingly crude. See David Morley, *The Nationwide Audience*; 'The Nationwide Audience: A Postscript,' *Screen Education* No. 39 (Summer, 1981).

48. See the famous analysis in terms of 'scopophilia' in Laura Mulvey, 'Visual Pleasure and Narrative Cinema,' *Screen*, vol. 16, no. 3 (Autumn 1975).

49. Is it significant, for instance, that Barthes does not mention 'internal' narrative in his view of the omnipresence of the narrative form, *Image–Music–Text*, p. 79? Does this absence suggest a larger structuralist difficulty with inner speech?

50. The ideas of the last few paragraphs are still in the process of being worked out in the CCCS Popular Memory Group. For some preliminary considerations about the character of oral-historical texts see Popular Memory Group, 'Popular Memory: Theory, Politics, Method' in CCCS, *Making Histories*. I have found some of the essays in Daniel Bertaux, *Biography and Society: The Life History Approach in the Social Sciences* (Sage, 1981) useful to argue with, especially Agnes Hankiss, 'Ontologies of the Self: on the Mythological Rearranging of One's Life History.'

51. Some of the best and most influential work in cultural studies has been based on personal experience and private memory. Richard Hoggart's *The Uses of Literacy* is the most celebrated example, but, in general, students of culture should have the courage to use their personal experience more, more explicitly and more systematically. In this sense cultural studies is a heightened, differentiated form of everyday activities and living. Collective activities of this kind, attempting to understand not just 'common' experiences but real diversities and antagonisms, are especially important, if they can be managed, and subject to the caveats which follow.

52. This is forcefully argued by Paul Jones in an article in *Thesis Eleven* (Monash University, Australia, 1983).

53. See Dave Morley and Ken Worpole (eds.), *The Republic of Letters: Working Class Writing and Local Publishing* (Comedia, 1982). For a more external and critical view see 'Popular Memory' in *Making Histories*. Also instructive is the debate between Ken Worpole, Stephen Yeo and Gerry White in Raphael Samuel (ed.), *People's History and Socialist Theory* (Routledge and Kegan Paul, 1981).

54. Some CCCS work is not exempt from this difficulty. Some of these criticisms apply, for instance, to *Resistance through Rituals*, especially parts of the theoretical overviews.

55. What follows is based, in rather too composite a way perhaps, on the work of Paul Willis, Angela MacRobbie, Dick Hebdige, Christine Griffin, and Dorothy Hobson and on discussions with other ethnographic researchers in the Centre. See especially, Paul Willis, *Learning to Labour*, Paul Willis, *Profane Culture* (Routledge and Kegan Paul, 1978); Angela MacRobbie, 'Working-Class Girls and Femininity' and Dorothy Hobson, 'Housewives: Isolation as Oppression,' in *Women Take Issue*; Dick Hebdige, *Subculture*; Christine Griffin, CCCS Stencilled Papers, Nos. 69 & 70. For an all-too-rare discussion of method in this area see Paul Willis, 'Notes on Method' in Hall *et al.*, *Culture, Media, Language*.

Fredric Jameson (1934–)

Fredric Jameson received his undergraduate degree from Haveford College and his doctorate from Yale University. He has taught at Yale University, University of California at San Diego and Santa Barbara, and currently teaches at Duke University. Jameson is one of America's strongest Marxist critics, almost paralleling the stature of Raymond Williams in Britain. He has written: *Sartre: The Origins of a Style* (1961), *Marxism and Form: Twentieth Century Dialectical Theories of Literature* (1971), *The Prison-House of Language: A Critical Account of Structuralism and Russian Formalism* (1972), *Fables of Aggression: Wyndham Lewis, The Modernist as Fascist* (1979), *The Political Unconscious: Narrative as a Socially Symbolic Act* (1981), and *Postmodernism, or the Cultural Logic of Late Capitalism* (1989). He has also written numerous essays, famous among them are 'Metacommentary' (1971, winner of the PMLA prize), and his recent 'Third World Literature in the Era of Multinational Capitalism' (1986), created a big *furore* in the post-colonial camp.

The essay re-printed here, 'On Cultural Studies', takes a critical view of the 'production' of this discipline (in projecting a diffuse, amorphous form) by using an American anthology, *Cultural Studies* (eds. Nelson, Grossberg, and Treichler). Pointing to the lack of any clear definition of the subject/discipline as it is presented in this anthology, he faults its practitioners who showcase it simultaneously as multi-disciplinary and politically correct, such that the boundaries between high/low culture, historicized/contemporary readings, and theoretical/empirical methodologies become blurred. Listing the various concepts raised by cultural studies as represented in this text, Jameson takes the example of 'group identity [which] would best open up a space for Cultural Studies . . . in a kind of United Nations plenary session, and was given respectful (and "politically correct") hearing by all the others: [is] neither a stimulating nor a very productive exercise.' However, in the concluding segment of this essay he does propose a revised agenda for cultural studies in specific Marxist terms. He writes:

it is therefore clear that the hermeneutic appropriate for social class also demands to be applied here, in a situation in which stable cultural objects, works, or texts, as dialogically antagonistic moves in the struggle between groups (which very specifically includes the achievement of group consciousness as one of its aims), moves which tend to express themselves affectively in the form of loathing or envy.

G.R.

On 'cultural studies'

The desire called Cultural Studies is perhaps best approached politically and socially, as the project to constitute a 'historic bloc,' rather than theoretically, as the floor plan for a new discipline. The politics in such a project are, to be sure, 'academic' politics, the politics within the university, and, beyond it, in intellectual life in general, or in the space of intellectuals as such. At a time, however, when the Right has begun to develop its own cultural politics, focused on the reconquest of the academic institutions, and in particular of the foundations and the universities themselves, it does not seem wise to go on thinking of academic politics, and the politics of intellectuals, as a particularly 'academic' matter. In any case, the Right seems to have understood that the project and the slogan of Cultural Studies (whatever that may be) constitutes a crucial target in its campaign and virtually a synonym for 'political correctness' (which may in this context be identified simply as the cultural politics of the various 'new social movements': antiracism, antisexism, antihomophobia, and so forth).

But if this is so, and Cultural Studies is to be seen as the expression of a projected alliance between various social groups, then its rigorous formulation as an intellectual or pedagogical enterprise may not be quite so important as some of its adherents feel, when they offer to begin the left sectarian warfare all over again in the struggle for the correct verbal rendering of the cultural studies party line: not the line is important, but the possibility for social alliances that its general slogan seems to reflect. It is a symptom rather than a theory; as such, what would seem most desirable is a cultural-studies analysis of Cultural Studies itself. This also means that what we require (and find) in the recent collection, *Cultural Studies*,[1] edited by Lawrence Grossberg, Cary Nelson, and Paula A. Treichler, is merely a certain comprehensiveness and general representativity (something forty contributors would seem to guarantee in advance), and not the absolute impossibility of the thing being done some other way or staged in a radically different fashion. This is not to say that absences from or gaps in this collection, which essentially reprints the papers delivered at a conference on the subject held in Urbana-Champaign in Spring 1990, are not significant features deserving of comment: but the comment would then take the form of a diagnosis of this particular event and the 'idea' of Cultural Studies it embodies, rather than of a proposal for some more adequate alternative (conference, 'idea,' program, or 'party line'). Indeed, I should probably lay my cards on the table at once and say that, as important (indeed, as theoretically interesting) as I think it is to discuss and debate the matter of Cultural Studies right now, I don't particularly care what ultimate form the program ends up taking, or even whether an official academic discipline of this kind comes into being in the first place. That is probably because I don't much believe in the reform of academic programs to begin with; but also because I suspect that once the right kind of discussion or argument has taken place publicly, the purpose of Cultural Studies will have been achieved anyway, regardless of the departmental framework in which the discussion has been carried out. (And I specifically mean this remark to have to do with what I take to be the most crucial practical issue at stake in the whole matter, namely the protection of the younger people writing articles in this new 'field,' and their possibility of tenure.)

I guess I also have to say, against definitions (Adorno liked to remind us of Nietzsche's dismissal of the attempt to *define* historical phenomena as such), that I think we already know, somehow, what Cultural Studies is; and that 'defining' it means removing what it is not, removing the extraneous clay from the emergent statue, drawing a boundary by instinct and visceral feel, trying to identify what it is not so comprehensively that finally the job is done whether a positive 'definition' ever ends up emerging.

Whatever it may be, it came into the world as the result of dissatisfaction with other disciplines, not merely their contents but also their very limits as such. It is thus in that sense postdisciplinary; but despite that, or perhaps for that very reason, one of the crucial ways in which Cultural Studies continues to define itself turns on its relationship to the established disciplines. It may therefore be appropriate to begin with the complaints from allies in those disciplines about the neglect by an emergent Cultural Studies of aims they consider fundamental; eight further sections will deal with groups; Marxism; the concept of articulation; culture and libido; the role of intellectuals; populism; geopolitics; and, in conclusion, Utopia.

It's not my field!

The historians seem particularly perplexed by the somewhat indeterminable relationship of the cultural people to archival material. Catherine Hall, the author of one of the more substantive pieces in this collection—a study of the ideological mediation of English missionaries in Jamaica—after observing that 'if cultural history isn't a part of cultural studies, then I think there's a serious problem' (272), goes on to say that 'the encounter between mainstream history and cultural studies in Britain has been extremely limited' (271). That could, of course, fully as much be the problem of mainstream history as of Cultural Studies; but Carolyn Steedman goes on to examine the matter more pointedly, suggesting some basic methodological differences. Collective versus individual research is only one of these: 'Group practice is collective; archive research involves the lone historian, taking part in an undemocratic practice. Archive research is expensive, of time and of money, and not something that a group of people can practically do, anyway' (618). But when she tries to formulate the distinctiveness of the Cultural Studies approach in a more positive way, it comes out as 'text based.' The cultural people analyze handy texts, the archival historian has to reconstruct, laboriously, on the basis of symptoms and fragments. Not the least interesting part of Steedman's analysis is her suggestion of an institutional, and more specifically educational, determinant in the emergence of the 'text-based' method: 'Was the "culture concept" as used by historians . . . actually invented in the schools, between about 1955 and 1975? In Britain, we do not even have a social and cultural history of education that allows us to think that this might be a question' (619–620). She does not, however, say in which discipline such a research question might properly belong.

Steedman also suggestively names Burckhardt as a precursor of the new field (no one else does); and she briefly engages with the New Historicism, whose absence from these pages is otherwise very significant indeed (save for a moment in which Peter Stallybrass denies having any kinship with the rival movement). For the New Historicism is surely basic competition, and on any historical view a kindred symptom with Cultural Studies in its attempt to grapple analytically with the world's new textuality (as well as in its vocation to fill the succession to Marxism in a discreet and respectable way). It can of course be argued that Cultural Studies is too busy with the present and that it cannot be expected to do everything or to be concerned with everything; and I suppose there is a residual afterimage here of the more traditional opposition between the contemporary concerns of students of mass or popular culture and the tendentiously backward-gazing perspective of literary critics (even where the canonized works are 'modern' and relatively recent in time). But the most substantial pieces in this collection—besides Catherine Hall's essay, these include Lata Mani's study of widow-burning, Janice Radway's essay on the Book-of-the-Month Club, Peter Stallybrass's investigation of the emergence of Shakespeare as an *auteur*, and Anna Szemere's account of the rhetoric of the 1956 Hungarian uprising—are all historical in the archival sense, and *do* tend to stand out like sore thumbs. They ought to be welcome guests, so why does everyone feel awkward?

Sociology is another allied discipline, so close that translation between it and Cultural Studies seems at best difficult if not altogether impossible (as Kafka once observed about the analogous kinship of German and Yiddish). But did not Raymond Williams suggest in 1981 that 'what is now often called "cultural studies" [is better understood] as a distinctive mode of entry into general sociological questions than . . . a reserved or specialized area' (quoted, page 223)? Still, this cross-disciplinary relationship seems to present analogies with that to history: 'text-based' work over here, professional or professionalized 'research' over there. Simon Frith's complaint is emblematic enough to be quoted in full:

> Now what I've been talking about up to now is an approach to popular music which, in British terms, comes not from cultural studies but from social anthropology and sociology (and I could cite other examples, like Mavis Bayton's [1990] work on how women become rock musicians). One reason I find this work important is because it focuses on an area and issue systematically (and remarkably) neglected by cultural studies: the rationale of cultural production itself, the place and thought of cultural producers. But what interests me here (which is

616

why this paper is now going to be a different narrative altogether) is something else: compared to the flashy, imaginative, impressionistic, unlikely pop writing of a cultural studies academic like, say, Iain Chambers, the dogged ethnographic attention to detail and accuracy is, as Dick Hebdige once remarked of my sociological approach in contrast to Chambers', kind of dull. (178)

Janet Wolff suggests more fundamental reasons for this tension: 'The problem is that mainstream sociology, confidently indifferent if not hostile to developments in theory, is unable to acknowledge the constitutive role of culture and representation *in* social relations' (710). Only it turns out that the feeling is mutual: 'Poststructuralist theory and discourse theory, in demonstrating the discursive nature of the social, operate as license to *deny* the social' (711). Quite properly, she recommends a coordination of both ('an approach which integrates textual analysis with the sociological investigation of institutions of cultural production and of those social and political processes and relations in which this takes place' [713]); but this does not do away with the discomfort still felt in the presence of the beast, any more than Cornel West's suggestion that the main advantage of Cultural Studies is that familiar old thing called 'interdisciplinary' ('cultural studies becomes one of the rubrics used to justify what I think is a highly salutary development, namely interdisciplinary studies in colleges and universities' [698]). This term spans several generations of academic reform programs, whose history needs to be written and then reinscribed in it in some cautionary way (virtually by definition it is always a failure): but one's sense is that the 'interdisciplinary' effort keeps taking place because the specific disciplines all repress crucial but in each case different features of the object of study they ought to be sharing. More than most such reform programs, Cultural Studies seemed to promise to name the absent object, and it does not seem right to settle for the tactical vagueness of the older formula.

Perhaps, indeed, it is *communications* that is the name required: only Communications programs are so recent as to overlap in many ways (including personnel) with the new venture, leaving only communications technology as a distinguishing mark or a feature of disciplinary separation (rather like body and soul, or letter and spirit, machine and ghost). It is only when a specific perspective unifies the various items of study of communications as a field that light begins to be shed, on Cultural Studies as well as on its relations with Communications programs. This is the case, for example, when Jody Berland evokes the distinctiveness of Canadian communication theory as such: nor does this merely amount to some homage to McLuhan and his tradition and precursors, but emerges in a more contemporary form, in her paper, as a whole new theory of the ideology of 'entertainment' as such. But she also makes it clear why Canadian theory is necessarily distinct from what she euphemistically refers to as 'mainstream communications research' (43), by which U.S. communications theory is meant. For it is clearly the situation of Canada in the shadow of the U.S. media empire that gives our neighbors their epistemological privilege, and in particular the unique possibility of combining spatial analysis with the more traditional attention to the media as such:

> The concept of 'cultural technology' helps us to understand this process. As part
> of a spatial production which is both determinant and problematic, shaped by both

617

disciplinary and antidisciplinary practices, cultural technologies encompass simultaneously the articulated discourses of professionalization, territoriality, and diversion. These are the necessary three-dimensional facets of analysis of a popular culture produced in the shadow of American imperialism. In locating their 'audiences' in an increasingly wider and more diverse range of dispositions, locations, and contexts, contemporary cultural technologies contribute to and seek to legitimate their own spatial and discursive expansion. This is another way of saying that the production of texts cannot be conceived outside of the production of spaces. Whether or not one conceives of the expansion of such spaces as a form of colonialism remains to be seen. The question is central, however, to arriving at an understanding of entertainment that locates its practices in spatial terms. (42)

What Berland makes clear is that attention to the situation of theory (or the theorist or the discipline) now necessarily involves a dialectic: 'As the production of meaning is located [by Anglo-American media theory] in the activities and agencies of audiences, *the topography of consumption is increasingly identified as (and thus expanded to stand in for) the map of the social.* This reproduces in theory what is occurring in practice' (42). The dramatic introduction of a geopolitical dimension, the identification of a certain cultural and communicational theory as Canadian, in sharp opposition to a hegemonic Anglo-American perspective (which assumes its own universality, because it originates in the center and need not mark itself nationally), now radically displaces the issues of the conference and their consequences, as we shall see at greater length later on.

On the other hand, it is unclear what kind of relationship to an emergent Cultural Studies is being proposed here. The logic of collective or group fantasy is always allegorical.[2] This one may involve a kind of alliance, as when the labor unions propose working together with this or that black movement; or it may be closer to an international treaty of some kind, like NATO or the new free trade zone. But presumably 'Canadian communication theory' is not intent on submerging its identity altogether in the larger Anglo-American movement; equally clearly, it cannot altogether universalize its own program, and ask for a blanket endorsement by the 'center' of what is necessarily a situated and 'dependent' or 'semi-peripheral' perspective. I suppose that what emerges here is then the sense that at a given point the analysis in question can be transcoded or even translated: that at certain strategic junctures a given analysis can be read, either as an example of the Cultural Studies perspective, or as an exemplification of everything distinctive about Canadian communication theory. Each perspective thus shares a common object (at a specific conjuncture) without losing its own specific difference or originality (how to name or better to describe this overlap would then be a new kind of problem specifically produced by 'Cultural Studies theory').

Nothing better dramatizes this overlap of disciplinary perspectives than the various icons brandished throughout these pages: the name of the late Raymond Williams, for example, is taken in vain by virtually everyone and appealed to for moral support in any number of sins (or virtues).[3] But the text that repeatedly resurfaces as a fetish is very much a book whose multiple generic frameworks illustrate the problem we have been discussing here. I refer to the study of English youth culture by Paul Willis (not present at this conference, incidentally) entitled *Learning to Labor* (1977). This book can be thought of as a classic work in some new sociology of culture; or as a precursor text from the 'original' Birmingham school (of which more below); or yet again as a kind of ethnology, something which now lights up as an axis running from the traditional terrain of anthropology to the new territory claimed by Cultural Studies.

Here, however, what enriches the interdisciplinary 'problematic' is the inescapable sense (it may also be so for the other disciplines, but can there equally well be overlooked) that if Cultural Studies is an emergent paradigm, anthropology itself, far from being a comparatively 'traditional' one, is also in full metamorphosis and convulsive methodological and textual transformation (as the presence of the name of James Clifford on the Cultural Studies roster here suggests). 'Anthropology' now means a new kind of ethnology, a new textual or interpretive anthropology, which—offering some distant family likeness with the New Historicism—emerges fully grown in the work of Clifford and also of George Marcus and Michael Fischer (with the appropriate acknowledgment of the precursive examples of Geertz, Turner, et al.). 'Thick description' is then evoked by Andrew Ross, in his pioneering work on New Age culture: 'the more exhaustive, or deep, "ethnographic" study of cultural communities that has produced one of the most exciting developments in recent cultural studies' (537); while the very rhetoric of thickness, texture, and immanence is justified by a memorable period of John Fiske, which has the additional merit of bringing out some of the practical stakes of the debate (which are far from boiling down to a battle of mere disciplinary claims and counterclaims):

> I would like to start with the concept of 'distance' in cultural theory. Elsewhere I have argued that 'distance' is a key marker of difference between high and low culture, between the meanings, practices, and pleasures characteristic of empowered and disempowered social formations. Cultural distance is a multidimensional concept. In the culture of the socially advantaged and empowered it may take the form of a distance between the art object and reader/spectator: such distance devalues socially and historically specific reading practices in favor of a transcendent appreciation or aesthetic sensibility with claims to universality. It encourages reverence or respect for the text as an art object endowed with authenticity and requiring preservation. 'Distance' may also function to create a difference between the experience of the art work and everyday life. Such 'distance' produces ahistorical meanings of art works and allows the members of its social formation the pleasures of allying themselves with a set of humane values that in the extreme versions of aesthetic theory, are argued to be universal values which transcend their historical conditions. This distance from the historical is also a distance from the bodily sensations, for it is our bodies that finally bind us to our historical and social specificities. As the mundanities of our social conditions are set aside, or distanced, by this view of art, so, too, are the so-called sensuous, cheap, and easy pleasures of the body distanced from the more contemplative, aesthetic pleasures of the mind. And finally this distance takes the form of distance from economic necessity; the separation of the aesthetic from the social is a practice of the elite who can afford to ignore the constraints of material necessity, and who thus construct an aesthetic

619

which not only refuses to assign any value at all to material conditions, but validates only those art forms which transcend them. This critical and aesthetic distance is thus, finally, a marker of distinction between those able to separate their culture from the social and economic conditions of the everyday and those who cannot. (154)

But the contents of the present volume do not particularly bear out Ross's claim, except for his own lucid study of that uniquely ambiguous 'interpretive community' which is the new yuppie culture of the New Age people; whereas Fiske's clarion call does not so much lead us down the road to anthropology as an experimental discipline (and mode of writing), as to a whole new politics of intellectuals as such.

Indeed, Clifford's own paper—a description of his exciting new work on the ethnology of travel and tourism—already implicitly redefines the polemic context by offering a displacement of the traditional ethnographic conception of 'fieldwork': 'ethnography (in the normative practices of twentieth-century anthropology) has privileged relations of dwelling over relations of travel' (99): this squarely redefines the intellectual and the anthropologist-ethnographer-observer as a kind of traveler and a kind of tourist, and it now at once rewrites the terms of this conference, whose attempt to define that thing called Cultural Studies—far from being an academic and a disciplinary issue—in fact turns on the status of the intellectual as such in relationship to the politics of the so-called new social movements or microgroups.

To put it this way is to make clear the discomfort necessarily triggered among many of the other participants by Clifford's 'modest proposal': far from being mere 'tourists' or even travelers, most of them want to be true 'organic intellectuals' at the very least, if not something more (but what would that 'something more' be exactly?). Even the cognate notion of the exile or neo-exile, the diasporic intellectual invoked by Homi Bhabha (whose remarks on the Rushdie affair—'Blasphemy is the migrant's shame at returning home' [62]—struck me as being extraordinarily pertinent and suggestive), proposes an intermittency or alternation of subject and object, of voice and substance, of theorist and 'native,' which secures an equally intermittent badge of group membership for the intellectual that is not available to the white male Clifford (or to the present reviewer either).

Social groups: popular front or united nations?

But the desire called the organic intellectual is omnipresent here, although it is not often expressed as openly as it is by Stuart Hall himself when, in one of the grandest Utopian moments of the conference, he proposes the ideal of 'living with the possibility that there *could* be, sometime, a movement which would be larger than the movement of petit-bourgeois intellectuals' (288). Here is what Hall says about Gramsci in this respect:

> I have to confess that, though I've read many, more elaborated and sophisticated accounts, Gramsci's account still seems to me to come closest to expressing what it

is I think we were trying to do. Admittedly, there's a problem about his phrase 'the production of organic intellectuals.' But there is no doubt in my mind that we were trying to find an institutional practice in cultural studies that might produce an organic intellectual. We didn't know previously what that would mean, in the context of Britain in the 1970s, and we weren't sure we would recognize him or her if we managed to produce it. The problem about the concept of an organic intellectual is that it appears to align intellectuals with an emerging historic movement and we couldn't tell then, and can hardly tell now, where that emerging historical movement was to be found. We were organic intellectuals without any organic point of reference; organic intellectuals with a nostalgia or will or hope (to use Gramsci's phrase from another context) that at some point we would be prepared in intellectual work for that kind of relationship, if such a conjuncture ever appeared. More truthfully, we were prepared to imagine or model or simulate such a relationship in its absence: 'pessimism of the intellect, optimism of the will.' (281)

The Gramscian notion, however, whose double focus structurally includes intellectuals on the one hand and social strata on the other, is most often in the present collection and in the present context not interpreted as a reference to alliance politics, to a historic bloc, to the forging of a heterogeneous set of 'interest groups' into some larger political and social movement, as it was in Gramsci and still seems to be in this formulation by Stuart Hall.

Rather, its reference here seems universally to be that of the 'identity politics' of the new social movements or what Deleuze calls microgroups. Certainly Cultural Studies has widely been felt to be an alliance space of just this kind (if not exactly a movement in the Gramscian sense, unless you understand its academic ambitions— to achieve recognition and institutional sanction, tenure, protection from traditional departments and the New Right—as a politics, indeed, the only politics specific to Cultural Studies as such.)[4] Thus, it welcomes together feminism and black politics, the gay movement, Chicano studies, the burgeoning 'postcolonial' study groups, along with more traditional aficionados of the various popular and mass cultures (they can also, in traditional academia, be counted as a kind of stigmatized and persecuted minority), and the various (mostly foreign) Marxist hangers-on. Of the 41 (published) participants, there is a relatively even gender distribution (24 women, 21 men); there are 25 Americans, 11 British, 4 Australians, 2 Canadians, and one Hungarian and Italian, respectively; there are 31 white people, 6 black people, 2 Chicanos, and 2 Indians (from the subcontinent); and there seem to be at least 5 gay people out of the forty-one. As for the disciplines or departments themselves, they seem to fall out as follows: English takes the lion's share with 11, as might have been predicted; Communications, Sociology, and Art History are distant runners-up with 4 each; there are 3 representatives of Humanities programs; 2 each from Women's Studies; Cultural Studies proper, History of Consciousness, and Radio, Television, and Film; while Religion and Anthropology have one representative each.

But these (admittedly very impressionistic) breakdowns do not reflect the group, subgroup, or subcultural ideological positions very accurately. As opposed to only four 'traditional' feminist papers, for example, there are at least two gay statements. Of the five black statements, one also raises feminist issues (or rather, it would be more accurate to say that Michele Wallace's paper is a statement of a black feminist position as such), while two more raise national questions. One of the two Chicano papers is also a feminist statement. There are ten recognizably mass-cultural or popular-cultural topics which tend to displace emphasis from 'identity' issues to media ones.

I indulge this exercise as much to show what seems to have been omitted from the Cultural Studies problematic as what is included in it. Only three papers seem to me to discuss the issue of group identity in any kind of central way (while Paul Gilroy's attack on the slogan, which he translates as 'ethnic absolutism,' is best examined in another context, below); and of those only Elspeth Probyn's intricately referenced essay makes a stab at a theory of collective identity or at least of collective enunciation, as such: asking us 'to go beyond discrete positions of difference and to refuse the crisis mode of representation . . . to make the sound of our identities count as we work to construct communities of caring' (511). Such sounds seem to be rather wild ones, however, as when we are told 'how images of the self can work successfully to annoy, to enervate discursive fixities and extra-discursive expectations' (506).

But the papers by Kobena Mercer and by Marcos Sanchez-Tranquilino and John Tagg are already en route toward something rather different from classic identity theory. Mercer, indeed, opens a path-breaking exploration into the way in which the sixties image of black militancy was able to serve as a suggestive and a liberating model for the politics of other groups; while Sanchez-Tranquilino displaces the more psychological or philosophical problematic of 'identity' back onto the social matter of nationalism: 'What is at issue in this resurrection of the *pachuco* in the late 1970s is . . . the representation of . . . militancy through the articulation of the *pachuco* into the politics of identity of a *nationalist* movement. The problems here are the problems of all nationalisms . . .' (562)

Maybe so: but the nationalisms—let's better say the separatisms—are not present here: feminist, lesbian, gay separatisms are not represented as such, and if there are still any black separatisms left, they are certainly not here either; of the other ethnic groups, only the Chicanos are here, to represent themselves and perhaps stand in for some of those other movements (but not for the more traditional national *ethnies*, whose problems are interestingly different from these, as witness the debates about Greece as a minor culture[5]); while the 'postcolonials' tirelessly make the point (as in the Homi Bhabha essay already referred to) that the diasporic fact and experience is the very opposite of one of ethnic separatism.

This is to say, then, that this particular space called Cultural Studies is not terribly receptive to unmixed identities as such, but seems on the contrary to welcome the celebration (but also the analysis) of the mixed, per se, of new kinds of structural complexity. Already Bakhtinian tones were invoked to dispel the monologic (and is not cultural separatism the longing for a certain monological discourse?): Clifford wishes 'not to assert a naive democracy of plural authorship, but to loosen at least somewhat the monological control of the executive writer/anthropologist' (100), while Stalleybrass's remarkable piece on the invention of 'Shakespeare' replaces the modern 'single author' with a 'network of collaborative relations,' normally between two or more writers, between writers and acting companies, between acting companies and printers, between compositors and proofreaders, between printers and censors such that there is also no single moment of the 'individual text' (601). The problematic of the *auteur* then reminds us to what degree the narrative notion of a single, albeit collective, agency is still operative in many garden-variety notions of 'identity' (and indeed returns on the last page of this anthology in Angela McRobbie's stirring invocation of the mission of Cultural Studies in the 1990s to act 'as a kind of guide to how people see themselves . . . as active agents whose sense of self is projected onto and expressed in an expansive range of cultural practices' [730]). But that isolationist conception of group identity would at best open up a space for Cultural Studies in which each of the groups said its piece, in a kind of United Nations plenary session, and was given respectful (and 'politically correct') hearing by all the others: neither a stimulating nor a very productive exercise, one would think.

The 'identities' in question in the present volume are, however, mainly dual ones: for them black feminism is the paradigm (but also Chicana feminism, as in Angie Chabram-Dernersesian's lively essay). Indeed, I'm tempted to suggest that Cultural Studies today (or at least that proposed by this particular collection and conference) is very much a matter of dual citizenship, of having at least a dual passport, if not more of them. The really interesting and productive work and thought does not seem to happen without the productive tension of trying to combine, navigate, coordinate several 'identities' at once, and several commitments, several positions: it's like a replay of Sartre's old notion that the writer is better off having to address at least two distinct and unrelated publics at the same time. Once again, it is in Stuart Hall's reflective and wide-ranging remarks (as one of the precursor or founding figures of the older, Birmingham 'Cultural Studies') that the necessity for living with these tensions is affirmed as such (284). To be sure, in this particular passage he means the tension between text and society, between superstructure and base, what he calls the necessary 'displacement' of culture out of the social real into the imaginary. But he had also before that recalled the tensions involved in multiple ideological influences and commitments, to Marxism but also to feminism, to structuralism or the 'linguistic turn,' as so many distinct forces of gravity, which it made up the richness of the school to respond to, rather than to achieve the final synthesis, iron out the contradictions, and flatten these multiple operations out into a single program or formula. The tensions between group identities, one would think, offer a more productive field of force than the interdisciplinary ambivalences discussed earlier, but all this then threatens to be flattened out and defused in a rather different way by the competing disciplinary formula of postmodernism and its version of pluralism, a topic which is here on the whole systematically avoided and eluded, for a reason that now becomes obvious.

Cultural studies as a substitute for Marxism

To stage a frontal assault on postmodernism as such, indeed, and to argue for the philosophical necessity of a Cultural Studies that was something other than a postmodern celebration of the effacement of the boundaries of high and low, the pluralism of the microgroups and the replacement of ideological politics with image and media culture, would require a reassessment of the traditional relationship of the general Cultural Studies movement with Marxism that evidently exceeded the ambitions of the present conference. Marxism is there for the most part evidently understood as yet another kind of group identity (but then of a very tiny group indeed, at least in the U.S.) rather than as the kind of problematic—and problem!—which Stuart Hall evokes ('the questions that Marxism as a theoretical project put on the agenda . . . questions [which] are what one meant by working without shouting distance of Marxism, working on Marxism, working against Marxism, working with it, working to try to develop Marxism' [279]). Yet it would be all the more important to come to grips with these issues, insofar as, in the U.S., Cultural Studies, as Michael Denning has argued for its precursor and competitor American Studies,[6] can equally well be seen to be a 'substitute' for Marxism as a development of it. But not even Raymond Williams's strategic British reformulation of Marxism as 'cultural materialism' receives attention here (nor have the Americans shown much anxiety in general about the problem of avoiding 'idealism'); nor is the political will implicit in the Birmingham group fully as much as in Williams generally in much evidence in these pages, about which it needs to be stressed again and again (for both) that Cultural Studies or 'cultural materialism' was essentially a political project and indeed a Marxist project at that. When foreign theory crosses the Atlantic, it tends to lose much of its contextual political or class overtones (as witness the evaporation of so much of that from French theory). Nowhere is this process more striking, however, as in the current American reinvention of what was in Britain a militant affair and a commitment to radical social change.

The usual American anti-Marxian litanies are, however, in the current volume only occasionally and perfunctorily intoned. A systemic transformation (which they do not, however, want to call 'postmodern' for some reason) is evoked with gusto by Sanchez-Tranquilino and Tagg: 'As long as the Museum could be conceived as an Ideological State Apparatus . . . it was possible to imagine another place, another consciousness . . . Now, with the undermining of these categories and logics, both sides seem to have been flung out or sucked into a gravity-less space. . . . Such forms of sociological explanation have themselves been caught in the internal collapse of the discipline they claim to critique' (556–7).

There is fortunately very little of the silliest of the usual claims, that Marxism is antifeminist or excludes women; but 'high feminism' also seems enveloped in another familiar reproach, namely that Cultural Studies does not do Grand Theory anymore ('in which massive, world-historical problems are debated on such a level of generality that they cannot possibly be solved' [Morris, 466]): a reproach that is specifically directed against Marxism, but seems also to secure the fairly thoroughgoing evacuation of any number of other grand theories and grand names besides feminism, psychoanalysis, Lacanianism, deconstruction, Baudrillard, Lyotard, Derrida, Virilio, Deleuze, Greimas, etc. (with Raymond Williams—but no longer with Gramsci, Brecht, or Benjamin—an exception, and one of the still minimally operative icons of the new movement).

Still, it seems possible that as the noisiest detractors of 'grand theory' are the

Australians, this particular move may owe something to the idiosyncratic and anarchist roots of Australian radicalism. It is, indeed, from Australia that another even more sinister variant of this otherwise harmless anti-intellectualism comes, in Tony Bennett's specifically political and 'activist' critique of Marxism. After hastening to except the 'new social movements' from his own reformist structures on political activity, he describes his position as follows:

> What it *is* to argue against are ways of conducting both of these aspects of political processes [alliances and single-issue politics], and of connecting them to one another, in ways which anticipate—and are envisaged as paving the way for—the production of a unified class, gender, people, or race as a social agent likely to take decisive action in a moment of terminal political fulfillment of a process assigned the task of bringing that agent into being. And it is to do so precisely because of the degree to which such political projects and the constructions which fuel them hinder the development of more specific and immediate forms of political calculation and action likely to improve the social circumstances and possibilities of the constituencies in question. (32)

Laclau/Mouffe versus Gramsci? Versus Lenin? Bennett versus Laclau/Mouffe? The frame of reference is impossible to determine, particularly since no one (on the Left) has ever believed in any 'unified class, gender, people, or race' in the first place (and certainly not Gramsci, who has been summarily sent packing in the preceding pages as being no longer 'of much service politically' [29]). Bennett's is a genuine 'thought of the other,' busy tracking down and denouncing the ideological errors of all these enemies on the Left in the shrillest traditions of Althusserian hectoring. Nor does he seem to realize how obscene American left readers are likely to find his proposals on 'talking to and working with what used to be called the ISAs rather than writing them off from the outset and then, in a self-fulfilling prophecy, criticizing them again when they seem to affirm one's direst functionalist predictions' (32). The invitation to stop mouthing Marxist slogans (grand theory) and to enter the (presumably vaguely social-democratic) government may have some relevance in a small country with socialist traditions, but it is surely misplaced advice here (and in any case quite impossible to fulfill). The tone of this essay, given pride of place for alphabetical reasons at the very opening of the volume, is remarkably misleading as to the spirit of the collection as a whole; what is more distressing is the ignorance it betrays about the structural differences of the various national situations today, one of the strong themes of the present volume and paradoxically one which the Australian contributors themselves play a central role in establishing, as we shall see shortly.

But this particular formulation by Bennett leads on to the fundamental anti-Marxian stereotype, for the passage quoted can readily be translated back into the hoariest of all negative buzzwords, 'totalization'—namely some kind of totalitarian and organic homogenization to which the 'Marxists' are supposed to subject all forms of difference. In Sartre, however, this originally philosophical term simply meant the way in which perceptions, instruments, and raw materials were linked up and set in relationship to each other by the unifying perspective of a project (if you don't have a project or don't want one, it obviously no longer applies). I'm not sure whether this concept projects a model exactly (or is constructed according to the image of one); but I suspect it would not matter much, since conceptions of *relationship*—however they attempt to keep their terms distinct and separate—tend to slip into images of an undifferentiated mass. Witness the fortunes of the at least pop-philosophical concept of the 'organic' which once designated the radical difference in function between the various organs (one of Marx's fundamental figures in the *Grundrisse* was that of 'metabolism'), but now seems to mean turning them all into the same thing. The 'organic' has thus, along with 'linear history' (a construction I believe we owe to McLuhan), become one of the fundamental poststructural indices of error (at least until 'totalization' came along). Of course, one can stop using these words for tactical reasons (and to abridge lexical and philological explanations such as this one); but surely on any dispassionate view the present collection is crammed full of various acts of totalization which it would serve no good purpose to track down and eliminate unless your aim is to return to that kind of simon-pure, solid-color theorization which has, in connection with the politics of an unmixed identity, been argued to be incompatible with the essentially mixed nature of Cultural Studies in the first place.

Articulation: a truck driver's manual

These acts of totalization are, however, camouflaged by a new figure, which—unlike the Sartrean coinage of totalization itself—has a respectable poststructural theoretical correctness about it (and which, like all figures, displaces the terms of the old one just slightly). This is the omnipresent concept of *articulation*, about which we urgently need a lexical entry in some larger ideological dictionary of the objective spirit of the period. Derived, like 'organic,' from the body as a reference, it rather designates the bony parts and the connections of the skeleton, than the soft organic organs (and perhaps the rigor and mechanical quality plays some part in its current favor); but is then quickly transferred to speech, as in a very allegory of the 'linguistic turn' itself. My sense is that we owe its compulsive use to Althusser (whose influence may then have had some effect on Foucault's even more compulsive figures of segmentation and spatial divisibility), with generalization via Ben Brewster's elegant English-language reinvention, and Poulantzas's political extensions, along with Pierre-Philippe Rey's anthropology, thence to Hindess and Hirst, and on into a generalized theoretical lingua franca, shortly to be rejoined by such current favorites as 'to erase,' 'circulation,' 'constructed,' and the like. What is less often remembered is that Althusser actually found this seemingly Althusserian and structuralist-sounding word in Marx himself, and specifically in the great unfinished program essay of August 1857 which was to have served as the introduction to the *Grundrisse*.[7]

Here *Gliederung* designates the articulation of the categories (and realities) of production, distribution, and consumption among each other (in the form it is a suggestive model whose application remains to be explored). Meanwhile, it is important to stress the well-nigh independent and extraordinarily rich development of the concept of articulation by the Birmingham School itself, at a crucial moment in its history when the intersections of race, gender, and class became an urgent theoretical problem. Catherine Hall's formulation is here canonical:

> I don't think that we have, as yet, a theory as to the articulation of race, class, and gender and the ways in which these articulations might generally operate. The terms are often produced as a litany, to prove political correctness, but that does not necessarily mean that the forms of analysis which follow are really shaped by a grasp of the workings of each axis of power in relation to the others. Indeed, it is extremely difficult to do such work because the level of analysis is necessarily extremely complex with many variables in play at any one time. Case studies, therefore, whether historical or contemporary, which carefully trace the contradictory ways in which these articulations take place both in historically specific moments and over time, seem to me to be very important. (270–271)

Perhaps the suggestion of what theory ought to be ('we do not yet have a theory') gives a little too much aid and comfort to those who are allergic to 'grand theorizing,' since one would have thought that the concept of articulation as referenced here is already very precisely a theory in its own right. It implies a kind of turning structure, an ion-exchange between various entities, in which the ideological drives associated with one pass over and interfuse the other—but only provisionally, for a 'historically specific moment,' before entering into new combinations, being systematically worked over into something else, decaying over time in interminable half-life, or being blasted apart by the convulsions of a new social crisis. The articulation is thus a punctual and sometimes even ephemeral totalization, in which the planes of race, gender, class, ethnicity, and sexuality intersect to form an operative structure. Here is a fuller statement by Stuart Hall:

> The unity formed by this combination or articulation, is always, necessarily, a 'complex structure': a structure in which things are related, as much through their differences as through their similarities. This requires that the mechanisms which connect dissimilar features must be shown—since no 'necessary correspondence' or expressive homology can be assumed as given. It also means—since the combination is a structure (an articulated combination) and not a random association—that there will be structured relations between the parts, i.e., relations of dominance and subordination. (579–580)

In reality, a whole poetic is implicit in such analytic terminology, since the very 'representation' of such complexes is always problematic. It is not merely the structure of the complex that is not given in advance (as, for example, whether race or gender happen to come first, which one stands as some provisional ultimately determining instance to the other); it is also the language in which the 'elements' and their connections are to be described which must be invented. Descriptions of articulation are thus also necessarily auto-referential in that they must comment on and validate their own linguistic instruments—only preserving the flimsiest and most tenuous survival of an older figural content (the joints or bones operating together, the mechanical sense of sheer connection as such).

Articulation thus stands as the name of the central theoretical problem or conceptual core of Cultural Studies, exemplified over and over again in this volume where it

627

is less often foregrounded as such. It can be sensed at work in Constance Penley's rather more Freudian (and also Marxian) notion of lack, contradiction, substitution, and compensation-formation, when, in her essay on women's *Star Trek* porn, she places on the agenda

> the fact that the women fans can imagine a sexual relation only if it involves a childless couple made up of two men, who never have to cook or scrub the tub, and who live three hundred years in the future. I would also argue that *Star Trek* fandom in general is an attempt to resolve another lack, that of a social relation. *Trek* fan culture is structured around the same void that structures American culture generally, and its desire too is that fundamental antagonisms, like class and race, not exist. (495)

But here the public/private or social/sexual articulation is grasped as a kind of dualism that folds the description back into more familiar Freudo-Marxisms like that of Deleuze and Guattari in the *Anti-Oedipus*. One can also represent articulation in terms of models and suggestive influences, as in Kobena Mercer's piece on the sixties (already mentioned), in which the black movement and the very ideological and libidinal structure of black militancy is articulated as a 'signifying chain' that can be reproduced in other constituencies. (That it is also a 'reversible connecting factor'— and can be rewired back into original new forms of racism—is another point he makes forcefully, in a timely rebuke to a certain omnipresent Cultural Studies triumphalism.) But articulation also implies and indeed grounds allegory as its fundamental expressive structure: thus Janice Radway reminds us of the way in which mass or popular culture has consistently been fantasized as feminine (513): the rotating allegorical structures of collective fantasy are surely in fact the basic text of any approach to articulation as symptom or as political program. But these dynamics of articulation will not be clarified until we more fully grasp the consequences implicit in seeing culture as the expression of the individual group.

Culture and group libido

For culture—the weaker, more secular version of that thing called religion—is not a 'substance' or a phenomenon in its own right, it is an objective mirage that arises out of the relationship between at least two groups. This is to say that no group 'has' a culture all by itself: culture is the nimbus perceived by one group when it comes into contact with and observes another one. It is the objectification of everything alien and strange about the contact group: in this context, it is of no little interest to observe that one of the first books on the interrelationship of groups (the constitutive role of the boundary, the way each group is defined by and defines the other), draws on Erving Goffman's *Stigma* for an account of how defining marks function for other people:[8] in this sense, then, a 'culture' is the ensemble of stigmata one group bears in the eyes of the other group (and vice versa). But such marks are more often projected into the 'alien mind' in the form of that thought-of-the-other we call belief and elaborate as religion. But belief in this sense is not something we ourselves have, since what we do seems to us natural and does not need the motivation and rationalization of this strange internalized entity; and indeed the anthropologist Rodney Needham has shown that most 'cultures' do not possess the equivalent of our concept, or pseudo-concept, of belief (which is thus unmasked as something the translators illicitly project back into nonimperial, noncosmopolitan languages).

Still, it happens that 'we' also often speak of 'our own' culture, religion, beliefs, or whatever. These may now be identified as the recuperation of the Other's view of us; of that objective mirage whereby the Other has formed a picture of us as 'having' a culture: depending on the power of the Other, this alienated image demands a response, which may be as inconsequential as the denial whereby Americans brush off the stereotypes of the 'ugly American' they encounter abroad, or as thoroughgoing as the various ethnic revivals whereby, as in Hindu nationalism, a people reconstructs those stereotypes and affirms them in a new cultural-nationalist politics: something which is never the 'return' to an older authentic reality but always a new construction (out of what look like older materials).

Culture must thus always be seen as a vehicle or a medium whereby the relationship between groups is transacted. If it is not always vigilantly unmasked as an idea of the Other (even when I reassume it for myself), it perpetuates the optical illusion and the false objectivism of this complex historical relationship (thus the objections that have been made to pseudo-concepts like 'society' are even more valid for this one, whose origin in group struggle can be deciphered). Meanwhile, to insist on this translation-program (the imperative to turn concepts of culture back into forms of the relationship between collective groups) offers a more satisfactory way of fulfilling the objectives of the various forms of a sociological Heisenberg principle than does the current individualistic recommendation to reckon back in the place of the observer. In reality, the anthropologist-other, the individual observer, stands in for a whole social group, and it is in this sense that his knowledge is a form of power, where 'knowledge' designates something individual, and 'power' tries to characterize that mode of relationship between groups for which our vocabulary is so poor.

For the relationship between groups is, so to speak, unnatural: it is the chance external contact between entities which have only an interior (like a monad) and no exterior or external surface, save in this special circumstance in which it is precisely the outer edge of the group that—all the while remaining unrepresentable—brushes against that of the other. Speaking crudely then, we would have to say that the relationship between groups must always be one of struggle or violence: for the only positive or tolerant way for them to coexist is to part from one another and rediscover their isolation and their solitude. Each group is thus the entire world, the collective is the fundamental form of the monad, windowless and unbounded (at least from within).

But this failure or omission of a plausible, let alone a 'natural' set of attitudes whereby group relations might be conducted means that the two fundamental forms of group relationship reduce themselves to the primordial ones of *envy* and *loathing*, respectively. The oscillation back and forth between these poles can at least in part be explained by prestige (to use one of Gramsci's categories): an attempt to appropriate the culture of the other group (which as we have already seen in effect means inventing the 'culture' of the other group) is a tribute and a form of group recognition, the expression of collective envy, the acknowledgment of the prestige of the other group. It seems likely that this prestige is not to be too quickly reduced to matters of power, since very often larger and more powerful groups pay this tribute to the groups they dominate, whose forms of cultural expression they borrow and imitate. Prestige is thus more plausibly an emanation of group solidarity, something a weaker group often needs to develop more desperately than the larger complacent hegemonic one, which nonetheless dimly senses its own inner lack of the same cohesion and unconsciously regrets its tendential dissolution as a group as such. 'Groupie-ism' is another strong expression of this kind of envy, but on an individual basis, as members of the dominant 'culture' opt out and mimic the adherence to the dominated (after all that has been said, it is probably not necessary to add that groupies are thus already in this sense potential or protointellectuals).

As for group loathing, however, it mobilizes the classic syndromes of purity and danger, and acts out a kind of defense of the boundaries of the primary group against this threat perceived to be inherent in the Other's very existence. Modern racism (as opposed, in other words, to postmodern or 'neo' racism) is one of the most elaborated forms of such group loathing—inflected in the direction of a whole political program; it should lead us on to some reflection on the role of the stereotype in all such group or 'cultural' relations, which can virtually by definition not do without the stereotypical. For the group as such is necessarily an imaginary entity, in the sense in which no individual mind is able to intuit it correctly. The group must be abstracted, or fantasized, on the basis of discrete individual contacts and experiences which can never be generalized in anything but abusive fashion. The relations between groups are always stereotypical insofar as they must always involve collective abstractions of the other group, no matter how sanitized, no matter how liberally censored and imbued with respect. What it is politically correct to do under such circumstances is to allow the other group itself to elaborate its own preferential image and then to work with that henceforth 'official' stereotype. But the inevitability of the stereotypical—and the persistence of the possibility of group loathing, racism, caricature, and all the rest it cannot but bring with it—is not thereby laid to rest. Utopia could therefore, under those circumstances, only mean two different kinds of situations which might in fact turn out to be the same: a world in which only individuals confronted one another, in the absence of groups: or a group isolated from the rest of the world in such a way that the matter of the external stereotype (or 'ethnic identity') never arose in the first place. The stereotype is indeed the place of an illicit surplus of meaning, what Barthes called the 'nausea' of mythologies: it is the abstraction by virtue of which my individuality is allegorized and turned into an abusive illustration of something else, something nonconcrete and nonindividual. ('I don't join organizations or adopt labels,' says a character in a recent movie. 'You don't have to,' replies his friend, 'You're a Jew!') But the liberal solution to this dilemma—doing away with the stereotypes or pretending they don't exist—is not possible, although fortunately we carry on as though it were for most of the time.

Groups are thus always conflictual; and this is what has led Donald Horowitz, in the definitive study of international ethnic conflict,[9] to suggest that although what he takes to be Marxism's economic or class account of such conflicts is unsatisfactory,

Marx may have unwittingly anticipated a fundamental feature of modern ethnic theory in his notion of the necessarily dichotomous structure of class conflict as such: ethnic conflicts, indeed, are for Horowitz always tendentially dichotomous, each side ending up incorporating the various smaller satellite ethnic groups in such a way as to symbolically reenact a version of Gramscian hegemony and Gramscian hegemonic or historic blocs as well. But classes in that sense do not precede capitalism and there is no single-shot Marxian theory of 'economic' causality: the economic is most often the forgotten trigger for all kinds of noneconomic developments and the emphasis on it is heuristic and has to do with the structure of the various disciplines (and what they structurally occult or repress), rather than with ontology. What Marxism has to offer ethnic theory is probably, on the contrary, the suggestion that ethnic struggles might well be clarified by an accompanying question about class formation as such.

Fully realized classes, indeed, classes in and for themselves, 'potential' or structural classes that have finally by all kinds of complicated historical and social processes achieved what is often called 'class consciousness,' are clearly also groups in our sense (although groups in our sense are rarely classes as such). Marxism suggests two kinds of things about these peculiar and relatively rare types of groups. The first is that they have much greater possibilities for development than ethnic groups as such: they can potentially expand to become coterminous with society as a whole (and do so, during those unique and punctual events we call revolutions), whereas the groups are necessarily limited by their own specific self-definition and constitutive characteristics. Ethnic conflict can thus develop and expand into class conflict as such, whereas the degeneration of class conflict into ethnic rivalry is a restrictive and centripetal development.

(Indeed, the alternation of envy and loathing constitutes an excellent illustration of the dialectic of class and group in action: whatever group or identity investment may be at work in envy, its libidinal opposite always tends to transcend the dynamics of the group relationship in the direction of that of class proper. Thus, anyone who observed the deployment of group and identity hatred in the recent Republican National Convention—the race and gender hostility so clearly marked in the speeches and the faces of characteristic 'cultural counterrevolutionaries' like Pat Buchanan—understood at once that it was fundamentally class hostility and class struggle that was the deeper stake in such passions and their symbolisms. By the same token, the observers who felt that symbolism and responded to the Republican Right in kind can also be said to have had their smaller group-and-identity consciousness 'raised' in the direction of the ultimate horizon of social class.)

The second point follows from this one, namely that it is only after the modulation of the ethnic into the class category that a possible resolution of such struggles is to be found. For in general ethnic conflict cannot be solved or resolved; it can only be sublimated into a struggle of a different kind that *can* be resolved. Class struggle, which has as its aim and outcome, not the triumph of one class over another but the abolition of the very category of class, offers the prototype of one such sublimation. The market and consumption—that is to say, what is euphemistically called modernization, the transformation of the members of various groups into the universal consumer—is another kind of sublimation, which has come to look equally as universal as the classless one, but which perhaps owes its success predominantly to the

631

specific circumstances of the postfeudal North American commonwealth, and the possibilities of social leveling that arose with the development of the mass media. This is the sense in which 'American democracy' has seemed able to preempt class dynamics and to offer a unique solution to the matter of group dynamics discussed above. We therefore need to take into account the possibility that the various politics of Difference—the differences inherent in the various politics of 'group identity'— have been made possible only by the tendential leveling of social Identity generated by consumer society; and to entertain the hypothesis that a cultural politics of difference becomes itself feasible only when the great and forbidding categories of classical Otherness have been substantially weakened by 'modernization' (so that current neo-ethnicities may be distinct from the classical kind as neoracism is from classical racism).[10]

But this does not spell a waning of group antagonisms but precisely the opposite (as can be judged from the current world scene), and it is also to be expected that Cultural Studies itself—as a space in which the new group dynamics develop—will also entail its quotient of the libidinal. The energy exchanges or ion formations of 'articulation' are not, indeed, likely to take place neutrally, but to release violent waves of affect—narcissistic wounds, feelings of envy and inferiority, the intermittent repugnance for the others' groups. And in fact this is precisely what we observe to be at work in some of the most remarkable papers in the present collection.

Thus, in one of its most dramatic moments, Douglas Crimp traces a liberal-tolerant practice of AIDS cultural politics through to the point at which it becomes clear that the photographic and video documentation in question, ostensibly intended to inspire pity and sympathy for what are always called the 'victims,' in reality constitute '*phobic* images, images of the terror at imagining the person with AIDS as still sexual' (130). This liberalism, then, comes with a price, namely the possibility for the liberal middle-class sympathizer to omit an imagination of the sick person as a sexual being; the implication is that a liberal tolerance for gays and lesbians generally requires this more fundamental imaginative repression of awareness of sexuality as such. Here the sexual or gender plane lends a powerful anticathexis or loathing to the social one, and enables a development of mass reaction and hatred that can be mobilized well beyond this particular target group and made available for alliance politics of a different and more alarming type.

For loathing and envy are very precisely the affective expressions of the relations of groups to one another, as has been argued above: insofar as the object of Cultural Studies can be defined as the cultural expression of the various relationships groups entertain with each other (sometimes on a global scale, sometimes within a single individual), the semiotics of disgust and of group envy ought to play a larger part here than it does. In that respect, the central exhibit is a remarkable article by Laura Kipnis, whose title '(Male) Desire and (Female) Disgust: Reading *Hustler*,' does not make it clear enough that one of its central theses has to do with the way in which— following the spirit of Bourdieu's *Distinction*—class consciousness here borrows the trappings of physical repugnance:

the transcoding between the body and the social sets up the mechanisms through which the body is a privileged political trope of lower social classes, and through which bodily grossness operates as a critique of dominant ideology. The power of grossness is predicated on its opposition from *and to* high discourses, themselves prophylactic against the debasement of the low . . . (376)

But Kipnis goes even further than this (and than Bourdieu himself) in the way in which, as is appropriate in dealing with a class consciousness that is by definition a relationship and a form of struggle, she takes on the intricate matter of the 'subject positions' involved in this act of cultural aggression (in which, at least for openers, women are allegorized as gentility and high culture and men, by way of what Jeffrey Klein calls 'a blue-collar urge' [391], as lower class):

> . . . there is the further discomfort at being addressed as a subject of repression— as a subject with a history—and the rejection of porn can be seen as a defense erected against representations which mean to unsettle her in her subjectivity. In other words, there is a violation of the *idea* of the 'naturalness' of female sexuality and subjectivity, which is exacerbated by the social fact that not all women *do* experience male pornography in the same way. (380)

But this analysis of intercollective subjectivities and subject positions leads us virtually to the borderlines of a whole new field, which is no longer either anthropology or sociology in the traditional sense, but which certainly restores to culture its hidden inner meaning as the space of the symbolic moves of groups in agonistic relation to each other. One other essay, bell hooks's 'Representing Whiteness in the Black Imagination,' occupies this area as its own; its account of the visceral fear of white people in the black imagination has something of the vividness of a work of art in its own right (not necessarily the highest compliment in the present context, I realize).

Yet such a new field is neither so accessible nor so easy of realization as I may have unwittingly suggested: there are barriers, and they are not automatically overcome even by the least self-indulgent introspection or the most controlled autobiographical exploration. To see what these are we need to return to Marxism again (indeed, the preceding section constituted a description of the forms taken by totalization in Cultural Studies). What has not yet been said is the role played by social class in Cultural Studies as currently constituted, which may not be an altogether obvious one, although it has been hinted at in passing.

Free-floating intellectuals

Class here essentially takes two forms, in addition to the shifting and aleatory participation of a class 'factor' in the various cultural constellations in question (as when class reappears in Kipnis's analysis of a pornographic cultural object, or is fantasized according to a gender allegory). The first form in which class reappears here, charged with an anxiety that is omnipresent in these pages, is through the inconspicuous backdoor of the role of the intellectual as such. Simon Frith designates it with some uncharitable bluntness when he says, 'from my sociological perspective, popular

·music is a solution, a ritualized resistance, not to the problems of being young and poor and proletarian but to the problems of being an intellectual' (179). Nor is the professional reference to a 'sociological perspective' an idle one, for it conveys a very different conception of the relationship of the intellectual to society than anything Cultural Studies could envisage (when indeed it is willing to conceptualize this embarrassing question), namely, what I am tempted to call 'the tragic sense of life' of the great sociologists, from Weber and Veblen to Bourdieu—that glacial disengagement from social phenomena as such which is the very condition of the sociologist's disabused knowledge and which excludes any activist participation in the social—indeed any political commitment in the usual sense—on pain of losing the very insights, the very power of demystification, paid for by just this epistemological separation from the human.

This is, I believe, a 'bourgeois' (or pre-Marxist) view of the matter, but it expresses the conviction of a very real truth, which is none other than the 'Heisenberg principle' of the status of the intellectual as observer, the sense that it is precisely that status—itself a social reality and a social fact—that intervenes between the object of knowledge and the act of knowing. Such sociology is in any case constituted by a passion for seeing through the ideologies and the alibis which accompany the class and group struggles of the social and entangle those in ever higher levels of cultural complexity; if now we become aware that such lucidity as to the real mechanisms of social relationship demands the price of a single white lie, a strategic blind spot in the area of the intellectual, the occupation of everything that is social about our own observer's viewpoint itself, the renunciation of social commitment, the attempt to surrender social knowledge from action in the world, indeed the very pessimism about the possibility of action in the world in the first place, will come to seem an act of atonement for this particular (structural) original sin. For the intellectual is necessarily and constitutively at a distance, not merely from her or his own class or origin, but also from the class of chosen affiliation; even more relevant in the present context, she is also necessarily at a distance from the social groups as well; and the ontological security of the militants of the new social movements is deceptive, who were able to feel that because they were women, blacks, or ethnics, as intellectuals they counted as members of those 'peoples' and no longer had to face the dilemmas of the classic intellectual with his Hegelian 'unhappy consciousness'. But we now know this is impossible, particularly since the question of the intellectual has been rewritten in the new paradigm as the problem of representation as such, about which there is some agreement that it is neither possible nor desirable. On the older paradigm, however, the intellectual was most lucidly conceived of as what Sartre called an 'objective traitor,' an impersonal and unintentional Stalinist crime for which no solution can be found, but only expiation or bad faith. Where Sartre was always closest to Marxism was in this conviction that when you cannot resolve a contradiction, it is best and most authentic to hold onto it in wrenching self-consciousness; or at least, that is preferable, as anything else always is, to repression and the artificial working up of this or that form of good conscience. This is not inconsistent with a Utopian position, in which, with Stuart Hall, we can try to act as though the group whose 'organic intellectual' we try to be already existed; or, remembering that other remark of Gramsci that 'everyone is an intellectual,' we can also suffer the class and blood guilt of the contemporary intellectual situation, in the hopes of some future abolition of classes altogether, and thus, with them, of everything now conflicted about the smaller groups now buffeted by the force field of class struggle.

In the light of this dilemma, Foucault's ad hoc invention of the category he calls 'the specific intellectual' seems trivial; while beyond it, the old Maoist solution itself seems a tragic impossibility, in which by going back to the factory or the field the intellectual is promised some reimmersion in the group which will cleanse him of that particular original sin which is the crime of being an intellectual. But this is also called populism, and it remains very much alive, not least in these pages. The negative symptom of populism is very precisely the hatred and loathing of intellectuals as such (or, today, of the academy that has seemed to become synonymous with them).[11] It is a contradictory symbolic process not unlike Jewish anti-Semitism, since populism is itself very precisely an ideology of intellectuals (the 'people' are not 'populist'), and represents a desperate attempt on their part to repress their condition and to deny and negate its facts of life. In the Cultural Studies area, it is of course the name of John Fiske that has primarily been associated with a certain populist stance toward culture:

> Politics have never been far below the surface in my attempt to think critically about the relationships between dominant and subordinated habituses in cultural theory. I hope we can narrow the gap and increase the travel between them because by doing so I believe we can help change the relationship between the academy and other social formations, in particular those of the subordinate. Many of those living within such subordinated formations find little pertinence between the conditions of their everyday lives and academic ways of explaining the world. It is in none of our interests to allow this gap to grow any wider, particularly when we consider that many of the most effective recent movements for social change have involved allegiances between universities and members of repressed or subordinated social formations. (164)

Here and throughout a few hardy souls dare to express the opinion that academics are also people; but no one seems particularly enthusiastic about the prospect of undertaking an ethnology of *their* culture, fearing perhaps rightly the anxieties and the dreariness of such self-knowledge, which Pierre Bourdieu has unremittingly pursued in France (but after all there is a way in which populism and anti-intellectualism are a specifically—one even wants to say an exceptionally—American matter). The primary reproach to Fiske's work lies elsewhere, and seems to turn very precisely on the ambiguity of culture or the superstructure about which Stuart Hall warned, on its tendency, as an object, to displace itself away from the social, to reaffirm its semi-autonomy, 'to instantiate a necessary delay . . . something decentered about the medium of culture . . . which always escapes and evades the attempt to link it, directly and immediately, with other structures' (284). Fiske's work builds on this very gap, affirming the presence of economic oppression and social exploitation, at the same time that it reads culture as a set of 'resources to fight against those constraints' (157). The fear is not only that, as with Marx's supposedly infamous view of religion,[12] that fight may be only an imaginary one; it is even more the suspicion that it is the intellectual himself who may here be using the celebration of mass culture as a ritual to conjure his particular structural 'distance' and to participate, like Edward Curtis, in the dances and solidarity of the ethnic tribe itself. (Interestingly, one of the really interesting 'textual' studies in this collection, William Warner's paper on *Rambo*, affirms the operativity of pain in this mass-cultural text, as a way in which the American public assuages its guilt at the loss of the war by way of images of the physical suffering of its hero; in general, a little more attention to the 'negative emotions,' in popular culture as well as in its analysis, would have enhanced the credibility of this volume.)

But it is Michele Wallace who raises these issues most sharply in her exploration of the ironies of representation in the micropolitics of Cultural Studies: after repudiating the claims of others to 'represent' black feminism, and after describing the tensions within it between subversion and institutionalization (or commercial stardom, as in the actors of *The Color Purple*), she goes on to problematize the thing itself, following Gayatri Spivak's famous query, 'Can the subaltern speak?':

> What I am calling into question is the idea that black feminism (or any program) should assume, uncritically, its ability to speak *for* black women, most of whom are poor and 'silenced' by inadequate education, health care, housing, and lack of public access. Not because I think that black feminism should have nothing to do with representing the black woman who cannot speak for herself but because the problem of silence, and the shortcomings inherent in any representation of the silenced, need to be acknowledged as a central problematic in an oppositional black feminist process. (663)

This modesty, along with Cornel West's forthright call to the participants to recognize and acknowledge themselves as *American* intellectuals (and to take up the burden of American cultural history, which, along with 'American Studies,' is also strangely absent here), may offer the most satisfactory way of working through or working out the dilemma of the cultural intellectual.

It is, however, not the only one, and surely the most innovative treatment of the intellectual in this conference lies in the new model of the intellectual as 'fan': 'Some of the most exciting work being done in Cultural Studies, as you know, is ethnographic, and positions the critic in some respects as a "fan" ' (Ross 553). It is at least a somewhat more attractive image and role than that of the 'groupie' of sixties vintage, and implies the transformation of group or ethnic identity (to which the 'groupie' was attracted as a moth to the flame) into practices and performances which one could appreciate like a not unparticipatory spectator. This surely reflects the properly postmodern transformation of ethnicity into neo-ethnicity, as the isolation and oppression of groups is lifted up (in a properly Hegelian *Aufhebung*, which preserves and cancels that at one and the same time) into media acknowledgment and the new reunification by the image. But it is not an unproblematical solution either: for the new fan is something like a fan of fans, and both Constance Penley, in her account of *Star Trek* culture, and Janice Radway (in her classic book on the romance) are careful to document the distance that has to be overcome between the 'real' fans and their academic ethnographer. Simon Frith goes even further than this: 'if, as is variously suggested in this book, fans are "popular" (or organic) intellectuals, then they may well have the same anxieties about being fans (and take comfort from the

636

same myths) as the rest of us' (182). This is to underscore a peculiarly Derridean turn in the transformation of the 'people' into 'fans': where the first of these was a primary substance, calmly persisting in its essence, and exercising a powerful gravitational effect on the insubstantial intellectuals who fluttered near it, the new version opens up a hall of mirrors in which the 'people' itself longs to be a 'people' and be 'popular,' feels its own ontological lack, longs for its own impossible stability, and narcissistically attempts, in a variety of rituals, to recuperate a being that never existed in the first place. That would, to be sure, lead us on to a more psychoanalytic view of groups and ethnic conflict (perhaps along the lines proposed by Slavoj Žižek); but it would also considerably dampen the enthusiasm of populist intellectuals for a collective condition not much better than their own.

All of which supposes that the 'people' in question still somehow refers to that television-watching, beer-drinking population of middle-to-lower-class jobholders (or unemployed) who, black or white, male or female, are generally fantasized to constitute some larger fundamentally ethnic social reality. But what if it were otherwise? Indeed, Meaghan Morris remarks ominously, 'this process does not extend to involvement with the one figure who in fact remains . . . quite unredeemably "other"—the bureaucrat' (465). Andrew Ross, meanwhile, seems at various moments in his contribution to realize that what is more ambiguous, for a Cultural Studies public, about his own object of study ('New Age technoculture') is that the New Age people may not really any longer be 'popular' in this populist sense, but rather, far more fatefully, *middlebrow*. (Indeed, the originality and importance of Janice Radway's work-in-progress, on the Book-of-the-Month Club, lies in its promise to show the very construction of the middlebrow as such, and the social and political function of that construction as a kind of repression or displacement of the popular). Finally, in one of the truly chilling and comical moments in this conference, Ian Hunter describes just this ultimate First Contact with the bureaucratic Other:

> The problem with aesthetic critique—and with cultural studies to the degree that it is still caught in its slipstream—is that it presumes to comprehend and judge these other cultural regions from a single metropolitan point, typically the university arts faculty. To travel to these other regions though—to law offices, media institutions, government bureaus, corporations, advertising agencies—is to make a sobering discovery: They are already replete with their own intellectuals. And they just look up and say, 'Well, what exactly is it that you can do for us?' (372)

Populism as doxa

One cannot, however, leave the matter of populism without a final, more general complaint, which touches on a few of the theoretical and verbal rituals of this ideology. Raymond Williams's *Keywords* being so crucial a reference throughout, it might be desirable to think of a companion volume, to be called *Buzzwords* (and which one imagines looking, for our era, something like Flaubert's twin *Dictionary of Received*

637

Ideas and *sottisier* of commonplaces). Failing that, one might propose as a form of philosophical hygiene that for ten years or so we simply stop using the two words, *power* and the *body*. Nothing is more disembodied than such references to the body, except where, as in Laura Kipnis's article on *Hustler* already referred to, or in Douglas Crimp's, it generates some real visceral effects; materialism is scarcely achieved by the corporeal litany, which seems if anything to be a sop thrown to the (admittedly) materialist culture of the masses under Bourdieu's watchful eye. The materialism of the body is the eighteenth-century mechanical materialism and is fashioned on the medical model (whence the role of Foucault in both these obsessional conducts); it should not be confused with a historical materialism that turns on *praxis* and on the mode of production.

But in a more general way, we must be very suspicious of the reference to the body as an appeal to immediacy (the warning goes back to the very first chapter of Hegel's *Phenomenology*); even Foucault's medical and penal work can be read as an account of the construction of the body which rebukes premature immediacy. In any case, structuralism and psychoanalysis both work energetically at the demystification of the illusions of bodily intimacy most strongly suggested by 'desire'; the theme of torture does not refute this but rather confirms it by making the worldless individual bodily experience the most isolated of all and the most difficult of access. But the fascination today with pornography, torture, and violence is the sign of the loss of that immediacy and the longing for the impossible physically concrete, rather than the proof by the Zeitgeist that it lies all around us ready to hand: in fact what lies all around us are rather images and information stereotypes of the body, which are themselves the most powerful source of interference when it comes to a full phenomenological approach to the body itself. This last is therefore a theme that is always to be historically problematized, and never taken as an interpretive code in its own right, at least not for us, here and now.

As for *power*, about which it is frequently suggested in these pages that it is what Cultural Studies is all about ('share a commitment to examining cultural practices from the point of view of their intrication with, and within, relations of power' [Bennett 23]), it is an even more dangerous and intoxicating slogan for intellectuals, who thereby feel themselves closer to its 'reality' than they may actually be. My sense is that interpretations in terms of power must come as punctual demystifications, de-idealizations, and involve thereby a certain shock, a painful rebuke to our own habits of idealization in the first place. Certainly the realm of culture is a privileged space for such shock effects, for given the amphibiousness of the superstructures (and that tendency to be displaced away from their context of which Stuart Hall spoke), the revelation, at this or that historical point, that culture is socially functional, that it stands in thrall and service to the institutions, and that its veneer of the aesthetic or of leisure time, the restorative or even the Utopian, is false and a lure—this kind of timely reminder can only be a healthy one, particularly for cultural intellectuals. But if everything is power, then we neither require that reminder, nor can it retain any of its demystificatory force (which also had the benefit of calling us into question as intellectuals in the process). In that case 'power' is as satisfactory an explanation as the 'vertu dormitive' of opium; if it is everywhere, then there is not much point talking about it (Foucault could do so only because as a historian he sought to trace out the *emergence* of a new scheme of modern power). What is indeed the advantage in stigmatizing the power of that corporate bureaucrat who made his unexpected appearance in these pages a moment ago? Wouldn't it be more useful to look at the structure of the multi-national corporations themselves, with a view toward determining the mode of influence and production of a properly corporate culture? But there is a confusion when the individual experience of domination, in acts of racism or *machismo*, authoritarianism, sadism, conscious or unconscious personal brutality, is transferred to social phenomena which are a good deal more advanced and complicated than that: Konrad and Szelenyi indeed pointed out some time ago that the realm of experience of capitalist cultural production is a relatively old-fashioned or underdeveloped, retrogressive enclave within late capitalism.[13] It hearkens back to the entrepreneurial moment, elsewhere in corporate society long since vanished and present only as nostalgia (the yuppie rhetoric of the market is thus a cultural symptom which demands textual analysis in its own right). It is therefore not surprising that a kind of feudal picture of personal domination and subordination is sometimes carried over into the faceless corporate universe; but in that case it is a text to be analyzed, rather than an interpretive code still useful in the deciphering of other contemporary social texts (forms of personal or symbolic brutality, however, probably tending to reflect an absence of power in the social sense, rather than its acting out).

But by way of this anachronism, a whole liberal political theory and ideology then pours into Cultural Studies (and other disciplines); for the rhetoric of 'power' carries a good deal more in its baggage—a repudiation of economic analysis, for example, a kind of forthright anarchistic stance on the thing itself, the unholy marriage between the heroism of dissidence and the 'realism' of 'talking to the institutions.' The problematic of power, as systematically reintroduced by Weber and then much later by Foucault, is an anti-Marxist move, designed to replace analysis in terms of the mode of production. That opens up new fields and generates rich and fascinating new material; but users should be aware of its secondary ideological consequences; and intellectuals should above all be wary of the narcissistic intoxications of its knee-jerk invocation.

The geopolitical imperative

This is then the moment, not merely to say what ought to be done in the void left by these two buzzwords, and in the ideological loose ends at which the critique of populism may well leave us, but also to show how in fact many of the papers in this collection are already moving in just that direction.

This is the fundamentally spatial dimension of Cultural Studies (already underscored by Jody Berland), which can at first be sensed in the discomfort with American parochialism and exceptionalism tactfully voiced by some of the foreigners. Thus Stuart Hall, who pronounces himself 'dumbfounded': 'the enormous explosion of cultural studies in the U.S., its rapid professionalization and institutionalization, is not a moment which any of us who tried to set up a marginalized Centre in a university like Birmingham could, in any simple way, regret. And yet I have to say, in the strongest sense, that it reminds me of the ways in which, in Britain, we are always aware of institutionalization as a moment of profound danger' (285). And we have already seen some of the Australians reflecting on the different meaning and significance of cultural institutions in the U.S. (which unlike their own are mostly private), without necessarily drawing differential consequences (but see also Graeme Turner on Australian and Canadian differences [644–645]). To talk about it this way seems to introduce the theme of the nation as such (which indeed becomes a significant preoccupation here); but that may be too restricted and misleading.

It is rather a specific global constriction that Meagham Morris has in mind in a splendid and illuminating outburst:

> This exchange makes me realize that I haven't been explicit enough about why 'Eurocentrism' should worry me at a rudimentary level at a conference like this. It's a restlessness I have, rather than a position I can expound, and maybe it came through in my speech rather than in the text of my paper. I'm restless about the map of cultural studies being constructed at this conference, about what's not *on* that map, rather than what is. We've talked about local and global relations in a world where Japan, South Korea, Hong Kong, Taiwan, Singapore, or Indonesia simply don't exist, certainly not as *forces* in emergent structures of world power. The one time I heard somebody mention the Pacific Rim, it turned out to be a way of talking about relations between North and Central and South America— another way of staying on the American land mass, not a way of crossing the ocean. I'm not making a plea for inclusiveness, it's just that certain globalizing structures have potential, if 'only' on the economic level, to affect people's lives everywhere in the future, and they aren't 'centered' now in quite the same old *doubled* way (UK/USA, or USA/USSR), that traditional critiques of Eurocentrism sometimes Eurocentrically assume. To ignore this seems to me to be a political error. (476)

There is much to be said about this moment, in some ways one of the climaxes of the conference. One might remark that 'Eurocentrism' does not quite seem the word anymore, for what is surely an American parochialism: even if informed by European canonical perspectives (and very much imbued with the return of the repressed of a scarcely unconscious Anglophilia—after the Francophilia of the preceding moment of high theory), these are now the perspectives of an American NATO view of the world for which the old Europe is not much more significant for us than Birmingham for the new U.S. Cultural Studies. Europe and Britain are surely live-wire issues for the Australians, and even the Canadians here, more than they are for the Americans; and perhaps this is a deeper undertone and implication of Meaghan Morris's reproach, that we are not sufficiently worried about our European and Oedipal link, we are too complacent about it. But in the same sense the new Pacific Rim culture she celebrates here may be a different kind of liberation for Australia than for Americans intent on at least sharing it with the Japanese. And she dismisses Latin America, an oversight remedied by Donna Haraway, whose picture of an analogous Pacific culture it is instructive to juxtapose at this point:

I grew up in a town in Colorado where I thought the Atlantic Ocean began some-where in Kansas and that anything that happened East of Kansas City counted as the East Coast. And I know Cornel grew up in California, but I think maybe you've been in the East too long. Paul's Atlanticist reformulation of African herit-age, African culture, and African-Americans reformulated a lot of issues for me. But it's a California statement I want to make. It has to do with seeing the world in relationship to Latin America, Central America, Mexico, living in conquest terri-tory so that it almost seems like Quebec is part of California rather than part of the world you're talking about. It's the sense of the Pacific. I think of Bernice Johnson Reagon's speech on coalition politics which took place at a West Coast women's music festival and is an absolutely canonical text in U.S. feminism and in the con-structions of the category, 'women of color,' but also of a feminist cultural politics and a vision of a new world cultural politics. None of this is caught by the ten-dency to build the world as black/white and America/Britain, with a little bit of Australia and Canada thrown in. This particular global mapping leaves out these really crucial questions. (703)

All of which may seem to confirm the Clifford view of Cultural Studies as a model based on travel and tourism: but this would be to neglect deeper and more interesting tensions, those for example expressed in a sharp exchange between Morris and Paul Gilroy, whose remarkable proposal to acknowledge and reconstruct a properly black Atlantic culture seems on first glance to present some symmetrical analogies to the Pacific Rim vision. But Gilroy has a somewhat different agenda: 'The specificity of the black Atlantic can be defined on one level through this desire to transcend both the structures of the nation-state and the constraints of ethnicity and national partic-ularity' (194–5; we have already seen that Gilroy's is an explicit repudiation of the 'politics of identity' or of cultural separatism). But Gilroy can (and must) resist the divisive pull of a celebration of British or U.S. cultural exceptionalism (even when that is staged in terms of the exceptionalism of Black-British or African-American culture): the great floating decentered archipelago of the Caribbean is there to authorize such resistance. Perhaps, however, the Australians and the Canadians can-not so easily jettison the determinant problem and category of the nation, as Jody Berland thinks: 'The reason I refused the idea of identity in terms of a historical tra-dition in the struggle around communications was that, in Canada, it's both impossible and compulsory to talk about the problem of identity. It's a complete double-bind: one has to talk about it constantly because it's a problem, but you can't talk about it because as soon as you start you're in danger of imposing a singular def-inition on something which isn't singular at all' (52).

The discomfort seems to have to do in part with the words 'nation' and 'national,' which evidently still vehiculate the baggage of the older autonomous nation-state and give rise to the apprehension that one is still talking about the national culture, the national *topoi* (as Morris calls them in her interesting sketch of the Australian version of these), the national allegories, in a kind of separatist or cultural-nationalist way. For that structural allergy of Cultural Studies to the 'unmixed' which I mentioned above, this is clearly decisive, and it plays a greater role in Gilroy's reaction than in Morris's remarks. But it should be added that autonomy is the great political question of the postmodern age: communism itself foundered on the impossibility of autarchy (even of socialism in several countries) in the multinational era. We should thus see nationalism, not as the vice and the toxic symptom of the immediate post-World War II era, but rather as itself a kind of nostalgia for a social autonomy no longer available for anyone; while 'nation' today ought to be used as the word for a term within a system, a term which ought now always to imply relationality (of a more than binary type). Indeed, it is the need for some new relational discourse on these global and spatial matters which makes itself felt through such uneasy debates.[14] The new requirement is not—as with the multiple subject-positions and, as it were the internal structural problems of cultural identity—a matter of articulation, so much as it is one of the superposition of incommensurable dimensions: Morris quite rightly asks us 'to think of cultural studies as a discipline capable of thinking the relations between local, regional, national, and international frames of action and experience' (470): but the word 'representation' might be even more suggestively substituted for the notion of merely 'thinking' those relations. It is then curious that she should so insistently refuse the model offered by David Harvey in his splendid *Condition of Postmodernity*: it need not be the final word on anything, to be sure, but it is one way of mapping the new global system from which we can begin (indeed, she says herself that her alternate models 'use similar economic arguments to Harvey's' [474]), but maybe the Marxism is just a bit too much; and perhaps it is Eurocentric as well? (Indeed, in one remarkable moment [455] she seems to be attributing the seemingly feudal battle cry 'For England and Marxism!' to Terry Eagleton, something the Irish comrades need never hear about.) Still, hers is far and away the richest and most stimulating discussion both of a national cultural self-representation and of the urgent international dimensions still missing from Cultural Studies: it is embarrassing that none of the Americans think any of these thoughts (which Clifford, to be sure, echoes in a more reflective/contemplative way).

Conclusions and Utopia

It is time to sum up the lessons of this book (the lessons I have learned from this book): something best done in the form of future tasks, of an agenda, although not necessarily an agenda for 'Cultural Studies' in the narrower institutionalized or would-be disciplinary sense we have also seen emerging from this collection. That agenda would include groups, articulation, and space; and it would also open a new entry (so far mostly blank) for commodification and consumption. The phenomenon of group struggle—in bell hooks and in Mercer, for example—reminds us that, no less than for class, cultural texts, when properly decoded, can always be expected to constitute so many messages in this symbolic process, and to stand as so many distinct strategic or tactical moves in what is an enormous agon. It is therefore clear that the hermeneutic appropriate to social class also demands to be applied here, in a situation in which stable cultural objects, works, or texts, are to be rewritten as dialogically antagonistic moves in struggle between groups (which very specifically includes the achievement of group consciousness as one of its aims), moves which tend to express themselves affectively in the form of loathing or envy.

This methodology no longer seems quite so useful when, as in so many of the contributions here, the phenomenon of group relationship is interiorized and becomes a matter for mixed feelings, multiple subject positions, productive schizophrenia, or unhappy co-consciousness: it being understood that all these things can characterize the collective condition of a group as well. Here, then, the model of articulation seems again to reimpose itself, and we pass from the dialectical (in the case of inter-group struggle) to the structural, in this particular field which is that of group interrelationship, intra-group phenomena, or the construction of larger molar group units. The poetics of this moment also seems relatively distinct from that of the first one, where a text could be translated into a symbolic and strategic value which it possessed simultaneously with its surface value or organization. Here translation takes the form of transcoding, or synonymity within a given term: for it is the possibility of any given term to bear several distinct meanings at the same time that allows the sharing of a text between several distinct codes (and the groups whose language they constitute). Here group connection is enabled by the transfer of a crucial seme or atom, which binds the codes together momentarily by way of its own polysemousness.

But these first two zones of meaning and analysis are still safely contained within 'Cultural Studies,' now understood as some vast Popular Front or populist carnival. The third dimension emerges only when we reach the edge of that and look out upon the true Other, the bureaucrat or corporate figure who stands in late capitalism itself and its now global institutions. It is because this Other can no longer be assimilated into the structures previously described that relations with it must be modeled on an external or spatial mode, and demand a kind of geographical analysis for which we have as yet no particularly adequate language (my implication that it will turn out to be neither dialectical nor structural is little more than an impression and a possible starting point). This is then the moment when our own social role and status as intellectuals returns with a vengeance, since it is a role which is mediated by geopolitics, its value conferred by the world system itself and by our positioning within it. It then returns upon our individual readings and analyses to enforce a new requirement of geographic reflexivity or geopolitical self-consciousness, and to demand the validation of some account of the 'national' situation from within whose standpoint the analysis has been made: it being understood that 'national' is now merely a relational term for the component parts of the world system, which might also be seen as the superposition of various kinds of space (local and regional as well as national, the geographical bloc as well as the world system itself). In that case, U.S. Cultural Studies, as here, would have to sign its address a little more self-consciously to its contributions.

But who says the U.S. says global capitalism itself: and the move on into the culture of that, and the dynamics of that truer Other than any of the microgroups at play here, demands the return to some form of commodity analysis, of which save for Jody Berland's suggestive pages on the ideology of 'entertainment', there is little enough trace here. Perhaps, in a kind of populist way, it is felt that to treat these cultural products as commodities about to be swept off in the purely formal process of

643

consumption is somehow to demean them and to diminish their dignity, to overlook their other social and group functions (outlined above). But that need not be the case for an analysis of the right complexity, although it is certain that for consumption, as a culture and a collective form of addiction, the act of consumption is an empty one, indifferent to the specific contents of a given object and thus relatively unpropitious for an analysis that would want to do it justice in substantive detail. Still, conflict, alienation, reunification, what used to be called the inauthentic, have to be given their due; nothing truly interesting is possible without negativity; error or ideology, false appearance, are also objective facts that have to be reckoned back into truth; the standardization of consumption is like a sound barrier which confronts the euphorias of populism as a fact of life and a physical law at the upper reaches of the spectrum.

Beyond that lies Utopia, also secretly at work everywhere in these pages, wherever the most obscure forms of enjoyment and group celebration or narcissism are to be found. But it must also be named, without which its half-life decays with unbelievable speed on exposure to the smog-filled light and polluted air of current reality. Donna Haraway names it here, in an essay of such range and complexity that I cannot do it justice here, let alone in these concluding pages: suffice it to say that in an immense wheeling and slowly rotating movement, she designates a succession of radically Other or alternative spaces to aspects of our own—the rain forest to our social space; the extraterrestrial to our physical one; the biomedical microcosm to our still conventional bodies; and the science fictional macrocosms to our still conventional minds. Let these Utopias then move as a kind of starry firmament over this collection, as indeed over Cultural Studies in general.

NOTES

1. Lawrence Grossberg, Cary Nelson, and Paula A. Treichler, eds., *Cultural Studies* (New York: Routledge, 1992), internal page references to this text.
2. As in 'the unhappy *marriage* of Marxism and feminism': see Jane Gallop's recent *Around 1981: Academic Feminist Literary Theory* (New York: Routledge, 1992) for a more elaborate exploration of the allegorical models by way of which an emergent feminism has sought to tell itself the story of that emergence.
3. One must also mention Dick Hebdige's *Subculture*, which more than any other single work invented the style and stance repeatedly adopted in the present conference.
4. See in particular the rather triumphalistic program article by one of the organizers of the present conference: Cary Nelson, 'Always Already Cultural Studies,' *Journal of the Midwest Modern Language Association* 24, no. 1 (1991), 24–38.
5. Fredric Jameson, 'Commentary,' *Journal of Modern Greek Studies* 8 (1990), 135–39.
6. Michael Denning, ' "The Special American Conditions": Marxism and American Studies,' *American Quarterly* 38, no. 3 (1986), 356–80.
7. See the 1857 Preface to the *Grundrisse*, as well as Louis Althusser and Etienne Balibar, *Reading Capital* (London: Verso, 1970), 174ff, 207. I am indebted to Perry Anderson and Ken Surin for their assistance in this hit-and-run genealogy; Jose Ripalda Crespo assures me that the history of the concept beyond Marx is banal and lost in the night of medieval scholasticism. Meanwhile, the latest and most familiar use of this term, in Ernesto Laclau and Chantal Mouffe's remarkable anatomy of alliance politics, *Hegemony and Socialist Strategy* (London: Verso, 1985), 105ff, does not attribute the concept historically (it is, however, not to be found in Gramsci). Finally, I am told by both Michael Denning and Andrew Ross that the fundamental image whereby this was always conveyed in Birmingham— shades of the locomotive of history!—was what in Britain is called the 'articulated lorry.'
8. Harald Eidheim, 'When Ethnic Identity Is a Social Stigma,' in *Ethnic Groups and Boundaries*, ed.

Fredrik Barth (Boston: Little, Brown, 1969), 39–57. See also Bernard McGrane, *Beyond Anthropology* (New York: Columbia University Press, 1989), which breaks new ground in analyzing the succeeding figures of the Other in the Renaissance (in which the Other is an infernal being, on the level with gold and spices), the Enlightenment (in which the Other is pagan and 'unenlightened' in the specific sense of being ignorant of 'unknown causes'), and in the nineteenth century (where the Other is positioned backward at an earlier point in historical time).

9. Donald Horowitz, *Ethnic Groups in Conflict* (Berkeley: University of California Press, 1985), 90–92. And see also Perry Anderson's interesting survey of the concept of 'national character' in 'Nation-States and National Identity,' *London Review of Books* 9 (May 1991), 3–8.

10. Etienne Balibar, 'Is There a "Neo-Racism"?' in Etienne Balibar and Immanuel Wallerstein, *Race, Nation, Class* (London: Verso, 1991), 17–28.

11. See for example Constance Penley's telling remarks on the popular feeling that intellectuals—in this case, feminists—are somehow upper class: 'The slashers do not feel they can express their desires for a better, sexually liberated, and more egalitarian world through feminism; they do not feel they can speak as feminists, they do not feel that feminism speaks for them' (492).

12. But it is important to stress, as Cornel West does, that religion (and in particular fundamentalism) is a very large and basic component of American mass culture, and in addition, that it is here decidedly underanalyzed and underrepresented.

13. Gyorgy Konrad and Ivan Szelenyi, *Intellectuals on the Road to Class Power* (New York: Harcourt Brace Jovanovich, 1979).

14. That this also holds for cultural production as such is suggested by Simon Frith's work on music culture; for example, 'the tension in this world is less that between amateurs and professionals . . . than between local and national reference groups' (176).

Henry Giroux, David Shumway, Paul Smith and James Sosnoski

'The Need for Cultural Studies: Resisting Intellectuals and Oppositional Public Spheres', first published in the *Dalhousie Review* (1985), discusses the opposition between the role of the specialist and the role of the intellectual in relation to specialized disciplines and departments in North American universities as it is structurally opposed to the interdisciplinarity of cultural studies. Following Foucault, the authors discuss the capacity of disciplinary technologies to 'normalize and hierarchize, homogenize and differentiate' their elements in ways that rigorously define disciplines and distinguish them absolutely from one another. Not only does disciplinary specialization eliminate collaboration among departments, but it also removes intellectuals from public spheres. Consequently, 'critique is ... disabled and the mechanisms of both social and cultural reproduction enabled.'

The essay asserts that cultural studies 'needs to develop a curriculum and a pedagogy that stresses the mediating and political role of intellectuals' who 'develop and work with movements outside of the limiting contours of the disciplines, symposia, and reward systems that have become the sole referent for intellectual activity.' This is a call for 'resisting intellectuals' who can establish a common language between the general public and the so-called intellectual. It encourages political readings of the so-called intellectual and of popular culture which makes disciplines peripheral to the main concern of cultural studies. The authors urge students to see aspects of culture relationally and to continually analyse the cultural practices as lived-in experiences, instead of viewing culture through a pre-determined set of values and class categories. They conclude that 'Cultural Studies' cannot afford to have intellectuals select certain aspects of culture as their subject because this limits discussions and 'restrict[s] that subject arbitrarily.'

K.M.S.

646

The need for cultural studies: resisting intellectuals and oppositional public spheres

Introduction

In North American Universities the study of culture[1] is so fragmented through specialization that concerted cultural critique is almost impossible. The historical development of insulated disciplines housed in segregated departments has produced a legitimating ideology that in effect suppresses critical thought. Rationalized as the protection of the integrity of specific disciplines, the departmentalization of inquiry has contributed to the reproduction of the dominant culture by isolating its critics from each other.[2] Under the banner of the academic freedom of experts to direct their own activity, specialists now bind themselves in discursive formations that generally circumscribe the nature of their inquiries.

The practitioners of disciplines investigating cultural phenomena—e.g., anthropology, sociology, history, literary studies—are limited in their ability to communicate with each other about their common concerns. Traditional literary study, for instance, has developed within formalistic parameters that set an almost impassable boundary between the study of a society and the study of a novel; similarly, sociologists make use of literature in ways that alienate traditional literary critics. And so on. The conventional wisdom for academics is to let members of other departments do whatever they say is their work in whatever way they choose—as long as this right is granted to them. As a consequence of these developments, the study of culture is conducted in fragments. And, in so far as experts must define themselves over and against a public comprised of amateurs, specialization removes intellectuals from other public spheres.[3] Critique is thus disabled and the mechanisms of both social and cultural reproduction enabled.

The role of the specialists is not altogether compatible with the role of the intellectual. As Paul Piccone remarks,

> unless one fudges the definition of intellectuals in terms of purely formal and statistical educational criteria, it is fairly clear that what modern society produces is an army of alienated, privatized, and uncultured experts who are knowledgeable only within very narrowly defined areas. This technical intelligentsia, rather than intellectuals in the traditional sense of thinkers concerned with the totality, is growing by leaps and bounds to run the increasingly complex bureaucratic and industrial apparatus. Its rationality, however, is only *instrumental* in character, and thus suitable mainly to perform partial tasks rather than tackling *substantial* questions of social organization and political direction.[4]

The argument of our essay is that there is a need for cultural studies to engage critically exactly those social and political issues to which Piccone alludes, and to promote an understanding of both the enabling and constraining dimensions of culture. This suggests both the development of a critique and the production of cultural forms consonant with emancipatory interests. One important task for such a transformative critique is to identify the fissures in the ideologies of the dominant culture. In the absence of intellectuals who can critically analyze a society's contradictions, the dominant culture continues to reproduce its worst effects all the more efficaciously. And, without a sphere for cultural critique, the resisting intellectual has no voice in public affairs.

This essay begins by showing how definitions of disciplines are historically arbitrary. It then goes on to argue that attempts to cut across the arbitrary boundaries set by disciplines and to develop interdisciplinary programs—American or Canadian Studies, Womens Studies, Black Studies, etc.—have failed. Next, the essay argues that the traditional humanist rationale for the disciplinary study of culture is inappropriate in that it masks the role that members of a culture can play as agents in its formation. This leads us to argue for the necessity of a counter-disciplinary praxis. At this point, we introduce the notion of the resisting intellectual as an educational formation necessary to restore to academics their roles as intellectuals. The sections that follow sketch out some of the implications of our argument: a return of intellectuals from ivory-towered departments to the public sphere; and a movement away from individualist, esoteric research towards collective inquiries into social ills. The essay concludes by outlining conditions for the development of Cultural Studies.

I. The arbitrariness of disciplines and the failure of interdisciplines

Most of us think of academic disciplines as the reflection of more or less 'natural' categories of things which we call subjects. English is different from history because literature and history are two distinct sorts of thing. But if we consider the matter further we soon recognize that the identification of a discipline with natural objects doesn't explain very much. In the first place, a particular group of objects is the subject of any number of disciplines. The same text, *Uncle Tom's Cabin* for example, can be studied by both literary scholars and historians. Secondly, the particular objects which a discipline studies do not remain the same throughout its history. 'Literature' has had its current reference—fiction, poetry, and drama—only since the early 19th century. Furthermore, the way in which categories are defined regularly changes. English has been recognized as a legitimate area of study only since the late nineteenth century, and new subdisciplines in physics or chemistry have been emerging at an ever increasing pace.

What is studied under the aegis of an academic discipline at any given time is not a natural subject matter, but a field which is itself constituted by the practice of the discipline. Such a field is not arbitrary in the sense that it develops randomly or on whim; rather, a field can be called arbitrary because it is contingent on historical circumstance. Hence it reflects cultural, social, and institutional demands. This is true of all academic fields, but especially so in fields outside the natural sciences. To understand why this is the case, it is necessary to look more closely at the formation of academic disciplines.

Michel Foucault has shown that discipline[5] as a particular strategy of social control and organization began at the end of the Classical age and came into dominance in the modern period. Though Foucault is not directly concerned with academic disciplines, much of his analysis applies to these enterprises. What is characteristic of disciplinary technologies is their capacity simultaneously to normalize and hierarchize, to homogenize and differentiate. This paradox is explained by the control which discipline asserts over difference. Because norms are carefully established and maintained, deviation can be measured on a scale. The goal of the professional in a discipline is to move up this scale by differing only in the appropriate ways.

It does not require Foucauldian analysis to understand that a discipline limits discourse. To be part of a discipline means to ask certain questions, to use a particular set of terms, and to study a relatively narrow set of things. But Foucault's work does help us to see how these limitations, this discipline, are enforced by institutions through various rewards and punishments most of which pertain to hierarchical ranking. The ultimate punishment is exclusion. If one ceases to speak within the discourse of the discipline, one will no longer be considered part of it. This does not usually mean that heretics will be prohibited from teaching or even from publishing; rather, they are simply marginalized. The situation is similarly severe for the new Ph.D. for whom the price of admission into the academy is the same conformity with dominant academic discourses.

Even though the development of normal science in Kuhn's sense distinguishes the natural sciences from other disciplines, 'The human sciences constantly try to copy the natural sciences' exclusion from their theories of any references to the [social and historical] background.'[6] In the social sciences and humanities there has been an increasing normalization consistent with the professionalization of the various disciplines, but it is clear that no discipline has succeeded in completely excluding 'background' from its theories. Formalizing techniques can make normal science possible in the social sciences and the humanities only by excluding the social skills, institutions, and power arrangements that make the isolation of attributes possible. This practice ignores the social practice and cultural interaction of social scientists and humanists.

Because social practice is not one of the objects constituted by the natural sciences, 'it is always possible and generally desirable that an unchallenged normal science which defines and resolves problems concerning the structure of the physical universe establish itself, [but] in the social sciences such an unchallenged normal science would only indicate that an orthodoxy had established itself, not through scientific achievement, but by ignoring the background and eliminating all competitors.'[7] Although humanistic disciplines allow a wider variety of activities than do the disciplines of the natural sciences, these activities themselves are hierarchically valued. In English, for instance, normal study under the New Critical 'paradigm' was the acontextual interpretation of individual texts of the literary canon. Other kinds of scholarship were permitted and sometimes rewarded, but were never allowed to overshadow normal New Critical practice. Historical scholarship, in this instance, had its place, but it was regarded as subsidiary to New Criticism.[8]

Although work in the humanities does not pose as normal science, its disciplinary structure aims at producing specialists. The disciplinary structure of study in literature, history, sociology, and other divisions that often focus on culture, tends to prohibit these specialists from relating their knowledge to public spheres. Disciplinary study requires constant attention to those few questions that constitute its current specialized concern. These questions are inevitably far removed from the genuine controversies in a given culture.

Interdisciplinary movements such as American Studies and Women's Studies have often developed out of the sense that the most important issues were being lost in the cracks between the rigid boundaries of the disciplines. As a consequence, American Studies began with the agenda of retrieving such issues. It should be remembered that the nationalism which spawned American Studies and Canadian Studies was openly political, and that American Studies books were critical of the ideological interests embedded in canonical documents of American culture. Nevertheless, American Studies should be regarded as a cautionary example to those who would try to establish Cultural Studies as an interdisciplinary enterprise within the academy. The problem is that no solid alternatives to disciplinary structure have evolved within the academy and, as a result, movements such as American Studies paradoxically must strive to become disciplines. Thus, while these movements often begin with a critical perspective, they retreat from radical critique as they become more successful. To the extent that such movements resist disciplines, their seriousness is questioned. Practitioners are regarded as dilettantes rather than real scholars, and their enterprises are written off as mere fads. In American Studies, the idea of interdisciplinarity became a means for practitioners to challenge a particular hierarchy, but it did not offer an alternative to hierarchical order. And as American Studies became more entrenched, interdisciplinarity receded in importance in the rhetoric of the movement.[9]

It would be a mistake to regard the failure of interdisciplinary movements to remain critical enterprises as the result of the suppression of political ideas. Because an intellectual's political views are posited as irrelevant to the work of disciplines themselves, speaking and thinking about political and social questions is construed as merely eccentric to the disciplinary study of culture. This failure to engage historical contexts and social particularities can be seen most clearly in the type of pedagogy that traditional disciplines institute.

Difficulties with the traditional rationale of the study of culture

Broadly speaking, the rationale of traditional humanistic education is that it offers students assured access to a storehouse of cultural materials which is constituted as a canon. Such a canon is, of course, relatively flexible in its definition insofar as it can incorporate and take cognizance of both marginal and recondite materials; as a thesaurus of sorts it cannot pass up anything of value. The values that are operational here do fluctuate according to specific ideological needs—witness the now quite secure incorporation of a women's studies canon or even a literary theory canon into some university curricula. But, at the same time, there is an always implicit 'gold standard' by which these provisional incrementations and fluctuations are regulated. Just recently, the head of NEH, William Bennett, conducted an *ad hoc* survey to discover what books every high school student 'might reasonably be expected to have studied' before graduation. The list of such books, thirty in all, ranged from Plato's *Republic*, through some Virgil, Chaucer, Dickens and Tolstoy, to *Catcher in the Rye*.[10] These books and authors represent the regulatory standard of a certain cultural currency by which the humanities and their productions are measured. A familiarity with the stable central core of the canon is said to enable students to absorb the values enshrined there, to the point that they could apply those values to its more marginal or provisional components. Most importantly, students would have access to a wealth which is 'humanizing' in its effect; but that effect is a complicity with the economy which has produced that wealth for humanity.

Leaving aside the not unimportant questions of how this project for the humanities is effected ideologically, and of how it relates in practice to students' lived lives (their individual socio-economic histories), it is important to ask whether or not it would be desirable or even necessary for Cultural Studies to appropriate or exploit in any way the same kind of educational rationale. After all, and as the new right is quick to point out, that rationale has always taken seriously the ideological effect and function *for* students of what is taught. By learning the dominant culture, or imbibing its representative values, students are theoretically *enabled* in that they are given the wherewithal for particular manners of action and behaviour within that culture. The argument can easily be made (as it is often made in Women's Studies, for example) that the teaching of an alternative substance, of a new canon, can effectively produce new ideological positions and thence political actions.

However, it must be remembered that the humanist rationale for the canon is based upon an hierarchical economy where cultural objects are ranked. Certain of those objects (Shakespeare's writing, for example) are assumed to be 'the best' of western culture; they thus represent, synecdochally, the *essence* of the culture. It is exactly this symbolic view of culture against which Cultural Studies should fight. The installation of a new canon, constructed on assumptions about what is most important and valuable for students to know or be familiar with, merely replicates the traditional hierarchical view of culture, albeit in a novel and perhaps minimally subversive form. Cultural Studies, on the other hand, should be built upon a different economy, one which sees that cultural objects are, in fact, disposed *relationally*.

This is to say that Cultural Studies should look with suspicion upon any hierarchizing project through which culture is synecdochally delimited to certain of its parts, whether such parts represent the culture's essential 'best' or even if they represent what has been predetermined as politically or ethically important and valuable. Cultural Studies should, in short, abandon the goal of giving students access to that which represents a culture. Instead, Cultural Studies has the possibility of investigating culture as a set of activities which is lived and developed within asymmetrical relations of power, or as irreducibly a process which cannot be immobilized in the image of a storehouse.

By investigating and teaching the claim that culture is in a real sense *unfinished*, Cultural Studies can secure its own political effectiveness. Students—particularly those marginalised by the values of the dominant culture—can be disabused of the notion that the culture they actually inhabit is somehow not theirs or available to them only through proper initiation into the values enshrined in representative texts. Cultural Studies, taking new (i.e. necessarily non-canonical) objects and implicating them in a relational rather than hierarchical view, encourages a questioning of the premises of dominant educational and political practices. Most importantly, Cultural Studies can refuse to agree that 'literature [and any other cultural object] . . . is distinct from politics'[11] and can thus re-consider the ideological and political appurtenance of a text or any set of texts.

Clearly, what is at stake here is the possibility that Cultural Studies could promote in students, not a striving after a predetermined or a once-and-for-all complacent accession to a given set of cultural values, but rather a continual analysis of their own conditions of existence. Such a praxis, founded in an overthrowing of the preassumptions of traditional disciplinary approaches to culture, is a pre-requisite for self-conscious and effective resistance to dominant structures.

II. The need for a counter-disciplinary praxis

In the first section of the essay we pointed out that disciplines concerned with the analysis of culture, including those called humanistic, have attempted to model themselves on the pattern of 'normal science.' Their aim is to describe culture, to accumulate a knowledge about a culture. In the preceding section we argued that such an aim leaves the impression on students that a culture has a permanent character and that specific structures can be described in an essentialist manner. Such procedures are especially pernicious in those disciplines associated with the humanities since they suggest that the culture has already been formed rather than that it is in the process of transformation.

Cultural Studies should resist such tendencies. This requires a movement away from our de-contextualized *conception of disciplinary practices* toward a *'conception of human Praxis*, emphasising that human beings are neither to be treated as passive objects, nor as wholly free subjects,' since the study of human life is properly 'the study of definite social practices, geared to human needs.'[12]

Given the disciplinary mechanisms at work in the structure of Western universities, such a praxis is necessarily counter-disciplinary in the sense that it resists the notion that the study of culture is the accumulation of knowledge about it. In our view, the proper study of culture is 'intrinsically involved with *that which has to be done*'[13] in societies rife with oppression. The precondition of such action is critical resistance to prevailing practices. However, resistance will not be effective if it is random and isolated; intellectuals must play the crucial role of mobilizing such resistance into a praxis that has political impact.

Resisting intellectuals
Central to the emancipatory project that informs our notion of Cultural Studies is a reformulation of the role of the intellectual both within and outside the university.

We concur with Gramsci that it is important to view intellectuals in political terms.[14] The intellectual is more than a person of letters, or a producer and transmitter of ideas. Intellectuals are also mediators, legitimators, and producers of ideas and social practices; they perform a function eminently political in nature. Gramsci distinguishes between conservative and radical organic intellectuals. Conservative organic intellectuals provide the dominant classes with forms of moral and intellectual leadership. As agents of the status quo, such intellectuals identify with the dominant relations of power and become, consciously or unconsciously, the propagators of its ideologies and values. They provide the ruling classes with rationales for economic, political and ethical formations.

According to Gramsci, conservative organic intellectuals can be found in all strata of advanced industrial society—in industrial organizations, in universities, in the culture industry, in various forms of management, and so on. He claims that radical organic intellectuals also attempt to provide the moral and intellectual leadership for the working class. More specifically, radical organic intellectuals provide the pedagogical and political skills that are necessary to raise political awareness in the working class, and to help it develop leadership and engage in collective struggle.

Gramsci's analysis is helpful in formulating one of the central goals of Cultural Studies: the creation of what we want to call *resisting intellectuals*. This differs from Gramsci's notion of radical organic intellectuals; we believe that such intellectuals can emerge from and work with any number of groups which resist the suffocating knowledge and practices that constitute their social formation. Resisting intellectuals can provide the moral, political and pedagogical leadership for those groups which take as their starting point the transformative critique of the conditions of oppression. The epithet 'organic' in our case cannot be reserved for those intellectuals who take the working class as the only revolutionary agent.

The notion of the resisting intellectual is important in the most immediate sense because it makes visible the paradoxical position in which radical intellectuals in higher education find themselves in the 1980s. On the one hand, such intellectuals earn a living within institutions that play a fundamental role in producing the dominant culture. On the other hand, radical intellectuals define their political terrain by offering to students forms of oppositional discourse and critical social practices at odds with the hegemonic role of the university and the society which it supports. In many cases, this paradox works in favor of the university:

> More often than not, [the] goal has been to elaborate disciplines, rather than
> develop projects, to meld the bloodless tenets of semiology, systems theory, prag-
> matism and positivism with the archaicisms of historical materialism. The
> unflagging appetite of these leftist intellectuals to gain credibility within their
> respective disciplines, to be *au courant* and appreciated as its 'left wing' and its
> most 'forward looking tendency,' is appalling evidence that what we lack is . . . a
> revolutionary intellectual movement.[15]

Bookchin's remarks remind us that critical scholarship is generally removed from any relation to concrete political movements; radical social theory becomes a mere commodity for academic journals and conferences; and radical intellectuals get safely

653

ensconced within a tenure system that offers them as proof of the university's commitment to liberal pluralism.

Rather than surrender to this form of academic and political incorporation, Cultural Studies needs to define the role of the resisting intellectual as a counter-hegemonic practice that can both avoid and challenge it. In general terms, we can point to the following pedagogical and strategic activities. *First*, Cultural Studies needs to develop a curriculum and a pedagogy that stress the mediating and political role of intellectuals. This means providing students with the critical tools they will need to both understand and dismantle the chronic rationalization of harmful social practices, while simultaneously appropriating the knowledge and skills they need to rethink the project of human emancipation. *Secondly*, resisting intellectuals must actively engage in projects which encourage them to address their own critical role in the production and legitimation of social relations. Such projects are necessary not only to fight against conservative intellectuals and the multiple contexts in which legitimation processes occur, but also to broaden the theoretical and political movements outside the university. Resisting intellectuals must develop and work with movements outside of the limiting contours of the disciplines, symposia, and reward systems that have become the sole referent for intellectual activity. More importantly, such a project broadens the notion of education and takes seriously Gramsci's notion of all society as a vast school.[16] In addition, it encourages resisting intellectuals to play an active role in the many public spheres that are developing around various ideological conflicts.

Cultural Studies thus posits the need for resisting intellectuals who can establish new forms of political relations within and outside the university. In this theoretical context, Cultural Studies echoes Gramsci's call for radical intellectuals to forge alliances around new historical blocs. Intellectuals can play an important role in empowering individuals and groups within oppositional public domains.

Public spheres, popular culture and cultural studies
The importance for Cultural Studies of participating in oppositional public spheres is an underlying premise of this essay. A counter-disciplinary praxis undertaken by resisting intellectuals would not be effective if it had as its only audience people in universities. Rather, it should take place more extensively in *public*. Although many universities are public institutions, we rarely consider them part of the public sphere. If Cultural Studies is to be understood as an oppositional public sphere, it should not be conceived as a 'department' or as part of the boundary separating professional activities from those of amateurs. Instead of thinking of Cultural Studies in terms which more properly characterize disciplines, we should reconceive traditional rationales in an effort to create counter practices. The classroom, to take one instance, is viewed traditionally as a place where information is transmitted to students. Experts in a discipline impart to apprentices the received knowledge about a particular subject matter; students are not agents in this process, but passive and overtly uncritical receptacles. However, as we have argued, if we grant students an active role in the process of cultural formation, they can become agents in the production of social practices. To accomplish this we should become involved in fostering forms of resistance; a critical pedagogy is required which will promote the identification and

analysis of the underlying ideological interests at stake in the text and its readings. We are then engaged together as resisting intellectuals in a social practice that allows both parties to construe themselves as agents in the process of their own cultural formation. An obvious concretization of this praxis might be a woman resisting the view of women proffered in a canonical novel. This instance is a reflection of resistance to large-scale social practices that oppress women. Such resistance needs to be produced.

Rather than abandon scholarship, resisting intellectuals need to repoliticize it. Scholarly *public*-ations, the disciplinary criterion used to establish the merit of professional opinions against those of a public made up of amateurs, do not reach the public. Though it is not appropriate to argue the point here, we contend that the disciplines presently concerned with the study of culture are unduly bound to the premise that their task is to do disciplinary research, that is, to accumulate and store in a retrievable way descriptions of cultural phenomenon. But, if we reconceive our activity as the production of (rather than the description of) social practices, then what we do in our classrooms is easily extended into public spheres. We cannot capitulate to the disciplinary notion that research has as its only audience other experts in the field. Resisting intellectuals must legitimate the notion of writing reviews and books for the general public, and they must create a language of critique balanced by a language of possibility that will enable social change.[17]

This means that we need to become involved in the political reading of popular culture. As Stanley Aronowitz remarks in 'Colonized Leisure, Trivialized Work,' 'It remains for us to investigate in what way mass culture becomes constitutive of social reality.'[18] Training in disciplinary practices leads us away from the study of the relation between culture and society and toward the accumulation of descriptions of cultural material cut off from its connection to everyday life. As Aronowitz points out:

> To fully understand the ideological impact and manipulative functions of current media presentations, it is necessary to appreciate the multi-layered character of contemporary mass culture. In addition to the *overt* ideological content of films and television—transmitting new role models, values life styles to be more or less consciously emulated by a mass audience—there is also a series of *covert* messages contained within them which appeal to the audience largely on the unconscious level. . . . Typically, [these] define the character of the spectator's experience of the spectacle in terms of the . . . gratification of his or her unconscious desires. . . . By creating a system of pseudo–gratifications, mass culture functions as a sort of social regulator, attempting to absorb tensions arising out of everyday life and to deflect frustrations which might otherwise actualize themselves in opposition to the system into channels which serve the system.[19]

It is because the effects of culture are so often unconsciously absorbed, that the need for a Cultural Studies emphasising critique arises. As we pointed out earlier in this essay, the disciplines that claim selected aspects of culture as their subject restrict that subject arbitrarily—for instance, by constituting the field of literary study as a canon. Simultaneously, they have placed a wedge between professionals and the public in the service of the ruling classes as in the case of literary study where so-called,

655

'low' culture is excluded from the research domain. Nor should we now continue to be fooled by the admission of films, popular novels, soap operas and the like into the curricula of literature departments. As long as such cultural artifacts are examined as merely the materials that make up a fixed culture, their disciplinary description will do no more than create storehouses of knowledge having almost nothing to do with lived culture, much less its transformation. Only a counter-disciplinary praxis developed by intellectuals who resist disciplinary formation is likely to produce emancipatory social practices.

The problem with suggesting that Cultural Studies be counter disciplinary is that it cannot be housed in universities as they are presently structured. Hence the need for counter-institutions. There would be various sorts of collectives, variously membered—study groups, counter-disciplinary research groups, even societies and institutes.

It is unlikely that the disciplinary structures and mechanisms of universities will disappear in the near future. However, it would be a mistake to locate Cultural Studies within them. Our alternative would be to treat disciplines as peripheral to our main concerns while nonetheless obtaining some important concessions from their administrators. This is a tactical matter which has to be negotiated situation by situation. However, we can go even further and develop models of collaborative inquiry that extend beyond the university in order to combat hegemonic public spheres and to form alliances with other oppositional public spheres. In the context of Cultural Studies it will not be appropriate simply to generate idiosyncratic interpretations of cultural artifacts. The most important aim of a counter-disciplinary praxis is radical social change.

We should not be resigned to the roles that universities assign us. The resisting intellectual can develop a collective, counter-disciplinary praxis within the university that has a political impact outside it. The important tactical question at this moment in the history of North American universities is how to get Cultural Studies established as a form of cultural critique. Our suggestion has been the formation of institutes for cultural studies that can constitute an oppositional public sphere.

Conclusion

If Cultural Studies is to be informed by a political project that gives a central place to critique and social transformation, it will have to begin with a dual recognition. First, it is imperative to recognize that the university has a particular set of relations with the dominant society. These relations define the university as neither a locus of domination nor a locus of freedom. Instead, the university, with relative autonomy, functions largely to produce and legitimate the knowledge, skills and social relations that characterize the dominant power relations in society. Universities, like other public institutions, contain points of resistance and struggle, and it is within these spaces that the ideological and material conditions exist to produce oppositional discourses and practices. Such a recognition not only politicizes the university and its relation to the dominant society, it interrogates the political nature of Cultural Studies as both a sphere of critique and as a medium of social transformation. This leads to the second point.

If it is to be a radical social project, Cultural Studies must develop a *self-regulating discourse*: by this we mean a discourse that contains a language of critique and a concomitant language of possibility. In the first instance, it must lay bare the historically specific interests that structure the academic disciplines, the relations among them, and the manner in which the form and content of the disciplines reproduce and legitimate the dominant culture. This is a central task for Cultural Studies. For, if it is to promote an oppositional discourse and method of inquiry, it will have to embody interests that affirm rather than deny the political and normative importance of history, ethics and social interaction.

The discourse of Cultural Studies must resist the interests contained in the established academic disciplines and departments. It must interrogate the knowledge-claims and the modes of intelligibility central to the defense of the academic status quo in various departments and disciplines. Equally importantly, Cultural Studies must indict the interests embedded in the questions *not* asked within academic disciplines. That is, it must develop methods of inquiry into how the present absences and structured silences that govern teaching, scholarship, and administration within academic departments deny the link between knowledge and power, reduce culture to an unquestioned object of mastery, and refuse to acknowledge the particular way of life that dominant academic discourse helps to produce and legitimate.

In order to retain its theoretical and political integrity, Cultural Studies must develop forms of critical knowledge as well as a critique of knowledge itself. Such a task demands resistance to the reification and fragmentation that characterizes the disciplines. Because of their constitution, disciplinary structures obstruct the overthrowing of technical and social divisions of labor of which they are part and which they help to produce. Cultural Studies needs to develop a theory of the way in which different social formations are both produced and reproduced within the asymmetrical relations of power characterizing the dominant society. Similarly, it needs to develop a language of possibility, one in which knowledge would be viewed as part of a collective learning process connected to the dynamics of struggle both within and outside the university. Cultural Studies, in this sense, must develop an oppositional discourse and a counter-disciplinary praxis to deal with struggles over different orders of representation, conflicting forms of cultural experience, and diverse visions of the future. Clearly, the interests that inform such a problematic cannot be developed within traditional departments. Currently, the structure of universities is inextricably tied to interests which suppress the critical concerns of intellectuals willing to fight for oppositional public spheres. Such interests can be dismantled in favor of more radical practices only through the collective efforts of resisting intellectuals.

NOTES

1. Our working definition of culture is taken from John Clarke, Stuart Hall, Tony Jefferson and Brian Roberts, 'Subculture, Culture and Class' in *Resistance Through Rituals*, edited by Stuart Hall and

657

Tony Jefferson (London: Hutchinson Publications, 1976): 'By culture we understand the shared principles of life characteristic of particular classes, groups or social milieux. Cultures are produced as groups make sense of their social existence in the course of everyday experience. Culture is intimate, therefore, with the world of practical action. It suffices, for most of the time, for managing everyday life. Since, however, this everyday world is itself problematic, culture must perforce take complex and heterogeneous forms, not at all free from contradictions,' pages 10–17.

2. This remark is based on the work of several members of the Group for Research into the Institutionalization and Professionalization of Literary Study (GRIP) who have been examining the relationship between the historical development of disciplines and their departmentalization. See also Thomas S. Popkewitz, 'Social Science and Social Amelioration: The Development of the American Academic Expert,' in *Paradigm and Ideology in Educational Research* (Philadelphia: The Falmer Press, 1984), pp. 107–128.

3. See Burton Bledstein's *The Culture of Professionalism: The Middle Class and the Development of Higher Education in America* (New York: Norton, 1976).

4. Paul Piccone, 'Symposium: Intellectuals in the 1980's,' *Telos* 50 (Winter, 1981–82), p. 116.

5. Michel Foucault, *Discipline and Punish* (New York: Pantheon), Part Three, pp. 135ff.

6. Hubert L. Dreyfus and Paul Rabinow, *Michel Foucault: Beyond Structuralism and Hermeneutics* (Chicago: University of Chicago Press, 1982), p. 163.

7. Dreyfus and Rabinow, pp. 163–4.

8. See J. Sosnoski's 'The *Magister Implicatus* as an Institutionalized Authority Figure: Rereading the History of New Criticism,' *The GRIP Report*, Vol. I, (Oxford: Ohio Research in Progress circulated by the Society for Critical Exchange).

9. See D. Shumway's 'Interdisciplinarity and Authority in American Studies,' *The GRIP Report*, Vol. I.

10. See *New York Times*, August 13, 1984, p. 7. One wonders at the inclusion in this canonical list of *The Communist Manifesto*: a symptom of paranoia or cautious liberalism, or both?

11. See *PN Review* 10:6, p. 4–5—a piece which is a quite typical expression of the new right's emergent views on the ideological relations of literature.

12. Cf. Anthony Giddens, *Central Problems in Social Theory* (Berkeley, University of California Press, 1983), pages 150–51.

13. Giddens, p. 4.

14. Gramsci, *The Prison Notebooks* (New York: International Publications, 1971), pp. 5–27.

15. Murray Bookchin, 'Symposium: Intellectuals in the 1980's,' *Telos* 50 (Winter, 1981–82), p. 13.

16. Gramsci, *The Prison Notebooks, passim.*

17. See Peter Hohendahl's *The Institution of Criticism* (Ithaca: Cornell University Press, 1982), 44ff. and 242ff. for a discussion of this point.

18. Stanley Aronowitz, *False Promises* (New York: McGraw-Hill, 1973), p. 97.

19. Aronowitz, p. 111.

Interview with Professor Stuart Hall (by Roger Bromley)

In 1992 Stuart Hall kindly agreed to an interview with Roger Bromley for this publication. The interview has been transcribed by the editors; square brackets indicate the editors' explanations, a row of asterisks indicates that editorial cuts have been made to the transcript.

Stuart Hall (1932–) was born in the West Indies and educated at Oxford. He is currently professor of sociology at the Open University and for over a decade was the director of the Centre for Contemporary Cultural Studies in Birmingham. For a more detailed description of Hall's contribution to cultural studies, see Section 3, Cultural Studies in Britain.

Roger Bromley (1942–) Roger Bromley was educated at the University of Wales, the University of Illinois at Urbana-Champaign, and the University of Sussex. He has lectured in literary and cultural studies at the University of Portsmouth, and was formerly head of humanities at the Cheltenham and Gloucester College of Higher Education. Currently, he is a professor working in media and cultural studies at the Nottingham Trent University. For a number of years he was an executive member of the Association for Cultural Studies and corresponding editor of the *European Journal of Communications*. He has published a book, *Lost Narratives* (1988), and numerous essays, including 'The Boundaries of Hegemony: Thomas Hardy and the *Mayor of Casterbridge*', *Literature, Society and the Sociology of Literature* (1976), 'The gentry, bourgeois hegemony and popular fiction: *Rebecca* and *Rogue Male*' in *Popular Fictions: Essays in Literature and History* (1986). Roger Bromley has also selected, edited and introduced the section in this *Reader* on Cultural Studies in Britain.

R.B.   Was there anything specific in your early experience as a young person in a colonized society which led you to an emphasis on the cultural, rather than the economic, political or social, as an 'academic' priority? I know you cannot really separate these, but was there anything that would have programmed the cultural? Were you conscious, self-conscious of being in an Anglo-centric society?

S.H.   Yes, there certainly was. You know this was a period in Jamaica and the Caribbean Islands before the society had become Black in terms of their cultural consciousness. I was born into a lower-middle-class/middle-class family in which the tensions around class and colour and culture were very sharp indeed. My mother came from a poor background but had been adopted by relatives who were, if not white, nearly white, oriented towards England, etc. She was formed in that milieu, and she maintained that pole of aspiration in our family right from the very beginning. My father was from a much poorer, country family, much darker in colour, although his own aspirations were socially upwards, culturally upwards, because he worked all his life for the United Fruit Company, which was the big, fine company etc., etc. Nevertheless, there were already those differences reflected in the culture of my own family, and I was in colour darker than any other member of my family. The first family story that I remember—I don't know if it's true or not, and it hardly matters, it is the necessary imaginary myth of origin as it were—is my sister saying to my parents about me 'Where did you get this coolie baby from?' 'Coolie' is a word for an Indian, a derogatory word for an East Indian, she couldn't bring herself to say 'where did you get this Black baby from?' But 'coolie' clearly meant that in the cultural colour codes of the society.

I was aware from the very beginning of the grades of colour, the orientation towards America, and the UK and British culture, as opposed to the orientation towards the indigenous Black culture. I was aware of the fact that our entire family would grade our friends in this way. I mean, the people I was encouraged to be with would always be the ones moving up the class-colour-culture grade. I felt completely torn by that. I was torn between this internal culture of my family and the friends and people that I knew outside whom I would never have dreamt of taking home. When I was seventeen, my sister became extremely ill as a consequence of precisely having a relationship with someone whom on cultural and colour grounds my father would not accept. So when I left Jamaica as a student at eighteen to come to England to study, although I did not know it, I was in complete flight from these tensions, which I found unbearable. I rejected those aspirations, but I had to live with them.

R.B.   Did school compound these tensions?

S.H.   To some extent, not quite, not exactly in that way. School was a big boys' school, rather an imitation English public school, so classwise it was certainly stratified, but already by then it was quite mixed. Provided you were bright and got a scholarship, it didn't matter what colour or background you came from. So, already, institutions like that were beginning to move faster than my own family! My family was deeply anachronistic, stuck sort of in the period before that, so that even when Independence came, which didn't in itself provoke a cultural revolution, many things remained intact, the differences between ordinary folk, country folk, and this aspiring Kingston middle-class were not resolved by Independence, but there was a sort of notion that the indigenous middle-class had taken power—my father was out of step even with *that*! They really imagined that they had come from, well, somehow my mother really did think that she'd come from Europe. On that side my family I guess was about two generations away from the Scots, or whatever they were, although my father was also two generations away from being African, and there was East-Indian blood, and Portuguese—I'm the absolute cultural hybrid, I'm a mongrel culturally. So, I was always aware of cultural questions, and political questions. I never thought about imperialism and colonialism. I would think about it in terms of the way these were lived, in terms of rival cultural images, this struggle to identify with one or another pole in this divided society.

R.B. Did you find coming to England a filling out of the experience, or was it mixed?

S.H. Well, first of all, it was a relief to get away from the psychic pressure of these tensions which I was destroyed by. I felt it was a relief, an escape: it was an interesting experience, an escape to Britain at the moment of the early migration. The milieu into which I dropped was the milieu of Caribbean students, and civil servants doing economics and development economics, etc., looking forward to the spirit of Independence. I really became a West-Indian, as opposed to a Jamaican, in England. That's the first time I met Barbadians, and Trinidadians, and Grenadans, and Ascencions, and in the West-Indian Students Union, which was a quite militant, anti-colonial outfit, and gradually making contact with people who came to work with the students. I think although I was in England, I was able to make more contact with a wider range of West Indian people there than my own family culture had allowed me.

R.B. Was there any sort of consciousness in your time of getting ready for a return? You've talked about people studying development economics, getting ready for Independence.

S.H. Yes, and we were all then West-Indian Federationalists. We all believed we had to transcend the culture of the individual islands. We looked for the possibility of creating a wider market, first amongst the British-speaking, but we were also beginning to be aware that we came from the Caribbean, but none of us had ever been to Spanish-speaking Islands, the Dominican Republic, etc. We did not think of ourselves as part of the Central-American or Latin-American basin. But we were beginning to open those connections, looking for the possibility of federation, and federation was on the political agenda when Britain started, finally, to grant independence to various independence movements. They sort of tried to encourage them, in East Africa, common-market federations, to harness them into the Commonwealth to create larger markets. Well, that foundered, it foundered on inter-island jealousies . . .

I mean the islands were so separate in their individual development, the link was to British culture rather than to one another. They may have made economic arrangements for the sake of their mutual benefit, but there wouldn't have been anything like cultural integration. I mean really, you know, I was taught by the Scots, by the British, by the Jamaicans, by the English, by the Welsh. But in the sixth-form, there appeared a Barbadian to teach me classics, he had an external degree from Durham or somewhere in classics, he came to teach me Latin, well I had never heard an accent which sounded so strange. He was *really* the outsider. The English, we made jokes about them, but they were our *intimate* enemies; these Barbadians, they were like from Mars, they were Black, we didn't know where they had come from or anything about them.

Then there is the sixties, and there is a huge cultural revolution, in the Caribbean, in Jamaica especially, linked to Rastafarianism, Reggae, and all that. And the society, culturally for the first time discovers that it is largely a Black society. It discovers a language, through Rastafarianism, through which it is able to speak its own history, to speak its transportation, to speak slavery, slave-origin, to try to imaginarily reconstruct its African connections. That transforms the society and culture: I mean economically and politically it doesn't have much odds.

R.B.   What were the major forces? Partly academic, partly intellectual?

S.H.   No, it's broader than that. Intellectuals were sort of classical Marxists waiting for the proletariat to march forward. No, it was really the hugely suppressed folk culture, the culture of large amounts of ordinary people with connections to slavery, and to the slave period and colonialism, who had hoped, or imagined, that political independence would bring them to power. But it didn't do that, what it brought was the indigenous middle class, the national bourgeoisie, to power, and then the question was, 'Well you've had independence, but you are still in Babylon.' So the language is from below, of the urban poor, masses of poor people in Kingston, people in the countryside who've been left out, not shopping in Miami—the stuff that went on amongst the middle-class in that period—it's a kind of revolution from within the revolution, within the Independence movement a kind of cultural revolution. It's very connected with Black power, with the Civil Rights movement in the early sixties.

R.B.   Over here, did you feel close to that, or did you feel more UK socialist?

S.H.   We have to reconstruct the connections, with Marxism, with the New Left and so on. But this is a kind of continuing thread for me, I was very excited by the impact of what was happening in Jamaica; if it had happened in Jamaica before I left I would have gone back, because *that* was a Jamaica I could have gone back to. By then though, I was involved in other things, it wasn't possible any longer. I'd made the transition, but that was the society that I would have wanted to grow up in. So I was very excited . . .

R.B.   The influence of Hoggart must have been rather different. The CCCS [Centre for Contemporary Cultural Studies] was established by then wasn't it? How did you fit into Birmingham? How did that work with people outside the university, like young Black kids?

S.H. I suppose that for a long time they were slightly two different facets of my own interests, because Cultural Studies, obviously, had another kind of history, which I was also very closely connected with. That begins in Oxford, with my rejection of the dominant models of literary study, my rejection of that as maintained in the Oxford English School of Literature, *belles lettres* as a sort of accomplishment—it was *so* British. What you needed to do to get a First in English, you absorbed through the genes. [A First is the highest grade for degrees in the UK] I hated that and the social implications of that for pedagogy, and, of course, I couldn't do that, and I didn't have those genes. I couldn't find Englishness. So we were in the first instance, Leavistes, left Leavisites. We were rejecting the élitism of a lot of the Leavis programme, but drawn to Leavis because Leavis took literature seriously, as a *deadly serious issue*, with questions about language and the culture, about the dissociation of language in the seventeenth century. All of those debates—Queenie Leavis's work on popular fiction—raised cultural questions for us. So we created a kind of alternative culture around our literary studies.

R.B.   This movement was quite extensive, several people were doing this?

S.H.   Yes, many of those were people who 'ran' in '56, came together to form the early New Left. They were involved with socialist activities, or involved with the Socialist Club, which was a kind of meeting place for people in the Labour Party, and the Labour movement, and in the Communist Party, all mainly students. We were in conversation with the Party—*they* thought we were going to join them and *we* thought they were going to leave and join us! The Socialist Club was a meeting place for a lot of this debate. It was in that milieu that I first met Raymond [Williams]. Raymond was doing extra-mural studies, I'd stayed on to do post-graduate work, I was in Oxford for six years, but met Raymond in that milieu of left literary studies. There was quite an interesting group of people, who were third world independent Marxist or left people. A really interesting independent left cultural milieu.

Because of our studies, but also partly because cultural questions started to be raised about the society outside, we were trying to make sense of Britain, and trying to see how the Marxist and socialist models applied to Britain, and whether they could explain cultural change, as it appeared in Americanization and so on. So, trying to make sense of all that, we also came in that milieu to define cultural questions as much more important, much more central, than normally they had been assumed to be. Questions about the middle class, could it survive post-war affluence? Questions about class structure, but aware of the fact that cultural issues were important and that they weren't subordinate or superstructures, etc., etc. Therefore, someone like Raymond, who was writing *Culture and Society* at that time—we read some of the chapters and discussed them with him—was thinking about class cultural questions. Then there was Hoggart's book, which cuts through that, cuts across that debate. So we read those books as partly cultural questions, partly political questions.

Then '56 occurred, the Communist Party disintegrates, that left the Labour Party. There's that conjunction of Hungary and Suez. Suez brings those people who are arguing that Imperialism is bad to the left, but it liberates those people who are Stalinists, Hungary etc.—a double-conjunction there which creates a space for the

New Left. So we started this journal called *Universities Quarterly* which is parallelled by the starting-up outside that of the *Left Review*.

Our generation of communists left when Edward [Thompson] and the others were expelled. But our milieu was not entirely composed of those people. There were a lot of people like us who had never been, and never ever had any intention of being on the left. There was a big conversation going on around political questions, cultural questions, etc.. The New Left, for me, was formed in that milieu, which is why cultural studies is a take-up of many of those questions in another context.

R.B.   The traditional histories, such as they are, neglect '56, they start in '65.

S.H.   They tend to start in '65, and they tend to start with the great books. But the great books are partly formed on an earlier moment and partly came out of it. *The Long Revolution* was then written in the period when Raymond was a member of that group, the two journals fused in 1959 and I became the first editor, and on the board is Raymond, Edward, Richard Hoggart was never on the board but he was very close, published in the journal.

R.B.   Perry Anderson, was he involved?

S.H.   That was the next generation, the Socialist Club in Oxford was the place where we met the next generation of people, like Perry and Robin Blackburn and Gareth Stedman Jones, and Mike Rustin, the whole slew of the next generation. When we finally left Oxford, Raphael Samuel, and myself, Chuck Taylor, in about '57, '58, there was another generation, who then formed their own left student union, so there is a sort of continuity going on there. That moment, the formation of that milieu into a kind of political new left is very important. All of that was at large very much in English culture, it had come out of English writing, its object of inquiry was what is happening to British society, and how far are the old socialist projects valid in this changed milieu, and how much and how little of Marxism, as a theoretical position, explains what is going on. Of course, there is a kind of imperialist interest and edge to that, but that is not at the centre of the early new left point of view, in *Culture and Society* and *Long Revolution*, or *The Making of the Working Class*, or *The Uses of Literacy*, that question is nowhere near the centre. So that at the same time as I'm involved in that, I'm involved in these other things. They don't come together in my own mind and in my own work for a while. I don't try to harness them together in the same space until later.

I then came to London in '57 and worked as a supply teacher in South London, mainly in Brixton, and I taught extra-mural studies. I taught for the Oxford Extramural Dept., and I worked for the British Film Institute, because I'd become interested in film and the media, and Paddy Whannel in the Education Dept. there was beginning to develop an interest in film through extra-mural and other teaching; and I edited *Universities and Left Review*, unpaid, so that was the life that I put together. Then, when I became editor of *New Left Review*, that became a full-time job, though I went on doing other teaching and that went on until '61. At that point I left and I went to Chelsea College of Science, teaching Complementary Studies, and

I guess I may have been one of the first full-time appointments teaching film and media studies. The head of department there was in conventional literary studies, nevertheless, was sensitive to these cultural debates going on and opened a space, within the framework of complementary studies, for what, in fact, we would now call 'cultural studies', work on media, and British culture and so on, and we used to teach this stuff, unexamined, to dentists.

R.B.   What resources did you have, what material?

S.H.   Mainly we used a lot of stuff from the British Film Institute, a lot of film, we had television, and that got me back into teaching in a completely different area. Although I'd make the break into questions of culture earlier than that. When I started graduate work it was on Henry James, on the relationship between Europe and America, as kind of moral, cultural poles, how these two were articulated as points of reference, it was about the clash of cultures. But I spent most of the time reading about culture, that was when I read anthropology and sociology for the first time and realized that this was the missing concept and that anthropology was where one could find it. I was then trying to make the bridge between the way culture was discussed in the Leavisite debate and these wider ways of life, anthropological definitions of culture that Raymond was picking up on, and which I came on by reading a lot more about the Caribbean, about syncretism; there's a lot of syncretism in Latin America and the Caribbean. As you get older you discover you're only interested in the same things, you keep saying the same things.

Then Hoggart went to Birmingham as professor and decided that he wanted to use his position there to get graduate students to work on the stuff he'd being doing in *Uses of Literacy* rather than just in straight literary studies. The university said 'ok but we don't have any money.' Hoggart had got a lot, *Uses of Literacy* had made enormous sales for Penguin Books, Hoggart had been a key witness for the *Lady Chatterley* trial, and Allen Lane gave a bit of money to hire a research fellow and to get a few books, to take a group of graduate students. I gave up Chelsea College in '64, published the *Popular Arts* book, with Paddy Whannel, got married and went to Birmingham. I went to Birmingham and thought this will be OK for a few months and stayed fifteen years, '64 to '79.

R.B.   Then, when you were there, you discovered this region, a major centre of migrants, a working-class community. How far was the Centre involved with the community beyond the university?

S.H.   Those things were not very connected, there was not a single Black student in the university or in the Centre. All that is really created in '68, because in the student movement of '68 and in the student occupation in '68, which radicalized and politicized the undergraduate population, a lot of the undergraduates who came to the Centre after that were students who had been involved in '68, and the Centre was kind of involved. And those students had a lot of connections with the city; for instance, there were people like Chas Critcher, who was one of the graduate students who worked with me on *Policing the Crisis*, who ran a Community Centre in

665

Painswick. So gradually they came into the Centre, Black students, well not many at first, but people who had connections in those community affairs. *Policing the Crisis* begins because Chas Critcher's group called in when the three kids in Birmingham were arrested for mugging and given twenty years in prison, and they filmed the defence committee. Suddenly we became aware that there was beginning to be this thing about Black crime, very excessively punished and so on. That was the origin of *Policing the Crisis*. I mean it comes from the outside, suddenly we felt, well these are political, cultural questions, how come the Centre has never been maintained outside the university framework and boundary—let's do some work on this, and that's the first time, I think, that the Centre appropriates those themes, rather than sort of keeping inside the Centre.

R.B.   Looking back and on from the outside, I always thought there was a very tense collective mode of working, organic to the Centre, are you suggesting that people brought those modes, and wishes to work in that way, and the Centre gave them the chance?

S.H.   Well, no, I've always worked in that collective way, in the formation of the New Left group, I tried to create a grouping like that around *New Left Review*; I've always worked in informal collectives. But what gave the thrust to that was the whole student movement critique of dominant forms of knowledge, compounded by the fact that since cultural studies was not a discipline, established etc., we could hardly pretend that we were transmitting any finished traditions since we were making it up. So you just couldn't maintain the old relationships of teacher and taught in a field where everyone was constructing the field as they studied. One of the ways in which we framed the question earlier on, reminds me, and perhaps I'd better say something about this now, the Centre did never try itself to be a kind of unified political body that intervened in different places.

R.B.   That's sometimes how it was seen by some people.

S.H.   Yes, indeed, sometimes people criticized me, but I intervened on several occasions to prevent that image of the Centre. Various elements within the Centre sometimes bid for the Centre to do that. It seemed to me that we were not in a position to do that, from within the university, you know, we would have lasted about three months. Secondly, we were within a left milieu, but we had different positions within that milieu. There were one or two people who were still in the communist party, a whole great variety of New Left people, some beginning to be feminists, there were one or two Trotskyists—we would never have agreed! We would have spent our whole time trying to solve our political line. So what I said is, there are a number of different tasks, one of which is cultural analysis, cultural critique, theory etc. Of course, theory has an active relation to politics, but it doesn't all have to happen in the same space, in the same milieu, we all belong to a much wider variety of social, cultural movements, the Arts Lab, cultural movements like that, as well as political movements, and community work, and this enriches the Centre.

R.B.   Did you at the Centre initiate any of these contacts?

S.H.   Not often, what I said was, we are the conduits between them, and you ought to bring in to the Centre the experiences, connections, links, insights that you've won outside and what we do within the Centre are ideas, individually and as groupings, informal groupings, which you can take back. But that's a different thing from saying the Centre organizationally is going to lead this or that project—it was not a political party.

R.B.   In the early days was it even Marxist, could you describe it easily or readily in that way?

S.H.   No, that's another great mystification. You can see from what I've said, certainly, I've always been in conversation with Marxists, but I've never in my life been a classical, orthodox Marxist. In the Caribbean, it always seemed to me that there were certain problems where the application of Marxism, in the classic classism-Marxism, was silent. Marxism was not very good about imperialism; it was not very good on those societies which had been moved into capitalism through the conquest and slavery routes rather than the unfolding of feudalism. So, of course, Marxism is an important thing one needed to know about, but I was using it and arguing with it. When I got to Oxford, the communists there held a rather more orthodox position about Marx, and I remember when I finished my undergraduate work, the first political meeting I went to was to argue about whether class remained as it was. So Marxism was a presence, but '56 could not be described as a Marxist moment, it was a moment of the left, but it was a moment *against* Stalinism, against the invasion of Hungary, against active existing socialism, against official Marxism, etc.

I've always occupied a milieu, which I would say is at best dissident to Marxism. When you come to questions of culture, my position there was very much the position that Raymond Williams outlined in the debate between Leavis and the Marxists. The available models in Marxism to understand culture, questions of the so-called superstructure, the very superstructure model, were *so* reductionist, *so* over-simplified, *so* mechanistic, that our view was that Leavis, though also wrong from another direction, won, and deserved to win. He gave a more complex account of cultural relationships than was available in Marxism. If you wanted to remain Marxist and be interested in questions of culture, you had a lot of work to do and you could never only draw on Marxist ideas. So when one gets into those debates, one is drawing on Marxism but one is also drawing on other things. When you get to the Centre, there is not the imposition of Marxism, we went around the clock to find other things. We read sociology, we read sociology of literature, to try and find models which would enable us to make those links but an orthodox, base-superstructure model—never ever. People tell the story, it started there and *then* we moved away from it. *We never were in it*, and the closest approach was in the '70s, rather than the '60s—post '68— and it was only because, first Althusser and then Gramsci, allowed us to raise Marxist questions in a non-classical Marxist way. Which is only because Althusser shifted the base-superstructure model where determination was possible, determination by the economic was not tenable—and even Althusser was a bit too structuralist for me—so

667

I became a Gramscian rather than an Althusserian. It was precisely Gramsci, who in raising questions of culture, was displacing exactly those things in Marxism implausible on cultural questions. The '70s is a kind of convergence, when a Marxist-structuralism is making it possible for people who wouldn't have dreamt of being Marxists in a communistic sense to find a way of being in a more radical political milieu.

R.B. So that's the legacy of '68.

S.H. Yes, the legacy of '68, it's the legacy of suddenly there being these works available in translation. Before that you had a rather mechanistic Marxism, then you had the founding of critical theory, Lukács. During the late '60s a lot of that becomes translated, in New Left books, when (Stanley) Mitchell translates *History and Class Consciousness*, and Benjamin and Sartre, and then Gramsci. A lot of the literature of an alternative Western Marxism, which is more a base on which cultural studies could build, becomes available in the wake of '68 and in the early '70s. That's when it becomes possible to teach that stuff, for students to read it for themselves, and the arguments can develop around Marxism. So, it's quite late. There's a whole discourse of cultural studies up to then which is quite explicit, aware of Marxist questions, especially the question of ideology, but aware of the limitations and problems which classical Marxism presents.

R.B. Some people, I think, found offensive a kind of terrorism which surrounded the language. It seems difficult to translate European conceptual terms into English. I mean a lot of people found *On Ideology* [a CCCS Working Paper publication, 1976], which was about '76, '77, very inaccessible, but *Policing the Crisis* not. *Policing the Crisis* is not theoretically simple, but does have accessibility, it's in part an ethnographic work isn't it?

S.H. I think it's absolutely true that there is something deeply hostile towards that kind of conceptual theory in English, in the culture, and therefore it presents a real problem. There's a real problem in the social environment. I think you see it with Raymond. In the first part of *The Long Revolution* he's trying to theorize, but he's still very much afraid and not at home in a wholly conceptual language.

R.B. And then there's the awkwardness of the clumsy language.

S.H. Absolutely, awkwardness. Clifford Geertz, the American anthropologist talks about 'thick description', I think it's 'thick' theorizing. There's this problem in the culture intellectually with that kind of theoretical work, a real suspicion of it, that presents difficulties not just for cultural studies but in general. In the '70s there is a kind of theoreticists' deluge, in which, because it is so difficult to think indigenously within an English idiom at that kind of conceptual level, what people do is mimic it. Trying to make French puns in English, which absolutely drove me insane, because the languages never work like that. Talk about sliding signifiers, sliding puns, there was a lot of very good work which ended on sliding puns which could only make a kind of Franglais. So, there was a real problem, and I know in the '70s at the Centre, a number of students who were reduced to silence. They could not write a sentence, commit themselves to a thought —that would be to take a position—but then did the 'real' really exist and so on. They had to know *everything* before they could say *anything* at all.

Paradoxically, I had not thought of this before, but in a way this made people more reliant on the group, the arguments went on in the groups, and each group had a slightly different culture in a way. Some groups were more exclusively into theoretical issues, some were less so, for instance, the media group, found a way through some of those debates by taking on ideology. And they always had some concrete base to bite on, something to analyse, that had a slightly different milieu. I say that, because *Policing the Crisis* arises in what was the old sub-cultures group, and *it* had a particular milieu, drawing a little bit on social interactionism, on ethnographic work etc., as its concrete object, it's very much the group which had produced *Resistance through Rituals* and so on, working on group culture etc.. Because the kids who'd been arrested in Painswick were young and Black, that group picks it up and that group always had a more concrete, almost sociological, anthropological, ethnographic feel to it. It was one of the groups at the Centre more resistant to the Althusserian-Gramscian thing. As the work developed, and as *Policing the Crisis* is being researched and written over a long period of time and with lots of spin–offs from it, gradually it becomes more theorized. But it becomes theorized from *within* and around this concrete problem, with a tradition of concrete work running along beside it. I think it's a more organic theorizing, it doesn't begin from 'let's write an Althusserian book about race', but let us try to understand why crime and race and Englishness are so wrapped up out there in Birmingham—and in order to do that, we can draw on theories about the media, and theories about the state, and theories about hegemony, etc. I think that's why this comes off that way in that particular area of cultural-studies work, but alongside that there's other kinds of work going on, partly feminist which is bringing psychoanalysis, Lacanian theory—a completely different theoretical tradition. These theories are being taken up slightly in different milieus within the Centre.

* * *

By '79 I can go; at the Centre someone else will be made the director. I wouldn't have gone before. What I couldn't see was the onslaught on the universities, and on graduate work, Thatcherism, but what that did was to clobber the Centre from on top, and so cultural studies could not have been generated from out of the Centre in the '80s; it was being hammered all the time. What seems to me to happen in the '80s is that it proliferates outside, it becomes autonomous outside; now that's not because people are appointed to cultural studies, people are appointed to history or literature, or to sociology or whatever, but they are cultural-studies people and this network begins in institutions, in the Polys, in FE [Further Education] etc. of cultural studies being taught. That is the moment of autonomy, because these people can't depend on the Centre any longer to give them their definition; for instance, Portsmouth [Polytechnic] harnessed a tradition in literature and history in a way which was not exactly the disciplinary mix out of which cultural studies arose in the Centre, whereas PCL [Polytechnic of Central London] had another tradition, design, and art history and communications, rather than literature and history, so in each place it begins to be located in a different disciplinary milieu, but that's a moment of auto-nomization. It looks like dispersal, and these centres are very weak, but actually it gives them an indigenous root in their own intellectual life rather than travelling to Birmingham to find out the news. We didn't need to tell them how to do it, do it! I understand why they came to Birmingham to see what was going on. In the '80s you couldn't, I think this was very good, this wasn't planned, it was the result of an onslaught, but nevertheless it happened. And in those different spaces, it contracted other intellectual-critical links, feminism, critical theory, a kind of movement back to literary theory and literary theory itself is transformed by some of these conceptual models, deconstruction and so on, so it's the moment of the fusion of Cultural Studies with other strands of critical intellectual work.

R.B.   Quite a lot of that comes from the States and has a big impact here, literary critical theory comes a lot from the States, deconstruction particularly, rather perhaps than from Europe, and then returns to the States.

S.H.   Yes, it is the impact of American literary culture of the European connection, but it's different from the way in which Europe impacts on Britain. It doesn't take up Gramsci, it doesn't take up Althusser, but it takes up Barthes, it takes up deconstruction, it takes up a certain kind of Lacanian psychoanalysis etc. then it begins to make an impact back on Britain. I think it is, nevertheless, what I would call a European moment for both of us. But it's differently appropriated, and then it has a further impact when it comes to us, because American universities are so huge that once they start on anything there's a big generation, and the publishers . . .

R.B.   I don't know how it seems to you, but it's not strong historically yet.

S.H.   No, that's another difference, it's not historical, it's not Althusserian, it's never Althusserian, they have a Gramscian moment but it's different from ours—it's intellectual, it's not a Gramsci who is active in the factories as it were, it's not a Gramsci grounded in a political reality.

*   *   *

S.H.   Insofar as there is a philosophical rationale and theorization of the work we were doing at the Centre, as part of the larger movement in education, very Gramscian, one is that the Centre did come to think of itself as producing organic intellectuals. That's not what we did, not what we were, but that was the image, to produce intellectuals, who were intellectuals, so they occupied a place in the intellectual conversation. They were intellectuals in the larger sense in that they could articulate themselves with a wider group, and the second thing, that Gramsci says about that, it is that it is necessary for organic intellectuals to be at the forefront, you have to know *more, better*, that's the condition of being an intellectual. At the same time the organic intellectual has a responsibility for translating, for mediating it, the function of the organic intellectual is not to be an intellectual in a narrow professional sense, but to address the intellectual function, which is enormous. So these two fronts were always there.

Many times we weren't able to do that, we got lost, in jargon, in the language of a particular school, but at the same time, in the idea of publishing that stuff in working papers, etc. and the books, there was always an attempt at trying to connect with some wider audiences out there, to take some of these ideas out. That was always a pressure. There was a lot of debate at the Centre between intellectualism and publishing, there was always a strand at the Centre of 'let us go to the people', *narodnik*, and I had to hold that back, rein that in, because that was making too easy a translation between theory and politics. But then there's always an intellectualist version of that, where if you just think the right thoughts that will do it.

* * *

R.B. Wasn't there a sense in which working-class culture and popular culture were seen as identical?

S.H. On the question of the popular, which was not a code word for the working class, it's always what you are trying to theorize about, even if you are theorizing about it in a very arcane manner. There's the sort of didactic, socialist tradition, but then there are also TV, games, and both of these are popular. The popular is for us from the beginning a site of contestation, even at our most sort of 'popular equals working class' moment we realized work has to be done on the people to get them to appear in this authentic disguise! We never had a folk notion, a working-class folk notion of the people.

R.B. But I think Richard Hoggart has treated it like this.

S.H. Yes, and there are other elements, there is a kind of Arnoldian, de Tocquevillian suspicion of the people. Playing on the evidence that we all have, there is not one culture there just being suppressed, being over-laid by the middle class, because there are already these contentions and different traditions are operating inside the popular desire. The very notion of popular is deliberately a way a kind of blurring those class delineations. That's why we liked Gramsci; Gramsci's national popular is not collapsible into any one empirically observable or theoretical class, but is about a wider formation. We were always addressing that issue as a problem, but of course, we don't yet have any notion that it can be so contradictory. If you read *Policing the Crisis* carefully, we talk about the conservative elements into which the lower middle class feed. For instance, Gramsci does not say that there is a conspiracy of the state, he talks about the attempt to hegemonize from the top which is matched by the whole notion of moral panic, which classic Marxist critics hate, which was generated because there is no way of talking about a formation which harnesses a political drive from the state apparatus with a popular feeling of 'we are losing our bearings, the world is changing too fast for us, save us from freedom.'

* * *

R.B.   For some time now, your writing has been getting more accessible.

S.H.   I have had so little time to do consistent intellectual work that people have read more of my writing of that kind [journalism] than any other. And I think my own writing has been transformed. I no longer try to write that way. It's a flat reaction against that '70s—it is a mark of being trapped in a university milieu, talking only to one audience, which is I think reinforced by the American influence. Their universities are so big, you don't have to move outside the university all week, so that they really do think politics take place in the university. When I go to the States now, I have only one song, whatever I'm talking about ends with a peroration about how they ought to be dealing with concrete problems and then discover which theoretical concept will help them to understand that rather than the other way around. I mean you must understand me, it's not that I'm opposed to theory, in some ways now I'm a very theoretical person, but I don't believe theory is self-sufficient, I don't want to produce theory as an object. It's a shield for thinking with but it's not an end product. The pressure writing for other journals means you can't just put down concepts, you can't start with Derrida.

R.B.   What about the post-'89 situation, nationalisms, local identities?

S.H.   I think that's very mixed. I think there are both regressive and positive features. Certainly, there is a whole persistence of nationalism, the return of the particular— the notion that even though the identity is not fixed and complete it will also always be attached to particular histories, particular moments—there's the return of specificity and difference. Marxism is one of the last great universal rationalisms—the march of capital will defeat every particular—and it's just not true. The particularity of gender keeps returning inside the most advanced divisions of labour, the particularity of place keeps returning, particularism and difference reassert themselves and in that sense I think we are in a new kind of very complicated cultural dialectic.

* * *

R.B.   Have you ever had any experience of 'Stuart Hall' being seen as a kind of cultural icon, both positively and negatively; has there ever been any problem of your own complexity being ignored, of people wanting to use you for particular purposes?

S.H.   Being used and tokenized? A bit, a bit, at one stage, for instance, television and radio wanted to work with me to do things like chair discussions, chair a session, I thought I was very much on the edge of being incorporated, I had to take quite a conscious decision to refuse. As a cultural icon I don't feel that's so.

R.B.   But possibly in the States more, you're thought of as UK cultural studies.

S.H.   Ah, yes that is, I suppose, the only place where I feel it. I do feel that in the States, and I have to resist it like crazy. Now, I have a problem about that in the States because I'm mainly identified as one of the father figures of British cultural studies and the Birmingham School. Very often, the way in which that history is understood is extremely truncated and overlaid by their interest and their own take on it, very different from my own. Now, my problem is this, that I try to refuse that, so I refuse the authority of being able to speak for cultural studies, what I'm really trying to say is that there isn't any one theory about that. The Centre for cultural studies was full of different rows and arguments, different tenets, that was what the real intellectual work was like, not the evolution of a school . . . of what? On the other hand, because there's something at stake in that debate, in terms of defining what cultural studies is, I do find myself drawn in to producing my own narrative, and then I have to say, of course, my story may be no more accurate than anybody else's. But I do have a story to tell about that. So it is quite difficult, and I notice that much more in the States than anywhere else.

One of the most important aspects of my struggle there with the American definition of cultural studies is how narrow it is. It talks about only some of the things we have studied, there's a whole slew of work being done there which doesn't realize that a lot of people from Birmingham, whom they are still writing about, have gone, have gone on to do other work, and then they don't know about all the other people, people like yourself, who were never institutionally at Birmingham at all, but have always been working in cultural studies in some other place. They have a very narrow definition of it and a very narrow view of cultural studies as well.

Interview with
Professor J. Hillis Miller

J. Hillis Miller (1928–) is an eminent scholar and critic of English literature. He has taught at Johns Hopkins University and Yale University, and is presently a Distinguished Professor of English and Comparative Literature at the University of California at Irvine. When he was at Yale, J. Hillis Miller together with Geoffrey Hartman and Paul de Man was instrumental in introducing the American academy to deconstruction and post-structuralist criticism. For J. Hillis Miller the defining aspect of contemporary critical theory is its potential to engage in the act of 'reading' with a sense of ethics in the dissemination of knowledge. In fact, in his presidential address to the Modern Language Association a decade ago, at a time when universities were sceptical about deconstruction and its threat to the integrity of the written word, he emphasized precisely a combination of ethics and responsibility in handling a text. His preoccupation with reading and ethics as a mode of cultural critique is seen in the interview printed below. J. Hillis Miller's major works are *Charles Dickens: The World Of His Novels* (1958), *The Disappearance of God* (1963), *The Poets of Reality: Six Twentieth-Century Writers* (1965), *The Form of Victorian Fiction* (1968), *Thomas Hardy: Distance and Desire* (1970), *Fiction and Repetition*, (1982), *The Ethics of Reading* (1987), and *Tropes, Parables, Performatives: Essays on Twentieth-Century Literature* (1990). His most recent publication is *Illustration* (1992), an investigation into both deconstructive and cultural-studies approaches to the materials of art and literature. A hallmark of J. Hillis Miller's work is his ability to wed a systematic textual analysis to contemporary critical theory such that subtle nuances of both are brought to light. As he says in *Fiction and Repetition*, 'A theory is all too easy to refute or deny, but a reading can be controverted only by going through the difficult task of reading the work in question and proposing an alternative reading.' While some critics tend to see J. Hillis Miller as an Arnoldian figure speaking from within a liberal, humanist tradition, it is vital to point out that he pushes the very limits of that tradition by constantly engaging in critiques. Unlike Arnold, democratizing culture in J. Hillis Miller's opinion does

not always lead to 'anarchy'.
G.R.

G.R. and J.M.   In *The Ethics of Reading* (1987), you lay the groundwork for a theory
of reading for an individual, as a consciously responsible and culturally acceptable act
or performance. You say, for example: 'I mean that aspect of the act of reading in
which there is a response to the text that is both *necessitated*, in the sense that it is a
response to an irresistible demand, and it is *free*, in the sense that I must take
responsibility for my response and the further effects, "interpersonal", institutional,
social, political, or historical, of my act of reading. For example, as that act takes the
form of teaching or possible commentary on a given text. What happens when I read
must happen, but I must acknowledge it as my act of reading' (43).
   Could you elaborate on the freedom you refer to in the book, and which is related
to personal responsibility? Could you also comment on the 'I' 'my'/reader, which is
itself a cultural construct, and whose 'ethicity' could be called into question with
relation to any text but, perhaps, particularly with multi-cultural texts.

J.H.M.   You ask about my notion of freedom and personal responsibility in the ethics of reading, as well as about the 'I' as reader. As you know, *The Ethics of Reading* is
an attempt to think out the questions I pose at the beginning of that book through
readings of particular texts, writers, writing about their own work. The general formulations, for example the one you cite, are developed in the course of the readings
and are difficult to detach from those readings. It is difficult to repeat in a sentence
or two in answer to an interviewer's question the careful development, in response to
a particular text, of my thinking in that book. Nevertheless, I'll try. 'Freedom' is of
course a complex and overdetermined concept. For me, there cannot be a concept of
ethics or of responsibility without some notion of freedom. My attempt in *The Ethics
of Reading* and in other subsequent books has not been to detach works of literature
and the act of reading, teaching, or writing about them from the surrounding historical context. Of course that context is always there, vast, powerful, heterogeneous,
overdetermining. But the work of literature always has some excess over that determining context. That excess is carried over to the reader. I mean by that excess
something so simple and obvious as the fact that a work by a given writer, let's say
Shakespeare or Toni Morrison, cannot be fully determined by the class, race, gender,
and subject position of the author. It is that excess most readers, I think, especially
value, the margin of unpredictability and strangeness. The reader, any reader,
responds in one way or another to that strangeness and unpredictability. The most
unexpected things happen when you pick up a work of literature and read. I experience that strangeness and unpredictability both as a necessity, that is the power of the
work over me when I read it, and also as a mode of freedom—freedom, for example,
from what I was before I began the reading. But this transformative freedom imposes
a new responsibility on me, a responsibility to act in one way or another in response
to it, for example, in teaching the work or writing about it. Some of that inaugurating
or initiating excess in the work is passed on through me to my readers or students.
For what happens then I must take responsibility, since it is something I have done.
   You ask then about the 'I' as reader, taking it for granted that the 'I' is itself a cul-

tural construct. No, if you mean it is massively determined once and for all by social surroundings. Of course, the very idea of an ego or subject or 'I' is a cultural construct, determined by all sorts of religious, metaphysical, cultural, and linguistic presuppositions. And any person's particular 'I', mine for example, is no doubt to be defined as a result of my particular 'subject position', that is my race, class, gender, and so on. It can change from time to time, even from moment to moment. Nevertheless, as many people of differing critical persuasions would probably now agree, the 'I' or ego is not an eternal given, something I am born with, but, precisely, as you say, a 'social construct'. One of the things that constructs it is the reading of works of literature. This means that the reading of any new work of literature or even a re-reading of one already read will, in however small a degree, re-make the 'I' or subject of the reader. Otherwise, I do not see any reason to read literature at all. Information about the historical and cultural context can be obtained much more accurately in other ways. Anyone who tries to go directly from Shakespeare, Melville, or Toni Morrison to the surrounding culture will make some strange and inaccurate assumptions about that culture. Reading, like going to the movies or watching television, has a power to change the 'I' of the viewer in ways that are by no means wholly predictable. A classroom for literature has always seemed to me potentially a dangerous place in the university, dangerous to the university, I mean, insofar as the university is defined as the guardian of fixed values transmitted from generation to generation.

You then go on to suggest that since the 'I' is a social construct, its 'ethicity' can be put in question, perhaps particularly in relation to multicultural texts. I particularly meant to call that 'ethicity' into question in my book by defining it as a responsibility not to be predicted or controlled by any general rules but a responsibility to act in a certain way generated by the reading itself. The ethicity of the 'I', like the rest of the 'I', is re-made, altered, re-oriented by the act of reading. I do not see that multicultural texts are different from any others from this point of view. I suppose you may mean that a white reader has a different relation to an African-American text from the one an African-American does. That is certainly true, but it does not keep me from reading that work or any other work outside my own ethnic limitations. Most so-called 'canonical works', Homer, Dante, Milton, or Shakespeare, for example, are far outside the boundaries of my own ethnic enclave. To read them is almost like reading a work of science fiction. When I read any work, in any case, what happens, happens, and I would hold that that combination of necessity, freedom, and responsibility is the arena of a particular kind of ethics, namely 'the ethics of reading'.

G.R. and J.M.   In the same book commenting upon the role of 'literature', you discuss the construction and formation of a culture, 'there must be an influx of the performative power from the linguistic transaction involved in the act of reading into the realm of knowledge, politics, and history. Literature must be in some way a cause and not merely an effect, if the study of literature is to be other than the relatively trivial study of one of the epi-phenomena of society' (5). You also say, 'Nothing is more urgently needed these days in humanistic study than the incorporation of the rhetorical study of literature into the historical, social, and ideological dimensions of literature' (7).

You would seem to be suggesting that the responsible reader needs to translate the effects of the reading into acts in the realm of the 'real', knowledge, politics and history. How congruent is ethical reading and ideological analysis? Further, is there an implication that rhetorical study is itself ideology free and therefore able to engage in unmasking?

J.H.M.   I did not mean to say that 'the responsible reader needs to translate the effects of the reading into acts in the realm of the "real", knowledge, politics and history.' I meant that the reader could not help doing that. If reading, as I have just argued above, remakes the reader, changes his or her subject position, then everything the reader does thereafter, which includes the modest way in which the individual is involved in society, politics, and history, will be different. It is not a matter of need or intent but of inevitable necessity. That doesn't mean some reflection about that transition might not be in order for the teacher. If I have been made different by reading, I will behave differently. No, I do not mean to imply that rhetorical study is itself 'ideology free and therefore able to engage in unmasking'. No one at any time, as we all know, can be 'ideology free'. 'Rhetorical criticism' is a name for the effort to identify in the work itself the power it has to change me, to be inaugural or constitutive. Some forms of cultural criticism or of the so called 'new historicism' seem to me in danger of taking the meaning and value of works of literature a little too much for granted. A scrupulous return to the words on the page in an attempt to find out how those meanings and values are generated is always a necessity. Otherwise we would be free to say anything we like about a given work of literature. It is not so much that we unmask literature as that it unmasks us, if my ascription to it of strangeness and inaugural power is correct. Another way to put this would be to say that literature frees us to some degree and momentarily from our own ideological prison, or, if you like, puts us in a different cell.

G.R. and J.M.   When you contextualize the study of literature through *The Ethics of Reading* as a social construction of knowledge where do you see the authority of the reader in contemporary culture?

J.H.M.   You ask where I 'see the authority of the reader in contemporary culture'. The authority of the reader in contemporary culture is getting weaker all the time. Reading can have the social effects I have described in the answer to your first question—only if reading occurs. These days, reading clearly occurs less and less. That is the obvious fact that justifies all the new attention to other media, such as film and television. We may deplore this change and wring our hands about it, but it is probably irreversible. Nothing, that I can see, requires that a vigorous culture be maintained by printed books rather than by visual and auditory cultural forms like movies, television, and CDs. But the latter would be a big change from a print culture.

G.R. and J.M.   In your *TLS* article (1988) on Heidegger and de Man, you ascribe one of the possible reasons for the outcry against de Man to his deconstructive poetics rather than to his early neo-fascist leanings. You comment on 'a conservative climate, a xenophobic moment in history that attacks not de Man the man, but his thinking, and thus deconstruction, and by extension the progressive schools with curricula that include critical theory'. Do you see the recent attacks on cultural studies as a similar phenomena with C.S. taking over the 'foreign' and theoretical mantle of deconstruction?

J.H.M.   Yes, I think attacks on cultural studies are to a considerable degree a displacement of the hostility to European theory and deconstruction. This is clear from the way the attacks [generally from the right] often conflate the two. This ignorance of the difference between so-called deconstruction and cultural studies is no doubt in part evidence of the profound ignorance of those attackers, who often seem not to have read a single word of what they attack. Nevertheless, there may be something more to it than that. Both deconstruction and cultural studies share a critical rather than a blindly reverent attitude toward the Western tradition. Both pose a threat to the conventional organization of the university. In spite of the tensions between so-called deconstruction and cultural studies, for example the frequent repudiation by the latter of the former as a 'sterile or reactionary formalism', nevertheless cultural studies, feminism, African-American studies, Chicano/a studies, ethnic studies, and so on, would surely not have taken the form they are taking without the prior existence of structuralism and poststructuralism, including deconstruction. So though many of those attacking cultural studies and theory write from an amazing and profound ignorance, nevertheless they may be right in feeling that there must be some similarity in the threat each one poses.

G.R. and J.M.   In the preface to *Tropes, Parables, Performatives: Essays on Twentieth-Century Literature*, you emphasize the inherent indirection of literary language ('tropes and parables') and its 'failure' to take the reader to the 'somewhere' to which it elusively, and performatively, points—a failure which produces both dissatisfaction and desire. You go on to say that 'Nevertheless, this tropological, parabolic, performative dimension enables writing and reading to enter history and be effective there, for better or for worse' (ix). Could you elaborate on what you mean by reading and writing entering history? And what would be 'the better or worse' manifestations of this entry? How do the points you make here about the performative aspect of literature connect to your warnings about purely effect based readings and the 'ethicity' of the reader referred to in our first question?

J.H.M.   Your question begins with an interrogation of my assumption that the figurative dimension of language has something to do with its performative power. How can that be? My emphasis in my answer to your first question on the excess of literature over its context or its unpredictable strangeness may help explain. Even the most literal and straightforward language of narration, as Valéry, Kafka, and Blanchot recognized, has that strangeness . . . Your question then goes on to ask how reading and writing enter history. I have already said something about that. It is a mistake to exaggerate the degree to which you or I as teachers make history, but in some small way we do in effects on our students and in effects on the readers of what we write. I mean readers of Shakespeare, Melville, or Morrison behave differently, in however small a way. Our students and those who read us behave differently, in however small a way, as a result of that reading. History is material. It is embodied in houses, roads, monuments, utensils, artifacts of all kinds, but all those are results of behavior by their makers. Reading is one of the things that influences that making, for better or for worse.

When I say for better or worse, I mean the following: If we allow that reading literature can have a good social effect, measured by one or another concept of good, we must allow that the effects might be bad, according to one or another measure of bad. If I am right in thinking that the effects of reading literature are to some degree unpredictable, one has to conclude that whether or not the effect will be good or bad cannot be told beforehand for certain. That's what I meant by saying that a classroom where literature is taught is a wild place, or, to put this another way, a wild card in the university game. I think these remarks would at least implicitly answer your last question about my 'warnings.'

G.R. and J.M.   At the conclusion to your preface to *Tropes*, you remark that 'To say that prosopopoeia is a speech act giving a name, a face, and a voice to the absent, the inanimate, or the dead is to confront the ultimate question. Is it the face of a pre-existent other we encounter through the transport of literature or is that face only invoked by the performative spell of the work, charmed into phantasmal existence by the words? It seems the face is already there, but how would one know for sure?' (x). In the last essay in the book, 'Prosopopoeia in Hardy and Stevens', you disagree with Kant's aesthetics and state that prosopopoeia is always there; 'personification . . . is fundamental, original, there from the beginning. It cannot be erased or suspended by a return to clear, philosophical, reasonable, non-figurative first principles' (245). How does such a statement relating trope and idea connect to the query you raise in the preface which seems to suggest the possibility of some formation—'the face of the pre-existent other'—prior to the language that describes it? Is it your contention that any language must always give the impression of an otherness lurking beyond language? Are we not, more specifically, also encountering forms of cultural programming, distinctly European forms, which have developed tropes, parables to express culturally specific yearnings?

J.H.M.   I did not mean to say that prosopopoeia was prior to the language that describes it, but that it is already always there in language prior to any overt tropological substitutions in that language. In this, prosopopoeia is like catachresis. It is a trope and not a trope. It is a trope in that the 'face' of the mountain is not really a face, but it is not a trope in that it does not substitute for some literal word. Prosopopoeia is woven into the fabric of ordinary non-tropological language.

Yes, I do think, in answer to your second question here, 'that any language must indeed always give the impression of an otherness lurking beyond language.' This is an exceedingly difficult issue, one at the borders or edges of my ability to articulate it. It is easier, for me at least, to talk about it in relation to some particular text that gives me a glimpse of that otherness that inhabits language while not being wholly within it, like a ghost or guest haunting the house of language. I have tried here and there, and will go on trying to find ways to express this sense of an otherness within

679

language but invading it from without. It might be connected to a sense of the heterogeneity of any given text, the way it cannot be reduced to a wholly perspicuous and rational system. The sense that a person of another gender, race, or culture is 'other' seems to me no more than a displacement of this primordial otherness.

Your final question is an extremely important and difficult one. I would agree that the array of available tropes in a given language is related to the 'culturally specific yearning' of that culture, though it would be difficult to know whether the language makes the culture or the other way around. Those speaking, writing, and reading any one of the European family of languages are bound together by a certain historical consistency of tradition and by certain historical boundaries in the available repertoire of 'tropes, parables'. Nevertheless, there is a good bit of differentiation even within European languages, as any American will discover who tries seriously to read German philosophy in the original. The relation between figurative and conceptual language in German is quite different from that in English. This means that Hegel, Nietzsche, or Heidegger is to a considerable extent untranslatable. I am ashamed to say I do not know more than a little of any non-European language, but I would suspect that there might be even more difference between Chinese, say, and English, from this point of view, than there is between English and German. I think this should be a major area for investigation by cultural critics and critics of post-colonial culture. This would require the kind of deep knowledge of some non-European languages that is taken for granted in the discipline of anthropology. One thing I much hope for as a result of current developments in cultural studies and multi-culturalism is learning of Chinese, or Japanese, or Arabic, or African languages, or Hindi by scholars whose primary language is one of the European languages. I am sure that a real answer to the last of your questions can only be given by scholars who can juxtapose European and non-European languages with your question in mind. Is, for example, prosopopoeia as intrinsic a part of the fabric of Chinese as it is of English, French or German? Only someone who knows Chinese as well as English, French, or German could answer that question authoritatively.

G.R. and J.M.   Now, to move to a new area. The seemingly romanticized notion that computer technology has the potential to redefine human consciousness and the character of our culture was the frame of your plenary address to the Semiotic Society of America at the University of Oklahoma in 1990. Could you elaborate on the applications of such a technology to the humanities scholar in three areas: (a) the creating and manipulating of texts, (b) researching potential that transcends the physical boundaries of libraries, and (c) the immediacy and free-floating nature of knowledge produced by computer technologies, like E-mail for example?

J.H.M.   I didn't quite say in that Oklahoma lecture, that 'computer technology would redefine human consciousness', though I did say and do believe that it is changing and will change more and more 'the character of our culture'. In revisions and considerable extensions of that paper, now to come out as the first part of a little book entitled *Illustration*, I have modified what I said there about the effects of the computer in the direction of being a bit more sceptical. I am not at all sure, for example, that certain apparently innovative techniques for research using the computer do not reinforce extremely old-fashioned notions about contextual determination of works of literature or other cultural artifacts. How much change there will be and what that change will be depends on how the technology is used. Nevertheless, much more of the reception of signs by scholars, including cultural critics, as well as by people in general, will come by way of electronic devices like film, television, CD-ROMs, VCRs, E-Mail, and so on. For the cultural critic, this will gradually make possible quite new ways of studying, editing, and splicing together visual material, for example film clips or segments of television. This is bound to have a considerable effect on the possibilities of research in these areas. As I said in my Oklahoma lecture, the availability at a computer terminal almost anywhere of vast data bases will in the near future to a considerable degree democratize university research. One will no longer need to be at the places where this material is stored, but can work in a small college or even outside the university altogether. The development of modems and E-mail is already putting cultural critics and other scholars in touch with one another in a new way and making much more possible new forms of collaborative research in that area. It would be a good idea to remain sceptical about the ways the computer will 'redefine human consciousness', but there can be no doubt that the new technologies will make profound changes in the way research and teaching in the humanities are carried on.

G.R. and J.M.   Thank you for your carefully thought out responses.

Index

683